Enhance your learning experience with the accompanying interactive e-book, featuring video clips, exercises, quizzes and more!

Visit **www.wileyopenpage.com** to access your interactive e-book.

CW00556809

PSYCHOLOGY
RONALD COMER, ELIZABETH GOULD AND ADRIAN FURNHAM

INCLUDES INTERACTIVE E-BOOK
LOOK FOR THIS ICON AS YOUR GUIDE TO THE EMBEDDED MEDIA

Easily navigate your e-book using the chapter menu, search and bookmark options.

You can save notes or voice annotations as a reminder of key points.

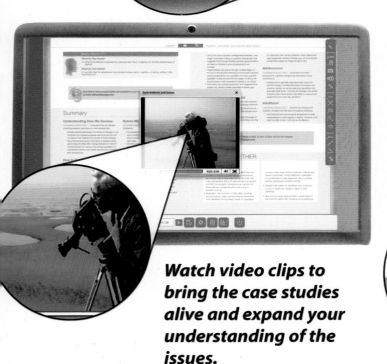

Watch video clips to bring the case studies alive and expand your understanding of the issues.

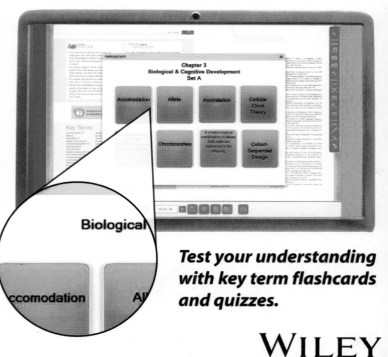

Test your understanding with key term flashcards and quizzes.

WILEY

Psychology

Psychology

Ronald Comer
Princeton University

Elizabeth Gould
Princeton University

Adrian Furnham
University College London

WILEY

ISBN 9781119941262 (pbk)
ISBN 9781118686478 (iebk)
ISBN 9781118686362 (ebk)

A catalogue record for this book is available from the British Library

Set in 10/13 pt Minion Pro by MPS Limited, Chennai, India

Printed in Italy by Printer Trento, Trento

Senior Commissioning Editor:	Andrew McAleer
Senior Media and Development Editor:	Deborah Egleton
Marketing Managers:	Fran Hunt and Jo Underwood
Project Editor:	Juliet Booker

FSC MIX Paper from responsible sources FSC® C015829

Brief Contents

Contents

About the Authors

Ronald Comer has taught in Princeton University's Department of Psychology for the past 35 years and has served as Director of Clinical Psychology Studies for most of that time. He has also received the President's Award for Distinguished Teaching at the university. Comer is the author of the textbooks *Abnormal Psychology* and *Fundamentals of Abnormal Psychology* and the coauthor of *Case Studies in Abnormal Psychology*. He has published numerous journal articles in clinical psychology, personality and social psychology and is also the producer of a range of educational videos.

Elizabeth Gould has taught in Princeton University's Department of Psychology for the past 14 years. An international leader in the study of neurogenesis (the production of new neurons in the mammalian brain), Gould was the winner of the 2006 NARSAD Distinguished Investigator Award and the 2009 Royal Society of the Arts Benjamin Franklin Medal. She serves on the editorial boards of *The Journal of Neuroscience, Neurobiology of Learning and Memory*, and *Biological Psychology*.

Adrian Furnham has been Professor of Psychology at University College London since 1992. He is also Adjunct Professor of Management at the Norwegian School of Management. He has written over 1000 scientific papers and 70 books *including People Management in a Downturn* (2011), *The Talented Manager* (2012) and *Humanitarian Work Psychology* (2012). He is also a regular newspaper columnist at the *Sunday Times*.

Contributors

This is the first adaptation from Europe of a successful text by Ronald Comer and Elizabeth Gould in the US. A project of this size could not be achieved without the contribution of teaching experts in all areas of psychology. The following contributors used their expertise to adapt chapters in their fields of teaching and research and are also acknowledged on the chapters themselves.

Trevor Archer	University of Gothenburg, Sweden
Pam Blundell	University of Leeds, UK
Helen Driscoll	University of Sunderland, UK
Daniel Farrelly	University of Sunderland, UK
Mark Forshaw	Adelphi Values, UK
Trevor Harley	University of Dundee, UK
David Holmes	Manchester Metropolitan University, UK
Chris McVittie	Queen Margaret University, Edinburgh, UK
Chris Moulin	Université de Bourgogne, Dijon, France
Alan Porter	University of Westminster, UK
Corriene Reed	Institute of Education, University of London, UK
David Simmons	University of Glasgow, UK
Alastair Smith	University of Nottingham, UK
Stuart Wilson	Queen Margaret University, Edinburgh, UK

To the Instructor

Psychology is all around us. If ever there were a subject that permeates our everyday lives, it is psychology. Behaviour occurs everywhere, and the study of behaviour can help shed light on the widest range of events and issues. This textbook, *PSYCHOLOGY*, helps to open students' minds to the notion that psychology is around them every day and that its principles are immediately applicable to a whole host of life's questions.

We have always been struck by how differently students react to various subjects of psychology. For example, most students find Abnormal Psychology fascinating, relevant, and 'alive', while many consider other areas of psychology to be flat and removed from their lives.

This gap between the appeal of abnormal behaviour and that of everyday behaviour occurs throughout psychology. Students are fascinated by instances of 'lost memories' yet take for granted that people can remember in the first place. They love to follow the activity of serotonin and dopamine when studying mood disorders and schizophrenia, but not so much when learning about these neurotransmitters in an introductory psychology course. Students are captivated by failures in attention (ADHD), thought (schizophrenia), communication (autism), or coping (posttraumatic stress disorder), yet almost nonchalant about the fact that people usually attend, think, communicate, and cope quite well. They keenly appreciate the importance and effects of psychotherapy, yet almost overlook everyday instances of attitude, behaviour and mood change.

Our textbook is dedicated to helping students appreciate that all human behaviour can be fascinating, and to energize, excite, and demonstrate for them the enormous relevance of psychology. It encourages students to examine what they know about human behaviour and how they know it; and opens them up to an appreciation of psychology outside of the classroom.

About the Text

While implementing the traditional introductory psychology concepts and theories, this textbook also introduces a variety of unique pedagogical tools that help to demonstrate how psychology topics are relevant to each other and also to everyday life.

TYING IT TOGETHER

All introductory psychology textbooks present the various subfields of psychology in a chapter-by-chapter format, but what is missing from most books are tools to help students move beyond a compartmentalized view of the field. Each chapter focuses on the nature, explanations, and applications of each subfield, but they typically do not explore how such areas of psychological functioning *develop* or what *disorders* may occur in each area.

One of the most important ways that this text will help students see a more complete picture of psychology are recurring sections that highlight how different subfields of psychology interconnect and interrelate. We highlight human development, brain function, abnormal psychology, and individual differences as themes that work well to tie together topics and present psychology as an integrated science.

Every chapter on a substantive area of psychology not only offers a thorough presentation of the nature, explanations, and applications of that area, but also includes sections with the icons 'How We Develop', 'How We Differ', 'What Happens in the Brain' and 'Out of the Ordinary'.

YOUR BRAIN AND BEHAVIOUR

Many introductory psychology students consider the study of neuroscience to be difficult and at times irrelevant to the study of human behaviour. In recent years, however, neuroscience has been tied to virtually every subfield of psychology. Remarkable brain imaging studies, in conjunction with animal studies, have helped us to identify the neural mechanisms of everyday experience. Accordingly, *PSYCHOLOGY* incorporates information on neuroscience into chapters where it has been traditionally absent such as Social Psychology and Consciousness. In addition, the text offers a key teaching feature that helps bring neuroscience directly into the lives of readers. 'Your Brain and Behaviour' layouts appear throughout the book illustrating what happens in the brain when people are performing such common behaviours as eating pizza, playing a video game, acquiring a second language, and more. These 'visual essays', which include neuroimages and findings from both human studies and relevant animal experiments, draw students into the brain and provide them with up-to-date information about the neural mechanisms at work during their everyday experiences.

Instructor Resources

Instructor Resources can be found on the text's companion website:
www.wiley.com/college/comer

Videos

The ***Psychology Around Us series of videos*** help bring lectures to life and, most importantly, captivate their students. They help demonstrate the most important theme of an introductory psychology course – that psychology is all around us and that behaviour, from everyday normal behaviour to abnormal behaviour, is truly fascinating. Averaging 3–5 minutes in length, this collection covers a range of relevant topics.

Each video is a high-quality excerpt, many from the BBC archive, illustrating a particular study or lecture point such as animal communication, the development of moral thinking or hypnosis and pain.

Instructor's Manual

Adapted by Gemma Philips-Pike, GP (Psychology) Consultancy

This **Instructor's Manual** is designed to help instructors maximize student learning and encourage critical thinking. It presents teaching suggestions for every chapter using the book's objectives as well as including ideas for lecture classroom discussions, demonstrations, and videos. This manual will also share activity-based applications to everyday life.

Lecture PowerPoint Presentation

Adapted by Gemma Philips-Pike, GP (Psychology) Consultancy

Every chapter contains a **Lecture PowerPoint Presentation** with a combination of key concepts, figures and tables, and problems and examples from the textbook.

Test Bank

Adapted by Nikki Newhouse, Oxford Brookes University

The **Test Bank** is available in a word document format or through Respondus. The questions are available to instructors to create multiple versions of the same test by scrambling the order of all questions found in the test bank. Respondus allows users to customize exams by altering or adding new questions. It is compatible with Blackboard, Moodle and all other major Learning Management Systems.

Mind Maps

Adapted by Nikki Newhouse, Oxford Brookes University

Each chapter is summarized in a detailed **mind map.** This is a great resource for students who like to visualize the information as they learn.

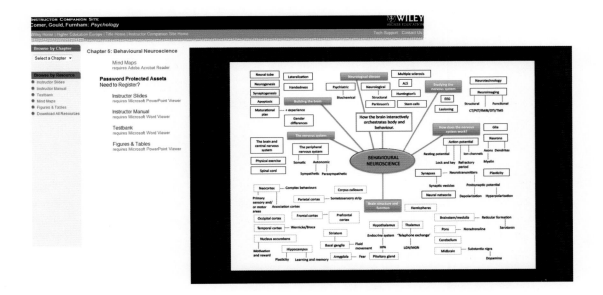

Lecture PowerPoint Presentation

Adapted by...

Every chapter contains a Lecture PowerPoint Presentation with a combination of key concepts, highlighted notes, and problems and examples from the text itself.

Test Bank

Authored by...

The Test Bank is available in a word document or through Respondus. The questions are available in full measure to create multiple versions of the author test by assembling the order of all questions found in the test bank. Respondus allows instructors to customize exams by filtering, adding new questions, and compacting with blackboard, Moodle, and all other major Learning Management Systems.

Mind Maps

Adapted by...

Each chapter is summarized into a detailed mind map. This is a great resource for students to use to visualize the information as they learn.

To the Student

The features in this book promote your reading comprehension, reflection, problem-solving skills, and critical thinking skills. Let's walk through the pedagogical features that will help you learn the material in this book.

Guided Learning

Chapter Learning Objectives summarize what you should be able to do once you have studied the chapter. You can use the learning goals in two ways. First, study them before reading the chapter to get an overall picture of how the concepts in the chapter are related to each other and what you will be learning. Then, after reading the chapter, use the learning goals to review what you have learned, either individually or in peer study groups. Advance organizers can improve learning and retention without significantly increasing study time.

Chapter-Opening Vignettes

Every chapter begins with a **vignette** that shows the power of psychology in understanding a range of human behaviours. This theme is reinforced throughout the chapter, celebrating the extraordinary processes that make the everyday possible.

Social Cognition: Attitudes

LEARNING OBJECTIVE 1

Explain how attitudes form and change and what role they play in behaviour.

There are few things in our world that we do not evaluate in some form or another. On some evaluations, people tend to agree. For example, most people believe that poverty is bad, that horror movies are scary and that Olympic Games pro-

component) and believed they were safe (cognitive component). Similarly, before the earthquake in 2011, most residents of north-east Japan felt relatively safe and secure and went about their lives accordingly. Clearly, the attitudes of those living in the United States and in Japan would change markedly following the impact of these major events. Attitudes, then, can and do change. We will explain how that can happen later in this section; but first, let us discuss how attitudes form in the first place.

Nature or Nurture?

What shapes our mental life? Are we the product of our genetic heritage (nature) or our upbringing and environment (nurture)? This has been a fundamental philosophical question since Antiquity, when Plato espoused the view that children were born with innate knowledge, and is not one that can be easily answered. Consider, for example, Chang and Eng, the conjoined siblings who gave us the term *Siamese Twins*. Born in 1811 in the Kingdom of Siam (now Thailand), the twins became world-famous medical curiosities, touring many countries and eventually settling in the United States. As you might expect, there was much in their behaviour to demonstrate how alike they were: they shared many beliefs, opinions and habits, and were rarely heard talking to each other (fuelling stories that they were telepathic). However, there were also striking differences between them. Chang was more dominant, with a quick intellect and a short temper, whereas Eng was a quieter, more considered individual, with a wider range of interests. ∎

Helpful study tools . . .

Following each section is a **Before You Go On** feature that helps you check you mastery of the important items covered. **What Do You Know?** questions ask you to stop and review the key concepts just presented. **What Do You Think?** questions encourage you to think critically on key questions in the chapter.

Before You Go On

What Do You Know?

1. What is sensory transduction?
2. What are absolute and difference thresholds?
3. Compare and contrast bottom-up and top-down processing.

What Do You Think?

Describe examples of sensory adaptation that you have experienced in two or more of your sensory modalities.

Intersecting with the text material at just the right points on each page are **features boxes** highlighting research findings, real life examples and practical suggestions, and selected photos.

PSYCHOLOGY AROUND US   Living by the Railway

Tassi *et al.* (2010) investigated the long-term effects of living next to a railway on sleep and cardiovascular reactivity. They took 20 men who lived next to a railway track and 20 men who lived in a quiet environment and compared their sleep in the laboratory on both a quiet night and a night with 30 simulated trains passing by. They found that those who lived next to the railway showed less sleep disturbance, and less of a cardiovascular response to the noise of the trains, than those who did not live next to the railway line. This is because of a long-term habituation to the noise of the trains in those who lived by the railway.

PRACTICALLY SPEAKING   Using Punishments and Rewards to Teach Children

Although both reinforcement and punishment are effective ways of altering behaviour in laboratory learning studies, evidence from real-life situations suggests these two approaches may not be equally effective. Positive reinforcement seems to be more effective than punishment for teaching young children, for example. One exception to this general rule is in cases where children put themselves in immediate danger. At such times, a harsh telling-off may be much more effective at stopping the behaviour.

One reason that positive reinforcement seems more effective may be because punishment is often misused. Research suggests the following guidelines for using punishment effectively to promote learning:

- Positive punishment is most effective when it occurs immediately after the incorrect behaviour.
- Punishment is effective only when it is clear that the punishment is a consequence of a specific behaviour, rather than, say, a result of the teacher or caregiver's bad mood or general dislike for the child.
- Punishment works only when its aversive component outweighs any reward obtained by the behaviour. It is difficult and often unethical to devise a punishment that far outweighs the rewarding aspect of the behaviour.

Margin Definitions define the key terms discussed in the text.

important that psychologists can disentangle developmental changes from practice effects.

Seeking to obtain the advantages and avoid the drawbacks of cross-sectional and longitudinal designs, some developmental researchers design studies that combine the two. One such combined research method is the **cohort-sequential design**. Here, researchers look at how age groups compare with one another at various points in the research, but they also look at how any differences between the groups vary over time (de Haan *et al.*, 2010). For

cohort-sequential design a blended cross-sectional and longitudinal research design that follows at least two different age groups over time.

Another approach is known as **developmental trajectory** analysis (see Thomas *et al.*, 2009). This method of study is particularly useful for understanding developmental disorders (such as Down syndrome or Williams syndrome, both of which result from genetic abnormalities and have associated cognitive profiles). When testing special populations such as these it is often difficult to find an appropriate control sample of typically developing children to compare them with. Instead, this method takes measurements on the same task from a

developmental trajectory an approach that measures how a group or population follow a common developmental course (i.e., between chronological age and another variable).

Seeing the 'big picture' in Psychology

Tying It Together

Every chapter on a substantive area of psychology not only offers a thorough presentation of the nature, explanations, and applications of that area, but also includes *recurring* sections on the *development, brain function, individual differences,* and *disorders or rarities* that occur in that realm of mental life. At the end of each chapter these themes are brought together in a Tying It Together summary section.

WHAT HAPPENS IN THE BRAIN?

- Low activity of the neurotransmitter GABA has been linked to several anxiety disorders.
- Low serotonin and low noradrenaline activity have been linked to depression.
- High dopamine activity accompanies schizophrenia.
- Improper functioning of various brain structures and brain circuits has also been linked to psychological disorders.

OUT OF THE ORDINARY

- Around 18% of adults suffer from one or more of the anxiety disorders, making them possibly the most common of psychological disorders.
- Around 7% of adults experience major depressive disorder, whereas 1% display bipolar disorder.
- Around 1% of adults suffer from schizophrenia, but that includes 3% of all divorced or separated people.

HOW WE DIFFER

- Poor people experience more psychological disorders than wealthy people.
- Women with depression and panic disorders outnumber men with these disorders by at least two to one.
- Those in the East tend to somatize their anxiety, whereas those in the West present psychological symptoms.
- People with high sensitivity to bodily cues are more likely to develop certain anxiety disorders and somatoform disorders.

HOW WE DEVELOP

- Traumas and significant losses during childhood can increase the likelihood of adult depression developing.
- People who acquire dysfunctional attitudes early in life are more at risk of developing generalized anxiety disorder, social anxiety disorder and depression in adolescence or adulthood.
- Individuals whose childhoods are filled with uncontrollable events increase their risk of developing depression.
- People who develop resilience in life can overcome early risk factors for psychopathology.

Your Brain and Behaviour

It's our hope that you will come to see the fascination of normal behaviour and develop a passion for this field of study. One example of how we demonstrate this to you is a regular feature throughout the textbook — called **Your Brain and Behaviour**. Focusing on a common everyday activity, these lively spreads clarify the remarkable brain events that help give life to the activity and serve as fascinating reminders that psychology is everywhere.

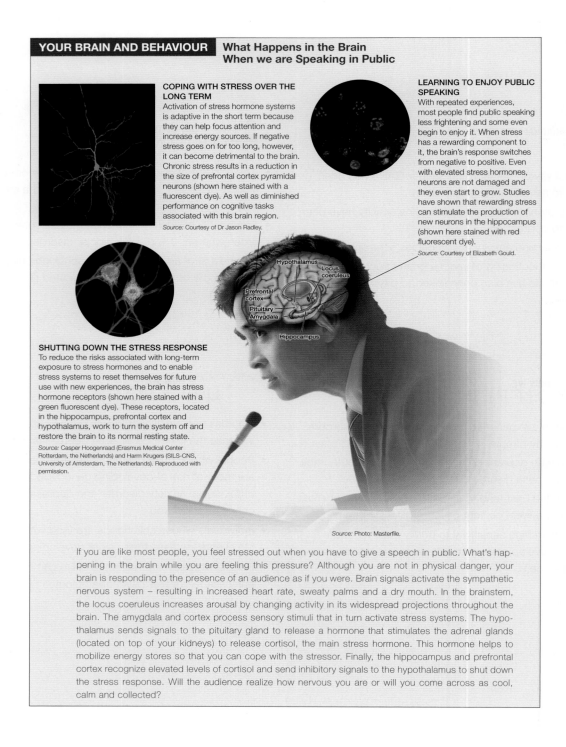

YOUR BRAIN AND BEHAVIOUR   **What Happens in the Brain When we are Speaking in Public**

COPING WITH STRESS OVER THE LONG TERM
Activation of stress hormone systems is adaptive in the short term because they can help focus attention and increase energy sources. If negative stress goes on for too long, however, it can become detrimental to the brain. Chronic stress results in a reduction in the size of prefrontal cortex pyramidal neurons (shown here stained with a fluorescent dye). As well as diminished performance on cognitive tasks associated with this brain region.
Source: Courtesy of Dr Jason Radley.

LEARNING TO ENJOY PUBLIC SPEAKING
With repeated experiences, most people find public speaking less frightening and some even begin to enjoy it. When stress has a rewarding component to it, the brain's response switches from negative to positive. Even with elevated stress hormones, neurons are not damaged and they even start to grow. Studies have shown that rewarding stress can stimulate the production of new neurons in the hippocampus (shown here stained with red fluorescent dye).
Source: Courtesy of Elizabeth Gould.

SHUTTING DOWN THE STRESS RESPONSE
To reduce the risks associated with long-term exposure to stress hormones and to enable stress systems to reset themselves for future use with new experiences, the brain has stress hormone receptors (shown here stained with a green fluorescent dye). These receptors, located in the hippocampus, prefrontal cortex and hypothalamus, work to turn the system off and restore the brain to its normal resting state.
Source: Casper Hoogenraad (Erasmus Medical Center Rotterdam, the Netherlands) and Harm Krugers (SILS-CNS, University of Amsterdam, The Netherlands). Reproduced with permission.

Hypothalamus
Locus coeruleus
Prefrontal cortex
Pituitary
Amygdala
Hippocampus

Source: Photo: Masterfile.

If you are like most people, you feel stressed out when you have to give a speech in public. What's happening in the brain while you are feeling this pressure? Although you are not in physical danger, your brain is responding to the presence of an audience as if you were. Brain signals activate the sympathetic nervous system – resulting in increased heart rate, sweaty palms and a dry mouth. In the brainstem, the locus coeruleus increases arousal by changing activity in its widespread projections throughout the brain. The amygdala and cortex process sensory stimuli that in turn activate stress systems. The hypothalamus sends signals to the pituitary gland to release a hormone that stimulates the adrenal glands (located on top of your kidneys) to release cortisol, the main stress hormone. This hormone helps to mobilize energy stores so that you can cope with the stressor. Finally, the hippocampus and prefrontal cortex recognize elevated levels of cortisol and send inhibitory signals to the hypothalamus to shut down the stress response. Will the audience realize how nervous you are or will you come across as cool, calm and collected?

Review Main Concepts

Chapter Summary

The end-of-chapter **Summary** reviews the main concepts presented in the chapter with reference to the specific Learning Objectives. It provides you with another opportunity to review what you have learned as well as to see how the key topics within the chapter fit together. The **Key Terms** are grouped together with the page numbers where they appear in the chapter.

Summary

Theories of Motivation

LEARNING OBJECTIVE 1 Compare and contrast major theories of motivation.

* Several theories offer explanations for our motivation but no single theory can explain all our behaviour.
* Instinct theory, which suggests that environmental cues stimulate innate behavioural instincts, best explains motivation that serves basic biological drives, such as eating, drinking and sex.
* Drive-reduction theory suggests that internal homeostatic mechanisms produce balance within the body by reducing arousal stemming from unmet basic biological needs.
* Arousal theory explains why we sometimes seek to increase, arousal levels. The Yerkes–Dodson law proposes that task performance is best if our arousal level matches that needed for a task.
* Incentive learning produces extrinsic motivation to engage in experiences that do not fulfil basic biological drives. Primary and secondary incentives may both be involved. Different incentives motivate different people.
* Incentive motivation involves brain systems associated with pleasure, incentive learning and the neurochemical opiate dopamine.
* Maslow proposed that we are motivated by a hierarchy of needs, in which basic survival needs must be satisfied before higher-level needs for belonging, achievement and self-actualization.

Biological Motivations: Hunger

LEARNING OBJECTIVE 2 Summarize physical and psychological factors that affect our levels of hunger and our eating behaviour.

* Hunger, our motivation to eat, is created by the interaction of signals from our stomachs, levels of food-related chemicals in our blood and brain activity, particularly in the hypothalamus.
* Culture and individual differences interact with our basic biological need for food to determine what foods we will eat, when and with whom we like to eat and how much we eat.

* Obesity is a major public health problem in the United States. It is usually caused by overeating, which can result from an interaction between genes and the environment.
* Anorexia nervosa is an eating disorder in which individuals believe they are fat and eat too little. Bulimia nervosa is an eating disorder in which people binge on food to then purge themselves of the food before it can add weight to their bodies.

Biological Motivations: Sex

LEARNING OBJECTIVE 3 Describe factors that affect our sexual motivation and behaviour.

* Sexual practices vary widely as a result of cultural influences. Research consistently shows much variety in normal sexual behaviour throughout healthy adulthood.
* Sex researchers have described a four-stage sexual response cycle.
* Testosterone and other hormones affect our motivation towards sexual behaviour. Many parts of our brains become active during sexual arousal and behaviour.
* Four types of sexual problems may occur: sexual dysfunctions, paraphilias, gender identity disorder and medical problems.

Psychological Motivations: Affiliation and Achievement

LEARNING OBJECTIVE 4 Describe factors that influence our psychological motivations for affiliation and achievement.

* Affiliation represents our need to interact with others, not only for survival but also for self-worth.
* Isolation puts people at risk of psychological impairments.
* Self-determination theory suggests that we need competence, relatedness and autonomy to realize our potential.
* Achievement through intrinsic motivation does not involve incentives.
* Individuals who are able to delay gratification can focus on goals and ignore distractions.

Key Terms

basic emotions 420
bipolar disorder 428
Cannon–Bard theory of emotion 416
cognitive-mediational theory of emotion 418
depression 428
differential emotions theory 421

display rules 426
emotion 408
emotion dysregulation 424
emotional intensity 423
facial efference 418
facial-feedback theory of emotion 418
generalized anxiety disorder 428

James–Lange theory of emotion 415
major depressive disorder 428
mania 428
obsessive-compulsive disorder (OCD) 428
panic disorder 428
phobia 428

Schachter and Singer's two-factor theory of emotion 416

Online Study Tools

- Student companion website at **www.wiley.com/college/comer**

On this website you will find tools for every chapter that will allow you to assess your understanding of chapter concepts. You can study and revise using Self Test Quizzes, drag and drop interactivities, mind maps, crosswords and key term Flash Cards.

- Interactive e-book at **www.wileyopenpage.com**

An interactive e-book is included with every copy of the book (via the access code inside the front cover). The e-book has embedded media including videos, quizzes and activities that are found in the text right where you need it. Putting students in the driver's seat, this enables easy access to tools that will help you absorb key concepts and test your understanding. You can also personalize your e-book by making notes, voice annotations, creating links to the text or to websites and by highlighting sections.

Look for these icons in the text that show you where media has been embedded.

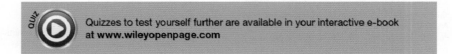

Quizzes to test yourself further are available in your interactive e-book at www.wileyopenpage.com

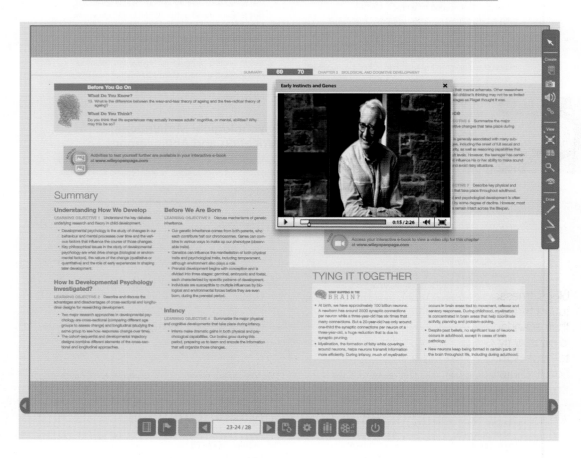

CHAPTER 1

Psychology: Yesterday and Today

Adapted by Alan Porter,
University of Westminster, UK

CHAPTER OUTLINE

- What Is Psychology?

- Psychology's Roots in Philosophy

- The Founding of Psychology

- Psychology in the 21st Century: Cognitive Psychology, Neuroscience and Evolution

- The Diversity of Psychology and Psychological Literacy

 Access your interactive e-book to view a video clip for this chapter at **www.wileyopenpage.com**

The Rise of Information Technology

The idea for a World Wide Web was first proposed by Tim Berners-Lee in 1989. Since then, information technology has extended into all of our worlds. People keep in touch through social networks, blogs, messaging services and video calls; students get course information and interact with their tutors through virtual learning environments; businesses sell goods and services online and promote their brands through online advertising campaigns; and so on. The reach of information technology is constantly being extended and evolving into new and unexpected forms. We are currently getting to grips with understanding the consequences of this new technology for how we process information and interact with each other. Already we are seeing how videos posted on the Internet can make powerful political propaganda. Micro blogging services were used to organize resistance during the Arab Spring revolts and, apparently, to coordinate looting and rioting in the United Kingdom in 2011. A completely new vocabulary, including 'tweeting', 'FBing' and 'sexting', has been coined to describe activities that were unknown only a generation ago.

How do these technologies fit in with our basic cognitive and emotional make-up? Do they fundamentally change us or does their use fit in with processes that were fixed thousands of years ago? ■

These are the types of questions that the science of psychology tries to answer. Of course, they are not the only questions; indeed, there are many. In this book, for example, we will examine questions of human development, asking how we mature from birth, through childhood to old age. We will look at what drives and motivates us, how we characterize and understand the wide range of emotions and feelings that we all experience. Along the way, our goal is to help you get insights not only into the attention-grabbing things that can go wrong but also into the often-overlooked but miraculous things that

usually go right. Many interesting examples are highlighted in 'Psychology around Us' boxes. We have also included several 'Practically Speaking' boxes, which we hope will help you in your academic and working life. Every journey needs a first step. In this chapter, the first step is to learn how the science of psychology has been defined in very different ways and with fundamentally different assumptions and goals. This has led to the development of different approaches and perspectives within psychology. To understand these different approaches and perspectives we will examine the origins of the discipline.

PSYCHOLOGY AROUND US Myth vs. Reality

Go to a party and tell strangers that you are a psychologist, and they will most likely ask you if you can read their body language or if you know what they are thinking. It is quite likely that they will tell *you* what psychology is all about and start sharing their diagnoses of their friends and of themselves. They may well tell you all about their anxieties or phobias. Most people believe that all psychologists are therapists, when, in fact, clinical psychology is but one speciality in a field that includes cognitive, social, developmental and sports psychology, among many others. Like most scientific fields, many myths surround psychology, myths that lead to inaccurate stereotypes about psychologists and the phenomena that they study. Here are a few of them:

MYTH #1: The nature versus nurture debate was put to rest years ago. *In fact, it is still very much alive in psychology.*

MYTH #2: Most mental disorders have clear and dominant biological causes. *It just seems that way because so many drug treatments are available for people with psychological problems. In fact, we still have much to learn in this realm.*

MYTH #3: The brain does not produce new neurons after childhood. *Actually, current research indicates that new neurons continue to be formed throughout life, even in old age.*

MYTH #4: As most people age, all of their mental functions decline. *In fact, in normal ageing, many mental functions hold up very well, and some actually improve, for example vocabulary and certain other verbal skills.*

What Is Psychology?

LEARNING OBJECTIVE 1

Give definitions of psychology, and describe the goals and levels of analysis of different approaches to psychological sciences.

Chances are that you, like Marc below, often find yourself reflecting on why people, including you, think and act as they do. You may wonder, for example, why you cannot seem to settle down and start your assignment. You may be curious about why a

friend of yours is attracted to someone you find repulsive. You may sense that a family member is depressed and may try to think of ways you can help. All of us, in short, have an interest in understanding other people and ourselves either for practical reasons or simply because it is such a fascinating subject.

The systematic, empirical study (or science) of selves and others is known as **psychology**. Psychology jostles for room amidst other sciences such as sociology, linguistics, anthropology and economics and borrows ideas

psychology the systematic study of selves and others.

PSYCHOLOGY AROUND US More than a Train Ride

Marc looked around the train. He noticed a child watching his mother expectantly, while the mother stared out of the train window, looking tired and distracted. He saw a man bobbing his head ever so slightly to the sound of whatever was playing on his iPod. And he observed a woman who looked sad and downcast.

Marc also noticed that all of these passengers acted in similar ways. For example, no one made eye contact. If someone

happened to catch Marc's eye, the passenger would quickly cast his or her eyes down, like pulling a hand from a hot stove. When someone sat down next to an already seated passenger, the passenger always seemed to move his or her body—sometimes a little, sometimes a lot, but always immediately. Was there meaning in these patterns, Marc wondered, or was each person on the train making an individual choice?

from and lends them to the neurosciences and medical sciences, including psychiatry. Psychology is not just an academic subject taught and learnt for its own sake; it also refers to a profession with carefully considered entrance qualifications, ethical standards and rules of conduct providing expert advice and guidance based on research evidence in realms of human life, including mental disorders, education and business.

Psychology as the Science of Mind or Behaviour, or Both?

What unites psychologists is their commitment to building accounts of selves and others on the foundations of systematic, empirical research. It is not enough to simply cite authority or opinion. Theories in psychology must be backed up by research evidence and logical argument. As we shall see when we look at the history of psychology, some psychologists begin their account of what it is to be human by looking inwards and examining **mental**

mental processes activities of our brain when it is engaged in thinking, observing the environment and using language.

introspect to study one's own mental states and feelings, hence introspection.

processes. These mental processes include complex experiences, such as anger love and even the act of lying. During psychology's early history, the primary method for exploring internal mental processes was to **introspect** (i.e. to carefully describe one's experiences). For these early psychologists, psychology was primarily a science of

mind. Other psychologists distrusted introspection and attempted to build a science of psychology not on how an individual privately *experiences* the world but on what any individual, irrespective of their background, opinions or motivations could directly observe when looking at themselves or others, in other words publicly observable behaviour.

For much of the history of psychology these two perspectives have been mutually exclusive; psychologists were either for *mind* or for *behaviour*, but not both! Some psychologists have tried to build bridges between the two approaches or have tried to show that mind is really behaviour or that behaviour is really mind.

When you read the upcoming chapters, you can try to identify which perspective is taken in particular theories or research studies.

When psychologists study mental processes and behaviour, irrespective of whether they are more interested in mind or behaviour, they generally have one of the six following goals in mind:

- *Description*. Psychologists seek to *describe* very specifically the things that they observe. As you

read this book, you will see that psychologists have described phenomena ranging from how babies learn to talk to how humans fall in love, make decisions and more.

- *Explanation*. Telling what, where, when and how are sometimes not enough. A key goal for many psychologists is to answer the question 'Why?' As we will see in Chapter 2, psychologists have developed hypotheses and theories to *explain* a huge variety of events, from why we get hungry to why we either like or do not like parties.

- *Prediction*. Psychologists also seek to *predict* the circumstances under which a variety of behaviours and mental process are likely. You will learn later in this book, for example, about research that predicts the conditions under which we are most likely to offer help to a stranger in need.

- *Control*. We often encounter situations in which we want to limit or increase certain behaviours or mental processes, be they our own or those of others. Psychology can give people advice on controlling behaviours, ranging from how to limit unhealthy stress to how to remember more from a class.

- *Understanding*. Sometimes, we encounter people or situations that we find completely incomprehensible. This may be the case when we study people from very different cultures who engage in practices we find perplexing. For example, in some cultures female circumcision is seen as a natural part of growing up, while for those of us not brought up in that culture the practice is both criminal and abhorrent.

- *Personal Development*. Some psychologists argue that prediction and control miss some of the important dimensions of human existence. They argue that becoming a more rounded and happier person is the central focus of psychological research. The humanistic psychologists, who we will discuss later, are examples of this point of view.

In order to describe, explain, predict, control and understand mental activity and behaviours or, for that matter, change or develop oneself, we need to recognize how these processes are embedded in complex webs of influence. We can categorize these influences in a series of levels, starting from what goes on within the individual (*intra-personal*), such as brain and cognitive process, then moving to explanations that use processes that go on between individuals (*inter-personal*) to explanations which depend on group

TABLE 1.1 The Levels of Analysis in Psychology

Level	What Is Analysed
Intra-personal processes	Processes that go on 'under the skin' or in the brain. The biological correlates of intelligence or personality would fit in here
Inter-personal processes	Processes that occur once an individual encounters someone else. The phenomenon of social facilitation when the mere presence of another person improves performance on a wide variety of tasks would fit in here
Inter-group processes	Processes that are affected by group membership. A football fan will react differently to meeting a rival fan from how they will react to meeting an individual who supports the same team
Cultural / Societal processes	Processes that are related to broad cultural factors. Social psychologists have found that in Western countries which embrace an individualistic way of thinking judgements about success and failure are different from those in cultures which stress the importance of communal life

membership (*inter-group*) and finally cultural factors (*cultural/societal*) (Table 1.1).

These levels of analysis are not mutually exclusive. Consider, for example, the psychology of inter-personal attraction. To fully understand why we find some people more attractive than others, we may need to look at a genetic contribution since evolutionary psychologists have argued that certain physical attributes indicate fitness to breed and that we are therefore 'pre-programmed' to find them attractive (intra-personal level). We may need to look at reciprocity in a relationship: we find people attractive if they find us attractive. This would be at the inter-personal level of analysis. At the inter-group level, we may have to consider the social background of the individuals; social class, for example, may influence how we dress, which in turn identifies us as belonging to certain groups. At the cultural level we may have to consider their shared beliefs about appropriate conduct for men and women and the expression of interest in the opposite sex.

We have examined what kinds of phenomena psychologists study. Next, we will consider how the different approaches and perspectives we find in contemporary psychology started life. We will discuss how psychology got its start, how historical and societal factors have affected what psychologists do and how psychologists have shifted their energies among the different goals and levels of analysis over time. We will then consider where the field of psychology is today and where it may be going tomorrow.

Before You Go On

What Do You Know?

1. How is behaviour different from mental processes?
2. What are the four levels of analysis in psychology?

What Do You Think?

Why might understanding the use of social networks need to include intra-personal, inter-personal, inter-group and cultural levels of explanation?

Psychology's Roots in Philosophy

LEARNING OBJECTIVE 2

Describe how from the time of the Ancient Greeks to the mid-19th century philosophers and scientists viewed the relationship between mind, body and soul.

In a time before universities and specialist subjects, Ancient Greek thinkers knew no academic boundaries and mixed topics and debates that today we think of as belonging to specific areas of inquiry, such as psychology, moral philosophy, the philosophy of science, theology, physics, biology and medicine. One topic that concerned many Ancient Greeks thinkers was identifying what it is that distinguishes the living from the dead and distinguishes human beings from other living beings. They speculated that these differences were the result of humans having or being *psuche*, or 'souls', and put forward different accounts of the relationship between the soul and the body, the persistence or otherwise of the soul after death and how the soul can come to know the world. It is from the Ancient Greek word *psuche* that we eventually got the 'psych-' of psychology.

The most well known of the Ancient Greek thinkers are Socrates (*c.* 470–399 BCE), Plato (*c.* 427–347 BCE) and Aristotle (*c.* 384–322 BCE). These thinkers have influenced generations of Western thinkers, and many psychologists still refer to them to this day. Socrates left no written work so we only know of him through the writings of his pupil Plato. Socrates cultivated the idea of living an 'examined' life, during which one must

FIGURE 1.1 Hippocrates' psychological theory. This medieval manuscript illustrates the psychological effects of the humours proposed by the Greek physician. The illustration on the left demonstrates the melancholia produced by black bile, while the one on the right depicts the joyous, musical and passionate personality produced by blood.

Source: The Granger Collection, New York. Reproduced with permission.

question authority and receive opinion and put arguments to the test through the employment of logic. Plato argued that we live in a world of endlessly shifting shadows and that philosophers could show us how to move out of these shadows to a sunlit world of pure, eternal knowledge. Plato likened the human predicament to a charioteer trying to drive and control two wild and powerful horses. One horse represented our appetites; the other, pride and passion; the charioteer represented reason. For Plato, the bodily seat of reason was in the brain. He deemed the world around us as temporary and cruel and something to be escaped. This was not the case for Aristotle, the son of a medical doctor, who took a keen interest in natural history. Aristotle found the world to be a never-ending source of wonder. One of his basic theories was that there were different kinds of souls and that these souls could be placed in a hierarchy. The simplest soul is the 'vegetative' soul found in plants, which allows them to grow and reproduce. Animals have a 'vegetative' soul and a 'sensitive' soul, which allows them to perceive the world around them. Humans have a 'vegetative', 'sensitive' and, crucially, a 'rational' soul. This rational soul is capable of reflection and language.

Ancient Greek physicians, or medical doctors, contributed to debates on the nature of the soul. Hippocrates (c. 460–377 BCE), a Greek physician, argued that the universe was built up from four elements: fire, water, earth and air. These elements were found in the body in the form of *humours* – four bodily fluids (blood, phlegm, yellow bile and black bile). A person's particular combination of humours, argued Hippocrates, determined their character and well-being and predicted their responses to various situations. Hippocrates

also correctly identified the brain as the organ of mental life (Figure 1.1). Ancient Greek philosophy was kept alive by the Romans, but after the fall of the Roman Empire many Greek and Latin texts were lost. The vigorous debate of the Ancient Greeks was replaced by reverence for God and the authority of the Church. Christian thinkers developed philosophical ideas within the bounds of Christian thinking and fused the philosophy of the Ancient Greeks with Biblical teaching. St Augustine produced a version of Platonism compatible with the Church, and St Thomas Aquinas produced a Christian version of Aristotle. These teachings formed the core curriculum of the newly formed universities and persisted for centuries.

The Scientific Revolution

During the 16th and 17th centuries, some of the accepted teachings of the Church about the world and, in particular, the reliance on the rote learning of Aristotle, was questioned by thinkers such as Francis Bacon (1561–1626) in England and René Descartes (1596–1650) in France. Isaac Newton (1642–1727) revolutionized physics by showing how diverse events such as the falling of an apple and the motion of the planets could be understood using the concept of gravitation and that the theory could generate predictions that could be tested through observation. Two great philosophical traditions emerged. Following Descartes, the *rationalists* stressed the importance of clear and distinct ideas which could only be identified by ignoring our senses. This view was often associated with the theory that knowledge was innate and simply needed working out through the application of reason. A good

Charles Darwin (1809–1882) The theories by the English naturalist about human evolution opened the way for later psychologists to understand the mind as a natural phenomenon.

example of a rationalist philosopher is Gottfried Leibniz (1646–1716). In contrast, the *empiricists* argued that sensory information is all that we have and that all knowledge must be traced back to the sensations that cause them. A good example of an empiricist philosopher is John Locke, who popularized the blank slate, or *tabula rasa*, hypothesis, which states that our mind is empty of content at birth and must be filled with the knowledge gained from experience. The implications of rationalist and empiricist accounts of knowledge, and the types of minds we must have to have that knowledge, were worked out over the following centuries. Immanuel Kant's (1724–1804) ultimately failed attempt to reconcile the two traditions helped to continue the development of Western thought.

During the 18th and 19th centuries, physiological and medical knowledge was developing and anatomists began to map the brain and the structure of the nervous system. This process was advanced when German scientists began to use the methodological techniques employed by physicists in the field of physiology. Johannes Müller (1801–1858) showed that some nerves delivered impulses from the sense receptors to the brain while others delivered motor impulses from the brain to the muscles. A student of Müller's, Hermann von Helmholtz (1821–1894), managed in 1850 to measure the speed of the nervous impulse by timing how long it took for a frog's muscle to contract after the nerve connected to it was stimulated. In England, Charles Darwin showed that the development of different species could be explained in terms of natural variation and selection and that there was no reason for supposing that human attributes could not be explained in the same way. Post Darwin, a non-religious account of the development of the *psuche* was available.

Before You Go On

What Do You Know?

3. What are the major differences between Plato's and Aristotle's views of the relationship between the body and the mind?

4. Compare and contrast rationalist and empiricist accounts of the mind.

What Do You Think?

Another word for 'black bile' is 'melancholia'. When people are sad or depressed, they can be described as melancholic. When people are cheerful, they can be described as sanguine. In English, we use the language of the humours to describe people. Is this evidence that Hippocrates was correct after all?

The Founding of Psychology

LEARNING OBJECTIVE 3

Name important early psychologists and describe the main schools of psychological theories: introspection, psychoanalysis, functionalism, psychometrics, Gestalt, behaviourism and humanistic.

Against this background of increasing technical sophistication and an increasing willingness to think of humans as 'natural' rather than 'spiritual' beings, psychology by the end of the 19th century had emerged as a separate scientific field of investigation and by the mid-20th century distinctive approaches and perspectives on the subject had developed. We will now consider seven of these approaches, or perspectives, that have been particularly influential.

Wundt and Introspection (1)

In 1879, a former assistant to von Helmholtz, Wilhelm Wundt (1832–1920), opened a laboratory in Leipzig,

Germany dedicated to the study of psychology. Wundt had wide interests encompassing philosophy, history, ethics and anthropology. Psychology was, for Wundt, the foundation for these other disciplines because it was based on immediate or direct experience. The data for other disciplines, such as physics or history, were abstracted from these immediate data so a study of psychology was a logical priority. Fundamental to Wundt's psychology was his idea that the mind is not a thing but an activity and that when we experience the world we do so from a particular perspective that we construct on the basis of our history and situation. Our experience is therefore a result of selection and is an action of the will rather than a passive recording of what is in front of us. This approach to the mind is known as **voluntarism**.

voluntarism the doctrine that states that all our mental life is motivated, that our mental life is not a passive reflection of the world around us.

To study psychological processes Wundt advocated the use of introspection in very carefully controlled conditions. He believed that psychology could only study simple mental phenomena and that more complex phenomenon which relied on language or culture needed different methods of research. He therefore made a clear distinction between experimental psychology and a form of cultural psychology he called *Völkerpsychologie*. Wundt's experimental psychology generated huge interest and his students went around the world founding their own psychology laboratories. Wundt wrote many volumes on *Völkerpsychologie* in which he analysed the writings of anthropologists, linguists and historians in an attempt to understand how cultures develop.

Psychoanalysis: Psychology of the Unconscious (2)

Wundt was instrumental in founding psychology in the academic setting of the university. A close contemporary of Wundt did not work in an academic environment but instead worked in the *psychiatric hospital* and the *private consulting room*.

Sigmund Freud (1856–1939) was a Viennese neurologist who suggested that many of our thoughts and feelings existed beyond the realm of conscious awareness and could not be revealed by *introspection*. This **unconscious** mind is organized around basic and often socially unacceptable desires. To stress how alien these desires are to our normal selves, Freud called this part of the mind the **id**, or the 'it'. These desires are kept in check by a part of the mind that is geared to self-protection and dealing with reality. This part of the

unconscious a hypothesized repository of thoughts, feelings and sensations outside human awareness, thought in some theories to have a strong bearing on human behaviour.

id according to psychoanalytic theory, the personality element representing basic instinctual drives.

mind Freud called the **ego**. To reveal these hidden parts of the mind that the ego represses Freud invented the technique of **psychoanalysis**. When we are sleeping, our mind is at its most relaxed and, therefore, the ego is at its weakest. By talking about one's dreams to an analyst the patient could understand what was going on in his or her unconscious. Finally, Freud recognized that we are not just governed by blind desire and self-protection: we can act morally. The part of the mind that generates moral judgements Freud called the **superego**. Freud explained the development of these parts of the mind. He argued that the child is born into the world as a little bundle of simple and pressing desires for food and comfort (id processes) and through processes of maturation and interaction with parents and others develops an ego and superego.

ego a personality element that works to help satisfy the drives of the id while complying with the constraints of the environment.

psychoanalysis the theory, developed by Freud, suggesting our psychological functioning is the result of the dynamic interplay of forces of which we are largely unaware.

superego a personality element in charge of determining which impulses are acceptable to express openly.

Freud's theories have been controversial since they were first published. This controversy is, in part, because of Freud's direct discussion of the development of sexuality through childhood and adulthood. It is still the case that psychoanalysis has a firmer foothold in the clinic than the university.

Functionalism: The Practical Application of Psychology (3)

William James (1842–1910) set up the first psychology laboratory in the United States at Harvard University and wrote one of the first important psychology texts, *Principles of Psychology*. James was both a psychologist and a philosopher. As a philosopher, he is associated with **pragmatism**, the doctrine that knowledge is to be evaluated in terms of its usefulness rather than by eternal standards. As a psychologist, James described himself as a **functionalist** in order to stress the purposefulness of mental life. In this sense he agreed with the voluntarism of Wundt. James did not produce a systematic overarching theory of psychology but was highly influential. He stressed that psychological knowledge should be used to benefit humanity and emphasized the need for research to include animals, children and persons with mental disorders in order to understand both normal and abnormal psychological functioning (Stam, 2010; Richardson, 2006).

pragmatism an American philosophical movement that argued that our theories are evaluated by examining their practical consequences.

functionalists someone who believes that mental processes have purpose, and that the focus of study should be on how the mind adapts those purposes to changing environments.

Spurred on by the functionalists' efforts to provide more useful information, psychology began to tackle socially relevant topics. The researchers William Lowe Bryan and Noble Harter (1897), for example, performed a famous investigation of how quickly telegraph operators could learn necessary typing skills. Their findings were used to improve training for railroad telegraphers, and the study is now widely regarded as one of the first to have a major social and commercial impact. Functionalism also marked the beginning of exploration into socially important issues such as learning and education. Indeed, *educational psychology* remains a key area of research in the field today.

Psychometrics: Measuring the Mind (4)

An approach to psychology that was also influenced by Darwinian ideas about the 'adaptive' function of the mind began life in England at around the same time as James was writing his famous textbook. Francis Galton (1822–1911), a cousin of Charles Darwin, was consumed by a passion for measurement, statistics and the theory of evolution. He put these passions together to found the **psychometrics** approach to psychology. Galton hoped to measure natural variation amongst people and to use this information to provide evidence for human evolution and to provide practical advice about human breeding. He called the latter project **eugenics**, which is a Greek term for 'good genes'. Galton assumed that many human characteristics such as ability and health were distributed according to a bell-shaped distribution that could be described in mathematically precise terms. From 1884 to 1885, Galton set up a laboratory at the South Kensington Museum in London to collect anthropometric (human measurement) data. While Galton's measurements in his laboratory were not found to be related to ability and his eugenics programme was used to justify

psychometrics an approach to the mind that uses tests to measure differences between people.

eugenics the controversial approach that attempts to use scientific principles to guide human breeding.

forced sterilizations of people deemed unfit to breed in both Europe and America, making his ideas controversial to this day, Galton's assumptions about the distribution of characteristics and the possibility of measuring human attributes influenced many psychologists, who went on to found their own anthropometric or psychometric laboratories.

Gestalt Psychology: More than Putting Together the Building Blocks (5)

Wundt's approach to psychology sharply distinguished between experimental psychology and *Völkerpsychologie*. His experimental psychology focused on a controlled introspection of simple processes. Other psychologists in Germany questioned this approach. They argued that Wundt's psychology experiments were artificial and the elements of consciousness they identified were abstractions and did not really exist in our experience. Exponents of **Gestalt psychology** – Max Wertheimer (1880–1943), Wolfgang Köhler (1887–1967) and Kurt Koffka (1886–1941) – argued that we perceive things as broad 'perceptual units' rather than as individual sensations. Indeed, the word *Gestalt* means 'whole' or 'form'. The school subscribed to the idea that 'the whole is greater than the sum of its parts'.

Gestalt psychology field of psychology arguing that we have inborn tendencies to structure what we see in particular ways and to structure our perceptions into broad perceptual units.

For example, when you watch TV, you see complete pictures. In fact, each picture is made up of thousands of small dots, called *pixels*. If you get close enough to the screen, you can see the picture break down. Even so, your brain still favours blending those dots into a whole picture. Similar findings have been gathered regarding our tendency to group eyes, noses and mouths into recognizable human faces. Children three months of age or younger show a preference for human faces, but only when the various parts of those faces are arranged correctly into a facial appearance (Turati *et al.*, 2010; Morton & Johnson, 1991).

PSYCHOLOGY AROUND US 'Music is My Religion'

This famous line is attributed to the legendary guitarist and songwriter Jimi Hendrix. Clearly, for Hendrix, music was a phenomenon whose wholeness was greater than the sum of its parts. Music is defined, fairly simply, as an arrangement of sounds that produces a continuous and unified auditory experience. Its elements include melody, tone, harmony, rhythm, pitch and timbre. But, of course, music is much, much more than the sum of these elements.

Like Hendrix, many musicians and songwriters have described music's broad, special and almost mystical powers.

Billy Joel said, 'Music in itself is healing.' Ray Charles claimed, 'Music [is] a necessity for me – like food or water.' Bono asserted that 'music can change the world because it can change people'. And Paul Simon proclaimed that 'music is forever'.

And let's not forget the impact of music on scholars, scientists and everyone else. Physicist Albert Einstein once said, 'I often think in music. I live my daydreams in music. I see my life in terms of music . . . I get most joy in life out of music.'

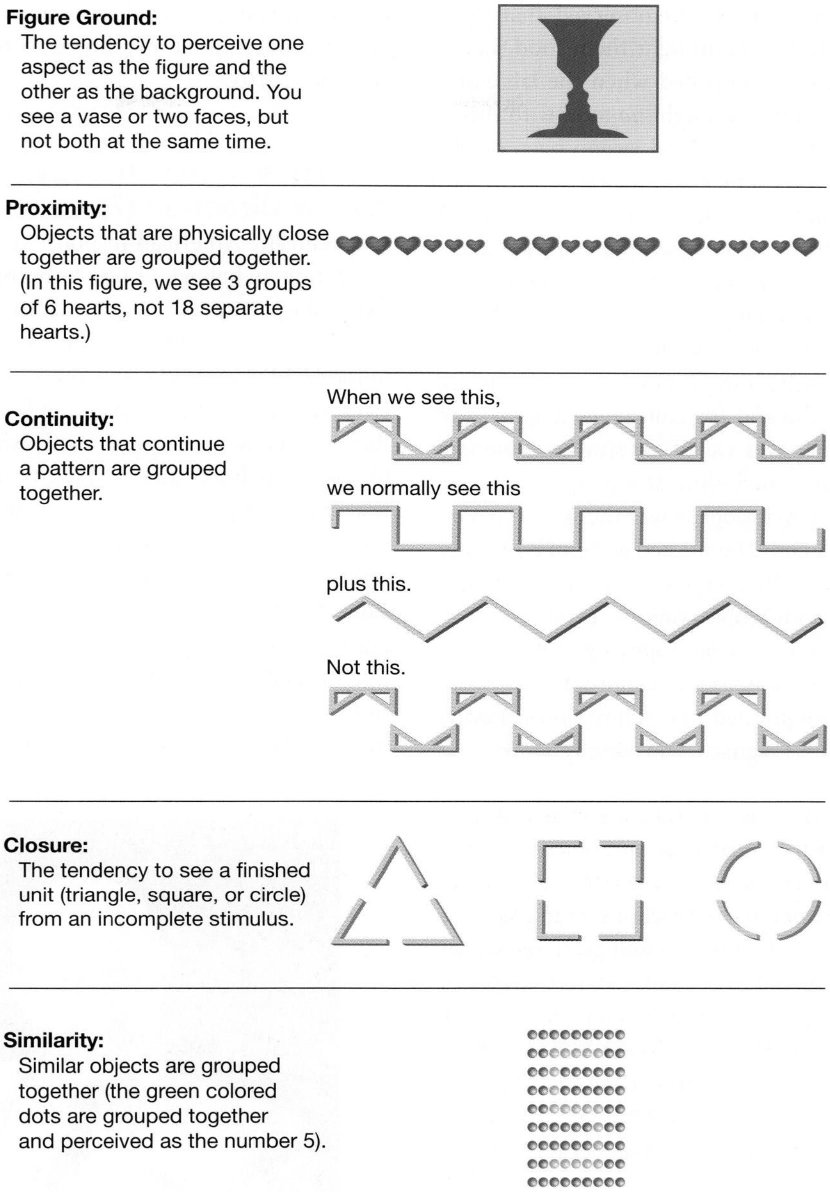

Figure Ground:
The tendency to perceive one aspect as the figure and the other as the background. You see a vase or two faces, but not both at the same time.

Proximity:
Objects that are physically close together are grouped together. (In this figure, we see 3 groups of 6 hearts, not 18 separate hearts.)

Continuity:
Objects that continue a pattern are grouped together.

When we see this,

we normally see this

plus this.

Not this.

Closure:
The tendency to see a finished unit (triangle, square, or circle) from an incomplete stimulus.

Similarity:
Similar objects are grouped together (the green colored dots are grouped together and perceived as the number 5).

FIGURE 1.2 Gestalt laws. Gestalt psychologists studied how we perceive stimuli as whole forms or figures rather than individual lines and curves.

Gestaltists developed over 100 principles to describe how the brain and sensory systems perceive environmental stimuli. Some of the Gestalt laws are shown in Figure 1.2. Gestaltists viewed learning as tied to *perception*: the recognition and identification of stimuli that come through our senses. (We will discuss perception later in this text: see Chapter 7.) They also believed that problem-solving occurs when a person develops a sudden and complete insight into a solution. Indeed, they believed that problems remain in an unsolved state until such insights occur. The Gestaltists took psychology to be a science of the mind and placed great emphasis on the importance of examining conscious experience.

Behaviourism: Psychology of Adaptation (6)

Another school of thought that emerged in the early 20th century took a very different approach to those of both psychoanalysts and Gestalt psychologists. This area of psychology, called **behaviourism**, was founded on the belief that psychology should study only publicly observable events rather than private, conscious processes. This approach to psychology has its roots in *laboratory* studies of animal behaviour.

Behaviourism originated in the United States and Russia. In Russia, the Nobel Prize-winning

behaviourism a branch of psychological thought arguing that psychology should study only directly observable behaviours rather than abstract mental processes.

physiologist Ivan Pavlov (1849–1936) observed that dogs salivated when his lab assistants brought them food. Later, he noticed that the dogs also salivated when the lab assistants appeared, even when they brought *no* food with them. The dogs had learnt, or in the technical jargon been *conditioned*, to associate one stimulus (food) with another (lab assistants) and to respond in the same way to both. You will read more about Pavlov's work in Chapter 9. By manipulating such factors such as how many times **stimuli** needed to be paired together for learning to take place or how learning could be extinguished by 'un-pairing' stimuli, Pavlov and his colleagues mapped the mechanisms of what later was called *classical conditioning* in a number of organisms, including sheep, apes and rats. Of particular interest to psychologists was the way in which relations between stimuli could be studied without bothering with introspective reports. In everyday language we might say that the dogs in Pavlov's observations 'expected' food when they saw the lab assistants or stopped getting excited and salivating when the lab assistants came into the room after they had been 'disappointed' too many times. Pavlov could dispense with this language and simply count and measure behaviours.

> **stimuli** an environmental trigger that changes our internal or external states.

John Watson (1878–1958) is generally credited with pioneering the school of behaviourism as an approach to the whole of psychology. He extended Pavlov's animal work to young children and extended the reactions that could be measured from physiological **responses** like salivating to emotional responses and motor responses such as moving one's leg.

> **responses** the ways we react to stimuli.

B. F. Skinner (1904–1990) emerged as the leading behaviourist after World War II. He developed the methods and theories of Edward Thorndike (1874–1949), who conceptualized learning not so much as an association between stimuli presented to a passive animal but as an association between a behaviour and its consequence. Skinner developed this idea and studied how an organism 'operated' on the environment, hence his labelling this kind of learning as **operant conditioning**. The details of classical conditioning and operant conditioning are described in Chapter 9.

> **operant conditioning** a form of associative learning whereby behaviour is modified depending on its consequences.

Behaviourism was not embraced by all, however. Some psychologists criticized John Watson and other prominent behaviourists for popularizing and, in their view, cheapening psychology by removing all reference to the mind and by suggesting that human behaviour, including art, poetry and philosophy, was no different except in complexity from the behaviour of a rat learning to run through a maze. In 1929, for example, psychologist Joseph Jastrow wrote that behaviourism's portrayal in popular magazines and newspapers undermined psychology's role as a valid science (Jastrow, 1929).

Humanistic Psychology: A New Direction (7)

A specifically American response to the perceived cheapening of human behaviour was **humanistic psychology**, which was orchestrated in the 1950s and 1960s by the so-called humanistic psychologists. These theorists rejected behaviourism and what they saw as the more pessimistic aspects of psychoanalysis, such as Freud's insistence that he could not make anyone happy, just reconciled to their ordinary, mundane lives. Instead, they focused on what they saw as a uniquely human capacity for growth and development. Carl Rogers (1902–1987) and Abraham Maslow (1908–1970) argued that all people have the potential for creativity, positive outlook and the pursuit of higher values. If we could fulfil our full potential, these theorists believed, we would inevitably lead a positive life of psychological growth.

> **humanistic psychology** a theory of psychology that sought to give greater prominence to special and unique features of human functioning.

Humanistic pioneer. Carl Rogers was the founder of client-centred therapy, which promotes an equal relationship between therapists and clients and helps clients to achieve their full potential.

Source: © Michael Rougier/Time & Life Pictures/Getty Images, Inc.

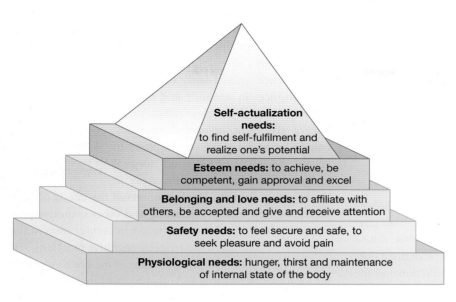

FIGURE 1.3 Maslow's hierarchy of needs. Maslow prioritized our numerous needs and believed that we must satisfy basic physiological and safety needs first. Only then could we progress up the hierarchy and achieve self-actualization.

PSYCHOLOGY AROUND US   Top Self-Actualizers

Maslow believed that only around 2% of all people achieve full self-actualization. Such people could be rich or poor, famous or unknown and from just about any walk of life. To help clarify the notion of self-actualization, however, he listed famous individuals whom he believed to be self-actualizers. His list included Albert Einstein, Eleanor Roosevelt (first lady), Frederick Douglass (American social reformer), Abraham Lincoln and Thomas Jefferson (both presidents of the United States), Jane Addams (first American woman to receive the Nobel Peace Prize), Albert Schweitzer (physician and humanitarian), Walt Whitman (American poet and essayist), Mahatma Ghandi (spiritual leader and leader of Indian nationalism movement), Martin Luther King (civil rights activist) and George Washington (the first president of the United States). Why might Maslow have considered these people fully self-actualized? What well-known people in today's world might be considered fully self-actualized?

Maslow, in fact, proposed that each of us has a basic, broad motive to fulfil our special human potential, which he called the drive for *self-actualization*. He suggested that anyone who achieved this broad motive would indeed lead a positive and fulfilling life. Maslow's hierarchy of human needs summarized his theory and is shown in Figure 1.3.

Carl Rogers developed a humanistic alternative to the psychoanalytic approach to psychotherapy, which he called **client-centred therapy**. According to Rogers, therapists should respect their clients as equals (not as a scientist observing a specimen). In this approach, the therapist establishes a trusting and warm relationship with the client by 'mirroring' feelings and conveying unconditional support and positive regard for the client. This very human approach to therapy played an important role in the establishment of the fields of clinical and counselling psychology after World War II.

client-centred therapy an approach to therapy founded by Carl Rogers, based on the notion that the client is an equal and positive gains are made by mirroring clients' thoughts and feelings in an atmosphere of unconditional positive regard.

Before You Go On

What Do You Know?

5. Which theorist is most closely associated with psychoanalysis (the theory that unconscious conflicts, rooted in childhood, affect much of our behaviour)?

6. What is operant conditioning?

7. What did the Gestalt psychologists study?

What Do You Think?

Which early school of psychology most closely resembles the way you view the human mind? Why?

Psychology in the 21st Century: Cognitive Psychology, Neuroscience and Evolution

LEARNING OBJECTIVE 4

Summarize the major principles of the cognitive, psychobiological and neuroscience approaches to psychology.

Up until the end of World War II, no single approach to psychology dominated the field. In America, psychoanalysis and behaviourism and, to a lesser extent, humanistic psychology competed for students and influence. European psychology followed in the footsteps of Wundt, Freud, the Gestalt psychologists and the psychometricians. In the 1950s, a new school of psychology emerged with roots in work done during the war to enhance human/machine interaction and the mechanical processing of information. Drawing on the work of information and computer scientists such as John von Neumann (1903–1957) and Norbert Wiener (1894–1964), the mind was conceived as an information processor that functioned in the same way as a digital computer. Cognitive researchers were able to observe the 'inputs' and 'outputs' of the mental system through carefully controlled experimentation. They then theorized about the internal mechanisms that must underlie such mental functioning, likening mental processes to the mind's *software* and the human nervous system to the system's *hardware*.

In 1967, Ulric Neisser published the influential book *Cognitive Psychology*. In it, he describes *cognition* as 'all the processes by which . . . sensory input is transformed, reduced, elaborated, stored, recovered, and used' (Neisser, 1967, p. 4). Neisser went on to define **cognitive psychology** as the study of **information processing**, the means by which information is stored and operates internally. Today, the field of cognitive psychology continues to greatly influence the study of memory, perception and consciousness, among other areas that we will discuss in this text.

cognitive psychology a field of psychology that studies mental processes.

information processing the means by which information is stored and operated internally.

Psychobiology/Neuroscience: Exploring the Origins of the Mind

The cognitive psychologists treated the mind as a digital computer linking input behaviour to output behaviour. On the whole they argued that information processing could be studied independently of the 'machine' it was running on. The implication was that cognitive psychology could be studied independently of the underlying brain. However, as we have seen, interest in the neurological basis of psychological phenomena can be traced through the work of Hippocrates, Aristotle, Pavlov and even Freud.

The study of psychobiology, now **neuroscience**, gained early momentum with advances in scientific and medical techniques. Karl Lashley (1890–1958), one of the most influential neuroscientists, based his work on the study of animal brains. Lashley used surgical techniques to destroy certain areas in the brains of animals. He then observed the effects of such destruction on memory, learning and other cognitive processes. Lashley found that the tissues in certain areas of the brain were often linked to particular cognitive functions. His ultimate goal was to pinpoint all areas of the brain responsible for memory, learning and other higher functions. He was never able to accomplish this goal fully, and it continues to be of major interest in contemporary research.

neuroscience the study of psychological functions by looking at the biological foundations of those functions; previously known as psychobiology.

Roger Sperry (1913–1994), a researcher who was influenced greatly by Lashley, pioneered *split-brain* research on animals. Sperry and his colleagues cut the connections responsible for relaying information between the left and right hemispheres, or halves, of animal brains. They found that even after the brain is split surgically, the two hemispheres can often function and learn independently. Later investigators found similar results when they studied human beings who had undergone split-brain surgery to treat severe seizures (Gazzaniga, 2010, 2005). Split-brain research on both animals and humans made it possible to study the separate functioning of the brain's hemispheres. As we will see in Chapter 5 such research remains a popular topic in psychology today.

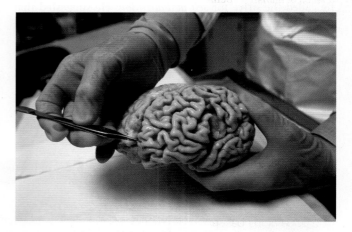

Studying the human brain. Neuroscientists examine brain structure and brain activity to determine how they are related to behaviour. Here a researcher dissects the brain of a former patient with dementia as part of a study to learn more about memory and memory disorders.

Source: © Karen Kasmauski/Corbis Images.

A number of psychological subfields has been influenced by the field of neuroscience, as well as by Darwin's early work on evolution. **Behavioural genetics**, for example, studies the influence of genes on cognition and behaviour. Another related field is sociobiology. **Sociobiologists** theorize that humans have an innate sense of how social behaviour should be organized, a sense brought about partly by evolutionary principles. In 1975, Harvard biologist Edward O. Wilson, a specialist on ants, brought great attention to this view with his book *Sociobiology: The New Synthesis*. He and other sociobiologists suggested that humans are genetically more predisposed than other organisms to learn language, create culture, protect territory and acquire specific societal rules and regulations. Sociobiologists did not claim that genetic and evolutionary influences are necessarily more important than environmental factors, such as parenting or the mass media. Rather, they proposed that our social behaviour is the result of both biological *and* cultural influences. One sociobiologist, David Barash (1979, p. 45), commented, 'For too long social science and biological science have pursued "nothing but" approaches. Sociobiology may just help redress that imbalance.'

Sociobiology is now better known under the title of **evolutionary psychology**. Evolutionary psychologists hold that the body and brain are largely products of evolution and that inheritance plays an important role in shaping thought and behaviour (Table 1.2). The laws of evolutionary psychology are thought to apply to all organisms and to all kinds of mental functions and behaviours at intra-personal, inter-personal, inter-group and cultural levels of analysis.

Evolutionary psychology has become a very popular and controversial topic in psychology today (Confer *et al.*, 2010;

behavioural genetics a subfield of psychology looking at the influence of genes on human behaviour.

sociobiologists theorists who believe humans have a genetically innate concept of how social behaviour should be organized.

evolutionary psychology the field of study that applies evolutionary ideas, including the importance of adaption over millions of years, to the explanation of human behaviour.

TABLE 1.2 The Major Perspectives in Psychology Today

Perspective	Major emphases
Psychoanalytic	Interactions between the conscious and unconscious mind govern virtually all behaviour Childhood experiences set the stage for later psychological functioning
Behaviourist	Only observable behaviour can be studied scientifically Perspective focuses on stimulus–response relationships and the consequences for behaviour
Humanist	People can be helped to realize their full and grand potential, which will inevitably lead to their positive psychological growth
Cognitive	Mental processes are studied using an information processing model (inputs/outputs)
Neuroscience/Psychobiological	Psychobiological functions are explained primarily in terms of their biological foundations
Evolutionary	Behaviour and mental processes are explained in terms of evolution, inheritance and adaptation
Psychometric	Problem-solving and personality are studies using batteries of tests to identify patterns of functioning and to allow comparisons between individuals

PSYCHOLOGY AROUND US   Did Our Ancestors Prefer Blondes?

One of the criticisms of evolutionary psychology is that it is fairly easy, and often inaccurate, to produce theories about how certain current behaviours, traits or emotions may have evolved from earlier times. Evolutionary psychologist Matthew Rossano, for example, writes, 'It is quite tempting to observe a current behaviour and construct an evolutionary story [a "just so" story] about how that behaviour evolved for some adaptive purpose.

'One of the best examples of this comes from the neuroscientist V. S. Ramachandran, who became so frustrated with what he considered to be the excess of unsubstantiated "just so" stories in evolutionary psychology that he made one up himself and called it "Why do gentlemen prefer blondes?"

He proceeded to weave an imaginative tale about how, in our evolutionary history, fair-skinned females would have been preferable as mates because indicators of health, fertility, and sexual fidelity would have been more clearly visible than on their darker complexioned counterparts. He had no evidence, of course – just a plausible story. Much to his amazement, the article was accepted for publication! Critics of evolutionary psychology contend [that "just so"] stories have proliferated in the field, straining the credibility of the discipline.

'On the other hand, this criticism is often used unfairly to smear the entire field of evolutionary psychology as nothing but "just so" stories.' (Rossano, 2003, pp. 44–45)

That certain look. Facial expression of sadness (left two photos) and happiness (right two photos) are universal across all cultures. Are these commonalities related to our evolutionary history?

Source: Far left: Mitchell Kanashkevich/Getty Images, Inc.; Left: Victoria Blackie/Getty Images, Inc.; Right: Theo Allofs/Masterfile; Far right: Daniel Milnor/Masterfile.

Buss, 2009, 2005, 1999). Evolutionary psychologists suggest that some behaviours and mental processes are more effective than others at solving problems of living, namely ones that help people to survive and reproduce. These successful strategies are passed on to people's children, and they eventually become important parts of each individual's inborn make-up.

One goal of evolutionary psychologists is to identify **cultural universality**, human behaviours and practices that occur across all cultures. Just as behaviourists study animal behaviour to identify simple actions that form the basis of more complex human behaviours, evolutionary psychologists believe that uncovering universal human behaviours will help identify inborn functions common to all humans. Theoretically, such knowledge will answer important questions about the relative impact of biological factors and life experiences on our development.

cultural universality those behaviours and practices that occur across all cultures.

Throughout this book, we will be observing a number of common practices displayed by people across all cultures, such as using certain facial expressions to express emotions, displaying a fear of snakes, telling stories and giving gifts. But are such common practices the direct result of evolutionary forces? Have these behaviours and reactions been passed on from generation to generation largely because they remain highly adaptive? Two evolutionary biologists, Stephen Jay Gould and Richard Lewontin (1979), do not think so. They argue that some of the traits and behaviours seen across cultures no longer serve an evolutionarily advantage and instead may be *by-products* of behaviours that did serve adaptive functions a long time ago. Initially, for example, the human smile may have represented an aggressive baring of teeth often seen in animals, designed to ward off attacks by enemies. Over many years, however, it has instead come to be used in human social environments to signal the presence of a friend or to signal humour.

Before You Go On

What Do You Know?

8. What counts as 'inputs' and 'outputs' when we are thinking about human activity?

9. What is meant by a 'just so' story in the context of evolutionary explanations? Why are they problematic?

10. Which of the theories presented here depend largely on biological principles?

11. Which of the theories seem to be based more on environmental explanations? And which appear to rely on an interaction of factors?

12. What is cultural universality, and what kinds of psychologists are interested in it?

The Diversity of Psychology and Psychological Literacy

LEARNING OBJECTIVE 5

Describe the major professional branches of psychology and summarize key trends in psychology.

Today, in the field of psychology, we can recognize the influence of various schools of thought that date back to the days of the Ancient Greek philosophers. The psychological approaches or perspectives we have discussed in this chapter, such as psychoanalysis, behaviourism and cognitive psychology, have not disappeared. Rather, they continue to develop and interact with one another. Indeed, there is now broad recognition that psychology is a diverse field where there is little consensus as to a single method, theory or approach that could do justice to all psychological phenomena. For the practitioner, student or consumer of psychology the challenge is to make sense of this diversity. It is here that **psychological literacy** is of vital importance. In this book we are showing you how to *read* psychological research so that you can understand where it is coming from and how it is linked (or not!) to other research and then go on to make informed evaluations of its scope and value. Remember: you may not become a professional psychologist but you will have many people at home, school, work and surgery giving you advice based on psychological theories and research. You need to be able to make your own decisions about its usefulness.

> **psychological literacy** having the research skills and vocabulary allowing one to evaluate, communicate and apply psychological principles.

Psychology as a Profession

Many students take a psychology degree because they want to become professional psychologists, such as clinical psychologists, educational psychologists, health psychologists, occupational psychologists, counselling psychologists and sports psychologists. Others want to pursue pure research in an academic environment.

If you wish to make a career of psychology and become a professional psychologist then be aware that an undergraduate degree is just the first step: you will need to undertake postgraduate training, and usually to doctorate level. In the United Kingdom, professional psychologists are chartered members of the British Psychological Society (BPS) and have completed postgraduate programmes approved by the Health & Care Professions Council (HCPC).

In Scandinavia, students need to follow a five- or six-year course leading to a master of science in psychology degree followed by, or including, a stage of internship or practical experience under supervision. After this, they are eligible to apply for registration with the relevant psychological association of their country.

Current Trends in Psychology

The field of psychology is growing more diverse, continuing to profit from technological advances and to give birth to new schools of thought.

Growing Diversity Early in the history of psychology, few women or members of racial minority groups were able to obtain the advanced education and professional status necessary to work in the field. As psychology itself has grown more diverse, however, so have psychologists. Psychology now has more women earning graduate degrees than does any other science. In the United Kingdom, about 85% of undergraduates studying psychology are female.

With growing diversity among psychologists has come increased interest in the diversity of the people they study, treat and influence. **Cultural psychology** has, for example, become an important area of investigation. As we observed earlier, this field of study seeks to uncover mental processes that exist across all cultures, as well as important cultural differences.

> **cultural psychology** the study of how individual behaviour can be shaped or affected by societal processes.

Cultural psychologists often focus on differences between **collectivist** cultures and **individualistic** cultures. Members of collectivist cultures emphasize the needs of the group – the community, family or peer group, for example – over the desires of the individual. In contrast, individualistic cultures stress the needs of persons over those of the group. One study of differences between these two types of cultures examined positive emotions, such as happiness. Individuals from Eastern cultures, which tend to be more collectivist, and Western cultures, which tend to be more individualistic, appear to hold different beliefs about the sources of happiness. When asked to talk about events that made them feel happy, Chinese

> **collectivist** a culture that focuses more on the needs of the group and less on individual desires.

> **individualistic** a culture that places the wants or desires of the person over the needs of the group.

PSYCHOLOGY AROUND US   Choosing Wisely

As she comes closer to graduation, Jasmine, who is taking an undergraduate psychology degree, is beginning to have more and more worries about what she is going to do after university. She is certain that she wants to become a professional psychologist but she is not sure she is particularly interested in clinical work. For one thing, she tends to get irritated when friends assume that just because she is studying psychology she is interested in their problems or has good advice for them.

At first, Jasmine was interested in understanding how issues like race and class influence clinical disorder rates in urban communities. But, as she moved through her studies, she became less interested in these broader social influences and increasingly interested in studying the impact of biological and developmental factors on individual stress levels and on the emergence of psychological problems, particularly in poor communities. Recently, she has been gathering more information about what studying to be a clinical psychologist entails. Still, she is not sure that clinical psychology is the right fit for her. And she is not sure how to go about getting all the answers she is looking for.

PRACTICALLY SPEAKING What Can You Do with a Psychology Degree?

Psychology's wide influence. Psychologist Daniel Kahneman (left) is awarded the 2002 Nobel Prize in Economics.
Source: Jonas Ekstromer/Pool/AP/World Wide Photos.

Psychology is the study of behaviour and mental life. Students who graduate in psychology gain a broad understanding of what makes people 'tick' from a wide range of perspectives, including developmental, social, clinical and biological. They also acquire a body of knowledge and set of skills that help qualify them for a range of career choices.

In the United Kingdom, only about 20% of psychology graduates go on to become professional psychologists. Others find that their psychology degree can help open the door to graduate study in many other fields, such as law, business management, economics and medicine.

Even if graduate study is not for you, an undergraduate degree in psychology can lead to interesting jobs and careers. Psychology graduates are typically viewed by prospective employers as well qualified to work in fields that require people skills, as well as analytical, research and writing abilities. An undergraduate degree in psychology particularly qualifies individuals for entry-level jobs in people-orientated careers such as communications, marketing, human resources, sales and business. Beyond people skills, the analytic, research and writing skills of psychology graduates may make individuals good candidates for careers in law, management consulting, computer game design or investment banking.

In short, psychology is related to so much in our world that a degree in this discipline can lead to work and careers in more areas and fields than you might imagine. Keep in mind, for example, that the psychologists Daniel Kahneman (2002) and Herbert Simon (1978) are Nobel Laureates in *economics*, while the neuroscientists Eric Kandel (2000), Rita Levi-Montalcini (1986) and Roger Sperry (1981) won their Nobel Prizes in *medicine* and *physiology*.

---

research participants focused on interpersonal interactions and evaluations from others. Western participants, in contrast, pointed to personal achievement and self-evaluation (Lu & Shih, 1997).

Even within a broad culture, subcultures may differ with regard to happiness. Studies have shown, for example, that certain levels of positive emotions, such as strong feelings of self-acceptance, are, on average, a bit lower among individuals from southern parts of the United States than among those from the West or Midwest. Some researchers have hypothesized that these lower levels of well-being and self-acceptance may reflect a subculture that is relatively more concerned with showing hospitality and respecting tradition than with fostering positive self-concepts and promoting personal growth (Markus *et al.*, 2004). Given psychology's growing interest in these and other differences among people and groups, we have included throughout the textbook sections called HOW WE DIFFER. These sections examine how memory, emotions, social values and the like differ from situation to situation, person to person and group to group.

Advances in Technology As we observed earlier, technological shifts also contribute to shifts in psychological theory. The development of computers in the 1950s and 1960s contributed to the cognitive psychology revolution. Technology has continued to change the face of science and psychology more recently. Innovations such as brain imaging and effective *pharmacological*, or drug, treatments for mental disorders have revealed a great deal about human mental processes and behaviour. As you will see in Chapter 5, for example, the development of neuroimaging technology has made it possible for researchers to observe activity in the brain directly.

In fact, in recent years a new area of psychological study and theory has emerged: **cognitive neuroscience** focuses not only on mental processes but also on how mental processes interact with the biological functions of the brain; that is, what happens in the brain when we are remembering something, making a decision or paying attention to

cognitive neuroscience the study of mental processes and how they relate to the biological functions of the brain.

PSYCHOLOGY AROUND US   Pioneering Women Psychologists

Since the beginnings of psychology as a science, women have made important discoveries and contributions to it. Here are but a few of the field's female pioneers.

The work of Mary Whiton Calkins (1863–1930) was noteworthy for her emphasis on the self, consciousness, emotions and dreams, which stood in stark contrast to John Watson's behaviourist movement at the time. Calkins was the first woman president of the American Psychological Association (APA).

Margaret Floy Washburn (1871–1939) was the first woman to receive a PhD in psychology (1894) and the first woman elected to the National Academy of Sciences (1932). She was one of the earliest experimental psychologists to insist that mental phenomena were as important for scientific study as observable behaviours.

Karen Horney (1885–1952) was one of the most influential early psychoanalytic theorists, a pioneer in the discipline of 'feminine psychiatry' and a leader in the Neo-Freudian movement that challenged traditional Freudian views. She was especially critical of Freud's theory of sexuality.

Leta Hollingworth (1886–1939) was best known for her studies of 'mentally deficient' and 'mentally gifted' individuals and for her views on gender differences in mental functioning. She was one of the first theorists of her time to challenge the notion that women were biologically inferior, arguing instead that women were victims of a male-dominated social order.

Mamie Phipps Clark (1917–1983) and her psychologist husband Kenneth Clark were two of the first well-known African-American psychologists. She and her husband were best known for their work on the effects of segregation on the self-images of minority children.

Brenda Milner (1918–) has been a pioneer in the study of memory and other cognitive functions in humans. She was the first to investigate how damage to the brain's hippocampus affects memory through her study of a famous amnesia patient known as H. M. in the research literature.

Carol Gilligan (1936–) is best known for her pioneering work on gender differences, which has forever changed society's understanding of the human experience.

Anne Treisman (1935–) has been a leading researcher of visual attention, perception and memory. She was the first psychologist to propose that different kinds of attention enable people to combine the observed separate features of an object into a consciously experienced whole.

Uta Frith (1941–) is a developmental psychologist who is best known for her work on understanding autism. She has argued that autistic children lack a 'theory of mind'.

---

something. One goal of cognitive neuroscientists is to link specific mental processes to particular brain activities. Similarly, a field called **social neuroscience** seeks to link social functioning to particular brain activities. Recent studies have, for example, found that a network of nerve cells in the brain is activated when we show *empathy*, the ability to understand the intentions of others.

social neuroscience the study of social functioning and how it is tied to brain activity.

Cognitive and social neuroscience are currently among psychology's more active areas of theory and research. Given the enormous growth and impact of such areas, we have also included throughout the book a section called **WHAT HAPPENS IN THE BRAIN?** In these sections, you will learn about the neuroscience of memory, emotions, social behaviour and the like. You will discover, for example, what happens in the brain when you are learning new material before an important test and then what happens when you get together with friends to celebrate the completion of that test.

The development of imaging tools, computer technology and a number of biological techniques has also helped enhance our understanding and treatment of mental disorders in recent years. These tools have enabled researchers to look directly at the brains of disturbed persons while they are feeling sad or anxious, hearing voices or recalling repressed memories. Such studies have helped reveal that depression, for example, is related not only to traumatic childhood experiences, major losses in life and feelings of helplessness but also to abnormal activity of key chemicals in the brain. Given such wide-ranging insights, we have included in most chapters a section called **OUT OF THE ORDINARY**. We discuss in these sections what happens when normal psychological processes – such as memory, emotional coping and social engagement – go astray.

At first glance, psychology's increased focus on the brain may make it appear that technology and biology are now dominating psychology. However, it is unlikely that psychology will ever be overtaken by biology. Indeed, recent findings in cognitive neuroscience and other areas suggest that our insights about mental functions (and dysfunctions) and about behaviour are most complete when the different branches of the field intersect and cooperate. In clinical psychology, for example, it is now clear that many mental disorders are best understood and treated when explanations and techniques from different schools of thought are combined.

One important area of psychology that has intersected with other areas for many years is developmental psychology, the study of how we change over the course of our lives. Developmental psychology has both incorporated and contributed to research in such as our use of language, our emotions, our personalities and the structure of our brains. We emphasize the intersection between development and other areas by including in most chapters a section called **HOW WE DEVELOP**.

New Schools of Thought As we saw earlier, historical schools of thought in psychology sow the seeds for related but new ideas. Consider, for example, a relatively new movement called **positive psychology**. In this movement, we can see influences of both the functionalists, who were interested in applying psychological research, and the humanists, who were interested in helping people achieve their highest potential. Positive psychology gives special attention to more upbeat features of human functioning, including happiness, meaning in life and character strengths. It also focuses on how those features of positive living might be developed more readily (Biswas-Diener, 2011).

Happiness seems to have become a buzzword of our times. It has been embraced particularly by the popular media, fuelling a self-help industry that claims to give people tools for achieving emotional well-being. Whenever you visit a bookstore, you can easily see media interest in this area. Happiness has been used, for example, to help market nutritional advice – as in the book *The Good Mood Diet: Feel great while you lose weight* (Kleiner & Condor, 2007) – and has appeared even in fields not associated primarily with psychology – as in the book *The Architecture of Happiness* (Botton, 2006). Positive psychologists have applied the use of scholarly discussion and scientific methods to the study of happiness and other positive variables (Cooper, 2010). Further information on courses in positive psychology can be found at www.positivepsychology.org.uk.

A growing body of research does indeed suggest that positive emotions can have a powerful effect on development and behaviour. As you will see in a later chapter when we discuss stress, coping and health (Chapter 18), a number of studies have found that having a positive outlook promotes *resilience*, the ability to bounce back in the face of misfortune (Garbarino, 2011). Similarly, studies indicate that positive emotions may boost the functioning of our body's immune system. Research even suggests that our emotions help influence how well we resist common colds (Cohen *et al.*, 2008, 2003)!

> **positive psychology** a movement in psychology that focuses on the positive features of human functioning and examines how they might be developed more readily.

Accentuating the positive. Residents of a small Spanish village cry out with joy as they are drenched with 30 tons of water during a water festival. Positive psychologists study the impact that happiness and positive emotions have on human functioning.
Source: Ian Berry/Magnum Photos, Inc.

In Chapter 14, on emotions, we will come upon research that suggests that each of us has a particular 'set point' on our happiness thermometer. We carry this stable level of well-being with us to each situation in our lives. We may depart from our set point for short periods of time, but many of us return to our typical level of happiness within weeks or months of an upsetting event (Headey, 2008).

What Changes and What Remains Constant? Since the early years of Greek philosophy, theorists have attempted to explain themselves and other people. Psychologists have asked whether there are universal laws that link mental and physical phenomena. Those questions remain at the forefront of psychology today. Neuroscientists, cultural theorists and other psychologists still try to determine how the mind and body are related, whether there are knowable universal truths about mental processes and human behaviours and whether such truths are best understood by focusing on the brain, the individual or the group, or a particular combination of the three. It is not likely that psychology can ever provide complete answers to these complex questions but we can articulate partial answers by looking at how different levels of analysis can be stitched together to produce a range of interesting theories and research findings.

As you read about these theories and findings throughout this textbook, you will do well to keep asking yourself a question raised by Carl Jung (1875–1961), one of the field's most famous clinical theorists: 'How much truth [is] captured by this [particular] viewpoint?' Ideas move in and out of vogue, and what is accepted today as a useful or accurate outlook may not be seen the same way tomorrow.

Both historical and social forces help determine where scientists focus their energy. Psychology, perhaps more than any other field, struggles constantly to achieve a proper balance between popular trends and interests, societal influences and scientific objectivity (Leahey, 2000, p. 544). Fads and fashions will likely continue to exert some influence on the field of psychology in the coming years. It is important, though, to recognize that such fads hardly make up the substance of the field. Moreover, we must always keep in mind the limitations of psychology (or of any discipline) in answering the basic questions of human existence. As we noted at the beginning of this chapter, scientific knowledge serves as a *means* for exploring such questions rather than an end.

Before You Go On

What Do You Know?

13. What new forms of psychology are in the process of development?

14. What is cultural psychology and how can it help us to explain differences between groups?

15. What is the focus of positive psychology?

What Do You Think?

How can psychology influence the way you live your life? Are there any areas of your life you would not like psychologists to explore?

Activities to test yourself further are available in your interactive e-book at
www.wileyopenpage.com

Summary

What Is Psychology?

LEARNING OBJECTIVE 1   Give definitions of psychology, and describe the goals and levels of analysis of different approaches to psychological sciences.

- Psychology studies what people do from different perspectives. Psychology as the science of the mind and psychology as the science of behaviour have been the dominant ways of approaching the subject.
- The goals of psychology are to *describe*, *explain*, *predict* and *control* behaviour and mental processes. Psychologists vary in the degree to which they focus on some of these goals more than others. Some psychologists argue that we also need to study how people *understand* and *develop*.
- The study of psychology must occur at multiple levels, including the level of the *brain* (intra-individual), the level of the *person* (inter-individual), level of the *group* (inter-group) and the level of *culture* (societal).

Psychology's Roots in Philosophy

LEARNING OBJECTIVE 2   Describe how from the time of the Ancient Greeks to the mid-19th century philosophers and scientists thought about the relationship between mind, body and soul.

- Early explanations of human behaviour were rooted in superstition and magic.
- Theorizing how mind and body were related became a major theme in Western philosophy.
- The work of such early philosophers as Hippocrates, Socrates, Plato and Aristotle contributed to the later formation of psychology as a systematic, empirical science.
- 19th-century physiologists began to investigate the functions of the brain and nervous system.

The Founding of Psychology

LEARNING OBJECTIVE 3   Name important early psychologists and describe the main schools of psychological theory: introspection, psychoanalysis, functionalism, psycho-metrics, Gestalt, behaviourism and humanistic.

- The first psychology laboratory was founded in Leipzig, Germany by physiologist/philosopher Wilhelm Wundt. Wundt was interested in human consciousness and will, which he studied by asking trained experimental participants to observe their conscious activity under carefully controlled conditions.
- Wundt distinguished between experimental psychology, which was limited to the study of simple sensory processes, and *Völkerpsychologie*, which studied higher cognitive processes that were the product of cultures, language and history.
- William James established the first psychology laboratory in the United States at Harvard and helped shift the field's focus to the functions of mental events and behaviours, forming a school of thought known as functionalism.
- Gestalt psychologists, rather than divide consciousness into its smallest parts, studied human tendencies to perceive pattern, putting together the 'parts', or individual sensations, to create a 'whole' or perception that went beyond the sum of the parts.
- Over the years, different fields of psychology emerged, with different ideas about what was the appropriate area of study for human psychology. Some of the most influential fields were the psychoanalytic, behaviourist, humanistic, cognitive and neuroscience schools of thought.
- Sigmund Freud's psychoanalytical theory focused on the importance of unconscious mental processes.
- Behaviourists believed strongly that psychology should restrict its focus to the careful study of observable behaviours.
- Francis Galton began the systematic study of individual differences in intelligence and personality.
- Psychometricians focused on measuring individual differences within such areas as intelligence and personality.
- Humanistic psychologists reacted against the mechanical portrayals of people by the behaviourists and emphasized individuals' potential for growth and self-actualization.

Psychology in the 21st Century: Cognitive Psychology, Neuroscience and Evolution

LEARNING OBJECTIVE 4   Summarize the major principles of the cognitive, psychobiological and neuroscience approaches to psychology.

- Cognitive psychologists reignited interest in the study of mental processes, comparing the workings of the mind to the workings of computers.
- Cognitive psychologists replaced the behaviourist language of stimulus and response with the language of information processing, input, output, hardware and software.
- Experiments by Roger Sperry on people who had undergone surgery that split their brain into two fully independent hemispheres showed how functioning at the psychological level was related to underlying brain organization.
- Sociobiologists such as E. O. Wilson applied the principles of evolution to explain complex social behaviour in terms of adaptation, leading to the development of evolutionary psychology as an emerging field of study.

The Diversity of Psychology and Psychological Literacy

LEARNING OBJECTIVE 5   Describe the major professional branches of psychology and summarize key trends in psychology.

- The theoretical and cultural diversity of the field of psychology has increased dramatically over recent years.
- There are several major branches of professional psychology: clinical, counselling, educational, occupational, sports and exercise, forensic, teaching and research.
- Across these professional areas psychologists are united by their shared values. Psychologists generally agree that psychology is *theory-driven*, *empirical*, *multilevel* and *contextual*.
- Currently, psychology appears to be developing as a science in response to a growing *diversity* throughout the field, advances *in technology* (such as neuroimaging) and the development of relatively *new schools* such as cultural psychology, cognitive neuroscience, social neuroscience and positive psychology.

Quizzes to test yourself further are available in your interactive e-book at **www.wileyopenpage.com**

Key Terms

behavioural genetics 13

behaviourism 9

client-centred therapy 11

cognitive neuroscience 16

cognitive psychology 12

collectivist 15

cultural psychology 15

cultural universality 14

ego 7

eugenics 8

evolutionary psychology 13

functionalist 7

gestalt psychology 8

humanistic psychology 10

id 7

individualistic 15

information processing 12

introspect 3

mental processes 3

neuroscience 12

operant conditioning 10

positive psychology 18

pragmatism 7

psychoanalysis 7

psychological literacy 15

psychology 2

psychometrics 8

responses 10

social neuroscience 17

sociobiologists 13

stimuli 10

superego 7

unconscious 7

voluntarism 7

Flashcards to test yourself further are available in your interactive e-book at **www.wileyopenpage.com**

CHAPTER 2

Psychology as a Science

Adapted by Mark Forshaw,
Adelphi Values, UK

CHAPTER OUTLINE

- What Is a Science?
- Is Psychology a Science?
- How Do Psychologists Conduct Research?
- How Do Psychologists Make Sense of Research Results?
- What Ethical Research Guidelines Do Psychologists Follow?

 Access your interactive e-book to view a video clip for this chapter at **www.wileyopenpage.com**

Ugly Reality?

Reality television has become an increasingly common part of the world's media over the past decade. Shows such as *Big Brother*, *American Idol*, *The X Factor*, *Survivor*, *Strictly Come Dancing* and *Dancing with the Stars* currently dominate television. There are local versions of most of these programmes in most nations around the globe. Actually, there are various kinds of reality shows: for example, the competition realities, in which people compete for a job, recognition or a dream mate; the real-life realities, which have people conduct their lives as usual, for all the world to see; and the advice realities, in which professionals tell individuals how to change their lifestyles or behaviours.

Among the most popular reality shows are the giveaway/makeover programmes: shows in which people who are poor, down on their luck or who believe themselves unattractive are chosen to receive special gifts, opportunities that will improve their lives markedly or makeovers.

Many criticisms have been levelled at reality TV (Pozner, 2010; Hirschorn, 2007). Its detractors say it takes advantage of people and encourages audiences to take pleasure in the humiliation of other human beings.

Defenders of reality TV counter that such criticisms reek of snobbery. They point out that participants on reality TV include individuals from a variety of racial and socio-economic backgrounds who rarely receive much exposure on scripted television shows. At their best, defenders argue, reality shows, particularly the giveaway/makeover ones, bring out admirable qualities in viewers, tapping into positive feelings such as generosity, empathy and concern for others, and, in turn, offer insights into social behaviours and interactions. ■

Is reality TV a negative force in society? Is it a force for good, giving a voice to the voiceless and providing insights into human behaviour? Or is it, after all, just television?

Viewers may base their answers to these questions on their personal experiences. Journalists and media critics may use comparisons to other televisions shows or look at trends over time. Sociologists may look for large-scale shifts in societal, cultural and moral standards. Psychologists try to answer questions like these by using scientific research methods to look for relationships between reality TV and systematic changes in individuals' mental processes and behaviour.

In this chapter, you will find out exactly what the scientific research methods of psychologists are and how psychologists use them. We will begin the chapter by defining what science is. Then, we will consider just how well psychology fits with the definition of a science, particularly in comparison to other fields. Next, we will examine in some detail the methods that psychologists use to conduct research, including, by way of example, research into the nature of television viewing habits. Finally, we will look at the statistics that help researchers interpret their results and the ethical rules that guide them when working with humans or animals.

What Is a Science?

LEARNING OBJECTIVE 1

List two core beliefs of science, and describe the steps in the scientific method.

Before we look at psychology in particular, take a moment to try to answer the general question 'What is a science?' You may answer by listing types of sciences, such as chemistry, biology or physics. An image may come to your mind of a white-coated person in a laboratory, mixing strangely bubbling chemicals or lecturing students on how to dissect the frog in the tray in front of them. Such things are only *sometimes* tied to science. For example, you may define science as something carried out by a 'boffin' or a 'geek'. Many scientists are boffins and geeks, but it is not a useful defining feature. Two characteristics that all sciences do share, however, are similar beliefs about how best to understand the world and a reliance on the *scientific method* as a way to discovering knowledge.

Scientific Principles

Science is built on a set of core beliefs about the world. Two key principles are that:

- *The universe operates according to certain natural laws.* Scientists believe that things happen in and around us in some kind of orderly fashion that can be described using

rules or laws. The natural law of cause and effect, for example, suggests that when something is set in motion it has an effect on other things. Psychologists look for the laws that describe mental processes and behaviour.

- *Such laws are discoverable and testable.* By carefully observing what happens in the natural world, we can deduce the laws governing those events. In turn, we can use these laws to make predictions about what could happen, and we can then experiment to see whether those predictions come true. This is also tied to the belief that things are measurable. Without measurement, there can be no science.

As a natural science, psychology operates according to these two core beliefs. Psychology also shares with other sciences a similar logical approach to discovering and testing laws about how things happen: the scientific method (Lalasz, 2011).

The Scientific Method

The scientific method relies upon a process of logical reasoning that was first used in the field of philosophy. Early views on human knowledge were governed by **deductive reasoning**, a process that starts with broad basic principles and applies them in specific situations to prove hundreds and thousands of other, smaller truths. If you ever applied the Pythagorean theorem to calculate the length of a side of a right-angled triangle, you were using deductive reasoning; you were applying a broad principle to a specific case.

> **deductive reasoning** the reasoning proceeding from broad basic principles applied to specific situations.

The British philosopher Sir Francis Bacon (1561–1626) was one of the first to question the deductive reasoning

Law seeking. This meteorologist relies on physical laws to describe and predict the force and path of hurricanes. Similarly, psychologists seek out laws to describe and predict mental processes and behaviour.

Source: Joe Raedle/Getty Images, Inc.

approach. Bacon felt deductive reasoning was too easily influenced by the thinker's **biases** – personal beliefs or conventional wisdom that a particular thinker mistakenly accepts as broad, basic truths. We will see throughout this book that psychological research has shown many times that widely accepted conventional wisdom can be biased. For example, people typically consider themselves free and independent thinkers who will always stand up for what they believe to be right. As we will discuss in Chapter 17, however, scientists have been able to demonstrate that, when

biases distorted beliefs based on a person's subjective sense of reality.

faced by an authority figure or even just a small group of people with opposite views, many people go along with the higher authority or the crowd rather than follow their own beliefs.

Bacon argued that, to avoid bias, science and philosophy should proceed in the opposite direction to deductive reasoning, using a process called **inductive reasoning** instead. Here, thinkers use careful direct observations to produce broad conclusions, and over time such conclusions are combined to reach truths about the laws of the universe.

inductive reasoning the reasoning process proceeding from small specific situations to more general truths.

PSYCHOLOGY AROUND US   Dying for the Cause of Science

In the spring of 1626, Francis Bacon was being driven in an open horse-drawn carriage to his country estate. It was a bitterly cold night and snow covered the ground. Bacon noticed that when the carriage wheels passed over the grass under the snow, the exposed grass looked fresh and new. In a flash, he wondered whether freezing cold might be able to preserve food, just as the frozen snow seemed to be preserving the grass that it covered.

Bacon decided to do an experiment (Aubrey, 2000). He ran from the carriage to a nearby house and bought a

gutted chicken from a local villager. Using his bare hands, he stuffed the chicken with snow, placed it in a bag and packed more snow around the dead chicken. In short, he created the world's first frozen chicken.

As Bacon had expected, the chicken was indeed preserved by the refrigerated process – ready for cooking and eating at a later time. But Bacon himself was not so lucky. He quickly became ill as a result of running around in the freezing temperatures and using his bare hands to collect snow. He contracted pneumonia and died a few days later at the age of 65.

Psychologists using inductive reasoning would begin the search for natural laws by making **empirical** observations of mental processes and behaviours; that is, observations that can be tested in objective ways. Their observations would in turn lead them to develop **theories**; namely, ideas about the laws that govern those processes and behaviours.

empirical able to be tested in objective ways.

theories ideas about laws that govern phenomena.

Inductive reasoning is still a key idea in much scientific research. There are so many factors governing human behaviour, however, that if psychologists were to rely entirely on induction, or observation, they could never discover and specify all of them. Thus, to build on the best of both deductive and inductive reasoning approaches, psychologists today typically employ a blended model known as the **hypothetico-deductive approach** (Sprenger, 2010; Locke, 2007).

Using a hypothetico-deductive approach, psychologists begin with a deductive process: they identify a **hypothesis**, a specific statement that can be tested objectively and be assessed as

hypothetico-deductive approach a process of modern science where scientists begin with an educated guess about how the world works and then set about designing small controlled observations to support or invalidate that hypothesis.

hypothesis a general statement about the way variables relate that is objectively falsifiable.

being likely to be wrong or right. According to the famous philosopher Karl Popper (1902–1994), a sound scientific theory must establish, in advance, the observations that could prove it wrong (Popper, 1963, 1959). In other words, a useful theory runs the risk of being proven false. To test the soundness of their theories, researchers create hypotheses. A physicist, for example, might produce a hypothesis, based on the theory of cause and effect, which states that hitting a baseball with a bat causes the ball to move in a new direction. If researchers were then to discover that baseballs keep going straight into the catcher's mitt, even after being hit, the hypothesis would be disproved and scientists would have to reconsider their theory of the law of cause and effect.

Similarly, in the hypothetico-deductive approach, psychologists set out to create controlled observations that will verify or disprove their hypotheses. Note that we do not talk of 'proof', because that is a logical impossibility. We can disprove something quite easily, whereas absolute proof is not possible. We can demonstrate that something is highly likely to be true to an ever-increasing degree, but we never reach 100% proof. In many cases, research results do indeed disprove their hypotheses. Psychologists may then reject or change their theories and produce

FIGURE 2.1 Reasoning and the scientific method. Several different kinds of reasoning may be used as scientists carry out their work. Most psychological researchers use the hypothetico-deductive approach.

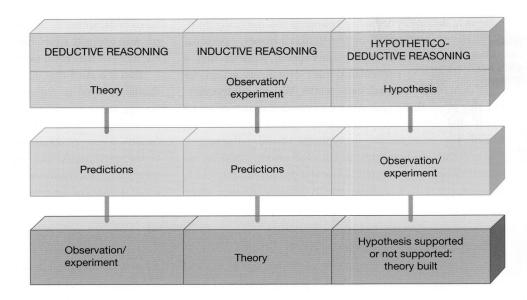

new hypotheses for further testing. Through repetition of this process, increasingly accurate explanations of human thought and behaviour keep evolving. This approach is outlined in Figure 2.1.

We must keep in mind two things as we test our hypothesis: validity and reliability. *Reliability* refers to the notion that if something is true it will keep happening. Therefore, when we replicate a study, we should get the same or similar findings, over and over again. If we do not, the results are not reliable. One of the reasons that this may happen is if our measurements are not valid. *Validity* refers to whether we are testing what we mean to test. People have argued for a century, for example, about whether intelligence tests of various kinds actually measure intelligence. If a question you ask a respondent means different things to different people, or different things to different people on different days, then you have a problem with both reliability *and* validity.

As we discussed at the beginning of the chapter, many people have ideas about whether reality TV has good or bad effects or indeed any effects at all on viewers. To produce a scientific theory about the effects of reality TV, a person would need to step outside his or her personal beliefs in order to avoid bias. A scientific approach would involve the steps described below:

- *Make observation.* We might first examine what viewers do after watching a reality TV show. For example, do they display moral behaviour after watching an episode of a reality TV show? That is, do they behave in ways that suggest increased empathy and awareness of others' beliefs and needs? Particular care should be taken to ensure that our observations are valid and

reliable. Does everyone agree on what moral behaviour is, and do different raters agree when they have seen examples of it?

- *Develop hypotheses.* After making such observations, we would produce hypotheses about what led to the behaviour we observed. If viewers acted more morally, for example, did positive behaviour on the show cause viewers to think of their fellow human beings in a more positive or caring light? Or were the viewers simply modelling themselves after the television cast? Whatever our explanation, we would be producing a hypothesis that could be tested. One hypothesis, for example, might be that viewers change their behaviour to be more like the people they see on reality TV shows.

- *Test hypotheses.* As we will see in this chapter, there are several kinds of research studies we could conduct to see whether this hypothesis could be disproved.

- *Build a theory.* If the hypothesis were, indeed, disproved, we might change it or even throw it out and develop and test a new hypothesis. If, however, our study does not disprove the hypothesis that people who watch reality TV change their behaviour to be more like the cast of the show, we might test the hypothesis further. We might, for example, decide to study the viewers of other reality shows as well. If the results continue to support our hypothesis, the hypothesis can become a theory. The theory, in turn, can be used to produce additional hypotheses.

Before You Go On

What Do You Know?

1. What are the two core beliefs of a science?
2. What is the difference between inductive and deductive reasoning?
3. What is the difference between a hypothesis and a theory?
4. What is the hypothetico-deductive method?

What Do You Think?

Based on what you know about the scientific method, do you think psychology is a science in the same way that chemistry, biology and physics are sciences?

Is Psychology a Science?

LEARNING OBJECTIVE 2

Compare and contrast psychology with other natural sciences, such as biology, chemistry and physics, and with pseudo-psychologies, such as astrology.

As we saw in Chapter 1, prior to the 19th century, psychology was a field based largely on philosophy, religion and even mysticism. With a rise in the popularity of animal research in the 19th century, however, scientists began to develop an increased interest in physiology and how human actions are tied to innate biological functions. Charles Darwin's theories on evolution, along with advances in the field of biology, raised questions about the interactions between humans and their environments. Given this journey, many credit the influence of biological science for shifting psychology from a philosophy towards becoming a science (Hergenhahn, 2005).

Psychology is now defined as a natural science that uses experimental methods to study mental processes and behaviour. It does, however, differ from the physical sciences, such as biology, in key ways, including how it pursues scientific goals and its ability to influence personal and social values.

Goals of Psychology

All sciences share the goals of describing, explaining, predicting and controlling the phenomena they study. However, the emphasis each field places on these goals varies. One key difference between psychology and the physical sciences, for example, is in the area of description. A core goal of many physical sciences is to isolate and describe the smallest elements that contribute to a larger whole. Biologists look at how a cell contributes to the overall functioning of an organism, for example. Chemists and physicists examine how atoms and subatomic particles make up the structure of, well, everything. Psychology also attempts to identify basic elements of behaviour and mental processes. However, psychologists face an additional task because behaviour is determined by so many such factors simultaneously: it is what we call *multivariate*, i.e. governed or influenced by many variables at once.

The basic factors that affect behaviour can be temporary or permanent parts of a person's life. The atomic structure of gold, for example, is the same in all gold all over the world, but a complex behaviour, such as reading this textbook, cannot be broken down into a standard set of elements that always work the same for every person. The reading behaviour of a student can be influenced by a temporary factor, such as knowing that an exam is coming up, a factor that obviously does not affect the reading behaviour of non-students. Furthermore, someone whose second or third language is English may read this from a different perspective than a native English speaker. The idea behind psychological research is both to *separate out* the relative contribution of factors such as these and to think about how various factors *come together* to influence human behaviour.

Psychologists also face an additional challenge, namely much of what they study does not have the clear and observable physical reality that the basic units of study in other scientific fields have. With the help of special tools, scientists in those fields can observe even the tiniest bits of matter, including atoms and DNA. Of course, this is also true of psychology *to some degree*. Certain behaviours, sensations or physiological responses, for example, can be directly observed, measured and explained. This allows us to mirror aspects of empiricism, which is one of the key defining factors of science. **Empiricism** is the belief that our knowledge should be derived from the evidence of our senses. It does not mean that one should believe everything one sees or hears, but rather that we should test our senses systematically, forming hypotheses based upon them. In his review of science, the great German philosopher Immanuel Kant suggested that when psychology is studying phenomena such as these it is indeed

empiricism the view that our knowledge of the world should come from testing out what our senses perceive.

empirical and very close to a 'real' science (Kant, 2003). Other psychologists, such as the behaviourist B. F. Skinner, also advocated this view of psychology. Indeed, as we saw in Chapter 1, many behaviourists have stated that, as scientists, psychologists should study *only* what is directly observable.

On the other hand, as Kant himself observed, many of the processes that form the basis of psychology cannot be observed or described directly. We have no microscopes or tests that will allow us to see a thought or an emotion, for example, with the same clarity as a cell. Granted, good scientific work and sound experimental study have enabled us to look at many of the ways thoughts and feelings can influence behaviours, and psychologists are always seeking out new ways of objectively defining these and other features of mental functioning. But direct observation continues to be a difficult task in the field of psychology.

Science and Qualitative Research So far, we have concentrated on the quantitative end of psychology, with its traditional focus on measurement, which in many ways mirrors the development of science itself. However, it would be disingenuous not to discuss the so-called qualitative turn. In recent years (some would say at least 50), we have begun to call into question the view that psychology should be scientific and all about numbers and measurements, since a great deal of human activity is actually about thoughts, feelings and experiences, which, as we have just discussed, can be notoriously difficult to capture using measurement tools per se. In addition to this, there is a deeper, philosophical issue concerned with somehow subjecting human beings to measurement and labelling. People are not rocks. Therefore, we have started to accept that sometimes talking to people, or at least listening to what they say or write, can be a very valuable way to approach understanding human behaviour.

There are many varieties of qualitative research that are used in psychology and the social sciences and humanities more widely, but they are mostly underpinned by some basic principles, the first of which is that there is added value to talking to people, over and above questionnaires or galvanic skin responses. If a person seems to be stressed, because the electrical conductivity of their skin has changed, or because they are dry in the mouth or because they are shaking, we perhaps do ourselves a disservice if we stop there. Why not ask that person what they feel, and why they feel it, in detail? In this rather obvious example we see the value of qualitative research instantly.

However, most human beings are extremely complicated, and so many of the big questions we may have are not easily answered by means of quantitative research methods. In fact, another characteristic of many qualitative approaches is to call into question the value of quantitative, statistically focused research in answering certain questions. Some qualitative researchers even go so far as to point out the harm that is done to participants, respondents and interviewees by certain traditional methods of research. A shaking and distressed participant rings alarm bells from an ethical point of view, for example! We will return to these qualitative approaches shortly.

Values and the Application of Psychology

Psychology is also different from other scientific fields inasmuch as it deals in major ways with issues such as values, morality and personal preference – issues that historically were addressed only by spiritual and political leaders. People are particularly inclined to use psychological information to decide philosophical, religious and legal issues, as well as issues from other such realms of life. For example, psychologists gave testimony to the Supreme Court in the US about adolescent brain function and risk-taking behaviour (*Roper* v. *Simmons*). They reported findings that many adolescents' brains are not yet developed enough to allow them to understand fully the consequences of their behaviours. Based on this testimony, the Court ruled on an important moral, ethical and legal question: adolescents who commit murder should not be faced with the possibility of the death penalty (http://www.supremecourt.gov/opinions/04pdf/03-633.pdf).

Of course, other sciences also influence the values and ethics of human beings to various degrees. Consider the field of genetic research, for example. This field was pioneered by biological scientists who were looking for better farming practices and better ways to carry out the breeding of farm animals. After a while, some of the scientists came to believe that selective breeding also could be applied to humans to increase the likelihood that they would produce desired offspring. Their ideas and research gave rise to a

Happy Birthday! Yangyang, a female goat cloned by Chinese scientists in 2000, wears a wreath at her sixth birthday party. Advances in genetic research and genetic engineering hold much promise but the ethical implications are important to consider.

Source: China Foto Press/Getty Images, Inc.

field eventually known as *eugenics*. It is a branch of science devoted to improving the genetic make-up of a population by eradicating faulty genes leading to disease. It is often seen as a right-wing approach to social problems. Eugenics, associated with Francis Galton, influenced not only many people's personal childbearing decisions but also the policies of governments and social agencies. In some locations, for example, governments required forced sterilization surgery for people deemed unfit to reproduce, people very low in intelligence, for example (Tartakovsky, 2011). Furthermore, eugenics often was associated with racism and homophobia.

Today, the field of genetic research sparks debates about food practices, stem cell research, human cloning and other such issues. Every scientific field must wrestle with questions of how to ethically apply the knowledge it discovers about the world, but few more so than the field of psychology. In addition, few sciences are as plagued as psychology is with popular imitations and misrepresentations of their work, as we will see in the next section.

Misrepresentation of Psychology

It is natural for people to seek guidance periodically on how to live their lives. And psychologists certainly do not shy away from helping people with their problems, as evidenced by the thriving areas of clinical, health and counselling psychology and other applied areas described in Chapter 1. Ultimately, however, science – even psychology – cannot

---

PSYCHOLOGY AROUND US   Psychology . . . Not!

Astrology is a good example of pseudopsychology. It uses Zodiac signs to predict the future and give advice about relationships and decisions. Astrology's guiding principle is that all human beings have particular personality traits that are based on the alignment of planets on the dates of their births. Moreover, astrologers believe that those celestial-based traits determine how people will react to events and interact with others. The predictions, connections and claims of astrology have no scientific foundation. Most of them cannot, by definition, be tested and falsified, while others have consistently failed to receive any support. Yet the methods and tests used in astrology bear some resemblance to psychological personality tests. Thus, astrologers often adopt the terminology and topics of psychology, confusing many individuals – including many astrologers themselves – into believing that their field is scientifically based.

PSYCHOLOGY AROUND US   Making Psychology More Popular

Within many scientific disciplines, there are charismatic researchers and practitioners who are able to describe their complex topics so that almost anyone can understand the concepts. These individuals present facts about science in ways that engage the public's imagination. As a result, some of them become well-known figures in the popular media, such as in mass-market books, magazines, television and radio. Psychology too has its share of such individuals.

Antonio Damasio, MD, PhD, for example, is an award-winning, internationally recognized neuroscientist. He is director of the University of Southern California's Brain and Creativity Institute. Damasio is also the author of best-selling books that explain the underlying neurobiological systems for emotion, memory, language, consciousness and ethics (Damasio, 2010, 2003, 1999, 1994). His books have made neuroscience accessible to a wide audience.

Another popular researcher is psychologist Steven Pinker, PhD, who teaches at Harvard University. His specialities include visual cognition and language development. He is the author of award-winning and best-selling books that explore the idea that language is instinctual for human beings (Pinker, 2010, 2007, 2002, 1997, 1994). Pinker was named one of *Time* magazine's 100 most influential people in the world in 2004 and received the Humanist of the Year award in 2006.

And then, of course, there are the celebrity practitioners – professionals who are very well known to the public as talk show hosts on radio and television. Some such practitioners are well trained and have appropriate professional credentials. For example, in the United Kingdom there is Professor Richard Wiseman, who has written popular books but all from an evidence-based perspective. His work is especially relevant here because his career is partly devoted to debunking paranormal phenomena and providing alternative explanations for 'spooky goings on' that people report.

However, for each Wiseman, who is well qualified, there are many more celebrity practitioners who do not have proper training or appropriate credentials in their supposed areas of expertise, including some of the media's most popular TV and radio advisers. Before listening too closely, it is always best to check the qualifications of a psychologist or other professional who is dispensing advice on radio, television or the Web.

answer fundamental and subjective questions about human nature.

People who claim that psychology can answer *all* of life's questions are confusing the science of psychology with *pseudopsychology* (Leahey, 2005). Pseudopsychology, or *pop psychology*, is not based on the scientific method, yet it takes on the appearance of science. Often, pseudopsychologists have hidden agendas, such as promoting certain moral or religious values (Hergenhahn, 2005).

Clearly, psychologists are forced to maintain a difficult balance. On the one hand, it is important to encourage the human drive to seek guidance about how to live effectively. On the other hand, psychology must distance itself from pseudoscience in order to remain a natural, empirically based science. As one researcher wrote, 'Mainstream psychologists have a problem differentiating themselves from . . . a pseudoscience without seeming dogmatically intolerant' (Hergenhahn, 2005, p. 532).

Before You Go On

What Do You Know?

5. What are the four goals of psychology?

6. What is the main difference between psychology and pseudopsychology?

What Do You Think?

Why do you think that pseudopsychology appeals to so many people even though it is not based on science and does not reflect the truth?

How Do Psychologists Conduct Research?

LEARNING OBJECTIVE 3

List steps in the research process and key characteristics of descriptive and experimental psychological research methods.

Let us return to the controversy over reality TV. Suppose that you often watch *Big Brother*, the show in which people live together in a house to compete to win a prize. The first ever season of *Big Brother* in the United Kingdom saw the winner, Craig Phillips, donate his £70,000 prize money to a girl with Down syndrome to spend on a heart and lung transplant. Let us say that after viewing the show you noticed that you were more charitable towards your friends. You wonder whether all people who watched this particular show became morally superior to those people who did not. Did Craig set an example for others? How would you, as a psychological researcher, study this question?

Well, you could subject people to hours of repeats of the show, or you could decide to test the idea that the show itself promotes helping behaviour, and Craig's example was only part of that, and so you could focus on the current run of the show instead of one that is years old. As we described earlier, the scientific method begins with observation. So, after noting your own reaction, you may decide to observe other viewers. Maybe you get together with some friends or sit in a common area when the reality show is on. And you watch how everyone interacts with each other during and after the show.

State a Hypothesis

After you have made such observations, you need to make a prediction; this is your research hypothesis (Figure 2.2). As we have noted, a hypothesis defines what you think will happen and states your prediction in a way that can be tested. Your hypothesis may be: Watching *Big Brother* typically increases viewers' charitable behaviour.

Notice in your hypothesis that you are saying that one thing results in another thing. The two things are called variables. A **variable** is a condition, event or situation. It can really be many things. A condition or event that is thought to be a factor in changing another condition or event is known as an **independent variable**. In this study, watching or not watching the show is an independent variable. A researcher could change this variable to see how it affects charitable behaviour. Charitable behaviour would be a **dependent variable**, the condition or event you expect to change as a result of variations the independent variable.

In addition to defining these variables, you also have to **operationalize** the variables: develop precise definitions of the independent and dependent variables that allow you to measure and test them (McGrath, 2011). In this case, you

> **variable** the condition, event or situation that is studied in an experiment.

> **independent variable** the condition or event that is thought to be a factor in changing another condition or event.

> **dependent variable** the condition or event that you expect to change as a result of variations in the independent variable.

> **operationalize** to develop a working definition of a variable that allows you to test it.

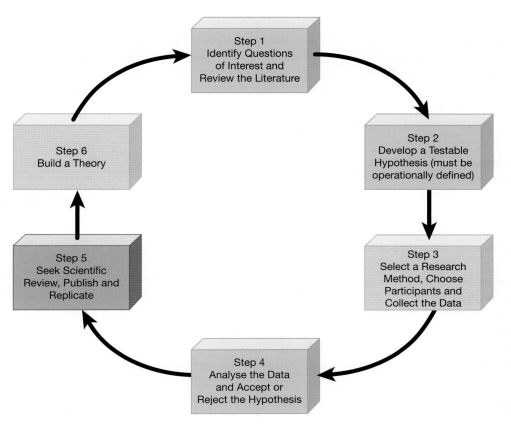

FIGURE 2.2 How do psychologists conduct research? Psychologists follow certain steps and confront a number of choice points as they study questions about mental processes and behaviours.

may define the independent variable as the length of time viewers watch the show. As a researcher, you may require the participants in your study to watch part of an episode, a whole episode or even a series of episodes.

It is pretty easy to create an operational definition of watching. But it is harder to operationalize the dependent variable in this study: charitable behaviour. You may have participants fill out a questionnaire asking about their charitable feelings. The questionnaires also may ask about their intentions to volunteer their time, give money to good causes or help friends. Of course, if you did this, you still would not know for sure that the attitudes and intentions stated on the questionnaire reflected actual charitable behaviour. Many people think a lot about volunteering or helping others without actually doing so.

Thus, you may prefer to have participants in your study demonstrate some kind of actual charitable behaviour. You could, for example, set up a situation in which each participant has to make a donation to other participants or to a charity, and then see who gives larger contributions. Even here, however, you would not be sure that your operational definition of charitable behaviour is on target. You may not be measuring 'true life' moral behaviour; the participants may be changing their research behaviour because they know they are being watched. There are yet other ways researchers can

operationally define charitable behaviour. Each definition will have advantages and disadvantages and each will have implications for the conclusions the researchers can draw.

Choose Participants

Once you have identified your variables, you need to select the people who will participate in your study. It generally is not possible for researchers to go out into the world and study the entire population of people whose behaviour interests them. Indeed, a population of interest could sometimes include everybody in the whole world. Or the desired population may be other large groups, such as all Europeans, adults, teenagers, men or women. In your reality show study, the population of interest includes everyone who watches and everyone who does not.

Because they cannot usually study an entire population, researchers must obtain a subset, or **sample**, from their population of interest. This subset stands in for the population as a whole. Population sampling of this kind is used very often. Political pollsters, for example, interview samples of the voting population in order to predict which candidate will win an election.

sample the group of people studied in an experiment, used to stand in for an entire group of people.

random selection
identifying a sample in such a way that everyone in the population of interest has an equal chance of being involved in the study.

Ideally, researchers choose their samples through **random selection**. Random selection means choosing your participants in such a way that everybody in the population of interest has an equal chance of becoming part of the sample. That way,

you can minimize *sampling biases*; that is, you will not select a group that is especially likely to confirm your hypothesis. If you include only your pro-reality show friends in your sample, the study will not be representative of the world at large. Similarly, a sample comprising television critics would not be representative of the full population of interest.

PSYCHOLOGY AROUND US   Wrong Sample, Wrong Conclusion

In 1936, President Franklin Delano Roosevelt ran for re-election against Kansas governor Alfred Landon. This was during the midst of the Depression. Landon ran on a platform of cutting government spending, and he seemed to be the favourite by quite a margin.

At that time, the *Literary Digest* was America's most popular magazine. It predicted that Landon would win, based on the largest number of people to ever reply to a poll: 2.4 million! In fact, the Digest had correctly called the winner in every presidential election since 1916.

But Landon did not win the 1936 election. The *Digest*'s prestige suffered and, partly because of this, it went bankrupt a few years later. The magazine had predicted that Roosevelt would get only 44% of the vote, when in fact he wound up with winning a total of 62% of the vote!

What went wrong? Simple. The *Literary Digest* picked its sample incorrectly. The magazine mailed 10 million questionnaires using addresses from the phone book and club membership lists. By doing so, they tended to miss poor voters who did not have phones and did not join clubs. (Only one household in four had a phone.) Poor people were overwhelmingly in favour of Roosevelt, but few of their voices were represented in the Digest poll. Hence, sampling bias created a sample that was non-representative.

A new polling organization run by George Gallup used 'random' methods of selection in that same election and predicted that Roosevelt would win with 56%. That was close enough to help launch the famous and still-going-strong Gallup Poll.

Genuine random selection can be difficult to achieve. The part of your population that does not watch *Big Brother* includes, for example, four-year-olds, who probably are not interested in adult-orientated programmes of any kind. Nor would four-year-olds be capable of making the same kinds of choices about charitable behaviour that 25- or 45-year-old persons might make. Thus, you may decide to narrow your sample to include adults only. Of course, such a choice would mean that your findings would be relevant to adults only, rather than to the entire human population. But, in this case, that is really the key population of largest interest.

Pick a Research Method

descriptive research methods studies that allow researchers to demonstrate a relationship between the variables of interest, without specifying a causal relationship.

Investigators have several options when designing studies to test their hypotheses (McGrath, 2011). Research methods differ in their goals, samples and the ability of researchers to generalize their results to a population. Researchers may, for example, use **descriptive research methods**, such as case studies, naturalistic observation and

surveys. These methods allow researchers to describe, or demonstrate, that a relationship exists between the variables of interest. As an alternative to descriptive methods, investigators may conduct *experiments*, a method that allows them to explain the *causes* of behaviour (Figure 2.3).

Case Studies A **case study** focuses on a single person. Medical and psychological practitioners who treat people with problems often conduct case studies to

case study a study focusing on a single person.

help determine whether therapeutic interventions produce changes in their clients' symptoms (Lee *et al.*, 2010). One disadvantage of a case study, however, is that it can be affected greatly by *researcher bias*, which occurs when investigators see only what they expect to see in their studies. Some clinicians/researchers may, for example, note only the healthy behaviours of persons after they have provided treatment to those individuals. Another disadvantage of case studies is that researchers cannot confidently generalize to other situations from the study of a single person (Lee *et al.*, 2010). Suppose, for example, that you conduct a case study in order to test your hypothesis that watching a giveaway/makeover

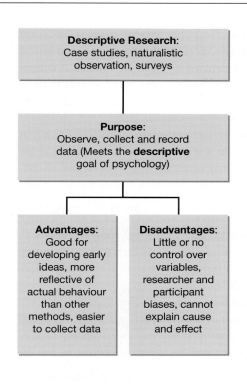

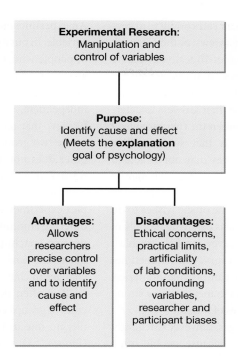

FIGURE 2.3 Descriptive versus experimental research
Because descriptive methods and experimental methods each serve particular purposes and have different advantages and disadvantages, psychological research includes both kinds of approaches.

Source: Adapted from p. 15, Carpenter & Huffman, *Visualizing Psychology*. John Wiley & Sons Inc. with permission.

reality show increases charitable behaviour. You closely observe one man who watches such a show, and you find that he later reports himself to be generous and charitable, giving hours of service to a homeless shelter every weekend. Your case study observation may indicate that your hypothesis is worthy of further research, but without including other participants in your study, it is impossible to say much about other viewers of the show. You would not know whether this person's behaviour after watching the show is the norm or an exception.

Naturalistic Observation In **naturalistic observation**, researchers watch while people behave as they normally do. Researchers often make naturalistic observations of children in schools or day-care centres. Perhaps as a researcher you could go into participants' homes and see whether they watched a particular giveaway/makeover show week after week. You could then observe whether those people who watch the show generally display more moral behaviour and whether those who do not watch behave less morally. Naturalistic observations have the advantage of being more reflective of actual human behaviour than most other research designs. However, a disadvantage of this type of research is that it too can be subject to researcher bias: observers may notice only what they expect to see (Goodwin, 2011; Connor-Greene, 2007). Another potential problem is that the mere presence of a researcher or even a video camera

naturalistic observation a study in which researchers directly observe people behaving as they normally do.

in an otherwise natural environment can change the behaviour of the participants. Many people become nicer or more considerate when they are aware that they are being watched, for example.

Surveys A third descriptive approach, frequently used in psychological research, is the **survey**. In a survey, researchers ask

survey a study in which researchers use a questionnaire or interview participants.

An observer's best friend. Computer monitors have made it easier and more accurate for researchers to conduct naturalistic observation. Rather than having to stand in a corner or use an expensive one-way mirror to observe school children at work, families interacting etc., the researcher can sit in another room, perhaps miles away, and watch the behaviours under investigation, all captured by an inconspicuous camera and microphone.

Source: moodboard/Corbis.

people a series of questions. Researchers can conduct surveys using in-person, telephone or email interviews, or they may ask the questions via a written questionnaire. To test your reality show hypothesis, for example, you may design a questionnaire that asks people about their *Big Brother* watching habits and about their charitable attitudes, and use their answers to determine whether a relationship exists between the two variables.

The advantage of this approach is that surveys allow researchers to obtain information that they may not be able to gather using case studies or naturalistic observations. It may be hard, for example, to determine whether a person in a case study is engaging in moral behaviour because he or she wishes to do the right thing or whether the individual is behaving morally in order to get some kind of reward. A survey can help establish the facts of such issues. Another reason surveys are sometimes favoured by psychologists is that they can provide numerical scores or ratings that enable researchers to measure how strong the relationship is between two variables of interest.

Surveys do suffer some disadvantages, however (McGrath, 2011). Their data can be unreliable because people often answer in ways that are socially acceptable rather than in ways that reflect their true attitudes, a problem known as *participant bias*. Thus, people in your giveaway/makeover show study may describe themselves on a survey as more charitable than they actually are because they know that being charitable is considered a socially appropriate trait. Similarly, participants in a survey study may have inflated views of just how charitable they are. Participant bias obviously is not only a common concern for survey researchers. It can also occur in experiments and other types of research as well, as we shall soon see.

Another problem is that survey data cannot tell us the *direction* of the relationship between variables. Do people who regularly watch a particular reality show become more charitable, or are highly charitable people drawn to watch that type of show? A survey cannot help you answer this question.

experiment a controlled observation in which researchers manipulate the presence or amount of the independent variable to see what effect it has on the dependent variable.

experimental group a group that is exposed to the independent variable.

control group a group that has not been or will not be exposed to the independent variable.

Experiments If you want to know what *causes* what, you have to design an experiment (McGrath, 2011). An **experiment** is a controlled observation in which researchers manipulate one variable – called the independent variable – and then observe any changes that occur in another variable – the dependent variable.

One way of experimentally testing your reality show hypothesis would be to divide your sample into two groups: an **experimental group** and a **control group**.

An experimental group is the one exposed to the independent variable. In our example, the experimental group would consist of people who are instructed to watch *Big Brother*. A control group, in contrast, consists of people who are similar to those in the experimental group but who are not exposed to the independent variable; for example, people not instructed to view that show. By comparing the charitable behaviour of the two groups after one group watches the show and the other does not, you may conclude with some degree of confidence that differences in charitable behaviour are caused by exposure to *Big Brother*. You could also create a more complex experiment, in which various experimental groups watch differing amounts of this reality show and compare them with the non-watching control group participants. This would help determine how much viewing of the show it takes to produce changes in charitable behaviour.

It is often difficult to make sure that experimental and control groups consist of the right participants. In our example, no one in the control group has ever seen *Big Brother* (Figure 2.4) and none will be instructed to do so for the study. But what about the experimental group? Should you include people who have watched the show previously, or should you begin with a group of participants who – like the control group – have never watched the show, and then expose the experimental group to a marathon of this reality

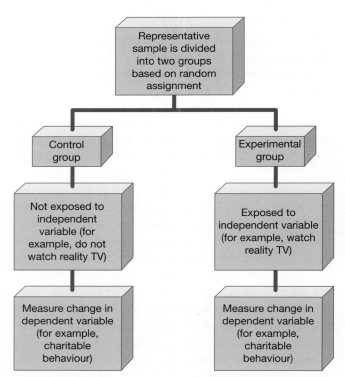

FIGURE 2.4 The experimental design. Key features of experimental designs are independent and dependent variables and random assignment of experimental and control groups.

show's episodes. Either approach is acceptable, but the two approaches may lead to different conclusions.

Other kinds of differences – past or present – between the experimental and control groups may also influence the results of an experiment. Researchers may use *random assignment* to make sure that everyone in their sample has an equal chance of being in either the control or experimental group (Remler & Van Ryzin, 2011). Even then, however, they still run the risk that the groups will differ in important ways. Suppose that you randomly assign your reality TV participants to each of your groups but nevertheless wind up with wealthy individuals in one group and poor individuals in the other group. Such an unintended group difference may affect the participants' later charitable behaviours and so may lead you to draw incorrect conclusions. Thus, before they begin running a study, some researchers interview or give questionnaires to participants in both the experimental and control groups. They then use this pre-study information as they are assigning participants to groups, making sure that the groups are comparable. In short, the use of such preliminary information helps guarantee that whatever effects emerge in the study are caused by the experimental manipulation of the independent variable and not by other variables, such as income level.

In addition, experimenters must be careful when deciding what tasks will be performed by participants in the control group. Researchers often have the participants in a control group take part in an activity of some kind. This makes sure that the changes seen in the experimental participants are indeed due to the impact of the independent variable and not the result of the experimental participants being especially active during the study. You may, for example, have your control group participants view another – non-reality – TV show that is just as entertaining as *Big Brother*. You could show an animated cartoon series such as *The Simpsons* to the control group. If the experimental participants still demonstrate more charitable behaviour than the control participants afterwards, you can be more certain that the reality show, rather than just any entertaining show, is in fact responsible.

Finally, experimenters must be careful to avoid bias in their studies. Once again, they must avoid participant bias and researcher bias (sources of bias that we discussed earlier). In addition, they must set up their studies so that they do not unintentionally communicate to participants the outcome that they (the experimenters) expect to see. If experimenters do somehow convey the expected outcome to participants, they are setting up what is called a *demand characteristic*. If a researcher were to tell participants in the experimental group that their answers to a charitability questionnaire would indicate how much reality TV contributed to positive real-life behaviour, the researcher might be creating a demand characteristic. Specifically, they might be encouraging those participants

to overstate their charitable inclinations. For this reason, many studies, particularly pharmaceutical drug studies, are designed so that the persons who run the study or who evaluate the behaviour of participants are unaware of the hypotheses of the study (Remler & Van Ryzin, 2011). Indeed, a number of studies use a specialized method known as a **double-blind procedure**, in which neither the participant nor the researcher knows which group – experimental or control – the participant is in (Wender *et al.*, 2011). Double-blind studies help keep researchers from creating what they want to observe. In addition, this keeps participants from intentionally acting in ways that confirm a researcher's hypothesis.

> **double-blind procedure** a study in which neither the participant nor the researcher knows what treatment or procedure the participant is receiving.

Almost everything we have just been discussing does not apply to qualitative research. It is time, therefore, to consider how qualitatively orientated psychology researchers go about their work.

Even from first principles some qualitative researchers differ in their ethos. For example, in the case of **grounded theory** (Glaser & Strauss, 1967), many argue that the researcher should try to approach the subject naively, without knowing about previous research in the area. In reality this is hard to achieve, but that blank slate approach can certainly prevent you from bringing baggage that directs and occasionally even determines what you are likely to discover. This is because many people believe that, when it comes to psychological research, you find what you look for. Instead, in the case of grounded theory, you allow the findings to emerge from the data. This is why it is called grounded theory (because the theories you produce are grounded in the data you collect). This is a very important distinction between this approach and traditional science, where you have a theory (or hypothesis) and then test it out by collecting data to confirm or disprove your theory. In the case of pure grounded theory, all you know is that you want to learn more about an issue, then you let the participants speak for themselves. You are not testing out anything.

> **grounded theory** an approach to qualitative research which emphasizes the need to collect data from interviews or texts and analyse those for themes which emerge from the text.

Of course, there are other qualitative approaches. The most simple, arguably, is **thematic analysis** (Boyatzis, 1998), which involves reading and re-reading texts or transcripts of interviews to identify recurring ideas, or themes, which a researcher then draws out. An increasingly common qualitative approach in psychology is **interpretative phenomenological analysis (IPA)** (Smith, 1996).

> **thematic analysis** a basic form of qualitative analysis involving derivation of themes from a text or interview transcript.

> **interpretative phenomenological analysis (IPA)** an approach to qualitative research that emphasizes interpretation and aims to understand the lived experience of the participants.

The two crucial words that define IPA are the first two. It is interpretative because, in order to use this, one accepts that it is impossible to approach something without interpreting it. Everything we perceive comes through the filter of our senses, and everything someone says to us is heard through the filter of our previous experiences. Rather than pretend otherwise, IPA researchers accept this and make it an explicit part of what they do. 'Phenomenological' refers to an attempt to understand the world of individuals through their reported experiences. By way of analogy, we could say that everyone lives in a house of their own making. It is not isolated from the rest of the world: it sits on the street, next to other people's houses. Also, with permission of the owner, you can visit it. You can look at the layout, inside and out, and you can make various judgements about the decor. Even if you try not to, you may find it difficult not to think about the wallpaper or the choice of carpets. However, what you cannot do is totally understand what it is like to live in that house, because you are only visiting. You can reflect on what you have been allowed to see, and that is why IPA is interpretative. You can write about what you feel living in that house, and other houses like it, would be like, based upon what you have seen. That is what makes IPA phenomenological.

All qualitative methods share this idea of examining what people say or write and drawing out themes. However, another method used in psychology, **discourse analysis**, is worth reflecting on because it has a different approach. For most discourse analysts, psychological phenomena are social constructs. We create our world around us, essentially. The words we use to describe the world are, effectively, the world itself, and shape it. We cannot separate the world from the words. This means that discourse analysts approach texts (interviews or written pieces) in a different way from that of most other qualitative researchers. They avoid interpreting texts and instead prefer to focus on the language used to express ideas. They would normally not go as far as to suggest what someone means by what they say. Instead, they present what they say, and analyse how they say it. For example, they analyse texts for forms of humour, or exaggeration, or even coughs and silences. They are often interested in the power relations that are set up between people, and that includes between the interviewer and the interviewee. They are constantly aware of the roles – social roles, of course – we all play and how these can shape, and be expressed through, language. As you can see, this is quite different from IPA.

Some researchers apply blends of various strands of qualitative research to their analysis. Therefore, it is not unusual to hear of a grounded theory/discourse analysis hybrid. One thing to remember, however, is that for many qualitative researchers the world of science is an irrelevance. They do not subscribe to the views that there is a truth out there to be discovered, or that we can measure it objectively and with a requirement that findings should be replicable. This is a substantially different ethos from that which guides traditional science, and the debates between hard-line qualitative and hard-line quantitative researchers can become heated.

> **discourse analysis**
> a qualitative research approach that focuses on the use of language to construct and shape the world around us.

Before You Go On

What Do You Know?

7. Which variable is controlled or manipulated by an experimenter?
8. What are three descriptive research methods used in psychology?
9. Which research method allows researchers to say that one variable causes another?
10. What are the main differences between any two qualitative approaches to data analysis?

What Do You Think?

What would you conclude if people's charitable behaviour increased after a single exposure to *Big Brother*? How would that conclusion be different if charitable behaviour only increased after a marathon viewing of the show?

How Do Psychologists Make Sense of Research Results?

LEARNING OBJECTIVE 4
Tell what information is conveyed by statistics, including correlation coefficients, means and standard deviations, and explain how psychologists draw conclusions about cause and effect.

Once researchers obtain results from a descriptive study or an experiment, what do they do with them? Can they simply look at their findings and say that there is a relationship between this and that variable, or that the two groups under study are different? No. Scientists cannot depend just on impressions. If they tried, they would have no way of knowing whether a relationship found between variables or a difference between groups actually mattered.

In quantitative psychology, psychologists use *statistics* to describe and measure relationships between variables. There are many statistical analyses that scientists use to look at the differences and similarities between groups (Goodwin, 2011). We will not go into a lot of depth about statistics here. We will, however, give you a few tips to help you understand the research findings you will read about in this book. First, we will discuss correlational analyses, statistical analyses that indicate how closely variables are related (Girden & Kabacoff, 2011). Then we will go on to discuss the statistical tests researchers use to ensure that their results do not occur simply by chance. And, finally, we will examine how researchers use statistical results to decide whether their hypothesis has been supported and to guide the next steps in the research process.

correlation a predictable relationship between two or more variables.

correlation coefficient a statistic expressing the strength and nature of a relationship between two variables.

Correlations: Measures of Relationships

A predictable relationship between two or more variables is called a **correlation**. To indicate correlations in descriptive studies psychologists use a statistic called a **correlation coefficient**. A correlation

coefficient can range from −1.00 to +1.00. The positive or negative sign in a correlation coefficient and the number itself each convey different information.

The positive or negative sign of a correlation tells you the *direction* of the relationship between variables. When scores on both variables get bigger together or smaller together, the relationship is known as a **positive correlation**, indicated by a positive sign. In our example of a reality show study, we predicted a positive correlation between *Big Brother* watching and charitable behaviour: as watching increases, so will charitable behaviour. If we had suggested that charitable behaviour does not increase, but actually drops, as people watch more reality TV, then we would be predicting a **negative correlation**, indicated by a negative sign. This is what many people might even suggest would happen given that the show was fundamentally about competition as much as it was about cooperation. When the variables are negatively correlated, higher scores on one variable are related to lower scores on another variable. Figure 2.5 shows various such relationships.

positive correlation a relationship in which scores on two variables increase together.

negative correlation a relationship in which scores on one variable increase as scores on another variable decrease.

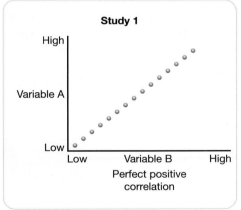
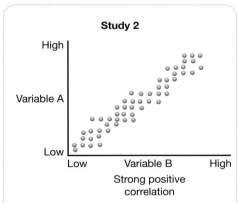
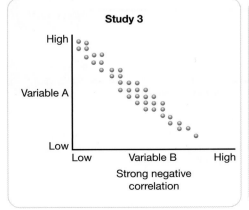
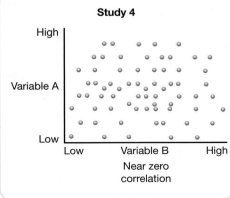

FIGURE 2.5 Graphing correlations. Were we to plot each participant's score on Variable A and Variable B on a graph, we would see that the variables display a perfect positive correlation in Study 1, strong positive correlation in Study 2, strong negative correlation in Study 3 and a near zero correlation in Study 4.

In addition to looking at the positive or negative sign, we must consider the number itself of the correlation coefficient. The number tells the size, or strength, of the relationship between variables, that is how strongly we can predict one variable if we know the other. The larger the number, the stronger the relationship. Thus, a correlation coefficient of 0.00 means that there is no relationship between the two variables. Knowing a person's score on one variable tells you nothing about the person's score on the other. The further a correlation coefficient gets from 0 in either the positive or negative direction, the stronger the relationship between the two variables. A high positive correlation coefficient means that scores on the two variables under examination *typically* rise and fall together, and a high negative correlation coefficient means that a rise in one of the variables *usually* is accompanied by a fall in the other. A correlation of +1.00 or −1.00 is known as a **perfect correlation**, one in which the variables' scores are always perfectly related. One score always rises or falls in direct proportion to the changes in the other variable.

Again, it is important to keep in mind that in correlation coefficients the positive and negative sign and the number itself provide two different pieces of information. A correlation with a negative coefficient is not weaker than one with a positive coefficient. In fact, the relationship may be stronger if, for example, the negative correlation is −0.7 and the positive correlation is +0.2. A negative correlation of −0.7 would mean that the two variables are quite strongly related in such a way that low scores on one variable very often are associated with high scores on the other (Figure 2.6).

In psychology, really exciting relationships are often reflected by a correlation coefficient of 0.3 and above. This is far from a perfect correlation, largely because relationships between behaviours, thoughts and emotions can be complex. Moreover, many other variables may also be at work in such relationships. Nevertheless, 0.3 or above typically means that the two variables in question have some kind of predictable relationship.

Correlations offer lots of useful information, particularly when we are interested in the scientific goal of *prediction* (Girden & Kabacoff, 2011). The correlation coefficient tells us just how well we can use one piece of information about someone, such as how often the person watches a giveaway/makeover reality show, to predict his or her behaviour in another realm, in this case charitable behaviour. A key piece of information that correlations do *not* tell us, however, is *causality* (Remler & Van Ryzin, 2011). That is, they do not shed light on whether a change in one variable actually *causes* the change in the other variable (Figure 2.7). As we mentioned earlier, only experimental studies and experimental analyses can tell us whether causality is at work.

perfect correlation one in which two variables are exactly related, such that low, medium and high scores on both variables are always exactly related.

+1.00	Perfect positive relationship
+0.88	Very strong positive relationship
+0.62	Strong positive relationship
+0.38	Moderate positive relationship
+0.12	Weak positive relationship
0.00	No relationship
−0.12	Weak negative relationship
−0.38	Moderate negative relationship
−0.62	Strong negative relationship
−0.88	Very strong negative relationship
−1.00	Perfect negative relationship

FIGURE 2.6 How to read a correlation coefficient. The sign of the coefficient tells us the direction and the number tells us the magnitude, or strength, of the relationship between two variables.

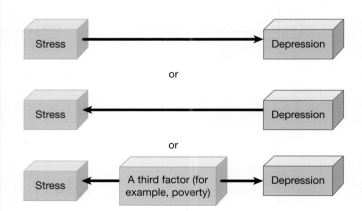

FIGURE 2.7 Correlation versus causation. Research has found a strong correlation between stress and clinical depression. However, this correlation does not tell us whether stress causes depression or whether depression causes stressful events, or that other factors, such as poverty, produce both stress and depression.

Correlation versus casualty.
The repeated co-occurrence of two events (correlation) does not necessarily mean that one is causing the other. Children who eat ice cream, for example, tend to have bike accidents. It may be that eating ice cream while riding causes young bikers to have more accidents. Or it may be that parents typically treat their children to ice cream whenever they have accidents. Or perhaps hot summer days lead to increases in both ice cream eating and bike riding.

Source: Left: Masterfile; Right: ©Mika/Corbis.

PSYCHOLOGY AROUND US   Do Not Be Fooled

Every month, it seems, studies tie happiness to certain kinds of jobs. One study, for example, found that people who work as clergy, fire-fighters, physical therapists, architects, special education teachers and airline pilots tend to be happier than other workers (GSS, 2007). Meanwhile, people who work as roofers, machine operators, labourers, hotel room staff and kitchen workers were found to be less happy than most other workers.

So what can we conclude from such studies? Not all that much, it turns out. Most important, we cannot conclude, despite the exclamations of news reports and popular magazines, that certain jobs produce more (or less) happiness than others.

The problem is that the findings from studies of jobs and happiness usually are correlational. As such, they do not tell us what causes the relationship. In fact, jobs and happiness may be correlated for any one of three reasons:

- Certain jobs do in fact cause more happiness, the preferred interpretation of news reports and magazines.

That is, working as a fire-fighter may in fact make you particularly happy in life, while working as a service station attendant may make you particularly unhappy.

- Happiness may cause people to seek certain jobs. Perhaps happy people are more likely than unhappy people to seek work as priests, special education teachers or airline pilots.
- Job choice and level of happiness may each be caused by a third variable, such as financial security. Perhaps a lack of money causes certain people to be unhappy and, independently, causes those same people to work in jobs such as machine operators, hotel maids and kitchen workers.

Of course, it may well be that some jobs are more satisfying and produce more happiness than others. It is just that we need more correlational studies to establish that causal relationship.

Experimental Analyses: Establishing Cause and Effect

If you want to examine differences between groups and determine the cause of such differences, you have to do a particular kind of statistical analysis, called an *experimental analysis*. As the first part of this analysis, researchers calculate the **mean** and **standard deviation** of each group.

mean the arithmetic average of a set of scores.

The mean is the arithmetic average of the scores of all participants in a group. This is the same average you have been calculating since your early days in school. Big differences between the mean – the average score – of an experimental group and the mean of a control group may indeed suggest big differences between the participants in the groups.

standard deviation the statistical index of how much scores vary within a group.

To be certain of this, however, researchers also look at the standard deviation, an index of how much the participants' scores *vary* from one another within each group. Let us say, for example, you have 10 control-group participants who watch *Pokemon* and then make donations to charity of 4, 5, 4, 6, 5, 4, 4, 7, 5 and 6 currency units in a charitability task. Let us further suppose that you also have 10 experimental-group participants in your study who watch *Big Brother*, who subsequently make donations of 1, 2, 12, 11, 5, 9, 4, 1, 3 and 2 units. Each group would have a mean donation of 5 units. Unless you also examine the standard deviations for both groups (1.05 for the control group and 4.20 for the experimental group), you may not realize that there are more extreme reactions in the reality show group than in the other group (Figure 2.8).

After determining the mean and standard deviation of each group, researchers can compare the two groups. Psychologists typically compare means by using statistical procedures known as *t-tests* (for two groups) or *analyses of variance* (for two or more groups, often abbreviated to ANOVA). These procedures take into account both the mean differences and the variance within the groups, as well as of the size of the groups. The statistical procedures are known as *significance tests* because they measure whether the collection of differences found between the groups is *statistically significant*.

In statistics, the word *significant* has a different meaning from its everyday use. A test of statistical significance tells us how probable it is that the differences found between groups are due to experimental manipulations rather than to chance. Each test of statistical significance yields a *probability statistic*, or *p level*. If a test of statistical significance produces a probability statistic of $p < 0.05$, it means that there is a less than a 5% probability that the differences found between the two groups in a study are due to chance. That is, if researchers were to conduct the same study 100 times, they would, by chance alone, get the same result found in the current study less than 5% of the time. In other words, there's an extremely low probability that the difference between groups found in the current study occurred simply as an act of chance. Most likely, it occurred because of a real difference between the two groups of participants in the study. By convention, when a test of statistical analysis yields a probability of less than 0.05 ($p < 0.05$), psychological researchers conclude that the difference they have found between groups in their study is statistically significant; that is, likely to be a real difference that is due to the manipulations carried out in the study.

Keep in mind that the numerical difference between group means and the probability statistic say nothing about how big an effect you are seeing in your study. Let us say that participants who watch *Big Brother* later display a higher mean charity score than do those who watch the cartoon *Pokemon*, and that the probability statistic is less than 0.01 ($p < 0.01$). This does not necessarily mean that the reality show viewers have become *much* more charitable than the non-viewers. It just means that there is less than one chance in 100 that you obtained that result by chance. If you want to know how big the effect of watching reality TV is, you need to calculate yet another statistic, known as the *effect size*. If you were to find a large effect size in your study, it would suggest that watching the reality show strongly increases charitable behaviour.

The Qualitative World

Once more, we should remember that in qualitative research all this talk of cause and effect and correlation is essentially meaningless. Qualitative researchers are approaching an understanding of human behaviour from a completely different angle. However, that is not to say that there is not a kind of middle ground. In fact, growing numbers of researchers treat qualitative and quantitative methods as different tools in the researcher's toolbox, to be chosen when they see fit, depending on the research question. Furthermore, we often find researchers conducting both qualitative and quantitative research at the same time and then looking to see whether they can draw conclusions across both types of method of inquiry. If we see similar things cropping up in interviews as when we take more formal measurements, we often describe this as *triangulation* (Denzin, 1978). The 'strength' of a quantitative finding can be increased if it resonates with

Charitable donations

Pokemon	Big Brother
4	1
5	2
4	12
6	11
5	5
4	9
4	4
7	1
5	3
6	2
5 ← Mean → 5	
1.05 ← Standard deviation → 4.20	

FIGURE 2.8 Variability and the standard deviation. Although these two sets of data have the same mean, or average, score of charitability in our fictitious study, viewers of *Big Brother* are much more varied in their charitable behaviours (high standard deviation) than are viewers of *Pokemon* (low standard deviation).

a qualitative finding, according to some researchers. In fact, Denzin describes four different types of triangulation: of these, the methodological version is only one. Not all qualitative researchers are happy with the notion of triangulation, especially those who entirely reject the view that research in the behavioural disciplines like psychology should be quantitative. If you were against 'measuring' people, then of course you would be unlikely to want to somehow verify your findings against such measurements. However, this raises another important issue in qualitative research: the purpose. Qualitative researchers are often opposed to trying to apply what they find to other populations. To them, their findings are one version of a reality that changes over time, and are unlikely to generalize. Therefore, they normally avoid talk of validity or generalization in this sense.

Using Statistics to Evaluate and Plan Research

If you get a result like this – a difference between groups that is very unlikely to have occurred by chance – does it mean you have fully supported your hypothesis and should sit back and toast your success? Well, not yet. Scientists need to be sure. They need to go back and test their hypotheses some more. It is only through **replication** – taking the data from one observation and expanding on it to see whether it holds up under a variety of conditions and in multiple samples – that we can determine whether what we hypothesize is correct. Over time, replication enables hypotheses to become theories and theories to become laws.

replication the repeated testing of a hypothesis to ensure that the results achieved in one experiment were not due to chance.

Another important feature of science is to use different research methods to explore the same research question (McGrath, 2011). If researchers use several approaches, including surveys, experimentation and independent observations, and obtain the same results, they can be more certain that their hypotheses are accurate and can be confident about incorporating those hypotheses into theories.

As we described earlier, in our discussion of the scientific method, theories also enable us to produce additional hypotheses. If your hypothesis about *Big Brother* proves correct, and people on average report themselves to be more charitable and display more charitable behaviours on experimental tasks, you have reason to continue your line of research. You can conduct the same experiment with other reality shows, and see whether the hypothesis continues to hold up for all kinds of reality shows. You may also decide to look at other forms of moral or pro-social behaviour besides charity, such as feelings of empathy or a sense of fair play. If you continue to replicate these results with other shows and other moral behaviours, you are effectively supporting the theory that watching reality TV in fact contributes to increased moral behaviour.

PRACTICALLY SPEAKING   Tips on Reading a Scientific Journal Article

As a psychology student, you will need to read journal articles. Initially, this task may seem overwhelming. The authors of journal articles tend to use unfamiliar language, condense complex concepts into a small space and make assumptions about the reader's knowledge of their topic. However, you can turn this task into something interesting and worthwhile by following a few simple steps.

When you read a research paper, try to understand the scientific contributions the authors are making. You should read the paper critically and not assume that the authors are always correct.

You do not need to read the paper sequentially to get the gist of it. First, you could read the abstract, the introduction and the conclusions. Next, look through the references to determine whose work is at the heart of the current research. After this first read-through, try to summarize the article in one or two sentences.

Then, go back and read the entire paper from beginning to end. Study the figures, re-read parts that are difficult to understand and look up unfamiliar words. Make notes in the margins or on separate sheets of paper. And answer the following questions as you work:

- Title: What does this tell you about the problem?
- Abstract: What does this general overview tell you about the current paper?
- Introduction: What are the authors' assumptions, important ideas and hypotheses?
- Methods: Do the methods seem to effectively test the authors' hypotheses?
- Related work: How does the current work relate to past work? What is new or different about the current study?
- Conclusions: What were the study's results, and do they make sense? What were the study's limitations? What do the authors propose for future research? How does the study contribute to a better understanding of the problem?

You also may choose to outline, summarize or keep more detailed notes, especially if you are using the article for a term paper.

Before You Go On

What Do You Know?

11. What two pieces of information does a correlation coefficient give about the relationship between variables?
12. What do the mean and standard deviation tell you about scores of a group?
13. What do *t*-tests tell experimenters?
14. What is triangulation?

What Do You Think?

Give some examples of positive and negative correlations that you have observed in everyday life.

What Ethical Research Guidelines Do Psychologists Follow?

LEARNING OBJECTIVE 5

Tell what ethical steps psychologists take to protect the rights of human research participants.

For 40 years between 1932 and 1972, the American government violated ethics in the now-infamous Tuskegee Syphilis Study, an extensive clinical study concerning the course and treatment of syphilis in African-American men. Many of the men in the study who tested positive for syphilis were not treated, or were treated only minimally for the disease, to ensure that they would not benefit from treatment. The reason for this was that researchers wanted to study the course of the disease when left untreated.

In a later interview, John Heller, one of the medical directors of the Tuskegee Syphilis Study stated, 'The men's status did not warrant ethical debate. They were subjects, not patients; clinical material, not sick people' (Jones, 1981, p. 179). Horrors such as this project alarmed the public and raised awareness and concern about the ethical practices of scientists, including psychologists, who conduct research with human and animal participants (Nagy, 2011; McGaha & Korn, 1995).

Today, psychological research must protect the needs and rights of participants involved in a study. Psychology researchers are bound by the same general ethical principles that guide doctors and other clinicians (Campbell *et al.*, 2010). The Code of Ethics of the American Psychological Association states it clearly: 'Psychologists . . . take care

PSYCHOLOGY AROUND US   A Notorious Project (MK-ULTRA)

The rights of research participants were also profoundly violated in a number of other celebrated studies during the 20th century. In the 1950s and 1960s, for example, almost 100 people unknowingly became participants in 'depatterning' experiments meant to test the feasibility of mind control. Both the Canadian government and the United States CIA funded experiments to learn more about mind control before potential foes could master the technique. Most of the research participants emerged from the experiments emotionally disabled, with limited memories of the life they had lived before they entered the hospital.

Linda Macdonald was one of those participants. In 1963, she checked into a Canadian institution to be treated for fatigue and depression. Six months later, she could not read, write, cook a meal or make a bed. She did not remember her husband, her five children or any of the first 26 years of her life.

During her stay, Ms Macdonald was given massive doses of various drugs, put into a drug-induced sleep for 86 days, given more than 100 electroconvulsive treatments and exposed to 'psychic driving', a technique in which repetitive taped messages were played to her for 16 hours a day. The purpose was not to treat this woman's depression but to gather information about the causes and effects of brainwashing (Davis, 1992; Powis, 1990).

Later many of the victims, including Macdonald, sued the Canadian and United States governments for subjecting them to these experiments without their permission. In 1988, the United States government agreed to compensate Macdonald and eight others with about $100,000 each, and in 1992, the government of Canada agreed to pay each of the 80 living victims $100,000.

to do no harm' (American Psychological Association, 2002). There are almost identical statements in the codes of conduct of the British Psychological Society, and indeed most of the psychological professional bodies worldwide.

To ensure that researchers follow proper ethical practices, **ethics committees** now oversee studies conducted in academic and other research settings across the world. Any institution (university, private corporation, government agency or medical school) conducting research involving human participants is expected to appoint an *ethics committee*. The committee often consists of a mixture of researchers from inside and outside the field and of individuals from the community. They examine research proposals and rule on the potential risks and benefits of each study's procedures. If the board concludes that a proposed study's risks or discomforts outweigh its potential scientific benefit, then the undertaking is not allowed to proceed. Ethics committees generally require that psychologists studying human participants take the following steps to protect those participants:

> **ethics committee** a research oversight group that evaluates research to protect the rights of participants in the study.

> **Informed consent** the requirement that researchers give as much information as possible about the purpose, procedures, risks and benefits of the study so that a participant can make an informed decision about whether to participate.

- *Obtain informed consent.* **Informed consent** from participants requires that researchers give as much information as possible about the purpose, procedures, risks and benefits of a study, so participants can make informed decisions about whether they want to be involved in the study (Nagy, 2011). If the participants are children, researchers must obtain informed consent from the parents or caregivers and the child.

- *Protect participants from harm and discomfort.* In addition to medical or physical risks, such as those faced by the men in the Tuskegee studies, researchers must avoid putting participants in situations that could cause them excessive emotional stress, for example.

- *Protect confidentiality.* Researchers must follow procedures that protect the identities of participants and ensure the confidentiality of their research responses (Nagy, 2011). In addition, they must explain these procedures to the study's participants.

- *Provide complete debriefing.* In some cases, were participants to have full knowledge about the purposes and goals of a study before it began, their responses during the study might be influenced by that very knowledge. They might, for example, try to behave

as the investigators predict they would behave. Thus, researchers often try to provide participants with enough information before a study to protect their rights, yet withhold certain information that may affect the participants' responses. At the end of a study, the researchers are required to offer a **debriefing** to participants – an information session during which they reveal any information that was withheld earlier.

> **debriefing** supplying full information to participants at the end of their participation in a research study.

In addition to ruling on the costs and benefits of the study, ethics committees also assess other issues. They look, for example, at the compensation individuals receive for taking part in a study. It is important, for example, that participants not be tempted by overly high levels of compensation to participate in potentially dangerous studies. In addition, ethics committees determine whether particular groups (such as men, women or members of minority ethnic groups) are singled out unnecessarily for a given study.

In a related development, the ethics of psychological research involving animals has received careful attention. Animal rights advocates point out that animals are especially vulnerable research participants, since they cannot give their consent to be part of a study. They also argue that animals may be exposed to more extreme risks than humans, for sometimes unclear benefits.

Although animal rights activists are certainly correct in pointing out that animal studies often pose special concerns, they are not so accurate when some of them suggest that the study of human psychology has gained little benefit from the study of animals. Much of our knowledge about learning and motivation began with studies of animals, such as Pavlov's famous dogs (which we will talk more about in Chapter 9). We also have gained enormous knowledge about the nervous system from work on animals, using research procedures that could never be conducted on human beings. And animal research has played a major role in the development of medications, including medications for psychological and neurological disorders.

The British Psychological Society and other societies worldwide have issued specific ethical guidelines regarding research with animals. These guidelines rule that the research must improve the welfare of both humans and animals, and that it should only be conducted when it advances our knowledge of behaviour or neuropsychological functioning. In addition, before conducting animal studies, researchers must first consider alternatives to the use of animals (such as the use of different procedures with human participants) (ILAR, 2011; American Psychological Association, 2002; British Psychological Society, 2012, 2009). Furthermore, in the

Source: I Dream Stock/Masterfile.

years. Thus, let's clarify some important facts and figures about animal research (American Psychological Association, 2002; ILAR, 2011; MORI, 2005, 1999).

- The welfare of animal subjects is of great interest and concern not only to animal activists but also to animal researchers, government agencies, scientific organizations and the public.

- Around 8% of psychological research involves the use of animals; 90% of the animals used are rodents and birds (mostly rats and mice); 5% are monkeys and other primates.

- Ethics committees oversee the work of animal laboratories and ensure that each study follows all ethical, legal and humane guidelines, and the committees pay close attention to such issues as the prevention or alleviation of animal pain, alternatives to the use of animals and the clinical and scientific importance of the study.

- In surveys, 7% of the public say that they can accept animal research as long as it is for scientific purposes (MORI, 2005). Most respondents even approve of experiments that bring some pain to animals when those investigations are seeking a cure for childhood leukaemia, AIDS or other significant problems.

United Kingdom, for example, the Home Office gives out the licences for carrying out animal research, which are closely protected and given out only where the research could not be conducted without the use of animals, and the number of animals used is minimized, and finally where the benefits of the research clearly outweigh the harm (which is always a subjective judgement, of course).

As you have seen in this chapter, research involving animals has been the focus of scrutiny and debate in recent

All such guidelines, for both animal and human research undertakings, help ensure not only more ethical procedures but also better science as well.

Before You Go On

What Do You Know?

15. What does an ethics committee do?
16. What is informed consent and how does it relate to debriefing?

What Do You Think?

Are ethical standards for psychology different from those for other sciences? Should they be?

Activities to test yourself further are available in your interactive e-book at **www.wileyopenpage.com**

Summary

What Is a Science?

LEARNING OBJECTIVE 1   List two core beliefs of science, and describe the steps in the scientific method.

- Science is an approach to knowing the world built on the core principles that (1) the universe operates according to certain natural laws and (2) these laws are discoverable and testable.
- Science is founded upon the scientific method, a process that moves from making controlled, direct observations to generating progressively broader conclusions and tests and attempting to disprove hypotheses.

Is Psychology a Science?

LEARNING OBJECTIVE 2   Compare and contrast psychology with other natural sciences, such as biology, chemistry and physics, and with pseudopsychologies, such as astrology.

- Psychology shares with every science the primary goals of describing, explaining, predicting and controlling the objects of study. The goals of psychology differ from those of other sciences because the search for elements of mental processes and behaviour is complicated by constantly shifting human factors.
- Psychology also shares more similarity with the fields of religion and philosophy than many sciences do because psychological findings are more often associated with values, morality and personal preference.
- Psychology is different from pseudopsychology. Although the latter also attempts to answer fundamental questions about human nature and behaviour, it has no basis in the scientific method.

How Do Psychologists Conduct Research?

LEARNING OBJECTIVE 3   List steps in the research process and key characteristics of descriptive and experimental psychological research methods.

- Psychological research is rooted in first generating a hypothesis, or prediction, about the relationship between two or more variables based on observations.
- Psychologists conduct research with a sample, a small group meant to represent the larger population of interest. The best means of selecting a sample is random selection, a procedure in which everyone in the population has an equal chance of being selected.
- Descriptive research methods include case studies, naturalistic observations and surveys.
- Case studies are in-depth observations of a single individual.
- Naturalistic observation involves observing people in settings outside of laboratories, where their behaviour occurs naturally.
- Surveys may be conducted in interviews or with questionnaires.
- Only experiments allow researchers to draw conclusions about cause-and-effect relationships.
- All research methods have advantages for particular uses and all are subject to various drawbacks. Researchers must plan carefully to avoid subject bias, researcher bias and demand characteristics.

Qualitative research methods are designed to add a different dimension to psychology through the understanding of texts, interviews and speeches in a richer way than numerical analysis can achieve. Various qualitative methods exist with a different ethos attached to each. In grounded theory, one allows the themes to emerge from the data, whereas in discourse analysis one concentrates on the construction of our world through the language used to describe it. In interpretative phenomenological analysis (IPA), the emphasis is on understanding and interpreting the world of the person.

How Do Psychologists Make Sense of Research Results?

LEARNING OBJECTIVE 4   Tell what information is conveyed by statistics, including correlation coefficients, means and standard deviations, and explain how psychologists draw conclusions about cause and effect.

- Correlations allow us to describe and measure relationships between two or more variables. A *correlation coefficient* tells the direction and size of a correlation.
- Researchers use the *mean* and *standard deviation* to describe and summarize their results.
- Researchers use *p values* to determine the statistical significance of results. *Effect size* gives an indication of how strong the relationship between variables is.
- Replication of experiments and repeated study of the same predictions using different methods help hypotheses become theories.

What Ethical Research Guidelines Do Psychologists Follow?

LEARNING OBJECTIVE 5 Tell what ethical steps psychologists take to protect the rights of human research participants.

- As egregious ethical practices came to light in the United States in the 1960s and 1970s, people took action to protect the rights of research participants.

- Today, ethics committees help to protect human rights.
- Psychological researchers must obtain informed consent from human participants, protect them from harm and discomfort, protect their confidentiality and completely debrief them at the end of their participation.
- The use of animal participants in research has also raised ethical concerns. Ethics committees help to protect animals' needs and comfort in experiments.

 Quizzes to test yourself further are available in your interactive e-book at **www.wileyopenpage.com**

Key Terms

biases 25
case study 32
control group 34
correlation 37
correlation coefficient 37
debriefing 43
deductive reasoning 24
dependent variable 30
descriptive research
   methods 32
discourse analysis 36

double-blind procedure 35
empirical 25
empiricism 27
ethics committee 43
experiment 34
experimental group 34
grounded theory 35
hypothesis 25
hypothetico-deductive
   approach 25
independent variable 30

inductive reasoning 25
Informed consent 43
interpretative
   phenomenological
   analysis (IPA) 35
mean 39
naturalistic observation 33
negative correlation 37
operationalize 30
perfect correlation 38
positive correlation 37

random selection 32
replication 41
sample 31
standard deviation 39
survey 33
thematic analysis 35
theories 25
variable 30

 Flashcards to test yourself further are available in your interactive e-book at **www.wileyopenpage.com**

CHAPTER 3

Biological and Cognitive Development

Adapted by Alastair D. Smith, University of Nottingham, UK

CHAPTER OUTLINE

- Understanding How We Develop
- How Is Developmental Psychology Investigated?
- Before We Are Born

- Infancy
- Early and Middle Childhood
- Adolescence
- Adulthood

 Access your interactive e-book to view a video clip for this chapter at **www.wileyopenpage.com**

Nature or Nurture?

What shapes our mental life? Are we the product of our genetic heritage (nature) or our upbringing and environment (nurture)? This has been a fundamental philosophical question since Antiquity, when Plato espoused the view that children were born with innate knowledge, and is not one that can be easily answered. Consider, for example, Chang and Eng, the conjoined siblings who gave us the term *Siamese Twins*. Born in 1811 in the Kingdom of Siam (now Thailand), the twins became world-famous medical curiosities, touring many countries and eventually settling in the United States. As you might expect, there was much in their behaviour to demonstrate how alike they were: they shared many beliefs, opinions and habits, and were rarely heard talking to each other (fuelling stories that they were telepathic). However, there were also striking differences between them. Chang was more dominant, with a quick intellect and a short temper, whereas Eng was a quieter, more considered individual, with a wider range of interests. ■

Siamese Twins: The most famous Siamese twins, Chang and Eng Bunker (1811–1874), after whom the rare condition is named. Born in Siam (modern Thailand), they married two sisters and had nine children each, eventually dying on the same day.

Source: Hulton Archive/Getty Images, Inc.

sophisticated techniques have been used to argue that differences between individuals (such as susceptibility to alcoholism) can be traced to the precise genes responsible. On the other hand, studies have shown that adopted children often develop very similar personalities and intellects to those of their non-genetic siblings in the household (Plomin & Daniels, 1987).

All of these factors demonstrate that we can only truly understand human psychology if we take development into account. We are certainly not born fully formed, nor do we emerge as simple versions of our adult selves. Instead, we go through many years of development both within the womb and outside it. Some of these processes will be influenced by our genetic make-up, and others will be influenced by the environment we are raised in. All the things that go together to make up our individual sense of self, from intellect to personality, are a direct result of this developmental process.

This chapter is the first of two that consider the fundamental role of development in human psychology. Here we will explore how psychologists have studied developmental change. We will then move on to the role of genetics in shaping who we are and will describes how psychologists have explored the development of cognitive abilities – the skills that enable us to understand and respond to the world.

What is Developmental Psychology?

Unlike other fields in psychology, which often focus on what a person is like at a particular moment in his or her life, **developmental psychology** is concerned with changes in our behaviour and mental processes over time, and how various factors affect the course of those changes. Thinking back to our discussion of Chang and Eng above, we often ask similar questions of ourselves: what happened to make us into the women and

> **developmental psychology** the study of changes in behaviour and mental processes over time and the factors that influence the course of those changes.

men we are? Was it genes, or parents, or friends, or other, more individualized, factors that led you to where you are right at this moment? Do changes occur because of biological factors or because of our experiences? Are we all doomed to turn into our mothers or fathers?

These questions are challenging: development is very complex and depends on a great many cultural and social influences (Jensen, 2011). This makes it difficult for developmental psychologists to state precisely what causes us to be the way we are. Instead, they try to identify several general factors that work together to influence how we grow and change across our lifespan.

How can we account for those important psychological differences? They shared the same genetic material (and, indeed, a liver) so they certainly received the same starting point in life. Furthermore, unlike the great majority of people, they shared the exact same environment until the day that they both died. If either nature or nurture were wholly responsible for human personality and intellect then we would expect Chang and Eng to have been identical. Yet they remained different personalities in their own right, which leads to the hypothesis that a more subtle interaction between genes and environment could be responsible for our eventual outcome. For example, people may have been more likely to respond to Chang's dominant personality than Eng's quieter one, meaning that Chang may have received more interaction (both good and bad) from the people around them. Thus, small differences may have large outcomes when all of life's influences are combined.

We can still see the prominence of this debate within modern experimental psychology. On the one hand,

TABLE 3.1 Developmental Stages over the Lifespan

Stage	Approximate Age
Prenatal	Conception to birth
Infancy	Birth to 2 years
Early childhood	2–6 years
Middle childhood	6–12 years
Adolescence	12–20 years
Young adulthood	20–45 years
Middle adulthood	45–60 years
Later adulthood	60 years to death

It is worth noting that the terms *developmental psychology* and *child psychology* have often been treated interchangeably. If you take a developmental psychology course, you will probably spend most of your time working on child psychology and will be unlikely to extend your studies into the psychology of adolescence. In some respects, this chapter will be very similar. We will spend much of this chapter discussing childhood, simply because that is what most of the pioneering theorists in developmental psychology spent their time thinking about and studying. Equally, however, we will not just stop at adolescence, as we will be looking at development in adulthood and what is now called *the third age*.

This inclusivity is because of a revolution that has gained momentum recently. Psychologists now acknowledge that developmental changes do not stop when we leave childhood (Table 3.1). As we will see later in the chapter, there is a trend towards a longer human lifespan, and this has given greater prominence to fields of study such as *gerontology* or the *psychology of ageing* (Overton & Lerner, 2010).

We will also think about how development can take an atypical course, an area in which another revolution has been brewing. A relatively new field of study called *developmental psychopathology* has provided a new way to help us focus on the factors over the course of a person's lifetime that contribute to their atypical development, a development that then follows a different developmental trajectory. This may result from brain damage, genetic disorder or a neuropsychiatric problem.

Understanding How We Develop

LEARNING OBJECTIVE 1

Understand the key debates underlying research and theory in child development.

Before we discuss what happens in development, it would be useful to consider some of the key issues that concern developmental psychologists. These issues are often foundations for theory, research and clinical work, but they are not always directly tested. As you work through the chapter, you may want to think about how the theories we will discuss later fit with these big ideas about human development.

What Drives Change? Nature versus Nurture

As we saw at the beginning of this chapter, the key debate in human development centres on how much of our growth, personality and behaviour is influenced by *nature* (i.e. our genetic inheritance) and how much is influenced by *nurture* (i.e., the environment around us as well as our experiences as we grow).

Scientists who take a strong view of the influence of genetics or biology on development are said to view development *endogenously* (Porges & Carter, 2010). They look at development as biologically programmed to happen sequentially, a process known as **maturation**. Other scientists believe that our experiences have a greater influence on how we develop, a perspective known as an *exogenous* view of development (Overton, 2010).

> **maturation** the unfolding of development in a particular sequence and timeframe.

In reality, however, our traits and behaviours are almost always influenced by an interaction between such factors (Overton, 2010). Still, researchers continue to have heated debates about whether endogenous or exogenous factors are more important. You will see in later chapters that the so-called nature/nurture issue applies not only to questions about cognitive development but also to ideas about intelligence, social behaviour and psychological disorders.

Qualitative versus Quantitative Shifts in Development

Throughout this chapter, whether we are referring to physical development, social development or cognitive development, you will notice that we sometimes talk about **stages**. A stage is a developmental period characterized by a certain level of functioning that is qualitatively different from the functioning that characterizes other stages.

> **stages** developmental periods that are characterized by a certain level of functioning that is qualitatively different from the functioning that characterizes other stages.

The fact that this shift is a *qualitative* one is particularly important here. A qualitative shift occurs when individuals make developmental jumps that cause them to be different than they were before (McNamara *et al.*, 2010). Stage theorists may argue that once we acquire language, for example, we think of the world in a different way because we are able to give things names and even to think about things that do not have a concrete reality. Without the word 'love', they argue, it would be hard to conceive of the various things that love means, because one cannot point to love or sense it in a direct way (at least not in the same way you do a ball or a favourite toy). Stage theories are largely endogenous. They hold that major qualitative shifts are biologically programmed to happen in a certain sequence and at a certain time, leading people to progress through development in the same general way and reach milestones at around the same time. For example, most humans begin to walk at around the age of one year.

However, not all theorists agree with the idea that development moves forward in distinct stages: the timing of developmental milestones does vary. For example, some children take their first steps months earlier than others do. Thus, some psychologists believe the individual variations in timing indicate that development represents more of a *quantitative* shift. According to this approach, development is the result of an ongoing acquisition of new information and new experiences. In this view, what may seem like a big, sudden developmental change actually results from a gradual accumulation of many small changes, often so small that they are

hard to notice. Theorists and researchers in the quantitative camp believe that walking comes as a result of a series of small developmental changes, including the steady growth of our muscles until they can hold our body weight and the development of our brains until they can control physical coordination (Lloyd *et al.*, 2010). As such, quantitative accounts of development have an easier time explaining individual differences in the timing of milestones but a harder time describing why most people go through similar patterns of development, despite considerable variations in their experiences. The two views are summarized in Figure 3.1.

Do Early Experiences Matter? Critical Periods and Sensitive Periods

Related to the question of stage theories versus continuous theories of development is the question of whether there are *critical* periods in development. A **critical period** is a point in development when the organism is extremely sensitive to a particular kind of environmental input, making it easier for the organism to acquire certain brain functions (Anderson *et al.*, 2011). If the environmental input does not occur at

critical period point in development when an organism is extremely sensitive to environmental input, making it easier for the organism to acquire certain brain functions and behaviours.

(a) Qualitative development   (b) Quantitative development

FIGURE 3.1 Does development represent qualitative or quantitative shifts in development? (a) Some theorists believe that individuals make qualitative jumps in development as they move from stage to stage. (b) Others think that development is a steady, continuous process.

PSYCHOLOGY AROUND US   Growing up Worldwide

The documentary *Babies* (2010) follows four babies, Ponjiao from Namibia, Bayarjargal from Mongolia, Mari from Japan and Hattie from the United States from the day they are born until the day they take their first steps. The movie includes no narration – it simply shows how each baby develops in response to his or her particular environment.

Not surprisingly, the child-rearing practices in these four countries are very different. Bayarjargal's farmer parents tie him to a post in their yurt, a tent-like home, and leave him alone for much of the day to fend for himself (and be tormented by his brother). Ponjiao plays with sticks and usually shares his mother's lap with another child. Mari, an only child, soaks in all of her parents' attention. Yet the movie suggests that Bayarjargal and Ponjiao are in the process of becoming more active and independent than the wealthier (and more closely watched) Hattie and Mari.

The filmmakers invite the audience to think about various issues. What makes for a happy, well-adjusted baby? Should parents take a more active, closely observant role in watching over their children or will that result in children who are overly dependent and less willing to step out on their own? Does a lack of resources necessarily lead to poor developmental outcomes?

The followers. By exposing these baby geese to him alone during their first day of life, ethology pioneer Konrad Lorenz manipulated them into viewing him as their mother. For geese the first 36 hours after birth are a critical learning period during which they become imprinted on their mother – or a mother substitute.

Source: Nina Leen/Time & Life Pictures/Getty Images, Inc.

that point, development will be thrown off track (hence the term *critical*). For example, the pioneering critical period theorist Konrad Lorenz (2002, 1971, 1970) found that goslings will forever connect with whatever moving stimuli they see most often during the first 36 hours of their lives. In Lorenz's work, he was able to get certain goslings to think of him (or more specifically his boots) as their mother. He used the term *imprinting* to describe the development of this attachment.

Psychologists have long been curious about whether people also have critical periods. Of course, it would be unethical for researchers to deprive human beings of their usual early experiences in order to see what would happen, but cases of human deprivation – resulting from, say, extreme poverty or the death of one's parents – do sometimes occur naturally. By studying the histories of children in these unfortunate situations, researchers have learnt that serious psychological disabilities may result from early deprivation (Pollak *et al.*, 2010; Rutter *et al.*, 2010). At the same time, however, other studies have found that subsequent changes in environmental input (e.g., removing deprived children from their early negative environments and placing them in more positive ones) can help the children recover partially or, in some cases, completely (Sheridan *et al.*, 2010).

Because individuals can recover at least partially even after deprivation during key periods in their lives, most of today's psychologists and biologists believe that critical periods are better defined as *sensitive periods*. During these times, we are especially receptive to environmental input, but not rigidly so (Baird, 2010; Michel & Tyler, 2005). Theorists today are less inclined to believe that input is essential during a critical period, as if a countdown were running out on your opportunity to develop particular traits or functions. Instead, they view sensitive periods as largely *experience-driven*, flexible enough to extend past typical timeframes for development (Armstrong *et al.*, 2006).

Before You Go On

What Do You Know?

1. How do quantitative theories of development differ from qualitative theories of development?
2. What is the difference between a critical period and a sensitive period?

What Do You Think?

Do you think biological or environmental factors play the major role in your development?

How Is Developmental Psychology Investigated?

LEARNING OBJECTIVE 2

Describe and discuss the advantages and disadvantages of different experimental designs for researching development.

As we have already noted, developmental psychologists are interested in learning about changes that happen as we age. How do they go about measuring those changes? One approach is the **cross-sectional design**. In this approach, researchers compare groups of different-aged people (Memmert, 2011). For example, they might compare a group of 60-year-olds with a group of 30-year-olds on a memory task to see how memory changes over time. A smaller age gap might be examined in children to assess when certain behaviours emerge – for example, between the ages of 5 and 7 years children acquire the ability to use spatial relational grammar (e.g., this object is to the left of that object) in their speech (Hermer-Vazquez *et al.*, 2001).

A potential problem with the cross-sectional approach is that one can make the assumption that any changes found in a study are the result of age. Researchers must remember to also consider other factors that may influence their results. In the case of the first example, let us say that the task used to measure memory differences between the two adult groups was computer-based. If the 30-year-olds performed better on the memory task, the researchers might conclude that the results were due to age-related changes in memory. But the findings could possibly be related more to the fact that 30-year-olds are more familiar with and less intimidated by using computers than 60-year-olds are. Effects like these are known as *cohort effects*. They result from the different life experiences of different age groups (or age *cohorts*).

For these reasons, many developmental researchers prefer another kind of approach, the **longitudinal design** (Figure 3.2). This research follows the same group of people over a given period, administering the same tasks or questionnaires to them at different points in their lives to see how their responses change. We will discuss one of the most famous of these studies in Chapter 12 when we talk about long-term longitudinal studies of extremely intelligent people (Jolly *et al.*, 2011; Feldhusen, 2003).

The main benefit of longitudinal research is that researchers can be reasonably confident that the observed changes are a function of time and developmental experiences. Unfortunately, longitudinal studies require considerable time and money. The study you will read about in Chapter 12 went on for 85 years! Moreover, many participants in longitudinal studies drop out of the studies over the course of their lives because they move away, lose interest, become ill or even die. Another important issue is that participants are likely to become better at the same task if they have multiple chances to complete it over the course of the study. It is therefore

cross-sectional design research comparisons of groups of different-aged people.

longitudinal design research following the same people over a given period by administering the same tasks or questionnaires and seeing how their responses change.

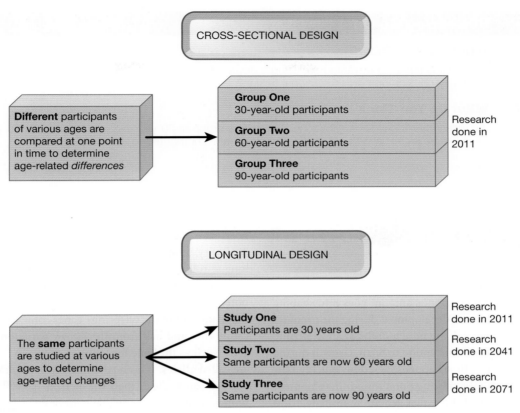

FIGURE 3.2 Cross-sectional versus longitudinal research design. Cross-sectional research uses participants of various ages to examine age-related differences. Longitudinal research studies the same participants over time to determine age-related changes.

Source: Adapted with permission of John Wiley & Sons, Inc., from Carpenter, S. & Huggman, K. (2008). *Visualizing Psychology*. Hoboken, NJ: John Wiley & Sons, Inc., p. 230.

important that psychologists can disentangle developmental changes from practice effects.

Seeking to obtain the advantages and avoid the drawbacks of cross-sectional and longitudinal designs, some developmental researchers design studies that combine the two. One such combined research method is the **cohort-sequential design**. Here, researchers look at how age groups compare with one another at various points in the research, but they also look at how any differences between the groups vary over time (de Haan *et al.,* 2010). For example, to compare patterns in alcohol use, one study followed children from three age groups for four years (Duncan *et al.,* 2006). One group was followed from ages 9 to 12, another from ages 11 to 14 and another from ages 13 to 16. By using this design, the researchers could measure any differences between the groups that persisted over time. However, because of the age overlap among groups over time, they could also look at differences that may result from age.

cohort-sequential design a blended cross-sectional and longitudinal research design that follows at least two different age groups over time.

Another approach is known as **developmental trajectory** analysis (see Thomas *et al.,* 2009). This method of study is particularly useful for understanding developmental disorders (such as Down syndrome or Williams syndrome, both of which result from genetic abnormalities and have associated cognitive profiles). When testing special populations such as these it is often difficult to find an appropriate control sample of typically developing children to compare them with. Instead, this method takes measurements on the same task from a variety of ages to create a typical developmental trajectory, which describes how performance on a task is related to age (i.e., we may expect children to improve as they get older). One can then establish how the performance of an individual with a developmental disorder compares with the typical trajectory. They may, for example, perform at a level that is reduced for their chronological age but is commensurate with that of a younger typically developing child: this would suggest a delay in their development.

developmental trajectory an approach that measures how a group or population follow a common developmental course (i.e., between chronological age and another variable).

Before You Go On

What Do You Know?

3. What is the main advantage of using a developmental trajectory approach as opposed to a longitudinal design or a cross-sectional design?

What Do You Think?

If a researcher today finds differences between a group of 20-year-olds and a group of 60-year-olds, what historical, social and cultural factors may have contributed to those differences?

Before We Are Born

LEARNING OBJECTIVE 3
Discuss mechanisms of genetic inheritance.

prenatal period the approximately nine months of development stretching from conception to birth.

An enormous amount goes into shaping human development during the **prenatal period**, the nine months or so stretching from conception to birth. Growth during this time happens incredibly quickly. Our biological parents are the starting point for our development by contributing parts of their own genetic inheritance, and we will see that the contributions from a mother and a father can form a variety of combinations – some matching exactly, some differing completely.

In the Beginning: Genetics

genes basic building blocks of biological inheritance.

deoxyribonucleic acid (DNA) molecules in which genetic information is enclosed.

chromosomes strands of DNA; each human being has 46 chromosomes, distributed in pairs.

genotype a person's genetic inheritance.

phenotype the observable manifestation of a person's genetic inheritance.

Genes are the most basic building blocks of our biological inheritance (Kagan, 2010). Each gene is composed of a specific sequence of **deoxyribonucleic acid**, or **DNA**, molecules. DNA and genes are arranged in strands called **chromosomes** and found in each cell of our bodies. Each of us has 23 pairs, or 46 total, chromosomes. Twenty-three chromosomes are contributed by each of our biological parents. The resulting combination is called our **genotype**, which broadly refers to our genetic inheritance. In contrast, our **phenotype** is the observable manifestation of that genotype. The physical and psychological characteristics that are on display in each individual make up that individual's phenotype.

It is difficult to determine a person's genotype solely based on his or her phenotype. Consider the ability to roll your tongue: this is genetically determined. As such, either you are

born with the ability or you will never have it (McDonald, 2010; Fry, 1988). If you can roll your tongue, you display a tongue-rolling phenotype, but without further information we cannot say exactly what your genotype is. As we have noted, each parent contributes half of a child's chromosomal make-up; half of the offspring's genes come from the biological mother and half from the father. Variations of the same gene, such as the gene for tongue rolling, are called **alleles**. If both parents contribute the same allele, then the person is **homozygous** for the trait; that is, he or she has two matching alleles of the same gene. If you can roll your tongue, you *may* be homozygous for the tongue-rolling gene.

alleles variations of a gene.

homozygous both parents contribute the same genetic material for a particular trait.

It turns out, however, that people can still roll their tongues if they inherit a tongue-rolling allele from one of their parents and a non-rolling allele from the other. In such instances, the individuals have the observable phenotype of tongue rolling, but their genotype is **heterozygous**, a combination of two different alleles. Thus, if you can roll your tongue, you are displaying a tongue-rolling phenotype, and this phenotype may reflect either a homozygous or a heterozygous genotype (Figure 3.3).

heterozygous parents contribute two different alleles to offspring.

Genotype:	Homozygous		Heterozygous		Homozygous	
Parent contribution:	Mother: tongue-rolling allele	Father: tongue-rolling allele	Mother: tongue-rolling allele	Father: non-tongue-rolling allele	Mother: non-tongue-rolling allele	Father: non-tongue-rolling allele
Phenotype:	Tongue-rolling trait will be expressed		Tongue-rolling trait will be expressed		Tongue-rolling trait will not be expressed	

FIGURE 3.3 Genotype versus phenotype. Individuals who are able to roll their tongues may have either a homozygous or a heterozygous genotype for tongue rolling. In contrast, people who cannot roll their tongues must have a homozygous genotype for non-tongue rolling.

Depending on the trait in question, any of three different phenotypes can result when a person has a heterozygous combination of different alleles (adapted from Truett *et al.*, 1994):

- One possibility is that the trait either will be expressed in its entirety or will not be expressed at all. This is the case with heterozygous tongue rolling. If you have one rolling allele and one non-rolling allele, you will be able to roll your tongue. Tongue rolling is a **dominant trait**, a trait that is expressed in your phenotype regardless of whether your genotype is homozygous or heterozygous for the trait. A **recessive trait**, on the other hand, is expressed in your phenotype only when you are homozygous for that trait. The inability to roll your tongue is recessive. You must have two matching non-rolling alleles in order to be prevented from rolling your tongue.

> **dominant trait** a trait that is expressed in a phenotype, no matter whether the genotype is homozygous or heterozygous for the trait.

> **recessive trait** a trait that is only expressed if a person carries the same two genetic alleles (e.g. is homozygous for the trait).

- For some traits, a person with a heterozygous pair of alleles may show a *mixture* of genetic coding. For example, children of couples who have different racial backgrounds can have features associated with the backgrounds of both parents, such as blended skin colour or eye shape.

- For yet other traits, persons with a heterozygous pair of alleles may express *both* of the parents' genes in their phenotype. This outcome is called **codominance**. An example of codominance is found in blood type. If one parent has blood Type A and the other parent has Type B, the child can express both in the form blood Type AB.

> **codominance** in a heterozygous combination of alleles: both traits are expressed in the offspring.

The thing that makes the study of genetics particularly challenging is that only a few of our traits are **discrete traits**, meaning the product of a single gene pair. Instead, most human traits are **polygenic traits**, which involve the combined impact of multiple genes. It is especially likely that traits affecting our behaviour are polygenetic.

> **discrete traits** traits that result as the product of a single gene pairing.

> **polygenic traits** traits that manifest as the result of the contributions of multiple genes.

Before You Go On

What Do You Know?

4. What are the possible phenotypic outcomes from a heterozygous genotype?

What Do You Think?

Which of your personal characteristics do you think may have been genetically inherited?

Infancy

HOW WE DEVELOP

LEARNING OBJECTIVE 4

Summarize the major physical and cognitive developments that take place during infancy.

To the untrained eye, newborn infants may seem to have very few abilities; for example, they are unable to feed themselves or move much distance on their own for many months. In many important ways, however, they also arrive with a wide range of sophisticated abilities.

Physical Development

Compared with the young of some other species, human infants are still relatively "unfinished" at birth. We grow at an amazing rate, our key senses develop fully during our first months, and we learn to walk after about a year or so. But our brains, although they also show amazing development during infancy, are not fully formed until we are young adults.

Patterns of Growth From birth to 1 year of age, babies go through a 'growth spurt'. Typically, their weight triples over that period, and their height increases by about one and a half times. Two particular patterns are apparent in babies' growth and development. First, they follow a **proximodistal pattern**. That is, parts closer to the centre grow and develop sooner than parts at the outer edges (the extremities) (Logsdon, 2011). Second,

> **proximodistal pattern** a pattern in which growth and development proceed from the centre to the extremities.

cephalocaudal pattern a pattern in which growth and development proceed from top to bottom.

they follow a **cephalocaudal pattern**, from head to foot. This is apparent in the bodily proportions of infants, as their heads are much larger in proportion to their bodies than the heads of toddlers are.

Senses and Reflexes The senses of taste, smell and touch are all highly developed at birth. A baby can distinguish the scent of his or her mother's milk from that of another woman's milk and can make fine distinctions between various tastes after only a few days out of the womb. In contrast, other senses are less developed. Hearing is still immature and affected by fluid from the mother's womb that continues to take up space in the newborn's ears. If you have ever spent a day swimming, you have probably had a sense of what it is like to hear like a baby – things sound a little muddled, with greater sensitivity to high- and low-pitched sounds. These limitations change quickly, however, and within a few days, the baby can distinguish familiar speech from new sounds and words that they have not heard before.

Vision is a newborn's least developed sense (Bedinghaus, 2010; Kellman & Arterberry, 1998; Maurer & Salapatek, 1976). Newborns cannot clearly see objects much more than seven to 10 inches away. Similarly, their ability to scan objects is limited, and they tend to fixate on local components of an object. For example, if they look at a triangle, they will probably focus only on one of its corners. Equally, if they look at a face, they will focus largely on the chin or hairline. Furthermore, they do not develop good colour vision until they are around three months of age. At first, these visual limitations do not have much impact upon the quality of an infant's life. After all, babies do not travel very far, and they can see far enough to make eye contact with their mother while nursing. Importantly, by the time they start moving around, at about seven to eight months of age, their vision has approached adult levels.

Despite the slow development of visual abilities, however, it is also clear babies emerge from the womb with strong preferences for particular visual stimuli and an uncanny ability to imitate. For example, Fantz (1961) demonstrated that

one-month-old babies preferred to look at a stimulus depicting a schematic human face, rather than another stimulus with identical facial features but in a different spatial arrangement. Perhaps more strikingly, Meltzoff and Moore (1983) found that babies as young as three months were very adept at imitating the facial expressions of adults, such as puckering their lips or poking their tongues out. This is not something that the child would have consciously practised, and yet they were able to control their facial muscles in order to produce an accurate imitation of another individual's expression. This therefore suggests that the infant already has a strong mapping between visual input and motor output; that is, they are able to rapidly transform perceptual information into an appropriate movement that they can then execute. This is very sophisticated for an organism that was very recently only able to focus on the odd detail.

In addition to our senses, we are also born with certain **reflexes**, programmed reactions to certain cues that do not require any conscious thought to perform. For example, babies pucker their lips and begin to suck whenever something brushes their cheeks or is put in their mouths. This response, called the *rooting reflex*, helps babies to begin feeding, and one can see why babies need to come into the world with this ability. Some other common reflexes and their functions are listed in Table 3.2.

reflexes programmed physical reactions to certain cues that do not require any conscious thought to perform.

Learning to Control Movements By the end of their first year, most babies are up and moving. **Motor skills**, the ability to control bodily movements, include achievements such as grasping objects, crawling and eventually walking.

HOW WE DIFFER

motor skills ability to control bodily movements.

Table 3.3 shows the typical ages at which Western children (in this case the United States) reach particular motor-development milestones. Most babies acquire motor skills in roughly the same order, which suggests that there may be a maturational explanation for the way in which they unfold.

TABLE 3.2 Common Newborn Reflexes

Reflex	Stimulation	Response	Function
Rooting	Touch the corner of the infant's mouth	Infant turns towards the stimulation and begins to suck	Helps infant begin feeding
Grasping	Press finger against infant's palm	Infant grasps finger and holds on	Allows infant to hold on to caregiver for safety
Moro	Let infant's head lose support	Infant flings arms outward and then inward in a hugging motion	May have helped infant to hold on to caregiver when support is lost
Babinski	Stroke sole of infant's foot	Toes spread apart	Unknown

TABLE 3.3 Milestones in Motor Development

Motor Milestone	Average Age Achieved	Age Range
When prone, lifts chin up	2 months	3 weeks–4 months
Rolls over	2 months	3 weeks–5 months
Sits alone	7 months	5–9 months
Crawls	7 months	5–11 months
Stands holding furniture	8 months	5–12 months
Stands alone	11 months	9–16 months
Walks alone	11 months, 3 weeks	9–17 months
Walks up steps	17 months	12–23 months

Source: Based on Laura E. Berk, Infants, Children, and Adolescents (6th edn). Boston: Allyn & Bacon, 2008. Table 5.2, p. 188.

At the same time, as the table also shows, children vary considerably in when they hit a particular milestone. The timing of motor development can be influenced by a number of environmental factors, including the social signals given by caregivers (Adolph *et al.*, 2010).

Negative influences, such as abuse, neglect or poor nutrition, can slow a child's motor development. Cultural practices that either encourage or discourage early motor development can also influence the timetable (Adolph *et al.*, 2010). On the one hand, for example, the Kipsigis people in Kenya begin working with babies shortly after birth to help them sit up, stand and walk (Super, 1976). In turn, Kipsigis children achieve these milestones about a month before children raised in the United States. On the other hand, the Ache parents in Paraguay worry about their children moving more than a few feet away, and they actively discourage independent motor development in their children. As a result, Ache children do not walk until an average of one year later than children in the United States (Kaplan & Dove, 1987).

The timetable for learning to walk provides an excellent example of the interaction of nature and nurture, which we discussed earlier in the chapter. It also underscores an important point. Although achieving a developmental milestone three months early or one year late is significant (particularly to a worried or proud parent), it is equally significant that almost everyone eventually hits this particular milestone.

Infancy **WHAT HAPPENS IN THE BRAIN?** Given the vast amount of knowledge and skills acquired by babies, it is no surprise that infancy is a time of remarkable change in our brains. Although a newborn's head is only about one-fourth the size of an adult's, it already contains a great deal of sophisticated neural apparatus. As you will discover elsewhere in this book, however, the brain continues to change and develop throughout our lives.

Two key processes are responsible for the remarkable development of the brain in the earliest years of life. The first is a sheer increase in connections among *neurons*, the brain's nerve cells. As we will describe in detail in Chapter 5, information is passed from neuron to neuron at transmission points called **synapses**. Born with 100 billion neurons, a child acquires synaptic connections at a staggering rate during the first few years, expanding from 2,500 such connections per neuron at birth to around 15,000 per neuron by age two or three years (Zelazo & Lee, 2010; Bock, 2005; Di Pietro, 2000). Many of these connections develop as a function of normal maturation, regardless of the baby's experiences. In fact, they serve as a way of helping the baby process new experiences.

synapses transmission points between neurons.

As a result of this amazing growth rate, babies develop far more synapses than they will eventually need. Over the course of childhood, a large proportion of these early synaptic connections fall away (Zelazo & Lee, 2010; Bock, 2005; Di Pietro, 2000). Experiences help to stimulate and strengthen some of the connections, while synapses that are not used weaken and dissipate. This process is called **synaptic pruning** because of its similarity to pruning, or cutting away, the dead branches of a tree or bush in order to help the healthy, live branches flourish (Keverne, 2010; Edin *et al.*, 2007).

synaptic pruning developmental reduction of neuronal connections, allowing stronger connections to flourish.

The other process that accounts for increased brain growth is **myelination**. Myelin is a fatty white deposit that forms around and insulates portions of many neurons, helping electric impulses pass through a neuron more efficiently. In general, during infancy, myelination occurs in the spinal cord and in areas of the brain primarily associated with movement, reflexes, sensory responses and certain low-level learning processes.

myelination development of fatty deposits on neurons that allow electric impulses to pass through neurons more efficiently.

Cognitive Development

Amazingly, in just two short years, people proceed from newborns that are completely dependent on others for their survival to toddlers who can often display quite astounding feats of independence. What happens during this period of time that triggers such a dramatic shift? We will talk about how we learn language in Chapter 11. Here, we discuss some of the important changes in thinking ability that happen during those first two years.

Piaget's Theory One of the world's most influential developmental psychologists, Jean Piaget, made his most important contribution with an account of **cognitive development**: how thinking changes as the child gets older (Piaget *et al.*, 2009; Piaget, 2003, 2000, 1985). Piaget's theory began with naturalistic observations of children, including his own, in real-life situations. On the basis of his observations, Piaget hypothesized that young children's thinking processes might differ from those of adults. He then proceeded to test his hypotheses by making small changes to a particular situation that the child was in and watching to see how the child responded to those changes (Phillips, 1975). Based on the results of these tests, Piaget developed a theory of how we acquire knowledge and the abilities to use it.

> **cognitive development** changes in thinking that occur over the course of time.

According to Piaget, all of us have mental frameworks or structures for understanding and thinking about the world. He called these frameworks **schemata**, and he believed that people acquire and continuously build schemata through their experiences in the world. For example, you may have acquired a schema about Indian restaurants, based on your experiences. When you go to an Indian restaurant in your community, you can predict some of the dishes that are going to be on the menu, and you know not to look for pizza or a burger. Equally, you will behave in a way that is consistent with your previous experiences, so when someone comes to take your order you will ask for the food you want rather than the haircut you would like.

> **schemata** Piaget's proposed mental structures or frameworks for understanding or thinking about the world.

Piaget believed that when children gain new knowledge, their schemata change. This can happen in two ways. The first, **assimilation**, was defined by Piaget as the inclusion of new information or experiences into existing schemata. During your first few visits to Indian restaurants, for example, you may have ordered only balti chicken. In later visits, however, you may have expanded, but not

> **assimilation** one of two ways of acquiring knowledge, defined by Piaget as the inclusion of new information or experiences into existing schemata.

drastically altered, your schema with new information by trying other chicken dishes.

Sometimes, we come across new information so different from what we already know that we cannot simply add it to our old schemata. We must alter an existing schema significantly to fit in new information or experiences. Piaget called this adjustment **accommodation**. Let's say that you travelled for the first time to Birmingham's Sparkbrook neighbourhood, in the UK. There you learnt not only that there are several different styles of Indian cooking but also that your favourite dish, balti chicken, is not even really a traditional Indian dish, but was actually created in Birmingham. Based on this experience, you would have to revise your mental framework for Indian restaurants.

> **accommodation** one of two ways of acquiring knowledge, defined by Piaget as the alteration of existing mental frameworks to take in new information.

According to Piaget, engaging in assimilation and accommodation helps us to reach a mental balance, or **equilibrium**. As a result of your experiences in Indian restaurants at home and in Birmingham, you may now feel comfortable in a variety of Indian restaurants.

> **equilibrium** balance in a mental framework.

Piaget's theory is a *stage theory*. He suggested that we travel through several stages of cognitive development in life, progressing from being, as babies, unable to even form schemata to being able, as teenagers and adults, to perform complicated mental feats of logic using schemata. Piaget believed strongly that, as we move from one stage to the next, *qualitative* shifts occur in our thinking. Children in one stage not only know more but also actually become different sorts of thinkers than they were at earlier stages (this is the very definition of a stage theory). Table 3.4 shows the four developmental stages proposed by Piaget.

At this point in the chapter we will focus on the earliest stage, the starting point of infancy. Piaget named this first stage sensorimotor because he thought that, early on, babies can think only about the world in terms of what they can sense directly or encounter through simple motor actions; that is, any object in the world, from a ball to a parent, is present only insofar as the baby can sense it directly or

TABLE 3.4 Piaget's Four Stages of Cognitive Development

Stage	Age	Description
Sensorimotor	Birth to 2	'Thinks' by using senses and motor skills; no thought beyond immediate experience
Preoperational	2–7	Able to hold ideas of objects in imagination; unable to consider another's point of view or distinguish between cause and effect
Concrete operational	7–11	Can think about complex relationships (cause and effect, categorization); understands conservation; unable to think abstractly or hypothetically
Formal operational	11+	Able to think abstractly and hypothetically

lay hold on it in some way. Once that ball has rolled under the settee, it has gone: out of sight, out of mind (we will return to this phenomenon very shortly). It is no wonder that babies find peek-a-boo so entertaining.

Piaget believed that much of our early learning happens as a result of our reflexes. He observed that even though they were hardwired into us reflexes could change. As the baby engages in reflex behaviours, he or she gets feedback about how those responses affect him or her and the surrounding world. The rooting reflex often brings food to a hungry infant, for example. In this way, babies are acquiring knowledge that contributes to the formation of schemata. The baby may come to develop a schema relating rooting behaviour to feeding.

A major cognitive milestone of the sensorimotor stage occurs at around eight months of age. It is the development of **object permanence**, the realization that objects continue to exist even when they are out of one's immediate sensory awareness. So, although the child can no longer see that ball when it has rolled under the settee, he/she knows it still exists, and wants it back. When children eventually begin to demonstrate awareness of things out of their sensory input, it suggests that they are beginning to hold concepts in mind. They have developed mental schemata of those objects. This is known as *representation,* literally a re-presentation of an object or concept that is held in mind rather than the external world. This is a fundamental component of human intelligence: it is how we know that our home occupies a point in space when we are elsewhere, or that the world is still there when we close our eyes.

> **object permanence** an infant's realization that objects continue to exist even when they are outside the infant's immediate sensory awareness.

Eventually, babies become able not only to represent objects in their minds but also to manipulate and make predictions about those objects and how they interact with other objects. A baby may try to lift a cloth to look under it for a hidden toy, for example. Piaget believed that by the end of the sensorimotor stage, the young child's schemata have changed in a fundamental way. The child no longer depends on a direct experience of the world. Instead, ideas and concepts have begun to stand in for those objects.

Information-Processing Views of Cognitive Development

Piaget often looked at what children could not do and then used their mistakes to determine their cognitive abilities. Today, however, psychologists who adhere to information-processing theory look to see what children *can* do, as opposed to what they cannot. **Information-processing theory** focuses on how children take in and use

> **information-processing theory** developmental theory focusing on how children take in and use information from their environment.

information from their environment. Theorists who adhere to this view have found that Piaget may have underestimated children's competencies at various developmental stages (Lourenç & Machado, 1996).

To ascertain whether a baby had developed object permanence, for example, Piaget would hide an object and observe whether the baby looked for it. Searching suggests that the baby still has the object in his or her mind. It takes some time, however, for babies to master control over their bodies enough to move purposely and conduct a search: clearly, if you cannot grab a cloth that is hiding a toy, you cannot lift it and look under it. Thus, other researchers have suggested that a better indicator of object permanence is whether babies react with surprise when hidden objects are revealed again (Charles & Rivera, 2009; Baillargeon, 1987). After all, to be surprised, you have to have an expectation that is challenged in some way. Such surprise implies that you have a mental representation of the situation. Studies focusing on the surprise reaction suggest that babies as young as three months may display some form of object permanence.

Researchers also have found evidence that babies can *learn* and *remember* right after birth. Throughout life, individuals often learn to perform and repeat certain behaviours by experiencing positive consequences after they first manifest the behaviours, a process called *operant conditioning.* (We will talk much more about this process in Chapter 9.) It turns out that even very young babies learn to perform certain behaviours when they are systematically rewarded by researchers. If babies can shift their strategies to bring about positive outcomes or avoid negative ones, they must have some concepts (and, by extension, memories) of the relationships between behaviours and outcomes. Babies also display **habituation**; that is, they stop responding over time to the same stimulus if it is presented repeatedly. If babies had no memory or no idea of external objects, they would not be able to become bored by repeated presentations. Habituation has therefore become a crucial research tool for measuring infant perceptions of colours, sounds, faces and other such abilities that we may otherwise find very difficult to measure.

> **habituation** the process in which individuals pay less attention to a stimulus after it is presented to them repeatedly.

Beyond what we may perceive as basic cognitive processes, the information-processing approach has even been able to demonstrate that babies may have some concept of mathematics! Psychologist Karen Wynn conducted a series of studies in which she showed five-month-old babies a sequence of events in which one doll is put in a case behind a screen followed by another doll (McCrink & Wynn, 2004; Wynn 2002, 1992). She found that when the screen was dropped, the babies expressed surprise and looked longer if only one doll was in the case than if both dolls were present. The babies seemed to know that the case should hold two dolls. This result has been replicated with even larger numbers (five to 10 dolls) in nine-month-old children.

By adjusting their approaches to focus more on the child's capacities, information-processing researchers have found that cognitive development may involve fewer qualitative shifts and more quantitative growth than Piaget believed. Nevertheless, Piaget remains very influential. His stages still provide a general guideline for the cognitive development of children. For that reason, as noted, we will continue to

look at his stages later in this chapter. In addition, his theory remains influential in generating research. If nothing else, the controversy ignited by Piaget's ideas has helped us think about how best to study children's thought processes. Perhaps most importantly, Piaget encouraged psychologists to stop thinking of children as organisms programmed by biology or by early experiences and start thinking of them as active interpreters of their world. Piaget considered children to be little scientists constantly drawing conclusions about the world based on their own personal research, conducted through their experiences.

Before You Go On

What Do You Know?

5. What is the role of synaptic pruning in the development of the brain?

6. According to Piaget's account of cognitive development, what are schemata?

7. How does the information-processing approach differ from Piaget's stage theory?

What Do You Think?

Do babies have more advanced cognitive abilities than we may think? If so, what stops them from demonstrating them?

Early and Middle Childhood

LEARNING OBJECTIVE 5

Summarize the major physical and cognitive developments that take place during early and middle childhood.

Physical Development

Growth during early childhood, which lasts from about the ages of two to six years, and middle childhood, which lasts from about age six until 12, is not as dramatic as it was during infancy. Although progress is more gradual, children's brains and bodies still experience major changes – as we will see, both become much more efficient.

How Does the Body Grow During Childhood? The dramatic physical growth that occurs from conception through our second year slows down during early childhood, such that we grow only about 2½–3 inches a year. In contrast, however, we master a much greater degree of motor and physical control during this period. Children develop basic control over their urination and bowel movements, and they solidify a preference for their right or left hand for most tasks. Of course, during early childhood

many aspects of development are still in progress. For example, although our coordination improves and we can work the buttons and zips necessary to dress ourselves, that does not necessarily mean that we can select the appropriate clothes for the day ahead.

As children move from early into middle childhood, around age six, things begin to gather pace again. Children's motor abilities improve dramatically as they gain coordination, agility and strength (Drummond, 2011). At the same time, the first major distinctions between boys and girls begin to appear. Girls experience a growth spurt in height and weight during their 10th or 11th year, while boys have to wait a couple of years more for their spurt. On the other hand, boys develop somewhat more muscle mass, meaning they can throw and jump a little further and run a little faster. Girls tend to be a bit more agile on average. As we will see later in the chapter, these average differences become much more pronounced as children move into adolescence.

WHAT HAPPENS IN THE BRAIN? Childhood Throughout early and middle childhood, the brain becomes more efficient through a continued combination of the myelination and synaptic pruning that began in infancy. During childhood, myelination is concentrated in the brain areas known as the *association regions*. These are the areas of the brain that coordinate the activity and operation of other regions of the brain (Bartzokis *et al.*, 2010; Paus *et al.*, 1999). The increased efficiency of the association regions as they become myelinated leads to more sophisticated planning and problem-solving abilities. Most four-year-olds cannot play chess very effectively, for example, but many children in their first few years of schooling will possess the strategic skills to make good players.

As we discussed earlier, synaptic pruning helps solidify the neural connections that are most beneficial to the child. As childhood draws to a close, the rate of pruning slows down. In turn, the numbers of synaptic connections between particular neurons and the overall electric activity in the brain both begin to stabilize.

Cognitive Development

One of the major activities of childhood is going to school, and in most countries, formal education begins around the ages of five to seven. We will see in this section that school entry coincides with the development of the cognitive skills that Piaget called **operations**, the ability to hold an idea in the mind and manipulate it mentally (Bialystok & Craik, 2010). Piaget suggested that between the ages of about two and 12 children go through two stages of cognitive development: the *preoperational stage*, which lasts from age two to seven, followed by the *concrete operational stage*, lasting from age seven to 12. Schools also provide rich social environments, a factor that another cognitive development theorist, Lev Vygotsky, believed is crucial to learning.

operations Piagetian description of a child's ability to hold an idea in his or her mind and mentally manipulate it.

Piaget's Preoperational Stage According to Piaget, as children move into the **preoperational stage**, they are able to hold memories, or representations, of objects in their imaginations and to work with them as ideas (Müller & Racine, 2010). This represents a dramatic shift from the earlier sensorimotor stage, in which they were able to manipulate actual objects only. The thinking of children at this stage still shows some limitations, compared with adult thinking, however.

preoperational stage according to Piaget, a developmental stage during which the child begins to develop ideas of objects in the external world and the ability to work with them in his or her mind.

One major limitation is what Piaget called *irreversibility*. Although they can work with symbols and concepts that stand in for real-world objects, children at the preoperational stage still think in rather simplistic ways about the relationships between those concepts and objects. For them, changes in relationships happen in one direction only. One

researcher offers the following example of a four-year-old who was asked about his family:

'Do you have a brother?'
'Yes.'
'What's his name?'
'Jim.'
'Does Jim have a brother?'
'No.'

(Phillips, 1975)

The boy is able to hold the idea of his brother Jim in his head, even though Jim is not there, indicating he has developed object permanence. At the same time, he has adopted this concept in one direction only: Jim is *my* brother. The boy is unable to think about the reverse relationship, that he is Jim's brother also.

The reason this child cannot think of himself as Jim's brother, according to Piaget, is because he cannot take Jim's point of view, an inability Piaget referred to as **egocentrism** (Kesselring & Müller, 2011). Piaget did not use the term *egocentrism* to mean the boy is arrogant. His use of the term refers strictly to children's flaws in logical reasoning. This boy cannot yet realize that other people also have brothers. Piaget believed that *perspective-taking*, the ability to take another person's point of view, is not mastered until a later stage. A more striking demonstration of this was made using the Three Mountains Task. Piaget presented children with a three-dimensional diorama containing three mountains, each with a distinctive feature atop them, and then positioned himself so that he was viewing the scene from a different vantage point from that of the child. Children were then shown several pictures of different views of the scene and asked to select which of them represented the view that the other person could see. Preoperational children would almost always select the picture that matched their own view, demonstrating that they were unable to take the perspective of another individual, or imagine that there could be another view of the same world.

egocentrism flaws in a child's reasoning based on his or her inability to take other perspectives.

Irreversibility is also related to a lack of **conservation**, the ability to understand that something can stay the same even though its appearance may change. Piaget used a now-famous task to demonstrate young children's problems with conservation. He gave a child two identical beakers with equal amounts of water in each and asked which of the beakers held more water. Children over two years old were usually able to say that both beakers held the same amount. Piaget would then

conservation the understanding that certain properties of an object (such as volume and number) remain the same despite changes in the object's outward appearance.

ask the child to pour the water into two new beakers that were shaped differently, one shallow and wide and the other tall and narrow. After the children poured the water, Piaget again asked which held more water. Children between the ages of two and seven, even after they themselves had poured the water into the new beakers, were more likely to say the tall, narrow beaker held more water. Piaget believed this indicated that the children could not mentally reverse the pouring of the water to imagine that the two amounts of water would once again match if both were returned to their original containers.

Children's lack of conservation may also be related to difficulty in making distinctions between *appearance* and *reality*. In one classic example of this confusion, researcher Rheta DeVries (1969) allowed children to play with her cat, Maynard. After a while, DeVries and her assistants would hide Maynard's front half from view while they strapped a dog mask onto the cat's face. DeVries then asked the toddlers what kind of animal Maynard was. Even though Maynard was never completely out of view, the majority of the three-year-old participants, and a good number of four- and five-year-olds thought the cat had magically become a dog. By the age of six, when they were nearing the concrete operational stage, none of the children made this mistake.

As we saw earlier, however, tasks such as these may underestimate children's ability to conserve at this age. It has been suggested, for example, that the way the task is framed may lead children to think that something must have changed. To explain, take one of Piaget's assessments of conservation for quantity: he would first show children two rows of counters, identically spaced and with an equal number in each. Naturally, when asked which row contained more counters, the child responded that they were the same. Piaget then rearranged one of the rows so that it was more widely spaced than the other. Once more, he asked child which row contained more, and the preoperational child (failing to conserve quantity) would state that the longer row was more numerous. McGarrigle and Donaldson (1975) reasoned that the younger child may state that there had been a change in quantity because the adult had deliberately manipulated the situation and then asked the same question (leading the child to assume that something must now be different). To assess this, they employed the assistance of Naughty Teddy, a puppet that would sometimes interfere with the counters during their game. When Donaldson rearranged one of the rows herself, children under six years would state that the longer of them contained more counters. However, when Naughty Teddy interfered with the counters without the experimenter's permission, the same child was more likely to report that the rows still contained the same quantity. McGarrigle and Donaldson (1975) argued that because it was Naughty

Teddy that had changed the situation, against the wishes of the adult, the child was no longer compelled to focus on the change that had happened.

A similar reconfiguration of a classic Piagetian task was also used to show that 'preoperational' children might indeed be able to take the perspective of another. Hughes (1975) devised a different version of the Three Mountains Task that contained a more familiar context for children to engage in. They were presented with a model containing four walls arranged as a cross. Hughes then introduced two policeman figures and positioned them each at an end of a different wall – for example, one was placed at the southern end of the cross and another was placed at the eastern end. Children were then told that a naughty boy doll was trying to hide from the policemen and that they had to place him somewhere in the model so that he could not be seen by the policeman. Since the policemen were overlooking three quadrants between them, there was only one place in the model that the boy could hide, and 90% of children aged from three to five years selected the correct quadrant. This demonstrates that they could correctly take the perspective of another individual. Why do younger children pass this task but not the Three Mountains Task? One possibility is that the context makes more sense to them: they are used to the game of hide and seek, and are therefore able to appropriately engage in the problem. The other is that the Three Mountains Task may also entail an imaginal rotation of viewpoint (i.e. imagining your viewpoint gradually changing, or rotating around the scene, until it matches that of another person). This may be much harder for younger children to achieve and therefore confounds our investigation of their perspective-taking abilities. Tasks such as this one, and McGarrigle and Donaldson's (1975) Naughty Teddy task, again make the important demonstration that the nature of the task itself may be responsible for the manner in which children respond.

Piaget's Concrete Operational Stage During the stage of **concrete operations**, children demonstrate the ability to think about ideas. They start to talk authoritatively about complex relationships, such as cause and effect and categorization. They can take others' perspectives and reverse operations. By now, they consider the notion that a cat can mysteriously become a dog ridiculous. They know dogs and cats fit into particular categories, and they can now extend those categories to other organisms that share the same features.

> **concrete operations**
> Piagetian stage during which children are able to talk about complex relationships, such as categorization and cause and effect, but are still limited to understanding ideas in terms of real-world relationships.

Children at this stage show a mastery of real-world relationships. This mastery is limited, however, to ideas that have real-world counterparts, such as family members, plants and animals, or weather conditions. That is why Piaget referred to the stage as *concrete* operations: concepts need to be firmly rooted in reality. Children in this stage have difficulty with relationships between objects that do not exist in the real world, such as abstract mathematical relationships. They also find it difficult to think about hypothetical, alternative possibilities and have trouble speculating on questions, such as 'In what ways can this situation play out?' A mastery of those kinds of relationships is left for the next stage of development.

Criticisms of the Preoperational and Concrete Operations Stages

Aside from the policeman task described above, many critics have more fundamentally challenged Piaget's belief that children in the preoperational and concrete operations stages have problems taking others' points of view. In fact, some researchers have become very interested in young children's beliefs about how their own minds and the minds of others work, a field of research called **theory of mind** (Carpendale & Lewis, 2010; Mar *et al.*, 2010).

> **theory of mind** a recognition that other people base their behaviours on their own perspectives, not on information that is unavailable to them.

Theory of mind was first studied in an experiment with children between the ages of three and nine. Wimmer and Perner (1983) told children a story about a boy named Maxi who tries to sneak some chocolate from his mother. According to the story, Maxi's mother brings home some chocolate to make a cake. While Maxi is watching, she puts the chocolate in a blue cupboard (Figure 3.4). Maxi then goes out to play. While he is outside, his mother makes the cake and puts the remaining chocolate in a green cupboard. Next, Maxi comes back in, wanting some chocolate. The researchers then asked the children in the study where Maxi would look for the chocolate.

This deceptively simple task actually requires a high level of thought. Children have to not only remember where the chocolate has travelled but also take the viewpoint of Maxi and realize that he has no way of knowing that his mother moved the chocolate. Three- and four-year-olds regularly fail such tests, suggesting this task is too complicated for them, while six-year-olds regularly succeed. Experiments such as these support Piaget's notion that young children are highly egocentric. They also suggest, however, that many children are able to take other people's thoughts and feelings into account much sooner than Piaget had predicted.

In part, Piaget's approach may have been limited by a failure to listen to his own theory. Piaget believed that thought precedes language – that our thinking develops faster than our ability to use words. Yet, many of his tests of those hypotheses rested on observations of children's performance in language-based tasks, such as the question about Jim's brother mentioned earlier. Other researchers, by focusing on nonverbal responses or by making their questions more age-appropriate or child-friendly, have found evidence that children develop certain cognitive competencies sooner than Piaget thought.

Still other critics have charged that Piaget's theory fails to account fully for *social* factors, the influences that other people may have on a child's cognitive development (Carpendale & Lewis, 2010; Freund & Lamb, 2010). Piaget's theory, instead, focuses on how children guide their own development through experimentation and reflection. Later in his life, Piaget himself also wondered whether his theory said enough about the role of social experiences in development (Inhelder & Piaget, 1979; Piaget, 1972). As we will see, a contemporary of Piaget's had more to say about social influences on cognitive development.

FIGURE 3.4 Theory of mind. Participants with a theory of mind recognize that the child in the story will look for the leftover chocolate in the blue cupboard, because the child is not aware of the mother's switch of locations.

What Do You Know?

8. In what areas of the brain is myelination concentrated during childhood, and how does myelination of these areas affect the child's cognitive functioning?

9. What are the key differences between Piaget's tasks and those used by later researchers?

What Do You Think?

How should we design the right experiments to test children's cognitive abilities?

Adolescence

HOW WE DEVELOP

LEARNING OBJECTIVE 6

Summarize the major physical, cognitive and emotional changes that take place during adolescence.

With the possible exception of the first couple of years of life, the amount of change that occurs during adolescence rivals that of any other developmental passage. Most crucially, puberty begins. In the cognitive sphere, adolescents display features of both children and adults, and they begin to learn how to function independently. In this section, we will describe some key biological, cognitive and social transitions that characterize this dramatic period.

Physical Development

HOW WE DIFFER

puberty development of full sexual maturity during adolescence.

Puberty refers to the physical development of primary and secondary sex characteristics (Herdt, 2010). **Primary**

sex characteristics are the body structures that have to do specifically with the reproductive system, including growth of the testes and the ovaries. **Secondary sex characteristics** are non-reproductive body events that differ according to gender, such as the deepening of the male voice or the increase in female breast size (Figure 3.5).

The onset and course of puberty are influenced largely by the *pituitary gland*, which coordinates the activities of the rest of the endocrine system (Blakemore *et al.*, 2010). As you will see in Chapter 5, the endocrine system includes the *adrenal glands*, *testes* and *ovaries*. During adolescence, events throughout this system stimulate the growth of body hair and muscle tissue and trigger the onset of the female menstrual cycle, among other changes. One of the most

primary sex characteristics changes in body structure that occur during puberty that have to do specifically with the reproductive system, including the growth of the testes and the ovaries.

secondary sex characteristics changes that occur during puberty and that differ according to gender, but are not directly related to sex.

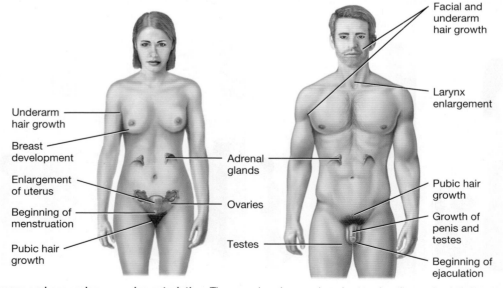

FIGURE 3.5 Primary and secondary sex characteristics. The complex changes in puberty primarily result when hormones are released from the pituitary gland, adrenal gland and ovaries and testes.

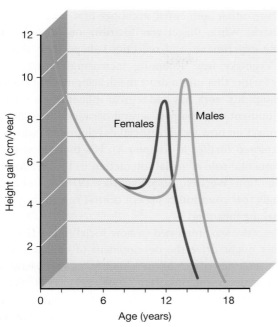

FIGURE 3.6 Adolescent growth spurt. The growth spurt of girls occurs, on average, two years before that of boys. Thus, between the ages of 10 and 14, the average girl is taller than most boys the same age.

Source: Adapted by permission from BMJ Publishing Group Limited. *Archives of Disease in Childhood,* J. M. Tanner, R. N. Whitehouse and M. Takaislu, vol. 41, pp. 451–471, 1966.

1992). The changes of puberty stabilize after a couple years. In the meantime, however, many of those changes can be very disruptive to adolescents. For both boys and girls, variations from age norms for puberty can be upsetting; girls who mature early and boys who mature late report more problems making the transitions through adolescence than those who hit puberty 'on time' (Blakemore *et al.,* 2010; Hayatbakhsh *et al.,* 2009).

The brain also goes through significant changes during adolescence (Roberson-Nay & Brown, 2011; Ernst & Hardin, 2010). Myelination continues to increase, and synaptic connections continue to decrease as a result of synaptic pruning. These changes make the brain work more efficiently. In addition, the *prefrontal cortex,* which is among the last parts of the brain to mature, further develops over the course of adolescence. It is widely accepted that improvements in abstract reasoning, planning and decision-making are related to the development of the prefrontal cortex during this time. The teenager's ability to control impulsive responses also improves as the prefrontal cortex matures. Even so, the prefrontal cortex is not completely mature even at the end of adolescence; it continues to develop through the early twenties.

important changes is a growth spurt triggered by the thyroid gland.

As we observed earlier, this growth spurt actually begins for girls in middle childhood and for boys during early adolescence (Drummond, 2011) (Figure 3.6). The growth spurt happens about two years before the primary sex characteristics kick in. It not only is a forerunner of those later changes but also helps prepare the body for them (Rekers,

Cognitive Development

Adolescent thinking has features of both child cognition and adult cognition. Teenagers show increased capacity for reasoning about abstract things, but they also have deficits in their abilities to see outside of the moment or to take others' points of view. These strengths and limitations both come into play in their social and emotional growth as adolescents attempt to define themselves as persons.

PSYCHOLOGY AROUND US   Road to Intelligence

Would you rather think of yourself as 'clever' or 'a hard worker'? During adolescence, our ability to theorize about ourselves becomes more complex and begins to have complicated implications for how we behave. Psychologist Carol Dweck has studied teens who have 'entity' theories of intelligence and those who have 'malleable' theories of intelligence. Teens with entity theories believe that intelligence is a resource that you either have a lot of or a little of – and that there is little you can do to change your intelligence. Teens with malleable theories, in contrast, believe that, with work, you can improve your intelligence level.

Based on Dweck's research, teens with entity theories of intelligence tend to feel better about themselves initially and

are more likely to be orientated towards goals that let them demonstrate how clever they are. They also tend to be more afraid of failure and less confident about their overall ability. In contrast, teens with malleable theories of intelligence tend to feel a little worse about themselves initially but also tend to persist at challenging tasks longer with the idea that they are building themselves up. By treating intelligence as a muscle that needs exercise to grow, these teens are able to improve their confidence and academic performance over the long term.

How would you prefer to think about yourself now?

Piaget suggested that at around the age of 12 we cross over into mature adult thinking processes, a final stage known as **formal operations**. Piaget believed that the hallmark achievement of this stage is the ability to think about ideas conceptually without needing concrete referents from the real world. The successful transition to formal operations means that teens are no longer bound by the concrete realities of their world. For example, in maths lessons they have moved beyond using real-life representations of numbers, such as counters, and now can use rules to solve problems, even algebra problems involving variables. They can conceive of other worlds and other possible realities, even ones that do not exist outside their own imaginations.

formal operations
Piaget's final stage of cognitive development; the child achieves formal adult reasoning and the ability to think about things that do not have a concrete reality.

The crossover into formal operations also opens the door to higher-level moral thinking, as we will study in more detail in the next chapter (Kohlberg, 2008, 1994, 1963). Teenagers may recognize, for example, that rules serve a societal purpose, not just a personal one. With this growth in cognitive and moral thought, teenagers begin looking at the validity of rules very closely. They realize, for example, that an 11:00 P.M. bedtime is, in many respects, an arbitrary rule that can be challenged and perhaps changed. Similarly, they become aware that adults often do things that contradict what the adults say. According to pioneering developmental psychologist David Elkind, these realizations may cause teenagers to feel angry and upset and may produce a desire to rebel (Elkind, 2007, 1978; Oda, 2007). And so the battle between adolescents and their parents (or other adults) begins.

Elkind noted that teenagers' mastery of formal operational thinking enabled them not only to tune into the flaws of other people but also to recognize their own flaws. They become very sensitive to what other people may be thinking about them. Correspondingly, they display a psychological phenomenon called *adolescent egocentrism*, the mistaken belief that everyone else is focusing largely on them and their behaviour.

One feature of adolescent egocentrism is the *personal fable*. Over the course of searching for a sense of identity and spending time in deep focus on their own thoughts and feelings, teens may become convinced that they are special – the first persons in history to have those particular thoughts and feelings. Another feature of adolescent egocentrism is the *imaginary audience*. Teenagers feel that everyone is scrutinizing them, a notion that leads to strong feelings of inhibition and self-consciousness.

Alternative Accounts of Cognitive Development

We have thus far explored cognitive development using Piaget's stage theory as a guiding framework. There are, however, other influential accounts that take a different approach. While Piaget was focusing on how children's private experiments and reflections shape their thinking, Lev Vygotsky was becoming increasingly interested in other factors that might drive the development of children. Although his work has had a great influence on cognitive development over the past several decades, it has also had an impact on how we view social development (which will be explored further in Chapter 4). His theories stress the fundamental role of social interaction in the development of cognition (Wertsch, 1985; Vygotsky, 1978), as he believed strongly that community plays a central role in the process of 'making meaning'.

Vygotsky was interested in how social interactions with parents might drive the development of children. Unlike Piaget, who viewed a child's development as a process of individual achievement, Vygotsky (2004, 1991, 1978) believed that constructive interactions with parents, older children, teachers and siblings help the child develop ways of thinking about, and functioning in, the world. In Vygotsky's view, an older mentor, such as a parent, helps the child by initially taking responsibility for the basic skills and capabilities the child is developing. Over time, the mentor takes less responsibility. Vygotsky referred to the mentor's step-by-step assistance as **scaffolding**. Vygotsky labelled the gap between what children can accomplish by themselves and what they can accomplish with the help of others as the **zone of proximal development**.

scaffolding developmental adjustments that adults make to give children the help that they need, but not so much that they fail to move forward.

zone of proximal development the gap between what a child can accomplish alone and what the child can accomplish with help from others.

Because of his death at the young age of 37 and the chilly political climate between the former Soviet Union and the West, Vygotsky's ideas have become known only in recent years. However, developmental psychologists have found numerous ways to apply Vygotsky's ideas (Trawick-Smith & Dziurgot, 2011), and he has become one of today's most influential developmental theorists (Eun, 2010; Feldman, 2003). Indeed, ideas of scaffolding and zones of proximal development are now an important part of educational systems throughout the United Kingdom, Europe and the United States. When helping children learn to read, for example, many teachers begin by reading books to them, and then gradually turn over responsibility for various reading skills. The children may first follow along with the pictures as the teacher reads the words, then point to letters. Eventually, they learn to read single words, then sentences and finally entire books on their own.

Whereas Piaget believed that thinking preceded language, Vygotsky believed that language is crucial to cognitive development because a great deal of mentoring relies on talking and listening (Eun, 2010). Both theorists noticed that preschool-aged children seem to talk to themselves a lot. Piaget regarded this incessant chatter as largely unimportant, egocentric babble. Vygotsky, however, called that chatter **private speech**. He believed that children use private speech to regulate their behaviour and internal experiences, to plan and to solve problems, often repeating or imitating the words of their mentors. Vygotsky believed that, eventually, these private chats turn into silent, internal dialogues, perhaps similar to the conversations adults have in their heads each morning about whether to hit the snooze button on their alarm clocks one more time and risk being late for that first appointment.

private speech a child's self-talk, which Vygotsky believed the child uses to regulate behaviour and internal experiences.

Because Vygotsky believed that other individuals are critical to a child's development, he also believed that there is a great deal more variability in how children develop. He believed that each culture has its own specific challenges, and that those challenges change over the course of life, meaning that development has to meet those challenges. Vygotsky's ideas have been very influential in the work of psychologists such as Jerome Bruner. His book *The Process of Education* (1960) had a huge impact on educational policy both in the United States and in the United Kingdom. Bruner's basic philosophy was that, although it was important that children learn and discover for themselves, others can also help in the learning process. Like Vygotsky, he also saw a much more fundamental role for language in cognitive development. Rather than language reflecting changes in thinking (as Piaget believed), Bruner saw it as a driving force: improvements in language ability are the reason why children are able to represent ideas in mind around the age of six years. As such, Bruner believed that cognitive development can be speeded up through training in the use of symbols, whereas Piaget thought that it follows the same biologically predetermined course irrespective of assistance or otherwise.

Before You Go On

What Do You Know?

10. If a child arrives at puberty significantly earlier or later than his or her peer group, how may that affect his or her adjustment?

11. Define *formal operations*.

12. How did the approaches of Vygotsky and Bruner differ from Piaget's?

What Do You Think?

Do we all undergo the same changes at the same time, or does our social world affect our individual development?

Adulthood

LEARNING OBJECTIVE 7

Describe key physical and cognitive changes that take place throughout adulthood.

Physical and Cognitive Development

With the end of adolescence comes maturity. Nevertheless, the body continues to go through changes during adulthood. And, as we will see, so does the brain.

What Happens in the Body During Adulthood?

Generally, physical attributes, such as strength, reaction time and overall body function, are at their peak during our 20s. As we move into our 30s, our bodies begin to decline slowly. Our metabolism slows, for example, so it takes a bit more work to keep some roundness from appearing around the waist.

During our 30s and 40s, we begin to show the first significant signs of ageing. Skin begins to lose some of its elasticity, and grey hairs begin to sprout. Although we are significantly past our sensory peak, we generally do not begin to notice declines in that area of functioning until we are in our 40s (Drummond, 2011; Fozard *et al.*, 1977). We become more farsighted, finding it hard to read or see small objects close to us, and we have difficulty seeing in the dark or recovering from sudden glares of light. We also become less sensitive to high-frequency noises.

menopause series of changes in hormonal function occurring in women during their 50s, which lead to the end of the menstrual cycle and reproductive capabilities.

Women in their 50s typically go through a major change called **menopause** (Nosek *et al.*, 2010). Menopause involves a series of changes in hormonal function that eventually lead to the end of the menstrual cycle and reproductive capabilities. The early phase of menopause is often associated with a variety of physical experiences, such as hot flushes, headaches and sudden shifts in mood.

As we move into late adulthood, during our 60s and 70s, we may become a bit shorter and thinner, owing to changes in our skeletal structure and metabolism (Drummond, 2011; Bord-Hoffman & Donius, 2005). Our immune systems also begin to decline in function, leaving us at higher risk for illness. Our vision and hearing continue to decline, joined by our sense of taste. Our pupils shrink, so that less light reaches the retina, making it harder for us to see in low light.

The story is not as simple as a long, slow, inevitable decline, however. Exogenous factors, such as exercise, stress, diet and life experience, can have a dramatic influence on the course and impact of these changes (Drummond, 2011; Larson *et al.*, 2006; Brach *et al.*, 2003). Although declines are common, many of the changes can be subtle and have minimal impact on how well we function in the world.

Adulthood — WHAT HAPPENS IN THE BRAIN?

Until recently, neuroscientists believed that our brains begin to shrink during adulthood, in terms of both volume and weight, and that much of this loss is attributable to the shrinkage and loss of active brain cells (Miller & O'Callaghan, 2005). Research over the past decade, however, has revealed that no significant loss of neurons occurs in adulthood, except in cases of brain pathology (Miller & O'Callaghan, 2005). Indeed, new neurons keep forming in certain parts of the brain throughout life, including during adulthood (Leuner *et al.*, 2006; Gould, 2007). These neurons may be the result of new learning or may play a role in further learning, or both (Leuner *et al.*, 2010, 2006). Given the stability and even addition of neurons during adulthood, it is not surprising that most of our broad intellectual capabilities remain intact throughout our lives.

As we move into our 40s and 50s, however, we do begin to see *some* intellectual shifts. Recovering information from long-term memory starts to take a little longer, and it takes a bit longer to learn new material. During our 60s and 70s, our memories decline, as does our confidence in our ability to remember and to solve problems (Ornstein & Light, 2010; Freedman *et al.*, 2001). Overall, as we will discuss in Chapter 10, such declines tend to have a more significant impact on our ability to recall information than on our skill at solving problems or dealing with new situations.

Some declines are more serious. In some types of dementia, severe memory problems combine with losses in at least one other cognitive function, such as abstract thinking or language (APA, 2000). The occurrence of dementia is strongly related to age. Around 1–2% of people aged 65 years have dementia, compared with some 50% of people over 85 (Apostolova & Cummings, 2008). This will also be discussed in greater depth in Chapter 10.

Why Do We Age? Scientists have offered many theories about why we age; no single explanation is widely accepted (Pierpaoli, 2005). One important theory of ageing, the **cellular clock theory**, suggests that ageing is built into our cells. Tiny structures on the ends of DNA strands, called *telomeres*, aid in cell reproduction but grow shorter each time they are used. Eventually, they become too short, and cells can no longer reproduce themselves. As a result, the body is less able to repair itself. The various changes of ageing – saggy skin and decreases in vision and memory, for example – are the direct result of those events.

cellular clock theory the theory suggesting that we age because our cells have built-in limits on their ability to reproduce.

Two other theories of ageing are rooted in our experiences and the impact that life events can have on us. The wear-and-tear and free-radical theories suggest that years of use help wear out our bodies. The **wear-and-tear theory** boils down to this: the more mileage we put on our bodies through living (augmented by factors such as stress, poor diet and exposure to environmental teratogens), the sooner we wear out (Hawkley *et al.*, 2005). The **free-radical theory** provides a chemistry-orientated explanation (Perluigi *et al.*, 2010; Boldyrev & Johnson, 2007). Free radicals are oxygen molecules that are negatively charged. A negative charge on a molecule can attract small particles of matter called *electrons* from other molecules. According to the free-radical theory of ageing, free radicals become more prevalent in our system as we get older, increasingly destabilizing cell structures and doing progressively more damage to our bodies, resulting in the ageing effects described above.

wear-and-tear theory the theory suggesting we age because use of our body wears it out.

free-radical theory the theory suggesting we age because special negatively charged oxygen molecules become more prevalent in our body as we get older, destabilizing cellular structures and causing the effects of ageing.

Summary

Understanding How We Develop

LEARNING OBJECTIVE 1   Understand the key debates underlying research and theory in child development.

- Developmental psychology is the study of changes in our behaviour and mental processes over time and the various factors that influence the course of those changes.
- Key philosophical issues in the study of developmental psychology are what drive change (biological or environmental factors), the nature of the change (qualitative or quantitative) and the role of early experiences in shaping later development.

How Is Developmental Psychology Investigated?

LEARNING OBJECTIVE 2   Describe and discuss the advantages and disadvantages of different experimental designs for researching development.

- Two major research approaches in developmental psychology are cross-sectional (comparing different age groups to assess change) and longitudinal (studying the same group to see how responses change over time).
- The cohort-sequential and developmental trajectory designs combine different elements of the cross-sectional and longitudinal approaches.

Before We Are Born

LEARNING OBJECTIVE 3   Discuss mechanisms of genetic inheritance.

- Our genetic inheritance comes from both parents, who each contribute half our chromosomes. Genes can combine in various ways to make up our phenotype (observable traits).
- Genetics can influence the manifestation of both physical traits and psychological traits, including temperament, although environment also plays a role.
- Prenatal development begins with conception and is divided into three stages: germinal, embryonic and foetal, each characterized by specific patterns of development.
- Individuals are susceptible to multiple influences by biological and environmental forces before they are even born, during the prenatal period.

Infancy

LEARNING OBJECTIVE 4   Summarize the major physical and cognitive developments that take place during infancy.

- Infants make dramatic gains in both physical and psychological capabilities. Our brains grow during this period, preparing us to learn and encode the information that will organize those changes.

- One of the most important developmental theorists, Jean Piaget, proposed a theory of cognitive development that suggested that through learning and self-experimentation we help our thinking to grow progressively more complex.
- Piaget believed we passed through multiple stages on the way to formal adult reasoning and that each transition was accompanied by the acquisition of a new cognitive capability. During the sensorimotor stage, in infancy, we become able to hold memories of objects in our minds.
- Information-processing researchers have suggested that babies may develop mental capacities at earlier ages than Piaget believed they did.

Early and Middle Childhood

LEARNING OBJECTIVE 5   Summarize the major physical and cognitive developments that take place during early and middle childhood.

- Physical growth continues at a generally slower pace in childhood than in infancy. Myelination and synaptic pruning continue to shape the brain.
- Piaget believed that children pass through the stages of preoperational and concrete operations thinking, learning

to manipulate their mental schemata. Other researchers have suggested children's thinking may not be as limited during these stages as Piaget thought it was.

Adolescence

LEARNING OBJECTIVE 6   Summarize the major physical, cognitive and emotional changes that take place during adolescence.

- Adolescence is generally associated with many substantial changes, including the onset of full sexual and physical maturity, as well as reasoning capabilities that approach adult levels. However, the teenager has certain limitations that influence his or her ability to make sound judgements and avoid risky situations.

Adulthood

LEARNING OBJECTIVE 7   Describe key physical and cognitive changes that take place throughout adulthood.

- Adult physical and psychological development is often characterized by some degree of decline. However, most basic faculties remain intact across the lifespan.

VIDEO   Access your interactive e-book to view a video clip for this chapter at **www.wileyopenpage.com**

TYING IT TOGETHER

 **WHAT HAPPENS IN THE** B R A I N ?

- At birth, we have approximately 100 billion neurons. A newborn has around 2500 synaptic connections per neuron while a three-year-old has six times that many connections. But a 20-year-old has only around one-third the synaptic connections per neuron of a three-year-old, a huge reduction that is due to synaptic pruning.
- Myelination, the formation of fatty white coverings around neurons, helps neurons transmit information more efficiently. During infancy, much of myelination

occurs in brain areas tied to movement, reflexes and sensory responses. During childhood, myelination is concentrated in brain areas that help coordinate activity, planning and problem-solving.

- Despite past beliefs, no significant loss of neurons occurs in adulthood, except in cases of brain pathology.
- New neurons keep being formed in certain parts of the brain throughout life, including during adulthood.

HOW WE DIFFER

- Only a few human traits are the product of a single gene pair. Most traits, particularly behavioural ones, are *polygenic*, helping to produce many variations in how traits are expressed from person to person.
- On average, Kipsigis in Kenya walk a month before babies in the United States, and Ache babies in Paraguay begin walking a year later than Western children: variations that are due to cultural differences in parenting.
- On average, girls experience a growth spurt during their 10th or 11th year, a couple of years prior to boys.
- Primary sex characteristics during puberty include growth of the testes for boys and growth of the ovaries for girls. Secondary sex characteristics include a deepening of the voice for boys and an increase in breast size for girls.

HOW WE DEVELOP

- At birth, the senses of taste, smell and touch are highly developed; hearing is somewhat immature; and vision is extremely limited.
- Babies may have some sense of maths as early as five months of age.
- Most children do not develop a *theory of mind*, the *ability* to recognize that other persons have a perspective different from their own, prior to three years of age.
- Although less egocentric than younger children, many teenagers often display personal fables in which they are convinced that they are special – the first persons to have various thoughts and feelings – and perceive an imaginary audience in which they believe everyone is scrutinizing them.
- It is not entirely clear why we age and grow old.
- The human lifespan has continued to increase with each generation.

Quizzes to test yourself further are available in your interactive e-book at **www.wileyopenpage.com**

Key Terms

Flashcards to test yourself further are available in your interactive e-book at **www.wileyopenpage.com**

CHAPTER 4

Social and Emotional Development

Adapted by Corriene Reed, Institute of Education, UK

CHAPTER OUTLINE

- Before We Are Born
- Infancy
- Childhood

- Adolescence
- Adulthood and Old Age
- Atypical Development

 Access your interactive e-book to view a video clip for this chapter at **www.wileyopenpage.com**

Growing Up Social

Did you ever think about what it takes to become a social person? What input is needed for us to understand the world around us, and to interact with the people in it successfully? Are these skills already part of our genetic make-up or do they develop as we interact with our environment? This argument is familiar to us when we apply it to language and how it develops, but it can also be applied to our development as social beings.

What happens in situations where very young children have been secluded for long periods, with no knowledge of the world and in circumstances of extreme deprivation? There are a number of reports on children who have spent their early years in exceptionally difficult and deprived environments. Many researchers (e.g., Skuse, 1993) have been concerned with how their language has developed, but it will be useful to investigate, in this opening vignette, how their social development was also negatively affected. Certain features were common to these children when they were found; they were lacking basic human skills such as speech and social skills. However, many children, when removed from their difficult environment, quickly developed their cognitive and social skills. The most famous case of severe deprivation was that of 'Genie', reported by Curtiss (1981). She had been confined to a small room from the age of 20 months, under conditions of extreme physical restraint, and was found at the age of 13 years and seven months. Curtiss comments,

'Genie was unsocialised, primitive, hardly human'. She was severely malnourished, had been left by her family in an impoverished environment with little or no stimulation, and had minimal exposure to language. Amazingly, when she was found, she was alert and curious, and eager for social contact. She did have great problems in expressing emotions and would have silent tantrums and show challenging behaviours. Although there is still a big debate about whether she ever acquired language, it is clear from later video footage that she was able to communicate using sign language and that her social development had improved after she was found. Thompson (1986) reports the case of 'Adam', who had been abandoned in Colombia, South America. He was raised in a windowless room in a girls' reform school until he was 16 months of age. When he was found he had severe malnutrition, was anaemic and infested with parasites. He was emotionally withdrawn and passive, crying when handled and disliking physical contact. By the time he was followed up, just before he was 14, he was functioning well socially and educationally. These case studies suggest that opportunities for play, physical contact with caregivers and family and an environment filled with language and love are clearly important for social development. ■

This chapter is the second of two that consider the fundamental role of development in human psychology. While the first chapter looked at biological and cognitive development, in this chapter we turn our attention to social and emotional development and consider issues such as temperament, moral development and atypical development.

Before We Are Born

HOW WE
DIFFER

LEARNING OBJECTIVE 1
Discuss the developmental origins of temperament.

Many psychological researchers are interested in trying to determine how much of the way we think and act is influenced by our genetic inheritance, a field of study called *behavioural genetics*. Developmental psychologists are often in a position to examine the influence of genetics. One of the key areas of focus of both behavioural genetics and developmental psychology, for example, has been **temperament**, often defined as a biologically based tendency to respond to certain situations in similar ways throughout our lifetimes (Bates *et al.*, 2010; Henderson & Wachs, 2007). In a longitudinal study that began in the 1950s, researchers Stella Chess and Alexander Thomas (1996) suggested that, as infants, people tend to fall into one of three temperament categories:

temperament biologically based tendencies to respond to certain situations in similar ways throughout our lifetimes.

- *Easy.* Babies with easy temperaments were described as playful, regular in bodily functions, such as eating and sleeping, and open to novelty.

- *Difficult.* Babies with difficult temperaments tend to be irritable and likely to have intensely negative reactions to changes or new situations.

- *Slow-to-warm-up.* Babies in this category are less active and less responsive than babies in the other two categories. In general, they tend to withdraw in the face of change, but their withdrawal is not as sharply negative as those babies with difficult temperaments.

Following Chess and Thomas's studies, many researchers have examined how our temperament relates to our later personality characteristics. In a famous line of work, biologist and psychologist Jerome Kagan (2010, 2008, 2001) conducted a longitudinal study examining the relationship between young children's levels of *behavioural inhibition*, the tendency to withdraw from new or different situations, and levels of shyness later in life. He found that children who were highly inhibited at 21 months of age were more likely than uninhibited toddlers to be shy when they were 12 to 14 years old.

Kagan's research seems to illustrate two key aspects of temperament:

- *Temperament is inborn.* For an attribute to be temperamentally based, it must appear early (e.g. shortly after birth). Considering that Kagan tested babies at such a young age, it is doubtful that they had much of an opportunity to learn to be fearful of new situations. Thus, many researchers believe that inhibited temperaments are biologically inherited.

- *Temperament is stable across situations and time.* The participants in Kagan's study who were most shy temperamentally were the ones who were most inhibited at different times and in different situations. Researchers have also established that other aspects of a person's temperament are stable over time and place (Bates *et al.*, 2010; Henderson & Wachs, 2007).

PSYCHOLOGY AROUND US   Lefties during the Middle Ages

People who were left-handed were believed to be possessed by the Devil. In later centuries, doctors thought left-handedness was linked with criminal behaviour. The derivation of the word *sinistrality* reflects this. It comes from the Latin word *sinistra*, originally meaning left, but took on later meanings of evil. Of course, we now know that left-handers are not inherently evil. We now know, too, that indications of left-handedness can be observed in the womb. In fact, foetuses show a preference for which hand they keep nearer their mouth.

Researchers have recently found that handedness is, at least partly, a genetically inherited preference. Still, our environment plays a role in how we express that preference. More than a few children, for example, have learned to be right-handed in response to their parents' disapproval of their natural left-handedness. Further complicating matters is the fact that

handedness usually is displayed along a continuum. We may prefer one hand to another, but it may not be an absolute preference. We may even shift hands between tasks.

What does appear to be clear from biological evidence is that handedness is linked with brain lateralization, or brain asymmetry. As you will see later in this book, the two halves of the human brain are *not* exactly alike, that is they are asymmetrical. In addition, each half has primary control over certain functions. It turns out that left-handers and right-handers differ in which hemisphere controls their particular handedness.

All that said, larger questions remain. Why should there be a connection between brain asymmetry and handedness? Why are our brains asymmetrical in the first place? And what about left-handers who learn to become right-handed?

PSYCHOLOGY AROUND US   Birth Order Effects: What Is Real?

Source: Rubberball/Getty Images, Inc.

Have you ever explained yourself by referring to your birth order? 'Oh, I'm the middle child, so I just don't feel like I belong.' Or perhaps, 'I'm spoiled and act out because I'm an only child.' In reality, the effect of birth order on personality is hotly debated by psychologists, and most of the 'effects' of birth order may be more anecdotal than they are actual.

In 1996, scientist and scholar Frank Sulloway published the book *Born to Rebel* in which he argues that first-borns tend to be more responsible, while later-borns tend to be more rebellious. He further hypothesizes that later-borns tend to be more open to experience and more agreeable than first-borns, and, at the same time, less neurotic, less extraverted and less conscientious (Jefferson *et al.*, 1998).

Although Sulloway's book was widely praised at first, many psychologists eventually questioned his methodology and noted inconsistencies in his data. Most notably, in 2000, the journal *Politics and the Life Sciences* attempted to publish a roundtable issue devoted to a discussion of Sulloway's book. The issue was to include articles and commentaries from a

number of scholars who rejected or questioned Sulloway's work (Townsend, 2000, p. 135). The debate became so heated that, according to the journal's editor, Sulloway threatened legal action and the publication of the issue was delayed for four years, eventually appearing in 2004.

Scientists typically subject research to peer review, in which an article is read by fellow scientists and intensely scrutinized and revised before it is published. Books, however, do not have to go through this process, which was one of the criticisms levelled against Sulloway's research (Townsend, 2000). In contrast to Sulloway's findings, a peer-reviewed article that examined over 1000 birth order studies has concluded that birth order does not influence personality in a clear and consistent way (Jefferson *et al.*, 1998).

Perhaps that is why birth order research seems to be shifting away from the area of personality and towards other areas, such as intelligence and physical features (Frank *et al.*, 2010; Skinner & Fox-Francoeur, 2010). It has been found, for example, that first-borns tend to score about three points higher on IQ tests compared to second-borns. Similarly, children born earlier in a family are, on average, taller and weigh more than those born later (Kluger, 2007).

Despite the fact that birth order studies have not yet yielded clear or compelling findings, the topic remains very popular in the public domain. Indeed, in recent years, *Time* and other news magazines have presented several cover stories on the relationship between birth order and psychological and social functioning, an indicator that, even as many psychologists believe birth order to be a subject unworthy of research, the public's fascination with the topic continues to grow (Kluger, 2007).

This is not to say, however, that there is no variability at all from time to time and situation to situation. Indeed, investigators have found greater stability of temperament when measuring behaviour across similar situations, such as in various family situations, than when comparing temperamental influences on children's behaviour across different situations, such as school versus home.

Despite the importance of biological factors, it is necessary to recognize that our environments also play impor-

tant roles in how we behave. Kagan's studies revealed, for example, that not all of the babies who were inhibited at birth later developed into shy teenagers. Similarly, being highly extroverted around new toys as a newborn did not always lead these infant participants to become 'party animal' teenagers. In fact, if genetics were destiny, we would all have a much easier time predicting how people would turn out, and this would be a much shorter chapter. As we will see, however, our environment plays a very strong role in determining our development, beginning before we are even born.

Before You Go On

What Do You Know?

1. How do Chess and Thomas categorize the temperaments of babies in their studies, and what are the major attributes of each temperament category?

2. What are the key things that identify a behaviour as temperamentally based?

3. What did Kagan's studies tell us about temperament and the nature—nurture debate?

What Do You Think?

How do you think environment may also influence a genetically influenced trait, such as behavioural inhibition? For example, what might parents or teachers of an inhibited toddler do that would either contribute to or decrease later shyness?

Infancy

LEARNING OBJECTIVE 2

Summarize the major social and emotional developments that take place during infancy.

Parents are at the centre of an infant's social world, and many psychologists have focused on the importance of the early experiences children have with their parents. *Attachment theory* has made the best empirical case for how crucial this relationship is (Allen, 2011a, 2011b; Nelson & Bennett, 2008). In this section, we will talk about the principles of this theory and how parent–child relationships may influence a child's social and emotional development.

Attachment theory

Theorist John Bowlby believed that human beings are born

attachment a close emotional bond to another person, such as a baby to a caregiver.

with a drive to form an **attachment**, to become emotionally close to one particular caregiver, usually their mother. He suggested that early positive experiences with that caregiver are critical to health and well-being and that they shape how well the individual will function emotionally, socially and even cognitively later in life.

Bowlby also argued that all the behaviours of infants are targeted at bringing them closer to their mothers. He believed, for example, that reflexes such as rooting or reaching out help babies build relationships with their mothers (Bowlby, 1958). To Bowlby, the presence of these reflexes provided evidence that attachment processes are inborn and crucial to the survival and well-being of babies. Bowlby also thought that children with strong attachments to their parents would actually feel safer than children who were more independent and less attached to their parents. Indeed, he suggested that steady, consistent responsiveness to a baby's needs is actually the best way for a mother to eventually bring about a truly independent and well-functioning child. Initially, the scientific community reacted to this assertion negatively. The psychological wisdom of Bowlby's day had held that parents who responded to children's needs by drawing the children in would succeed only in fostering neediness and dependence. However, his Maternal Deprivation Hypothesis did become very influential in the 1960s, having a strong practical impact on government policy implications to do with hospitalization and childcare. Bowlby's ideas have been strongly criticized (Rutter, 1981; Clarke & Clarke, 1998). His views on the importance of the attachment to the mother have been queried, as children often have several attachment figures,

(a) (b) (c) (d) (e)

FIGURE 4.1 The Strange Situation procedure.
(a) The baby plays while the mother is nearby.
(b) A stranger enters the room, speaks to the mother and approaches the child.
(c) The mother leaves and the stranger remains in the room with an unhappy baby.
(d) The mother returns and the stranger leaves.
(e) The baby is reunited with the mother.

who could compensate. Research on children brought up in institutions was compromised because other confounding variables, such as an unstimulating environment and social deprivation, were not considered. On balance, although his work may have made mothers returning to work feel unnecessarily guilty, it also had a very positive impact on hospital care and institutional care for children.

Mary Ainsworth, a student of Bowlby's who had conducted naturalistic observations in Uganda, supported Bowlby's ideas that mother–child attachment occurs around the world (Ainsworth, 2010, 1993, 1985, 1967). In addition, like Bowlby, Ainsworth argued that babies attach to their mothers because that is how their needs get met (Hughes, 2009; Bretherton, 1992). Ainsworth further noticed that some mothers, whom she labelled 'highly sensitive', seemed to form attachments that were more successful in fostering their children's independence.

Ainsworth developed a way to test the attachment between babies and their mothers in a laboratory setting. In Ainsworth's procedure, called the *Strange Situation* (Figure 4.1), a baby plays in a laboratory room with his or her mother nearby. After a time, a stranger enters the room, speaks with the mother and attempts to interact with the baby. Then the mother leaves the room. The baby, left alone with the stranger, generally is in some distress. The researchers are most interested in how the baby reacts to the mother when she returns, as well as how willing the baby is to explore when the mother is present.

Based on her experimental findings, Ainsworth identified three basic attachment styles:

- *Secure attachment.* The infant uses the mother as a secure base from which to explore and as a support in times of trouble. The infant is moderately distressed when the mother leaves the room and happy when she returns.

- *Anxious/avoidant attachment.* The infant is unresponsive with the mother and is usually indifferent when she leaves the room and when she returns.

- *Anxious/ambivalent attachment.* The infant reacts strongly when the mother leaves the room. When she returns, the infant shows mixed emotions, seeking close contact and then squirming away angrily.

Later, psychologist Mary Main noted that some children fail to show any reliable way of coping with separations and reunions, exhibiting features of all of the three attachment styles (Main *et al.*, 2005; Main & Solomon, 1990). She therefore added a fourth category to describe this pattern:

- *Disorganized/disoriented attachment.* The infant displays confused and contradictory behaviour when the mother returns. For example, the infant may ignore the mother while being held, appear flat and depressed, look dazed, cry out and/or show a rigid posture.

The incidence of all four styles is shown in Figure 4.2.

Do attachment types predict other aspects of development? Secure attachment has been associated with curiosity and problem solving, social confidence and later

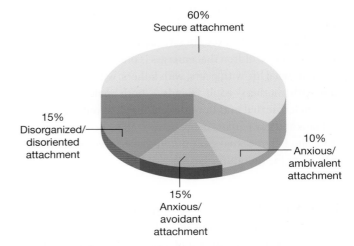

FIGURE 4.2 Styles of Attachment. Ainsworth and Main identified four styles of attachment. Secure attachment is by far the most common.

independence (Oppenheim *et al.*, 1988). The problem is that attachment is reciprocal: it is a relationship and not a specific characteristic of a young child. There have also been questions about whether the Strange Situation is valid in different cultural settings. Takahashi (1990) showed that Japanese infants got very upset in the infant alone episode, because they are never usually left alone at the age of 12 months. So it may be that many Japanese babies were being labelled as insecurely attached, when in fact they were not.

Based on Ainsworth's work, Bowlby (1969) later suggested that early attachment experiences help people create an *internal working model* of the world and themselves. Children with sensitive mothers, in Bowlby's view, will come to think of other people as supportive and helpful. In turn, this positive model will influence their later relationships in a healthy way. In contrast, children who develop a working model that the world is insensitive may be at risk of poor adjustment or difficult relationships later in their lives.

The vast majority of attachment research has focused on mothers. Indeed, cultural practice bears out the importance of the mother–child relationship; in almost every society, mothers are primarily responsible for childcare. Evidence also indicates, however, that fathers are capable of responding in highly sensitive ways (as defined by Ainsworth). If a father is highly sensitive, a baby generally turns out to be securely attached (Veríssimo *et al.*, 2011; Howes, 1999). We will explore the importance of fathers to children's social and emotional development later in the chapter.

What about other caregivers? The results of existing research comparing lesbian and gay parents to heterosexual parents and children of lesbian and gay parents to children of heterosexual parents (Allen & Demo, 1995; Patterson, 2000) are quite clear: stereotypes about them being poor parents and role models are not supported by the data. Empirical evidence suggests that children of lesbian and gay parents have positive relationships with peers and that their relationships with adults of both sexes are satisfactory. The picture of lesbian mothers' children that emerges is one of general engagement in social life with peers, with fathers, with grandparents and with mothers' adult friends – both male and female, both heterosexual and homosexual. Fears about children of lesbians and gay parents being ostracized by peers or isolated from the heterosexual community have received little support from the literature.

Parenting Styles  HOW WE DIFFER

Researchers have also looked at factors such as parenting styles, parenting practices and parental involvement, what are known as family-related factors, to tease out the links between these factors and children's psychological outcomes

and adjustment. There is much empirical research that indicates the importance of parental influence.

Hill *et al.* (2004) observed a group of over 450 adolescents, from around 12 years through to 16 years of age. Their longitudinal study found that parental academic involvement at 12 was negatively correlated with behavioural problems at 13 and positively correlated to the aspirations of 16-year-olds. There were variations depending on parental education levels, and ethnicity was also a factor. Among the higher parental education group, parent academic involvement was related to fewer adolescent behavioural problems, achievement and then aspirations. For the lower parental education group, parent academic involvement was related to their adolescent's aspirations but not to their behaviour or achievement. Parent academic involvement was positively related to achievement for African-Americans but not for European Americans. It may be that different demographic groups see parental academic involvement differently, in terms of its purpose and importance.

Locke & Prinz (2002), in an American study, reviewed the measurement of parental discipline and nurturance from over 20 years' worth of research. Although these two factors are commonly used constructs in parenting research literature, there are a bewildering number of ways to measure them: questionnaires that could be used face to face, for telephone-structured questions or in the form of a vignette. They also evaluated over 30 observational schedules for both discipline and nurturance. They pointed out that there were methodological difficulties, with so many measures of parental influence, in comparing different studies using different methods of measurement. They indicated that there was a need for greater attention to cultural variation and questioned whether these different measurement techniques were equivalent to each other.

Normal genetic variability will also have an effect on parental behaviour. Maccoby (2000) cites evidence that children's genetic make-up affects their behaviour and influences the way they are treated by their parents. However, she argues that knowing the strength of genetic factors was not enough to estimate environmental ones, and if we tried to do this we could underestimate parenting effects on children's development. Maccoby considers that children's genetic predispositions and their parenting regimes should be seen to be very closely linked, and they both affect children's development. So both nature and nurture can affect the relationship between parents and children.

Attachment theory gave psychologists a way of *operationalizing* (or defining in a measurable way) the relationship between parents and children. After that, researchers began applying those insights to understanding how parent behaviours may contribute to development. For example,

TABLE 4.1 Parenting Styles

Parental style	Parental behaviour	Associated outcome in children
Authoritative	Warm, sensitive to child's needs, nurturing Makes reasonable demands and encourages appropriate autonomy	High self-esteem, cooperativeness, self-control, social maturity
Authoritarian	Cold, rejecting Makes coercive demands Frequently critical of child	Low self-esteem, anxious, unhappy, often angry and aggressive
Permissive	Warm, accepting but overindulgent and inattentive	Impulsive, disobedient, overly dependent on adults, low initiative
Uninvolved	Emotionally detached and depressed Little time or energy for child rearing	Anxious, poor communication skills, antisocial behaviour

Diana Baumrind, a psychologist at the University of California–Berkley, studied the parental environment of primarily white, middle-class preschool children. She found that two characteristics of parental behaviour seem particularly important: how many demands the parent puts on the child and how responsive the parent is to the child (Baumrind *et al.*, 2010; Baumrind, 1991). Combining those two dimensions, Baumrind identifies four parenting styles: authoritative (high demand, high responsiveness), authoritarian (high demand, low responsiveness), permissive (low demand, high responsiveness) and uninvolved (low demand, low responsiveness). As you can see in Table 4.1, the authoritative style produces the most positive outcomes for children.

A key question about Baumrind's theory has been how well it applies outside white, individualistic cultures, those in which people are expected to be self-reliant and self-achieving, in contrast to *collectivist cultures*, which expect people to be focused primarily on the needs of the group. Cross-cultural research has found that parents in a variety of cultures can be classified into the same four styles. It is not clear, however, that the outcomes of the four parenting styles are the same across different cultures. Research has suggested, for example, that in Asian cultures the authoritarian parenting style may not always lead to negative child outcomes, as it typically does in Western cultures (Pong *et al.*, 2010; Chao, 2001). Research also suggests that outcomes of parenting styles vary among cultural groups within one country. Studies show that authoritarian parenting style, for example, seems to be more harmful to middle-class boys than to middle-class girls, to white preschool girls than to African-American preschool girls and to white boys than to Hispanic-American boys (Baumrind *et al.*, 2010; Baumrind, 1991).

Leung *et al.* (1998) conducted a study on parenting style and academic achievement using Chinese high school students in Hong Kong, and Australian and European American high school students. They found that authoritarian parenting was positively associated with the academic achievement among Hong Kong Chinese high school students. There was no relationship between authoritative parenting style and academic achievement among Hong Kong Chinese high school students. However, authoritative parenting style was positively associated with academic achievement among Australians and European American high school students. It is clear that the link between parenting styles in different cultures needs further exploration.

Another important question researchers have examined is how children's behaviours affect parenting styles, a transaction known as **reciprocal socialization**. The direction of causality is unknown, in that the behaviour of the child can be affected by parenting style, but parenting style could also be dependent on the behaviour of the child. Very rowdy children are, for example, more likely to evoke authoritarian control behaviours in their parents (Chan, 2010; Caspi, 1998). Most of today's research on reciprocal socialization emphasizes the transaction between the parent and the child and holds that the *fit* between a parent and child's behavioural styles is more important than some objectively right or wrong style.

reciprocal socialization the transactional relationship between parent and child.

Critical psychologists such as Erica Burman (2008) have questioned the assumption that the traditional middle-class family (consisting of a married heterosexual couple with a father who works outside the home and a mother who devotes herself to caring for the couple's two or three biological offspring) is necessary for the good social and emotional development of a child. Children growing up under alternative arrangements have often been perceived to be at more at risk than if they grew up in the more traditional nuclear family. What research evidence is there to show that this is, indeed, the case? What is the relationship between family arrangements and development? Many researchers have interpreted findings that characteristics of parents and parenting are associated with children's outcomes as

PSYCHOLOGY AROUND US   Worth a Thousand Words

One thing most parents seem to share, regardless of parenting style, is a love for baby photos. As a result, the embarrassing baby photo is a fact of life for many of us. We all dread the first time we bring a friend (or worse, boyfriend or girlfriend) home and a family member whips out the photo album or turns on the computer. And, given the new age of social media, a new level of embarrassment may be about to strike the next generation.

In 2010, AVG, an Internet security firm, polled mothers with Internet access in Europe, North America, Australia, New Zealand and Japan. Their survey found that 92% of newborns have some level of presence on the Internet. That includes 23% with uploaded birth scans, their Internet presence preceding their actual birth, and 7% with their very own email address. Growing up is becoming a much more public and potentially embarrassing experience.

One has to wonder: will this new connectedness have an impact on the way in which children grow up and develop?

PSYCHOLOGY AROUND US   What Do Fathers Have to Do With Development? A Lot!

It takes both a sperm and an egg to create a child. Yet if you looked at child development research conducted prior to the mid-1970s, you would have thought that researchers were unaware of this fact. Case in point: upon reviewing the existing literature in 1975, psychologist Michael Lamb declared that fathers were 'forgotten contributors to child development' (Lewis & Lamb, 2003). Why were fathers so long ignored, and what do we now know about their impact on children?

Fathers were left out of developmental research for decades for both pragmatic and stereotype-based reasons. Mothers were more likely to be the primary caregivers of children, leading researchers to believe that their impact was more important to study. In addition, fathers were more difficult to recruit for research because they tended to work outside of the home during regular business hours. Early childhood educators also tended to have more frequent contact with mothers than fathers, leading mothers to be more salient when those educators conducted studies of 'parenting' effects (Gadsden & Ray, 2003). There were also implicit biases driving the oversight, such as the widely held belief that fathers lacked the sensitivity towards children that could only come from 'maternal instinct' (Lamb, 2010; Solantaus & Salo, 2005).

In recent years, however, it has been found that parenting styles are largely equivalent between the sexes. Moreover, while mothers in more conventional family structures do tend to be slightly more sensitive caregivers than fathers, particularly after the child reaches one year of age, the amount of parenting experience seems to underlie much of this effect. That is, if a father spends more time taking care of the child, his sensitivity tends to be higher (Newland & Coyle, 2010). For a variety of cultural reasons, fathers in Western societies tend to be more involved in play with their children than in caretaking. In fact, given the choice, infants prefer playing with their fathers to playing with their mothers. Such differences in interaction styles, however, are not large (Lamb, 2010; Lewis & Lamb, 2003).

Research suggests that, on average, children from families in which two parents are present and active have many advantages over those raised in mother-only families (Lamb, 2010; Newland & Coyle, 2010; NFI, 2009; Cuffe et al., 2005). They have, for example, fewer accidents as toddlers, are less likely to be depressed as children and adults and display lower rates of juvenile delinquency, teenage pregnancy, drug use or incarceration.

Although developmental research still focuses more heavily on mothers than on fathers, the field has come a long way over the past 30 years. Moreover, the number of articles and books devoted to fathers seems to be on the increase (Lamb, 2010; Lamb & Day, 2004; Tamis-LeMonda & Cabrera, 2002).

though they show parental influence, but many psychologists have argued against this (Clarke-Stewart & Dunn, 2006; O'Connor, 2002).

Cowan and Cowan (2002), in their research based in California, looked at family-based interventions that had been designed to improve parent–child and/or marital relationships as a way of helping development and reducing psychological problems in children and adolescents. Their summary of correlational studies showed that the difficult and ineffective parent–child and poor marital relationships were risk factors for children's cognitive, social and emotional problems in childhood and adolescence, and they reviewed prevention studies and therapy evaluation studies that were helpful in mediating these risk factors. O'Connor (2002) considers research findings on the quality of parent–child relations and their usefulness as predictors of behavioural and emotional adjustment in children. He suggests that researchers need to look at the impact of larger social systems on children's well-being, as described by Bronfenbrenner (1989), and be aware of the bi-directional nature of parent–child interactions. O'Connor considers that there are strong links between the quality of the relationship between parents and children and their well-being, but that it is important not to draw causal connections and say with absolute certainty that poor parent–child relations cause major problems in children's development. We need to consider the methodological difficulties in measuring parental attitudes and how these measures can be applied in a clinical setting.

Jaffee *et al.* (2003) critically evaluated the impact of father absence on children's development. They show that the assumption that being raised by two married biological parents is the best way is a simplistic view. Their twin study found that the less time fathers live with their children, the more conduct problems these children will have, but only if these fathers do not show high levels of antisocial behaviour. If fathers are highly antisocial, then the more time they live with their children, the more conduct problems these children will have. Thus, Jaffee *et al.*'s research indicates that fathers are important in children's social development, but it very much depends on the type of father a child has; that is, someone who can provide reliable emotional and economic support.

In recent years, there has been considerable research from the United States on positive outcomes for children whose fathers become involved in their care. There is also current UK research on fathers' parental influence. Welsh *et al.* (2004), in a UK study, used longitudinal data from the National Child Development Study (NCDS) on 17,000 children who were born in England, Wales and Scotland in one week in 1958. They explored fathers' involvement with their children when the children were aged seven, 11 and 16 years of age. How would an 'involved' father be defined? He would be defined as someone who reads to his child, takes his child on outings, is interested in his child's education and takes a role equal to the mother's in managing his child. He may or may not live with the child's mother, and he may or may not be the biological father to the child. The NCDS findings showed that fathers were important to a child's social development. Usually, the higher the level of a father's education, the greater was the likelihood of his involvement with his children. The study showed that once a father was involved with his child he remained involved throughout childhood and adolescence. Father involvement was associated with good parent–child relationships in adolescence and with later satisfactory partnerships in adult life. Good father–child relations were associated with an absence of emotional and behavioural difficulties in adolescence and greater academic motivation. Children, particularly boys, with involved fathers were less likely to be in trouble with the police. The involvement of fathers also protected children in separated families against later mental health problems. Father involvement was also found to be strongly related to children's later educational attainment at age 20, for both girls and boys.

Friendship and Peer Relations

It is not just parents who are an important part of the social development of the child. As children develop and go to school, the time they spend with their peer group increases and relationships with their peers become more important (Hartup, 1996). Much research has focused on friendship and sociometric status. Blatchford and Baines (2010), in particular, have studied children's relationships and their implications for development, learning and adjustment to school. They focus on the social dynamics of peer groups, playground behaviour and social relations. They point out the positive aspects of break time for the child's social development, where so much of social life goes on. Children spend much of break time talking to each other or playing with others, often in rule-based games such as football and skipping. Why are these play activities so important in the development of social relations? Pellegrini and Blatchford (2002), in their work in primary schools, suggest that play activities serve as a social scaffold for children: they help to maintain friendship groups, are useful for social exploration, 'allow' girls to play with boys and can bring children together and help with the integration of different ethnic groups.

However, there can be negative aspects to social relations. Research has been done on peer influence and bullying, where links have been made between bullying, victimization, involvement in peer groups and social competence (Garandeau & Cillessen, 2006).

Smith *et al.* (2008) investigated cyber bullying in secondary-school pupils. Cyber bullying is a newer form of bullying that involves mobile phones and the Internet, where bullying is done by text messaging and emails. Smith *et al.*'s research, using surveys and focus groups, reported that cyber bullying was less frequent than traditional bullying. It tended to happen more outside of school than in a school setting. Phone call and text message bullying were the most frequent form of cyber bullying along with instant messaging. Children felt that the impact of this cyber bullying was comparable to traditional bullying. Mobile phone/video clip bullying was a less frequent form of cyber bullying, but was perceived to have more negative impact. Many cyber victims were traditional 'bully-victims'. Pupils recommended blocking/avoiding messages, and telling someone, as the best coping strategies; but many cyber victims had told nobody about it.

Before You Go On

What Do You Know?

4. What is the Strange Situation?

5. What are the major parenting styles, and what are the major child outcomes associated with each style?

6. Why are break times really that important for children's social development?

What Do You Think?

How do you think the various attachment styles correlate with Baumrind's parenting styles? Do you think there is one optimal form of parenting?

Childhood

LEARNING OBJECTIVE 3

Summarize the major social and emotional developments that take place during childhood.

Although physical growth slows somewhat during childhood, our social and emotional lives also become more complex and the social circle expands as much more time is spent with peers and teachers. In this section, we will focus on how the world gets a lot bigger during childhood and how children manage to keep up.

Moral Development

One of the most important tasks for a child is to try to work out how to behave, and start to learn what constitutes good and bad. In other words, *moral* development: how children acquire an understanding of right and wrong and how to function in a complex society.

Theories of Moral Development

Piaget believed that, as with general logical reasoning, children learn how to reason morally by translating their behaviours and experiences into general moral principles that they then apply across different situations. He proposed that children's morality is based initially on obeying adults. As they get older, the basis of their moral reasoning shifts towards cooperation with peers (Piaget, 1965). Piaget described several stages of children's reasoning about right and wrong. Up to the age of three or four, Piaget thought of children as *premoral*. He considered that children of this age do not yet understand rules, so they do not make judgements about rule violations. The first stage of actual moral reasoning, according to Piaget, is *heteronomous morality* or *moral realism*, characteristic of pre-school children (aged 3–6 years). Children at this stage are moral absolutists who think that rules are sacred and unchanging. Piaget presented children with

several pairs of stories that posed a problem of moral judgement. Then the child would have to make a judgement as to which child in the two stories was the naughtiest. He found that before nine or 10 years of age children often judged on the basis of the amount of damage done. They tended to be more focused on outcome than intention.

Lawrence Kohlberg was a student of Jean Piaget, and was interested in his ideas on moral development. He expanded upon Piaget's ideas and developed a method to evaluate the moral reasoning processes of children. He presented them with stories about moral dilemmas and asked them to say what the main characters in the stories should do and why. The story of Heinz, presented in Figure 4.3, is a good example. Heinz's wife is dying of cancer, but Heinz cannot afford the medicine that might save her. Should he steal the medicine or let his wife die?

On the basis of his studies, Kohlberg developed a stage theory of moral development (Kohlberg, 2008, 1994, 1963). He labelled the major stages *preconventional*, *conventional* and *postconventional*, as shown in Table 4.2. Younger children, up to about the age of nine, show preconventional thinking. They believe we should obey rules to keep out of trouble or to get rewards. In older children and adolescents, conventional morality becomes dominant. These young people adopt society's rules as their own and follow the rules in order to be seen as good people. Rules are rules, in this view, and must be obeyed. Not everyone reaches the final stage, the postconventional level. At this level, society's rules are no longer the last word. Instead, the focus is on abstract ethical principles of right and wrong.

The focus of Kohlberg's theory is *moral reasoning* – how children come to their decisions about what is right and wrong – rather than on the particular decisions that they make. Like Piaget, Kohlberg believed that young children make moral choices that seem likely to ensure the least amount of trouble with authority figures. However, Kohlberg also looked beyond childhood to adolescence and described how older children and adults become more independent in their moral reasoning.

Heinz and the Drug

In Europe, a woman was near death from a special kind of cancer. There was one drug that the doctors thought might save her. It was a form of radium that a druggist in the same town had recently discovered. The drug was expensive to make, but the druggist was charging ten times what the drug cost him to make. He paid $400 for the radium and charged $4,000 for a small dose of the drug. The sick woman's husband, Heinz, went to everyone he knew to borrow the money and tried every legal means, but he could only get together about $2,000, which is half of what it cost. He told the druggist that his wife was dying, and asked him to sell it cheaper or let him pay later. But the druggist said, "No, I discovered the drug and I'm going to make money from it." So, having tried every legal means, Heinz gets desperate and considers breaking into the man's store to steal the drug.

Question: Should Heinz steal the drug? Why should he steal it or why should he not?

FIGURE 4.3 Kohlberg's moral dilemma story.

Source: Paragraph excerpted from Scott Lilienfield, Steven Lynn, Laura Namy and Nancy Wolf, *Psychology from Inquiry to Understanding* (Boston: Pearson: Allyn & Bacon).

TABLE 4.2 Kohlberg's Stage Theory of Moral Development

Stage	Reason to steal drug	Reason not to steal drug
Preconventional: Morality centres on what you can get away with	He can get away with it	He will be caught and go to jail
Conventional: Morality centres on avoiding others' disapproval and obeying society's rules	If he does not steal the drug, people will think he is a terrible person	If he steals, people will think he is a criminal It is against the law
Postconventional: Morality is determined by abstract ethical principles	Sometimes the law is unjust, and it is right to break it	He will not have lived up to his own standards of honesty and will lose his self-respect

Although Kohlberg believed that moral reasoning is often correlated with other areas of development, such as cognition or intelligence, he held that it develops along its own track. As the ability of children to take another person's point of view grows, their moral reasoning also becomes more complex. To reach the highest stages of moral reasoning, Kohlberg believed, individuals must be exposed to complex social situations, such as working at jobs that involve dealing with many different people or going to college.

Like Piaget's theory of general cognitive development, Kohlberg's theory suggests that each stage of moral development represents a new framework for making moral decisions. Each stage forms a foundation for the next stage, and children must travel through the stages of moral development in sequence. A child may be delayed or perhaps even fail to reach some of the higher stages, but he or she must go through each earlier stage to reach the next one.

Finally, Kohlberg considered that the process of moral development is universal and happens the same way in every culture. Kohlberg's original research included boys only, but he later studied girls as well. He also conducted moral dilemma interviews in villages in Mexico, Taiwan and Turkey. On the basis of this work, Kohlberg insisted on the cross-cultural invariance of his stage sequence, on the grounds that his theory was not concerned with specific beliefs but with underlying cognitive capabilities.

Eisenberg's Theory of Prosocial Moral Judgement

Eisenberg and Mussen (1989) point out that when children respond to Kohlberg's story about Heinz's moral dilemma they are choosing between two acts that are wrong. Heinz would either have to steal the drug, in the hope of keeping his wife alive, or decide to allow her to die. Eisenberg and Mussen suggest that there are other moral dilemmas where the choice is between personal advantage and fairness to others.

Children were presented with stories where they had to choose between helping someone (prosocial behaviour) or doing something that would please themselves.

Eisenberg and Mussen (1989) found that children were using five stages of prosocial moral reasoning, similar to Kohlberg's stages. These stages were also found cross-culturally, for example in Brazilian children (Carlo *et al.*, 1996) and in Japanese children (Munekata & Ninomiya, 1985). The only difference was that children's reasoning that reflected thinking about others happened earlier using Eisenberg's prosocial stories than when using Kohlberg's traditional moral dilemmas.

Gilligan's Theory of Moral Development

One of Kohlberg's collaborators, Carol Gilligan (1993), also questioned some of his findings and ideas. She notes, as we have mentioned, that his studies initially focused on boys alone. She takes issue with the fact that his later studies seemed to suggest that girls are morally less developed than boys. Kohlberg believed that girls do not have as many complex social opportunities as boys and, as a result, are excessively concerned with the standards of others and often fail to achieve the highest stages of moral reasoning; his suggestion would need reappraisal today.

Gilligan interprets the boy/girl findings differently. She argues that the moral reasoning used by girls is indeed different from that of boys, but not inferior. She noticed that boys tend to base their decisions about moral dilemmas on abstract moral values, such as justice and fairness. Many girls look at the situations differently. Instead of the abstract values involved, they focus more on the value relationships between the principal players. A boy's answer to the Heinz dilemma might centre on the importance of property value for the druggist, for example. A girl's answer might stress that Heinz would not be able to help his wife if he were jailed for stealing the drug. Gilligan argues that the reasoning of boys and girls is equally sophisticated but that their goals and the aspects of the dilemma that they notice differ. Gilligan went on to conduct her own interviews with men and women and found further support for her theory that women are inclined to make moral judgements based more on caring and managing relationships than on Kohlberg's notions of justice and fairness.

Other studies have not always supported Gilligan's theory that women and men differ in their moral orientation. Nor have they always supported Kohlberg's notions of moral superiority among males (Turiel, 2010; Walker, 2006). Some studies, for example, suggest that differences in the education levels of their research participants may have accounted for the apparent moral differences between males and females observed by these two investigators. When education level is controlled for, females and males often earn similar moral stage scores (Dawson, 2002).

Gilligan's ideas have had a broad influence on psychology, anthropology and other social sciences. In her classic book, *In a Different Voice*, Gilligan (1993) notes that over the years many psychological theorists have embraced male development patterns as the norm and viewed differences from that norm as inferior. Similarly, she argues that women have been underrepresented in many of psychology's most influential studies and theories. Of course, the gender imbalance would not be an issue in psychological research today. If anything, there is an over-representation of females in much of the research, as the majority of psychology undergraduates are female. In addition, most of today's researchers think of differences among participants as individual variations rather than positive or negative characteristics (Jensen, 2011).

Current Directions in Moral Development

Much research in moral development over the past 50 years has been influenced by Kohlberg's and Gilligan's theories (Turiel, 2010). Many researchers have focused on Kohlberg's notion that the stages of moral development are the same for everyone. Indeed, one review of 45 studies conducted across a wide range of cultures found that Kohlberg's claims of universality hold up pretty well for the early stages of moral development (Snarey, 1985). Such research has also suggested that people from different cultures rarely skip stages or revert to previous ones.

Cross-cultural researchers have also noted cultural differences that support Gilligan's ideas. Some researchers have found, for example, that respondents from *collectivist* cultures tend to score lower on the Kohlberg scales than do those from *individualistic* cultures (Gibbs *et al.*, 2007). Close examinations indicate, however, that these score differences reflect differences in the kinds of moral problems faced by people in each of these cultures, not moral superiority or inferiority (Jensen, 2011). As described in Chapter 1, collectivistic cultures put greater emphasis on society and relationships than individualistic cultures, which tend to emphasize individual justice and fairness.

Finally, a number of moral development researchers have wondered how much the expressed moral attitudes of people reflect their actual decision-making (Krebs & Denton, 2006). As we will see in our discussion of attitudes in Chapter 16, people do not always actually do what they say they will do (an experience you have probably had once or twice in your own life). Because the vast majority of research into moral reasoning has relied on Kohlberg's moral dilemma interviews, many researchers argue that we may be able to say a fair amount about people's moral *philosophies* but little about their *behaviour*.

Children's Developing Understanding of Deception

Understanding about right and wrong goes hand in hand with understanding about deception and lie-telling. The study of deception dates back as early as Charles Darwin (1877), who observed his two-year-old son telling lies. In a short essay, 'A Biographical Sketch of an Infant', he concludes that when children disobey and leave behind evidence, even at a very young age, they try to cover up their disobedience by lying. He also observed that young children are not very good at telling lies. This is because they do not yet know how to use language to strategically cover up; they fail to make their statements consistent with evidence of their wrongdoing.

Following Darwin's initial examination of young children's lie-telling and later work with older children the study of children's deceptive behaviours remained neglected for nearly 50 years, until it received renewed attention from developmental psychologists, from the 1980s onwards. They became more interested for several reasons:

- Theoretically, research on the issue has implications for current debates about children's theory of mind.

- Research also has theoretical implications for the universality of moral development.

- Research on the issue also has practical implications for developing moral education programmes in schools.

- There are practical implications for assessing children's testimony in legal settings.

In a classic study, Sodian (1991) examined the ability of three- to five-year-old children to deceive a competitor in a hiding game. In the first experiment the child had to deceive a nasty robber puppet in order to get a reward (a star). There was also a nice king puppet, who, if he found the reward, would give it to the child. The child was asked to point to the location of the star for both puppets. Sodian found that children below the age of about three years consistently failed to deceive a competitor. Sodian considered that her experimental work showed that three-year-olds' difficulty with false belief representation made it difficult for them to be successful deceivers.

However, psychologists have found that very young children of three and four can engage in deception, and do so quite regularly! Newton et al. (2000) were able to monitor children's lie-telling behaviour by getting mums to keep a diary and observe deceptive behaviour. There were several categories of deception encountered (see Table 4.3).

Children certainly give into temptation. Talwar and Lee (2002) left children alone in a room with a music-playing toy placed behind them, and they were asked not to peek. Most children could not resist having a quick look while the experimenter was out of the room. Naive adult evaluators who watched the video clips of the children's responses had to rate whether they were lie-telling or not. They found this very difficult to do based on children's body language, but found it much easier based on what children said, as children often came up with things that contradicted their lie.

Sometimes children lie to be nice, as not all lies are anti-social. These nice lies are told with the intention to help, rather than harm, and are prosocial in nature. For example, children may pretend to like a gift, when they do not really like it. Talwar et al. (2007) used a disappointing gift experiment to examine children's prosocial lie-telling. Children played a game where they were promised a gift from a basket that contained a range of different toys and gifts. After the task, children were given a gift of soap; something that they were decidedly unimpressed with! When asked if they liked it, the majority of the children were very polite and said that they did. School-aged children were more likely to lie than preschool children.

There are practical implications for research on children's development of deception, because in a legal setting we need to know whether young children understand the difference between the truth and a lie, and whether they are more likely to tell lies than adults, or whether there is no difference. All of these issues need to be considered when evaluating the testimony of a child in court. The sorts of question that a child is asked can have an effect on whether they make false statements. A child might be asked a recognition question or a recall question. Children found very simple recall questions where they had to provide the same answer every time the easiest to make false statements about. It was only at the age of three and a half years that young children were capable of maintaining false claims across question types (Ahern et al., 2011).

Three-year-old children are very trusting. They will continue to believe somebody who has repeatedly misled them. In a clever trust experiment by Mascaro and Sperber (2009),

TABLE 4.3 Categories of children's deceptive behaviour (from a longitudinal study by Newton et al., 2000)

Type	Example	Notes
Bravado	*'That didn't hurt.'*	When a child was hurt after being warned of the danger
False 'nothing' assertions	*'I'm not doing anything.'*	
Feigned ignorance	*'I don't know who messed it up.'*	
False assertions of permission	*'Dad said yes.'*	

a naughty puppet told children that a marble was hidden in one box, when it was actually in the other. Four-year-olds quickly learnt to look in the box that was not mentioned by the puppet. However, three-year-olds continued to trust what the puppet had said, even after six trials where they had been misled, and even when reminded after each trial that the puppet had told them a lie. Jaswal *et al.* (2010), in a similar 'naughty puppet' experiment, wanted to find out whether children trusted people or whether what people said was more important. In a game that involved hiding stickers under upside down cups, children were misled by a tricky experimenter, who told them to look in the wrong place. Then a big black arrow was used to indicate in which of the two cups the sticker was hidden. All the children were initially misled by what they were told by the tricky experimenter, and by the black arrow. However, children found it very difficult to disregard what they were told, but found it easier to ignore the big black arrow pointing in the wrong location. Jaswal *et al.* suggest that three-year-olds have a very specific bias to trust deceptive testimony; that is, it is not that young children trust people: they specifically trust what other people say.

Before You Go On

What Do You Know?

7. In what ways is Kohlberg's theory of moral development different from Piaget's theory of moral development?

8. How do contemporary theories of moral reasoning differ from Piaget's, Kohlberg's and Gilligan's theories?

9. What is a prosocial lie?

10. Looking at the research on deception, at what age are children usually able to lie?

What Do You Think?

Do you think that men and women reason differently about morality? If the outcome is the same in our moral choices, does the reasoning we use to achieve that outcome matter?

Adolescence

LEARNING OBJECTIVE 4

Summarize the major social and emotional changes that take place during adolescence.

We are all familiar with the fact that adolescents spend a lot of time trying to figure out who they are and how they fit into the world. Because this is such a central task of adolescence, we will focus on it here. We will pay particular attention to the work of German psychologist Erik Erikson, an important contributor to our understanding of the social and emotional life of adolescents.

Erikson did not restrict himself to theorizing about adolescents. Indeed, he is one of the few major developmental theorists to look at development across the *entire* lifespan (Erikson, 1985, 1984, 1959). He divided the span from birth to old age into eight stages. Each of Erikson's stages is associated with a 'main task' – a challenge the person must meet and reconcile. An individual's achievement at each stage has a direct impact on how he or she meets the challenges of the next stage. Erikson believed that relationships and culture play strong roles in personality formation, and so he referred to his work as a stage theory of *psychosocial* development (Clark, 2010).

As Table 4.4 shows, Erikson believed that each stage of development is associated with a potentially positive outcome versus a potentially negative outcome. For example, the conflicts and challenges associated with infancy determine whether a baby will develop a basic trust in the world (positive outcome) or mistrust (negative outcome). Babies whose parents respond attentively when they cry with hunger learn that the world is a good place and that other people can be trusted.

The key developmental task faced by adolescents is to resolve the conflict between *identity* and *role confusion*. During adolescence, teenagers start making decisions that affect their future roles, such as whether they want to go to university or what they want to do with their lives, as well as decisions about abstract aspects of their identities, such as political or religious beliefs.

According to Erikson, if we do not reach a successful resolution of the conflict confronted at a particular stage, we may find it harder to meet the challenges of subsequent stages. Teenagers who did not effectively resolve the conflicts of their earlier psychosocial stages may enter adolescence with heightened feelings of mistrust and shame. These lingering feelings may render the teens particularly confused

TABLE 4.4 Erikson's Stages of Psychosocial Development

Stage	Age (years)	Type	Description
One	birth–1	Trust versus mistrust	Infants develop a basic trust in others If their needs are not met by their caregivers, mistrust develops
Two	1–3	Autonomy versus shame and doubt	Children exercise their new motor and mental skills If caregivers are encouraging, children develop a sense of autonomy versus shame and doubt
Three	3–6	Initiative versus guilt	Children enjoy initiating activities and mastering new tasks Supportive caregivers promote feelings of power and self-confidence versus guilt
Four	6–12	Industry versus inferiority	Children learn productive skills and develop the capacity to work with others If not, they feel inferior
Five	12–20	Identity versus role confusion	Adolescents seek to develop a satisfying identity and a sense of their role in society Failure may lead to a lack of stable identity and confusion about their adult roles
Six	20–30	Intimacy versus isolation	Young adults work to establish intimate relationships with others If they cannot, they face isolation
Seven	30–65	Generativity versus stagnation	Middle-aged adults seek ways to influence the welfare of the next generation If they fail, they may become self-absorbed
Eight	65+	Integrity versus despair	Older people reflect on the lives they have lived If they do not feel a sense of accomplishment and satisfaction with their lives, they live in fear of death

about which roles and beliefs truly reflect their own values and which ones reflect excessive peer and family influences. Peer relationships are extremely important to all teenagers, and Erikson believed that vulnerable teens are particularly likely to be confused about where their own beliefs start and the wishes of others end.

A number of other theorists and researchers have also highlighted the critical role that identity formation plays while teens are seeking to negotiate their way through adolescence successfully (Phinney & Baldelomar, 2011). James Marcia, for example, expanded Erikson's theory, suggesting that a combination of *explorations*, which involve active questioning aimed at reaching decisions about goals and values, and *commitment*, which involves making choices and working to implement them, help to define a teen's identity (Kroger *et al.*, 2010; Marcia, 2010, 2007, 1994). To better understand the identity formation process, Marcia developed the *Identity Status Interview*, a method of semi-structured interviews with young people. He asked whether the participants in his study had established a commitment to an occupation and ideology and, secondly, had experienced, or were presently experiencing, a decision-making period (adolescent identity crisis). Interview material was evaluated using a scoring manual developed by Marcia and colleagues yielding four identity statuses: foreclosure, identity diffusion, moratorium and identity achievement.

- *Foreclosure.* This is when a commitment is made without exploring alternatives. Often these commitments are based on parental ideas and beliefs that are accepted without question. Foreclosure is an endorsement of authoritarian values, with commitment but no exploration.

- *Identity Diffusion.* This is when some adolescents become overwhelmed by the task of identity development and neither explore nor make commitments and may become socially isolated and withdrawn. They may or may not have experienced a crisis, with some reporting having little interest in identity status and others reporting repeated indecision.

- *Moratorium.* This is the status of individuals who are in the middle of a crisis but whose commitments are either absent or only vaguely defined. This status is characterized by the active exploration of alternatives. Marcia noted that adolescents report experiencing more anxiety than in any other status. The world for them is not, currently, a highly predictable place; they are vitally engaged in a struggle to make it so.

- *Identity achievement.* This is the status of individuals who have typically experienced a crisis, undergone identity explorations and made commitments. Marcia suggested that adolescents who have achieved an identity as having developed an internal, as opposed to external, locus of self-definition.

David Elkind provides interesting theories on adolescence in his 1967 work 'Egocentrism in adolescence', in which he coins the term *personal fable*. His work stemmed from Piaget's theory of cognitive development, and according to Elkind, in conjunction with Piaget's theory, adolescent egocentrism is to be understood in the context of ontogeny (i.e. development across the lifespan). These ontogenetic changes in egocentrism are thought to drive the development of logical and formal operational thinking. Elkind proposes that the onset of adolescent egocentrism is brought on by the emergence of the formal operational stage, which allows the adolescent to mentally construct hypotheses that are contrary to reality.

Elkind argues that the adolescent period fosters adolescent egocentrism. This is a stage of self-absorption where the world is seen only from one's own perspective. Thus, adolescents are highly critical of authority figures, unwilling to accept criticism and quick to find fault with others. Elkind suggests that adolescent egocentrism helps to explain why teens often think they are the focus of everyone's attention. He proposes that adolescent egocentrism leads to two distortions: an *imaginary audience*, where adolescents think they are the focus of everyone else's attention and construct elaborate scenarios about others' thoughts/intentions. Their other distortion is that of *personal fables*, the belief that they are unique and exceptional and their thoughts are shared by no one else, which may lead to their thinking that nobody understands them and risk-taking behaviour.

Before You Go On

What Do You Know?

11. Describe what Erikson believed was the major dilemma and risk for adolescence.

12. What do you think would happen to an adolescent who remained in an identity moratorium state, as described by Marcia?

What Do You Think?

Do you think that every adolescent goes through the adolescent egocentrism described by David Elkind? Did you?

Adulthood and Old Age

HOW WE DEVELOP

LEARNING OBJECTIVE 5
Describe key social and emotional changes that take place throughout adulthood.

Traditionally, developmental psychology viewed adulthood as an outcome rather than a period worthy of study. Indeed, many of today's theorists further divide adulthood into a series of stages: *early adulthood*, *middle adulthood* and *old age*. Let us look at some of the developmental changes that happen over the course of adulthood.

Social and Emotional Development in Adulthood

Although the social and emotional changes that occur in adulthood are more gradual than those that characterize childhood, adults do in fact experience multiple transitions in these spheres of functioning (Aldwin *et al.*, 2010; Freund & Lamb, 2010; Holcomb, 2010). As shown in Table 4.4, Erikson proposed that individuals confront important psychosocial conflicts as they travel from early adulthood to old age. A number of other theorists have made similar claims.

Social and Emotional Features of Early and Middle Adulthood

According to Erikson (1985), during early adulthood (20 to 30 years of age), people form intimate relationships and sexual unions that call for self-sacrifice and compromise. In fact, he believed that the primary goal of this period is to attain love. The ethical convictions developed in adolescence and the sense of moral obligation formed in childhood contribute to ethical strength in young adulthood. These early acquisitions are important, he believed, because a sense of morality is required for the truly loving relationships of adulthood. Erikson further believed that people who are unable to successfully meet the challenges of young adulthood tend to become isolated and may actually avoid the contacts that create and sustain intimacy. Thus, he concluded that young adulthood is dominated by a conflict between *intimacy* and *isolation*.

Erikson proposed that during middle adulthood (30 to 65 years of age) people are inclined to turn their attention to younger people. Their focus is to help create, or at least contribute to, the next generation. Erikson used the term *generativity* to describe this focus. Caring for younger people, whether through parenthood or by mentoring junior colleagues at work, is a major concern. This process enriches individuals who engage in it. Erikson believed that people who fail to develop such activities may experience stagnation and boredom. Middle adulthood, then, is dominated by a conflict between *generativity* and *stagnation*.

Several theorists have extended Erikson's work on early and middle adulthood. One particularly broad investigation of these life stages was conducted by psychologist Daniel Levinson (Levinson, 1986a, 1986b). Levinson's research, written up in his book *The Seasons of a Man's Life*, examined men's development throughout the adult life cycle by exploring the lives of 40 men from early adulthood through middle adulthood, using a methodology of extensive biographical interviewing. Specific biographies of four men – a manual labourer, an executive, a biologist and a novelist – were described in more detail with a little reconstruction of their lives. Through these means, Levinson created a theory of adult development presented in a sequence of distinct developmental periods, which are progressive in nature. According to Levinson's findings, the stage of *early adulthood* (which he defined as 22 to 40 years of age) is characterized simultaneously by high energy and abundance and by contradiction and stress. The aspirations of individuals in this age range tend to be youthful. They establish a niche in society, they may raise a family and ultimately they reach a relatively senior position in the adult world.

For many, this period brings great satisfaction and creativity. But early adulthood can also be a period of enormous stress. The burden of becoming a parent, undertaking an occupation, incurring financial obligations and making other critical decisions about marriage, family, work and lifestyle often fills people with anxiety and tension.

Levinson described *middle adulthood* (40 to 65 years of age) as a stage in which biological functioning, although less than optimal, is still sufficient for an 'energetic, personally satisfying and socially valuable life'. During this stage, people usually become 'senior members' of their particular world. They take responsibility for their own work, that of others and the development of younger adults. This, too, can become a period of self-satisfaction and peace of mind. At the same time, growing biological problems, numerous responsibilities and anticipation of upcoming old age may also produce considerable stress and tension.

Although the stages of early and middle adulthood may themselves be sources of stress, Levinson believed that the periods of *transition* that people must pass through as they move from one stage to another can be even more pressure-filled. During such transitional periods, people confront particularly difficult career, marital and family issues and reflect on and adjust their dreams.

The *early adult transition*, often called 'emerging adulthood', bridges adolescence and early adulthood. During this period, which lasts from approximately 17 to 22 years of age, people may go through a very unsettled time. They take steps towards individuation and modify their relationships with family, friends and social institutions, but they may feel insecure in these efforts and, correspondingly, may experience anxiety and confusion. However, Daniel Levinson collected the data for his study many decades ago, and, owing to the period, the participants in his study had three things in common: they came from stable families, they had realistic goals for their life and they became adults in an expanding economy. Because of this, it is not so easy to generalize from Levinson's studies to today's generation.

Arnett (2007) was the first to propose that 'emerging adulthood' was a very useful way of conceptualizing this period from the late teens to mid-twenties, in industrialized societies. He points out that young people's lives have changed: there are more people staying on in education or further training after secondary school, and people are entering into steady relationships, marriage and parenthood later than they used to. Because of this, Arnett suggests that the transition from adolescence to adulthood is now long enough to be a separate stage of the life course. He considers that there are five features that make emerging adulthood distinct:

- It is the age of identity exploration.
- It is the age of instability.
- It is the self-focused age.
- It is the age of feeling in-between.
- It is the age of possibilities.

On the whole, Arnett sees emerging adulthood as being a positive experience for most people. The fact that it takes longer to become an adult now than it did in the past does not mean that growing up is in some way harder than it used to be. However, it would be simplistic to think that emerging adults are a homogeneous group, characterized by high self-esteem and well-being. Osgood *et al.* (2005) found that emerging adults struggle if they are part of especially vulnerable populations, for example in foster care, coming out of the criminal justice system or experiencing disability. More research needs to be done on whether emerging adulthood is a useful concept in different countries and different cultures, as Arnett's research is based mainly on North American emerging adults.

PSYCHOLOGY AROUND US   The Usefulness of the Concept of Emerging Adulthood: The Emperor's New Clothes?

Arnett's rejoinder to Hendry and Kloep

In their critique of Arnett's theory of emerging adulthood, Hendry and Kloep borrowed a metaphor from the Hans Christian Andersen story about the emperor's new clothes. Not surprisingly, Arnett was not keen on this metaphor, as he was cast in the role of the naked, deluded emperor. A major point that Hendry and Kloep made was that Arnett's portrayal of generally increasing well-being during emerging adulthood was too positive and applied mainly to emerging adults who are from social class backgrounds that are middle class or higher: wealthy middle-class youths with supportive parents do have better options. Hendry and Kloep (2007) claimed that their research on adolescents and emerging adults (ages 16–20) in Wales showed that emerging adulthood was experienced quite negatively by many of them, and that they were pessimistic and frustrated. Arnett considered that this was a difficult claim to evaluate because they had restricted their sample to those who were either working or unemployed and not in school, and it is unclear how well this sample represents the Welsh population of 16- to 20-year-olds (Arnett *et al.*, 2011). He suggested that it remained an open question how much social class is related to experiencing emerging adulthood positively or negatively, and how much this may vary among societies. Even working-class emerging adults may have high hopes for their adult lives, and even upper-middle-class emerging adults have anxieties about whether their hopes will be realized. In subsequent research, Hendry and Kloep (2010) still wondered whether emerging adulthood was a universal phenomenon. Their empirical work examined the concept of emerging adulthood in a small sample of Welsh young people (aged 17–20 years) who were not in higher education; that is, either working or unemployed. In their exploratory study, young people were questioned about their lifestyles and their perceptions of 'being adult' in semi-structured interviews lasting about 40 minutes. Results indicated that Arnett's concept of the emerging adulthood stage held good for only one subgroup of those participants that they interviewed. They also noted that many other participants claimed to perceive themselves as adult and to be perceived by others as adult. They continue to question the value of Arnett's stage theory to young people in a European society, based on their findings.

Hendry and Kloep (2007) question the need for Arnett's concept of emerging adulthood. First, they point out that young people may reach adult status earlier in some domains than others. They also note that development can be nonlinear and reversible. Second, they suggest an alternative scenario to emerging adulthood, that of perpetual youth, where adults undergo cosmetic surgery, maintain a youthful physical and mental outlook and have children later. They also point to many countries where young people do not experience adolescence, let alone emerging adulthood. They also stress the heterogeneity of this age group, with some young people in a state of 'prevented adulthood' through lack of opportunities, and an 'early maturing' subgroup, who have had to grow up quickly because they have had to care for parents who became ill. They recommend a move away from age-bound stage theories to more comprehensive lifespan approaches, as proposed by Baltes (1997).

PSYCHOLOGY AROUND US   Moving Ahead?

Generally, when we think of 20-somethings, we think of young people making their initial journey into independence. But increasingly, and around the world, young adults are returning home after college or never leaving in the first place. In some countries, the trend is so strong that it has inspired specific names: in Germany, for example, young adults who live with their parents are called *Nesthocker*, or birds that stay too long in the nest. In Italy, they are *bamboccioni*, or overgrown babies. In the United Kingdom, they are kippers, or 'kids in parents' pockets, eroding retirement savings'.

This group has received the most negative attention in Japan, where sociologist Masahiro Yamada coined the term *parasite singles* to describe them. Young people have been accused of being unwilling to take on the responsibilities of adulthood. In their defence, many of these young adults point out that entry-level jobs are hard to come by, and those that are available do not pay enough. The average rent in Japan constitutes two-thirds of the average young adult's salary.

Some researchers have begun to study this widespread phenomenon and have argued that a new stage of development may be emerging, much as adolescence developed initially in response to social changes that outlawed child labour and made education more widely available.

Even more stressful for some people, according to Levinson (1986a), is *middle life transition*, a period lasting from ages 40 to 45 that bridges early and middle adulthood. During this period, individuals experience significant changes in the character of their lives. On the positive side, they may become more compassionate, reflective and judicious, less conflicted and more accepting and loving of themselves and others during these years. On the negative side, however, some individuals feel overwhelmed as they increasingly recognize that they are no longer young and vibrant, that time is passing, that life's heaviest responsibilities are falling on them, that they must prepare for the future and that some of their dreams may not be met. These persons may question their accomplishments in life and conclude that they have achieved and will continue to achieve too little. In certain cases, they may even try to deny the passage of time and to recapture their youth, a phenomenon popularly labelled the *midlife crisis*.

Social and Emotional Features of Old Age

'Old age' in our society typically refers to people who are at least 65 years old. Psychologists further distinguish between the young-old, people between 65 and 74; the old-old, those between 75 and 84; and the oldest-old, individuals aged 85 and above.

By this account, around 10.3 million people in the United Kingdom in 2012 are old, as they are 65 years or older. This is an 80% increase over six decades (since 1951). Older women outnumber men, and the greater number of women than men is most pronounced among the very old, as women tend to live longer than men. Population ageing is an international phenomenon: in 2005, just 10% of the world's population was aged 60 years or over, and it is expected to more than double over the next 40 years, reaching 22% in 2050 (Office for National Statistics, 2010).

Old age brings special pressures, unique upsets and profound biological changes. People become more prone to illness and injury as they age. They also are likely to experience the stress of loss, of spouses, friends and adult children as well as the loss of former activities and roles (Etaugh, 2008).

Despite such difficulties and despite their awareness that death eventually awaits them, older people do not necessarily become depressed or feel overwhelmed (Edelstein *et al.*, 2008). Indeed, Erikson (1985) believed that, for many, old age is characterized by accumulated knowledge and understanding and by mature judgement. The goal of old age, he proposed, is to attain wisdom, a detached yet active concern with life in the face of death; he considered that wisdom is achieved by integrating insights based on reflecting on past experience, and on one's present situation. Furthermore, he

believed that those who do not effectively meet the challenges of this stage may experience an extreme fear of death or despair, show bitterness and disgust and feel that life is too short. He therefore categorized old age as a conflict between *integrity* and *despair*.

Research indicates that many older persons do indeed use the changes that come with ageing as opportunities for learning and growth. One case in point: the number of older, often physically limited, people who use the Internet to connect with people of similar ages and interests doubled between 2000 and 2004, doubled again between 2004 and 2007, and doubled yet again by 2011. Individuals such as these Web searchers seem likely to remain involved and active right up to the end of their lives, health permitting.

It is also worth noting that, despite the common themes of old age, the population of older adults is actually quite heterogeneous. That is, older adults are more *unlike* than similar to one another. Older people have very different life experiences, adapt to change in uniquely personal ways and age at different rates. Thus, psychologists make a point of distinguishing between chronological age and functional age. *Chronological age*, or the number of years one has lived since birth, is regarded as little more than a 'short-hand variable' because it is not a true indicator of an older person's functional capacity. *Functional age*, however, reflects the individual's capacity to adapt his or her behaviour to the changing environment.

The Third Age/Fourth Age Distinction

This is an important stage theory that has structured both academic and popular discourse on old age. It relates to two very different parts of old age. The Third Age is after retirement and after any children have left home. The Fourth Age is when old age leads to dependency and prevents old people living independently. Laslett (1994) proposes getting rid of the category of 'old age', and coins the term 'Third Age', the stage of personal fulfilment. Third Agers are fit in body and sound in mind. They do not fit the traditional stereotypes about old people. The Fourth Age is more about growing dependence, increasing ill health and death. Laslett considers that this stage theory would have a positive impact on public and private attitudes, policy and practice on employment, pensions and widespread ageism. However, as is the case with most stage theories, putting ages to stages is not a straightforward matter. People who are 75 are considered Fourth Agers, but plenty of 75-year-olds are fit and well. Clearly, life course divisions do not fit in neatly with chronological age. Laslett also makes the point that the Fourth Age does not necessarily occur for every individual at the same time: it can occur at any point in the lifespan.

There are a number of theories that are relevant to the final stage in the lifespan. These include Wisdom Theory (Baltes, Sternberg), Socio-emotional Selectivity Theory (Carstensen) and Selection, Optimism and Compensation Theory (Baltes).

Baltes' Wisdom Theory How does wisdom develop over the lifespan and why are some people wiser than others? Do implicit beliefs about wisdom differ across cultural groups? In order to try to answer these intriguing questions, Baltes and his colleagues developed the *Berlin Wisdom Paradigm*, in which they brought together philosophical concepts of wisdom with theories and methodologies from lifespan psychology. Baltes and Smith (2008) defined wisdom as encompassing a domain of knowledge that they called 'the fundamental pragmatics of life'. This knowledge could be applied to life planning (e.g., what future goals to pursue and how); life management (e.g., how to deal with a critical problem like a family conflict); and life review (e.g., how to make sense of life history and past experiences). In order to try to measure wisdom, they gave adult participants life management problems, such as, 'A 14-year-old girl is pregnant. What should she do? What should one consider and do?' They stressed to participants that there were no right or wrong answers to these dilemmas. They found from the answers that very few people displayed high levels of wisdom. They also found that measures of intelligence overlapped with, but were not identical to, measures of wisdom. From the answers collected they formulated a *Wisdom Theory*, proposing that three factors help in making wise decisions: general person factors, expertise-specific factors, and facilitative experiential contexts. Baltes and Smith considered that one of the most important components of wisdom was lifespan contextualization (knowledge about the context of life experiences and their temporal relationships, and something that many older people can be rather good at). Although wisdom was one domain in which older people excelled, just getting older did not necessarily mean the automatic acquisition of wisdom. Baltes and Smith suggest that future research could look at the opposite side of the coin: foolish behaviours.

Sternberg's Balance Theory of Wisdom Sternberg (1998) presents a *Balance Theory of Wisdom*, in which wisdom is defined as the application of tacit knowledge, a 'knowing how' rather than a 'knowing that'. This tacit knowledge is mediated by wanting to achieve the common good, through a balance of factors that Sternberg considers important: intra-personal factors, inter-personal factors and extra-personal interests. This Balance Theory of Wisdom ties in well with Piaget's proposal that the development of intelligence involves an equilibrium or balance between assimilation and accommodation (Piaget, 1985). Wisdom is related to constructs like social intelligence, but Sternberg considers the differences. Social intelligence is to do with understanding and getting along with others, sometimes for selfish purposes, whereas Sternberg maintains that wisdom seeks out a good outcome for everyone, through balancing interests. He proposes that if schools put more effort into the development of wisdom, as they do in developing academic skills, then there would possibly be less conflict in society.

The Socio-emotional Selectivity Theory Another theory that is relevant to the final stage in the lifespan is *Socio-emotional Selectivity Theory* (Carstensen *et al.*, 1999). According to Socio-emotional Selectivity Theory, some people do not realize that time is limited, and they feel they have the time to gather knowledge and status and expand their horizons. Others are more aware of time constraints on their lives and so are more likely to focus on their relationships with others and attend more to emotionally meaningful aspects of their lives. Carstensen *et al.*'s theory hypothesizes that older people will resolve inter-personal conflicts quickly, whereas younger people may feel this is not so much of a priority. The theory suggests that when time is seen as unlimited people focus their attention on the future rather than on the present. Clearly, there are exceptions to this rule, as Carstensen (1995) found in her research. Young people facing terminal illness, like older participants, chose to spend time with familiar social partners, given a choice from someone in their immediate family, a recent acquaintance with whom they had a lot in common or the author of a book they had read. This work supported Socio-emotional Selectivity Theory, which proposes that people grow increasingly selective in their choice of social partners, depending on how much time they think they have left.

A person's temporal perspective will therefore determine their goals, and indirectly their behaviour. Someone who sees the future as open ended will have a negativity bias, focusing on long-term goals at the expense of immediate emotional experiences. They are less inclined to attend to cues that result in positive emotions. Carstensen and Mikels (2005) note that the portrayal of human ageing as a period of loss and decline is not altogether accurate. Their research produced a robust finding that emotional functioning is preserved, or even increases, in older people. They predicted that memory for emotional information would be better than for non-emotional information in older people, a positivity effect. Indeed, their results show exactly this. There was better performance in memory tasks for positive emotional information (operationalized by recognition and recall of cute pictures of babies and animals) in older participants.

There was also greater activation in the amygdala, a brain area involved in the processing of emotion. Thus, age-related preferences were shown to occur at the attentional level, as well as for memory. The Socio-emotional Theory has proved a very useful theory for understanding social behaviour across the lifespan.

Baltes' Selection, Optimism and Compensation Theory (SOC)

In terms of human development, how can we define successful development? Psychologists such as Baltes and Carstensen have defined it as 'the relative maximization of gains and the minimization of losses'. Baltes (1997) suggests that the *Selection, Optimism and Compensation Theory (SOC)* was an effective strategy for successful ageing. He uses the example of the famous concert pianist Arthur Rubenstein to illustrate his theory. Rubenstein was 80 when he was interviewed on television about how he still managed to play at such an extraordinarily professional level. He said he played fewer pieces (selection), he practised those pieces more frequently (optimization) and he deliberately played much slower before faster segments, to make them appear faster (compensation). Baltes considers Selection, Optimism and Compensation to be a metatheory which could be applied to a number of areas. He maintains that SOC Theory could be applied to language acquisition and intellectual development across the lifespan, where it would help regulate cognitive ageing. Certainly, it is a theory that helps to explain how people deal with the challenges that they face in old age with dignity.

The Changing Face of Adulthood and Old Age

The journey through the stages of adulthood features many rites of passage, including marriage, parenting, retirement and death – events that we will discuss throughout this textbook. It is worth noting that, in many societies, the timing and form of such milestones of adulthood are now more variable than they were in earlier days. In the past, for example, the length of time a couple would spend married before having their first child was relatively short. That time has extended greatly in recent decades. Moreover, the number of couples who choose to remain childless has more than doubled since 1982 (Rubino, 2011; Demo *et al.*, 2000). It also has become acceptable in some societies for people who are not married to raise children (Weinraub *et al.*, 2002).

Similarly, the average human lifespan continues to increase, lengthening the time that older adults remain part of the workforce, as well as part of the retired population, before dying (Elrod, 2010; Volz, 2000). Such cultural shifts have opened new areas of study for psychologists, who are seeking to understand how these shifts may affect adult development.

Before You Go On

What Do You Know?

13. Is 'emerging adulthood' part of a psychology of affluent middle classes in Western society?

14. Describe and define Erikson's major crises of adult development.

15. A number of theories are relevant to the final stage in the lifespan. Which one do you consider the most useful?

16. How easy is it to measure wisdom? How would you do it?

What Do You Think?

Do you think that life experiences may actually increase adults' emotional, as well as cognitive, or mental, abilities? Why might this be so?

Atypical Development

 OUT OF THE ORDINARY

LEARNING OBJECTIVE 6

Understand how the atypical development approach uses a developmental perspective to look at challenging behaviours.

atypical development when children do not develop in line with typically developing peers.

Atypical development occurs when children do not develop in line with typically developing peers in one or more areas of development. One of the difficulties in definition is whether a "delay" or a "deficit" approach is taken. Throughout the text, we will consider the ways that different psychological attributes and faculties develop and how those attributes and faculties may not develop in the usual fashion. For now, however, we will offer just a broad understanding of atypical development.

Psychologists in the field of are interested in how patterns of challenging behaviour evolve, based on both genetics and early childhood experiences, and in how those early patterns affect functioning as individuals move through later life stages (Cicchetti, 2010a, 2010b; Santostefano, 2010; Hinshaw, 2008). Developmental psychologists also compare and contrast problematic behaviour patterns with more typical behaviour patterns, seeking to identify **risk factors**, biological and environmental factors that contribute to children's outcomes. In addition, they seek to identify other factors that can help children avoid or recover from such negative outcomes.

risk factors biological and environmental factors that contribute to problematic outcomes.

conduct disorder a clinical disorder in children and adolescents associated with emotional and behavioural problems, such as rule-breaking, trouble with limit-setting from authority figures, bullying, fighting and cruelty.

One disorder of special interest is called **conduct disorder**, a diagnosis applied strictly to children and adolescents. Conduct disorder (and its less severe cousin, *oppositional defiant disorder*) is characterized by a number of emotional and behavioural problems, including frequent rule-breaking, trouble following the limits imposed by authority figures, bullying, fighting and cruelty. Looking at how developmental psychologists approach this disorder can help us understand how they approach all psychological disorders.

Developmental psychologists focus first on the various behaviours shown by children with conduct disorders (Murray & Farrington, 2010; Hinshaw, 2002) to distinguish the conduct disorder from other disorders and to see whether it has any relation to milder problems, such as impulsiveness and distractibility. The negative behaviours of conduct disorder, such as defying authority, breaking rules and fighting, are categorized as *externalizing behaviours* (as opposed to *internalizing behaviours*, such as fearful responses, crying or withdrawal).

PSYCHOLOGY AROUND US   Bullying: A Continuing Problem

Reports examining the many school shootings that have occurred across the United States over the past few decades found that bullying was a factor in most of them (Gonzalez, 2010; Crisp, 2001). Sometimes, the shooters had been bullies; more often, they had been the *victims* of bullying.

One survey asked children aged eight to 15 what issues in school troubled them most, and the children pointed to teasing and bullying as 'big problems' that ranked even higher than racial discrimination, AIDS and sex or alcohol peer pressures (Cukan, 2001). Overall, over one-quarter of students report being bullied frequently and more than 70% report having been victimized at least once, leading in many cases to feelings of humiliation or anxiety (Smith, 2010; Jacobs, 2008; Nishina et al., 2005). In addition, our online world has broadened the ways in which children and adolescents can be bullied, and today cyber bullying – bullying by email or text-messaging – is increasing (Smith & Slonje, 2010; Jacobs, 2008).

In response to these alarming trends, many schools have started programmes that teach students how to deal more effectively with bullies, work to change the thinking of bullies, train teachers, conduct parent discussion groups and apply classroom prevention measures (Rigby & Bauman, 2010; Jacobs, 2008; Frey et al., 2005; Twemlow, 2003). Furthermore, there have been campaigns to educate the public about anti-bullying programmes.

Although recognizing the negative, and potentially tragic, impact of bullying, some experts worry that the sheer prevalence of bullying may make it a very difficult problem to overcome. It is hard, for example, for educators and clinicians to identify which bullies or bullied children will turn violent given that a full 70% of children have experienced bullying. Can we really rid our schools and communities of a problem as common as this?

Some studies, looking for patterns and changes over time, have suggested that when externalizing behaviours begin in early childhood they are more likely to be due to biological factors, such as genetic inheritance (Taylor et al., 2000). This places children with early-onset conduct disorders at greater risk for problems later on in life than those whose conduct problems begin in adolescence. Other studies indicate that, although they tend to be moderately stable over time, the specific forms of externalizing behaviours do shift with age. For example, explicitly aggressive acts, such as picking fights, typically decrease over time, while less overt acts of aggression tend to increase during early adolescence (Hinshaw, 2002). It seems that many children with conduct disorder learn as a result of the negative consequences for their bad behaviour, but they do not really change internally. They learn primarily to hide their aggressive behaviour so that they do not get into as much trouble.

Other psychologists consider that behaviour can be analysed in a variety of ways. According to this view, a full account of how children can go off the rails (or stay on-track) requires looking at how genetics, environmental influences and the children's own psychological processes collaborate to bring about their pattern of behaviour and functioning.

Autistic Spectrum Disorders

A very different example of atypical development is that of autistic spectrum disorders. Autistic spectrum disorders will be described elsewhere in this book, but it is important to be aware of a developmental condition where there can be a profound problem with social aspects of life. Autistic spectrum disorder is a life-long developmental disability affecting social and communication skills. People with autistic spectrum disorder can also have accompanying learning difficulties but, whatever their general level of intelligence, everyone with the condition shares a difficulty in making sense of the world. There is a rising number diagnosed with autism compared with other conditions (Baird *et al.*, 2006), with a possible under diagnosis in girls and women.

It is because autism occurs in differing degrees of severity and a variety of forms that the term *autistic spectrum disorder* is often used to describe the whole range. This term includes the condition Asperger syndrome, which is a form of autism and describes people at the higher functioning end of the autistic spectrum. People with Asperger syndrome are of average or above-average intelligence and generally have fewer problems with language, often speaking fluently, though their words can sometimes sound formal or stilted.

The current diagnostic criteria used now are the DSM-IV, where it is seen as a broad spectrum developmental disorder including Pervasive Developmental Disorder (PPD); Autism, PDD-NOS, Asperger Syndrome and Rett's Syndrome.

The difficulties are often evident from birth but a formal diagnosis is usually not made until a child is two to three years old, when the difficulties in verbal communication become apparent. As our understanding of autistic spectrum disorders increases, there have been more tests developed that can provide early indicators for this condition – for example, CHAT (the Checklist for Autism in Toddlers) and CARS (Childhood Autism Rating Scale).

Two Useful Concepts for Atypical Development: Equifinality and Multifinality

equifinality the idea that different individuals can start out from different places and end up with the same outcome.

multifinality the idea that children can start from the same spot and end up in any number of other outcomes.

Two concepts that psychologists have provided to the field of atypical development are **equifinality** and **multifinality** (Fanti & Henrich, 2010; Mitchell *et al.*, 2004). The concept of equifinality holds that individuals can start out from all sorts of different places and yet, through their life experiences, subsequently function (or dysfunction) in similar ways. Multifinality follows the opposite principle. It suggests that children can start from the same point and end up in any number of different psychological places. Applying these two concepts to conduct disorders, it appears that various roads may lead

TABLE 4.5 Risk Factors that Link Conduct Disorders to the Commission of Violent Crimes during Adolescence or Adulthood

Family violence	Multiple clinical disorders
Family dysfunction/conflict	Risky behaviour/impulsiveness
Family distress	Gun availability/risk
Childhood exposure to violence	Antisocial parent
Childhood maltreatment	Gang membership
Childhood neglect	Peer violence
Childhood adversity	Personality disorder
Substance abuse	Academic failure
Hyperactivity	Social incompetence

Source: Murray & Farrington, 2010; FAS, 2008; Weaver *et al.*, 2008; González *et al.*, 2007; Lahey & Waldman, 2007; Mueser *et al.*, 2006; Panko, 2005.

to the development of a conduct disorder during adolescence (Litschge *et al.*, 2010). A child with conduct disorder may have been born with a difficult temperament, experienced poor parenting or developed poor social skills. Table 4.5 lists risk factors that link conduct disorders to the likelihood of committing serious and violent crimes during adolescence or adulthood. As suggested by the notion of equifinality, regardless of which set of risk factors is at play, the outcome is often similar.

At the same time, multifinality assures us that not every difficult baby and not every baby with ineffective parents will develop a conduct disorder. Indeed, the vast majority will have no emotional and behavioural problems at all. Developmental psychologists are very interested in the biological, psychological and environmental factors that help buffer against or negate the impact of risk factors – factors that help produce **resilience**, an ability to recover from or avoid the serious effects of negative circumstances (Dudley *et al.*, 2011; Flouri *et al.*, 2011; Hudziak & Bartels, 2008). In short, according to this viewpoint, it is just as critical to understand what goes right as it is to understand what goes wrong. Sameroff and Chandler's concept of a 'continuum of caretaking casualty' is still as useful today as when they introduced it in 1975. It describes the ways in which the environment can heighten or decrease the vulnerability of a child born at biological risk (e.g., factors such as homelessness). There are so many physical and social factors that can have a negative impact on early development, that it is very difficult to pinpoint which single risk is most harmful. However, Sameroff and Chandler suggest that there are environmental influences, such as loving parents and sensitive teaching, which may have a positive effect in helping children at biological risk, who can prove surprisingly resilient.

resilience the ability to recover from or avoid the serious effects of negative circumstances.

Before You Go On

What Do You Know?

17. How do externalizing behaviours differ from internalizing behaviours?

18. What is the difference between equifinality and multifinality?

19. Why is resilience important to the study of atypical development?

What Do You Think?

Consider problems such as anxiety and depression. Do you see any advantages to looking at emotional or mental problems from a developmental perspective, as the product of a lifetime of biological and environmental experiences, rather than just examining the symptoms displayed by people with these problems? Do you see any disadvantages to this approach?

Activities to test yourself further are available in your interactive e-book at **www.wileyopenpage.com**.

Summary

Before We Are Born

LEARNING OBJECTIVE 1   Discuss the developmental origins of temperament.

- Behavioural genetics focuses on how much of the way we think and act is influenced by our genetic inheritance.
- Chess and Thomas (1996) suggest that we fall into one of three categories: easy, difficult and slow to warm up.
- Temperament was also considered to be inborn, a biologically based tendency that was stable across time.
- Our environment plays an important role in how we behave, from expressing a preference for which hand we use to how birth order effects can explain behaviour, although this explanation is controversial.

Infancy

LEARNING OBJECTIVE 2   Summarize the major social and emotional developments that take place during infancy.

- Attachment theory suggests that the baby is biologically predisposed to bond and form a relationship with a key caregiver, thus ensuring that his or her needs are met. The security of the attachment relationship will have later implications for how secure the person feels in his or her emotional and social capabilities.
- Baumrind (1991) found evidence that different parenting styles could also affect the overall well-being of the child,

although subsequent research suggests that outcomes may vary depending on other environmental and cultural influences.

- Clearly, parental influence is important at this stage, but there is an increasing acknowledgement of the role that fathers play. Also, it is not just the type of caregiver who is key (e.g. grandparents, lesbian and gay parents) but also the quality of the parenting that is important.
- Friendships and peer relations are of increasing importance and it is useful to investigate their positive and negative effects on children.

Childhood

LEARNING OBJECTIVE 3   Summarize the major social and emotional developments that take place during childhood.

- Theories of moral development have often focused on moral reasoning (the reasons why a child would do one thing or another) rather than values. Generally, research supports the movement from morality rooted in submitting to authority to morality rooted in more autonomous decisions about right and wrong.
- Eisenberg and Mussen (1989) suggest that there are moral dilemmas where the choice is between personal advantage and fairness to others.
- Some researchers suggest that moral reasoning may vary across gender and culture. Other researchers have

questioned whether morality theories would be better served by measuring behaviour instead of expressed reasoning or attitudes.

- As children develop, they gain an increasingly sophisticated understanding of deception.

Adolescence

LEARNING OBJECTIVE 4   Summarize the major social and emotional changes that take place during adolescence.

- Erikson (1959, 1984, 1985) proposes a highly influential theory of social and emotional development that stretches across the lifespan and incorporates various dilemmas that need to be successfully reconciled in order for development to stay on track. The key task for adolescents is to resolve the conflict between identity and role confusion.
- Marcia (2007) elaborates on Erikson's ideas about identity formation and used semi-structured interviews to study the process of identity formation.
- Marcia suggests that there are four identity statuses: foreclosure, identity diffusion, moratorium and identity achievement.
- Elkind (1967) considers that adolescent egocentrism gives rise to two interesting concepts: the personal fable and the imaginary audience.

Adulthood and Old Age

LEARNING OBJECTIVE 5   Describe key social and emotional changes that take place throughout adulthood.

- According to Erikson, the challenge of early adulthood is to resolve the conflict between intimacy and isolation; of middle adulthood, to resolve the conflict between generativity and stagnation; and of old age, to resolve the conflict between integrity and despair. Levinson (1986b)

points out that transitions from one stage to the next can also cause conflicts.

- The ages at which adults are expected to reach major social and emotional milestones, such as marriage and parenting, are more flexible now in many societies than they were in the past.
- Arnett (2007) provides the concept of emerging adulthood and Levinson (1986a) charts the life stages of man as a lifespan approach.
- Old age has been reconfigured to provide a Third Age/Fourth Age distinction and there is a proliferation of theories which are relevant to the final stages of the lifespan, such as those proposed by Baltes and Smith (2008).

Atypical Development

LEARNING OBJECTIVE 6   Understand how the atypical developmental approach uses a developmental perspective to look at challenging behaviours.

- The atypical developmental approach studies how early challenging behaviours evolve as a function of a person's genetics and early experiences and how those behaviours affect the person in later life.
- Developmental psychologists are particularly interested in identifying the risk factors that contribute to developmental outcomes.
- The concept of equifinality holds that although children may start out at different places through their life experiences they end up functioning (or dysfunctioning) in similar ways. The concept of multifinality holds that children can start out at the same place but may end up in a number of different psychological places.
- Developmental psychologists are also interested in the factors that contribute to resilience, the ability to recover from or avoid the serious effects of negative circumstances.

Access your interactive e-book to view a video clip for this chapter at **www.wileyopenpage.com**

TYING IT TOGETHER

HOW WE DIFFER

- Babies may display a *secure*, *anxious/avoidant*, *anxious/resistant* or *disorganized attachment* style – a style that helps predict later relationship needs.
- According to some research, the higher stages of moral development of males tend to focus on justice, fairness and other abstract moral values, whereas those of females factor in relationship needs and responsibilities.

HOW WE DEVELOP

- Young children tend to make moral decisions that help ensure they will not get into trouble with parents or adults. In contrast, the moral decisions of adolescents and young adults tend to be more complex and guided by broader principles of right and wrong.
- Although less egocentric than younger children, many teenagers often display personal fables in which they are convinced that they are special – the first persons to have various thoughts and feelings – and perceive an imaginary audience in which they believe everyone is scrutinizing them.

OUT OF THE ORDINARY

- Developmental psychologists seek to identify biological, psychological and environmental *risk factors* that contribute to the development of behavioural problems and psychological disorders.
- Risk factors for the development of *conduct disorders* in children and adults include family violence or dysfunction, childhood maltreatment, substance abuse, peer violence and personality disorders.
- Despite the appearance of such risk factors, many children do not develop conduct disorders, a phenomenon attributed to their *resilience*. Like risk factors, the biological, psychological and environmental factors that help produce resilience are of enormous interest to developmental psychologists.

Quizzes to test yourself further are available in your interactive e-book at **www.wileyopenpage.com**

Key Terms

attachment 76
atypical development 93
conduct disorder 94

equifinality 95
multifinality 95
reciprocal socialization 79

resilience 95
risk factors 93
temperament 74

Flashcards to test yourself further are available in your interactive e-book at **www.wileyopenpage.com**

CHAPTER 5

Behavioural Neuroscience

Adapted by Trevor Archer,
University of Gothenburg, Sweden

CHAPTER OUTLINE

- How Do Scientists Study the Nervous System and the Brain?

- How Does the Nervous System Work?

- The Brain's Structural and Functional Organization

- Neurons and the Communication Systems of the Brain, Nervous System and Body

- Building the Brain

- Brain Side and Brain Size

- Neurological Diseases

 Access your interactive e-book to view a video clip for this chapter at **www.wileyopenpage.com**

Your Brain in Facebook

Most students use Facebook, logging on to keep in touch with friends and to keep up with events. One may keep track of several different conversations at a time, check other Facebook pages to see what one's friends are up to, switch over to YouTube to watch a video someone recommended and then hook up Skype to chat in person with a friend abroad. Most students find all these Internet options easy to use: once tried a few times, communicating this way becomes second nature. Nevertheless, although these behaviours are generally fun and easy, they require the involvement of a large proportion of one's brain and nervous system. The sensory neurons in the body's receptor organ (eyes, ears, fingers) receive information about sight (what you see on the screen), sound (what you hear when you play a video, listen to music or talk to a friend over Skype) and touch (how the keyboard feels to your fingers). This information is transmitted along nerves to particular regions of the brain and spinal cord. This sensory input induces the brain to engage a large number of circuits to help you process and respond appropriately to the information you gather. Brain regions that process sensory input are activated, along with those important for reading, controlling emotions, making judgements, solving problems, learning, recalling, typing and talking. The use of many programs simultaneously or switching back and forth to participate in several conversations simultaneously activates regions of the brain that allow flexible thinking. In fact, every behaviour performed during the day leading up to sitting down at the computer, and even after one closes down for the night and goes to sleep, involves the brain and nervous system. ■

neuroscience the study of the brain and nervous system.

behavioural neuroscience the study of how the brain and nervous system control our behaviour.

Neuroscience is the study of the brain and nervous system. **Behavioural neuroscience** is the study of how the brain and nervous system control our behaviour and orchestrate *in an interactive fashion* our organs, glands, skeletal muscles, immune system, etc. This study involves comparative analyses of the brain and central nervous system with the peripheral and autonomic nervous systems. It is of critical importance to bear in mind that the brain and nervous system collaborate intimately with the various glands of the endocrine system and the different tissues, for example lymph and bone marrow, that contribute to the body's immune system.

The complexity of the adult human brain is huge and probably consists of several universes we do not even know about. The present state of our knowledge may at best be described as insightful and at worst as rudimentary. Despite hundreds of years of progress, we are still unable to conceptualize how the actions of brain cells (neurons) may produce single thoughts, never mind complex chains of behaviour. Even the generation of a single thought which may or may not involve the 'activation' or 'inhibition (inactivations)' of millions of neurons remains impossible for our meagre powers of description and formulation in spite of the stupendous resources invested. Structural-functional considerations of how mammalian and human brains developed originally, that is phylogenetically, provide hints regarding our sensory-motor, cognitive and emotional domains. Thereafter, how the ontogenetic development of individuals' brains may proceed is determined to a large extent by those developments: for example, areas of the frontal lobe that are selective (and on a species level a novelty) for human brains are also the regions that develop latest in the human individual. Even before birth, many millions of brain cells are arranged in an orderly fashion, and order is a functional prerequisite; this is important since analyses of the brains of schizophrenic patients post mortem shows much disorderliness. Each one of them must link up with other appropriate brain cells in order to transmit the messages that will let us breathe, eat, see, hear and think. Throughout the perinatal, infant, childhood, adolescent and adult stages of brain development, scientists are seeking to understand how and where these cellular events occur. Continual development is a major arena for study, be it for describing normal functioning or for determining the pathogenesis of neural disorders.

Perhaps the most amazing aspect of studying the myriad agents that disturb brain development and function is that this highly complicated process works more or less sufficiently and necessarily most of the time in so-called normal individuals and even episodically in those afflicted by disorder. Although accidents do happen even in the brain and nervous system, as described below, the overwhelming majority of individuals present normally functioning brains even under conditions where structural integrity is compromised. Taking into account all of the various activities, be they implicit or explicit, that one embarks upon during the course of a single day, it is highly impressive what our brains accomplish. We are not even aware of most of these activities.

How Do Scientists Study the Nervous System and the Brain?

LEARNING OBJECTIVE 1

Understand the key methods that scientists use to learn about brain anatomy and functioning.

If there were a single defining characteristic of a brain, it would be to allow us to survive in an ever-changing and highly variable environment, be it physical, social or virtual. For human beings, the brain is highly developed for handling social contexts in ever-changing social environments. It is important at the outset to distinguish between sensory systems, which are designed to detect alterations in an ever-changing environment, and motor systems, which are designed to allow humans and animals to alter or manipulate their environment; the former represent an input, the latter an output. The progressive development of **neurotechnology** for the study of the brains of humans and laboratory animals has provided great leaps in the understanding and description of the structure and function of a central nervous system so that we may understand physical entities, events and their outcomes more or less non-invasively, thereby avoiding structural damage.

neurotechnology the technology on which our understanding of neurons is based.

Previously, human neuroscience relied on one of the following methods:

- *Examining autopsy tissue.* This method allows examination of the gross and microstructure of the brain without providing any information regarding how the brain functions.

- *Testing the behaviour of patients with damage to certain parts of the brain.* Neuropsychologists have learnt much about the brain from studying patients with brain damage. Patients with localized brain damage often

PSYCHOLOGY AROUND US   Traumatic Brain Injury (TBI)

OUT OF THE
ORDINARY

A blow to the head, violent shaking or penetration of the brain tissue usually causes traumatic brain injury (TBI). Headache, dizziness, loss of consciousness, blurred vision, confusion, memory loss, seizures, paralysis and coma are predominant amongst the initial symptoms, while apoptosis and loss of blood–brain barrier intactness may be expected. The severity, whether mild, moderate or severe, depends on the extent and depth of the injury together with the type of structural insult and its location, as well as the distribution and magnitude of inflammation and loss of cerebrovascular integrity, and the eventual efficacy of intervention. Exercise intervention exerts multiple positive effects upon the patient afflicted by TBI, including anti-neurotoxic and anti-apoptotic effects, the augmentation of neuroplasticity and neuronal repair, and both neurogenesis and angiogenesis. *Apoptosis* is programmed cell death; brain trauma can accelerate this process. *Angiogenesis* involves the development and arborization of cerebral blood vessels.

A Swedish National registry-based study reported about 250 per 100,000 individuals sustain a TBI annually and it is estimated that across the United Kingdom there are around 500,000 people aged 16–74 living with long-term disabilities as a result of TBI (Brain Injury Group, 2012).

TBI diagnosis can cover a wide range of short- and long-term impairments in physical, cognitive, behavioural and emotional domains, depending upon injury extent, severity and location. In mild sport-related TBI, memory problems, not least spatial navigation memory deficits and alterations in brain networks, can cause widespread behavioural changes. For example, regarding affective status, TBI patients report significant changes in self-concept with the post-injury self-image experienced negatively in comparison with pre-injury self-image. Anxiety following childhood TBI appears to be part of a broader problem of affective dysregulation related to a damaged dorsal frontal lobe and frontal white-matter systems. Therefore, quality-of-life issues are critical to considerations of post-injury recovery (Borg *et al.*, 2011).

Psychiatric disorders are common following TBI, and the timing of onset may differ according to pre-injury history with different trajectories for anxiety and depressive disorders, thereby posing implications for identifying the time individuals are most at risk for psychiatric disorders post-injury (Archer, 2012; Archer *et al.*, 2012).

---

lose some function. The loss of function then suggests what the brain region does when it is undamaged. The obvious drawback to this approach is that it involves inferring information about the normally functioning brain from the damaged brain. Even patients with localized brain damage may have smaller undetectable abnormalities in other areas of the brain. Also, the damaged brain may undergo reorganization over time, so abnormalities in behaviour may not reflect what goes on in the intact brain.

- *Recording brain activity, or brain waves, from the surface of the scalp.* The *electroencephalogram*, or EEG, provides information about the activity of our brains during certain states of consciousness (awake and asleep) as well as during the performance of certain behaviours. One drawback of this type of analysis is that surface recordings only provide a summary of activity over a large expanse of tissue; pinpointing the location of activity using this method can only be done in a general sense. Another drawback pertains to the level of structural and functional resolution.

Research findings using these older methods have been combined with those from animal studies in which specific brain regions are examined microscopically, recorded from electronically or targeted for destruction, a process called lesioning. Taken together, these approaches have provided us with a sufficiency of information about the brain and the nervous system in general, but they all share drawbacks. There is very limited information assembled regarding activity in specific regions of healthy, living human brains.

Over the past few decades, however, several new techniques, collectively referred to as **neuroimaging**, have been developed to study brain activity in awake, healthy humans. These techniques enable researchers to identify the activity of brain regions under different conditions, for example in a resting state or during the performance of a cognitive task. *Structural* imaging involves the structure of the brain and the diagnosis of gross (large-scale) intracranial disease (such as tumour or haemorrhage)

neuroimaging
involves the application of various brain imaging techniques that provide images of the structure and function of awake (or not) humans either directly or indirectly; some of these techniques are invasive (e.g. PET); others non-invasive (e.g. fMRI).

and other damage (such as TBI). On the other hand, *functional imaging* is applied to diagnose metabolic diseases and lesions on a finer scale (such as in attention-deficit hyperactivity disorder, or ADHD) and neurological and neuropsychological studies. Although these techniques allow researchers and clinicians to 'visualize' the brain, a very high level of experience and expertise is necessary to obtain accurate interpretation of the brain images. Computerized tomography (CT), which is often a preliminary examination of a patient's brain, generates an enormous amount of data that may be manipulated to assess the integrity of various structures based on their ability to block x-ray beams. Nevertheless, the images obtained from CT scans are relatively blurred and generally only useful for obtaining gross anatomical abnormalities, such as large brain tumours.

Among the most commonly used neuroimaging methods are *positron emission tomography (PET)* and *functional magnetic resonance imaging (fMRI)*. PET (Figure 5.1) scans enable the detection of uptake and metabolism of certain molecules (e.g. fluorodeoxyglucose (FDG)) so that brain areas of increased activity may be identified. PET offers a nuclear medicine imaging technique that produces a three-dimensional image of functional processes in the brain. The system detects pairs of gamma rays emitted indirectly by a positron-emitting radionuclide (tracer agent), which is introduced into the body

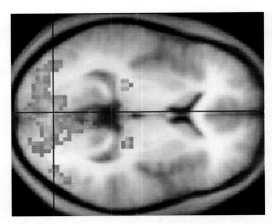

FIGURE 5.2 An fMRI image of the human brain. Regions of activation including primary visual cortex (V1, BA17), extrastriate visual cortex and lateral geniculate body in a comparison between a task involving a complex moving visual stimulus and rest condition (viewing a black screen). The activations (yellow/red)? are shown (as is typical) against a background based on the average structural images from the subjects in the experiment.

Source: Zhang, H., *et al.* (2010). High-resolution fMRI mapping of ocular dominance layers in cat lateral geniculate nucleus. *Neuroimage, 50*(4), 1456–1463.

on a biologically active molecule marked with a radioactive isotope generally via the carotid artery. Three-dimensional images of tracer concentration within the body are then constructed by computer analysis. Owing to the short half-lives of most radioisotopes, the radiotracers have traditionally been produced using a cyclotron in close proximity to the PET imaging facility, which essentially decides the expensiveness of PET.

FMRI (Figure 5.2) allows for the detection of changes in blood flow, a presumed indicator of changes in the activity of neurons. MRI makes use of the property of nuclear magnetic resonance to image nuclei of atoms inside the brain. An MRI instrument applies a powerful magnetic field to align the magnetization of certain atoms in the brain and radio frequency fields to alter, in a systematic manner, the alignment of that magnetization. This procedure causes the nuclei to produce a rotating magnetic field detectable by the MRI scanner. This image is recorded to construct an image of the scanned region of the brain. Three-dimensional spatial information may be obtained by providing gradients in each direction. Dr Paul Lauterbur and Sir Peter Mansfield were awarded the Nobel Prize for Medicine in 2003 for developing the MRI technique for studying the brain.

Another neuroimaging method, *diffusion tensor imaging (DTI)*, uses MRI technology to examine the connections between brain regions. Many brain disorders are characterized by dysconnectivity between brain regions. *Single photon emission computed tomography (SPECT)* is a nuclear medicine

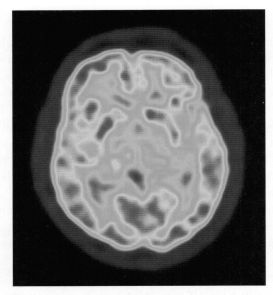

FIGURE 5.1 A PET scan of the human brain (transaxial slice of the brain of a 56-year-old male patient). The injected dose was 282 MBq of 18F-FDG and the image was generated from a 20-minute measurement with an ECAT Exact HR + PET Scanner. Red areas show more accumulated tracer substance (18F-FDG) and blue areas are regions where low to no tracer have been accumulated.

Source: Langer (2008), Event-Driven Motion Compensation in Positron Emission Tomography: Development of a clinically applicable method, PhD thesis, University of Technology Dresden, Germany.

tomographic imaging technique that applies gamma rays. In many respects, it is similar to conventional nuclear medicine planar imaging using a gamma camera; it is able to provide three-dimensional information but like PET it has that disadvantage of being invasive, requiring injection of a gamma-emitting radioisotope (radionuclide) into the bloodstream. *Transcranial magnetic stimulation (TMS)* offers a non-invasive method to induce depolarization or hyperpolarization in brain neurons. TMS applies electromagnetic induction to initiate weak electric currents using a rapidly changing magnetic field; the induction may cause activity in specific or general parts of the brain with minimal discomfort, allowing the functioning and interconnections of the brain regions to be studied.

The availability of these neuroimaging technologies has produced an explosion of research that has infused neuroscience into virtually every area of psychology. The results have confirmed many previously held claims about brain function and raised infinite numbers of enigmatic notions, contradictory issues and new questions, in addition to questioning certain strongly held beliefs. With the rapid development in structural and functional resolution, neuroimaging techniques are applied in close alignment with other instruments measuring performance over several domains (e.g. cognitive, emotional) that advance current notions under both normal conditions and brain disease conditions. Also, it is necessary that methods and procedures for study, observation and analysis keep pace with theoretical notions and clinical realities. Thus, rapid improvements in structural and functional resolution place incremental demands on the competence of neuroscientists in formulating the essential and critical questions that need answering.

Before You Go On

What Do You Know?

1. Describe how studies of people with brain damage and EEGs have contributed to our knowledge of the brain and nervous system.

2. What are the main advantages of neuroimaging methods over earlier neuroscience research methods?

What Do You Think?

Do you think it will be possible to use neuroimaging techniques to determine what a person is thinking? What are the ethical implications of using this technology?

How Does the Nervous System Work?

 **WHAT HAPPENS IN THE BRAIN?**

LEARNING OBJECTIVE 2

Describe the two major types of cells in the nervous system, and explain how communication in the nervous system works.

neuron a nerve cell.

The **neuron**, or nerve cell, provides the fundamental structural and functional unit of the nervous system (Jones, 2007). Communication (signalling) among neurons is essential for all parts of this complex system, which comprises several universes within each other, to function normally. Along with neurons, the nervous systems also contain *glia (glial cells)* whose functions are broader than was once assumed. One indication of the importance of glial cells is that there are about 10 glial cells to every neuron.

The structure and function of individual neurons, as well as how these cells work individually and in groups, called *networks*, has been the subject of considerable scientific inquiry for over a century (Jones, 2007). It has been shown that neurons have specialized structures that enable them to communicate with other neurons using both electrical and chemical signals. In essence, the whole business of communication within the brain and nervous system may be expressed simply as an electrochemical process.

Neurons and Glial Cells or 'Those Who Act and Those Who Serve'

The human brain contains about 100 billion neurons. The basic structure of a neuron is shown in Figure 5.3. Similar to most other cells of the body, neurons have a cell body filled with cytoplasm that contains a nucleus (the residence of chromosomes that contain the genetic material). In addition, neurons contain organelles that enable the cell to make proteins and other molecules, produce energy, as well as permit the breakdown and elimination of toxic substances. However, as Figure 5.3 shows, neurons are different from other cells, in that they have specialized structures called *dendrites* and *axons* that are important for communication with other neurons, the former providing an input region; the latter an output region.

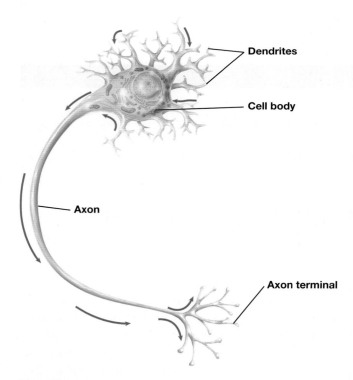

FIGURE 5.3 The neuron. The major parts of the neuron include the cell body, the axon and the dendrites. Dendrites typically receive information from other neurons, while axons send information away from the cell body to communicate with other neurons. Arrows indicate the direction of information flow.

Dendrites extend like branches of a tree, hence the term *arborization*, from the cell body to collect inputs from other neurons. Neurons can have many dendrites and, indeed, some have very extensive dendritic 'trees' that allow a single neuron to receive more than 200,000 inputs from other neurons.

dendrites the parts of neurons that receive input from other neurons.

Axons also extend from the cell body. Unlike dendrites, however, axons typically function to carry information away from the cell body, towards other neurons. Axons have a specialized region at the end, called the **axon terminal**. Unlike the case with dendrites, neurons usually have only one axon. The axon can be very long. One of your axons, for example, runs from your spinal cord all the way to the end of your big toe. In addition, axons can be highly branched. These branches, or collaterals, greatly increase the number of neurons that the axon comes into contact with.

axons the part of the neuron that conducts information away from the cell body towards other neurons.

axon terminal the end of a neuron's axon that provides the output through which neurotransmitters are released.

There are many different kinds of neurons. Some are large, while others are relatively small. Some have very elaborate dendritic trees, while others possess a single unbranched dendrite. Although these cells all look quite different from one another, they have two features in common. All neurons are covered by a membrane that surrounds the entire neuron, including its axon and dendrites, and all have the capability of communicating with other cells by producing and sending electrical signals.

At a fundamental level, three types of neuron are referred to: monopolar, bipolar and multipolar neurons.

In addition to neurons, as mentioned, the nervous system contains a large number of non-neuronal cells called **glia**. In fact, in some parts of the human brain, glia outnumber neurons by a factor of about 10. Their vast numbers make it surprising that glia have, until recently, received relatively little attention from neuroscientists. In the past, glia were considered to be support cells, which implies a passive structural function. Discoveries over the past two decades, however, have confirmed that these cells are diverse and actively serve many purposes that are critical for the normal functioning of neurons. Although most of the rest of this chapter focuses on neurons and systems made up of neurons, glia are actively involved in the functioning and integrity of the nervous system. For example, under conditions where the metabolic output of neurons in the production of high-energy ATP (adenosine-triphosphate) molecules is insufficient, astrocytic glycogenolysis and glycogen mobilization are implicated in normal brain function. We will return to glial cells periodically throughout the rest of this chapter.

glia the cells that, in addition to neurons, constitute the nervous system.

PSYCHOLOGY AROUND US   The Arborization of Neurons

Arborization, the collection of branches, as the branching terminus of a nerve-cell process, is an essential structural aspect of individual neurons. Although it is much more convenient to draw or imagine simple and straightforward shapes of neurons, in fact the shapes and forms that neurons may take can be very complicated and convoluted indeed; furthermore, the more complex the structure of individual neurons, the greater the extent to which they branch, the greater the degree of arborization and the more effective the functioning of the brain to which these neurons belong. Cellular or neuronal arborization is an aspect of communication within the brain and central nervous system that it is difficult to overestimate, and is to a great extent modulated during early life experience. A plethora of excellent studies (see below in the section on plasticity: 'Communication across the Synapse') has been carried out over several different species that demonstrates the enormous and critical difference between having had the good fortune to be fostered in an enriched environment or the misfortune to have been fostered in an impoverished environment. One of the earliest and mostly highly documented differences between an enriched, in contrast to an impoverished, environment pertains to the degree of neuronal arborization (whereby the former provides a much greater extent). Environmental enrichment and degree of arborization have been shown to affect directly the functional capacities, for example in cognition, of individuals in later life. Environmental enrichment also affects the production and availability of several growth factors, such as *nerve growth factor (NGF)*, *brain-derived neurotrophic factor (BDNF)* and *glial-derived neurotrophic factor (GDNF)*, in conjunction with arborization. Accepting that the purpose of each neuron is to maintain communication and signalling through the electrochemical process, it is astounding to consider the numbers of other neurons that a single neuron may be in connection with. Some years ago, estimates suggesting that a single neuron may connect to several hundred or a thousand others sounded impressive, but that is not nearly enough; nowadays, estimates like 10,000 or 20,000 sound quite reasonable. This enormity of communicative potential is the consequence of cellular arborization.

The Action Potential

As mentioned above, communication among neurons is vital to the functioning of the nervous system. In describing the basic events leading to the electrochemical signals used by the nervous system to initiate, conduct and transmit the information, which are the basis of knowing, feeling, desiring and creating, it is essential to array the major actors in this drama: the cell membrane, neurotransmitters, receptor sites, the key-and-lock principle, the membrane potential, the distribution of ions on the inside and outside of the cell membrane and the resting state of the cell membrane. Neurons send messages to one another via electrochemical events. A sudden change in the electrical charge of a neuron's axon causes it to release a chemical that can be received by other neurons. There follows one description of how the signal communication proceeds.

Neurons are covered by a neuronal membrane (that may be referred to as an 'axon membrane', 'dendritic membrane', 'presynaptic membrane', 'postsynaptic membrane', etc., depending on site) with *extracellular fluid* surrounding the outside of the nerve cell. Both the extracellular and intracellular (inside the neuron) fluids contain charged particles called *ions*. Ions can be either positively or negatively charged. The main ions found on the outside and inside are: Na^+, K^+, Cl^- and Ca^{2+} (see below). Owing to relative differences in the amounts of these ions intracellularly and extracellularly, as well as the preponderance of negatively charged ions (protein molecules) on the inside, measuring the electrical potential from the outside to the inside using appropriate instruments reveals a negative charge. That is to say, this charge, called the *resting potential*, is negative; the fluid inside the neuron is more negatively charged than the fluid outside the cell. When a neuron is not sending a message, it is said to be 'resting'. A recording microelectrode can be placed inside the axonal membrane and will be shown to read a negative charge of around –50, –60 or –70 millivolts (mV), relative to outside of the cell, depending on the species or type of nerve cell.

Neuronal membrane exhibits *selective permeability* to ions. Embedded in the membrane are specialized **ion channels**, or pores, that only allow the passage of certain ions into and out of the cell. These ion channels can open or close depending on information the cell receives from other neurons. Some of the key ions that are involved in determining the resting potential

> **ion channels** pores in the cell membrane that open and close to allow certain ions into and out of the cell.

are the positively charged ions sodium (Na$^+$) and potassium (K$^+$) and the negatively charged chlorine (Cl$^-$) ion. It is important to note that if the ion channels are open, some are voltage-gated and some open and close on a lock-and-key basis (see below). When the neuron is at rest, Na$^+$ ions are proportionally higher in concentration outside of the cell whereas K$^+$ ions are proportionally higher in concentration on the inside. Cl$^-$ and Ca^{2+} ions are more concentrated outside the cell. These concentration gradients change dramatically when the cell is activated by other neurons. The resting potential of the neuron is maintained by two purely physical factors: (1) force of diffusion and (2) electrostatic pressure. The former implies that ions will move down a concentration from high to low, whereas the latter implies that similarly charged ions reject each other, and oppositely charged ions attract each other. The negative value of the resting potential, say from −50 to −80 mV, is described as a state of polarization. Events that increase the level of polarization from the resting potential level are said to induce hyperpolarization, whereas events that decrease (or reverse the negative value to a positive value) the level of polarization from the resting potential level are said to induce depolarization.

When information received from other neurons induces positively charged, or *excitatory*, events, these are termed *excitatory postsynaptic potentials (EPSPs)*. Sometimes this information causes negatively charged events termed *inhibitory postsynaptic potentials (IPSPs)*. The point at which the axon starts at the cell body of the neuron is the axon hillock. This region is the starting point for all the electrical events conducted from the cell body to the axon terminals; that is, the initiation of electrical conductance. At any given moment, EPSPs and IPSPs are summated at the axon hillocks and it is quite likely that there are equal numbers of each so that they cancel each other out without any threshold of stimulation being reached. However, if the number of EPSPs exceeds the number of IPSPS significantly, thereby reaching a certain *threshold (a threshold of stimulation)*, an event begins at the axon, known as the **action potential** (or impulse or signal depending on the context). The action potential is presented in Figure 5.4. During an action potential (also known as a *spike*), ion channels that allow the passage of sodium (Na$^+$) through the membrane open rapidly. This follows the opening of voltage-gated Na$^+$ channels starting from the section of the axon closest to the axon hillock shortly after the threshold of stimulation was reached. This enables Na$^+$, which is present in higher concentrations outside of the axon, to rush through the Na$^+$ channels into

action potential a sudden positive change in the electrical charge of a neuron's axon. Also known as a spike, or firing, action potentials rapidly transmit an excitatory charge down the axon.

the axon. The sudden influx of positive ions shifts the electrical charge of the axon from negative to positive. At the peak of the action potential, the membrane charge is about +50 mV.

Seven 'Lock-and-Key' Principles of Receptors and Neurotransmitters

One simple way of envisioning the events leading up to the events termed EPSPs, IPSPs and action potentials is to imagine that the neurotransmitter plays the role of a key and the receptors positioned over the dendrites and their spines are the locks that give access to ion channels. When the right key enters the right lock, the channel is opened. The opening of this channel may allow the influx of Na$^+$ or Cl$^-$, or the outflow of K$^+$ thereby leading to expression of EPSPs or IPSPs, respectively. Glutamic acid, an excitatory acid neurotransmitter, acts as a key that opens a receptor lock that provides access to a Na$^+$ 'lock and key' channel through which, once opened, Na$^+$ ions may flow into the cell and initiate EPSPs. Gamma-amino butyric acid (GABA), an inhibitory neurotransmitter, acts as a key that opens a receptor lock that provides access to a Cl$^-$ 'lock and key' channel through which, once opened, Cl$^-$ ions may flow into the cell and initiate IPSPs. Glutamic acid always induces EPSPs whereas GABA always induces IPSPs. There are four other neurotransmitters: serotonin, noradrenaline, dopamine and acetylcholine. These neurotransmitters may induce EPSPs or IPSPs depending on neuropharmacological circumstances. It is important, and sobering, to bear in mind that of the 100 billion or so neurotransmitter-producing neurons in the brain, glutamic acid and GABA account for over 95%, whereas serotonin, noradrenaline, dopamine and acetyl choline, together with about 200 other neurotransmitter-producing neurons, account for less than 5%.

As Figure 5.4 depicts, the action potential travels down the axon, in the direction away from the axon hillock of the cell body towards the axon terminal area. As each portion of the axon spikes, or *fires*, the Na$^+$ channels on the next patch of membrane open, letting the spike continue its progress towards the axon terminal. As the action potential develops with continued depolarization of the membrane and positive value 'peak amplitude' (of, say, +50 mV) voltage-gated K$^+$ channels open at about the same time as voltage-gated Na$^+$ channels close.

Action potentials are not graded: there cannot be weaker or stronger action potentials. They follow an *all-or-nothing* principle. If the stimulation reaching the neuron – essentially, the number of EPSPs minus the number of

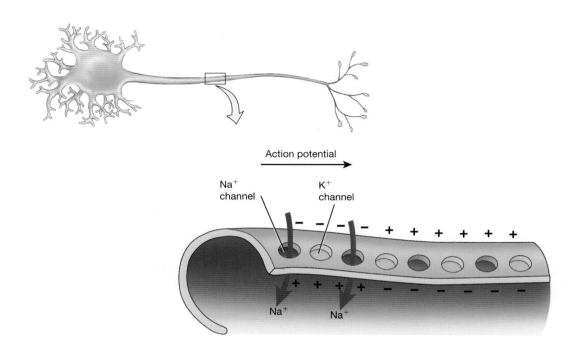

Action potential

Na$^+$ channel   K$^+$ channel

Na$^+$ Na$^+$

(a) This figure shows an action potential occurring along a segment of the axon membrane. During an action potential, Na$^+$ channels in the axon membrane open and Na$^+$ enters the cell, giving the membrane a more positive charge.

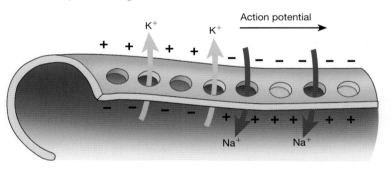

Action potential

K$^+$ K$^+$

Na$^+$ Na$^+$

(b) As the action potential moves past a certain patch of membrane, the membrane works to restore the resting potential by closing the Na$^+$ channels so no more Na$^+$ enters the cell. K$^+$ channels are opened and K$^+$, which is more concentrated inside the cell, exits through the channels. Thus, the resting potential is restored.

FIGURE 5.4 The action potential.

IPSPs – exceeds a certain threshold (i.e. the threshold of stimulation), it fires; otherwise, it does not. To facilitate and accelerate the conductance of the action potential down the axon, the axons of many neurons are insulated by **myelin**, produced by specialized glial cells. Wrapped areas of the axon are broken up at regular intervals by regions that expose the neuronal membrane to the extracellular fluid. These regions are called *nodes of Ranvier*. As shown in Figure 5.5, action potentials travel very quickly down myelinated axons by jumping from node to node.

myelin a fatty, white substance, formed from glial cells, that insulates the axons of many neurons.

After it fires, the neuron cannot fire again for a short time, known as a *refractory period*. Immediately following an action potential, the axon is unable to fire no matter how strong the stimulus to the neuron. This time is called the **absolute refractory period**. During the **relative refractory period**, which begins a little later, the cell can fire if it is given a strong enough stimulus, but the threshold for spiking is higher than usual.

absolute refractory period a short time after an action potential during which a neuron is completely unable to fire again.

relative refractory period time just after the absolute refractory period during which a neuron can only fire if it receives a stimulus stronger than its usual threshold level.

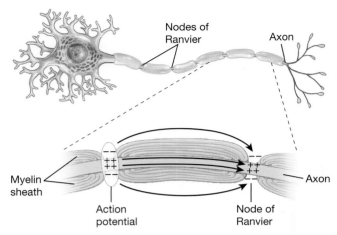

FIGURE 5.5 Nodes of Ranvier. The nodes of Ranvier are the regions of bare axon that are between areas wrapped in myelin. Action potentials travel down the axon by jumping from node to node.

Since action potentials are all-or-nothing, the information conveyed is not specific. Nevertheless, the pattern of action potentials – whether they occur in rapid succession or at a slow pace, whether they are regular or more sporadic, as well as their 'peak amplitude' – can provide a neural code that endows a degree of specificity.

Communication across the Synapse

On arrival of the positive charge of an action potential at the axon terminal and its various boutons, the configuration of the axonal membrane is altered, whereby voltage-gated Ca^{2+} channels are opened, thereby allowing Ca^{2+} ions that have a much higher extracellular concentration compared with the inside to enter the axon terminal. The net result of this influx of ions is to markedly increase the concentration of Ca^{2+} ions in the axon terminal. These events stimulate the activity of the vesicles stored in the axon terminal boutons so that they move in the direction of the presynaptic membrane. Neurons are not physically connected to one another. They are separated by small gaps. These gaps, called synapses, are tiny spaces (about 20 nm or 0.00002 mm wide) usually between the axon terminal of one cell and the dendrite of another cell. Communication across these spaces involves specialized chemicals called **neurotransmitters**. Neurotransmitter molecules are usually contained within small **synaptic vesicles** in the axon terminal, also known as the *presynaptic terminal*, of the neuron sending the information.

neurotransmitters specialized chemicals that travel across synapses to allow communication between neurons.

synaptic vesicles membrane-bound spheres in the axon terminals of neurons where neurotransmitters are stored before their release.

PSYCHOLOGY AROUND US   Neurotransmitters and Their Functions

There are vast numbers of different neurotransmitters (about 200+ including both small and large molecules), and most are associated with selective brain functions, though the relationships are complicated and variable. Many drugs that alter psychological functioning are designed to interfere with or enhance neurotransmitter functions. For example, the neurotransmitter *serotonin* has been implicated in a number of important functions, such as activity levels and mood regulation (Lowry *et al.*, 2008). Several popular drugs used to treat depression and anxiety increase the action of serotonin, thereby improving mood. Table 5.1 lists some major neurotransmitters, their associated functions and some drugs that can be used to manipulate these systems. Later in the chapter, you will see that certain neurotransmitters are also associated with specific brain regions.

TABLE 5.1 The Functions of the Major Neurotransmitters and Their Associated Drugs

Neurotransmitter	Function	Associated Drugs
Glutamate	Learning, movement	Ketamine (an anaesthetic)
GABA	Learning, anxiety regulation	Valium (diazepam, used to relieve anxiety, muscle spasms), Ambien (zolpidem, used to treat insomnia)
Acetylcholine (ACh)	Learning, attention	Nicotine
Dopamine	Movement, reward learning	Cocaine, heroin, methamphetamine
Serotonin	Mood regulation	Ecstasy (MDMA), LSD (hallucinogens); monoamine oxidase inhibitors (MAOIs), selective serotonin reuptake inhibitors (SSRIs) (antidepressants)
Noradrenaline	Attention, arousal	Adderall (a stimulant made up of dextroamphetamine and amphetamine)

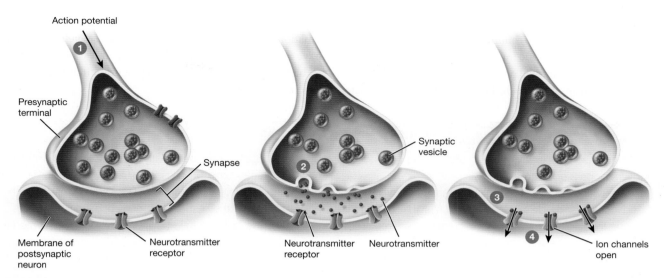

FIGURE 5.6 Communication across the synapse. (1) A positive charge reaches the end of the axon; (2) the positive charge stimulates release of neurotransmitters contained in membrane-bound vesicles into the synapse; (3) neurotransmitters bind to receptors on the post-synaptic neuron; (4) ion channels open and an electrical charge in the postsynaptic neuron is generated.

Eventually, when the spike reaches the presynaptic axon terminal, it causes the release of neurotransmitter molecules into the synaptic cleft. As Figure 5.6 shows, the neurotransmitter then diffuses across the synapse and binds to neurotransmitter receptors on the dendrite (or dendritic spines) of the receiving, or *postsynaptic*, neuron. **Neurotransmitter receptors** are proteins in the cell membrane that recognize specific molecules. They operate in a lock-and-key fashion, so that receptors can only receive the specific neurotransmitter that 'fits' them.

> **neurotransmitter receptors** proteins in the membranes of neurons that bind to neurotransmitters.

As described above, when a neurotransmitter binds to a receptor, the combination stimulates an opening of an ion channel inducing influx of either Na^+ or Cl^- ions. These **postsynaptic potentials**, *excitatory* or *inhibitory*, determine the electrical response of the postsynaptic cell. If the receptor has an excitatory action, then the postsynaptic cell will be depolarized: the membrane potential will become less negative. *Depolarizations* that arise from inputs of a single neuron may not be great enough to trigger an action potential in the postsynaptic neuron, but when summed with other excitatory inputs to the same neuron the threshold will be reached and the neuron will fire. This will then send the information on to the next neuron in the chain. Alternatively, if the neurotransmitter has an inhibitory action, then the postsynaptic cell will be hyperpolarized: its membrane potential will become more negative. *Hyperpolarization* makes it less likely that the postsynaptic neuron will fire an action potential.

> **postsynaptic potentials** electrical events in postsynaptic neurons that occur when a neurotransmitter binds to one of its receptors.

Compared with the action potential, which is an all-or-nothing depolarization, postsynaptic electrical events, EPSPs and IPSPs are much more varied, and in the greater order of events of much less consequence. As described above, they can be depolarizing or hyperpolarizing and graded in strength. In addition, postsynaptic events at individual synapses may be altered through experiential factors.

The repeated release of neurotransmitter into the synapse can result in long-lasting changes in neurotransmitter receptors located on the postsynaptic membrane (Costa-Mattioli *et al.*, 2009); these changes may be referred to as *receptor adaptation*. Glial cells also release chemicals, called *gliotransmitters*, that can cause long-term changes in postsynaptic membranes (Angulo *et al.*, 2008), and indeed modulate the quality of functional expressions. These receptor changes may make the postsynaptic response stronger or weaker, depending on the characteristics of the input. Change in the nervous system is generally referred to as **plasticity**. Plasticity at the synapse, such as the changes that occur from repeated release of neurotransmitters, is called *synaptic plasticity*. Neuroscientists have studied synaptic plasticity extensively because evidence suggests that it may explain some types of learning, as we will describe further in Chapter 9.

> **plasticity** change in the nervous system.

Neural Networks

In the brain, the number of neurons involved in a neural circuit is typically much greater than two. Collections of neurons that communicate with one another are referred to as *neural circuits* or *neural networks*. Given that the human brain contains about 100 billion neurons, each of which receives numerous synaptic inputs from a multitude of other neurons, the computational power of this organ is vast. Some clusters of neurons in specific brain regions communicate more heavily with those of other specific regions; these combinations participate in certain functions. Neuroscientists have focused attention on individual neural systems in order to better grasp the functioning of neural circuits related to specific behaviours.

PSYCHOLOGY AROUND US Artificial Neural Networks

Some neuroscientists have tried to understand how neural networks operate by creating their own versions: artificial neural networks, or ANNs. Artificial neural networks are simplified computer models made up of units that represent neurons together with values that represent the strength of the connections between the neuron units. The first artificial neural network, called *Perceptron*, was created in 1958 by psychologist Frank Rosenblatt. It was intended to model how the human brain processes visual data and learns to recognize objects. Since then, other researchers have used ANNs to study other aspects of human behaviour, especially cognitive behaviour. Experiments have demonstrated that models of this kind can learn face recognition, reading and simple grammatical structure, among other things.

Before You Go On

What Do You Know?

3. What are the main functions of the two types of cells in the nervous system?
4. What happens in the axon of a neuron during an action potential?
5. How does a postsynaptic neuron receive and respond to messages from other neurons?

What Do You Think?

Long axons are vulnerable to damage. What do you think some advantages may be of having a neuron with a very long axon (e.g. one with a cell body in the spinal cord and axon terminal in the toe or finger)?

The Brain's Structural and Functional Organization

 **WHAT HAPPENS IN THE BRAIN?**

LEARNING OBJECTIVE 3
List key structures of the brain, and describe their relationships to our behaviour.

The brain is divided into regions that serve varying functions. Figure 5.7 shows the major structures of the brain. The following descriptions present a bottom–top, old/new account of the brain starting from structures that made up the reptile brain to those that are phylogenetically very new: the brains of human beings. The old structures are important to life; the new ones ensure quality of life.

The Brainstem

The part of the brain closest to the spinal cord is called the **brainstem** or **medulla**. The brainstem is important for basic bodily functions, including respiration and heart rate regulation. Although most of the actions of the brainstem occur without our conscious/explicit awareness or involvement, this part of the brain is critical for survival and normal functioning. Damage to the brainstem, as a result of stroke or trauma, is often fatal.

The brainstem is also important for integrating information about pain and touch from the head and neck with motor output. Neurons from the face, mouth and tongue related to touch, pain, pressure and vibration send inputs into the central nervous system that connect first in the brainstem. Parts of the brainstem are important for controlling eye movement, tongue movement and facial expressions.

Several neuron groups, or *nuclei*, in the brainstem work together to form an area known as the **reticular formation**, which is important for sleep and

brainstem or **medulla** the area of the brain closest to the spinal cord that serves basic functions.

reticular formation a brain structure important for sleep and wakefulness.

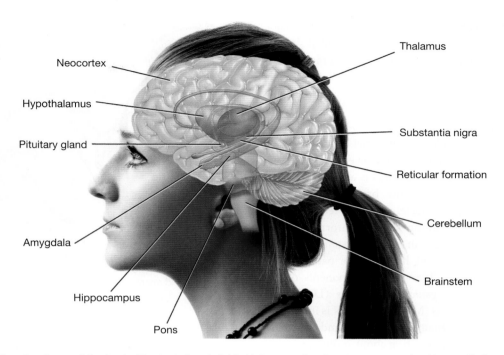

FIGURE 5.7 Major structures of the brain. The brain is subdivided into several major structures, each with specific functions.
Source: © iStockphoto.com/Eduart Titov.

serotonin a neuro-transmitter involved in activity levels and mood regulation.

wakefulness. Groups of neurons in the reticular formation are the major brain source of the neurotransmitter **serotonin**, with the associated cell body region, the *raphe nuclei*. Serotonin and noradrenaline interactions modulate sleep/wakefulness in the brainstem.

The Pons

Above (anterior to) the brainstem is a region called the **pons**. This part of the brain also contains cell body area for the *locus coeruleus*, which belongs to the reticular formation. Neurons producing the neurotransmitter **noradrenaline** are to be found in the locus coeruleus and communicate with many other neurons in the brain and spinal cord. Noradrenaline neurons are important for arousal and attention (Viggiano *et al.*, 2004).

pons the area of the brain anterior to the brainstem that includes the locus coeruleus.

noradrenaline the neurotransmitter important for arousal and attention.

The Cerebellum

Sitting at the back of the brain (dorsal), connected to the brainstem by the pons, is the highly convoluted **cerebellum**. This part of the brain is important for motor coordination and fine-motor control. Individuals presenting cerebellar damage often

cerebellum the area of the brain, near the back of the head, that is important for motor coordination.

have an awkward gait and difficulty reaching for objects without trembling. In addition to its role in motor coordination, the cerebellum is important for certain types of learning involving not only movement but also selective attention. For example, when you learn to tie your shoelaces or to play the piano, your cerebellum is at work. Other parts of the brain participate as well, particularly in cases where the task involves paying attention to a complicated series of instructions. The cerebellum then stores the learnt motor information to be recalled automatically once it is completely learnt. Individuals afflicted by ADHD show marked deficits in cerebellar function.

The Midbrain

Anterior to the pons sits a collection of brain regions collectively called the midbrain. The midbrain contains a number of different nuclei, including an area called the **substantia nigra** (which literally means 'black substance') that contains the cell bodies for the production of the neurotransmitter **dopamine**. Like the cerebellum, the substantia nigra is important for movement, but this area serves different functions from those of the cerebellum. Dopamine neurons communicate with other brain regions located in the forebrain. These pathways are critical for fluidity of movement as well

substantia nigra the region of the brain concerned with fluidity of movement and inhibiting movements.

dopamine neurotransmitter with various brain functions, including movement and reward learning.

as inhibition of movement. This brain region is the major structure damaged in a neurological disorder called *Parkinson's disease* (Cenci, 2007), which we discuss in more detail later in this chapter.

The Thalamus

The **thalamus** is a large collection of nuclei located anterior to, or in front of, the substantia nigra. One easy way to conceptualize thalamus is as the 'telephone exchange' of the brain. Many of the thalamic nuclei serve as relay stations for incoming sensory information. In fact, all of our sensory systems, with the exception of the sense of smell, have a major pathway that synapses in the thalamus. Two major components of the thalamus are the *lateral geniculate nucleus* (LGN) and the *medial geniculate nucleus* (MGN). The LGN is important for relaying information about visual stimuli and the MGN is important for relaying information about auditory stimuli.

thalamus the area of the brain that serves as a relay station for incoming sensory information.

The Hypothalamus

The **hypothalamus** is aptly named because this collection of nuclei sits beneath the thalamus (the prefix *hypo-* comes from the ancient Greek for 'below' or 'under'). The hypothalamus is located below the thalamus, just above the brain stem. In neuroanatomical terminology, it forms the ventral part of the diencephalon. Regions of the hypothalamus are important for a number of motivational processes, including eating, drinking, sex and maternal behaviour. Damage to discrete parts of the hypothalamus can alter these basic behaviours dramatically. The hypothalamus is also critical for the control of the **endocrine, or hormonal, system**. Finally, the hypothalamic–pituitary–adrenal (HPA) axis is critical to our stress reactions and the mobilization of resources to deal with situations. Disruptions in the functioning of the HPA axis have profound consequences for health and disease.

hypothalamus the brain structure important for motivation and control of the endocrine system.

endocrine, or hormonal, system the system that controls levels of hormones throughout the body.

The Pituitary Gland and the Endocrine System

The hypothalamus is connected through myriad blood vessels to the anterior and posterior parts of a structure called the **pituitary gland**. The pituitary functions, in conjunction with the hypothalamus,

pituitary gland the brain structure that plays a central role in controlling the endocrine system.

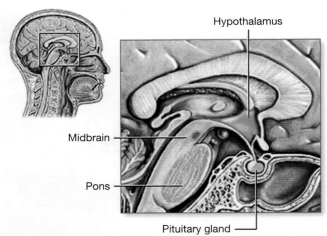

Brain section, showing pons, hypothalamus, pituitary gland and midbrain. Also present, but not labelled, are the thalamus, pineal gland and mamillary bodies.

Source: Medline, nlm.nih.gov.

to control a particular class of chemical messengers in the body (*hormones*) that are important for growth, reproduction, metabolism and stress. The pituitary protrudes ventrally and anteriorly from the base of the hypothalamus, resting in a small bony cavity (sella turcica) within a dural fold (diaphragma sellae). It weighs 0.5 g and has functional connections to the hypothalamus through myriad blood vessels.

There are two parts of the pituitary gland, the *anterior pituitary* and the *posterior pituitary*. The anterior pituitary is connected to the hypothalamus via blood vessels that allow it to receive signalling molecules from specific neuron groups of the hypothalamus. These parts of the hypothalamus communicate with the anterior pituitary to release various *peptides*, which are chemicals that can act as hormones themselves (such as growth hormone) or that can work to stimulate the release of hormones from endocrine glands in the periphery.

There are a number of key endocrine glands. The anterior pituitary produces releasing factors that control endocrine glands, such as the ovaries, the testes, the thyroid and the adrenal glands. The ovaries and testes are sex glands, or gonads. They produce our reproductive hormones: oestrogen and progesterone for the ovaries, testosterone for the testes. The thyroid gland produces thyroid hormones that are important for metabolism.

Following arrival of releasing factor (see below) from the hypothalamus, the pituitary gland releases adrenocorticotrophic hormone (ACTH) into the bloodstream, which is taken up by the adrenal glands. ACTH acts upon the *adrenal glands*, specifically the adrenal cortex (outer region), to produce hormones, called glucocorticoids. On the other hand,

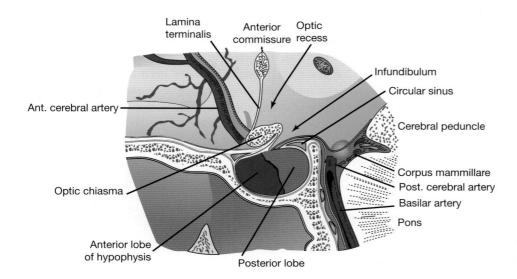

Anterior and posterior
lobes of the pituitary and its
position in the sella turcica.

the adrenal medulla (inner region) releases noradrenaline in response to the sympathetic nervous system (see below) that is critical for responding to stressful situations. As shown in Figure 5.8, the hypothalamus, pituitary and adrenals work together in a system called the HPA axis, which is an important component of the stress response. The HPA axis works in concert with activation of the sympathetic nervous system to maximize our chances of survival under adverse conditions through mobilization of available resources. It must be

borne in mind, however, that there is a price to pay: all the so-called stress hormones – glucocorticoids, including cortisol, adrenaline and noradrenaline – are 'anti-inflammatory' compounds: that is, they combat infections, and when one is under stressful pressures this is an advantage. Eventually, the stressful pressure decreases and hormone release is reduced but now the body's own immune defence system is poorly regulated because of the presence of high levels of circulating anti-inflammatory stress hormones. So, what is a common scenario? After an intense period of work pressure and stress when one finally takes a few days off work one succumbs to a head cold, sore throat and runny nose. It is essential always to bear in mind the close links between the HPA stress axis and the body's immune system.

Hormones not only affect organs and muscles throughout the body but also provide feedback and interact with the brain. Hormones of the ovaries, testes, thyroid and adrenals are small molecules that readily cross the blood/brain barrier. In the brain, one of their major actions is to provide a negative feedback signal. For example, when high enough levels of adrenal stress hormones (*glucocorticoids* or *cortisol* in humans) reach the hypothalamus, they provide a feedback signal to stop further stimulation to the HPA axis. In this regard, too, high concentrations of circulating glucocorticoids are monitored by the hippocampus, which sends negative feedback to the hypothalamus that inhibits its release of *corticoid-releasing hormone (CRH)*, thereby reducing eventual stress hormone release. In addition to their actions in negative feedback, hormones of the ovaries, testes, thyroid and adrenals have been shown to influence the functioning of our neurons as well as biochemistry and growth, both during development and in adulthood. Thus, the appropriate control of the pituitary releasing factors by the anterior pituitary is critical for numerous functions.

FIGURE 5.8 The hypothalamic–pituitary–adrenal gland (HPA) axis. In response to stress, the HPA axis is activated. The hypothalamus produces a hormone that stimulates the anterior pituitary to release another hormone into the blood stream. The adrenal gland then releases the stress hormone cortisol. Cortisol travels to the brain and shuts off the HPA axis via negative feedback.

Source: Hola Images/Getty Images, Inc.

Similar to the anterior pituitary, the posterior pituitary is also connected to the hypothalamus, this time by neuronal connections. The parts of the hypothalamus that communicate with the posterior pituitary do so by sending nerve impulses to the posterior pituitary. The posterior pituitary also plays a role in the endocrine system. Activation of the posterior pituitary leads to the release of hormones called *neuropeptides* into the bloodstream. These hormones are *oxytocin*, important for nursing, and *vasopressin*, important in regulating blood pressure. Brain oxytocin and vasopressin have been implicated in social behaviour, including forming a strong bond with your mate and caring for infants, as well as in stress responses (Donaldson & Young, 2008).

PSYCHOLOGY AROUND US   The Hippocampus as a Primary Site of Neurogenesis

The concept of neurogenesis has contributed a completely different understanding to previously held notions of brain development in a life-long perspective. The subventricular zone lines the lateral ventricles, where neural stem cells and progenitor generate new neurons (neuroblasts). Neurogenesis has been characterized in the cerebellum and in certain areas of the neocortex; the role of glial cells has been implicated. Figure 5.9 depicts neurogenesis in the subgranular zone, which is part of the dentate gyrus. Several studies have linked neurogenesis to the beneficial actions of specific antidepressants, suggesting a connection between decreased hippocampal neurogenesis and depression. Adult cell proliferation and neurogenesis are regulated differentially by genetic and epigenetic processes, and it has been established that the presentation of adult rodents to exercise regimes induces neurogenesis in hippocampal regions, such as the dentate gyrus, with overexpression of *brain-derived neurotrophic factor (BDNF)* with increased hippocampal dendritic arborization. BDNF is a neuroprotective agent critical for the survival, function and plasticity of neurons and has been linked to the age-related decline in neurogenesis with reductions in nerve growth factor as age increases. Physical exercise is involved with the regulation of neurogenesis in both the adult brain and the ageing brain. For example, it has been demonstrated that in 17- to 18-month-old female mice of the C57Bl/6 strain, housed under single or group housing arrangements with sedentary or running conditions, that a programme of voluntary exercise reduced stress and enhanced hippocampal cell proliferation (Kannangara *et al.*, 2011). It has been found that the rate of production of 'new cells' in the dentate gyrus of the hippocampus (which is something of an exception to the 'neurogenesis-unfriendly' environment of the adult brain) is reduced markedly in aged animals (Kuhn *et al.*, 1996). Since there are strong implications that neurogenesis may promote neuroplasticity, it is important to consider the necessity of interventions optimizing neurogenesis as treatment for Parkinson's disease, Alzheimer's disease and even for normal ageing.

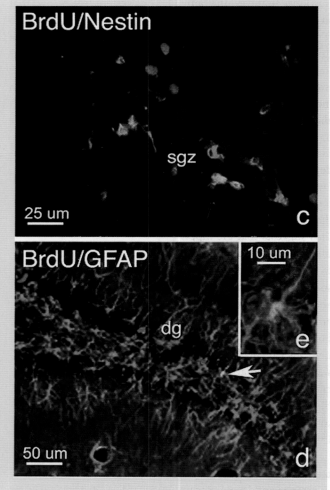

FIGURE 5.9 BDNF overexpression marking neurogenesis in mouse hippocampus.

The Amygdala

amygdala the area of the brain involved in processing information about emotions, particularly fear.

The **amygdala** is located deep within the brain, in a region referred to as the *temporal lobe* within the medial part of these lobes. Like the thalamus and hypothalamus, the amygdala is not a homogeneous structure. Instead, it is a collection of nuclei that serve different functions. The amygdala is involved in recognizing, learning about and responding to stimuli that induce fear (LeDoux, 2007). This region has been the focus of considerable attention by neuroscientists because it may be involved in the development of *phobias*, or abnormal fears, and is implicated also in the generation of various aggressive behaviours. In addition, the amygdala has been implicated in processing information about more positive emotions.

The Hippocampus

hippocampus the region of the brain that is important for certain types of learning and memory.

The amygdala communicates with the **hippocampus**, a proximal brain region important for certain types of complex learning and memory. Neuroscientists have extensively studied individuals with damage to the hippocampus and found that they are incapable of forming new *episodic* memories, or memories about events (described in more detail in Chapter 10). The hippocampus is intimately involved in the generation and maintenance of explicit or conscious memory that we are dependent upon on a daily basis for adequate functioning. Destruction of the hippocampus in adulthood does not wipe out all memories of early life or one's identity, merely those that occurred relatively close to the time of brain damage. This suggests that the hippocampus only temporarily stores information about events (Squire *et al.*, 2004). In addition to its role in the formation and transient storage of episodic memories, the hippocampus is important for learning about one's spatial environment. Learning how to navigate around a new campus, for instance, requires the hippocampus. Animal research shows that the hippocampus has neurons called *place cells*, groups of which are more active when the animal is located in a specific location (Moser *et al.*, 2008). Unlike the situation of the temporary role of the hippocampus in episodic memory, the hippocampus seems to retain its critical role in the storage of spatial navigation information for a long time, perhaps an entire lifetime.

The hippocampus appears not to consist of well-delineated collections of neurons or nuclei. Instead, it is organized in regions and layers. Because of the layered structure of the hippocampus, neuroscientists have been able to both record from and stimulate individual parts of the hippocampus, so that much of the function and connectivity of this brain region has been studied. The hippocampus is a major site of plasticity, or the ability of neurons to change, as we described earlier. Neurons in the hippocampus show both synaptic and structural plasticity. In fact, it is a region known to produce entirely new neurons in adulthood (Gould, 2007; Cameron & McKay, 2001). The function of these new neurons remains unknown, but their presence suggests that the adult brain is capable of regenerative processes, and furthermore that the process of neuron birth, or neurogenesis (which we discuss in more detail later in this chapter), may be harnessed for purposes of brain repair. We will return to the hippocampus at length when we discuss learning and memory in Chapters 9 and 10.

The Striatum and Basal Ganglia

striatum an area of the brain that works with the substantia nigra to enable fluid movements.

Located more towards the midline of the brain are the **striatum** and its related structures, the basal ganglia (Figure 5.10). This brain region works with the substantia nigra to produce fluid movements, such as those needed to jump up quickly while immersed in Facebook to answer the door. Damage to either of these brain regions produces a collection of debilitating motor symptoms, such as uncontrollable shaking (tremors). In addition to its role in movement, the striatum is important for certain types of learning and memory (Grahn *et al.*, 2008), namely those that do not require conscious awareness. The basal ganglia are associated with various more-or-less essential functions, including voluntary motor control, procedural learning relating to routine behaviours or 'habits' such as bruxism, implicit, non-conscious memory tasks (such as using a knife and fork or tying shoelaces), eye movements and cognitive or emotional functions. Current notions

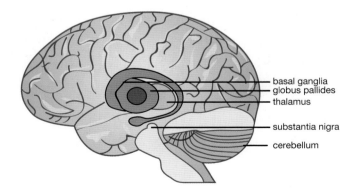

FIGURE 5.10 The basal ganglia and related structures of the brain. Includes thalamus, globus paladus, substantia nigra and cerebellum.

Source: John Henkel, from the Food and Drug Administration.

implicate the basal ganglia primarily in action selection; that is, the decision of which of several possible behaviours to execute at a given time.

The Nucleus Accumbens

Anterior to the striatum is a brain region called the **nucleus accumbens**, an area important for motivation and reward learning (Goto & Grace, 2008). It receives important communications from neurons in the midbrain. This circuitry is important for reward learning and has been implicated in drug abuse (Nestler, 2004). The nucleus accumbens presents a collection of neurons and forms the main part of the ventral striatum. It is thought to play an important role in reward, pleasure, laughter, addiction, aggression, fear and the placebo effect. The nucleus accumbens also receives important inputs from the prefrontal region of the frontal cortex (PFC); these inputs are covered by glutamatergic neurons and modulate the activity of dopamine (DA) neurons. It has been established that every single type of reward or pleasure results in the release of DA from the DA neuron terminal and the glutamatergic inputs from the PFC control this release. Damage to the PFC or excessive abuse of drugs like cocaine or heroin weakens the modulatory effects of the PFC and leads to serious behavioural problems.

> **nucleus accumbens** an area of the brain that is important for motivation and reward.

All of the above-mentioned brain regions are collectively referred to as *subcortical* because they are located beneath the largest and most complex part of the human brain: the neocortex.

The Neocortex

The human **neocortex** is huge, much too large to fit in the skull if it were stretched out. This is the reason why the human brain is all folded on the surface. The neocortex has many *convolutions*, or folds, that enable it to cram a large number of neurons into a head small enough to be supported by the human neck.

> **neocortex** the largest portion of the brain, responsible for complex behaviours, including language and thought.

The neocortex is highly developed in humans and is responsible for many of our most complex behaviours, including language and thought. Although some of the functions of neocortical regions are not well understood, there is consensus among neuroscientists that within the neocortex there is localization of function. This means that certain parts of the neocortex are important for specific behaviours or abilities.

At the most macroscopic level, the neocortex can be subdivided into four different parts, or *lobes*, as shown in Figure 5.11: occipital, temporal, parietal and frontal. Within each of these regions, there are two major classifications:

- *Primary sensory and/or motor areas.* These areas are responsible for processing basic information about the senses as well as for producing signals that lead to voluntary movement. As we will see, many of the primary sensory and motor parts of the neocortex process information related to the opposite, or *contralateral*, side of the body.

- *Association cortex.* **The association cortex** in each region is responsible for many complex functions, including higher-order sensory processing, integrating information from different senses (how you know that an object that looks like a violin is producing the music), thinking, planning and other complex functions.

> **association cortex** those areas of the neocortex responsible for complex functions, including higher-order sensory processing, thinking and planning.

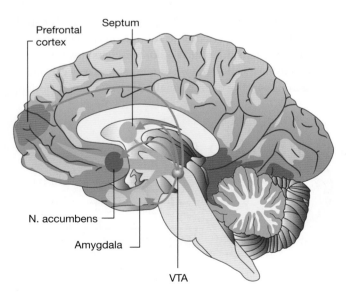

Prefrontal cortex — Septum — N. accumbens — Amygdala — VTA

Projections of the ventral tegmental area (VTA) to the prefrontal cortex, nucleus accumbens, septum and the amygdala; projection from the nuclear accumbens to the VTA via the medial forebrain bundle (MFB).

Source: http://lecerveau.mcgill.ca/flash/pop/pop_copy/pop_copy_i.html.

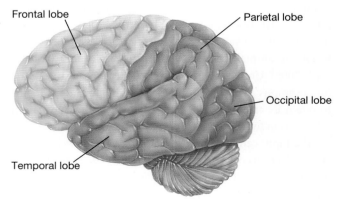

Frontal lobe — Parietal lobe — Occipital lobe — Temporal lobe

FIGURE 5.11 The lobes of the neocortex. The neocortex can be subdivided into four lobes: occipital, temporal, parietal and frontal.

The Occipital Cortex The **occipital cortex**, the cortical area at the back of the skull, contains primary sensory regions important for processing very basic information about visual stimuli, such as orientation and lines. As shown in Figure 5.12, visual information arrives in the occipital cortex via partially crossed connections. The visual information from each eye that is closest to the midline between the two eyes is actually projected to the opposite side of the

occipital cortex the lobe of the neocortex at the back of the skull, important for processing visual information.

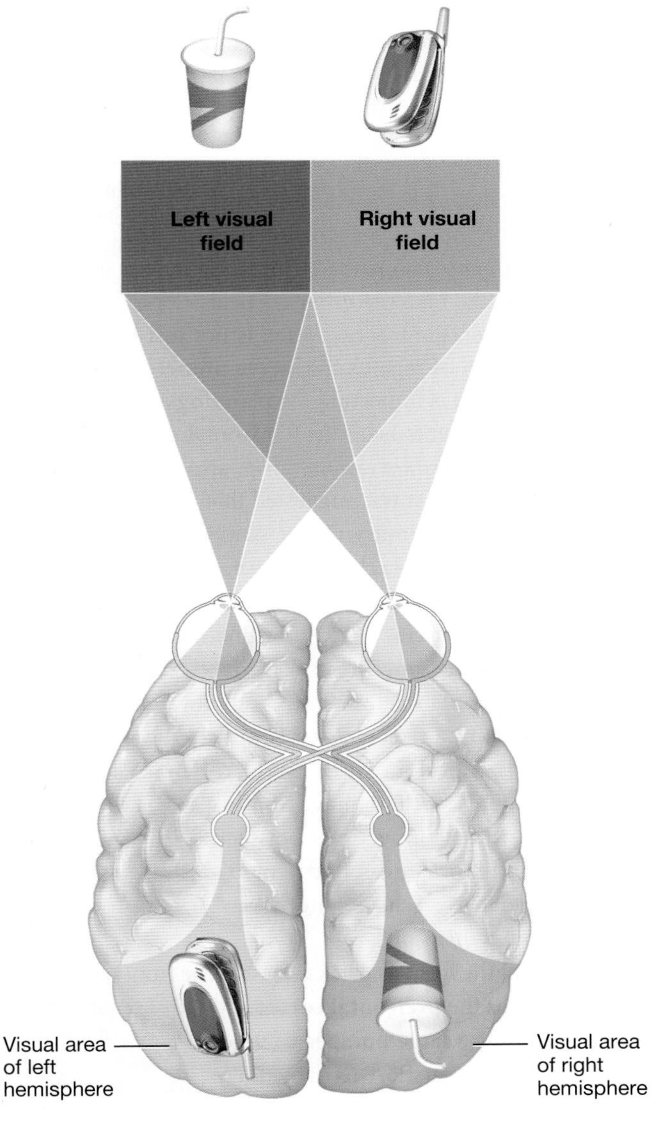

brain. As a result, the representation of your left visual field is on your right primary visual cortex, and vice versa.

Association areas in the occipital cortex integrate information about colour, complex patterns and motion. Since vision is such an important sense for primates, the occipital cortex is very well developed in humans. Although the occipital cortex is often referred to as the visual cortex, it is important to realize that visual information is also processed in other parts of the neocortex. In fact, some estimates suggest that 50% of the human neocortex is devoted to some sort of visual task. Connections to other parts of the neocortex enable us to connect visual information with information from other sensory modalities as well as with our memory stores (e.g. connecting the sight of a potato chip with its smell, taste, sound when crunched, feel and memories of having that type of food before). This serves as an important reminder that no brain region operates entirely on its own. Each receives input from other areas and communicates with many other regions to produce integrated responses.

The Temporal Cortex The **temporal cortex** is located on the sides of the head within the temporal lobe. It wraps around the hippocampus and amygdala. The temporal cortex includes areas important for processing information about *auditory stimuli*, or sounds. Abnormal electrical activity in the temporal cortex, such as what occurs with seizures or epilepsy, has been shown to result in auditory hallucinations. People who have epileptic seizures centred in this region sometimes 'hear' in their minds very loud music during seizures. Neurosurgery to remove a region causing seizures is particularly dangerous in this part of the brain since there are so many critical functions that may be disrupted.

temporal cortex the area of the neocortex important for processing sounds, speech comprehension and for recognizing complex visual stimuli, such as faces.

For instance, the temporal cortex also contains regions important for language comprehension (Damasio *et al.*, 2004). Shown in Figure 5.13, this area, called **Wernicke's area**, is located on the left side of the brain in the vast majority of humans (over 90%). (This is a good example of a phenomenon called *lateralization of function*, which means that the particular ability is localized to one side of the brain. We will return to this general issue later in the chapter.) Wernicke's area communicates with other areas, including a region located in another cortical area important for the recognition of appropriate syntax (language rules) and the production of speech.

Wernicke's area an area of the temporal cortex important for language comprehension.

In addition to the temporal cortex's involvement in hearing and language comprehension, this lobe plays important roles in learning and memory as well as in the recognition

FIGURE 5.12 The visual system is a partially crossed pathway. Visual cues from the temporal (towards the side) part of the visual field are sent to the opposite side of the brain, while those of the medial (towards the nose) part of the visual field are transmitted to the same side of the brain.

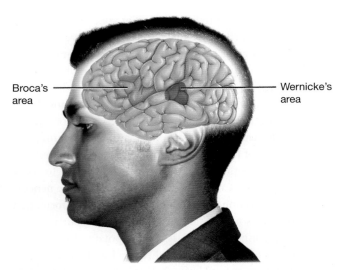

Broca's area

Wernicke's area

FIGURE 5.13 Major brain regions important for speech production and language comprehension. Broca's area, located in the frontal lobe, is critical for speaking and Wernicke's area, located in the temporal lobe, is critical for understanding language.

Source: Asia Images Group/Getty Images, Inc.

of objects using visual cues. Regions of the temporal cortex respond to complex visual stimuli, such as faces (Gross, 2005). Neuroimaging studies have shown that parts of this neural region are activated when people view photos of faces, particularly those of familiar faces. These findings are strengthened by the fact that recording electrodes placed into these same brain regions show changes in neuronal activity, or firing rate, when the same complex visual stimuli are presented (Seeck *et al.*, 1993). At first consideration, the presence of neurons that respond to faces in the temporal cortex may suggest that direct projections from the eye activate a set of cells in the temporal lobe that are programmed to respond to complex visual stimuli. This is not the case, though. The 'face cells' in the temporal cortex respond to faces because they receive inputs from visual areas in the occipital cortex as well as memory centres in the brain, allowing the recognition of faces previously seen.

parietal cortex the lobe of the neocortex involved in processing information related to touch and complex visual information, particularly locations.

somatosensory strip an area of the parietal cortex that processes tactile information coming from our body parts.

The Parietal Cortex The **parietal cortex** is localized on the upper-middle area of the brain. The primary sensory parts of this cortical region are critical for processing information about touch or somatosensory stimuli: our senses of touch, pressure, vibration and pain. The parietal cortex contains a region known as the **somatosensory strip**, a band of cortex that processes tactile information about different body parts. As Figure 5.14 shows, this area of the brain forms a systematic body map, but one in which some parts of the body are represented more than others. For instance, somatosensory information about the lips (which are particularly sensitive) occupies a greater amount of cortex than does somatosensory information about the elbow.

In addition, the parietal cortex plays an important role in the higher-order processing of visual stimuli. As we will see in Chapter 7, processing visual stimuli involves localizing visual cues in space. The parietal cortex contains a system known as the *where pathway* that enables us to see and respond to visual information in a spatially appropriate way. People with damage to the where pathway can find it impossible to pour water from a jug into a glass. This deficiency is not due to a motor disturbance but rather to an inability to properly determine where the glass is located relative to the jug.

The Frontal Cortex Located at the front of the brain (behind the forehead) is the **frontal cortex**. The frontal cortex is a relatively large cortical region and is proportionately larger in humans compared with less complex animals. Like the other cortical regions, however, the frontal cortex is not just one area but a large collection of regions that serve numerous functions. The frontal cortex is important for planning and movement. Voluntary movements begin in the frontal cortex, in a part referred to as the *primary motor strip*, also shown in Figure 5.14. For a long time it was suggested that stimulation of different parts of the primary motor strip invoked movement in specific groups of muscles. However, recent research suggests that parts of motor cortex are not just involved in contracting specific muscles but in coordinating the use of these muscles in complex movements (Graziano, 2006).

frontal cortex the lobe of the neocortex involved in many functions, including movement and speech production.

In addition to its role in controlling movement, the frontal cortex contains a region called **Broca's area**, which is critical for speech production. Individuals with damage to this region, or to the connections between Wernicke's and Broca's areas, find it impossible to generate speech, despite normal language comprehension.

Broca's area the region of the brain located in the frontal lobe that is important for speech production.

The part of the frontal cortex closest to the front of the head is referred to as the **prefrontal cortex** and is important for a large number of functions. Among them is short-term memory, or working memory (Soto *et al.*, 2008). When you are given a phone number and hold that number in your mind while you

prefrontal cortex the portion of the frontal cortex involved in higher-order thinking, such as memory, moral reasoning and planning.

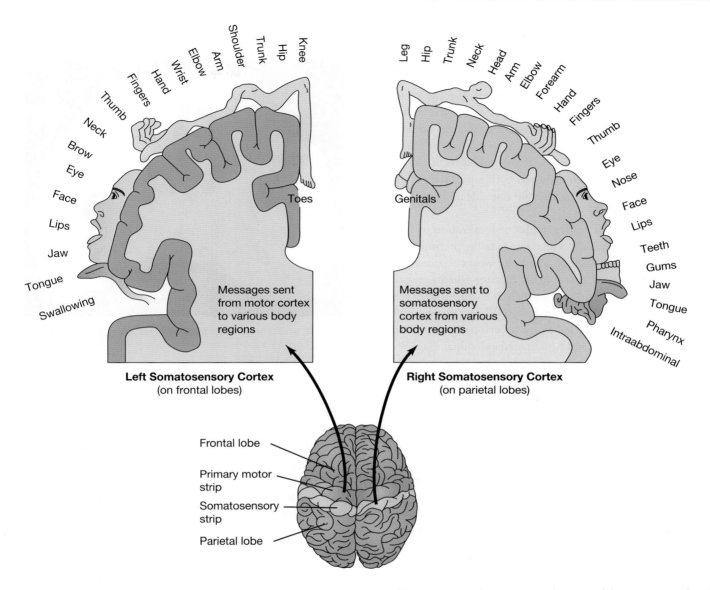

FIGURE 5.14 Motor and sensory cortices are organized according to body parts. Areas of motor cortex that control the movement of specific body parts and those of somatosensory cortex that receive tactile information are grouped according to body parts. Some regions are overrepresented, including the mouth and hands.

PSYCHOLOGY AROUND US   Brain Implants

With their ever-more-sophisticated knowledge of brain structure and function, neuroscientists are developing new methods to treat malfunctions in the brain. For example, scientists at the University of Pittsburgh are testing brain implants that they hope will enable paralysed patients to move prosthetic arms with their thoughts. In some of these experiments, electrodes implanted in the motor cortex will interpret patients' brain signals and send them to a computer, which will in turn control the movement of a prosthetic arm and hand. Persons who have suffered spinal cord damage, as discussed earlier in this chapter, may ultimately benefit from this research.

dial, you are using your prefrontal cortex. In addition, when you execute complex plans, such as planning a party and inviting friends, you are using your prefrontal cortex.

Moral reasoning (discussed in Chapter 4) has also been localized, at least in part, to a component of the prefrontal cortex. Children with damage to the prefrontal cortex can have difficulty understanding ethical principles despite normal IQ (Anderson *et al.*, 1999). The prefrontal cortex has also been implicated in some aspects of mood regulation. Studies have shown that individuals with a positive outlook on life tend to have more activity on one side of their prefrontal cortex (Urry *et al.*, 2004).

One of the earliest examples of localization of function involved an individual with damage to the prefrontal cortex. In the mid-19th century, a railroad worker named Phineas Gage experienced severe brain damage when a metal railroad spike penetrated his frontal lobes during an explosion. Gage miraculously recovered physically, but those who knew him previously reported that his personality was never the same again. Once a mild-mannered individual, Gage became short-tempered and prone to outbursts of anger. Cases such as this, as well as some experimental data, led to the suggestion that the prefrontal cortex is important for personality. Such claims, which did have some basis in fact but were perhaps overstated, led to the development of a once-popular procedure called a *prefrontal lobotomy*, which was used to treat individuals with problems ranging from severe mental illness to nonconformity and rebellion (Heller *et al.*, 2006). Owing to the lack of scientific basis and the side effects of its application, this surgery has (appropriately) fallen out of fashion. However, more limited destruction of the prefrontal cortex is still used for a small number of patients suffering from severe depression or other forms of mental illness who do not respond to drug therapy (Abosch & Cosgrove, 2008).

The four general regions of the neocortex can be further subdivided into many areas, which serve different functions and have different neural connections. However, all parts of the neocortex share some neuroanatomical features. The neocortex consists of six layers, whether occipital, temporal, parietal or frontal. Although some variations exist in the composition of the layers across regions, in general the output neurons (those that project to subcortical structures) are located in the deepest layers.

The Corpus Callosum

Communication from one side of the neocortex to the other occurs through a large structure called the **corpus callosum** (Figure 5.15).

corpus callosum the region of the brain that allows communication from one side of the neocortex to the other.

The corpus callosum appears to connect two relatively equal halves of the brain, called **hemispheres**, but the brain

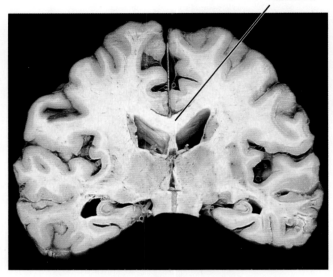

Corpus Callosum

FIGURE 5.15 The corpus callosum. This cross-section of the human brain shows the structure that allows communication between the two hemispheres.
Source: Courtesy of Mark Nielsen.

is actually not completely symmetrical, nor do the hemispheres work quite the way you might expect. For instance, you

hemispheres halves of the brain.

might expect the right hemisphere to control things that happen on the right half of the body, and the left to control the left. Things are not that simple, however. There are many crossed connections to and from the primary cortex, leading to asymmetries, or differences, in function between the hemispheres. Input from our visual, auditory and somatosensory systems is at least partially crossed, for example. The left part of the somatosensory cortex receives tactile input from the right part of the body, and vice versa. Crossed connections also contribute to asymmetries in the primary motor cortex. The left part of the primary motor cortex controls movement on the right part of the brain, and vice versa. Furthermore, as we describe later in this chapter, not everybody's hemispheres are the same. There are some fascinating individual differences in the two halves of our brain.

A treatment sometimes used when people have severe epilepsy is to sever the corpus callosum, to stop the spread of seizures from one side of the brain to the other. People who have undergone this surgery are called *split-brain patients*. These patients are normal in many respects, but they lack the ability to integrate information from the two hemispheres (Gazzaniga, 2005). Studies on these patients have highlighted the fact that the two hemispheres need the corpus callosum to communicate. Preventing this can sometimes result in one part of the brain acting in opposition to the other.

PSYCHOLOGY AROUND US   Do We Really Use Only 10% of Our Brains?

A popular claim about brain function is that we only use a small fraction of our brains while the rest lies dormant. Many claim that we could transcend what we commonly consider human limitations if we could only tap into the potential of this large, 'unused' percentage of the brain. The idea that we only use 10% of our brain is false and has no support at all in the scientific literature of today. In fact, scientists have shown that large parts of our brains are activated at all times, both during wakefulness and sleep.

The myth that we use very little of our brains was probably based, in part, on neuroscience studies done by the psychologist Karl Lashley in the early part of the 20th century (Lashley, 1929). Lashley showed that rats could learn some mazes even after very large parts of their brains had been removed. Those who supported this myth also pointed

out that in some instances large parts of the brain could be damaged in humans with little functional deficit; people with major brain damage often seemed wholly unaffected by their injuries.

It is important to consider that, although it may not be critical for solving a maze or carrying out another task, a brain region may be active nonetheless. Neuroimaging studies have shown that even when humans engage in relatively simple tasks, such as pressing an elevator button, visual, motor, memory and attention areas are activated. Thus, people without brain damage are actually using large areas of the brain in these tasks (Bédard & Sanes, 2009), even though we could get along without some of those regions if we had to.

The research is clear about the brain's activity: most of the brain is active, much of the time.

Before You Go On

What Do You Know?

6. Which part of the brain is essential to basic functioning, such as respiration?
7. Describe the role of the brain in regulating hormones throughout the body,
8. Which part of the brain has been linked with our fear responses?
9. What behaviour is most closely linked to the hippocampus?
10. Which of our senses is linked primarily with the occipital cortex? Which with the temporal cortex? Which with the parietal cortex?
11. What are the primary functions of Broca's and Wernicke's areas, and where are they located?
12. What mental functions are associated with the frontal cortex?

What Do You Think?

What are the potential pitfalls in making inferences about brain function from studying a single brain area?

Neurons and the Communication Systems of the Brain, Nervous System and Body

WHAT HAPPENS IN THE
BRAIN?

LEARNING OBJECTIVE 4

Describe the functions and subdivisions of the two major parts of the nervous system.

The human nervous system may be divided into two main parts: the central nervous system, which is made up of the brain and spinal cord, and the peripheral nervous system,

which is made up of the somatic and autonomic nervous systems (Figure 5.16). The *central nervous system*, with the brain and spinal cord, is concerned with analysis and decision-making. The *peripheral nervous system*, with nerves extending throughout our bodies, ensures that information is brought and sent back and forth between the periphery (for instance, your fingers) and the central nervous system.

The Integrated Brain

It is important to remember that many of the above-mentioned brain areas, including the cortical regions, can be divided into

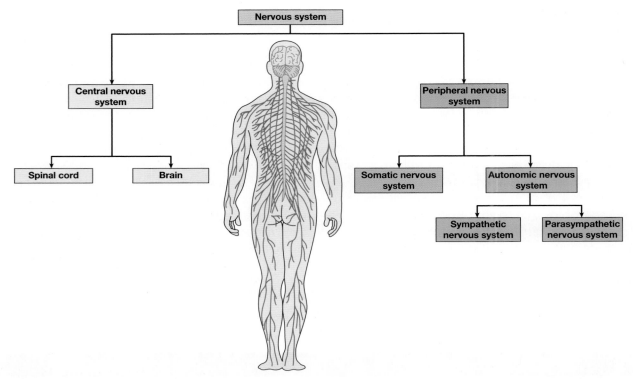

FIGURE 5.16 Organizations of the nervous system. The nervous system is divided into the central nervous system (consisting of the brain and spinal cord) and the peripheral nervous system (consisting of the somatic nervous system and the autonomic nervous system). The autonomic nervous system is further divided into the sympathetic and parasympathetic nervous systems.

Source: Adapted with permission of John Wiley & Sons, Inc., from Huffman, K. (2010). *Psychology in Action* (9th edn). Hoboken, NJ: John Wiley & Sons, Inc, p. 64.

multiple areas or nuclei, each of which is involved in different functions. However, no brain region works alone. To process information, integrate it with previous information and then formulate and execute a reaction requires neural circuitry undoubtedly not contained within a single brain region. For example, a person whose brain contained only a hippocampus would not be able to store information about anything because it would lack the sensory pathways necessary to provide stimuli about events or the spatial environment. Understanding how a brain region works requires sophisticated knowledge about information that flows into the area, that which flows out of the areas and, of course, the important computations that occur within the neurons of the given brain region.

The Spinal Cord The *spinal cord* extends from the base of the brain down the back. The spinal cord is very important for gathering information from the body and sending it to the brain as well as for enabling the brain to control the movement of the body.

As described earlier, the somatic nervous system works together with the central nervous system to integrate sensory information with motor output. In most cases, this integration involves the brain (voluntary movement, for example,

requires the brain). However, some very basic functions, including reflexes, involve just the somatic nervous system and the spinal cord.

Have you ever stepped on something sharp, possibly a tack, and pulled your foot back before you even got a chance to yell 'ouch'? Shortly afterwards, you felt the pain, which may even have brought tears to your eyes. The rapid reaction of withdrawing your foot is the result of activity in the pain reflex circuit of your spinal cord. The delayed emotional reaction comes from activation of brain regions that produce a much larger, and therefore slower, circuit. As shown in Figure 5.17, simple circuits consisting of three neurons can control pain reflexes without any communication with the brain. These simple circuits include a sensory neuron that communicates with the spinal cord; a connecting cell, called an interneuron; and a motor neuron that connects to muscles in the body.

Spinal Cord Injuries OUT OF THE **ORDINARY**

In addition to controlling simple reflexes, the spinal cord is very important for carrying sensory information up to the brain and motor information back out to the body. When the

Exercise Intervention for Neurogenesis Regarding Brain Structure and Function

Daily physical exercise holds great benefits, not only because it improves our quality of life and physical strength but also because it offers manifest benefits for brain regional structure integrity (not least hippocampus) and improved functional performance (such as cognition and emotional resilience), as observed from both human and laboratory animal studies (Kramer *et al.*, 1999; Fordyce & Weiner, 1993). The generality of benefits endowed by physical exercise/activity have been established in a variety of settings, over species, age and health conditions. For example, in the laboratory setting, Clark *et al.* (2011) show that regular wheel-running exercise increased neurogenesis in mice from 12 different isogenic strains, although the magnitude of effect depended markedly on genotype. The authors suggest that genetic contributions to hippocampal neurogenesis imply eventual identification of genes and pathways associated with enhanced neuroplastic responses to exercise. Physical exercise has been defined as planned, regular and structured physical activity that fulfils the purpose of improving one or more aspects of physical fitness, health and functional capacity. It may be any

or all activity that generates force through muscular activity that disrupts a homeostatic state. The advantages offered by regular physical exercise have been demonstrated both in structure/function domains and in brain biomarker integrity (Archer, 2012, 2011; Archer *et al.*, 2012, 2011a, 2011b, 2010; Archer & Fredriksson, 2011, 2010; Archer & Kostrzewa, 2011; Fredriksson *et al.*, 2010). Adherence to physical exercise schedules facilitates the efficacy and longevity of healthy functioning in both cognitive and emotional domains. Several mechanisms and a range of moderating factors attest to the utility of physical activity in childhood and adolescence and maintained through early, middle and late adulthood. Neurogenesis, neurotrophic factors and angiogenesis (the development of cerebral vascular systems) or stress and depression during ageing may facilitate or compromise the palliative effects of physical exercise upon health variables in young and old individuals The principle of either maintaining (through exercise) or losing (through a lack of exercise) healthy brain tissue remains the beacon that guides current notions of the essential role of exercise.

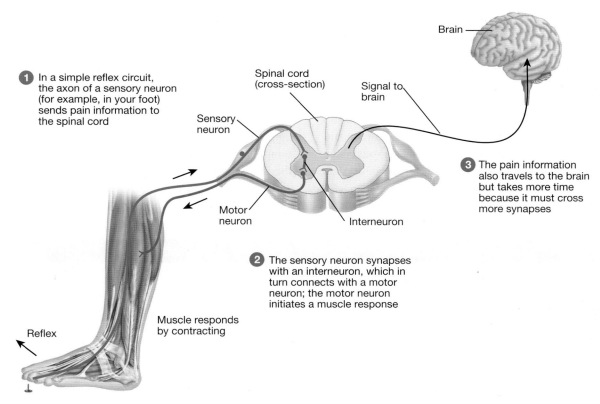

1 In a simple reflex circuit, the axon of a sensory neuron (for example, in your foot) sends pain information to the spinal cord

Spinal cord (cross-section)

Signal to brain

Brain

Sensory neuron

3 The pain information also travels to the brain but takes more time because it must cross more synapses

Motor neuron

Interneuron

2 The sensory neuron synapses with an interneuron, which in turn connects with a motor neuron; the motor neuron initiates a muscle response

Muscle responds by contracting

Reflex

FIGURE 5.17 The reflex circuit of the spinal cord. Sensory information travels into the spinal cord, where it communicates with interneurons. Interneurons send information to the motor neurons, which then send impulses back out to the body to induce movement.

spinal cord is damaged such that the flow of information to and from the brain is disrupted, individuals become paralysed, as well as incapable of noticing touch or pain sensations on the body. The higher up the spinal cord the damage occurs (the closer it occurs to the brain), the larger the proportion of the body that is paralysed. Thus, when people break their necks and permanently damage the spinal cord close to the brain, they lose touch and pain sensation everywhere but their heads and faces, and they become *quadriplegic* (paralysed everywhere but the head and neck). If the damage occurs farther down the back, then they may retain sensation and use of the upper limbs and torso but not of the lower limbs.

Since spinal cord damage is so devastating and affects such a large number of young people, scientists have directed attention to finding ways to enhance regeneration of connections in the spinal cord, as well as the potential replenishment of motor neurons destroyed by injury (Barnabé-Heider & Frisén, 2008). Although some progress has been made in the treatment of spinal cord injury, there is much work to be done. In most cases, spinal cord injury results in permanent loss of function.

The Peripheral Nervous System

The peripheral nervous system includes the somatic nervous system and the autonomic nervous system. The **somatic nervous system** consists of all of the nerves that gather sensory information (typically about touch and pain) from all over the body, neck and head and deliver it to the spinal cord and brain, as well as the nerves that send information about movement from the central nervous system to the muscles of the body, neck and head. As we will soon see, the somatic nervous system does not serve any function without the integrating capacity of the central nervous system. Even very simple reflexes require the central nervous system.

By contrast, parts of the **autonomic nervous system** operate, in large part, without help from the central nervous system. The

> **somatic nervous system** all the peripheral nerves that send information about the senses and movement to and from the central nervous system.

autonomic nervous system can be divided into two parts: the *sympathetic nervous system* and *parasympathetic nervous system*. Both parts of the autonomic nervous system consist of nerve cells and their axons distributed throughout the body. However, they serve opposing functions. The sympathetic nervous system is activated under conditions of stress, whereas the parasympathetic nervous system is inhibited during those times but active during more restful times.

The **sympathetic nervous system** is responsible for the 'fight-or-flight' reaction, the physiological response that enables us to respond to potentially life-threatening situations. The **parasympathetic nervous system**, on the other hand, is important for controlling basic functions that occur when the individual is not at immediate risk. For instance, digestion is a function under the control of the parasympathetic nervous system. Not surprisingly, when stressful situations occur and the sympathetic nervous system is activated, digestion stops. This makes good adaptive sense. Energy spent digesting food could be used for other functions (such as increasing blood flow to the leg muscles) so that you can escape the threatening situation.

Sometimes, the sympathetic nervous system is activated when we are not necessarily at risk of bodily harm. We may instead be in social situations where our major fear is humiliation, such as responding appropriately when a friend posts an embarrassing photo of us on their Facebook page.

Some aspects of the autonomic nervous system, such as the components that regulate digestion, are active without input from the central nervous system. Activation of the sympathetic nervous system definitely requires input from the brain, however, since we need our brains to recognize and respond to an experience as stressful. We talk more about the role of the brain in stress in Chapter 18.

> **autonomic nervous system** the portion of the peripheral nervous system that includes the sympathetic and parasympathetic nervous systems.

> **sympathetic nervous system** the division of the autonomic nervous system active during times of stress.

> **parasympathetic nervous system** the division of the autonomic nervous system active during restful times.

Before You Go On

What Do You Know?

13. What are the two parts of the central nervous system?

14. What happens when the sympathetic nervous system is operating? How does that compare to the operation of the parasympathetic nervous system?

15. How do the brain and spinal cord work together?

16. What neuron types are important for simple reflexes?

17. What determines how much disability will result from a spinal cord injury?

What Do You Think?

Describe an occasion when you have experienced the workings of the sympathetic nervous system. Have you ever been able to control your sympathetic or parasympathetic reactions? If so, how?

Building the Brain

LEARNING OBJECTIVE 5

Describe neurogenesis, synaptogenesis and programmed cell death, and explain their roles during development and throughout the lifespan.

Development of the nervous system begins during the embryonic phase of prenatal life, before we are born, and continues throughout the lifespan.

Brain Development Before We Are Born

Embryos have three layers of rather undefined tissue that later specialize to become all of our recognizable body parts. Nervous tissue originates from one of the layers, called the *ectoderm*. A portion of the ectoderm thickens and eventually folds to form a tube called the **neural tube**. As cells lining the wall of the neural tube divide and produce more cells, eventually the process of *differentiation* begins. Differentiation refers to the achievement of characteristics specific to a certain type of cell, in this case a neuron. The production of new neurons is called **neurogenesis**.

Progenitor cells are formed near the centre of the neural tube and migrate away from their original 'birth-site' to create new brain regions (Figure 5.18). The migrating young neurons can travel in several different ways, including moving along the specialized glia, called *radial glia* (Marín & Rubenstein,

> **neural tube** area of an embryo from which the central nervous system arises.

> **neurogenesis** the production of new neurons.

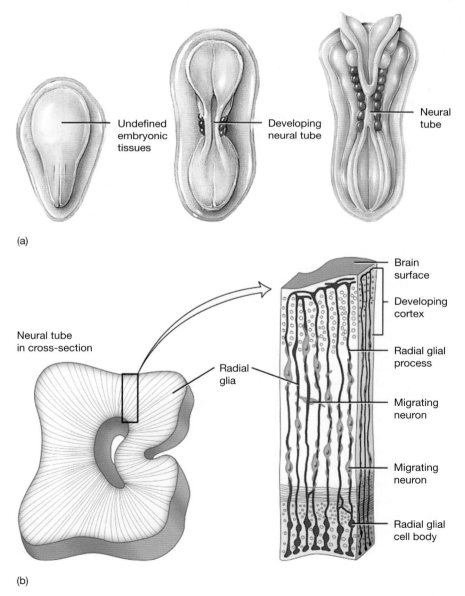

(a)

(b)

FIGURE 5.18 How the nervous system develops. (a) The brain and spinal cord originate from the embryotic neural tube. (b) Neurons are born in tissue that surrounds the central canal (the ventricle) and migrate away from the centre to build the central nervous system.

2003). They can also move along axons of other neurons that have already been formed or travel through the extracellular space itself.

As these progenitor cells become established in areas where certain brain regions are forming, they grow axons and dendrites and quickly make synaptic contact with other neurons. It is important to consider that progenitor cells must become established in programmed positions accord-

apoptosis cell death that is preprogrammed.

synaptogenesis the process of forming new synapses.

ing to a predetermined pattern. Failure to do will result in **apoptosis**, preprogrammed cell death. The process of forming new synapses is called **synaptogenesis**. Gradually, through neurogenesis and synaptogenesis, a young brain is formed. Many of its functions, including hearing and touch, work even before we are born.

It seems most intuitive that brain development would require mostly constructive processes: a new brain needs to synthesize new neurons and those new neurons need to make dendrites, axons and synapses. However, neuroscientists were surprised to find that destructive cellular events are just as important for brain development as are constructive cellular events. During development, our brains overproduce neurons in large numbers. The extra, unused neurons are culled in the process of apoptosis (Levi-Montalcini, 1988). In some brain regions, cell death claims the lives of over three-quarters of the neurons originally produced by the brain.

Why would the brain waste so much energy making neurons only to kill them off? The answer seems to be that producing a large number of neurons will ensure that a reasonable number make appropriate connections. Those that fail to make the necessary connections ultimately die. Developmental cell death is special because it involves the activation of a programme of suicide genes within the neuron itself (Steller, 1995). Importantly, it does not trigger any of the inflammation or reactive events that occur with other types of cell death as a result of trauma. For example, developmental cell death does not attract microglia or astroglia, nor does it lead to the formation of a glial scar. This ensures that the young neurons that did not make an appropriate connection were eliminated without adversely affecting that region of the brain.

Of those neurons that survive, most undergo some form of regressive structural remodelling before development is complete. That is, many neurons initially develop more dendrites and synapses, or more elaborate axons, than they will eventually need. Only those that are necessary and make appropriate connections survive (Luo & O'Leary, 2005). The rest are retracted and reabsorbed, so that in the long-term the brain spends energy only on those circuits that work most efficiently.

Drinking for Two Rapid brain development puts the foetus at risk of exposure to toxins that can disrupt the coordinated format ion of neural circuitry. One of the most common problems associated with exposure to a developmental toxin is *foetal alcohol syndrome (FAS)*. Babies whose mothers drank a lot of alcohol during pregnancy are often born with stunted growth and cognitive deficits. FAS can range from moderate to severe and is often associated with other symptoms that indicate abnormal brain development, such as impulsive behaviour and lack of motor coordination. Alcohol is known to have growth-inhibiting effects on the brain, stopping the production of neurons and their formation of connections. It has been shown that alcohol is an effective antagonist of the neurotransmitter glutamic acid and, during the brain's development, alcohol blocks the glutamic acid signal in the foetus that is essential for the prevention of apoptosis. Since scientists have no clear idea about how much alcohol is too much, the general advice given to pregnant women is to avoid drinking alcohol completely during pregnancy.

Brain Development across the Lifespan

For humans, many of the cellular events, such as neurogenesis, neuronal migration, dendrite formation, axon extension, synaptogenesis and their regressive counterparts that take place before birth reflect the unfolding of a programmed, maturational plan that can only be altered by toxic influences, such as the ingestion of drugs or alcohol by a pregnant woman. Although there are some interesting exceptions, presented in Chapters 7 and 9, that describe evidence of foetal sensation and learning, our brains are generally much more open to being physically shaped by our experiences after rather than before we are born. Both progressive and regressive developmental events occur after birth, too; these are affected by experience. For example, our experiences may determine which synapses are maintained and which are pruned during infancy and childhood.

Other events, such as myelination, occur at different points in our development, depending on the brain region. As described in Chapter 3, myelination in humans occurs mostly after we are born. It begins relatively rapidly in some of the primary sensory areas and continues through late adolescence or early adulthood. Myelination of the prefrontal cortex, for example, is not finished until after puberty, which may explain why adolescents are generally less efficient at planning and executing complex behaviours than adults are.

You may think that developmental events in the nervous system stop once you become an adult. In fact, a very common myth about the brain is that you have

PSYCHOLOGY AROUND US   Dying Cells in a New Brain?

Early neuroanatomists studied growth and development of the nervous systems in a variety of species. One important developmental phenomenon they overlooked, however, was the role of cell death in sculpting the brain. It was not until the 1940s that an Italian medical doctor, Rita Levi-Montalcini, began investigating this possibility.

Ousted from her post at the Turin medical school during World War II because she was Jewish, Levi-Montalcini (1988) made a discovery that changed how we view brain development and eventually led to her winning a Nobel Prize. Though she was under constant threat of deportation and death, Levi-Montalcini continued to study neural development in her apartment, using fertilized eggs from a nearby farm as her experimental animal. Through careful microscopic work, she was the first to discover that neurons are overproduced during development and that neural circuits are sculpted by cell death, as we described in this chapter.

She was also able to determine which neurons were most likely to survive. The survival of a new neuron, she found, was critically dependent on whether it made contact with an appropriate target site. Levi-Montalcini found that amputating a limb bud from a developing chick embryo resulted in the survival of fewer motor neurons, whereas grafting an extra limb to a developing chick embryo led to the survival of more neurons.

Levi-Montalcini eventually made it to the United States, where she was the first to identify trophic factors, the chemicals that promote neuron growth. In 1986, she was awarded the Nobel Prize in medicine. She later returned to Italy, where she continues her active life, serving in the Italian Senate past the age of 100.

all of the neurons you will ever have once you are born and any that die cannot be replaced. Neuroscientists have overturned this fallacy by showing that some populations of neurons continue to be produced well into adulthood (Gould, 2007).

As discussed earlier in this chapter, a brain region that exhibits substantial neurogenesis in adulthood is the hippocampus (Cameron & McKay, 2001). Adult neurogenesis may be important for the functions of the hippocampus, which, as we saw earlier, is involved in learning and memory (Leuner *et al.*, 2006). Although still a controversial issue, it is possible that the plastic nature of new neurons may provide the substrate needed for us to change as a result of our experiences; in other words, to learn.

In addition to the incorporation of entirely new neurons into existing neural circuits, the adult brain also shows evidence of ongoing dendritic remodelling (McEwen, 2001) and synaptogenesis, or forming of new synapses (Cooke & Woolley, 2005). Although evidence for these changes was first observed decades ago, using traditional methods of examining brain sections under the microscope, subsequent studies using genetically engineered mice with fluorescent neurons have allowed researchers to examine and determine the size and shape of individual neurons in live animals through transparent windows implanted into their skulls. These studies have confirmed the earlier reports by showing that dendrites and synapses change in shape, size and number throughout adult life (Knott *et al.*, 2006).

The extent to which this structural plasticity contributes to normal brain function remains unknown, but its occurrence indicates that the adult brain is not a rigid, static place. Researchers studying structural plasticity in the adult brain hope that identifying the mechanisms controlling these events may someday help us to actually change the shape and connections of neurons in order to repair circuits that are abnormal as a result of brain damage or birth defects.

Before You Go On

What Do You Know?
18. How are neurons formed before we are born?
19. What is synaptogenesis? Does it ever stop?

What Do You Think?
What advantages does cell death have for the developing brain?

Brain Side and Brain Size

LEARNING OBJECTIVE 6

Discuss what neuroscience evidence tells us about brain lateralization and the significance of brain size.

You may have heard popular theories about 'left-brained' or 'right-brained' types of people, or jokes about the female brain versus the male brain. Neuroscience tells us that, although the importance of them may be exaggerated in the public mind, there are, indeed, some differences among the brains of different groups of individuals.

Differences in Brain Lateralization

In most people, there are some parts of cortex that exist only on one side of the brain. Wernicke's and Broca's areas related to speech and language, for example, are on the left side of most people's brains, but not everybody's. The exceptions occur most often in left-handed individuals. Left-handers are more likely to have these language areas located on the right side of their brains, or on both sides, than are right-handers, suggesting that lateralization of more than one function (handedness and language) may be linked in some way.

Right or Left? Are you one of those people who are so right-hand dominant that they cannot really use their left hands for anything that involves fine coordination? (You can test this by trying to write neatly with your left hand.) If so, the chances are that your language areas are located exclusively on the left side of your brain. You are also a member of a large majority: worldwide, it is estimated that around 90%

of people are right-hand dominant. Handedness has generally been considered an inherited trait, but environment may also play a role in its development.

In addition to these rather clear-cut functional and anatomical asymmetries, many people believe that more general thought processes are lateralized, such that people who think a certain way are using proportionately more of one side of their brain than they are the other side. Although this remains controversial, the conventional view has always been that individuals who rely heavily on their right brain are more likely to be creative and use abstract reasoning and imagery to solve problems. This side of the brain is thought to be dominant in artists and engineers. By contrast, the left side of the brain is thought to be dominant in individuals with strong analytical and verbal skills. This distinction is so popular that it is difficult to separate fact from fiction.

What then is the scientific evidence for right-brain and left-brain dominant thinking? Neuroscientists have been able to temporarily inactivate one hemisphere, by infusing drugs into the circulatory system that feeds that side of the brain, in order to determine which functions are affected most and fastest. Another way neuroscientists study the hemispheres is by taking advantage of the fact that part of the visual field of each eye crosses over to the opposite side of the brain. Researchers can present visual stimuli to only one hemisphere by requiring the participant to fixate on a point and/or use a special contact lens. They then ask participants to complete a task using just one side of the brain.

Studies such as these have shown that the right-brain/left-brain dichotomy is only a general theme, and there are notable exceptions. For instance, the right brain, which is typically believed to excel at spatial perceptual tasks, is actually less accurate at making some spatial perceptual distinctions,

---

PRACTICALLY SPEAKING   How Can You Prevent Age-Related Decline in Brain Function?

A common adage used today with regard to the ageing brain is 'Use it or lose it!' Stories in the media encourage ageing individuals to keep their brains active by spending time on crossword puzzles, Sudoku or other brainteasers. Some companies have even developed and marketed brain puzzles they claim are specifically designed to keep the brain agile and prevent declines in a wide range of general cognitive abilities, such as day-to-day problem-solving and memory.

Unfortunately, the scientific evidence available does not support these claims. While it is true that people with a higher level of education and those with multiple interests and socially active lives seem somewhat protected from age-related cognitive dysfunction (Perneczky et al., 2008), there

is no evidence that engaging in brain puzzles is beneficial for any purpose other than making you better at solving similar brain puzzles. In other words, mastery of these tasks does not generalize to overall cognitive performance.

One type of experience, however, that does seem to make a difference in cognitive performance is physical exercise. In humans, aerobic exercise increases blood flow to the brain, improves performance on cognitive tasks and elevates mood (Pereira et al., 2007). Studies in experimental animals have shown that physical exercise increases the birth of new neurons in the hippocampus and stimulates the growth of neurons in general throughout brain structures that support cognitive function (Stranahan et al., 2006, 2007).

such as determining the location of objects in relation to one another. Overall, the research shows that, aside from the language areas noted above, the two hemispheres are more similar than they are different. Indeed, even when right/left differences are detected in function, these differences are usually relative. For example, the left brain can accomplish what the right brain can accomplish; it is just less efficient at some tasks and more efficient at others.

Gender Differences

On average, the brains of women are smaller than those of men. Does this mean men are smarter than women? It does not. The overall size of the brain appears to be more closely related to the size of the body than to function. In fact, a relationship between brain size and intelligence does not exist, except at the two ends of the spectrum; people with

abnormally small or abnormally large brains are both more likely to exhibit mental deficiencies than those with brains whose size falls within the normal range.

In addition to the overall size difference, researchers have reported some differences in the size of certain brain regions in humans. For example, part of the corpus callosum, the bundle of axons connecting the two hemispheres of the brain, has been shown to be larger in women (Johnson *et al.*, 1994). This finding has contributed to the much-overstated suggestion that women are more likely to use both sides of their brains than men. Even in cases where differences have been reported in the size of brain regions, the overall differences between men and women are very small, so much so that they really do not tell us much about the individual person of either gender. An exception to this exists in the hypothalamus, where certain nuclei that control the release of reproductive hormones differ in men and women.

Before You Go On

What Do You Know?

20. What does research show about 'right-brained' creative thinking versus 'left-brained' analytical thinking?

21. On which side of the brain do most people have their language-related areas? What about left-handed people?

22. Does overall brain size matter in how well brains function?

What Do You Think?

What are some of the ethical problems associated with searching for structural differences in the brains of different groups of people?

Neurological Diseases

 OUT OF THE ORDINARY

LEARNING OBJECTIVE 7

Describe four neurological disorders and the current directions in research for treating them.

In general, diseases of the nervous system can be divided into two broad classes characterized by the type of physician designated to care for the patient. These classes are psychiatric illnesses and neurological illnesses. In the case of psychiatric illnesses, such as depression and schizophrenia, the underlying problem is often thought of as primarily a biochemical or neurotransmitter imbalance. In the case of neurological illnesses, such as Parkinson's disease and Alzheimer's disease

(discussed in Chapter 10), the main problem is thought to be structural, generally involving the degeneration of neurons. Although there is certainly overlap between these two classes of brain diseases – for example, persons with depression are known to have a smaller hippocampus (Sheline *et al.*, 2003) and persons with Parkinson's disease have a deficiency in the neurotransmitter dopamine (Jankovic & Aguilar, 2008) – this general distinction holds true. Because psychiatric diseases are taken up in other chapters of this book, we will focus here on some key neurological diseases.

- **Multiple sclerosis** involves demy-elination, or loss of myelin, on the axons of neurons. This leads to

multiple sclerosis
neurological disease that causes a loss of myelin on the axons of neurons.

the inefficient transmission of electrical information among neurons and a range of symptoms, including vision loss, pain and muscle weakness, depending on where the demyelination occurs. Research on multiple sclerosis has focused on finding ways to stimulate myelination (Franklin & Ffrench-Constant, 2008).

amyotrophic lateral sclerosis (ALS or Lou Gehrig's disease) a neurological disease that causes degeneration of motor neurons in the spinal cord, leading to loss of movement and eventual death.

- **Amyotrophic lateral sclerosis** (ALS, also called Lou Gehrig's disease) is another condition that affects movement. People with ALS experience degeneration of motor neurons in the spinal cord. The symptoms of this disease begin with localized muscle weakness and, ultimately, the entire body is afflicted. People with ALS typically die when the motor neurons that control basic functions, including breathing, die.

- Interestingly, some populations of motor neurons appear to be more resistant to ALS than others. Examples of the resistant populations include the cells that control eye movements (Laslo *et al.*, 2001) and those that are involved in motor control of the anus and genitals (Mannen *et al.*, 1982). Investigators are studying these neuron groups to determine whether molecular differences between vulnerable and resistant populations of cells can be used to stimulate protective mechanisms in motor neurons that degenerate in this devastating disease.

PSYCHOLOGY AROUND US   **The Importance of Helmets**

Lou Gehrig was a legendary baseball player who was a member of the New York Yankees from 1925 to 1939, when he retired because of failing health. Gehrig had developed symptoms of ALS, which was later named Lou Gehrig's disease for that reason. However, scientists now think that Lou Gehrig may not have had ALS. Instead, he may have developed symptoms that were similar to those of ALS because he was so often hit in the head with baseballs (he played before batting helmets were required). Gehrig lost consciousness on many such occasions, as well as during fights on the baseball field. Repeated head trauma, particularly when associated with loss of consciousness, can lead to the death of motor neurons. Head trauma can kill other groups of neurons, too, and produce a different set of symptoms. Many athletes, including football players and boxers, have been initially diagnosed with Parkinson's disease or Alzheimer's disease but have later had these diagnoses changed when it became clear that their symptoms were due to repeated brain damage.

Parkinson's disease a neurological disease that involves the death of dopaminergic neurons in the substantia nigra, leading to tremors, muscle rigidity and other motor problems.

- **Parkinson's disease** is a neurological condition that involves the death of dopaminergic neurons (those that rely on the neurotransmitter dopamine) in the substantia nigra. Patients with this condition often have a tremor in their hands and muscle rigidity. Parkinson's disease can have many different causes and affects a relatively large percentage of the population. In most cases, however, the cause is not known and thus the disorder is referred to as *idiopathic*. What is well known is that the disorder involves a massive loss of the neurotransmitter dopamine.

People with Parkinson's disease can be treated with drugs that replace the dopamine that is lost when the neurons in the substantia nigra die. However, this replacement is only temporary. As time passes, patients become resistant to the dopamine drugs and/or develop intolerable side effects to the drugs. Because drug therapy is only temporary and so many people suffer from the condition, scientists have spent considerable effort searching for novel therapies. Among them are the transplantation of stem cells, which can be induced to produce new neurons that make dopamine. Although these treatments are promising, there is much work to be done before they can be used routinely (Isacson & Kordower, 2008).

- **Huntington's disease** is an inherited condition that results in the death of neurons in the striatum. People suffering from this disease exhibit awkward movements and, often, symptoms of psychosis (Paulsen, 2009). Like ALS and Parkinson's disease, Huntington's disease is progressive and, as yet, there is no cure.

Huntington's disease an inherited neurological condition that results in the death of neurons in the striatum.

Transplanting Stem Cells to Treat Neurological Disorders

Medical and neuroscience researchers have not yet developed truly effective medicines for these devastating neurological diseases, so some neuroscientists have turned their attention to the possibility of repairing damaged brain regions by transplanting new tissue into the brain.

Early work ruled out the possibility of transplanting fully differentiated brain tissue into a damaged region. In most cases, these transplants did not survive or integrate properly into the existing circuitry. Subsequent attempts to transplant foetal brain tissue into the brains of adults suffering from Alzheimer's or Parkinson's disease also met with limited, if any, success. Foetal tissue may integrate into the damaged brain, but it remains foreign and often does not function normally for extended periods.

stem cells
undifferentiated cells that can divide to replace themselves and create new cells that have the potential to become all other cells of the body, including neurons.

Thus, transplantation research has focused primarily on the possibility of restoring damaged circuits by transplanting stem cells. **Stem cells**, as described earlier, are undifferentiated cells that have the potential to grow into any cell type if given the appropriate environmental cues. The most versatile stem cells come from embryonic tissue (Srivastava *et al.*, 2008). Researchers have obtained stem cells from embryos created as part of in vitro fertilization, a procedure sometimes used to help infertile couples have babies. Eggs are fertilized with sperm in the laboratory, and some of the resulting embryos are implanted into a woman's uterus. Remaining, or extra, embryos, at very early stages of development, can provide a source for stem cells. This source, however, is very controversial among those who question whether the embryos could be considered humans yet. Because, as we will see, stem-cell research has shown great promise, researchers are now working to find other sources of stem cells, including reproducing them from adult tissue.

Thus far, stem-cell transplantation studies in animals have been successful in some cases, particularly in animal models of Parkinson's disease (Takahashi *et al.*, 2009; Hovakimyan *et al.*, 2008). The effectiveness of stem-cell treatment may depend on what kind of brain cell is damaged and where the damaged cells are located. For instance, Parkinson's disease arises predominantly from the death of dopaminergic neurons in the substantia nigra. Thus, restoring this population of neurons, providing they make appropriate connections and synthesize the correct neurotransmitter, is likely to repair the deficit. Other neurological diseases that cause more widespread damage may not respond as well. For example, patients with Alzheimer's disease (which we discuss in some detail in Chapter 10) lose neurons throughout their brains. The disease also causes the formation of abnormal clusters of non-degradable protein that interfere with neuronal function (Rafii & Aisen, 2009). Replacing only certain types of dead neurons may not be sufficient to overcome the widespread devastation characteristic of this disease.

Before You Go On

What Do You Know?

23. What goes wrong in the nervous system to cause multiple sclerosis, ALS, Parkinson's disease and Huntington's disease?

24. What have neuroscientists learnt to date about transplants of brain tissue as a way to treat neurological diseases?

What Do You Think?

What are the technical and ethical pitfalls stem-cell researchers must contend with?

ACTIVITY

Activities to test yourself further are available in your interactive e-book at **www.wileyopenpage.com**

Summary

How Do Scientists Study the Nervous System and the Brain?

LEARNING OBJECTIVE 1   Understand the key methods that scientists use to learn about brain anatomy and functioning.

- Neuroscientists examine autopsy tissue and patients with localized brain damage to learn about brain anatomy and brain function.
- EEGs and neuroimaging, such as PET scans and fMRI, allow us to study brain function in the living brain.

How Does the Nervous System Work?

LEARNING OBJECTIVE 2   Describe the two major types of cells in the nervous system, and explain how communication in the nervous system works.

- The two major types of brain cells are neurons and glia.
- Neurons are the fundamental units of the nervous system. Communication among neurons is necessary for normal functioning of the nervous system.
- Glia are involved in various functions, such as forming the blood/brain barrier, producing myelin and clearing the brain of debris.
- Communication within a neuron occurs electrically by means of the action potential, whereas communication between neurons occurs at the synapse via chemical signals called neurotransmitters.
- Neurotransmitters are released by the presynaptic neuron, diffuse across the synapse and bind to receptors on the postsynaptic site.
- The response of a receiving neuron to a neurotransmitter is determined by the receptor on the postsynaptic, or receiving, neuron's membrane. Depending on the type of receptor, the postsynaptic neurons will fire or not.

The Brain's Structural and Functional Organization

LEARNING OBJECTIVE 3   List key structures of the brain, and describe their relationships to our behaviour.

- The brain can be divided into many regions, each of which serves one or more specialized functions.

- The brainstem participates in movement and sensation of the head and neck as well as in basic bodily functions, such as respiration and heart rate.
- The midbrain includes the substantia nigra, an area important for movement.
- The hypothalamus controls basic drives (hunger, thirst, sex) and hormones, while the thalamus serves as a relay station for sensory information on its way to the cerebral cortex.
- Many brain regions participate in different types of learning. The hippocampus is important for spatial navigation learning and learning about life events, the amygdala is important for fear learning, the cerebellum and striatum are important for motor learning and the nucleus accumbens is important for reward learning.
- A large part of the brain consists of the neocortex. The neocortex can be subdivided into the frontal, parietal, temporal and occipital regions. The neocortex controls movement, integrates sensory information and serves numerous cognitive functions.

Neurons and the Communication Systems of the Brain, Nervous System and Body

LEARNING OBJECTIVE 4   Describe the functions and subdivisions of the two major parts of the nervous system.

- The two major divisions of the nervous system are the central nervous system, which consists of the brain and spinal cord, and the peripheral nervous system, which consists of nerves that extend throughout the body outside the central nervous system.
- The peripheral nervous system has two divisions: the somatic nervous system, which sends information about the senses and movement, and the autonomic nervous system, which controls involuntary functions and responses to stress.
- The autonomic nervous system is divided into the sympathetic nervous system, which responds to stress, and the parasympathetic nervous system, which is responsible for digestion and other processes that occur when the body is at rest.

Building the Brain

LEARNING OBJECTIVE 5 Describe neurogenesis, synaptogenesis and preprogrammed cell death, and explain their roles during development and throughout the lifespan.

- Cellular processes that build the brain are neurogenesis, which produces new neurons, and synaptogenesis, which forms new synaptic connections with other neurons.
- Cellular processes that sculpt or fine-tune the brain are cell death, axon retraction and synapse elimination.
- Changes in brain structure, including neurogenesis and synaptogenesis, occur throughout life, into old age.

Brain Side and Brain Size

LEARNING OBJECTIVE 6 Discuss what neuroscience evidence tells us about brain lateralization and the significance of brain size.

- Research shows that the two hemispheres are more similar than different and that any differences are usually relative.
- Brain size appears to be related to overall body size and not to brain function.

Neurological Diseases

LEARNING OBJECTIVE 7 Describe four neurological disorders and the current directions in research for treating them.

- Multiple sclerosis involves the loss of myelin on the axons of neurons.
- In amyotrophic lateral sclerosis, the motor neurons in the spinal cord degenerate.
- Parkinson's and Huntington's diseases are primarily the result of neuronal destruction in the substantia nigra and striatum, respectively.
- Some regeneration occurs in the brain after it is injured, but repair is typically not complete and functional impairment often remains. Researchers believe transplantation of brain tissue, particularly embryonic stem cells, may provide relief for some neurological diseases.

 Access your interactive e-book to view a video clip for this chapter at **www.wileyopenpage.com**

TYING IT TOGETHER

 **WHAT HAPPENS IN THE BRAIN?**

- The human brain contains about 100 billion neurons. In addition, some parts of the brain contain 10 times that many non-neuronal cells, called glia.
- If you put a recording electron into a 'resting' neuron, it will read a negative charge of approximately −70 mV. At the peak of a neuron's action potential, the membrane charge is around +50 mV.
- Action potentials of neurons follow an all-or-nothing principle. When sufficiently stimulated, a neuron fires; otherwise, it does not.
- Synaptic spaces are about 20 nanometres wide. A nanometre is one billionth of a metre.
- The sympathetic nervous system is responsible for the 'fight or flight' reaction; the parasympathetic nervous system helps control the basic functions of life, such as digestion.
- The hypothalamus helps regulate eating, drinking, sex, maternal behaviour and the endocrine system.
- Although the two halves of the brain are called hemispheres, the brain is not completely symmetrical.

HOW WE DIFFER

- Although the speech and language areas – Wernicke's and Broca's areas – are on the left side of most people's brains, these areas may be located on the right side or both sides for some people, particularly left-handed people.
- On average, the brains of women are smaller than those of men, although such size differences have no relationship to intelligence or other faculties.
- Some theorists believe that women are more likely than men to use both sides of their brain.

HOW WE DEVELOP

- Over the course of development, a process of programmed cell death, or cellular pruning, results in the death of over 75% of the neurons initially produced by the brain.
- Our environmental experiences help determine which synapses are maintained and which are pruned during infancy and childhood.
- Myelination of the frontal cortex is not completed until after puberty.
- Contrary to past beliefs, some populations of neurons continue to be produced well into adulthood (e.g. neurons in the hippocampus).
- Adult brains continue to undergo dendrite remodelling and synaptogenesis.

OUT OF THE ORDINARY

- When the spinal cord is damaged and information to and from the brain interrupted, individuals become paralysed. The higher up the damage – and so the closer it occurs to the brain – the larger the proportion of body affliction.
- People with damage to the frontal cortex region called Broca's area cannot generate speech but can understand language.
- With some notable exceptions, psychiatric disorders (e.g. clinical depression) seem tied most often to biochemical imbalances in the brain, while neurological disorders (e.g. Parkinson's disease and Alzheimer's disease) seem tied to brain-structure abnormalities, including the degeneration of neurons.
- Many neuroscientists are currently trying to develop treatments for certain neurological diseases in which they restore damaged neural circuits by transplanting new tissue into those areas of the brain, particularly by transplanting stem cells, undifferentiated cells that can grow into particular cell types.

Quizzes to test yourself further are available in your interactive e-book at **www.wileyopenpage.com**

Key Terms

absolute refractory period 107
action potential 106
amygdala 115
amyotrophic lateral sclerosis (ALS or Lou Gehrig's disease) 130
apoptosis 126
association cortex 116
autonomic nervous system 124
axon terminal 104
axons 104
behavioural neuroscience 100
brainstem or medulla 110
Broca's area 118
cerebellum 111
corpus callosum 120

dendrites 104
dopamine 111
endocrine, or hormonal, system 112
frontal cortex 118
glia 104
hemispheres 120
hippocampus 115
Huntington's disease 130
hypothalamus 112
ion channels 105
multiple sclerosis 129
myelin 107
neocortex 116
neural tube 125
neurogenesis 125
neuroimaging 101

neuron 103
neuroscience 100
neurotechnology 100
neurotransmitter receptors 109
neurotransmitters 108
noradrenaline 111
nucleus accumbens 116
occipital cortex 117
parasympathetic nervous system 124
parietal cortex 118
Parkinson's disease 130
pituitary gland 112
plasticity 109
pons 111
postsynaptic potentials 109

prefrontal cortex 118
relative refractory period 107
reticular formation 110
serotonin 111
somatic nervous system 124
somatosensory strip 118
stem cells 131
striatum 115
substantia nigra 111
sympathetic nervous system 124
synaptic vesicles 108
synaptogenesis 126
temporal cortex 117
thalamus 112
Wernicke's area 117

Flashcards to test yourself further are available in your interactive e-book at www.wileyopenpage.com

CHAPTER 6

Genes, Environment and Evolution

Adapted by Daniel Farrelly and Helen Driscoll, University of Sunderland, UK

CHAPTER OUTLINE

- The History of Evolutionary Approaches to Psychology

- The Principles Behind Evolutionary Psychology

- Main Areas of Research in Evolutionary Psychology

- Criticisms and Misunderstandings of Evolutionary Approaches to Human Behaviour

- The Future of Evolutionary Psychology

 Access your interactive e-book to view a video clip for this chapter at **www.wileyopenpage.com**

Do You Have a Sweet Tooth?

Many individuals today face difficult battles with both their weight and health. Most health professionals are unequivocal in the guidance they give about things that are bad for us, which include sugary foods. The advice clearly states that we should all follow a healthy diet. However, given that many of us love chocolate, fizzy drinks, sweets and cakes, many of us do not follow this advice. So, why do so many of us have such a strong, almost overwhelming, desire for sweet foods when they cause so many health problems? ■

evolution the process by which species modify and change over time.

The answer lies in our **evolution** and can best be understood by exploring our past. Our ancestors lived in far harsher environments than those most of us live in now, where various nutrients vital for survival were in short supply. These included sugary foods (such as ripe fruits) that provided an excellent source of calories, which all organisms need. As a result, those

innate characteristics that have biological or genetic origins.

of our ancestors who had an **innate** preference (in other words, one with a genetic or biological origin) for sugar and experienced psychological pleasure from such foods would be more likely to explore and search their environments for them than those who did not. Therefore, a sweet tooth would have been advantageous as their owners would have been more likely to get the calories needed every day to survive in severe environments. Furthermore, as these preferences were innate, their offspring would inherit this advantageous behaviour. This would continue into following generations until preferences for sugary foods became widespread in our species. In other

adaptation a characteristic that improves the survival and reproductive prospects of an organism in its current environment.

words, preference for sugar is an **adaptation** that evolved in humans to solve the problem of getting necessary nutrients from the environment.

However, these preferences persist today, and with fast and processed foods easily and cheaply available in our current environments such a

maladaptive an adapted characteristic that no longer improves survival and reproductive prospects, owing to changes in the environment.

desire is now **maladaptive**. This mismatch between the environments we evolved in and the one we live in now illustrates the power of evolutionary and genetic approaches to behaviour for understanding human nature. This chapter will introduce you to this fascinating and enlightening perspective that has flourished recently. To begin with, you will learn about Charles Darwin's theory of evolution by natural selection, and how it has developed and been applied to psychology. You will then discover the main areas in which evolutionary psychologists work, as well as being introduced to the different debates and controversies of this field. Finally, the future of this field will be discussed. It is hoped that, having read this chapter, you will not only appreciate the fundamentals of evolutionary and genetic approaches to behaviour but also be armed with the necessary tools to explore the role of evolution in all areas of psychology.

The History of Evolutionary Approaches to Psychology

LEARNING OBJECTIVE 1

Understand the historical and scientific discoveries that have shaped how evolutionary theory is applied to human behaviour.

Charles Darwin and *On the Origin of Species*

Although Darwin's name is now synonymous with the term *evolution*, the notion that species evolve had long been accepted. However, Darwin's contribution was important because for the first time it explained *how* evolution could occur (in other words, what the mechanism was). The best starting point for explaining the role of Darwin is his voyage on HMS *Beagle*, where he observed, noted and collected numerous samples of different species during the ship's voyage. Upon his return, he began to notice many interesting phenomena in these different species. Of particular interest were his findings about the beaks of different finches that inhabited the Galapagos archipelago. Darwin found that different species had formed on different islands, and although they clearly shared a common ancestor each species differed from the others.

This led Darwin to ponder why these differences had occurred, and from this he began to formulate his theory of natural selection. According to this theory, there are three necessary requirements for evolution to occur. First, there must be **variation** in a particular characteristic within a population (such as height, beak shape or behaviour). Second, this variation must be **heritable**. Finally, there must be some form of **selection**. By applying this to finches' beaks, Darwin saw that there was great variation in their size and shape and that chicks inherit similar forms to their parents. Importantly, he realized that the different forms could aid survival: for example, larger beaks allowed individuals to manage hard seeds. In these instances, larger-beaked finches would be more likely to survive and leave more larger-beaked offspring in future generations. That the particular finches on the different islands had beaks that were adapted to the island's environment (such as the abundance of different foods) further supported Darwin's view that natural selection could account for how different species evolved. Darwin fully explained this theory in *On the Origin of Species* in 1859, a book that revolutionized not only the field of biology but also our entire understanding of the natural world.

variation the different varieties of a characteristic within a population.

heritable characteristics that can be transmitted to offspring.

selection certain variants of the characteristic will aid survival or reproduction better than others.

The Modern Synthesis

Following its publication, many were drawn to the power and strength of Darwin's theory. However, it was not without criticism, and one major criticism was that, although he spoke of it, Darwin did not know what the mechanism was that ensured inheritance occurs. According to Darwin, characteristics may be inherited by a process of *blending* of the mother's and father's characteristics, which we now know is not the case. Therefore, a clear understanding of how characteristics are inherited was necessary.

Such a breakthrough came from an Austrian monk, Gregor Mendel. Working on pea plants in his Moravian monastery, Mendel explored how their characteristics (e.g. pod colour, texture) were passed between generations by carefully controlling the fertilization of different plants. He found that when he crossbred a plant with yellow pods with one with green pods all the offspring had yellow pods. Furthermore, when he crossbred two of these new plants he discovered that now approximately three-quarters of this new generation had yellow pods and one-quarter had green pods (even though neither of their parents had green pods).

How could this be explained? Mendel concluded that 'particles of heredity' (which we now call **genes**) exist that are passed on intact from parents to offspring. In the above example, there would be a gene for 'green pod' and another for 'yellow pod'. Furthermore, it was clear to Mendel that if a plant could possess both colour genes then there must be a further process that determines which colour is expressed. The results showed that one colour gene (or **allele**) was *dominant* and the other was *recessive*. In this case the yellow allele was dominant, and would be expressed if the plant inherited yellow alleles from both parents (in other words it was *homozygous* for pod colour) or if it inherited a yellow allele and a green allele (*heterozygous* for pod colour). However, because the green allele was recessive, it would only be expressed when it was homozygous (both green alleles present). To Mendel, this explained not only the relative number of plants with either yellow or green pods but also why a plant could have green pods even if both parents had yellow pods.

genes basic unit of biological inheritance.

allele different variations of the same gene.

The eventual combination of Darwinian evolution and Mendelian genetics led to the *Modern Synthesis*, a movement that would guide and shape understanding of all factors in biology that emerged in the twentieth century.

Tinbergen, the Birth of Ethology and the Four 'Whys' of Behaviour

One such area that has benefited from the advancements of the modern synthesis is our understanding of how behaviour has evolved. **Ethology** was founded by notable field biologists, including Konrad Lorenz and Nikolaas Tinbergen. According to Tinbergen (1951), ethology was concerned with understanding the causes of behaviours in terms of four different levels of

ethology the scientific study of the evolutionary origins of behaviour.

TABLE 6.1 Why Do We Eat Chocolate?

Tinbergen's 'Why'	Answer
Proximate/mechanistic	'It tastes nice and I'm hungry'
Developmental/mechanistic	'I have always liked eating chocolate, since I was young'
Phylogenetic/historical	'Humans have manufactured and consumed chocolate for years, and we are able to digest and enjoy it'
Ultimate/functional	'I will gain energy and certain nutrients from it, which will aid my survival and reproductive prospects'

explanation (called Tinbergen's 'four whys' or 'four questions'). These are:

1. the *proximate* or *mechanistic* cause (the immediate explanation)

2. the *developmental* or *mechanistic* cause (how the organism's lifetime development can explain behaviours)

3. the *phylogenetic* or *historical* cause (explanations based on the species' evolutionary history)

4. the *functional* or *ultimate* cause (the adaptive or evolutionary explanation).

Table 6.1 gives an example.

All are valid and explain the causes of the behaviour, but for the purposes of ethology (and, later on, evolutionary psychology) it is perhaps the ultimate explanation that is most important as it explains their adaptive origin.

Inclusive Fitness

One of the most important advancements is from the theoretical work of William Hamilton. Hamilton (1964) first theorized that organisms have evolved to increase the likelihood that their genes will survive and be passed on to future generations. However, he also realized that this does not necessarily have to be through the increased direct survival and reproductive prospects of the individual organism; it may also be through others who possess the same genes. This theory of **inclusive fitness** helps explain why organisms often help close relatives (e.g. parental care), as it is these individuals that they are most likely to share particular genes with. Furthermore, Hamilton devised a measure called

inclusive fitness the reproductive success of a particular gene in different organisms.

relatedness the probability that any particular gene is shared between two individuals.

relatedness. Such relatedness is 0.5 between parents and offspring and between siblings, 0.25 between uncles/aunts and niece/nephews, and grandparents and grandchildren, and so on. This measure is a valuable tool in helping understand who we direct help to and under what conditions, to maximize our inclusive fitness. (This is covered more in the section on kin selection below.)

Adaptations, and the Demise of Group Selection

George Williams (1966) applied the logic of inclusive fitness to the then-popular view that evolution selected for groups, so that members evolved certain characteristics that enhanced the survival of their group. Williams correctly noted that it was rather the individual that was being selected, as behaviours such as group members' restraining their food intake so that resources were not unduly depleted would not be adaptive. Although group selection would predict that it would be beneficial for a group to contain only individuals who restrained their feeding, any new individual who 'invaded' the group and did not restrain their feeding would be very successful (because of the reduced competition for food supplies) at the expense of existing members. As a result, the predominant view switched from the role of group selection to the more accurate view of individuals being selected.

Williams (1966) also provided an insight into how best to define adaptations. Williams noted that although many characteristics are adaptations owing to their contribution to the survival and reproductive success of an organism (e.g. preference for sugary foods), it is important that there are clear guidelines for determining an adaptation. He proposed three criteria. First, it must be *economical*, in that it solves the problem in a simple and frugal manner. Second, it must be *efficient*, so that it is relatively successful (but not necessarily perfect) in solving the problem. Finally, it must be *reliable*, meaning it is consistent in solving the problem in different contexts. We shall see the importance of these criteria throughout the chapter.

The 1970s: Robert Trivers, E. O. Wilson and the Dawn of Sociobiology

The influence of the modern synthesis continued and can be seen in the work of the biologist Robert Trivers. Trivers first developed his theory of reciprocal altruism (Trivers, 1971), which was the first explanation of how altruism between unrelated individuals could be adaptive. Following this, Trivers (1972) explored how differences in the investment each parent makes in their offspring subsequently shape the **sexual selection**

sexual selection a form of natural selection for characteristics that improve an individual's reproductive success.

of males and females of all species (further details below). Finally, his interpretation of inclusive fitness theory showed how it could lead to conflict as well as helping, in particular between parents and offspring owing to the different ways they can maximize their inclusive fitness (Trivers, 1974).

In 1975, E. O. Wilson published *Sociobiology: The new synthesis*, and with it a new term, and later a whole new field of psychology was created. The book examined the biological and evolutionary basis of behaviour in all animals. However, it is the final chapter on humans that the book is probably best known for. Here, Wilson outlines how sociobiology would shape our understanding of human psychology. Controversial and criticized from the start, the field of sociobiology was no doubt influential in shaping how we apply evolutionary theory to psychology today, and the modern field of evolutionary psychology owes a great deal to Wilson's contribution.

Evolutionary Psychology

 WHAT HAPPENS IN THE BRAIN?

Leda Cosmides and John Tooby of the University of California, Santa Barbara are widely recognized as the founders of the modern field of evolutionary psychology. Outlining this field's main principles, Cosmides and Tooby (1992) first proposed the notion that the human brain is best considered as consisting of a number of tools (or 'modules') that have evolved to solve specific problems, rather than being a general processor. This new approach of **modularity** differs from sociobiology by emphasizing the evolution of cognitive processes.

modularity a view that different processes in the brain function independently and specifically.

The main assumptions of evolutionary perspectives on cognitive mechanisms are:

- The human mind consists of many evolved information-processing mechanisms.

- These mechanisms are adaptations (via natural selection) to our ancestral environments.

- They are specialized to produce behaviour that solves specific problems (e.g. predator avoidance).

- They may be richly structured in content-specific ways.

This view of the mind as a series of tools that solve specific problems (akin to a Swiss army knife) was important to the new field of evolutionary psychology, and although it is not followed by all evolutionary psychologists it did lead to further key pioneering research from the likes of Steven Pinker, David Buss, Margo Wilson and Martin Daly.

Before You Go On

What Do You Know?

1. Explain Darwin's theory of evolution by natural selection.
2. What are the developments in evolutionary theory relevant to psychology since Darwin?

What Do You Think?

Do you think the work of these early evolutionary theorists can rightly be applied to human psychology?

The Principles Behind Evolutionary Psychology

LEARNING OBJECTIVE 2

Gain knowledge of how findings from different areas of scientific research have shaped our understanding of human evolutionary psychology.

Human Evolution

In order to appreciate how evolution has shaped human nature, it is important to have an understanding of how we have evolved. It is through fields such as palaeontology and archaeology – and findings from fossil records, ancestral living areas and other artefacts – that we can piece together our history. Most experts agree that our species split from the common ancestor we share with our closest living relative, the chimpanzee, approximately six to eight million years ago. Table 6.2 lists the different species of **hominids** we currently know of that were ancestors of modern humans.

hominids organisms that belong to the Hominidae family.

TABLE 6.2 Details of Early Hominid Species

Species	When (approximately)?	Characteristics	Cranial capacity[1] (in cubic centimetres)
Ardipithecus ramidus	4.4 million years ago	Ape-like in appearance, bipedal[2]	300–350
Australopithecus africanus, Australopithecus robustus	2–4.5 million years ago	More human-like, larger jaws, increased bipedal locomotion	375–550
Homo habilis	2.4 million years ago	Shift in diet towards meat-eating, used tools	500–800
Homo erectus	1.8 million–300,000 years ago	Increased tool use, capable of speech/language abilities	900–1,200
Homo heidelbergensis	500,000 years ago	Increased tool use and cognitive abilities, heavier than modern humans	1,350

[1] **Cranial capacity** is the calculated volume of the cranium (skull); in modern humans, 1355 cubic centimetres.
[2] **Bipedalism** is the ability to walk upright on two legs.

PSYCHOLOGY AROUND US   Our Origins: Multiregional Evolution or Out of Africa?

Controversy and debate surround the origins of modern humans, with two competing hypotheses. The *multiregional evolution* view suggests that *Homo erectus* migrated out of Africa and into Europe and Asia approximately two million years ago. Alternatively, the *Out of Africa* hypothesis states that, following earlier waves of *Homo erectus* that migrated out of Africa but then became extinct, *Homo sapiens* arose in Africa approximately 200,000 years ago and then migrated out of Africa approximately 130,000 to 35,000 years ago.

Which hypothesis is correct? Currently, there is more support for the 'Out of Africa' hypothesis from fossils and DNA evidence. However, as with many theories relating to our evolutionary history, results are not conclusive and scientists continue to search for and find evidence that is improving our understanding of our origins.

The Environment of Evolutionary Adaptedness (EEA)

The term *environment of evolutionary adaptedness (EEA)* refers to the ancestral environment of a species where their specific characteristics evolved and adapted, in response to specific problems they faced then. In other words, the unique physical and psychological traits we have were selected for in our EEA. Because of this, the term is regularly used when discussing evolutionary origins of human behaviours.

When and where was the EEA? This is an important and debated issue. First, it need not be a specific time or place, as Tooby and Cosmides (1990, p. 386) state that the EEA can be thought of as 'a statistical composite of the adaptation relevant properties of the ancestral environments encountered by members of ancestral populations'. However, the predominant view is that the EEA was during the **Pleistocene** era in the savannahs of eastern Africa (now Ethiopia, Somalia and Kenya). This, therefore, means that the EEA incorporates the rapid increase in brain size among early humans as well as the development of other unique traits such as bipedalism, tool use and language. Furthermore, it would place later developments such as cultural advances (approximately 40,000 years ago) and agriculture (approximately 10,000 years ago) and the spread of modern humans across the globe as occurring after the EEA. This is an important issue, as it implies that any changes since the EEA have not affected our evolved characteristics.

> **Pleistocene** period between two million and 10,000 years ago.

The EEA is important for evolutionary approaches to psychology, as the conditions and problems humans faced then need to be considered. Once these are known, testable hypotheses can be generated about what adaptations humans possess that evolved to solve these problems. For example, we can reasonably deduce that our ancestors lived in close groups during the EEA and would need to interact with other group members successfully for their own benefit (such as for sharing important information about food sources). Because of this, Cosmides and Tooby (1992) suggest that humans have evolved 'cheater detection' mechanisms (or modules) to make sure we detect individuals who are costly to interact with, and through their research (discussed later) they show experimentally that humans do show heightened abilities to detect cheats, particularly in social contexts.

However, as mentioned above, the concept of the EEA is controversial for a number of reasons. First, it could be argued that we do not know enough about the EEA to reliably develop hypotheses about human adaptations. Ancestral savannahs were different from those observed today and would have varied greatly between different areas. Similarly, it is difficult to accurately assess the lives of early humans. We can infer certain aspects by drawing comparisons with contemporary hunter-gatherer societies (such as the ¡Kung San of Africa); however, these will not be the same as those in the EEA due to changes in environment and culture that have certainly occurred since then. Also, it relies on the premise that since the EEA there have been minimal effects of natural selection (an *adaptive lag*) on humans. This is believed to be due to advances made in terms of technology and culture that mean current environments are rapidly changing (making it difficult for particular adaptations to evolve) and lessening any impact of natural selection owing to increased survival rates (such as advancements in medicine). However, there is evidence that some adaptations have evolved since the Pleistocene, such as Lactose tolerance in Northern European populations (Durham, 1991). This suggests that evolutionary change since the EEA is possible and may have occurred. This means that using only the EEA when considering human evolution may be inaccurate and lead to the formulation of false hypotheses.

Despite these criticisms, the EEA remains a useful theoretical concept for generating testable hypotheses on the evolution of behaviour, when it is treated cautiously and conservatively. Indeed, as our understanding increases, a more accurate description of the EEA should be formed, thus reducing criticism of it.

Genetics

The Modern Synthesis with Mendelian genetics allowed Darwin's theory of evolution to be fully accepted and integrated into modern biology. Therefore, it is important that anyone seeking to understand the role of evolution in human psychology understands the role of genetics.

Introduction to Genetics

Since Mendel first discovered the existence of genes, we now know a great deal more about their make-up and how they work. Genes are arranged into pairs of chromosomes within a cell's nucleus, with one chromosome from each parent. In humans, there are 23 pairs of chromosomes. It is your 23rd chromosome that determines your biological sex; females have XX chromosomes, whereas males have XY chromosomes (the names of these are based on their shape).

Genes are made of deoxyribonucleic acid (DNA), and each chromosome is made of long chains of these molecules in two separate strands that are bound together to form a double helix shape. Each strand is made of different combinations of four different bases, called adenine (A), thymine (T), cytosine (C) and guanine (G). The two strands are connected by pairs of bases forming bonds, with A pairing with T and C with G. Each gene is made of thousands of bases, and the specific sequence of bases code for individual amino acids (e.g. alanine is an amino acid formed by the base sequence GCA). Amino acids combine to form proteins, which then create the phenotypic trait that the gene is responsible for.

Genetic material is passed down generations via sexual recombination. Here, sex cells (gametes) contain only one of an individual's chromosomes, and are formed into sperm (males) and eggs (females) by a process called *meiosis*. Sexual recombination occurs when a sperm and an egg fuse to form an embryo, and the individual chromosomes in each sex cell pair up to create a new genotype. As there are a huge number of possible combinations of chromosomes in each embryo, this recombination leads to a great deal of variation between individuals in a species (which we know is a vital component of natural selection).

Further variation is created because the above processes do not always work perfectly. Sometimes, there are slight errors in recombination, which leads to **mutations** of the genetic code. We each have a number of mutations; most mutations have little, if any, noticeable effects, though some can have damaging effects when expressed, but a very small number of mutations can improve the survival and/or reproductive prospects of the holder. It is the latter that are an important component in the development and evolution of new traits in a species.

> **mutations** alterations to the sequence of DNA within an organism's genome.

Behavioural Genetics

Although we know much about *molecular genetics* (what genes are made of and how they work), links between genes and the specific phenotypic traits they create are hard to determine. This is because any physical trait is likely to be the result of many genes working together (except for traits such as eye colour, which is controlled by only one gene). This is even more of a problem for psychological traits, as we know little about the physical structures that cause them (but we can guess that they are somewhere in the brain). As a result, the links between individual genes and behaviour are pretty much impossible to deduce.

However, that does not mean we do not know how genetics can affect behaviour. For example, we know that there is a positive relationship between parents' and their offspring's IQ scores, and this will partly be due to genetics but also partly due to the environment (e.g. diet, life events). Behavioural

genetics help us separate the heritable (genetic) component from other influences.

Twin studies are the main tool for calculating the **heritability** of a trait. There are two types of twins: *monozygotic (MZ)* twins are identical as they grow from the same egg, and *dizygotic (DZ)* twins grow from different eggs and are equivalent to full siblings. MZ twins share 100% of their genes, whereas DZ twins share 50%. It is assumed that each pair of twins will have a shared environment in their development (including diet, parental relationships and schooling). Also, the concordance rates between twins for a trait (i.e. how similar it is between them) will be a combination of both their shared genes and shared environment. From this, the genetic causes of a trait can be estimated from the different concordance rates between MZ and DZ twins. Therefore, if the concordance rates for a trait are much larger for MZ than for DZ twins, it follows that the genetic component is large, as this difference is only due to the higher number of shared genes in MZ twins (as both sets of twins' shared environments will be equal).

> **heritability** an estimate of the contribution that genetics can have on a particular trait.

Estimating heritability is not without its criticisms. First, it assumes shared environments between all pairs of twins, but this may not be so, owing to unique events that only affect one twin (e.g. accidents) that have a profound influence on their development. Likewise, it assumes that the shared environments are the same between different twin types, whereas it is entirely probable that identical twins are treated differently by carers, peers and other family members than non-identical twins are (particularly if the latter are a boy and a girl). Therefore, care must be exercised when using heritability measures, and it must be remembered that these are estimates only.

Regardless, heritability estimates show how genetics can affect the development of traits. A trait does not need to have 100% heritability (i.e. be entirely due to genetics) for it to have a genetic origin, and any trait that has above-zero heritability can be shaped by natural selection. Most human psychological traits have at least some heritability, but few will be entirely due to genetics. Why might this be? Humans are a highly social and intelligent species, and our cognitive abilities are too complex to be entirely innate, so we rely heavily on developmental learning to support the heritable component of these traits. Take language, for example. This is not entirely innate, as language is far too expansive and complex. Instead, the *ability to learn a language* is influenced by the environment we grow up in, and this determines how we develop language (more on this later).

Before You Go On

What Do You Know?

3. Describe the evolutionary history of humans.

4. How can genetics affect our behaviour?

What Do You Think?

Do you think the concept of the EEA is suitable to use to study human evolutionary psychology? Do you think we need to fully understand genetics before we can view psychological traits as being evolved?

Main Areas of Research in Evolutionary Psychology

LEARNING OBJECTIVE 3

Gain knowledge of the main areas of research in evolutionary psychology.

Sexual Selection

Natural selection gives rise to traits that provide a survival advantage, which is important for inclusive fitness. However, inclusive fitness is not determined by survival, because survival alone is not enough to pass on one's genes to future generations; it must be accompanied by **reproductive success**.

> **reproductive success** the number of fertile offspring an individual has.

The evolution of traits which specifically contribute to reproductive success is known as *sexual selection*. Selection should strongly favour traits that promote successful reproduction and should do so even when those traits are detrimental to survival. There are many examples of physiological traits within the animal kingdom that cannot be explained by natural selection because they hinder (rather than promote) survival. A classic example of this is the peacock's tail. The peacock has a large, brightly coloured tail that is clearly detrimental to survival because it attracts the attention of predators and impairs the peacock's ability to escape. Furthermore, the tail is very costly to grow and maintain. Given the substantial survival disadvantage, such a trait must have evolved to be beneficial in some other way, by providing a reproductive advantage. Petrie *et al.* (1991) demonstrate that males with smaller, less ornamental tails are more likely to be shunned by peahens. But this raises two important questions. First, why is it typically males who have costly sexual ornaments? Second, why do females choose these males? We will deal with these two questions in turn.

Why Do Males Have Elaborate Ornaments? While peacocks have enormous, decorative tails, peahens are rather drab-looking; they are predominantly brown with no elaborate feathers. Likewise, there are many examples of exaggerated ornaments only in males in other species. For example, the now-extinct Irish elk males had huge, cumbersome antlers. In many bird species, the males are brightly coloured, but the females are not. To understand why sexual ornaments occur more commonly in males, we need to consider one of the most fundamental theories in evolutionary biology: *parental investment theory* (Trivers, 1972).

Parental investment theory is based on sex differences in the minimum obligate investment needed to successfully rear offspring. This is due to *sex differences* in the size of the sex cells (gametes). In humans and other mammals, males produce vast quantities of highly mobile sperm that simply carry the DNA necessary for fertilization. In contrast, the female sex cell (the ovum, or egg) is relatively large and limited in number. This sex difference in the size of the sex cells is known as **anisogamy**. From conception, women provide greater investment

> **anisogamy** sex differences in the size of sex cells (gametes).

A peacock attempts to impress a peahen by displaying his highly ornamental tail.

Source: Alexey Repka/Shutterstock.com.

in offspring than men do, and this continues throughout the offspring's life. Owing to internal fertilization and female lactation, the minimum investment for a mother in the ancestral environment comprised a nine-month gestation, followed by perhaps three to four years of breastfeeding. In contrast, the minimum investment required from the father was simply the energy needed to achieve fertilization. This sex difference in minimum (obligate) parental investment further results in differences in the number of potential offspring the two sexes can produce. Owing to their high investment, women can bear only a limited number of offspring in their lifetime. Women therefore have low **fitness variance**. In contrast, owing to their much lower minimum investment, it is possible for men to produce large numbers of offspring. Men therefore have high fitness variance. Greater maternal investment in offspring is found throughout the animal kingdom. In most mammal species, relative maternal (to paternal) investment is more extensive than in humans, since most male mammals provide little or no investment (Geary, 2000).

> **fitness variance** the amount of variance in the number of offspring produced.

One important consequence of females' greater parental investment is that, as the higher-investing sex, they are a valuable reproductive resource and males compete for access to them. This is known as *Bateman's principle* (Bateman, 1948). Consequently, males typically *court* and females *choose*. Parental investment theory is therefore able to explain why sexual ornaments tend to evolve in males, as they allow males to provide females with information on which they can base their mate choices. Displays of mate quality towards the opposite sex were termed **intersexual selection** by Darwin (1871).

> **intersexual selection** competition via sexual display to attract members of the opposite sex.

Why Do Females Choose Males Who Possess Survival Disadvantages?

Fisher (1930) proposes that preferences for elaborate sexual ornaments develop by a process called **runaway selection**. A runaway trait is (naturally) selected initially because it provides some survival advantage. For example, slightly longer tail feathers in peacocks might have allowed faster motion. A *preference* for longer tail feathers may then be selected in peahens so that such traits are passed on to sons, who will both be faster and preferred by females. The preference and the trait become linked, and it becomes a runaway process, with females preferring larger and larger tails. This preference is passed on to daughters and genes for larger tails are passed on to sons. The trait becomes exaggerated beyond its original function and is no longer advantageous to survival but is for reproduction, owing to the strength of the female preference.

> **runaway selection** the tendency for exaggerated sexual ornaments to evolve because of their attractiveness to the opposite sex.

Fisher refers to this tendency for females to seek heritable sexual ornaments which can be passed on to sons as the **sexy sons hypothesis**.

The **handicap principle** (Zahavi, 1975) offers a somewhat different explanation of how sexual ornaments evolve. According to this principle, for a peacock to grow a large, ornamental tail, and to survive with such an impediment, he must have good genes. Thus, the tail is a handicap, but a male can demonstrate his fitness by surviving despite it. If a female chooses such a male, his genes will be passed on to her offspring. Any sons will also have the genes required to grow and survive with large tails, allowing them to attract females. According to this theory, sexual ornaments are not arbitrary; they are *honest signals* of genetic quality.

> **sexy sons hypothesis** females will choose males who possess genes most likely to enhance their sons' reproductive success.

> **handicap principle** the theory that males develop handicaps to demonstrate their genetic quality to females.

It is important to note that these two theories (runaway selection and the handicap principle) are not necessarily in competition. They are two possible ways in which sexual ornaments may evolve; however, both may be involved in their selection. Traits such as the peacock's tail may be selected as an honest display of fitness because it is a handicap while also subject to runaway selection as there is a selection pressure on females to favour large tails.

Sex Differences in Humans

Evolutionary psychologists draw on the same principles of parental investment and fitness variance to provide ultimate explanations for sex differences in human mating. Indeed, this is one of the most heavily researched areas in evolutionary psychology.

Female mate preferences Because women's fitness variance is low, sexual selection has favoured women who invest highly in their offspring, meaning women are more concerned with quality of offspring than quantity. As a result, there is a fitness advantage associated with acquiring a long-term partner to assist in the difficult task of raising children. In a large-scale study of 37 cultures with over 10,000 participants, Buss (1989) found that women show strong preferences for men who are willing and able to invest. They consistently rated economic resources as important as well as reporting preferences for male status, which signals the ability to provide protection and is associated with higher levels of resources. Additionally, women reported a preference for slightly older men as long-term partners, reflecting the ability of men to accrue greater status and resource levels as they get older.

Women also prefer partners who are physically attractive. Buss (1989) reports female preferences for athletic prowess, which signals both good health and good genes, as well as the ability to provide protection. Women also prefer symmetrical features (Gangestad & Thornhill, 1997). Any deviation from symmetry is known as *fluctuating asymmetry*, which may indicate developmental instability and high mutation load. However, women's preferences for long-term partners prioritize men's ability to invest in offspring over their physical attractiveness. This reflects the high resource costs involved in raising children and corresponding selection for paternal investment in humans, something which is extremely rare in other mammals (Geary, 2000).

Male mate preferences Whereas women's primary concern is long-term mate quality, men's higher fitness variance means that they have much to gain (in fitness terms) from pursuing numerous partners. If successful, they could leave behind many copies of their genes in future generations. Indeed, men show a stronger preference for short-term mating (Buss & Schmitt, 1993). However, a man's ability to successfully implement a short-term mating strategy is dependent on his own mate quality. If only high-quality males can successfully engage in short-term mating, the interests of the majority of men are likely to be better served by acquiring a long-term partner and providing investment.

From an evolutionary perspective, female beauty is evidence of good health, good genes and fertility.

Source: Maksim Toome/Shutterstock.com.

This largely guarantees reproduction of some offspring, and investment in them ensures their quality.

Three key selection pressures have shaped men's mate preferences. First, to achieve reproductive success, males need to be sensitive to cues of health and fertility, which signal females' ability to bear children. This means that human females (unlike most mammals) display sexual ornaments designed to influence male mate choice. From an evolutionary perspective, female beauty provides adaptively useful information that advertises good genes, health and fertility. Because female fertility declines with age, youth is a powerful signal of fertility, and cross-culturally men show a strong preference for younger women (Kenrick & Keefe, 1992; Buss, 1989). Aspects of female body shape provide further information about health and fertility. *Waist-to-hip ratio (WHR)* is the diameter of the waist divided by the diameter of the hips, and a WHR of 0.7 (an hourglass shape) is associated with better fertility and health, and is rated as most attractive by men (Singh, 1993). However, *body mass index (BMI)*, weight divided by height squared, is a measure of overall fatness or thinness and appears to be a more reliable cue to health and fertility, as Tovee and Cornelissen (2001) found that BMI was a more powerful predictor of attractiveness than WHR was. A second selection pressure acting on the mate preferences of males is the need to pass on good genes to offspring. Like women, men are sensitive to cues of genetic quality, such as low fluctuating asymmetry (Gangestad & Thornhill, 1997). Finally, when seeking a long-term partner and offering investment, men's reproductive success will be reliant on their ability to avoid **cuckoldry**. Men therefore seek cues of fidelity in potential long-term partners (Buss & Schmitt, 1993).

> **cuckoldry** when males raise another male's offspring in the mistaken belief they are their own.

Sex differences in other social behaviours Sex differences in parental investment and fitness variance underlie sex differences in many aspects of social behaviour beyond those in mate choice. For example, evolutionary theories of sex differences in aggression are able to successfully account for men's greater involvement in direct aggression. Wilson and Daly (1985) propose that men have evolved a *taste for risk* which facilitates aggressive male competition for status. The evolution of traits which facilitate competition between members of the same sex for mates is known as **intrasexual selection**. Campbell (1999) has subsequently argued that sexual selection has acted to limit women's involvement in direct aggression because of the high costs to offspring in the ancestral environment as a result of maternal death or injury. Together, these two theories provide an account of how the different selection pressures acting on men and women have resulted in sex differences in aggression.

> **intrasexual selection** the selection for traits which provide advantages in same-sex competition for mates.

Sexual selection has been a fundamental process in human evolution and is ultimately responsible for many of the sex differences that psychologists seek to explain. It is therefore essential to an accurate understanding of human nature, as without this such accounts cannot adequately explain the universal nature of many sex differences in behaviour.

Kin Selection

As mentioned above, inclusive fitness theory explains why individuals are likely to help those they are related to, as they are likely to share a number of genes with them. This directing of help to genetic relatives is known as **kin selection**, which has favoured a tendency to behave altruistically to close relatives only when there is a net inclusive fitness benefit to the helper. Hamilton (1964) defines the conditions under which the tendency to help relatives could evolve. He proposes that helping would occur when the cost of helping (c) is less than the benefit of helping (b) multiplied by relatedness to the recipient (r), that is when $c < rb$. This is known as *Hamilton's rule*. As a result of this, we are more likely to help close relatives such as siblings or offspring with whom we have higher relatedness ($r = 0.5$) than first cousins ($r = 0.125$), even when the cost of doing so is quite high. However, when costs are low (and benefits to the recipient are high), we will then be more willing than at other times to help those with whom we share lower levels of relatedness. The great evolutionary biologist put it far more succinctly when he stated: 'I would lay down my life for two brothers or eight cousins.' Hamilton's rule therefore shows how we may make decisions about helping relatives (albeit unconsciously) in terms of what is best for our genes, by explaining the circumstances under which we are likely to provide help to relatives. As a result, we behave in ways that maximally enhance our inclusive fitness, by helping the largest possible number of our genes to be passed on to future generations.

> **kin selection** altruistic behaviour towards close relatives which increases an individual's inclusive fitness.

Evidence for kin selection in humans is widespread. Smith *et al.* (1987) found that people bequeathed more in their wills to direct descendants than spouses or other relatives with whom they shared lower relatedness than their offspring. There is further evidence from many different cultures that help is directed more to relatives, such as labour (Berté, 1988; Hames, 1988) and food (Betzig & Turke, 1986). A laboratory-based study showed that individuals are more likely to endure painful tasks to benefit close relatives (Madsen *et al.*, 2007). Furthermore, cues of relatedness in strangers such as physical resemblance (DeBruine, 2002) and having a shared surname (Oates & Wilson, 2002) lead to more trust and helping behaviours directed towards them.

Hamilton's rule explains the circumstances under which we are likely to provide help to relatives. This basic principle has profound implications for our relationships with family members. Because we share a large proportion of our DNA with relatives (but not usually 100%), inclusive fitness theory predicts that family relationships will be characterized by both cooperation and conflict. From an inclusive fitness perspective, we should not expect families to be entirely harmonious. Below the implications for relationships between parents and offspring are considered.

Parent–Offspring Conflict Parental care is the most powerful example of kin selection. However, resources for investment are finite and from the outset (conception) parents must decide how much to invest in individual offspring. Such decisions are the result of complex (usually unconscious) economic considerations. We have already seen that mothers typically invest more in offspring than fathers do; however, a mother's investment in each offspring is not limitless. Mothers seek to maximize their own reproductive success, and they do so by allocating resources so as to maximize the fitness of their entire group of offspring. This includes potential future as well as current offspring. From the perspective of each individual offspring, however, they would prefer their mother to invest more resources in them than in any sibling. Trivers' (1974) theory of parent–offspring conflict predicts that conflicts occur because each offspring desires more investment in itself than parents are willing to give.

A very common time of conflict is weaning (Trivers, 1974). In the ancestral environment, diets did not allow further pregnancy to occur during lactation, and mothers might have breastfed infants up to around the age of three or four (Sear & Mace, 2008). At that stage, the mother's fitness interests were better served by reducing investment in the current offspring (stopping breastfeeding) to allow fertility (and therefore the possibility of conceiving another offspring) to return. This is a source of conflict because the existing offspring would prefer further investment and might resist weaning attempts. Infants have various psychological weapons at their disposal to allow them to extract more investment. Mothers rely on babies' crying to communicate hunger and distress, but crying can also be used to manipulate parents and divert attention from siblings. In the toddler years, tantrums are a particularly effective means of forcing parental intervention and demanding resources, and occur around weaning time (Barrett & Dunbar, 1994).

Sibling Rivalry **Sibling rivalry** refers to conflict between siblings, essentially associated with disagreement over the amount of parental investment each receives.

> **sibling rivalry** the competition between siblings for parental investment.

It is common in animals, and can even result in death (siblicide); chicks may throw siblings out of the nest or peck them to death to gain more resources for themselves (Mock *et al.*, 1990). While it is generally less extreme in humans, many parents of young siblings are perpetually frustrated by their refusal to share and their squabbles over apparently trivial issues. However, such rivalry reflects a genuine biological reality. Sibling relationships are inherently paradoxical as although they have a relatedness of 0.5 (and thus a certain amount of cooperation is to be expected between them owing to inclusive fitness benefits) they will still have a greater fitness interest in themselves than in each other. Each would prefer their parents to invest more in themselves than their siblings. The rivalry may be exacerbated when parents do not always invest equally in offspring. Selection would have favoured parents who were sensitive to cues from offspring regarding their ability to convert investment into successful reproduction (Daly & Wilson, 1995). Parents may therefore engage in differential investment to maximize their own reproductive success, thus increasing the rivalry between siblings.

Cooperation and Altruism

The traditional view of evolution selecting behaviours that benefit survival has difficulty in explaining the existence of cooperative or altruistic behaviours. These should not be selected for; however, their near ubiquity in many species suggests such acts are the result of evolution. Even Darwin (1871) notes the 'problem' of **altruism** to his theory of evolution by natural selection. Therefore, it is necessary to explore how cooperative behaviours can be adaptive, and under what conditions.

altruism acts that benefit other individuals but are costly to the actor.

Traditional Explanations Hamilton (1964) first identified how cooperative acts between closely related individuals can be adaptive, because of enhancing the inclusive fitness of the cooperator. This concept of kin selection being important in the evolution of cooperation has been outlined in more detail previously.

Kin selection cannot, however, account for cooperation between non-related individuals. As mentioned above, Trivers (1971) introduced **reciprocal altruism** to explain such behaviours. Evidence for reciprocal altruism is widespread; we can see it in how food is shared between traditional hunter-gatherer societies (Gurven, 2004), and countless examples exist in other human societies, such as the exchange of goods and services that we all engage in. Other examples from animals include findings that low-ranking male baboons will help one another usurp higher-ranked males (Packer, 1977). Also, vampire bats that have recently fed on blood regurgitate blood meals for other unrelated bats (who they regularly interact with) to feed on (Wilkinson, 1984).

reciprocal altruism an individual incurring a cost to help another provided the recipient will return the act in the future.

Reciprocal altruism will, however, only occur under specific conditions; first, the cost of incurring the act must be less than the benefit that is received later; second, the species it occurs in must be highly social (thereby guaranteeing continued interactions between individuals); and finally it will involve species that have appropriate cognitive capacities, such as long-term memory and face recognition. Therefore, it is not surprising that most observations of reciprocal altruism occur in humans and other primates who meet the latter conditions owing to their advanced cognitive abilities compared with other animals (with vampire bats perhaps an exception).

The Prisoner's Dilemma and Tit-for-Tat For reciprocal altruism (and other forms of cooperation) to be adaptive, it must be more beneficial to the altruist than not cooperating at all, and it must be resistant to exploitation. In other words, there must be suitable strategies or procedures in place to ensure that a cooperator is not cheated by performing a cooperative act that is not reciprocated. As such, it is possible to compare cooperative interactions in real life with behaviour in an economic game called the *Prisoner's Dilemma*.

PSYCHOLOGY AROUND US   **The Prisoner's Dilemma**

In this game, two players must choose between two different tactics to play, which in this example we shall call 'cooperate' or 'defect' (these can be called anything; what matters is what each tactic means for the outcomes of the games). The decisions that both players make will affect their returns from the game.

If both player 1 and player 2 choose 'cooperate', they both receive £4 [*R*]. However, if player 1 chooses 'defect' when player 2 chooses 'cooperate', then player 1 now receives £6 while player 2 receives nothing [*T*] (and vice versa if player 2 chooses 'defect' and player 1 chooses 'cooperate' [*S*]). Finally, if both choose 'defect', they each receive only £2 [*P*].

The payoffs to players always follows the same formula of $T > R > P > S$. In single, one-off trials, the rational decision is to choose 'defect' as this guarantees a return of either £2 or £6), whereas choosing 'cooperate' may leave a player with nothing. However, over repeated trials between the same players it pays to choose 'cooperate', as this means that both have a higher overall return from the game.

If the Prisoner's Dilemma can be viewed as similar to real cooperative interactions, then it is important to know what the best strategy is for playing the game. To answer this, Robert Axelrod and William Hamilton (1981) organized a computer-based tournament for different strategies that would compete with one another in the Prisoner's Dilemma game. Of the various strategies that were played, *Tit-for-Tat* was the most successful, and formed an **evolutionarily stable strategy**.

evolutionarily stable strategy a strategy that cannot be out-competed by others.

Tit-for-Tat was unusual compared with other strategies, owing to its simplicity. It consisted of only two different rules; always choose 'cooperate' on the first move and always choose the tactic the other player chose in the previous trial. Therefore, it initiates and continues to cooperate with a cooperative partner but will punish any defection by defecting in return and will continue to defect with a defecting partner. However, if the partner attempts a reconciliation (by returning to cooperating after defecting), then the strategy is forgiving and will start cooperating again. The success of Tit-for-Tat shows not only that being cooperative can bring adaptive benefits but also that cooperation can be stable, providing the rules of the strategy (i.e. be cooperative, punish cheats, accept reconciliations) are maintained in real-world interactions. We will discuss the evolved mechanisms we have to deal with one of these rules (detecting cheats) later in this chapter.

Contemporary Theories of the Evolution of Cooperation Although kin selection and reciprocal altruism help us understand the problem of cooperation, there are clear examples for which these theories cannot account. For example, why do humans donate money to charities where the recipient is very unlikely to be a relative or be able to reciprocate? A number of new theories have sought to explain such behaviour. Each of these has in common the notion that cooperation is adaptive due to *indirect* reciprocity (Alexander, 1987). As a result, you will see that each theory shows how a cooperator's reputation can be enhanced, for different reasons.

In Nowak and Sigmund's (1998) *image scoring model*, all individuals in a group will have an image score that represents their cooperativeness and is displayed to all other group members. In future interactions, a partner will make a decision to cooperate or not with an individual based on what their image score is, with higher image scores more likely to elicit help from others. Similarly, Roberts' (1998) *competitive altruism theory* suggests that the adaptive benefits of a good reputation lead to individuals in a group competing to be seen as cooperative. Individuals will enter many cooperative interactions in an initial assessment stage, which is followed by a partnered stage where they are able to choose a partner and interact solely with them. As being in a cooperative alliance in the partnered stage will be beneficial to an individual, it is important to gain a highly cooperative partner, which is more likely if the individual was similarly highly cooperative in the assessment stage.

Being cooperative can also bring reputational benefits when it acts as a costly signal (Gintis *et al.*, 2001) of the cooperator's ability as a coalition partner or competitor. For such signals to be honest (Zahavi, 1975), they must be directly linked to the quality of the trait, costly to produce, beneficial and effectively broadcast (Smith & Bleige Bird, 2000). This can help explain large charitable donations, particularly when they are clearly linked to the donor (e.g. having a hospital wing named after them). Cooperation may also be used as a costly signal of quality to potential mates. This is because cooperation can signal desirable traits in mate choice, such as the ability to cope with the cost of the handicap (which would signal 'good genes') or kindness and the ability to be a reliable parent or partner (signalling 'good parent' skills). This has been recognized as being a possible explanation for the evolution of cooperation (Miller, 2007, 2000; Roberts, 1998; Tessman, 1995; Zahavi, 1995) and is supported by findings that individuals find cooperative behaviour attractive in potential mates (Farrelly, 2011; Barclay, 2010; Farrelly *et al.*, 2007; Jensen-Campbell *et al.*, 1995) and that individuals use cooperation to signal their quality to potential mates (Jonason *et al.*, 2009; Iredale *et al.*, 2008; Farrelly *et al.*, 2007; Griskevicius *et al.*, 2007).

The Evolution of Cognition

Cognition can explain the main processes related to abilities such as reasoning, decision making, memory and attention. Evolutionary psychology has aided our understanding of these, and more specifically for what purposes these may have evolved. In this section we will concentrate on two areas in human cognition that have benefited from an evolutionary perspective: reasoning and problem solving.

Reasoning, Social Contracts and Cheater Detection
We like to think of ourselves as logical, rational and accurate decision makers. However, we now know that our abilities are far from perfect. A classic example of this is performance on the Wason (1966) *selection task* (Figure 6.1). Here individuals are presented with four cards and are told that on one side of each card is a letter and on the other is a number. They are asked which cards they would need to turn over to check the rule 'If there is an even number on one side, there is a vowel on the other.' In this abstract form of the task, people perform very poorly. Only about 4% would correctly

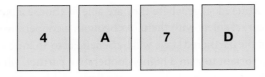

FIGURE 6.1 Abstract version of the Wason selection task.

FIGURE 6.2 Social version of the Wason selection task.

recognize that in this example they need to turn over the 4 and the D card. It is believed that people perform so poorly at this because of their innate overreliance on confirming rules when they should be trying to falsify them. This means people are far more likely to check that a rule is being adhered to (by checking the vowel (A) card) rather than looking to see whether it has been violated (by checking the consonant (D) card, as if there were an even number on the other side it would show the rule has been broken). So why do we struggle with such seemingly straightforward tasks?

Cosmides and Tooby (1992) believe we do not always have problems with these tasks: how the question is framed affects our performance. They state that our minds have not evolved to solve abstract problems; instead, we should be able to reason much better when it is relevant to the problems we faced in our evolutionary history. They show that this is the case with an alternative version of the task (Figure 6.2). Here individuals are now told that each card represents a person, on one side of the card is their drink and on the other is their age, and that they should imagine that they are a bouncer at a local bar who needs to check that no one is breaking the rule 'If a person is drinking alcohol, then they must be over 18.' Cosmides and Tooby found performance on this task was much better than for the abstract one (with the correct response being the 'beer' and '15' cards), even though the underlying format was the same.

The reason for this is that the latter version represents a **social contract**. Such contracts would have been extremely important to our ancestors as part of the cooperative alliances they formed with different individuals. As a result, Cosmides and Tooby (1992) believe we have evolved specific reasoning abilities that help us detect cheats in these contracts, in order to avoid further interactions with them and/or to punish them.

This proposed **cheater** detection module is one of the earliest examples of evolutionary psychology using the modular view of our cognitive abilities. It is **domain-specific**, which explains why our reasoning is so much better here than the more generic abstract version.

social contract individuals only receive a benefit when they incur a cost.

cheater an individual who receives a benefit without incurring a cost.

domain-specific the ability of a particular mental module is only present in relevant tasks.

Cosmides and Tooby (1992) also show that the cheater detection module is activated even with novel contracts (e.g. 'If you get married, you must have a tattoo on your forehead'), and individuals who have never encountered the drinking rule before (the Shiwiar in Ecuador) also show similar accuracy to American college students (Sugiyama *et al.*, 2002).

Neurobiological Evidence WHAT HAPPENS IN THE BRAIN?

Further evidence of a cheater detection mechanism comes from neuroscience. Stone *et al.* (2002) examined brain functioning in a patient with brain damage to his cortex and his amygdala. The patient performed worse than other individuals on social contract versions of the task; however, on versions that were based on precautionary rules (e.g. 'If you enter a building site, then you must wear a hard hat'), his performance was similar to that of others. This is taken as evidence that cognitive abilities relating to social contracts are separate, thus giving more support to the domain-specificity of the cheater detection module.

Similarly, Fiddick (2004) found differences in the emotions that social contract and precautionary rule violators provoked in observers. Cheats in social contract rules elicited anger, whereas cheats in precautionary rules elicited fear, providing more evidence for separate evolved mental mechanisms. Finally, it has been found that we are better able to remember the faces of cheats than non-cheats (Farrelly & Turnbull, 2008; Chiappe *et al.*, 2004; Oda, 1997; Mealey *et al.*, 1996). However, not all studies found this (Mehl & Buchner, 2008; Barclay & Lalumière, 2006) and Barclay (2008) suggests it is not necessarily cheats that we remember better but those individuals whose behaviour is the rarest.

Further Problems with Human Problem-Solving As mentioned above, Tooby and Cosmides (1992) state that cognitive mechanisms have evolved to solve specific problems rather than to be perfect general problem-solving tools. With this in mind, the common existence of heuristics and biases in human cognition makes sense. These include the *base-rate fallacy*, *conjunction fallacy* and the *availability heuristic* (for more details, see Kahneman, 2011), each of which is usually successful for solving problems but can be shown to be erroneous in other cases.

Cosmides and Tooby (1996) state a further example that early humans would observe how regularly certain events occurred in their environment, such as how often rain followed thunder or illness followed a snake bite. This is called *ecological structure*, and mental mechanisms would use these for problem solving (creating *ecological rationality*). Therefore, to properly judge human cognition, we must use only evolutionarily relevant stimuli in tasks. Furthermore, how information is presented to individuals also reveals the evolved nature of our decision making. In our past, we would have gathered information based on the frequency rather than the probability of certain events occurring. In other words, information-processing mechanisms would be designed to incorporate information as frequencies, such as, 'I have been down to that valley 10 times and it has provided me with food four times' rather than the same information being presented as a probability percentage, such as, 'That valley has a 40% chance of providing food.'

Cosmides and Tooby (1996) show this from the results of the *medical diagnosis problem*. This is the original form that was presented to individuals:

> If a test to detect a disease whose prevalence is 1/1,000 has a false positive rate of 5%, what is the chance that a person found to have a positive result actually has the disease, assuming that you know nothing about the person's symptoms or signs?_____%.

The correct answer (2%) was only selected by 18% of medical students, with almost half of them instead stating the answer was 95%. However, when probability information in the problem was replaced with frequency information (e.g. '1 out of every 1,000 Americans has disease X' rather than 'a disease whose prevalence is 1/1,000'), performance increased dramatically. Now 76% (or 76 out of every 100!) got it right. Furthermore, performance increased even further when information was also presented visually (e.g. squares representing each individual in the sample were presented).

This shows humans are far better at reasoning when details were presented in more ecologically valid ways (i.e. frequencies not probabilities or visually), and that base-rate information is less likely to be ignored when it is in a similar format to the input that our ancestors would have used. Cosmides and Tooby (1996) suggest that evolutionary pressures also shaped the importance of other information we receive. They believe that information relating to events close to us as well as those that occurred recently will be more important. For example, it would have been adaptive for our ancestors to pay more attention to information about food sources that are local and recent, rather than about those that are further away and/or occurred a long time ago (particularly foods that fluctuate over seasons, such as vegetation). Overall, we need to think about human cognitive abilities in terms of our evolutionary history first, as this will reveal the most interesting and relevant findings about how we think.

The Evolution of Language

Few phenomena are as important as language to human nature. This ability is unique to us and has undoubtedly affected every area of our societies and cultures. As such, scientists have sought to fully understand details of how it has evolved.

Why Is Language Useful to Our Species?
Language is an open-ended system of communication, made up of grammatical structure, syntax, symbolic representation and vast vocabularies. It allows the transfer of information between individuals, such as facts, ideas and beliefs. Information can be shared with many individuals at the same time. Language therefore is a flexible and efficient communication tool, suggesting it may have been shaped by natural selection. However, is this the case?

Is Language an Evolved Trait?
The debate about language being a product of natural selection originates from how this ability develops. Noam Chomsky (1957) was the first to suggest that there was something special about how infants learn language that went beyond simple learning or behavioural responses. He claimed that infants have an innate ability to understand the underlying rules of language. This he called the *language acquisition device (LAD)*, and it is an ability used with all languages (in other words it is like a *universal grammar*). The LAD allows infants to understand the syntactic properties of their parents' language, as well as increase their vocabulary at a time when other complex intellectual capabilities are beyond them. The LAD can be viewed as akin to a set of switches that are set by the rules of the particular language in an infant's environment.

Chomsky (1991), however, is sceptical about the adaptive basis of language. Instead, he believes it is a **by-product** that emerged by chance from our increased brain size. This view is shared by Gould (1987), who believes that unknown laws of growth and form within the brain led to language spontaneously appearing, rather than natural selection.

> **by-product** a characteristic that emerged alongside an adaptation but is not adaptive itself.

Others (e.g. Pinker, 1994; Pinker & Bloom, 1990) believe differently, and argue that language meets the necessary requirements of an evolved trait. First, it has a complex design for a specific function, making it unlikely to have arisen by chance. Pinker and Bloom (1990) also highlight that it solves a particular adaptive problem humans would have faced: the need to transmit large amounts of information effectively. They suggest that the LAD could have existed in intermediary forms; in other words, even in its most basic form it would have been selected for.

Theories of the Origins of Language There are a number of *adaptationist* theories of the origins of language evolution, which differ in terms of the key selection pressure solved by early forms of language. Robin Dunbar (1993, 1996) believes the origins of language lie in challenges we faced living in large groups. There is a positive correlation between group size and neocortex size in primates, highlighting the increased cognitive capacities needed to cope with the interactions and relationships between different group members. Dunbar believes the key behaviour in primates that allows this is *grooming*. Grooming is a social act, rather than having any practical use, which promotes group cohesion via the initiation and maintenance of pair bonds. However, it is different for humans, as the expected group size for humans based on neocortex size would be around 150 individuals, far more than other primate groups. Consequently, it would be impossible for humans to maintain the social bonds in such groups via grooming alone, as it would be too time-consuming. So how can we manage it? Dunbar believes that language first evolved to solve this problem, as it acts as a far more efficient method of maintaining social interactions with different group members. It was adaptive as it allowed individuals to interact with more than one group member at a time, and share more detailed and rich information such as what had happened in the past, ideas and beliefs and details about others. This theory shows that *gossip* is therefore a vital use for language in our evolutionary history, allowing us to keep track of the dynamics of relationships within a group. It is perhaps no surprise, then, that social topics (in other words gossip) make up to two-thirds of all conversations (Dunbar *et al.*, 1997).

Problems of living in large groups are also a key feature of Terrence Deacon's (1997) *social contracts theory* of language evolution. However, for Deacon it was the nature of long-term pair bonds within groups that were important. Early humans would have been hunter-gatherers, with males mainly hunting in large groups away from their female partners. Such social systems would have been problematic, as males risked being cuckolded, whereas females risked being deserted because of the long periods each spent apart from their partners. Deacon believes that to overcome this the use of 'symbolic' contracts between partners evolved in early humans. These contracts were early forms of marriage, which would be recognized by all group members. As a result,

although a pair-bonded couple spent time apart, there would be some recognized social symbol to show that they were in an exclusive relationship. What this early symbol would have been is unknown (it might even have been a ring). However, once it came into use it allowed early humans to understand symbolic representations. Once humans had evolved this ability, owing to social contracts, it opened up the possibility that symbolism could be used elsewhere, and eventually in early forms of language.

Geoffrey Miller's (2000) *Scheherazade effect theory* of the origins of language states that language evolved because of sexual selection for its use in attracting and maintaining mates. This is because linguistic abilities are honest signals of genetic quality, making language use a reliable fitness indicator. He points to the extensive human vocabulary, which is far more costly than would have evolved by natural selection. Therefore, sexual selection has shaped language to act as a costly handicap in much the same way as a peacock's tail. Miller states that males predominantly use language skills to attract mates, and as evidence he points out that males produce more poetry, books, scientific and philosophical output than females, and that this productivity peaks around the age of 30, which coincides with peak competition between males for access to females. However, he also states that females, too, will evolve complex and advanced language abilities, as these would be necessary to judge the language use (and thus fitness) of potential suitors.

Each theory offers a plausible account of why language first evolved, and it is important to note that each of these theories highlights that the social world of our species is vital. However, they are not without criticism. For example, we do not know much about the evolutionary history of language, which can lead to accusations of these theories being just-so stories (see below). Because of this, we may never know conclusively why language first evolved. However, this does not mean that the search for the answer is fruitless, as they have and will continue to unearth many important elements of human language.

Cultural Evolution

Within psychology, culture has often been viewed as separate from biology, and the extent to which behaviours or traits are the product of environmental (or cultural) influences or biological influences is frequently debated. Perhaps surprisingly then, the study of culture is currently one of the fastest-growing areas of research within evolutionary psychology. Culture is ultimately a product of biology because genes build brains, and brains generate culture. A key question for evolutionary psychology therefore is why humans have culture.

Dual Inheritance Theory: Why Do Humans Have Culture?

Dual inheritance theory (Boyd & Richerson, 1985) is the dominant approach to the study of culture within evolutionary psychology. Dual inheritance theorists propose that human nature results from the interaction of genetic and cultural inheritance. They also argue that culture has adaptive value. Owing to the length of a human generation, biological evolution is a slow process and humans face difficultly in evolving genetic adaptations to rapidly changing environments. However, cultural change can occur extremely quickly, and cultural evolution has been rapid and has dramatically changed the world. The variety and complexity of human cultural practices and products are staggering. Examples include the complexity of technology (modern cars, the World Wide Web, landing on the moon) and the richness of human creativity (epic works of fiction such as *War and Peace*, great works of art, fabulous architecture such as the pyramids). These are the products of rapid cumulative cultural evolution over a very short space of evolutionary time. Culture has evolved at a much faster rate than biology, and therefore cultural change can occur quickly in response to new selection pressures. Another advantage of culture is that the resulting knowledge, skills and technology can be passed on from one individual to another. This is important because many cultural products could not be devised by a single individual within their lifetime (e.g. the skills, design and technology needed to build a car). However, with accumulated knowledge, an individual can acquire the results of years of work undertaken by many others within a short space of time.

Mechanisms of Cultural Learning

Making adaptive use of cultural information requires cognitive mechanisms designed for effective learning, and a prerequisite for this is the ability to imitate others. It is easy to take imitation for granted, because humans find it so easy. However, imitation is very rare in other species (Tomasello, 1999). It requires complex cognitive processes that allow us to form a representation of a behaviour performed by someone else, and to then translate it into our own behaviour (Blackmore, 1999). Imitation differs from direct copying, as the acquisition and retention of information can be manipulated for future use.

The ability to imitate is not sufficient for efficient learning, however. Effective cultural learning also requires mechanisms for deciding what kind of information is most useful, and from whom it is most appropriate to learn. A number of mechanisms have been proposed by which humans acquire useful information from those around them (Boyd & Richerson, 1985). These include *content biases*, which are preferences to attend to particular kinds of information and guide us towards what to learn about, and *context biases*, which guide our choices about who we should be attending to (i.e. which cultural role models are adaptively useful to follow).

In terms of whom to learn from, it is adaptive to identify and learn from people who signal ability and success because this is likely to save time and to provide useful information. One mechanism is to directly observe individuals and to make a personal judgement about their ability. However, better indicators of ability are signals of success and prestige, because their acquisition requires a high level of skill over a sustained period. Humans are sensitive to such cues and use them to guide their choice of cultural models. This is known as **prestige bias** (Henrich & Gil-White, 2001). A further consideration when choosing who to learn from is the learner's own abilities, as this must to some extent be consistent with those of their preferred role model for any chance of success. Finally, learners must decide what aspects of their chosen role model's behaviour to copy, as it will be important to identify only those traits that led to the latter's success.

> **prestige bias** a preference for imitating individuals judged to be prestigious.

Memes: Culture for Culture's Sake

While dual inheritance theorists argue that culture is adaptive, not all cultural theorists agree that culture serves biological fitness benefits. While it is easy to see the adaptive benefits of cultural practices which permit rapid adaptation to changing environments (e.g. learning how to make and use tools), other aspects of culture appear to be fitness-neutral: what is the fitness benefit of that annoying song you cannot get out of your head? Indeed, some aspects of cultural learning appear to be detrimental to biological fitness. For example, use of contraception is a cultural practice that limits the number of offspring, and directly impairs reproductive success.

One such theory of cultural evolution that does not view culture as always being biologically adaptive is introduced by Dawkins (1976). He provides a different (and controversial)

The world has changed rapidly and dramatically as a result of cultural evolution.

Source: Songquan Deng/Shutterstock.com.

perspective on the 'purpose' of culture. He argues that every time imitation occurs, something is passed on. What is passed on is a unit of cultural information, which he calls a **meme**. Memes can be, for example, ideas, songs, catchphrases and fashion trends. The important thing about memes is that they are *replicators*. They meet the criteria for a replicator because (like genes) they are subject to variation, selection and heredity. If you consider songs as memes, there is clearly a great deal of variety. There is selection: some songs are popular and some struggle to ever be heard. There is also heredity because successful song memes are passed on; they are played on the radio, bought and repeated by people who have listened to them. If these criteria are met, the process of natural selection will occur, and evolution will happen. This is an example of **universal Darwinism** in action. Dawkins suggests that the human brain with its capacity for imitation has unleashed a new replicator. Just like genes, memes will selfishly replicate for their own benefit, not ours or our genes'. Just as genes group together to build organisms, memes could combine together into *memeplexes*, groups of mutually reinforcing memes that are more likely to be replicated in combination than alone. For example, Dawkins considers Christianity to be a memeplex. It is composed of individual memes (such as belief in God, the devil and an afterlife) that replicate more successfully together.

> **meme** a unit of cultural selection analogous to a gene.

> **universal Darwinism** the idea that natural selection will occur whenever an entity is subject to variation, selection and heredity.

Susan Blackmore (1999) extends Dawkins' ideas and uses meme theory to explain fundamental aspects of human nature. Blackmore suggests that competition between memes for human attention is the reason we cannot stop thinking, and memes create an illusion of consciousness and sense of self in their attempt to inhabit the human brain so that they can achieve successful replication. These ideas are interesting, but speculative. Meme theory has received widespread attention and has a cult following online, yet the response within academia has been weak. Meme theory has been subject to a number of criticisms. It is difficult to precisely specify the unit of a meme: is a meme a line in a song or the entire song? This criticism is a little unfair because it is no more possible to precisely specify the length of a piece of DNA that constitutes a gene. However, a more important criticism regards the extent to which memes meet the criterion of heredity. Because memes, unlike genes, are not always copied with high fidelity (e.g. when you repeat a story you are likely to change it in some way), the extent to which they can be inherited is questionable.

Is Biology or Culture more Important? Evolutionary theories of culture agree that culture initially evolved for biological advantage. However, they disagree regarding the subsequent power of culture to evolve regardless of biological fitness. Wilson (1978) argues that genes hold culture on a leash, meaning that cultural replicators can only be successful if they also benefit genes. However, memeticists tend to view cultural evolution as benefiting memes, regardless of biological fitness. The reality may be somewhere between these two views. Clearly, some aspects of culture are not biologically adaptive and their persistence may be due to their own successful replication. However, it also seems clear that culture has a better chance of success if it is associated with biological fitness, and therefore relates to survival and reproductive success. The relationship between biology and culture is interdependent and it is difficult to disentangle their influences on human nature. Because culture is the product of biology, biological explanations may to some extent subsume cultural explanations. However, once culture arises, it creates new selection pressures for genes, and has an impact on biological evolution. Additionally, cultural evolution may occur regardless of genetic benefit. If this is the case, some behaviours may require explanation from a meme's eye (rather than a gene's eye) view.

Before You Go On

What Do You Know?

5. Explain the principles of kin selection.

6. How is sexual selection different from natural selection?

7. What are the main theories that explain how cooperative behaviour could have evolved?

8. Why are humans so poor at some reasoning and problem-solving tasks?

9. Why do some people think language is an evolved trait?

10. What are the differences between biological and cultural evolution?

What Do You Think?

Why do you think it is in the above six areas of psychology that evolutionary approaches have been used the most? What are the strengths and weaknesses of the evolutionary approaches to them?

Criticisms and Misunderstandings of Evolutionary Approaches to Human Behaviour

LEARNING OBJECTIVE 4

Understand the criticisms and misunderstandings of evolutionary approaches to psychology, as well as the responses by proponents in the field.

The application of evolution and genetics to psychology has illuminated our understanding of psychology. Research in this domain has blossomed and is now beginning to become a major contribution to this academic field. However, this has not been universally popular, and some of the main criticisms of using Darwinian evolution to explain human behaviour are described below, as well as the responses from advocates of evolutionary psychology.

Criticism 1: Evolutionary psychology too often believes a behaviour is an adaptation (panadaptationism)

The concept of adaptations is crucial to identifying psychological traits that have evolved to solve a survival or reproductive problem our ancestors faced. However, not all traits will be adaptations, and many will be by-products of other adaptations. So, evolutionary psychologists must be careful when describing behaviours as adaptations, as critics will accuse them of creating **just-so stories**.

just-so story an account of why a characteristic is adaptive that seems plausible (or in some cases entertaining or interesting) but is actually incorrect.

Panadaptationism is potentially an issue. However, evolutionary psychologists generally are reluctant to call something an adaptation without supporting evidence. This discipline relies on understanding our evolutionary history to hypothesize about which behaviours would be adaptive and which would not, and testable hypotheses are then formed from this, which have been and are currently being tested. As a result, some theories of why a particular behaviour is believed to be an adaptation are supported, whereas others are not. This leads to the latter theories eventually being rejected, and it is such testing of hypotheses that rebuffs these criticisms of panadaptationism.

Criticism 2: Evolutionary psychology is guilty of biological determinism

This common criticism argues that evolutionary psychology places too much emphasis on biology and ignores the role of the environment. By doing so, critics believe that evolutionary psychology cannot fully understand the complexity of many of our unique abilities and behaviours. However, this is a false perception of evolutionary psychology, and misrepresents its position within the nature/nurture debate. Although they are more concerned with the nature side of the debate (i.e. the biological/genetic origins of behaviours), evolutionary psychologists fully recognize the role of the environment. In fact, it is believed that the highly social lives of humans were important in shaping many adaptive behaviours, and the flexibility of these in response to the environment is itself an adaptation. A good example of this is the language acquisition device (LAD), which is an innate ability that combines with the language in an infant's environment to produce fully formed linguistic skills.

Criticism 3: Evolutionary psychology tries to explain things too simply (reductionism)

In a similar vein to biological determinism, many critics argue that evolutionary psychology uses too few underlying principles (i.e. natural and/or sexual selection) to explain complex psychological traits. They believe that this leads to other important principles being ignored, such as the role of culture and the environment. However, all science is reductionist, and there is merit in attempts to understand the world in the simplest way possible. Problems arise when reductionism goes too far, at the expense of accuracy. This is known as *greedy reductionism* (Dennett, 1995), but is evolutionary psychology guilty of it? Its proponents would say no, and again stress that this is a false view of the discipline. Few, if any, psychological traits that are considered adaptations are believed to be due to biology alone. Instead, as mentioned before, evolutionary psychology regularly integrates the roles of learning, culture and environment as well. Therefore, evolutionary psychology can be seen as reducing our understanding of psychology, but not too far.

Criticism 4: Evolutionary psychology justifies immoral behaviours

Critics often view the findings of evolutionary psychology as allowing individuals to justify or excuse their behaviour, stating things like, 'I can't help it; my genes made me do it' or 'It's only natural.' This is particularly concerning as many behaviours researched by evolutionary psychologists are negative and immoral (e.g. aggression, infidelity, rape). If such behaviours have an evolutionary origin, does that mean that they are justified? No. People who use this criticism are committing the **naturalistic fallacy**. This is certainly not the view

naturalistic fallacy the false belief that if something occurs naturally it ought to occur.

of evolutionary psychologists, who emphasize that their sometimes disturbing findings about human nature are by no means meant to condone them. Instead, they emphasize how an understanding of the evolutionary origins of negative behaviours can help in the reduction or prevention of their actually occurring.

A similar criticism is that research into possible sex differences in psychology implies the researchers are being discriminating or sexist. Again, this is an unfair accusation, as evolutionary psychologists are only interested in understanding why such differences exist rather than in supporting them. Also, if sex differences do exist, it does not imply that one sex is better than the other, just that there were differences in the adaptive problems that men and women faced in our evolutionary history. Overall, this criticism possibly stems from the belief that evolutionary psychologists are ideologically driven, when in fact, like all good scientists, evolutionary psychologists seek only to explain the natural world rather than use it to support particular world views.

PSYCHOLOGY AROUND US   Is Evolutionary Psychology a Separate Area of Psychology?

No. As this new field grows and matures, we are starting to see its principles being applied to all areas in psychology. This reinforces the view that evolutionary psychology should not be viewed as a separate area (such as cognitive psychology). Instead, it serves as a theoretical perspective with which we can further understand all aspects of our psychology, and can guide future research. As such, it can offer a different level of explanation of different phenomena. As mentioned earlier, the evolutionary perspective offers the ultimate explanation for behaviours, which can complement and sit alongside existing psychological research that investigates proximate explanations (Scott-Phillips *et al.*, 2011).

Before You Go On

What Do You Know?

11. Explain the main criticisms of evolutionary psychology.

12. What are the responses from evolutionary psychologists to these criticisms?

What Do You Think?

Do you agree with the critics, or do you agree with evolutionary psychologists? Are some of these criticisms more valid than others?

The Future of Evolutionary Psychology

LEARNING OBJECTIVE 5

Gain understanding of the new areas of evolutionary psychology research, and an appreciation of future directions.

Further Understanding of Genetics

Our understanding of the role of genetics is increasing rapidly, and one of the most important breakthroughs was the sequencing of the human **genome** (Lander *et al.*, 2001), which raised important issues that shaped how we view the biological basis of human behaviours. First, it was made up of fewer genes than were expected (it is only about twice as many as in a fly or worm), which can be viewed as problematic if we view the

genome the entire genetic code that makes up an organism.

genetic components of psychological traits as being important (which evolutionary psychology does). However, this finding shows that the link between biological complexity and amount of DNA is not straightforward and further supports the view that the link between traits and individual genes is complex. Furthermore, when compared with the chimpanzee genome it turns out that humans share approximately 98% of their genes with them. Does this suggest that we are virtually identical to our closest living relatives, and that the vast majority of our differences are due to cultural/environmental reasons? No, because the difference (2%) is actually quite large (approximately 32 million base pairs) and it must still be able to explain many unique human traits (e.g. bipedalism, bigger brains, language). Also, the difference is relative (we share 50% of our genes with bananas!) and again highlights the complex and non-linear relationship between genes and phenotypic traits.

PSYCHOLOGY AROUND US   Epigenetics

Further proof of the complex relationship between genes and psychological traits comes from recent discoveries in epigenetics. Epigenetic changes are changes to DNA that happen within an individual organism's lifetime, but which can then be passed on to their offspring and even on to further generations. It has been found that Dutch mothers who themselves were born during famines in the Second World War went on to have offspring that were smaller than offspring of mothers born outside of the time of famine. This was a surprising finding, as it went against the accepted wisdom that we inherit the exact same genes from our parents (barring the odd mutation), and that evolution acts only on this genetic inheritance. Instead, epigenetics shows that the environment can also affect this, by causing certain genes to be switched on or off over an individual's lifetime. Does this finding oppose Darwin's theory of evolution? Not necessarily, as most scientists would agree that epigenetics furthers our understanding of genetic inheritance. However, by doing so it also increases the complexity and difficulty in understanding how genes may cause different behaviours.

If the link between genes and the behavioural traits we believe to be the result of evolutionary processes is so complex, can we be certain that they really exist? This is something we can be fairly certain of, as genes are vital for building brains, and results from behavioural genetics show that many psychological traits have significant genetic components. However, does the complicated link between genes and behaviour mean we should just assume these links exist, without attempting to discover more? This assumption is known as the *phenotypic gambit*, and has been a fundamental part of the study of the evolutionary basis of behaviours in all organisms. However, such assumptions may become more and more precarious as further advances are made in genetics. Therefore, it is important not only that evolutionary psychologists are knowledgeable about these advances but also that they embrace them as providing further validity to their claims.

Hormones

As with advances in genetics, our understanding of the function of various hormones will prove invaluable in furthering our knowledge of the evolutionary basis of many behaviours. This is because hormones are the result of biological mechanisms, and therefore any behaviour that is hormonal in origin can be under the scrutiny of natural selection. As technological advances allow cheaper and easier ways to measure hormones in humans (e.g. saliva sampling rather than blood sampling), evolutionary psychologists are increasingly coupling behavioural with endocrinological research.

testosterone an androgen hormone primarily found in males.

For example, research on **testosterone** (T) has helped our understanding of male competitive behaviours from an evolutionary perspective. As females are the choosier sex, owing to parental investment differences, evolutionary theory predicts that males will exhibit and invest more in competition in order to increase their reproductive success. As a result we now know how T may be the underlying mechanism that drives this, as T levels rise before contests and are higher in winners (Mazur & Booth, 1998) and T levels are higher in males than in females during competition (Mazur *et al.*, 1997). Also, males' T levels increase following interacting with attractive females (Roney *et al.*, 2003). Furthermore, it will be predicted that a male's motivation to compete will decrease once they are no longer actively seeking further mating opportunities (and thus competing with other males). Again, this is borne out by findings that married males and males in long-term relationships have lower T levels than single males do (Burnham *et al.*, 2003; Gray *et al.*, 2004).

Similarly, research in cooperation may be supported from recent findings relating to the hormone **oxytocin**. Oxytocin has generally been linked to social bonding in animals, particularly between mother and offspring (van Leengoed *et al.*, 1987) and between males and females in long-term pair bonds (Bales & Carter, 2003). However, subsequent research has shown that oxytocin can lead to increased trust in cooperative situations (e.g. Kosfeld *et al.*, 2005), which may be due to oxytocin making individuals less averse to betrayal in such situations (Baumgartner *et al.*, 2008). Also, oxytocin has been shown to increase trust of strangers (Theodoridou *et al.*, 2009) and also increase the judgements of the emotional expressions of others (Domes *et al.*, 2007). It is possible that research into oxytocin will help us better understand the proximate mechanisms behind why we as a species are so cooperative and social, and as a result help us further appreciate the ultimate explanations for this.

oxytocin hormone produced in pituitary gland that plays a role in different social interactions.

Individual Differences

Explanations of individual differences are possibly the least straightforward to apply evolutionary theory to. This is due to the perception that natural selection will have led to certain adaptive behaviours in the EEA reaching **fixation** due to the benefits they bring (Tooby & Cosmides, 1992). Individual differences instead emphasize the variation in traits, such as personality and intelligence. This is at odds with the traditional view that there should be no variation in these as they would be fixed at optimal levels of fitness (in other words we should all have the same levels of intelligence and types of personality).

> **fixation** occurs when only one allele remains within a population, usually because of its adaptive benefits.

Can this explain the reluctance of evolutionary approaches being adopted by individual differences researchers? Possibly, but the **universality** of individual differences in these measures (and their high heritability) needs to be explained. First, the notion that natural selection will always lead to characteristics being fixed is not correct, as there will always be some variation remaining, and even if this is low it will still be of interest. Furthermore, variation within a characteristic itself may be adaptive, as there is no fixed or optimal human nature and the best behaviour will depend on the environment and others' behaviour (e.g. should we always be selfish or kind?). Nettle (2007) further shows that variation in a number of individual differences characteristics (e.g. handedness) can bring fitness benefits for different reasons (e.g. handedness may have affected combat success). He also explains why variation would have been favoured by natural selection, and puts forward a number of explanations, including responding to changing environments, fitting into niches and indicating fitness.

> **universality** describes a characteristic that is shared by all members of a species.

As a result, research in individual differences has begun to use an evolutionary perspective. It has been shown that ultimate explanations can account for variation in the Big Five (Costa & McCrae, 1992) personality measures (Nettle, 2006), trustworthiness (McNamara *et al.* 2009) and empathy and systemizing abilities (Baron-Cohen, 2003). Penke *et al.* (2007) use the principles of evolutionary genetics to propose a model for the heritability of individual differences in personality and general intelligence. The interesting findings these early investigations have produced suggest a fruitful future for evolutionary individual differences research.

Neuroscience

WHAT HAPPENS IN THE BRAIN?

Evolutionary psychologists are interested in how natural selection affects the frequency of genes in a population that account for different behaviours. However, little attention is paid to how these genes physically create the behaviour, which is by producing particular brain structures and

systems. Neuroscience is therefore a key area in which we can use an evolutionary perspective, and was touched upon in the research on the modular view of the human brain (Cosmides & Tooby, 1992). With advances made in neuroscience techniques (e.g. fMRI), we are now better placed to see how such workings are represented physically.

The main benefit an evolutionary perspective can provide is a coherent way of approaching brain functioning. By first understanding what the brain has evolved to do, we can then see how it works. One example of this is the *social brain hypothesis* (Dunbar, 1998), which challenged the conventional belief that primate brains evolved to process factual information. Instead, Dunbar showed via positive correlations between brain size and group size in primates that brain evolution reflects the demands of complex social systems. Similarly, the functioning of the amygdala suggests to some researchers that it does not exist as a single structure (Swanson & Petrovich, 1998). However, when an evolutionary perspective is used to understand its role and how it has evolved, we find strong evidence to suggest that it is a separate structural and functional unit (Barton *et al.*, 2003).

Attempting to understand neuroscientific phenomena will, incidentally, teach us more about the mysteries of the human brain. We are constantly finding strange and interesting processes within the brain, for example the existence of **mirror neurons** (e.g. Rizzolatti *et al.*, 1996). Such findings can be difficult to interpret and understand; however, this is helped when we consider the need to

> **mirror neurons** a set of motor neurons that are activated by perceiving motor acts.

understand and recognize the social world that has shaped primate evolutionary history. This knowledge of the role of evolution can not only aid our understanding but also shape future research in neuroscience.

Applied Evolutionary Psychology: Darwinian Medicine and Evolutionary Psychopathology

 **OUT OF THE ORDINARY**

The application of evolutionary principles to the understanding of health and disease, otherwise known as *Darwinian medicine*, is a burgeoning area. Nesse and Williams (1995) laid the foundations for this important area of study. They considered why the human body, apparently so intricately designed by natural selection, is so susceptible to physical and psychological illness. Modern medicine has provided a great deal of information regarding the proximate causes of illness, but much less is known about why we are so susceptible to ill health at all. Darwinian medicine offers ultimate explanations for illness, challenging our notions of disease, offering adaptive explanations for their origins and

A phobia of spiders would have been adaptive in the ancestral environment.

Source: Peter Waters/Shutterstock.com.

explaining why some degree of ill health is inevitable. These ultimate explanations have significant implications for effective treatment.

From the perspective of evolutionary psychology, one of the most interesting areas of Darwinian medicine is evolutionary psychopathology, the application of evolutionary principles to mental health problems. Within psychology and psychiatry, mental illness is usually considered maladaptive, the result of something gone wrong. While this is often the case, it is argued that many aspects of psychopathology may have adaptive origins. Some of the most common phobias (such as spiders and snakes) are adaptive responses to fitness threats in the ancestral environment. Individuals who did not fear spiders and snakes in the EEA (where they were more prevalent than in many environments humans currently live in) would be at a significant survival disadvantage.

One of the most endemic forms of psychopathology is depression. The central symptoms of depression (low mood, lack of interest in activities) appear to be maladaptive; however, the *social competition hypothesis* (Price *et al.*, 1994) proposes that depression may be an adaptive response to loss in a status struggle, promoting yielding and reconciliation with the victor. Other models consider depression an adaptive response to loss more generally, promoting reflection and loss-limiting behaviour in the future (see McGuire *et al.*, 1997). Depression is currently considered a mood disorder, and is treated as such. However, if depression is sometimes an adaptive response to loss, drugs that treat low mood may not always be appropriate.

A further perspective offered by evolutionary psychopathology concerns the impact of the mismatch between modern and ancestral environments for psychological health. Culture has evolved at a much faster rate than biological evolution (see above on cultural evolution). Human psychology has changed little since hunter-gatherer times, but the world we inhabit is very different. To name but a few of the differences, we now live in much larger groups, are often separated from kin, work longer hours and have less leisure time. In short, we inhabit a world that we are not adapted to. The mismatch between ancestral and modern environments is likely to underlie much psychopathology. For example, depression and anxiety may result from lack of kin support, crowded living conditions and the highly competitive environment in which we live. Buss (2000) argues that the environmental mismatch is responsible for a great deal of human unhappiness.

Darwinian medicine is in its infancy but has the potential to transform our understanding of health and disease, and contribute to effective treatment.

Before You Go On

What Do You Know?

13. Describe the role of evolutionary approaches to these future areas of research.

14. What are the benefits to these areas of using an evolutionary perspective?

What Do You Think?

Will evolutionary theory help our understanding of all areas of psychology in the future? What do you think are the main reasons that could prevent this?

Activities to test yourself further are available in your interactive e-book at **www.wileyopenpage.com**

Summary

The History of Evolutionary Approaches to Psychology

LEARNING OBJECTIVE 1 Understand the historical and scientific discoveries that have shaped how evolutionary theory is applied to human behaviour.

- Charles Darwin first explained evolution by natural selection in *On the Origin of Species,* which showed that the key principles of variation, inheritance and selection were vital for evolution to occur.
- The modern synthesis combined Mendel's discoveries on genetic inheritance with Darwinian evolution.
- William Hamilton produced the notion of inclusive fitness, which explains kin selection. This was then used by George Williams to show that the individual is selected for and not the group.
- Niko Tinbergen used his 'four whys' of behaviour to found the field of ethology, which examined the evolutionary origins of behaviour.
- Further understanding of the evolution of behaviour was provided by the findings of Robert Trivers (reciprocal altruism, parental investment and parent–offspring conflict) and E. O. Wilson (sociobiology).
- This led to the founding of evolutionary psychology by Leda Cosmides and John Tooby, who viewed the brain as consisting of evolved modules.

The Principles Behind Evolutionary Psychology

LEARNING OBJECTIVE 2 Gain knowledge of how findings from different areas of scientific research have shaped our understanding of human evolutionary psychology.

- Evidence from different sources can be used to show human evolution, including the differences between species and details about their physical structure and other artefacts that can be used to assess their possible mental and cognitive abilities.
- The environment of evolutionary adaptedness (EEA) can be used to produce theories about human evolution; however, there are a number of criticisms of using this.
- An understanding of genetic inheritance and the possible links between genes and behaviours can show the biological causes and origins of different psychological traits.

Main Areas of Research in Evolutionary Psychology

LEARNING OBJECTIVE 3 Gain knowledge of the main areas of research in evolutionary psychology.

- Sexual selection gives rise to traits that provide reproductive (rather than survival) advantages.
- Sexual selection results in sex differences in mate preferences and other social behaviours due to the different selection pressures that have acted on men and women, primarily resulting from sex differences in fitness variance and parental investment.
- Kin selection describes the tendency for individuals to provide help to genetic relatives in order to increase their own inclusive fitness.
- However, because parents and offspring do not share 100% of their DNA, there is 'disagreement' regarding the extent of parental investment. Siblings also compete for investment, resulting in sibling rivalry.
- Altruistic behaviour was originally problematic to Darwin's theory of natural selection; however, kin selection (cooperation between relatives) and reciprocal altruism (where any help is returned in the future) were early theories that solved this problem.
- Contemporary theories of the evolution of cooperation (e.g. image scoring, competitive altruism, costly signalling) emphasize the reputational benefits of indirect reciprocity.
- Language is a unique form of communication, and it has many potential adaptive benefits.
- Infants have an innate ability to learn language (language acquisition device).
- There is disagreement as to whether language is an evolved trait or just a by-product of overall brain growth.
- The main theories of why language first evolved (grooming and gossip, social contracts and marriage, language as a fitness indicator) emphasize the strong role of the social environment on language evolution.
- Humans are poor at some abstract, logical reasoning tasks (e.g. Wason selection task). However, when we look at the same task under evolutionarily relevant conditions (social contracts), we see that our cognitive abilities have evolved to solve those problems instead.
- Our ability to understand statistics and other information is influenced by whether the stimuli are evolutionarily relevant.

- Dual inheritance theorists argue that culture and cultural learning have genetic fitness benefits because they allow rapid responses to changing environments and equip individuals with useful knowledge and skills.
- Memeticists have argued that cultural evolution can occur, regardless of genetic fitness benefit.

Criticisms and Misunderstandings of Evolutionary Approaches to Human Behaviour

LEARNING OBJECTIVE 4   Understand the criticisms and misunderstandings of evolutionary approaches to psychology, as well as the responses by proponents in the field.

- Evolutionary psychology is criticized for too easily believing that behaviours are adaptations (panadaptations). However, it is argued that the testing of different hypotheses can reduce this possibility.
- Evolutionary psychology is considered guilty of placing too much emphasis on biological explanations (biological determinism), although evolutionary psychologists often recognize the importance of the environment or culture in shaping adapted behaviours (e.g. LAD).
- Evolutionary psychology maybe tries to explain things too simply (reductionism); however, evolutionary psychologists would argue that reductionism is good, and that they do not reduce explanations too far.
- Critics believe that by showing the existence of certain negative behaviours, evolutionary psychology is condoning them. This is strongly denied by evolutionary psychologists, who state that such criticisms are guilty of the naturalistic fallacy and are false.

The Future of Evolutionary Psychology

LEARNING OBJECTIVE 5   Gain understanding of the new areas of evolutionary psychology research, and an appreciation of future directions.

- Advances in research in genetics (genome sequencing, epigenetics) show the complex link between genes and behaviour, therefore highlighting the importance of understanding the role of genetics in shaping evolved behaviours in the future.
- Hormones research can show that the mechanisms that lead to evolved behaviours (such as testosterone affecting male competition, and oxytocin affecting trust and cooperative behaviours) are biological, therefore providing further evidence of their adaptive origin.
- The traditional view of natural selection fixing characteristics makes understanding the existence of individual differences difficult. However, this may not necessarily be an issue and the variation itself may be adaptive.
- Recent research in individual differences has shown the value of an evolutionary perspective in understanding the Big Five personality traits, empathy, trustworthiness and more.
- An evolutionary approach to neuroscience can help us understand different properties of the brain by examining how and why they evolved (e.g. primate brain size, amygdala).
- Evolutionary neurosciences can also help us understand unusual yet fascinating properties and systems in the brain, such as mirror neurons.
- Darwinian medicine provides an ultimate perspective on the origins of physical and mental illness. The insights provided by this relatively new area of study have important implications for effective treatment.

 Access your interactive e-book to view a video clip for this chapter at www.wileyopenpage.com

TYING IT TOGETHER

HOW WE DEVELOP

- Human infants rely on substantial parental investment to reach maturity. Parents provide investment in order to increase their own inclusive fitness (kin selection).

- Humans are born with a language acquisition device (LAD) that develops during infancy and gives us the ability to learn and understand the structure and grammar of the language we are exposed to at a rapid rate when we are very young.

- Evolutionary approaches to psychology do not suggest that evolved behaviours are completely innate; instead, they often recognize the roles of culture, learning and the environment as well.

- Epigenetics recognizes that the environment can also cause changes to genetic structure that are related to behaviours that can be inherited by future offspring.

WHAT HAPPENS IN THE BRAIN?

- Evolutionary psychology assumes that the human brain is made up of a series of modules that have evolved to solve specific problems our ancestors faced.

- Reasoning on different types of tasks (social, hazards) has been shown to use different areas of the brain, which suggests there are specifically evolved brain mechanisms (modules) for detecting cheats.

- The social brain hypothesis argues that the best way to understand brain functioning is to look at what the brain has evolved to do, which is to deal with complex social systems.

- The existence of mirror neurons can help us understand further what our brains evolved to do, and help explain how they can do this.

HOW WE DIFFER

- Behavioural genetics uses the differences in how traits are expressed in twins as a means of estimating how much of that trait is due to genes and how much is due to environment.

- Evolutionary approaches to individual differences recognize that psychological traits do not have to be fixed, and that variation in these traits can be adaptive.

- Variation can be adaptive if there are survival and/or reproductive benefits to different forms of a trait, or if it is necessary to have different expressions of traits due to changing environments.

- The evolutionary approach to individual differences in humans is a growing area, and research has already explored personality and intelligence from such a perspective.

- As a result of differential selection pressures in the ancestral environment arising from sex differences in fitness variance and parental investment, sexual selection has shaped many of the psychological mechanisms of men and women in different ways.

- Evolutionary psychology has provided ultimate explanations for sex differences in a number of social behaviours, including mate preferences, mating strategies and aggression.

OUT OF THE ORDINARY

- The relatively new discipline of Darwinian medicine provides an ultimate perspective on human health problems, showing how perceived 'symptoms' are often adaptations to combat disease.

- The sub-discipline of evolutionary psychopathology examines mental health problems through an evolutionary lens, and suggests that they often arise from adaptive responses to selection pressures in the ancestral environment, while others arise from the mismatch between modern and ancestral environments.

Quizzes to test yourself further are available in your interactive e-book at **www.wileyopenpage.com**

Key Terms

adaptation 138
allele 139
altruism 148
anisogamy 144
bipedalism 141
by-product 151
cheater 150
cranial capacity 141
cuckoldry 146
domain-specific 150
ethology 139
evolution 138
evolutionarily stable
   strategy 149

fitness variance 145
fixation 158
genes 139
genome 156
handicap principle 145
heritability 143
heritable 138
hominids 141
inclusive fitness 139
innate 138
intersexual selection 145
intrasexual selection 146
just-so story 155
kin selection 147

maladaptive 138
meme 154
mirror neurons 158
modularity 140
mutations 143
naturalistic fallacy 155
oxytocin 157
Pleistocene 142
prestige bias 153
reciprocal altruism 148
relatedness 140
reproductive success 144
runaway selection 145
selection 138

sexual selection 140
sexy sons hypothesis 145
sibling rivalry 147
social contract 150
testosterone 157
universal Darwinism 154
universality 158
variation 138

Flashcards to test yourself further are available in your interactive e-book at **www.wileyopenpage.com**

CHAPTER 7

Perception and the Senses

Adapted by David Simmons, University of Glasgow, UK

CHAPTER OUTLINE

- Introducing Perception: Common Features of the Senses

- The Chemical Senses: Smell and Taste

- The Tactile Senses: Touch, Pressure, Pain, Vibration

- The Auditory Sense: Hearing

- The Visual Sense: Sight

 Access your interactive e-book to view a video clip for this chapter at **www.wileyopenpage.com**

On and Off Sensation

Have you ever noticed how enticing the aroma of your favourite restaurant is when you first walk through the door? The smell of foods you enjoy coming from the kitchen makes your mouth water. Depending on how long it has been since you last ate a meal, you may develop an urgent craving to order as soon as possible.

After you order, while you wait for your meal to arrive, you may not even notice it, but your awareness of the food odours in the room is probably gradually decreasing. By the time your meal comes to your table, you are probably not even noticing the smells that seemed so strong when you first got to the restaurant. When the server places your plate on the table, right under your nose, however, you may suddenly begin to notice the smell of food again – this time your own. ■

Our sense of smell contributes greatly to our enjoyment of a good meal. In fact, all of our senses work at the same time when we enjoy a meal. We use vision, our sense of sight, to admire the food on the plate. We use hearing to listen to the sizzle of a particularly hot dish or enjoy conversation with our friends and family. Obviously, our sense of taste is involved once we actually take a bite of food, but so are our senses of touch, as we notice the temperature and texture of the food. Without our touch (tactile) senses, we could not tell a rough, cool salad from a smooth, warm soup.

Psychologists have generally agreed that there are five senses: smell, taste, touch, sound and sight. Touch is actually several senses, together called the *cutaneous senses* or the *somatosenses*. These include pressure, vibration, pain, temperature and position. Although we will discuss each of these five major senses separately in this chapter, in most of our day-to-day experiences, we do not use only one sense at a time. We actually use each of these sensory systems, or *modalities*, together to experience the world.

Some psychologists argue that our senses engage in two important and interacting processes. One process is **sensation**, the act of using our sensory systems to detect stimuli present in the environment around us. Once detected, sensory information must be interpreted or compared with past and present sensory stimuli. This process, which also involves recognition and identification (e.g. the realization that you recognize a smell and are able to identify that smell as pizza cooking in a restaurant), can be broadly defined as **perception**. Other psychologists argue, however, that the distinction between sensation and perception is an artificial one. They argue that the physical structure of our sense organs and the way that we choose to use them by, for example, moving our eyes to predict the future position of an object, mean that the interpretation of sensory stimuli begins as soon as, or even before, the stimulus activates sensory receptors. We should therefore rename the whole process as *perception*, which is what we will do for the remainder of this chapter, reserving *sensation* as a general term for certain kinds of perception.

> **sensation** the act of using our sensory systems to detect environmental stimuli.

> **perception** recognition and identification of a sensory stimulus.

Perception is critical for our understanding of and interaction with the world around us. In some situations, accurate functioning of our sensory systems is necessary for survival. Imagine how greatly diminished your chances of survival would be, for example, if you could not see a fire, feel its heat, hear others crying 'Fire!' or smell the smoke, or if you did not realize that these sensations meant you needed to run from harm's way quickly. Our ability to perceive the world is clearly adapted to help us in life-threatening situations, but our other life experiences are also greatly enriched by these processes. Let us explore perception in more detail.

Introducing Perception: Common Features of the Senses

LEARNING OBJECTIVE 1

Describe characteristics shared by all the senses, including receptor cells, transduction and thresholds, and differentiate between top-down and bottom-up processes of perception.

Our sensory systems obviously differ from one another. You would not try to use your ears to taste the dinner you ordered at your favourite restaurant, for example. But all of our sensory systems also share some common processes. We start the chapter by looking more closely at these processes, and then we turn to the processing of sensory information.

Translating Stimuli: Sensory Transduction

Each of our sensory systems is set up to 'translate' the physical stimuli we receive from the world outside our bodies into the 'language' of neural information. Each of the senses has a set of specialized cells called *sensory receptor cells* that convert a specific form of environmental stimuli into neural impulses, the form of communication used in our brains and nervous systems (Figure 7.1). This process of conversion is called *sensory transduction*. For each sensory system, the different physical stimuli that are converted to brain activity through sensory transduction are listed in Table 7.1.

Here is what happens. Whenever you encounter a stimulus, though you are not always aware of it, your brain receives information that helps you know how to respond. For example, the instant a fly lands on your arm, the sensory receptor cells in your skin respond by sending neural impulses to your brain. That is when you 'sense' something on your arm. You look down in that direction, and sensory transduction occurs again as you see the fly. The information

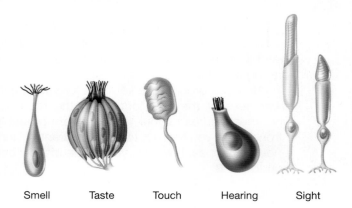

Smell   Taste   Touch   Hearing   Sight

FIGURE 7.1 Sensory receptor cells. Each sensory system contains specialized cells that are activated by particular physical stimuli.

TABLE 7.1 Sensory Transduction Converts Environmental Stimuli into Neural Activity

Sensory system	Physical stimuli
Olfactory (smell)	Odorants (airborne chemicals)
Gustatory (taste)	Chemicals in contact with the tongue (typically in food)
Somatosensory (touch, heat, cold, pain)	Pressure, temperature change or damage to the skin
Auditory (hearing)	Sound waves
Visual (sight)	Light (photons)

TABLE 7.2 Absolute Thresholds for Various Senses

Sense	Absolute threshold
Smell	A drop of perfume diffused into the entire volume of a large room
Taste	One teaspoon of sugar in 7.5 litres of water
Touch	An insect's wing falling on your cheek from a height of one centimetre
Hearing	The tick of a watch six metres away in a quiet room
Sight	A candle flame 50 kilometres away on a clear, dark night

that you have received from your sensory systems tells you to swat the fly away. All this happens in only a few seconds. In fact, it usually seems to happen before you can even 'think'.

The Limits of the Senses: Thresholds

Our sensory receptors can be activated by very weak stimuli. A stimulus must, however, reach a certain level of intensity before we can detect it. The process of sensory transduction occurs only when the stimuli reach this level, or *threshold*. If a stimulus were too weak, we would not even know it was there. The minimum stimulation necessary for detection is called the **absolute threshold** (Table 7.2). Although the absolute threshold is different for every person, in most cases it is surprisingly small. For instance, many people are capable of detecting a candle flame many kilometres away on a clear night (Galanter, 1962).

absolute threshold the minimum stimulation necessary for detection by a person.

Researchers have also worked to determine the smallest difference that we are able to notice between two stimuli of the same type, such as the smells wafting from two different meals. This measure is called the **difference threshold** or **just noticeable difference**. When sensory systems are working well, the difference threshold is also remarkably small.

difference threshold or **just noticeable difference** the smallest difference between two stimuli necessary for detecting a difference between the two.

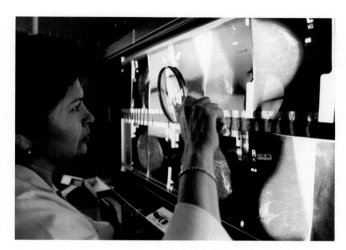

A critical difference. A radiologist carefully examines a mammogram, looking for the slightest indication of a tumour. An individual's ability to detect a difference between two visual stimuli (such as normal versus abnormal tissue) can be increased by special training, practice and instruments, but it is still limited to some degree by sensory difference thresholds.
Source: ©ER Productions/Corbis.

Thresholds may limit our abilities in some ways, but they are also very useful to us. Imagine if you noticed every little change in wind pattern or each individual fibre in your clothing. You probably would not be very comfortable if you noticed all of these small details. Many individuals with autism appear to do this, however.

PSYCHOLOGY AROUND US   Sensory Processing in Autism: An Eye for Details

Although the condition *autism* is generally considered (and largely defined) in terms of problems with social interaction, most individuals with a diagnosis of autism report or display signs of difficulties with sensory processing (Leekam *et al.*, 2007). These usually take the form of a combination of hyper- (increased) or hypo- (reduced) levels of sensitivity to environmental sensory stimuli compared to typical individuals. Sometimes this can be advantageous. The life of Temple Grandin, the famous autistic and pioneer of innovations in humane animal husbandry, makes this very clear (Grandin & Scariano, 1986). Grandin's ability to

observe the behaviour of beef cattle in exquisite detail allowed her to propose radical changes to the way they were handled that have become standard across the United States. However, Grandin's difficulty with filtering out irrelevant sensory stimulation became problematic in other situations (especially social ones) where she would become anxious and panic-stricken. Recent studies have suggested a link between the sensory symptoms of autism and social behaviour (see Robertson & Simmons, 2012). The underlying cause of these sensory differences in autism, as with autism itself, is currently unknown.

Surrounded by Stimuli: Sensory Adaptation

Our senses are generally organized to detect change. In other words, we use our senses to notice what is changing around us, more than to pay attention to what stays the same over time. This makes sense, because most stimuli we are exposed to are not important enough to demand our constant attention (but see the 'Sensory Processing in Autism' box). Imagine how difficult it would be to concentrate on reading this chapter if the odours of your surroundings, the taste of your mouth, the sound of the clock ticking and the touch of your clothing were all competing with your ability to read. We avoid such distractions and enhance our ability to focus on more important cues through a process called **sensory adaptation**. What happens is this: when some stimulus in our surroundings stays the same for a period of time, such as the pressure of our clothing on our skin, our sensory cells respond to it less and less. Sometimes, in fact, we no longer notice the stimulus at all. All of our sensory systems exhibit some form of adaptation, but the sense of smell seems especially prone to this response.

> **sensory adaptation** the process whereby repeated stimulation of a sensory cell leads to a reduced response.

Let us return to our restaurant example. Although it is possible that the diminished sense of smell people experience as they sit in a restaurant may be due to blocked sinuses, it is much more likely that it happens as a result of sensory adaptation. Our ability to detect odours gradually fades as they surround us for a long time. When a much stronger stimulus presents itself, however, sensory adaptation is diminished. This is what happens when your restaurant meal is delivered to your table. Now that the source of the smell is more concentrated just under your nose, your ability to smell is renewed. This change in concentration is a change in your environment – a new opportunity to gain information to bring you up to date with the world around you. Your new awareness of the smell of food is one of the things telling you that your meal has arrived and it is time to eat.

Processing Sensory Information

Researchers have identified two different ways in which information from our senses is processed: *bottom-up* and *top-down processing*.

Bottom-up processing begins with the physical stimuli from the environment and proceeds through transduction of those stimuli into neural impulses. The signals are passed along to more and more complex brain regions, ultimately resulting in the recognition of a stimulus. For example, when you look at the face of someone you know, your eyes convert light energy into neural impulses, which travel into the brain to visual regions. This process allows you to detect the visual stimulus and to ultimately understand that you are looking at someone's face and that the face belongs to someone close to you. In other words, bottom-up processing starts from the *bottom* – with the stimulus you are trying to perceive. Sensory cells then transduce the stimulus into neural impulses that travel *up* into your brain.

> **bottom-up processing** the perception that proceeds by transducing environmental stimuli into neural impulses that move on to successively more complex brain regions.

Equally important to perception is **top-down processing**, which involves memories, expectations and other higher-level processes. When people look at their grandmother's face, for example, brain regions that store information about what faces look like, particularly those that are familiar, can help them to perceive and recognize the specific visual stimulus. Information from their memory moves from their brain at the *top* and helps them understand what is happening *down* at the sensory level. Even if a stimulus is unfamiliar – that is, someone has no memory of it – they can probably work out something about it from what they know about other things.

> **top-down processing** the perception processes led by cognitive processes, such as memory or expectations.

The power of top-down processing goes far beyond just using our memories to recognize our grandmother's face. Our perceptual expectations, or **perceptual sets**, actually prepare us to perceive certain things in particular ways. For example, a photo showing a fuzzy UFO will look very different to you depending on whether you believe

> **perceptual sets** readiness to interpret a certain stimulus in a certain way.

FIGURE 7.2 Old or young? What you see when you look at this drawing depends in part on what you expect to see.

there is such a thing as UFOs. And perceptual sets do not relate only to vision. Consider, for example, whether a dish in your favourite restaurant would taste exactly the same to you if you thought it was chicken as it would if you thought it was rat. Many elements – our experiences, our cultures, the contexts in which we find ourselves – affect our perceptual sets.

Perceptual sets may come into play when we are faced with *ambiguous stimuli*, stimuli that could be interpreted in different ways. A well-known visual example is presented in Figure 7.2. Looked at one way, the drawing shows a young woman looking over her shoulder – you can see her jawline, her ear and a bit of her nose. Looked at another way, it shows an old woman with her chin to her chest. If someone pointed out this drawing to you by saying, 'Look at this picture of an old woman with a big nose,' that is most likely what you would see – because that is what you would expect to see.

Typically, perception involves both bottom-up and top-down processing occurring at the same time. As we have seen, when these two processes occur together, they let us rapidly recognize familiar faces and other visual stimuli. Similarly, recognizing familiar songs involves not only information carried from the ear to the brain but also the matching of information about the sound of the music with memories about the music. We also combine bottom-up and top-down processes to help us recognize the smell or taste of a familiar food and the feel of a familiar fabric.

PSYCHOLOGY AROUND US   Superstitious Perception: If It's Not There, Make It Up!

Have you ever had the experience of imagining you see a face in a pattern of wood grain? Or seen what you think is a person only to realize that it is a tree? Perception researchers have taken this to the extreme in experiments on *superstitious perception*. In these experiments, they presented experimental participants, over the course of a few days, with thousands of very slightly different but nevertheless random patterns of black-and-white dots. But, ingeniously, they told them that there was a very faint image in half of these random patterns and their task was to spot which ones. By analysing the images for which the participants said 'yes', they were able to generate a picture of 'pure' top-down perception – in other words the internal image of the picture that the participants were looking for (in some cases an 'S', and in others a face). They argued that it is precisely this process that accounts for superstitious perceptions like the man in the moon (Figure 7.3; Gosselin & Schyns, 2003).

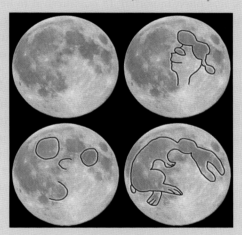

FIGURE 7.3 Example 'superstitious' perception of faces and other figures in the patterns made by the shadows of moon craters.

Source: Adapted from Wikipedia.

Before You Go On

What Do You Know?

1. What is sensory transduction?
2. What are absolute and difference thresholds?
3. Compare and contrast bottom-up and top-down processing.

What Do You Think?

Describe examples of sensory adaptation that you have experienced in two or more of your sensory modalities.

The Chemical Senses: Smell and Taste

LEARNING OBJECTIVE 2

Summarize the biological changes that underlie smell and taste.

Smell and taste are usually called the *chemical senses* because they involve responses to particular chemicals. Smell, our

> **olfactory sense** our sense of smell.

> **gustatory sense** our sense of taste.

olfactory sense, and taste, our **gustatory sense**, emerged early in our evolutionary history (Doty, 1986). The sense of smell, in particular, is more sensitive in, and of greater significance to, animals that are less evolved than humans. Rodents, for example, use their sense of smell for social communication as well as finding food and avoiding predators (Mech & Boitani, 2003; Yahr, 1977). The sense of smell is less essential for humans, who rely more heavily on vision. Nevertheless, both smell and taste are important to safety, social communication and overall quality of life for humans. It is often important to our survival to be able to detect dangerous odours, such as smoke or a gas leak, or dangerous flavours, such as tainted food or poison. Our senses of taste and smell also contribute to our enjoyment of life, as when we smell a rose or eat a good meal.

In this section, we will explore the environmental stimuli that create smells and flavours, the organs we use to sense those stimuli and how environmental stimuli are transformed into brain signals that eventually help us perceive different smells and tastes. We will also discuss the development of these abilities, some very interesting differences among people in their ability to taste and smell things and some things that can go wrong in the olfactory and gustatory systems.

Smell and Taste

Smell and taste are two separate senses. Nevertheless, they work closely together, as you will see.

Smells around Us

Sensation in the olfactory system begins

> **odorants** airborne chemicals that are detected as odours.

when chemicals called **odorants** enter the nose, as shown in 'What Happens in the Brain When We Eat Pizza' on the following pages. Odorants are converted to neural signals at sensory receptors in the mucous membranes lining the nose. These sensory receptors are located on the

> **olfactory receptor neurons** sensory receptor cells that convert chemical signals from odorants into neural impulses that travel to the brain.

cilia, or hairlike structures, of **olfactory receptor neurons** (McEwen *et al.*, 2008).

When odorants enter the nose, these chemicals bind to specific receptors located on the olfactory receptor neurons. These chemicals bind to receptors as a key fits into a lock: the chemical is the key, the receptor the

lock. Only certain airborne chemicals bind to specific receptors (Buck, 1996). In other words, only certain chemicals can 'unlock' specific receptors. When enough odorant molecules have 'unlocked' these receptors, the combination sets off an action potential in the olfactory receptor neuron. As we described in Chapter 5, the action potential, or *firing*, of a neuron sends a message to other neurons. The firing of olfactory receptor neurons is transmitted to the brain, as we will see next.

Continuous binding of the same odorants to receptors, such as those contained in the main ingredients of a restaurant dinner, will result in fatigue of the olfactory receptor neurons to which they bind. In other words, as described earlier, the cells will stop responding to the odorants unless they are given a chance to recover so they can fire again (Dalton, 2000). If you were to step outside the restaurant to make a phone call, for example, you would probably notice the food smells again when you stepped back inside, because your olfactory receptor neurons would have had a break from constant exposure to the odorants. If you remain in the restaurant, however, the olfactory receptor neurons will respond to the odorants only if the smell becomes stronger. This is what happens when the food is brought directly to your table. Many more odorant molecules are now available to your nose and its olfactory receptor neurons.

Types of Tastes

In humans, the sense of smell is very closely tied to that of taste. In fact, what we normally call *taste* is really *flavour*, which is a combination of smell and taste. Taste, the gustatory sense, is itself independent of smell. The tongue, the major organ of taste, is covered with bumps, called **papillae**. As shown in Figure 7.4, papillae contain

> **papillae** bumps on the tongue that contain clumps of taste buds.

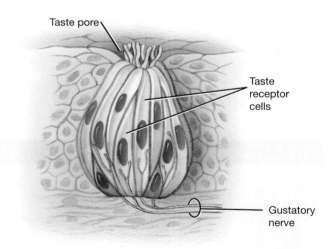

FIGURE 7.4 A taste bud. The receptor cells for taste are located within the taste buds found in the bumps, or papillae, covering your tongue.

Labels on figure: Taste pore; Taste receptor cells; Gustatory nerve

taste buds clusters of sensory receptor cells that convert chemical signals from food, drink, etc. into neural impulses that travel to the brain.

clumps of **taste buds**, each of which contains sixty to one hundred sensory receptor cells for taste. Taste receptor cells have cilia that contain the actual receptors. These cilia extend through the pores of the taste receptor and come in contact with anything in your mouth.

There are four major kinds of taste receptors. Each responds to a specific taste in our food: (1) sweet, (2) sour, (3) bitter and (4) salty (Sugita, 2006). A fifth type of taste receptor has also been discovered: *umami*. Umami is the taste of monosodium glutamate (MSG). It is a chemical additive used in cooking some Asian food and American fast food. Each of these five types of taste receptor uses a slightly different mechanism to transduce the chemicals in food into neural impulses. For example, salt activates its taste receptors by sending sodium ions into the channels on the taste receptor cell. Since sodium ions are positively charged, the electrical charge of the taste receptor then becomes more positive. Taste buds are not evenly spread out across the tongue but most tastes can, more or less, be recognized on most parts of the tongue, contrary to the common misconception of specialized tongue regions for specific tastes (Halpern, 2002).

Eating: It Is More than Smell and Taste The overall sensations we experience when we eat food result not only from the combined interactions between olfactory and gustatory senses. Much of the information we get about food comes to us through one of the touch, or *tactile*, senses. For example, we use the tactile sense to recognize the consistency, spiciness and temperature of what we eat. The consistency of a particular food is relayed to the brain by inputs from touch receptors located on the tongue. Food consistency largely affects what foods we prefer to eat. Many people reject certain foods, such as raw oysters or cooked okra, because, to them, those foods have a slimy texture, for example.

In addition, the sensation we experience when we eat a hot (i.e., spicy) meal is related to a component of the tactile system that communicates information about pain. A chemical called *capsaicin*, from chili peppers, activates pain receptors in the tongue (Numazaki & Tominaga, 2004). These pain impulses, along with tactile information about the food texture, and the flavours (smell and taste) associated with the food, can combine to produce a sensation that many people find enjoyable.

Suppose a food is not spicy but is hot because it just came out of the oven. We have all had the experience of burning our mouths, which can damage the taste receptors on the tongue. The sensory receptors of taste are unusual because they regenerate when this happens.

Smell and Taste: How They Work

 **WHAT HAPPENS IN THE BRAIN?**

Next, we will follow the path of neural signals as they travel from the sensory receptors to the brain. Again, we start with the sense of smell. Signals from our olfactory receptor neurons travel to the brain via the olfactory nerve. As Figure 7.5

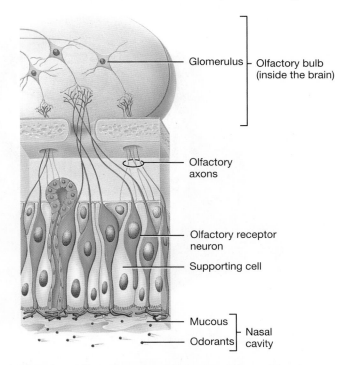

FIGURE 7.5 The smell route. Olfactory receptor neurons (shown here in blue) transduce information from odorant molecules that enter the nose. This information is carried by the olfactory nerve into the brain where it synapses on neurons called *glomeruli* in the olfactory bulb.

YOUR BRAIN AND BEHAVIOUR　What Happens in the Brain When We Eat Pizza

Is this the best pizza you have ever had, or does it fall short? When you dig into a slice of pizza, several neural circuits are activated to give you the overall experience. The appearance of your food can play an important role in how you enjoy it. Photoreceptors in the eye transmit this information to the brain via the optic nerve, which synapses in the thalamus and finally the visual cortex. Taste receptor cells, as well as sensory cells that respond to touch and temperature, are activated on your tongue. These nerves carry impulses into the brain where they synapse in the brainstem, thalamus and sensory cortex (gustatory cortex and somatosensory cortex). Taste is combined with smell information to produce flavour. Olfactory receptor neurons transduce pizza odorants and send this information to the olfactory bulb and then the olfactory cortex (smell is the only sensory modality that bypasses the thalamus on its way to the cortex).

Information about taste, smell, texture, temperature and appearance is integrated in various association regions of the neocortex. These circuits, together with those that store memories related to your previous pizza experiences, work together to produce your perception of this particular slice.

Sensing more than taste.
A large part of somatosensory cortex (shown here with neurons genetically engineered to produce fluorescent dyes) is devoted to processing information about texture, temperature and pain from the tongue. Somatosensory information from the tongue is critical for the enjoyment of food – many people prefer their crust crispy, while others like it soft.

Source: Drs Hang Hi and Ariel Agmon, Sensory Neuroscience Research Center, West Virginia University. Reproduced with permission.

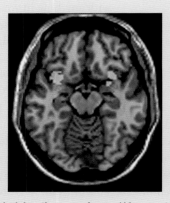

Maximizing the experience. When you eat something delicious and close your eyes, you may maximize the experience by turning up the activity in certain parts of the cortex. When your eyes are open, activity in parts of cortex serving nonvisual parts is decreased. Closing your eyes increases activity in these areas, including in taste and smell cortex. This fMRI image shows such increased activation in the olfactory cortex (yellow).

Source: Reproduced from M. Wiesmann et al., *NeuroImage* 32:293–300, Figure 4 (2006) with permission.

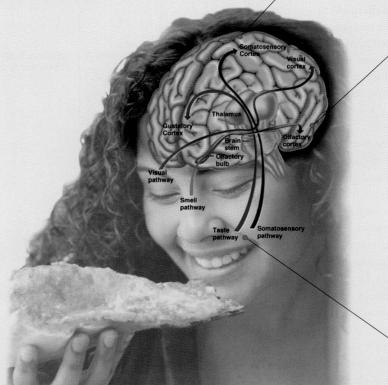

Somatosensory Cortex
Visual cortex
Thalamus
Gustatory Cortex
Brain stem
Olfactory cortex
Olfactory bulb
Visual pathway
Smell pathway
Taste pathway
Somatosensory pathway

Burning your tongue. Taste buds contain taste receptor cells (shown here marked with fluorescent dyes) that continually regenerate. The process is hastened when the tissue is damaged, such as when you burn your tongue.

Source: Marco Tizzano et al. Expression of Galpha 14 in sweet-transducing taste cells of the posterior tongue, *BMC Neuroscience* 2008 9:110, Figure 5. Reproduced with permission.

Source: Masterfile.

olfactory bulb the first region where olfactory information reaches the brain on its way from the nose.

shows, information carried along the olfactory nerves travels first to a structure called the **olfactory bulb**, located at the base of the front of the brain, beneath the frontal lobes. Olfactory information is then sent to regions of the cerebral cortex that are important for recognizing and distinguishing different odours, including the pyriform cortex (Wilson, 2001).

The ability of our cortex to recognize patterns of information from a variety of olfactory receptors is most likely responsible for our detection of certain odours. Studies have shown that the pyriform cortex is *plastic*, or changeable, in adulthood (Li *et al.*, 2008). That is, the parts of pyriform cortex that normally recognize specific odorants can change with experience, actually remapping this brain region. The chemical structures of some pairs of molecules are so similar that untrained humans cannot tell them apart (the two odours are usually below the just noticeable difference). However, if exposure to one of the chemicals is paired with a painful shock to the leg, humans can be taught to tell the difference between the odours (Li *et al.*, 2008). This is a remarkable example of top-down processing, where people recognize a smell because of the memory of pain they associate with it. Learning about associations between odours and other experiences (such as a shock) can influence our ability to perceive sensory information in the future. Along with the new ability to differentiate between the odours of closely related molecules, the areas of the pyriform cortex that are activated by each of these molecules become more distinct from each other.

The olfactory bulb also sends information to the amygdala, an area important for emotions (particularly fear), as well as indirectly to the hippocampus, an area important for learning and memory. Many people say that certain smells are evocative of past events (Lehrer, 2007). For example, the smell of baking may remind you of visiting your grandmother as a young child or the smell of floor polish may remind you of your old school. The ability of smells to bring back memories is probably partly related to olfactory connections to the hippocampus and amygdala.

Taste receptor cells do not have axons but instead synapse with sensory neurons in the tongue to send information to our brains. Taste information is sent to the *thalamus* and, eventually, the cerebral cortex. We will see throughout this chapter that the thalamus is a relay station for incoming sensory information of many kinds; all of our sensory systems except smell have a main pathway through the thalamus.

Taste information is integrated with reward circuits in the brain (Norgren *et al.*, 2006). Rewarding or pleasing tastes seem to be processed separately from aversive or unpleasant tastes. Tastes that are considered rewarding, such as salty and sweet, activate overlapping areas in the taste cortex. Tastes generally considered less pleasurable, such as bitter and sour, activate regions that overlap more with one another in the taste cortex, and not with rewarding tastes (Accolla *et al.*, 2007). Taste and smell information is processed through separate pathways, but that information converges in the association parts of the neocortex, namely in the prefrontal cortex.

In addition to integrating information about taste in general, part of the cortex that receives taste information, called the *insula*, is associated with the emotion of disgust. Neuroimaging studies have shown that this brain region becomes activated not only when we smell or taste something revolting but also when we view repulsive images (Schienle *et al.*, 2008; Calder *et al.*, 2007).

PSYCHOLOGY AROUND US   Regeneration in the Taste and Smell Systems

If you, like most people, have had the experience of burning your tongue on hot food, you have probably noticed that by the next day or so your ability to taste has returned and your tongue is no longer painful. This is due to the remarkable regenerative abilities of the taste buds. Taste receptor cells normally *turn over* – they die and are replaced – in a matter of days. The process happens even faster when they are damaged. Our olfactory receptor neurons are also constantly turning over under normal circumstances (Farbman, 1997).

The ability to regenerate on such a large scale and so rapidly is probably necessary because the receptor neurons for both taste and smell are exposed to the external world. Unlike the sensory receptors of the eye, which are protected by the eyeball, or those of the ear, which are protected by the eardrum, the surface of the tongue and the mucosa of the nose are directly exposed to any number of noxious chemical molecules that may enter our mouths or noses. Because destruction of receptors is likely under such circumstances, we need to constantly regenerate receptor cells just to continue normal functioning of our smell and taste systems.

Neurobiologists study the regenerative capabilities of the taste buds and olfactory receptor neurons in the hope of understanding exactly *how* these cells are constantly rejuvenating. Scientists and medical professionals hope that understanding these mechanisms may, in the future, allow us to replace other types of cells; ones that currently do not seem capable of repair when they are damaged.

PSYCHOLOGY AROUND US   'Eat Your Greens!'

Perhaps the phrase 'Eat your greens!' is familiar to you from your childhood. Many children dislike the tastes of fruits and vegetables that are bitter, such as Brussels sprouts, grapefruit, cabbage and spinach. It turns out, though, that the bitter taste in these foods comes from chemical substances that have health benefits. Although our parents' urging may have had little effect on us as children, most of us learn to make healthy choices about what we eat as we grow older. But many of us also eat more of these nutritious foods when we are older because we begin to enjoy bitter tastes.

Smell and Taste as we Grow

A number of our senses are relatively well developed at birth. The sense of smell is a good example. Research suggests that, within hours of birth, a newborn baby can tell his or her own mother from another woman using only the sense of smell. In fact, the sense of smell seems to exist even before birth. Newborn infants have a learnt preference for the odours of their mother's amniotic fluid. After birth, infants quickly learn to recognize the smell of their mother's milk. Smelling their mother's milk has a calming effect on infants when they are experiencing brief, minor pain, such as a needle stick in the heel (Nishitani *et al.*, 2009). This calming effect probably occurs because the baby associates the milk with the mother – exposure to other odours that the baby has associated with the mother has the same calming effect as the odour of their mother's milk (Goubet *et al.*, 2007).

The ability to taste is also well formed at birth in humans. Newborn babies show a natural preference for sugar and a dislike for bitter or sour tastes. Babies move their faces towards a sweet substance and make sucking movements with their mouths, but turn away and grimace when presented with a sour or bitter substance (Rosenstein & Oster, 1988).

Researchers have shown that by about seven years of age children begin to like sour tastes (Liem & Mennella, 2003). However, the tendency to dislike bitter tastes typically lasts until adulthood, when people begin to enjoy bitter foods and drinks, such as blue cheese, beer and dark chocolate.

Many developmental changes in taste preference are the result of learning. As children grow, they become accustomed to different tastes through trying different foods. However, there is some evidence to suggest that the gustatory system itself changes from infancy to adulthood. We form taste buds before we are born, and as newborns we have higher concentrations of them than we will as adults.

The fact that children have more taste buds may explain why they are often fussy eaters. The tastes of certain foods may seem too strong to children, because they have more taste buds to produce more neural impulses than adults would produce from eating the same food. Some researchers suggest that this may actually be adaptive, to help us survive.

For example, if young children enjoyed strong or bitter tastes they might be drawn towards dangerous substances and be at higher risk of poisoning.

Children often refuse or eat very little of foods that are unfamiliar to them (Koivisto Hursti, 1999). Although neuroimaging has not yet been used to study taste in developing humans, it is tempting to speculate that as individuals grow and develop a taste for more kinds of food, areas in the taste cortex represented by certain tastes are changed. It is likely that increased exposure to certain foods, especially when paired with positive social interactions and encouragement from parents, results in a remapping of previously aversive taste information on the gustatory cortex.

Sensitivity to Smell and Taste

Have you ever felt a bit faint when you were in a lift with someone wearing perfume, while others in the lift seemed not to notice? Humans vary greatly in their ability to detect certain odours. Some people seem relatively insensitive to even very strong smells, while others seem very sensitive. Some of these individual differences are related to learning. Exposure to particular odours during childhood lessens the reaction to those odours in adulthood.

In addition to these learnt differences, research suggests that females are generally more sensitive to smell than males are. Women's sensitivity also varies with the stage of the menstrual cycle (Pause *et al.*, 1996). Around the time of ovulation, women are more sensitive to odours than during other stages of the cycle. Women also become less able to detect different odours after menopause (Hughes *et al.*, 2002). The exact biological mechanisms that underlie these differences are not known, but it is possible that the presence of reproductive hormones, such as oestrogen, makes olfactory neurons less likely to fire.

There is also much variability among individuals' ability to taste. Researchers group people into three different categories of taste sensitivity: non-tasters (25% of people), medium tasters (50%) and supertasters (25%). These groups are distinguished based on their ability

A special gift? Perfumer Jean Kerléo the 'nose' of Jean Patou fragrances, determines whether a new perfume produces a pleasant result. People who are highly sensitive to odours often find employment that puts their special ability to use.

Source: ©Anna Clopet/Corbis.

to detect and dislike a specific bitter substance (Bartoshuk *et al.*, 1996). Supertasters are repulsed by this bitter chemical. Non-tasters do not notice the bitter taste, even though they can detect other tastes. Medium tasters notice the taste but do not find it particularly strong or unpleasant. These functional differences arise because individuals have different concentrations of taste buds on the tongue. More women than men are supertasters (Bartoshuk *et al.*, 1994).

We have seen that women tend to be more sensitive than men to both smell and taste. The heightened sensitivity of both these systems is likely to have had adaptive significance for women. The chemicals in the foods women choose to eat are passed along to their children when they are pregnant or nursing. Thus, the ability to detect and avoid potentially harmful odours and tastes may have helped the species survive by protecting infants from toxic substances.

Smell and Taste Disorders

OUT OF THE **ORDINARY**

Ageusia In some rare cases, typically as a result of head trauma or oral surgery, humans lose the ability to taste, a condition called **ageusia**. True taste disorders are rare, however. In fact, most people who seek medical assistance complaining that they cannot taste are actually suffering from problems with their sense of smell.

ageusia the inability to taste.

Anosmia Some people with a condition called **anosmia** lose the ability to smell. They can often still taste sweet, salt, sour, bitter and umami, but they can no longer detect other flavours that require the information from the odorants of food.

anosmia the inability to smell.

Head trauma is a leading cause of anosmia (Haxel *et al.*, 2008). Sometimes the nerves that carry olfactory information from the olfactory receptor neurons to the olfactory bulb can be damaged, cutting off the pathway for information about smell to reach the brain. People with Alzheimer's disease also suffer from a diminished sense of smell. This probably happens because of a combined degeneration of olfactory receptor neurons and neurons located in olfactory brain regions (Djordjevic *et al.*, 2008).

Although humans can certainly survive without the ability to smell, quality of life without it is considerably diminished. Many people with anosmia report feelings of depression. In addition, the inability to smell can have effects on our safety and social contact. Since we use our sense of smell to detect dangers, such as smoke or spoiled food, anosmia can increase the risk of injury from these sources. Basic practices of hygiene expected by others may be difficult to follow with anosmia, since humans often use olfactory cues to make decisions about bathing, washing clothes and brushing teeth. People with anosmia can learn to cope effectively with their condition by using other senses to detect danger. They may, for example, use sound cues, such as a blaring smoke detector to notice smoke, or visual cues, like the appearance of their food and expiration dates, to notice spoiled food.

Migraines, Epilepsy and the Sensory Systems The chemical senses are also involved in the symptoms of some people with migraine headaches or epilepsy. For instance, a specific odour can initiate the onset of a migraine (Kelman, 2007). Likewise, patients with a certain type of epilepsy, called *reflex epilepsy*, will experience a seizure only if they smell a specific odour. The reasons why this happens remain unknown, but these individuals must avoid specific intense odorants. In other patients suffering from migraines or epilepsy, stimuli from the other sensory systems, such as touch, sound and sight, can initiate headaches or seizures.

Some people experience hallucinations, called *auras*, either before or during migraine headaches or epileptic seizures. Auras can involve any of the sensory systems. People with these conditions can have touch, sound or sight hallucinations, and some sense strong, often unpleasant, smells or tastes. The involvement of different senses indicates which brain circuits are affected by these conditions. For example, if a person has strong olfactory hallucinations before a seizure, it is likely that his or her olfactory pathways are setting off the seizure, or at least contributing to it.

The Tactile Senses: Touch, Pressure, Pain, Vibration

LEARNING OBJECTIVE 3
Describe how the different senses of touch work and what can happen when things go wrong.

- *Tactile*, as we mentioned earlier, means 'touch'. As with the chemical senses, there are also rewarding and aversive types of tactile stimuli. The pleasure associated with a relaxing back massage or stroking a baby's cheek contrasts greatly with the discomfort of getting a scrape or burn, for example. The tactile, or somatosensory, system is actually a complex sense. As shown in Figure 7.6, our skin contains a variety of sensory receptors to register different types of physical stimuli (Johnson, 2002; Munger & Ide, 1988).

- *Free nerve endings* are located mostly near the surface of the skin and function to detect touch, pressure, pain and temperature.

- *Meissner's corpuscles* transduce information about light touch and are found in the hairless (glabrous) regions

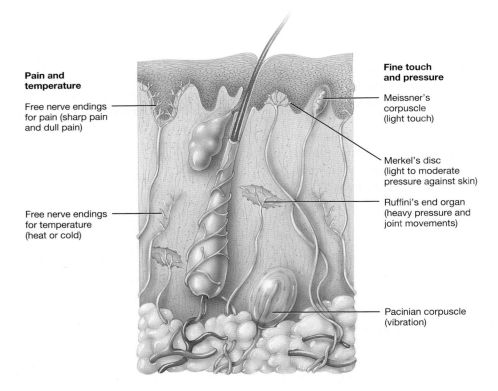

Pain and temperature

Free nerve endings for pain (sharp pain and dull pain)

Free nerve endings for temperature (heat or cold)

Fine touch and pressure

Meissner's corpuscle (light touch)

Merkel's disc (light to moderate pressure against skin)

Ruffini's end organ (heavy pressure and joint movements)

Pacinian corpuscle (vibration)

FIGURE 7.6 Sensory receptors in the skin. The tactile senses rely on a variety of receptors located in different parts of the skin.

of the body, such as the fingertips, lips and palms. They are particularly important for handgrip control.

- *Merkel's discs* transduce information about light-to-moderate pressure against the skin and are involved in sensing fine details like tactile form and texture.

- *Ruffini's endings* are located deep in the skin. They register heavy pressure and movement of the joints (especially stretching of the skin).

- *Pacinian corpuscles* are also buried deep in the skin. They are sensitive to high-frequency vibrations usually transmitted through objects held in the hand.

Pressure on the skin activates free nerve endings that give us the sense of being touched. As you may have noticed, your skin is not equally sensitive to tactile stimuli over your whole body. Certain parts of your body, like the skin on your elbow, are much less sensitive to touch than other areas, like the face and hands. These sensitivities are probably different because of different densities of free nerve endings. Areas that are more sensitive have more free nerve endings.

We can also experience sensory adaptation, resulting in a reduced tactile sensation from depression of the skin that remains for some time. This happens to you every day when you put on your clothing; shortly after getting dressed, you are no longer aware of the tactile stimulus of your clothing on your skin (unless, of course, it is too tight).

Tactile Senses

 **WHAT HAPPENS IN THE BRAIN?**

Our brains use a variety of related processes to help us perceive general information about a range of non-painful touch sensations, including pressure, temperature and general touch. Pain perception is also an important, but not yet fully understood, function.

The Touching Brain When we touch something, or something touches us, our free nerve endings send tactile information into the spinal cord. The signals travel up the spinal cord to the brain, as shown in Figure 7.7. In the brain, touch information is first received in the thalamus and then transferred to the somatosensory cortex (located in the parietal lobe). Information about pressure and vibration is generally transmitted to the brain in a similar way, after being converted to neural impulses by the specialized receptors described above.

Our brain processes tactile information *contralaterally*, or on the opposite side of the brain from the side of the body

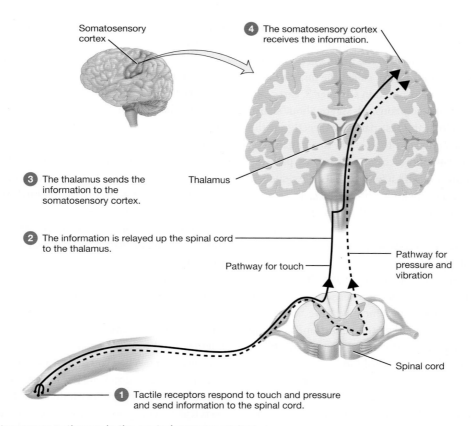

FIGURE 7.7 Somatosensory pathways in the central nervous system.

where the touch occurred. So, if you touch something with your left hand, the information is eventually processed by the somatosensory cortex on the right side of your brain.

As we discussed in Chapter 5, the parts of the body are not equally represented in the somatosensory cortex (Kakigi *et al.*, 2000). For example, tactile inputs from the hands take up proportionately more space in the somatosensory cortex than those from the back. This seems reasonable, since we use our hands so much and need to process information from them in great detail. Information about pressure and vibration is generally similarly transmitted to the brain after being converted to neural impulses by the specialized receptors described above.

PSYCHOLOGY AROUND US **The Nose Knows**

Just as humans have a very high concentration of tactile receptors on their hands, other mammals, particularly those without hands, have concentrated tactile receptors on different parts of their bodies. They rely on these specific body parts for fine-touch information, much in the same way we rely on our hands. The star-nosed mole, for example, is named for its specialized nose, shaped like a star (Figure 7.8). This creature lives mostly underground and is almost completely blind. It navigates throughout its dark environment by using its star-shaped nose, as a blind person would use his or her hands, to accomplish such tasks as finding food and exploring its environment. Accordingly, the nose representation in the star-nosed mole's somatosensory cortex is proportionately larger than that devoted to other body parts.

FIGURE 7.8 The star-nosed mole. The very special nose of this excellent-swimming mole guides it as the animal forages along the bottoms of streams and ponds, sniffing for prey.
Source: ©Ken Catania/Visuals Unlimited/Corbis.

Pain and the Brain Like general touch information, painful sensations are also transmitted to the brain via free nerve endings. Pain information travels to the brain via two different types of pain fibres. One system, called the *fast pathway*, uses myelinated axons that, as noted in Chapter 5, carry signals faster than unmyelinated axons. Messages about sharp, localized pain travel along the fast pathway directly up the spinal cord to the thalamus and to areas of the somatosensory cortex. Pain information received via the fast pathway helps us to respond quickly with a withdrawal reflex, such as pulling a hand away after touching a hot surface. The slower pain pathway uses more unmyelinated axons. These inputs communicate with brain regions that help to process emotions. Pain we perceive via the slow pathway is more often burning pain than sharp pain.

Like the other sensory systems we have discussed so far, the pain system shows evidence of sensory adaptation. A common example is the experience we have when eating a spicy meal. Remember that the sensation of eating chili peppers is mostly due to the activation of pain fibres on the tongue. Often, when a very hot food is first ingested, the pain response seems intense. As the meal progresses, the response is less powerful and we are less likely to experience discomfort. The pain fibres become adapted to the stimulus, and they become less active. However, when pain is associated with actual tissue damage or an abnormality in the pain system, as discussed later, pain can be persistent and agonizing.

Development of the Tactile Senses

HOW WE DEVELOP

Like smell and taste, the tactile senses are generally in place at birth. In fact, studies have shown that foetuses can respond to the touch of a hair at a relatively early stage in prenatal development (Lagercrantz & Changeux, 2009). However, the ability to recognize and respond to many different somatosensory stimuli occurs only after birth and involves further brain development and learning.

For children, one of the most enjoyable somatosensory inputs is being tickled. Although rough or prolonged tickling can become unbearable, under the right circumstances children often explode with laughter from tickling. The reaction we have to tickling is a result of activation of somatosensory pathways in an uneven, uncontrollable and unexpected way. Not only are our sensory systems organized to detect change but they are also most responsive to stimuli that are unexpected and surprising. When you move your body and produce tactile sensations, these stimuli are less noticeable to you than are sensations produced by another individual. The sensations of your own legs touching one another when you cross your legs, for example, is generally less noticeable than a similar touch would be if someone sitting next to you brushed a leg against yours.

Likewise, your reaction to your cat jumping onto your lap is probably much greater if you have your eyes closed when it happens. These different responses to surprising tactile stimuli appear to involve a defence mechanism. It is probably also the reason why being tickled by someone else is more effective at producing a reaction than trying to tickle yourself (Blakemore *et al.*, 2000). Our enjoyment of being tickled generally diminishes as we age.

Pain Thresholds

Individuals have very different levels of ability to detect physical stimuli on the skin. In addition, they differ in the degree to which they find certain tactile stimulation pleasurable or aversive. For example, some people enjoy an intense back massage, while others do not. Of all the somatosensory experiences, the one that has received the most research attention is that of pain. Pain management for surgical procedures and other medical conditions is a critical part of patient care. People's pain thresholds differ dramatically, as does the degree to which pain causes them emotional suffering. Some of these differences can be attributed to ethnicity. For example, studies have shown that Japanese people have a lower pain threshold than Caucasians. These differences are also related to differences in the ability to detect non-painful stimuli (Komiyama *et al.*, 2009).

Learning plays a role in the perception of pain, but groups of people could also differ because of physical differences in their sensory systems. Studies have shown, for example, that women have a lower threshold for detecting some types of pain than men, although the field is highly controversial (Racine, et al., 2012; Garcia *et al.*, 2007). While no cause for this difference has yet been found, it has been speculated that women and men may have different relative numbers of pain receptors in some parts of their body.

Neuroimaging studies have shown that people's brains react differently depending on their sensitivity to pain (Dubé *et al.*, 2009). One theory, the **gate control theory of pain**, attempts to explain the relationship of brain activity to pain by suggesting that some patterns of neural activity can actually create a 'gate' that prevents messages about painful stimuli from reaching parts of the brain where they are perceived as pain (Melzack, 1999). Early versions of this theory hypothesized that pain signals were blocked in the spinal cord, but later research has focused on neurochemicals or patterns of activity in the brain itself. Individual differences in gating mechanisms may explain wide range of pain sensitivity experienced by different people.

gate control theory of pain suggests that certain patterns of neural activity can close a 'gate' to keep pain information from travelling to the parts of the brain crucial for pain perception.

Difficulties with Tactile Senses

As we have seen, sensing and perceiving pain are normal, and important, functions of our tactile senses. Some people, however, experience either too much pain or too little. Sometimes, people even feel pain and other sensations in limbs or other body parts that have actually been removed.

Chronic Pain The most common abnormality associated with the somatosensory system is chronic pain (pain that lasts longer than three months). In Europe, a relatively large portion of the population, about 19%, suffer from chronic pain (Breivik *et al.*, 2006). There are multiple causes of chronic pain, and in some cases the cause cannot be identified. In all cases, however, pain management is a critical issue, since prolonged pain sensations can interfere with daily functioning and may lead to depression or even suicide.

Researchers have identified two groups of chemicals naturally produced by our nervous systems that have pain-relieving properties: **endorphins** and **enkephalins**. Endorphins and enkephalins belong to a class of molecules called *opiates*. As we will see in Chapter 8, this class of chemicals also includes painkilling drugs, such as morphine and heroin. Sometimes, opiates are present in the nervous system naturally, in which case they are referred to as *endogenous opiates*. These molecules are released by neurons after intense physical exercise, stress and sexual experience. They are thought to be responsible for the so-called *runner's high*, as well as for the ability some people have to perform extraordinary physical actions under extreme pressure.

endorphins naturally occurring painkilling chemicals in the brain.

enkephalins naturally occurring painkilling chemicals in the brain.

Medical practitioners use opiate drugs that mimic or stimulate the endogenous opiate system for pain relief. However, this approach has caused problems because people easily become addicted to opiate drugs. Opiate drugs are addictive not only when they are abused illegally, as by heroin users, but also when they are prescribed medically, as happens with morphine. Repeated use of these drugs to treat chronic pain can produce a physiological dependence that is very difficult to overcome. In addition, these drugs become less effective with continual use, so higher and higher doses are needed to achieve pain relief. This can become dangerous because opiates suppress breathing, especially at high doses. Eventually, people with chronic pain can reach a point where the dose of medicine needed to actually reduce their pain would be enough to stop their breathing and kill them while lower doses do not provide them with pain relief. Scientists continue to explore new ways to relieve pain that do not produce addictions or unwanted side effects. In extreme, debilitating cases of chronic pain, some doctors have turned to neurosurgery.

Intentionally destroying the pathways that carry information about pain stimuli to the brain can be effective for some people (Cetas *et al.*, 2008).

No Pain Some people are incapable of detecting painful stimuli. While the idea of feeling no pain may sound appealing at first, our ability to recognize and respond to discomfort is critical to prevent physical damage to the body. Consider how often you shift position in your chair when you are studying or sitting in a lecture. If you were unable to receive signals of discomfort from your body, you would not move to relieve pressure on your skin. The parts of your skin under continuous pressure could develop sores or bruises, which can happen to people who are immobile owing to medical conditions, and is why they have to be turned in bed by medical staff. Since many everyday experiences would be damaging to our bodies if we were not able to detect discomfort, an inability to detect pain can be very dangerous.

Some people are born unable to feel pain. A rare genetic condition called *familial dysautonomia* is associated with an inability to detect pain or temperature (Axelrod, 2004). Children with this disorder are at serious risk of life-threatening injuries and must be monitored very carefully (Figure 7.9). Loss of pain sensation can also be acquired later in life. Some medical conditions, including diabetes, can cause *neuropathies*, or nerve dysfunction, that block pain sensations from the person's extremities. People with such neuropathies may not notice if they sustain an injury in an affected area, such as a toe. Sometimes tissue can be so damaged that it must be amputated.

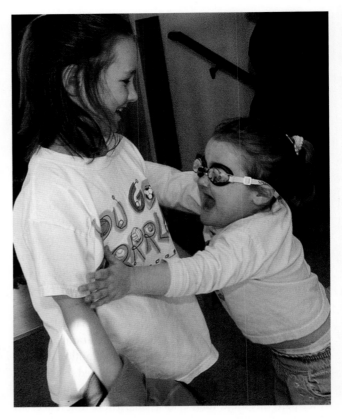

FIGURE 7.9 She feels no pain. The child on the right looks like any other three-year-old welcoming her big sister home from school, except for the goggles she is wearing. The child, who suffers from a severe case of familial dysautonomia, cannot detect any pain to her body and must wear goggles to protect her eyes from excessive rubbing and scratching and the effects of various injuries. She has lost one eye, damaged the other and inadvertently chewed apart portions of her tongue and mouth.
Source: Jim Mone/©AP/Wide World Photos.

PRACTICALLY SPEAKING **Quick Ways to Reduce Acute Pain**

As we discuss in this chapter, medical practitioners are constantly seeking ways to provide relief to patients in chronic, or continuing, pain. But what about acute pain, the short-term pain you feel when you bump your shin on a table, for example?

Gate control theory suggests that touch sensations, which frequently travel along fast fibres, can help prevent some pain sensations travelling along the slow pathways from reaching areas of your brain crucial for pain perception. According to this theory, the brain only processes so much input, so touch can help to set up a 'gate' that stops pain. This explains why we have a tendency to rub the skin of areas of our body that have been injured. For example, if you walk into a piece of furniture, you might rub your leg to dampen the pain.

Focusing on your breathing may also help. We often tend to gasp and then hold our breath when we injure ourselves, such as stubbing a toe. Formal methods of pain control, such as the Lamaze method for childbirth, work in part by altering this natural tendency, by teaching people to breathe in short, panting gasps (Leventhal *et al.*, 1989).

Distraction can also help, whereas anxiously focusing on pain can make it worse (al Absi & Rokke, 1991). Some studies have suggested that simply looking at a pleasant view can affect pain tolerance (Ulrich, 1984). Other evidence suggests that in order for a distraction to be effective the experience must be active. Studies have shown that playing an interesting videogame can dampen pain detection, whereas passive watching of a TV show has little effect. Stress and sexual experience also decrease the perception of pain. So, if you bump your leg on the way into a job interview, perhaps you would not notice the pain as much as you would under other circumstances.

Phantom Limb Sensations Many individuals with amputated limbs report tactile hallucinations or *phantom sensations* of touch, pressure, vibration, pins and needles, hot, cold and pain in the body part that no longer exists. Some people even feel the sensation of a ring on the finger or a watch on the wrist of an amputated arm. Similar phantom sensations have been reported in women who have undergone mastectomy for the treatment of breast cancer (Björkman *et al.*, 2008).

Researchers believe that phantom sensations result from abnormal activity in the somatosensory cortex of the brain. When a body part is removed, the part of somatosensory cortex that previously received its input does not become inactive.

Instead, somatosensory inputs from intact body parts expand to occupy those regions of the cortex (Ramachandran, 2005). Although researchers do not fully understand how reorganization of the somatosensory cortex produces phantom sensations, memory clearly contributes to these sensations. People are more likely to experience phantom sensations that they actually felt before on the missing body part, as opposed to random sensations. For example, someone who previously wore a ring or a watch is more likely to have the sense of wearing one after an amputation than a person who did not wear a ring or a watch. Similarly, people who previously experienced considerable pain in their now-missing body part are much more likely to feel phantom pain.

Before You Go On

What Do You Know?

8. List the different types of tactile receptors in the skin and the primary functions of each.
9. Compare and contrast slow and fast pain pathways.
10. Why is it so difficult to tickle yourself?
11. What are some possible explanations for individual differences in people's sensitivity to pain?

What Do You Think?

Have you experienced an occasion when your senses have worked together to either enhance or diminish pain or another touch sense? For example, did certain sights or sounds make pain better or worse?

The Auditory Sense: Hearing

LEARNING OBJECTIVE 4
Summarize what happens when we hear.

Hearing, the auditory sense, plays a crucial role in our ability to communicate socially. Humans, after all, are social creatures who have evolved to live and work together. Furthermore, whether through a warning shout or a crash in the distance, hearing helps us to detect danger. In addition to these clearly adaptive roles, the ability to hear enriches our lives through music and other pleasurable sounds. Imagine what life would be like if you could not hear your favourite song or the lapping of waves on the seashore.

From Sound Waves to Sounds

sound waves vibrations of the air in the frequency of hearing.

The auditory system is designed to convert **sound waves**, usually vibrations of the air, into neural impulses. Sound waves have two major qualities that produce our perceptions of different sounds:

- *Frequency*. The *frequency* of a sound wave refers to the number of cycles the wave completes in a certain amount of time. Frequency of a sound wave is measured in units called *Hertz (Hz)*, which represent cycles per second. The frequency of a sound wave is responsible for producing the *pitch* of a sound. The voice of Mickey Mouse, for example, is a high-frequency sound wave that produces a high-pitched sound. Although the range of human hearing is quite large, we hear sounds best within the range of 2,000–5,000 Hz, which encompasses the frequencies of most sounds that humans actually make, such as babies crying and people talking.

- *Amplitude*. The *amplitude* of a sound wave refers to the strength of a given cycle. Waves with higher peaks and lower troughs are higher amplitude than those that do not reach such extremes. The amplitude of a sound wave is responsible for our detection of *loudness*. Waves with high amplitudes produce loud sounds, while those with low amplitudes produce sound soft. Loudness is measured in units called *decibels (dB)*.

Our detection of sound begins, of course, in the ear. Sound waves are converted to neural impulses in the ear through several steps, as shown in Figure 7.10.

1. First, sound waves enter the outer ear and, at its deepest part, cause distortions of the eardrum, or **tympanic membrane**.

tympanic membrane the eardrum.

2. Vibrations of the tympanic membrane set in motion a series of three tiny bones, or ossicles, called the *hammer, anvil* and *stirrup*. The stirrup, which is the last bone in the chain, transfers these vibrations to the **oval window**, a membrane separating the ossicles from the inner ear.

oval window a membrane separating the ossicles and the inner ear, deflection of which causes vibrations in the cochlear fluid.

3. Vibration of the oval window causes pressure waves to form in the fluid-filled **cochlea** of the inner ear. When fluid vibrates in the cochlea, it causes movement in the **basilar membrane**, which runs down the middle of the cochlea. The basilar

cochlea fluid-filled structure in the inner ear containing the hair cells.

membrane is covered with rows of **hair cells**, the auditory sensory receptors. Movement of the basilar membrane bends the hair cells that transduce the 'fluid sound wave' into electrical activity.

basilar membrane structure in the cochlea where the hair cells are located.

hair cells sensory receptors that convert sound waves into neural impulses.

4. The hair cells communicate with nerves in the cochlea. These nerves, in turn, send the neural impulses to the brain. Damaged hair cells in the bird cochlea are regenerated, but humans lack this ability. Scientists are studying the regeneration of bird hair cells to find ways to repair hearing loss in humans.

There are two major theories about how the auditory system converts sound waves into all the various sounds we can perceive. The first, called *frequency theory*, suggests that different sound frequencies are converted into different rates of firing in our auditory nerves. According to this theory, high-frequency sounds produce more rapid firing than do low-frequency sounds. Although there may be some truth to frequency theory – different firing rates contribute to sound perception of low tones – researchers agree that this theory cannot fully explain sound perception.

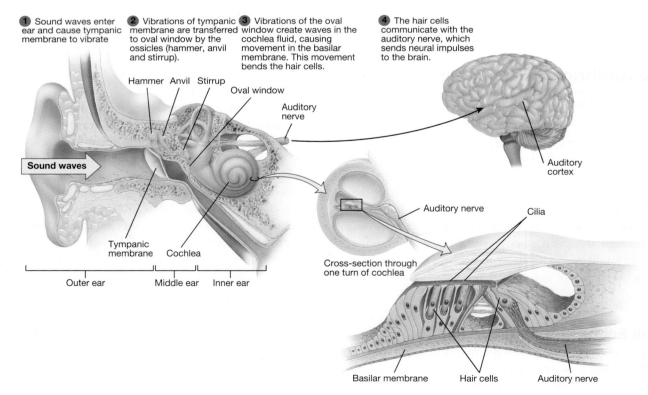

1. Sound waves enter ear and cause tympanic membrane to vibrate

2. Vibrations of tympanic membrane are transferred to oval window by the ossicles (hammer, anvil and stirrup).

3. Vibrations of the oval window create waves in the cochlea fluid, causing movement in the basilar membrane. This movement bends the hair cells.

4. The hair cells communicate with the auditory nerve, which sends neural impulses to the brain.

Hammer   Anvil   Stirrup

Oval window

Auditory nerve

Sound waves

Tympanic membrane   Cochlea

Outer ear   Middle ear   Inner ear

Auditory cortex

Auditory nerve   Cilia

Cross-section through one turn of cochlea

Basilar membrane   Hair cells   Auditory nerve

FIGURE 7.10 How the ear hears.

The second theory, called *place theory*, seems to account for a greater degree of auditory perception. Place theory holds that differences in sound frequency activate different regions on the basilar membrane. Regions along the basilar membrane send inputs to the brain that are encoded according to the place along the membrane where the inputs originated.

Drowning Out the Noise

As with the other sensory systems we have discussed, adaptation occurs in the auditory system when we continuously hear sounds. We can adapt to sounds in several ways. First, our ears respond to a very loud noise by contracting muscles around the ear's opening so that less of the sound wave can enter the ear. This also happens when you talk, so that the sound of your own voice, which is so close to your ear, is not deafening.

Second, the hair cells of the ears become less sensitive to continuous noises. Unfortunately, if the noise is loud enough, it can actually damage the hair cells (Petrescu, 2008). Unlike receptors for the chemical senses, sensory receptors in the ear are not readily replaced, so damage to the hair cells makes the ear permanently less sensitive.

Finally, the brain can filter out many sounds that are not important, even if they are relatively loud. You have probably noticed that you can usually carry on a conversation with your friends at a noisy party. This phenomenon, often referred to as the *cocktail party effect*, is another example of top-down processing. The brain is able to attend to and pick up relevant sounds even in a very noisy environment. These relevant sounds, such as your name or the names of people who interest you, grab your attention and focus your auditory perception because you have previously learnt their importance. So background noise, even if it is also the sounds of people talking, interferes minimally with hearing a conversation, as long as the conversation is of interest to us.

Sounds in Space

To determine the importance of a particular sound, it is necessary to *localize* it in space, to work out where it is coming from. For example, if you are driving in a car and hear the sound of an ambulance siren, you need to determine whether the ambulance is far away or close by in order to decide whether to pull over to the side of the road to let the ambulance pass. You also need to determine from which direction the sound is approaching. The auditory system uses several cues to help localize sound:

- *General loudness.* We learn from many early experiences that loud sounds are usually closer to us than are soft sounds, so that eventually we automatically use the loudness of a sound to assess the distance between ourselves and the source of the sound.

- *Loudness in each ear.* Because of the distance between our ears, the ear closer to the sound hears a louder noise than the ear farther from the sound. This difference is particularly useful in detecting the location of high-frequency sounds.

- *Timing.* Another cue used to localize sound is differences in the time at which sound waves hit the two ears. Sound waves will reach the ear closer to the source of the sound before they reach the ear farther away. Since the ears are separated in space, a sound wave will also hit each ear at a slightly different part of its wave cycle, creating what is called a *phase difference*. This cue is particularly useful to us in localizing sounds with low frequencies.

We also adjust our heads and bodies to locate where sounds are coming from. As we adjust ourselves, we hear how the sound changes with our changes in position. We use these changes to help make a reasonable approximation of the sound's original location. Finally, we may use other sensory systems. For instance, you might confirm the location of the ambulance when you look in your rear-view mirror and see it approaching.

Hearing and the Brain  WHAT HAPPENS IN THE BRAIN?

We have discussed how auditory information is transduced from sound waves by the hair cells in the basilar membrane of the cochlea. After that, it travels as a series of signals from nerves in the cochlea to the brainstem, the thalamus and then the auditory cortex, which is located in the temporal lobe. Part of the primary auditory cortex is organized

tonotopic map the representation in the auditory cortex of different sound frequencies.

in a **tonotopic map**. That is, information transmitted from different parts of the cochlea (sound waves of different frequency and, hence, sounds of different pitch) is projected onto specific parts of the auditory cortex, so that our cortex maps the different pitches of sounds we hear. Information from sounds heard in one ear is sent to the auditory cortex areas on both sides of the brain. This allows us to integrate information heard from both ears and helps us to locate the sources of sounds.

From the primary auditory cortex, auditory information moves on to the auditory *association areas* in the cortex. As we described in Chapter 5, association areas of the brain's cortex are involved in higher-order mental processes. Association areas help to link the sounds we hear with parts of the brain involved in language comprehension.

They can't fool the brain (yet). MIT professor Neil Gershenfield and a graduate student work on project Digital Stradivarius, an attempt to build a digital model that can match the sound of the great violins of Stradivarius. When digital-produced and instrument-produced sound waves are converted into neural impulses in the brains of musical experts, the experts can detect the difference. The instrument remains the champion.
Source: ©George Steinmetz/Corbis.

PSYCHOLOGY AROUND US   Sensory Fusion: Synaesthesia

OUT OF THE ORDINARY

Can you see noise or taste words? Some people can. This condition is called *synaesthesia*. The name comes from two Greek words: *syn*, meaning 'together', and *aesthesis*, meaning 'perception', and therefore refers to 'joined perception'. People who have synaesthesia experience a stimulus that normally would be perceived by one sense in a different sensory modality (or sub-modality). For example, they may actually see colours or images when they hear music.

The most common form of synaesthesia is called *grapheme-colour synaesthesia*. A person who has this form always sees a colour in response to visual presentation of a specific letter or number. There are also synaesthetes who smell particular odours in response to touch, hear noises in response to smell or feel a tactile stimulus in response to sight. There are even some individuals who possess synaesthesia involving three or more senses, but this is especially unusual (see Spence, 2011).

People who experience synaesthesia may not simply be imagining their unusual sensations. Neuroimaging studies have suggested that sensory areas normally not affected by particular stimuli are activated if that sense is involved in the synaesthetic experience (Nunn *et al.*, 2002). For example, the auditory cortex of sight–sound synaesthetes, as well as the visual cortex, becomes active in response to particular visual stimuli that cause

synaesthesia. The brain of a person who can hear a picture or colour really does respond as though the stimulus were producing sound waves, as well as reflecting light waves. However, some of these results have recently been disputed (Hupé *et al.*, 2012).

The best kaleidoscope ever. Performer and songwriter Tori Amos has said that she often experiences the notes and chords in her music as colours and light filaments. She says, 'Try to imagine the best kaleidoscope ever.'
Source: Paul Warner/Getty Images, Inc.

Association areas also integrate, or coordinate, auditory information with signals from other senses. You have probably noticed how distracting it is to watch a movie that has an audio slightly out of synch with the video image. This is because the brain is set up to integrate information from multiple sensory systems. Over time, we learn to have expectations about certain visual stimuli that coincide with specific sounds. When the sounds in a movie do not match the visual images the way they would in real life, our expectations are violated and our attention is drawn to this discrepancy from the norm.

In some people, the integration of sensory systems in the brain can lead to 'crosstalk' between the senses. As described in the 'Psychology Around Us' box on the previous page, people who experience a condition known as *synaesthesia* can perceive sensations in a modality different from the one that is actually being activated. For example, they may 'see' music or 'hear' smells. Synaesthesia is not a debilitating condition. In fact, it has sometimes been described as enriching, particularly when it occurs in artistic or musical individuals.

Hearing and Learning HOW WE DEVELOP

Our ears are formed and capable of transducing sound waves before we are even born. In fact, human foetuses have been shown to respond to noises long before birth. Research has shown that foetuses respond to loud noises with a startle reflex and that, after birth, they are capable of recognizing some sounds they heard while in the womb. However, the ability to recognize and respond appropriately to a wide variety of sound stimuli is acquired over many years after birth. Sounds associated with language, for example, become recognizable as infants develop, as do those associated with music. We describe language development in more detail in Chapter 11.

There are sensitive periods of development for both language and music learning (Knudson, 2004). As described in Chapter 3, we acquire certain abilities during sensitive periods of development much more easily that we do after the sensitive period has ended. The tonotopic map in the primary auditory cortex of the brain is organized during a sensitive period of development in this way (de Villers-Sidani *et al.*, 2007). Studies in experimental animals have shown that exposing animals to pure tones during a certain time in development leads to larger representations of those sounds in the auditory cortex. The same exposure after the sensitive period is over has no such effect. If a sound is made important to the animal, however, by pairing it either with a reward, such as water, or with a punishment, such as an electric shock, the primary auditory cortex can be reorganized so that more of it responds to the relevant tone (Bakin *et al.*, 1996). Such top-down processing of tones indicates that this

region of the brain is still plastic after the sensitive period is over. It is not as easy, however, to remap the brain after a sensitive period as it is during one. The stimuli needed to produce changes in older animals must be very strong and important compared with those needed for younger animals (Kuboshima-Amemori & Sawaguchi, 2007). In humans, the auditory brain is set up to acquire information about speaking and music most readily relatively early in life, during the preschool years. It is more difficult, but by no means impossible, for us to learn additional languages or certain music skills after we mature.

Identifying Pitch  HOW WE DIFFER

We differ greatly in the extent of our ability to detect specific sounds. People show particular differences in their ability to identify certain notes in a musical scale. **Perfect** or **absolute pitch** refers to the ability to recognize an individual note in isolation. This is very difficult for most people. Only about one in 10,000 people in Western countries has perfect pitch. This ability seems to originate in childhood, between the ages of three and six years, through musical training, and it is associated with differences in brain anatomy (Zatorre, 2003). Research has shown that portions of the cortex are actually thinner in individuals with perfect pitch (Bermudez *et al.*, 2009). Although it is not clear whether people with perfect pitch start out with a thinner cortex or whether they develop it through training, it is possible that synaptic pruning contributes to this structural difference.

> **perfect (absolute) pitch** the ability to recognize or produce any note on a musical scale.

Studies have shown, too, that people who speak tonal languages – languages in which differences in tone convey meaning, such as Vietnamese and Mandarin Chinese – are more likely to develop perfect pitch than those speaking Western languages. This again suggests the possibility that early learning of auditory information related to tones can have a permanent effect on the functioning of this sensory system.

Just as some people have perfect pitch, others are tone deaf, or unable to discern differences in pitch. Although tone deafness, or *amusia*, is sometimes the result of damage to the auditory system, it can be present from birth, and researchers believe it may be related to genetics (Peretz *et al.*, 2007). Tone deafness is thought to affect up to 4% of the Western population, although this figure has recently been brought into question (Henry & McAulay, 2010). Not surprisingly, these people are less likely to have an appreciation for music, but they are not affected in other aspects of life. This condition only presents serious problems when it occurs in cultures where the language is tonal and the individual is unable to communicate normally in social interactions (but see Liu *et al.*, 2012).

Difficulties with Hearing

OUT OF THE ORDINARY

Many conditions can lead to abnormalities in the auditory system. Some cause either partial or total **deafness**, the loss of hearing. Abnormalities in the auditory system can also add unwanted auditory perceptions.

> **deafness** the loss or lack of hearing.

Deafness Deafness has a variety of causes. It can be genetic or caused by infection, physical trauma or exposure to toxins, including overdose of common medications like aspirin.

Since speech is an important way humans communicate with each other, deafness can complicate socialization. This is of particular concern for children, because young children need auditory stimulation in order to develop normal spoken language skills. For this reason, doctors try to identify auditory deficits at an early life stage. If a child is found to have hearing deficits, parents can decide among different options to help the child as soon as possible. Some deaf individuals learn to use sign language and other methods of communication that rely on senses other than hearing. In a relatively new development, cochlear implants have been constructed to help individuals with deafness to hear sounds (Sharma *et al.*, 2009). This research work is developing quickly, but there are still many deaf people who cannot be helped by cochlear implants (Battmer *et al.*, 2009). This is one reason that many individuals and families choose to avoid them. Some in the deaf community also believe that hearing is not necessary in order to lead a productive and fulfilling life. They believe that the potential benefits of implants may not outweigh the potential risks of surgery required to place them in the cochlea (Hyde & Power, 2006).

Hearing Unwanted Sounds About one in every 200 people is affected by *tinnitus*, ringing in the ears. Tinnitus has multiple causes, including some that are related to abnormalities in the ear itself (Lanting *et al.*, 2009). Most people are able to cope with the noise, but some find it too loud and distracting to ignore.

Patients with epilepsy in the temporal cortex have reported the perception of hearing complex auditory stimuli, such as a musical tune (Wieser, 2003). This symptom, which can be completely distracting and disturbing, is the result of abnormal electrical activity in brain circuits that store complex memories of sounds. Treatment for epilepsy sometimes involves neurosurgery to remove the part of the brain that is responsible for starting the seizures. Brain surgery in the temporal lobes, where auditory information is processed, is particularly dangerous, however. This is because the temporal lobe also houses Wernicke's area, which is critical for understanding language.

Before You Go On

What Do You Know?

12. What happens in the ear to transduce sound waves into neural signals?
13. What is a tonotopic map?
14. What are sensitive periods, and how are they important for hearing?
15. What is tinnitus?

What Do You Think?

What would you suggest including in an ideal early-school curriculum to develop children's auditory systems to their maximum capabilities?

The Visual Sense: Sight

LEARNING OBJECTIVE 5

Describe key processes in visual perception.

All the senses already discussed in this chapter play important roles in our ability to make sense of the world around us. For many of us, though, the ability to see is especially useful and enriching. We use our vision in virtually all of our activities, including our interactions with other people. Vision helps us communicate: we use facial expressions and body language to communicate without words and express information that cannot be said, because it is lost in spoken language. The visual sense is particularly well developed in humans because it so important to us. Some estimates suggest that about half of the cerebral cortex of our brains is devoted to processing visual stimuli. Whether this is true or

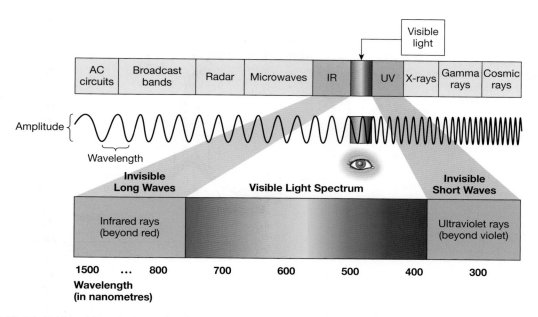

FIGURE 7.11 Visible light and the electromagnetic spectrum. The part of the electromagnetic spectrum that our visual receptors can detect is restricted to a narrow range.

Source: Based on Carpenter, S. & Huffman, K. (2013). *Visualizing Psychology*. Hoboken, NJ: John Wiley & Sons, Inc., p. 91.

not, it certainly seems to be the case that many parts of the brain have inputs derived from the eyes, and must therefore at least *use* visual information in some way.

The stimulus for vision is light. Light is made up of particles called *photons*. The light that we can see is part of the electromagnetic spectrum of energy that also includes many forms we cannot see, such as X-rays and radio waves. Like sound, light travels in waves. The visible spectrum of light ranges from about 400 to 700 nanometres in wavelength (a nanometre is 1/1,000,000,000 (10^{-9}) metres). As shown in Figure 7.11, different wavelengths within our visible spectrum appear to us as different colours. Objects in the world absorb and reflect light in varying levels and patterns; and those that reflect more light are usually perceived as brighter.

Seeing the Light

Vision begins when light enters the eye, as shown in Figure 7.12. Muscles in the iris – the coloured part of the eye that you can see – adjust the size of our pupils to let in more or less of the light reflected from objects around us. These muscles also adjust the shape of the lens, focusing the light that enters the eye onto a specialized sheet of nerve cells in the back of the eye, called the **retina**. The retina is where we transduce light waves into neural impulses that the brain can process. The retina has

retina a specialized sheet of nerve cells in the back of the eye containing the sensory receptors for vision.

two major classes of visual receptors, or **photoreceptors**: the **rods** and the **cones**. Most of our photoreceptors are rods. There are over 100 million rods in the human retina. Rods are important for detecting light; they are very sensitive to small amounts of light and help us to see at night when light levels are low. There are fewer cones, only about six million per human retina. Cones respond differently to light of different wavelengths, and thereby support colour vision. They are less sensitive than rods, but wired differently, enabling the detection of fine detail at higher (i.e. daytime) light levels (see below).

photoreceptors the sensory receptor cells for vision, located in the retina.

rods photoreceptors most responsive at low light levels.

cones photoreceptors necessary for colour vision and perception of fine detail.

When light reaches the photoreceptors, a series of chemical reactions take place. The rods and cones stimulate the bipolar cells, which in turn cause ganglion cells to fire. The axons of the ganglion cells are bundled together to form the **optic nerve**. Signals from the ganglion cells travel along the optic nerve out of the eye and into the brain.

optic nerve the bundle of axons of ganglion cells that carries visual information from the eye to the brain.

Rods and cones are not spread evenly throughout the retina. Cones are concentrated more in the centre. The **fovea**, the region at the centre of the retina where our vision is at its sharpest, is largely made up of cones. In contrast, rods are concentrated more at the outer edges of the retina. Have you ever noticed that your peripheral

fovea centre of the retina, containing only cones, where vision is most clear.

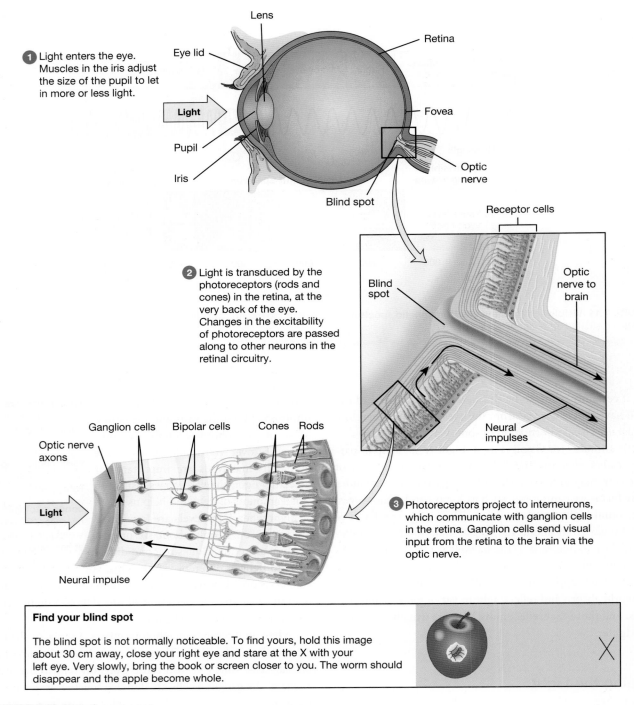

1 Light enters the eye. Muscles in the iris adjust the size of the pupil to let in more or less light.

Lens
Eye lid
Retina
Light
Fovea
Pupil
Iris
Optic nerve
Blind spot

2 Light is transduced by the photoreceptors (rods and cones) in the retina, at the very back of the eye. Changes in the excitability of photoreceptors are passed along to other neurons in the retinal circuitry.

Receptor cells
Blind spot
Optic nerve to brain
Neural impulses

Ganglion cells   Bipolar cells   Cones   Rods
Optic nerve axons
Light
Neural impulse

3 Photoreceptors project to interneurons, which communicate with ganglion cells in the retina. Ganglion cells send visual input from the retina to the brain via the optic nerve.

Find your blind spot

The blind spot is not normally noticeable. To find yours, hold this image about 30 cm away, close your right eye and stare at the X with your left eye. Very slowly, bring the book or screen closer to you. The worm should disappear and the apple become whole.

FIGURE 7.12 How the eye sees.

vision is not particularly clear? It mostly enables you to detect movement, not details. This is because rods dominate the peripheral parts of the retina. The retina also contains a region that does not have any rods or cones. This area creates a blind spot in your vision. The *blind spot* is the location where your optic nerve leaves your retina. Because the visual parts of the brain are very good at filling in incomplete images, the blind

spot is not normally noticeable. You can experience your blind spot, however, by manoeuvring and controlling visual stimuli as instructed in Figure 7.12.

Like the other sensory systems discussed above, the visual system undergoes sensory adaptation. Dilation and constriction of the pupil, the opening in the centre of the iris, is one way that the visual system adapts to the light. When

PSYCHOLOGY AROUND US | Artificial Pupil Dilation

Have you ever had your pupils dilated? Eye-care professionals, like optometrists and ophthalmologists, use special eye drops to make your pupils *dilate*, get bigger, so they can see inside your eyes. Normally, your pupils adjust automatically to the amount of light available. When you step outside into daylight, your pupils therefore become smaller. When your pupils are dilated artificially, however, they cannot adjust themselves for some time. Patients with dilated pupils are especially sensitive to light and need to wear sunglasses until the effect of the drops wears off – usually in three to four hours. Interestingly, the effect wears off faster in dark-eyed people than in people with lighter-coloured eyes. Asymmetric pupil dilation, sometimes caused by one eye recovering from the drops faster than the other, can cause some strange visual phenomena (Heron *et al.*, 1995).

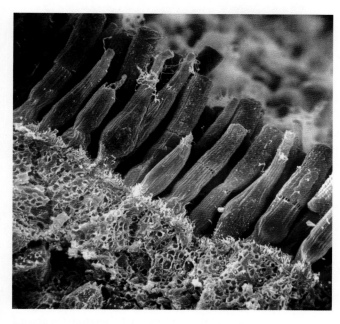

The photoreceptors. This colourized scanning electron micrograph shows the retina's photoreceptors – the rods and cones – which help pass visual signals through the optic nerve to the brain. Rods (*pink*) are the photoreceptors that detect light. Cones (*olive*) are photoreceptors that detect colour.

Source: Omikron/Photo Researchers, Inc.

you go from inside a building to outside on a bright, sunny day, you may immediately feel the need to squint and shade your eyes. Your eyes quickly adapt to light, however, in part because your pupil constricts to decrease the amount of light entering the eye. In dark places, the pupil will open more to let in more light to allow you to see.

Seeing in Colour

As noted earlier, cones enable us to see colour. Exactly how the perception of colour works, though, is not yet perfectly understood.

Characteristics of Colour The colour of a visual stimulus can be described by three features: hue, saturation and brightness. The variety of colours we see is related to various combinations of these three characteristics.

- *Hue* is closely linked to the wavelength of light that the visual stimulus contains. This is the most basic aspect of colour, whether the stimulus is red, blue, yellow or some other colour.

- *Saturation* refers to how pure and deep the colour appears – colours that appear whitish, or greyish, are less saturated (e.g. 'pastel' colours).

- *Brightness* of a colour refers to how much light emanates or is reflected from the visual stimulus.

Theories of Colour Perception As suggested earlier, no single theory can entirely explain how we perceive colour. Historically, there were two (apparently contradictory) theories of colour vision: trichromatic theory and opponent process theory.

The **trichromatic theory** of colour vision states that there are three different sensors for colour and that each type of sensor responds to a different range of wavelengths of light (Balaraman, 1962). Obviously, of course, we can see more than just three colours. The rich variations we can detect in colour arise from the many ways in which these three types of sensors can be activated in combination with one another. The trichromatic theory is largely correct, in that people with normal colour vision do have three different kinds of cones. One type responds best to light containing longer (yellowish-red) wavelengths, another to the medium (greenish) wavelengths and the third to light containing shorter (bluish-purple) wavelengths. Typically, at least two of the cone types will respond to a certain wavelength of visible light, but how much they respond varies between them. As noted, the combination of the signals produced by cones is what enables the brain to respond to lots of colours.

> **trichromatic theory** a theory of colour perception holding that the human eye has three sensors of colour, each of which responds to a different range of wavelengths.

opponent process theory a theory holding that colour perception depends on the actions of three systems of colour opposites: blue/yellow, red/green and black/white.

An (apparently) alternative theory about colour vision is called the **opponent process theory** (Buchsbaum & Gottschalk, 1983). This theory maintains that three sets of colour pairs work to inhibit one another in the perception of colour. Specifically, red inhibits the perception of green (its 'opponent'), yellow inhibits the perception of blue and black inhibits the perception of white. There is also some truth to this theory because we cannot mix certain combinations of colours. For example, we cannot see reddish-green or bluish-yellow (although see Billock & Tsou, 2010, for a different view). Opponent processing is now thought to be due to different classes of ganglion cell in the retina combining the outputs of different classes of cone photoreceptor in opposing pairs.

You can observe opponent processing at work by staring at the white dot in the middle of the green and black flag in Figure 7.13. After about 30 seconds, stare at a white sheet of paper. You will see an *afterimage* that is red and white. This also works with other colours in the opponent pairs. A white-on-black image will produce a black-on-white afterimage, and a yellow image will produce a blue afterimage. Afterimages happen when one colour in an opponent pair inhibits the other. We end this inhibition by looking away from the first colour, and then the previously inhibited colour overcompensates and creates an afterimage made up of the colours that were inhibited before.

The two theories can be used together to explain what is commonly known as *colour blindness*, but more correctly termed *colour deficiency*. Very few people are actually unable to see any colours at all. Most people who have colour blindness are really just unable to distinguish certain colours. Most

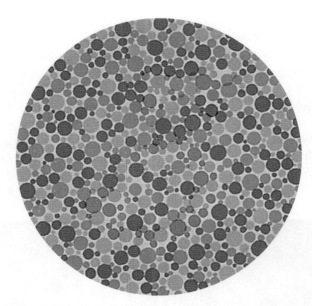

FIGURE 7.14 Colour deficiency. Most people who are colour deficient cannot easily distinguish between red and green; they would see a different number in this figure (usually a 5) from someone without colour deficiency, who would see a 3. However, this example might be affected by colour reproduction and is not a definitive test. Always consult an eye-care professional if you are concerned about your colour vision or any other aspect of your sight.

Source: Carpenter, S. & Huffman, K. (2008). *Visualizing Psychology*. Hoboken, NJ: John Wiley & Sons, Inc., p. 107.

common is red/green colour deficiency, which is tested with images such as the one shown in Figure 7.14. Studies suggest that people with this problem have a shortage of cones that respond to either the greenish or the reddish wavelengths. (This relates to the trichromatic theory.) Therefore (in accord with opponent process theory), inputs to retinal ganglion cells are imbalanced and people find it harder to distinguish the two colours (Goldstein, 2010).

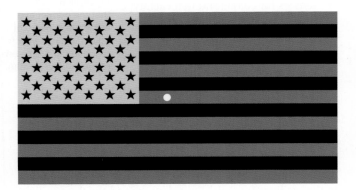

FIGURE 7.13 The afterimage effect. Afterimages occur when one colour in an opponent pair inhibits the other. When you look away from the first colour, the previously inhibited colour is turned on. To see opponent processing in action, stare at the white dot in the centre of the flag for about 30 seconds, and then look away at a white sheet of paper.

Source: Carpenter, S. & Huffman, K. (2008). *Visualizing Psychology*. Hoboken, NJ: John Wiley & Sons, Inc., p. 106.

How Sight Works

 **WHAT HAPPENS IN THE BRAIN?**

From the rods and cones of the retina, most visual information travels via the optic nerve to the thalamus, synapsing on neurons in the **lateral geniculate nucleus (LGN)**. From the LGN, visual input travels to the primary visual cortex, located in the occipital lobe.

Visual information is transmitted throughout the brain via a partially crossed set of axons (Figure 7.15). This is organized in such a way that information from the left half of each retina, which corresponds with the right half of the **visual field**, goes to the left half of the primary visual cortex, and information

lateral geniculate nucleus (LGN) the part of the thalamus which processes visual information.

visual field a term used to describe how the world looks from the point of view of the visual system. Positions in the visual field correspond with points on each retina.

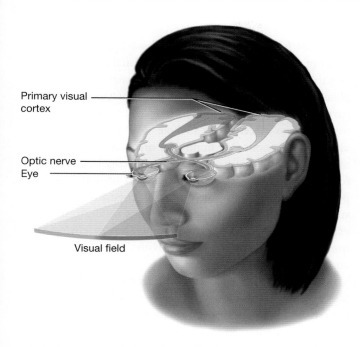

FIGURE 7.15 The crossed visual pathway. Before entering the brain, the optic nerves partially cross. Visual information dealing with the left visual field travels to the right side of the visual cortex, while information from the right visual field travels to the left side of the visual cortex.

from the right half of each retina, corresponding to the left visual field, goes to the right half of primary visual cortex. There is a bit of overlap in the middle.

Once visual information reaches the primary visual cortex, it is processed to allow the detection of very simple features, such as lines and edges (Hubel & Wiesel, 1959). However, we do not see the world as a collection of lines and

edges. Instead, we see a rich set of complex visual stimuli that change as we move and the world around us transforms. We are able to see complex visual stimuli as a result of circuitry that elaborates on these lines and edges by joining them together, involving additional visual information, such as motion and colour, and eventually linking them with other areas of the brain dealing with the higher-order cognitive processes, like memory.

It has been suggested that the pathways that process information about complex visual stimuli can be roughly divided into the *what* and the *where* pathways, as shown in Figure 7.16 (Ungerleider & Haxby, 1994). That is, the regions that process visual information to help us determine *what* is the identity of an object (is it an apple, a car or a house?) are different from those that process the visual information to figure out *where* the object is located in space (is the apple on the table, under the table or behind the table?). The what pathway involves axons that travel from the occipital cortex to the temporal cortex. The where pathway involves axons that travel from the occipital cortex to the parietal cortex. Other scientists have suggested that the where pathway is more accurately termed the *how* pathway as its main role is to guide movements, such as aiming, reaching or tracking with the eyes (Milner & Goodale, 1995).

How do researchers know about the brain regions that serve these complex functions? Recall from Chapter 5 that one way scientists have determined the function of certain brain regions is by examining the processing deficits that people have after damaging particular areas of their brains. This type of damage usually occurs as a result of stroke, disease or head trauma. Patients with damage to certain parts of the temporal cortex, which houses the what pathway, have

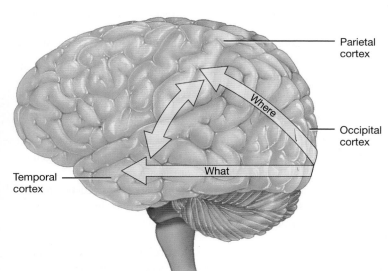

FIGURE 7.16 The what and where pathways. The what pathway of the brain processes information that helps us identify an object, while the where pathway helps us identify its location in space. Communication between the two pathways allows us to integrate complex visual stimuli.

a condition called *visual agnosia*. In this case, their vision remains intact, though they cannot recognize objects visually. For example, when shown a rose, they can describe it, but they cannot name the object as a rose. If they are allowed to touch or smell the rose (thus using other senses to detect it), they can immediately identify it as a rose. A more specific form of visual agnosia that happens to people with damage to a certain part of the what pathway is called *prosopagnosia*. Individuals with prosopagnosia cannot recognize faces (Farah *et al.*, 1995). Sometimes these patients can recognize familiar individuals by concentrating on some visual characteristic that is not really a facial feature, such as the person's hairstyle or spectacles, but their ability to recognize the face itself is lost (Sacks, 1985).

Patients with damage to the where pathway also have normal vision, but they have lost the ability to locate objects in space. For example, when given the task of pouring water from a jug into a glass, they will almost always miss and pour the water onto the table or floor. A very interesting form of damage to the where pathway results in a condition called *hemi-neglect* (Mesulam, 1981). Patients with hemi-neglect completely ignore one side of their visual field. Because nerves that carry visual information cross to the opposite sides of the brain, people with damage to the left side of their where pathways do not notice the right side, and vice versa. When asked to copy a drawing, people with hemi-neglect will leave out one half of it. Women with this condition have been known to apply make-up and do their hair only on one side.

In addition to the information researchers have gained from studying patients with brain damage, neuroimaging studies of people without brain damage have confirmed that there are what and where pathways. Indeed, these types of studies have shown that brain activity changes in specific parts of the what pathways when the participants are viewing objects (Reddy & Kanwisher, 2006).

Visual Perception from the Top Down

So far, we have discussed vision from a bottom-up perspective. Light comes in through the eye and the neural impulses generated are passed to more and more complex brain regions, ultimately resulting in the perception of a visual stimulus. Equally important to visual perception, however, is top-down processing, which involves previously acquired knowledge. Like perception involving the other sensory systems, visual perception involves bottom-up and top-down processing occurring simultaneously. Brain regions that store information about what objects look like can help us to perceive visual stimuli even when they are partially hidden.

Putting Together the Parts: Gestalt Principles We do not see images as a series of small patches of colour or a series of simple features. Instead, our visual system assembles this information into objects and scenes that are complete so we can understand them. Even when we see a small part of an object or scene that is blocked by another object, we are able to perceive it as a whole, if we have just enough visual information. Our brains are organized to fill in the missing parts so that we perceive and recognize meaningful stimuli. As we described earlier, part of our ability to perceive images comes from our use of cognitive processes, such as memory and learning, to help us recall from prior experience images that match the stimuli we are sensing. We use these memories to fill in the missing parts of the object and understand what it is.

The area of study focused on understanding the principles of how we perceive and recognize visual stimuli in their entirety with only limited information is called *Gestalt psychology*. As mentioned in Chapter 1, Gestalt psychologists believe that perception helps us to add meaning to visual information, so that 'the whole is greater than the sum of the parts' of what we see. Gestalt psychologists have identified several laws that organize visual information into coherent images:

- *Proximity*. The law of proximity indicates that visual stimuli near to one another tend to be grouped together. For example, AA AA AA is seen as three groups, while AAA AAA is seen as two groups despite the fact that each set has six As.

- *Similarity*. The law of similarity indicates that stimuli resembling one another tend to be grouped together. So AAaa is viewed as two groups because of the dissimilar appearance of upper- and lower-case letters.

- *Continuity*. The law of continuity indicates that stimuli falling along the same plane tend to be grouped together. AAA ^{AAA} would be organized into two perceptual groups because two sets of As are not on the same line.

- *Good form*. The law of good form indicates that stimuli that form a shape tend to be grouped together while those that do not remain ungrouped. Compare ☺ to O:). The former stimuli are perceived as a smiley face while the latter are perceived as three separate symbols.

- *Closure*. The law of closure indicates that we tend to fill in small gaps in objects so that they are still perceived as whole objects.

These laws of visual organization put together all the 'pieces' of visual stimuli to complete a 'puzzle' to build meaningful information from everything we see when we look at something. Sometimes, however, the fact that our brain tends to create order amongst the things we are seeing can lead us to perceive sights that are illusions.

Getting in Deep: Binocular and Monocular Cues

When you look at the items on the table in a restaurant, how do you know which items are closer to you and which are farther away? This question relates to *depth perception*, determining how far objects are from us and from one another. We use a number of methods to perceive depth.

Because our eyes are set a slight distance apart, we do not see exactly the same thing with both eyes. This **retinal disparity**, the slightly different stimuli recorded by the retinas of the eyes, provides us with a *binocular* cue to depth. Our brains use the discrepancies between the visual information received from our two eyes to help us judge the relative distances of objects from us. You can observe your own retinal disparity by looking at your finger when at arm's length from your face. Close first one eye, then the other, and notice how your finger seems to change position relative to objects in the background behind your finger.

> **retinal disparity** the slight difference in images processed by the retinas of the two eyes.

PSYCHOLOGY AROUND US   How Do 3D Movies Work?

A now-familiar real-world application of the power of retinal disparity as a depth cue is found in 3D movies. The 3D glasses that you need to see the movie properly use an optical technique to separate the images intended for the left and right eyes. These are very slightly different and are intended to mimic the differences found in real scenes viewed from slightly different directions. Of course, 3D movie makers play all sorts of tricks to exaggerate these depths to intensify the audience's film-going experience. But 3D movies are not for everyone.

Many people can feel nauseous while watching fast-moving scenes, possibly because the depth illusion, although powerful, is not *quite* the same as the real world (because it is all projected onto a single screen at a fixed viewing distance). Another issue is that about 10% of the population cannot see depth from retinal disparity, usually because of an imbalance between the two eyes. It remains to be seen whether the current fad for 3D movies will be sustained or fade away as other 3D innovations have in the past.

Another binocular cue to depth is actually tactile. We feel changes in the muscles around our eyes as we shift them to look at objects at different distances from us. Closer objects require more **convergence**, which involves turning our eyes inward towards our noses. Use your finger again to demonstrate convergence. Start with the finger at arm's length from you and watch it as you bring it closer and closer to your face. Note the sensations you feel as you do so.

> **convergence** the inward movement of the eyes to view objects close to oneself.

We also use other cues to determine depth. The following are sometimes called **monocular** or **pictorial cues**, because, if needed, they can help us judge depth based on information from only one eye (Figure 7.17):

> **monocular (pictorial) cues** visual clues about depth and distance that can be perceived using information from only one eye.

- *Interposition*. When one object blocks part of another from our view, we see the blocked object as farther away.

- *Elevation*. We see objects that are higher in our visual plane as farther away than those that are lower.

FIGURE 7.17 Monocular depth cues. How many monocular depth cues can you identify in this photograph of the Taj Mahal in India?
Source: Margo Silver/Getty Images, Inc.

- *Texture gradient.* We can see more details of textured surfaces that are closer to us. For example, when sitting at a wooden table in a restaurant, we can see the grain of the wood more clearly than we could from across the room.

- *Linear perspective.* Parallel lines seem to converge in the distance.

- *Shading.* We are accustomed to light, such as sunlight, coming from above us. We use differences in the shading of light from the top to the bottom of our field of view to judge the size and distance of objects.

- *Familiar size.* Once we have learnt the sizes of objects, such as people or restaurant plates, we assume that they stay the same size, so objects that look smaller than usual must be further away.

- *Relative size.* When we look at two objects we know are about the same size, if one seems smaller than the other, we see it as being further away than the other.

Some studies show that we can perceive depth at very early ages, and we may even be born with some depth perception abilities (Banks & Salapatek, 1983). Nevertheless, top-down processing also plays an important part in depth perception, for example we use our memories of the sizes of objects around us to help judge depth.

Artists use monocular depth cues to help us 'see' depth in their two-dimensional depictions. Essentially, they create an illusion of depth. Because visual perception happens nearly automatically, we are easily influenced by such visual tricks. For example, people from cultures that have a lot of architecture and structures featuring straight edges, such as the United States, are easily fooled by the Müller-Lyer illusion and the Ponzo illusion, shown in Figure 7.18, which both appear to take advantage of our tendency to use linear perspective to judge distance (Berry *et al.*, 1992; Brislin & Keating, 1976).

Seeing What We Expect to See: Perceptual Constancy

Top-down processing also contributes to **perceptual constancy**, our tendency to view objects as if they were unchanging, even though the actual visual sensations we receive are constantly shifting. There are several kinds of perceptual constancies, including:

perceptual constancy the perception that objects are unchanging, despite shifts in the environmental stimuli we receive.

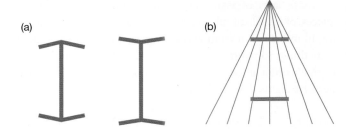

FIGURE 7.18 Perceptual illusions. (a) The Müller-Lyer illusion: the line on the right appears longer, but both lines are the same length. (b) The Ponzo illusion: the converging lines make the upper bar seem larger, but both bars are actually the same length.

- If you are sitting in a restaurant when the manager dims the lights for the evening, you are not likely to look down at your dessert and believe that its colour has changed, even though the light waves your eyes are receiving have changed in intensity and wavelength content. This phenomenon, known as *colour constancy* (Schiffman, 1996), depends in part on how we perceive the entire scene. When the lights dim in the restaurant, your brain makes adjustments based on information coming from all the objects that you can see.

- Another constancy, *size constancy*, helps us to perceive depth. Once we have learnt the size of an object, we expect it to stay the same; this is an example of top-down processing. If the object looks smaller than usual, we do not conclude that it has somehow shrunk. Instead, we assume that it is further away. Like other perceptual processes, perceptual constancies, while usually very useful in helping us understand the world, can sometimes lead us to 'see' illusions. A common illusion of size, for example, is the moon illusion. The image of a full moon on the retina stays the same size all the time, but when we view it close to the horizon it appears much bigger than when we see it farther from the horizon (Figure 7.19) (Kaufman & Rock, 1989).

- Once we have formed expectations about the shape of an object, we also experience *shape constancy* (Gazzaniga, 1995). We may get visual input of only the edge of a plate as the waiter carries it towards us, for example, but we perceive the plate as a round disk. A famous illusion based on both shape and size constancy involves the Ames room, shown in Figure 7.20. The person on the right-hand side looks huge compared with the one on the left. Why? First, we expect the room to be square, but it actually is

FIGURE 7.19 The moon illusion. The moon is the same size all the time but it appears larger near the horizon than higher in the sky, partly because no depth cues exist in space.

Source: ©Ron Watts/Corbis.

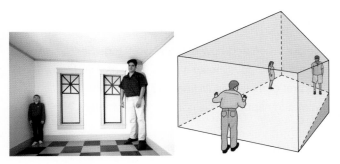

FIGURE 7.20 The Ames room. This specially constructed room is trapezoidal in shape, with sloping floors and ceilings. An observer can see inside only through a peephole, using one eye, so that the room appears normal. Because the observer assumes both people in the room are the same distance from him, he 'sees' the people as being very different in size.

Source: Field Museum Library/Getty Images, Inc.

irregularly shaped. Second, because we think the room is square, we believe that both people are the same distance from us, leading us to perceive one as much larger than the other. You may notice that even when you know how this illusion works, the people's respective sizes still do not look right – indicating how strongly our expectations affect our perception.

Developing Sight

Sight is less developed than other senses in newborns. Newborn infants are capable of seeing, but their vision is much less sharp than it will be after a few months. For a short time after birth, human babies focus mostly on contrasts. For example, a baby will stare at the hairline of his or her caregiver, instead of the face.

By the time they are about two months old, visual perception has improved, and infants seem to focus intently on faces. The range of objects on which they can focus is limited, though. They see objects best that are within 30 cm. Perhaps not coincidentally, this is about the distance people tend to put their faces when interacting with babies. Over the next several months, the ability to see fine detail improves, so that by the end of the eighth month, vision in babies is quite similar to that of normal adults. These early life changes in vision are due to the development of the visual nervous system after birth. As we shall see next, proper development of the visual system also requires visual experience during a specific part of early life.

Difficulties with Sight

Many common vision problems can be corrected today. Laser surgeries and corrective lenses have become more and more common to help people cope with visual deficits. Some common problems that can be corrected this way include *myopia* (short-sightedness), or difficulty seeing things clearly that are further away, and *hyperopia* (long-sightedness), problems seeing close objects clearly. Eye-care practitioners help with a variety of other problems as well. Sometimes, however, there is no treatment available, or patients start treatment too late to prevent the loss of vision in one or both eyes.

Amblyopia To see the world as a whole, both eyes must work together to produce not two separate images but one integrated image. Motor control of both eyes is important so that the eyes move together, for example while following a particular object. Newborn infants often have not mastered this ability. It is not uncommon for parents to report concern that their young infants sometimes appear to have crossed eyes. This is a normal characteristic that typically resolves itself within a few months after birth as the eye muscles and the motor system that controls them mature.

Some people, however, do not naturally develop coordinated movement of both eyes. This condition is called *strabismus* and affects about 2% of the population. To avoid seeing double images, children with strabismus will rely on what they can see from only one eye while ignoring information from other. Strabismus is commonly treated by having the child wear a patch over the stronger eye, thus forcing the child to use the weaker one, or by surgery. If children are treated during early life, their normal binocular vision can sometimes be preserved.

If strabismus is not corrected by the age of about six years, however, it will eventually lead to a loss of visual abilities in the weaker eye, or *amblyopia*. Amblyopia can be a permanent condition that results from abnormal development of the brain's visual cortex. As we discussed in Chapter 3, many developmental psychologists suggest that there are not only sensitive periods, when we can develop certain skills with greater ease than at other times in our lives, but also critical periods, which are the *only* times during which certain developments can take place. Amblyopia develops if we do not receive visual stimulation from both eyes during the critical period in which humans normally develop the visual brain. After about the age of six, the brains of children with strabismus seem to lose the ability to use information from both eyes and instead process inputs only from one eye. However, some very recent clinical studies suggest that it may be possible to improve binocular vision in older children with amblyopia using visual training techniques (Knox *et al.*, 2012).

Blindness According to the Royal National Institute for the Blind, almost two million people in the United Kingdom suffer from 'sight loss', with 360,000 being registered blind or partially sighted. Most of the people with sight loss not on the register are older people with age-related visual problems. There are many potential causes of blindness. Some are *congenital* (present at birth), while others are acquired later in life. Diseases that can produce blindness include diabetes, glaucoma and macular degeneration.

Since humans rely so heavily on visual information, living without adequate visual input is very challenging. A number of devices have been created to help blind people live independently. Braille, a system of reading that involves touch, has significantly improved the quality of life for blind people. Braille uses various combinations of raised dots to replace traditional printed letters and numbers.

Visually impaired individuals can become so proficient at reading Braille that they can actually read faster than people with normal vision typically read printed material. Researchers have found that blind individuals who become experts at reading Braille are actually using parts of their visual brain to process the sophisticated tactile information. Neuroimaging studies have shown that parts of the occipital and temporal cortices that normally process visual information are activated in blind individuals while they read Braille. It is also noteworthy that individuals with congenital blindness use more of their visual brains to read Braille than do those who become blind later in life. This may be another example of a critical period at work. The acquisition of Braille reading skills as a child may allow for the reorganization of the visual system to serve some new function. Learning Braille later in life may lead to less dramatic reorganization because those parts of the visual brain have already become hard-wired, or less plastic and open to change.

Before You Go On

What Do You Know?

16. What are rods and cones?

17. Historically, what were the two theories of colour vision and how did they work together?

18. What do the 'what' and 'where' pathways in the brain do? Should it really be 'what' and 'how'?

19. How do the Gestalt principles help us to interpret complex visual images?

20. What is strabismus, how is it treated and what can happen if it is not treated promptly?

What Do You Think?

Is the cliché 'seeing is believing' really true? Why or why not?

Access your interactive e-book to view a video clip for this chapter at **www.wileyopenpage.com**

Summary

Perception is the process of interpreting the neural signals provided by our senses to understand the information we receive.

Introducing Perception: Common Features of the Senses

LEARNING OBJECTIVE 1   Describe characteristics shared by all the senses, including receptor cells, transduction and thresholds, and differentiate between top-down and bottom-up processes of perception.

- Our sensory systems convert physical stimuli into neural information with specialized cells called *sensory receptor cells* that convert a specific form of environmental stimuli into neural impulses by a process called *sensory transduction*.
- The conversion of physical stimuli into neural impulses only occurs when the stimuli reach a certain level, or threshold. The absolute threshold is the minimum level of a stimulus we can detect. The difference threshold is the smallest difference we can detect between two similar stimuli.
- Our sensory systems are set up to detect change. With continuous exposure to a stimulus, adaptation occurs.

The Chemical Senses: Smell and Taste

LEARNING OBJECTIVE 2   Summarize the biological changes that underlie smell and taste.

- Smell, our olfactory sense, converts chemical odorants into neural signals that the brain can use. Taste, our gustatory sense, is closely intertwined with smell. Most flavours are a combination of scents with the five basic tastes we can discern: sweet, salty, sour, bitter and umami.
- Our tactile sense combines with taste and smell to help us appreciate, or dislike, the textures of foods and to experience temperature and hot sensations from capsaicin in spicy foods.
- Taste buds in papillae on the tongue convert chemicals in our food to neural signals the brain can use. Taste receptors and smell receptors are routinely replaced, since they are more vulnerable to damage than other sensory receptors.

- Information about smell goes directly from the olfactory bulb to the olfactory cortex. Areas of the brain that process smells and tastes are plastic (changeable). The processing of smells also sometimes overlaps with emotions and memories.
- Our preferred tastes change as we mature, probably from a combination of learning and physical changes in the mouth.
- True disorders of taste are rare; people more frequently lose part or all of their sense of smell. Anosmia can present safety risks and diminish pleasure in life.

The Tactile Senses: Touch, Pressure, Pain, Vibration

LEARNING OBJECTIVE 3   Describe how the different senses of touch work and what can happen when things go wrong.

- A variety of sensory receptors throughout our bodies convert touch, pressure or temperature stimuli into neural impulses that our brains can perceive.
- The sensory cortex of the brain maps touch sensations. Especially sensitive or important body parts receive disproportionately large representation in the cortex.
- Pain travels to the brain via both a fast pathway and a slow pathway.
- People differ greatly in the perception of pain. Some of the differences are related to culture and gender. Others are individual.
- The gate control theory of pain suggests that certain patterns of neural activity can close a 'gate' so that pain information does not reach parts of the brain where it is perceived.
- Medical professionals continue to search for ways to relieve people's chronic pain. Opiate drugs that simulate natural painkilling endorphins or enkephalins are addictive. Sometimes, practitioners resort to neurosurgery, which stops a patient from receiving all touch signals.
- The inability to feel pain can put people at high risk for injuries.
- People who have lost body parts surgically or through accidents often feel phantom sensations in the missing body part. These may be related to the reorganization of the somatosensory cortex after an amputation.

The Auditory Sense: Hearing

LEARNING OBJECTIVE 4 Summarize what happens when we hear.

- The frequency and amplitude of sound waves produce our perceptions of pitch and loudness of sounds.
- When sounds enter the ear, they move the eardrum, which sets in motion the ossicles. The last of these, the stirrup, vibrates the oval window, setting into motion fluid in the cochlea. Hair cells on the basilar membrane in the cochlea transduce movements along the basilar membrane into neural signals the brain can interpret.
- Frequency theory suggests that patterns in the firing rates of the neurons are perceived as different sounds. Place theory suggests that information from different locations along the basilar membrane is related to different qualities of sound.
- Top-down processing lets us use the general loudness of sounds, as well as differences in the signals received from each ear, to determine location of a sound.
- Different pitches are represented in a tonotopic map in the auditory cortex of the brain. Association areas of the cortex help us recognize familiar sounds, including speech.
- The brain integrates information from multiple sensory systems to enable the appropriate recognition and response to stimuli. Some people experience an overlap of sensory systems known as synaesthesia.
- As young children, we experience a sensitive period during which it is especially easy for us to learn auditory information, including language and music. Some people, particularly those exposed to pure tones during this sensitive period, develop perfect pitch.
- Common hearing problems include hearing loss and deafness, as well as hearing unwanted sounds, such as tinnitus.

The Visual Sense: Sight

LEARNING OBJECTIVE 5 Describe key processes in visual perception.

- Vision is very important to humans, and a great deal of our brain is involved in processing visual information.
- Rods and cones in the retina at the back of the eye change light into neural impulses. Cones provide detailed vision and help us perceive colour, while rods provide information about intensity of light, particularly at low light levels.
- Two different theories in combination – trichromatic theory and opponent process theory – explain a good deal of how we perceive colour.
- The fovea at the centre of the retina contains only cones and provides our sharpest vision. We have a blind spot where the optic nerve leaves the retina to carry information to the brain.
- In the brain, visual information is processed through the what and where/how pathways.
- Damage to certain areas of the brain can produce abnormal perceptual experiences like visual agnosia and visual neglect.
- Top-down processing is involved in much visual perception. Gestalt theorists have identified several principles by which we recognize stimuli, even when visual inputs are limited. We use binocular and monocular cues for depth perception. Perceptual constancies, based on learning from previous experiences, help us to see things as stable despite constant shifts in our visual inputs. These top-down processes can be fooled by visual illusions.
- Without adequate visual stimulation through both eyes during a critical period of life, we may not develop binocular vision, a condition known as amblyopia.
- Blind individuals can use other sensory modalities to compensate for the loss of visual information. Learning Braille with touch involves the use of brain areas normally used for vision.

Activities to test yourself further are available in your interactive e-book at
www.wileyopenpage.com

TYING IT TOGETHER

WHAT HAPPENS IN THE
BRAIN?

- The brain normally integrates information from multiple sensory systems. In people who experience synaesthesia, brain areas for one sense are activated by stimuli related to different senses (or sub-modalities of the same sense), so that they might, for example, hear colours.
- Different parts of our brains are active in working out what we see from those that help us work out where things are when we see them.
- Blind people who learn to read Braille at an early age actually use parts of their visual cortex to do so, in addition to areas normally associated with touch.

OUT OF THE
ORDINARY

- People rarely lose their sense of taste. Most problems with taste are related to the loss of the sense of smell.
- When we damage taste buds or odour receptors in the nose, they are replaced, but damage to other sensory receptors, such as photoreceptors and hair cells, is permanent. They are not replaced.
- People who experience phantom sensations in missing body parts usually feel things they actually felt before losing the body part.

HOW WE
DIFFER

- About a quarter of all people are supertasters, able to discern bitter tastes that many others do not even notice.
- Only about one person in 10,000 in Western countries develops perfect pitch, the ability to identify tones heard in isolation. More people who speak tonal languages have perfect pitch.
- About four people in 100 in Western countries are tone deaf.

HOW WE
DEVELOP

- All of our sensory systems begin to develop during foetal life. We can hear, feel, smell and taste before we are born.
- Sight is our least-developed sense at birth.
- Children have more taste buds in more locations in their mouths than adults do, which may explain in part why they dislike many new foods.

Quizzes to test yourself further are available in your interactive e-book at **www.wileyopenpage.com**

Key Terms

absolute threshold 167
ageusia 175
anosmia 175
basilar membrane 182
bottom-up processing 168
cochlea 182
cones 187
convergence 193
deafness 186
difference threshold or just
    noticeable difference 167
endorphins 179

enkephalins 179
fovea 187
gate control theory of pain
    179
gustatory sense 170
hair cells 182
lateral geniculate nucleus
    (LGN) 190
monocular or pictorial
    cues 193
odorants 170
olfactory bulb 173

olfactory receptor
    neurons 170
olfactory sense 170
opponent process theory 190
optic nerve 187
oval window 182
papillae 170
perception 166
perceptual constancy 194
perceptual sets 168
perfect or absolute pitch 185
photoreceptors 187

retina 187
retinal disparity 193
rods 187
sensation 166
sensory adaptation 168
sound waves 181
taste buds 171
tonotopic map 184
top-down processing 168
trichromatic theory 189
tympanic membrane 182
visual field 190

Flashcards to test yourself further are available in your interactive e-book
at **www.wileyopenpage.com**

CHAPTER 8

Consciousness

Adapted by Stuart Wilson, Queen Margaret University, Edinburgh, UK

CHAPTER OUTLINE

Part 1: The Philosophy of Consciousness

- Defining Consciousness

- Is Consciousness 'Mysterious'?

- What's in the World? Part 1: Material Stuff *or* Mental Stuff

- What's in the World? Part 2: Material Stuff *and* Mental Stuff

Part 2: Studying Conscious States

- When We Are Awake: Conscious Awareness

- Preconscious and Unconscious States

- Hypnosis

- When We Are Asleep

- Psychoactive Drugs

 Access your interactive e-book to view a video clip for this chapter at **www.wileyopenpage.com**

'Take your right hand and pinch the skin on your left forearm. What exactly happened when you did so? Several different sorts of things happened. First, the neurobiologists tell us, the pressure of your thumb and forefinger set up a sequence of neuron firings that began at the sensory receptors in your skin, went into the spine and up the spine through a region called the tract of Lissauer, and then into the thalamus and other basal regions of the brain. The signal then went to the somatosensory cortex and perhaps other cortical regions as well. A few hundred milliseconds after you pinched your skin, a second sort of thing happened, one that you know about without professional assistance. You felt a pain. Nothing serious, just a mildly unpleasant pinching sensation in the skin of your forearm. This unpleasant sensation had a certain particular sort of subjective feel to it, a feel which is accessible to you in a way that it is not accessible to others around you . . . you can know about your pain in a way that others cannot. [T]he mode of existence of the sensation is a first-person or subjective mode of existence, whereas the mode of existence of the neural pathways is a third-person or objective mode of existence; the pathways exist independently of being experienced in a way that the pain does not.' ∎

Source: Searle, *The Mystery of Consciousness*, 1997, pp. 97–98

Everything in the example above is linked to consciousness, one of the most important topics to anyone studying the mind, and the topic of this chapter. Explaining consciousness is one of the most difficult problems in science, and in this chapter we will explore why, beginning with some of the philosophical issues before moving on to more empirical concerns.

Answer the following question. How could you prove that the next person you meet is conscious? What would you do? You could ask them 'Are you conscious?' and see what they say. They will probably say 'Yes', but is this good evidence? Perhaps they are a very sophisticated robot that has been programmed to respond to questions in the English language with various different verbal responses. (OK – they are probably *not* a robot, but how would you know for sure?) You could pinch them and see whether they experienced pain, but isn't that open to the same objection? How would you know that they had actually experienced pain and were not merely producing a host of behavioural outputs that made it *look* like they were in pain, but without the pain itself? You really have absolutely no way of knowing whether anyone else you meet is conscious in the same way you are, because you cannot climb out of your own head and experience the world as someone else experiences it. We have no 'consciousness meter' that we can use to determine when some collection of molecules has conscious experiences and when another collection of molecules does not.

As psychologists, we are all trying to understand people, and there are many things to keep us busy. We can focus on observable behaviours, as the behaviourists did, or we can try to understand mental processes, as cognitive psychologists do. We can attempt to understand intelligence and personality, how brains develop, how we interact with other people and so on. All of these pursuits are worth while and will certainly contribute greatly to our understanding of the mind and behaviour. But there is something else. Much of our behaviour and our cognitive processing is accompanied by experience. It is easy to take this for granted because we are so familiar with it, but it is a rather amazing thing. We experience the world around us. We look at a rose and we experience its redness; we step on a sharp object and we experience the pain in our foot; we take our first spoonful of strawberry ice cream and we can taste the delicious flavour.

qualia the raw material of conscious experience. Qualia is the name philosophers use to describe the experiences that make up our consciousness. What it is like to experience the redness of a red object, for example, is a quale (singular).

The experiences of seeing 'redness', of feeling pain or of tasting strawberry are known as *qualia* (singular: quale). **Qualia** are one of the central problems in understanding consciousness. There is a certain quality attached to your experience, and this is usually quite hard to put into words. What does it actually *feel* like to experience red or to taste strawberry ice cream? Could you describe the experience to someone who had never had it? There are certain things you could say (e.g., 'It is quite sweet' or 'It smells fruity'), but these things are unlikely to accurately convey the actual experience you have of tasting it for yourself (i.e. the quale). There appears to be something intensely private about your own experience; nobody knows what it is like to have the kinds of experiences that you do, and you do not know what anyone else's private subjective world is like.

Any serious attempt to understand consciousness must have something to say about how and why a physical system can have first-person qualitative experiences. This is not an easy thing to do. The way we understand the world is by studying it. Most investigations happen in the third person. What this means is that there is a *thing* to be studied. That thing is usually *out there* in the world. Two people studying that thing can usually agree on what it is and how to study it. Conscious experience seems different. It is not out there. It is not objective. It is, by definition, subjective. It is your own (and everyone else's) personal experience. Why is this a problem? It is a problem because it is the only type of data that we know of that is purely subjective in nature. Of course, there are things that are *linked* to consciousness (and we will come to those soon), but as to whether these things actually *are* consciousness is one of the central debates in the field.

Consciousness really is one of the most puzzling features of our world. It is hard to define, it is hard to explain and it is hard to study. As the philosopher David Chalmers pointed out in 1995, it is a 'hard problem'. Yet there is nothing you know more intimately than your own consciousness. It is your inner world. It is what makes you *you*. It is a perplexing problem because we do not really understand what it is, what it is for or how it arises in the brain. We know that it is *linked* to our brains. That is not really in doubt. But why is it that our brains, which are material objects, are able to *experience* things? Most material objects are not conscious. Mountains do not experience the world around them. Computers do not reflect on the processes they carry out. But human brains do these things. What is it about the human brain (and maybe brains in general) that gives rise to experience? Is it sheer complexity? Is it the amount of information that is processed? If so, why is complexity or processing capacity associated with phenomenal experience? Does that mean that we could artificially create a complex information processor that was conscious in the same way that we are? Could we create a conscious machine? Would this machine have a will of its own? If it were conscious just like us, could it fall in love as we can?

These are just some of the questions that students of consciousness wrestle with and in this chapter we will attempt to give you a tour of some of the main issues. To do this, we have divided this chapter into two parts. In Part One, we will cover some of the more abstract, philosophical issues that surround consciousness. It is important not to neglect this, because consciousness is a topic that straddles the boundary between psychology and philosophy. In Part Two we will look at some of the psychological topics, an understanding of which will be required if we are ever to achieve an understanding of consciousness.

PART 1: THE PHILOSOPHY OF CONSCIOUSNESS

Defining Consciousness

LEARNING OBJECTIVE 1

Define consciousness and identify why it is both central to the study of the mind and such an elusive topic of investigation.

Defining consciousness is notoriously difficult, and serious progress is frequently hampered by differences of opinion concerning the definition of the thing that we are trying to explain. Discussion of consciousness often produces much heat and very little light, and one of the reasons for this is that different people define it in different ways. The result of such variability in definition is different people trying to explain different things, using different assumptions to do so, all of which makes progress (and worthwhile debate) very difficult to achieve. Philosopher Thomas Nagel (1974) defined consciousness as 'what it is like to be' in some state. This definition places emphasis on the experiential nature of consciousness. There is *something it is like to be*

you, there is *something it is like to be* me and (to use Nagel's famous example from 1974) there is *something it is like to be* a bat. This 'what it is like'-ness is what many refer to as consciousness. Some, however, would cast doubt on this, and we shall be hearing from them in other parts of this chapter.

Consciousness is often closely linked to the concept of the *mind* and the *mind/body problem*. It is easy to see why this is the case, because there can be little doubt that your experience is necessarily linked to your mind. Additionally, when we reflect on our own minds, our natural intuition leads us to think that our mind is something different from our physical body; in much the same way, our intuitions about consciousness often lead us to similar conclusions.

Despite the close links between mind and consciousness, we need to be careful not to conflate the two things entirely, because there are aspects of mind that are almost certainly not conscious. Many of our mental processes happen outside of our conscious awareness, which means that *the mind* is probably too broad a definition for what we are talking about when we use the term *consciousness*. More traditional definitions of consciousness will mention 'wakefulness', 'awareness' or 'self-reflective-ness'. Again, these things are all linked to consciousness in important ways, but they cannot themselves be a complete definition. For example, 'there is something it is like' to be in a dream-state, even though you are not awake or self-reflecting (you may be 'aware' in some sense, although this is arguable). We will return to these aspects of consciousness later in the chapter, but for now we are going to stick to the more general 'what it is like-ness' definition that Nagel (1974) suggested.

Before You Go On

What Do You Know?

1. What is it about consciousness that makes it such a difficult problem?

What Do You Think?

If you were researching consciousness, what kinds of things would you give priority to?

Is Consciousness 'Mysterious'?

LEARNING OBJECTIVE 2

Describe why some philosophers have found it hard to place consciousness within a physical framework.

We live in a physical universe. This universe is made up of physical things and physical processes. Some of these

physical things are familiar to us: rocks, water, books. Other physical things are harder for us to see, but we know that they are out there. These may be things like oxygen, magnetic fields and atoms. Physics is the branch of science that tries to make sense of the physical world, and physicists have done an impressive job so far, modelling the universe that we live in and figuring out how it works. There are unanswered questions, of course, but the story they tell is mostly comprehensible and is largely supported by observation and evidence.

To many people, however, there is a problem. There is nothing in our physical story of the universe that says anything about why some physical things should be conscious and other things not. Our best theories about the physical world work without any reference to consciousness whatsoever. There is nothing in physics to suggest that the material from which our world is made (which includes the material from which we are made) should ever be conscious of anything. The material world, from rocks to planets to galaxies, can be described physically without suggesting that any part of it is conscious. Qualia are not part of the picture.

Our consciousness is linked to our brain. Our brain is also a physical object in which physical events happen. Does understanding our brain give us any clues about consciousness? This is where much of the debate lies. To put it in the simplest form possible, our brains are physical systems. We can confidently say that our brain is the seat of our conscious experience. The big question is: 'How does it do this?' This is not a trivial question. This is the key question for everyone who studies consciousness. The human brain is perhaps the most complex thing in the known universe, but it is still a physical thing. Electrochemical signals and electrical fields are physical processes that allow the brain to go about its business. But none of these physical things is conscious. A neuron is not conscious. A collection of one hundred neurons would not be conscious – or would it? (One of the problems inherent in dealing with consciousness is that we have no way of knowing at what point a collection of neurons 'becomes conscious'.) But somehow, all of these non-conscious things lead to consciousness when put together in a certain way inside a head. Is this surprising? To some people, it is not surprising at all. To others, it is the most surprising thing imaginable. The debate between them is fierce, and is a long way from being settled. Let's explore some of the issues.

What's in the World? Part 1: Material Stuff *or* Mental Stuff

LEARNING OBJECTIVE 3

Summarize the monist positions, particularly those involving materialism, and the objections to approaching consciousness in these ways.

As we mentioned previously, we live in a physical universe. If we take that at face value, then it would mean that everything could be explained in physical terms. If we understand enough about the constituent parts of our universe and the way that they interact, then we should (at least in principle) understand everything. This is **materialism**. Materialism is a branch of **monism**, which is a position that states that there is only one type of fundamental substance, or *stuff*, in the world. Materialists claim that the one type of stuff is physical, and things like mental phenomena and consciousness must necessarily be explained in physical terms. Idealists, on the other hand, think that there is only 'mental' stuff in the world and anything that we consider physical is merely an illusion caused by our minds (or our consciousness). There are not many idealists around these days, because most people accept that material objects have an existence that is independent of our minds. When it comes to consciousness, materialists claim that a complete understanding of the brain and its processes will provide us with a full and satisfying explanation. The only reason that consciousness seems such a mystery, according to materialists, is because we simply do not yet have a complete understanding of brain function. Once we understand brain function, an explanation of consciousness will follow and we will find that consciousness is nothing more than physical matter carrying out physical processes. This type of materialism comes in different forms, but for now we will describe two: *identity theory* and *eliminativism*.

Identity Theory

Identity theory holds that mental states are *identical* to brain states. Brain states *are* the whole story. In other words, there is a one-to-one correlation between physical processes in the brain and everything we associate with 'the mind' (including consciousness and qualia). So, just as a concept like temperature is identical to kinetic energy (which is physical), so consciousness is just another name for the physical processes in the brain. Feeling pain, for example, is simply a specific pattern of neural activity, and once you have explained the neural activity, then, according to identity theorists, you have explained everything; including the experience of the pain. Any talk of *experience* is clouding the issue, because experience can be completely explained by looking to states of matter in brains. Identity theory can be traced back to Place (1956), but its most prominent contemporary proponents are Patricia and Paul Churchland, the latter of whom famously wrote, 'the human species and all of its features are wholly the physical outcome of a purely physical process. We are notable only in that our nervous system is more complex and powerful than that of our fellow

materialism a philosophical position in which it is held that everything can be explained in physical/material terms.

monism the idea that there is one type of fundamental substance from which everything else is made. This can be either *physical* substance (i.e. *materialism*) or mental substance (i.e. *idealism*).

identity theory a position in the philosophy of mind that holds that brain states are identical to mental states.

creatures. We are creatures of matter. And we should learn to live with that fact' (Churchland, 1988, p. 21).

Eliminativism

Eliminativism (sometimes known as *eliminativist materialism*) is another materialist view. Eliminativists deal with many of the core challenges (such as qualia) by claiming that they do not exist or that they are not problems of such huge magnitude as some would like to insist. Eliminativists would argue that, when studying consciousness, all we have to go on are our objective observations about the physical world. When we look objectively at the brain, we see nothing that would equate to conscious experience and so conscious experience as we usually think of it must not exist (or is an illusion). If we cannot find something in the material world, it makes no sense to speak of that thing as having a real, quantifiable existence. One proponent of this position is Daniel Dennett. Dennett wrote a book called *Consciousness Explained* in 1991, and in it he attempts to demolish the idea that much of what we call consciousness (including qualia) actually has a real, independent existence. For Dennett, what we think of as consciousness is actually the output of a massively complex information-processing system. Any system that has such an enormous number of components must be organized in such a way that only certain pieces of information can influence behaviour and 'high-level' processing at any one time.

> **eliminativism** a viewpoint within materialism which does not accept that qualia are 'things' that have an independent existence. Eliminativists attempt to get rid of such notions (eliminate them) by explaining them in purely physical terms.

There will always be competition for attention amongst the various components, and only the ones that 'shout the loudest' will have prominence in guiding further processing and behaviour. This, according to Dennett, is where our feeling of being conscious comes from. In other words, we are tricked into thinking that consciousness is something special (e.g. qualia) when in actual fact there is nothing beyond the information processing. Linked to this, Dennett also takes issue with the common feeling that there is an *I* that looks out on the world, having experiences. He calls this the *Cartesian Theatre* and his opinion is that it is also an illusion caused by the complex way our brains deal with information. It is in these ways (by denying the reality of qualia and a subjective I) that Dennett can be said to be an eliminativist.

Objections to Identity Theory and Eliminativism

Identity theory has been criticized in a few ways. The strict adherence to a one-to-one relationship between mental states and physical states has been criticized for being too inflexible. This is known as the problem of **multiple realizability**. Identity theory states that there is a direct one-to-one correlation between brain states and mental states, but if it can be shown that certain mental states can exist via more than one brain state, then this one-to-one relationship cannot hold. For example, language comprehension is usually associated with certain brain areas in the left hemisphere. However, in some people (e.g. some left-handers), the language centres are found to be in other areas. Also, if a person has their language centre damaged (through a stroke or other brain injury), then it is sometimes possible for them to regain language function by shifting it to another area in the brain. Both of these cases suggest that the same mental state can be achieved by *different* brain states, throwing doubt on the identity theorists' insistence on one-to-one correlation. Second, identity theorists would have to say something meaningful about what makes some brain states mental states, while other brain states are not. There are many things going on in your brain, and only some of them are related to brain states. At the moment, there is no convincing account that explains the difference between those brain states that are also mental states and those that are not.

> **multiple realizability** the idea that identical mental states can be realized by different brain processes (or different brain regions).

Eliminativism has been criticized because of its attempts to deny that consciousness is as hard a problem as many people make it out to be. As we have seen, the thing about consciousness that is hardest to explain is the subjective, phenomenal experience that we all feel; the redness of red, the taste of strawberries and so on. Eliminativists want to deny that these qualia exist, but critics question whether this is a valid position given that rich subjective experiences seem to be the most obvious data that we have about our mental life. We all have these experiences, and these experiences demand an explanation, so to deny that they are what they appear to be is (according to critics) unhelpful. Eliminativists would also have to give a coherent account of exactly how our brains trick us into thinking we have subjective experiences when in actual fact we do not, which is something that they have not done entirely (despite several attempts, of which Dennett's account is one).

The Rise of Functionalism

Identity theory was criticized for being too inflexible because of its insistence that mental states (including qualia) have a direct one-to-one relationship with brain states. There is a way around this objection, however, that still counts as a version of materialism. Functionalists place emphasis on the causal relationships between mental states and what mental states actually do (i.e. their function). Focusing on function has an important consequence: there is no need to be strictly bound to the physical constitution of mental states.

Think of a clock. A clock can take many different forms. It can be an analogue tick-tock clock that you have to wind up every day. It can be a digital clock that runs on batteries. It can be a piece of software on your computer that displays the time at the bottom right corner of your screen. All of these things perform the same function (displaying the current time) in completely different ways. What is most important about them is not the physical medium in which they do it but the fact that they all do the same thing. Displaying the time is their function, regardless of how that is achieved.

Functionalists view the mind in similar terms. To them, the most important things are the functions of mental states, not the physical medium in which they happen. They view the brain as being like a computer and the mind as being like a computer program. A word-processing program, for example, is not necessarily tied to a specific type of computer; it may be able to run on many different machines. What is most important is not the actual hardware but the function of the program itself (i.e. word processing). A functionalist account of mental states, therefore, holds that a mental state is a mental state by virtue of what it does rather than the machine in which it does it.

PSYCHOLOGY AROUND US   The Consequences of Functionalism: Conscious Machines?

A functionalist account of the mind opens up some intriguing possibilities. If the function is important rather than the hardware, this suggests that it may be possible to create something that performs identical functions to human minds, but does not require a biological brain. This is not possible at the moment (and probably will not be possible in the near future), but a functionalist view of mental processes does, in principle, allow for what John Searle (1997) calls 'strong artificial intelligence'. A full understanding of function in terms of causal relationships and so on would not rule out the possibility that a machine could be created that runs 'human mind' software in a machine made of silicone (rather than the one made of meat which is in your head). The implications of this are huge. If functionalism is correct and if mind states are equivalent to computational states, then it is conceivable that a computer could run a functionally equivalent version of your mind. An important question then follows: would this computer experience the world in the same way that you do (assuming that it processes sensory information in exactly the same way that you do)? Does the computer-you feel the same things you do when it receives your favourite song as input? Strict functionalists would say that it would, because mental states are functional states, and the computer-you is functionally equivalent to the actual-you and processes information from its environment in exactly the same way that the actual-you does.

Criticisms of Functionalism

Functionalism can be criticized in a similar way to other materialist approaches to consciousness, in that it does not specifically state how particular functions should be accompanied by experience. If you ask a strict functionalist whether a machine that is functionally equivalent to a human would have human experiences, they would most likely say that it would. However, they cannot explain *why* functions equal experiences (or why some functions are associated with experience while others are not). This is not to say that functionalism is definitely wrong. It may be the case that functionalism (or some other materialist approach) *does* explain consciousness, and once all the material facts are in place, consciousness necessarily follows, but at the moment we are not in a position to make this claim with confidence. (Question: will we ever be able to make this claim with confidence? How would you know if a machine

was conscious? Even if it acted as if it were, and even if it said 'yes' to the question 'Are you conscious?', would you ever be able to conclusively demonstrate that the machine was actually having conscious experiences rather than just running a program that responded to various inputs with various types of behaviour?)

One critic of functionalism over the years has been the philosopher John Searle. Searle's famous objection to functionalism is known as the *Chinese Room*. Before we describe Searle's objection, let's first think about what functionalism entails. Functionalism holds that the mind is an information processor. Information processors work by performing computations. Computations involve the manipulation of symbols. A computer performs computations on symbols (in the very simplest form, these symbols would be 0s and 1s). The computations are carried out by applying a set of rules that determine the various ways in which the symbols are manipulated. These rules are called *syntax*. When a program uses syntax to manipulate symbols to perform some function, this is what we mean by *computation*. The functionalists think that this is what our minds are like. They argue that our minds are like computer programs that process information according to syntactical rules.

John Searle disagreed with this, and he did so because he thought there was something missing from this picture: *semantics*. When you speak (or think) in your own language, you are doing something more than manipulating symbols according to the rules of the language (grammar). You also understand the meaning of the words. According to Searle, a computational view of the mind that is based on the syntactical manipulation of symbols cannot account for the fact that our minds can represent meaning. Our minds are also semantic. To illustrate this, Searle employed an old favourite of philosophers: a thought experiment.

Imagine a big information processor. We tend to think of computers as small things, but for the moment imagine one that is big enough for you to climb inside: a room, in other words. Now, imagine that instead of all the processing being done by electronic signals it is done by you. You are the *processor* in this computer. You need a function, and the function is to produce an output in the Chinese language. You do not speak Chinese, but this is not a problem because in this room is a big book of rules (the program). Also in the room are a lot of cards with Chinese symbols on them. You have everything you need to produce outputs in Chinese. There is a letterbox on the door of the room, and every so often, cards come through this letterbox with a variety of Chinese symbols arranged in various ways. This is the *input*. You carefully follow the rules, and you perform the operations on the symbols. This allows you to produce an output using the Chinese symbols available to you, and post this newly constructed Chinese phrase back out through the letterbox. It is quite time consuming, but if you and the person on the outside are patient enough, then you can start to have a conversation. In other words, you are a computer that is implementing a program that has been specifically designed to produce intelligible sentences in Chinese based on intelligible inputs. To the person on the outside it may look as if he or she is having an intelligent conversation with a Chinese speaker, but you still do not understand Chinese.

This, according to Searle, is a huge problem for functionalist accounts of the mind because it demonstrates that programs running syntactical operations on symbols do not have semantics: a computer program alone does not (and cannot) extract meaning when implementing its rules. Minds clearly do have semantics so, according to Searle, minds cannot be mere programs. This criticism argues that it does not matter how complex your program is, because you cannot get to a semantic understanding through syntax alone.

Assessing the Materialist Approach

The idea that a full understanding of the brain or the functions of the brain will tell us all we need to know about consciousness is an appealing one, but is it correct? The problem, of course, is that we will not know if it is correct until we have a full understanding of the brain, but there are a couple of things we can think about to test whether this is a viable position. The assumption of materialism is that the physical story explains all the facts. With specific reference to consciousness, materialism states that the physical story (about the brain or about the functions of the brain) fully encompasses everything we could ever need to know about conscious experience. In other words, there is nothing left over once the physical story is complete.

How likely is this? A rudimentary analysis suggests that it may not be as straightforward as that. If materialists manage to describe all the physical facts about your body and about your brain, does this mean that they know everything there is to know about your beliefs, your desires, your passions and your conscious experiences? Even if we accept that mental phenomena like beliefs and desires can be explained physically, what about your conscious experience? Doesn't it seem as if there are some facts that are left over once the physical account is in? In philosophy, this is known as an *explanatory gap*. Even a complete physical story of brain function still has to explain why brain processes are associated with conscious experience. There needs to be some kind of explanation that we can point to and say, 'And *this* is why consciousness happens.' At the moment, we do not seem to be close to such an explanation. Some of the more pessimistic consciousness researchers would go even further, and say that not only are we nowhere near an explanation but also we *do not even know what an explanation would be like*. This may turn out to be a trivial problem. Perhaps a complete understanding of the brain will see the hard problem melt away. But it is just as likely that bridging the explanatory gap and solving the hard problem remains as elusive as ever, despite a fuller understanding of brain processes.

Why might this be the case? Critics of strict materialism have come up with a number of ingenious objections, many of them involving thought experiments.

PSYCHOLOGY AROUND US

What Mary Didn't Know

Philosopher Frank Jackson (1986) suggested the following scenario as a way of testing the assumptions of the materialist position. Imagine that we are living in a time in which the physical story about the brain is complete. The world's leading expert on the brain is called Mary. Mary has dedicated her entire life to studying the brain. She knows everything there is to know about the workings of neurons, neurotransmitters, synapses and so on. She is particularly interested in colour vision, and she has a full understanding of everything that happens when we process visual information. She understands the physics involved in receiving information from the external world into the visual system and she knows exactly how the optical system processes information and how the brain makes sense of this information. However, Mary has spent her entire life living in a black and white room. All the books she has read have been black and white. Everything she has ever experienced has been black and white. She has never actually experienced colour, despite being the world's leading expert on the neurophysiology of colour vision. Now imagine that Mary leaves her black and white world for the first time, and she sees something red. Does she learn something new? There are (at least) two

responses to this. Either Mary leaves the room, sees something red and says, 'Yes, I knew that's what it would be like; it is *obvious* to me' (because she fully understands the physical story) or she leaves the room, sees something red and says, 'Ahhh, so *that's* what it is like to see red.' In other words, either the experience of seeing red is entailed by the physical facts or it is not.

What Is It Like to Be a Bat?

Thomas Nagel (1974) was making a similar point when he asked 'What is it like to be a bat?' Bats have smaller brains than humans, so it is not inconceivable that someone may achieve a full understanding of the workings of bat brains. The thing about bats is that they use echolocation to navigate the world. They use auditory information in (very loosely) the same way we use visual information. If you were to achieve a full understanding of bat brains and all the processing that they do, does that mean that you will also understand what it is like to be a bat? Does the physical knowledge also entail an understanding of the experience – the 'what it is like-ness'? Many people doubt that it does, which means experience (i.e. consciousness) is something that is left over once all the physical facts are in.

What these thought experiments actually show (if anything) has been the subject of much debate. But what their originators were attempting to do with them was to show how experience might not be entailed by the physical facts. If Mary learns something new when she leaves the room, then this suggests that the actual subjective *experience* of seeing something red is a different thing from the physical story that can be told about how the sensory system and the brain perceive colour. One of the key questions, therefore, is whether there is anything left to explain once the physical story is complete. If there is, where does this leave materialism?

Before You Go On

What Do You Know?

2. What are the main similarities and differences between the approaches to consciousness described in the previous sections?

What Do You Think?

In your opinion, which of the above approaches has the most to offer? Why?

What's in the World? Part 2: Material Stuff *and* Mental Stuff

LEARNING OBJECTIVE 4

Summarize the dualist positions, including why some philosophers adopt dualism, and give an account of the objections to approaching consciousness in these ways.

Materialism holds that everything in our world can be explained through an understanding of the material that makes up the world and the various forces that interact with that material. But this does not sit well with some people. At the moment, there is nothing in physics, chemistry or biology that suggests consciousness is a part of the physical story that we are constructing about our world. Even studying a brain does not reveal anything about why that brain, with all its physical processes, should have conscious experiences. There still seems to be a lot of other things left over once you have told the physical story. To put it bluntly, there are only two possibilities to explain this. Either current science is incomplete and needs to be extended in order to incorporate consciousness, or consciousness is something that is not part of the physical story. Materialists prefer the first option; dualists prefer the second.

Dualism

To many people (including some philosophers), there appear to be two different types of things in the world. There are the physical things that can be explained by materialism and there are also minds and consciousness, and these do not seem to be material in nature. It certainly does not *feel* to us that our minds are merely physical things. Our minds feel different. Many people's intuition tells them that consciousness is a different type of thing altogether. Is this an illusion, or is this real? Could there really be two fundamentally different kinds of thing in our universe: material stuff and consciousness stuff? The suggestion that consciousness is not part of the physical world is known as **dualism**, of which there are two broad forms.

> **dualism** a position in the philosophy of mind that states that the world consists of two distinct kinds of thing.

Substance dualism   Modern **substance dualism** can be traced back to the French philosopher René Descartes (1596–1650). According to Descartes, humans bodies were physical machines made out of the same material substances that made up other aspects of the physical world (he called this *res extensa*, which is a reference to the fact that material substances are extended in space). Descartes, however, thought that there was another component to humans that was not part of the physical body. He called this second thing *res cogitans*, which refers to a (non-material) thinking substance. For Descartes, humans were a duality: they consist of both a material body (which includes a brain) and an *immaterial* mind (or soul). This was the birth of modern substance dualism: the suggestion that there are two different kinds of thing in the universe; things that are material and things that are not. If you agreed that Mary learns something new when she leaves her monochrome dwelling, then you may be a dualist. One implication of taking this stance is that the *experience* is something that is not entailed by the physical story: experience is something else, something that is not physical. There are very few substance dualists these days, because it has some critical flaws, some of which we will mention below.

> **substance dualism** a position that holds that there are two distinct and independent substances that constitute our world: material things (the physical world) and immaterial things (consciousness/mind/soul).

Property Dualism   **Property dualism** is a weaker form of dualism, because it does not try to oppose materialism as strongly as substance dualism does. Property dualists agree that there is probably only one type of substance (i.e. material). However, they say that material can have different properties: physical properties and non-physical properties. It is in this sense that property dualism is in disagreement with materialism, because materialists want to reduce consciousness (and other mental states) to physical states, while property dualism rejects this by suggesting that consciousness is *not* reducible to physical states of the brain, but is instead an *emergent property* of brains. Property dualism, therefore, holds that humans have two properties: physical properties and mental properties (e.g. consciousness).

> **property dualism** the idea that there is probably only one type of substance, but this can have both physical and non-physical properties.

There are various versions of property dualism. Most (but not all) hold that there is something uniquely special about brains that allow this 'consciousness property' to emerge. This may be the way they are organized biologically, which would make 'consciousness' loosely analogous to the way in which 'life' is a property of matter when arranged in a very specific (and complex) way. The oldest version of property dualism is **epiphenomenalism**. Epiphenomenalism suggests that consciousness and other mental phenomena emerge when brains surpass some criteria of complexity. When this happens, consciousness arises and 'rides on top' of the physical processes without ever being reducible to the physical processes. This may seem like a strange position, but it is not hard to see why it could be appealing. Neuroscience and cognitive neuroscience do a very good job of furthering our understanding of the brain and how it works. Yet despite continued advances, there have been little or no clues as to where consciousness fits into this picture. On one hand we have a third-person, objective account of brain function, but on the other hand we *know* that this is accompanied by consciousness through our own experience. Substance dualism is not justified (for the reasons given below) and so suggesting that brains can have a second, first-person property is one way to resolve the paradox.

> **epiphenomenalism** an explanation for consciousness based on the idea that it emerges from physical processes but is not reducible to them.

At least one version of property dualism has some very odd consequences. David Chalmers (1996) attempts to reconcile property dualism with functionalism. Chalmers is a functionalist in the sense that he believes that it is the functional organization of a system that is a necessary condition for consciousness. In this respect, Chalmers sees no reason to afford the brain any special privilege, and holds that functional organization in *any* medium (e.g. silicon computing devices etc.) has the capacity to be conscious. But he does not leave it there. He states that functionally organized systems give rise to consciousness on account of the way they deal with information. The definition of *information* that Chalmers employs is slightly different from how we usually use the term. He defines it as a 'difference that makes a difference' (p. 281). So, any system that has its state changed by something else is said to be an *informational system*.

Chalmers uses the example of a light. A light can be in one of two states, on or off (ignore dimmer switches for the moment). It is a two-state information space and you can make a difference to this state by flicking a switch. This is a very simple version of an informational system. Our brains can be in any of an enormous number of states, and there are an equally enormous number of things that can influence brains to change states.

To Chalmers, it is this capacity for a functionally organized system to change information states that is the key to consciousness. He argues that the difference between the light and our brains is one of degree, not one of kind. Our brains are vastly more complicated than a light that can be on or off, but essentially they are both functionally organized informational systems. Some readers may have already worked out the consequence of this. Chalmers speculates (and he admits it is speculation) that consciousness might be found in *any* system that has changes in informational states. The light is, in a sense, conscious. It would be conscious in a very different way from us, but Chalmers would argue that is purely because it is a much simpler system. This remarkable

panpsychism the view that consciousness is pervasive and exists in everything.

suggestion is known as **panpsychism**, which is the view that consciousness is *everywhere* and is a fundamental feature of the universe.

Problems with Dualism Substance dualists are very rare in modern philosophy and psychology, despite its being the most pervasive view of consciousness in most cultures. The reason that there are not many dualists left is because it faces some very serious problems when subjected to scrutiny. Substance dualists, remember, claim that consciousness is something entirely different from (and separate from) the physical world. That is a huge claim. It is slightly baffling as well, because it claims that consciousness is immaterial. If it is not physical, what is it? What is it made of? It is not made of anything, but it is still a thing. How can something be made out of nothing? More basically, *where* would a non-physical consciousness be?

It is tempting to say that it would be inside your head, because that is where you feel your consciousness resides.

But inside your head is part of the physical universe, and consciousness (in this view) is most definitely *not* part of the physical universe, which means that it cannot have a location within the physical universe (whether it is inside your head or anywhere else). Substance dualists have no convincing answer to these questions, because their definition of consciousness is entirely negative. They tell us what it is *not* (i.e. it is not physical) but they do not tell us what it *is*. Without any positive definition, it becomes extremely difficult to take substance dualism seriously, because how can we find out about something if we have not got any clue what that thing actually is?

There are more problems. If consciousness is not part of the physical universe, then how could it have any causal influence on the physical universe? We like to think that our conscious experience has a causal role to play in our lives. We feel sad, so we cry. It is the experience of feeling sad (which is not physical, according to substance dualists) that influences the physiological (hence physical) mechanisms that eventually lead tears (which are also physical) to come out of our physical tear-ducts and roll down our physical cheeks. Our understanding of the physical, material world is that all effects have causes. Substance dualism claims that consciousness is *not* part of this physical story, but given that our understanding of cause and effect relies on the physical story it becomes very problematic to start positing that something that is completely separate from the physical universe can have any kind of causal role to play within that physical universe. To suggest that it does begins to sound a little bit too 'magical' or 'supernatural'.

Property dualism manages to avoid many of the most serious objections to substance dualism by being careful not to make any claims about consciousness being a different kind of thing. However, property dualism does not completely escape the pitfalls of substance dualism, especially when it comes to the causal role of consciousness. If our consciousness is an emergent property of our brains and 'rides on top' of the physical processes, then it becomes difficult to see how it could have any causal effects. As we saw above, it is counterintuitive to suggest that our experiences have no role to play in causing our actions. The liquidity of water is an emergent property of how the constituent parts of water behave in a certain configuration, but nobody would suggest that liquidity itself had a causal role to play in the world. Some property dualists have attempted to address this problem by suggesting what might be called *interactionist property dualism*, but these attempts have never offered an entirely convincing account of how the emergent consciousness can interact with (and thus have a causal influence on) the brain and behaviour.

A further problem emerges when we consider the property dualists' insistence that consciousness as a property of matter is irreducible. This is the claim that puts the 'dualism' into property dualism, because it suggests that consciousness is a unique property that cannot be explained in physical terms. If this were indeed the case then, as Paul Churchland (1988) points out, we would require a completely new type of science that explains mind and consciousness without relying on any of the material sciences that currently exist; we would need a science of consciousness, with its own language methods, fundamental (non-physical) principles and so on. That is how radical property dualism really is. It suggests an entirely new type of science that is not based on materialism.

Chalmers' amalgamation of property dualism and functionalism falls foul of similar objections. One of John Searle's problems with Chalmers' panpsychism is that it seems absurd.

It admittedly does seem absurd to suggest that consciousness is in things like light bulbs, but just because something seems absurd does not necessarily make it wrong. Dennett (1996) criticizes Chalmers by asking us to consider an imaginary, but analogous, argument to the one Chalmers makes: 'We can see this by comparing Chalmers' proposal with yet one more imaginary non-starter: cutism, the proposal that some things are just plain cute, and other things are not cute at all'. With his tongue firmly in his cheek, Dennett goes on to suggest that 'we had better postulate cuteness as a fundamental property of physics alongside mass, charge and space-time' (p. 6). There may ultimately be no way of knowing whether Chalmers is correct, but until there is good evidence (whatever that may be) suggesting that consciousness is a fundamental feature of the universe, then no conclusion can be drawn.

Before You Go On

What Do You Know?

3. What is dualism?
4. Why might someone seeking to understand consciousness be drawn to a dualistic approach?
5. What are the main objections to dualism?
6. What are the main differences between substance dualism and property dualism?

What Do You Think?

Both dualism and materialism have important consequences for the way we think about the world. In your view, which of these positions is less problematic, and why?

Summary of Part 1

Consciousness is a unique problem in psychology, philosophy and science in general because at the moment it seems to be a uniquely first-person subjective phenomenon that resists an objective third-person analysis. There is nothing else like this in the world that scientists study. This has some profound implications for how we think about it and study it, and philosophers continue to argue about its nature. Current opinion seems to favour a materialist approach, insisting that consciousness is inextricably linked to brain function, and a better understanding of brain function will bring with it an understanding of conscious experience. But this is just current opinion, and, as we have seen, there are some serious objections to such an account. Additionally, until scientists can actually claim to have made progress in understanding consciousness, then the claim that we will eventually understand it remains to be optimistic speculation. On the other hand, taking a non-materialist position is itself fraught with difficulties. It may seem as though our consciousness is non-physical, and we may be convinced by thought experiments like Mary's Room, but it really is a radical step to suggest that consciousness is not entirely part of the physical world. This radical step may be a step too far for most scientists. Again, though, this remains speculation. The truth is, when it comes to consciousness, we are a long way off a final explanation.

PART 2: STUDYING CONSCIOUS STATES

Although the 'hard problem' (of being unable to define consciousness satisfactorily) appears to be a long way from being resolved, there are still a great number of things to be learnt about the mind that can contribute to our understanding of consciousness. Most experimental psychologists and cognitive scientists acknowledge the hardness of the hard problem, but put it to one side while they conduct research on the vast number of factors that are associated with conscious experience. The implicit hope is that by gradually furthering our knowledge of all the psychological and neurological phenomena that are linked to consciousness, we will eventually make some progress on the bigger questions. The second part of this chapter will look at some of this research.

Many of psychology's early pioneers named consciousness as their primary area of concern, and the study of consciousness has undergone many historical shifts since then. The influential American psychologist William James, for example, notes that our conscious awareness continually shifts based on what we are paying attention to and how intensely we are attending (Schooler, 2011; Singer, 2003).

At the same time, we feel continuity from moment to moment. If you simply reflect upon your conscious experiences, it is easy to see that many thoughts and experiences – all different in meaning and feeling – can occur within a short period, yet we maintain a sense of sameness. We have a sense of ourselves as the same person from moment to moment, regardless of what we happen to be thinking of at the time. James coined the term *stream of consciousness* to signify how we experience our conscious life, because consciousness, like a running stream, keeps moving, yet seems to be the same. You may recall from Chapter 1 that one of psychology's most famous early theories was Sigmund Freud's psychoanalytic theory. Sigmund Freud popularized the idea that we can have *unconscious* thoughts and feelings of which we are not aware. Right up to his death in 1939, Freud kept defining and revising his ideas about states of consciousness, but one of his key insights was this notion of the unconscious (Elisha, 2011). If we are ever to understand consciousness, then we will also have to understand the difference between conscious and unconscious mental states.

During the latter part of the 20th century, consciousness re-emerged as a topic of major interest in psychology, partly because of important developments in neuroscience and computer technology. With the help of neuroimaging techniques, investigators have been able to explore the relationship between brain activity and various states of consciousness (Baars & Gage, 2010). Indeed, a considerable body of research is now directed at the study of conscious, less conscious and non-conscious states (Revonsuo, 2010).

When We Are Awake: Conscious Awareness

LEARNING OBJECTIVE 5

Define different levels of conscious awareness and describe key brain structures and functions associated with those levels.

As the opening story illustrates, *attention* plays a key role in conscious awareness. Psychiatric researcher John Ratey (2001) points out, 'Before we can be conscious of something . . . we have to pay attention to it.' Although attention is important, it is not the same as consciousness. We need something more. To be fully conscious of something, we must also be *aware* that we are attending to it (Lewis, 2010).

Clearly, conscious awareness involves elements in addition to attention, and a number of such elements have been suggested by theorists. Three of the most prominent are *monitoring*, *remembering* and *planning*:

- We *monitor* ourselves and our environment as we decide (implicitly) what items to be aware of (Kannape et al., 2010; Glaser & Kihlstrom, 2005). A quickly moving car coming towards us might capture our awareness, for example.

- In order to be aware of a current event, we often must use *memories* of past experiences and previously acquired knowledge and skills (Johannsdottir & Herdman, 2010; Baars, 2003). These memories establish a context for our current situation, provide us with the motivation and ability to focus on it and may even become part of the present situation. A driver has to have a memory related to traffic lights in order to be aware that an amber light is a signal to slow down.

- *Control* and *planning* are also often at work. In fact, to help us plan for the future – from which route to take to the dry cleaners to our choice of a partner or career – we often bring into conscious awareness images, events and scenarios that have never occurred. In such cases, conscious awareness may help us to initiate more effective behaviours or make wiser decisions.

PSYCHOLOGY AROUND US   A Different Kind of Thoughtlessness

Human beings have a remarkable ability to multitask – to keep whole sets of complicated tasks and ideas in mind while still managing to engage in the basic activities of living. On the other hand, consciousness sometimes has blind spots, episodes in which conscious behaviours and intentions seem to break down.

Dr Baba Shiv, a marketing professor, conducted a study with undergraduates at the University of Iowa. He asked students to memorize a number that was either two digits long or seven digits long. After the memorization task, the students were asked to go down a hall to another room where they were to be tested on their recollections. On the way down the hall, however, a stranger (actually a confederate of Shiv's) stopped them and offered them a snack – either a nutritious, healthy fruit salad or a decadent, tempting chocolate cake.

Shiv found something interesting: people who had been required to hold a seven-digit number in mind chose the chocolate cake twice as often as the people who were holding on to only a two-digit number. Shiv believed that this happened because the cognitive processes of people holding seven-digit numbers in mind were too overloaded to have the conversations we usually have with ourselves when we are offered chocolate cake. That is, their minds were too overloaded to consider notions such as 'Chocolate cake is not good for me'. Shiv also believed that this is the kind of thing that happens to our cognitive processing whenever we get stressed or overloaded in life.

When We Are Awake

WHAT HAPPENS IN THE BRAIN?

In order for us to be conscious, there must be multiple brain processes operating simultaneously. Research has shown that when we are awake, most if not all of the neurons in our brains are constantly active. Of course, certain neurons become particularly active when we are stimulated by objects or events, but even in the absence of such stimulation, neurons are still active at a steady, low level and are communicating with other neurons (Hopkin, 2010; Llinás & Ribary, 2001).

Neurons tend to work together in groups, or *networks*, and those networks become more and more efficient with repeated use. For us to experience conscious awareness of something, such as a thought or a car speeding towards us, many of these networks must become active at once. While one set of networks enables us to pay attention to the stimulus, other biological events must also be at work, enabling us to be aware and recognize that we are attending. Still others are allowing us to monitor, remember and control.

Researchers have not yet pinpointed all of the brain areas and events that are responsible for such complex *parallel processing*, but research has suggested that there are two areas of great importance to consciousness: the *cerebral cortex*, which is the brain's outer covering of cells, and the *thalamus*, the brain structure that often relays sensory information from various parts of the brain to the cerebral cortex.

The Cerebral Cortex Evidence has accumulated that some areas of the brain are responsible for attention, while other areas – particularly ones in the cerebral cortex – are in charge of our awareness of that attention. Investigations by Lawrence Weiskrantz on *blindsight* illustrate how this works in the visual realm (Sahraie *et al.*, 2010; Weiskrantz, 2009, 2002, 2000). Weiskrantz studied people whose visual areas in the cerebral cortex had been destroyed, leaving them blind (so far as they were aware). When Weiskrantz presented these people with a spot of light on a screen and asked them to point to it, they were totally unaware of the light and could not fulfil the request. However, when he told the same people to 'just point anywhere', they typically pointed in the direction of the light. Similarly, these individuals could generally avoid chairs, tables and other objects as they walked through a room, denying all the time that they were seeing anything at all. The patients in Weiskrantz's studies could attend to visual objects, yet because the visual areas in their cerebral cortex had been destroyed they were completely unaware of those objects. Weiskrantz and others have concluded that the areas of the brain that help us *attend* to visual stimuli are different from the visual areas in the cerebral cortex that help us to be *aware* that we are attending to such stimuli.

Remarkable studies of *split-brain patients*, conducted by investigators Roger Sperry and Michael Gazzaniga, also point to the cerebral cortex as being implicated in conscious awareness (Gazzaniga, 2010, 2005; Colvin & Gazzaniga, 2007; Sperry, 1998, 1982). In certain circumstances, people with severe seizure disorders can sometimes be helped by cutting the nerve fibres of their *corpus callosum*, the brain structure that connects the two hemispheres of the brain, to keep abnormal activity from travelling from one side of the brain to the other. By carefully studying such split-brain patients, Sperry and Gazzaniga learnt that the left and right sides of the cerebral cortex may play different roles in conscious awareness.

As shown in Figure 8.1, in split-brain patients the objects in the left visual field project only to the visual area in the right hemisphere (Thompson, 2000). Similarly, visual

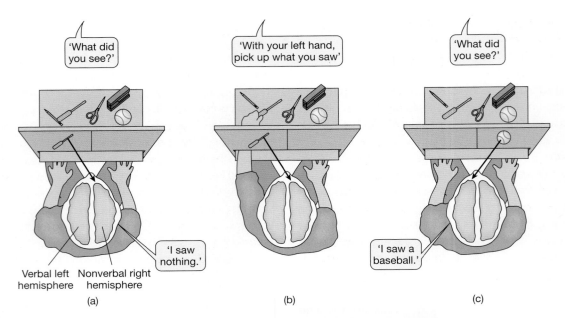

FIGURE 8.1 Split-brain research. (a) When a picture of a screwdriver is flashed to a split-brain patient's left visual field, the information goes to his nonverbal right hemisphere and he cannot name the object. (b) When instructed to feel behind a screen among a variety of objects and select the one that matches the picture just seen, the patient correctly selects the screwdriver. (c) When a picture of a baseball is flashed to the patient's right visual field, he easily names it.

information presented to the right visual field projects only to the visual area in the left hemisphere.

Using this information, the investigators found that when they showed a word to a patient's left hemisphere, the individual was able to say and write the word. When a word was flashed to the right hemisphere, however, the individual could *not* say what it was or write it. Apparently, the left cerebral cortex is responsible for *verbal awareness*.

In contrast, the right cerebral cortex seems to be responsible for nonverbal forms of conscious awareness. In one study, for example, the experimenters flashed a picture of a screwdriver to each patient's right hemisphere. The individuals were then instructed to feel, from behind a screen, a variety of real objects, including a real screwdriver and, on the basis of touch, to select the object that matched the picture they had just seen: all correctly selected a screwdriver. Apparently, the right cerebral cortex can produce tactile awareness and perhaps other kinds of nonverbal awareness as well, but not verbal awareness. Of course, for most of us, our two hemispheres are connected and these various kinds of awareness occur simultaneously, helping to produce a broad and complete sense of conscious awareness.

The Thalamus One way to think of the networks of neurons in the brain is that they are similar to the different train lines in a complicated railway system. In order for trains to get from place to place on time and without collision, a train conductor (or even a group of them) must oversee the process. Researchers have nominated several brain areas as potential conductors, involved in routeing messages along the proper neural network 'railway lines' of our brains. Two candidates are the *intralaminar nuclei* and *midline nuclei* of the *thalamus* (Benarroch, 2011, 2008; Van der Werf *et al.*, 2003, 2002; Ratey, 2001). Research indicates that the intralaminar and midline nuclei receive and project long axons to neurons throughout the cerebral cortex, including areas that, as we have seen, are involved in conscious awareness.

Consistent with this theory, investigators have observed that people actually lose all consciousness and enter a deep coma if their intralaminar and midline nuclei are broadly damaged. If, however, the damage to the nuclei occurs in only one hemisphere, individuals lose awareness of only half of their bodies. They become unaware of all events that occur on one side of their visual field, for example, or unaware of all objects that touch one side of their body. In short, the intralaminar and midline nuclei seem to play an important role in conscious awareness, with different nuclei responsible for different dimensions of consciousness.

Alert Consciousness

Are toddlers conscious? What about babies? There have been a number of attempts to identify consciousness in infants. There is evidence that, even before the age of two, babies may be able to direct their attention, hold concepts in mind and engage in planned or intentional behaviours – all things that we would consider key components of consciousness. Because babies are not yet able to talk very well, it is difficult to determine just how aware they are that their experiences are things happening to them, or even whether they are fully aware of themselves as separate beings from others (a concept known as *sense of self*).

Researchers have developed some ingenious ways to try to determine when babies first experience a sense of self. In one test, experimenters secretly dabbed red make-up on babies' foreheads while pretending to wipe them. Then they placed the babies in front of a mirror. The researchers reasoned that babies who had developed a sense of self would see the make-up and touch their own heads, while those who did not understand they were looking at themselves in the mirror would try to touch the make-up by touching the mirror. Based on such tests, it seems that most children develop a stable concept of the self by around 18 months of age (Lewis, 2010).

Some researchers suggest that the early cognitive development we discussed in Chapter 3 and the development of consciousness contribute to one another. That is, if infants demonstrate the ability to develop concepts and to think through their behaviours – even if they cannot verbally express such thinking – then they should be viewed as having a raw sense of self-consciousness. Without this basic sense of consciousness, babies would not be able to develop any concepts at all (Lewis, 2010; Mandler, 2004).

Other theorists suggest that consciousness is rooted in language. Because babies do not have language, they cannot reflect on their thoughts and behaviours and do not have consciousness yet (Neuman & Nave, 2010; Zelazo, 2004). These theorists suggest that a shift happens at around 22 months of age, when babies show the abilities to reason inductively

Hello there. When babies look into a mirror and realize they are looking at themselves, it means that they finally experiencing a sense of self. That is, they are aware of themselves as separate beings from others.

Source: Charles Gullung/Getty Images, Inc.

and to name and categorize concepts, which in turn enable them to represent concepts in a richer and deeper way.

What is clear is that the way in which we attempt to describe how consciousness develops during awake states is influenced in large part by how we define consciousness (a problem that we encountered in the first part of this chapter). The matter is further complicated by another question: Just how aware is 'aware'? We will see next that there may be levels of alert consciousness at which we are not fully aware of all our thoughts.

Before You Go On

What Do You Know?

7. List the core cognitive processes of consciousness.

8. What is blindsight?

What Do You Think?

What characteristics do you believe are essential to define alert consciousness? At what point in an infant's life would you consider it to be conscious? Why?

Preconscious and Unconscious States

LEARNING OBJECTIVE 6

Summarize the ideas of preconscious and unconscious states, including Freud's thinking on the unconscious.

Theorists often talk about different *levels of consciousness* or *degrees of consciousness*, and some believe that consciousness should be distinguished from two alternative states: *preconsciousness* and *unconsciousness*.

Preconsciousness is a level of awareness at which information can become readily available to consciousness if necessary. Have you ever tried to remember something that you are certain you know but just cannot recall at the moment?

preconsciousness the level of awareness at which information can become readily available to consciousness if necessary.

When something is on the tip of your tongue, it is in your preconsciousness. When (or if) you finally do remember it, the memory has reached conscious awareness.

Most of our most familiar behaviours occur during preconsciousness. Can you remember exactly what your morning ritual was this morning? What song was playing when you woke up? Did you count every tooth as you brushed it? For many morning activities, you probably do things in the same order, but you do not necessarily need to plan all the steps or think about what you are doing as you move through your ritual. Preconscious behaviours of this kind are sometimes called *automatic behaviours*.

> **unconscious state** the state in which information is not easily accessible to conscious awareness.

An **unconscious state** is one in which information is not easily accessible to conscious awareness. Information, feelings and memories held in the unconscious are, by definition, not readily available to conscious awareness.

Cognitive Views of the Unconscious

Throughout much of the 20th century, scientists paid little attention to the unconscious. Rejecting Freud's psychoanalytic ideas, they also rejected the notion that our behaviours, thoughts and feelings may be influenced by mental forces of which we are unaware. This dismissal of the unconscious has shifted dramatically in recent decades. Today, most psychologists believe that unconscious functioning does occur and a number of explanations – particularly cognitive explanations – have been proposed.

One of the most prominent of recent developments in understanding the cognitive unconscious has been the concept of **implicit memory** (Manelis *et al.*, 2011; Kihlstrom, 2007; Kihlstrom *et al.*, 2000). Cognitive psychologists distinguish two basic kinds of memory: *explicit memory* and *implicit memory*. Explicit memories are pieces of knowledge that we are fully aware of. Knowing the date of your birth is an explicit memory. Implicit memories refer to knowledge that we are not typically aware of – information that we cannot recall at will – but that we use in the performance of various tasks in life.

> **implicit memory** the knowledge that we have stored in memory that we are not typically aware of or able to recall at will.

Implicit memory is usually on display in the *skills* we acquire, such as reading, playing an instrument, driving a car or speaking a second language. Our performance of these skills improves as we gain more and more of the knowledge, motor behaviours and perceptual information required for the skills. These gains – that is, these implicit memories – are usually revealed to us indirectly by our improved performances. It is unlikely that we would be able to consciously pinpoint the skills we have gained and the experiences that led to the improvements. Shortly after learning to drive, you may realize one day that you are able to drive and talk to a passenger at the same time. However, it is unlikely that you will be able to recall the exact moment you learnt how to control the wheel and pedals well enough to add the additional activity of carrying on a conversation.

Implicit memory may also involve factual information. When we vote for a particular candidate in an election,

---

PSYCHOLOGY AROUND US Snap Decisions

Freud once said: 'When making a decision of minor importance, I have always found it advantageous to consider all the pros and cons. In vital matters, however, such as the choice of a mate or a profession, the decision should come from the unconscious, from somewhere within ourselves.'

Many psychologists have begun to look at the benefits of unconscious decision making, quick, intuitive judgements. Psychologist Gary Klein, for example, has examined decision making in fire-fighters. Klein had expected that, given the huge stakes involved in fighting fires, fire chiefs typically must consider a range of scenarios and carefully weigh their pros and cons before acting. What he found instead was that, when fighting fires, fire chiefs typically identify one decision immediately, run the scenario in their head and if it does not have any glaring errors, they pursue that cause of action. Basically,

the fire chiefs let their experience automatically generate a solution.

In contrast, neuroscientist Antonio Damasio has worked extensively with patients who have suffered damage to certain parts of their prefrontal cortex. Damasio has found that these perfectly intelligent individuals are only able to make deliberate decisions. They can only make decisions in which they have time to systematically weigh options and arrive at a clearly advantageous course of action. If they are required to make a quick choice, like when to schedule an appointment or where to go for dinner, they become paralysed and simply cannot decide. Damasio argues that it is intuition and unconscious decision making that allow us to operate effectively under situations of uncertainty, and that most of life's decisions, even the big ones, involve a lot of uncertainty.

a wealth of past experiences and information may be at the root of that behaviour: childhood discussions with our parents about political parties, websites we have seen, articles we have read, classes we have taken, interviews or news items we have heard and so on. In the voting booth, however, we typically are not aware of all these past experiences or pieces of information, even though they may be influencing how we vote.

Cognitive and cognitive neuroscience theorists see implicit memories as a part of everyday functioning rather than as a way to keep difficult information from reaching our awareness (Czigler & Winkler, 2010; Kihlstrom, 2007; Kihlstrom *et al.*, 2000). They have implemented research methods to test our unconscious – implicit – memories and have gathered evidence that explicit and implicit memories are stored in different pathways in the brain (Sheldon & Moscovitch, 2010).

Before You Go On

What Do You Know?

9. What is the difference between preconscious and unconscious states?

10. What is the importance of implicit memory to the notion of the unconscious?

What Do You Think?

Do you think there are unconscious forces driving people's behaviours? If not, is it all conscious choice, or do you believe there are other explanations?

Hypnosis

LEARNING OBJECTIVE 7

Define hypnosis and discuss theories and evidence about what it is, how it works and how it can be used.

hypnosis a seemingly altered state of consciousness during which individuals can be directed to act or experience the world in unusual ways.

Being under **hypnosis** is what some people call an *altered state of consciousness* (Lynn *et al.*, 2010; Kihlstrom, 2007). If we are to reach a full understanding of conscious experience, we will have to investigate those situations in which our consciousness is altered in some way, because knowledge about what influences something can help us build a picture of what that thing is and how it works.

People are usually guided into the hypnotic state by a trained hypnotist or hypnotherapist. The process involves relinquishing control over certain behaviours. In most cases, hypnosis will work most efficiently if the individual is open and responsive to suggestions made by the hypnotist. Even then, there are individual differences, and some people are more open to a hypnotist's suggestions than others are, a quality that often runs in families (Barnier & Council, 2010; Gfeller & Gorassini, 2010). Approximately, 15% of adults are very susceptible to hypnosis, while 10% are not at all hypnotizable. Most adults fall somewhere in between. People who are especially suggestible, in touch with their fantasy worlds and comfortable playing with their imaginations, are particularly likely to approach the experience with a positive and receptive attitude. Perhaps not surprisingly, therefore,

The power of suggestion. People can be directed to experience unusual sensations and act in unusual ways when in a hypnotic state – a trance-like altered state of consciousness marked by extreme suggestibility. Here a hypnotized young man believes that a balloon is tied to his left hand and that his right hand is extremely heavy.

Source: Francoise Sauze/Photo Researchers, Inc.

children tend to be particularly open to hypnotic suggestion (Olness & Kohen, 2010).

Hypnotic Procedures and Effects

Hypnotists use various methods to induce the hypnotic state (Gibbons & Lynn, 2010). Sometimes a person is asked to relax while concentrating on a single small target, such as an item in a painting on the wall. At other times, the hypnotist induces a *hyperalert* hypnotic trance that actually guides the individual to heightened tension and awareness. In either case, the hypnotist delivers *suggestions* to the subject, which are different from the strict authoritarian commands we see when hypnosis is depicted in the movies.

One area of functioning that can be readily influenced by hypnotists is motor control. If the hypnotist suggests that a person's hand is being drawn like a magnet to a nearby stapler, the individual's hand will soon move to the stapler, as if propelled by an external force.

In some cases, people can be directed to respond *after* being roused from the hypnotic trance. A predetermined signal prompts such *posthypnotic responses*. During hypnosis, the hypnotist may suggest, for example, that the person will later stand up whenever the hypnotist touches a desktop. After being roused, and with no understanding of why, the person will stand when the hypnotist touches the desk.

Some practitioners have even applied hypnosis to help control pain during dental and other forms of surgery (Auld, 2007). Although only some people are able to undergo surgery while anesthetized by hypnosis alone, combining hypnosis with chemical forms of anaesthesia apparently helps many individuals (Hammond, 2008; Fredericks, 2001). Beyond its use in the control of pain, hypnosis has been used successfully to help treat problems, such as anxiety, skin diseases, asthma, insomnia, stuttering, high blood pressure, warts and other forms of infection (Covino & Pinnell, 2010; Mellinger, 2010).

Many people also turn to hypnosis to help break bad habits, such as smoking, nail biting and overeating. Does hypnosis help? Research has shown that hypnosis can help some people to quit smoking (Green, 2010). It also helps many people to better control their eating and lose weight, particularly if hypnosis is paired with *cognitive treatments*, interventions that help people change their conscious ways of thinking.

Why Does Hypnosis Work?

Hypnosis is such a strange thing that many people refuse to believe that it is actually real. Assuming that it is a valid phenomenon, how might we explain it? There are various theories about why hypnosis works (Lynn *et al.*, 2010). One views hypnosis as a state of *divided consciousness* (Sadler & Woody, 2010; Hilgard, 1992). Another theory (Spanos, 1996) sees it as an implementation of *common social and cognitive processes* (Figure 8.2).

As a professor, Hilgard hypnotized a student to become deaf during a classroom demonstration. The student could not hear even loud noises. Another student asked Hilgard whether 'some part' of the hypnotized student could still hear noise. In response, Hilgard instructed the hypnotized student to raise his finger if some part of him could still hear. Surprisingly, the student did raise a finger.

From this experience, Hilgard concluded that consciousness splits into two parts and that both act at once during hypnosis, an experience called **dissociation** (Sadler & Woody, 2010; Hilgard, 1992; Hilgard's account was actually named *neodissociation* to distinguish it from psychiatric dissociative states). One part of our consciousness becomes fully tuned into and responsive to the hypnotist's suggestions. The second part, which Hilgard called the *hidden observer*, operates at a subtler, less conscious level, continuing to process information that is seemingly unavailable to the hypnotized person's conscious awareness. According to Hilgard, the hidden observer was the part of the student's mind that was still able to hear while hypnotized, with one 'self' controlling the person's actions with the other self being unaware of this control. Obviously, such explanations (if true) have huge implications for the study of consciousness, because they suggest that our experience of our consciousness as being a unitary thing is possibly a fragile illusion.

Another leading theory of hypnosis is that, instead of resulting from a divided consciousness, hypnotic phenomena

> **dissociation** a splitting of consciousness into two dimensions.

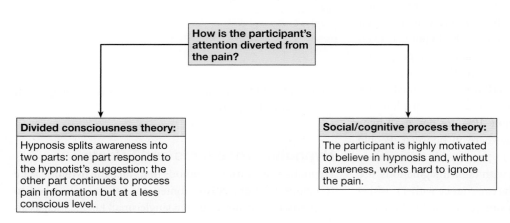

How is the participant's attention diverted from the pain?

Divided consciousness theory:
Hypnosis splits awareness into two parts: one part responds to the hypnotist's suggestion; the other part continues to process pain information but at a less conscious level.

Social/cognitive process theory:
The participant is highly motivated to believe in hypnosis and, without awareness, works hard to ignore the pain.

FIGURE 8.2 Explaining hypnosis. Two theories explain how a hypnotized individual is able to ignore pain.

consist simply of highly motivated people performing tasks, being extra attentive and enacting roles that are asked of them (Dienes *et al.*, 2010). Because of their strong beliefs in hypnosis, these people fail to recognize their own active contributions to the process. The main proponent of this view was Nicholas Spanos (e.g., see Spanos, 1996) who argued that hypnosis was not an altered state of consciousness, a phenomenon that relies on the social context in which it happens and the motivations, expectations and beliefs of the people involved.

Hypnosis in the Brain

 **WHAT HAPPENS IN THE** B R A I N ?

Neuroimaging studies show that hypnosis affects neuron activity in brain areas previously implicated in conscious awareness, suggesting to some theorists that the procedure does indeed produce altered consciousness (Naish, 2010; Oakley & Halligan, 2010; Rainville *et al.*, 2002, 1999, 1997).

When people are hypnotized, they are usually first guided into a state of *mental relaxation*. Studies have found that during this state neural activity in key areas of the cerebral cortex and thalamus – brain regions that are implicated in conscious awareness – slows down significantly (Rainville *et al.*, 2002). Hypnotized individuals are next guided into a state of *mental absorption*, during which they focus carefully on the hypnotist's voice and instructions and actively block out other sources of stimulation, both internal and environmental. In fact, mental absorption has often been described as a state of *total focus*. During this state, cerebral blood flow and neural activity actually pick back up in key areas of the cerebral cortex, thalamus and other parts of the brain's attention and conscious awareness systems (Rainville *et al.*, 2002).

Neuroimaging research suggests that one part of the brain's cerebral cortex, the *anterior cingulate cortex*, may be

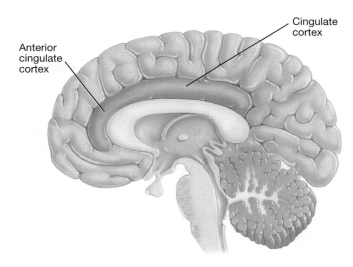

FIGURE 8.3 The anterior cingulate cortex is thought to be involved when hypnosis is used to reduce awareness of pain.

involved when hypnosis is used to anaesthetize or reduce pain (Figure 8.3). This region has been implicated both in general awareness and in the unpleasantness we feel during pain. In one study, participants were hypnotically induced to ignore their pain while placing their hands in painfully hot water (Rainville *et al.*, 1997). While the individuals were in a hypnotic pain-free state, neurons in their anterior cingulate cortex became less active. Although the activity of other neurons that receive pain messages continued as usual in these people's brains – suggesting that they were indeed receiving sensations of pain – the decreased activity in the anterior cingulate cortex seemed to reduce their *awareness* of the pain. They did not perceive the pain sensations.

Before You Go On

What Do You Know?

11. How does Hilgard use the idea of a divided consciousness to explain hypnosis?

What Do You Think?

What are the ethical implications of using hypnosis to control behaviour?

When We Are Asleep

LEARNING OBJECTIVE 8
Describe what happens when people sleep, key theories of why we sleep and dream, and problems with sleep and how they affect functioning.

Hypnosis is one kind of altered state, but you do not have to be hypnotized to alter your consciousness: you just need to tuck yourself up in bed. When we fall asleep, we lose the consciousness that is most familiar to us, and enter into a different realm of experience. Again, if we are ever going to understand consciousness, we need to understand the things that can alter it (or inhibit it). Sleep is so central to our lives – indeed, most people spend 25 years of their lives asleep – that we first need to ask what important purpose it serves.

Why Do We Sleep?

Interestingly, despite considerable research into the matter, no consensus exists about why people need to sleep (Thakkar & Datta, 2010). After all, as we will see, the brain does not rest when we are sleeping, nor, on the surface, does sleep offer the body much more rest than it would get by sitting down and relaxing for a while. Yet all animals sleep, and they would, in fact, die if they were deprived of sleep for too long.

adaptive theory of sleep the theory that organisms sleep for the purposes of self-preservation, to keep away from predators that are more active at night.

One theory, the **adaptive theory of sleep**, suggests that sleep is the evolutionary outcome of self-preservation (Worthman, 2011; Rial *et al.*, 2010). Proponents of this view suggest that organisms sleep in order to keep themselves away from predators that are more active at night. Our ancestors, for example, tucked themselves away in safe places to keep from being eaten by nocturnal animals on the prowl. Animals that need to graze and so have less chance of hiding from predators tend to sleep less (Figure 8.4). An elephant, for example, sleeps only two or three hours a day, whereas a bat sleeps around twenty. This evolutionary argument, however, seems to account more for why we sleep at night than for why we sleep in the first place.

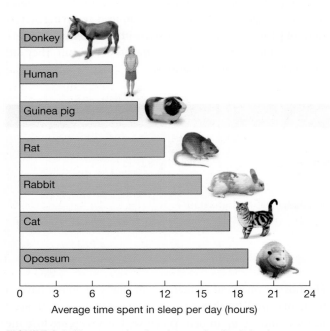

FIGURE 8.4 Sleep needs of various animals. Animals vary greatly in how much sleep they need each day. Their sleep needs are related in part to how much awake time is needed to obtain food and protect themselves from predators.

Several biological theories of sleep have also been proposed. One suggests that sleep plays a role in the growth process, a notion consistent with the finding that the *pituitary gland* releases growth hormones during sleep (García-García *et al.*, 2011; Gais *et al.*, 2006). In fact, as we age, we release fewer of these hormones, grow less and sleep less.

Researchers have also observed changes in neuron activity in other areas of the brain during sleep, including the *reticular formation* and the *pons*, as well as the *forebrain region*, which are important for alertness and arousal. Researchers have not established, however, that changes in the activity of these areas *cause* us to sleep.

restorative theory of sleep theory that we sleep in order to allow the brain and body to restore certain depleted chemical resources and eliminate chemical wastes that have accumulated during the waking day.

Another biological theory, the **restorative theory of sleep**, suggests that sleep allows the brain and body to restore certain depleted chemical resources, while eliminating chemical wastes that have accumulated during the waking day (Dworak *et al.*, 2010; Irwin, 2001). Which chemicals might be depleted, and which ones might build to excess? We do not really know (Thompson, 2000). While we may not yet know exactly what causes sleep, we do know that sleep occurs in regular patterns, or *rhythms*, and that these rhythms reflect changes in the body's chemistry.

Rhythms of Sleep

circadian rhythm the pattern of sleep/wake cycles that in human beings roughly corresponds to periods of daylight and night.

Human beings' basic pattern is called the **circadian rhythm** (Figure 8.5). Within each 24-hour period, we experience a sustained period of wakefulness that gives way to a period of sleep. Although we tend to be awake during the day and to sleep at night, our circadian rhythms are not fully dependent on the cycles of daylight (Cartwright, 2010; Schultz & Kay, 2003).

During the circadian cycle, we also experience other, more subtle patterns of biochemical activity. As morning nears, for example, our temperature rises and continues to rise until it peaks at midday. Then it dips and we feel fatigued. Many people around the world take naps during this early-afternoon lull. Later in the afternoon, body temperature rises once more, only to drop again as we approach our full evening sleep (Danovi, 2010; Johnson *et al.*, 2004). Research has suggested that, on average, we are most alert during the late-morning peak in the circadian rhythm. This 'rule', however, varies with age (Yoon *et al.*, 2003). Younger people tend to peak later in the day, while older people peak earlier.

Along with shifts in body temperature, we also experience changes throughout the 24-hour period in blood pressure, the secretion of hormones, and sensitivity to pain.

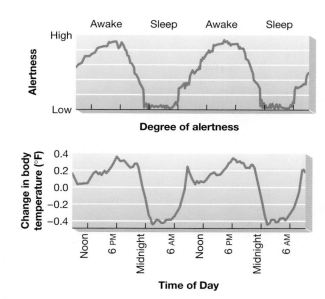

FIGURE 8.5 Circadian rhythms. Two prime examples of circadian rhythms are our cycles of alertness and shifts in body temperature.

The circadian rhythm has been called our *biological clock* because the pattern repeats itself from one 24-hour period to the next. This clock, however, can be disrupted by certain events (Cartwright, 2010; Waterhouse & DeCoursey, 2004). For example, the clock can be disrupted by long-distance aeroplane flights when we are awake at times that we should be sleeping – a problem compounded by crossing time zones. The result: jet lag. Similarly, people who work nightshifts, particularly those who keep irregular schedules of dayshifts and nightshifts, may experience sleep disorders and, in some instances, develop problems such as depression or health difficulties. People with a pattern called *circadian rhythm sleep disorder* experience excessive sleepiness or insomnia as a result of a mismatch between their own sleep–wake pattern and the sleep–wake schedule of most other people in their environment (Ivanenko & Johnson, 2010; Lack & Bootzin, 2003).

When We Sleep

 **WHAT HAPPENS IN THE BRAIN?**

Research has uncovered what happens in our brains to control the circadian rhythms of when we wake and sleep, as well as what happens in the brain while we sleep.

suprachiasmatic nucleus (SCN) the small group of neurons in the hypothalamus responsible for coordinating the many rhythms of the body.

Controlling the Clock The **suprachiasmatic nucleus (SCN)**, a small group of neurons in the *hypothalamus*, is ultimately responsible for coordinating the many rhythms of the body (Danovi, 2010; Kalsbeek *et al.*, 2010). As daylight

fades into night, the SCN notices the change and directs the *pineal gland* to secrete the hormone *melatonin* (Figure 8.6). Increased quantities of melatonin, travelling through the blood to various organs, cause sleepiness. Melatonin production peaks between 1.00 and 3.00 a.m. As dawn approaches, this production decreases and sleepers soon wake up.

During the day, photoreceptors in the retina of the eye communicate the presence of sunlight to the SCN and melatonin secretions remain low. Photoreceptors are also sensitive to artificial light. In fact, the invention of the light bulb just over a hundred years ago has disturbed the human experience of the circadian rhythm by increasing the number of hours of light people are exposed to in a given day. This may be one reason why many people today sleep much less than our forebears.

What happens if a person is entirely deprived of access to environmental shifts in sunlight and darkness? In a number of sleep studies, participants have been placed in special settings where they are totally deprived of natural light. In such settings, the SCN extends the body's 'day', by as much as an hour, to about 25 hours (Lavie, 2001). When we are deprived of light, the various circadian rhythms also become out of synch with each other. The normal cycles of body temperature and melatonin production, for example, no longer coordinate with one another.

If we speak of a biological clock, we should also be able to speak of *setting*, or *resetting*, the clock (Waterhouse & DeCoursey; 2004). In fact, when a person who has been kept in an environment without sunlight is returned to normal living conditions, the usual 24-hour circadian rhythm is quickly restored.

Patterns of Sleep Every 90 to 100 minutes while we sleep, we pass through a sleep cycle that consists of five stages. Researchers have identified these stages by examining people's brain-wave patterns while they sleep, using a device called an *electroencephalograph* (*EEG*) (Fedotchev, 2011; Lavie, 2001). EEG readings indicate that each stage of sleep is characterized by a different brain-wave pattern, as shown in Figure 8.7.

When we first go to bed and, still awake, begin to relax, EEG readings show that we experience what are called *alpha waves*. As we settle into this drowsy pre-sleep period, called the **hypnagogic state**, we sometimes experience strange sensations. We may feel that we are falling or floating in space, or 'hear' our name called out, or we may hear a loud crash. All of these sensations seem very real, but none actually has happened. Such sensory phenomena are called *hypnagogic hallucinations* (Jones *et al.*, 2010). Also common during this pre-sleep stage is a *myoclonic jerk*, a

hypnagogic state a pre-sleep period often characterized by vivid sensory phenomena.

FIGURE 8.6 The suprachiasmatic nucleus detects the onset of nightfall and directs the pineal gland to secrete melatonin.

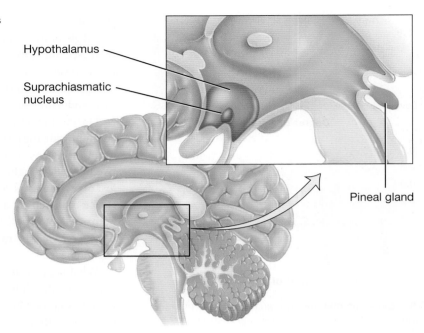

Hypothalamus

Suprachiasmatic nucleus

Pineal gland

sharp muscular spasm that generally accompanies the hypnagogic hallucination of falling.

When we finally doze off, EEG readings show that our brain waves become smaller and irregular, signalling that we have entered *Stage 1 sleep*. Alpha-wave patterns are replaced by slower waves, called *theta waves*. This first stage of sleep actually represents a bridge between wakefulness and sleep; it lasts only a few minutes. Our conscious awareness of street noises or the hum of an air conditioner fades. If we are roused from this stage, we may recall having just had ideas that seem nonsensical.

Falling deeper into sleep, we next pass into *Stage 2 sleep*. A still further slowing of brain-wave activity occurs during this stage, although we may also exhibit **sleep spindles**, bursts of brain activity that last a second or two.

sleep spindles bursts of brain activity lasting a second or two; occur during Stage 2 sleep.

During Stage 2, breathing becomes steadily rhythmic. Occasionally, the body twitches, although generally our muscle tension relaxes. During this stage, which lasts 15 to 20 minutes, we can still be awakened fairly easily. Towards the end of Stage 2 sleep, our brain waves slow even further and *delta waves* start to appear in addition to the theta waves. Delta waves indicate *delta sleep*, or deep sleep.

The next two stages of sleep, *Stage 3* and *Stage 4*, are characterized by very deep sleep. In Stage 3, between 20 and 50% of our EEG waves are delta waves. During Stage 4, the percentage of delta waves increases to more than 50% (Bertini *et al.*, 2007). During Stage 4, heart rate, blood pressure and breathing rates all drop to their lowest levels and the sleeper enters deep sleep. Interestingly, although our muscles are most relaxed during this deepest phase of sleep, this is also the time that people are prone to sleepwalking.

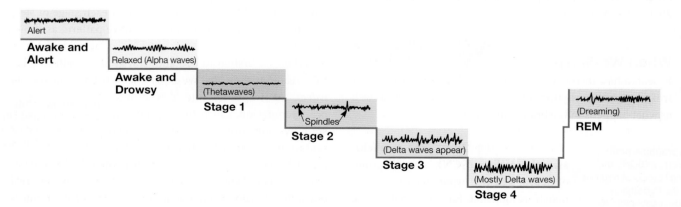

Alert

Awake and Alert

Relaxed (Alpha waves)

Awake and Drowsy

(Thetawaves)

Stage 1

Spindles

Stage 2

(Delta waves appear)

Stage 3

(Mostly Delta waves)

Stage 4

(Dreaming)

REM

FIGURE 8.7 The stages of sleep. As people move from an awake state to a state of deep sleep, their brain waves become less and less frequent, and at the same time, larger and larger. REM sleep waves resemble alert-state brain waves.

Similarly, children who wet their beds tend to do so during this stage.

Passing through all of the first four stages takes a little more than an hour of each 90- to 100-minute sleep cycle. After that, we experience the most interesting stage of sleep, **rapid eye movement (REM) sleep**. In fact, all the preceding stages (Stages 1–4) are collectively called **non-REM (NREM) sleep**. During REM sleep, we experience rapid and jagged brain-wave patterns, in contrast to the slow waves of NREM sleep. REM sleep has been called *paradoxical sleep* because, even though the body remains deeply relaxed on the surface – almost paralysed – we experience considerable activity internally (Thakkar & Datta, 2010; Wickwire *et al.*, 2008). The rapid brain-wave pattern of REM sleep is accompanied by increased heart rate and rapid and irregular breathing, for example. Moreover, every 30 seconds or so, our eyes dart around rapidly behind our closed eyelids. Perhaps most interestingly, our brains behave during REM sleep just as they do when we are awake and active.

rapid eye movement (REM) sleep stage of sleep associated with rapid and jagged brainwave patterns, increased heart rate, rapid and irregular breathing, rapid eye movements and dreaming.

non-REM (NREM) sleep Stages 1 through 4 of normal sleep pattern.

As we will discuss shortly, dreams usually occur throughout REM sleep. If people are awakened during this stage, they almost always report that they have been dreaming. Unlike the hypnagogic hallucinations of pre-sleep, which are often fleeting and isolated images, dreams tend to be emotional and are experienced in a story-like form. Dreams are less common during NREM sleep, and when they do happen, they are less vivid or fantastic than REM dreams.

Many researchers believe that REM sleep serves a particularly important function: the consolidation of memories of newly learnt material (Diekelmann & Born, 2010; Legault *et al.*, 2010). In fact, REM sleep tends to extend longer than usual in both animals and humans if the organisms go to sleep after just having learnt a new task (Smith, 2006, 1996). In one study, a group of volunteers was trained on a perceptual task just before going to sleep (Karni *et al.*, 1994). Half of the sleepers were awakened during REM sleep, while the other half were awakened later, during the next cycle of NREM sleep. The next day, those who had been awakened during REM sleep performed more poorly on the perceptual task than those who had been awakened during the later NREM phases. Presumably, the REM-awakened volunteers had not yet had the opportunity to fully consolidate their memories of the newly learnt task.

This memory consolidation theory has, however, been challenged by some studies showing that when animals are administered antidepressant drugs, which typically disrupt REM sleep, they nevertheless continue to learn and

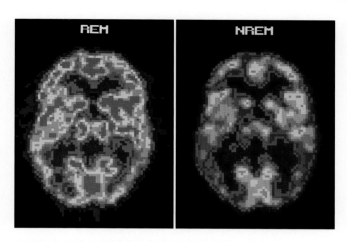

Almost like being awake. When we are in REM sleep our brains behave much like they do when we are awake and active, and indeed it is during this stage of sleep that we dream. The PET scan of a brain during sleep (left) reveals much more activity (indicated by the colours 'red' and 'orange') than does the scan of a brain during NREM sleep (right).

Source: Hank Morgan/Photo Researchers, Inc.

remember quite well (Vertes & Eastman, 2003). Research also finds that people with lesions to the *pons* portion of the brain – which is active during REM sleep – learn, remember and function quite normally.

It is worth noting that every kind of mammal whose sleep patterns have been studied experience both NREM and REM sleep. The same is true of birds. Thus, many theorists believe that animals also dream. Of course, this comes as no surprise to dog owners who have, no doubt, frequently observed their pets twitch their paws in a regular rhythm during REM sleep, as if running in a dream (Thompson, 2000).

Dreams *Dreams* – emotional, story-like sensory experiences that usually occur during REM sleep – are a very special kind of experience. That dreams represent 'conscious' experience is open to debate. In one sense, they are not conscious in that we are rarely consciously aware when we are dreaming, and we usually lack the self-reflective abilities that we have when we are awake. However, if we are adhering to the definition for consciousness that we used in the first part of this chapter (the 'what it is like-ness' of an experience), then dreams certainly are a component of consciousness, as there is definitely 'something it is like' to be in a dream state, even though this may be better described as an *altered state* of consciousness. Dreams have proven to be endlessly fascinating to scientists, clinicians, philosophers, artists and laypeople, probably because of how vivid and mysterious they are.

Freudian dream theory Sigmund Freud argued that dreams represent the expression of unconscious wishes or desires. He believed that dreams allow us to discharge internal energy associated with unacceptable feelings (Freud, 2010). Freud suggested that *dream interpretation*, in which a psychoanalytic therapist facilitates insight into the possible meaning behind a dream, may help clients appreciate their underlying needs and conflicts with the goal of being less constrained by them during waking life. For example, if a lonely and morally upstanding man is sexually attracted to his brother's wife, he might have a dream in which he goes swimming in a private pool that is marked 'No Trespassing'. His therapist might help the man arrive at the conclusion that the dream about swimming in an off-limits pool symbolizes his wish to be with his sister-in-law. Such an insight eventually might help the man to overcome inhibitions he feels about finding a suitable partner for himself.

Freud called the dream images that people are able to recall the *manifest content*. The unconscious elements of dreams are called the *latent content*. In our example, the young man's desire for his sister-in-law (latent content) – a scandalous idea that he would never allow himself to have – is symbolized in the dream by a swim in the pool (manifest content). His dream of a happy swim in forbidden territory is his mind's solution to a problem that he could not work out consciously.

Many of today's theorists, including a number of psychoanalytic ones, criticize Freud's theory. For example, *object-relations theorists*, psychoanalytic theorists who place greater emphasis on the role of relationships in development, focus more on relationship issues when interpreting dream material.

Information-processing theory Information-processing **theory** offers an alternative, more cognitive, view of dreaming. According to this view, dreams are the mind's attempt to sort out and organize the day's experiences and to fix them in memory. Consistent with this, studies have revealed that interrupting REM sleep – and so interrupting dreams – impedes a person's ability to remember material that he or she has learnt just before going to sleep (Empson, 2002). Also, in support of this view, researchers have found that periods of REM sleep (during which we dream) tend to extend longer when individuals' days have been filled with multiple stressful events or marked by extensive learning experiences (Fogel *et al.*, 2011; Palumbo, 1978).

> **information-processing theory** the hypothesis that dreams are the mind's attempt to sort out and organize the day's experiences and to fix them in memory.

Activation-synthesis hypothesis Researchers J. Allan Hobson and Robert W. McCarley have proposed a more biological hypothesis about dreaming: the **activation-synthesis model** (Hobson, 2009, 2005; Hobson & McCarley, 1977) (Figure 8.8). They argue that as people sleep their brains activate all kinds of signals. In particular, when dreams occur, neurons in the *brainstem* are activated. These, in turn, activate neurons in the *cerebral cortex* to produce visual and auditory signals. Also aroused are the emotion centres of the brain, including the *cingulate cortex*, *amygdala* and *hippocampus*. Neuroimaging scans of people who are experiencing REM sleep confirm heightened activity and neuron communication in each of these brain regions.

> **activation-synthesis model** the theory that dreams result from the brain's attempts to synthesize or organize random internally generated signals and give them meaning.

Hobson and McCarley suggest that the activated brain combines – or *synthesizes* – these internally generated signals in an attempt to give them meaning. Each person organizes and synthesizes this random collection of images, feelings, memories and thoughts in his or her own way – in the form of a particular dream story (Hobson *et al.*, 2011, 2003, 1998). What remains unclear in this model is why different people synthesize their onslaught of brain signals in different ways. Freud, of course, would suggest that each person's particular synthesis is influenced by his or her unfulfilled needs and unresolved conflicts.

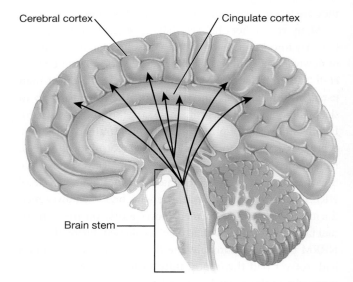

Cerebral cortex

Cingulate cortex

Brain stem

FIGURE 8.8 Activation-synthesis. According to the activation-synthesis theory of dreaming, neurons in the brainstem activate neurons in other areas throughout the brain. The brain combines these various signals into a story, or dream.

Dream Stories. People often experience similar stories. For example, 80% of all people have had repeated dreams of running towards or away from something.

Source: Harald Sund/Getty Images, Inc.

Nightmares, Lucid Dreams and Daydreams Dreams evoke many different feelings. Dreams filled with intense anxiety are *nightmares*. The feeling of terror can be so great that the dreamer awakens from the dream, often crying out. Nightmares generally evoke feelings of helplessness or powerlessness, usually in situations of great danger. They tend to be more common among people who are under stress. People who experience frequent nightmares and become very distressed by their nightmares are considered to have a *nightmare disorder*.

It appears that nightmares are more common among children than adults, although there is some dispute on this issue. When children have a nightmare, simple reassurances that they are safe and that the dream does not reflect real danger are usually helpful. It is important to help the child appreciate the difference between inner and outer reality (Gonzalez, 2010; Halliday, 2004).

In contrast to nightmares, during which dreamers feel they are caught in a real and terrifying situation, **lucid dreams** are dreams in which people fully recognize that they are dreaming (Blagrove *et al.*, 2010; Baars *et al.*, 2003). Some lucid dreamers can even wilfully guide the outcome of their dreams (Erlacher & Schredl, 2010).

A third dream-related phenomenon is actually associated with waking states of consciousness: the *daydream*. Fantasies that occur while one is awake and mindful of external reality, but not fully conscious, are called *daydreams* (Delaney *et al.*, 2010; Schon, 2003). Sometimes a daydream can become so strong that we lose track of external reality for a brief while. Although we may be embarrassed when caught daydreaming, such experiences may also afford us opportunities for creativity; we are, after all, less constrained during the fantasies than we would be if attending strictly to the outside world.

> **lucid dreams** dreams in which the sleeper fully recognizes that he or she is dreaming, and occasionally actively guides the outcome of the dream.

Sleep at Different Ages HOW WE DEVELOP

Parents or older siblings know all too well that young babies do not sleep quite like older children or adults. Through the first four months of life, babies sleep between 14 and 17 hours each day. The amount of time that they spend sleeping declines steadily as they get older (Blumberg & Seelke, 2010; Sadeh *et al.*, 2009). Although babies spend a lot of time asleep overall, their sleep can last anywhere from minutes to hours before they are stirred and crying out for attention. For parents, the good news is that sleep tends to become more structured at around six months of age.

Babies appear to spend a great deal more time than adults do in REM sleep – around eight hours per day for infants, compared with two hours for adults (Sankupellay *et al.*, 2011; Siegel, 2005). The size of this difference has led theorists to suspect that infant sleep patterns are crucial to development in various ways. Several have speculated, for example, that REM sleep aids in the development of the central nervous system by facilitating synaptic pruning and preventing the formation of unnecessary connections, although research has not yet confirmed this. Also, by slowing body activity, the extended REM sleep of babies may help to regulate the temperature of their developing brains. REM sleep tends to decrease to adult levels somewhere between the ages of two and six years (El-Sheikh, 2011; Curzi-Dascalova & Challamel, 2000).

By early childhood, an individual's total daily sleep requirement also decreases significantly (Figure 8.9). Most children sleep around nine hours each day, although paediatricians recommend between 12 and 15 hours of sleep for anyone between two and five years of age (Crisp, 2010; Acebo *et al.*, 2005). Teenagers average around seven hours

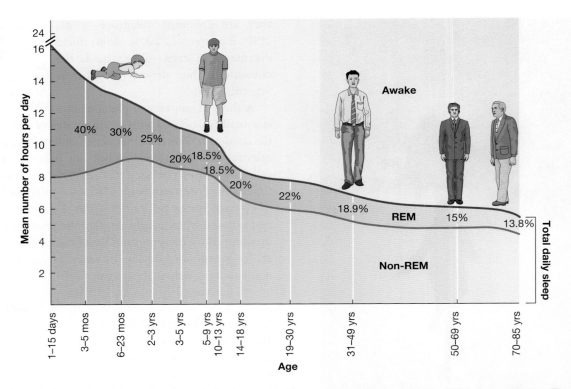

FIGURE 8.9 The effects of ageing on the sleep cycle. As we get older, our total daily sleep and our REM sleep decrease. The largest shifts occur during out first three years of life.

of daily sleep, although paediatricians recommend at least eight hours for them. As adults, our sleep patterns continue to change. As we age, we spend less and less time in deep sleep and REM sleep, our sleep is more readily interrupted, and we take longer to get back to sleep when awakened (Bliwise, 2010; Garcia-Rill *et al.*, 2008).

As discussed earlier, our sleep–awake cycle is tied to our bodies' circadian rhythms. These biological clocks are also affected by environmental demands and expectations (Worthman, 2011). Studies have, for example, contrasted parenting practices in different cultures. For example, many Western parents structure their babies' sleep by putting them down at designated times and not responding to their cries. In contrast, mothers from the Kipsigis people of Kenya keep their babies with them constantly. As a result, Kipsigis babies sleep for much shorter periods of time later into infancy than do babies from many Western cultures; in many cases, they do not sleep for long stretches even as adults (Super & Harkness, 2002, 1972). The body clocks of teenagers also seem to be compromised by the increased social and academic pressures that they encounter (El-Sheikh, 2011; Crowley *et al.*, 2007). Many adolescents, for example, stay up late largely because that's what it takes for them to finish their homework or to keep up with their friends (Payne, 2010).

Sleep Deprivation and Sleep Disorders   OUT OF THE ORDINARY

How much sleep a person needs varies, depending on factors such as age, lifestyle and genetic disposition. The amount of sleep a person actually gets may also be different from how much they need. Their lifestyles deprive many people of sleep, and sleep disorders may also make it impossible to sleep properly.

Sleep Deprivation Left alone, most people would sleep for nine or ten hours a day in order to awaken alert and refreshed. However, we have all had the opposite experience – that of not getting enough sleep. We become generally tired and irritable. After a while, we may yearn for sleep.

Researchers have found that without enough sleep, people also experience a general malaise (Orzel-Gryglewska, 2010). They display lower productivity and are more apt to make mistakes (Gunzelmann *et al.*, 2011). Not surprisingly, accidents and deaths sometimes occur when drivers and pilots do not get enough sleep. While it is possible to make up for the lost sleep of one night by sleeping a little longer the next night, it becomes increasingly difficult for persons to 'pay off' their 'sleep debt' if they chronically miss sleep (Moorcroft, 2003).

Adolescents are particularly likely to be sleep-deprived (Wolfson & Richards, 2011; Carskadon, 2002). Interestingly,

PSYCHOLOGY AROUND US   'Give me five more minutes!'

George woke up exhausted . . . yet again. Personally, he blamed getting home late from football training and excessive homework for his tiredness. But he knew his parents would blame playing games and chatting online with his friends. Since George certainly was not ready to give up those activities, he splashed water in his face and tried to look as awake as possible when he first saw his parents.

Like most other teenagers, George runs on at least some level of chronic sleep deprivation. Much of today's research on teenage sleep deprivation seeks to identify environmental factors for this problem. For example, teens these days tend to be overscheduled and overworked for a variety of reasons. And

such patterns clearly have an impact on sleep. However, scientists have also found evidence for a phase shift associated with puberty. This means that George's body clock makes him want to go to bed a couple of hours later than he did when he was younger. The problem is that he still needs the same amount of sleep he did in the past. And school tends to open at the same early hours as in the past.

Basically, in all conflicts between a teenager's biological needs and the demands of the environment, sleep deprivation is the only possible outcome. This losing battle has led some major paediatricians to suggest that a later start time for school or college may be an appropriate intervention.

teenagers today get about two hours less sleep per night than teens did 80 years ago. In fact, the distinguished sleep researcher William Dement has asserted that 80% of students at his institution, Stanford University, are 'dangerously sleep deprived' (Dement & Vaughan, 1999).

Ironically, students who pull all-nighters in order to complete their work actually wind up working less efficiently and effectively than they would if they were to sleep the eight or nine hours that they needed. Despite such problems among young persons, researchers have not conducted much research on how sleep deprivation specifically affects physical, cognitive and emotional development (Kopasz et al., 2010; Loessl et al., 2008).

Sleep researchers used to spend most of their time examining the impact of lost sleep on simple or monotonous tasks. Today's researchers, however, often look at the impact of sleep deprivation on more complex activities (Anderson & Platten, 2011; Moorcroft, 2003; Harrison & Horne, 2000). Studies suggest, on the one hand, that sleep deprivation does *not* necessarily lower one's performance on complex logical tasks. Sleep-deprived participants in such tasks often are able to avoid poor performances by being highly interested in the complex tasks at hand. Many sleep-deprived university students, for example, seem able to conduct research or write papers, particularly if their level of interest is high.

Problems arise, on the other hand, when a sleep-deprived person faces unexpected turns of events, distractions or innovations while working on a complex task, or needs to revise the task. If, for example, someone turns on the television while you are studying in a sleep-deprived state, your learning is likely to suffer.

In an important set of findings, researchers have also learnt that sleep loss can lower the effectiveness of people's immune

systems (Bollinger et al., 2010; Dement & Vaughan, 1999). Sleep-deprived people apparently have a more difficult time fighting off viral infections and cancer, for example. Thus, it may not be surprising that people who average at least eight hours of sleep a night tend to outlive those who get less sleep.

Sleep Disorders Sleep disorders occur when normal sleep patterns are disturbed, causing impaired daytime functioning and feelings of distress (Ivanenko & Johnson, 2010; Espie, 2002). Almost everyone suffers from some kind of sleep disorder at one time or another in their lives. The sleep disorder may be part of a larger problem, such as tress, a medical condition or substance misuse. Or it may be a *primary* sleep disorder, in which sleep difficulties are the central problem. Primary sleep disorders typically arise from abnormalities in the person's circadian rhythms and sleep–wake mechanisms.

People who suffer from **insomnia**, the most common sleep disorder, regularly cannot fall asleep or stay asleep (Bastien, 2011; Horne, 2010). Up to one-third of people suffer from insomnia (lack of sleep or poor quality sleep). It is a huge public health problem, and the most commonly reported mental health complaint in the United Kingdom (Mental Health Foundation, 2011).

> **insomnia** a sleep disorder characterized by a regular inability to fall asleep or stay asleep.

As you might expect, many cases of insomnia are triggered by day-to-day stressors. In particular, job or school pressures, troubled relationships and financial problems have been implicated. For many people, a subtle additional stress is worrying about not getting enough sleep while trying to fall asleep. This vicious cycle can further intensify anxiety and make sleep all the more elusive (Jansson-Fröjmark et al., 2011).

Insomnia is more common among older people than younger ones (Jaussent et al., 2011). Elderly individuals are particularly prone to this problem because so many of them have medical ailments, experience pain, take medications or grapple with depression and anxiety – each a known contributor to insomnia (Taylor *et al.*, 2008). In addition, some of the normal age-related sleep changes we described earlier may heighten the chances of insomnia among elderly people. As individuals age, for example, they naturally spend less time in deep sleep and their sleep is interrupted more readily (Bliwise, 2010; Edelstein *et al.*, 2008).

Beyond insomnia, there are a number of other sleep disorders. Obstructive *sleep apnoea* occurs in approximately 3–7% of adult men and 2–5% of adult women. It is more common in older people and in those who are overweight (Punjabi, 2008).People with this condition repeatedly stop breathing during the night, depriving the brain of oxygen and leading to frequent, perhaps dozens of, awakenings.

Another two sleep disorders, *narcolepsy* and *hypersomnia*, are marked by extreme daytime sleepiness. People with narcolepsy experience an uncontrollable urge to fall asleep and may suddenly fall into REM sleep in the midst of an argument or during an exciting football game (Goswami *et al.*, 2010), while hypersomnia sufferers complain they never feel fully refreshed and may not feel fully awake for several hours after waking. Both hypersomnia and narcolepsy are rare, estimated at 0.3% of the general population for hypersomnia and 0.045% for narcolepsy (Ohayon, 2008).

Two other sleep disorders are particularly common among children. Up to 5% of children *sleepwalk* (Dogu & Pressman, 2011; Wickwire *et al.*, 2008). They sit up, get out of bed and walk around while still in a sleep state. Individuals who suffer from another sleep disorder, *night terror disorder*, awaken suddenly, sit up in bed, scream in extreme fear and agitation and experience fast heart and breathing rates. They appear to be in a state of panic and their talk is often impossible to understand. Night terror disorder is much more than the periodic experience of nightmares that we discussed earlier.

Before You Go On

What Do You Know?

12. What are the major theories of why people sleep?

13. What is the difference between the manifest content of a dream and its latent content?

14. What is the role of the suprachiasmatic nucleus (SCN) in human consciousness?

15. What is the difference between a nightmare and a night terror?

What Do You Think?

Which of the theories of dreams described in this section seems to make most sense to you and why? Could another idea or a combination of theories better explain dreaming?

Psychoactive Drugs

LEARNING OBJECTIVE 9

Define and describe common depressant, stimulant and hallucinogenic psychoactive drugs and their effects.

What is one of the first things you do every day? For millions of people, the answer is to have a cup of coffee (maybe more than one). Why do so many people do this? For most, it is to give themselves a bit of a jolt and to get the day going. Similarly, people often use other substances to help improve, or at least change, how they feel or function. Many people smoke cigarettes to feel more alert, less anxious or both. Others may have a glass of wine or beer in the evening in order to wind down from a hectic day.

All of these substances – coffee, cigarettes and alcohol – along with many others, have one thing in common: they alter our consciousness in some way. Collectively, they are examples of **psychoactive drugs**, chemicals that affect awareness, behaviour, sensation, perception or mood. Some such drugs are illegal chemicals (heroin, ecstasy, marijuana), while others are common and legal. Table 8.1 shows the three categories of drugs and lists examples of specific drugs that fall within those categories.

Some of the changes brought about by psychoactive drugs are temporary, lasting only as long as the chemicals remain in the brain and body. But certain psychoactive drugs can also bring about long-term changes. People who regularly ingest them may develop problematic patterns of behaviour and changes in their body's physical responses, a pattern commonly called **addiction**. We will also be discussing addiction in Chapter 13, where we examine the motives and drives that direct behaviour, and in Chapter 19, the chapter on psychological disorders.

psychoactive drugs chemicals that affect awareness, behaviour, sensation, perception or mood.

addiction psychological or physical compulsion to take a drug, resulting from regular ingestion and leading to maladaptive patterns of behaviour and changes in physical response.

TABLE 8.1 Psychoactive Drugs and Their Effects

DRUG CLASS	EFFECTS
Depressants	**Depress activity of the central nervous system**
Alcohol	Slows down brain areas that control judgement, inhibition and behaviour (speech, motor functioning, emotional expression)
Sedative-hypnotics (benzodiazepines)	Produce relaxation and drowsiness, relieve anxiety
Opioids (opium, heroin, morphine, codeine, methadone)	Reduce pain and emotional tension, produce pleasurable and calming feelings
Stimulants	**Increase activity of the central nervous system**
Caffeine	Increases alertness
Nicotine	Increases alertness, reduces stress
Cocaine	Increases energy and alertness, produces euphoric feelings of well-being and confidence
Amphetamines	Increase energy and alertness, reduce appetite, produce euphoric feelings
Hallucinogens	**Enhance normal perceptions**
LSD	Dramatically strengthens visual perceptions (including illusions and hallucinations) along with profound psychological and physical changes
Cannabis (marijuana, THC)	Produces a mixture of hallucinogenic, depressant and stimulant effects
MDMA (Ecstasy)	Enhances sensory perceptions, increases energy and alertness and produces feelings of empathy and emotional well-being

Depressants

depressants a class of drugs that slow the activity of the central nervous system.

Psychoactive drugs that slow down the central nervous system are called **depressants**. Two widely used groups of depressants are *alcohol* and *opioids*.

Alcohol Alcohol, a depressant that is taken in liquid form, is one of the most commonly used psychoactive drugs. All alcoholic beverages contain *ethyl alcohol*, a chemical that is quickly absorbed into the blood through the lining of the stomach and the intestine. The ethyl alcohol immediately begins to take effect as it is carried in the bloodstream to the central nervous system (the brain and spinal cord). At first, ethyl alcohol depresses, or slows down, the brain areas that control judgement and inhibition. People become looser and more talkative, relaxed and happy. When more alcohol is absorbed, it slows down additional areas in the central nervous system, and affects the person's state of consciousness. For example, it causes the drinkers to make poorer judgements, become careless, feel more emotional and remember less well.

As drinking continues, the motor responses of individuals decline and their reaction times slow. They may be unsteady when they stand or walk, for example. Their vision becomes blurred and they may misjudge distances. They can also have trouble hearing. As a result, people who have drunk too much alcohol may have enormous difficulty driving or solving simple problems.

As summarized in Table 8.2, the *concentration*, or proportion, of ethyl alcohol in the blood determines how much

TABLE 8.2 Alcohol's Effects on the Body and Behaviour

Number of drinks[a] in two hours	Blood alcohol content (%)[b]	Effect
(2)	0.06	Relaxed state; increased sociability
(3)	0.09	Everyday stress lessened
(4)	0.10	Movements and speech become clumsy
(7)	0.20	Very drunk; loud and difficult to understand; emotions unstable
(12)	0.40	Difficult to wake up; incapable of voluntary action
(15)	0.55	Coma and/or death

[a] A *drink* refers to a 341 ml (0.6 pints) beer, a 125 ml (0.2 pints) glass of wine or a 37.5 ml (0.065 pints) shot of spirits.
[b] In the United Kingdom, the legal blood alcohol level for 'drunk driving' is 80 mg of alcohol per 100 ml of blood, which translates to 0.08%.

Cultural endorsement? Five men and hundreds of others around them celebrate at Oktoberfest, Germany's annual 16-day festival, marked by eating, special events and, perhaps most prominently, drinking. Almost seven million litres (12 million pints) of beer are served to thousands of revellers at each year's festival, an excessiveness that many believe contributes to binge drinking and alcoholism.

Source: ©Murat Taner/Corbis.

it will affect a person (Hart *et al.*, 2010). When the alcohol concentration reaches 0.06% of the blood volume, a person usually feels relaxed and comfortable. By the time the alcohol concentration reaches 0.09% of the blood volume, the drinker crosses the line into *intoxication*.

Opioids The term **opioids** refers to *opium* and drugs derived from it, including *heroin*, *morphine* and *codeine*. Opium, a substance taken from the sap of the opium poppy, has been used for thousands of years. Scientists have learnt over the years that this substance and its derivatives are all addictive, some more than others. Each of the drugs has a different strength, speed of action and tolerance level.

opioids a class of drugs derived from the sap of the opium poppy.

Outside of medical settings, opioids are smoked, inhaled, snorted (ingested through the nose), injected by needle just beneath the skin ('skin popped') or injected directly into the blood stream ('mainlined'). An injection quickly produces a *rush*, a spasm of warmth and joy that is sometimes compared with an orgasm. The brief spasm is followed by several hours of a pleasant feeling and shift in consciousness called a *high* or *nod*. During a high, the opioid user feels very relaxed and happy and is unconcerned about food or other bodily needs.

Opioids depress the central nervous system, particularly the brain areas that control emotion. The drugs attach to brain receptors that ordinarily receive **endorphins** that help reduce pain and emotional tension

endorphins neurotransmitters that help relieve pain and reduce emotional tension.

(Hart *et al.*, 2010). When neurons receive opioids at these receptors, the opioids produce the same kinds of pleasant and relaxing feelings that endorphins would produce.

The most direct danger of opioid use, particularly heroin use, is an overdose. An overdose shuts down the respiratory centre in the brain, almost paralysing breathing and in many cases causing death. Each year 2% of those addicted to heroin and other opioids are killed by the drugs, usually from an overdose (Theodorou & Haber, 2005; APA, 2000).

Stimulants

Psychoactive drugs that speed up the central nervous system are called **stimulants**. They produce increases in blood pressure, heart rate, alertness, thinking and behaviour. Among the most problematic stimulants are caffeine, nicotine, cocaine and amphetamines.

stimulants substances that increase the activity of the central nervous system.

Caffeine, a mild (and legal) stimulant, is the world's most widely used stimulant. It is found in coffee, tea, chocolate, cola and so-called *energy drinks*. It heightens a person's attention and awareness. Caffeine is addictive, in its particular way. Quitting it can quickly cause unpleasant withdrawal symptoms for chronic users, including tiredness, anxiety, irritability, depression, constipation and headaches.

Although legal, *nicotine* is one of the most highly addictive substances in the world (Hart *et al.*, 2010). Most commonly, it is taken into the body by smoking tobacco. Nicotine proceeds to activate nicotine receptors located throughout the brain and body.

Regular smokers develop a tolerance for nicotine and must smoke more and more in order to achieve the same results (Hymowitz, 2005). When they try to stop smoking, they experience withdrawal symptoms such as irritability, increased appetite, sleep disturbances and a powerful desire to smoke (APA, 2000).

Cocaine, the key active ingredient of South America's coca plant, is the most powerful natural stimulant currently known. The drug was first separated from the plant in 1865. For many centuries, however, native people have chewed the leaves of the plant to raise their energy and increase their alertness.

Processed cocaine – a white, fluffy powder – is snorted and absorbed through the mucous membrane of the nose. Some users, however, prefer the more powerful effects of taking cocaine intravenously or smoking it in a pipe or cigarette. Cocaine brings on a rush of euphoria and well-being – an orgasmic-like shift in consciousness if the dose is high enough. Initially, cocaine stimulates the higher centres of the central nervous system, shifting users' levels of awareness and making them excited, energetic and talkative. As more cocaine is taken, it stimulates additional areas of the central nervous system, resulting in increases in heart rate, blood

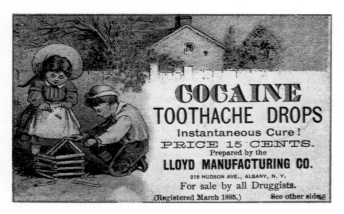

The early days. In the early 20th century, cocaine was an ingredient in such products as Cocaine Toothache Drops and Coca-Cola soft drinks.

Source: The Granger Collection, New York. Reproduced with permission.

pressure, breathing, arousal and wakefulness. Cocaine apparently produces these effects largely by increasing activity of the neurotransmitter *dopamine* at key neurons throughout the brain (Haney, 2008).

Regular use of cocaine may lead to a pattern of addiction. Tolerance to the drug may develop, and suddenly withdrawing from it results in depression, severe fatigue, sleep problems and anxiety (Hart *et al.*, 2010). Cocaine also poses serious physical dangers (Kosten *et al.*, 2008). Use of the drug in powerful, smokeable, forms known as *freebasing* and *crack*, has caused the annual number of cocaine-related emergency room incidents in the United States to increase 100-fold since 1982 (SAMHSA, 2008). The greatest danger of cocaine use is an overdose, which may impair breathing, produce major – even fatal – heart irregularities or cause brain seizures (Doweiko, 2006).

Amphetamines are manufactured in the laboratory. These stimulants are most often taken in pill or capsule form. Like cocaine, amphetamines increase energy and alertness and lower appetite in small doses, produce intoxication and psychosis in higher doses, and cause an emotional letdown when they leave the body. Also like cocaine, these drugs produce such effects by increasing the activity of the neurotransmitter dopamine (Haney, 2008).

Tolerance to amphetamines builds very rapidly, thus increasing the chances of users becoming addicted (Acosta *et al.*, 2005). When people who are addicted to the drug stop taking it, they fall into a pattern of deep depression and extended sleep identical to the withdrawal from cocaine.

One powerful kind of amphetamine, *methamphetamine*, like other kinds of amphetamines, increases activity of the neurotransmitter dopamine, producing increased arousal, attention and related effects. Users are often seduced by their perception, correctly or incorrectly, that the drug makes them feel more sexual and less inhibited (Jefferson, 2005).

The drug is, however, very dangerous to one's health, leading to rapid deterioration in one's physical condition and to rapid addiction.

Hallucinogens

Hallucinogens, or *psychedelic drugs*, are substances that can dramatically change conscious experience. They may, for example, enhance a person's normal perceptions and produce illusions and hallucinations. The substance-induced sensory changes are sometimes called *trips*. These trips may be exciting or frightening, depending on how a person's mind reacts to the drugs.

> **hallucinogens** substances that dramatically change one's state of awareness, causing powerful changes in sensory perception.

Lysergic acid diethylamide, or *LSD*, is a very powerful hallucinogen that was derived by the Swiss chemist Albert Hoffman in 1938 from a group of naturally occurring substances. During the 1960s, a period of rebellion and experimentation, millions of users turned to the drug in an effort to raise their consciousness and expand their experiences. Within two hours of being swallowed, LSD brings on *hallucinosis*, a state marked by a strengthening of visual perceptions and profound psychological and physical change. People may focus on small details – each hair on the skin, for example. Colours may seem brighter and users often experience illusions in which objects seem distorted and seem to move, breathe or change shape. Such effects take place while the user is fully alert.

A key problem is that LSD is so powerful that any dose, no matter how small, is likely to produce very strong reactions. Sometimes the reactions are quite unpleasant, an experience called a *bad trip*.

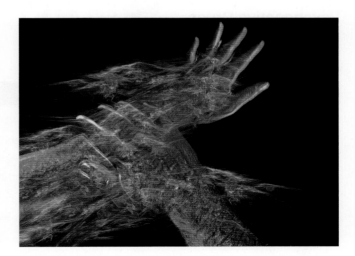

Bad trip. Ingesting LSD brings on hallucinosis, a state of sensory and perceptual distortion. Sometimes this state can be very frightening and disorientating, as captured in this photo illustration of the hallucination of hands and arms burning.

Source: Carol and Mike Werner/Phototake.

Cannabis is considered by many to be a kind of hallucinogen. The hemp plant *Cannabis sativa* grows in warm climates. Collectively, the drugs produced from varieties of hemp are called cannabis. The most powerful of them is *hashish*; the weaker ones include the best-known form of cannabis, *marijuana*, a mixture derived from the buds, crushed leaves and flowering tops of hemp plants.

Although there are several hundred active chemicals in cannabis, *tetrahydrocannabinol (THC)* is the one most responsible for its effects. The greater the THC content, the more powerful the cannabis. Owing to changes in growing patterns, today's marijuana is at least four times higher in THC content than was the marijuana of the early 1970s (Doweiko, 2006; APA, 2000).

When smoked, cannabis changes one's conscious experiences by producing a mixture of hallucinogenic, depressant and stimulant effects. At low doses, the smoker typically has feelings of happiness and relaxation, although some smokers become anxious or irritated, especially if they have been in a bad mood. Many smokers have sharpened perceptions and become fascinated with the heightened sounds and sights that they are experiencing. In strong doses, cannabis produces particularly unusual visual experiences, changes in body image and even hallucinations (Mathew *et al.*, 1993).

Because marijuana can interfere with complex sensorimotor tasks and cognitive functioning, it has been tied to many automobile accidents (Kauert & Iwersen-Bergmann, 2004). In addition, many people on marijuana fail to remember information, especially recently learnt material. Thus, heavy marijuana smokers may function poorly at school or work (Lundqvist, 2005).

Psychoactive Drugs

WHAT HAPPENS IN THE BRAIN?

An ingested drug increases the activity of certain neurotransmitters in the brain – chemicals whose normal purpose is to reduce pain, calm us, lift our mood or increase our alertness. And these neurotransmitters, in turn, help produce the particular effects of the drug. Alcohol, for example, heightens activity of the neurotransmitter *GABA*, opioids raise *endorphin* activity, cocaine and amphetamines increase *dopamine* activity and cannabis increases the activity of a neurotransmitter called *anandamide*.

It used to be thought that each drug, along with its corresponding neurotransmitters, sets in motion a *unique* set of brain reactions. However, recent brain-imaging studies suggest that while each drug has its own starting point in the brain most of them eventually activate a single **reward learning pathway**, or pleasure pathway, in the brain (Haney, 2008). This brain reward learning pathway apparently extends from the midbrain to the nucleus accumbens and on to the frontal cortex (see Chapter 5).

> **reward learning pathway** brain circuitry that is important for learning about rewarding stimuli.

The key neurotransmitter in this pathway appears to be *dopamine*. When dopamine is activated there, a person wants – even craves – pleasurable rewards, such as music, a hug or, for some people, a drug (Higgins & George, 2007; Higgins *et al.*, 2004). Certain drugs apparently stimulate the reward learning pathway directly. You will recall that cocaine and amphetamines directly increase dopamine activity. Other drugs seem to stimulate it in roundabout ways. Each biochemical reaction triggered by alcohol and opioids, for example, sets in motion a series of chemical events that *eventually* leads to increased dopamine activity in the reward learning pathway.

Research also suggests that people prone to abuse drugs may suffer from a **reward-deficiency syndrome** – that is, their reward learning pathway is not activated readily by the events in their lives (Blum *et al.*, 2000) – so they are more inclined than other people to turn to drugs to keep their pathway stimulated.

> **reward-deficiency syndrome** the theory that people may abuse drugs because their reward centre is not readily activated by usual life events.

Before You Go On

What Do You Know?

16. What are the major drug categories and the characteristics of each category?

17. What is addiction, and what are two key features of addiction to a drug?

18. What is the brain's reward learning pathway, and what role may it play in drug use and drug abuse?

What Do You Think?

Why do you think alcohol is more acceptable culturally than some of the other drugs we are discussing here?

VIDEO

Access your interactive e-book to view a video clip for this chapter at **www.wileyopenpage.com**

Summary

Defining Consciousness

LEARNING OBJECTIVE 1 Define consciousness and identify why it is both central to the study of the mind and such an elusive topic of investigation.

- Consciousness is defined in different ways by different theorists and researchers. This is often why there is so much debate about its nature.
- Consciousness is closely linked to the *mind* and the *mind/body problem*, but there are subtle differences. Not all things we associate with the mind are necessarily associated with consciousness. Unconscious mental processes are an example of something that is linked to the notion of the *mind* but not *consciousness*.

Is Consciousness 'Mysterious'?

LEARNING OBJECTIVE 2 Describe why some philosophers have found it hard to place consciousness within a physical framework.

- Some researchers claim that consciousness is extremely difficult (if not impossible) to study objectively because it is inherently subjective in nature. This is one reason that it has been called *mysterious*: it is the only thing we know of that has so far eluded attempts to objectively study it.
- A consequence of its subjective nature is that our consciousness does not feel to us as if it is part of the physical world. Most people's intuition is that consciousness is something other than physical processes. This is another reason why it has been tagged as mysterious in nature.

What's in the World? Part 1: Material Stuff *or* Mental Stuff

LEARNING OBJECTIVE 3 Summarize the monist positions, particularly those involving materialism, and the objections to approaching consciousness in these ways.

- Monism is the position that the world is made of one type of fundamental thing.
- Idealism is a form of monism that holds this 'thing' is purely mental, and the physical world is a construction of our minds. Idealism is no longer popular in philosophy and science, although another form of monism is materialism.
- Materialism contends that the world and everything in it (including consciousness) can be explained in terms of physical matter and physical processes.

- Identity theory is a materialist explanation for consciousness in which conscious states are thought to be identical to states of the brain.
- Eliminativism is another materialist position that argues against the idea that conscious is mysterious by attempting to reduce (and thus eliminate) things like qualia to physical processes. Both of these positions have been criticized. Certain mental states have been found to have more than one physical instantiation (what researchers call multiple realizability), which challenges identity theory. Eliminativism has been criticized because it cannot (yet) fully explain the exact ways in which physical processes are linked to subjective states.
- Functionalism was suggested as an alternative perspective. Functionalists maintain that the most important thing to consider is what mental states actually do (i.e. their function). Certain functions can be achieved in a number of different ways (and potentially in mediums other than brains), which means that the problems associated with identity theory are avoided. Functionalism has been criticized, however, because there seems to be no way to explain why certain functions (e.g. manipulation of syntax rules) are associated with actual semantics (meaning). We clearly know what certain words and phrases mean, and it seems that this is a step too far for a purely functional account to explain.

What's in the World? Part 2: Material Stuff *and* Mental Stuff

LEARNING OBJECTIVE 4 Summarize the dualist positions, including why some philosophers adopt dualism, and give an account of the objections to approaching consciousness in these ways.

- Dualism is the position that the world consists of two distinct kinds of thing. Substance dualism claims that there are material things (i.e. the physical world) and there are non-material things (e.g. consciousness). This has been widely criticized on a number of grounds, but primarily because it is difficult to define exactly what a non-material thing actually is. Moreover, substance dualism also runs into problems because of its lack of any explanation for how these two distinct types of 'thing' interact with each other.
- Property dualism suggests that there is only one type of substance, although this unitary substance can have both physical and non-physical properties.

- Epiphenomenalism is a form of property dualism that claims consciousness emerges from physical processes but cannot be completely reduced to them. Both of these positions have been criticized because it is not entirely clear what the *second thing* or *second property* actually is and how it interacts with everything else.
- Generally, most philosophers with an interest in consciousness would agree that there is an *explanatory gap* – a missing piece of the puzzle that explains how and why physical processes are linked to subjective conscious states. Much of the subsequent debate concerns whether and how this gap will be reduced.

When We Are Awake: Conscious Awareness

LEARNING OBJECTIVE 5 Define different levels of conscious awareness and describe key brain structures and functions associated with those levels.

- Attention is one of the key aspects of conscious awareness. Other key cognitive activities underlying cognitive awareness include monitoring (our implicit decisions about what to attend to), memory and planning.
- Most biological investigators believe that consciousness results from a combination of brain activities in several brain regions.
- Two key brain structures appear to be the cerebral cortex, which helps regulate our awareness of attentional processes, and the thalamus, which relays sensory information from various parts of the brain to the cerebral cortex for processing.

Preconscious and Unconscious States

LEARNING OBJECTIVE 6 Summarize the ideas of preconscious and unconscious states, including Freud's thinking on the unconscious.

- In addition to our conscious level of awareness, many psychologists believe there are other levels or degrees of consciousness, and distinguish conscious awareness from two other states: unconsciousness and preconsciousness.
- Preconsciousness is a level of awareness in which information can become readily available to consciousness if necessary.
- Unconsciousness is a state in which information is not easily accessible to conscious awareness.
- Freud viewed the human unconscious as an important storehouse for knowledge and experience, which

although not directly accessible to our conscious awareness still influences our behaviour.
- Although Freud's ideas fell out of favour for several years, in recent years, scientists have begun to re-examine the unconscious from different points of view. For example, implicit memory describes knowledge that we have and are able to apply to various tasks, without being able to recall it at will.

Hypnosis

LEARNING OBJECTIVE 7 Define hypnosis and discuss theories and evidence about what it is, how it works and how it can be used.

- Hypnosis is a suggestible state during which people can be directed to act in unusual ways, experience unusual sensations, remember forgotten events or forget remembered events.
- Ernest Hilgard's theory suggests that hypnosis divides consciousness into two parts: one focused on the suggestions of the hypnotist and the other a hidden observer. Other theorists suggest that motivated role-playing is at work in hypnosis.
- Hypnosis has been used to successfully help control pain, as well as treat problems, such as anxiety, skin diseases, asthma, insomnia, stuttering, high blood pressure, warts and other forms of infection.

When We Are Asleep

LEARNING OBJECTIVE 8 Describe what happens when people sleep, key theories of why we sleep and dream, and problems with sleep and how they affect functioning.

- Every 90 to 100 minutes when we sleep, we pass through a sleep cycle consisting of five different stages. The fifth stage of sleep, rapid eye movement, or REM sleep, is characterized by rapid and jagged brain-wave patterns and eye movements and irregularities in heart rate and breathing. Dreaming usually occurs during this phase of sleep.
- Scientists have identified brain activities that maintain the regular rhythms of life. Our move from a sustained period of wakefulness into a period of sleep during each 24-hour period is known as a *circadian rhythm*.
- Scientists have not reached a definitive conclusion about why people sleep, although some scientists have suggested sleep serves an evolutionarily adaptive function, keeping our ancestors away from predators that hunted

at night. Others have suggested that sleep plays a role in growth, or allows us time to restore depleted chemical resources in the brain and body and eliminate chemical wastes that have accumulated throughout the day.

- We also do not understand why people dream. Freud believed that dreams represent expressions of the internal desires and wishes that have been repressed and stored in the unconscious.
- Recent theories about dreams emphasize more cognitive approaches. The information-processing theory of dreams suggests that dreams are the mind's attempt to sort out and organize the day's experiences and fix them in memory. The attention-synthesis hypothesis suggests that dreams are the mind's attempts to give meaning to internally generated signals firing throughout the brain during deep sleep.
- Sleep deprivation can lead to feelings of fatigue, irritability and malaise, resulting in lower productivity and a tendency to make mistakes. Loss of sleep can also affect the functioning of the immune system. The regular

inability to fall asleep or stay asleep is called insomnia. Other sleep disorders include sleep apnoea, narcolepsy, sleepwalking and night terrors.

Psychoactive Drugs

LEARNING OBJECTIVE 9   Define and describe common depressant, stimulant and hallucinogenic psychoactive drugs and their effects.

- The three main classes of psychoactive drugs are depressants (substances that slow down brain activity), stimulants (substances that excite brain activity) and psychedelic or hallucinogenic drugs (substances that distort sensory perceptions).
- Regular ingestion of some drugs can lead to problematic changes in a person's behaviour patterns and physical responses, a pattern known as *addiction*. Signs of addiction can include increased tolerance, the need for larger and larger doses of a substance to get the desired effect and symptoms of withdrawal when one discontinues the drug.

Activities to test yourself further are available in your interactive e-book at **www.wileyopenpage.com**

TYING IT TOGETHER

WHAT HAPPENS IN THE
BRAIN?

- Although we know that consciousness is closely linked to brain function, we do not yet have a full picture of how or why certain processes in the brain give rise to subjective awareness. Despite this, we can study the various ways in which consciousness is affected when brain function is altered.
- People who are blind because of damage to visual areas in the cerebral cortex are still able to point in the direction of light projected onto a screen, even though they are not aware of attending to the light. That's because the areas in the cerebral cortex that are in charge of *awareness* of attention are not the same as the areas responsible for attention itself.
- Similarly, hypnosis used to anaesthetize or reduce pain does not keep sensations of pain from reaching neurons. Instead, it reduces awareness of the pain by

decreasing activity in a particular part of the cerebral cortex.
- Humans are probably not the only animals that dream. Dreaming takes place during rapid eye movement (REM) sleep, the final stage of the brain's five-stage sleep cycle, and every kind of mammal that has been tested experiences these sleep stages.
- There are various theories to explain dreaming. Some researchers, for instance, believe that we dream because the brain, while we sleep, produces a variety of visual and auditory signals and then tries to combine these self-produced signals in a way that makes sense.
- Most, or perhaps all, psychoactive drugs eventually work by activating a single reward centre, or pleasure pathway, in the brain. The key neurotransmitter in this pathway is dopamine. Music can activate dopamine, and so may a big hug – and so may drugs.

OUT OF THE ORDINARY

- Adolescents are especially likely to suffer from sleep deprivation. In fact, teenagers today get about two hours less sleep per night than teens 80 years ago.
- Going without sleep, over time, causes a variety of problems: general malaise, lower productivity and an increased tendency to make mistakes, and even lower immune system functioning.
- The most common sleep disorder is insomnia. Insomnia sufferers, who are generally older people, have trouble falling asleep, staying asleep or feeling rested by sleep.

HOW WE DEVELOP

- The question of when babies develop alert consciousness is a matter of debate. On the one hand, some researchers argue that early cognitive development such as that discussed in Chapter 3 shows that babies do have a rudimentary sense of consciousness. Others argue that consciousness comes later, with the development of language.
- During the first four months of life, babies sleep between 14 and 17 hours a day, and the time spent sleeping declines steadily as people get older.
- Environmental demands and expectations affect babies' sleep–awake cycles. In the Kipsigis tribe, for example, babies sleep for much shorter periods longer into infancy than Western babies do. That's because Kipsigis mothers keep their babies with them constantly, while Western parents structure their babies' sleep by putting them to bed at regular times.

Quizzes to test yourself further are available in your interactive e-book at **www.wileyopenpage.com**

Key Terms

activation-synthesis model 224
adaptive theory of sleep 220
addiction 228
circadian rhythm 220
depressants 229
dissociation 218
dualism 209
eliminativism 205
endorphins 230

epiphenomenalism 209
hallucinogens 231
hypnagogic state 221
hypnosis 217
identity theory 204
implicit memory 216
information-processing theory 224
insomnia 227
lucid dreams 225
materialism 204

monism 204
multiple realizability 205
non-REM (NREM) sleep 223
opioids 230
panpsychism 210
preconsciousness 215
property dualism 209
psychoactive drugs 228
qualia 202
rapid eye movement (REM) sleep 223

restorative theory of sleep 220
reward learning pathway 232
reward-deficiency syndrome 232
sleep spindles 222
stimulants 230
substance dualism 209
suprachiasmatic nucleus (SCN) 221
unconscious state 216

Flashcards to test yourself further are available in your interactive e-book at **www.wileyopenpage.com**

CHAPTER 9

Learning

Adapted by Pam Blundell,
University of Leeds, UK

CHAPTER OUTLINE

- What Is Learning?
- Classical Conditioning
- Operant Conditioning
- Observational Learning
- Factors that Facilitate Learning

- When We Learn
- Prenatal and Postnatal Learning
- Learning and Gender
- Learning Difficulties

 Access your interactive e-book to view a video clip for this chapter at **www.wileyopenpage.com**

Name that Tune

If you have a favourite band, you probably wait impatiently for the release of their latest album and search the Internet for signs that they will be touring in your area. When you first hear a new song the group has just recorded, it is likely to feel a little familiar, because you know the group's style well. The lyrics and tune will be new, however, and you will not know them right away. If you listen to the album several times on your iPod, even if you are not intently concentrating on the music and are instead working out or studying while listening, the music will seem increasingly familiar each time you hear it. You may find yourself humming or whistling the tune without realizing it. After you have heard the song a few times, you will probably know most, if not all, of the lyrics. All of this learning is likely to occur without much effort. For most people, it is much easier than learning a poem or an essay of comparable length. Learning a song like this seems easy for many different reasons. Often, you feel an emotional connection with the lyrics, and the fact that they are set to music makes them catchy, so you remember them effortlessly. ■

This type of automatic learning experience may stand in stark contrast to your efforts to master the information presented in a difficult course that requires you to remember many facts and figures, such as statistics. For a course like this, students often use specific study techniques to learn the material. At the very least, concentration and extensive studying are critical for learning in such a course.

Why are these two learning experiences so different? There are most likely several reasons. First, there is the difficulty factor. Material in your most challenging courses is likely to be conceptually difficult. It may be hard to understand certain ideas, let alone remember them clearly. Thus, learning the material requires first gaining an understanding of it and then finding a way to remember it. By contrast, information presented to you in a song is relatively simple and usually does not require concentrated effort to understand.

Second, attention probably plays an important role. Sustaining attention is critical for certain types of learning, and it is probably not difficult to pay attention to the lyrics of a new song from your favourite group. After all, they already have your interest. Even for statistics aficionados, however, it may be hard to pay attention long enough to learn labour-intensive course material well in just one sitting. Remembering this type of material often requires repeated exposure, perhaps first in a lecture, then by reading in your textbook and finally by studying your notes.

Third, emotional factors help people to learn information. Numerous studies have shown that emotionally charged material is easier to learn (although this can sometimes present a problem, as we will see later in the chapter). Most likely, when your favourite group releases new music, you have an emotional reaction to it. Often, you feel excited and happy, and you will learn the new song more readily.

Finally, differences between these two types of learning experiences may be related to our biology. Humans evolved living in groups where social cooperation was essential for survival. Thus, we are biologically ready to learn about social interactions and relationships, the subject matter of many song lyrics. Facts about statistics, on the other hand, were not critical information for the survival of early people, and as a result our brains are not as prepared to learn this type of information.

All of these variables – task difficulty, attention, emotions and biological readiness – are important for learning. The study of each will come up later in this chapter. The overall picture underscores how learning is complex and multidimensional.

What Is Learning?

LEARNING OBJECTIVE 1

Define learning, and distinguish between associative and non-associative learning.

Put simply, **learning** is defined as a lasting change caused by experience. In the laboratory, scientists study learning by measuring changes in behavioural responses. This is particularly true for studies of animals, where it is impossible to ask subjects what and how much they have learnt. However, it is clear that considerable learning occurs even when no obvious changes in behaviour can be observed. For example, when you eat mint chocolate, there will be an association formed between the mint flavour and the chocolate flavour, such that if you smell mint it may remind you of chocolate. However, this association is behaviourally silent: being reminded of chocolate may not change your observable behaviour.

> **learning** a lasting change caused by experience.

It may seem strange to separate a discussion about learning from a closely related subject – memory, which is covered in the next chapter. Although learning and memory are indeed interrelated, and many of the biological mechanisms (and brain regions) that underlie learning are also critical for memory, these topics have been studied differently in the laboratory. Traditionally, studies of learning used animals (dogs, monkeys, pigeons, rats and mice), whereas studies of memory focused on humans. Today, with the advent of neuroimaging technology and a greater public concern for understanding learning disabilities, as well as a desire to move away from animal research where possible, more research on learning is focused on humans as well. Wherever possible throughout this chapter, we will discuss information that scientists have gained from animal experimentation to explain questions about human learning.

Scientists typically display data from learning studies in a **learning curve**. This type of graph shows how performance on a particular learning task changes over time, as shown in Figure 9.1. The learning curve can be used to determine whether mastery of the task occurs rapidly, as it does when the task is relatively easy, or gradually, which is the case when the task is, relatively difficult. A typical learning curve is *negatively accelerated* – that is, the curve will be very steep initially, but will then level out, as performance reaches the *asymptote*.

> **learning curve** a graph that shows change in performance on a learning task over time.

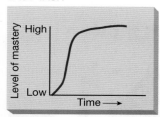
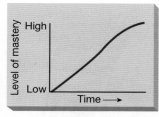

FIGURE 9.1 Learning curves. Learning study data are typically displayed on learning curve graphs that show the mastering of a task over time. The learning curves reveal whether the task was an easy or a difficult one.

associative learning a type of learning that involves forming associations between stimuli.

non-associative learning a type of learning that does not involve forming associations between stimuli.

In general, learning can be divided into two major categories: *associative* and *non-associative*. **Associative learning** is a change that occurs as a result of experiences that lead us to link two or more stimuli together. In other words, we learn by associating one stimulus with another. An example of associative learning would be learning that a tone predicts a food pellet. **Non-associative learning** also involves change based on experience, but happens without associations forming: for example, habituation.

Non-Associative Learning

Non-associative learning is by far the simpler of the two types; the most basic forms of learning are non-associative. This means that they do not involve linking information about more than one stimulus. Rather, non-associative learning involves a change that occurs as a result of our experiences with a single sensory cue. There are two major types of non-associative learning: *habituation* and *sensitization*.

Habituation We discussed habituation of our senses in Chapter 7. Habituation happens when our senses begin to respond less strongly to repeated presentations of the same sensory cue. A smell, such as fresh coffee, may be very powerful when you first walk into your home, but after a while you will barely notice it. Even though the coffee continues to give off just as much aroma, you have become habituated. You respond less and less strongly, though the same stimulus repeatedly reaches the sensory receptors in your nose. In most cases, we are unaware when sensory habituation occurs. You may notice you were habituated to the stimulus afterwards, but your attention is not required for learning to occur.

When we use the term **habituation** to talk about learning, it also refers to a decrease in response after repeated stimulus presentation. Learned habituation, however, is not just the result of sensory adaptation or fatigue of neurons in the sensory receptors. Instead, learning theorists study habituation that involves changes in neurons in our central nervous system. If a decrease in response occurs because of a change in neurons in the brain or spinal cord, then learning has taken place.

habituation a form of non-associative learning whereby repeated presentation of a stimulus leads to a reduction in response.

Sensitization **Sensitization** is another form of non-associative learning that involves an altered response after the presentation of a single sensory cue. Unlike habituation, sensitization involves an increase, as opposed to a decrease, in response with learning. A good example of sensitization is the sound of a dripping tap, particularly if you are concentrating hard. The dripping noise appears to become louder, and gets more irritating.

sensitization a form of non-associative learning whereby repeated experience of a stimulus results in an increasingly bigger response to that stimulus.

Both habituation and sensitization make good adaptive sense. In the case of habituation, when harmless stimuli are repeatedly presented, continuing to respond to them is a waste of energy and may prevent you from noticing an important change in the environment. In the case of sensitization, an extreme unexpected stimulus may signal danger, so noticing smaller stimuli more easily afterwards may be helpful for survival.

PSYCHOLOGY AROUND US   Living by the Railway

Tassi *et al.* (2010) investigated the long-term effects of living next to a railway on sleep and cardiovascular reactivity. They took 20 men who lived next to a railway track and 20 men who lived in a quiet environment and compared their sleep in the laboratory on both a quiet night and a night with 30 simulated trains passing by. They found that those who lived next to the railway showed less sleep disturbance, and less of a cardiovascular response to the noise of the trains, than those who did not live next to the railway line. This is because of a long-term habituation to the noise of the trains in those who lived by the railway.

Habituation in action. When this child is first given letter blocks, she responds to them happily and learns various ways to play with them (left). However, after months of repeated presentations with the blocks, she is less enthusiastic and excited by the stimuli (right).

Source: Left photo: ©Mango Productions/Corbis. Right photo: ©Simon Jarraett/Corbis.

Non-Associative Learning

 **WHAT HAPPENS IN THE BRAIN?**

Since habituation and sensitization are very basic forms of learning, they occur in animals with very simple nervous systems. Neuroscientists have taken advantage of this and used one of the simplest – the nervous system of *Aplysia* (a sea slug) – to study the biological basis of non-associative learning (Kandel, 2001).

Aplysia do not have brains or spinal cords. They do, however, have some of the largest neurons in the animal kingdom. Their neurons can actually be seen with the naked eye. This makes it easy to record from the neurons using electrodes, as described in Chapter 5. Researchers have been able to use electrode recordings from *Aplysia* to develop a thorough understanding of how simple nervous systems change in response to learning.

If you touch an *Aplysia* once lightly, it will withdraw two vulnerable parts of its body: the gill and the siphon. If you touch it multiple times lightly, eventually this response will diminish because the slug becomes habituated to the touch. Recordings from the *Aplysia*'s neurons have shown that when habituation occurs the amount of neural activity in the motor neurons (the neurons that control the gill and siphon muscles) goes down as the animal is repeatedly touched (Gingrich & Byrne, 1985). The neural activity decreases because the neurotransmitter in the synapse between the *Apylsia*'s sensory neuron and the motor neuron becomes depleted when repeatedly presented with the tactile stimulus.

Eventually, the amount of neurotransmitter is so diminished that the synapse can no longer be activated. At this point, the same level of sensory stimulus no longer causes the *Aplysia* to withdraw the gill and siphon (Figure 9.2).

To study sensitization, scientists apply an electric shock to the tail of the *Aplysia*. It responds to this shock with a strong reflex, withdrawing the gill and siphon. Then they apply a very mild tactile stimulus to the *Aplysia*'s body. It still strongly withdraws its gill and siphon because it is sensitized. The withdrawal is much stronger than in an animal that did not have the initial shock to the tail.

Sensitization can occur even when an *Aplysia* has become habituated to a stimulus (Hawkins *et al.*, 2006). If habituation occurs as a result of neurotransmitter depletion, how can activity in the same motor neuron be restored so that sensitization results? The answer lies in the fact that the tail shock activates another set of neurons, called *interneurons*. Interneurons work to enhance and intensify the weakened sensory neuron input to the synapse of the sensory and motor nerves. With the help of interneurons, the motor neurons can produce the strengthened withdrawal response.

Although there are many important differences between *Aplysia* and humans, it is likely that these basic mechanisms, or something very close to them, also operate in more complex nervous systems, such as our own. We, too, may experience habituation because of depleted neurotransmitter and sensitization because of the activation of interneurons.

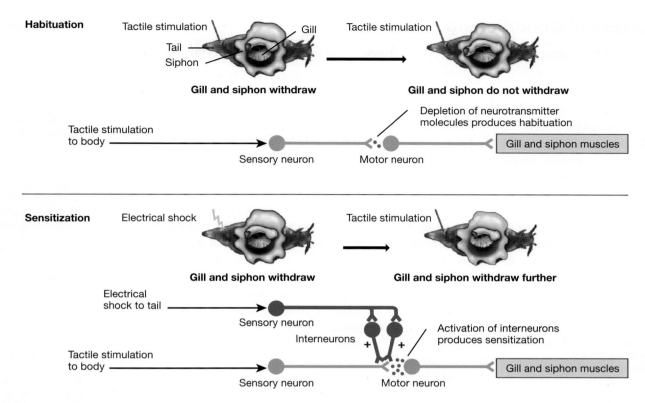

FIGURE 9.2 Habituation and sensitization in the sea slug. (Top) The sea slug gill and siphon withdrawal reflex becomes habituated to a repeated tactile stimulus when the neurotransmitter needed to activate its motor neurons has been depleted. (Bottom) After habituation, the sea slug can experience sensitization to mild tactic stimulation if it is first exposed to a particularly powerful and unpleasant stimulus like electric shock – a stimulus that activates a group of neurons called interneurons, which stimulate the animal's motor neurons, which in turn produce responses to even mild tactile stimuli.

Associative Learning

Much learning in more complex organisms, like humans, is not non-associative learning. Rather, it is associative learning that involves making connections between two or more stimuli. Most of the learning you engage in as a student is highly associative. Learning course material involves connecting many concepts and facts to gain an overall understanding of a certain subject. Two major types of associative learning are *Pavlovian* (or classical) conditioning and *operant* (or instrumental) conditioning. In classical conditioning, as we will see next, we come to associate two stimuli, eventually responding in a similar way to both. We will then examine instrumental conditioning, by which we come to learn the relationship between our behaviours and their consequences.

Before You Go On

What Do You Know?

1. What is learning?
2. What happens in synapses during habituation?
3. What happens in synapses during sensitization?

What Do You Think?

Give an example from your own life of non-associative learning.

Classical Conditioning

LEARNING OBJECTIVE 2

Describe the basic processes of classical conditioning, and explain how classical conditioning is relevant to learning.

One type of associative learning was accidentally discovered, around the turn of the previous century, by a Russian physiologist named Ivan Pavlov. His discoveries paved the way to a systematic investigation of associative learning in the laboratory, and versions of his original research methods are still being studied in psychology laboratories today.

Pavlov was interested in understanding the role of the salivary reflex in digestion. To do so, he conducted research on dogs; his laboratory method is shown in Figure 9.3. During his studies, Pavlov noticed that his dogs were salivating even when food was not present: what he termed 'psychic salivation' (Pavlov, 1927). They salivated when the laboratory assistants arrived or when they heard noises that signalled their arrival. Pavlov recognized this as evidence that the dogs had learnt that the laboratory assistant was a signal for food. Thus, they were demonstrating a behavioural response (salivation) in anticipation of getting food. Pavlov investigated this basic form of associative learning

Pavlovian or **classical conditioning** a form of associative learning whereby a neutral stimulus is paired with a salient stimulus so that eventually the neutral stimulus predicts the salient stimulus.

using a systematic approach that is now called **Pavlovian** or **classical conditioning** (Windholz, 1987). He used a variety of stimuli, including a metronome, tactile stimulation, a buzzer and heat.

How Does Classical Conditioning Work?

In classical conditioning, a person or animal learns to associate a previously neutral stimulus with an **unconditioned stimulus (US)**, one that normally elicits a physiological response. Because this response does not have to be learnt, it is called the **unconditioned response (UR)**. After being repeatedly paired with the unconditioned stimulus, the neutral stimulus alone eventually elicits the physiological response. After that happens, the stimulus is no longer neutral. The person or animal has now formed an association between the two paired stimuli. The previously neutral stimulus is now called the **conditioned stimulus (CS)**, and the physiological response it elicits is called the **conditioned response (CR)**. This process is summarized in Figure 9.4.

unconditioned stimulus (US) a stimulus that on its own elicits a response.

unconditioned response (UR) a physical response elicited by an unconditioned stimulus; it does not need to be learnt.

conditioned stimulus (CS) a neutral stimulus that eventually elicits the same response as an unconditioned stimulus with which it has been paired.

conditioned response (CR) a physical response elicited by a conditioned stimulus; it is usually the same as the unconditioned response.

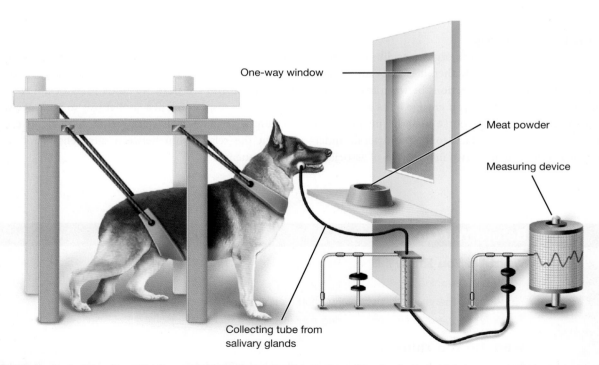

One-way window

Meat powder

Measuring device

Collecting tube from salivary glands

FIGURE 9.3 Pavlov's setup for collecting and measuring salivation in dogs. The dog is placed in a harness and given a bowl of meat powder. A tube from the salivary gland collects the saliva, which is measured and recorded.

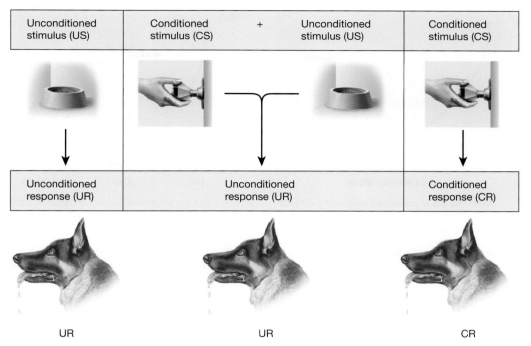

Unconditioned stimulus (US)	Conditioned stimulus (CS) + Unconditioned stimulus (US)	Conditioned stimulus (CS)
Unconditioned response (UR)	Unconditioned response (UR)	Conditioned response (CR)
UR	UR	CR

FIGURE 9.4 Classical conditioning. The sequence of classical conditioning is shown here, from left to right. (1) The US (meat powder) produces the UR (salivation). (2) During conditioning the US is paired with a CS, a neutral or conditioned stimulus (a sound such as a door-knob being turned). (3) After conditioning, the CS alone produces the conditioned (learnt) response of salivation.

For Pavlov's dogs, the unconditioned stimulus was food. Their unconditioned response was to salivate. While initially it was the arrival of a laboratory assistant that was a neutral stimulus to the dogs, in his further experiments it was the use of discrete and controllable stimuli such as metronomes. After repeated pairings of the metronome with food, the metronome became a conditioned stimulus. The dogs salivated when they heard the metronome. Their salivation, once an unconditioned response to the food, was now a conditioned response to the metronome.

Classical conditioning is not just for the dogs, however. It happens to people, too. When cancer patients receive chemotherapy (US) which makes them sick (UR), the hospital itself (CS) can elicit nausea and vomiting (CR). This phenomenon of anticipatory nausea and vomiting is distressing for the patients, and can interfere with treatment. However, by understanding the learning mechanisms responsible, we can try to find ways of stopping the learning, and improving outcomes for these patients (Symonds & Hall, 2012).

Timing plays an important role in the formation of learnt associations. When the US and the CS are paired together, the CS must come slightly before the US. The appearance of the CS allows the prediction that the US will soon appear. Patients attend hospital, and then they receive the nausea-inducing chemotherapy, for example. If a neutral stimulus follows an unconditioned one, the neutral stimulus has little or no predictive value, making it unlikely that an association between the stimuli will form. If the patients went to the hospital after feeling nauseous, the hospital would never provoke anticipatory nausea and vomiting. Not surprisingly, learning is usually more robust when there are many CS–US pairings.

Pavlov also showed that the learnt response to the CS could be eliminated, by presenting the CS over and over again without also presenting the US. Pavlov trained a dog that a 30 s metronome signalled food, and the animal salivated during presentation of the metronome signal. The metronome was then played seven times, with no food delivered. At the end of this *extinction training*, the dog then did not salivate when the metronome was played. Current theory suggests that extinction does not represent 'unlearning' or forgetting but rather a process by which the previously learnt CR is actively inhibited (Baeyens *et al.*, 1995).

Evidence that the CS–US pairing is not really 'unlearnt' after extinction training can be observed by allowing time to pass with no training after extinction has occurred. In this case, the CR will often re-emerge at a later date – a phenomenon called **spontaneous recovery** (Figure 9.5). In Pavlov's experiment, when the metronome was played again 23 minutes after

> **spontaneous recovery** re-emergence of a conditioned response some time after extinction has occurred.

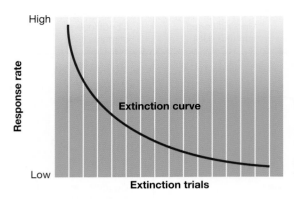

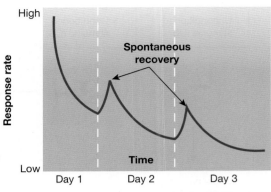

When the CS is presented repeatedly without the US, the individual's learnt response gradually decreases until extinction occurs.

But the information about the previous CS–US pairing is not lost, and the extinguished response spontaneously reappears.

FIGURE 9.5 Extinction and spontaneous recovery.

the last extinction trial, he found that the dog salivated again, demonstrating spontaneous recovery, and providing evidence that extinction is not unlearning: it is obvious that the previously learnt information has not been lost or forgotten, because it can be spontaneously recovered without any further learning.

Examples of Classical Conditioning

Autoshaping In *autoshaping*, a CS such as a light is presented to the animal. That stimulus is paired with a food reward. The animal will approach that stimulus, indicating that the stimulus has come to signal the food. There are several interesting features of autoshaped responding. The form of the response depends on the US, suggesting that the identity of the US is somehow encoded in the association. This suggests that there is a CS–US association, rather than simply a stimulus–response (S–R) association.

Conditioned Fear In *conditioned fear* experiments, animals are given a neutral stimulus, such as a tone, which is followed by a mild foot shock. The shock causes pain, and so the neutral stimulus becomes a conditioned stimulus (CS) for fear. An animal obviously cannot tell us it is frightened, but we can observe a number of changes in its behaviour. A frightened animal will *freeze* – stop all movement. By videoing the animal's behaviour, we can compare the amount of freezing when the CS is present and the amount when it is not. This will give us a measure of the strength of the association between the CS and the US.

Conditioned Taste Aversion It makes evolutionary sense that animals can learn to avoid foods that cause them

to be ill, and this has been exploited in the laboratory, where animals are given distinctively flavoured food or drink, followed by an injection of lithium chloride, which makes them feel ill. This allows the animal to learn an association between the flavour and the illness, and the animal will subsequently avoid any food or drink with that flavour.

Classical Conditioning WHAT HAPPENS IN THE BRAIN?

Extinction training and spontaneous recovery show that classical conditioning creates lasting changes in the nervous system in order for us to make a CS–US association. After extinction training, these changes persist; the nervous system does not go back to the way it was before conditioning. Instead, the extinction training is a type of newer learning in itself, creating further changes that allow us to suppress the conditioned response.

Researchers have used another form of classical conditioning, conditioning of the eye-blink response, to learn more about where nervous system changes occur in classical conditioning. In this procedure, humans or animals are conditioned to associate a tone (CS) with a US, such as a mild shock to the eyelid or a puff of air to the eye, that normally elicits an eye blink. Eventually, eye blink becomes a conditioned response, elicited in response to the CS tone alone (Figure 9.6). By studying animals subjected to eye-blink conditioning, scientists have found that the cerebellum is critical for this type of learning (Attwell *et al.*, 2001). Inactivation of the cerebellar cortex in rabbits during training abolishes learning. Ramnani *et al.* (2000), using fMRI, found that following eye-blink conditioning in humans there were learning-related changes in the cerebellum and in motor/premotor cortex.

Training →	Tone (CS)	Puff of air (US)	Blink (UR)
After training →	Tone (CS)	Blink (CR)	Puff of air (US)

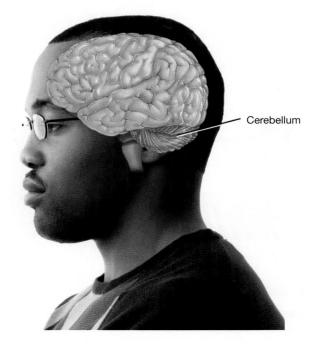

Cerebellum

FIGURE 9.6 Eye-blink conditioning. Researchers have relied on eye-blink conditioning in animals to learn more about the brain processes involved in classical conditioning. In this procedure, a CS or neutral stimulus (a tone) is followed by a stimulus (such as a puff of air) that causes the animal to blink (UR). After conditioning, the animal will blink after hearing the tone and before receiving the stimulus. Researchers found that the cerebellum is critical for learning the association between the CS and UR.

Source: Jose Luis Pelaez/Blend Images/Getty Images, Inc.

Experiments in rats and humans have demonstrated that many neural structures are involved in classical conditioning, and that the communication between the structures is very important. In a series of experiments using autoshaping in rats, Parkinson *et al.* (2000) demonstrate that limbic structures such as the nucleus accumbens, anterior cingulate cortex and central nucleus of the amygdala are all necessary for Pavlovian conditioning. They suggest that the structures work together in functional circuits.

Classical Conditioning and Fears

Although the work on classical conditioning of the salivary reflex and the eye-blink response was groundbreaking, you may have trouble seeing how classical conditioning is relevant to human learning outside of the laboratory. Some of us experience a mild version of classical conditioning when we feel hungry around a certain time of day, but other forms of classical conditioning are probably much more relevant to human life.

Phobias One such example is called *fear conditioning*. Fear conditioning was first studied by the American psychologist John Watson. Perhaps Watson's best-known study involved the classical conditioning of a human baby named *Little Albert*. Watson presented baby Albert with a white rat, an initially neutral stimulus. Albert initially reached for the rat, but as soon as he touched it, he was subjected to a loud crashing noise that startled him, causing him to jump violently and bury his face in a mattress. This pairing of the rat and the noise was repeated once more. A week later, the rat was presented again, but this time Albert did not reach for it, and was very cautious even when the rat was moved nearer. This suggested that the two training trials a week earlier had changed Albert's response to the rat. Watson and Rayner gave a further five conditioning trials with the rat and the loud noise, following which Albert would cry and crawl away from the rat, demonstrating a clearly conditioned emotional response to the rat. This conditioned emotional response persisted over a number of days. However, there is no good control condition in this experiment, and as a single case study it must be interpreted cautiously. Little Albert is a very famous case, but is frequently misreported in textbooks. Serious ethical problems are associated with Watson's line of research. Little Albert's mother was never informed of the studies, which were carried out without regard for their cruelty or the possibility that they would have a lasting negative effect on his emotional state (Field & Nightingale, 2009). Subsequent research by Fridlund *et al.* (2012) suggests that,

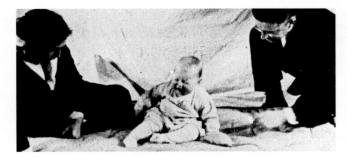

Teaching a child to fear. In a study that is ethically questionable by today's standards, John Watson and his colleague Rosalie Rayner used classical conditioning principles to teach 11-month-old little Albert to fear white rats.

Source: Courtesy Benjamin Harris.

contrary to the reports of Watson and Rayner, Albert was not a healthy or normal infant but was suffering from substantial behavioural and neurological deficits. He died aged six, of hydrocephalus. However, this is one of the first recorded examples of classical conditioning in humans and of fear conditioning in any species.

Watson's studies also led to the discovery of **stimulus generalization**, which refers to the fact that similar, but not identical, stimuli can take the place of a CS. In other words, a stimulus similar to the CS can come to produce the same response as the CS. Albert, for example, came to fear not only the white rat but also other stimuli with similarities (i.e. white and furry, including a rabbit, a seal fur coat and a Santa Claus mask). Further studies with animals in the laboratory have shown that fears are very easily learnt. Fear conditioning of laboratory rodents involves training them to associate a neutral cue (such as a tone) with a painful stimulus, such as a mild electric shock to the feet (Figure 9.7). Rodents will respond to foot shock by stopping and standing in a 'frozen' position, keeping very still. This response probably reflects the adaptive behaviour of small mammals when confronted with a predator and no way to escape; they try to minimize body movement to escape the predator's detection so they will not be eaten. Typically, just a few pairings of a tone with foot shock are needed to lead to a lasting CS–US association. The rat will freeze at the CS tone alone (LeDoux, 2003). This type of learning involves the central nucleus of the amygdala (LeDoux, 2000).

> **stimulus generalization** the situation in which similar stimuli elicit the same response as a conditioned stimulus after classical conditioning has occurred.

Rat is given electric shock to the feet in combination with a tone.

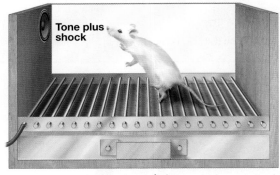

Tone plus shock

Later
Rat freezes in fear to the tone alone.

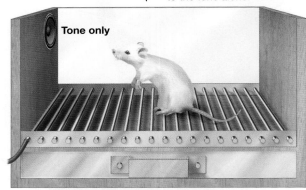

Tone only

FIGURE 9.7 Fear conditioning in rats. In fear conditioning, a laboratory rat is given an electric shock (US) to the feet just after exposure to a neutral stimulus (CS), such as a tone. Only a few pairings of the US and CS are needed for the rat to freeze in fear at the tone alone.

Phobias

OUT OF THE ORDINARY

Some scientists believe fear conditioning is the basis for a category of anxiety disorders called **phobias** (Edwards & Salkovskis, 2006; Davey, 1992). Phobias are exaggerated fears of stimuli, many of which are not dangerous. Little Albert was conditioned to have a phobia of white rats. People who suffer from phobias are believed to have learnt an association between neutral and dangerous stimuli, thus being conditioned to fear something relatively harmless.

> **phobia** an abnormal fear, often of a stimulus that is not inherently dangerous, that may arise as a result of fear conditioning.

Given the negative effects a phobia can have on a person's life, it is important that they receive therapy to enable them to lead a normal life. The theory that phobias arise from fear conditioning has led to the development of therapies that are also based on classical conditioning. In one common process, known as **systematic desensitization**, people who suffer

> **systematic desensitization** a process used to condition extinction of phobias through gradual exposure to the feared object or situation.

phobias undergo a series of extinction trials, to try to eliminate the fear response. Therapists attempt to desensitize clients to the stimuli through repeatedly exposing them to the feared object or situation *without* pairing it with a US. While exposed to the feared object, the patient ideally comes to realize that the object is not causing something painful or unwanted to happen. If little Albert had been treated with systematic desensitization, Watson might have created a pleasant, quiet situation and placed Albert and the white rat together in this situation many times until Albert no longer cried at the sight of the rat.

Systematic desensitization sometimes helps people with phobias to overcome their anxiety and function normally in the presence of the fear-inducing cue. Remember, however, that extinction trials do not produce *unlearning* but instead involve active inhibition of the previously learnt association (Baeyens *et al.*, 1995). This means that the previously learnt fear may reappear. Neuroimaging studies suggest that phobias involve abnormal activity in the amygdala, a part of the brain that is active when we experience emotions, including fear. People with phobias show rapid activation of this

PSYCHOLOGY AROUND US   Learning to Love Pain?

Some researchers made an interesting discovery when attempting to use olfactory cues to fear condition very young rat pups. Adult rats will avoid stimuli that are associated with punishment. If an odour is paired with a shock, rats will learn to distinguish that odour and avoid it in the future. This response to olfactory learning, however, is not present during the first week of life for rats. Instead, rat pups will display the opposite effect of such conditioning. Odour pairings with shock produce an approach response in the pups (Moriceau & Sullivan, 2006). Why would rat pups learn to move towards, instead of away from, an odour that predicts pain?

The answer may lie in rats' normal lifestyles. Rat pups live in the nest, staying close to their mothers for the first two weeks of life, until they start weaning. During this early time in the nest, the mother is likely to do many things to the pups that elicit pain. Mothers retrieve pups by picking them up with their teeth, and they routinely step on their babies. Thus, a tendency to form avoidant reactions to odours associated with pain would be detrimental to the survival of a very young rat.

As time passes, however, the pups become less dependent on the mother and more capable of avoiding her sharp teeth and heavy feet, and they develop a healthy aversion to painful stimuli. Around this time, avoidance becomes the natural response to odour pairings with noxious stimuli; rats at this age learn, for example, to avoid smells associated with electric shock.

Tough love. This peaceful domestic scene belies the fact that female rats are often very rough with their young pups – perhaps explaining why many rat pups are attracted to, instead of repelled by, stimuli associated with pain.
Source: Alan and Sandy Carey/Photo Researchers, Inc.

Some investigators have speculated that a similar conditioning process may contribute to the development of *attachment disorder* in humans. This condition is characterized by an inability to form healthy emotional relationships with others. People with attachment disorder do not respond positively to nurturing behaviour, and they often seek out situations that are likely to result in physical and emotional pain. Since a major cause of this condition is early childhood abuse and neglect, it is possible that excessive strengthening of associations between painful stimuli and one's caregiver during development lead to persistent maladaptive responses to social interactions.

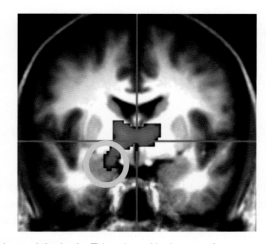

Phobias and the brain. This coloured brain scan of a cross-section of the brain reveals increased activity in a phobic individual's amygdala (region circled in yellow) while the person is looking at a feared object.
Source: L. Goossens *et al.* (2007). Amygdala Hyperfunction in Phobic Fear Normalizes After Exposure. *Biological Psychiatry, 62*(10), 1119–1125, Figure 1. Reproduced with permission.

brain region when exposed to the stimuli they fear most. As phobias diminish with extinction training, by contrast, the prefrontal cortex becomes activated. (Quirk *et al.*, 2006). The prefrontal cortex is involved in inhibiting the fear response, but the association that previously produced the response is not forgotten. Thus, phobias that have been desensitized still exist. As a result, like other classically conditioned behaviours, they are prone to spontaneous recovery.

Classical Conditioning and Taste Aversions

As mentioned above, another type of classical conditioning that has been studied in the laboratory is **conditioned taste aversion**. This involves learning an association between a particular food and a subsequent stomach illness (Garcia *et al.*, 1985). Many of us have had this type

conditioned taste aversion a form of classical conditioning whereby a previously neutral stimulus (often an odour or taste) elicits an aversive reaction after it is paired with illness (nausea).

of experience, after eating a certain type of food and then feeling nauseated. Whether the symptoms are related to the food itself, an aversion to that particular dish can persist for some time afterwards. In this case, the US is whatever caused you to feel sick, whether it is a bacterial, viral or chemical agent. The food is the CS. The unconditioned physiological response (UR) is the nausea itself. You will have this same experience of nausea again as a CR if you are exposed to this food in the future.

Some people are especially vulnerable to conditioned taste aversions. Pregnant women with severe morning sickness may develop intense aversions to foods that are followed by nausea. As mentioned above, people undergoing chemotherapy for cancer treatment can develop aversions to foods they ingest right before a chemotherapy session, owing to their association with the nausea that is a side effect of the drug.

Conditioned taste aversions happen very quickly. Laboratory research has shown that just one pairing of food and nausea are sufficient to induce an aversion. Maybe you still feel queasy at the thought of a food that you ate once before feeling sick. It is particularly impressive that these aversions form so easily, given the length of time that may pass between being exposed to the CS and starting to feel sick – sometimes several hours. Separation of a tone from a shock by several hours would make it very difficult, if not impossible, to produce fear conditioning, and yet conditioned taste aversion is highly successful with just one pairing, even when the US does not immediately follow the CS.

Scientists suggest that we are biologically ready to learn certain associations (Gaston, 1978). Clearly, the link between taste and stomach illness is physiological. This biological readiness may be rooted in our evolutionary history. The ability to associate potentially tainted food with a subsequent illness was most likely highly adaptive during human evolution. Those who could not learn by association were more likely to be poisoned and to risk poisoning members of their families. Those who readily formed such associations and avoided potentially risky food were more likely to survive and successfully reproduce. We would expect that those who survived because they could make this association would have passed this trait on to their offspring. As a result, eventually most people in the population would form conditioned taste aversions – which, indeed, is what we see today.

Biological preparedness also may help explain why animals that use odour and taste to detect food learn taste aversions so easily. These same animals have difficulty forming associations between visual or auditory cues and nausea. For some other animals, however, just the opposite is true. Animals that select their food using visual cues, such as birds, have difficulty forming conditioned aversions to flavours or odour. They can, as you would expect, be more readily conditioned to avoid visual cues (such as a coloured bead) when those cues have been paired with stomach illness. Since birds often search out food using vision (consider the bird searching for a wiggly worm), it is more natural for them to associate a visual cue, rather than a gustatory or olfactory one, with a subsequent stomach illness.

Before You Go On

What Do You Know?

4. You take your dog in the car when going to the vet. After several visits, the dog cowers and whimpers whenever he sees the car. Identify the US, UR, CS and CR in this example of conditioned fear.

5. What is conditioned taste aversion? How does it happen?

What Do You Think?

How might the principles of classical conditioning be used in advertising?

Operant Conditioning

LEARNING OBJECTIVE 3

Describe the basic processes of operant conditioning, and explain how shaping can be used to teach new behaviours.

Classical conditioning is a passive form of learning that does not involve the active participation of the learner.

In everyday life, however, the majority of our learning is active. Most of us are not passive participants in the environment. Instead, we seek out pleasurable experiences, such as good food, good company and good grades, and we do our best to avoid unpleasant experiences. We react to our environments and change our behaviour according to the responses we receive. As we continue to learn more about the environment, we change our behaviour accordingly. Psychologists use the term **operant** or **instrumental conditioning**

operant or **instrumental conditioning**
a form of associative learning whereby behaviour is modified depending on its consequences.

to describe learning that occurs when we seek to receive rewards and avoid punishment.

For some of the earliest laboratory studies of operant conditioning, psychologist Edward Thorndike created a contraption called a *puzzle box*. This was a wooden box into which Thorndike placed a hungry cat. As shown in Figure 9.8, the animal could escape from the box by pressing a pedal that pulled a string. Escape from the box led to a food reward. The first escape from the box probably happened when the cat pressed the pedal randomly. In moving about the cage, the cat would accidentally step on the pedal and would then be temporarily freed and receive a food reward. Once this occurred, however, Thorndike's cats began to more quickly find the pedal when he put them back into the box. Eventually, the cat would immediately step on the pedal when placed into the puzzle box. This work led Thorndike to develop a theory known as the **law of effect** (Thorndike, 1933). This theory states that behaviours leading to rewards are more likely to occur again, and behaviours producing unpleasant results are less likely to occur again. He proposed that the law of effect applied not only to other animals but also to humans.

> **law of effect** behaviours leading to rewards are more likely to occur again, while behaviours producing unpleasantness are less likely to occur again.

How Does Operant Conditioning Work?

Thorndike's ideas about instrumental conditioning eventually became highly influential. For several decades of the 20th century, the dominant school of thought in psychology was **behaviourism**, the systematic study and manipulation of observable behaviour (Gantt, 1980). A major goal of behaviourist psychologists was to understand the principles of instrumental, or operant, conditioning. Many researchers, such as leading behaviourist B. F. Skinner, conducted learning research with laboratory animals such as rats and pigeons.

> **behaviourism** the systematic study and manipulation of observable behaviour.

Reinforcement and Punishment In typical experiments, stimuli are provided in response to the animal's behaviour. These stimuli make it more or less likely that the animal will engage in the same behaviour again. For example, if a laboratory rat presses a lever and receives a food pellet reward, the food works as a **reinforcer**, a consequence that increases the likelihood that the rat will repeat the behaviour, or press the lever again. If, on the other hand, the rat receives an electric shock in response to a lever press, the shock works as a **punishment**, a consequence that decreases the likelihood that the rat will press the lever again.

> **reinforcer** an experience that produces an increase in a certain behaviour.

> **punishment** an experience that produces a decrease in a certain behaviour.

What happens in the brain during instrumental conditioning? It appears that somewhat different areas of our brains respond to reinforcement and punishment. Regions important for reward include the ventral tegmental area (Matsumoto & Hikosaka, 2009), the nucleus accumbens and the prefrontal cortex (Kalivas & Nakamura, 1999). These are regions that all rely on the neurotransmitter dopamine (we will return to this subject in Chapter 13 on motivation). Learning from punishment involves some of the same brain regions (Matsumoto & Hikosaka, 2009). In addition, learning from punishment involves regions important for fear and pain, including the amygdala and somatosensory cortex (Figure 9.9).

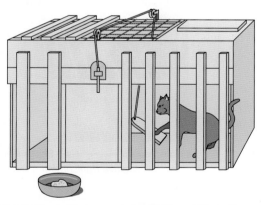

FIGURE 9.8 Thorndike's puzzle box. Edward Thorndike used a puzzle box to study operant conditioning in cats.

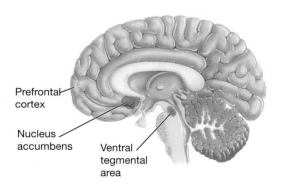

Prefrontal cortex

Nucleus accumbens

Ventral tegmental area

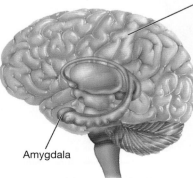

Primary somatosensory cortex

Amygdala

FIGURE 9.9 Brain areas involved in instrumental learning. Different regions of the brain are involved in reward and in punishment. Learning from reward (left) involves the ventral tegmental area, nucleus accumbens and prefrontal cortex. Learning from punishment (right) involves the amygdala and the somatosensory cortex.

positive reinforcement the presentation of a pleasant consequence following a behaviour.

negative reinforcement the removal of a negative consequence as a result of behaviour.

positive punishment the presentation of an unpleasant consequence following a behaviour.

negative punishment the removal of a pleasant stimulus as a consequence of a behaviour.

Reinforcement and punishment can be either negative or positive. Both forms of reinforcement – positive and negative – increase the likelihood that a response will occur, and both forms of punishment decrease the likelihood of a response recurring.

- **Positive reinforcement** is what we consider to be a reward – providing a motivating stimulus.
- **Negative reinforcement** involves removing an aversive stimulus.
- **Positive punishment** involves administering an unpleasant consequence for behaviour.
- **Negative punishment** takes away something pleasant.

If we take the case of our lever-pressing rat, as shown in Figure 9.10, positive reinforcement would provide a food reward, and negative reinforcement would turn off an electric shock. Both would likely increase the rat's rate of lever pressing. Positive punishment would provide an electric shock, and negative punishment would remove food. Both would decrease lever pressing. We frequently encounter reinforcers and punishments in our day-to-day lives. Suppose you download a song by a new band and really like it, for example. Your pleasure in listening to the song works as a positive reinforcer that makes you likely to buy more of the band's songs in the future.

Types of Reinforcers Most reinforcers used in the laboratory fulfil basic biological needs. Rats are trained to press levers to get access to food, water or mates. These rewards are examples of a **primary reinforcer**: they are intrinsically pleasurable; they are rewarding by their very nature. Outside

primary reinforcer a reinforcer that is intrinsically pleasurable.

Increases Behaviour

Lever pressed ⟶ Food delivered
Positive Reinforcement

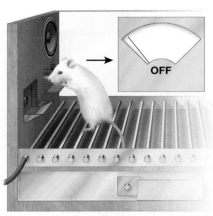

Lever pressed ⟶ Shock removed
Negative Reinforcement

Decreases Behaviour

Lever pressed ⟶ Shock delivered
Positive Punishment

Lever pressed ⟶ Food removed
Negative Punishment

FIGURE 9.10 Reinforcement and punishment. The apparatus shown here is called a Skinner box. The rat can press a lever to receive a food pellet. The floor of the box is wired to give an electric shock. The box is used to test the effects of positive and negative reinforcement and punishment on behaviour.

TABLE 9.1 Intermittent Reinforcement Schedules

Schedules Based on Number of Responses

	Definition	Response rate	Example
Fixed ratio	Reinforcement occurs after a predetermined number of responses	High	Field workers paid by the amount they harvest
Variable ratio	Reinforcement occurs after an average number of responses	High	A slot machine pays out after an average of 20 tries but the payout intervals are unpredictable

Schedules Based on Time Intervals

	Definition	Response rate	Example
Fixed interval	Reinforcement occurs after a fixed period of time	Increases with time	A worker receives a pay packet every week
Variable interval	Reinforcement occurs after varying lengths of time	Low	Work breaks occur at unpredictable intervals, such as 60 minutes, 72 minutes and 54 minutes

the lab, however, most (but not all) of our own actions do not involve behaviour designed to directly increase the likelihood of getting a primary reinforcer. For example, most people work for money, not food. In this case, money is considered to be a **secondary reinforcer**. Because secondary reinforcers are associated with primary reinforcers, they also increase the likelihood that people will engage in certain behaviours, such as work.

> **secondary reinforcer** a reinforcer that is associated with primary reinforcers.

Schedules of Reinforcement In real-life situations, we are not usually reinforced or punished every single time we perform a behaviour. You may, for example, hold the door open for the person who walks in behind you many times a day, but only receive a pleasant 'thank you' once or twice. How often a behaviour is reinforced is called the *schedule of reinforcement*. Researchers have studied the effects of different schedules of reinforcement on behaviour (Skinner, 1958; Skinner & Morse, 1958). A behaviour that is reinforced every single time it occurs is said to be an example of **continuous reinforcement**. In contrast, there are also several possible schedules of **intermittent** or **partial reinforcement**, by which the behaviour is only sometimes reinforced. The most common types of intermittent reinforcement schedules are described in Table 9.1.

> **continuous reinforcement** when behaviour is reinforced every time it occurs.

> **intermittent** or **partial reinforcement** a schedule of reinforcement where the behaviour is only followed by reinforcement some of the time.

PRACTICALLY SPEAKING   Using Punishments and Rewards to Teach Children

Although both reinforcement and punishment are effective ways of altering behaviour in laboratory learning studies, evidence from real-life situations suggests these two approaches may not be equally effective. Positive reinforcement seems to be more effective than punishment for teaching young children, for example. One exception to this general rule is in cases where children put themselves in immediate danger. At such times, a harsh telling-off may be much more effective at stopping the behaviour.

One reason that positive reinforcement seems more effective may be because punishment is often misused. Research suggests the following guidelines for using punishment effectively to promote learning:

- Positive punishment is most effective when it occurs immediately after the incorrect behaviour.
- Punishment is effective only when it is clear that the punishment is a consequence of a specific behaviour, rather than, say, a result of the teacher or caregiver's bad mood or general dislike for the child.
- Punishment works only when its aversive component outweighs any reward obtained by the behaviour. It is difficult and often unethical to devise a punishment that far outweighs the rewarding aspect of the behaviour.

Negative punishment seems to be less problematic ethically than positive punishment, but still may fail in some circumstances. Many parents and preschool teachers use a negative punishment technique called *time out* as a consequence of unwanted behaviour. This method involves removing the child from his or her surroundings and putting them in a separate location in the classroom or home. The child has thus had a pleasurable stimulus (access to playthings and classmates) removed. Time out also removes the child from the environment that may have contributed to the bad behaviour and allows them time to reflect on their behaviour. The effectiveness of time out depends on the circumstances and the individual. If the child was acting out to gain attention, then intervening, even in a negative manner, may not effectively eliminate the behaviour. Also, removal from a certain environment, such as the classroom or the dinner table, may not be sufficiently negative to alter the offensive behaviour. It may even be rewarding to some children. In general, educators and child psychologists conclude that, wherever possible, positive reinforcement of desired behaviour is the best motivator for behavioural change.

In a *ratio schedule*, reinforcement is based on the number of behavioural responses. Ratio schedules can be fixed or variable. In a **fixed ratio schedule**, people or animals are rewarded every time they make a predetermined number of responses. The loyalty card at your local coffee shop may offer you a free cup of coffee after you pay for a dozen other cups, for example. In a **variable ratio schedule**, reinforcement occurs for a predetermined average number of responses. You may have a new message on average every three times you look at your phone, but sometimes you can look six times in a row and see no messages, and other times you may have a message twice in a row.

> **fixed ratio schedule** reinforcement occurs after a specific number of responses.

> **variable ratio schedule** the number of responses required for reinforcement varies.

In an *interval schedule*, reinforcement is based on elapsed time, rather than on the number of behavioural responses. Here again, the schedule may be fixed or variable. In a **fixed interval schedule**, such as occurs with a monthly salary, you are reinforced every time a certain period of time passes. Like a variable ratio schedule, a **variable interval schedule** provides reinforcement after varying lengths of time have passed.

> **fixed interval schedule** reinforcement occurs every time a specific time period has elapsed.

> **variable interval schedule** reinforcement occurs after varying amounts of time.

Intermittent or partial reinforcement schedules are more effective than continuous reinforcement schedules at maintaining behaviour. With continuous reinforcement, the behaviour is always paired with the reward. If reinforcement stops, the elimination signals a major change in the relationship between stimulus and response. If the reward is no longer present, behaviour will probably change. By contrast, with intermittent reinforcement, the behaviour is only followed by reinforcement some of the time. When a response occurs but is not reinforced, it is not readily apparent whether the reward has stopped altogether. Continuing to engage in the behaviour makes sense in case a reward will happen.

The principles of partial reinforcement can be applied to **behaviour modification**, a planned effort to change behaviour, in children. Parents, teachers and caregivers should avoid providing intermittent reinforcement for behaviours they want to stop. When parents are trying to wean children off a bottle, for example, experts agree it is best to do so in an absolute manner. If parents sometimes allow a child who cries or whines to have the bottle, he or she will be more likely to cry or whine again in the future than if the crying and whining are never reinforced.

> **behaviour modification** a planned effort to change behaviour.

What Is Learnt in Instrumental Conditioning?

Thorndike's law of effect suggests that when a behaviour is followed by a desirable outcome that behaviour is more likely to happen again, and a behaviour that is followed by an unpleasant outcome is less likely to happen again. A consequence of this account of instrumental conditioning is that the animal does not have knowledge of the outcome of its responding. Although it makes the action – the lever press, the key peck, etc. – it has no representation of the likely consequence of that action. Researchers have tested whether this is the case by changing the value of the outcome of the action. Rats were trained to press a lever to get food, and then the food was devalued by pairing it with nausea – so that the food was no longer palatable. Animals that had undergone limited training on the instrumental action reduced their lever pressing, suggesting that they understood that the lever press would earn them the food and no longer wanted the food. However, animals that had undergone extensive lever press training carried on making responses for the food, showing that they had developed a *habit* (Adams, 1982). Further research has demonstrated that habits, and goal-directed actions, are mediated by separate neural systems. Killcross and Coutureau (2003) found that rats with lesions of the infralimbic region of the prefrontal cortex remained sensitive to the value of the food, even after they had extensive training, whereas those with lesions of the prelimbic region of the prefrontal cortex were never sensitive to the value of the food. A similar double dissociation has been found in the dorsal striatum, with lesions of the dorsolateral striatum preventing the development of habitual responding, but lesions of the dorsomedial striatum impair sensitivity to food value in instrumental responding (Yin *et al.*, 2008). These results suggest that there are multiple independent circuits within the brain that control instrumental actions.

Using Operant Conditioning to Teach New Behaviours

Until now, we have described how operant conditioning can lead people and animals to increase or decrease behaviours that they already display at least some of the time. Thorndike's cats, for example, learnt to press the pedal in the puzzle box more often than they would have by chance, but they already pressed the pedal at least once in a trial-and-error fashion before learning the association. Operant conditioning can also be used to teach people and animals entirely new, complex behaviours.

This method, called **shaping**, rewards actions that are increasingly closer to a desired final behaviour, rather than waiting for the exact behaviour to happen before providing reinforcement. Consider training a dog to roll over. First you could provide a treat if the animal lies down on its stomach. Eventually, you would require the dog to perform something closer to rolling over in order to get the same reward. You could offer a treat only when the dog lies down and turns a bit to the side. You would then carry on in this way, rewarding *successive approximations* of the desired behaviour until the dog performed the complete behavioural task. Shaping is highly effective in modifying the behaviour of animals and can be used to teach people, too. Humans regularly learn behaviour through shaping. If you are learning to dance the tango, for instance, your instructor may give you a lot of praise at first for simply moving your feet in the correct order. Later, you may win praise only for moving them without stepping on your partner's toes and so on, until only graceful, coordinated steps earn positive remarks.

> **shaping** introducing new behaviour by reinforcing small approximations of the desired behaviour.

PSYCHOLOGY AROUND US — A Whale of a Story

The entertainment establishment SeaWorld has long used shaping methods to train dolphins and killer whales, or orcas, to perform impressive tricks, including doing mid-air flips, clapping their fins and coming out of the water onto the side of the pool on command. Animal trainers begin by giving food rewards in response to minor movements in the direction of the desired behaviour. As the animal masters that component of the task, trainers make the food reward dependent on the animal completing more of the task. The result is impressive shows featuring marine mammals that appear to be having fun performing tasks that are unnatural to their species but of interest to ours. Despite the fact that these animals are smart enough to be shaped to perform tricks, some unfortunate incidents have highlighted the difficulty in using very large and powerful animals with a natural instinct to kill for entertainment purposes. In 2010, a killer whale at SeaWorld aggressively drowned his trainer. Over the many years of his captivity, this same animal had been responsible for two other human deaths. These events underscore the fact that, although shaping can profoundly modify behaviour, the underlying instinctual responses remain.

As with classical conditioning, we should note that biology plays a role in determining how easy or difficult a particular learning task will be for a certain species. To be sure, some trainers appear to be quite capable of teaching animals to engage in a wide range of behaviours that these animals do not naturally perform. Nevertheless, it turns out that there are limits to this kind of learning.

Some of Skinner's students tried to train raccoons to put coins in a piggy bank, for example. Through shaping techniques, raccoons can be trained to pick up a single coin and place it in a piggy bank. However, raccoons are known for their natural tendency to wash food before eating it. If they are given more than one coin at a time, their natural tendency to wash objects seems to interfere with the shaping techniques. Instead of putting the coins into the bank, they rub them together (Breland & Breland, 1961). Biology also places constraints on language learning. Other than humans, only certain species of birds, like parrots, can be taught to speak (and their speech is generally thought to be a form of mimicry). No matter how much reinforcement or punishment is provided, biological factors make speech impossible for most animals. (We will return to this topic in Chapter 11.)

Learned Helplessness

Sometimes, our prior learning experiences can cause problems with later learning. One problem that can arise as the result of operant conditioning is a phenomenon known as **learned helplessness**. In this situation, people (or animals) are conditioned by past experiences in which they were unable to escape punishment. This conditioning then leads them to accept punishing consequences in later situations

> **learned helplessness** a situation in which repeated exposure to inescapable punishment eventually produces a failure to make escape attempts.

YOUR BRAIN AND BEHAVIOUR What Happens in the Brain in Spatial Learning: Taxi Drivers

Source: Jupiter Images/Thinkstock/Getty Images, Inc.

London taxi drivers must learn and remember a large amount of spatial information, known as *the Knowledge*, to perform their jobs efficiently. Perhaps it is not surprising, then, that this job has been linked to differences in brain regions that are important for spatial navigation learning. MRI studies of London taxi drivers, for example, showed that they have a slightly larger hippocampus than people of the same age who do not have taxicab training (Maguire *et al.*, 2000), and larger than bus drivers, who simply follow the same route every day (Maguire *et al.*, 2006)

In a follow-up study, Woollett and Maguire (2011) examined the brains of trainee taxi-drivers, before and after the Knowledge training. They found that those who successfully passed the Knowledge increased the volume of the grey matter in their posterior hippocampus. Those who did not succeed, and control participants, did not. There have been similar findings in animals, where living in a complex environment, learning and physical activity all increase the size and number of neurons in the hippocampus in laboratory animals (Shors, 2009; Leuner *et al.*, 2006; Mirescu & Gould, 2006).

---

when they could actually avoid them (Seligman *et al.*, 1980). For instance, research with rats has found that, after repeated inescapable shocks to the tail, if rats are given the option of escaping a foot shock by moving to a different area in the testing cage many of them fail to do so (Weiss & Glazer, 1975). The rats that could not escape the tail shocks failed at first to learn how to stop a shock to the foot. Instead, they stayed put and took the punishment. Learned helplessness is thought by some researchers to be an animal model of depression (Porsolt, 2000). Humans with depression are often unmotivated to act in order to change the stimuli negatively affecting their lives, and some theorists suggest that these people have learnt this pattern of inaction from earlier, perhaps unrelated, experiences in which they were unable to make the changes they wanted. Learned helplessness also may partially explain some of the characteristics of battered spouse syndrome (Clements & Sawhney, 2000). Repeated, inescapable abuse may cause learned helplessness. The victims can become withdrawn and unable to respond to protect themselves, even if there is a way to escape the abusive situation.

Learning and Thinking

Strict behavioural psychologists have argued that all types of learning are forms of conditioning. Indeed, during the 20th century, some prominent behaviourists argued that everything we do results from either classical or operant conditioning. Many also suggested that only observable changes in behaviour should be taken as evidence of learning. This interpretation, however, seems overly simplistic when you consider how much knowledge you have collected throughout your life without clearly identifiable reinforcement. Indeed, research has shown that learning does seem to happen without any obvious reinforcement.

Spatial Navigation Learning Let's look at an example of a study that showed how learning could occur without reinforcement. This study was designed to assess how well reinforcement works to teach rats **spatial navigation**. Perhaps not surprisingly, researchers can train laboratory rodents to navigate through a

spatial navigation a type of learning that involves forming associations among stimuli relevant to navigating in space.

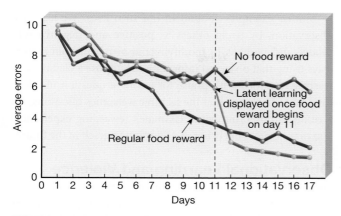

FIGURE 9.11 Latent learning in rats. Rats are motivated to explore a maze without reinforcement. When given a food reward, they make fewer errors in finding the quickest route to the end of the maze and the reward. When the reward is introduced after the rats have explored the maze, the error rate drops sharply, indicating that learning occurred during exploration.

Source: Based on Gazzaniga, M. S. & Heatherton, T. F. (2006). *Psychological Science* (2nd edn). New York: WW Norton, p. 230.

maze by providing them with reinforcement along the way. This approach, which is a form of shaping, involves providing food rewards as rats move in the correct direction.

Without reinforcers, rats typically explore a maze, but are not motivated to find the quickest route from start to finish. However, when rats are first allowed to explore the maze and then provided with reinforcement, they learn the task much faster than rats who have never explored the maze before. Studies of this type show that the rats were learning information about the spatial environment inside the maze while they were randomly exploring it – even though they were not receiving any reinforcement for learning. The fact that they were able to navigate the maze much faster than rats that had not explored it earlier showed that they had learnt and retained information about the layout of the maze as they explored it without reinforcement. When reinforcement was introduced, the rats demonstrated their previous, or *latent*, learning (Figure 9.11) (Tolman & Gleitman, 1949).

You can probably imagine yourself in a similar situation. Say, for instance, you have a job interview in a particular part of town. You will find the office where your interview is to take place much more easily if you have already explored the neighbourhood while riding your bicycle or driving than if you have never been to that area before.

This particular example of learning spatial navigation without obvious reinforcement probably represents another form of biological readiness for certain types of learning. Rodents, and probably humans, seem naturally ready to form maps of the spaces around them through learning (O'Keefe, 1990). Learning spatial information about their environments would have had adaptive value to our ancestors, who would have needed this information to find food, shelter and escape routes from threats. The ability to learn information about spatial navigation requires an intact hippocampus, a brain region that is also important for learning about other non-spatial information (Morris, 1990).

Insight Learning Another type of learning that cannot be readily explained in behaviourist terms is **insight learning**. Most of us have had this experience. We may puzzle and struggle over a difficult problem. Then, some time later – perhaps while we are not even working on the problem – we may have an 'ah-ha!' or 'eureka' moment, when we suddenly realize how to solve the problem. Indeed, the solution may seem obvious. Some individuals even report solving problems in their dreams. The Nobel laureate Otto Loewi, who discovered the actions of neurotransmitter chemicals, claims to have come up with his definitive study while sleeping, after pondering the question over and over while awake (Loewi, 1957). Although finding the solutions to our problems in our dreams is fairly rare, insight learning is widespread and is another type of learning that does not involve any obvious reinforcement.

> **insight learning** a sudden realization of a solution to a problem or a leap in understanding new concepts.

Language learning is yet another kind of learning that does not neatly fit into a behavioural explanation. As we discuss in detail in Chapter 11, the principles of association and reinforcement cannot fully explain a number of aspects of how we learn to understand and use our native languages.

Before You Go On

What Do You Know?

6. What are positive reinforcement and negative reinforcement? What are the effects of each on behaviour?

7. What is learned helplessness?

8. What is spatial navigation learning, and why is it difficult to explain using operant conditioning?

What Do You Think?

How could you use operant conditioning principles to get a flatmate or child to regularly hang up his or her coat instead of throwing it on the floor?

Observational Learning

LEARNING OBJECTIVE 4

Define observational learning, and summarize concerns about observational learning from the media.

In both classical and operant conditioning, we learn through experiencing something ourselves. But we can also learn by observing others. Not only humans but also other animals have this ability.

Observation and Modelling

Studies of animal behaviour in natural habitats have shown that members of certain species learn tasks by watching each other. A good example of this can be seen with a troop of Japanese macaques. Monkeys in this troop routinely wash sweet potatoes before eating them. This is not a natural behaviour practised by macaques all over the world. It began with one innovative monkey, who first started washing sweet potatoes after the potatoes were given to the macaques by researchers. After observing this behaviour, other members of the group started to wash their own sweet potatoes. Similar behaviour has been observed with other foods (Nakamichi *et al.*, 1998). Other studies have reported that **observational learning** – learning from watching the behaviour of others – has led dolphins and members of certain primate and bird species to use innovative tools (Krützen *et al.*, 2005). Rats that have to push a joystick left or right to get food were more likely to push it left if they had seen a demonstrator animal push it left (Heyes *et al.*, 1992). Through observational learning, behaviours can be passed between generations of animals. That is, parents or older members of a group engage in behaviour that the young observe. Observation leads to mimicry, or **modelling**. This change in behaviour is concrete proof that learning has occurred.

> **observational learning** a type of learning that occurs without overt training but in response to watching the behaviour.

> **modelling** mimicking the behaviour of others.

In addition, observation can affect other types of behaviour that indirectly signal that learning has occurred. A good example of this can be seen with reward studies in capuchin monkeys (Brosnan & De Waal, 2003). This species can be trained rather easily to perform a task for a food reward, such as a cucumber slice. If, however, the trained monkey observes another monkey receiving a more desirable reward (e.g. a grape) for performing the same task, the monkey will respond by refusing to carry out the task again. This suggests not only that capuchin monkeys have an internal representation of reward value but also that they have used the experience of observing the consequences of another monkey's behaviour to modify their own.

Similar examples abound in our own lives. We learn by observation, by using others as positive and negative role models and, perhaps, by modifying our own behaviour in new ways using that observed information. Suppose a classmate is warmly rewarded with praise for asking a question in a lecture. You now know that the lecturer welcomes questions. As a result of observing your classmate's rewarding experience, you may be more likely to ask a question yourself in the future.

Observational Learning and Violence

Some of the most famous experiments of observational learning in children were carried out by Albert Bandura. Bandura was interested in whether children learnt violent behavioural responses by observing aggression. He showed children a movie of a woman beating up an inflatable clown punching bag, called a Bobo doll (Figure 9.12) (Bandura *et al.*, 1961).

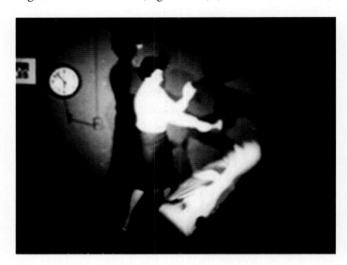

FIGURE 9.12 Aggressive modelling. Bandura found that children learnt to abuse an inflatable clown doll by observing an adult hit the doll.

Source: Courtesy of Albert Bandura.

After the movie, the children were allowed to play in a room full of toys, including a Bobo doll. Those who had previously watched the Bobo video were twice as likely as those who did not watch it to behave violently towards the doll.

The researchers further investigated whether observational learning would be influenced by information about reward and punishment. Indeed, they found such a relationship. The children who saw a video in which beating up the Bobo doll led to rewards, such as candy and praise, were more likely to act aggressively towards the doll than those who observed the woman being punished for beating Bobo.

Bandura's studies, and a great deal of research that followed, have raised concerns that violence on television, in movies and in video games promotes aggressive behaviour among viewers, especially children (Bandura, 1978). Some studies have demonstrated a convincing link between excessive television watching and aggressive behaviour in children (Johnson *et al.*, 2002). The number of violent acts in a short stretch of children's programming can be disturbingly high. The number of such acts is typically highest in cartoons, where there are no real consequences of violent actions. In fact, cartoon characters seem to have many lives, often returning unscathed after experiencing what would be horribly damaging events in reality. Cartoons use falling anvils and such for humour, but the research suggests we should consider the possible impacts of cartoon watching on aggressive behaviours.

Although there is strong correlational evidence that television watching is associated with aggressive behaviour in children, remember from our discussion of correlations in Chapter 2 that a correlation can only tell us that two variables are related. Correlations do not tell us whether one variable causes the other. Some studies suggest that kids who already behave aggressively may prefer to watch more violent TV. Recall, too, that correlations only describe the relationship between the two variables specified. Other factors may influence both of those variables. In the studies of TV watching, for example, it is clear that media violence is not the only factor contributing to children's aggression. Some studies have shown that children who watch excessive television are also less likely to have other positive influences in their lives than children whose viewing is limited. Heavy TV watching is associated with low socioeconomic status and low parental involvement, so these children may lack parental or neighbourhood influences against aggression.

PSYCHOLOGY AROUND US　A Positive Influence

A great deal of research has focused on how observational learning and modelling can teach socially unacceptable behaviours, like violence, to young children. Fewer studies have focused on the opposite situation – where non-aggressive and affiliative behaviours are passively learnt by observation. An interesting example of this situation was detected in a troop of baboons living in Africa. As a result of feeding at a rubbish dump associated with a tourist area, the adult male baboons in one particular troop died. Since adult male baboons are often aggressive, the frequency of violent interactions in the group declined considerably when the adult males died. Over the years, new adolescent males joined the group from outside (around the time of puberty, male baboons typically leave their original group to seek a new social scene). As they matured, they adopted the peaceful culture of their new companions. These baboons groomed one another and were able to be in close physical contact and fought less than had they been in a typical baboon troop. This observation is an interesting example of cultural transmission of prosocial behaviour through observational learning (Sapolsky & Share, 2004).

Before You Go On

What Do You Know?
9. What is observational learning and what does it demonstrate when it happens?
10. What has research shown about media violence and aggressive behaviour in child viewers?

What Do You Think?
How might the media be used to get children – or adults – to mimic positive social behaviours?

Factors that Facilitate Learning

LEARNING OBJECTIVE 5
Define massed and spaced practice, and tell what conditions are best for learning semantic material.

It is clear that we can learn in a variety of ways: through simple habituation and sensitization, by linking stimuli in classical conditioning, by associating our behaviour to its consequences through operant conditioning or by using our observations of the consequences of another's behaviours as a model for our own. We also know that several factors can affect how well each of these learning methods works. Timing, as we have seen, is crucial in classical conditioning. It can also affect other types of learning. Other important factors in learning include the context in which we learn, the amount of attention we pay when trying to learn and the amount of rest we get.

Timing

You have probably noticed that you learn more information when you study for an exam over an extended period, as opposed to cramming for the test by 'pulling an all-nighter.' Why is this?

Much of the learning that you, as a student, undertake on a daily basis involves acquiring information about facts. Psychologists distinguish between this type of learning, called *semantic learning*, and *episodic learning*, which is learning about events in our own lives. We will return to the distinction between episodic and semantic learning in the next chapter, dealing with memory, but we can offer some advice now about how to better learn semantic material.

Most importantly, repetition helps. Semantic learning is easier when you are exposed to the same material many times, rather than just once. For example, you are more likely to learn the material from a class if you read the textbook, then listen carefully in class and then review your notes and textbook than if you only read the book or only go to class.

You will also learn better if some time passes between these exposures. When learning trials occur close together, as they do when you try to cram all your reading and reviewing into the night before a big test, they are referred to as *massed*. When they are separated in time, they are referred to as *spaced*. The difference in efficiency between massed and spaced trials for learning has been demonstrated not only in the laboratory but also in real life. Massed studying, or cramming, is ineffective for two reasons. First, it does not allow enough time between learning trials to maximize learning and, second, it leads to sleep deprivation.

Context

Psychologists have long recognized that context plays an important role in learning and remembering. For example, if you take a test in the same location in which you learnt the material, you are more likely to do your best. Godden and Baddeley (1975) investigated this by having divers learn lists of words either on land, or underwater, and then remember the lists either in the same context or the different context. The divers remembered words best in the same context in which they had learnt them. However, when you are tested on material, you invariably do the test in a different place than you do the learning. Therefore, if you want to recall information in a new context, you need to overcome the context-dependency of learning. Evidence from Smith (1984) suggests that this may be the opposite of what your parents or school teachers have advised: the longstanding recommendation has been to find a quiet place with good lighting in which to do your nightly homework. However, Smith (1984) demonstrates that studying in several different locations increases the likelihood that you will recall that information in a new context. Smith and Rothkopf (1984) tested this explicitly using an eight-hour statistics course that was delivered by video. Students learnt better when they split the eight hours across four rooms than if they had all of the videos in one room.

Awareness and Attention

We are often unaware that we are learning. Non-associative learning and some forms of associative learning – including some forms of classical conditioning and procedural, or motor-skill, learning – often occur without the individual realizing that information has been acquired. There is fierce debate about the role of awareness in human evaluative conditioning. Associations are important in the formation of many of our preferences: for example, our liking of foods depends upon our previous experiences with those foods, but we are often unaware of those associations (De Houwer *et al.*, 2001). Observational learning also often occurs without awareness, as in the case of children who model aggressive behaviour they see on television. Indeed, in some instances, awareness and excessive attention can actually interfere with learning. Gymnasts, for example, sometimes find that mentally rehearsing a new move actually breaks their concentration and interferes with their performance when they are trying to learn a new move.

In most instances, however, greater awareness and attention enhance learning. Many forms of associative learning, including semantic and episodic learning, require awareness and are greatly enhanced by attentional processes. You have probably experienced this first-hand on days when you are feeling tired and have difficulty concentrating on your coursework. The information you read or hear in lectures at these times is much less likely to be learnt than material presented at a time when you are more attentive.

Because attention is so important to learning, it is worth considering an important question: how does attention work? Scientists have found that the answer to this question depends on the circumstances. Some attentional processes are automatic and occur when a particular stimulus is very different from those that surround it. Psychologist Anne Treisman studied attention to visual stimuli and showed that in the case of a simple scene if one stimulus differs considerably from others it will immediately grab our attention, a phenomenon referred to as *pop-out*. In order for pop-out to work, the stimulus must be singularly different from the surroundings (Treisman & Kanwisher, 1998). As scenes become increasingly complicated, pop-out is less likely to help guide attentional processes. Instead, we must rely on an active searching method, where we examine material in search of the most relevant stimuli. Anyone who has enjoyed children's books like *Where's Wally?* or *I Spy*, where the object you are searching for is buried in a complex visual scene, has used an *active searching* attentional process. Recall from Chapter 7 the distinction between bottom-up and top-down processing. Pop-out, because of its simplicity and speed, employs bottom-up processing, while active searching, because of the need to draw on cognitive processes and memory, uses top-down processing.

Sometimes attentional processes can get in the way: if information is inherently contradictory, for example, attending to one stimulus can block our ability to attend to the relevant one. A good example of this is the *Stroop effect*, a psychological test that involves presenting a list of words printed in different colours. Each of the words is a colour word (green, red, black, blue), but each is printed in colour that differs from the colour the word refers to. For example, the word *black* may be printed in green ink. Participants are asked to list the colours of the ink, thus ignoring the word content. This is very difficult to do quickly, because bottom-up attentional processing interferes with the ability to focus on just one of the contradictory stimuli (Herd *et al.*, 2006).

What can we do, then, to maximize our attention to relevant information while trying to learn? First, it is a good idea to identify relevant pieces of information and focus on those throughout your reading. If your professor mentions topics repeatedly in class, you may use an active searching method to find similar material in your readings. Second, avoid dividing your attention. Our attentional processes are generally at their best when they are focused on one task. Performing other behaviours, such as answering text messages or watching TV while trying to study usually interferes with our ability to attend to relevant material. In fact, one study showed that people who engaged in a high degree of multi-tasking are less likely to perform well overall (Ophira *et al.*, 2009).

PSYCHOLOGY AROUND US   Too Much Social Networking?

According to one report, students who use Facebook while they study get lower grades than those who do not (Kirschner & Karpinski, 2010). Specifically, the research found that students who had Facebook running while they studied – even if it was simply running in the background – tended to have lower grade point averages and fewer study hours than students who were not similarly distracted. Unfortunately, the students themselves do not seem to be aware of the problem. About three-quarters of the Facebook users said they did not think the practice had any negative effects on their studying. Although one reasonable interpretation of these results is that Facebook is so distracting that it prevents the focused attention necessary for effective studying, it is also possible that students who use Facebook while studying are weaker students with poorer study habits in general to begin with. Remember: correlation does not mean causation! And it is not clear which would have a worse impact on learning: having Facebook running while studying or rushing through studying in an effort to get back to your electronic social scene!

Sleep

Studies have shown that sleep is important for learning and memory. Sleep deprivation impairs our abilities to pay attention and learn. In addition, sleep deprivation can prevent learnt information from moving into more permanent long-term memory storage. Studies in experimental animals have confirmed that sleep deprivation interferes with learning and memory. During slow-wave sleep and rapid eye movement sleep, hippocampal place cells in the rat replay sequences previously observed during waking (Lee & Wilson, 2002; Louie & Wilson,

2001) These findings suggest that the brain replays information learnt while awake, presumably to strengthen those connections and form longer-lasting memory traces. (As you will see in Chapter 10, memories are thought to leave physical traces in the brain – so-called *memory traces* – when they are acquired.) So while staying up late to study may be inevitable, make sure you get a decent amount of sleep so that you do not forget what you are learning. Getting enough sleep will also help you to process information you encounter for the first time the next day.

When We Learn

 **WHAT HAPPENS IN THE BRAIN?**

LEARNING OBJECTIVE 6
Discuss synaptic changes that occur in learning.

Throughout this chapter, we have mentioned different brain regions and neural mechanisms that may underlie certain types of learning. One general conclusion we can draw about the neuroscience of learning is that a single 'learning centre' does not exist. Even one type of learning will involve multiple brain systems, from perception of stimuli through to carrying out actions. However, we do know that particular neural systems are involved specifically in some types of learning. For example:

- Habituation and sensitization arise from changes in the sensory neurons themselves and their related corresponding interneurons and motor neurons.

- Classical conditioning of the eye-blink response is associated with the cerebellum, while fear conditioning involves the amygdala.

- Reward learning relies on the midbrain dopamine system, and motor learning involves activation of the basal ganglia, a region near the thalamus.

- Spatial navigation learning and episodic learning in general involve the hippocampus.

The evidence that some kinds of learning can take place without our awareness, while others require close attention, also emphasizes the fact that there is no single learning system in the brain. See, for example, 'What Happens in the Brain When We Learn to Play a Video Game' after the end of this section.

Although there are multiple neural systems that underlie different types of learning, neuroscientists suspect that all

Complex environments and learning. Humans exposed to stimulating environments, as well as animals raised in stimulating cages, seem to perform better on many learning tests than those living in more deprived settings. This is consistent with what we now know about how the brain changes during learning (Rosenzweig & Bennett, 1996).

Source: left photo: Photolink/Getty Images; right photo: imagebroker/Alamy Limited.

learning involves some kind of change in the strength of the synapse, the connection between neurons. One of the first ideas about learning involving changes in synaptic strength was put forth in the 1950s by the Canadian psychologist Donald Hebb. Hebb suggested that cells that were activated at or around the same time as one another would have stronger synapses than those that were out of step with one another (Cooper, 2005). So if cells are activated at the same time, the synapses become stronger and learning occurs.

Scientists have gathered considerable evidence to support Hebb's view. Many forms of associative learning have been linked to a form of synaptic plasticity, or change, called **long-term potentiation (LTP)**. Recall from Chapter 5 that a synapse is the tiny gap across which neurons communicate via neurotransmitters. Long-term potentiation refers to a change in activity at the synapse that results in a long-term enhancement in the activity of the postsynaptic neuron – the one that receives the neurotransmitter message (Figure 9.13) (Bliss & Lomo, 1973). LTP has been demonstrated in the synapses in brain areas involved in eye-blink conditioning, fear conditioning and spatial navigation learning (Scelfo et al., 2008; Whitlock et al., 2006; Maren, 2005). LTP can be associative in nature, in that it increases the strength of a weak synapse between two neurons when both of them are active at the same time. Moreover, researchers have

long-term potentiation (LTP) a form of synaptic change that involves increased activity in the postsynaptic cells after strong, repetitive stimulation.

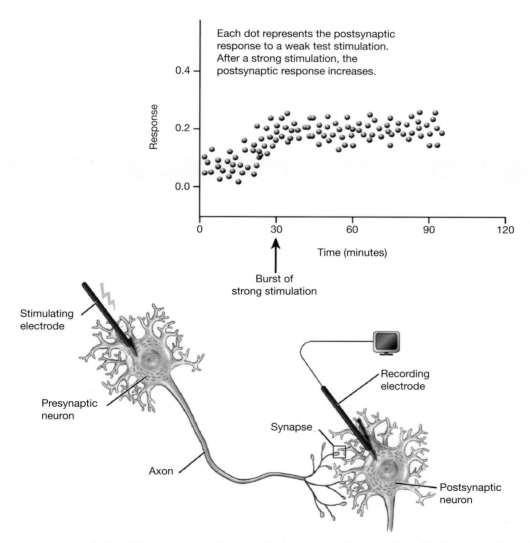

FIGURE 9.13 Long-term potentiation. When a presynaptic neuron is given a strong burst of stimulation, it changes the activity at the synapse of the postsynaptic neuron. Subsequently, a weak stimulation reaching the postsynaptic neuron produces a greater effect than would have occurred before.

demonstrated, by blocking the neurotransmitter receptors in the postsynaptic neuron, that preventing LTP inhibits some forms of learning.

Another possible mechanism for learning, one that could actually work along with LTP, is the formation of new synapses in our brains. The possibility that learning is accompanied by growth of synapses was first suggested by the early neuroanatomist Ramón y Cajal in the late 19th century (DeFelipe, 2002). Since then, numerous studies have shown that Ramón y Cajal was correct. Changes in the number, size and shape of synapses and dendritic spines – sites of excitatory synapses – have been observed with learning (Leuner *et al.*, 2003; O'Malley *et al.*, 1998; Moser *et al.*, 1994). Even the number of entirely new neurons in our hippocampus can increase with certain types of learning (Shors, 2009). These studies present the possibility that structural change may not only occur with learning but also actually underlie learning.

Before You Go On

What Do You Know?

13. Which brain regions are associated with reward and punishment?

14. Name and describe a process referred to in the expression, 'Cells that fire together, wire together.'

What Do You Think?

Why are so many different brain regions involved in learning?

Prenatal and Postnatal Learning

HOW WE DEVELOP

LEARNING OBJECTIVE 7

Summarize the types of learning that occur before we are born and during the newborn period.

Several studies suggest that non-associative learning can occur before we are even born. Foetuses show habituation and sensitization to smells and other sensory stimuli. In one set of studies, for example, infants who had been exposed to garlic in the womb – through their mothers' digestion – recognized the garlic odour after they were born. They did not try to avoid the smell, as babies who have not been exposed to garlic typically do. Habituation studies of newborns also show that they can distinguish between new and familiar sights and sounds. Even very soon after birth, babies typically stop moving for a brief time when they are exposed to a new visual or auditory stimulus, indicating that they are paying attention to the stimulus. This response suggests that they have already become accustomed, or habituated, to 'old' sights and sounds.

We are also capable of basic associative learning before birth. One team of researchers reported that human foetuses

YOUR BRAIN AND BEHAVIOUR   What Happens in the Brain When We Learn to Play a Video Game

You need to find that key, but watch out for those obstacles!

How do we learn to navigate through virtual reality, avoiding dangers that prevent us from moving through the game to mastery? What parts of the brain enable us to learn the rules of the game and respond to changes in the electronic world as we play?

When we learn a new video game that involves spatial navigation through a virtual three-dimensional space, trying to avoid punishments and obtain rewards all along the way, we are engaging a number of neural circuits throughout the brain. First, spatial navigation learning requires inputs from the visual cortex to the hippocampus and temporal lobe. Second, learning about rewards involves dopamine projections extending from the ventral tegmental area to the nucleus accumbens and prefrontal cortex. And third, integration and long-term storage of the information from these systems involves other cortical regions, including the parietal and temporal cortex. Will you make it to the next level?

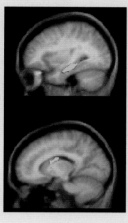

Picking a strategy. People use different strategies to solve tasks that involve navigating in space. Some people use a 3D strategy; use their position relative to the environment to find their way. Others use landmarks and numbering strategies (for example, enter the second door on your right). The different strategies engage different neural systems, shown on these fMRI images. Special 3D strategies activate the hippocampus (top, yellow) while landmark strategies activate the basal ganglia (bottom, yellow).

Source: Iaria, G., Petrides, M., Dagher, A., Pike, B., & Bohbot, V. D. (2003). Cognitive strategies dependent on the hippocampus and caudate nucleus in human navigation: Variability and change with practice. *Journal of Neuroscience, 23*(13), 5945–5952. Reproduced with permission.

Strengthening Your Synapses. When you learn a task that involves spatial navigation and rewards, synapses in a number of brain regions, including the hippocampus and nucleus accumbens, likely undergo long-term potentiation (LTP), a form of synapse strengthening. Most postsynaptic sites that undergo synapse strengthening are located on small extensions that protrude from dendrites, called dendritic spines (shown here labelled with a green florescent tracer).

Source: Courtesy of Elizabeth Gould.

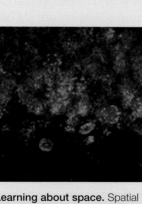

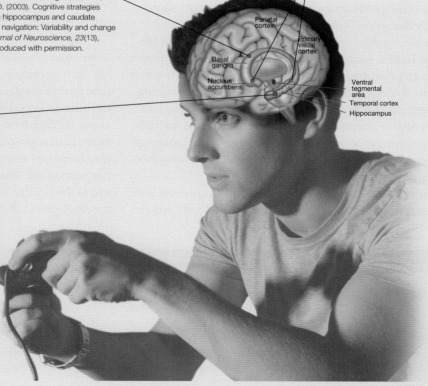

Learning about space. Spatial navigation learning leads to an increase in the number of new neurons in the hippocampus, shown here stained with florescent dyes (red). Engaging the hippocampus in this way prevents newly born neurons from dying.

Source: Courtesy of Elizabeth Gould.

Source: Masterfile.

PSYCHOLOGY AROUND US · Cat in the Hat

A classic study revealed that infants not only hear their mother's speech in the womb but also pay attention to what they are hearing and remember it (DeCasper & Spence, 1986). The researchers had pregnant women read aloud the Dr. Seuss book *The Cat in the Hat* each day during the last several weeks of pregnancy. Soon after the babies were born, they learnt to suck on a nipple that would turn on a voice recording. Babies sucked harder to hear their mothers' voices than the voices of others – and they sucked hardest to hear their mothers read *The Cat in the Hat*.

could learn by classical conditioning. Recall from Chapter 7 that hearing is partially developed before birth. These researchers paired specific music (initially a neutral stimulus) with relaxation exercises done by the mother. The maternal relaxation exercises served as an unconditioned stimulus, often leading to a slowing of foetal physical activity (an unconditioned response). After enough pairings of the music and the relaxation, the music became a conditioned stimulus, leading directly to a decrease in foetal movement (CR), with or without the relaxation exercises.

Newborn humans also demonstrate olfactory learning by showing an almost immediate preference for their own mother's odour – a preference they show by turning their heads towards their mother's odour much more often than towards the odours of strangers (Porter & Winberg, 1999). The preference for maternal odour has clear adaptive consequences. Throughout our evolutionary history, mothers have been the primary source of food and care for infants, and the ability of infants to identify that source by smell is obviously to their benefit.

As we develop from infancy onward, it is clear that biological factors, such as brain development, guide the development of learning. Psychologists and paediatricians often refer to *developmental milestones*, such as crawling, walking, language comprehension and speech. Many of these milestones require learning. The fact that these abilities typically emerge during specific time windows suggests that biological changes affect when specific types of learning can take place during development.

The types of learning that occur during the prenatal and early postnatal periods are simple forms that do not require

Early olfactory learning. In this study infants are exposed to bottles containing smells of their mothers, their fathers and other people. In such research undertakings, babies consistently show the highest preference for the smell of their mothers and second highest for that of their fathers.

Source: LookatSciences/Phototake.

brain regions that develop later. More complex forms of learning, such as episodic and semantic learning, are not efficient until forebrain regions, such as the hippocampus and neocortex, have developed to a greater extent. This is one reason why young children have a difficult time learning about facts and events in an organized and accurate way. Most of us do not have clear memories about our lives before the time we were around four years of age. This phenomenon, called *infantile amnesia*, is tied to the fact that learning episodic information depends on the development of the hippocampus and neocortex.

Before You Go On

What Do You Know?
15. What kinds of learning can happen before we are born?

What Do You Think?
What are the advantages and disadvantages of having only very simple forms of learning intact during foetal life? What consequences would arise if we possessed intact learning about events before birth?

Learning and Gender

LEARNING OBJECTIVE 8

Summarize gender differences in learning, and discuss their potential sources.

Within the range of what is considered normal, learning abilities vary greatly. You have likely experienced this first-hand by comparing how you learn best with how some of your friends and family learn. Some individuals are gifted at certain subjects, for example, and are capable of acquiring information in that subject area much more readily than in others. Studies of twins have suggested a genetic factor in certain forms of learning, but that does not account for the majority of variability in people's learning abilities. Other factors clearly play a role. Environmental factors, as well as non-genetic biological factors, are likely to affect learning abilities.

One highly controversial topic in the study of individual differences in learning is the issue of gender. Many individuals have preconceived notions about learning performance in boys and girls. For instance, it is a relatively common claim that boys are better at mathematics, while girls excel at languages. Since these claims affect how boys and girls are treated in social and educational settings, it is important to carefully evaluate scientific evidence related to them. The first question we need to ask is whether significant sex differences in learning actually exist. If so, then the cause of these differences becomes the critical issue. Are the differences caused by biological factors, such as chromosomes or hormones, or do they arise as a result of environmental influences?

Numerous studies have claimed that gender differences exist in a number of different learning tasks. Tasks that require mental rotation of images tend to favour males, while verbal-learning tasks sometimes favour females. These overall differences are sometimes statistically significant when relatively large numbers of individuals are tested. Nevertheless, there is a substantial overlap between the two genders in performance on both tasks. In addition, the difference between the averages for the two sexes is smaller than the range within a given sex. We can thus conclude that reports of these gender differences in learning ability do not mean much for the individual. In other words, there are plenty of spatially gifted girls and verbally talented boys.

In the mathematical domain, it is a mixed picture. Two meta analyses of mathematical ability, and a major longitudinal study published in 2010, reached very different conclusions (Stoet & Geary, 2012). However, there seem to be critical differences in the ratio of men to women at higher levels of performance (Geary, 1996).

Even though the differences just discussed are small, and even though there is a lot of overlap between genders, the evidence of gender difference is enough to raise issues about whether biological or environmental factors are responsible. One environmental explanation has focused on socialization. That is, cultural expectations, as shown in families, schools and the media, may influence what and how boys and girls learn. Teachers, for example, may form attitudes based on a belief that girls and boys differ in mathematical ability. The teachers may unintentionally discourage girls who are learning maths because they have lower expectations of their performance.

As the teachers just mentioned, many people have traditionally thought about girls' mathematical abilities in terms of *stereotypes*, generalized ideas about certain groups of people based on the social category they occupy. Studies done by social psychologist Claude Steele (Steele & Aronson, 1995, 2004) have identified a phenomenon called **stereotype threat**, in which awareness of negative stereotypes about oneself can interfere significantly with test performance. In these studies,

> **stereotype threat** an awareness of a negative stereotype that affects oneself and often leads to impairment in performance.

PSYCHOLOGY AROUND US   Maths and Theories of Intelligence

In Chapter 3, we mentioned Carol Dweck's work on teens who have entity theories of intelligence and those who have malleable theories of intelligence. Recall that teens with entity theories believe that intelligence is a resource that you either have a lot or a little of and can do little to change. Teens with malleable theories believe that, with work, you can improve your intelligence level. These theories can apply to any type of intelligence. It is interesting to note that, where maths is concerned, girls are more likely than boys to hold entity theories. This difference may result at least in part from differential treatment in the classroom. Traditionally, teachers have given boys more feedback on the quality of their work than they have given girls, as well as more encouragement to persist on mathematical problems that they initially get wrong. When boys are having trouble with maths, they are more likely to be told they need to try harder, while girls may be encouraged to believe that they simply are not good at maths. With this type of feedback, it is not surprising that girls learn to attribute their failures to a lack of ability and boys learn to attribute theirs to a lack of effort (Gutbezahl, 1997).

Steele and his colleagues observed that mentioning, before a test, a gender difference disadvantaging one gender led to poorer performance on the part of the group experiencing the bias. Members of stereotyped groups performed worse, even if researchers called attention to the stereotype in an encouraging way, such as, 'Come on, girls: I know you can score well on this test and disprove the belief that boys are better at maths!' In fact, trying hard to overcome such a stereotype seems to worsen performance. This phenomenon, which is not completely understood, does not apply only to stereotypes about gender differences in mathematical performance. Stereotype threat can also impair the performance of white males on an athletic test if they are informed of the stereotype that white people are less athletically gifted than black people. In Chapter 12, we will discuss additional effects of stereotype threat on IQ test performance.

Stereotype threat has been shown to have a negative impact on test performance when it is specifically mentioned in a laboratory test, but could it have an effect when stereotypes are not specifically mentioned? Many female students are undoubtedly aware of the stereotype that women are not as good at maths as men are. Stereotype threat may negatively affect such students' performance in maths-related tasks, even though the negative stereotype is not explicitly mentioned. However, Stoet and Geary (2012) question whether stereotype threat alone is sufficient to explain gender differences in maths.

A biological factor that could affect learning may be our differing responses to stress. Some studies have shown that gender differences in response to stress can affect not only learning but also test performance. On average, girls are more emotionally perturbed than boys by the anxiety of taking a test. These studies also show that helping girls to reduce test stress by teaching them relaxation exercises or exposing them to the testing environment before they sit a test can eliminate many gender differences in performance (we discuss stress and coping techniques in further detail in Chapter 18.) This work emphasizes the need to consider other factors, such as stress, when we evaluate claims of individual differences in learning ability.

Before You Go On

What Do You Know?

16. What is stereotype threat, and what effect does it have on learning?

What Do You Think?

What are the ethical problems associated with investigating gender differences in learning abilities? How may positive or negative findings of sex differences in learning affect society's attitude towards men and women in the workplace?

Learning Difficulties

 OUT OF THE ORDINARY

LEARNING OBJECTIVE 9

Describe dyslexia, dyscalculia and attention disorders.

A **learning difficulty** is a specific deficiency in one aspect of cognitive functioning, while other aspects function nor-

> **learning difficulty** a specific deficiency in one aspect of cognitive function while other aspects function normally.

mally. Learning difficulties are different from intellectual disability, which involves most or all intellectual abilities. Individuals with learning difficulties can have very high IQs with impairment only in one type of learning. Here, we discuss the most common learning disability, dyslexia, as well as a somewhat less common one, dyscalculia. We also look at attention deficit disorders, which are not learning disabilities but are often associated with them.

Dyslexia

The most common learning difficulty is **dyslexia**, which involves the processing of written language. Children with dyslexia have trouble learning to read and, sometimes, to write. Some estimates sug-

> **dyslexia** involves difficulties in learning to read not caused by deficits in general intelligence.

gest that between 5 and 10% of school-age children have dyslexia.

Contrary to popular belief, dyslexia is not primarily experienced as a reversal of letters in words. Reversal of letters or words is common in young children in the process of learning to read. Most children outgrow this tendency as they acquire reading skills. People with dyslexia display this characteristic for longer, in part because their learning skills do not progress as quickly. Thus, letter reversal is a symptom of their larger problems in learning to read, not the cause of their difficulty.

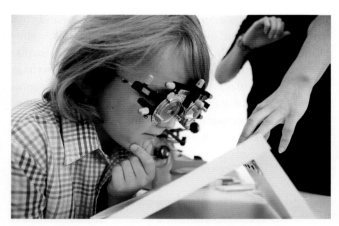

Studying dyslexia. A range of factors has been proposed to explain dyslexia, including deficits in visual processing, speech skills, auditory processing and object or letter identification. Here a young boy with the disorder undergoes a reading test with prism glasses.
Source: Olivier Voisin/Photo Researchers, Inc.

There is some evidence that people with dyslexia have visual-processing deficits that may produce perceptual problems. These deficits contribute to their difficulty in recognizing written words. Neuroimaging studies comparing children with dyslexia to those without the disability have shown that some children with dyslexia have reduced blood flow in brain regions associated with the acquisition of reading skills, such as the left parietal and temporal cortex (Hoeft *et al.*, 2006). Most people with dyslexia can deal with their difficulties in learning to read with the help of extensive tutoring and specific educational programmes.

Dyscalculia

A somewhat less prevalent learning difficulty, which may exist with or without dyslexia, is a condition known as **dyscalculia**. This refers to an inability to readily process mathematical computations.

> **dyscalculia** an inability to readily process mathematical computations.

Dyscalculia can occur in individuals whose reading abilities are normal or even higher than average, suggesting a deficit in specific brain circuitry associated with the acquisition of mathematical skills. Less information is available about dyscalculia than about dyslexia, but some evidence suggests that parts of the left parietal and frontal cortex of the brain are less active in individuals with dyscalculia (Price *et al.*, 2007). As with dyslexia, intensive tutoring and specific educational programmes can help students with dyscalculia learn mathematical information.

Attention Deficit Disorders

As we have noted, attention greatly aids some types of learning, especially the semantic learning required in school. Two attention disorders often contribute to difficulties in learning. **Attention deficit disorder (ADD)** is characterized primarily by an inability to concentrate. **Attention deficit hyperactivity disorder (ADHD)** is a similar disorder in which problems concentrating are accompanied by problematically high activity levels. These attention disorders are sometimes associated with dyslexia and dyscalculia.

> **attention deficit disorder (ADD)** a disorder characterized by an inability to concentrate.

> **attention deficit hyperactivity disorder (ADHD)** a disorder characterized by an inability to concentrate, accompanied by problematically high activity levels.

Neuroimaging studies have identified some brain regions that appear to be different in children with ADD or ADHD, compared with children without these disorders. Some evidence suggests that ADHD is associated with structural abnormalities in the cerebral cortex (Qiu *et al.*, 2009; Wolosin *et al.*, 2009; Shaw *et al.*, 2007). Studies have also shown decreased blood flow in the basal ganglia (Bush *et al.*, 2005) as well as a portion of the prefrontal cortex called the *anterior cingulate* (Smith *et al.*, 2008). Some studies have even shown an overall decrease in the size of these brain regions in people with ADHD (Hill *et al.*, 2003).

ADD and ADHD can be successfully treated with stimulant drugs, including methylphenidate, widely known by the trade name Ritalin, and dextroamphetamine, which has the trade name Adderall. Both drugs enhance attention and, even though they are stimulants, paradoxically diminish hyperactivity. The extent to which these drugs correct abnormalities in the cerebral cortex of people with ADD and ADHD remains undetermined.

Issues in Treatment

The identification and treatment of learning difficulties and attention deficit disorder raise important considerations. First, it is paramount that diagnoses be made early, so that intervention can occur before a child falls significantly behind in the normal course of schooling and development. As is often the case, the earlier intervention begins, the better the result is likely to be. Second, it is equally important that diagnoses are accurate, so that children with other problems are not incorrectly labelled or medicated.

A third issue concerns the misuse of the stimulant drugs often prescribed for attention disorders. For one thing, there has been some concern that attention deficit disorders may have been overdiagnosed. If so, it is likely that some children who take prescription medications do not have attention disorders, even though they have been diagnosed as having them. Needless to say, taking unnecessary medications can lead to problems. In the case of the stimulant drugs prescribed for attention disorders, these problems include the drugs' possible side effects.

In addition, some recent studies have estimated that a significant percentage of university students have used Ritalin and similar drugs without a prescription. Most students surveyed report that they use the drugs to help them study.

Since attention-disorder drugs enhance attention and thus learning in normal individuals, this practice raises ethical questions (Greely *et al.*, 2008). Do stimulants provide an unfair advantage to students who take them in settings such as universities where success is determined by cognitive function? Is stimulant use among people without attention disorders comparable, for example, to athletes using performance-enhancing drugs to improve their competitive standing?

Before You Go On

What Do You Know?

17. What are dyslexia and dyscalculia?

What Do You Think?

What, in your opinion, are the ethical pros and cons of taking attention-enhancing drugs when they are not needed to treat a disorder?

VIDEO

Access your interactive e-book to view a video clip for this chapter at
www.wileyopenpage.com

Summary

What Is Learning?

LEARNING OBJECTIVE 1   Define learning, and distinguish between associative and non-associative learning.

- Learning is a lasting change in the brain caused by experience.
- Non-associative learning is a lasting change that happens as a result of experience with a single cue. Types of non-associative learning include habituation, in which we display decreased responses to familiar stimuli, and sensitization, in which we display increased responses to stimuli after repeated experience of those stimuli.
- Associative learning is a lasting change that happens as a result of associating two or more stimuli. Types of associative learning include classical and operant conditioning.

Classical Conditioning

LEARNING OBJECTIVE 2   Describe the basic processes of classical conditioning, and explain how classical conditioning is relevant to learning.

- As a result of classical conditioning, a previously neutral stimulus comes to elicit a response by being paired with an unconditioned stimulus (US) that already generates the response, known as an unconditioned response (UR). The neutral stimulus becomes a conditioned stimulus (CS) when it elicits the same response as the US. The response to the CS is known as a conditioned response (CR).
- Repeated presentation of the CS without the US can lead to extinction, or suppression of the CR. Extinction does not mean we forget the CS–US association, however. The CR can be spontaneously recovered.

- Eye-blink conditioning shows that classical conditioning requires changes in the cerebellum.
- Phobias and conditioned taste aversions can result from classical conditioning. Systematic desensitization uses classical conditioning to extinguish phobia responses. Conditioned taste aversions suggest that we are biologically prepared to quickly learn responses important to our survival.

Operant Conditioning

LEARNING OBJECTIVE 3 Describe the basic processes of operant conditioning, and explain how shaping can be used to teach new behaviours.

- Operant conditioning is a learnt association between stimuli in the environment and our own behaviour. The law of effect states that we learn to repeat behaviours that will increase our rewards and help us avoid punishment.
- Reinforcers are rewarding stimuli from the environment. Positive reinforcement provides a desired stimulus; negative reinforcement takes away an unpleasant stimulus. Both increase the chance a behaviour will be repeated. Primary reinforcers are reinforcing in and of themselves. Secondary reinforcers become reinforcing because of their association with primary reinforcers.
- Positive punishment provides an unpleasant stimulus; negative punishment takes away a rewarding one. Both types lower the chances that a behaviour will be repeated.
- Schedules of intermittent reinforcement provide reinforcements after either fixed or variable intervals of time or numbers of responses. Any intermittent reinforcement modifies behaviour more effectively than continuous reinforcement.
- Shaping, or rewarding successive approximations of a behaviour, uses operant conditioning principles to teach new behaviours. People and animals are limited in the behaviours they can learn, however, by their biological endowments.
- Learned helplessness occurs when previous learning that punishment is inescapable interferes with the subsequent ability to learn how to avoid escapable punishment. It may be related to depression or the behaviour of abuse victims.
- Insight learning and spatial navigation learning seem to take place in the absence of any obvious reinforcement.

Observational Learning

LEARNING OBJECTIVE 4 Define observational learning, and summarize concerns about observational learning from the media.

- Observational learning is learning by watching the behaviour of others. We are likely to model, or imitate, others' behaviour that we see rewarded.
- Many people are concerned that high levels of violence in the media encourage viewers to model such aggression. Studies about the causal nature of media encouraging violence have been inconclusive.

Factors that Facilitate Learning

LEARNING OBJECTIVE 5 Define massed and spaced practice, and tell what conditions are best for learning semantic material.

- Repeated, spaced practice aids learning of semantic material, such as classroom information.
- According to the context effect, if you learn information in only one context, or location, you may be less likely to recall it when you are in a different context.
- We can learn without paying attention, and some tasks are easier to learn that way, but focused attention aids semantic learning.
- Sleep deprivation impairs our ability to pay attention and to learn.

When We Learn

LEARNING OBJECTIVE 6 Discuss synaptic changes that occur in learning.

- Long-term potentiation (LTP) is a change in the ability of networks of neurons, in which the postsynaptic neuron becomes more active in response to certain presynaptic inputs.
- Learning may also be linked to the addition of more synapses in the brain, either through growing new neurons or by adding dendritic material to existing ones.
- Many regions of the brain, including the hippocampus, neocortex and cerebellum, are involved in different types of learning and have been shown to exhibit long-term potentiation and neuron growth.

Prenatal and Postnatal Learning

LEARNING OBJECTIVE 7 Summarize the types of learning that occur before we are born and during the newborn period.

- We are capable of non-associative learning, both habituation and sensitization, before birth, as well as basic associative learning, such as classical conditioning.
- We become capable of increasingly complex forms of learning as relevant areas of our brains mature after we are born.

Learning and Gender

LEARNING OBJECTIVE 8 Summarize gender differences in learning, and discuss their potential sources.

- Studies show small, but consistent average differences between males and females in learning, with males performing better at spatial rotation tasks and females performing better at verbal learning. Males also tend to average higher mathematics scores on standardized tests. However, the range of abilities within a sex is much greater than the difference between males and females.
- Environmental factors, such as stereotype threat, may contribute to these gender differences. Biological differences in stress reactions may also play a role in test-score differences.

Learning Difficulties

LEARNING OBJECTIVE 9 Describe dyslexia, dyscalculia and attention disorders.

- A learning disability is a specific deficiency in one area of learning, while learning in other areas takes place normally. Dyslexia is a common disability in learning to read. Dyscalculia is a disability in learning mathematics.
- Attention deficit disorder (ADD) and attention deficit hyperactivity disorder (ADHD) affect concentration and can impair learning. Both are commonly treated with stimulant drugs. The use and misuse of these drugs raises many ethical concerns.

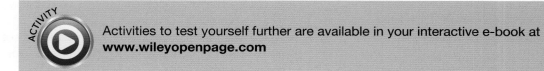

Activities to test yourself further are available in your interactive e-book at **www.wileyopenpage.com**

TYING IT TOGETHER

 **WHAT HAPPENS IN THE BRAIN?**

- All types of learning actually involve changes in our brains, although different types of learning involve different brain regions.
- London taxi drivers, who have intricate spatial knowledge of the city, tend to have a larger hippocampus than people without similar geographical knowledge.
- Some research suggests that our brains may rehearse new information in our sleep, which could explain why sleep deprivation makes learning more difficult.

 **HOW WE DIFFER**

- There are very small average differences in learning between males and females, but average differences cannot help you predict how well any individual will learn.
- If we learn about a negative stereotype about a group to which we belong, our learning and performance often change to reflect that stereotype.

OUT OF THE ORDINARY

- Phobias may result from classical conditioning, in which we learn to respond with fear to something that is not necessarily threatening. We can learn to extinguish phobic behaviour, but cannot 'unlearn' the phobia.
- We can learn a long-lasting aversion to a food if it makes us sick only once, even several hours after we eat it.
- Learned helplessness may play a role in depression. If people have previously been unable to escape punishment, they may fail to act to escape unpleasant situations, even when it becomes possible.

HOW WE DEVELOP

- We can learn simple associations before we are even born.
- Very early in life, we fail to display efficient complex learning, such as episodic or semantic learning. These forms of learning depend on further development of the hippocampus and neocortex.
- Reinforcement is generally more effective and ethical than punishment for teaching children.

QUIZ Quizzes to test yourself further are available in your interactive e-book at **www.wileyopenpage.com**

Key Terms

associative learning 239
attention deficit disorder (ADD) 267
attention deficit hyperactivity disorder (ADHD) 267
behaviourism 249
behaviour modification 252
conditioned response (CR) 242
conditioned stimulus (CS) 242
conditioned taste aversion 247
continuous reinforcement 251
dyscalculia 267
dyslexia 266

fixed interval schedule 252
fixed ratio schedule 252
habituation 239
insight learning 255
intermittent or partial reinforcement 251
law of effect 249
learned helplessness 253
learning 238
learning curve 238
learning difficulty 266
long-term potentiation (LTP) 261
modelling 256
negative punishment 250

negative reinforcement 250
non-associative learning 239
observational learning 256
operant or instrumental conditioning 248
Pavlovian or classical conditioning 242
phobia 246
positive punishment 250
positive reinforcement 250
primary reinforcer 250
punishment 249
reinforcer 249
secondary reinforcer 251
sensitization 239

shaping 253
spatial navigation 254
spontaneous recovery 243
stereotype threat 265
stimulus generalization 246
systematic desensitization 246
unconditioned response (UR) 242
unconditioned stimulus (US) 242
variable interval schedule 252
variable ratio schedule 252

FLASHCARDS Flashcards to test yourself further are available in your interactive e-book at **www.wileyopenpage.com**

CHAPTER 10

Memory

Adapted by Chris Moulin,
University of Bourgogne, France

CHAPTER OUTLINE

- What Is Memory?
- How Do We Encode Information into Memory?
- How Do We Store Memories?
- How Do We Retrieve Memories?
- Why Do We Forget and Misremember?
- Memory and the Brain
- Memories in the Young and Old
- Disorders of Memory

 Access your interactive e-book to view a video clip for this chapter at **www.wileyopenpage.com**

Life Is All Memory

Memory is a fundamental psychological entity, the store of everything we are, and the means by which we string events together into a continuous experience. In the *Milk Train Doesn't Stop Here Anymore*, the American playwright Tennessee Williams wrote, 'Life is all memory, except for the one present moment that goes by you so quickly you hardly catch it going.' By this view, memory is going to play a large part in all human thought and behaviour.

What would it be like to have no memory at all? We get a window into such experiences through people with severe *amnesia*, or memory loss. PJM (the people in case studies are usually referred to by their initials) had a cycling accident while on holiday in France, and as a result spent several weeks in a coma, and six months in hospital. PJM describes her experience: 'I remember my life up until a couple of years ago . . . it's weird that the accident just sort of knocked out the two years before it' (Rathbone *et al.*, 2009). In fact, the period of amnesia 'knocked out' several key life events, like the decision to have a second child and the birth of that child, as well as moving to a new house, where PJM said, 'We must have chosen to move here, because we needed more space. But I have no memory of choosing to move here.' Imagine having no memory for such important things but having to reason with yourself and work out the facts of your current existence like a detective. But then turn to the more mundane things that memory lets you do, and think about how with a memory deficit it is difficult to work (PJM lost her job as an academic following the accident), and to function independently at all. ∎

Consider everything that memory lets you do. Obviously, there are the everyday tasks, such as passing tests, handing in coursework on time or remembering a friend's birthday. But go deeper: think of the things memory lets you do that you take for granted. Because of memory, you can have favourite foods, favourite musicians, favourite movies and favourite TV shows. Not only can you remember friends' birthdays but you can also remember their typical behaviours and preferences and, for example, predict what they might want for their birthday.

You can go deeper still. If you did not somehow store events and people in your mind, you would not know about anything that you were not directly sensing at that moment. You would only know what was in your line of sight and have no idea how the things that you were seeing connected to you or had any significance or meaning. Without memory, you may be, like PJM, a stranger to yourself, unable to link the present to the past and using this information to make decisions about the future (Kihlström, 2001). By keeping a record of our past, our memory takes us out of an infinite present.

What Is Memory?

memory the faculty for reproducing past events and past learning.

encoding a basic activity of memory, involving the recording of information in our brain.

storage a basic activity of memory, involving retention of information for later use.

retrieval a basic activity of memory, involving recovery of information when we need it later.

LEARNING OBJECTIVE 1
Define the basic activities of memory and describe two major models of memory.

Simply put, **memory** is the faculty for reproducing past events and past learning. This definition is perhaps the only thing about memory that is simple. Although psychologists can differ in their ideas about how memory works, they generally agree that it involves three basic activities:

- **Encoding** – Getting information into memory in the first place.

- **Storage** – Retaining memories for future use.

- **Retrieval** – Recapturing memories when we need them.

These three stages work together. For any single memory event, all three need to have been achieved. In memory clinics, neurologists sometimes ask people to report what they had for breakfast. You can consider this simple question now, and form an answer. To be able to report this information, you need to have been paying attention to breakfast in the first place in order to encode it, then information concerning breakfast needs to have been meaningfully stored and, finally, when asked, you need to successfully travel back (mentally) to the right time point and to the right information. This may even involve some mental effort, or the sensation that information is rushing back. But a disruption to any of these three stages will mean that the information is lost, even if only temporarily.

How do we manage to encode, store and retrieve information? Psychologists have developed a number of models of explanation, including the *information-processing model* and the *parallel distributed-processing model*, or *connectionist model*.

The **information-processing model** of memory holds that information must pass through three stages, or systems, of mental functioning in order to become a firmly implanted memory: sensory memory, working memory and long-term memory (Figure 10.1) (Dudai, 2011; Nee *et al.*, 2008). When we first come across a stimulus, we retain a sensory image – or *sensory memory* – of it for less than a second. Sensory memories help us to keep alive items that we have experienced briefly a bit longer, so that we can, in a sense, decide whether to pay further attention to them. If, for example, we are copying from one piece of text while typing, we will store a brief sketch of where in the document we are looking, before turning to the computer and turning back again. The sensory information stores the place where we were looking long enough to switch our attention from one thing to another.

To understand the next stages in memory we need to think more about the processes that draw upon memory. Sensory memory is basically brief and low level, unintelligent almost. If we look up a person's e-mail address, our sensory

information-processing model a view of memory suggesting that information moves among three memory stores during encoding, storage and retrieval.

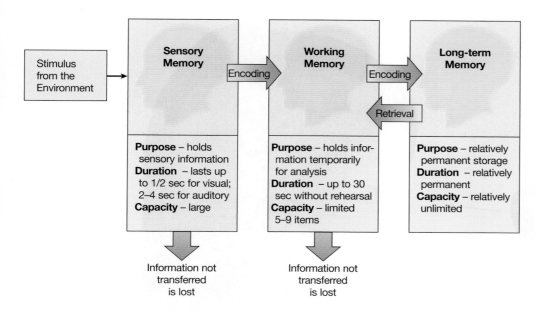

FIGURE 10.1 The three-stage memory model. This model is a useful framework for thinking about the three basic memory stages. Each stage differs in purpose, duration and capacity.

memory undoubtedly records a snapshot of the address, but to make sense and to use this information it needs to quickly pass to *working memory*. We can help retain the new address in working memory by concentrating on it and repeating it over and over as we begin the e-mail or type it into our address book. But working memory itself can hold only so much information at a time. It will eventually fail us and the information will disappear unless it is further passed on to our *long-term memory* system, the system that can retain an enormous amount of information for a seemingly endless period.

Do you watch the progress bar as you retrieve a You-Tube clip from the Internet? The way the different stores in memory interact is similar to this. YouTube works by downloading the movie while it is being watched. A little portion of upcoming information is stored very briefly to allow the film to play smoothly. But the YouTube clip is not downloaded completely or stored permanently, although it is sometimes possible to download clips from the Internet and store them for the long term. *Sensory memory* works in a similar way, giving us a quick copy of the information in our environment, allowing us to string together the stream of consciousness which is the present moment, *buffering* our experiences like the YouTube clip does. In addition, information saved to *working memory* is like the information that a computer retains for as long as a document or website is open, but which disappears if you do not save it. And the final memory system, *long-term memory*, is the equivalent of the computer hard drive, storing information until something causes the disruption or loss of the memory. These three systems are sometimes referred to as *memory stores*.

The information-processing model has produced a great deal of research, which we will explore further in the sections of this chapter that focus on encoding, storage, retrieval and forgetting.

Although the information-processing model suggests that sensory memory, working memory and long-term memory correspond roughly to computer memory structures, we need to be clear that this is but a metaphor (Silva, 2011). If a computer were to be opened up, the various forms of memory would be easily seen. This is not the case with the human brain, however, as equivalent specific structures where short-term memory and long-term memory exist have not yet been identified.

Unlike the information-processing model, which suggests that information is stored and retrieved piece by piece, an alternative model of memory, the **parallel distributed-processing (PDP) (or connectionist) model** holds that newly encountered pieces of information immediately join with other, previously encountered, pieces of information to help form and grow networks of information (McClelland, 2011). Such networks result in sophisticated memories, broad knowledge and the ability to make better decisions and plans in life by generalizing. Look, for example, at Figure 10.2. When the person in the figure sees an apple, links to relevant kinds of information are activated – connections to concepts such as shape (roundness), colour (red) and grandmother (because of the apple tree in her garden) – while other, less relevant connections are *inhibited*, or shut

> **parallel distributed-processing (PDP) (or connectionist) model** a theory of memory suggesting information is represented in the brain as a pattern of activation across entire neural networks.

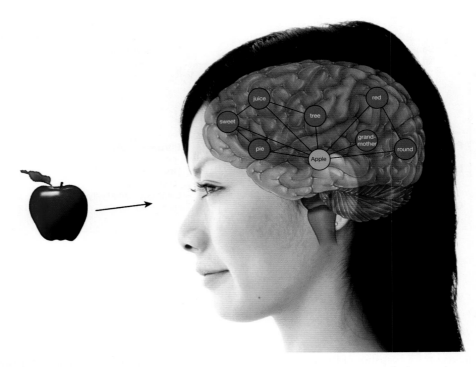

FIGURE 10.2 The PDP model of memory. The PDP, or connectionist, model of memory suggests that memories are stored in a network of associations throughout our brains.
Source: Digital Vision/Getty Images, Inc.

down. These activated connections are all part of the net-work of information related to apples that this person has stored. When one part of the 'apple network' is activated, related neurons throughout the brain become active and richer memories spring forth. The PDP model of memory has gained many proponents, largely because its principles fit well with the field's growing recognition that neurons throughout our brains form networks of association as we respond to repeated learning experiences and events in life (Changeux, 2011).

Before You Go On

What Do You Know?

1. What are encoding, storage and retrieval?
2. What are the three memory stores suggested by the information-processing model of memory?

What Do You Think?

Judging from your own experiences, do you think memory works more like a computer, with different memory stores, or more in a connectionist fashion? Could the two ideas both be useful in explaining some of your experiences?

How Do We Encode Information into Memory?

LEARNING OBJECTIVE 2
Describe how information is encoded and transferred among different memory stores and what we can do to enhance encoding.

How many steps are there from the front door of your build-ing to your room? Can't remember? How about an easier question: what was the first word you said yesterday morn-ing? Most of us probably cannot recall an answer to either of these questions.

Your lack of recall may be because the information was never *encoded*, or entered into your memory, in the first place.

PSYCHOLOGY AROUND US   Living by Post-It Notes

Contestants in an annual US Memory Championship are asked to memorize thousands of numbers and words, pages of faces and names, and decks of cards (Schacter, 2001). Yet one recent winner considers herself dangerously forgetful in her normal life, 'I'm incredibly absentminded,' winner Tatiana Cooley told a reporter. Fearful that she will forget to carry out everyday tasks, Cooley depends on to-do lists and notes scribbled on sticky pads: 'I live by Post-its,' she admitted.

Why does someone with a capacity for amazing recall need to write down anything at all? Can't she call on the same memory abilities and strategies that she uses to memorize hundreds of words or thousands of numbers to help remember that she needs to pick up some milk on the way home? Apparently not.

The kinds of everyday memory failures that Cooley seeks to remedy with Post-it notes – errands to run, appointments to keep and the like – reflect absentmindedness: lapses of memory caused by inattentiveness, improper encoding or carelessly overlooking available memories at the time of information retrieval, a phenomenon we will come to shortly.

Because we fail to encode many pieces of information that we come across in life, we do not actually remember most of the things that we experience. Encoding requires *attention*, that is we need to focus on or notice the information. We can encode only what we attend to (Eysenck *et al.*, 2010).

Using Automatic and Effortful Processing to Encode

We are not always aware that we are attending to things in our environment. Sometimes we attend to information – particularly, information about *time*, *space* or *frequency* – without much conscious awareness and indeed with little or no effort. Even though you may not know how many steps there are from the front door of your building to the door of your room, you probably do not get lost very often along the way and you probably did not need to practise the route to work out how to get to your room. The encoding process that allowed you to learn this basic route is called **automatic processing**.

automatic processing encoding information with little conscious awareness or effort.

Although we use automatic processing to encode many kinds of information, the encoding of other information requires us to make conscious effort and pay very close attention (Gilchrist & Cowan, 2010). This is the type of processing that hopefully you are engaging in right now as you read this chapter, if you are preparing for tomorrow's lecture or studying for a test. As you read through the present material, you should try to find ways to bring this new information into your existing knowledge, because the facts – or memories – will be better stored there with your careful attention. This kind of encoding, – which is typically necessary when learning new information – such as names, songs or tasks – is called **effortful processing** (Hasher & Zacks, 1979). The difference between effortful and automatic processing is a fundamental issue in

effortful processing encoding information through careful attention and conscious effort.

memory and has given rise to many different theories and experimental manipulations.

Keep in mind that whether we are encoding information through automatic or effortful processing we must pay attention. Our attention may be less apparent in automatic processing, but if we do not attend sufficiently to information, in one way or another, we will simply not be able to encode it. If a digital photo is taken of a particular scene, no amount of processing or zooming in or out will change the direction that the camera was pointed in when the photo was taken. The image may be retained in more or less detail, with different resolutions, be blurred or not blurred; but a photo taken of your friend smiling at the camera will record nothing of the person who was behind you when you took the photo.

There are key differences between effortful and automatic processing. First, the encoding of information by effortful

Memory buster. This student's upcoming test performance is at risk. *Effortful processing*, such as acquiring new information from a textbook, is easily disrupted when one also attends to other tasks during the encoding process.

Source: Masterfile.

processing tends to be disrupted when a person is forced to perform other tasks or to attend to other information while trying to encode the information at hand. You will not gather much from this book if you try to read it while carrying on a lively SMS or phone conversation about something else, for example. In contrast, automatic processing, being so effortless, is disrupted only slightly by the performance of other tasks.

Second, as the name suggests, putting the effort into effortful processing makes it more effective. Automatic processing is not greatly improved by a person's extra efforts to attend and encode. You could go and rehearse the path from your front door to your room and count the steps, but it is unlikely that you will know any more about the route than you knew this morning. In contrast, extra effort can make a big difference in effortful processing. Reading over the material in this chapter again and again – especially if you are paying particular attention to it – will affect considerably your ability to recall it on a test.

Encoding Information into Working Memory: Transferring from Sensory Memory into Working Memory

As was described earlier, when we first come across a stimulus, we retain a very brief sensory image of it – an image called a **sensory memory** (Magnussen *et al.*, 2010). If, for example, we are shown a photograph for just a moment, we retain a detailed image of all the shapes and items in the photograph for a few hundred milliseconds. Studies by researcher George Sperling in the late 1950s and early 1960s offered important clues about how sensory memories operate (Sperling, 1960).

sensory memory a memory involving a detailed sensory image or sound being retained for a brief period.

Sperling wanted to demonstrate the presence of a brief visual storehouse, like the memory buffer of a computer, that would hold a picture of our environment for a very brief period. He also wanted to measure how long this buffer would last. To do so, he exposed participants to a list of random letters, similar to what you would see on an eye chart (although always the same size) (Figure 10.3). They were presented extremely quickly and he found that, generally, participants were successful in recalling the letters they saw, as long as they were asked to do so immediately. The greater the time between showing the letters and saying what they had seen, the less well the participants performed. After about half a second, participants had trouble remembering any letters from the grid.

If we do not pay much attention to our sensory memories, as is usually the case, they will disappear forever.

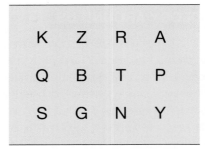

FIGURE 10.3 Test of sensory memory. In his study of the duration of sensory memory, George Sperling flashed a chart of letters, similar to this one, for 1/20 of a second. He found that participants could recall almost all the letters in a particular row if asked to do so immediately, but half a second later, their performance was much worse.

Those that are attended to, however, may enter **working memory**, the second system of memory. The phrase was introduced by the British psychologists Baddeley and Hitch (1974) in a very influential paper. Working memory is a fundamental concept, and one to which we shall return several times in this chapter. Working memory serves several important functions in our day-to-day lives (Baddeley, 2004). One of the most important is that of enabling us to hold onto information – such as a website address or a phone number – that we need for short periods. We use working memory in this way much of the time. Whenever we read, for example, our working memory enables us to keep the beginning of a sentence in mind while we are reading the last part of the sentence, so that the whole phrase will make sense to us (Just & Carpenter, 2002). It also enables us to relate new sentences, such as this one, to previous sentences we have just read. Similarly, in a conversation, working memory helps us link new comments to previous ones so that we can follow what we are hearing.

working memory a form of memory that allows the simultaneous manipulation and storage of information in the short term.

One way of helping to make sure that information is encoded into working memory is **rehearsal**, consciously repeating the information. As far back as 400 BC, Greek philosophers recognized the value of rehearsal in memory. Assuming that hearing and saying the same things would transfer new information into memory, the philosophers advised students to repeat whatever they heard (Turkington & Harris, 2009). We are rehearsing when we keep repeating a phone number we have just heard until we can call it or add it to our phone's contact list. Such rehearsal means that the information will be available to working memory as we key in the phone number.

rehearsal conscious repetition of information in an attempt to make sure the information is encoded.

Encoding Information into Long-Term Memory: Transferring Working Memory into Long-Term Memory

Although concentrated efforts, such as rehearsal, can lengthen the availability of information in working memory, eventually that information is either passed on to the long-term memory system or lost (Jonides *et al.*, 2008, 2003). It is in **long-term memory** that we hold all of the information we have gathered, available for use – often at a moment's notice – in a new situation or task. When we retrieve past events, previously gathered information, people we once met, past feelings or even just carry out previously acquired skills, we are using long-term memory.

long-term memory the system that holds previously gathered information ready for retrieval and use in a new situation.

Just as rehearsal can help move information from the sensory memory system to the working memory system, it can help us move short-term, working memories into the long-term memory system (Neuschatz *et al.*, 2005). Most of us rehearse information from a course's textbook and lectures, for example, when we are revising for an examination. Information passes into long-term memory best when our rehearsal sessions are spread over several sessions rather than attempting to take in a great deal of information all at once. This phenomenon is known as the **spacing effect**. Thus, *distributed practice*, such as studying material weekly, followed by reviews closer to the time of an exam is usually more profitable than *massed practice*, such as studying in one session just before the exam (Greene, 1989).

spacing effect the facilitated encoding of material through rehearsal situations spread over time.

As we saw in Chapter 9, sleep can help or hurt rehearsal. Information acquired in the hours before falling asleep tends to be encoded into long-term memory, as long as we have time to process it before sleep sets in (Stickgold, 2011; Backhaus *et al.*, 2008). Information learnt just as sleep is approaching is rarely retained, however, partly because we fall asleep before we can rehearse. Furthermore, information that comes to us during sleep – a language CD, for example – does not typically enter our memories at all.

In What Form Is Information Encoded?

We must use some kind of code or representation to encode information. Different codes are available to us (Martin, 2009). When encoding information into working memory – for example, trying to keep a phone number in memory long enough to dial it – we can use a *phonological code*, repeating the *sounds* of the numbers over and over and again, or we can employ a *visual code*, holding an *image* of how the digits would look if written down. Research suggests that people tend to favour phonological codes when recording verbal information, such as digits, letters and words. We rely more on visual codes for nonverbal information, such as a person's face or a speeding car (Just & Carpenter, 2002).

Although adequate for most purposes, the phonological or visual codes that people use to record information in their working memory tend to be flawed. Some people, however, produce visual images with remarkable detail and near-perfect accuracy. When recalling an object or scene that they have just witnessed, these people almost seem to be looking at a photograph. Thus, their detailed images are called *eidetic memories*, or photographic memories. Eidetic memories usually occur among children: as many as 5% of children encode images with this level of detail. Eidetic images can last for several minutes (Hochman, 2010, 2001).

When we encode *nonverbal information* into long-term memory, we once again tend to use phonological or visual codes. Similarly, we may use olfactory, gustatory or tactile codes to help record smells, tastes or physical sensations. Long after a concert, for example, audience members may remember its intensity by visualizing images of the stage and the lighting effects, re-experiencing the smells of the arena and the crowd and calling to mind the sounds of the musical instruments, the performers' voices and the crowd's cheers.

In contrast, to encode *verbal information* into long-term memory, people tend to use a **semantic code**, a representation based on the *meaning* of information. Because we often rely on the meaning of information when transferring items into long-term memory, our later recall of events may be flawed to some degree. Many a family gathering has been spent sharing different versions of an important event, for example. Everyone at a gathering like a wedding may remember the key elements of that special day, but the specific memories of each person may differ dramatically. Why? In part, it is because each member used semantic coding to record the important family event into their long-term memory. But the day will also mean different things to different people and they will have their own bias in encoding and retrieving the results. People in the same family may, for instance, retrieve the same event with very different emotions: it was a good day for one person but not another. These different perspectives for each person are one of the things that make memory research so interesting and revealing about the individual.

semantic code cognitive representation of information or an event based on the meaning of the information.

It is worth noting that the various codes may operate simultaneously when information is being encoded (Kessels & Postma, 2002). One of these codes – semantic, phonological or visual – may be used more actively than the others in particular instances, but when we use multiple codes the combined impact of the these codes increases the likelihood and strength of the memory.

Meaning and Encoding Inasmuch as meaning often plays a key role in long-term memory, we should not be surprised that the more meaningful information is, the more readily it is encoded and later remembered. In one study, for example, people were asked to memorize 200 words of poetry, 200 nonsense syllables and a 200-word prose passage (Figure 10.4). The poetry took 10 minutes to learn and the prose less than 20 minutes, but the nonsense syllables took an hour and a half.

Similarly, the more meaningful a personal event, the more readily it is encoded and later remembered. A student's acceptance into medical school is recognized by everyone in the family as a significant turning point in her life. Thus, the student, her parents and her siblings all remembered the day of her acceptance. A lesser event, such as a day at the circus or a trip to a department store, may not be encoded as readily. Of all meaningful events, it is often public events, such as the death of Diana, Princess of Wales, in Paris in 1997 or the death of Michael Jackson in 2009 which are particularly strongly burnt into memory.

Possibly the most well-known study of how encoding pertains to memory is the classic Levels of Processing effect (e.g. Craik & Lockhart, 1972), whereby the depth to which information is studied massively affects its later recall. In a standard version of this experiment, participants are given lists of words to read and asked either to rate how pleasant the word is (which has to activate the meaning of the word) or they report how many vowels that the word has (which is only a perfunctory assessment of the written form

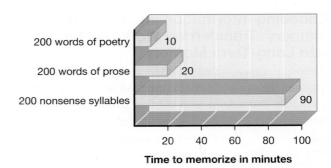

FIGURE 10.4 Meaning matters in memory. Meaning helped people memorize poetry and prose much faster than nonsense syllables.

Source: Based on Turkington & Harris, 2009.

of the word). Experiments with these sorts of instructions robustly find that words encountered in the context of assessing meaning (invoking a deeper level of processing) yield much higher memory performance on subsequent tests, even when the test is unexpected, and people do not wilfully memorize the information.

Helping Memory: Elaboration and Mnemonics Of course, people can also help ensure that less meaningful information proceeds into long-term memory by artificially *adding* meaning to it or by wilfully elaborating on the meaning of the information. Such efforts are known as **mnemonic devices**, cognitive techniques that impose additional or intensified meaning on various pieces of information (Cavallini *et al.*, 2003). Throughout this book, we include relevant examples that we hope will make the information more applicable and more relevant and, in turn, make your memories more available.

mnemonic devices techniques used to enhance the meaningfulness of information to make them more memorable.

PSYCHOLOGY AROUND US **Mnemonics**

Many a new music student has come to appreciate that the five lines of printed music of the treble clef are called *E-G-B-D-F*, by first tying those letters to a sentence such as 'Every Good Boy Deserves Favours'. The first letter of each word in the sentence is the same as one of the lines of printed music. By giving more meaning to the musical language, the sentence helps the students to encode the information into their long-term memory. (The notes between the lines are easily remembered too, with just the word that the letters spell: FACE.)

One of the best ways to elaborate is by making the target information personally meaningful. For example, if you want to remember the difference between the spelling of the words dessert (a treat that follows a meal) and desert (a hot, arid place), you could say to yourself, 'I like something **s**uper **s**weet after dinner', to remind you that the food item is spelled with a double 's'.

As we have seen, you can use mnemonic techniques – efforts at *elaboration*, or *elaborative rehearsal* – to impose meanings on seemingly unrelated pieces of information, such as the names of musical notes. Two other mnemonic techniques involve *imagery*, taking a mental picture of something meaningful to you and using information from the picture to increase your memory potential.

Key Word Method

This visualization method was developed by researcher Richard Atkinson (1975) for the learning of foreign-language words. A student trying to learn Spanish, for example, will think about an image that ties the Spanish word to an English key word that sounds similar to a portion of the foreign word. The Spanish word *caballo*, which means 'horse', sounds like *eye* in its middle syllable. So a student could imagine a horse kicking a giant eye. When confronted with the word *caballo*, the sound of the key word, *eye*, should cue the student to see the image in his or her mind and to retrieve the information that *caballo* means 'horse'. In one experiment, students who were instructed to use this method of study scored an average of 88% correct on a test, while those who studied by repetition alone for the same duration scored only 28% (Pressley *et al.*, 1982; Raugh & Atkinson, 1975). The method has also proven helpful in studying unfamiliar vocabulary within a student's native language, such as medical terms (Trout-Ervin, 1990).

Method of Loci

This method (*loci* is Latin for 'places') can help you remember information that must be recalled in a specific order, such as a list of words. First, imagine a place that you know well, such as your home. Visualize the layout of that place as you walk through it. At home, for example, you could imagine yourself walking through the front door, past a sofa, towards a round table, then past a television set and finally into the kitchen. Next, form a picture in your mind that connects each word or object to a location in the house. If the first word on a list to be remembered is *cat*, you may imagine a cat scratching at the front door, for example. Once you have tied the items on the list to these images and practised them, you can mentally walk through the 'place' and list the items one by one in the correct order.

As you know by now, organizing information is necessary for the proper storage and retrieval of memories. *Chunking* is one way of organizing information to help enhance memory. Another organizational technique – organizing a list of unrelated words into a story – has also been shown to be very successful. In one study, participants who used this approach were able to recall, on average, over 90% of the words presented to them from 12 lists, compared with only 10% recalled by participants who did not use this approach.

A third way to organize new material is to create a *hierarchy* of the information, separating it into sections and subsections, much like the chapter of a textbook. For example, if you needed to memorize the names of all the muscles of the body for an anatomy class, you might group them according to their locations or by their actions.

One very useful study technique for helping readers to learn and remember textbook information is, once again, based on the principle of organization (West *et al.*, 2008). The *PQRST method* is named for its five steps, which are to be undertaken in order.

- *Preview*. Skim the entire section you are required to learn. Look for the basic themes, and try to get an idea of the information you will have to process when reading the section in more detail. If you were reading a section of a textbook about the events surrounding the creation of the European Union (EU), your preview might focus on figuring out the principal events and people involved in the build-up.

- *Question*. Examine the organization of the section and turn each subsection into a question that you want to answer over the course of your reading. If one of the sub-heads was 'The Founding Six Countries', ask yourself, 'Which six countries were influential in setting up the EU?'

- *Read*. Read the section with the goal of finding the answers to your questions.

- *Self-Recitation*. Ask yourself and answer aloud a set of questions that arose from the reading material, such as, 'In what year was the Treaty of Rome signed?', 'What year did Greece join the EU?' and 'What is the significance of the Maastricht treaty?'

- *Test*. Test yourself by trying to recall as much of the learnt information as possible.

By organizing your reading in this way – by asking yourself questions about the information at hand before, during and after reading – you stand a better chance of retaining the information than if you were to spend your time simply reading through the section several times.

Finally, one of the most powerful organizational structures in memory is the self. Try relating all the material you read to your own thoughts, views, feelings and memories (this is easier with history or politics than biochemistry). It will help you retrieve it later. For instance, do you remember when euro coins were introduced or using one for the first time? Have you visited any European countries? If so, are they a member and when did they enter. Do you hold any views on the Union? In what ways are they relevant to the story?

Organization and Encoding Another important variable that can enhance the encoding of information into long-term memory is *organization*. Actually, when people add to or elaborate on the meaning of certain pieces of information or events, they are organizing them: that is, they are giving the information a structure that is more familiar and available to them. As such, they are making it easier to encode into long-term memory. Typically, people do this intuitively. If we asked you to memorize a list of words that included 'fox', 'bear', 'Italy', 'England', 'rabbit', 'Spain' and 'mouse', you might naturally sort the words into rough categories of 'Animals' and 'European countries'.

Organization by categories can be particularly useful in helping us to encode complicated situations. Cognitive psychologists have identified structures called **schemas** (Brewer & Treyens, 1981), bases of knowledge that we develop based on prior exposure to similar experiences or other bases of knowledge. Schemas can be helpful in allowing us to attend to and encode a lot of information in a hurry. Think about the first time you walked into a new restaurant. Did it feel awkward or strange because you were not sure of the rules or what to order? If you had visited other, similar restaurants before that one, the schemas you developed during your

> **schemas** knowledge developed from prior exposure to similar experiences or other knowledge bases.

In need of a schema. This young boy enjoys watching a model train at Round House Restaurant in Brno, Czech Republic. The Round House's unusual use of a model train to deliver food and drinks to its customers will not feature in its customers' schemas of visiting a restaurant.
Source: Tomas Hajek/isifa/Getty Images, Inc.

experiences at those restaurants probably helped you know what to do and what to order in the new restaurant with less effort than you would have needed if you had never been in a restaurant at all.

Before You Go On

What Do You Know?

3. How does increased attention affect automatic and effortful processing?

4. Why is it more effective to study all term long, rather than in one massive session right before a final exam?

5. Which type of coding would most people use to remember someone's face? Which type would most people use to remember a person's name?

What Do You Think?

What sort of things do you struggle to remember? How could you help yourself to remember them?

How Do We Store Memories?

LEARNING OBJECTIVE 3

Describe how we organize and store information in working and long-term memory and how we can enhance our long-term memory.

As you have seen, after entering the working memory system, information remains there for only a short time, sometimes only a matter of seconds. In contrast, when information moves to the long-term memory system, it can remain there for hours

or a lifetime. The retention of information, whether brief or long, in either of these memory systems is called storage.

Storage in Working Memory

Information may enter working memory from two major sources. New information, as we have seen, can be encoded after a short trip through the sensory memory system. In addition, we can bring back into the working memory system information that previously has been encoded in the long-term memory system, for use in a current situation or task.

During the time that information from either of these sources is residing in the working memory system, it can, as we have seen, serve many important functions in our daily lives, from enabling us to read or carry on conversations to helping us solve current problems (Hofmann *et al.*, 2011). The information stored in working memory also helps us do mental computations, such as mathematical problems (Maybery & Do, 2003). We could not, for example, add together the numbers 12 plus 13 if our working memory were not reminding us that we are computing those particular numbers, that addition is the task at hand and that $3 + 2 = 5$ and $10 + 10 = 20$. In fact, because working memory helps us do mental computations, it is often characterized as a *temporary notepad* that briefly holds intermediate information while we think and solve larger problems (Baddeley, 2004).

The Storage Limits of Working Memory

Once information enters working memory, it can be stored for just a limited period (Courage *et al.*, 2010). Concentrated efforts, such as rehearsal, can lengthen the availability of information in working memory, but eventually it is either passed on to the long-term memory system or lost (Jonides *et al.*, 2008, 2003).

Just as striking as the limited *duration* of working memory is its limited *capacity* (Hofmann *et al.*, 2011). On average, only five to nine items can be stored there at a given moment. This number was first uncovered back in 1885 by the German researcher Hermann Ebbinghaus (1850–1909), who pioneered memory research by studying his own memory, and it was confirmed over 70 years later by psychologist George Miller (1956).

In a typical study of this phenomenon, researchers present people with a sequence of unrelated digits, letters, words or the like, and then ask them to restate the items in the correct order. Because the items are unrelated and presented rapidly, it is likely that this procedure is tapping into working memory only, not into some related information that has been stored in long-term memory, because, as we have seen above, meaning massively influences memory encoding and retrieval. In study after study, almost every adult can recall sequences that consist of five items, but very few can recall lists consisting of more than nine items. Each individual displays his or her own **memory span** – the maximum number of items that can be recalled in the correct order – but no memory span strays very far from seven. Because research shows that almost everyone has a working memory capacity in this range, Miller described it as the magical number seven, plus or minus two.

memory span maximum number of items that can be recalled in their correct order.

Enhancing Working Memory Actually, the storage capacity of working memory is not quite as limited as it may seem from the Ebbinghaus and Miller studies. Each of the seven or so items that working memory holds can consist of more than a single digit, letter or word. An item can consist of a *chunk* of information. **Chunking** pieces of information together into larger units enables us to encode more information in our working memory system, and enables our working memory to store more information at a given moment.

chunking grouping bits of information together to enhance one's ability to hold that information in working memory.

Let us say that we are presented with a long string of numbers, 9-1-1-1-9-6-6-1-9-3-9-1-4-9-2-1-2-7. Because our capacity in working memory is only 7 ± 2 items, we would, on the face of it, be unable to store this sequence of 18 items. If, however, we split it into more manageable chunks, such as 911-196-619-391-492-127, our task changes. We now need to store only six items (i.e. six chunks of digits) in working memory, and the task becomes manageable, but still quite difficult. In fact, these digits can be further chunked according to meaning: 911 (September 11th), 1966 (Year England won the Football World Cup), 1939 (Outbreak of the Second World War), 1492 (Columbus' 'discovery' of America, 127 (Danny Boyle's 2010 film, *127 Hours*). Chunking in this way massively increases the amount of information you hold in memory. But you will notice it in more subtle ways too, like the way you read aloud numbers to someone else – not in a monotone, but by chunking into sets by using pauses and intonation in your voice. Without realizing it, we may be taking advantage of chunking when we first try to master a song's lyrics. Rather than learn the song letter by letter or word by word, we may hold onto seven new lines at a time, repeating the lines until we have successfully learnt them.

Our ability to chunk actually comes from our long-term memory system (Cowan & Chen, 2009). Information may enter working memory as either new information arriving from sensory memory or through retrieval from long-term memory. In chunking, we use our stored, long-term knowledge that certain letters spell certain words or that words can be organized to form sentences to guide us in chunking new information.

Storage in Long-Term Memory

Whereas the sensory memory and working memory systems deal only with a limited number of short-term memories, our long-term memory system retains a seemingly unlimited number of pieces of information for an indefinite period, extending from minutes to a lifetime (Voss, 2009). Indeed, an oft-cited estimate is that our long-term memory system may hold as many as one quadrillion, i.e. 1,000,000,000,000,000, separate pieces of information (e.g. see Loftus & Ketchum, 1991). This expansive capacity and duration is critical to our functioning, for it is in this vast memory store that we hold – ready for use – all of the information that we have ever gathered. When we remember previously gathered knowledge, past events and people, or acquired skills, we are using our long-term memory system.

Several factors influence whether particular events are stored in long-term memory. As we have observed, new information must first be attended to in order to have any chance of eventually winding up in this memory system. Furthermore, items that are attended to must be encoded and briefly stored in working memory and then encoded into long-term memory before they can be stored in this memory system (Baddeley, 2010). Any shortcomings in these attention and encoding activities may prevent the information from being stored in the long-term system (McGaugh, 2006, 2003). Moreover, even after information is successfully stored in long-term memory, some of it may become unavailable (Loftus & Loftus, 1980). That is, some of the information that we have previously acquired cannot be retrieved from long-term memory. Most of the research on long-term memory storage, including the loss of stored information, has been conducted in the biological realm, as we shall soon see.

We have observed that the number of items that can be stored in working memory is rather similar from person to person (7 ± 2). The capacity for long-term memory storage, while enormous for most of us, does, however, vary greatly among people.

What Types of Memories Do We Store in Long-Term Memory? Various kinds of information are stored in long-term memory, as shown in Figure 10.5. **Explicit memory** is the type of memory that you can consciously bring to mind, such as your mother's birthday, or your travel to foreign countries. But there are other types of memories that we are not consciously aware of – such as learnt reactions, learnt motor behaviours and perceptual information – that help us to develop various skills. For instance, an **implicit memory** could include reacting with disgust when you are given a plate of food that made you sick sometime in the past – you may not recall the initial bad meal, but you will remember to avoid the food.

explicit memory a memory that a person can consciously bring to mind, such as one's date of birth.

implicit memory a memory that a person is not consciously aware of, such as learnt reactions, motor behaviours and skills.

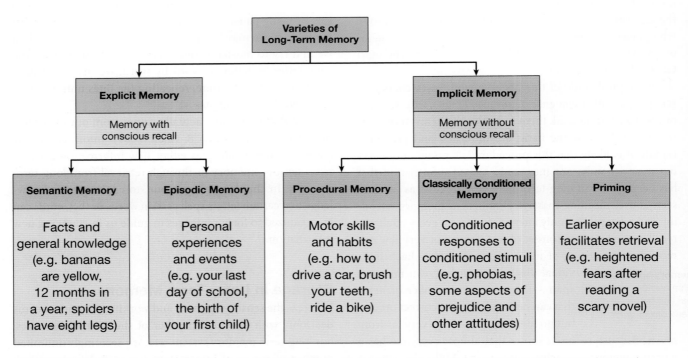

FIGURE 10.5 A diagram outlining some general classifications of long-term memory. Our long-term memories are of two main types, with various subdivisions within each.

PSYCHOLOGY AROUND US   Where Do Feelings of Disgust Come From?

In a series of studies, researchers Andrea Morales and Gavan Fitzsimons found not only that some products – rubbish bags, nappies, cat litter, tampons – evoke a subconscious feeling of disgust, but also that they can transfer their general 'ickiness' to anything they come in contact with (Lemonick, 2007).

Where do feelings of disgust for certain products come from? In part from early-life experiences with the products and perhaps, say the researchers, through evolution, from the negative experiences of our ancestors. Either way, the idea that negative qualities can be passed on by a touch has become hardwired, says Fitzsimons. So he and Morales set out to see whether toilet paper and other products could psychologically contaminate food in a shopping basket. They used real shopping baskets and told shoppers that the study had to do only with product preference.

Strong preferences were just what the shoppers exhibited. Any food that touched something perceived to be disgusting became immediately less desirable itself, though all of the products were in their original wrapping. The appeal of the food fell even if the two products were merely close together; an inch seemed to be the critical distance. 'It makes no sense if you think about it,' said Fitzsimons.

'We'd take cookies out of the basket and offer them to the subjects,' said Fitzsimons, 'and we had some really tempting-looking cookies.' No takers. Moreover, he added, 'Everything we did suggested that these feelings were below the level of awareness. If we told someone, "You didn't take the cookie because it touched the cat litter," they would say, "That's ridiculous,"' (Lemonick, 2007).

Neuroimaging studies of patients with brain damage suggest that explicit and implicit information are stored in different brain regions (Mecklinger *et al.*, 2011; Squire & Schacter, 2002). Explicit memories are converted into long-term memories in the hippocampus and then stored permanently in various areas of the neocortex. (In a sense, the hippocampus serves as a temporary storage site within the long-term explicit memory system.) In contrast, the striatum, the region located towards the midline in the brain, plays a key role in the storage of implicit memories. When implicit memories are activated to help people carry out various skills and habits, their striatum and its related structures become particularly active. In fact, an individual whose striatum is damaged by injury or disease may have great difficulty performing long-time skills and habits, yet retain most of his or her explicit memories.

To further explore the complexities of long-term memory, there are two types of explicit memories: **semantic memory**, your general knowledge of the world, and **episodic memory**, memories of personal events or episodes from your own life. Some studies further hint that these two subgroups of explicit memories may be stored in different ways from one another, but this is far from certain (Christman & Propper, 2010; Markowitsch *et al.*, 2010).

> **semantic memory** a person's memory of general knowledge of the world.

> **episodic memory** a person's memory of personal events or episodes from his or her life.

Explicit versus implicit memories. (Left) The many details of *Star Trek* movies that this onlooker and other Trekkies love to recall are *explicit* memories. (Right) In contrast, the learnt motor behaviours and perceptual information that enable this skateboarder to artfully do her thing are *implicit* memories.

Source: (left photo) Ethan Miller/Getty Images, Inc.; (right photo) AAGAMIA/Getty Images, Inc.

How Are Long-Term Memories Organized? How does the long-term memory system organize the many pieces of information that are stored there? Is it set up like a bookshop in which the various items are organized first by broad categories, such as fiction and non-fiction, then by subcategories (e.g. in the case of non-fiction, 'art', 'health', 'nature', 'science' or 'travel'), and finally by sub-subcategories (e.g., art books whose authors' names begin with A, B and so on)? Despite years of study, we do not fully understand how pieces of information are organized when stored in long-term memory.

At the same time, psychologists do now know that, regardless of their precise organization, the pieces of information stored in long-term memory are indeed linked to each other, forming a *network of interwoven associations*.

Thus, when we retrieve one piece of information from long-term memory, a related one will often spring forth, and that piece of information may, in turn, trigger another one. This web of associations enables us to travel rapidly through our long-term memory to retrieve much of the information we need for a current situation or task. As we saw earlier, the PDP, or connectionist, model of memory helps explain such networks by suggesting that our neurons also are activated in networks. One such network is the *Self Memory System* (Conway, 2005), where personal memories are organized into a meaningful network of experiences and lifetime periods, by which we can have a representation of our self in the past. When we think about a certain period in our life, like when we lived in Paris, it activates relevant memories and knowledge from that time and location.

Before You Go On

What Do You Know?

6. What is chunking, and why would you want to use it?

7. What kind of information is stored in semantic memory and episodic memory? Are semantic and episodic memories implicit or explicit memories?

What Do You Think?

What are some examples of elaboration and organizational strategies that have helped you in school or other areas of your life? What new ones are you going to try after reading this chapter?

How Do We Retrieve Memories?

LEARNING OBJECTIVE 4

Describe how we retrieve information from memory and how retrieval cues, priming, context and emotion can affect retrieval.

As we have noted, when information is successfully encoded from working memory into long-term memory, it is not only stored there but also is available for retrieval later. When we retrieve information from our long-term memory, it moves to the front and centre of our thinking and becomes available once again for use in our working memory system. Upon its return to working memory, the retrieved information may be used to help clarify current issues, solve new problems or simply re-experience past events (Baddeley, 2010; Hambrick & Engle, 2003). Retrieved memories of well-learnt multiplication tables help us calculate new mathematical problems, and retrieved 'memories' of how to drive guide us to park our cars in tight spaces. Even evolutionarily, retrieving a memory of an attack from a sabre-toothed tiger will have an impact on our behaviour when we revisit the location where it happened – how useful is that? The kind or amount of information stored in long-term memory would mean little if we were unable to retrieve it. Like a library or the Internet, the information in long-term memory must be navigated efficiently and accurately in order to produce necessary information.

Just as researchers do not fully understand how information is organized when stored in long-term memory, they do not know for sure how retrieval is carried out. Some theorists propose that it is a kind of 'search' process (Raaijmakers & Shiffrin, 2002, 1992). In other words, the person focuses on a specific question and scans his or her memory for the specific answer to that question. Other theorists believe that retrieval is more like an 'activation' process in which the questions people pose to themselves activate relevant pieces of information that have been stored in long-term memory, after which this activation then spreads *simultaneously* to every other associated piece of information. The difference between these two operations is like the difference between the specific results you get on a Wikipedia search versus the hundreds of results you get from a Google search.

If we fail to locate a particular book in a library or bookshop, it can mean either that the book is not there or that we are looking for it in the wrong section. Similarly, our failure to locate a piece of information in our long-term memory may mean that it is not stored there (encoding failure or storage loss) or that we have committed a *retrieval failure* of some kind.

We experience many retrieval failures in our daily lives. Often we find ourselves unable to recall a face, an event or a scheduled appointment, yet it comes to mind later. Obviously, the information was available in our memory all along, or we would not recall it later. Similarly, all of us have experienced the frustration of being unable to recall the answer to an exam question, only to remember it soon after the test. And in some instances we may become particularly frustrated when a piece of information feels right at the edge of our consciousness, an experience called the *tip-of-the-tongue* phenomenon.

retrieval cues words, sights or other stimuli that remind us of the information we need to retrieve from our memory.

The retrieval of information from memory is aided by **retrieval cues** – words, sights or other stimuli that remind us of the information that we need. Essentially, when we come across a retrieval cue, we enter our long-term memory system and activate a relevant piece of information. Because the pieces of information in this memory system are linked to each other in a network of associations, the activation of the first piece of information will trigger the activation of related pieces until a complete memory comes forth.

Priming and Retrieval

If the pieces of information stored in long-term memory are indeed linked together in a network of associations, then

priming activation of one piece of information, which in turn leads to the activation of another piece and ultimately to the retrieval of a specific memory (Tulving *et al.*, 1982).

the key to retrieving a specific memory is to locate one piece of information and follow associated pieces until arriving at the memory. In implicit memory, this activation of one piece of information, which then triggers the activation of other pieces and leads to the retrieval of a specific memory, is called **priming** (Was,

2010; Ramponi *et al.*, 2007). A similar process occurs in long-term memory, where it is usually referred to as *cueing*. We can consciously try to cue a memory, whereas priming is an automatic process that does not need attention. If, for example, we are having trouble remembering the name of a woman whom we met last week, we may bring the letter M to mind, recalling vaguely that her name began with that letter and hoping that the M sound will lead to (or cue) her name. Or we may try to recall our conversation with the nameless acquaintance, hoping that this recollection will eventually lead us back to her name.

Priming will take place without our conscious awareness. For example, you might be shopping one day and one shop you entered was playing the classic jazz standard *Summertime*. If you were to walk out of the shop and a friend were to ask you what song had just been playing on the store's speaker, you might not be able to recall it. However, if a short while later, in an unlikely turn of events, a quiz show host were to pop up and ask you to name three classic jazz songs for a large sum of money, research suggests that you would be particularly likely to include *Summertime* in your answer. Although you had no choice in the matter and were not even aware that it was happening – and even if you disliked jazz and were trying to ignore the song while in the store – it would have served as a retrieval cue and primed you to recall *Summertime* when later quizzed about jazz hits.

Given the operation of cueing and priming, we should not be surprised that the more cues and primes we encounter, or the more informative they are, the better our retrieval of memory. This is why people perform better on **recognition tasks**, ones in which they must report whether they have seen a particular item before (multiple-choice exams are an example of this, during which one selects the correct answer from a set of alternatives; you do not need to reproduce it, just 'recognize' which is the correct answer), than on **recall tasks**, those in which they are forced to produce memories using no or few retrieval cues (Figure 10.6) (Wixted & Squire, 2010; Tulving, 1974).

recognition tasks memory tasks in which people are asked to identify whether they have seen a particular item before.

recall tasks memory tasks in which people are asked to reproduce information using little or no retrieval cues.

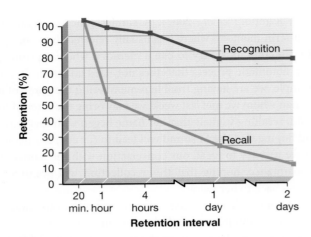

FIGURE 10.6 Recognition versus recall. In one study of retrieval, participants were tested for either recognition or recall of nonsense syllables over the course of two days. Retrieval on the recognition test was far superior to that on the recall test.

Source: Adapted from Schwanenflugel *et al.* (1992) and Luh (1922).

Context and Retrieval

It is often easier to retrieve particular information when we return to the setting or situation in which we first encoded it. The general idea is that memories are best retrieved when the cues overlap with the original trace, an idea put forward by Tulving (1974) as the *encoding specificity principle*. As the name suggests, this principle applies to how well items can be retrieved according to their encoding. Most of us have had personal experiences that attest to this. Upon returning to our old home or school, for example, we may find ourselves almost overrun by memories of events that we have not thought about for years. Similarly, a return to the scene of an argument or romantic encounter may bring forth detailed memories of the original event. Not surprisingly, then, some educators believe that people perform best on exams when the exams are administered in the same rooms where the material was taught. Can you think of other reasons why this may be the case? Or what good it may be to the student?

Clearly, returning to or duplicating the *context* in which information was learnt may help us to retrieve it (e.g. Postle, 2009, 2003). Why? Once again, the answer appears to be retrieval cues. The original context – the location or situation in which we learn material – is loaded with retrieval cues, each of which activates a piece of information, setting off the activation of related pieces and leading to memories of the original event. The likely impact of these many retrieval cues is an increase in the number, intensity and accuracy of relevant memories.

Emotion: A Special Retrieval Cue

Just as a letter, word, song or setting may serve as a retrieval cue and lead to specific memories, so may an emotional state or mood. If people learn something while in a particular state of mind, they may recall it more readily when they are in that state again. Gordon Bower was one of the first psychologists to recognize this phenomenon, called **state-dependent memory** (Bower, 2008, 1981; Forgas, 2008). In one study, he had people learn a list of words while they were in a hypnotically induced happy state of mind. He found that they remembered the words better if they were in a happy mood when tested later than if they were in a sad mood. Conversely, those who learnt the words when in a sad mood recalled them better if they were sad during later testing than if they were happy. Apparently, a feeling can serve as a cue for retrieving information that was encoded while experiencing that feeling.

> **state-dependent memory** a memory retrieval facilitated by being in the same state of mind in which you encoded the memory in the first place.

Some theorists further believe that a person's emotions may be more than just another retrieval cue (Rolls, 2011; McGaugh, 2003). As we shall see in the following sections, they suggest that strong emotions may enhance memories by leading to increased *rehearsal*, *elaboration* and *organization* of a particular event, or that intense emotions may trigger a *special memory mechanism*, producing emotional memories.

Emotional Memory: Rehearsal, Elaboration and Organization If an event makes us particularly happy, or for that matter very upset, we will probably think about it again and again. We are likely to talk about highly emotional events with relatives, perhaps send an SMS to our friends, maybe write about the events in a diary or even try to revisit the scene. Such behaviours are commonly displayed by people who have achieved a special personal accomplishment, observers of exciting sporting events or victims of accidents, hurricanes or other catastrophes. Together, responses of this kind amount to repeated rehearsals, elaborations and organization of the emotionally charged events. Think back to the example of a family wedding. Talking about the day with relatives not only helps people repeat an event, but probably also helps link it to other important events in the family's history and to organize recall of the event. We have seen already that rehearsal, elaboration, and organization are all ways to improve the encoding and storage of memories; thus, we should not be surprised that exciting or upsetting events tend to be retrieved more readily than ordinary ones (McGaugh, 2006, 2003).

Special Emotional Memory Mechanisms: Flashbulb Memories If we were asked where we were at a specific time, a few Tuesdays back, what we were doing and who we were talking to, few of us would be able to answer off the top of our heads. Yet, if we were asked the same questions about our whereabouts on Tuesday, September 11, 2001, when two planes crashed into and brought down the twin towers of the World Trade Center, many of us could state with apparent accuracy and great confidence these and other details (Denver *et al.*, 2010). Such detailed and near-permanent memories of emotionally significant events, or of the circumstances surrounding our learning of the events, are called **flashbulb memories**, and include events such as the death of Diana, Princess of Wales. Beyond widely shared events, such as the 9/11 attacks, people also have flashbulb memories of emotional events that have more personal significance, such as the birth or death of a loved one.

flashbulb memory detailed and near-permanent memories of an emotionally significant event, or of the circumstances surrounding the moment we learnt about the event.

The kinds of details retained in flashbulb memories seem unavailable to us in our memories of other events (Edery-Halpern & Nachson, 2004). What is it about these special events that enables us to retrieve such details? According to some theorists, it is the extraordinary level of emotionality that we experience during the event. Specifically, our intense emotions may help trigger a *special memory mechanism* – a mechanism beyond the usual memory processes – that produces a near-permanent record and more likely retrieval of nearly everything we experienced during the event (McGaugh, 2006, 2003).

Psychologists have yet to fully identify this proposed memory mechanism, but certain studies do support the notion that emotionally charged memories involve mechanisms beyond those operating for more neutral memories (LeDoux & Doyère, 2011; Kensinger & Corkin, 2003). In one study, for example, some participants were given a tranquilizer drug while hearing an emotional story about a boy who received emergency surgery, whereas other participants were given a placebo drug during the same story (Cahill

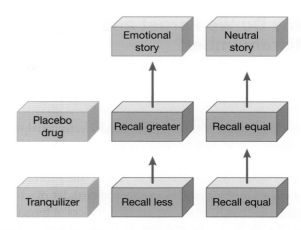

FIGURE 10.7 Emotional arousal and memory. In Cahill's study of emotion's role in memory, participants heard either an emotional or a neutral story. Those given a tranquilizer while hearing the emotional story recalled less than those given the placebo. However, both groups recalled the same amount of information for the neutral story.

et al., 1994). One week later, the participants who had been tranquilized – and owing to the tranquilizer, had experienced little emotionality during the intense story – remembered less about the story than did the placebo participants, whose emotions had been allowed to rise during the story. In contrast, when the study's participants were asked to recall a more neutral story, participants from both groups showed equal accuracy in their later recollections (Figure 10.7).

On the other hand, other research has called into question whether flashbulb memories are, in fact, as highly accurate as previously believed. One study, for example, compared undergraduates' memories of the 9/11 attacks with their memories of everyday events (Talarico & Rubin, 2009, 2007, 2003). Although the participants in the study reported a high level of confidence in the accuracy of their 9/11 memories, the data indicated that, in fact, such memories were no more accurate than those of more neutral events.

Before You Go On

What Do You Know?

8. What is the difference between priming and cueing?

9. If researchers show people several pictures of small rodents, then find that many people include hamsters and mice when asked to name animals that make good pets, what has happened? Why did it happen?

10. Why do many educators believe it is helpful to take an exam in the same room where you learnt the material?

11. How do strong emotions affect our memory processes?

What Do You Think?

Have you experienced flashbulb memories or state-dependent memory? If so, when?

Why Do We Forget and Misremember?

LEARNING OBJECTIVE 5

Summarize key theories of why we forget information and sometimes distort or manufacture memories.

Throughout most of this chapter, we have considered which variables help us to accurately remember events and information. But people do not always remember things as well as they would like (Tsukiura *et al.*, 2011). The elusive name, the missed meeting and the overlooked birthday of a friend or relative are all instances of **forgetting**, the inability to recall information that was previously encoded. Sometimes we not only forget information, we also distort or manufacture memories. We recall events differently from the way in which they occurred or we remember things that never occurred at all.

> **forgetting** the inability to recall information that was previously encoded into memory.

Theories of Forgetting

As we have observed, some apparent losses of memory are not really instances of forgetting at all, but rather *failures of attention*. If our mind is elsewhere when we are putting down our set of keys or the remote control, we simply cannot encode such acts. Correspondingly, the location of such items will not be stored in memory and available for later retrieval. At the other end of the spectrum, some material is indeed stored and available, but has weak or few retrieval cues attached to it, making it difficult for people to activate – or cue – the relevant memories from storage.

Beyond these common causes of forgetting, theorists have uncovered a number of variables that may actively interfere with memory and, in turn, produce forgetting (Macleod *et al.*, 2010; Wixted, 2010, 2004). Each of today's leading explanations of forgetting has received some research support, but, as you will see, each also has key limitations and raises important questions.

Decay As we observed earlier, German researcher Herman Ebbinghaus pioneered the study of forgetting over a century ago by systematically testing his own memory of lists of nonsense syllables (e.g., *lin, pav, sul*). After rehearsing and mastering a particular list, Ebbinghaus would measure how well he had retained the syllables after various intervals of time: 20 minutes, two days, a month later, and so on. He found that there was a huge drop in his memory of a list soon after learning it. However, the amount that he forgot eventually levelled off; in fact, most of the information that had been retained 10 hours after first memorizing a list remained in his memory three weeks later. Known as the *forgetting curve*

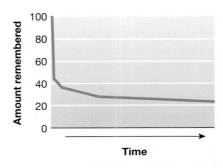

FIGURE 10.8 The forgetting curve. We forget a great deal very rapidly but the forgetting levels off and the amount of information we retain stabilizes.

(Figure 10.8), this pattern of rapid memory loss followed by a stable retention of the remaining information has been supported repeatedly by research (Erdelyi, 2010).

Many theorists explain patterns of forgetting, such as that observed by Ebbinghaus, by pointing to *decay*. According to the **decay theory**, memories often fade away on their own simply because they are neglected or not used for a long period (Wixted, 2010, 2004; McGaugh, 2006, 2003). This theory is built on the notion that memories leave a physical trace in the brain – a so-called *memory trace* – when they are acquired. Theoretically, these traces fade away over time if the person does not use them.

> **decay theory** the theory of forgetting, suggesting memories fade over time owing to neglect or failure to access over time.

Decay theory is not as popular an explanation for forgetting as it once was. It cannot account for the repeated finding that people learn seemingly forgotten information or skills much more rapidly the second time around than the first time. In other words, *relearning* is faster than initial learning. If forgotten information has, in fact, worn away because of lack of use – that is, if memory traces have been lost – relearning should be occurring from scratch, and it should take just as long as the initial learning did.

Interference According to the **interference theory**, forgetting is affected mainly by what happens to people before or after they learn information. This theory holds that information will be retained in memory as long as competing, similar information does not interfere with it (Tillman *et al.*, 2011; Wixted, 2010, 2004). Suppose your friend moves to a new house and receives a new landline phone number in which the first three digits are the same as the old number. Perhaps when dialling the new number, you find yourself mistakenly dialling her old number. According to the

> **interference theory** the theory that forgetting is influenced by what happens to people before or after they take information in.

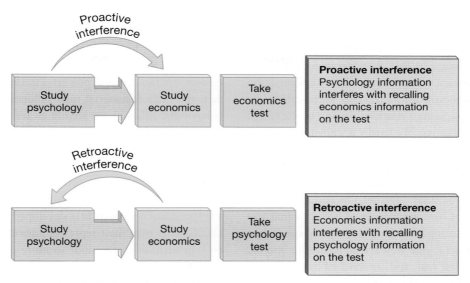

FIGURE 10.9 Proactive and retroactive interference. Forgetting is affected by interference from other information. Proactive interference occurs when information already learnt interferes with learning new information; retroactive interference occurs when new information disrupts recalling previously learnt information.

interference theory, the new landline number was forgotten because competing information – the old number – interfered with its retrieval.

When the competing information that prevents recall has been learnt before the forgotten item, as in the case of the forgotten phone number, the process is called **proactive interference**. Alternatively, **retroactive interference** occurs when new information prevents the retrieval of previously learnt information (Figure 10.9). Suppose you wish to call your friend's old number – perhaps to reach her mother who is still living at the old location – but you mistakenly dial the new number. In this scenario, you forgot the old number because competing information – the new number – interfered with its retrieval.

We should keep in mind that old information does not always interfere with the learning or remembering of new

proactive interference competing information that is learnt before the forgotten material, preventing its subsequent recall.

retroactive interference learning of new information that disrupts access to previously recalled information.

information. Sometimes it can even help us learn and hold on to new information. People who know how to roller-skate often pick up ice-skating faster than other people. Within European languages, shared Latin or Greek etymologies may help people learn new vocabulary in a foreign language more easily than starting a completely new unrelated language, like Japanese. Interference occurs only when old and new information conflict with one another, which of course can also happen with language learning, and with *false friends*, words which look similar but are not. In French *coin* means a corner or an area, whereas in English it is a metal disc used as currency.

We have observed how emotions – both positive and negative – often improve memory by either providing powerful retrieval cues, setting up additional rounds of rehearsal or triggering special memory mechanisms. At the same time, all of us have had experiences in which negative emotions, such as anxiety, actually interfere with memory and cause us to forget (Hawley *et al.*, 2011; Eysenck *et al.*, 2010; McGaugh, 2006, 2003).

PSYCHOLOGY AROUND US   Exam Nerves

Many students experience test anxiety. They may prepare fully for an examination, retain all of the necessary information and score highly on practice tests. Yet, on the day of the examination, they experience feelings of anxiety that grow from butterflies in their stomach to a strong fear that they will not do well in the exam . . . not pass the course . . . perhaps not even obtain their degree. Their anxiety grows so out of control as the test sits in front of them that they are unable to retrieve many of the answers that had been so available to them during practice tests the evening before. Many counsellors who work with such people suggest that the negative thoughts accompanying their anxiety (e.g. 'I will not pass this course') interfere with the retrieval of memories and cause the students to forget.

Motivated Forgetting Sometimes we seem to almost purposely forget information that is unpleasant, embarrassing or painful (Erdelyi, 2010; Mather, 2009; Kennedy *et al.*, 2004). Suppose, for example, that during your first year, you nervously and awkwardly stumble through a conversation with a classmate who you find attractive. Humiliated, you give up all hopes of pursuing a relationship, and by the end of the semester, the two of you are hardly acknowledging each other. Fast-forward three years. By now, you have become much more socially skilled and confident, and, as it turns out, you and your former 'crush' meet again at a graduation party. As the two of you laugh together, talk comfortably and discover shared tastes, you wonder aloud how it is that you never got together during your four years at college. Taken aback by your comment, your new friend recalls for you the conversation in the first year. You are shocked by this disclosure. On reflection, you recall vaguely that a discussion took place three years ago, but, for the life of you, you have no recollection of the stammering, falling and other embarrassing moves you made. In fact, you do not even recall having been all that interested in this person in the first place, you have put to one side the memory which was harmful to your self-esteem.

Clearly, you have forgotten an incident and related information that was unpleasant. But why? One possibility is that because the event was so painful you actively worked to forget it. You avoided opportunities for rehearsal, such as discussing the terrible experience with relatives or friends, sending a tweet about it or writing about it in your diary. You may have even avoided retrieval cues, such as the corridor where the catastrophic interaction occurred. In short, you avoided rehearsing, elaborating or organizing the information, making it less available for later retrieval from memory.

Of course, anyone who has *actively* tried to forget an upsetting event knows that this is not so easy to do. Even if we do not share the event with others, we often find ourselves thinking about it (i.e. privately rehearsing it) repeatedly. Moreover, like a flashbulb memory, the special emotional component of such an event often increases, rather than decreases, the likelihood of our remembering it.

repression a process in which we unconsciously prevent some traumatic events from entering our awareness, so that we do not have to experience the anxiety or blows to our self-concept that the memories would bring.

How then might we manage to forget certain unpleasant events or information? The leading explanation of such motivated forgetting is Sigmund Freud's theory of **repression**. Freud held that all people employ repression on occasion, a process in which we unconsciously prevent some traumatic events from entering our awareness, so that we do not have to

experience the anxiety or blows to our self-concept that the memories would bring. According to Freud, the repressed material is not lost, but rather *hidden* from consciousness. He believed that our experiences, especially childhood experiences, are too rich and powerful to slip away altogether. In fact, the hidden material may influence later decisions or behaviours, although we are not aware of its impact in such cases. In short, the repressed information takes on the form of an implicit memory.

According to Freud, repressed memories may be jogged and brought forth under certain circumstances. Indeed, as we saw in Chapter 1, a key feature of psychoanalytic therapy, the treatment approach first developed by Freud, is to help clients rediscover their repressed memories of past traumas and, in turn, open the door to more effective functioning. Despite the wide influence of this theory and of psychoanalytic therapy, it is important to recognize that research has failed to demonstrate consistently that people repress unpleasant events (Erdelyi, 2010; Kihlström, 2006). But the idea of motivated forgetting is one where Freud has had a clear and lasting influence on the understanding of how people might think, even where there are clear scientific weaknesses in some of his work.

Distorted or Manufactured Memories

Our memories can be subject to distortions. In large part, this is because, as we observed earlier, we tend to rely on semantic codes when we encode information into long-term memory. That is, we encode the *meaning* of an event, rather than its specific words or images. In turn, when we later retrieve the memory, we have to *reconstruct* it. We must fill in details from our earlier recollection. Thus, when five people later try to remember the same event, they may each recall the details of the event quite differently.

A number of factors may contribute to faulty reconstructions of memory; that is, to the distortion or manufacture of memories (Erdelyi, 2010). Three of the most common are *source misattributions*, *exposure to misinformation* and the *effects of imagination* (Table 10.1).

Source Misattributions When we encode and store information in long-term memory, we often forget or are confused about where it came from originally, its *source*.

Source misattribution can produce memories that are distorted, or in some cases manufactured (Lindsay *et al.*, 2004). Is our detailed recollection of getting lost at the supermarket when we

source misattribution remembering information, but not the source it came from; can lead to remembering as true information from unreliable sources.

Years ago in the United States, millions of viewers watched a popular television game show, *To Tell the Truth*. On this show, three contestants would claim to be an individual who was famous for a particular skill or accomplishment, for example a famous dog trainer. Only one of the three was, in fact, the real expert; the other two were imposters. A panel would ask questions of the three contestants. They might ask questions about dogs, dog instincts, effective training techniques, and so on and they would try to decide who the real expert was.

During the questioning period, viewers were exposed to a good deal of information. In the case of a famous dog trainer,

for example, viewers would hear answers about which breeds are easier to train, which training techniques are most effective, how long training typically takes, and so on. The problem was that only one-third of this information was necessarily accurate. Only the actual trainer was sworn to tell the truth. It was often impossible for viewers to remember whether a particular piece of information came from the expert (and was therefore accurate) or from one of the impostors (and was inaccurate). Unable to remember that the information came from a dubious source, many viewers carried away from each programme false information.

TABLE 10.1 Common Reasons Why We Distort or Manufacture Memories

Source misattribution	We often fail to record where the information came from when we encode and store the information in long-term memory
Exposure to misinformation	New information that is inaccurate or misleading can distort our recall or lead us to manufacture new memories
Effects of imagination	Our own imagination can lead us to recall events that never took place

were six years old a direct memory of that event? Or, are we actually remembering our parents' many stories about the event? Or are we confusing our own life with something we saw on television? We may have supreme confidence in our memory of the event and even 'remember' vivid details about it, yet the memory may be inaccurate or even entirely false. We feel we are remembering something, but it may not be the event itself.

Exposure to Misinformation Earlier we noted that retroactive interference often causes us to forget something when we are later exposed to new competing information. For example, an old phone number may be lost from memory when a fairly similar, new phone number is mastered. Similarly, exposure to new information, particularly misinformation, can lead to the distortion or the manufacture of memories (Wixted, 2010, 2004).

Consider a situation in which a man witnesses a robbery. If a week later the eyewitness is asked, 'Could you

please describe the robber?', he is being called upon to rely exclusively on his memory for a description. If, however, the eyewitness is told in passing, as part of the questioning process, 'We've had a number of similar robberies lately, involving a heavy, blond-haired guy with a beard', this new information may greatly influence the witness's recall of the robber and the robbery. Such exposures to new information, often misinformation, are of great concern in police cases. Many a defendant has been accused or even convicted of a crime based on testimony from witnesses whose memories were unintentionally distorted or manufactured (Devenport *et al.*, 2009; Wells & Loftus, 2003). (See 'What Happens in the Brain When We Give Eyewitness Testimony' at the end of this section for more information.)

The impact of misinformation on memory has received considerable attention in psychology laboratories. How do researchers plant misinformation in memory studies? A clever investigation by psychologist Elizabeth Loftus and her colleagues (1978) illustrates how this is done. Participants in her study observed a film of a traffic accident and were then asked to remember certain details of the accident. One group of participants was asked, 'How fast were the cars going when they *smashed* into each other?' A second group was asked, 'How fast were the cars going when they *hit* each other?' The experimenter's use of the word *smash* implies a very severe accident, whereas the word *hit* implies a milder accident. Not surprisingly, people who were given the *smash* description remembered the cars going at a faster speed than did those in the *hit* condition. The researchers also asked, 'Did you see any broken glass?' Those who were read the sentence with *smash* were significantly more likely to say yes than those who were read the sentence with *hit*. In fact, there had been no broken glass in the film.

Study after study has demonstrated the distorting effects of misinformation on memory. In each, participants first observe an event and later receive from experimenters new, misleading information about the event (Zhu *et al.*, 2010; Loftus, 2005). A short while after observing an uneventful interaction between two spouses, for example, participants in a study may be told, in passing, that one of the spouses is a rather hostile person, or passionate or devious. Sure enough, in their later recollections of the observed interaction, many participants 'remember' hostile, passionate, or devious acts by the spouse in question. Similarly, people have been misled by subsequent exposures to misinformation, to 'remember' objects – glasses, paintings, revolvers – that were not actually present in an observed event.

A particularly powerful way of being exposed to misinformation is through *hypnosis*. As we first saw in Chapter 8, people who are hypnotized enter a sleep-like state in which they become very suggestible. While in this state, they can be led to behave, perceive and think in ways that would ordinarily seem impossible. They may, for example, become temporarily blind, deaf or insensitive to pain. Hypnosis can also help people remember events that occurred and were forgotten years ago, a capability used by many psychotherapists. On the other hand, in recent years, it has come to the attention of researchers that hypnosis can also make people forget, distort or manufacture memories by supplying misinformation (Erdelyi, 2010; Mazzoni *et al.*, 2010; Barnier *et al.*, 2004). Witnesses who are hypnotized to help them remember an observed crime are, in fact, likely to remember details offered or implied by the hypnotist. These details – such as the time of the crime, the clothes worn by the perpetrator or the presence of a weapon – may be inconsistent with their actual observations. Courts in the United States no longer admit as evidence eyewitness recollections that have been gathered initially under hypnosis.

The Effect of Imagination It turns out that our memories can be distorted not only by misinformation supplied by others but also by false information that comes from within, from our imaginations. Researchers have found repeatedly that when people are instructed to imagine the occurrence of certain events, many come to believe that they have in fact experienced those events (Richardson, 2011; Thomas *et al.*, 2007).

In one study, a team of researchers asked the parents of college students to list events that had, in fact, occurred during the students' childhoods (Hyman & Kleinknecht, 1999). In later interviews, the students themselves were instructed to recall those real events, along with another event, one that had not actually occurred according to the parents' reports. The students were not told that this event was false. A student might, for example, be instructed to recall the false event of accidentally knocking over a table at a wedding, as well as a number of events that actually had occurred. When interviewed some days later, about one-fourth of the students fully believed that the false events had occurred during their childhood, and, in fact, they could 'remember' many details of the unfortunate experiences. Clearly, misinformation from others or from our own imaginations, or from a combination of the two, can greatly influence our recollections, leading at times to forgetting, the distortion or even the manufacture of memories.

Before You Go On

What Do You Know?

12. How does the decay theory explain forgetting?

13. What is repression?

14. In playing a joke on you, a friend tells you that they won a lot of money in a bet on a tennis match. A few minutes later, after they have enjoyed the look on your face, you learn that they were lying, and that they have not won anything. A few days later, you find yourself thinking of the friend and how they are spending the money, and how clever they were to predict the tennis score. What has happened to your memory?

What Do You Think?

What examples of proactive and retroactive interference or memory distortions have you experienced in your own life? Have you ever been certain of your version of an event only to be proved wrong by a more trustworthy or credible source?

YOUR BRAIN AND BEHAVIOUR What Happens in the Brain When We Give Eyewitness Testimony

Imagine you witnessed a car accident where someone was injured. You dialled for help and stayed at the scene to tell the police officer what happened. A few months later, you were called to testify as an eyewitness at the trial. How accurate do you think your memory would be?

When people give eyewitness testimony, many regions of their brains are involved, including the hippocampus, amygdala, prefrontal cortex, visual cortex, thalamus and mammillary bodies, among others. Let's see how several of these regions are involved in such eyewitness testimony.

Recalling the event. Eyewitness retrieval and recall of the observed event depends largely on neuron activity in the cerebral context, shown here in this image of a florescent pyramidal neuron. In addition, protein synthesis in the pyramidal neurons of the prefrontal cortex enables memories to be stored again after they have been used.

Source: Courtesy of Elizabeth Gould.

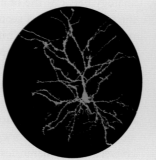

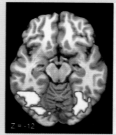
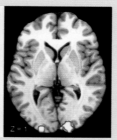

Retrieving an incorrect memory. Different parts of the visual cortex are activated when eyewitnesses remember an observed event accurately versus when they remember it inaccurately. Association parts of the visual cortex are at work in both true and false memories (orange areas on the left brain scan), whereas only true memories activate the primary visual cortex (orange areas on the right).

Source: Cabeza, Differential Contributions of Prefrontal, Medial Temporal, and Sensory-Perceptual Regions to True and False Memory Formation, *Cerebral Cortex*, 2007, Figure 4. Reproduced with permission.

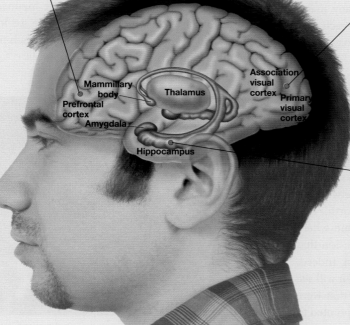

Mammillary body
Thalamus
Prefrontal cortex
Amygdala
Association visual cortex
Primary visual cortex
Hippocampus

Source: Masterfile.

Storing the memory. A major role in the formation and storage of memories about the observed event is played by the hippocampus, shown here in this image of neurons genetically engineered to make fluorescent dyes. The synapses in this brain region are changed by experience and are activated when we remember.

Source: Courtesy of Prof. Jeff Lichtman.

Memory and the Brain

WHAT HAPPENS IN THE
B R A I N ?

LEARNING OBJECTIVE 6

Describe how the brain is involved in memory.

Much of what we know about the biology of memory has come from studies of people who have suffered injuries to specific locations of the brain (Matthews, 2011). Important information has also been gained through experiments in which researchers surgically or chemically change the brains of animals and then observe the effects on old memories and new learning (Schwarting, 2003). In addition, over the past decade, studies using brain scans have enabled investigators to observe brain activity and structure at the very moment that people are thinking and remembering (Matthews, 2011). Finally, molecular biology studies have shed light on specific changes that may occur in our brain cells as memories form (Sweatt, 2010).

What Is the Anatomy of Memory?

Memories are difficult to locate. Recall from Chapter 5 that back in the 1920s neurological researcher Karl Lashley undertook a series of experiments with rats, in search of the specific places in the brain where memories are stored (Lashley, 1948). He would train a rat to run through a maze, then cut out a snippet of its brain tissue and set the rat loose in the maze again, checking to see whether it still remembered how to navigate through the maze. Lashley operated on many, many rats, cutting out different sections of brain tissue for each one. He found that all rats retained at least some memory of the maze, no matter what part of the brain he removed.

Based on studies such as this, researchers have concluded that there is no single place – no storehouse – in the brain where memories reside (Dudai, 2011). Information in the brain is distributed across various networks of neurons throughout the brain. As we have seen, for example, connectionist theorists see memory as a *process* rather than a place, an activity that involves changes in networks of multiple neurons throughout the brain. When such networking is activated, a memory is triggered and comes forth. This conclusion that there is no single place in the brain where memories reside is similar to the Chapter 9 conclusion that a single learning centre in the brain does not exist. Indeed, because memory and learning go hand in hand, you will see that several of the brain structures and activities that were discussed in Chapter 9 to account for learning are pointed to again here as we examine the neuroscience of memory.

Although today's theorists believe that neurons located throughout the brain are involved in memory, research has clarified that some brain areas are particularly important in the formation and retrieval of memories. Among the most important structures in working memory, for example, is the **prefrontal cortex**, a key structure within the neocortex that is located just behind the forehead (Öztekin *et al.*, 2009; Wang, 2005). When animals or humans acquire new information, the prefrontal cortex becomes more active (Chein *et al.*, 2011). Apparently, this activity enables them to hold information temporarily and to continue working with the information as long as it is needed. To refer back to our analogy between the brain and a computer, the neurons in the prefrontal cortex seem to operate like a computer's central processor, drawing information from various parts of the brain and holding it temporarily for use in a task, yet able to switch whenever necessary to other information and tasks.

Among the most important structures in long-term memory are the *hippocampus* (Figure 10.10) and other parts of the neocortex (Tsukiura *et al.*, 2011). In our earlier discussion of explicit memories, we noted that the hippocampus converts such memories into long-term status, stores the memories temporarily and then sends them on to various areas of the neocortex for genuine long-term storage. As we saw in Chapter 5, destruction of the hippocampus in adulthood does not wipe out all long-term memories, only those that occurred just prior to the brain damage (Jeneson *et al.*, 2010; Wixted & Squire, 2010). In contrast, destruction of certain parts of the neocortex results in the loss of older memories. These findings suggest that the hippocampus is indeed an important temporary storage site for long-term memories and a key player in the transfer of such memories into genuine long-term status in the neocortex.

prefrontal cortex important brain structure located just behind the forehead and implicated in working memory.

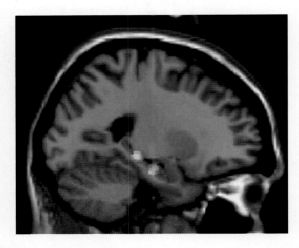

FIGURE 10.10 A key to memory. The hippocampus is a crucial structure for memory. It is activated when people recall information about facts and events (shown on this fMRI scan in yellow).

Source: Cabeza, Differential Contributions of Prefrontal, Medial Temporal, and Sensory-Perceptual Regions to True and False Memory Formation, *Cerebral Cortex*, 2007, Figure 4. Reproduced with permission.

What Is the Biochemistry of Memory?

As we have discussed, the PDP, or connectionist, model of memory describes the storage of information in long-term memory as a network of associations (McClelland, 2011) referred to as a *neural network*. When we activate one piece of information, related ones spring into action, enabling us to travel through our long-term memory system rapidly and retrieve particular memories. But how, in fact, does the brain manage to link such pieces of information to each other? Research increasingly points to biochemical and electrical changes in certain neurons, particularly those neurons located in the key brain regions that we have just noted.

Neural Circuits As we observed in Chapter 5, communication throughout the brain proceeds from neuron to neuron in a particular way. A given message arrives at a neuron as an impulse, travels down the axon of the neuron and is then carried by a chemical – a *neurotransmitter* – across the synaptic space to another neuron. The next neuron is then triggered and, like the preceding neuron, passes along a message to yet another neuron, and so on. When we talk about certain pieces of information being closely linked to other pieces of information in long-term memory, this is very likely to mean that certain neurons in the brain become predisposed to trigger other neurons, within a large neural network of interconnected neurons.

The question for memory researchers is how such neural circuits form (Changeux, 2011). How is it that some neurons become predisposed to trigger other neurons, enabling us to retrieve a given memory? It appears that the repeated stimulation of certain neurons greatly increases the likelihood that these neurons will respond, and respond strongly, to future stimulation of the same kind, a phenomenon called *long-term potentiation* (LTP) that was defined in Chapter 9 (Wixted, 2005). The effects of LTP can last quite a long time (hence the name *long-term* potentiation), long enough to be a key factor in the formation and retrieval of memories. Think of many sledges ridden one after another down a snowy slope, creating a groove that later sledgers can easily find. LTP seems to create a kind of groove that helps memories form, so a person can more easily retrieve a memory later by following the well-worn path.

You already know from Chapter 9 that LTP plays a role in learning. Researchers have gathered considerable evidence that it also plays a role in long-term memory. If experimental animals are given substances known to block the development of LTP, they have difficulty transferring information into long-term memory. Conversely, drugs that increase the development of LTP seem to improve the acquisition of long-term memories. Rats that are given an LTP-enhancing drug learnt and remembered a maze better than rats that were not given the drug (Glaser *et al.*, 2010; Sanberg *et al.*, 2006; Lynch *et al.*, 1991).

Many of the neurons and neural circuits that use *glutamate* as their neurotransmitter are particularly likely to exhibit LTP. Correspondingly, glutamate is a key neurotransmitter in the formation of memories, as you shall soon see. Moreover, neurons that display LTP are commonly located in the hippocampus and neocortex, brain regions that play such important roles in the formation of long-term memories, as we have just observed (Glaser *et al.*, 2010; Thompson, 2000).

Proteins Still other memory researchers have tried to identify biochemical changes that occur within neurons as memories are forming (Matthews, 2011; Sweatt, 2010; Rosenzweig, 1996). When neurons receive neurotransmitters at their receptor sites, chemical changes immediately begin to occur within the neurons, including the manufacture of proteins (Fioravante & Byrne, 2011). Proteins are believed to help memories form. Although researchers have yet to identify all of the proteins involved in memory formation, they have found that disruptions in the production of proteins often interfere with the proper encoding, storage, or retrieval of memories (Chen *et al.*, 2010).

All of these findings suggest that memory occurs as a result of changes both within and among neurons. Clearly, although no one has yet discovered all of the biological changes that account for memory, researchers are shedding more and more light on how the brain manages to provide this critical faculty.

Before You Go On

What Do You Know?

15. Which parts of the brain are most active in memory? How are these parts related to neurotransmitters involved in memory?

16. What is a neural network and how may long-term potentiation contribute to its formation?

What Do You Think?

What side effects might occur if drugs were taken that could manipulate memory-related neurotransmitters and proteins? Should such drugs be legally available to anyone who wants them?

Memories in the Young and Old

LEARNING OBJECTIVE 7

Describe the kinds of memories and memory changes that characterize early life and later life.

As you have seen in previous chapters, the brains of infants and young children seem to soak up information like sponges. Indeed, from the word go, the very young begin acquiring information, learn vocabularies and motor skills, and so on. All such feats of learning require the use of memory of one kind or another, and the different forms of memory develop at different times, as described below (Gathercole, 1998).

Young babies can remember what certain objects look like (even if they do not know what they are) and can discriminate between a novel object and a familiar one. Researchers assess this type of memory by measuring the amount of time a baby spends looking at an object. Babies prefer to look at, and so focus longer on, objects that they have not seen before. This task, called *preferential looking*, is a useful way to study memory in babies who are too young to speak or perform complex motor tasks that may otherwise reveal what they remember. Based on such research, we now know that the ability to remember objects increases from several minutes in the very young infant to several days in the toddler.

As babies gain control over their movements, they become able to learn new skills, skills that also require memory, although a different kind of memory. Memories of skills form during the first year of life as well. For example, one-year-olds can remember how to stack blocks or to successfully play with toys that require specific movements, such as winding a crank handle to get the jack-in-the-box to pop up. Once learnt, even in very early life, this type of procedural knowledge is rarely forgotten. That is why you will never forget how to tie your shoelaces, even if you go for years wearing only flip-flops. Procedural knowledge is stored, among other places, in the brain region called the *striatum*. The early ability to store procedural information for the long term suggests that the striatum matures quickly.

In short, babies and toddlers demonstrate many memories, from memories of faces, places and objects, to memories of skills and procedures. As a result, they can recognize a particular face as Daddy, a particular house as Nana's and a particular animal as a giraffe. Similarly, once they get going, they can remember how to walk and get from here to there, how to use a fork and, often, how to get their own way. On the other hand, their specific memories of the *events* that occur in their lives are not very impressive, and unlike the sorts of vivid recollections we are able to form when we are older. Prior to the age of four years, children do not hold onto memories of life events for very long. Correspondingly, most adults do not have any recollections of the events that occurred during their first four years of life; the early years of life are referred to as a period of *infantile amnesia*.

Why is it that young children can remember factual information, like the names of animals, from one day to the next, and remember how to play games and perform often complex motor skills, but they cannot form a permanent memory of life events? There are several possible reasons, a most persuasive one being that brain regions holding different types of memories do not develop at the same rate. That is, the brain circuits responsible for storing memories of events seem to develop more slowly than the brain regions responsible for storing information about language, motor skills and simple associations.

As you learnt in the previous section, in adults, memories about life events, often called *episodic memories*, are initially stored in the hippocampus. Only after temporary storage in the hippocampus is that information then distributed more widely throughout neocortical regions for long-term storage. We know that the hippocampus is a late-developing brain structure. It is one of the brain regions where a lot of neurogenesis occurs even in adulthood, and this late development may contribute to the inability to form episodic memories early on. Alternatively, it may not be a late-maturing hippocampus that is responsible for infantile amnesia, but rather the brain's early inability to transfer information out of the hippocampus to other locations in the neocortex (e.g. Squire, 1992).

Of course, if you spend any time with talkative two- or three-year-olds, you will notice they have a lot to say about what has been happening in their lives. They may tell you about what a friend said at nursery school, that a sibling took their toy or that they are expecting their Mummy to come home from work later in the day. This shows that young children are in fact *forming* memories of life events but that the information is not being stored permanently. If you ask those same two-year-olds a few months later about the same life events, unless the events have been repeated many times, the children will not recall them.

Think back to your earliest memory of a childhood event. If the memory is accurate (and not a manufactured one), it probably has an emotional component. The emotionally charged event that you remember may be positive, such as receiving a special birthday present, going on an exciting holiday or experiencing the arrival of your younger brother or sister. Or the remembered event may be negative, such as travelling to hospital after a fall off a scooter, being the victim of bullying in a nursery school class or experiencing the arrival of your younger brother or sister (depending on

PSYCHOLOGY AROUND US   First Memories

'One of my first, scariest memories I can recall was when I got stuck in my dress. It was super scary. I was playing with my gigantic doll who had a very nice dress on that used to belong to me at some point in time. I remembered that I used to wear it and thought that it would be a great idea to put it on. I didn't realize that I was way too big for that dress and kept squeezing it on until I got stuck. I could not take it off or put it on. My hands were stretched up and my elbows were somewhere by my ears. I felt very uncomfortable and it was dark, since the material of the dress was covering my head. I thought I would have to stay in that position forever. That was scary! My Mummy rescued me.'

how you viewed this event initially!). It is unlikely that the earliest event you remember is a neutral one, particularly if it occurred before the age of four years. The fact that most early-life memories are emotional suggests that the episodic memory system is helped along at early stages by brain regions that process emotional information, particularly the amygdala (LeDoux & Doyère, 2011).

Having looked at memory during the earliest years of life, let's take a look at memory during the later years. As we travel through middle adulthood and old age, we become more susceptible to forgetting, distortions and misremembering. Researchers suggest that older adults rely more on gist memory – the *gist* of things rather than hard facts – and older adults also tend to remember positive information while ignoring the negative (Park & Reuter-Lorenz, 2009; Jacoby *et al.*, 2005). For these reasons, some older individuals can fall prey to scams, often described as *doorstep crimes*, where people trick older adults into parting with money for work that does not need doing on their house, etc.

Although the age-related changes in the way our memory functions are gradual, they actually begin in our 20s (Park & Reuter-Lorenz, 2009). Certain parts of the brain, such as the hippocampus, begin to shrink. A study of the brains of older adults found that the hippocampus was about 20% larger in those who had retained memory function than those people with Alzheimer's disease (Winningham, 2010; Erten-Lyons *et al.*, 2009), but it is important to note that the memory problems in healthy ageing are not one and the same as Alzheimer's disease, even though cell loss in the hippocampus is responsible for both (see Learning Objective 8 below).

Indeed, as the older population continues to grow, an increasing amount of research is focusing on how to improve memory and prevent, or at the very least lessen, the impact of memory disorders such as Alzheimer's disease. Brain fitness approaches – using computer exercises and various mental games to keep the mind active – have become very popular and are often recommended by healthcare professionals. Although this approach has received support in a few studies (Basak *et al.*, 2008), many of today's researchers remain sceptical about whether brain puzzles and the like can in fact prevent memory decline. On the other hand, as we observed in Chapter 5, research has demonstrated repeatedly that *physical* exercise does indeed help to prevent or slow down deficiencies and impairments of memory and other forms of cognitive functioning (Hoveida *et al.*, 2011; Smith *et al.*, 2011).

Before You Go On

What Do You Know?

17. Why are toddlers able to effectively remember faces, places, objects and certain skills but not able to remember the events of their lives very well?

18. Why do the memories of older people tend to decline and what might help prevent or slow down memory problems? And, based on reading from earlier in the chapter (pp. 280–281), how might older people compensate for their memory problems?

What Do You Think?

Think of three of your earliest memories in life. Did the remembered events share certain characteristics, such as the arousal of great emotion or your age at the time? Think of conversations with your grandparents. What do they remember from their life (and what do they tell you about)? What period of life do they remember best? How may this relate to what happens to the hippocampus as you get older?

Disorders of Memory  OUT OF THE ORDINARY

LEARNING OBJECTIVE 8
Describe physical and psychological disorders that disrupt memory.

At times, each of us has been inconvenienced by flawed memories or by outright forgetting. When our memories fail to operate as we would like, we may experience dismay, frustration or embarrassment. Imagine how upsetting and confusing life would be if memory failure were the rule rather than the exception.

Such issues are recurring themes in Hollywood. Now a cult classic, the 2000 film *Memento* fascinated viewers with a series of harrowing situations that confronted the main character, Leonard. In the movie, Leonard is looking for the people who attacked him and brutally murdered his wife. His search is hard and frightening, however, because the attack left Leonard unable to form new memories. To cope, Leonard takes photos and makes notes as he acquires new information, and most notably he also tattoos his body with information. Despite these efforts, however, scenes in the movie frequently open with Leonard being attacked by people he does not know or chased for reasons he cannot explain until he has time to piece the information together. Leonard finds himself confronted with other characters who may – or may not – have his best interests at heart as they try to 'help' him along his way. But Leonard has doubts. Given his own memory loss, how can he be sure that he did not kill his wife and then somehow cause his own memory loss to protect himself from his guilt? Leonard's case is, of course, fiction; and his amnesia, rather pure. Not many people with such profound amnesia would have such clear-cut deficits in memory, or so unsubtle, and like our real case at the beginning of the chapter, PJM, find it difficult to work at the same level as before the amnesia, let alone solve a complex crime.

As you will see in Chapter 19, there are two basic groups of memory disorders: *organic memory disorders*, in which physical causes of memory impairment can be identified, and *dissociative disorders*, in which the disruptions in memory lack a clear physical cause. By a large margin, it is memory deficits of organic origin that are most frequently encountered by clinicians.

Organic Memory Disorders

Some changes in memory have clear organic causes, such as brain injuries or medical conditions. These injuries or conditions damage one or more of the brain regions or brain chemicals that are important in the formation, storage or retrieval of memories (Matthews, 2011). The most common kinds of organic memory disorders are *amnestic disorders*, which primarily affect memory, and *dementias*, which affect both memory and other cognitive functions.

Amnestic Disorders People with **amnestic disorders**, organic disorders in which memory loss is the primary symptom, experience retrograde amnesia, anterograde amnesia or both (Figure 10.11). **Retrograde amnesia** is an inability to remember things that occurred before the organic disorder or event that triggered amnesia. **Anterograde amnesia** is an ongoing inability to form new memories after the onset of the disorder or event.

In severe forms of anterograde amnesia, new acquaintances are forgotten almost immediately and problems solved one day must be tackled again the next. The person may not remember anything that has happened since the physical problem first occurred. A middle-aged patient who suffered a physical trauma more than 25 years ago, for example, may still believe that Margaret Thatcher is the prime minister of Great Britain or that the currency of Italy is the lira. People with very severe anterograde amnesia, such as the British amnesic Clive Wearing, have been described as prisoners of consciousness, since their memory disorder is such that they cannot string the present moment together into a meaningful continuous experience (Wilson & Wearing, 1995).

> **amnestic disorders** organic disorders in which memory loss is the primary symptom.
>
> **retrograde amnesia** the inability to remember things that occurred before an organic event.
>
> **anterograde amnesia** the ongoing inability to form new memories after an amnesia-inducing event.

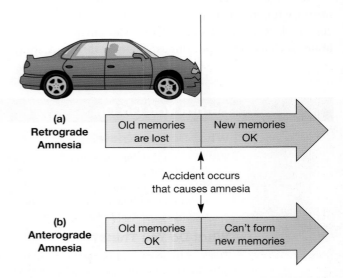

FIGURE 10.11 Two types of amnesia. An organic event can lead to two types of inability to remember. In retrograde amnesia, the individual loses memories of things that occurred before the event. In anterograde amnesia, the individual can recall the past but cannot form new memories.

Head injuries are a common cause of amnestic disorders. Although *mild* head injuries, for example a mild concussion, rarely cause much memory loss, almost half of all *severe* head injuries do cause some permanent learning and memory problems (Sadock & Sadock, 2007). Brain surgery can also cause amnestic disorders. The most famous case of memory loss as a result of brain surgery is that of HM (Henry Molaison), a man whose identity was protected for decades until his death in 2008 (Kensinger *et al.*, 2001; Corkin, 1984). HM suffered from severe epilepsy, a disorder that produced seizures in his temporal lobes. To reduce his symptoms, doctors performed surgery in 1953 that removed parts of both his temporal lobes, the amygdala and the hippocampus. At that time, the role of these brain areas in the formation of memories was not known. (Today temporal lobe surgery is usually done on only the right or left side of the brain.) HM experienced severe anterograde amnesia from the time of his surgery until his death. He kept failing to recognize anyone he met after the operation.

Dementias

In **dementia**, severe memory problems combine with losses in at least one other cognitive function, such as abstract thinking or language (APA, 2000). Between 3 and 9% of the world's adult population suffer from some form of dementia (Berr *et al.*, 2005). Among people 65 years of age, the prevalence of dementia is around 1.5%, increasing to as much as 50% of those over the age of 85 (Apostolova & Cummings, 2008).

> **dementia** severe memory problems combine with losses in at least one other cognitive function, such as abstract thinking or language.

Alzheimer's disease, named after Alois Alzheimer, the German physician who first identified it in 1907, is the most common form of dementia. This gradually progressive disease usually begins with mild memory problems, lapses of attention and difficulties in language and communication. As symptoms worsen over the years, patients also have difficulty with simple tasks and forget distant memories. Eventually, they may lose almost all knowledge of the past and fail to recognize the faces of even close relatives.

> **Alzheimer's disease** the most common form of dementia.

People with Alzheimer's disease form far more than ordinary numbers of **neurofibrillary tangles** and **senile plaques**, brain changes that are normal features of ageing up to a point (Selkoe, 2011, 2000, 1991). Neurofibrillary tangles are twisted protein fibres found within the cells of the hippocampus and several other brain areas. Senile plaques are sphere-shaped deposits of a protein known as *beta-amyloid protein* that form in the spaces between cells in

> **neurofibrillary tangles** twisted protein fibres found within the cells of the hippocampus and certain other brain areas.

> **senile plaques** sphere-shaped deposits of a protein known as beta-amyloid that form in the spaces between cells in the brain.

the hippocampus, cerebral cortex and several other brain regions, as well as in some nearby blood vessels. The presence of so many tangles and plaques indicates that very destructive processes take place in the brains of people with Alzheimer's disease (Meyer-Luehmann *et al.*, 2008; O'Connor *et al.*, 2008). Researchers do not yet fully understand what those processes are, but they have begun to focus on several possibilities.

One line of research suggests that two proteins involved in memory formation – *beta-amyloid protein* and *tau protein* – take an abnormal form and run amok in people with Alzheimer's disease, contributing to the formation of plaques and tangles in the hippocampus and other brain areas (Ramirez *et al.*, 2011; Apostolova & Cummings, 2008). Other studies suggest that Alzheimer patients may display abnormalities in the breakdown of calcium, a metallic element that helps produce proteins that are related to memory. And yet another line of research points to reduced activity of neurotransmitters, such as glutamate, that are typically related to memory (Chin *et al.*, 2007).

Gender and Dementia

Depending on whether you are male or female, you may be susceptible to different risk factors for dementia and Alzheimer's disease. Older women are more likely to develop dementia than men are. Although this may be because women tend to live longer, natural age-related declines in oestrogen, which is known to have a protective effect in the brain, could also be a factor (Sun, 2007).

As we age, certain conditions in men and women may increase the likelihood of developing dementia. A study of adults with mild cognitive impairment showed that stroke in men and depression in women increase the risk of dementia (Artero *et al.*, 2008). In addition to risk factors, Alzheimer's disease also may 'look' different in men and women. The brains of women with the disease, for example, typically have many more neurofibrillary tangles than do those of men (Barnes *et al.*, 2005). Also, men with Alzheimer's disease tend to be more aggressive, while women are more likely to become depressed (Lovheim *et al.*, 2009).

Dissociative Disorders

People with **dissociative disorders** experience major losses of memory without any clear physical cause. Many acclaimed books and movies have portrayed such disorders (Vidal, 2011), although they are relatively rare, but reveal important ways in which memory works. There are several

> **dissociative disorders** psychological disorders characterized by a major loss of memory without a clear physical cause.

different kinds of dissociative disorders, including *dissociative amnesia*, *dissociative fugue* and *dissociative identity disorder*:

- **Dissociative amnesia**. People with dissociative amnesia are unable to recall important information, usually of an upsetting nature, about their lives (APA, 2000). The loss of memory is much more extensive than instances of normal forgetting and is often triggered directly by a traumatic event – typically a serious threat to health and safety – as in wartime and natural disasters (Hunt, 2010; Cardena & Gleaves, 2007).

dissociative amnesia psychological disorder characterized by an inability to recall important information, usually of an upsetting nature, about one's life.

- **Dissociative fugue**. In addition to forgetting their personal identities and details of their past lives, people with dissociative fugue flee to an entirely different location. Although some individuals travel but a short distance and make few social contacts in the new setting, others travel far from home, take new names and establish new identities, develop new

dissociative fugue psychological disorder characterized by loss of memory of personal identities and details of one's past life and flight to an entirely different location.

relationships and even seek new lines of work (APA, 2000; Kihlström, 2001).

- **Dissociative identity disorder**. People with dissociative identity disorder, formerly known as multiple personality disorder, develop two or more distinct personalities – called **subpersonalities** – each having a somewhat unique set of memories, behaviours, thoughts and emotions. Often one of the subpersonalities has little or no recall of the experiences, thoughts, feelings or behaviours of the others: it is amnesic for the other subpersonalities. During activities and interactions, one of the subpersonalities takes centre stage and dominates the person's functioning. Women receive this diagnosis at least three times as often as men (APA, 2000).

dissociative identity disorder psychological disorder characterized by the development of two or more distinct personalities.

subpersonalities alternative personalities developed in dissociative identity disorder, each with a unique set of memories, behaviours, thoughts and emotions.

PSYCHOLOGY AROUND US | **The Three Faces of Eve**

In a famous case depicted in the book and movie *The Three Faces of Eve*, a woman had three subpersonalities: Eve White, Eve Black and Jane (Thigpen & Cleckley, 1957). Eve White, the primary personality, was quiet and serious; Eve Black was carefree and mischievous; and Jane was mature and intelligent.

According to the book, these three subpersonalities eventually merged into a single, integrated personality named Evelyn. However, in an autobiography decades later, this woman revealed that altogether twenty-two subpersonalities had come forth during her life, including nine subpersonalities after Evelyn (Sizemore, 1991).

A variety of theories have been proposed to explain dissociative disorders, but none of them has received much research support. Some psychologists in fact suggest that the symptoms of dissociative disorders may originate not from within the individual but from the therapist's consulting room. We have seen how easy it is for people to distort or manufacture memories based on even casual suggestions.

Perhaps therapists unintentionally create dissociative disorders, particularly dissociative identity disorders, by subtly suggesting to their clients over the course of treatment that they may have other personalities or by asking the clients to produce different personalities while in a hypnotic state (Loewenstein, 2007; Piper & Merskey, 2004).

Before You Go On

What Do You Know?

19. Compare and contrast retrograde and anterograde amnesia. What are the likely causes of both?
20. What changes happen in the brains of people with Alzheimer's disease?
21. How might state-dependent memory and self-hypnosis be linked to dissociative disorders?

What Do You Think?

Do you think that media portrayals of amnesia and dissociative disorders have actually influenced psychotherapists and members of the public to increase the number of diagnoses of these conditions? What other reasons may explain increased diagnoses?

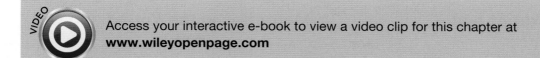

Access your interactive e-book to view a video clip for this chapter at **www.wileyopenpage.com**

Summary

What Is Memory?

LEARNING OBJECTIVE 1   Define the basic activities of memory and describe two major models of memory.

- Memory is our faculty for holding onto past events and past learning. It involves three basic activities: encoding, storage and retrieval.
- Researchers typically take an information-processing approach to memory, talking about different memory stores that work together in a similar way to part of a computer, each serving particular functions and holding information for varying lengths of time.
- Parallel distributed-processing (PDP) or connectionist models of memory suggest that information is stored not in a particular neuron or location in the brain but instead across a network of connections.

How Do We Encode Information into Memory?

LEARNING OBJECTIVE 2   Describe how information is encoded and transferred among different memory stores and what we can do to enhance encoding.

- Encoding refers to taking information in and putting it into memory.
- Encoding can happen either automatically or through effortful processing. Either way, however, a person must attend to something to put it into memory.
- One of the most common means of effortful processing is rehearsal of material.
- Encoding takes place in the form of phonological, sound or visual codes.

How Do We Store Memories?

LEARNING OBJECTIVE 3   Describe how we organize and store information in working and long-term memory and how we can enhance our long-term memories.

- The retention of information in memory is known as storage. Information can be stored in memory for anywhere from fractions of a second to a lifetime.

- Sensory memory is the equivalent of the small buffer on your computer, holding a very brief visual or auditory copy of information so you can decide whether to encode it into working or long-term memory. Sensory memory may also help maintain the continuity of your sensory input.
- Working memory is a short-term store of slightly more information that allows us to simultaneously store and manipulate information, so as to conduct simple calculations, such as memorizing a phone number so we can dial it immediately, or remembering the beginning of a sentence as we come to the end of the sentence.
- It appears that, without rehearsal, we can hold 7 ± 2 pieces of information in working memory, although we can expand that capacity through techniques such as chunking.
- Long-term memory appears to be infinite both in capacity and storage time.
- Information taken from working memory and placed into long-term memory appears to be organized according to its meaningfulness and relation to other concepts in long-term storage.
- Information in long-term memory may be stored in the form of explicit memories of facts or in implicit memories, knowledge about how to do something. A person cannot always articulate implicit knowledge.

How Do We Retrieve Memories?

LEARNING OBJECTIVE 4   Describe how we retrieve information from memory and how retrieval cues, priming, context and emotion can affect retrieval.

- The access of information from memory is known as retrieval. Retrieval can be facilitated by retrieval cues that make memories easier to access.
- Retrieval cues can include priming, context and enhancing meaningfulness of the memory by making them more personally or emotionally relevant.

Why Do We Forget and Misremember?

LEARNING OBJECTIVE 5 Summarize key theories of why we forget information and sometimes distort or manufacture memories.

- Forgetting is the inability to recall information that has previously been encoded.
- Initially, researchers believed that failure to access information regularly led to its loss from awareness, a theory known as decay theory. This theory is less popular now, and researchers instead emphasize other problems with remembering.
- Interference theory suggests that information gets in the way of the proper encoding of information, preventing it from being remembered later. Retroactive interference comes from new information that interferes with previous memories. Proactive interference comes from earlier memories that interfere with new ones.
- Motivated forgetting hypothesizes that we try to purposely forget information that is unpleasant, embarrassing or painful.
- In addition to being forgotten, memories can also be distorted or manufactured. We can make source misattributions, where we forget where information came from. We can also be exposed to new information that distorts previous information (as described in interference theory). Also, our own imaginations can play a role in distorting how our memories play out.

Memory and the Brain

LEARNING OBJECTIVE 6 Describe how the brain is involved in memory.

- Because scientists have not been able to pinpoint the place where memories are stored in the brain, they have concluded that there is no single storehouse. Instead, memory appears to be a process, resulting from activation patterns throughout the brain.
- However, structures like the prefrontal cortex are extremely important in helping people hold information in working memory and to work with it as long as it is needed. Also, the hippocampus and other parts of the neocortex appear to be important in the transfer of memories into long-term memory.
- Memory itself appears to be a neural circuit, a network of neurons predisposed to trigger one another whenever one is activated. Through a phenomenon called long-term potentiation (LTP), repeated stimulation of certain nerve cells increases the likelihood that the neurons will respond strongly whenever stimulated.

Memories in the Young and Old

LEARNING OBJECTIVE 7 Describe the kinds of memories and memory changes that characterize early life and later life.

- Babies and toddlers display many memories, from memories of faces, places and objects to memories of skills and procedures. But they do not retain memories of life events for very long.
- The slow development of the hippocampus may be responsible for the slow development of life event memories.
- Physical exercise seems to help prevent or slow down memory decline more than cognitive exercise does.

Disorders of Memory

LEARNING OBJECTIVE 8 Describe physical and psychological disorders that disrupt memory.

- Disorders of memory can come about through ageing, brain trauma, or the experience of traumatic events. Organic memory disorders, involving physical causes, include amnestic disorders and dementia. Major losses of memory without a clear physical cause are known as dissociative disorders.
- People with amnestic disorder are unable to remember things that have occurred before (retrograde amnesia) or after (anterograde amnesia) an organic event, such as a head injury or brain surgery.
- The other major class of organic memory disorders is dementia, characterized by severe memory problems combined with losses in at least one other cognitive function, such as abstract thinking or language.
- The most common form of dementia is Alzheimer's disease, a severe progressive form of dementia that accounts for at least half of all dementia cases.
- The brains of people with Alzheimer's disease have an extraordinarily high number of neurofibrillary tangles and senile plaques. The disease may stem from malfunctions of certain proteins or neurotransmitters involved in the normal formation of memories.
- Most of the time, dissociative disorders are triggered by a serious trauma or upsetting event and the memory loss is specifically related to that trauma.
- Dissociative amnesia refers to the inability to remember important, upsetting information about one's life.
- Dissociative fugue involves the complete loss of one's identity, combined with a flight to another location.
- Dissociative identity disorder describes a disorder in which a person develops two or more distinct personalities, each with a unique set of memories, behaviours, thoughts and emotions.
- Some theorists suspect that dissociative identity disorder may be inadvertently triggered by therapy discussions or events.

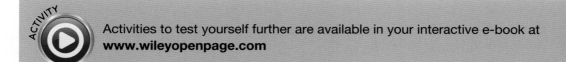

Activities to test yourself further are available in your interactive e-book at
www.wileyopenpage.com

TYING IT TOGETHER

WHAT HAPPENS IN THE BRAIN?

- In his pioneering neurosurgical studies, Karl Lashley found that rats retained at least some memory of their mazes, even when he removed large parts of their brains.
- Memory is not confined to any single area of the brain, although the prefrontal cortex is especially active in working memory and the hippocampus and other parts of the neocortex are heavily involved in long-term memory.
- If experimental animals are given substances that block the development of long-term potentiation (LTP) in their neurons, they have difficulty transferring information from working memory into long-term memory.
- The brains of people with Alzheimer's disease form an unusually large number of plaques, although these deposits may not be the actual cause of the disease.

HOW WE DIFFER

- The storage capacity of everyone's working memory seems to be about the same, but storage capacity in long-term memory varies greatly from person to person.
- Everyone uses phonological, visual and semantic codes to encode information into meaning, but individuals may differ in how much they use of each of these codes.
- The hippocampus size of older adults with excellent memories is, on average, 20% larger than that of people with Alzheimer's disease.
- Women are somewhat more likely than men to develop dementia.

OUT OF THE ORDINARY

- Head injuries are a common cause of amnestic disorders, organic disorders in which memory loss is the key symptom.
- From the moment that he had both of his temporal lobes surgically removed, the famous patient HM was never again able to form and hold new long-term memories.
- Only 1 to 2% of 65-year-olds experience Alzheimer's disease and other forms of dementia, compared with as many as 50% of those over the age of 85.
- The symptoms of dissociative identity disorder, formerly known as multiple personality disorder, usually begin in early childhood, often after episodes of abuse.

HOW WE DEVELOP

- Most adults cannot remember any life events that occurred before the age of three and a half to four years of age.
- Children are more likely than adults to have eidetic, or photographic, memories.
- As we age, we become more susceptible to forgetting, distortions and misremembering.
- Physical exercise helps prevent or improve memory problems in older people more than cognitive exercise does.
- Although changes in the functioning of our memories unfold gradually throughout adulthood, specific declines in memory may actually begin in our 20s.
- Although forgetfulness becomes increasingly common as we age, dementia is not a normal part of ageing.

Quizzes to test yourself further are available in your interactive e-book at
www.wileyopenpage.com

Key Terms

Alzheimer's disease 301
amnestic disorders 300
anterograde amnesia 300
automatic processing 277
chunking 283
decay theory 290
dementia 301
dissociative amnesia 302
dissociative disorders 301
dissociative fugue 302
dissociative identity
  disorder 302
effortful processing 277
encoding 274

episodic memory 285
explicit memory 284
flashbulb memory 289
forgetting 290
implicit memory 284
information-processing
  model 274
interference theory 290
long-term memory 279
memory 274
memory span 283
mnemonic devices 280
neurofibrillary
  tangles 301

parallel distributed-processing
  (PDP) (or connectionist)
  model 275
prefrontal cortex 296
priming 287
proactive interference 291
recall tasks 287
recognition tasks 287
rehearsal 278
repression 292
retrieval 274
retrieval cues 287
retroactive
  interference 291

retrograde amnesia 300
schemas 282
semantic code 279
semantic memory 285
senile plaques 301
sensory memory 278
source misattribution 292
spacing effect 279
state-dependent
  memory 288
storage 274
subpersonalities 302
working memory 278

Flashcards to test yourself further are available in your interactive e-book at
www.wileyopenpage.com

CHAPTER 11

Language and Thought

Adapted by Trevor Harley,
University of Dundee, UK

CHAPTER OUTLINE

- Language
- Language and Thought

- Thought

 Access your interactive e-book to view a video clip for this chapter at **www.wileyopenpage.com**

'I'd Like to Phone a Friend, Please.'

The average person of university age sends nearly 1,000 text messages every month; they average more text messages than they do phone calls (Keane, 2008; Elliott, 2007). Yet, today's mobile phones, of course, are not just for receiving calls and messages. As you are well aware, mobile phones have an amazing number of capabilities and features: you can use them to take and share pictures, get your e-mail, search the Internet or use an ever-expanding variety of other applications. Mobile phones sometimes even save lives. News reports often tell stories of lost walkers or others who were rescued after calling for help from their mobile phones, or when rescuers tracked them using the automatic GPS information generated by their phones. Once you choose a phone, all you need to do to get benefits from your handy device is to figure out how to use it.

Using your mobile phone requires language skills. You need to speak and understand the speech of your callers. When you text or scroll through the menus, you need to read, and perhaps write. You are also using language if you happen to read the instructions that come with your phone. Not only are you using language skills, you are also using a variety of different thinking skills. You may be mentally envisioning the person you are calling or texting. You may use what you know about their habits to try to determine when would be the best time to reach them, or to leave a voice mail if you do not really want to reach them. Of course, as we have noted, the process of acquiring the device and learning to operate it in the first place also involved some key thinking skills. You had to make several key decisions and possibly solve some problems, such as how to make sure that you could transfer all of your contacts from your old phone to your new one. ∎

Language and thought distinguish humans from other creatures. Language enables us to communicate in a precise and often creative way, to explain complex ideas and to express opinions or emotions. We use language, for example, to specify to a phone salesperson exactly what phone we want to buy, including its colour and accessories. We also use language to tell stories or jokes in exciting ways that make our friends gasp or laugh with us. Language has allowed us, as a species, to learn from past generations, originally by oral storytelling and then by written language. Language is critical for humans because it allows us to interact in complex settings, as when architects, engineers and others collaborate on large-scale building projects. Consider how difficult it must have been to organize a large group of people to build an ancient city. Such a feat would have been nearly impossible without the use of language.

Although language is communicative, sometimes we use language only in our own heads. We often think using words, and we do not always share our thoughts with others. Similarly, some people write extensively for their own pleasure, never intending or wanting others to read their written words. Although the processes of language and thought overlap, a clear difference exists between them. In general, psychologists study these processes separately.

Human thought is highly complex, varies from individual to individual and takes on many different forms. While much thought involves the use of words, some does not, instead relying on visual imagery or sounds. Consider, for example, what happens when a particular tune is stuck in one's head. Even if we cannot remember the lyrics, we can often imagine the music.

The study of thought is a major component of cognitive psychology. As we saw in Chapter 1, the word **cognition** refers to a variety of mental processes that contribute to thinking and knowing. Cognition is involved in learning and memory, as well as thinking. In this chapter, we will discuss a number of different types of thinking that can involve accumulating knowledge, solving problems, making decisions and even thinking about thinking.

cognition mental processes of thinking and knowing.

Language

LEARNING OBJECTIVE 1

Define language, describe how we learn languages, describe parts of the brain that are involved in language and discuss differences and problems that can affect people's language skills.

language a set of symbols used to communicate.

Language is a set of symbols used to communicate. These symbols can be spoken, signed or written. We use symbols, mainly words, to convey our thoughts and desires to others who share an understanding of the symbols. For instance, we communicate with you in this book using the symbols in the English written language. Language can be divided into two main components: language production and language comprehension.

Language production occurs when we generate communicative vocalizations or gestures: that is, when we use the symbols in our shared language to communicate thoughts and ideas. Human language production is generative, or creative; we make new sentences whenever we speak, rather than just restating old ones. In fact, humans have a remarkable capacity for producing new sentences, and we rarely repeat previously heard sentences exactly. We often produce sentences that have never been produced before. The ability to produce new sentences almost automatically is an important feature of human communication. We know that many other species communicate with sounds, but most species are born with the ability to make these particular sounds, and the sounds do not change. A lion does not need to learn how to roar, for example, and it does not phrase its roar differently every time.

language production the process of using movement to produce speech. Language production can also encompass signing by using hand signals.

Very few species other than humans can learn new vocalizations, sounds produced in an effort to communicate (Pinker & Jackendoff, 2005). Vocal learning occurs in some species of songbirds (canaries, zebra finches), bats, aquatic mammals (whales and dolphins) and humans. It may come as a surprise to you that no primates other than humans learn language naturally, although monkeys and apes have an extensive repertoire of species-specific vocalizations. These vocalizations are used to communicate but they are not learnt: they are innate, and there is little to no evidence that they change over time. In other words, a macaque monkey from Asia will make the same vocalizations, and those sounds will have the same meaning, whether the monkey lives in Asia or North America. Humans are also endowed with an impressive capacity for **language comprehension**, the ability to understand communicative vocalizations or gestures. We often can even fill in the blanks when not all information is provided precisely. For example, we can generally comprehend fragments of sentences or words that are mispronounced. We can understand people who speak with accents, people with speech impediments, such as lisps or stutters, and even the speech of toddlers. Our ability to understand speech that is incomplete or unclear is related to the fact that much of language comprehension is automatic. Typically, we understand spoken language without concentrating, which is the reason we are able to carry on a conversation without stopping to think about our responses.

language comprehension the process of understanding spoken, written or signed language.

Language Structure

The study of speech can be divided into four general areas: phonology, semantics, syntax and pragmatics. The building blocks of language are shown in Figure 11.1. In any language, the smallest unit of sound is called a **phoneme**, and the study of how sounds are put together to form words is called **phonology**. For example, the word tip has three phonemes: *t, i* and *p*. Different languages have different phonemes, and so the number of phonemes differs from language to language (Halle, 1990). The English language has approximately 40 phonemes (depending on the dialect). Some languages have very few phonemes, and some have many more phonemes than English. At the two ends of the spectrum are the language Pirahã (an indigenous language of Brazilian people living in the Amazon), which has only 10 phonemes, and the Taa language (also known as !Xóõ), a language of indigenous people of Botswana and Namibia, which has 141 phonemes.

phoneme the smallest unit of language, an individual sound.

phonology the study of how individual sounds or phonemes are used to produce language.

Speakers of one language often cannot distinguish phonemes that do not exist in their language (Dietrich *et al.*, 2007). For example, Spanish does not include the sound used in English to pronounce the letter J. Spanish speakers pronounce J like English speakers pronounce H, as in the case of the boy's name Juan. For children learning Spanish as their only language, the ability to make the English /j/ sound decreases. Spanish speakers who are exposed to both English and Spanish early in their lives, however, acquire the correct pronunciation for the English phoneme of the letter *J* much more readily. We discuss later in this chapter how it is much easier for us to learn languages during an early stage of life.

morpheme the smallest unit of meaning in language.

While phonemes are sounds, **morphemes** are the smallest units of language that convey meaning (Miller, 1978). For example, the word tips has two morphemes. One is tip and the other is s, which is used to communicate that the word is plural. The study of the meaning of words is referred to as **semantics**. The meaning of a word as given in a dictionary is referred to as its **lexical meaning**. Lexical meaning changes over time. Consider the word gay, which, prior to the 20th century, meant 'happy'. Now not only has *gay* an additional meaning of homosexual but also its original meaning has fallen largely into disuse.

semantics the study of how meaning in language is constructed of individual words and sentences.

lexical meaning dictionary meaning of a word.

Knowing the meaning of individual words is important, but a word's meaning is often communicated through its context. Depending on its context in a sentence, for example, the word blue can mean a colour or a depressed emotional state. When heard alone, it is impossible to tell the intended meaning, but when we hear blue in the context of a particular sentence, such as 'She wore a beautiful blue dress' or 'He's feeling blue today', the distinction becomes instantly clear. The way in which words are combined into sentences is referred to as **syntax**.

syntax the grammatical positioning of words in a sentence.

Phonology, semantics and syntax bring us to the point where we have sounds, words and sentences. Communication also requires adhering to social norms, such as speed of speech, responding at appropriate intervals, making eye contact and using acceptable body language. These aspects of communication are called **pragmatics**, because they refer to the practical use of language.

pragmatics the practical aspects of language usage, including speech pace, gesturing and body language.

One aspect of pragmatics is our use of body language, or **nonverbal communication**. The way we move our hands, bodies and faces can change the connotations of our speech. Suppose your lecturer said, 'I would like to meet with you after class.' If this statement were delivered with one raised eyebrow, a sneer and arms folded across the chest, you would likely interpret it to mean your lecturer was unhappy with you about something. You would interpret it differently if the lecturer said the same thing with a warm smile, while leaning

nonverbal communication body language.

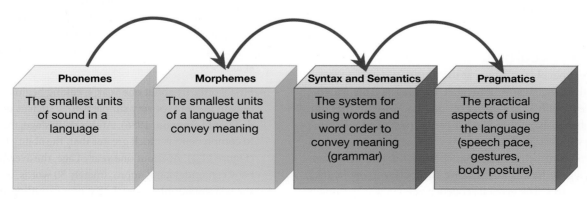

Phonemes	Morphemes	Syntax and Semantics	Pragmatics
The smallest units of sound in a language	The smallest units of a language that convey meaning	The system for using words and word order to convey meaning (grammar)	The practical aspects of using the language (speech pace, gestures, body posture)

FIGURE 11.1 The building blocks of language.

Getting his message across. The facial expression, hands on hips, body posture and other nonverbal cues of President Barack Obama, as he talks to his chief of staff, help communicate his feelings of concern and unhappiness.

Source: ©Pete Souza/White House/Handout/CNP/Corbis.

TABLE 11.1 Typical Outline of Language Development, but Note that There Can Be a Great Deal of Variation

Age	Type of sounds produced
0–6 weeks	vegetative sounds such as cries and burps
6 weeks	cooing
16 weeks	laughter
6–10 months	babbling
10–18 months	single word utterances
18 months	two-word utterances
24 months	telegraphic speech
30 months	full sentences, but development continues for many years

forward with hands on the desk. Sometimes, people are not aware of the body language they are using and unwittingly send the wrong messages when they attempt to communicate. An employee may believe, for example, that a boss is making inappropriate advances because the boss is unaware of the message he or she sends by standing close and touching the worker's arm while talking.

Nonverbal communication seems to be acquired automatically, often by observing the actions of others. Nonverbal communication is related to, but not identical with, gesturing, which refers to communicative movements of the arms and hands. Gesturing helps with speech production. While the ancient Greeks provided orators with explicit lessons in gesturing to enhance their speeches, studies have shown that gesturing occurs naturally (Acredolo & Goodwyn, 1988). For example, people blind from birth who have not had the chance to learn gestures by watching others nevertheless use gestures. Gesturing is often difficult to inhibit; blind people will gesture even when they realize they are talking to another blind person (Goldin-Meadow, 1999).

Language Learning  HOW WE DEVELOP

You were probably too young at the time you started to speak your native language to remember learning it. Your parents may have proudly kept a record of your first words. If they did, they probably abandoned the list pretty quickly, as it became too long very fast. Within just a few years, almost every human baby goes from being incapable of speaking or understanding language to having an extensive vocabulary in one of over 4,000 languages. The general sequence of language learning is the same for most people and is shown in Table 11.1.

- Prevocal learning. Between two and four months of age, babies are capable of perceiving all possible phonemes, including those that are not needed for the language(s) they will ultimately learn (Aslin *et al.* 1998). During this time, babies have a remarkable ability to distinguish among these sounds. Researchers investigated babies' abilities to distinguish among different phonemes by training the babies to turn their heads towards an interesting visual reward when they hear a change in speech sounds. Results of studies using this type of training (which is a form of operant or instrumental conditioning, as described in Chapter 9) suggests that young babies can discern a much wider range of phonemes than older children or adults can (Werker, 1989). This ability declines, however, as babies begin to learn their native languages (Eimas *et al.*, 1971). With practice in only the phonemes of our native languages, we lose the ability to distinguish among sounds that are only heard in other languages (Eimas, 1975).

- Babbling. By about six months, babies start to babble (Sachs, 2009). **Babbling** refers to the production of meaningless sounds that enable the infant to experiment with vocalizations. Babbling often consists of a sequence of duplicated syllables, such as *ba-ba-ba-ba-ba*. All babies babble, including those who are deaf (Wallace *et al.*, 1999).

  babbling babies' production of meaningless sounds.

- First words. By about one year, speaking begins, typically in the form of very simple words, such as mama, dada or hi (Ingram, 1986). At this early stage, the ability to comprehend is much greater than the ability to speak (Figure 11.2). At about one year of age, the average baby can understand approximately 50 words, but he or she will not be able to speak that many until about six months later (Fenson *et al.*, 1994). One-year-olds can

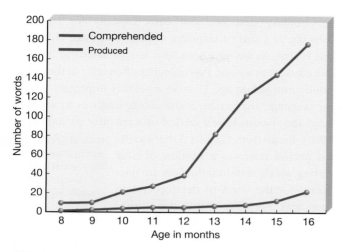

FIGURE 11.2 Babies' comprehension of words. Babies can comprehend more words than they speak. One-year-old babies understand about 50 words but will not be able to speak them until about six months later.

Source: Adapted from Fenson, L., Dale, P., Reznick, S., Bates, E., Thal, D., & Pethick, S. (1994). Variability in early communicative development, *Monographs of the Society for Research in Child Development, 59* (242), 1–185. With permission.

- Pragmatics. By three years of age, the average toddler has naturally acquired some practical information about language use, including the need to pause between sentences and the knowledge that certain sentences are statements, whereas others are requests (Garvey, 1974). The average English-speaking three-year-old has a vocabulary of about 1,000 words.

- Grammar. By age four, children have automatically absorbed many of the rules of grammar, even though they have received no formal teaching about the grammar of their native languages (Tager-Flusberg, 2001). As discussed below, some of the early stages of reading often emerge around this time when children are exposed to written words at home or preschool. By age six, the average child uses almost 3,000 words and likely understands a great many more (about 14,000 words, depending on the amount of language they were previously exposed to). By age nine, practical aspects of language – such as inferring meaning of obscure language, interpreting metaphors and understanding sophisticated humour – emerge (Wellman & Hickling, 1994).

Even though the majority of language learning occurs relatively early in life, we can still expand the size and sophistication of our vocabularies for decades. Many teenagers find themselves learning words they have not used before when studying for higher or further learning examinations. Vocabulary can increase throughout adulthood and seems to be one type of memory that does not diminish during the normal ageing process. Even when older people have slowed reaction times and impaired memory for events in their own lives, they often score as high, if not higher, than young adults on vocabulary tests.

often follow commands, such as, 'Get the ball and bring it to Mummy,' even though their spoken vocabulary may only include ball and mama.

- Telegraphic speech. By age two, most toddlers speak in very short (typically two-word) sentences (Bloom, 1970). This is called **telegraphic speech** because, as in old-fashioned telegraph messages (for which senders were charged by the word), only the essential words are used. Instead of saying, 'I want a biscuit,' a two-year-old is more likely to say simply, 'Want biscuit.'

telegraphic speech a type of speech that consists of minimalistic sentences. It characterizes early toddlerhood and is the first evidence of sentence formation.

PSYCHOLOGY AROUND US   Poverty and Language Development

Children from socioeconomically disadvantaged backgrounds often struggle with schoolwork. Several studies suggest that poor children have deficient vocabularies when they first enter primary school. These differences often become exaggerated over time because vocabulary builds on itself (Hart & Risley, 1995). The initial language deficits of poor children apparently result from environmental differences. On average, children from households with *lower socioeconomic status (SES)* are exposed to fewer words than are students from households with higher socioeconomic status. One study found that, in any given hour, children in poor homes heard less than half as many words as children in high-SES homes did (Hart & Risley, 1995). In addition, much more of the speech was prohibitive: 'Stop it!' or 'Don't touch that'. Exactly why poor parents communicate less, and less positively, with their children remains unknown. The stress of poverty and the potential lack of suitable role models for parents (parenting skills are largely acquired through one's own upbringing) are two likely causes. The good news is that the problem of reduced vocabularies in lower-SES children can be prevented by preschool intervention that includes educating parents about the benefits of talking and reading to their children at home.

Theories of Language Development Recall recent experiences you have had building your vocabulary, perhaps in readiness for exams in school or when studying generally. You may also have had experience learning a second or third language later in your education, in late primary or secondary school. In either situation, whether expanding your vocabulary in your first language or adding an entirely new language, you probably learnt at a much slower rate than you did when you learnt your first language as a very young child. You possibly also had to concentrate hard on your language learning; it most likely did not occur automatically.

The ease with which language is acquired by human infants has led many researchers to speculate that language has a biological basis. The linguist Noam Chomsky was among the first to suggest that language learning is built into our brains (Chomsky, 1964). The brain does appear to be set up to understand and communicate using language. As we have noted, the ability to detect all phonemes used in any human language exists in all human babies (as long as their hearing is intact). Other studies have also shown that the very young brain is wired to acquire language rapidly and automatically, because it is in a highly plastic, or changeable, state, ready to absorb new information about language. As humans grow and reach adulthood, the brain maintains the ability to change, but that ability has diminished (Johnson & Newport, 1989): language learning becomes much slower and requires more effort.

Chomsky described our early capacity for language learning as a sort of language acquisition device built into our brains. As we have seen, this 'device' seems to become less efficient as we age. Psychologists often refer to the childhood years before age 13 as an especially important period for language acquisition. Some debate exists as to whether language systems have a critical or a sensitive period (Kyle, 1980). Recall from Chapter 3 that a **critical period** refers to a window of time during which certain influences are necessary for the brain to develop certain capacities normally. After the critical period, these influences are no longer capable of having as profound an impact on the brain. A **sensitive period** refers to a developmental time during which the brain is more susceptible to influences. After the sensitive period, change can still occur but it does not happen as readily. Since we can still expand our vocabularies or learn new languages later in life, we probably go through more of a sensitive period than a critical period for language learning. Some evidence, however, such as that described in the accompanying box on the case of Genie, suggests that there is a critical period during which we must have some language input or we will not be able to acquire normal fluency with speech.

> **critical period** a time during development after which we cannot develop certain capabilities.

> **sensitive period** a time during development after which it becomes more difficult to develop certain capabilities.

PSYCHOLOGY AROUND US Critical Period for Language Learning? The Case of Genie

In the opening of Chapter 4 we mentioned the case of Genie, a severely neglected girl delivered to a welfare office in California with her blind mother in 1970 (Rymer, 1994). At the hands of her sadistic father, Genie had spent her entire life in isolation chained to a potty chair. She was rarely spoken to except in a punitive way ('stop it'). Her father communicated with her mostly by grunting and barking. At age 13, when her mother finally left her father, Genie had been exposed to almost no speech and appeared to be nearly mute. Her vocabulary consisted of about 20 words.

Age 13 was the time at which most researchers had assumed that the critical period for language acquisition was over. This assumption was based on the fact that, after this age, people learn new languages with greater difficulty and typically do not lose their accents. Because Genie was 13 years old at the time when she was rescued, she was an interesting, although tragic, test case of whether a critical period for language existed.

Genie's experiences tended to provide support for the theory that a sensitive period for language learning does exist. During the years that followed her rescue, Genie received extensive, interactive language training. Although she did initially show progress in expanding her vocabulary, it was always limited and did not include the acquisition of grammatical rules. Unfortunately, Genie's vocabulary regressed even further when she was under stress.

Although the case of Genie seems to support the language critical period theory, it is important to keep in mind that Genie was not only deprived of language but also subjected to extreme physical and emotional abuse that may have contributed significantly to her inability to learn (Kyle, 1980).

It is clear that our brains are biologically prepared to help us acquire at least one language, but the process of language learning is not exclusively hardwired in us. Much evidence suggests that the environment plays a critical role, too. Early behaviourists, including B. F. Skinner (1957), suggested that language is acquired as a result of instrumental conditioning. Toddlers are rewarded with praise for producing appropriate speech and ignored or scolded for failure to do so. As you may have noticed, however, parents, caregivers and other older people do not usually systematically reward toddlers for correct speech. The two-year-old who says 'Want biscuit' is just as likely to get one as another child who can say 'Please may I have a biscuit?' Conditioning alone, therefore, cannot explain language learning.

Interactive theories suggest that experience works along with biological developmental periods to enhance and guide language learning (Goldberg, 2008). These theories emphasise the fact that biology and experience together facilitate language acquisition. As we have described, for instance, if a baby is not exposed to certain phonemes, his or her capacity to distinguish among these sounds diminishes.

Babies and young children are typically exposed to very interactive speech. Most adults talk to babies with a special intonation in their voices: a high-pitched and sometimes exaggerated speech that is called **child-directed speech** (Fernald *et al.*, 1989). Child-directed speech may help babies learn words by keeping them interested. The patterns of child-directed speech are often rich in emotions, which may have the added benefit of fostering a close emotional relationship between caregiver and child, thus enhancing the quality and quantity of communication. Child-directed speech is also observed when parents use sign language to communicate with babies. Whether the adult, child or both are deaf, the use of sign language during the learning phase naturally follows the pattern of child-directed speech: slower in the formation of the hand signs, with longer pauses in between signs and exaggeration of facial expressions to show emotions (Masataka, 1998). Child-directed speech arises naturally; people adopt it without any formal instruction, suggesting that humans seem to have a biological predisposition to teach effective communication to the very young (Cooper & Aslin, 1994; Bornstein *et al.*, 1992).

The development of syntax, or grammatical rules, also suggests that language learning involves an interaction between biological factors and environmental conditions. As we noted earlier, young children acquire many of the rules of grammar without any formal instruction. Even in children with hearing loss who are not formally trained in sign language but develop their own form of signing, there is evidence of a grammatical structure. These findings suggest that the brain is predisposed to create a set of rules by which language will be used.

Even with such a strong biological basis, however, grammar is still affected by environment. We can see the effects of environment when children acquire the ability to form

child-directed speech
a speech characterized by exaggerated emotional responses and a slow pace that is common among caregivers communicating with babies and young children.

grammatically correct sentences (usually before the age of four), generally before they receive formal training in grammar (Tager-Flusberg, 2001). Even though preschool children are not specifically taught grammatical rules, they are implicitly learning them by mimicking what they hear. Once children acquire grammatical rules through this experience, they begin to make mistakes related to irregular words. For example, children who correctly use the suffix -ed to refer to the past tense apply -ed to verbs that are irregular, for example saying 'runned' instead of 'ran'. Such mistakes are referred to as **overregularization** (Maratsos, 2000). They provide evidence that, while the tendency to readily pick up syntax exists in the very young, some aspects of grammar are learnt. Children automatically absorb information about grammatical structure and begin to generalize that information. Of course, the problem of overregularization typically corrects itself as children gain more sophistication in language and become able to deal with exceptions to the rules.

overregularization
the process by which preschool children apply general grammatical rules to words that are exceptions.

Learning to Read As we noted earlier, many children begin formal education and start learning to read at around the age of five or six years old. Reading is a complicated behaviour that emerges considerably after the foundations of language production and comprehension have been laid down.

Identical genes, different reading skills. These five-year-old identical twins are reading as part of a study in Australia investigating how much of one's reading and spelling abilities are related to genes and how much are related to upbringing and schooling.
Source: Joe Castro/©AP/Wide World Photos.

Children typically begin the process of learning to read by telling stories from looking at pictures in a book and attempting to recognize a few simple words (Senechal & LeFevre, 2001). In schools in the United Kingdom, reading and writing are usually a main focus of the first few years at school. By around age eight, reading becomes much less difficult for most children, as it becomes an automatic process that requires little or no conscious thought (Ely, 1997). Parents may notice that during car trips children of this age begin to make exclamations of surprise when the printed words on posters and shop signs suddenly make sense.

Once reading becomes automatic, most people become very skilled at it. Just as we are capable of understanding spoken fragments of sentences or words spoken in foreign accents, we can understand written abbreviations with ease. Consider the abbreviated writing of the text message: 'U R L8.' It is very easy to determine that this means 'You are late' because the phonemes are identical to those that are used to correctly spell out these words. More complicated and non-phonetic written messages require explicit learning. Consider the abbreviated writing of the text message: 'I ctn I g2g ttyl.' Without prior knowledge of the acronyms *ctn*, *g2g* and *ttyl*, the message 'I can't talk now, I have got to go, I'll talk to you later' would remain a mystery.

Reading is a complex process. Skilled adult readers can read *regular* words, like STAKE, where there is a regular correspondence between the letters (or *graphemes*) and sounds (called *phonemes*); it is regular because all words ending in -AKE are pronounced the same way (BAKE, RAKE, WAKE, for example). But we can also read *irregular* words, such as STEAK, where there is an irregular correspondence between graphemes and phonemes (other words ending in -EAK are pronounced differently: BEAK, LEAK, SNEAK, for example). English is difficult to learn to read because it is full of irregular words; think of YACHT and GHOST. (Try to solve the old problem of how GHOTI spells *fish*!). But we can also read aloud strings of letters we have never seen before, such as PAKE or ZEAK.

One influential idea of how we accomplish all of these things is that the mind has two reading routes (Harley, 2010; Coltheart, 2005). One is called the *direct route* and is the route most used by skilled readers, and takes us straight from the printed form to the sounds. In that way we can read irregular words correctly as well as regular words. But for more difficult words, for less skilled readers and for reading new or non-words, there is a slower, less direct route that assembles the pronunciation of the words by taking each letter and translating it into its corresponding sound. That way we can build up pronunciations of strings of letters such as ZEAK that we have never seen before.

How Language Works  WHAT HAPPENS IN THE BRAIN?

In most people, language production and comprehension centres are located in the left hemisphere of the brain. In a small percentage of people (approximately 5%), the language centres are lateralized to the right hemisphere of the brain. In some cases, language involves both hemispheres. Broadly speaking, one area of the left hemisphere of the brain, known as *Broca's area*, is important for our ability to speak, while another area, called *Wernicke's area*, is important in language comprehension. In a typical conversation, which involves listening to others speak and responding appropriately, both areas would be active at once, along with other parts of the brain.

Broca's Area **Broca's area** is located in the frontal lobe in what is technically the motor association cortex (Damasio & Geschwind, 1984). This area was named after the neurologist who first described patients with damage to this region, Paul Broca. People who suffer damage in or near Broca's area develop a set of symptoms called **Broca's aphasia**. The term aphasia can refer to an inability either in language production or in language comprehension. In Broca's aphasia, the problem is with production: people have great difficulty speaking. They speak unusually slowly and have trouble with pronunciations.

> **Broca's area** a region in the frontal lobe near the motor cortex that is important for speech production.

> **Broca's aphasia** a neurological condition arising from damage to Broca's area where the patient is unable to produce coherent speech.

Because Broca's area is located in the motor association cortex, many researchers believe that the difficulty in speaking that characterizes Broca's aphasia is caused by difficulties in making the necessary movements. Speaking requires

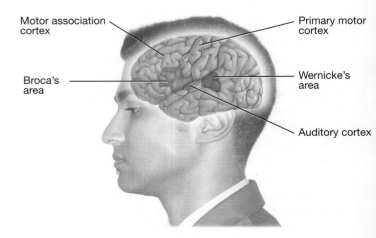

The main language areas of the brain.

Source: Asia Images Group/Getty Images, Inc.

a complex set of movements of the lips, tongue and larynx, and movements are largely controlled by the primary motor cortex in the brain. The content of patients' speech supports the theory that difficulties in movement, rather than in thinking, are the major problems when Broca's area is damaged. Although difficult to follow, the speech of most people with Broca's aphasia makes sense. They have clear thoughts to communicate, but they have great difficulty getting them out.

Damage to Broca's area can, however, also produce an inability to speak with proper grammar, a condition referred to as **agrammatism**. This deficit suggests that our ability to use grammar is stored close to or within the same neural tissue that is responsible for the movements necessary for speech production. This close neuroanatomical relationship probably explains how, once learnt, grammar is automatic. When we speak, we do not need to carefully construct grammatically correct sentences.

agrammatism a neurological condition arising from damage to a brain region just anterior to Broca's area where the patient is incapable of using words in grammatical sequence.

People with Broca's aphasia who suffer from agrammatism also tend to have a mildly impaired ability to comprehend language, particularly syntax. For instance, people with Broca's aphasia who were asked to point, from a group of pictures, to the correct one that showed in which 'the cat ate the food' could do so. If researchers asked these people to point to a nonsense picture illustrating the phrase 'the cow was on the car', however, they were almost as likely to choose a picture of a car on a cow as to choose the correct one. The researchers concluded that people with Broca's aphasia were not able to use clues such as grammar and word order to determine the meaning of a sentence that was not obvious from its individual words. Given the words *cat* and *food*, one can reasonably assume, from prior knowledge of what

cats do, that a cat would eat the food. Cows have no obvious relationship to cars, however, and the intended connection between them is unclear without language rules.

Neuroimaging studies of people without brain damage have confirmed much of what neurologists and neuropsychologists have discovered from studying the behaviour of people with Broca's aphasia (Gernsbacher & Kaschak, 2003). Broca's area itself is active during speaking, and a closely located area just in front of Broca's area becomes active when we try to comprehend sentences with complicated grammar.

Sign language uses brain areas similar to those important in spoken language. Neuroimaging studies show that, in people with intact brains, Broca's area and Wernicke's area are activated during signing. Since producing sign language does not require actual speech production, it does not involve as much activation of Broca's area. Even so, as noted earlier, sign language does use grammar rules to construct meaningful sentences, and using sign language activates the same neural tissue near Broca's area that is involved in the use of grammar when speaking. Deaf people with brain damage around Broca's area can experience deficits in grammar use with signing.

Wernicke's Area Although the brain tissue near Broca's area seems to contribute to the comprehension of grammar in language, other parts of the brain are even more important for language comprehension. Because speech comprehension begins when we hear, it is not surprising that the brain regions most important for understanding speech are located near the auditory cortex in the upper part of the left temporal lobe. **Wernicke's area** was first identified by a neurologist named Carl Wernicke. People who suffer destruction to this part of the

Wernicke's area a brain region located in the temporal lobe that is important for language comprehension.

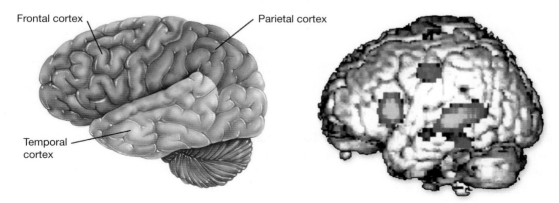

Scanning for language comprehension. This PET scan displays the brain activity of a person who is repeating the words of another individual. Such vocal repetitions activate (*red* and *orange*) his Broca's area for speech production (*left*), Wernicke's area for language comprehension (*right*) and a motor region tied to vocalizations.

Source: Right image: WDCN/Univ. College London/Photo Researchers, Inc.

Wernicke's aphasia a neurological condition associated with damage to Wernicke's area where a person cannot understand language.

brain have **Wernicke's aphasia**. They have difficulty in understanding speech. Patients with Wernicke's aphasia are fully capable of talking, but their speech often makes no sense.

Other Brain Regions In addition to Broca's and Wernicke's areas, other brain regions have important functions in specific aspects of language. For instance, the box on swearing accompanying this section describes how the amygdala, a brain region important for fear and aggression, appears to be involved in the use of profanity.

Most people also typically use regions in the right hemisphere to understand figurative language, such as metaphors. In figurative language, the meaning of a phrase is different from the literal meaning of the words used in the phrase. Damage to the right hemisphere can lead to taking figurative language literally. For instance, a person with such damage may think the phrase *hold your horses* means to grab hold of an actual horse. Metaphors are figures of speech that compare unlike things. Damage to the right hemisphere may lead a person to think that you live with an actual farm animal when you say 'My roommate is a total pig.' Perhaps because understanding humour requires a grasp of abstract language – humour often

involves the use of puns and metaphors – right-hemisphere damage can also disrupt the ability to understand jokes.

The role that the right hemisphere plays in processing information about metaphors has been demonstrated using a relatively new technique in brain science called transcranial magnetic stimulation, or TMS. Researchers can aim TMS, which delivers a strong magnetic signal, into a participant's head to inactivate temporarily a specific brain region. One such study found that TMS of the right hemisphere temporarily impaired the ability of humans to understand metaphors and that this impairment was greatest when the metaphors were unfamiliar to the participants (Pobric *et al.*, 2008).

If a person learns two or more languages simultaneously as a child, Broca's and Wernicke's areas are involved in the use of all languages. Interestingly, however, if we do not learn a second language (or third or fourth) until adulthood, the brain does not rely as heavily on Broca's and Wernicke's areas. Instead, it recruits other circuits to aid in the learning process. Among these are parts of the prefrontal cortex, important for working memory, and the temporal lobe, active in the acquisition of semantic information. The recruitment of additional brain regions not involved in language learning early in life may contribute to the greater difficulty of learning a language later in life.

PSYCHOLOGY AROUND US   What the @#?! Why Swear?

All languages have taboo words, those that are controversial and not considered to be part of neutral conversation. Across cultures, taboo or swearwords seem to fall into one of three general categories: religious references, sexual references or scatological references. The relative weight of each of these categories of swearwords differs according to cultural beliefs. Religious profanity (such as *G** damn it*) is considered to be much milder in more secular countries than those cultures in which belief in God is widespread.

People swear for a variety of reasons, including for intimidation, to show off, to emphasize a point and to express negative emotions in response to a mishap. Expletives are often used to get attention and intimidate. They are

commonly associated with anger. It is not surprising that the brain regions activated by swearing or hearing swearwords are those that are involved in aggression and fear. Use of profanity involves activation of the amygdala, a primitive brain region that is important for emotions, including fear and rage.

It appears that the same neural circuitry humans use for swearing is also important to other animals for responding to basic emotions, even though the manner of expressing these emotions is different. The amygdala is involved in expressions of fear and aggression in nonhumans, including monkeys, cats and rats. While these animals are known to vocalize loudly under threatening circumstances, they do not use language and they cannot speak. We can only imagine what they would say.

Reading also involves a wide range of brain regions. The physical actions required to read activate areas of the brain that aid in visual processing and motor functions. Since reading involves eye movements, for example, it recruits a brain region in the frontal lobe called the frontal eye fields. The content of what we read also affects which brain areas become more active during reading. Words of particular emotional importance, such as obscenities or disgust words, activate the amygdala. When we read words that evoke odours, such as garlic or

cinnamon, the primary *olfactory*, or smell-related, regions of the brain become activated (González *et al.*, 2006).

Recall that there are two reading routes in the brain: a direct route that takes us directly from the printed word to the sound and an indirect route where we have to assemble the pronunciations for new words or non-words. Each of these routes can be damaged, leaving the other intact, and when this happens we observe different types of reading disorder known as *dyslexia*. When the direct route is damaged, we are forced to rely on the indirect route; that means patients are going to have great difficulty with the irregular words that we depend on the direct route for. Damage to the direct route results in a condition known as *surface dyslexia*. People with surface dyslexia can read regular words without much difficulty, and can read non-words, but have great difficulty with irregular words, often trying to *regularize* them, by producing STEAK as though it rhymes with SPEAK, for example. When the indirect route is damaged, we can only use the direct route, resulting in a condition known as *phonological dyslexia*. People with phonological dyslexia can read most words, including irregular words, but have great difficulty with pronounceable non-words, such as ZEAK or TROP. Note that in practice it is very unusual to find clear-cut examples of these reading disorders because brain damage resulting from accidents or strokes very rarely affects only the parts of the brain responsible for one particular psychological process.

A third type of dyslexia acquired by brain damage, called *deep dyslexia*, happens when the interface between the reading and meaning systems is damaged. People with deep dyslexia make reading errors based on the word's meaning, such as saying 'flower' instead of 'rose' and reading aloud 'church' as 'pray'.

Language Variation

People learn language at different speeds, and the size of vocabulary and overall verbal skills of individuals varies widely. Some evidence suggests that males and females may differ in language skills. There are even differences in the number of languages that we acquire. Although all normal people become proficient in at least one language, some people are multilingual and can become fluent in many different languages.

Differences among Individuals Some of the variability in the rate of language acquisition is due to our environments. Our vocabulary size, for example, is affected by our exposure to language, particularly early in life. As described earlier in the chapter, children in low-income households often hear fewer words and have smaller vocabularies when they start school than those from more affluent families.

Reading and writing skills also vary a great deal in the normal population. For instance, people read at a range of different speeds. This skill seems to be tied to eye movements. In English, words are written on the page from left to right, and reading speed is fastest for individuals whose eyes move in the same left-to-right direction as the printed words, with no backtracking. Slower readers tend not only to pause longer over individual words but also to backtrack, moving their eyes back to words already passed (Lahey *et al.*, 1982). It is not clear whether the less fluid eye movements occur because reading is more difficult or whether the backtracking eye movements are a distraction that interferes with rapid reading.

Gender Differences in Language One difference in verbal learning and overall skills that may be related, at least in part, to genetics is a notable gender difference in early language learning. Girls tend to learn to talk earlier. On average, girls acquire speech and language comprehension at a faster rate than boys do (Figure 11.3) (Reznick & Goldfield, 1992). These early differences often diminish by about age two, however, when those slower to acquire language catch up.

Although boys may catch up in speaking skills, girls still seem to have an advantage over boys in the language skills used in elementary school. During this time, girls as a group seem to score higher on tests of English ability. It is not clear, however, whether this difference is directly related to language ability or to a gender difference in some of the skills necessary to be a good student, such as paying attention, taking legible notes and studying. By young adulthood, these differences seem to disappear. There are no substantial male/female differences in overall reading or writing performance.

As discussed in Chapter 9, when considering gender differences, remember to keep in mind that, even though statistical differences may exist between average scores of boys and girls or men and women, these differences may not mean much for any individual. Many boys acquire language skills very rapidly and become talented writers and speakers as adults.

Another important point to consider is that the gender difference in language acquisition may be related to different experiences girls and boys have when they are young. Because boys tend to, or are encouraged to, be more active

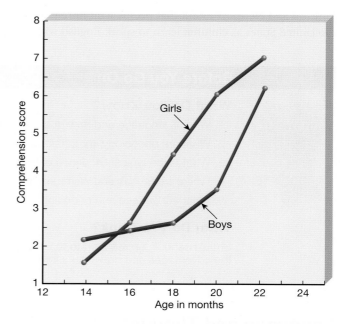

FIGURE 11.3 Gender differences in speech comprehension. Early on, there is a notable difference in language comprehension between girls and boys. Girls comprehend language at a faster rate, but this gender gap disappears by about age two.

Source: Adapted from Reznik, J. S. & Goldfield, B. A. (1992). Rapid change in lexical development in comprehension and production. *Developmental Psychology, 28,* 406–413. With permission.

than girls and girls tend to be more social than boys, it is possible that girls are exposed to a higher degree of interactive language than boys. If young boys are constantly on the move, exploring the environment, they may spend less time in social situations that facilitate language learning.

Despite the fact that there do not appear to be significant differences in overall verbal ability between adult men and women, some evidence suggests a difference in the way that women and men process language information. Neuroimaging studies have shown that, on average, women are more likely to use both hemispheres of the brain to process language information, whereas language processing in men tends to be more lateralized (Clements *et al.*, 2006). The extent to which these differences affect brain functioning during language processing has not yet been determined.

Learning More Than One Language Many children grow up in multilingual homes, where two or more languages are spoken. Such children tend to learn to speak and understand language at slightly later ages than children who only need to learn a single language. This very slight lag in learning could be explained by the greater amount of information and decoding necessary to learn two or more languages.

Like first languages, multiple languages are most readily acquired by the very young. In adulthood, the language-learning process is labour-intensive and often remains incomplete. By the age of 13, our language-learning ability has declined substantially (Figure 11.4) (Johnson & Newport, 1989). The difference can be seen with accents. Johnson and Newport found that people who immigrate to the United States as children learn to speak English without

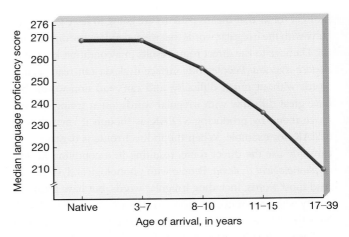

FIGURE 11.4 The earlier we learn a new language, the more proficient we become. Immigrants' mastery of English depends on when they began the learning process. The proficiency of those adults who started learning their new language before age seven is comparable to that of native speakers. However, the proficiency of those who started acquiring the language in young adulthood is much poorer.

Source: Johnson, J. S. & Newport, E. L. (1989). Critical period effects in second language learning. The influence of maturational state on the acquisition of English as a second language. *Cognitive Psychology, 21,* 60–99. With permission.

an accent, whereas those who immigrate as teens or adults speak English less fluidly and typically with the accent of their native tongue. A similar phenomenon exists for deaf children learning sign language. After about the age of 13, it becomes more difficult to learn this skill. Knowing this, many of us wish we had been exposed to multiple languages as youngsters. Those fortunate enough to have this experience can become fluent in several languages without any formal study. See 'What Happens in the Brain When We Learn a Second Language' on the following pages.

Before You Go On

What Do You Know?

1. What is language and how does language production differ from language comprehension?
2. What are phonology, morphology, syntax and pragmatics?
3. What is the typical sequence of language acquisition for most babies?
4. Where are Broca's and Wernicke's areas located in the brain and what is the primary function of each?
5. What are surface and phonological dyslexia and why do they arise?

What Do You Think?

Should schools be required to teach children multiple languages in their early years? What might be the advantages and drawbacks for children of such schooling?

Language and Thought

LEARNING OBJECTIVE 2

Define thinking that happens without words and summarize the linguistic relativity hypothesis.

Many of us associate our thoughts with the language we use to convey them. Since we often have no trouble responding automatically with words in a conversation, it can seem that language is the natural driving force of thought. One influential psychological theory suggests that our language controls

YOUR BRAIN AND BEHAVIOUR

What Happens in the Brain When We Learn a Second Language

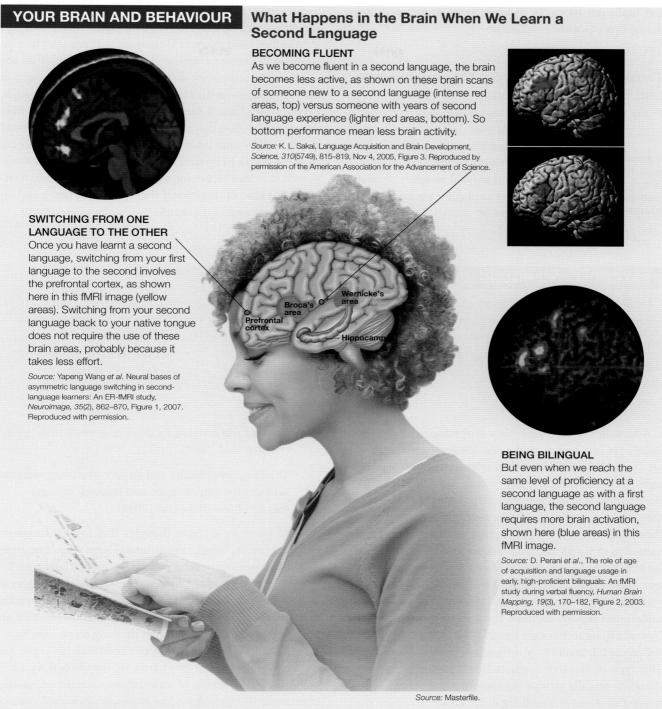

BECOMING FLUENT

As we become fluent in a second language, the brain becomes less active, as shown on these brain scans of someone new to a second language (intense red areas, top) versus someone with years of second language experience (lighter red areas, bottom). So bottom performance mean less brain activity.

Source: K. L. Sakai, Language Acquisition and Brain Development, *Science*, 310(5749), 815–819, Nov 4, 2005, Figure 3. Reproduced by permission of the American Association for the Advancement of Science.

SWITCHING FROM ONE LANGUAGE TO THE OTHER

Once you have learnt a second language, switching from your first language to the second involves the prefrontal cortex, as shown here in this fMRI image (yellow areas). Switching from your second language back to your native tongue does not require the use of these brain areas, probably because it takes less effort.

Source: Yapeng Wang *et al*. Neural bases of asymmetric language switching in second-language learners: An ER-fMRI study, *Neuroimage, 35*(2), 862–870, Figure 1, 2007. Reproduced with permission.

Prefrontal cortex

Broca's area

Wernicke's area

Hippocampus

BEING BILINGUAL

But even when we reach the same level of proficiency at a second language as with a first language, the second language requires more brain activation, shown here (blue areas) in this fMRI image.

Source: D. Perani *et al*., The role of age of acquisition and language usage in early, high-proficient bilinguals: An fMRI study during verbal fluency, *Human Brain Mapping, 19*(3), 170–182, Figure 2, 2003. Reproduced with permission.

Source: Masterfile.

Are you learning a second language now? If you are, then you probably know that it takes a lot of time to become fluent in a second language, particularly if you did not start to learn as a young child. Learning a second language not only engages brain regions that are involved in language production and comprehension but also activates areas important for learning semantic information, such as the hippocampus, and those important for working memory, such as the prefrontal cortex. As we acquire grammatical rules and become more fluent, the regions in our brain that are associated with learning a first language – such as Broca's area and Wernicke's area – become primarily involved. As we activate these language production and comprehension areas more and more, we rely less and less on semantic and working memory regions.

and limits our thoughts. In many cases, however, complex thoughts occur without language.

Thinking without Words: Mental Imagery and Spatial Navigation

In the run-up to spring, you may enjoy picturing yourself lying in a hammock sipping a cool drink while overlooking the Mediterranean coast or skiing down the slopes of the Scottish mountains. This is **mental imagery**, thoughts that involve conjuring up internal representations of stored sensory input.

mental imagery thoughts that involve conjuring up internal representations of stored sensory input.

Such mental imagery does not involve language, even if we can sometimes describe it with language.

Another good example of thinking that need not involve language is *spatial navigation thinking*. Some people do use narrative to remember directions, such as 'Turn right at the second light on the High Street.' In many cases, though, people instead use a form of visual imagery to get where they are going. You may remember the appearance of certain street corners and automatically turn right when you are triggered to do so by your visual system. In addition, some people use dead reckoning or a sense of direction to navigate. This kind of directional skill – knowing that a certain direction is north, for example – is not language-driven.

PSYCHOLOGY AROUND US Driving on Autopilot

For most people, spatial navigation becomes almost automatic, especially when this navigation is part of their routine. Consider a daily commute to work or university. You may climb into the car, turn on the engine and later find yourself at your destination without recalling the details of the drive.

In fact, some people become so lost in their thoughts while driving that they forget if they planned to go somewhere special or unusual at the end of the day. You may arrive at your house before even realizing that you had intended to go out to eat, for example.

Our ability to use imagery to solve problems is often based closely on our spatial memories. Studies have shown that we appear to search our actual relevant memories to solve tasks requiring mental imagery (e.g. Kosslyn *et al.*, 1978). For example, if researchers give participants photos of rooms that are long and narrow, with regularly spaced objects in them, and later ask the participants to describe the objects located in those rooms, the participants do so with a greater lag time between objects than if asked to carry out a similar task after looking at a photo of a smaller room.

Interestingly, using mental imagery activates many of the same brain regions used for the sensory experience itself. Neuroimaging technology has allowed us to observe which regions of the brain become most active when people think. This type of research suggests that thinking about something can actually activate the same brain regions as actually sensing or doing it (Goldberg *et al.*, 2006). There are many examples:

- When you visualize or picture in your mind an event or scene, your brain activates the visual areas that would be active if you were actually gazing at the event or scene (O'Craven & Kanwisher, 2000).

- Thinking about tastes and odours activates many of the same gustatory and olfactory brain regions

involved when you really do taste or smell something (Bensafi *et al.*, 2007).

- Thinking about fearful and anxiety-provoking subjects activates the amygdala, an area involved in anger, fear and stress (Shin *et al.*, 2004).

And when we do have thoughts that involve language, they activate the frontal and temporal lobes, the same areas used when we comprehend or produce spoken language.

Although some of our thinking involves mental imagery, it is obviously not sufficient for all of the complicated thoughts humans have. There are many concepts that do not have an adequate mental image. Consider thinking about love. Some symbols of love, such as a heart or Cupid with his arrow, are associated with love but they hardly tell the whole story. Even conjuring mental images of our loved ones does not adequately express our thoughts about love in general. As we will discuss in the rest of the chapter, much of our thinking does involve the use of words, often in combination with imagery.

The Influence of Language on Thought

Many psychologists believe that language influences our thinking a great deal. The **linguistic relativity hypothesis** suggests

linguistic relativity hypothesis the idea that the vocabulary available for objects or concepts in a language influences how speakers of that language think about them.

that the greater the number of words we have available to us related to a single concept, the more complex and detailed our thoughts are about that object or idea. The idea is sometimes known as the *Sapir–Whorf hypothesis* (Harley, 2010; Whorf, 1956), which says that our language affects the way in which we think, with different languages dissecting the world in different ways.

Evidence that supports the linguistic relativity hypothesis comes from cross-cultural studies showing that languages differ in the number of words they have to describe certain characteristics and objects. Studies have shown that extensive vocabularies for certain characteristics can lead to an ability to make finer distinctions along that dimension (Davies & Corbett, 1997). The English language, for example, has many words used to distinguish different colours. We can describe nuances of difference in shades of the colour blue, for example, by using words such as *azure, cobalt, cyan, indigo, turquoise, aquamarine* and more. By contrast, members of the Dani tribe of Papua New Guinea have in their entire language only two words to distinguish colour, one word for light and the other for dark. These people are not colour blind. They can perceive differences in colour, but they do not have words to describe them. The linguistic relativity hypothesis suggests that because English-speaking people have words for subtle concepts or distinctions regarding colour, they are encouraged to think more about them than they would if, like the Dani, their vocabulary did not include those words. The results, though, are quite complicated, with the biology of our visual system playing an important role in our sensitivity to different colours.

Before You Go On

What Do You Know?

6. What is mental imagery and what parts of the brain does it involve?

7. What research evidence suggests that we use mental imagery to solve problems involving our spatial memories?

8. What does the linguistic relativity hypothesis suggest about the influence of our language on our thinking and what research has been done?

What Do You Think?

In what ways do you believe your language influences your thoughts?

Thought

LEARNING OBJECTIVE 3

Define and summarize research on thinking processes, including problem-solving, decision-making and metacognition.

We can think in many different ways. The study of cognition includes, for example, mental imagery and spatial navigation, as we have seen. Cognitive scientists also study the development of our thinking abilities, how we solve problems, how we make decisions and even how we think about our own thoughts. We will look at some of their major findings in the remainder of this chapter. Our thinking abilities are truly impressive, but the variety and complexity of thought also means we are sometimes vulnerable to problems that interfere with our thinking. We will also discuss two psychological disorders that are characterized primarily by disruptions in thought processes.

Different forms of thinking develop at different rates. Thoughts that involve language emerge around the time that language capabilities are forming, whereas those that involve reasoning emerge later. Formulating long-term plans and carrying them out is a type of thought that develops relatively late (Chandler & Carpendale, 1998). Changes in our thinking continue to occur throughout life. Teenagers and young adults become increasingly capable of making and carrying out long-term plans for their futures.

Thinking and Effort: Controlled and Automatic Processing

The distinction between controlled and automatic thinking is an important concept in cognitive psychology. As we discussed in Chapter 10, on memory, controlled processing is effortful and relies on a limited-capacity system, while automatic processing seems effortless. Automatic processing is not usually disrupted very much if we are distracted by other tasks. Experienced drivers can carry on a conversation while driving a car, for example. However, automatic processing, such as skilled driving, can be severely disrupted by simultaneously engaging in a task that requires more attention than speaking, such as reading or sending a text message. Controlled processing requires more attention. Most of us cannot carry on a conversation while conducting multi-digit mental arithmetic. We must direct our thoughts towards the mathematical problem.

cognitive control the ability to direct thought in accordance with one's intentions.

Cognitive control refers to our ability to direct thought and action the way we intend to (Carter *et al.*, 1999). Some examples of this include:

- the ability to direct attention to a specific stimulus even when other, perhaps stronger, stimuli are competing for your attention, such as finding the face you are looking for in a crowd

- keeping a new piece of information in mind against distraction, such as remembering a telephone number until you dial it while in a crowded shopping centre

- overcoming a compelling behaviour, such as not scratching a very itchy mosquito bite

- pursuing a complex but unfamiliar behaviour, such as learning the rules and moves of a new sport

- responding flexibly and productively in new situations, such as playing a complex videogame that requires anticipating future consequences.

The brain's ability to exert control over mental processing is often referred to as executive function. People with damage to the frontal lobes often display a condition called dysexecutive syndrome, characterized by impairments in cognitive functions that depend on control, such as planning or the ability to flexibly respond in new situations. This deficit was dramatically documented in the classic case of Phineas Gage. As we discussed in Chapter 5, Gage was a railroad foreman who suffered damage to his prefrontal cortex when a metal spike was driven through his head in a construction accident. Before the accident, acquaintances described him as thoughtful, responsible and of sound judgement, but following his injury, he was considered erratic in his behaviour and unable to plan for the future. The damage to his prefrontal cortex affected his control over his mental processing, resulting in an inability to carry out plans. Changes such as these have been observed repeatedly in patients with damage to the frontal cortex.

As we age, we also develop more capacity for cognitive control. Very young children, for example, often make decisions based on impulse: if they want the biscuit and it is in view, they will grab it. Problems arise with social interactions for this reason. Preschool children will often fight over toys because they do not understand the concepts of waiting and fairness. As children grow, however, their decision-making process becomes more sophisticated. Usually, by the time they are six to eight years old, children are able to modulate their impulses for the good of their peers. During snack time, William may save a biscuit for Lydia, who is out of the room, rather than eat it himself. At an even later stage, between the ages of nine and 12, children become able to make decisions with the long-term future in mind. They are more willing to make sacrifices in the immediate future in order to get a larger pay-off later on. If given the option of getting one square of chocolate after completing a single mathematical problem or an entire chocolate bar after waiting for 24 hours, older children will often decide to hold out for the whole bar.

Automatic processing has its limits. Even automatic processing, such as that used when driving a car, can be severely interrupted by tasks that require significant attention, such as texting. Thus, to prevent car accidents, many countries have laws that allow people to talk (a relatively non-distracting activity) on a hands-free phone while driving but forbid them to use a hand-held phone.

Source: Left photo: ©Tom Grill/Corbis. Right photo: ©Image Source/Corbis.

Thinking to Solve Problems

One aspect of thinking that has received considerable attention from psychologists is that of **problem solv-ing**. Problem solving is triggered by our desire to reach a goal. We must figure out how to get from our current state of affairs, which is in some way unsatisfactory, to our desired end state (Bourne *et al.*, 1979). We use problem-solving skills in many avenues of life, from formal mathematical problems in school to informal day-to-day problems, such as how to get along with a roommate.

> **problem solving** determining how to reach a goal.

Defining Our Problems The first step when solving a problem is to figure out exactly what the problem is: to develop a representation of the problem.

On one end of the spectrum, we use formal problem-solving skills to solve mathematical problems. Our goal in arithmetic is usually straightforward: to move from not knowing the correct answer to knowing it. Researchers refer to problems such as arithmetic, with easily recognizable beginning and end states, as well-defined problems. We often find it fairly easy to find a strategy for solving well-defined problems, because we can easily define what outcome we want from the start.

On the other end of the problem-solving spectrum are ill-defined problems, such as how to deal with a less-than-helpful roommate. Our goal in this case may be difficult to define precisely. We may want to stop doing what we feel is an unfair share of housecleaning, but how will we know when we have reached that goal? As you may well imagine, it is often more difficult to find solutions for ill-defined problems than for well-defined ones, because it is hard to define the desired outcome.

To define a problem, you must figure out your current state and your goal, and identify the differences between them. Consider the following problem. When driving home on a particular road, you need to make a right-hand turn onto the High Street at a traffic light that is always very congested at that time of day. Your current state is frustration with the long wait at the light.

Your goal may be to find a faster way to make the turn. With this goal in mind, you could consider several ways to speed up the turn, such as altering the time of day you travel, driving faster to arrive at the intersection earlier or merging into the line of waiting cars closer to the crossroads. None of these solutions is ideal. If the problem is represented in a different way, however, a new solution may come to mind. You may, for example, change your question from 'How do I make a right turn onto the High Street?' to 'How can I get onto the High Street quicker?'

Adopting a new goal such as this may cause you to notice that you can turn right into the car park of a shopping centre at the corner, then quickly and legally exit onto the High Street in the direction you want to go – avoiding the right-hand turn and the traffic jam entirely. Changing how you think about a problem does not guarantee you will find a solution, but it increases your chances of finding one if your new representation triggers you to consider new alternatives.

Strategies for Problem Solving After you have defined the problem, you must choose a strategy for finding a solution. There are two major types of strategies: algorithms and heuristics. An **algorithm** is a strategy that, if followed methodically, will always lead to a solution. For example, an algorithm strategy could be used to solve an arithmetical problem that included adding up a series of 10 single-digit numbers by adding each number to the overall sum. Following this algorithm will produce a correct answer but it can be time-consuming. If you had to add up the total of 50 or 100 different numbers, you may begin to look for faster ways to solve the problem.

> **algorithm** a problem-solving strategy that always leads to a solution.

To save time and effort when solving problems, we often use a set of **heuristics**, or shortcut strategies. Instead of taking the time to add together a long list of numbers, you could just estimate the total. Heuristics often help us reach a satisfactory solution, but they do not guarantee a correct answer to a problem.

> **heuristics** shortcut thinking strategy.

Algorithm and heuristic strategies can be used to solve problems in everyday life. Consider the steps you would take to find out whether a particular lecturer would be a good teacher for you before enrolling in his or her course. Using an algorithm method, you might question every student enrolled in the class the previous term. This method would give you the maximum amount of information and the greatest chance of reaching the correct answer. You probably would not know everyone in the class, however. Even if you did, this method would be very time-consuming. Using a heuristic strategy, you might ask a few students you know who took the course or examine the drop rate in the class for evidence of how many students decided against the course once enrolled. The heuristic methods save time and effort, but they are also riskier. Your few acquaintances might not share your preference in teaching styles, for example.

Some helpful heuristic strategies in problem solving include working backwards, forming subgoals and searching for analogies:

- Working backwards is helpful for problems with well-defined goals. Starting from your goal, you think backwards, imagining a series of steps it would take you to move backwards from your goal to your current state. Once you have determined the steps between your current state and the goal, you can actually follow them in a forwards order. Working backwards to figure out if a lecturer is a good teacher for you, you may define your goal as enjoying the teacher's lectures. A good step to find out whether you would enjoy the lectures is to sit through one, so you might decide to visit and sample one of the lecturer's class sessions before registering for the next term.

- Forming subgoals involves dividing a larger problem into smaller ones (Catrambone, 1998). If your ultimate goal is to find out whether a lecturer would be a good teacher for you, you might decide to work on accomplishing two separate subgoals: asking three former students about the lecturer and arranging to sit in on one lecture.

- Searching for analogies involves recalling similar problems that you have encountered (Holyoak & Morrison, 2005). If you had successfully sought information about a film by asking friends and reading reviews, you might decide to use those same approaches to gather information about a lecturer: asking your friends and reading reviews posted online.

We are not always aware of using a method in order to solve a problem. Sometimes we seem to solve a problem quickly, without intensive effort or concentration, through a phenomenon known as insight. In fact, several groundbreaking scientific discoveries have been described as 'eureka moments' of insight. Sometimes sudden solutions occur after an incubation period, during which we have mentally set aside a problem that we have been working on. When we return to the problem after a while, the solution comes to mind without further conscious strategizing. Some studies suggest that type of problem solving is automatic (Novick & Bassock, 2005).

Problems in Problem Solving Sometimes we fall into patterns of thinking that make it difficult to solve problems to which those patterns do not apply. One common difficulty can happen early in representing the problem. We must define the problem using relevant information and ignore any irrelevant information. When trying to find out whether a lecturer has a good teaching style for you, for example, you may learn that the lecturer is engaged in a very interesting line of research. But if the lecturer's research has little impact on his or her teaching, it is not particularly relevant to your problem.

Other difficulties can occur when we get to the point of actually solving problems. Some of these are the result of

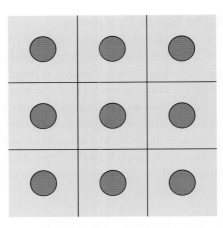

FIGURE 11.5 The nine-dot problem. Without lifting your pencil, draw no more than four straight lines to connect all the dots.

heuristics. When we use the heuristic of looking for analogies, for example, we risk falling into a **mental set**, a tendency to use problem-solving strategies that have always worked in the past. If you have a certain solution in mind, you may see the problem as fitting that solution, even when it does not. If you view getting onto the High Street with a mental set that sees the problem as how to make a right turn, you miss possible solutions that do not involve right turns. The nine-dot problem shown in Figure 11.5 is a good way to practise overcoming mental sets.

> **mental set** the tendency to use problem-solving strategies that have worked in the past.

One particular version of a mental set is referred to as **functional fixedness**, the tendency to view objects as having only one use or function. A coin, for instance, is a form of currency, used to buy things. It may not always occur to you that you can use a coin to turn the head of a screw when you do not have a screwdriver. You overcome functional fixedness when you realize that objects have more than one function, even if those other functions are atypical. The string problem, shown in Figure 11.6 is one test that psychologists have used to reveal when people are experiencing functional fixedness.

> **functional fixedness** tendency to view objects as having only one function.

We can also hamper our ability to solve problems by adopting a **confirmation bias**, a tendency to look for information that meets our expectations when problem solving. If you have heard that all of the lecturers in the department in which you are thinking of taking a class are good teachers, you may only seek out opinions from students who completed the class taught by the lecturer whose class you are thinking

> **confirmation bias** a tendency to look for information that meets our expectations when problem solving.

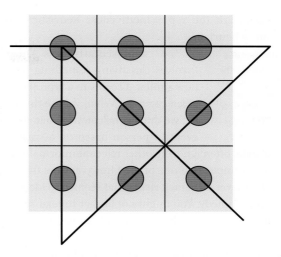

Solution to the nine-dot problem. Most people have difficulty with this problem because they see the arrangement of dots as a square and try to keep within the boundaries of the dots. This mental set limits their ability to solve the problem.

FIGURE 11.6 The string problem. Two strings are suspended from above and you cannot reach both of them at the same time. How can you tie them together?

of taking rather than undertaking the more difficult task of finding people who have dropped out of the course. The problem with this approach is that students who remained on the course throughout would be more likely to confirm what you expected to hear – that the lecturer was good – than to give you a negative, but potentially helpful, evaluation.

In one classic study, researchers revealed confirmation bias by giving participants a series of numbers: 2, 4 and 6 (Wason, 1960). They asked the participants to figure out the rule for that set by generating their own sets of numbers. Each time the participants offered a series, the experimenters told them only whether their set did or did not follow the same rule as the original set. Many participants became convinced that the rule was to increase each number by 2. They offered repeated sets of numbers, such as 8, 10 and 12 or 20, 22 and 24. The researchers told them that their sets conformed to the original rule, but when asked to state the original rule these participants got it wrong. The original rule was simply that each number had to have a numerical value larger than the one before it. The numbers the participants generated themselves conformed to the rules they created, but it did not occur to them that other rules were possible.

The way to overcome confirmation bias is to purposely look for information that disconfirms your ideas. People who generated random series of numbers, such as 54, 3, 12, would have been more likely to correctly work out the rule.

Thinking to Make Decisions

Decision making involves evaluating and choosing from among the alternatives available to us. Many of your everyday thoughts involve weighing options and making choices. First, you must decide what time to wake up. A series of decisions follow, including choices about what to wear, what to eat for breakfast, with whom to spend your time and what to do. Even when we are on a regular schedule, we do not behave like robots. We often have options to stick with our regular course of action or do something else, and we must decide which option to choose.

> **decision making** evaluating and choosing from among options.

Information for Decision Making To make decisions, we need to gather or recall information relevant to each option. Suppose you were trying to decide which of two films to go to see. You would not pick a film at random based on the title. You would probably like a little information about each film to help you make your choice. You could gather information from sources outside yourself, such as film reviews and the comments of your friends. You could also recall relevant information that you already had. You might, for example, recognize the names of some of the actors or one of the directors.

When we draw from our memories to get information, we often use heuristic shortcuts. The use of heuristics is sometimes successful but often leads us to reach an incorrect decision (Stanovich, 2008; Tversky & Kahneman, 1993, 1974). Two heuristics that have been described by researchers are the representativeness heuristic and the availability heuristic.

representativeness heuristic classifying something based on how similar it seems to a typical case in a given category.

The **representativeness heuristic** involves classifying something based on how similar it seems to a typical case in a given category. When we use this heuristic, we draw conclusions about an object, event or person based on a small set of specific data, often ignoring other relevant information. Suppose, for example, that one of the films you were thinking of seeing had several characteristics that seemed to identify it as a romantic comedy. You might not bother to read reviews or get other information about the film because, based only on its presumed identity as a romantic comedy, you had a set of expectations about what the movie would be like.

Two researchers, Amos Tversky and Danny Kahneman (1974), nicely demonstrated people's use of the representativeness heuristic by asking research participants to read a description of an individual that included personal attributes such as 'shows no interest in political and social issues' and 'spends most of his free time on mathematical puzzles'. After they read this, participants were also told that the individual was randomly selected from a pool that contained 70% lawyers and 30% engineers. Despite the fact that the individual was statistically more likely to be a lawyer than an engineer, most of the participants identified him as an engineer based on a few personal characteristics.

Another approximation used to make decisions is known as the **availability heuristic**. This refers to the likelihood that we will judge an event as more common if it is easier to call to mind (Keller *et al.*, 2006; Oppenheimer, 2004; McKelvie & Drumheller, 2001). You may easily remember the one really great film made by an actor in one of the films you are thinking about attending but not be able to recall the actor's so-so work in several other films. In reality, though, this actor makes so-so films more often than great films. The availability heuristic also explains why we tend to think that infrequent but highly salient and memorable events, such as plane crashes, are more common than they are. Because such events are easy to call to mind, we

availability heuristic judging easily recalled events as more common.

assume they commonly occur when, in fact, they are very rare (Foster, 2009).

Another aspect of the availability heuristic that affects decision making is the fact that we tend to rely on more recently stored memories to make judgements about events. For example, patients who underwent painful medical colonoscopy procedures are more likely to remember the event as excruciatingly painful if it is over quickly and ends at a time of maximal pain than if the procedure is extended for a longer period and they experience diminished pain at the end (Redelmeier *et al.*, 2003). Because it is easier to call more recent information to mind, we assume that it says more than in fact it does about the overall experience.

Rational Decision Making After we have gathered or brought to mind information about the options, how do we evaluate each one and go about picking one of them? For thousands of years, since the time of the ancient Greek philosopher Plato, philosophers have argued that it is better to rely on logical reasoning than on emotions or instinct when making decisions. And, until relatively recently, many of the theorists and researchers who studied decision making assumed that people's decisions – particularly financial decisions about what products to buy, whether to save or spend and how to invest – were based on purely logical reasoning. Many models of such rational decision-making processes exist. Many assume that we choose a set of criteria and rank each option on its utility, or its ability to satisfy each criterion (Edwards & Newman, 1986; Edwards, 1977). If you were looking for a new phone, for instance, you might evaluate its size, its cost and what apps were available. Some models of rational decision making suggest that we might go even further and give more importance to certain criteria. If, for example, it is very important to you that you have certain apps on your new phone, you may weigh that criterion more highly than the phone's size and cost. According to these models, after gathering and evaluating information on each phone, we could mathematically calculate which phone was the best for us. A model of such a calculation is shown in Table 11.2. According to this model, you would choose Phone C.

TABLE 11.2 Model of Rational Decision Making: Considering Both Rank and Weight (Importance)

Criterion	Weight of criteria	Phone A		Phone B		Phone C	
		Rank	Rank × weight	Rank	Rank × weight	Rank	Rank × weight
Size	+3	8	24	5	15	5	15
Cost	+6	8	48	6	36	4	24
Apps	+10	0	0	5	50	8	80
Total of rank × weight		**Phone A: 72**		**Phone B: 101**		**Phone C: 119**	

For some decisions, rational models of decision making suggest that we may also take into account the probability that we can attain our choices. If, for example, you are choosing classes for next term, the course that ranks as your top choice may be so popular on campus that your chance of getting into the class is low. In this case, you may decide to sign up for another course, instead of your top choice, as part of your rational decision-making process.

Reason-based decision-making methods such as these can help us when we have only a few choices and want to evaluate them based only on a few attributes (Payne & Bettman, 2004). Sometimes we cannot use such a model until we narrow down choices from a number of options (Slovic, 1990; Tversky, 1972). You may, for example, have eliminated 15 other phones that were entirely beyond your budget before choosing only three to decide among. Indeed, sometimes eliminating certain options leads us directly to a decision. If you can only afford one of the phones available, you do not need to perform a complicated analysis to make your decision, because there is only one option. In fact, research shows that we can be literally spoilt for choice, and find it easier to make decisions when there are fewer options available (Schwartz, 2005).

Rational decision-making models can be used only if we have information available to us about all the options and time to ponder this information. As you may have experienced, we often do not have enough information or time to make decisions this way (Gigerenzer & Goldstein, 1996). After you buy

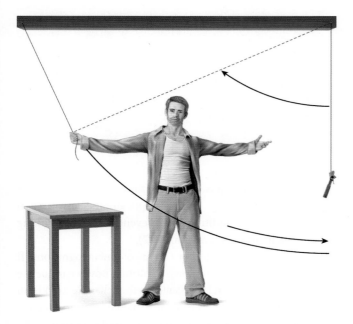

Solution to the string problem. Tie the spanner to one string and use it as a weight to swing the string closer to you. Functional fixedness can limit your ability to recognize this use for the spanner.

your phone, for example, you may want to stop in the food court at the shopping mall for a snack. With only a few minutes to decide, you may focus on only a few of the available options – maybe the first couple of restaurants you walk by – or a few attributes of the choices, such as whether they offer a vegetarian dish. You may still think rationally about your choice, but you are using a model, known as bounded rationality, that limits the cognitive effort you need to invest (Simon, 1957). Research suggests that we successfully use bounded rationality to make many of our decisions, doing the best we can with the cognitive resources and information that we have available at a given moment (Gigerenzer, 2004; Simon, 1990).

Emotions and Decision Making Suppose you were perusing the food court for your snack and you got a craving for some chips. You might just buy some and eat them, without putting much, if any, rational thought into your decision. For a long time, decisions made in this way troubled rational decision-making theorists, because such choices are not based on logical reasons. Because of the work of Kahneman, however, we now know that decision making often involves irrational processes that can be driven by our emotions. In fact, people often rely heavily on their emotions, or gut instinct, rather than pure reason to make decisions.

Because decision making involves emotions, it is hard to predict human decision-making behaviour. There are individual differences in emotional reactions, and many of these are driven by developmental experience and temperament. Even our moods can affect our decision making. Research suggests, for example, that when we are in a positive mood we tend to make more efficient decisions with less rational consideration of the alternatives. We also tend to be content with those choices (Schwartz et al., 2002).

Researchers have discovered a few situations in which we can predict that our emotions are likely to influence decisions. One of these is when we try to estimate risks in anticipating the consequences of our decisions. For example, if you buy the wrong new phone, you risk being unhappy with it or needing to take it in for lots of repairs. Research suggests that we base our decisions, at least in part, on how we expect we will feel if we make a bad choice (Mellers et al., 1998, 1997; Kahneman & Tversky, 1979). In general, we try hard to avoid making decisions we will regret later (Connolly & Zeelenberg, 2002). For many of us, *bad* outweighs *good* in our anticipation, so we may make less than optimal choices just to avoid the risk of feeling bad later. Given the option to receive 10 pence of a shared pound, for example, most people would opt out altogether, taking nothing instead of the 10 pence, because they would feel they had been treated unfairly if they had to share the pound. This is irrational behaviour since, clearly, 10 pence is better than nothing at all.

Understanding how emotions can affect people's purchasing decisions is of particular interest to advertisers. If the context that produces positive emotion can be identified, it can be used effectively to persuade consumers to buy. In many cases, language can play a role in producing this context by framing choices in positive or negative ways. We are more likely to buy a food that is labelled '75% fat-free' than one described as '25% fat' for example (Sanford *et al.*, 2002). Framing is especially effective in arousing emotions when we are estimating risks. Most college students would feel safer using condoms that prevent the transmission of HIV 95% of the time than the same condoms when they are described as failing to prevent HIV transmission 5% of the time (Linville *et al.*, 1993).

Emotions do not always affect decision making in a negative way. Although it is true that feeling upset, anxious, cheated or irrationally hopeful may impair our judgement and increase the chance that we will make an impulsive and unnecessary purchase, it is sometimes the case that emotions help us make better decisions. Research has shown that individuals often make better decisions in games with a chance

element when they claim to be operating on a hunch. Intuition is not well understood, but it is an irrational characteristic that sometimes improves decision-making capabilities. The Practically Speaking feature gives you some tips about when it can be helpful to 'go with your gut'.

Decision Making and the Brain Certain types of brain damage can lead to impairments in decision making (Ward, 2010). In particular, an area of the brain known as the *prefrontal cortex*, right at the front of the brain over the eyes, is involved in the executive processing underlying decision making. The prefrontal cortex is relatively larger in humans than in other animals. Patients with damage to the prefrontal cortex show poor planning and problems with making decisions. Neuroimaging techniques such as fMRI also show that the prefrontal cortex becomes activated when we plan and make decisions. The neurosurgical treatment of prefrontal lobotomy, carried out quite widely in the middle part of the past century for a range of psychiatric disturbances, left patients apathetic, docile and often unable to make even the simplest decisions.

PRACTICALLY SPEAKING   **When Is It Best to Rely on Emotions for Decision Making?**

Intuition, hunches, inner voice, gut instinct: emotional decision making goes by many names and its importance is often downplayed compared with rational thought. However, using emotion to make decisions is particularly important for interacting in social situations. In some cases, your survival may even depend on it.

For example, being able to judge a person by how you feel allows you to make quick decisions about interacting with them. You may conclude that you do not trust the individual but be unable to offer a rational explanation. After all, you do not even know them. Subtle characteristics about the individual from their body language to their facial expression may have led you to that conclusion. Researchers have

also discovered that the same areas of the brain that are activated when you make a negative judgement about a person are also activated in response to painful or aversive stimuli (Critchley et al., 2000).

Emotional decision making also comes into play when groups cooperate. When you and your friends are deciding on which movie to see, you do not make a pie chart. You gauge the interest of the others for the particular film choices and the choice with the most enthusiastic response is the film everyone usually decides to see (Thagard & Kroon, 2006). Of course, emotion alone rarely makes an appropriate decision: a combination of rational thinking and emotional processes probably leads to the best possible outcome.

Metacognition

One of the most complicated forms of thought is **metacognition**, or thinking about thinking. When we consider our own memories, for example, we engage in a form of metacognition. We may mull over specific facts we remember, thinking about where and when we learnt them. We may also think about how information we have learnt in the past is influencing our understanding of things happening now. Metacognition involving thinking about the source of memories involves activation of the frontal cortex of the brain, as

metacognition
thinking about one's thoughts.

well as the hippocampus, a region important for the storage of information. Damage to the hippocampus can result in source amnesia, a condition that prevents accurate thinking about one's memories (Lakhan, 2007).

Self-reflection is another form of metacognition. It involves thinking about our own identities, how we influence other people and our relative self-worth. Self-reflection is an important human behaviour because it enables us to evaluate and modify our responses based on our past experience. We may reflect on our behaviour at a recent party, for example, and decide that we would feel better about ourselves if we

Assessing metacognition in animals. Because chimps and gorillas cannot vocalize as humans do, researchers can assess their capacity for metacognition only with special strategies, such as by having them point to symbols on a keyboard or by observing their behaviour in certain learning tasks.

Source: Michael Nichols/NG Image Collection.

were more, or perhaps less, outgoing. Then we may take steps either to overcome shyness or tone down our party persona. Self-reflection can sometimes have negative consequences if it leads to repetitive thoughts of worthlessness and anxiety. For people with specific biological tendencies, excessive self-reflection can lead to psychological problems, such as depression and anxiety disorders (Takano & Tanno, 2009).

Another type of metacognition involves the theory of mind. As we discussed in Chapter 3, a theory of mind is the recognition that other people have their own perspectives and base their actions on these perspectives. Theory of mind is an important aspect of human thought. It enables us to infer what others are thinking by watching how they act. It also allows us to communicate and live peacefully with other people. If we did not have a theory of mind and instead needed explicit verbal information about the feelings and intentions of another person, social communication would be difficult. Thus, theory of mind is an adaptive trait.

PSYCHOLOGY AROUND US   Do Animals Have a Theory of Mind?

Dog owners have long noted that their pets seem to watch their faces and respond as if they were inferring the owners' thoughts. A dog that sees the owner smiling might eagerly approach with tail wagging, looking for a food treat, while one that sees the owner scowling might retreat, whimpering. But can animals really think? Evidence suggests that many animals are, indeed, capable of complicated thought and seem to possess a theory of mind (Hirata, 2009; Reid, 2009). Some

species of birds, for example, seem to infer the intentions of other birds. Western scrub jays will re-hide stored food if they notice they were being watched by another bird when the food was first hidden. This evidence suggests that the scrub jay has a theory of mind. The scrub jay seems to infer that a watching bird intends to steal hidden food. In response to this inference, the scrub jay moves the food to a new secret location after the watcher stops looking.

Once we acquire a theory of mind during development, it becomes automatic. You probably exercise your theory of mind many times a day, while assessing your roommate's mood based on his or her actions, gauging a lecturer's expectations based on his or her demeanour or trying to figure out what type of person your date is from the cues you receive on the first date.

Metacognition HOW WE DEVELOP Children develop a theory of mind gradually, starting during the toddler years. It is apparent that young children, aged two to three years, lack the ability to infer the thinking of the person who is searching for them when trying to play hide-and-seek. Children this age will often 'hide' by covering their eyes while remaining in a location that is in plain sight. Rather than think about the point of view of the searcher, they rely on their own experience: 'If I can't see because my

eyes are covered, no one else can see me.' This lack of theory of mind disappears within a few years (Sabbagh *et al.*, 2009; Aschersleben *et al.*, 2008).

When theory of mind is developing in young children, it may contribute to jealousy and an inability to share. A child may come to think of another child as a rival, with intentions to take away his or her toys. Another behaviour that is tied to thinking about what is going on in another person's head is *lying*. In general, people lie for two main reasons: to prevent themselves from being punished or to make someone else feel good. Children learn very early to lie in order to avoid punishment. This behaviour seems to emerge around the age of three for most children, and by the age of five it is a fairly universal phenomenon (Talwar & Lee, 2008). If backed into a corner by the expectation of punishment, almost all five-year-olds will lie. Their theory of mind allows people to lie in hopes of preventing punishment, even if they have not explicitly been warned about the punishment (Talwar *et al.*, 2007). Because the child is able to imagine that an adult believes the child's behaviour is wrong, he or she can then infer that the adult intends to punish the child for the wrong behaviour.

Lying to make another person feel better, such as giving false compliments or reassurances, is another behaviour that arises during the preschool years. Unlike lying to avoid punishment, however, this type of lying seems to increase in frequency as we get older. Have you ever complimented a friend on a new haircut or new outfit that you actually feel is less than flattering? The chances are you did not feel particularly guilty afterwards because your thoughts about how your friend feels are stronger than your desire to always tell the truth.

Although theory of mind seems to be present in young children, other forms of metacognition are not evident until later in development. For example, thinking about one's memories and evaluating current information in the context of the past is not common among young children. Young children often suffer from source amnesia (not remembering where they heard about certain information). This tendency not only makes them prone to develop false memories but also interferes with their ability to think about their memories in a meaningful way (Zola, 1998).

Theory of Mind — WHAT HAPPENS IN THE BRAIN?

Neuroscientists believe that the ability to think about another person's intentions is directly linked to a set of cells in the brain called **mirror neurons** (Rizzolatti & Fabbri-Destro, 2008). Mirror neurons are located in the frontal and parietal cortices. These cells are activated not only when an individual engages in a particular task but also when he or she watches another person engage in this same task. For example, the same neurons respond when you eat dinner and when you watch someone else eat. Since the same set of neurons are activated whether it is you or another person who acts, an overlap exists in the neural circuitry that probably allows you to make predictions about the other person's behaviour.

mirror neurons the neurons located in the frontal and parietal cortices that respond similarly when an individual engages in an activity or watches someone else engage in it.

Consider, for instance, what might happen in your brain were you to reach into a biscuit jar. Usually when you reach into a jar of biscuits, you are hungry and looking for something good to eat. This might activate several neurons in your frontal cortex, including those involved in movement, as well as those important for anticipation and for reward. For the sake of this discussion, let's refer to these neurons as A, B and C. Reaching into the jar activates neuron A, which in turn activates B and C. If neuron A is a mirror neuron, your neuron A can also be activated in your brain when you watch somebody else reach into a jar of biscuits. Activating your neuron A will, in turn, activate your neurons B and C, which carry information about intention. They tell you that the anticipated reward of reaching in the biscuit jar is finding the biscuit. Based on this activation in your brain, you may infer that the other person is reaching into the jar because they hope to find a biscuit inside.

Disordered Thought — OUT OF THE ORDINARY

Many disorders include problems with thinking. In many cases, however, these conditions are primarily associated with deficits in other psychological processes; impairments in the person's thinking are not the main problem. Individuals with Alzheimer's disease are often in a confused state, for example, but the reason they are not thinking clearly is because their memories are disrupted, not because of a problem with thinking itself. In other cases, problems with thinking are tied to irregular and undesirable emotional states. Depression often affects a person's thinking, as it is accompanied by repetitive thoughts about worthlessness and hopelessness. Cognitive therapy that targets these thoughts can often be a successful form of treatment (Rupke *et al.*, 2006). Although the thought components of dementia and mood disorders are real and significant symptoms, we discuss them in other chapters because these conditions are primarily associated with psychological processes other than thinking. Instead, we focus in this chapter on two disorders that are characterized primarily by difficulties in controlling one's thoughts: obsessive–compulsive disorder and schizophrenia.

Obsessive–Compulsive Disorder

Obsessive–compulsive disorder (OCD) is defined by having uncontrollable, anxiety-provoking thoughts called obsessions. Many people with this disorder feel compulsion*s*, or irresistible urges, to perform mental or physical ritual actions to help reduce their anxiety. People with OCD know that their thoughts are out of touch with reality, but they often find it impossible to stop or ignore these thoughts. The impulse to engage in compulsive behaviour, such as washing one's hands over and over or repeatedly checking whether the oven has been turned off, is so strong that anxiety builds with each passing moment if something prevents them from performing these actions (Magee & Teachman, 2007). OCD can range from relatively mild to extreme cases that make people unable to participate in normal everyday activities. Estimates of how prevalent OCD is in the population are uncertain because many people with mild OCD do not receive a formal diagnosis. Conservative estimates suggest that OCD affects about 1% of the population (Kessler *et al.*, 2009).

obsessive–compulsive disorder (OCD) a mental disorder associated with abnormal anxiety-provoking thoughts that can lead to ritualistic behaviours.

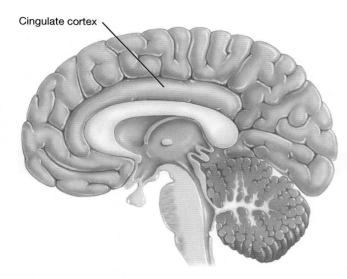

Cingulate cortex

FIGURE 11.7 Brain treatment for OCD. Surgery that selectively damages part of the cingulate cortex can bring relief to people with otherwise untreatable OCD.

The biological basis of OCD remains incompletely understood, but most researchers believe that an imbalance in the neurotransmitter serotonin may play some role. People with OCD often respond positively to treatment with antidepressant medications that target serotonin neurons, such as Prozac and Paroxetine (Soomro *et al.*, 2008). Behavioural therapy is also often effective in treating people with OCD. A typical behavioural therapy approach involves exposing the patient to conditions that provoke anxiety, such as touching food, while preventing the ritualistic behaviour that they would typically perform to diminish the anxiety, such as hand washing. With repeated exposures, the patient sometimes learns that withholding the ritual behaviour does not have negative consequences (Fenske & Schwenk, 2009). In turn, they may realize that their anxieties are uncalled for. In some cases, however, neither antidepressant treatment nor behavioural therapy helps relieve OCD. In extreme cases, where anxiety and ritualistic behaviour are preventing normal functioning, patients may undergo brain surgery. This treatment involves selectively damaging part of the prefrontal cortex, called the cingulate cortex (Figure 11.7). In about 30% of patients with otherwise untreatable OCD, cingulate damage is effective at reducing symptoms (Baer *et al.*, 1995).

schizophrenia a mental disorder characterized by disorganized thoughts, lack of contact with reality and sometimes auditory hallucinations.

Schizophrenia Schizophrenia is a relatively common psychotic disorder, characterized by extreme disorganization of thinking. About 1% of people in the West have been diagnosed with some form of schizophrenia (Regier *et al.*, 1993).

Although schizophrenia can exist in multiple forms, it generally involves a break from reality in thoughts and actions. People with schizophrenia experience distortions of reality in the form of hallucinations (usually auditory) and delusions, beliefs that are not based in reality (APA, 2000). They also exhibit a devastating inability to plan and control their own thoughts (Berenbaum & Barch, 1995). Furthermore, many people with this disorder suffer impaired working memory and find it impossible to keep track of information necessary to execute even a simple series of actions (Piskulic *et al.*, 2007).

Schizophrenia is typically diagnosed in the transition period between late adolescence and early adulthood. The disorder is progressive. In the beginning, schizophrenia can only be identified by what psychologists refer to as positive symptoms, such as active hallucinations and delusions (Gourzis *et al.*, 2002). As time passes, negative symptoms – behaviour stemming from the person's loss of thinking and memory abilities – present themselves and become even more devastating than the positive symptoms. Many people with schizophrenia find it impossible to hold down a job or participate in social or family relationships.

Schizophrenia often also includes a language component. Sometimes a person's speech and writing become entirely disorganized and out of contact with reality (Covington *et al.*, 2005). Despite living with schizophrenia, however, many people are able to write sentences with correct semantics and syntax (Covington *et al.*, 2005).

The causes of schizophrenia are still not completely understood, but there appears to be a genetic component (Sullivan *et al.*, 2003). Since some drugs have been discovered that can effectively treat schizophrenic symptoms, some scientists have suggested that people with schizophrenia may suffer from abnormalities in neurotransmitter activity (Goff & Coyle, 2001). Medications that block receptors for the neurotransmitter dopamine, called antipsychotics or neuroleptics, can reduce some of the symptoms of schizophrenia, including delusions and hallucinations (Tandon *et al.*, 2008). This has led researchers to speculate that schizophrenia may result from overactivity in the brain's dopamine systems or from an abnormal distribution of specific dopamine receptors in the brain (Carlsson & Lindqvist, 1963). New classes of drugs that target the neurotransmitter glutamate receptors have been used successfully to treat cognitive symptoms in schizophrenia that are not relieved by neuroleptic medications, suggesting that glutamate may also be involved in the disorder (Patil *et al.*, 2007).

One major problem with antipsychotic medications is the high rate of their side effects, some of which are permanent. In addition to weight gain, which can lead to other health problems, certain neuroleptics can produce a condition called tardive dyskinesia, a permanent motor disturbance of the mouth and tongue. Tardive dyskinesia often does not subside even when medication is stopped, and may be the result of a permanent restructuring of dopamine systems serving motor function (Larach *et al.*, 1997). Recall from the discussion of dopamine in Chapter 5 that this neurotransmitter is importantly involved in movement. Clearly, more research is needed to investigate the biological basis of schizophrenia with an aim towards its prevention and the development of new drugs that treat the symptoms without creating major side effects.

Before You Go On

What Do You Know?

9. Compare and contrast controlled and automatic cognitive processing.

10. What are the two main types of strategies for solving problems and how do they differ? Give at least one example of each type.

11. What are the representativeness and availability heuristics and how do they affect decision making?

12. How can emotions affect our decision making?

13. What are metacognition and theory of mind?

14. How is thinking disturbed in OCD and schizophrenia?

What Do You Think?

Which of the barriers to problem solving described in this chapter most often seem to affect you? Which problem-solving strategies seem to work best for you?

Access your interactive e-book to view a video clip for this chapter at
www.wileyopenpage.com

Summary

Language

LEARNING OBJECTIVE 1 Define language, describe how we learn languages, describe parts of the brain that are involved in language and discuss differences and problems that can affect people's language skills.

- Language is a set of symbols used to communicate. Language comprehension understands verbal messages, and language production is creating them.

- The study of language can be broken into phonology (sounds), semantics (meaning), syntax (grammar) and pragmatics (practical usage).

- Most people follow a typical sequence of language acquisition that includes the ability to distinguish, but not produce, all possible phonemes at about two to four months of age, babbling at about six months and speaking first words at around one year of age.

- The standard way we learn language suggests that we have an inborn capacity for language learning, although environment contributes as well. There appears be a sensitive or critical period before about 13 years old when it is easiest to acquire language.
- We make use of two routes when reading, a direct route for reading familiar words and an indirect route that enables us to read new words and non-words.
- In most people, the language centres in the brain are in the left hemisphere. The main brain region important for speech production is known as Broca's area. The main region for language comprehension is called Wernicke's area. Several other areas of the brain are also active in language, including the frontal eye fields when we read.
- Damage to different parts of the brain can give rise to different types of dyslexia called surface, phonological and deep dyslexia.
- There are small average gender differences in early language learning, with girls learning faster initially. These differences disappear with time.

Language and Thought

LEARNING OBJECTIVE 2   Define thinking that happens without words and summarize the linguistic relativity hypothesis.

- Some thoughts, including mental imagery and spatial navigation, require no words.
- The linguistic relativity hypothesis suggests that the amount of vocabulary we have available in our language for objects or concepts influences the way we think about those objects or concepts, and that different languages may dissect the world in different ways.

Thought

LEARNING OBJECTIVE 3   Define and summarize research on thinking processes, including problem solving, decision making and metacognition.

- We are capable of several different kinds of thought, and different types of thinking involve different brain regions, often including those related to specific thoughts. We develop various thinking abilities gradually with age.
- Controlled processing relies on the executive function of the brain. We become increasingly able to exert cognitive control as we age.
- Problem solving is finding a way to reach a goal. Algorithms, problem-solving strategies that guarantee a solution if followed methodically, work best for well-defined problems. Shortcut strategies called heuristics may help with ill-defined problems.
- Common problem-solving heuristics include working backwards, finding analogies to other problems and forming subgoals. Heuristics can lead to difficulties in problem solving, including mental sets, functional fixedness and confirmation bias.
- Decision making involves evaluating and choosing from among the options available to us. We often use heuristics to recall information in order to make decisions, but some, including the representativeness and availability heuristics, can bias our evaluations.
- Rational models of problem solving suggest that we make elimination options and/or make weighted evaluations of the utility and probability of options. We often lack time, information or cognitive resources for rational decision making, however, so we use a strategy of limited or bounded rationality.
- Emotions often play a role in decision making, sometimes interfering with our ability to make rational decisions, but other times helping us to make efficient choices.
- Metacognition is thinking about our own thoughts. It includes reviewing and evaluating our own memories, self-reflection and the theory of mind – inferring the intentions of other people. Mirror neurons in the brain contribute to theory of mind.
- Obsessive–compulsive disorder (OCD) and schizophrenia are two mental disorders that include a major thought disruption.

ACTIVITY

Activities to test yourself further are available in your interactive e-book at **www.wileyopenpage.com**

TYING IT TOGETHER

WHAT HAPPENS IN THE BRAIN?

- The main language areas are on the left side of the brain for most people – but not all.
- Thinking about images (or smells or tests) activates the same brain areas as if we were actually seeing (or smelling or tasting) them. Thoughts that involve language activate language areas of the brain.
- When we watch other people do things, mirror neurons in our brain can activate just as though we were doing the same things.

HOW WE DIFFER

- Girls tend to learn to talk earlier than boys. However, the difference soon disappears.
- Babies who learn two languages at home begin talking slightly later than those who learn just one.
- The number of words we have in our language for a certain object or concept (such as a colour) may influence how we can think about that object or concept.

OUT OF THE ORDINARY

- Damage near Broca's area of the brain can cause us to lose our ability to use grammar.
- Obsessive–compulsive disorder (OCD) involves unavoidable thoughts called obsessions and irresistible urges, or compulsions, to perform certain behaviours.
- About 1% of people in the West display schizophrenia, a disorder marked by disorganized thoughts and loss of contact with reality.

HOW WE DEVELOP

- Very young infants are able to perceive all the sounds of every language. As time passes, however, we lose the ability to distinguish phonemes of other languages.
- Our ability to learn languages is at its best before school age. After we pass age 13, it is much more difficult for us to learn new languages than it was earlier.
- We naturally tend to use child-directed speech with babies. It may be an evolutionary adaptation that helps humans learn language.
- One of the reasons toddlers do not play hide-and-seek very well is because their theory of mind abilities are still undeveloped.

Quizzes to test yourself further are available in your interactive e-book at
www.wileyopenpage.com

Key Terms

agrammatism 315
algorithm 323
availability heuristic 326
babbling 310
Broca's aphasia 314
Broca's area 314
child-directed speech 313
cognition 308
cognitive control 322
confirmation bias 324
critical period 312

decision making 325
functional fixedness 324
heuristics 323
language 308
language comprehension 308
language production 308
lexical meaning 309
linguistic relativity
   hypothesis 320
mental imagery 320
mental set 324

metacognition 328
mirror neurons 330
morpheme 309
nonverbal communication 309
obsessive–compulsive
   disorder (OCD) 330
overregularization 313
phoneme 309
phonology 309
pragmatics 309
problem solving 323

representativeness
   heuristic 326
schizophrenia 331
semantics 309
sensitive period 312
syntax 309
telegraphic speech 311
Wernicke's aphasia 316
Wernicke's area 315

Flashcards to test yourself further are available in your interactive e-book at
www.wileyopenpage.com

CHAPTER 12

Intelligence

Adapted by Adrian Furnham, University College London, UK

CHAPTER OUTLINE

- What Do We Mean by Intelligence?

- Additional Types of Intelligence

- How Do We Measure Intelligence?

- Is Intelligence Governed by Genetic or Environmental Factors?

- The Brain and Intelligence

- Extremes in Intelligence

Access your interactive e-book to view a video clip for this chapter at **www.wileyopenpage.com**

Two Smart Guys

Jack and Ben were at school together for many years. They were alike in many ways: they liked football and were both tall with blond hair. They both played the guitar and found, to their surprise, that when they had their IQ tested at school they both got exactly the same score: 125. Their teacher told them that this meant they were both very bright, but that they still needed to work hard to do well at school and in life. She was right because in his final years at school Ben joined a band and let his school work slip, while Jack became even more hard-working. Their final school results were very different and, while Jack went on to a famous university to study law, Ben went travelling after doing rather badly in his final school results.

They lost touch but met each other at a school reunion when they were 35. By this time, Jack was married and was well established as a lawyer, whereas Ben had become a brilliant software designer and a millionaire at 25. ■

What do we mean by *intelligence*? Does it mean the same thing in every instance? How do we understand it and how do we measure it? To these basic questions we must add several others. Can we distinguish between intelligence and talent? Are intelligence and wisdom the same thing? Are intelligence and creativity related? And, finally, how do we value intelligence? Our answers to such questions will influence how we define intelligence and whether we decide that anyone is particularly high in intelligence.

What Do We Mean by Intelligence?

LEARNING OBJECTIVE 1
Describe various ways in which intelligence has been defined and summarize the current thinking on whether intelligence is general or specific.

Some people are seen as astute, bright, brilliant, caring, keen, quick-witted and sharp. Others are perceived to be dim, dull, half-witted, slow or stupid. The former tend to be analytical and articulate: they learn fast, they remember things well and they can explain complex issues. The latter are the opposite. Smart people tend to do better at school and at work.

It was the famous Sir Francis Galton, who remarked 'When you can, count', who was the first clear advocate of intelligence tests. He seems to have believed that intelligence was a single general ability, that it was largely inherited and that it could best be measured in terms of the speed of problem-solving and other related mental processes

It was said by Thorndike in the 1920s that 'Intelligence is what an intelligence test measures and that is all.' Many laypeople and academics are deeply sceptical about the use of intelligence tests.

What, exactly, is intelligence? In 1921, Thorndike, who was a distinguished American researcher, asked 14 experts this question. Here are some of their answers:

- The ability to carry out abstract thinking.
- The ability to adjust to one's environment.
- The ability to adapt to new situations in life.
- The capacity to acquire knowledge.
- The capacity to learn or to profit from experience.
- Good responses from the point of view of psychological truth or fact.

Although experts still cannot agree on an exact definition of intelligence, themes common to many of their definitions are that intelligence is (a) the ability to learn from experience and (b) the ability to adapt to the environment.

The experts' difficulty in finding a totally satisfactory definition of intelligence reflects the fact that intelligence is a *psychological construct* – an abstract attribute that is *inferred* rather than observed directly.

Everyone has their own ideas about intelligence. The intelligent person is believed to solve problems well, reason clearly, think logically and have a good store of information, but also is able to balance information and show intelligence in worldly as well as academic contexts. Lay theories of creativity overlap with those of intelligence but tend to downplay analytical abilities, stressing rather unconventional ways of thinking and acting. Also, aesthetic taste, imagination, inquisitiveness and intuitiveness are part of lay theories, most of which go way beyond conventional psychological tests of creativity.

As well as academic definitions and disputes over the concept of intelligence, ordinary people also speculate about the topic. Two areas of research have been particularly interesting. The first concerns the question of whether intelligence is malleable: is it 'fixed' by late adolescence/early adulthood by genetic and biological factors or can you 'grow' your intelligence. Some people are *entity* theorists: what you see is what you get. Over the age of 20 or so just as you will not grow taller you will not or cannot grow brighter. On the other hand, there are *incremental* theorists who believe that with hard work, education and reading you can increase your IQ: you can increase your knowledge and vocabulary, which is all part of being intelligent.

The second area is sex differences in self-estimated intelligence. Studies by Furnham (2001) have shown that males give higher estimates than females for intelligence (cognitive ability), particularly spatial and mathematical intelligence, but that for estimates of emotional intelligence it is the other way around. Overall, however, people are not that good at estimating their actual scores, with some people showing *humility* – that is, underestimating their actual ability – and others showing *hubris* by overestimating the score that they actually achieved.

Defining **intelligence** in terms of our ability to learn, to adapt to the demands of our environment and to reflect on and understand our own mental processes makes intuitive sense. However, this definition encompasses a wide variety of notions about what intelligence may be.

> **intelligence** the ability to learn, to meet the demands of the environment effectively and to understand and control one's mental activities.

To develop a more precise definition, let's begin by considering a very basic question: is intelligence just one thing or a combination of many different skill sets? All current theories of intelligence in one way or another consider this question.

In 2011, IBM supercomputer Watson played Jeopardy! against the two greatest human players – Brad Rutter, who earned the most money on the programme, and Ken Jennings, who holds the record for consecutive wins. And, in fact, the supercomputer won. Won big. Watson had a final dollar amount of $77,147 compared with Jennings' $24,000 and Rutter's $21,600.

Now, obviously, the challenge for Watson's programmers was not the issue of knowledge. Watson's hard drive included Wikipedia, encyclopaedias, dictionaries and millions of pages of additional source material. No, the hard part was helping Watson figure out how to respond to the puns, clever turns of phrase and unique stylings of the 'answers' provided by Jeopardy!

In other words, whereas we think the smart part of playing Jeopardy! comes from knowing a lot about everything,

the tricky part for Watson was to learn to understand and respond to natural language – something a young child can do. Even more interesting, the hardest answers for Watson were often the simplest, with the fewest words. The supercomputer just did not have the context to narrow its choices.

Watson's undertaking seemed to please most viewers in one way or another. On the one hand, computer experts came away believing that the Watson prototype could form the basis for computers to become more directly responsive to natural language commands. On the other hand, everyday folks like us were comforted in knowing that as long as Watson thinks Toronto is a US city, we do not have to get ready for our robot overlords quite yet.

Is Intelligence General or Specific?

Suppose you were joining a challenging mountain-climbing expedition. Which of your team members do you think would be more likely to complete the climb successfully: a generally clearly intelligent, smart person or a person who had mastered, one by one, a large number of important tasks associated with mountain climbing? Maybe bright people tend to climb mountains faster or safely . . . or maybe it has little to do with intelligence.

Spearman and the *g* Factor   Charles Spearman (1863–1945) was a philosopher and soldier who became an influential figure in the study of intelligence. Spearman helped to develop a tool for analysing intelligence, called **factor analysis**. Factor analysis is a statistical method for determining whether certain items on a test correlate highly, thus forming a *unified set*, or cluster, of items. In the case of intelligence tests, for example, people who do well on vocabulary items also tend to do well on other verbal items, such as reading comprehension. Taken together, all of the test items relating to words and reading form a verbal-reasoning cluster that can be used to assess a person's overall verbal-reasoning skill. On Western intelligence tests, other clusters include those related to logical, spatial and mechanical reasoning.

While Spearman granted that some people have a particular strength in one area or another, he also noticed that those who scored high on one cluster tend to score high on other clusters as well. As he put it: 'A bright child tends to score

factor analysis a statistical method for determining whether certain items on a test correlate highly, thus forming a unified set, or cluster, of items.

higher on all aspects of an intelligence test than a dull one.' Thus, he hypothesized that a general factor, the **g factor**, of intelligence underlies all distinct clusters of mental ability. At the same time, he believed that each cluster of intelligence is further affected by a *specific factor*, an **s factor**, which is uniquely tied to that particular area of functioning (Figure 12.1) (Spearman, 1937, 1927, 1904).

Over the years, many theorists have embraced Spearman's notion of a *g* factor, and researchers have repeatedly found

g factor a theoretical general factor of intelligence underlying all distinct clusters of mental ability; part of Spearman's two-factor theory of intelligence.

s factor a theoretical specific factor uniquely tied to a distinct mental ability or area of functioning; part of Spearman's two-factor theory of intelligence.

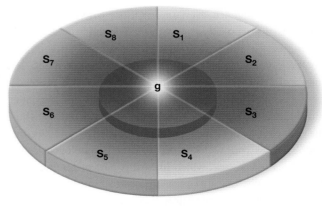

FIGURE 12.1 Spearman's two-factor theory of intelligence. In Spearman's model, the *g* factor of intelligence represents a broad and deep capability that underlies all other specific mental abilities, or the *s* factors.

indications that such a factor may indeed be at work (Castejon *et al.*, 2010; W. Johnson *et al.*, 2004). These theorists typically agree that the *g* factor is not merely book learning, a narrow academic skill, or test-taking smarts. Rather, it reflects a broader and deeper capability for comprehending our surroundings – 'catching on,' 'making sense' of things or 'figuring out' what to do (Gottfredson, 1997, p. 13). Indeed, most of the world's researchers who specifically study intelligence and cognitive ability support the concept of *g* or general intelligence.

Thurstone and Primary Mental Abilities Although many theorists continue to embrace Spearman's notion of a *g* factor of intelligence, the idea of such a general factor was controversial in Spearman's day and remains so to the present. An early critic of Spearman's ideas was Louis L. Thurstone (1887–1955), a pioneer in psychological measurement and statistics. He argued that intelligence is made up of *seven* distinct mental abilities: verbal comprehension, word fluency, numerical skill, spatial ability, associative memory, perceptual speed and reasoning (Thurstone, 1938). He termed these factors **primary mental abilities**.

primary mental abilities seven distinct mental abilities identified by Thurstone as the basic components of intelligence.

Observing such differences from person to person, Thurstone argued that each of the primary mental abilities on his list is *distinct*, not a reflection of general underlying intelligence. And, in fact, his initial work seemed to suggest that these abilities are not related. However, recognizing this theory as a direct challenge to the notion of the *g* factor, other researchers used factor analyses to re-evaluate Thurstone's ideas, and they detected at least a slight tendency of those who scored high in one mental ability to score high in another (Spearman, 1939). In short, Thurstone's work did not fully dispel the notion of the *g* factor.

Despite the limitations of Thurstone's theory, the idea of distinct areas of intelligence has continued to drive theorizing about intelligence, even among those who believe that a *g* factor is at least partly at play in intellectual functioning.

One of the most distinguished researchers in this area was Raymond B. Cattell, who famously distinguished between fluid and crystallized intelligence: the former is a problem-solving ability that declines with age in adults and the latter knowledge and vocabulary, which increases until old age. Thus, one may have a very specific general knowledge test like completing a crossword which is part of what psychologists called *crystallized intelligence*, which in turn is part of general intelligence. Equally, one can measure abstract problem solving as in sudoku, which measures *fluid intelligence*, or efficient problem solving. The implication is the more and more varied tests we give to an individual the better because we get a clearer, more reliable reading of their specific level of intelligence.

For many psychologists, the last word on this topic is the comprehensive and scholarly book by John Carroll, *Human Cognitive Abilities* published in 1993. He reviewed over 400 studies and found evidence of a general factor on intelligence, which he called *Stratum 1* (or Level 1). Under this were seven identifiable abilities like *General Learning and Memory* as well as *Processing Speed*. This was *Stratum 2* (or Level 2). Under that, he identified even more specific abilities. This describes the structure of intelligence but he clearly supported the general intelligence model, which he showed accounts for about half the individual differences scores for all people.

Let's turn next to the work of three modern theorists who have carried on Thurstone's quest to identify separate components of intelligence.

Current Multifactor Theories of Intelligence

Most of the early theorists on intelligence agreed with Spearman that intelligence has a *g* factor at its core. Some psychologists, however, have increasingly questioned the *g* factor or at least placed more emphasis on specific abilities, or *s* factors, that may affect intellectual performance. Three theorists in particular – Howard Gardner, Robert Sternberg and Stephen Ceci – have broadened the definition of intelligence and de-emphasized the *g* factor.

Howard Gardner's Theory of Multiple Intelligences

Are you equally successful in every academic subject? If you are like most people, you probably do better in some areas than others. If you are a good academic student, are you also a good artist? Musician? Cook? Do you know someone who does not do well on academic tests but nevertheless seems intelligent? Perhaps this person has strong leadership skills, social intuition or a razor-sharp sense of humour?

Psychologist Howard Gardner, influenced in part by the work of Thurstone, has advanced the **theory of multiple intelligences**, which argues that there is no such thing as a single unified intelligence (Gardner, 2011, 2008, 2004; Gardner & White, 2010). Instead, Gardner believes that there are several *independent* intelligences. Drawing on research from the fields of neuroscience and developmental, evolutionary and cognitive psychology, he claims that the different intelligences come from different areas of the brain. In support of this view, he notes that damage to specific areas of the brain does not necessarily lead to a universal collapse of

theory of multiple intelligences the theory that there is no single, unified intelligence but instead several independent intelligences arising from different portions of the brain.

Who is more intelligent? According to Howard Gardner's theory of multiple intelligences, each of these three extraordinary individuals has a different kind of intelligence. For Bruce Springsteen, it is musical intelligence. For Nobel Prize-winning author Toni Morrison, it is linguistic intelligence. And for physicist Stephen Hawking, it is mathematical intelligence.

Source: Left photo: Taylor Hill/FilmMagic/Getty Images, Inc. Centre photo: ©Lynn Goldsmith/Corbis. Right photo: Justin Sullivan/Getty Images, Inc.

mental functioning. Rather, some types of functioning may be affected while others remain intact.

Gardner's research regarding people of exceptional ability has also contributed to the notion of multiple and independent intelligences. His work with *savant syndrome* individuals, for example, seems consistent with this view. Individuals with savant syndrome often score low, sometimes extremely low, on traditional intelligence tests, yet possess startling ability in a specific area. Some have little verbal ability but are able to compute numbers with the speed of a calculator, others can draw with great skill, and still others have a keen memory for music.

Table 12.1 depicts the eight basic intelligences identified by Gardner: linguistic, logical/mathematical, musical, spatial, body kinaesthetic, interpersonal, intrapersonal and naturalistic. In addition, Gardner has raised the possibility that there may be two additional intelligences: spiritual intelligence, which enables people to focus on cosmic and spiritual issues; and existential intelligence, which is needed to consider ultimate issues, such as the meaning of life.

Although Gardner's theory has roots in Thurstone's ideas, it is, in fact, different from Thurstone's theory in several ways. First, Thurstone held that the mental functions he identified *collectively* constitute intelligence. He did not believe, as Gardner does, that each factor is itself an 'intelligence'. Further, Gardner believes that the various intelligences are best measured in the contexts in which they occur. Thus, assessments conducted in real-world settings are more useful than paper-and-pencil examinations for assessing several of the intelligences (Tirri & Nokelainen, 2008). Finally, Gardner's definition of multiple intelligences includes an important cultural component: each intelligence, he suggests, reflects 'the ability to solve problems, or to create products, that are valuable within one or more cultural settings' (Gardner, 1993).

TABLE 12.1 Gardner's Multiple Intelligences

Type of intelligence	Characteristics	Possible vocations
Linguistic	Sensitivity to the sounds and meaning of words	Author, journalist, teacher
Logical/mathematical	Capacity for scientific analysis and logical and mathematical problem solving	Scientist, engineer, mathematician
Musical	Sensitivity to sounds and rhythm; capacity for musical expression	Musician, composer, singer
Spatial	Ability to perceive spatial relationships accurately	Architect, navigator, sculptor, engineer
Body kinaesthetic	Ability to control body movements and manipulate objects	Athlete, dancer, surgeon
Interpersonal	Sensitivity to the emotions and motivations of others; skillful at managing others	Manager, therapist, teacher
Intrapersonal	Ability to understand one's self and one's strengths and weaknesses	Leader in many fields
Naturalistic	Ability to understand patterns and processes in nature	Biologist, naturalist, ecologist, farmer
(Possible) Spiritual/existential	Ability to focus on spiritual issues and the meaning of life	Philosopher, theologian

Source: Based on Gardner, H. (1993). *Multiple Intelligences: The theory in practice.* New York: Basic Books. Reproduced with permission of BASIC BOOKS in the format republish in a textbook via Copyright Clearance Center.

Because the various intelligences are thought to emanate from different areas, or modules, of the brain, Gardner's theory is often called a *modular model* of mental functioning. Nevertheless, according to Gardner, the various intelligences can influence one another. For example, in addition to a well-developed musical intelligence, a cellist might need a high body kinaesthetic intelligence to physically handle the instrument and a high interpersonal intelligence to work in perfect harmony with other players in an orchestra. Critics of Gardner's ideas, however, maintain that still deeper relationships exist among the various intelligences and mental functions (Gardner & Traub, 2010).

Despite the enormous popularity of Gardner's ideas, particularly among educationists, the theory has been consistently attacked for being short of supporting evidence. Where studies have attempted to test the theory, like that of Canadian psychologists Visser, Aston and Vernon (2006), it was found wanting. Most people agree that it is a very interesting theory but awaits empirical support.

Robert Sternberg's Triarchic Theory of Intelligence

Psychologist Robert Sternberg has proposed a **triarchic theory of intelligence** (Mandelman *et al.*, 2010; Sternberg, 2010, 2003). Sternberg shares Gardner's view that intelligence is not a unitary mental function. According to Sternberg, however, intelligence is made up not of numerous independent intelligences but of three interacting components, as shown in Figure 12.2 – the internal, external and experiential components – sometimes referred to as the *analytic, creative* and *practical* components.

triarchic theory of intelligence Sternberg's theory that intelligence is made up of three interacting components: internal, external and experiential components.

- *Internal (analytic).* This component of intelligence relates to the internal processing of information: acquiring information; planning, monitoring and evaluating problems; or carrying out directions. The internal aspect of intelligence is the one most often measured by today's intelligence tests – the sort of intelligence needed for straightforward tasks and problems that we confront at school, work or in life.

- *External (creative).* Sternberg notes that some tasks are novel and so require a special way of thinking. Travelling to Russia for the first time, for example, requires more creative thinking than purchasing a newspaper. Among other things, a traveller would have to figure out how to get through Russian customs, find his or her way to a hotel and order meals in restaurants – all, perhaps, without knowing the language. This component of intelligence clearly requires creativity and it must interact with the internal component of intelligence to bring about successful results.

- *Experiential (practical).* This type of thinking helps us adapt to, or improve, our environments or select new environments. Let's say you move into a new home and find that the neighbours make a lot of noise when you are trying to go to sleep. At first, you might try to solve the problem by moving to another bedroom in the house (adapting to the environment). If this does not work, you might try installing soundproof windows or complaining to the neighbours or to the landlord (changing the environment). And, finally, if that does not work, you might decide to move to another house (selecting a new environment).

Sternberg suggests that practical intelligence often relies on *tacit knowledge*, 'action-oriented knowledge, acquired without direct help from others, that allows individuals to achieve goals they personally value' (Sternberg *et al.*, 1995). A successful businessperson who earned only average qualifications in school has probably acquired considerable tacit knowledge, or know-how, by working in the business environment and figuring out what is needed to get the work done. Not surprisingly, research shows that tacit knowledge is related to job success (Joia & Lemos, 2010; Sternberg, 2003).

Sternberg argues that effective interactions among the internal, external and experiential components are key to achieving successful intelligence – an advantageous balance between adapting to, shaping and selecting problems encountered within one's environment. Because each intellectual component in Sternberg's theory actively relates to the others, his model is considered more dynamic, or interactive, than Gardner's.

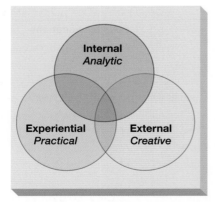

FIGURE 12.2 Sternberg's triarchic theory of intelligence. Robert Sternberg proposes that there are three components to intelligence, not multiple independent ones. In his model, intelligence is related to the successful interaction among these three: the internal (analytic), the external (creative) and the experiential (practical) components.

Again, Sternberg's ideas have provoked considerable interest and debate. However, they are not as yet supported by compelling evidence. One problem with testing the theory, however, is having to devise reliable and valid tests for things like creative and practical intelligence.

Stephen Ceci's Bioecological Theory of Intelligence

Psychologist Stephen Ceci has proposed the **bioecological model of intelligence**, which holds that intelligence is 'a function of the interactions between innate potential abilities, environmental context (ecology), and internal motivation' (Figure 12.3) (Barnett & Ceci, 2005; Ceci & Williams, 1997). According to Ceci, each person's innate abilities derive from a system of biological factors, or *resource pools*. These resource pools are independent of each other, and each is responsible for different aspects of one's information-processing capabilities. Further, Ceci claims that a person's innate abilities will develop more or less based on how they interact with the individual's environmental resources, or context.

> **bioecological model of intelligence** Ceci's theory that intelligence is a function of the interactions among innate potential abilities, environmental context and internal motivation.

Consider, for example, a girl whose biological resource pool endows her with the potential to succeed in mathematics. Her abilities may lead to early successes in arithmetic, prompting her parents to provide environmental changes – her own computer, special tutoring in mathematics, and so forth – that will help her to develop her innate mathematical potential. This encouraging environmental context will likely lead to further successes, which in turn may lead to additional environmental changes, such as enrolment in special classes.

Finally, according to the bioecological model, individuals must be internally *motivated* in order to fulfil their innate abilities and take advantage of their particular environments. When people feel motivated in certain areas, they tend to focus on their intellectual skills in those areas and to seek out environmental resources that are relevant. In an interesting study, Ceci found that men who were successful at race track betting and who produced complicated strategies for predicting winning horses did not demonstrate sophisticated thinking in other areas of functioning (Ceci & Liker, 1986). Clearly, such men were motivated by the desire to become rich and so developed complex intellectual processing and personal environmental opportunities that might lead to that particular result.

Self-Estimated Intelligence

IQ tests measure a person's intelligence. The average, or the mean, score on these tests is 100. Most of the population (about two-thirds of people) score between 85 and 115. Very bright people score around 130, and scores have been known to go over 145. Figure 12.4 shows a typical distribution of these scores.

But there are different types of intelligence.

How Intelligent Are You? We want you to estimate your overall IQ and your score on 14 basic types of intelligence:

- Overall intelligence
- Verbal or linguistic intelligence (ability to use words)
- Logical or mathematical intelligence (the ability to reason logically and solve a number of problems)
- Spatial intelligence (the ability to find your way around the environment and form mental images)
- Musical intelligence (the ability to perceive and create pitch and rhythm)
- Body kinaesthetic intelligence (the ability to use bodily functions or motor movements).

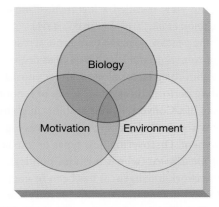

FIGURE 12.3 Ceci's bioecological model of intelligence. Stephen Ceci proposes that intelligence is the product of interaction among biological, environmental and motivational resources, and that each resource is responsible for a different aspect of intelligence.

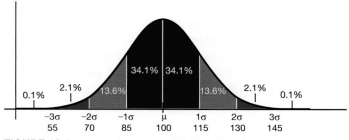

FIGURE 12.4 The bell curve: a normal distribution.

Source: http://en.wikipedia.org/wiki/File:Standard_deviation_diagram.png.

- Interpersonal intelligence (the ability to understand other people)

- Intrapersonal intelligence (the ability to understand yourself and develop a sense of your own identity)

- Existential intelligence (the ability to understand the significance of life, the meaning of death and the experience of love)

- Spiritual intelligence (the ability to engage in thinking about cosmic issues, the achievement of a state of being and the ability to have spiritual effects on others)

- Naturalistic intelligence (the ability to identify and employ many distinctions in the natural world, e.g. classifying animals and plants)

- Emotional intelligence (the ability to understand and manage your own and others' emotions)

- Creative intelligence (the ability to go beyond what is given to generate novel and interesting ideas)

- Practical intelligence (the ability to find the best fit between yourself and the demands of your environment)

Do you think you are brighter than the average person? Studies on the self-estimates of intelligence have shown some very interesting findings. First, nearly everyone thinks they are *above average* (i.e. over 100) on nearly everything, which simply cannot be the case Second, all over the world *males think they are overall brighter than do females*. This is called the *male hubris, female humility* effect. Males think they score higher on verbal and spatial intelligence, while females think they do better on emotional, inter- and intrapersonal intelligence. If you ask people to estimate their family, they think their father brighter than their mother, and parents sometimes think their sons are brighter than their daughters. All this despite the fact that, as we shall see, there is very little evidence to suggest there are any major sex differences in intelligence.

Consider the questions listed in Table 12.2.

Research by Adrian Furnham (2001) shows us some really interesting answers. About 10–20% of people (mostly men, of course) think males are brighter than females. A small number in most countries believe there are race differences in intelligence. Around a third to a half of young people believe that intelligence is inherited. On average, surveys have shown that over half of young people believe that traditional IQ tests measure intelligence fairly well and that they are therefore useful in educational settings. We also know that people's attitudes to tests do change once they have taken a reliable and valid test.

TABLE 12.2 Seven Questions about Intelligence

1. Have you ever taken an intelligence test?	YES / NO
2. Do you believe they measure intelligence fairly well?	YES / NO
3. Do you believe males are on average more intelligent than females?	YES / NO
4. Do you believe intelligence is primarily inherited?	YES / NO
5. Do you believe IQ tests are useful in educational settings?	YES / NO
6. Who do you think are more intelligent: males/females/neither?	Males / Females / Neither
7. Do you believe some races are more intelligent than others?	YES / NO

But of course, this is a very controversial issue, as we shall see. It can mean very different things to different people at different times.

Where Are We Today?

Many theories on the nature of intelligence have been proposed and investigated. Is there a basic view upon which today's theorists agree? On the one hand, it would be fair to say that the majority do believe that intelligence *includes* a *g* factor – an overriding intellectual ability (Hunt, 2011; Larsen *et al.*, 2008; Deary, 2001). On the other hand, few current theorists believe that the *g* factor is the be-all and end-all of intelligence. Most consider specific abilities (verbal, numerical and spatial skills, for example) and special factors (motivation, context, experience etc.) to also be important in the *expression* of intelligence. The *g* factor is at work in every task that we confront in life, while the specific abilities and special factors come into play for some tasks but not others. This prevailing view is called a *hierarchical model* of intelligence (Castejon *et al.*, 2010; Lubinski, 2004).

Because the *g* factor seems to play a role across all kinds of tasks, it is, of course, desirable to have a high degree of general intelligence. But the *g* factor alone will not consistently lead to outstanding performances or successes in school, work or other areas of life. Conversely, verbal ability, high motivation or proper environment alone rarely guarantees high intellectual achievement. Discovering new types of intelligence like *managerial intelligence* (which includes political, organizational and network intelligence) has been in vogue (Harvey *et al.*, 2002). Sceptics believe this effort is misplaced and putting the word 'intelligence' after some behaviour or skill does not necessarily mean that it exists as a separate entity.

Intelligence truly appears to be a complex, multifaceted phenomenon.

Before You Go On

What Do You Know?

1. Identify and define the two factors in Spearman's model of intelligence.
2. How does Thurstone's theory of primary mental abilities differ from Gardner's theory of multiple intelligences?
3. What are the three components of the triarchic theory of intelligence, and how do they contribute to mental functioning?

What Do You Think?

How would you define intelligence?

Additional Types of Intelligence

LEARNING OBJECTIVE 2

Discuss several proposed types of intelligence that go beyond intellectual functioning.

The ideas and work that we have encountered so far consider a wide range of intellectual skills. But have they captured all aspects of intelligence? A growing number of theorists are focusing on the role of intelligence in emotions, social functioning, wisdom, creativity and personality.

Emotional Intelligence

The concept of emotional intelligence is rather new: researchers began to actively study it in the 1990s. **Emotional intelligence** refers to an individual's ability to perceive, express and assimilate emotion, and to regulate emotion in the self and others (Cherniss, 2010; Roberts *et al.*, 2010; Goleman, 1995). Emotionally intelligent people are thought to be self-aware, sensitive to how they feel and how their feelings change and able to manage their emotions so that they are not overwhelmed by them. People with well-developed emotional intelligence also tend to be empathic, knowing how to comfort and encourage others. Not surprisingly, they often succeed in their careers and marriages, as leaders and as parents (Brackett *et al.*, 2011; Martin, 2008).

If we grant the existence of emotional intelligence, then the question arises: can it be measured? In fact, researchers have devised a number of ways to measure it (Roberts *et al.*, 2010). One test is the *Multifactor Emotional Intelligence Scale* (Maul, 2011; Mayer *et al.*, 2003; Salovey *et al.*, 2003). This test measures 12 emotional abilities that are, in turn, grouped into four *branches of abilities* – perceiving, facilitating, understanding and managing emotion. Although some theorists believe that certain individuals are inherently more skilled than others in the emotional sphere, other theorists argue that emotional intelligence can be learnt and they call for schools and businesses to offer systematic instruction in the understanding and management of emotions (Alegre, 2011).

> **emotional intelligence** an individual's ability to perceive, express, assimilate and regulate emotion.

PSYCHOLOGY AROUND US   Social Limits

Katniss Everdeen is a teenage girl forced to participate in a reality show in which teenagers must hunt and kill each other to entertain the masses. Katniss is the heroine of author Suzanne Collins' dystopian young adult novel *The Hunger Games*. Katniss is unquestionably brilliant when it comes to hunting and survival. She is a particularly deadly archer, and she is smart enough to know how to get an edge in the competition by destroying the food supply of wealthy rivals who are not used to going hungry.

That said, as ultracompetent as she is at surviving, she struggles with managing relationships. When her fellow tribute Peeta starts to show signs of interest in her, she has no idea how to respond other than to treat it as gamesmanship and strategy. Katniss is so locked into the idea of being a survivor that she cannot remember how to form a human bond with someone else.

Social Intelligence

Most people know someone who displays remarkable social ease: a person who can walk right into a party or a meeting and just take over the room. Unlike poor Katniss, such people seem to know intuitively what is important to others, how to charm their way out of difficult situations and how to gain the affection of everyone with whom they interact. Would you say these individuals are highly intelligent? Some theorists would say yes (Murphy & Hall, 2011; Goleman, 2006). Specifically, they would say that the individuals are high in *social intelligence*. To some extent, this was known in the past as *social skills* or *interpersonal skills*.

The notion of social intelligence is older than that of emotional intelligence. In fact, early in the 20th century, the learning pioneer Edward Thorndike (whom you may remember from Chapter 9) suggested that intelligence consists of three facets: the ability to understand and manage ideas (abstract intelligence), concrete objects (mechanical intelligence) and people (social intelligence) (Thorndike, 1920). By social intelligence, Thorndike meant 'the ability to understand and manage men and women, boys and girls – to act wisely in human relationships'. Other theorists have described social intelligence more simply as the ability to get along with others. Either way, it is clearly an important asset not only in interpersonal relationships but also at school and work and in leadership roles (Furnham, 2009, 2008; Bass, 2002). Many academic researchers would prefer the older term social skills applied to social intelligence because it implies culturally sensitive behavioural repertoires rather than intelligence.

Wisdom

In myth, art and popular culture, we often encounter characters who do not possess much formal education but who seem to have an insightful appreciation of life and the world. They are generally portrayed as experienced in the ways of the world; little about life appears to surprise them. These people are considered to possess *wisdom*, the ability to make sound judgements about important, difficult or uncertain situations and to choose the best course of action (Karelitz *et al.*, 2010; Fowers, 2005, 2003). Are intelligence and wisdom the same thing? The positive psychologists like Martin Seligman have defined wisdom as one of the six virtues and comprising curiosity and interest in the world, love of learning, good judgement, ingenuity, personal intelligences and a good perspective on life.

Robert Sternberg (2010, 2008, 2003) believes that wisdom is a special version of intelligence and has developed the *balance theory of wisdom* to account for this special capacity. Recall that in Sternberg's triarchic theory, intelligence consists of three aspects – analytic, creative and practical – with practical intelligence involving the ability to effectively apply one's experiences and learning to everyday decisions. According to Sternberg, wisdom is primarily (though not entirely) the product of practical intelligence. He says that wisdom is the application of tacit knowledge (know-how) to solve problems in such a way that a common good is achieved and a balance maintained among the interests of the individual, the community and society. Sternberg distinguishes wisdom from other expressions of practical intelligence by noting that wisdom involves a particular concern for the community at large and a careful balancing of interests.

More than any other dimension of intelligence, wisdom may be associated with age. When people are asked to name someone in their lives whom they consider wise, they are more likely to point to a grandparent, an uncle or aunt or a parent rather than to a teenager or young adult. Why? Because it typically takes years and repeated experiences to appreciate the needs of the community, the advantages of solutions in which everyone wins, the drawbacks of self-serving decisions and the delicate art of balancing multiple perspectives (Ardelt, 2011; Nair, 2003). That is, it takes time and experience to acquire a high degree of wisdom.

Research on the concept of wisdom has only really just begun. As yet, there seems no clear agreement on how to define or measure it.

Creativity

For many people, creativity is seen as a gift, a special ability, related to intelligence but more than intelligence. **Creativity** is the ability to produce ideas that are both original and valuable (Kaufman & Sternberg, 2010). Like wisdom, creativity reflects collective, as well as personal, values. Societies benefit from the creativity of their members; indeed, creativity plays a key role in technological, scientific and artistic advances. Thus, it is not surprising that different cultures define and appreciate creativity in different ways (Lubart, 2010; Runco, 2010, 2004). Creativity often requires verbal and mathematical skills in Western culture, for example, while it depends more on the ability to appreciate and interact with nature in certain other cultures.

Yet, creativity remains an academic backwater mainly because of how to decide whether a person, invention, work of art or science is *truly* creative. The question is *who makes the judgement* and the extent to which they have to agree before one can say 'it' is a real manifestation of creativity. Criteria could be based on patent awards, judgements made by professionals, social recognition or even sales. Different groups have different criteria and different levels of reliability. For the scientist, the whole enterprise hardly gets off the starting blocks. If one cannot adequately, robustly and

creativity the ability to produce ideas that are both original and valuable.

reliably describe the criteria or label the product, it remains particularly difficult to understand the process.

Some researchers, like Mark Batey at Manchester Business School, have adopted essentially one of four approaches to the problem:

- *The creative person.* Differential psychologists have attempted to delineate the particular and peculiar set of abilities, motives and traits that together describe the creative individual.

- *The creative process.* This is an attempt to understand the thought (cognitive) processes that go on in the process of creativity. It is not so much an attempt at the who but the how question.

- *The creative situation.* Social and business psychologists are particularly interested in cultural, environmental and organizational factors that inhibit or facilitate creativity. The idea is that one can therefore construct situations that induce creativity even in the not particularly creative.

- *The creative product.* This approach attempts to study all aspects of creativity by looking at those products that are clearly defined as creative.

Psychologists who study creativity and intelligence typically believe that a high intellectual aptitude is necessary but not sufficient for creativity (Silvia, 2008). People who score high on intelligence tests tend to score high on tests of creativity, but beyond a certain point (i.e. beyond an intelligence test score of about 120), the correlation between intelligence and creativity diminishes. Research has shown, for example, that on average, exceptionally creative architects, musicians, scientists and engineers do not score higher on intelligence tests than do their less creative colleagues. Thus, it appears that there is more to creativity than that which intelligence tests measure.

Theorists and researchers have pointed to various personal qualities as being essential to creativity (Cramond *et al.*, 2010; Sternberg, 2010, 2003). At the top of the list is *intrinsic motivation*, an internal drive to create. Also cited frequently are *imagination* – an ability and willingness to re-examine problems in new ways – and a *game personality*, one that tolerates ambiguity, risk and initial failure. Other useful qualities include complex thinking, broad attention, expertise in relevant fields, broad interests, high energy, independence and self-confidence.

Investigators have also found that creative thinking is, in fact, nurtured, inspired and refined by creative environments (Beghetto & Kaufman, 2010; Sternberg, 2010). Creative environments share several qualities: they encourage people to be innovative; are relatively free of criticism; and provide freedom, creative role models, sufficient resources and time to think and explore. Artist communities and schools for the performing arts aspire to be environments of this kind. Some such communities and schools succeed in this regard, while others become more demanding and competitive than nurturing. In addition, a creative environment need not be large or formal; it can exist in a supportive home, a positive work setting or a comfortable class.

Personality Characteristics

Even the earliest researchers of intelligence noted a relationship between intelligence and personality, our unique patterns of experiencing and acting in the world. Although intelligence

Creativity around the World. Different cultures encourage different kinds of creativity. A woman who can decorate a customer's hand with a beautiful henna design in India (left) is considered highly creative and intelligent in her country, while a man who addresses his firm's production needs by developing a complex computer model (right) is called a creative genius by his Western colleagues.

Source: Left photo: Bruno Morandi/Getty Images, Inc. Right photo: ©Paul Barton/Corbis.

tests often seek to separate intellectual functioning from personal style, many theorists argue that the division is artificial, that personality characteristics are inherent to intellectual functioning (Feist, 2010; Mayer, 2009, 2008). Indeed, David Wechsler, a pioneer in intelligence testing, considered intelligence to be a manifestation of personality (Wechsler, 1961). He thought that emotional, motivational and other personal characteristics (such as interest and volition) must be key components of any meaningful notion of intelligence.

Following Wechsler's lead, a number of today's theorists think of intelligence as the cognitive part of personality (Murphy & Hall, 2011; Furnham & Monsen, 2009). Others propose a complex reciprocal relationship between intelligence and personality, with intellectual, emotional and motivational variables repeatedly affecting each other in day-to-day behaviour (Hennessey, 2010; Mayer, 2008). Consistent with such notions, studies have found that negative emotional and motivational states can impair intellectual performance to some degree, especially when the intellectual tasks demand attention or quick recall. Conversely, certain personality factors, such as self-efficacy (the belief that one can master a demanding task) and a high need to achieve, often enhance performance on intellectual tasks (Freund & Holling, 2011; Lounsbury *et al.*, 2009, 2003).

Before You Go On

What Do You Know?

4. What is emotional intelligence and how is it best measured?

5. How does Robert Sternberg describe wisdom in relation to his triarchic theory of intelligence?

6. What are some factors that affect creativity?

What Do You Think?

Suppose you were given the job of making up a test to assess social intelligence. What kinds of questions would you include on the test?

How Do We Measure Intelligence?

LEARNING OBJECTIVE 3

Identify important considerations in the construction of intelligence tests, discuss the history of intelligence testing and describe some criticisms of intelligence tests.

The history of intelligence theory is completely intertwined with the history of intelligence testing. That is, both the theories psychologists propose and the tests they devise affect how they understand intelligence. It was only about a century ago that researchers and statisticians first fashioned standardized tests and statistical methods with which to assess intelligence. In the West, one of the oldest and most enduring approaches to understanding and assessing intelligence is the psychometric approach. The **psychometric approach** attempts to measure intelligence with carefully constructed psychological tests, called *intelligence tests*.

Before talking in detail about some of the ways people have measured intelligence throughout history, it would be salutary to think about what qualities make a good intelligence test. Knowing how psychologists build and use intelligence tests will help you make up your own mind about what these tests mean.

Intelligence Test Construction and Interpretation

Intelligence test constructors typically assume a comparative view of test scores. That is, intelligence is typically measured by comparing one person's test scores with another's. There is no absolute or independent measure of intelligence. Because of this comparative approach, a number of cautions arise. First, a test must function the same in different groups of people (so that individuals do not get different scores just because they are from different ethnic groups or different parts of the country). Second, the items on a test must relate both to one another and to the material of interest. To ensure that intelligence tests are grounded in sound scientific principles, psychologists design tests that adhere to three basic criteria: standardization, reliability and validity (Bowden *et al.*, 2011; Canivez & Watkins, 2010).

Standardization If you were the only person taking a particular intelligence test, your score would mean very

psychometric approach an approach to defining intelligence that attempts to measure intelligence with carefully constructed psychological tests.

little. For your score to have meaning, it must be compared with the scores of people who have already taken the same test. This group of people is referred to as a *sample population*. If all subsequent test-takers follow the same procedures as those used by the sample population, then each individual's test score can be compared with the scores of the sample. The process of obtaining meaningful test scores from a large representative sample population through the use of uniform procedures is called **standardization**. Good tests have good population norms. They need to examine whether there are systematic differences between men and women, younger and older people and those of different ethnic groups.

standardization the use of uniform procedures in administering and scoring a test.

Test results from large populations tend to follow particular patterns, called *distributions*. Scores on intelligence tests follow a **normal distribution** (or *normal curve*), a statistical pattern in which most people achieve fairly similar scores at or near the middle of the distribution while a small number earn low scores and an equally small number earn high scores. In graph form, these results form a bell-shaped pattern, often called a *bell curve* (Figure 12.5).

normal distribution a symmetrical, bell-shaped distribution in which most scores are in the middle with smaller groups of equal size at either end.

In a normal distribution, the scores of most people fall near the **median** score (i.e. the middle score). The scores that are higher or lower than the median keep declining in number as the scores extend further and further from the median. The very lowest and the very highest scores are found at the outer edges of the bell curve. The median score is but one indicator of a population's central tendencies. Others include the **mean**, or the average score, and the **mode**, the

median the score exactly in the middle of a distribution.

mean the average score in a distribution.

score that occurs most frequently in the population. If a sample is properly standardized into a normal distribution, the median, mean and mode should be the same.

mode the score that occurs most frequently in a distribution.

Reliability The second criterion that is needed for a test to be of value is **reliability**. When a test is reliable, it consistently produces similar scores for the same test-takers over time. Psychologists have developed several ways to show that a test is reliable. One approach is to administer it once and then a second time, in either the same version or a version that is slightly different. If the scores on the two administrations agree for each individual, they are said to correlate highly. Another approach is to divide the items on a single test among two groups, and see whether each individual's scores on the two halves of the test correlate highly. Whatever the approach, the higher the statistical correlation between scores, the greater the reliability. Remember from Chapter 2 that a correlation can vary from a value of −1.00 to +1.00. A correlation of +1.00 indicates the highest degree of reliability.

reliability the degree to which a test produces the same scores over time.

Validity A test with a high degree of reliability does not necessarily have high validity, but for intelligence a test with low reliability does mean that it cannot be valid. **Validity** is the extent to which a test accurately measures or predicts what it is supposed to measure or predict. Suppose, for example, we use a broken scale to weigh the residents of a town and we weigh each resident several times. Assuming that, for each person, the scale repeatedly yields the same weight, the resulting weights would be said to have a high degree of reliability. The results, however, would have low validity because the weights offered by the broken scales are not accurate: that is, although everyone's weight would be uniformly reported, no one's reported weight would be correct. We would not know how much anyone actually weighed.

validity the extent to which a test accurately measures or predicts what it is supposed to measure or predict.

But there are many different types of validity.

- *Predictive validity*, the extent to which selection scores predict future behaviour at school or work. Do IQ scores predict how successful you are in life measured by different measures?

- *Concurrent validity*, the extent to which selection scores predict current performance. It also means the extent to which scores on one (new) test concur (correlate) with scores on another.

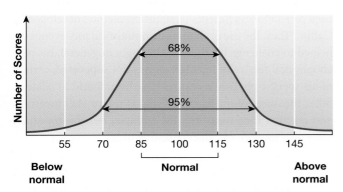

FIGURE 12.5 The bell curve of intelligence scores. The distribution of scores on intelligence tests follows a statistical pattern called the bell curve. Most people's scores fall in the middle range, with a small number scoring at the extreme ends.

- *Construct validity*, the extent to which selection accurately measures the constructs or dimensions it was designed to assess. This depends, of course, on how intelligence is defined.

- *Content validity*, the extent to which the measure adequately samples all the important dimensions of the intelligence like verbal, spatial and numerical intelligence.

- *Face validity*, the extent to which the test actually looks as if it is measuring intelligence.

How can we determine the validity, or accuracy, of a test? Often we can simply look at its content. If you were to administer a test on Chinese grammar to assess students' mastery of French, the test would not demonstrate much **content validity**. By contrast, if you were taking flying lessons and your instructor tested you on your understanding of the instrument panel and other kinds of relevant information, the test would demonstrate high content validity.

content validity the degree to which the content of a test accurately represents what the test is intended to measure.

We can also assess the validity of tests by correlating test scores with an external criterion that we have some confidence in – a correlation called a **validity coefficient**. If, for example, we believe that intelligent people will perform better at school (because of their higher intelligence), then we expect individuals' scores on a particular intelligence test to correlate with their school grades. The higher the validity coefficient, the more valid the test. A test need not just measure current performance. When high scores on an intelligence test continue to successfully predict high grades later in life, it is said to display high *predictive validity* (Gow *et al.*, 2011). *And they do!*

validity coefficient a correlation coefficient that measures validity by correlating a test score with some external criterion.

History of Intelligence Testing

The first systematic attempts to measure intelligence were developed during the second half of the 19th century. The most influential approaches were those of Francis Galton in England and Alfred Binet in France. Later, in the United States, Lewis Terman and David Wechsler made important contributions.

Galton and 'Psychophysical Performance' Profoundly affected by the work of his half-cousin Charles Darwin, Francis Galton (1822–1911) sought to apply Darwin's ideas about evolution to the study of intelligence. He believed that by studying intellectual development he could learn more about the evolution of the human species in general and the inheritance of intelligence in particular (Hunt, 2011; Fancher, 2009, 2004). In particular, Galton sought to understand why some people appear to be more intelligent than others. If he could understand the evolutionary factors at work in such differences, he reasoned, then steps could be taken to improve the species.

Galton, who believed in a general intelligence factor, proposed that two qualities distinguish more gifted from less gifted people: a kind of psychic energy and a heightened sensitivity to external stimuli. His theory, termed the *theory of psychophysical performance*, held that people with more energy can perform more work and, in turn, develop greater intelligence. In addition, inasmuch as people gather information from their five senses, individuals who have more highly developed senses can take in more information. To more accurately gauge intelligence, Galton developed tests of an individual's sensory processing, motor skills and reaction time.

Galton's work influenced many theorists. James McKeen Cattell, in particular, later designed 50 psychophysical tests, expecting that the tests would support and extend Galton's ideas (Sokal, 2010; Tulsky *et al.*, 2003). Cattell tested skills, such as how fast people could move their arm over a specified distance and how many letters in a series they could remember. Ironically, Cattell's tests eventually helped to discredit Galton's notions rather than support them.

In his doctoral dissertation, one of Cattell's students, Clark Wissler, hypothesized that people would perform consistently well or consistently poorly across the various psychophysical tests and that those who did consistently well would display a higher level of general intelligence than those who performed poorly (Wissler, 1961). However, Wissler found that a given person's various test performances did not necessarily correlate either with each other or with academic performance. To determine whether each research participant's performances on various psychophysical tests were in fact correlated, Wissler used *correlation coefficients* – a statistical method developed by Galton. Thus, the use of Galton's own statistical tool eventually helped to challenge his theory. Although, in general, his psychophysical theory of intelligence was not supported, certain of his specific physical measures have been found to relate to other measures of intelligence. Galton's motor skill measures and reaction time measures, for example, remain important aspects of modern intelligence testing today

Alfred Binet and the Binet–Simon Intelligence Test At the same time as Galton and his followers were developing psychophysical theories and tests, Alfred Binet (1857–1911), along with his collaborator Theodosius Simon, were viewing intelligence and its measurement in a different way.

In 1904, the French government mandated compulsory education, and the Minister of Public Instruction in Paris formed a commission to devise a way to distinguish children with learning disabilities from those who were unsuccessful in school for other reasons, such as behavioural problems. The idea was to assign intellectually capable children to regular classes and place those with learning disabilities in special classes. To help determine the most appropriate type of class for each child, Binet and Simon devised the first widely applied intelligence tests (Hunt, 2011).

Binet shared with Galton the notion of a general intelligence factor. However, regarding the psychophysical theory as wasted time, he argued that the basis of intelligence is judgment, otherwise called good sense, practical sense, initiative, the faculty of adapting one's self to circumstances. To judge well, to comprehend well, to reason well, these are the essential activities of intelligence. In short, Binet viewed intelligence as the ability to demonstrate memory, judgment, reasoning, and social comprehension.

The tasks on Binet's intelligence test focused largely on language abilities, in contrast to the many nonverbal tasks devised by Galton. Binet also introduced the idea of **mental age**, the intellectual age at which a child is actually functioning. Mental age does not necessarily match chronological age. A child's mental age is indicated by the chronological age typically associated with his or her level of intellectual performance. Thus, the typical 11-year-old has a mental age of 11. A more intelligent 11-year-old, however, may have a mental age of 13, while a less intelligent 11-year-old may have a mental age of nine.

> **mental age** the intellectual age at which a person is functioning, as opposed to chronological age.

Binet did not believe his intelligence test necessarily measured a child's *innate* level of intelligence. His goal was simply to predict a student's likelihood of success in school. And, in fact, he did find a strong correlation between performance on his test and performance in school. The test also correlated with scores on *achievement tests* – tests of knowledge about particular school subjects – although at a lower magnitude.

It is worth noting that Binet refused to use test scores to rank children. He felt that intelligence is too complex a phenomenon to draw meaningful conclusions about the *relative* intelligence among most children. It would be unfair to say, he argued, that one child of average intelligence, as measured by his test, was more intelligent than another child of average intelligence. However, Binet's concerns did not stop others from extending his test in ways that he neither anticipated nor advocated.

Lewis Terman and the Stanford–Binet Intelligence Test Interest in Binet's work spread throughout the world, and Stanford University professor Lewis Terman (1877–1956) adapted the Binet–Simon intelligence test for use in the United States. He realized that some of the test items, originally developed to test French children, needed to be changed to better assess the intelligence of children in the United States. The age norms, for example, did not apply to the American schoolchildren in Terman's sample. This was an important early recognition of the influence of culture in intelligence testing. Terman called his new test the Stanford–Binet Intelligence Test (Raid & Tippin, 2009).

In developing his version of Binet's test, Terman decided to state the results not simply in terms of mental age but in terms of a measure that would relate mental to chronological age. Thus, the famous **intelligence quotient (IQ)**, was devised. To arrive at this measure of intelligence, Terman calculated the ratio of mental age to chronological age and multiplied that ratio by 100 (in order to remove the decimal point). Thus, returning to our earlier examples, the 11-year-old with average intelligence would earn an IQ of 100 (11/11 × 100), the more intelligent child would post an IQ of 118 (13/11 × 100), and the less intelligent child's IQ would be 82 (9/11 × 100).

> **intelligence quotient (IQ)** Terman's measure of intelligence; the ratio of a child's mental age to his or her chronological age, multiplied by 100.

In addition to adapting Binet's test for use in American schools, Terman had a larger goal, a goal that today most people would consider reprehensible. He was an advocate of the 19th-century *eugenics movement*, which sought to discourage people deemed 'unfit' from reproducing while encouraging 'fit' individuals to have children (Leslie, 2000). He believed that his IQ test could help determine the 'fitness' of individuals to reproduce. He stated, 'the children of successful and cultured parents test higher than children from wretched and ignorant homes for the simple reason that their heredity is better.' More generally, Terman believed that his test demonstrated that some groups of people are inherently less intelligent than others (Hegarty, 2007; Feldhusen, 2003).

Working with agencies in the United States government, Terman also administered his test to newly arrived immigrants and to almost two million World War I army recruits. His student, Arthur Otis, developed nonverbal tasks for non-English-speaking individuals. Some psychologists at the time believed that the results of these alternative versions of the intelligence test proved the inferiority of people whose origins were not Anglo-Saxon. In fact, the mass testing of immigrants helped lead to a 1924 law that greatly lowered the number of people allowed to enter the United States from Southern and Eastern Europe, while increasing the number from Northern and Western Europe. Despite such misuse of the early Stanford–Binet test, it remained for many years the leading intelligence testing instrument in the United States.

David Wechsler and the WAIS As a young man inducted into the army during World War I, David Wechsler (1896–1981) was trained to administer and score the Stanford–Binet and other intelligence tests of the time. Over the course of his work, he came to recognize two key problems with the tests (Kaufman, 2009, 2000).

First, he realized that the distinction between mental and chronological age becomes less informative when testing adults. While it may be true that a considerable difference in intelligence is on display between an eight-year-old and a 13-year-old, a five-year difference between adults tends to be meaningless. How much difference is there, for example, between the mental ability of a typical 30-year-old and a typical 35-year-old? Not much. Second, Wechsler, who

was born in Romania and whose family immigrated to the United States when he was six years old, recognized the need for greater fairness when testing people who did not speak English or who spoke it poorly.

Over the course of his professional life, Wechsler devised a number of intelligence tests that took such problems into account. The first such test – the *Wechsler–Bellevue Intelligence Scale* – was published in 1939. Different versions of Wechsler's tests continue to be published by his associates to the present day (Watkins, 2010; Hartman, 2009). The best known of these tests are the *Wechsler Adult Intelligence Scale (WAIS)* and the *Wechsler Intelligence Scale for Children (WISC)*. Figure 12.6 shows sample items from the WAIS.

Wechsler Adult Intelligence Scale (WAIS) Sample Items		
Test	**Description**	**Example**
Verbal Scale		
Information	Taps general range of information	On which continent is France?
Comprehension	Tests understanding of social conventions and ability to evaluate past experience	Why do people need birth certificates?
Arithmetic	Tests arithmetic reasoning through verbal problems	How many hours will it take to drive 150 miles at 50 miles per hour?
Similarities	Asks in what way certain objects or concepts are similar; measures abstract thinking	How are a calculator and a typewriter alike?
Digit span	Tests attention and rote memory by orally presenting series of digits to be repeated forward or backward	Repeat the following numbers backward: 2 4 3 5 1 8 6
Vocabulary	Tests ability to define increasingly difficult words	What does repudiate mean?
Performance scale		
Digit symbol	Tests speed of learning through timed coding tasks in which numbers must be associated with marks of various shapes	Shown: 1 2 3 4 Fill in: 4 2 1 3 
Picture completion	Tests visual alertness and visual memory through presentation of an incompletely drawn figure; the missing part must be discovered and named	Tell me what is missing: 
Block design	Tests ability to perceive and analyze patterns presenting designs that must be copied with blocks	Assemble blocks to match this design: 
Picture arrangement	Tests understanding of social situations through a series of comic-strip-type pictures that must be arranged in the right sequence to tell a story	Put this picture in the right order:  1 2 3
Object assembly	Tests ability to deal with part/whole relationships by presenting puzzle pieces that must be assembled to form a complete object	Assemble the pieces into a complete object: 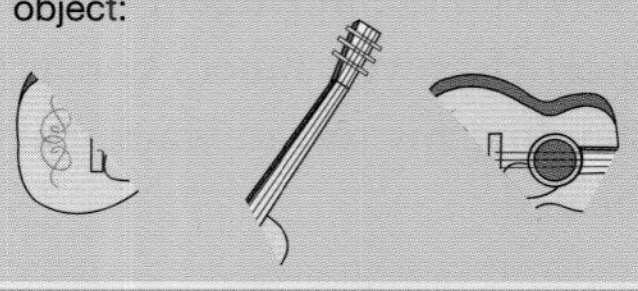

FIGURE 12.6 Items similar to those on the WAIS. The widely used WAIS gives separate scores for verbal intelligence and performance as well as an overall intelligence score.

Source: Harcourt Assessment, Inc.

Wechsler borrowed much from the Stanford–Binet and other tests; however, his tests were less dominated by tasks requiring verbal ability. There are 11 subtests on the WAIS, some requiring verbal ability and others requiring nonverbal reasoning. Each individual who takes the test receives specific subtest scores, which are grouped into two main categories: a verbal score and a performance score. The individual also receives an overall score that Wechsler associated with the *g* factor. Wechsler also discarded the old formula for calculating an IQ score. Although he still called a person's overall score an intelligence quotient, or IQ, he derived the score from a normal distribution (discussed earlier in this chapter) rather than from a ratio – a change that has been adopted in most other intelligence tests.

Wechsler's tests resulted from his clinical experience, not from a clear theoretical position. However, he did come to develop a broad view of what intelligence means. In particular, he believed that it is more than success on test scores. To him, intelligence is at work as individuals try to manage the day-to-day aspects of life, interact with others and perform at work. Wechsler's broad view of intelligence has gained momentum over the years. Indeed, as we suggested earlier, it lies at the centre of most current theories of intelligence. Indeed, it has been defined as a capacity for comprehending the social and physical environment, for *catching on* and *figuring out* all aspects of everyday life.

How Well Do Intelligence Tests Predict Performance?

The Stanford–Binet and the WAIS have very high degrees of reliability (Hunt, 2011). The correlation coefficient for retakes of each test is about +0.90. Furthermore, repeated measurements of IQ across the lifespan tend to correlate very highly (Gow *et al.*, 2011; Larsen *et al.*, 2008). People tested in their teens have been re-tested in their 80s. Today's leading intelligence tests are also highly correlated with school performance – a validity coefficient of about +0.50 (Lynn & Meisenberg, 2010; Sternberg *et al.*, 2001). The correlations are even higher between IQ scores and the number of years of schooling that people complete (Ceci, 1991). These findings are especially relevant considering that IQ tests were originally designed to assess for school performance.

Of course, IQ tests are meant to do more than predict school (or preschool) performance. When we talk about IQ, we often think about it in terms of defining general mental ability. Indeed, we measure IQ for adults far past school age. And we do this even though most of the tasks on any IQ test relate most strongly to school performance.

Intelligence and Longevity

Intelligence tests predict how long we live. This has been found by an American psychologist, Linda Gottfredson, and a Scottish psychiatrist, Ian Deary, using various different data banks. But the question is, why? Is it that brighter people get better jobs that have more pay and less stress and this is the major cause? Or is it that brighter people pay more attention to health warnings and what their doctors tell them? Does intelligence provide health-enhancing mental resources? Or is it that intelligence is a good metric of general physical fitness and more healthy people live longer? We do not know but certainly this is an interesting avenue for further research.

So what does IQ mean outside the classroom? Performance on intelligence tests correlates to some degree with other areas of functioning in life, such as occupational and social achievements, income and health-related behaviours (Hunt, 2011; Cramond *et al.*, 2010; Lubinski, 2004). In a massive undertaking, researchers administered the same intelligence test to every 11-year-old child in Scotland in 1932 and 1947 and then followed the children's development and achievements as they moved through the lifespan (Deary *et al.*, 2004). Performance on the IQ test at this young age was found to correlate to some degree with better health throughout life, greater independence during old age and a longer lifespan. It would appear, then, that IQ testing does have some relevance beyond the school ages.

Cultural Bias and Stereotypes in Intelligence Testing

Though widely used and respected, intelligence tests are subject to various criticisms, both fair and unfair. One set of concerns involves *cultural bias* (Tomes, 2010; Wicherts & Dolan, 2010). As mentioned earlier, different cultures may have different ideas of intelligence. For example, Western intelligence tests emphasize abilities such as logic, mathematical skill and verbal fluency over abilities such as getting along with others and fitting in with one's environment – abilities that are important in Chinese notions of intelligence. Such differences obviously make comparing intelligence across cultures challenging.

Should you use IQ tests to select people for university? Are they unfair to certain groups? Do they need to be supplemented by other tests? If so, which? For some, the IQ test offers a simple, cheap and reliable way to evaluate those who benefit most from higher education. But for others, they represent little more than a method that discriminates against certain groups.

Furthermore, problems are not limited to comparing people from different countries but extend to comparing members

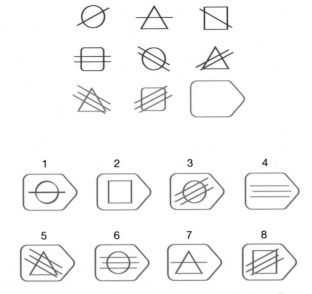

FIGURE 12.7 Item similar to the Progressive Matrices Test. This test emphasizes abstract, nonverbal skills. Here the respondent chooses which of the numbered boxes below finishes the sequence above. (Box #6 is the correct answer.)

threat to manipulate the performance of Asian women on a maths test (Ambady *et al.*, 2004, 2001; Shih *et al.*, 1999). Some participants were encouraged to focus on their female identity, and they tended to perform less well on the test (in keeping with the stereotype that women are not good at mathematics). Other participants had their attention focused on their Asian identity, and they tended to perform better (in keeping with the stereotype that Asians are good at mathematics).

As psychologists' awareness and ability to detect bias grows, they are becoming increasingly able to construct tests that are more sensitive and more effective. We have, for example, already noted the efforts of developers of the WAIS to make their tests less culture-specific. Overall bias can be assessed both at the general level we have discussed here and at a more detailed level. During test construction, today's tests are also assessed for *item bias*; if individuals from a particular gender or ethnic group miss an item with high frequency, that item is considered for elimination from the test. Similarly, certain questions may become less culturally relevant over time and must be exchanged for questions that better reflect current conditions. It appears that ongoing efforts to assess and challenge these sorts of bias have been somewhat successful in rendering generally nonbiased testing. In short, tests are becoming more reliable and valid.

of different subcultures within a single country. For example, although Wechsler made considerable efforts to standardize the WAIS and make it as unbiased as possible, critics noted several curious oversights in earlier versions of the test. Many of its problem-solving questions reflected problems confronted in middle-class settings, for instance (Hunt, 2011; Ford, 2008). In addition, until the most recent revisions of the WAIS, every time a picture of a person was used for a test item, the picture was of a white person.

Most people interested in the construction of intelligence tests have abandoned the idea of *totally* unbiased tests and instead try to design tests that do not put particular cultures at an absolute disadvantage. The Progressive Matrices Test attempts to achieve this goal in part by emphasizing abstract, nonverbal skills, for example. Some sample items from that test are shown in Figure 12.7.

stereotype threat when people in a particular group perform poorly because they fear that their performance will conform to a negative stereotype associated with them.

A related testing issue is **stereotype threat**, which occurs when people in a particular group perform poorly because they fear that their performance will conform to a negative stereotype associated with that group. Several studies have found that simply suggesting to students that they will not do well on a test because of their gender or race can lower their test scores (Owens & Massey, 2011; Steele & Aronson, 2004, 1995). In an interesting study, researchers were able to use stereotype

Is Human Intelligence Increasing?

We have observed that the median score on intelligence tests, such as the Stanford–Binet and the WAIS, is set at 100. To keep the median score at 100, the tests periodically must be *re-standardized*. People taking the WAIS today, for example, are taking a version that has been reconstructed in recent years – not the version that David Wechsler designed originally.

Upon reviewing test scores over time, researchers have noticed something startling: intelligence test scores from around the world seem to be increasing, even though scores from other kinds of educational tasks and tests, such as college aptitude tests, are dropping. Studies indicate that an average IQ score of 100 from 70 years ago would equate to a score of only 76 today. This puzzling phenomenon has been named the **Flynn effect**, after New Zealand researcher James Flynn (2007), who first discovered it (Figure 12.8).

Researchers do not fully understand why intelligence scores have increased over time (Ceci & Kanaya, 2010; Weiss, 2010).

Flynn effect an observed rise in average IQ scores throughout the world over time.

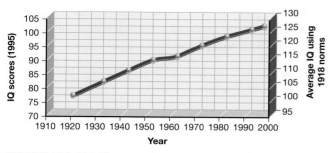

FIGURE 12.8 The Flynn effect. Flynn demonstrated that intelligence scores have increased from 1918 to 1995. The right axis of the graph shows that if the 1918 scales were used today, the average IQ score in the United States would be 125. The left axis shows that if the 1995 scales were used, the average IQ score in 1918 would equate to a score of 76 today.

Source: Adapted from Flynn, J. R. (1998). IQ gains over time: Toward finding the causes. In U. Neisser (ed.), *The Rising Curve: Long-term gains in IQ and related measures* (p. 37). Washington: American Psychological Association. Copyright © by the American Psychological Association. Reprinted by permission of the author.

Potential causes/explanations include:

- *Education.* In most countries with every generation people are spending longer at school and with better facilities. Schooling is compulsory and people from all backgrounds are used to learning and being tested. Intelligence is related to learning so as education is better and more widespread scores get higher.

- *Nutrition.* People are now better nourished, particularly in childhood, which reduces the incidence of developmental delay in the population. There are fewer people who had poor nutrition in youth so the bottom end of the distribution is removed, which means the average score goes up.

- *Social trends.* We are all now much more used to timed tests and performing against the clock. People are familiar with tests and testing and so do better overall.

- *Parental Involvement.* The idea is that parents provide richer home environments for their children and express a greater interest in their education than they used to. They have higher expectations and get involved more. The trend to have smaller families where parents invest more in their children may also be an important factor

- *Social Environment.* The world is more complex and stimulating. Modernization and new technology mean people have to manipulate abstract concepts more, which is essentially what intelligence tests measure.

Before You Go On

What Do You Know?

7. What three basic criteria are central to designing an intelligence test?
8. What was the original purpose of Binet's intelligence test?
9. How does mental age differ from chronological age?
10. What are some proposed causes of the Flynn effect?

What Do You Think?

How would you design a culture-free intelligence test?

Is Intelligence Governed by Genetic or Environmental Factors?

HOW WE DEVELOP

LEARNING OBJECTIVE 4

Review the contributions of heredity and environment to intelligence, and explain how emphasizing one factor or the other can affect social policy.

As you saw in Chapter 3, the nature/nurture debate centres on the question of whether particular qualities and behaviours result from genetic underpinnings or from the environment. Is a happy and healthy baby, for example, the result of robust genes, effective parental care and attention or both? A similar question can be asked about intelligence. Do we inherit our intelligence from our parents? And if we do, does that mean that the environment has no influence, or can experiences, such as parenting, schooling and familiarity with test-taking have an effect? Later in this section, we will examine how various psychologists answer these questions. First, though, we will consider important social questions that are raised by the search to identify the origin of intelligence.

What Are the Social Implications of the Nature/Nurture Debate?

If genes were clearly identified as the main determinant of intelligence, what might some of the social consequences be? In certain circles, such a finding might be taken to justify claims that some people were inherently superior to others. Perhaps some would even seek to create a social structure that assigned people to classes according to their parentage and restricted certain classes to certain social roles.

On the other hand, what if the environment were found to be more decisive in determining intelligence? Children from disadvantaged environments would be expected to lead disadvantaged lives and display, on average, lower intelligence; but, then again, their environments and their intellectual level could potentially be improved. Would people who possess environmental advantages be willing to share them with those who were deprived, however?

Other difficult questions involving the nature/nurture debate and intelligence have been asked with respect to gender, ethnicity and race. Perhaps the clearest example of the serious social consequences of such questions was the Nazi claim in the early 20th century that Aryans (Indo-Europeans who were supposedly Nordic in appearance and of German ancestry) were superior to all other groups. Although Nazi scientists failed to support this assertion, their efforts demonstrated that there will always be people who wish to use possible genetic differences in intelligence as a basis for oppressing and controlling people.

The Bell Curve Controversy

In 1994, two researchers published a book that ignited a firestorm of controversy regarding the issue of intelligence. In *The Bell Curve*, Richard Herrnstein and Charles Murray surveyed research on the origins and nature of intelligence as well as reporting their own analyses. From all of these data, the authors drew conclusions that most psychologists, educators and researchers take issue with, arguing that many of the authors' conclusions do not follow from the data. The conclusions offered by Herrnstein and Murray are:

- Conventional IQ tests measure intelligence accurately.

- IQ is an important predictor of many measures of success in life, including success at school, work, parenting and income. Higher IQ also predicts the avoidance of welfare dependence and criminality.

- Given such correlations, people who are high in intelligence form a cognitive elite – they reach the upper levels of society – whereas those with lower IQs fall towards the bottom.

- Given their predictive powers, intelligence tests can and should be used as a *gating* mechanism, to allow those with high IQs access to opportunities.

- IQ is largely heritable, passed on through the genes from one generation to the next.

- There are clear racial and ethnic differences in intelligence.

- It is likely, although not certain, that at least some of this difference between groups is due to genetic factors.

Herrnstein and Murray went on to argue for greater acceptance of these ideas and more paternalism towards those with lower IQs; that is, a benign recognition of the limitations of such individuals and greater efforts to help them in areas of life where lower intelligence holds them back.

As you may imagine, the debate over the book's conclusions and implications remains heated to the present day. As noted above, most psychologists and researchers have argued that many of the authors' conclusions do not follow from the data and may instead reflect the authors' ideology (Nisbett, 2009; Flynn, 2008, 2000). Furthermore, according to many critics, even if the authors' conclusions were justified in some places, the social policies they recommended on the basis of those conclusions would still be unfair and racist (Richards, 2004). Others have argued strongly in favour of the book's conclusions, like Canadian psychologist Phil Rushton. Politics aside, let us examine what scientists actually have learnt and not learnt about the nature/nurture debate on human intelligence.

Genetic Influences on Intelligence

A variety of studies has suggested that genetic factors can play a major role in intelligence. In particular, studies of twins and other relatives and research in molecular biology point to genes as a key contributor.

Family Studies Twins have received particular attention from intelligence researchers. If genetic factors are at work in intelligence, identical twins (who share all their genes) should have more similar intelligence test scores than fraternal twins (who share only about half of their genes). This expectation has been supported consistently by research (Bratko *et al.*, 2010; Plomin & Spinath, 2004). Studies have found, on average, a correlation of +0.86 between the intelligence test scores of identical twins, compared with a correlation of +0.60 between the scores of fraternal twins.

Do such findings mean that intelligence is related *primarily* to genes? Not necessarily. It turns out that parents treat identical twins more alike than they do fraternal twins. In fact, family studies find that identical twins are treated most alike of all siblings, followed by same-gender fraternal twins and then different-gender twins. Perhaps, then, the more closely related intelligence scores found among identical twins are, at least in part, a reflection of more similar interactions with parents.

To help sort out the relative influence of heredity and environment, we need to look at IQ scores for identical twins who have been raised apart from one another. If genetic factors are important determinants of intelligence, then the scores should remain closely related. Thus, researchers have looked at the IQ scores of identical twins who were adopted at birth and placed in separate homes. The correlation between the scores of these separated identical twins is +0.75 (Plomin & Spinath, 2004), an impressive statistic that seems to reflect once again the influence of genetic factors. At the same time, this correlation is not as large as the +0.86 correlation for the IQ scores of identical twins who are raised together, a difference that we could attribute to those twins' shared environments.

Another approach to the heredity and intelligence question is to examine the relationships between the IQ scores of adopted children and those of their biological and adoptive parents. If heredity is more influential than environment, the IQ scores of adopted children should be more similar to those of their biological parents than to those of their adoptive parents. If environment matters more, we should find the children's IQ scores closer to their adoptive parents' scores than to the scores of their biological parents.

Researchers have found, on average, a correlation of +0.22 between the scores of adopted children and the scores of their biological parents and a correlation of +0.19 between the children's scores and those of their adoptive parents (Plomin & Spinath, 2004). On the one hand, the children's IQ scores are somewhat related to the scores of their biological parents (correlation of +0.22), indicating a possible genetic influence. On the other hand, this correlation is not especially large, nor is it significantly higher than the +0.19 correlation found between the scores of the children and those of their adoptive parents. This pattern of findings indicates once again that the nature/nurture question is not a simple one to answer.

All of these family studies suggest that genes play a role in intelligence, but exactly how much of a role? Scientists have sought to answer this question by examining the specific data from many studies and arriving at an overall estimate of the heritability of intelligence. **Heritability** refers to the overall extent to which differences among people are attributable to genes.

heritability the overall extent to which differences among people are attributable to genes.

Evaluating the data from studies of twins and other relatives, researchers have determined that the heritability of intelligence is approximately 50% (Plomin & Spinath, 2004). Some have placed it as high as 70%; others, as low as 40%. It is important to note that the concept of heritability is used to explain the differences between groups of people, not to provide information about a single individual. Thus, the finding that the heritability of intelligence is around 50% does not mean that 50% of a particular individual's intelligence is inherited. Rather, it suggests that 50% of all differences observed in a population's intelligence test scores are due to genetic factors.

The statistical measure used to indicate the contribution of heredity to intelligence (or to any other characteristic) is the **heritability coefficient**, a number ranging from 0.00 to +1.00. A coefficient of 0.00 means that heredity has no impact on variations observed among people, whereas a coefficient of +1.00 means that heredity is the sole influence on the characteristic under investigation. The heritability coefficient for Huntington's disease, in which genetic factors are totally responsible for the emergence of the disorder, is +1.00. In contrast, as we have just observed, the heritability coefficient for intelligence is +0.50 – a figure that holds in studies conducted across the world, from the United States to Moscow, Japan and India (Plomin & Spinath, 2004).

heritability coefficient a correlation coefficient used to indicate the contribution of heredity to some characteristic, such as intelligence.

Findings from Molecular Biology We know that genes contribute to intelligence, but do we know which genes are important? Do we know the process by which this occurs? In recent years, new molecular biology techniques have enabled researchers to examine DNA sequences and genes. These techniques have already led to a detailed mapping (sequencing) of all genes in the human body, and they may lead eventually to the identification of the genes responsible for complex traits, such as intelligence. Although researchers do not yet know precisely which genes contribute to a person's intelligence, they have determined that more than one gene is involved (Pan *et al.*, 2011; Plomin & Spinath, 2004). In fact, early indications are that numerous genes from various chromosomes may be at work – a polygenic effect – with each such gene accounting for only a small amount of intellectual potential.

Environmental Influences on Intelligence

If the heritability of intelligence is 50%, then environmental factors of many types are responsible for the remaining 50% of differences in intelligence among people. The term *environment* can have a narrow or broad meaning. It can refer to our home setting, neighbourhood, extended family, school or socioeconomic group. It can even refer to biological events and experiences that a foetus confronts in its mother's uterus. Or it can refer to the sum of all such contexts. Four environmental influences have received particular attention in the study of intelligence: family and home, culture, occupation and schooling.

Family and Home Influences The first environment to which we are exposed in life, and the one that dominates our childhood, is the family and home. Our parents' childrearing methods and other characteristics, our interactions with siblings, the objects in our houses, family trips – these are all parts of our family and home environment. Some homes are full of books; others have none. Some parents read to their children daily; others never at all. The question is what effect this all has on the development of intelligence.

Research has suggested a link between family and home environment and children's intelligence scores. Several studies, for example, have examined the IQ scores of biological siblings and adoptive siblings. These investigations have found that when biological siblings are raised apart the correlation between their IQ scores is +0.22. In contrast, when children from different families are adopted and raised together, the correlation between their IQ scores is +0.32 (Plomin & Spinath, 2004). If family and home environment did not affect intelligence levels, we would expect a near-zero correlation between the IQ scores of adoptive siblings. Instead, they display a higher correlation than that displayed by biological twins who are raised apart.

PSYCHOLOGY AROUND US **Smart Parenting**

Early theories held that an individual's intellectual capacity was totally fixed at birth. As we have seen throughout this chapter, however, we now know that interventions of various kinds can improve intellectual functioning.

Researchers Robert Bradley and Bettye Caldwell have examined the impact of the home environment on intelligence and identified several parenting approaches that may help raise the IQ scores of preschoolers (Bradley et al., 2003; Bradley & Caldwell, 1984). In fact, they claim that such approaches are better predictors of IQ scores than factors such as socioeconomic class or family structure. Related research seems to support their assertions (Sidhu et al., 2010).

The parent to-do list includes:

- Be emotionally and verbally responsive and involved with the child.
- Avoid too much restriction and punishment.
- Organize the physical environment and the child's activity schedule.
- Provide appropriate play materials.
- Provide a variety of forms of daily stimulation.

Cultural Influences Most definitions of intelligence include how well people adapt to their environments. This criterion raises an important question: does the definition of intelligence change across different cultural environments? Many researchers say yes, the definition of intelligence varies from culture to culture (Smith, 2010; Georgas, 2003).

Note that this is different from asking whether people from different parts of the world (or from different racial or ethnic groups) have different levels of intelligence. That question relates more to the idea of comparing general intelligence, whereas we here are more concerned with comparing the specific skill sets that constitute intelligence in different cultures. Researchers have found that the values of a society or cultural group often have powerful effects on the intellectual skills of its members. Rice farmers in Liberia, for example, are particularly skilled at estimating quantities of rice (Cole et al., 1967) and children in Botswana, who are used to hearing stories, have good memories for the details of stories (Dube, 1982). These specific skills would improve individuals' ability to survive and thrive within their cultures and, thus, would be valued components of intelligence within each culture. Such principles can apply within subcultures as well: for example, a knowledge of fashion designers and the ability to walk a runway are prized skill sets in some subcultures within Western culture.

Most of the assumptions about intelligence that we have looked at thus far are Western-oriented. Western conceptions of intelligence tend to be influenced by the Western value of individualism, while some other cultures place more emphasis on the community as a whole. Moreover, Westerners tend to equate high intelligence with rapid mental processing, whereas other cultures may value depth of thinking, however slowly it occurs (Sternberg, 2007; Sternberg et al., 1981). One study found that

Taiwanese-Chinese theorists typically point to five factors at the root of intelligence (Yang & Sternberg, 1997):

- a general cognitive factor
- interpersonal intelligence (knowing about others)
- intrapersonal intelligence (knowing about oneself)
- intellectual self-assertion
- intellectual self-effacement.

While the first three qualities are similar to factors in some Western definitions of intelligence, the final two are not. Also, Westerners often believe that intelligence further involves verbal skill and the ability to solve practical problems, features absent from the Chinese list.

Occupational Influences Researchers have consistently found a relationship between intelligence and job complexity. People of higher intelligence tend to work in more complex jobs (Hunt, 2011; Ganzach, 2003; Ganzach & Pazy, 2001). An obvious explanation for this relationship is that individuals of higher intelligence can handle complex jobs more readily than less intelligent people can and so are more likely to obtain and succeed in such positions.

Psychologist Linda Gottfredson has made an extensive study of this topic and come to the following conclusions:

- Across all jobs and all ratings of success, intelligence is very important.
- The predictive power of intelligence rises with job complexity. The more intellectually and technically demanding the job, the more important is intelligence for success.
- The validity of intelligence is high compared with other factors, like personality, particular aptitudes or vocational interests.
- Differences between individuals do not decrease with training (the less good become better and the good remain much the same) but can increase. Intelligence is a major source of enduring, consequential differences in job performance.
- Higher levels of intelligence are required as people rise up the occupational ladder. Occupations both attract and accommodate individuals from a wide range of IQ levels but job incumbents are more homogeneous than applicants. But there appear to be minimum IQ thresholds that rise steadily with job level.
- Higher intelligence reflects higher trainability.
- The essence of intelligence at work is the ability to deal with complexity, which is an individual ability to acquire, apply, organize, recognize, select and update on salient work-related information. In other words, to mentally manipulate information and acquire and critique knowledge.

- Complexity is the key feature in the workplace. It is the major distinguishing factor between jobs. It is all about information processing.
- As social, cultural and work life become more complex, the role of intelligence inevitably increases.
- Where people have little time and ability to learn and be trained it is best to focus on specific training for specific skills.

Studies also suggest, however, that complex work may itself improve intelligence. In one study, for example, interviews with 3,000 men in various occupations seemed to indicate that more complex jobs lead to more intellectual flexibility and independent judgement among employees (Schooler et al., 2004; Schooler, 2001; Kohn & Schooler, 1973). A job that requires workers to organize and interpret detailed financial data, for example, may help produce more intellectual know-how than one requiring workers to simply add up customer bills.

Why would more complex jobs enhance intellectual skills? Perhaps because holders of such jobs are forced to acquire a greater amount of complex information and knowledge (Kuncel et al., 2010, 2004) – the very kinds of information and knowledge that are measured on intelligence tests. The complexity factor may also help explain differences in IQ scores between urban and rural populations. Several generations ago, studies found that urban residents scored, on average, six IQ points higher than rural residents (Terman & Merrill, 1937; Seashore et al., 1950). One possible explanation for this difference is the greater complexity of the urban environment. More recently, the difference declined to about two points (Kaufman & Doppelt, 1976; Reynolds et al., 1987). It could be that changes in rural environments – less isolation, increased travel, mass communication, Internet access, improvements in schools and increased use of technology on farms – have raised the level of complexity in these environments and, in turn, brought the IQ scores of rural citizens closer to those of city residents.

School Influences Researchers have determined that schooling is both a cause and consequence of intelligence (Shayer & Adhami, 2010; Fish, 2002; Sangwan, 2001). Brighter people tend to do better and go further at school. Children with higher intelligence test scores are more likely to be moved forward, less likely to drop out of school and more likely to attend university. In turn, schooling helps change mental abilities, including those measured on intelligence tests.

Researchers Stephen Ceci and Wendy Williams (2010, 2007, 1997) have demonstrated some interesting ties between intelligence scores and the amount of time spent in school. Students' IQ scores tend to rise during the school year and drop when schooling is discontinued or during the summer holidays. Students who complete secondary school perform higher on intelligence tests than those who leave school early. And young children whose birthdays just make the cut-off for beginning school early earn higher intelligence scores than those of almost identical age who miss the cut-off and remain at home for an extra year.

Why may schooling help improve intelligence scores? In part because schools provide the opportunity both to acquire information (Who wrote *Moby Dick*? What is a square root and how do you calculate it?) and to develop 'systematic problem-solving, abstract thinking, categorization, sustained attention to material of little intrinsic interest, and repeated manipulation of basic symbols and operations' – skills measured on intelligence tests (Neisser, 1998).

Researchers have also shown that the *quality* of the school environment affects intellectual performance. In financially poor schools, children tend to learn less and, in turn, tend to score significantly lower on IQ tests (Johnson, 2010; Nisbett, 2009). In a pioneering study conducted half a century ago, one researcher found that when African-American students from a poor school in Georgia moved to Philadelphia their IQ scores improved (Lee, 1961). Clearly, such findings argue for better schools so that each child can work in as enriching an environment as possible. The same has been found in Europe, with people moving from poor developing countries to advanced, rich countries in Northern Europe.

Group Differences in IQ Scores

Recall that at the beginning of this section we discussed *The Bell Curve* (Herrnstein & Murray, 1994), in which the authors argue that group differences in IQ may be due largely to genetic factors. We went on to discuss findings that intelligence is, indeed, heritable, but that environment plays a significant role as well. Let us now look more closely at group differences in IQ scores.

There are two trends on which most researchers of group differences in intelligence agree (Sackett & Shen, 2010; Lynn, 2008; Fish, 2002). First, racial groups do indeed differ in their average scores on intelligence tests. Second, high-scoring people (and groups) are more likely to attain high levels of education and income. In one review conducted decades ago, 52 researchers agreed that the IQ bell curve for Americans is centred around a score of 100 for white Americans and 85 for African-Americans, with scores for different subgroups of Hispanic Americans falling in between (Avery *et al.*, 1994). Similarly, researchers have noted that European New

Zealanders tend to outscore native Maori New Zealanders, Israeli Jews outscore Israeli Arabs and people with good hearing outscore the hearing impaired (Zeidner, 1990). The same pattern has been found in Europe with some, but not all, migrant groups scoring less well than the white natives. What can we make of such trends?

Two important issues about group differences can be clarified by means of an analogy offered by geneticist Richard Lewontin (Feldman & Lewontin, 2008; Lewontin, 2001, 1982, 1976). Suppose you start with 100 plant seeds from the same source and divide them into two groups. You plant one group of seeds in a flowerpot filled with poor soil and the other group in a flowerpot filled with fertile soil. What differences would you expect between the groups of seeds as they grow into plants? As shown in Figure 12.9, you should see two kinds of variation: variation between the two groups and variation within each group. When evaluating these variations, we need to keep in mind two principles that also apply to evaluating group differences in intelligence scores:

- *Environment contributes to variation between the groups.* The plants growing in poor soil vary from the ones growing in good soil, even though all of the plants came from the same mixture of seed. For example, the plants raised in poor soil are, on average, shorter than those raised in fertile soil. This difference is probably attributable to the environment. In short, optimal environments tend to produce optimal plants, and deficient environments tend to produce less successful plants. Similarly, on average, groups that now display lower average IQ scores have been raised in worse environments than the groups with higher scores.

- *An average variation between groups cannot be applied to individuals within each group.* In our plant example, even though on average the plants growing in poor soil are shorter than those growing in good soil, some of the poor-soil plants will be taller than others. Some will probably even be taller than the average plant in the good soil. These differences probably are attributable to normal genetic variation, since all the plants in a given pot share the same environment.

Again, this principle applies to people as well as plants. You cannot deduce anything about the intelligence of one person based on the mean scores of that individual's group. Even Herrnstein and Murray (1994), the authors of *The Bell Curve*, granted that 'millions of Blacks have higher IQs than the average White'. Failing to distinguish between individual performance and group norms can mislead people, produce incorrect expectations and cause social injustices.

With this analogy in mind, let us return to the question of IQ scores and group differences. In an important study, researcher

Group 1: poor soil   **Group 2:** fertile soil

FIGURE 12.9 Lewontin's plant analogy of intelligence. If two groups of plants start out from the same source of seeds (genetics), but one group is given a better environment, the differences in height between the two groups would be mainly determined by environmental conditions. The analogy applies when evaluating group differences in IQ scores.

Joel Myerson and his colleagues (1998) examined the intelligence scores of African-American and white American students from eighth grade through college and found that from the eighth grade through the early high-school years the average score of the white American students increased, whereas the average score of the African-American students decreased. The gap between the two groups was at its widest at about the time both groups took their college admission tests. During college, however, the scores of the African-American students increased more than four times as much as the scores of the white American students. The researchers concluded that 'as black and white students complete more grades in high-school environments that differ in quality, the gap in cognitive test scores widens. At the college level, however, where black and white students are exposed to educational environments of comparable quality . . . many black students are able to make remarkable gains, closing the gap in test scores.'

Such research suggests that public policy aimed at making more equitable resources available throughout society would lead to more similar intelligence test scores across different groups (Biswas-Diener, 2011; Williams *et al.*, 2004). Of course, this raises yet another important question: do efforts to equalize educational experiences and other environmental resources actually improve intelligence? We will consider next the effects of *environmental enrichment*, providing disadvantaged children with more stimulating environments at home and at school.

Men and Women Are Different (Cognitive Differences between the Sexes)
HOW WE DIFFER

You have to be courageous to even think about sex differences in intelligence. Many people want to believe that men and women are equal not only in potential but also in ability. They argue that even if there are small differences they should not be explored or explained because of the divisive effect that it has on both sexes.

Over the past century, there have been periods where both the 'difference' and 'non-difference' view occurred. The growth of environmentalism and feminism from the 1960s onwards perpetuated the idea that any observable differences between the sexes were the result of socialization. Further that they were iniquitous and could and should be changed. However, the pendulum from the 1990s onwards swung the other way, towards a more biological and evolutionary perspective, which recognized and explained sex difference as natural and inevitable.

There really are recognized sex differences at all stages of life. In infancy, we know boys are more active and spend more time awake; girls are more physically developed and coordinated; girls show R-hand preference at five months (not boys); girls have better hearing and are more vocal; girls make more eye contact and are more interested in social and emotional stimuli; boys are more interested in things and systems.

Glenn Wilson (1989) at the Institute of Psychiatry in London has shown that in the preschool period we know boys are more interested in block-building and vehicles; girls prefer doll play, artwork and domestic activities; boys like rough and tumble play; girls are more sensitive and sedentary; boys show narrow interests; girls a wider range, including boy-typical activities (asymmetrical sex-typing); gender segregation (same-sex playgroups) appears for both boys and girls. Boys groups are larger and more concerned with dominance issues; girls play in groups of two or three and are more sharing (concerned with fairness).

There are noticeable differences particularly in language. Girls acquire language earlier than boys do and remain more fluent throughout life; girls develop larger vocabularies, use more complex linguistic constructions, enunciate and read better. Boys are less communicative and use language instrumentally (to get what they want); brain localization of language is more bilateral for females than males (MRI and lesion studies); males suffer from bilingual development (e.g. memory deficit), while females seem unaffected.

If you give girls and boys at primary school different tests, there are clear differences. Boys can draw bicycles better than can girls, who in turn are more fluent with words. Boys are better at mathematical reasoning, dart throwing and mentally finding geometric forms in complex patterns and rotating objects. Girls are better at remembering displaced objects, recalling stories and precision tasks calling for good motor coordination.

Furnham (2008) proposes the following six positions of sex differences:

- Intelligence cannot be accurately measured and therefore it is difficult to prove or disprove the existence of sex difference. This view emerges every so often and is usually perpetuated by educators, journalists or politicians who are ideologically opposed to testing.

- There are no differences at all for one of two reasons. First, there are no good evolutionary or environmental theories or reasons to suppose there are. Second, the early tests were so developed to show no difference. That is, subtests were included and excluded so that neither sex was advantaged or disadvantaged.

- There are no mean or average differences between the sexes but there are differences at the extremes. Thus, men tend to be over represented both at the extremes of the bell curve. The most brilliant are men and so are the most challenged, meaning the average is the same but the distribution is wider for men.

- There are numerous, demonstrable and replicable sex differences in a whole range of abilities that make up overall intelligence.

- Sex differences that do emerge are not real. They occur for three reasons. Girls are taught humility and males hubris, and this social message leads them to approach tests differently. Next, it is less of a social requirement (particularly in mate selection) for girls to be intelligent, so they invest less in education and skill development. Females are less emotionally stable than males and thus anxiety impedes their test performance. So any differences that emerge do not reflect underlying reality.

- There are real differences between the sexes, with males having a four- to eight-point IQ advantage, which becomes noticeable after the age of 15. Before adolescence, females in fact have an advantage. The difference between the sexes is greatest for spatial intelligence. The difference is reflected in the brain size difference (corrected for body size) between men and women. Further this 'real' difference 'explains' male superiority in arts, business, education and science.

Glenn Wilson (1989) has shown that boys overall express more self-confidence in sport and mathematics, while girls do so in reading and music. Boys say any failure they experience is down to lack of effort, while often girls put their own failures down to lack of ability.

Girls show more concern for the feelings of others and are generally better at *mind-reading*. In a study of six-year-olds listening to the recorded sounds of a crying baby, girls expressed more sympathy and boys were twice as likely to turn the speaker off. Boys are more affected by bereavement, separation, maternal depression, etc. but are inclined to deny feelings of loss or sorrow.

There are those now who say that sex difference in intelligence is important and real. They tend to opt for five arguments:

- Similar differences observed across time, culture and species (hence unlikely to be learnt).

- Specific differences are predictable on the basis of evolutionary specialization (hunter/warrior vs. gatherer/nurse/educator).

- Brain differences are established by prenatal sex hormones; later on, hormones affect ability profiles (e.g. spatial suppressed by oestrogen, HRT maintains verbal memory).

- Sex-typed activity appears before gender-role awareness. At age two, girls speak better; boys are better at construction tasks. This is not learnt.

- Environmental affects (e.g. expectations, experience training) are minimal. They may exaggerate (or perhaps reduce) differences.

Does Environmental Enrichment Make a Difference?

Studies have indicated that young children from poor families typically receive less intellectual stimulation than do children from wealthier homes (Arnold *et al.*, 2008). They have, on average, far fewer books and educational toys, for example, and their parents read to them less. Only half of preschoolers from families on social welfare have alphabet books, compared with 97% of children from wealthy homes (Mason *et al.*, 1990; McCormick & Mason, 1986). It appears that their early environmental limitations may place poor children at a severe disadvantage when it comes to developing intellectual and academic skills.

We can see this problem particularly clearly in institutional settings, such as orphanages, and in foster homes. (Beckett *et al.*, 2010; Nelson *et al.*, 2009; Nelson, 2007). During the early 1980s, psychologist McVicker Hunt (1982) conducted work in a poor Iranian orphanage. In an effort to improve the lives of children in the orphanage and, in turn, improve their development, he offered a programme of 'tutored human enrichment'. He found that such early interventions did indeed help improve the cognitive functioning of the children. In other work, however, he clarified that early instruction of this kind helps to improve the intellectual capacities only of children who have been living in deprived environments, not of those who have already been living in enriched environments.

Based on findings such as McVicker Hunt's, *Project Head Start*, a US state-funded preschool programme, was launched in 1965. The programme, which has served more than 22 million disadvantaged children since its inception and now serves around one million each year, aims to enhance children's performances in school and beyond by helping to develop their cognitive and social skills as early as possible (USDHHS, 2011; Olsen & DeBoise, 2007; Ripple *et al.*, 1999). The programme continues to enjoy significant community and political support.

Does Head Start work? The results for many were rather disappointing: the effect was not as great as had been hoped, nor did it last for very long. Researchers have assessed its success by comparing children who have enrolled in the programme with same-aged counterparts who have not. Studies indicate that programmes such as Head Start do indeed produce at least *short-term* cognitive gains among disadvantaged children (USDHHS, 2011). Two past investigations found, for example, that children who participated in early childhood educational programmes were, by mid-adolescence, more than a year ahead of a matched control group of children who had not been in the programmes (Zigler & Berman, 1983; Lazar & Darlington, 1982). The early education participants also scored higher on various tests of scholastic achievement. Subsequent studies typically told a similar story (Sassi, 2011).

Head Start and similar programmes also appear to increase children's readiness for school, thus reducing the need for children to repeat years or to be placed in special-education classes. Although some research suggests that the IQ changes and academic benefits resulting from these early education programmes diminish over time, other studies indicate that, at the very least, the programmes enhance emotional intelligence, instil a more positive attitude towards learning, reduce school dropouts and even decrease later criminality (USDHHS, 2011; Siegler, 2003).

PSYCHOLOGY AROUND US   Is There Really a Mozart Effect?

For the past 20 years, a notion has been floating around that listening to the music of Mozart will significantly increase a person's intelligence. In addition, the earlier in life one is exposed to such music, the greater the intellectual impact is expected to be. The phenomenon is called the *Mozart effect*, and it has spurred many parents to surround their young children with such music. In some families, the composer's music is even introduced during the prenatal months.

The idea of a Mozart effect is exciting and even inspiring. But there is one small problem. It has no basis in fact (Pietschnig *et al.*, 2010). So where did the notion come from?

Back in 1993, a research team investigated whether performances by participants on a test of abstract spatial reasoning could be influenced by listening to classical music (Rauscher *et al.*, 1993). The participants were administered three different spatial tests: one after listening to a sonata by Mozart, another after listening to repetitive relaxation music and a third after sitting in silence. The researchers found that the spatial test scores of the participants rose by nine points after they had listened to Mozart. Almost immediately, exciting

reports about the Mozart phenomenon spread throughout the world.

It is critical to note that the effect of this music on the participants' performances was temporary – 15 minutes at most. Moreover, there was no effect on any other kind of intellectual task or on general intelligence. But such details were lost as the findings worked their way into the media. Hundreds of news stories and, later, books proclaimed the *permanent* impact of classical music, and particularly Mozart's music, on *general learning* and on *general intelligence*.

During the first decade of this century, many studies have been conducted on the relationship between music and cognitive functioning (Pietschnig *et al.*, 2010). The findings have been mixed, although some suggest that music, perhaps by its effects on mood and on arousal, can sometimes have temporary and modest effects on certain kinds of cognitive performances (Thompson *et al.*, 2001). But none of these studies has even come close to suggesting that classical music – by Mozart or anyone else – actually makes you smarter. Nevertheless, in the world of pop culture, this particular beat goes on.

Early intervention programmes can extend beyond school settings. They can include going into the homes of young children; working with their parents; adding stimulating toys, books and tools to the home; and otherwise enriching the home and community environments. It appears that such home-bound programmes often help increase children's cognitive achievements. One extensive research project has clarified that enrichment-intervention programmes of various kinds achieve greater success when they:

- begin earlier in life and continue

- are more intensive (more hours per day and more days per year)

- include programmes for maintaining positive attitudes and behaviours (Pungello *et al.*, 2010; Ramey & Ramey, 2007).

Short-term, superficial programmes appear to have little effect.

Before You Go On

What Do You Know?

11. What are the main arguments of *The Bell Curve*?

12. About what percentage of intelligence is thought to be genetically determined, and what evidence supports this?

13. What types of environmental factors have been shown to affect intelligence?

What Do You Think?

Considering the material you have read about test construction, heritability and cultural differences, what type of learning environment would maximize the intelligence of all individuals?

The Brain and Intelligence

WHAT HAPPENS IN THE BRAIN?

LEARNING OBJECTIVE 5
Describe how brain size, number of neurons, processing speed, brain activity and cortical thickness relate to intelligence.

So far in this chapter, we have explored several important questions concerning the nature, measurement and sources of intelligence. We now add another question: what brain differences underlie intelligence and thinking processes? Have researchers, for example, detected relationships between specific brain activities or specific brain structures and intelligence? To answer this question, let's look at four areas of investigation: brain size, brain speed, brain activity and cortical thickness.

Brain Size, Number of Neurons and Intelligence

Researchers have been exploring correlations between brain size and intelligence since the mid-19th century (Rushton, 2009; Ash & Gallup, 2008; Galton, 1948). Rushton (2009) claimed, for instance, that head size (which is easy to measure) is related to brain size, which is in turn related to intelligence.

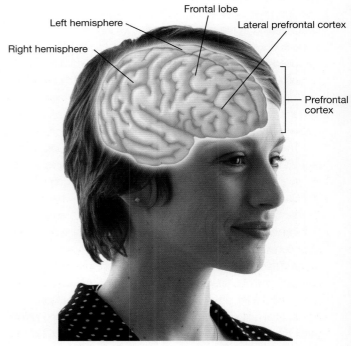

Source: Masterfile.

Initially, limitations in technology hampered meaningful outcomes. For example, researchers could only study the brains of corpses, which certainly make testing their intelligence impossible. Today's neuroimaging technologies, however, allow scientists to measure brain size and brain activity in living people.

Some neuroimaging findings over the past few decades have indeed suggested a possible correlation between brain size and mental functioning, but most studies of this issue fail to support this notion (Choi *et al.*, 2008; Vernon *et al.*, 2000; Vernon, 1990). As we noted in Chapter 5, the overall size of the brain appears to be more closely related to the size of the body than to intelligence. The main exception to this is people with extremely small or extremely large brains, each of whom are more likely to exhibit mental deficiencies than are people whose brain sizes fall within the normal range.

PSYCHOLOGY AROUND US   **When Smaller Is Better**

Sherlock Holmes once deduced the intelligence of a man by trying on his hat: '[The hat] came right over the forehead and settled upon the bridge of his nose. "It is a question of cubic capacity," said [Holmes]; "a man with so large a brain must have something in it."' As it turns out, however, human brains have shrunk over the past 30,000 years, not because we are getting dumber (fans of the movie *Idiocracy* should quiet down now), but because our brains are becoming more efficient.

Another potential reason for our shrinking brains is that our bodies are smaller than they once were. When you are more compact, you do not need as much brain space to regulate your movement and involuntary activities.

And there may be yet one more reason for the downward trend in brain size: *crowdsourcing*. Greater decreases in brain size appear to be correlated with increased population density. Some scientists believe that an individual brain does not need to be as big because people can rely on each other to help solve problems of living. In effect, we become part of a social network and approach problems as a unit, so more of our brain becomes devoted to social organizations rather than to holding onto the instincts that we once needed to survive.

Regardless of brain size, does the total number of neurons in a brain predict intellectual functioning? Apparently not. After all, there are, on average, 16% more neurons in male brains than female brains, but most research has found no systematic overall difference in IQ scores between men and women. On the other hand, intelligence may be related to the number of neurons in *particular* brain regions. Studies have suggested, for example, that general intelligence may be tied to the number of neurons in the brain's frontal lobes (Gläscher *et al.*, 2010; Tang *et al.*, 2010; Tranel *et al.*, 2008). All other things being equal, people with more such neurons seem to perform better on intelligence tests.

Brain Speed and Intelligence

Researchers often analyse the bioelectrical activity of the brain by using an *electroencephalogram (EEG)*, a device that places sensors on the outside of an individual's head and records his or her *brain waves*. EEG research has allowed investigators to see whether intelligence is correlated with brain speed – the speed with which the brain responds successfully to various stimuli, tasks and events (Sternberg, 2003; Deary & Stough, 1996).

One procedure, for example, involves the speed at which people process stimuli that are flashed before their eyes. In a typical study, the experimenter briefly flashes an incomplete stimulus on one side of a screen, then quickly flashes a more complete stimulus on the other side. Viewers are asked to indicate which side the complete image appeared

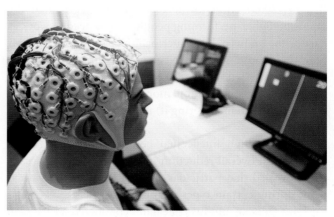

Speedier brains? People who score higher on intelligence tests tend to perceive correct images more quickly, as indicated by EEG readings.
Source: John MacDougall/AFP/Getty Images, Inc.

on. It typically takes only a fraction of a second for anybody to correctly answer this question. Still, some people are quicker than others, and those who perceive the correct image more quickly (as indicated by their EEG readings) tend to score higher on intelligence tests (especially on perceptual tasks) than those whose reactions are a bit slower. In short, people who are more intelligent may be physiologically wired to acquire and utilize information more quickly and efficiently than others.

In a related line of research, several investigators have found significant correlations between IQ scores and **nerve conduction velocity (NCV)**, the speed with which electrical impulses are transmitted along nerve fibres and across synapses (Sternberg, 2003; Reed & Jensen, 1992). Both the NCV and EEG findings fit well with studies showing that highly intelligent people are, on average, able to make decisions more quickly than less intelligent people are (Demaree *et al.*, 2010; Tulsky & O'Brien, 2008).

nerve conduction velocity (NCV) the speed with which electrical impulses are transmitted along nerve fibres and across synapses.

Brain Activity and Intelligence

Another biological approach to the study of intelligence examines how active people's brains are when solving intellectual problems. A *positron emission tomography (PET)* scan is a type of neuroimaging technology that can reveal where and how actively the brain is metabolizing, or breaking down, glucose at any given moment. Very active areas of the brain show up as red and orange on a PET scan's colour-coded pictures, while less active areas show up as green and blue. PET scans have generally revealed lower activity in the brains of people who are performing well on an intellectual task and higher activity in the brains of those who are performing poorly (Posner *et al.*, 2009, 2002; Raichle, 2005). Thus, some researchers suggest that the brains of higher-performing people do not need to work as hard as the brains of lower-performing people; that is, their brains are more efficient (Neubauer & Fink, 2010, 2003; Grabner *et al.*, 2003). The idea of smart (clever, bright) people processing information more efficiently (faster, more accurately and remembering it) underlies many theories of intelligence.

Although high intellectual performance seems to be related to an overall reduction in brain activity, PET scans have revealed that particular areas of brain activity are at work during certain types of intellectual tasks. Investigator John Duncan and his colleagues conducted a PET scan on 13 men and women while they were taking an intelligence test (Duncan, 2001; Duncan *et al.*, 2000). They found that for each individual the brain activity during the test

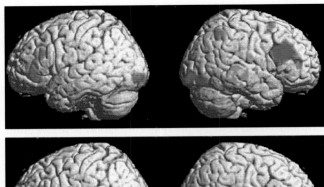
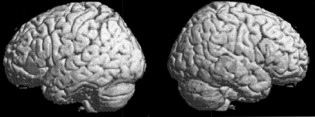

The prefrontal cortex and performance on intelligence tests. The study by John Duncan and his colleagues (2000) found that the left lateral prefrontal cortex is active during the performance of a range of cognitive tasks. These PET scans from the study reveal that the left and right lateral prefrontal cortices are both active during verbal special tasks (top row), while activity during verbal tasks tends to centre in the left lateral prefrontal cortex (bottom row).

Source: Brain scans from J. Duncan *et al.* A Neural Basis for General Intelligence, *Science,* 289(5478): 457–460, July 21, 2000, parts a and b. Reproduced by permission of The American Association for the Advancement of Science.

was concentrated in the left lateral prefrontal cortex and the right lateral prefrontal cortex – brain regions located towards the front and outer sides of the brain's two hemispheres. When a test-taker was performing verbal tasks on the test, the *left* lateral prefrontal cortex was activated (remember from Chapters 5 and 11 that language is processed predominantly in the left hemisphere of the brain). During spatial tasks, both the left lateral prefrontal cortex and the right lateral prefrontal cortex were activated. It is worth noting that the prefrontal cortex, which sends and receives information to and from numerous other brain sites, may help people keep track of several thoughts at the same time, solve problems, produce new ideas and filter out unimportant information.

The rapid development of technology in this area has given great impetus to this research.

While such studies are interesting, we must keep in mind that they do not clarify the causal relationships at work. For example, do people of higher intelligence display less brain activity overall, despite experiencing more activity in the prefrontal cortex, because they are smart, or are people smart because their brain activity is more efficient? Or are both brain activity and intelligence related to yet a third causal factor that researchers have yet to discover?

Cortical Thickness and Intelligence

HOW WE DEVELOP

We have seen that various brain features, such as the number of neurons, brain speed and brain activity, may be tied to intelligence. A related issue is whether *brain development* is related to the development of intelligence. A highly publicized study by researcher Philip Shaw and his colleagues sought to answer this question (Shaw *et al.*, 2008, 2006).

In a longitudinal study, the Shaw team performed brain scans on 309 children and teenagers between the ages of six and 19, with each participant scanned every two years. The scans revealed that throughout childhood and adolescence, individuals display changes in the thickness of the *cortex* – the folded outer layer of the brain. Such changes in thickness may well have implications for the development of intelligence (Karama *et al.*, 2011).

The study found that children begin with a thin cortex, which thickens over the years and then begins to thin down and continues thinning through adolescence. These changes in thickness are consistent with what is known about neural pruning during development. As we observed in Chapters 3 and 5, the brains of very young children produce a large number of neural synapses and neurons. Then, as the children grow older, their brains prune down the neural connections that are not being used and perhaps reduce the actual number of neurons as well, leaving the individuals with a much lower number of connections and, perhaps, neurons in their teenage and adult years. It is believed that a thick cortex may reflect a higher number of neural connections and neurons, whereas a thin cortex may reflect a lower number; so as adolescence approaches and pruning occurs, the cortex becomes thinner.

The study further found this pattern of changes in cortical thickness to be clearest in the prefrontal regions, the brain areas whose activity has been tied closely to intellectual activity. Thus, it appears that the development of intelligence may involve a process of synaptic and neural growth and then pruning, particularly in the prefrontal cortex – a process that is reflected by changes in cortical thickness throughout childhood and adolescence.

Beyond this general picture, Shaw and his colleagues (2008, 2006) found that the participants who were most intelligent showed a pattern of cortical thickening and thinning that was different from the pattern shown by participants with lower intelligence. That is, the highly intelligent individuals began with a rather thin cortex during early childhood, and the cortex gradually thickened until the age of 11 or 12, at which time thinning began and continued into the late teenage years. In contrast, the participants with lower intelligence began with a somewhat thicker cortex, which then further thickened until the age of eight, at which time the thinning began. Assuming that all of this reflects growth and pruning of synapses and perhaps of neurons as well, particularly in the prefrontal cortex, it may be that the processes of growth and pruning unfold over a much longer developmental span in highly intelligent people than they do in less intelligent individuals, perhaps because more complex and sophisticated neural circuits are being constructed.

Are such brain changes over the course of childhood and adolescence genetically predetermined? Once again, the answer is 'not necessarily'. We observed in Chapters 3 and 5 that the formation and pruning of neural networks are closely tied to interactions with the environment. Moreover, earlier in this chapter, we observed that enriching the environments of deprived young children often increases their intellectual performances. It could be that people with particularly high intelligence tend to be raised in rich social and learning environments and that this kind of environmental stimulation contributes heavily to the pattern of cortical thickness change that such individuals displayed in the study by Shaw and his colleagues.

Before You Go On

What Do You Know?

14. How are brain size and number of neurons related to intelligence?

15. How do researchers measure the speed of information processing in the brain?

16. Is efficient processing linked to relatively lower or relatively higher activity in the brain?

17. What is the role of cortical thickness in the development of intelligence?

What Do You Think?

Can you think of any other ways to explain why the brains of people who are performing better on intelligence tests are often less active than those of people who are doing poorly?

Extremes in Intelligence

LEARNING OBJECTIVE 6
Discuss intellectual disability and giftedness.

Earlier in the chapter, we mentioned that intelligence, as measured by IQ tests, follows a normal distribution; that is, a distribution shaped like a bell curve. At both ends of this curve are a small number of people who score either much lower or much higher than the people who make up the large middle. At the lower end are people who are diagnosed with intellectual disability, and at the higher end are those who are intellectually gifted (Figure 12.10).

Intellectual Disability

Most individuals demonstrate sufficient levels of intelligence to survive on their own and to succeed quite well. But the intellectual and adaptive functioning of some people is well below that of most other people. These individuals are said to display **intel-**

intellectual disability
a term describing individuals who have poor adaptive behaviour and display general intellectual functioning that is well below average.

lectual disability, a combination of general intellectual functioning that is well below average and poor adaptive behaviour. That is, in addition to having an IQ score of 70 or below, the individuals experience great difficulty in areas such as communication, home living, self-direction, work and safety.

Certainly then, diagnoses of intellectual disability based on such tests can be subject to error (Tomes, 2010;

Toth & King, 2010). Thus, to properly diagnose intellectual disability, mental health professionals must observe the functioning of an individual in his or her everyday environment, taking both the person's background and the community's standards into account.

The most consistent sign of intellectual disability is very slow learning (Toth & King, 2010; Hodapp & Dykens, 2003). Other areas of difficulty include attention, short-term memory, planning and language development (Edgin et al., 2010). These difficulties vary, of course, according to the level of disability.

The American Psychiatric Association (APA, 2000) describes four levels of 'mental retardation' (intellectual disability): mild (IQ 50–70), moderate (IQ 35–49), severe (IQ 20–34) and profound (IQ below 20).

Mild Intellectual Disability Around 85% of all people with intellectual disability fall into this category (Dusseljee et al., 2011; Harris, 2010; APA, 2000). Mild intellectual disability is not usually recognized until children enter school and take intelligence tests. These individuals have reasonable language, social and play skills, but they need assistance when under stress – a limitation that becomes increasingly apparent as academic and social demands increase. Often, the intellectual performance of individuals with mild intellectual disability improves with age; some even stop meeting the criteria for the label after they leave school (Toth & King, 2010; Sturmey, 2008). Their jobs tend to be unskilled or semiskilled.

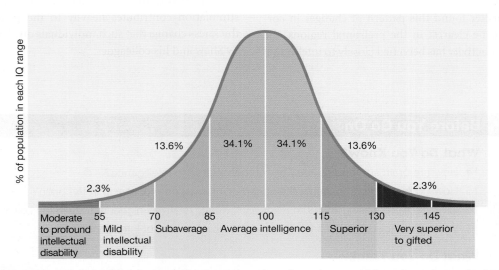

FIGURE 12.10 Extreme scores in intelligence. A small but equal number of people score at the extreme low and extreme high end of the IQ range.

Severe mental disability and special needs. A seven-year-old lies by his teacher at a training centre in China for children with disorders such as severe mental disability, autism and cerebral palsy.

Source: Liu Jin/AFP/Getty Images, Inc.

Research has linked mild intellectual disability mainly to the home environment, particularly early, poor and unstimulating environments, inadequate parent–child interactions and insufficient learning experiences during a child's early years (Martin, 2010; Sturmey, 2008). In addition, studies suggest that a mother's moderate drinking, drug use or malnutrition during pregnancy may lower her child's intellectual potential (Hart *et al.*, 2010; Stein *et al.*, 1972).

Moderate, Severe and Profound Intellectual Disability Although mild intellectual disability is considered a variation in human functioning by many psychologists, the other levels of intellectual disability – moderate, severe and profound – are viewed by most as disorders. Moreover, whereas the primary factors in mild intellectual disability seem to be related to the home environment, moderate, severe and profound levels of intellectual disability are caused largely by factors such as genetically based chromosomal and metabolic abnormalities, significant prenatal alcohol or drug use by mothers, prenatal maternal infections such as rubella and syphilis, complications during or after delivery and injuries and severe infections during early childhood (Martin, 2010; Sturmey, 2008).

In fact, severe and profound levels of intellectual disability often appear as part of larger syndromes that include severe physical disabilities. The physical problems are often even more limiting than the individual's low intellectual functioning and in some cases can be fatal. Given such causes, moderate, severe and profound levels of intellectual disability are typically viewed as neurological disorders.

Around 10% of people with intellectual disability receive a label of *moderate* intellectual disability. They receive their diagnosis early in life, typically demonstrating clear deficits in language development and play during their preschool years. By middle school, significant delays in the acquisition of reading and number skills and deficits in adaptive skills become apparent. By adulthood, however, many individuals with moderate intellectual disability are able to communicate and care for themselves adequately, benefit from vocational training and work in unskilled or semiskilled jobs. Most of these individuals also function well in the community if they have some degree of supervision (Trembath *et al.*, 2010; APA, 2000).

Many people with moderate intellectual disability have **Down syndrome**, the most common of the chromosomal disorders leading to intellectual disability (Hazlett *et al.*, 2011). Less than one out of every 1,000 live births results in Down syndrome, but this rate increases greatly when the mother's age is over 35. The syndrome usually is caused by the presence of extra chromosomal material on the 21st chromosome. The additional material disturbs normal development, resulting in characteristic features such as a small head, flat face, slanted eyes, high cheekbones and reduced intellectual functioning. Most individuals with Down syndrome are very affectionate people. More generally, they display the same range of personality characteristics as people in the general population.

> **Down syndrome** an inherited disorder, usually caused by the presence of extra chromosomal material on the 21st chromosome, that results in intellectual disability.

Approximately 3.5% of people with intellectual disability meet the criteria for *severe* intellectual disability. They typically demonstrate basic motor and communication deficits during infancy. Many have an increased vulnerability to brain seizure disorder. They usually require careful supervision, may profit from vocational training to some degree and can often perform only basic work tasks in structured and sheltered settings. Most are able to function well in the community if they live in group homes, in community nursing homes or with their families (Cain *et al.*, 2010; APA, 2000).

Around 1.5% of people with intellectual disability receive a diagnosis of *profound* intellectual disability. Their limitations are very noticeable at birth or early infancy. With training, the individuals may develop or improve basic skills such as walking, some talking and feeding themselves. They require a very structured environment, with close supervision and considerable help, including a close relationship with a caregiver, in order to develop adequately (Cain *et al.*, 2010; Sturmey, 2008; APA, 2000).

Giftedness

OUT OF THE ORDINARY

Psychologists do not agree on how to define *giftedness* (Sternberg *et al.*, 2011). Some use IQ tests as the sole criterion, defining the top 1 or 2% of the tested population as gifted. Lewis Terman, introduced earlier in this chapter, identified gifted people as those with IQ scores of above 140, and in a famous longitudinal study he followed a group of gifted research participants over the course of their lifetime (Simonton, 2010; Leslie, 2000; Terman, 1925).

Other researchers and educators have added criteria such as school success or career achievement to IQ scores when defining giftedness. Indeed, many of the participants in Terman's study, who became known as the *Termites*, achieved extraordinary success as scientists, scholars, businesspeople and professionals.

Other definitions of intelligence have led to still other definitions of giftedness. Howard Gardner, whom we also discussed earlier in the chapter, suggests that people can be gifted with high intelligence in any one of the multiple intelligences he has identified. He would consider a highly talented athlete or musician to be as gifted as a mathematical or verbal genius.

Some researchers use the words *genius* or *eminence* to describe gifted people, and many have attempted to look for common characteristics among gifted people (Sternberg *et al.*, 2011), such as:

- *Environment can contribute to giftedness.* Many gifted people are raised in nurturing and stimulating environments. Terman's Termites, for example, were typically members of upper-socioeconomic families, and they received many years of education. It is worth noting that, contrary to stereotype, most gifted children are not pushed by demanding parents. Families do, however, tend to centre much attention on such children. Typically, the parents first recognize the budding giftedness of their children and then support it by providing high-level intellectual or artistic stimulation. Parents of gifted children also tend to have higher expectations of themselves, model hard work for their children and grant the children high degrees of independence.

- *Gifted people are often intrinsically motivated.* It appears that children who are gifted at the piano, violin, chess, bridge, athletics and the like typically experience a deep, intrinsic motivation to master such domains and subject themselves to many hours of deliberate practice. Perhaps the high motivation of these children drives them and sustains their practice efforts. However, research has failed to show that gifted abilities necessarily precede extensive practice. Does this mean that a person of average intelligence and above-average motivation can readily become a concert pianist or astrophysicist? No. Other research indicates that hard work, intensive training, perseverance and practice alone rarely lead to giftedness. In short, motivation and hard work seem to be necessary but not sufficient requirements for the development of giftedness.

- *Some people gifted in academic or other forms of intelligence may not be equally gifted with social and emotional intelligence.* Some psychologists have observed that gifted children often display disproportionate social and emotional difficulties, especially during adolescence. Many are socially isolated and introverted. In fact, a number of academically gifted children try to hide their giftedness in an attempt to fit in with others. Girls seem more likely than boys to do this.

Before You Go On

What Do You Know?

18. What are the four levels of intellectual disability, and which is most common?

19. What are some causes of intellectual disability?

20. Is high IQ the only criterion for giftedness?

What Do You Think?

How might environment produce the effect of intellectual disability? Do you think this effect could be reversed? If so, how? If not, why?

Access your interactive e-book to view a video clip for this chapter at **www.wileyopenpage.com**

Summary

What Do We Mean by Intelligence?

LEARNING OBJECTIVE 1 Describe various ways in which intelligence has been defined and summarize the current thinking on whether intelligence is general or specific.

- Scholars early in the 20th century defined intelligence as the ability to learn and to meet the demands of the environment effectively. Later, other scholars added to this definition the ability to understand and control one's mental activities, called meta-cognition (see Chapter 11).

- A central issue in defining intelligence is whether it is a single, general factor or a cluster of different abilities. Charles Spearman hypothesized that a general factor, or *g* factor, underlies all mental abilities, while Lewis Thurstone argued that intelligence is made up of seven distinct primary mental abilities.

- Although most theorists today agree that intelligence does include a *g* factor, modern theorists such as Howard Gardner, Robert Sternberg and Stephen Ceci have tended to de-emphasize the *g* factor and focus on specific abilities, or *s* factors.

Additional Types of Intelligence

LEARNING OBJECTIVE 2 Discuss several proposed types of intelligence that go beyond intellectual functioning.

- Other theorists have broadened the definition of intelligence further to include emotional intelligence, social intelligence, wisdom, creativity and personality.

How Do We Measure Intelligence?

LEARNING OBJECTIVE 3 Identify important consider-ations in the construction of intelligence tests, discuss the history of intelligence testing and describe some criticisms of intelligence tests.

- The psychometric approach to studying intelligence attempts to measure intelligence with carefully con-structed psychological tests.

- To ensure that intelligence tests are grounded in sound scientific principles, psychologists design tests that adhere to three basic criteria: standardization, reliability and validity.

- Early pioneers of intelligence testing include Francis Galton, who proposed the theory of psychophysical performance, and Francis Binet, who developed a test to predict children's success in school.

- Adapting Binet's work for use in the United States, Lewis Terman constructed the Stanford–Binet Intelligence Test and devised the intelligence quotient (IQ).

- David Wechsler broadened the usefulness of intel-ligence testing by developing the Wechsler Adult Intelligence Scale (WAIS), along with several other tests.

- Both the Stanford–Binet and the WAIS have high degrees of reliability. Performance on intelligence tests also correlates highly with school performance and to some degree with other areas of functioning in life, such as occupational achievements.

- Although widely used, intelligence tests are subject to several criticisms. One issue involves the culture-specific nature of the tests, which may produce bias. A related problem is stereotype threat.

- Intelligence test scores from around the world have increased over time, a phenomenon known as the Flynn effect. Possible explanations include potential problems with the procedures, content or nature of the tests and improvements in education, nutrition, health or environments.

Is Intelligence Governed by Genetic or Environmental Factors?

LEARNING OBJECTIVE 4 Review the contributions of heredity and environment to intelligence, and explain how emphasizing one factor or the other can affect social policy.

- The nature/nurture debate as applied to intelligence has important social implications, exemplified by the contro-versial book *The Bell Curve*, whose authors argue that group differences in IQ are likely due at least in part to genetic factors.

- Family studies and research in molecular biology have indicated that heredity does play a major role in intelligence. Researchers estimate that the heritability of intelligence is about 50%.
- Environmental factors that affect intelligence include family and home, overall culture, occupation and schooling.
- Group differences in IQ scores enable us only to make distinctions between groups, not to reach any conclusions about an individual within a group.
- Studies have confirmed that environmental enrichment for members of disadvantaged groups is effective in producing at least short-term cognitive gains.

The Brain and Intelligence

LEARNING OBJECTIVE 5   Describe how brain size, processing speed, brain activity and cortical thickness relate to intelligence.

- Neuroimaging studies suggest that overall brain size is not correlated with intelligence. The number of neurons in certain brain regions, such as the frontal lobes, may be related to intellectual functioning.
- The speed with which the brain responds to stimuli, which can be measured by means of EEGs and nerve conduction velocity (NCV), also correlates with intelligence.
- PET scans, which show what areas of the brain are active at a particular moment, have generally revealed lower activity in the brains of people performing well on an intellectual task and higher activity in the brains of people performing poorly, suggesting that the brains of the higher performers may be more efficient.
- It appears that the development of intelligence involves a process of neuron growth and then neuron pruning, particularly in the prefrontal cortex – a process that is reflected by a distinct pattern of change in cortical thickness throughout childhood and adolescence.

Extremes in Intelligence

LEARNING OBJECTIVE 6   Discuss intellectual disability and giftedness.

- The two extremes of intelligence, as measured by IQ tests, are represented by intellectual disability and giftedness.
- Intellectual disability is classified as mild (IQ 50–70), moderate (IQ 35–49), severe (IQ 20–34) and profound (IQ below 20).
- Home environmental causes of intellectual disability include poor and unstimulating environments and inadequate parent–child interactions. These causes have been associated in particular with mild intellectual disability, though they may also be at work in more severe cases.
- Other causes of intellectual disability include genetically based chromosomal abnormalities, certain prenatal conditions in the mother, complications at delivery and injuries and infections during early childhood. These causes have been associated in particular with moderate to profound levels of intellectual disability.
- Down syndrome is a genetic abnormality resulting in intellectual disability.
- Psychologists do not agree on how to define giftedness but often identify gifted people as having IQs at the top 1 or 2% of the tested population.
- Environment can contribute to giftedness, and gifted people are often highly motivated. However, academically gifted people may not be equally gifted with social and emotional intelligence.

ACTIVITY

Activities to test yourself further are available in your interactive e-book at
www.wileyopenpage.com

TYING IT TOGETHER

WHAT HAPPENS IN THE BRAIN?

- A larger number of neurons in particular brain areas, such as the frontal lobes, may be associated with higher intellectual functioning.

- How fast the brain responds to stimuli also correlates with intelligence. It may be that some people are wired to acquire information more quickly than others are.

- PET scans have shown that the brains of people performing well on an intellectual task are less active than those of people performing poorly: that is, the brains of the high-performing people may not need to work as hard.

HOW WE DIFFER

- Intelligence, as measured by IQ tests, follows a distribution shaped like a bell curve. At one end of this curve are those diagnosed with intellectual disability and at the other are those considered intellectually gifted.

- Intellectual disability involves a combination of lower general intellectual functioning and poorer adaptive behaviour. The most consistent sign of intellectual disability is very slow learning.

- Mild intellectual disability, the most common kind, is linked primarily to home environmental causes, such as poor and unstimulating environments during early life.

- Often, intellectual giftedness is defined only in terms of IQ scores and does not take other forms of intelligence into account. Thus, an intellectually gifted person may be quite low in emotional or social intelligence.

OUT OF THE ORDINARY

- Most psychologists view moderate, severe and profound levels of intellectual disability as mental disorders.

- Biological factors are primarily responsible for moderate, severe and profound intellectual disability. Severe and profound intellectual disability often are part of larger syndromes that include severe physical disabilities.

- Although children with moderate intellectual disability display significant delays in school, special education programmes can help them to succeed in many areas. By adulthood, they can generally function well at work and in the community with support.

HOW WE DEVELOP

- As noted in Chapter 3, children's brains actually lose neurons and synapses as the children grow into adolescence. This developmental process is reflected in a thinning of the cortex.

- The developmental pattern of cortical thickening and thinning is different in more intelligent children than in less intelligent children. In highly intelligent children, the process takes longer.

- These brain changes may be the result of environmental interactions, genetic factors or both. Indeed, we know that enriching the environment of deprived children can improve their intellectual performance.

Quizzes to test yourself further are available in your interactive e-book at
www.wileyopenpage.com

Key Terms

bioecological model of
  intelligence 343
content validity 350
creativity 346
Down syndrome 369
emotional intelligence 345
factor analysis 339
Flynn effect 354
g factor 339

heritability 357
heritability coefficient 357
intellectual disability 368
intelligence 338
intelligence quotient (IQ) 351
mean 349
median 349
mental age 351
mode 349

nerve conduction velocity
  (NCV) 366
normal distribution 349
primary mental abilities 340
psychometric approach 348
reliability 349
s factor 339
standardization 349
stereotype threat 354

theory of multiple
  intelligences 340
triarchic theory of
  intelligence 342
validity 349
validity coefficient 350

Flashcards to test yourself further are available in your interactive e-book at
www.wileyopenpage.com

CHAPTER 13

Motivation

Adapted by Adrian Furnham, University College London, UK

CHAPTER OUTLINE

- Theories of Motivation
- Biological Motivations: Hunger
- Biological Motivations: Sex
- Psychological Motivations: Affiliation and Achievement

 Access your interactive e-book to view a video clip for this chapter at **www.wileyopenpage.com**

Hot Dogging: A Different Kind of Competition

Takeru Kobayashi is renowned throughout the world for eating hot dogs. The young Japanese man has repeatedly broken the world record, regularly consuming over 50 hot dogs in a single sitting, sometimes in as little as 12 minutes. Kobayashi reportedly suffers from arthritis of the jaw, related to incorrectly aligned wisdom teeth and years of competitive eating (he also holds the record for eating the most cow brains). He cannot open or close his mouth without pain. Nonetheless, he has been determined to continue his career in competitive hot dog eating.

In one recent year, Kobayashi's record was broken by an American competitor, Joey Chestnut. Kobayashi was determined to take back his crown. A month later, the two met. Kobayashi, reportedly in great pain, managed to eat 63 hot dogs in that contest. Unfortunately for him, Chestnut's personal best was 66. Kobayashi was unable to regain his title (Gilger, 2007). Despite his pain, Kobayashi remains determined to compete again (Hackworth, 2007). ■

Stories such as this make us wonder what motivates an individual to engage in such odd behaviour. Surely, no one eats that many hot dogs in one sitting because they are hungry? In fact, eating so much at one time is more likely to cause disgust and stomach pain than it is to produce a feeling of satisfaction. But the world famous *Guinness Book of World Records* is full of strange stories of human behaviour, from extreme endurance to people doing very odd things indeed. Is their only or main motivation fame? What sort of people endure pain, expense and years of practice to achieve these records? What motivates one person to extreme sports and another to extreme eating?

The topic of motivation is amongst the most interesting but also the most complex in psychology. We are very good and accurate at measuring things like personality and abilities but much less reliable at measuring motivation. Indeed, one of the problems for researchers is that people cannot, as opposed to will not, tell you what really motivates them. We are motivated by physiological needs for food and water. There is an increasingly sophisticated branch of neuropsychology that tries to understand these processes and why they sometimes go wrong, leading to addiction. We are also motivated to have sex and reproduce. We are motivated to be accepted by others and be respected for who we are. Sometimes we are motivated extrinsically by money and at other times to enjoy doing something for the sheer joy of the activity.

Inevitably, this most complicated of topics is amongst the most interesting in the whole of psychology.

motivation an internal state or condition that directs behaviour.

Psychologists define **motivation** as a condition that directs behaviour usually towards a goal. An individual experiences a motivational state that usually gives rise to a desire, an intention or a pressure to act.

motives one's needs or desires.

For any given circumstance, your behaviour is probably the consequence of a combination of several **motives**, your particular and specific needs or desires. Some motivations are sometimes related to the fulfilment of basic biological needs, but more often than not they are the result of complicated factors involving past experience and lifelong learning. Motivation also differs from person to person. Different students are more or less motivated to study, take part in extracurricular activities or earn extra money. But they tend to share the same physiological motivations for food, sleep and interpersonal activities.

We will see in this chapter that psychologists have developed a number of theories that attempt to explain how our motivation drives and guides our behaviour. Researchers have discovered a great deal about how the body and brain signals work to motivate us to fulfil some of our basic

Hot dogging. The driven former champion Takeru Kobayashi bites one of the many hot dogs that await him at the Nathan's Famous Fourth of July International Hot Dog Eating Contest.

Source: Mario Tama/Getty Images, Inc.

biological motives. We will look at how even common biological motives, such as hunger, can interact with our experiences and thoughts to lead to specific behaviours. We will discuss how these processes develop and what happens when things go wrong: when we become motivated to do things that are not in our best interests.

Theories of Motivation

LEARNING OBJECTIVE 1
Compare and contrast major theories of motivation.

Like all of us, psychologists are interested in explaining people's behaviour. There are several theories of motivation, each of which takes a different approach to explain what compels individuals to act as they do (Table 13.1). As we will see, however, no single theory has yet been able to provide a complete explanation for what motivates us to engage in our many different behaviours. Some psychologists have attempted to integrate many of these different theories, with varying degrees of success.

TABLE 13.1 Major Theories of Motivation

Theory	Approach
Instinct	Behaviour is motivated by instincts that are innate and which are activated by environmental stimuli
Drive-reduction	Motivation originates from biological needs to maintain the body in a state of balance or equilibrium
Arousal	Behaviour is motivated by the need to achieve optimum levels of arousal
Incentive	Behaviour is motivated by internal (intrinsic) or external (extrinsic) incentives or rewards
Hierarchy of needs	When different motives compete, basic survival needs must be satisfied first before we are motivated to satisfy higher-level needs, such as belonging and self-esteem

Instinct Theory

Instinct theory maintains that behaviours originate from a set of behavioural blueprints, or **instincts** (Fancher, 1996). Instinctive behaviours are innate and activated by particular environmental stimuli.

instincts innate behavioural tendencies, activated by stimuli in our environments.

Many of our own basic motives are *innate*, or inborn. Some of the most critical for survival, such as eating, are present at birth (Colson *et al.*, 2008).

Humans are also naturally motivated to form social contacts. As we saw in Chapter 7 babies are born with a well-developed sense of smell that lets them recognize the particular scent of their mothers (Porter & Winberg, 1999). We are also born with reflexes that allow us to engage in primitive social behaviour. The rooting reflex, discussed in Chapter 3, for example, involves turning the head and using the mouth to search for a nipple. Rooting not only helps a baby to eat but it also allows the infant to seek contact with other people. Combined with the ability to recognize their mothers by smell, rooting enables babies to start establishing close relationships with their mothers (Swain *et al.*, 2007). As the baby grows, new abilities emerge, such as smiling,

laughing, reaching arms out to be carried and talking. All of these further encourage the formation of social bonds, thus increasing the chance of survival (Messinger & Fogel, 2007; Broad *et al.*, 2006). As with eating, the nuances of this basic motivation change as we grow. For example, instead of seeking mother love, we seek romantic love. The motivation to be socially connected remains strong throughout life, however.

Although instinct theory can begin to explain some of our behaviour and much of animal behaviour, instincts do not account for all behaviour, even in relatively simple creatures, such as rats (Clark *et al.*, 2008). In fact, studies on learning and memory would be impossible to carry out on laboratory animals if all of their behaviour was innate.

Instinct theory has trouble explaining differences among individuals (Bevins, 2001). Among humans, for

Challenging a theory. This bungee jumper takes off from a bridge and begins a wild – and seemingly dangerous – free fall, challenging the instinct theory along the way.
Source: Denny Allen/Getty Images, Inc.

PSYCHOLOGY AROUND US | A Natural-Born Mother

A good example of instinctual motivation can be observed in the maternal behaviour of female rats. Virgin female rats typically ignore or avoid unfamiliar rat pups. In some instances, virgin females will even kill the pups. However, the same rat that reacted with indifference or violence when exposed to pups prior to giving birth will engage in a number of maternal behaviours once her own babies are born. She will build a nest and lick, groom, retrieve, huddle over and nurse her pups. These behaviours are not learnt by the animal, nor are there any external incentives for engaging in them. They occur automatically as a result of changes in hormone levels that coincide with delivering a litter of rat pups (Kinsley *et al.*, 2008).

example, some of us seek out experiences that others actively avoid or even find painful. Consider adventurers who have climbed Mount Everest, a gruelling and dangerous activity. Conversely, some individuals avoid experiences that others find rewarding and pleasurable. Catholic priests and nuns, for example, forgo marriage and biological parenthood to fulfil their obligations to their church. Clearly, these behaviours are not driven by instincts. We need other explanations to explain these more complex human motivations.

Drive-Reduction Theory

Drive-reduction theory also tries to explain motivation on the basis of internal biological factors. This theory is based

homeostasis a tendency of the body to maintain itself in a state of balance, or equilibrium.

on the concept of **homeostasis**, which is the body's tendency to maintain itself in a state of balance, or equilibrium (Figure 13.1). When an external factor alters the state of balance in the organism, a motivation arises to correct that balance (Stricker & Zigmond, 1986). A simple example of this can be seen in the response of the body to heat, which is called *thermoregulation*. When the temperature rises, your body perspires and you lose water. The perspiration evaporates and cools the surface of the skin, helping to maintain the temperature balance in the body. In addition, you may feel

motivated to remove layers of clothing or get a cool drink to return to an ideal body temperature.

Many of the major organs of the body (e.g. the liver and the kidneys) are designed to help maintain homeostasis by absorbing substances into the blood (like iron, sugar, fats) and disposing of wastes (like urea). When these organs fail, diseases like diabetes and problems like hypo/hyperglycaemia occur.

Most of us know the simple principle of energy balance. If we eat too much and exercise too little, we get fat; or eat too little and exercise too much we get (too) thin. Body weight is a function of the energy homeostatic system.

Drive-reduction theory works well to explain behaviours related to biological needs, such as cooling off when we are too hot. We engage in many behaviours, however, that do not appear to be motivated by a need to keep the body in a state of equilibrium (Schneider *et al.*, 2007). In fact, some human behaviour is designed to do just the opposite. Some people seek out adventurous situations that are designed to thrill and even terrorize for entertainment. Amusement park owners make millions every year providing an outlet for this sort of interest. It is difficult to explain the motivation to go on a very fast roller coaster using the drive-reduction theory because going on a roller coaster does nothing to restore the body to a state of equilibrium. In fact, the main purpose is to experience excitement by throwing riders suddenly *out* of a state of emotional equilibrium.

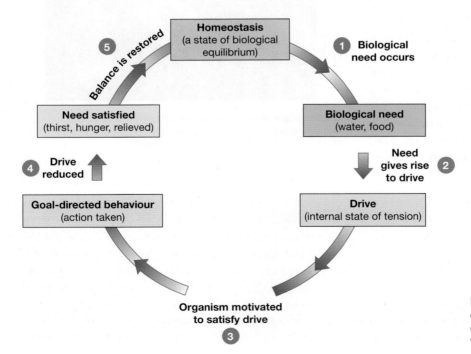

FIGURE 13.1 Drive-reduced theory. When external factors alter our body's normal state of equilibrium, we are motivated to behave in ways that restore the balance.

The Psychology of Pain and Pleasure There is still a debate as to whether pain and pleasure are at opposite ends of a continuum and whether we should accept a simple push–pull idea that people are simply motivated to avoid pain and seek out pleasure.

Researchers have explored parts of the brain that are chiefly associated with pleasure and reward. We have *hedonic hotspots* for various senses: sounds, sights, smells, sex and tastes. These are activated when we experience great pleasure. We know that there are neurochemical systems (opioid and dopamine) that regulate the relationship between pain and pleasure and can go wrong and are associated with addiction. Because we seek pleasure, we can soon discover everyday (alcohol, caffeine) as well as illegal (cocaine, marijuana) drugs that powerfully influence the neurochemistry of our bodies.

There are different theories that try to conceptualize the psychology of addiction.

Opponent-process theory This states that systems react and adapt to stimuli by opposing their initial effects. A desire, and then craving, for something that did not exist before any experience of the drug increases with exposure to it. People experience *affective pleasure* – a physical and emotional hedonic state that follows use or relaxation, or stress release, or just feelings of sudden energy. Then there is *affective tolerance*, which means that one needs more and more of the substance to have the same affect. Many experience *affective withdrawal*, which is what occurs if the drug is not taken.

So the drug causes a process that sets off an opposite reaction, which grows in strength with repeated exposure. This is *affective contrast*. With more use, the dominant reaction is negative. So one needs the drug to achieve a neutral state and little pleasure is derived from taking it.

Positive-reinforcement theory This idea suggests that drugs make one feel good, even euphoric. In the 1960s psychologists allowed monkeys to self-administer morphine and they showed all of the signs of addiction. They discovered drug reward pathways in the brain, particularly the brain regions and neurotransmitters that may be involved in so-called natural rewards, like food and sex, versus artificial stimulants, like drugs and electrical brain stimulation. We know that drugs like cocaine and amphetamine increase synaptic dopamine in the region called the *nucleus accumbens*. Other neurochemicals play a role, like endogenous opioids whose effects range from taste to stress. Many drugs give us real *highs* that we want to repeat.

Learning theories Drug-taking and the pleasures associated with it become associated with very specific situations, sights and sounds. Thus, people associate the drugs from alcohol to amphetamines with very specific situational reminders. Put people in particular settings and they will experience drug cravings. So pubs and clubs for alcoholics; the smell of smoke for nicotine addicts induces cravings. Cues that deliver impending drug delivery can induce strong desires which 'have to be' fulfilled. Indeed, perhaps the most exciting research at the moment is on the neurological aspects of motivation.

Arousal Theory

Arousal theory maintains that motivation comes from a need to achieve an appropriate level of arousal or stimulation (Jones, 2003). Unlike drive-reduction theory, in this particular theory the motivation does not always arise from a need to reduce arousal back to a neutral state like equilibrium. While some situations, such as hunger or thirst, can elevate our arousal to uncomfortable levels that we try to reduce (such as when we try to reduce our hunger through eating), arousal theory states that we can also be motivated to elevate our arousal levels if they fall too low. If we are under-aroused, we may be stimulated to seek out interesting and exciting situations (Maggini, 2000).

Eysenck's (1990) theory of extraversion is based on the concept of arousal. The extravert is under-aroused and under-stimulated, and so seeks out stimulation to satisfy that need. Extraverts are attracted to other people, noisy, exciting and often dangerous situations to satisfy their arousal needs. Introverts, on the other hand, are over-aroused and over-stimulated and therefore try to avoid any situation that increases their arousal. According to the theory, they avoid people and therefore gain a reputation for being shy.

In addition to providing motivation, our arousal levels can systematically affect our performance on tasks we undertake. The **Yerkes–Dodson law** (Yerkes & Dodson, 1908) states that ideal performance on a task occurs when our arousal level is right for the difficulty of the task. People who are over-aroused tend to be stressed; those who are under-aroused, bored.

> **Yerkes–Dodson law** holds that ideal performance on a task occurs when the arousal level is optimized to the difficulty level.

Task difficulty and arousal seem to be inversely related (Figure 13.2). That is, our performance on difficult tasks is optimal at relatively low arousal states, while our performance on easy tasks is optimal at high arousal states. This may be related to the fact that difficult tasks require more intense concentration that may be disrupted by highly arousing circumstances. Imagine, for example, that you are trying to finish writing a piece of coursework. You may find it easier to focus on your writing if you are not highly aroused by a

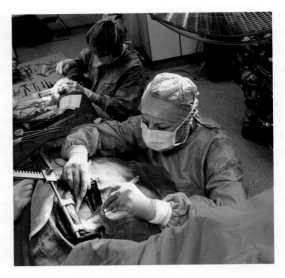

The Yerkes–Dodson law in action The worker on the left uses a sharp knife to cut bread at a restaurant in Italy, while the surgeon on the right uses her sharp instrument to perform open-heart surgery. According to the Yerkes–Dodson law, a high level of physical arousal will help the restaurant's worker's performance but probably not the surgeon's.

Source: Left photo: ©Atlantide Phototravel/Corbis. Right photo: Thierry Dosogne/Getty Images, Inc.

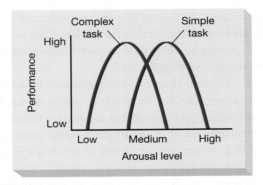

FIGURE 13.2 The Yerkes–Dodson law. Our optimal performance on tasks is inversely related to our arousal level. We perform difficult tasks best when our arousal level is low and simple or boring ones best when our arousal level is high.

Source: Based on Lillienfield, S., Lyon, S., Namy, L., & Wolf, N. (2009). Psychology: From inquiry to understanding. Boston: Pearson/Allyn & Bacon, p. 470.

deadline looming only a few hours away. If, however, you are trying to read some really boring material (something other than this book, of course), you may need to periodically raise your arousal levels with snacks, stretch breaks and the like, to help you focus on the task.

Incentive Theory

intrinsic motivation engaging in a behaviour simply for the satisfaction that is part of doing it.

Some behaviours arise from **intrinsic motivation**, which means that engaging in the behaviour is satisfying in and of itself (Schmitt & Lahroodi, 2008). For example, rats seem to find exploring mazes to be intrinsically motivating. For some people,

eating hot dogs is intrinsically motivating. Although they may never enter a hot-dog-eating contest, they occasionally eat hot dogs simply for the pleasure they get out of doing so, rather than to just satisfy their hunger. Most people have favourite foods that they likely eat even when they are not very hungry, simply because they love the taste of the food.

Other behaviours are driven by external motives, or **incentives**. Behaviour that is motivated by external incentives is known as **extrinsic motivation**. Rats can be extrinsically motivated: they learn their way through a maze more quickly if provided with an incentive (such as food) or a way to escape something unpleasant (such as water), than they do when no incentives are involved (Komaki, 2004).

incentives external motives that indirectly indicate reward.

extrinsic motivation engaging in a behaviour because of the influence of factors outside ourselves.

Even when our motivation to behave in a certain way involves instinct, a drive to maintain homeostasis or a motive to achieve an optimal level of arousal, it is clear that incentives play a major role in most human behaviour. *Incentive theory* highlights the influence of external stimuli in behaviour. Incentive theory would suggest that external rewards, such as public acclaim or financial prizes, contribute to the motivation of record-breaking hot-dog eaters, for example. This seems especially likely when one considers the upset stomach that results from eating so much. Though many students enjoy learning in itself, a good deal of your own behaviour as a student is probably also motivated by external factors, such as the desire to achieve high grades, graduate on time and obtain a good job.

Incentives can be either primary or secondary and they can be rewarding or punitive.

- *Primary incentives* are rewards or punishments that are innate; we do not have to learn to either like or dislike them. Food is a primary reward, and pain is a primary punishment, for example. Most humans instinctually find food rewarding and electric shocks punishing. For that reason, these stimuli are likely to influence our behaviour. There is an adaptive, or evolutionary, component to primary rewards and punishments. Typically, stimuli that increase our chances of survival and reproduction, such as food and sex, are rewarding, while those that are potentially harmful, such as anything painful, are punishing.

- *Secondary incentives* are cues that are viewed as rewarding or punishing as a result of our learning their association with other events. For example, most people are motivated to work to earn money. Money, in and of itself, is not rewarding. It becomes motivating to us when we learn its association with the rewarding goods, such as food, that it can buy.

Money as a Motivator The debate about the power of money to motivate is very old, extremely controversial and still unresolved. However, it is generally agreed that:

- Money is a good motivator for those who need or value it enough. People differ enormously in how much they value the symbolism, power and value of money. The greater the need, the greater the motivational power.

- Money is most effective when it has noticeable effects. Large, lump-sum increases make people feel materially better off and thus able to buy 'luxuries'.

- Money motivates when it is actually, and seen to be, rewarding performance. If people see a simple but direct relationship between input (hard work) and output (money), they feel able to control and predict their income. This is true of the individuals or groups working in gain-sharing programmes (e.g. worker cooperatives) that allow them to participate financially in the productivity gains they achieved.

If money *is* a powerful motivator or satisfier at work, why has research consistently shown that there is no real relationship between wealth and happiness? There are four good reasons why this is so:

- *Adaptation.* Although evidence suggests that people feel 'happier' after a pay rise, windfall or lottery win, one soon adapts to this and the effect disappears rapidly.

- *Comparison.* People define themselves as wealthy by comparison with others. However, on moving into more upmarket circles they find there is always someone else who is wealthier.

- *Alternatives.* As economists say, the declining marginal utility of money means that as one has more of the stuff, other things such as freedom and true friendship seem much more valuable.

- *Worry.* Increased income is associated with a shifting of concern from money issues to the more uncontrollable elements of life (such as self-development), perhaps because money is associated with a sense of control over one's fate.

The power of money as a motivator is short-lived. Furthermore, it has less effect the more comfortable the people are. Albert Camus, the French author, was right when he said it was a kind of spiritual snobbery to believe people could be happy without money. But given or earning a modest amount, the value of other work benefits becomes greater.

Although money is generally considered a strong motivator, every individual is differentially motivated by it. Why is this? Scientists attribute the different motivational power of certain cues to *incentive salience*; how noticeable or important a particular incentive is to us (Berridge, 2007). Incentives can become more salient and more motivating after they become associated with specific emotions (Robinson & Berridge, 2001). Consider a person's motivation to work hard at a job. The first time we receive a paycheque, the things we purchase with the money may lead to happiness. This association of money with happiness may, in turn, motivate us to engage in behaviours designed to improve the chance of earning even more money, such as working harder. Alternatively, if your first work experience is a very negative one that becomes associated with boredom and unhappiness, your drive to pursue happiness through hard work is less likely to flourish. You may seek to avoid work altogether, or you may be motivated to look for a better and more gratifying job. Particularly for complex behaviours, such as working at a job, there can be a number of different incentives that motivate different individuals. Some people work to avoid punishment, such as homelessness and shame, for example, while others work to receive rewards, such as money and pride.

Motivational theories that focus on incentives often take into consideration the distinction between *liking* and *wanting* (Berridge & Kringelbach, 2008). Liking refers to our experience of reward or pleasure that happens *at the moment* we are engaging in a particular behaviour, while wanting refers to the anticipation of an experience that we expect will cause us pleasure. Having a pleasurable experience in the past often leads to wanting to repeat that experience again in the future. If you really like your first coffee from a certain cafe, you may want more like it. You may even become motivated to walk an extra distance just to visit that particular cafe.

Neuroscientists have found that overlapping, but distinct, regions of our brains are involved in liking and wanting (Litman, 2005). Pleasure, or liking, is typically associated with systems of the brain that produce *opiates*. Opiates, such as endorphins, are naturally occurring neurochemicals that contribute to our feelings of pleasure. Eating, drinking and sex – biological motivations that we discuss later in this chapter – are all associated with a release of opiates. Other experiences, such as intense physical exercise (e.g. long-distance running) can also stimulate the release of brain opiates, producing a phenomenon called *runner's high* (Boecker *et al.*, 2008).

In addition to activating the brain-opiate system, rewarding stimuli typically stimulate the release of the neurotransmitter dopamine (Berridge & Kringelbach, 2008; Arias-Carrión & Pöppel, 2007). As discussed in Chapter 5, dopamine is present in two major systems of the brain. One region is mostly important for movement, and the other is important for reinforcement learning. The latter system consists of dopamine neurons in a region of the midbrain, called the *ventral tegmental area*, which send their axons to two key areas in the front of the brain: the *nucleus accumbens* and the *prefrontal cortex* (Figure 13.3). As we noted in Chapter 5, the nucleus accumbens is highly active in the experience of rewarding and pleasurable feelings (Carlezon & Thomas, 2009). The pathways of dopamine neurons from the ventral tegmental area to the nucleus accumbens and prefrontal cortex are not only activated during the reward experience; they also appear to be critical for future behaviour directed towards that reward. In other words, the dopamine system plays a critical role in *wanting*.

Although incentive theory explains how our behaviour is shaped by external stimuli, not all of our behaviour is motivated by wanting a reward or avoiding a punishment. Integrating incentive theory with other motivation theories is necessary to explain the complexity of motivation. For example, drive-reduction theory and incentive theory together more fully explain our motivation to eat than using just one theory does. Drive-reduction theory explains that eating to reduce the feeling of hunger maintains homeostasis and incentive theory explains the rewarding feelings associated with what you eat and the incentive to eat that food again in the future.

Multiple Motivations: Hierarchy of Needs

As we have seen, a combination of factors, including both innate and learnt motives, interact to drive behaviour. Psychologists have also recognized that different motives can compete with one another (LaGraize *et al.*, 2004). For instance, you may find it particularly difficult to concentrate on completing a homework assignment if you are hungry. The relative strength of certain motives and their ability to supersede or override the importance of one another led humanist psychologist Abraham Maslow to describe motives, or needs, in terms of a *hierarchy*, as we noted in the introductory chapter of this book (Maslow, 1970). Figure 13.4, which you also observed in Chapter 1, shows Maslow's hierarchy of needs.

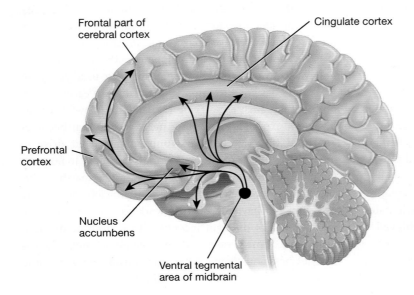

FIGURE 13.3 Reward pathways in the brain. Rewarding stimuli typically trigger dopamine neurons in the ventral tegmental area of the brain. The axons of these neurons project to the nucleus accumbens and the prefrontal cortex, activating rewarding and pleasurable feelings.

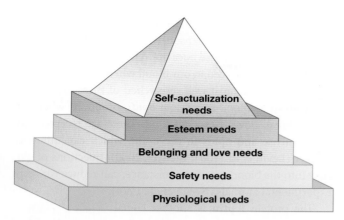

FIGURE 13.4 Maslow's hierarchy of needs. A combination of needs, both innate and learnt, drive our behaviour and sometimes are in competition. Maslow identified the relative strength of these needs and arranged them in a hierarchy. Basic survival needs at the base of the pyramid are the strongest and must be satisfied first before we are motivated to achieve our higher needs.

The most basic needs, such as the need to eat or drink, are at the bottom of the hierarchy pyramid. Unless these needs are satisfied, we find it difficult to generate motivation to engage in other behaviours. Above the basic needs are the safety needs: the need to feel secure and stable. It is important to realize that a balance exists between the first and second tier on the pyramid. It would not make sense for us to run out into traffic to stop the ice-cream van, acting primarily on our need to eat and bypassing the need for safety. That does not happen often, because food is usually not a matter of life or death in our culture. But humans, as well as other animals, will often take great risks to obtain food and water if they cannot be obtained in a safer setting.

Above the safety needs is the need to feel love and to belong to a social group. This need motivates us to seek companionship in the form of friends and romantic partners. It motivates the creation of families and the formation of clubs and other social organizations. The social need varies considerably from species to species. The tree shrew, for example, lives a solitary life and only interacts with other tree shrews for the purposes of mating. The mother tree shrew does not even sleep with her own babies! Humans vary from person to person, but as a species we are highly social and our needs for human contact are often very strong motivators of our behaviour.

Above the need to belong socially rests the need for a feeling of self-worth. This need motivates us to achieve at school, work and in the home. Finally, at the top of the pyramid, rests the need for self-actualization. As our highest need, the need for self-actualization motivates us to live up to our potential and become the best we can be. For many people, this involves engaging in selfless, altruistic behaviour, in the form of political activism or humanitarian behaviour.

According to Maslow's theory, it is difficult to meet this need without having satisfied the needs below it on the pyramid. Even so, many people sacrifice fulfilment of some of their basic needs to meet higher needs. Doctors who volunteer to work in war zones (members of Médecins Sans Frontières/Doctors without Borders, for example), sacrifice their safety needs to fulfil their needs for self-actualization.

Certainly, Maslow's theory was more comprehensive than previous approaches and it also stressed the positive aspects of human motivation. Yet researchers have found the concept of self-actualization both vague and difficult to measure. It has been argued that Maslow was over-optimistic in believing that everyone has potential to be realized. He also under-emphasized the role of environmental factors (schooling, parenting) that facilitate the development of self-actualization.

It should also be noted that Maslow's is not the only need theory. Henry Murray (1938) described 16 different needs of which three have been most thoroughly investigated: need for achievement (to accomplish something difficult and to surpass others); need for affiliation (to draw near to, befriend and win the affection and loyalty of others); and need for power (to influence, persuade and command others).

Before You Go On

What Do You Know?

1. What are some examples of instinctive motivations among humans?
2. How does drive-reduction theory differ from arousal theory?
3. What is intrinsic motivation and how does it differ from extrinsic motivation?
4. Give an example of a primary incentive and a secondary incentive.
5. What are the lowest level needs in the hierarchy of needs?

What Do You Think?

Consider one of your favourite hobbies, such as reading novels or playing videogames or a sport. Whatever the activity, describe how each of the motivational theories discussed in this chapter would explain why you do it. Does any one theory describe your motivation best?

Biological Motivations: Hunger

LEARNING OBJECTIVE 2

Summarize physical and psychological factors that affect our levels of hunger and our eating behaviour.

As we have noted, the drive to eat is *biologically ingrained*, or instinctual. Newborn babies show interest in feeding soon after they are born. The biological drive to eat remains in place throughout our lives since we need to eat to live. A person can generally last only about 40 days without food (Lieberson, 2004). Eating is not simply a matter of following an instinctive pattern of behaviour to satisfy an innate drive, however. As we will see, a number of other factors play a role in motivating how much, what, when and even where we are motivated to eat. First, let's explore what we know about the biology of eating.

Hunger Signals

WHAT HAPPENS IN THE BRAIN?

Hunger signals in our brains originate from several stimuli, including how full our stomachs are, the levels of nutrients circulating in our bloodstreams and interacting with both of those signals the activities of key parts of our brains.

Stomach Signals As you may have experienced, an empty stomach can trigger feelings of hunger. Doctors treating obese patients take advantage of the fact that physical signals produced by stretch receptors in the stomach are important for informing the brain to stop eating. These cues, called satiety signals, can be activated by surgically placing a balloon in the stomach. Since the stomach space is already partially occupied by the balloon, the stretch receptors will be activated even when the person eats a relatively small meal (Fernandes *et al.*, 2007; Rigaud *et al.*, 1995). Another technique that works on a similar principle is the surgical placement of a band around the stomach or physically stapling the stomach so that it is much smaller (Bowne *et al.*, 2006). Many individuals who have undergone these procedures first lose weight, but then eventually gain it back, suggesting that, although signals from the stomach can influence the degree to which we are motivated to eat, these signals alone do not control that motivation (Christou *et al.*, 2006).

Indeed, it turns out that satiety signals from the stomach are not even the most important hunger cues. People with no stomach at all, as a result of surgery for cancer, for instance, still experience hunger (Kamiji *et al.*, 2009). Also, as you may have experienced, eating a small amount of food often stimulates additional hunger.

Chemical Signals Eating occurs as a result of a complex interplay between hunger and satiety. Considerable evidence suggests that cues related to the metabolism of food can signal hunger or satiety (Erlanson-Albertsson, 2005; Wynne *et al.*, 2004). Some of these cues are related to levels of different chemicals produced in our blood when our bodies digest food. Two of the most well researched of these are *glucose*, also known as blood sugar, and *lipids*, produced when our bodies break down fats from food. There are receptors for both glucose and lipids in the brain, which can influence hunger (Levin *et al.*, 2004; Meister, 2000). Injections of glucose into the bloodstream, for instance, can reduce eating in experimental animals (Novin *et al.*, 1974).

The protein **leptin** is another signal that appears to be important for regulating the amount of food eaten over long periods. Leptin is released from our fat cells as they grow larger. When receptors in the brain sense high levels of leptin, they in turn send signals that inhibit us from eating (Dhillon *et al.*, 2006; Hommel *et al.*, 2006). Obese animals and humans may be insensitive to leptin. Some evidence suggests that although they have higher blood levels of leptin than normal-weight individuals they have fewer leptin receptors in their brains, which may prevent the signal to stop eating from being generated soon enough (Björnholm *et al.*, 2007; Farooqi *et al.*, 2007).

> **leptin** a protein produced by fat cells that is important for regulating the amount of food eaten over long periods.

Brain Signals Within the brain, the hypothalamus is a key mediator of eating. Specific subregions in the hypothalamus have been linked to both hunger and satiety. The **lateral hypothalamus (LH)** is important for hunger. Rodents with damage to this area dramatically under-eat; they need to be force-fed or they will starve to death (Petrovich *et al.*, 2002). A nearby brain region, the **ventromedial region of the hypothalamus (VMH)**, has been shown to play an important role in satiety. Destruction of this region leads to overeating and obesity in rats (Figure 13.5). Humans who develop brain tumours in the VMH also increase their food intake and become markedly heavier (Yadav *et al.*, 2009). A genetic condition in humans, known as *Prader–Willi syndrome*, is associated with an insatiable appetite, leading to obesity. This condition is believed to arise, at least in part, from dysfunction of the hypothalamus (Hinton *et al.*, 2006; Holland *et al.*, 1993).

> **lateral hypothalamus (LH)** a region of the hypothalamus important in signalling thirst and hunger.

> **ventromedial region of the hypothalamus (VMH)** a region of the hypothalamus important in signalling satiety.

The identification of these two brain regions as important for feeding behaviour led to the formation of the *dual-centre theory of motivation*. This idea proposes that activity in one area inhibits the area that serves the opposite function. For example, an empty stomach and low blood-glucose may

FIGURE 13.5 The VMH and obesity. The rat on the left had its ventromedial hypothalamus destroyed, which led to overeating and a dramatic increase in its body weight.

Source: Reproduced by permission of Prof. Philip Teitelbaum.

stimulate the LH to motivate us to eat, while at the same time inhibiting satiety signals from the VMH. Once the stretch receptors are activated and blood-glucose reaches a certain level, the VMH would once again become active and it would inhibit the LH.

Subsequent research, however, has shown that these brain regions influence eating in a more complicated way through the action of a hormone called *insulin* (Plum *et al.*, 2006; Woods *et al.*, 2006). The VMH appears to be important for modulating the levels of insulin in the blood. Insulin helps the body to metabolize and use glucose. Damage to the VMH can increase insulin levels. High insulin levels, in turn, cause our fat cells to store more glucose and grow. Studies of animals with lesions or damage in the VMH show that they experience increases in fat deposits, regardless of the amount of food they eat (Yadav *et al.*, 2009). So, it is not just a matter of the VMH failing to provide these animals with a satiety signal. They are actually short on blood sugar, or glucose, because glucose is metabolized quickly by high levels of insulin in the blood. Because they store energy from glucose as fat more rapidly than undamaged animals do, the signals of satiety, such as an increase in blood-glucose level, does not occur. As a result, the animals continue eating.

However, it is important to remember that no single area of the brain acts alone, especially in a complex behaviour, such as eating. Along with the hypothalamus, several additional brain regions participate in eating. Our ability to taste food certainly plays a role in eating, for example. As described in Chapter 7, taste information is processed in the prefrontal cortex. When we are presented with unpalatable food, like undercooked meat and mouldy bread, disgust cues involve the *insular cortex*, a region situated close to the prefrontal cortex (Roman *et al.*, 2009; Roman & Reilly, 2007).

Not only are many areas of the brain involved in eating, but the brain circuitry involved in our eating behaviour is also active in a variety of different motivational situations. Pathways important for general reward, punishment and disgust under other circumstances interact with brain regions that specifically process visual, olfactory, and gustatory information to modulate eating (Rolls, 2007; De Araujo *et al.*, 2003). For example, the same part of our brain that is active when we are enjoying the lovely scent of a flower may also be involved when we are enticed by the aroma wafting from a coffee machine.

Eating Behaviour

In addition to our basic biological need to eat, several psychological (that is non-biological) factors affect how hungry we feel and how much we eat. As we saw in the case of competitive hot-dog eaters, for example, people are sometimes motivated to eat even when they are not particularly hungry. Individual desires other than hunger obviously motivate competitive eaters and often affect the rest of us, too. Cultural and social influences also affect our eating behaviour.

Culture plays a role not only in the types of foods that people enjoy and what times of the day we prefer to eat but also in how much we eat. For example, in Korea, where a meal often consists of many communal side dishes, it is considered proper etiquette to try a little food from each. People in India often skip breakfast, but in Ireland, breakfast is often a large meal, and may include porridge, eggs and bacon. Food is also strongly associated with social interactions. Studies have shown that people eat considerably more when they are in a social setting, particularly when it is a relatively large gathering, compared to when eating alone (Lumeng & Hillman, 2007). People with schedules that involve business meetings and social engagements over meals are likely to eat more than those whose schedules do not include meetings at mealtimes, for example. This may be due to the fact that meals take longer with more participants, as well as the fact that people may pay less attention to restricting their diets when they are engaged in conversation (Pliner *et al.*, 2006).

Some researchers have also suggested that we each have an individual **body weight set point**. Researchers have long recognized that, as adults, our weights tend to stabilize near a certain general level. We may fluctuate in a small range around that weight, but we typically return to the original set point, even after major weight gain or loss (Pasquet & Apfelbaum, 1994). This is

> **body weight set point** a weight that individuals typically return to even after dieting or overeating.

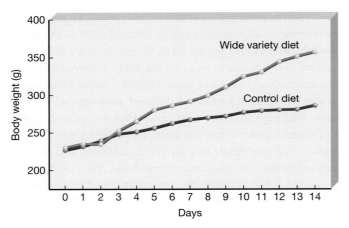

FIGURE 13.6 Food variety and obesity. Research suggests that body weight set point is not the only factor for determining the amount of food eaten by humans or animals. When rats in one study were given a wide variety of highly palatable foods, they ate more and became obese.

Source: Based on Sclafani, A. & Springer, D. (1976). Dietary obesity in adult rats; Similarities to hypothalamic and human obesity syndromes, *Physiology and Behaviour, 17,* 461–471. Reproduced with permission.

particularly evident when people diet. A reduction in body weight is often followed by a rebound back towards the original weight. . This is not always the case, however. Some people do undergo dramatic weight changes in one direction or another and maintain their new weights for a considerable period. People who maintain a lower body weight typically make permanent changes in their eating habits and persistently monitor their weight (Warziski *et al.*, 2008; Dansinger *et al.*, 2005). Fad diets often do not work because they do not involve life changes in eating patterns.

Other research suggests, however, that body weight set point is not the only factor at play in determining how much we eat. The availability of food we like also plays a role. Many individuals in Western societies, where food is plentiful, find their weights steadily creeping up over the years (Philipson, 2001). This can be seen with laboratory rodents, too. Presenting them with a wide array of highly palatable foods will cause more eating and weight gain (Figure 13.6) (Hagan *et al.*, 2003). This suggests that a firm body weight set point does not exist in experimental animals or humans. When presented with highly palatable food and reduced physical activity over the years, most people have a tendency to put on weight as they age.

Eating Issues

OUT OF THE ORDINARY

We have seen that our motivation to eat is very complex, affected not only by intricate biological processes but also by psychological, social and cultural influences. As with

any complex system, we face the potential for problems in our eating behaviour. Two of the most common problems include obesity, often related to too much eating, and eating disorders, which often involve eating too little.

Obesity, a condition of being extremely overweight, is determined on the basis of a weight-to-height ratio, called the **body mass index (BMI)**. Adults with a BMI of 30 or higher are considered obese, and those with BMIs between 25 and 30 are categorized as overweight (NIH, 2009). Obesity is a major health problem in the West. Nearly two-thirds of Americans and a similar number in Europe now fall into the categories of overweight or obese. Being overweight or obese is associated with a variety of health problems, most notably diabetes and heart disease (Poirier *et al.*, 2006; Huang, 2005). In addition to the physical risks they face, obese people are also more likely than those of normal weight to suffer from mood disorders, such as depression and anxiety. As the following 'Psychology Around Us' box describes, obese people are also often the victims of discrimination, particularly at work.

obesity overweight; characterized as a body mass index of over 30.

body mass index (BMI) weight-to-height ratio.

Some people become obese as a result of medical conditions. Researchers estimate, that medical conditions cause only about 1 to 5% of all cases of obesity and seem to be the result of a biological abnormality unrelated to overeating (Harvey *et al.*, 2005). In the majority of people, obesity is caused by overeating.

Why is it so common to overeat? One answer to this question may be found by considering the evolutionary perspective. Early people evolved under conditions of unpredictable food availability. At times, when food was plentiful, after a successful hunt or during a time when weather conditions led to an abundance of edible plants, it was certainly advantageous to overeat to prepare and compensate for a lack of food in the near future. Overeating would lead to fat storage that increased the chances of survival during periods of food scarcity. In many of today's developed cultures, where inexpensive high-calorie food is readily available, this built-in adaptive mechanism can lead to chronic overconsumption, working against its evolutionary purpose to increase chances of survival. Since high-calorie foods are available most of the time, we do not experience periods of fasting between bouts of overeating.

Bigger Portions, Bigger Waists The problem of overeating has intensified over the past few decades, as the food and restaurant industries have increased the size of portions and prepared foods have become a mainstay of the Western diet. Consumer behaviour research strongly suggests that many Europeans appreciate large-size portions because they appear to be of good value (Ledikwe *et al.*, 2005). It is very difficult to regulate the amount of food you ingest when the portions are so much larger than those recommended for maintaining a healthy weight. The over-sizing of portions common today has, for many of us, led to an increase in energy intake, as measured in calories, without a corresponding change in energy expenditure. In other words, we supply our bodies with more energy, but we do not compensate for increased energy by increasing our physical activity that would expend the energy, or 'burn calories'. As a result of the accumulation of unused calories, people gain weight.

PRACTICALLY SPEAKING   Too Much of a Good Thing

In 1955, when the fast-food chain McDonald's first opened, a regular-size drink like a Coke was seven ounces. In the new millennium, a child-sized drink serving is 12 ounces, and adults can choose from 16-, 21- and 32-ounce beverages (Young & Nestle, 2007). Burger King offers a Triple Whopper sandwich that has 1,140 calories, more than half the recommended daily calorie allotment for an average adult male (Burger King, 2012). Combine that with fries and a Coke, and you can easily end up with several thousand calories. Most such meals are consumed by people who do not realize just how much fuel they are taking in. Some fast-food restaurants now post the calorie content of all the foods they sell, but it is not clear that this is a significant deterrent. Publicity about the excessive calories present in fast food has had at least one benefit, though: many fast-food restaurants now offer healthier options, like salads, carrot sticks and apple slices.

Once people become accustomed to ingesting very large amounts of food, scaling back to sensible-sized portions can feel like deprivation. Many nutritionists often suggest that dieters eat their food from smaller plates to avoid feeling that the reduced portions are meagre. This trick alone is typically not sufficient to support a substantial weight loss, however. In fact, billions of pounds and euros are spent every year on dieting programmes and products that are designed to help overweight individuals lose weight and keep it off. However, diet programmes are often unsuccessful for long-term weight change. For this reason, many experts suggest that the best way to combat obesity is to prevent its occurrence (Bendelius, 2004; Mogan, 1984). Some approaches to obesity prevention may be suggested by identifying the risk factors for developing obesity. Although the majority of Americans and Europeans are now overweight, only about one-third are obese (CDC, 2009). Why are some people more prone to obesity than others? The answer, as always, involves many factors.

One substantial contributor to obesity is genes. Adoption and twin studies have shown that a good deal of the variation in obesity can be attributed to genetics. Adopted individuals studied tend to have the body mass indexes that more closely resemble the BMIs of their biological parents than those of their adoptive parents (Sørensen *et al.*, 1992; Moll *et al.*, 1991). Moreover, identical twins separated at birth are as similar in body weight as those that were raised together (Price & Gottesman, 1991). This strongly suggests that genetics play a major role in determining obesity.

Scientists do not understand exactly how our genes might predispose us to become obese. Some possibilities include inheriting a larger-than-normal number of fat cells, a lower metabolic rate (the speed at which we break down and burn the calories in food) or, as we saw earlier in the chapter, an abnormal leptin gene.

Genetics alone, however, cannot explain the rise in obesity over the past few decades. Genes may predispose people to become overweight, but the environment must be conducive to overeating in order for them to realize this potential. The social aspect of overeating is evident in recent findings that humans are much more likely to gain weight if they have an overweight friend, even if that person lives far away and the number of shared meals is minimal (Christakis & Fowler, 2007). This suggests that having overweight friends makes being overweight oneself seem more acceptable, perhaps because weight gain becomes associated with the positive stimulus of friendship. Obesity (especially among women) is also much more common among members of lower socioeconomic groups than in higher socioeconomic groups (McLaren, 2007). Researchers have suggested that this may be the result of less education about nutrition, fewer affordable healthy food choices and less social pressure to be thin (Monteiro *et al.*, 2004).

Although obesity can significantly reduce the quality of life, people can be overweight for decades before any negative health effects become evident. Eating disorders on the other end of the spectrum, those that involve eating too little, can lead rather abruptly to emergency situations and even death.

PSYCHOLOGY AROUND US   The Social Stigma against Obesity

Obesity is acceptable and even considered to be desirable in some cultures. For example, in the African nation of Mauritania, parents have been known to force feed their daughters with high-calorie food to make them gain weight so that they will be more attractive to prospective suitors. While this practice may be on its way out, given that nation's recent recognition that obesity is unhealthy, Mauritanians certainly hold a different standard of beauty from the ideals prevalent in the West.

In the West, the media often dictate a certain standard of beauty, particularly for women. Young, slender women are considered desirable. The thin standard of beauty is becoming increasingly extreme. Top female models weigh 23% less than the average woman, compared with 8% less 25 years ago (Sheppird, 2009). Ironically, as the ideal weight is shrinking, the actual weights on most people's scales are increasing (CDC, 2009).

Not only do people in the West consider overweight people to be less attractive than thinner people, they also seem to ascribe a number of other unfavourable characteristics to people who are obese. Although overweight people are often considered to be 'friendly' and 'happy', they are also judged more often as 'lazy', 'stupid' and 'incompetent' than are people of normal weight (Puhl et al., 2008; Friedman et al., 2005).

We know that overweight and obese people get lower wages and salaries, are less likely to be selected in recruitment campaigns and have a slower career progression (NAAFA, 2009). This discrimination can even affect normal-weight individuals associated with obese people. One study looked at the hiring rate of normal-weight job applicants who happened to be sitting next to an obese person just before their interview (Hebl & Mannix, 2003). Surprisingly, they were less likely to be hired. Perhaps unsurprisingly, obese people are also more likely than normal-weight people to suffer from depression and anxiety (Friedlander et al., 2003).

In recent years, several organizations in the United States have attempted to combat this prejudice by supporting the obese and lobbying the government to pass laws against obesity discrimination. There are no national anti-weight-discrimination laws yet but an antidiscrimination bill has been proposed in Massachusetts that would protect people from discrimination on grounds of weight and height and several cities have incorporated categories such as *personal appearance* into their existing human rights legislation (NAAFA, 2009).

Genes or environment? Research clearly suggests that obesity is related to genes, but there is also evidence that the eating habits of parents and other family members can play a major role in the development of this problem.

Source: Tim Boyle/Getty Images, Inc.

Eating Disorders: Anorexia Nervosa and Bulimia Nervosa **Anorexia nervosa** is a condition in which individuals are preoccupied with the notion that they are fat or will become fat. To combat these thoughts, people with anorexia engage in extreme dieting, often eating less than 500 calories per day (Sadock & Sadock, 2007). The restricted eating associated with anorexia generally leads to extreme weight loss, which can be very dangerous. People who lose too much weight are likely to suffer illnesses and imbalances in their blood chemistry. In as many as 10% of cases, anorexic weight loss leads to death (Steinhausen, 2002).

anorexia nervosa eating disorder in which individuals under-eat and have a distorted body image of being overweight.

It is important to realize that there are major differences between people who diet, even those who do so continually, and those with anorexia. People with anorexia have a distorted body image. Even when they are dangerously thin, they still think of themselves as fat and often cannot be convinced to increase their calorie intake.

Anorexia can begin as early as puberty (Hudson et al., 2007). Statistics suggest that about one in 100 young women in the West has anorexia and a higher number experience bouts of extreme and unhealthy dieting. It is much more common in females than males, although recent years have seen an increase in the number of males diagnosed with the condition (Hudson *et al.*, 2007).

The causes of anorexia are complex, but it is most common in cultures where food is prevalent and social pressure exists for people to be thin (Makino *et al.*, 2004). This makes sense because people in cultures where food is less readily available are likely to actively view food as a necessity for survival, rather than something impeding one's physical beauty. Similarly, many theorists have noted, with alarm, that today's media and fashion industry glamorize dangerously thin models. Anorexia often coexists with other anxiety disorders, such as obsessive–compulsive disorder (OCD), which we discussed in Chapter 11, suggesting that anorexia is just one of several possible outlets for a more general psychological disturbance.

There are many different academic theories of anorexia. First the *family systems theory* proposes that the roots of anorexia lie within the dynamics of the family. The *sociocultural theory* asserts that the promotion of thinness causes the development of anorexia nervosa, the media being seen as the source of external pressure on the individual. Chronic exposure to such thin ideals also leads to greater dissatisfaction with one's body as well as increasing the chances of developing an eating disorder, especially for susceptible individuals. *Biological theories* of the disorder have looked towards genetic predispositions, in which it has been suggested that there is 48–74% chance of the variance for eating disorder development from twin studies. A *feminist theory* views how the evolving roles and expectations of females may give rise to the development of anorexia nervosa.

Treatment of anorexia may involve hospitalization if extreme weight loss has occurred. Patients receive nutritional counselling to help restore a healthy weight. In addition, cognitive-behavioural therapy, which attempts to help patients develop a healthier body image, is used (Berkman *et al.*, 2006). Adolescents with anorexia may also benefit from family therapy (Keel & Haedt, 2008).

bulimia nervosa eating disorder in which individuals binge and then engage in purging behaviour.

Bulimia nervosa is a disorder in which individuals consume excessive calories and then go to extremes to prevent those calories from contributing to weight gain. People with bulimia typically rid themselves of excess food by inducing vomiting or diarrhoea or by engaging in intensive exercise. This cycle of bingeing followed by purging defines bulimia. Although people with anorexia often engage in bulimic behaviour in order to prevent weight gain, most people with bulimia do not appear to be underweight. Some are even overweight (Probst *et al.*, 2004). Like anorexia, bulimia is more common among females than males. The prevalence rates for bulimia nervosa are 1% and 0.1% for young women and young men, respectively (Hoek & van Hoeken, 2003).

Dangerous trend. Here Brazilian model Ana Carolina Reston models an outfit in a 2005 fashion show. She died one year later at the age of 21, weighing 88 pounds, of complications from anorexia nervosa. Her death underscores a dangerous trend in the fashion industry towards using increasingly thin models.
Source: Eugenio Savio/©AP/Wide World Photos.

The causes of bulimia are difficult to pinpoint. Like anorexia, bulimia is associated with other psychological disturbances, including OCD (Godart *et al.*, 2006). A significant number of people with bulimia have also engaged in other damaging behaviours, such as cutting themselves (Favaro *et al.*, 2008). There is evidence that traumatic life events and family factors, particularly pressure to achieve academically as well as poor interfamily relationships, have a role to play in the aetiology of bulimia.

Unlike anorexia, bulimia is typically not life-threatening. However, it can produce unwanted medical and dental problems, such as constipation from overuse of laxatives and tooth decay from excessive vomiting. The psychological effects of bulimic behaviour can be even more damaging than the physical ones. Because people with bulimia are generally ashamed of their binge/purge behaviours, they generally carry out these behaviours privately and make attempts to hide the evidence and keep their condition a secret. This secrecy, as well as the syndrome itself, often contributes to anxiety and depression (Hayaki *et al.*, 2002).

Treatment of bulimia requires that patients admit that the problem exists and talk openly about it. Effective treatments for bulimia include behavioural modification, in which healthier eating behaviours are rewarded, and cognitive therapy, which attempts to help people with bulimia develop healthier views of themselves and their eating patterns (Wilson & Shafran, 2005). Antidepressant drug treatments have also been found to be effective, particularly when combined with behavioural or cognitive therapy (Romano *et al.*, 2002).

Before You Go On

What Do You Know?

6. Describe the three main categories of biological hunger signals.
7. What non-biological factors affect our eating behaviour?
8. What is obesity and what factors can contribute to it?
9. What are the characteristics of anorexia nervosa and bulimia nervosa?

What Do You Think?

As a public-health effort to combat obesity, some restaurants now provide calorie and other nutritional information about food on their menus. What are some potential advantages and disadvantages of providing this information to customers?

Biological Motivations: Sex

LEARNING OBJECTIVE 3
Describe factors that affect our sexual motivation and behaviour.

Another basic motivation is sex. From an evolutionary perspective, engaging in sexual behaviour is highly adaptive. However, most sexual behaviour does not occur with the goal of procreating in mind. Actually, the opposite seems to be true. Humans often engage in sexual behaviour while taking steps to avoid conception. Humans, as well as other animals, seek out and engage in sexual behaviour because it is a primary drive: it is particularly pleasurable and therefore rewarding.

Sex: Psychological and Social Factors

Although there is a basic biological instinct to engage in sexual activity, sexual motivation is strongly governed by social cues. In some species of animals, only select members of the social group reproduce. Among honeybees, for example, only the queen bee of each hive reproduces, while the other bees work to maintain the living environment (Wenseleers *et al.*, 2004). In other groups, such as marmoset monkeys, dominant females in a social group procreate, and the other females help to raise the dominant's babies. Subordinate females must wait until a change occurs in the social order (perhaps the dominant will get old and sick and lose her rank) before they can reproduce (Barrett *et al.*, 1993).

Among humans, cultural factors play an important role in determining our choice and number of sexual partners, our range of sexual practices and the age at which sexual activity typically begins. For instance, some societies, such as certain Nigerian tribes, practise *polygamy*, an arrangement in which men have multiple wives. Other societies, such as the Nakhi of China, practice *polyandry*, an arrangement in which women have multiple male sexual partners.

Societies also vary in the sexual practices that are considered taboo or unacceptable. For example, in some Western countries, it is a crime for an adult to have sex with an under 16-year-old, but in some Middle Eastern countries, the earliest age of marriage (and its consummation) is 9 years old (Admon, 2009).

Some sexual taboos seem to be almost universal, however, suggesting that they may be rooted in human evolution. One example of this is the incest taboo. In most cultures, *incest*, defined as having sex with close relatives, is forbidden. It is illegal for siblings to marry in most countries throughout the world. In one case in Germany, for example, a biological brother and sister who were brought up separately, then met and fell in love as young adults were sentenced to prison after marrying (Connolly, 2007).

Why is sex between siblings so universally forbidden? From an evolutionary viewpoint, there are at least two possible reasons. First, procreation between closely related individuals increases the likelihood of passing on defective genes, particularly recessive ones. Early societies that forbade incest may have been genetically stronger than those that did not. Second, incest taboos put pressure on societies to interact with neighbouring cultures. Historically, this meant that tribal elders would bargain about marrying their children to one another. In the process, the two tribes might have increased general commerce and enhanced the access to food and other forms of wealth for both groups (Leavitt, 1989; Johnson & Earle, 1987). According to these views, avoiding sex with close relatives enhances the chances for survival of a group of people. Cultural regulation of our biological drive towards sexual behaviour may also have emerged because it serves the purpose of promoting our survival as a group.

Although norms vary from culture to culture, as we have seen, all cultures do approve certain sexual practices, while condemning others. Within nations, many religious, ethnic and other subcultural groups also influence the sexual behaviour of their members. In some societies, sex is not acceptable unless the couple's relationship is considered legitimate, in many cases until marriage. In the West, the sexual revolution of the 1960s and 1970s loosened many social restrictions on premarital sex. Today, over 95% of people in the West have sex before marriage (Finer, 2007) and the number of young adults with multiple sexual partners has also increased. By the time most individuals reach their early 20s, they have had three to four sexual partners (Mosher et al., 2005). Some sexual behaviours, such as homosexual relationships, remain controversial in many countries.

Sex: What Happens in the Body and Brain

Changes in societal views of sex and what is appropriate sexual behaviour grew, in part, from psychology research on the subject. One of the most influential sex researchers was biologist Alfred Kinsey. Realizing that many of his college students were uneducated about basic sexual practices, Kinsey switched his field of study from insect behaviour to human sexual behaviour in the 1940s (Bullough, 2004). He then undertook a massive project, interviewing thousands of people to collect data on the sexual practices of ordinary people. Kinsey's work was widely publicized and led to the realization that many 'normal' Americans engaged in sexual behaviour that was not considered to be conventional at the time, including oral sex, anal sex and having multiple partners (Brown & Fee, 2003). Kinsey's work helped to lessen taboos about discussing these sexual practices, because people realized they were not uncommon. He normalized sexual behaviour.

What Happens in the Body during Sex? During the 1950s and 1960s, researchers William Masters and Virginia Johnson brought the study of sexual behaviour into the laboratory. Masters and Johnson recorded some of the first physiological data in humans during sex. They studied the sexual responses of both men and women and described four phases of the human *sexual response cycle*, as shown in Figure 13.7 (Masters & Johnson, 1966).

- *Excitement.* This is the beginning of arousal and it can last up to several hours. Heart rate quickens.

- *Plateau.* At this phase, breathing and pulse rates increase. Muscles tense and a flush may appear across the chest.

- *Orgasm.* Muscle tension and blood pressure reach a peak. This is quickly followed by climax, which is

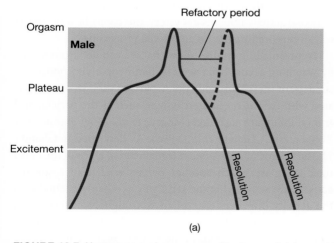

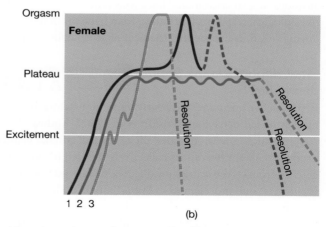

FIGURE 13.7 Human sexual responses. Masters and Johnson identified four phases in sexual response. Part (a) illustrates the typical pattern in males. Women experience greater variety in their sexual response. Part (b) shows three female patterns.

Source: Reprinted with permission from Masters, W. H. & Johnson V. E. (1966) *Human Sexual Response.* Boston: Little, Brown, p. 5. Copyright 1966 by the Masters and Johnson Institute.

a series of muscle contractions (the intensity varies, particularly among women).

- *Resolution*. Muscles relax and heart rate returns to normal. While men have a refractory period after an orgasm, during which they cannot ejaculate, women may have additional orgasms.

In the 1970s, sex therapist Helen Kaplan incorporated an additional element to the beginning of the sexual response cycle. Kaplan believed that *desire* – basically, whether you are 'in the mood' – was a necessary condition to motivate an individual to become excited (Kaplan, 1977). The research of Masters and Johnson and those that followed, such as Kaplan, was particularly influential to US society, because it encouraged women to enjoy sex, which was previously considered inappropriate (Weiss, 2000). Masters and Johnson's research also dispelled myths about ageing and sexual behaviour. Prior to their research, the conventional view was that sexual behaviour was the realm of young to middle-aged adults and that after a certain age sexual behaviour was minimal, if not physically impossible. As a result of Masters and Johnson's research, as well as others that followed, the current view is that sexual behaviour can continue throughout old age, providing a person remains physically healthy and has a willing partner (Waite *et al.*, 2009; DeLamater & Karraker, 2009).

Although the work of the early sex researchers was highly controversial at the time it was conducted and their methods have been questioned since then (Cochran *et al.*, 1953), the publicity these researchers received increased awareness of sexual behaviour, which had a lasting effect, altering society's standards of what is considered normal (Gagnon, 1975). This body of psychology research emphasized that sexual behaviour is a wholesome and healthy activity, another major change in thinking compared with earlier, more restrictive attitudes. It also encouraged later researchers to explore our physiological responses, including what happens in the brain during sex, thus broadening the field of acceptable research.

What Happens in the Brain during Sex?

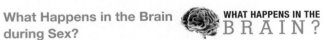

Reproductive hormones are clearly important factors in modulating sexual behaviour (Raskin *et al.*, 2009; Kudwa *et al.*, 2006; Berman, 2005). In males, the testes and adrenal glands produce male sex hormones collectively referred to as androgens. In females, the ovaries produce the female sex hormones (*oestrogen* and *progesterone*). Even though androgens are referred to as male sex hormones, they are produced by the adrenal glands of females too. Like all other hormones, these molecules are released in the bloodstream and travel throughout the body. In men, blood levels of androgens, particularly

testosterone, are linked positively to sex drive (Bancroft, 2005; Simon *et al.*, 2005). On average, sex drive in males declines with advancing age as testosterone levels drop, although, as we have seen, ageing does not preclude sexual interest and activity (Feldman *et al.*, 2002). In women, the story appears to be a bit more complicated: oestrogen levels are important for the physiological aspects of the sexual response (Frank *et al.*, 2008) as well as in determining feelings about one's attractiveness (Durante *et al.*, 2009). However, sex drive also appears to be stimulated, at least in part, by androgens in women.

In order for testosterone to enhance motivation for sex, it needs to act upon the brain. Sex hormones are all small molecules that readily cross the blood–brain barrier to act on many regions of the brain. One subregion of the hypothalamus, the *medial preoptic* area, is especially responsive to testosterone. This area is rich in sex hormone receptors and is important for sexual behaviour (Dugger *et al.*, 2007). Again, as with hunger, motivating people to have sex is not as simple as activating a single brain region. For humans, as well as for less complex animals, many brain regions are involved in sexual arousal and behaviour (Toates, 2009) and different regions are activated during different phases of the sexual response. Most research has focused on the excitement phase. Neuroimaging studies of people while they are viewing erotic films show that the hypothalamus, amygdala, prefrontal cortex, striatum and ventral tegmental area are all activated (Miyagawa *et al.*, 2007; Karama *et al.*, 2002). These last three regions are important components of the brain's reward system. The brain's reward system is also activated when we look at photos of our romantic partner's faces, suggesting that this area is importantly involved in responding to rewarding stimuli that are not necessarily erotic (Fisher *et al.*, 2005). During the orgasm phase, one study in males found that in addition to the ventral tegmental area the cerebellum is activated (Holstege *et al.*, 2003). While the involvement of the cerebellum in this phase of sexual activity remains a mystery, there may be links to the role of this brain region in emotional processing.

Neuroimaging studies show that we can get aroused just by watching sexual behaviour. When people view videos of sex acts, or merely imagine them, parts of their brains associated with the *mirror neuron system*, such as the parietal and frontal lobes, are activated (Mouras *et al.*, 2008; Shmuelof & Zohary, 2007; Gallese *et al.*, 1996). As described in Chapter 11, the mirror neuron system is made up of areas of the brain that, when we watch another person engage in a specific activity, are activated in the same way as when we actually do the activity ourselves (Rizzolatti & Craighero, 2004). Thus, watching other people engage in sexual behaviour activates some of the same regions of the viewer's brain that would be active if the viewer were actually having sex. This activation makes viewers feel sexually aroused simply from watching.

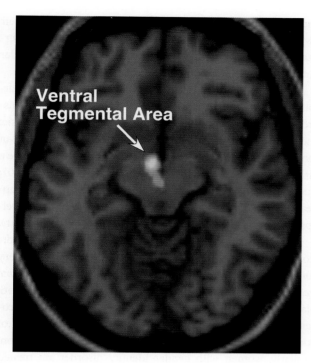

The brain, sexual arousal and rewards. Gazing at a photo of one's romantic partner activates the ventral tegmental area (VTA) (shown in yellow on this fMRI image). The VTA is activated during sexual activity as well as when looking at photos of loved ones in whom there is no sexual interest; this shows that this brain area is associated with learning about rewarding stimuli in general.

Source: Courtesy of Lucy L. Brown, Albert Einstein College of Medicine.

Even if we do not consciously see an erotic picture or film, we can become aroused. In one study, researchers presented a series of photos to participants. Some of the photos were sexual, and these were rapidly shown and removed before the viewer was consciously aware. Even though viewers did not remember seeing anything, neuroimaging showed activation of regions of the brain associated with arousal and reward (Childress *et al.*, 2008). Sexual behaviour is essential for the survival of the species, and the rapid activation of brain regions by subtle sexual cues ensures that we are motivated to have sex.

Gender Identity

Before we consider individual differences in sexuality, we need to address the most basic of differences in this domain, whether we are male or female. Early in prenatal life, it is impossible to tell whether the foetus is a boy or a girl (unless a chromosomal analysis is done). After a certain developmental stage, if the foetus is genetically male (its sex chromosomes are XY), it will develop testes. In the absence of testes and a Y chromosome, the foetus will develop ovaries.

In other words, development of a female foetus is a default programme that happens if the signals to masculinize are not present.

The testes release *testosterone*, which travels throughout the body. In certain organs, this hormone is converted to one of two other hormones, *dihydrotestosterone (DHT)* or, surprisingly, to oestrogen. DHT is important for masculinizing the external genitalia: this is the hormone that causes a male foetus to grow a penis. Testosterone can be converted to oestrogen in the central nervous system, and some evidence suggests that oestrogen along with testosterone then *masculinizes* the brain: they set up brain functioning that is, on average, characteristic of male brains. Since oestrogen is considered to be a female reproductive hormone, its involvement in *masculinization* seems contradictory, leading scientists to recognize that the traditional view of oestrogen as the female sex hormone and testosterone as the male sex hormone was probably an oversimplification. Oestrogen's role in masculinization also raises the question of why the female foetus, which produces oestrogen directly from its ovaries, does not end up with a masculinized brain. The answer to this question is that female foetuses are protected against their own oestrogen and the oestrogen produced by the mother, because they make a protein that binds to oestrogen and prevents it from masculinizing the brain.

Masculinization of the brain occurs in the hypothalamus, the brain region important for coordinating reproductive hormone release from the pituitary. Masculinization also occurs in brain regions important for non-reproductive behaviours, such as those important for regulating aggression. Exposure to specific hormones during foetal life may also determine whether humans identify with being a male or a female. Indeed, girls with a medical condition that exposes them during the foetal stage to masculine levels of hormones may later engage in play behaviour that is more like boys' than it is like girls' play behaviour (Hines & Kaufman, 1994).

In some cases, babies arrive with ambiguous genitalia, and the issue of gender identity is not readily resolved. Sometimes an XX baby, because of the hormones it was exposed to *in utero*, will be born with an enlarged clitoris that resembles a penis. Other times, an XY baby will arrive with a smaller-than-normal penis. People with ambiguous genitalia are now referred to as *intersex* (this term has largely replaced the old name *hermaphrodite*). After determining the genetic sex of the baby, physicians and parents need to make decisions about how to proceed.

In the past, psychologists and healthcare providers believed that gender identity was determined mostly by the environment. In other words, if a child is treated like a boy (or girl), then he/she will grow up to identify with that gender. As a result, several individuals with ambiguous genitalia received treatment to make their external genitalia appear to be more 'normal'. For example, boys without fully developed penises or where accidents happened in circumcisions underwent surgery and were raised as girls. In some cases, this treatment backfired and the surgically created 'girls' grew up very unhappy with their gender assignment and eventually underwent treatment to live the remainder of their lives as males. Today, doctors and scientists generally believe that gender identity is largely determined by biology and that hormones present early in life contribute to masculinization (or, by default, feminization) of the brain.

In still other kinds of cases, external gender characteristics appear to be the opposite of gender identity. That is, the individual appears to be one sex but identifies strongly with the other sex. Although it is not entirely clear how this disconnect occurs, it is possible that hormones responsible for masculinizing the body are not working synchronously with those that do so to the brain.

Psychologists have come to appreciate that many people do not always experience their own sense of gender in a clear way. They have *transgender experiences*: a sense that their actual gender identity is different from the gender category to which they were born physically, or that it lies outside the usual male versus female categories (Carroll, 2007). Many of today's psychologists believe that, in many cases, transgender feelings reflect alternative, rather than disordered, ways of experiencing one's gender identity. Numerous people with transgender experiences come to terms with their gender inconsistencies, blend gender in some way and become comfortable with their atypical gender identity. However, others experience extreme unhappiness with their given gender and may seek treatment for their problem. These individuals receive a diagnosis of *gender identity disorder*. People with gender identity disorder would like to get rid of their primary and secondary sex characteristics – many of them find their own genitals repugnant – and wish to acquire the characteristics of the other sex (APA, 2000). Men with the disorder outnumber women by around two to one.

Some children experience gender identity disorder (Carroll, 2007; Zucker & Bradley, 2005). Like adults with this disorder, the children feel uncomfortable about their assigned sex and deeply desire to be members of the opposite sex. Surveys of mothers indicate that about 1 to 2% of young boys wish to be a girl, and 3 to 4% of young girls wish to be a boy (Carroll, 2007; Zucker & Bradley, 2005). This childhood pattern usually disappears by adolescence or adulthood, but in some cases it develops into adult gender identity disorder (Cohen-Kettenis, 2001).

The causes of gender identity disorder are not well understood. In addition, treatment for the disorder has been very controversial. Many adults with this disorder receive *hormone treatments* to change their sexual characteristics (Andreasen & Black, 2006; Hepp *et al.*, 2002). Physicians prescribe oestrogen for male patients, causing breast development, loss of body and facial hair and a change in body fat distribution. Similarly, women with gender identity disorder are treated with *testosterone*. For other individuals, however, this is not enough, and they pursue one of the most hotly debated practices in medicine: *sex-change*, or *sexual reassignment, surgery* (Andreasen & Black, 2006; Hepp *et al.*, 2002). The operation itself includes, for men, amputation of the penis, creation of an artificial vagina and face-changing plastic surgery. For women, surgery may include bilateral mastectomy and hysterectomy. Studies in Europe have suggested that one in every 30,000 men and one in every 100,000 women may seek sex-change surgery (Carroll, 2007; Bakker *et al.*, 1993). Some clinicians consider such surgery to be a humane solution, while others believe that sexual reassignment is an inappropriate approach to a complex disorder (Olsson & Moller, 2003).

PSYCHOLOGY AROUND US   Ben Barres: A True Success Story

Ben Barres is a renowned neurobiologist at Stanford University. Ben was born a female and named Barbara. Ben has since transitioned to a male and has led a very successful career while actively engaging in the argument surrounding the relationship between sex and intelligence. He has provided abundant commentary on this issue, using his own experiences to illuminate lingering sexist attitudes in male-dominated fields, like maths and science. Ben argues that there are different expectations for women than for men, and one example from his own life seems to illustrate this fact pretty clearly. A colleague once heard a spectator remark after one of Barres's lectures that his work was so much better than his sister Barbara's. The spectator had unknowingly compared Barres's work as Barbara to Barres's work as Ben.

Source: Marcio Jose Sanchez/©AP/Wide World Photos.

Gender Differences in Sexuality Although each of us has our own preferences, beliefs and behaviours, there do seem to be some differences between men and women when it comes to sex. Males and females differ in characteristics they perceive as attractive in a mate and in the stimuli that arouse them. Their fantasies and desired numbers of partners may also differ.

Evolutionary psychologists suggest that much of how heterosexual men and women interact with the opposite sex is the result of thousands of years of evolution designed to maximize our chances of survival and reproductive success. Men desire youthful, attractive mates because those attributes signal good odds for reproductive success; women are attracted to men who are dependable and strong because they will most likely be able to protect and care for children. Men seek out women with a good hip-to-waist ratio (of around 0.7) and a BMI of around 22, as well as a good leg-to-torso ratio and other signs of health (clear skin, body symmetry). Women are interested in healthy males but are also interested in their social skills and capacity to earn money.

In addition to what makes someone attractive, men and women also differ in what arouses them. Men, on average, are aroused more quickly than women by visual stimuli (Stoléru *et al.*, 1999). Women, on the other hand, respond more strongly than men do to physical contact and verbal expression. This may be because arousal in women is more often influenced by their relationship with a partner, as well as their own self-image, than it is in men (Peplau, 2003).

Even women's sexual fantasies are on average more commitment-oriented (Ellis & Symons, 1990) and they tend to have fewer fantasies than men do (Byers *et al.*, 1998). In one study, surveyors asked university students, 'Have you had sex with over a thousand different partners in your imagination?' Males in the study were four times more likely than females to say yes (Ellis & Symons, 1990). The frequency of men's arousal and the number of their fantasies have led many psychologists to conclude that men generally have a higher sex drive. In fact, men tend to rate their own sex drives as higher than women rate theirs (Baumeister *et al.*, 2001).

It is important to realize that reported gender differences in sexual desire and sexual activity may reflect biases in reporting. On surveys and during interviews, women may downplay their sexual desires and behaviours because of perceived social constraints. Just as a woman's ability to enjoy sex was mostly considered inappropriate in the past, women may still feel that they are not supposed to have similar attitudes towards sex when compared with men. Conversely, males may be more likely to exaggerate such feelings and behaviours to fulfil imagined expectations for men. There is no question that women and men are judged differently by society when it comes to sex. In films, for example, women with high sex drives are often portrayed as dangerous or emotionally unstable, while men with low sex drives are often the subject of ridicule. These perceptions may influence the way that people respond to questions about their sex lives. In reality, though, women and men may be more alike than researchers once thought. For example, a study of undergraduates did not find a significant difference between women and men in their desired number of partners (Miller *et al.*, 2002).

Sexual Orientation Most people are **heterosexual**; they are sexually attracted to members of the opposite sex. Approximately 10% of males and 2% of females identify themselves as **homosexual**, or attracted to members of their own sex. Why are some people attracted to members of the opposite sex while others are attracted to members of the same sex? Arguments about this topic have been heated and often reflect a nature/nurture debate.

> **heterosexual** sexual attraction to members of the opposite sex.

> **homosexual** sexual attraction to members of one's own sex.

Since homosexuality is considered by some religious and political groups to be immoral, a common position of such organizations has been that homosexuality is a choice, or lifestyle, selected by an individual, as a result of being exposed to what they perceive as abnormal and unhealthy experiences while growing up (Lawson, 1987). Some theorists have suggested that homosexuals are more likely than heterosexuals to have experienced homosexual activity as youngsters or were not treated in a gender-appropriate way while growing up. Other theories explain homosexuality in terms of abnormal relationships with the opposite sex parent (Bieber *et al.*, 1962).

Alfred Kinsey believed that sexual orientation was on a continuum, with many people fitting between the two extremes of exclusively heterosexual and exclusively homosexual (Kinsey *et al.*, 1948). Kinsey's theory is controversial, but it does suggest that sexual orientation is changeable. Based on this idea, numerous organizations have devised treatment programmes to 'convert' homosexuals to heterosexuality. Such programmes assume that if a person living as a homosexual is, in fact, at least part heterosexual, intervention can cause the person to increase the heterosexual-to-homosexual ratio. In other words, with the help of the programme, individuals can learn to emphasize their heterosexual behaviours and thoughts in daily life and downplay and suppress homosexual behaviours and thoughts (Murphy, 1992; Pattison & Pattison, 1980). In fact, in the late 1960s, the Masters and Johnson Institute sponsored such a programme and reported conversions among the majority of participants (Masters & Johnson, 1979). These findings have not been supported, and current research strongly suggests that homosexuality is biologically based, not learnt and cannot be 'cured'. If anything, such attempts can be damaging to the individual, since they typically produce feelings of shame and embarrassment (Cramer *et al.*, 2008; Haldeman, 1994).

As part of a growing realization that homosexuality occurs naturally in some people, the American Psychiatric Association removed homosexuality from its designation as a psychological disorder in 1973. Additional evidence that homosexuality is a natural, biological phenomenon comes from repeated observations of homosexual behaviour throughout the animal kingdom. Homosexuality has been reported in both male and female birds (including one celebrated case of a homosexual penguin at the Central Park Zoo in New York City), as well as among bonobos, a type of chimpanzee (Roughgarden, 2004; Smith, 2004).

Although the exact influences leading to sexual orientation remain unknown, considerable evidence suggests our orientation has a biological basis. Researchers have studied the intertwined influences of genes, hormones and anatomical brain differences.

- *Genes*. Studies suggest a strong genetic influence on sexual orientation. In other words, homosexuality tends to run in families (Bailey & Pillard, 1991; Buhrich *et al.*, 1991). The correlation is greatest among monozygotic, or identical, twins. If one twin is homosexual, the other is also likely to have that orientation. Some evidence suggests this link exists even if the twins are raised apart (Eckert *et al.*, 1986). As with many other traits, however, genetics do not completely determine sexual orientation; even among pairs of identical twins who share the same genes, some pairs differ in orientation. Furthermore, a genetic link is not at all apparent for most people with homosexual orientations. Researchers have therefore considered other biological factors.

- *Hormones*. Some studies suggest that some homosexual males may experience different hormone levels before birth compared with heterosexual males. Studies have shown that having an older brother increases the odds of male homosexuality. With each additional older brother, the likelihood of homosexuality increases (Blanchard, 2004, 2001). In the case of younger brothers with homosexual orientations, some researchers suggest that the mother's immune system may sometimes react to male sex hormones while she is carrying a male foetus, such that in subsequent pregnancies maternal antibodies will lessen the masculinizing action of hormones on the brain of the younger brother. Although this hypothesis cannot account for the majority of homosexual individuals, studies examining brain differences support the possibility that prenatal hormone exposure may be an important factor for some individuals (Rahman, 2005; Williams *et al.*, 2000).

- *Brain anatomy*. A sex difference exists in the anterior, or front, part of the hypothalamus. This region is twice as large in heterosexual men as it is in women (Orikasa *et al.*, 2007). A similar size difference exists in this brain region between heterosexual men and homosexual men. The anterior hypothalamuses of homosexual men are, on average, more similar in size to those of women than to those of heterosexual men, suggesting that individual differences in masculinizing factors (most likely hormones) may contribute to changes in brain anatomy that ultimately lead to homosexual or heterosexual behaviour (LeVay, 1991).

Western society is gradually becoming more tolerant of homosexuality. Still, same-sex marriage is a hotly debated topic among religious and political groups. Roughly half of the population still believes it is wrong for two men or two women to marry (Pew Forum, 2003).

Difficulties with Sex   OUT OF THE ORDINARY

Although sexual activity brings great pleasure to most people, it can pose significant problems for some. Other than gender identity disorder (discussed above), there are three kinds of sexual problems or disorders: sexual dysfunctions, paraphilias and medical problems.

Sexual Dysfunctions *Sexual dysfunctions* are disorders in which people cannot respond normally in key areas of sexual functioning, making it difficult or impossible to enjoy sexual intercourse.

Two sexual dysfunctions – hypoactive sexual desire disorder and sexual aversion disorder – centre on how much sexual desire a person experiences. People with *hypoactive sexual desire disorder* lack interest in sex and, in turn, display very little sexual activity. As much as 16% of men and 33% of women may display this dysfunction (Maurice, 2007; Laumann *et al.*, 2005, 1999). People with *sexual aversion disorder* find sex distinctly unpleasant or repulsive. Indeed, the idea of sex may sicken, disgust or frighten them. Apparently, aversion to sex is relatively uncommon, particularly among men (Wincze *et al.*, 2008; Maurice, 2007).

There are two sexual dysfunctions that affect the excitement phase of the sexual response cycle: female sexual arousal disorder (once referred to as *frigidity*) and male erectile disorder (once called *impotence*). Women with a *female sexual arousal disorder* are persistently unable to attain or maintain proper lubrication or genital swelling during sexual activity (Heiman, 2007). Estimates of its prevalence vary, but most studies agree that more than 10% of women experience it (Laumann *et al.*, 2005, 1999, 1994; Bancroft *et al.*, 2003). Men with *male erectile disorder* persistently fail to attain or maintain an adequate erection during sexual activity. This problem occurs in about 10% of the male population (Laumann *et al.*, 2005, 1999). Most such men are over the age of 50, largely because so many cases are associated with ailments of older adults (Cameron *et al.*, 2005). However, according to surveys, half of all adult men experience erectile difficulty during intercourse at least some of the time.

Dysfunctions of the orgasm phase of the sexual response cycle are *rapid ejaculation, male orgasmic disorder* and *female orgasmic disorder*. A man suffering from *rapid*, or *premature*, *ejaculation* persistently reaches orgasm and ejaculates with very little sexual stimulation before, on or shortly after penetration, and before he wishes to. As much as 30% of men in the West experience rapid ejaculation at some time (Jannini & Lenai, 2005). Many young men experience this dysfunction, but it is not solely a young man's problem. Research suggests that men of any age may suffer from rapid ejaculation (Althof, 2007). A man with *male orgasmic disorder* is repeatedly unable to reach orgasm or is very delayed in reaching orgasm after normal sexual excitement. The disorder occurs in 8% of men (Hartmann & Waldinger, 2007; Laumann *et al.*, 2005, 1999). Similarly, women with *female orgasmic disorder* rarely reach orgasm or generally experience a very delayed one. Studies indicate that 10% or more of women have never had an orgasm, either alone or during intercourse, and at least another 9% rarely have orgasms (LoPiccolo, 2004, 1995; Bancroft *et al.*, 2003). In contrast, half of all women experience orgasm in intercourse at least fairly regularly (LoPiccolo & Stock, 1987).

Each of the sexual dysfunctions may be caused by a combination of biological and psychological factors. In the biological realm, for example, abnormal hormone activity can adversely affect sexual functioning and various medications have side effects interfering with sex drive and behaviour. Problematic psychological factors that contribute to sexual dysfunction include feelings of depression, anxiety or anger; inaccurate beliefs about sex; and stressors such as job pressure or relationship problems. Masters and Johnson (1970) found two psychological factors to be particularly common among men with sexual dysfunctions: *performance anxiety* and *spectator role*. They found that once some men experience erectile or orgasmic problems they start to worry about the possibility of failing to have erections or orgasms during their sexual encounters (performance anxiety). As a result, instead of relaxing during such encounters, they keep observing themselves and their performances. They become judges and spectators rather than sexually aroused participants, and their ability to engage in sexual activity declines.

Today's treatments for sexual dysfunctions can be traced to the publication of Masters and Johnson's landmark book *Human Sexual Inadequacy* in 1970. Their *sex therapy* programme has grown into a complex approach, which now includes a combination of cognitive-behavioural, couple and family techniques that you will read more about in Chapter 20 (Leiblum, 2007; Bach *et al.*, 2001). In recent years, drug therapies have been added to the sex treatment approaches, triggered by the enormous success of drugs such as *sildenafil* (trade name Viagra) in the treatment of male erectile disorder.

Paraphilias *Paraphilias* are disorders in which people have repeated and intense sexual urges or fantasies or display sexual behaviours in response to objects or situations that society considers inappropriate. Some of the most common paraphilias are fetishism, exhibitionism, voyeurism, paedophilia and sexual sadism. For most paraphilias, men with the disorders greatly outnumber women.

People with *fetishism* display recurrent intense sexual urges or behaviours that involve the use of a non-living object. The object – women's underwear, shoes and boots are particularly common – may be touched, smelled, worn or used in some other way while the individual masturbates or has intercourse (Marshall *et al.*, 2008).

A person with *exhibitionism* has recurrent urges to expose his genitals to another person, almost always a member of the opposite sex. He rarely attempts to initiate sexual activity with the person to whom he exposes himself; rather, he wants to produce shock or surprise. Sometimes an exhibitionist will expose himself in a particular neighbourhood at particular hours. In one survey of 2,800 men, 4.3% reported that they perform exhibitionistic behaviour (Långström & Seto, 2006).

An individual with *voyeurism* has recurrent and intense urges to secretly observe unsuspecting people as they undress or to spy on couples having intercourse. The person may also masturbate during the act of observing or when thinking about it afterwards but does not generally seek to have sex with the observed person.

People with *paedophilia* gain sexual gratification by watching, touching or engaging in sexual acts with prepubescent children, usually 13 years old or younger. Some individuals with this disorder are satisfied by material such as children's underwear ads; others seek out child pornography; and some are driven to actually watch, fondle or engage in sexual activities with children (Durkin & Hundersmarck, 2008). Both boys and girls can be paedophilia victims, but research suggests that two-thirds of them are girls.

Most paedophilic offenders are imprisoned or forced into treatment if they are caught. Some people with paedophilia can exhibit distorted thinking, such as 'It's all right to have sex with children as long as they agree' (Roche & Quayle, 2007). Similarly, it is not uncommon for paedophiles to blame the children for adult–child sexual contacts or to assert that the children benefited from the experience (Durkin & Hundersmarck, 2008).

A person with *sexual sadism* is intensely sexually aroused by the thought or act of inflicting suffering on others by dominating, restraining, blindfolding, cutting, strangling, mutilating or even killing the victim. Many carry out sadistic acts with a consenting partner; some, however, act out their urges on non-consenting victims (Marshall *et al.*, 2008). A number of rapists and sexual murderers, for example, exhibit sexual sadism. The key to their arousal is suffering by the victim.

A number of explanations have been proposed for the various paraphilias, but none has received much research support (Abramowitz, 2008). Moreover, none of the current treatments for these disorders has been clearly successful (Roche & Quayle, 2007).

Medical Problems Sexual activity is not without risks. People who have sex without contraception face the risk of unintended or unwanted pregnancies. Unprotected sex also leaves participants at risk of contracting *sexually transmitted infections (STIs)*, including HIV, the virus linked to AIDS. Other common STIs include chlamydia, which is the most frequently reported; gonorrhoea; genital herpes; and human papillomavirus (HPV). Most individuals with an STI have no symptoms. Using condoms can greatly reduce the chances of contracting most STIs, and women younger than 26 years of age can receive a vaccine to protect against most of the HPV strains that cause cervical cancers, but abstaining from sex is the only way to entirely prevent infection (CDC, 2008; Markowitz *et al.*, 2007).

Half of all new cases of HIV are contracted before the age of 25 (CDC, 2011). Because of the public health threats posed by HIV/AIDS, as well as other STIs and teen pregnancies, sex education for secondary school students has become a priority (Luker, 2007; Dailard, 2001).

Before You Go On

What Do You Know?

10. What aspects of sexual behaviour are affected by our cultural standards?

11. What are the phases of the sexual response cycle described by Masters and Johnson and what happens at each one?

12. What biological factors has research found to be related to sexual orientation?

13. Identify four kinds of sexual problems or disorders and give an example of each.

What Do You Think?

Describe the specific cultural standards for sexual behaviour that affect your peer group.

Psychological Motivations: Affiliation and Achievement

LEARNING OBJECTIVE 4

Describe factors that influence our psychological motivations for affiliation and achievement.

In the previous sections, we talked about biological motivations. Recall Maslow's hierarchy of needs, though, and you will see that we are also motivated by non-biological needs. The need to belong and the need for self-worth are psychological motivations that are just as important to our health and happiness. These motivations make sense when we consider that humans often live in tightly knit social groups, and as such our connection to our social group and our sense of worth within our group is very important.

Just as it may be difficult to focus on achieving in school if you are hungry, your focus may be affected if the more basic psychological need of *affiliation*, or belonging, is not met.

Affiliation

Going to university is, for many students, their first experience away from home for a prolonged period. Suddenly, you are on your own, without the support and comfort of your family. Those first few weeks can be quite stressful, until students become acquainted with their new surroundings and meet new people.

Being part of a social group, whether it is a family or a group of friends or an organization, helps us define who we are and allows us to feel secure about our place in the world. We derive security, identity and stimulation from social groups. We are social animals drawn to others who are like us. The need to live in a social group has evolved in humans because it is evolutionarily advantageous for groups to live together, being able to provide food and protection for one another, while individuals living alone must be self-sufficient, and are therefore less likely to survive (Diener & Seligman, 2002). Members of the species who were drawn to be a part of a social group were therefore more likely to survive than their individualistic counterparts.

From the moment we are born, we seek a connection with others. *Instinct theory* explains that infants automatically seek out their mother's breast and this *rooting* reflex reinforces the infant's chances of survival. As we develop, relationships with friends and, later, significant others help to raise our self-esteem. Men and women in long-term, healthy relationships

have less depression and live longer (Holt-Lunstad *et al.*, 2008). Even older spouses who provide more care to each other live longer than those who are less considerate of each other (Kaplan & Kronick, 2006). Good supportive social relationships are the key to good mental and physical health at any age.

Isolation and Exclusion

OUT OF THE ORDINARY

Our motivation to belong may also explain why some individuals remain in abusive relationships or join gangs. The fear of social exclusion is a powerful motivator. In fact, when people feel excluded, the anterior cingulate cortex in the frontal cortex is activated (Eisenberger *et al.*, 2003). Recall that this same area responds to physical pain. Social isolation and banishment is a punishment; solitary confinement is a form of torture.

PSYCHOLOGY AROUND US   Fitting in While Doing Good

Our need for affiliation can lead to morally abhorrent behaviour, such as gang violence. But it can also be used to encourage positive social behaviour. Communities have used it to their advantage when developing recycling programmes, for instance. Publicizing recycling and making it very obvious that neighbours are recycling (by using brightly coloured garbage cans, for example) can go a long way towards recruiting new recyclers. However, the drive to fit in has its limits, and one

of them seems to be related to the size of the social group. Psychologists have found that people respond more positively to arguments about the positive effects of recycling on small communities, such as a few residential blocks or a small town, than to claims about what impact recycling would have on the entire nation. It may be that very large social groups make individuals feel anonymous enough that they believe their individual efforts will not matter much.

The need to be affiliated with others is routinely exploited as a means of punishment or torture during war and even in prisons. So profound is our motivation to be around others that the effects of long-term isolation are not only disturbing but also often lead to permanent psychological damage. One study of inmates at a US prison (Haney, 2008) found that months of isolation could cause a person to become catatonic, or completely nonresponsive. Another study composed of over 200 interviews of prisoners who had been confined to solitary cells found that one-third became psychotic, losing contact with reality (Grassian, 1983).

Affiliation with others is an essential psychological need. When we are denied contact with other humans, we not only are unable to satisfy biological needs but also lose our motivation to pursue our highest level needs: self-worth and self-actualization. We are no longer driven to achieve.

Intrinsic and Extrinsic Motivation What is the difference between intrinsic and extrinsic motivation? It can be illustrated by the following story.

A professor was working at home. Things were going well, but it was a holiday and the local park nearby was

full of children laughing and playing. Their erratic, loud, uncontrollable noise was deeply disturbing. There was no easy alternative for the writer. Closing the windows did little to muffle the sound; it only made the room stuffy. There was no other room to decamp to.

So what to do, other than ask the children to move on? A number of possibilities arose: threaten the children or bribe them to go away. The children might accept the bribe but soon return to this lucrative source of money.

The academic, however, knew his motivation theory. He wandered outside. Mustering all the charm he could, he gathered the children around him and told them that he had observed them from his office and had admired and enjoyed their noisy games, high-spirited yells and laughter – so much so that he was prepared to pay them to continue.

Of course, they continued. The professor paid them again the next day and the next. But on the fourth day, when the expectant children gathered around, he explained that for various reasons he had no money so he could no longer continue to 'subsidize' their play. Speaking on behalf of the others, the oldest child said that if he thought the children were going to carry on playing for nothing he was sadly misinformed, and they left.

What the writer knew was that the essence of play is that it is intrinsically satisfying. It is a preposterous idea to pay people to play, because they love and volunteer for the activity. You only have to recompense people for doing things they do not really enjoy: things that are dangerous or mind-numbingly dreary, things that are tiring or difficult. People are intrinsically motivated by the joy and stimulation of the activity. However, they will do many other things less pleasurable (dirty, difficult, dangerous) if they are given sufficient incentive, like money.

Achievement

The fact that you are reading this book means that you are motivated to go to university, study and obtain a degree. You may even pursue additional degrees or you may graduate and find a job. No matter what path you take, to satisfy the needs at the top of Maslow's pyramid, self-worth and self-actualization, you need to feel competent, engage with others and possess control over your own life. **Self-determination** theory says that competence, relatedness and autonomy are instinctive and that they give purpose and meaning to life (Ryan & Deci, 2002). Not all psychologists agree with this theory, though. As you will see later in this section, other cultures, such as the Chinese, place less importance on autonomy, instead valuing collective effort.

self-determination competence, relatedness and autonomy thought necessary for us to achieve our potential.

As you might expect, incentives often play a role in motivating us to achieve. At university, you may be motivated intrinsically by curiosity to learn new information. In other words, the behaviour may be engaging and enjoyable for you in and of itself. Or you may be motivated to learn indirectly as a result of incentives. For instance, your reason for studying hard in this course may be because you are hoping to be rewarded with the top grade at the end of term. When achievement is motivated by incentives, it is often associated with competition. People who place too much value on rewards are more likely to suffer when they fail (Sheldon *et al.*, 2004). If they succeed, they may think that the reward, and not their motivation, was the reason for their success. In contrast, psychologists associate intrinsic motivation with the qualities of self-determination theory: competence, relatedness and autonomy. When you strive to do well for yourself, you enjoy yourself more (Blumenfeld *et al.*, 2006). See 'What Happens in the Brain When We Are Motivated to Run a Marathon' at the end of this section for a display of what happens in the brain when we strive to achieve in the realm of physical exercise.

We know that people who are high in achievement motivation:

- exercise some control over the means of production and produce more than they consume
- set moderately difficult goals for themselves
- try to maximize the likelihood of achievement satisfaction
- want concrete and regular feedback on how well they are doing
- like assuming personal responsibility for problems
- show high initiative and exploratory behaviour in their environment
- continually research the environment for opportunities of all sorts
- regard growth and expansion as the most direct signs of success
- continually strive to improve (the Japanese *kaizen* concept).

Delayed Gratification

Social, or non-biological, motivations, especially those that involve incentives, are not present at birth but are learnt. In fact, often, incentive motivations involve inhibiting basic biological drives to obtain the reward. Consider a restaurant waiter trying to earn money in his job. If the waiter acted on biological instincts and ate the food off the customer's plate, then it would be difficult to keep the job and earn money.

Delaying gratification is especially important for some of the goals you set as a student. Earning a degree takes a long time, during which you often set aside immediate pleasures, such as social activities, in favour of studying. This type of self-control is not present in very small children, but instead develops over time. The ability to delay gratification requires not just an understanding of the relative worth of the rewards but also an ability to control impulses. Impulse control also develops over time. While playing, toddlers often get into physical fights over sharing toys, whereas preschool age children react this way less and less.

Developmental psychologists have tested the ability to delay gratification in the laboratory by offering children of varying ages the choice of getting a reward right away or waiting some time to get a better reward.

Studies have shown that children display a wide range in the ability to delay gratification; some are much more able to do so than others (Lemmon & Moore, 2007). Related research also suggests that the ability to delay gratification in a laboratory setting may be predictive of success in other realms, including in academic and social settings (Mischel *et al.*, 1989).

PSYCHOLOGY AROUND US   Can you resist?

In the 1970s, an American psychologist called Walter Mischel played a simple game with 500 four-year-olds. He gave them a choice: eat one (delicious, tempting) marshmallow right away or wait for him to return in just 15 minutes and eat two marshmallows instead. Videos on how the children behaved are charmingly amusing, particularly of those who can be seen trying hard to fight their urges to gobble up the tempting treat. Some looked away the whole time; others fixated on the one available. Some held out for a few minutes but quite quickly gave in to temptation.

It is possible to see the effect of parenting in some of them. All those parental messages such as 'save it for later' or 'others first', for example, are attempts to control greed.

The test was about the importance of impulse control and emotional regulation, often called *the postponement of gratification*. But why this modest study has attracted attention is that the children now in their forties have been followed up.

The postponers did better in life. They were richer (and even thinner) than their impatient peers. They had achieved more at school and university. And they were less likely to experience all the negative aspects of life: addiction, divorce and such like (Shoda *et al.*, 1990).

One likely explanation for the fact that very young children lack the skills necessary to work towards long-term goals and delay instant gratification along the way is that their brains are not yet developed in key areas related to these tasks. The prefrontal cortex is not yet myelinated in children, and the adult levels of synapses connecting them to other neurons are not reached until after puberty. The prefrontal cortex is important not only for mediating reward signals but also for planning and carrying out complicated tasks that involve several steps towards the achievement of a long-term goal. This may provide some explanation for the common observation that, compared with adults, teenagers are more likely to engage in risky behaviour, jeopardizing their futures for instant gratification.

You may find that, as you get older, it is easier to set your sights on goals far in the future, including several years away. You realize that your actions in the present will contribute to your situation in the future. These are mature thought processes that cannot occur without an intact prefrontal cortex.

Achievement and Culture

Just as psychological and social factors influence our motivation to achieve, so does culture. For instance, one of the elements of self-determination theory, autonomy, does not seem to be essential to individuals who are part of collectivist cultures (Triandis, 2002). As we noted in Chapter 1, people from collectivist cultures tend to view achieving as a cooperative group preferable to achieving on one's own. Individuals may be motivated to succeed in order to make their organization, team or country proud, for example, rather than to garner individual recognition for themselves.

Motivation, be it biological or psychological, is complex and inextricably linked to other cognitive processes, such as memory and emotion. In trying to understand why we do the things we do, it is important to remember that society and culture play important roles as well. Whether undertaking the challenge of a hotdog eating contest or trying to pass a psychology course, our behaviours illustrate that our survival is dependent on the need for purpose.

Before You Go On

What Do You Know?

14. Why are we motivated to be socially connected?

15. What are the components of self-determination theory?

16. How do intrinsic and extrinsic motives influence achievement?

17. How does the delay of gratification help us reach goals?

What Do You Know?

Describe a long-term goal you have and how you might achieve that goal by dividing it into several smaller, short-term goals.

YOUR BRAIN AND BEHAVIOUR

What Happens in the Brain When We Are Motivated to Run a Marathon

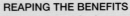

REAPING THE BENEFITS

Long-term exercise increases the number of glial cells (shown here stained with green fluorescent dyes) in the prefrontal cortex, a brain region important for reward learning and cognitive function. Glial cells assist with synaptic function and provide growth factors to sustain neurons, so an increase in their number may improve prefrontal function, potentially enhancing the rewards of running.

Source: Courtesy of Elizabeth Gould.

GROWING NEURONS WHILE YOU BUILD MUSCLE

One of the long-term benefits of getting in shape by running is that exercise stimulates the growth of new dendrites and new synaptic connections in the neocortex (shown here in this temporal lobe pyramidal neuron stained with a fluorescent dye). More connections likely translates into greater brain function, enhancing learning and memory.

Source: Courtesy of Elizabeth Gould.

Ventral tegmental area

Prefrontal cortex

Nucleus accumbens

Temporal lobe

Hippocampus

GETTING THE BLOOD FLOWING

Aerobic exercise increases your heart rate, which sends more blood throughout your body as well as to the brain. Increased blood flow in runners is particularly evident in the hippocampus, shown here in colours on this brain scan. Since the hippocampus is important for anxiety regulation, increased blood flow may contribute to the calming and mood-elevating effects often associated with exercise.

Source: S. Small, *et al.*, An *in vivo* correlate of exercise-induced neurogenesis in the adult dentate gyrus. *Proceedings of the National Academy of Sciences, 104*(13), 5638–5643, 2007. Reproduced with permission.

Source: Masterfile.

A marathon is a 26.2-mile race that generally requires months of preparation. Many people follow strict regimens to help them prepare. Runners eagerly sign up for marathons all across the world, in all kinds of weather. What might motivate people to run?

When we are motivated to run for personal achievement, the *reward learning pathway* – the brain regions involved in basic biological reward, such as the ventral tegmental area, the nucleus accumbens and the prefrontal cortex – is engaged. In addition, areas that are important for storing the memories of our past running experiences, such as the hippocampus and neocortex, are likely to be involved. The prefrontal cortex is also important for enabling us to attend to our goals and respond flexibly to changes in the terrain as we run. Will we beat our personal best?

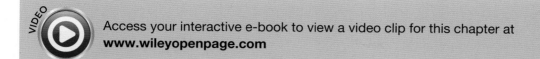

Access your interactive e-book to view a video clip for this chapter at **www.wileyopenpage.com**

Summary

Theories of Motivation

LEARNING OBJECTIVE 1   Compare and contrast major theories of motivation.

- Several theories offer explanations for our motivation but no single theory can explain all our behaviour.
- Instinct theory, which suggests that environmental cues stimulate innate behavioural instincts, best explains motivation that serves basic biological drives, such as eating, drinking and sex.
- Drive-reduction theory suggests that internal homeostatic mechanisms produce balance within the body by reducing arousal stemming from unmet basic biological needs.
- Arousal theory explains why we sometimes seek to increase, arousal levels. The Yerkes–Dodson law proposes that task performance is best if our arousal level matches that needed for a task.
- Incentive learning produces extrinsic motivation to engage in experiences that do not fulfil basic biological drives. Primary and secondary incentives may both be involved. Different incentives motivate different people.
- Incentive motivation involves brain systems associated with pleasure, incentive learning and the neurochemical opiate dopamine.
- Maslow proposed that we are motivated by a hierarchy of needs, in which basic survival needs must be satisfied before higher level needs for belonging, achievement and self-actualization.

Biological Motivations: Hunger

LEARNING OBJECTIVE 2   Summarize physical and psychological factors that affect our levels of hunger and our eating behaviour.

- Hunger, our motivation to eat, is created by the interaction of signals from our stomachs, levels of food-related chemicals in our blood and brain activity, particularly in the hypothalamus.
- Culture and individual differences interact with our basic biological need for food to determine what foods we will eat, when and with whom we like to eat and how much we eat.

- Obesity is a major public health problem in the West. It is usually caused by overeating, which can result from an interaction between genes and the environment.
- Anorexia nervosa is an eating disorder in which individuals believe they are fat and eat too little. Bulimia nervosa is an eating disorder in which people binge on food to then purge themselves of the food before it can add weight to their bodies.

Biological Motivations: Sex

LEARNING OBJECTIVE 3   Describe factors that affect our sexual motivation and behaviour.

- Sexual practices vary widely as a result of cultural influences. Research consistently shows much variety in normal sexual behaviour throughout healthy adulthood.
- Sex researchers have described a four-stage sexual response cycle.
- Testosterone and other hormones affect our motivation towards sexual behaviour. Many parts of our brains become active during sexual arousal and behaviour.
- Four types of sexual problems may occur: sexual dysfunctions, paraphilias, gender identity disorder and medical problems.

Psychological Motivations: Affiliation and Achievement

LEARNING OBJECTIVE 4   Describe factors that influence our psychological motivations for affiliation and achievement.

- Affiliation represents our need to interact with others, not only for survival but also for self-worth.
- Isolation puts people at risk of psychological impairments.
- Self-determination theory suggests that we need competence, relatedness and autonomy to realize our potential.
- Achievement through intrinsic motivation does not involve incentives.
- Individuals who are able to delay gratification can focus on goals and ignore distractions.

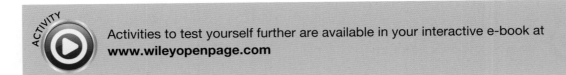

Activities to test yourself further are available in your interactive e-book at **www.wileyopenpage.com**

TYING IT TOGETHER

WHAT HAPPENS IN THE BRAIN?

- Rewards can lead our brains to release natural pain-killing neurochemicals called opiates, the same ones responsible for the so-called runner's high.
- Damage to different parts of the hypothalamus can lead to either severe overeating or under-eating.
- When we see erotic videos or pictures, mirror neurons in the brain activate just as though we were having sex ourselves.

OUT OF THE ORDINARY

- Restricted eaters, people who use external cues, such as calorie counts to control their eating, are more likely than non-restricted eaters to binge after they have eaten a small amount of a high-calorie food.
- Long-term isolation can lead people to develop severe psychological problems.
- At least 10% of men experience erectile disorder and at least 10% of women experience sexual arousal disorder.

HOW WE DIFFER

- We eat more in social settings, with other people, than we do when we are alone.
- Men are more likely to fantasize about having lots of sexual partners, but the number of partners men and women say they would like to have in real life is similar.
- People in collectivist societies value achievement that contributes to one's group more highly than that which benefits the individual.

HOW WE DEVELOP

- Even as young children, people vary in their ability to delay immediate gratification in exchange for larger rewards later. Some can do it; some cannot.
- Delaying immediate gratification in order to achieve long-term goals may get easier with age for most children and teenagers, because parts of their brain associated with planning are still developing.

Quizzes to test yourself further are available in your interactive e-book at **www.wileyopenpage.com**

Key Terms

anorexia nervosa 388
body mass index (BMI) 386
body weight set point 385
bulimia nervosa 389
extrinsic motivation 380

heterosexual 395
homeostasis 378
homosexual 395
incentives 380
instincts 377

intrinsic motivation 380
lateral hypothalamus (LH) 384
leptin 384
motivation 376
motives 376

obesity 386
self-determination 400
ventromedial region of the
  hypothalamus (VMH) 384
Yerkes–Dodson law 379

Flashcards to test yourself further are available in your interactive e-book at
www.wileyopenpage.com

CHAPTER 14

Emotion

Adapted by Adrian Furnham, University College London, UK

CHAPTER OUTLINE

- What Is Emotion?
- Where Do Emotions Come from?
- The Range of Emotional Experiences

Access your interactive e-book to view a video clip for this chapter at **www.wileyopenpage.com**

Emotion in the Driver's Seat

'Road-Rage Accusations Fly over Death,' trumpeted the headline. The story told how an outburst of violent emotion had sparked a fatal chain of events that resulted in the death of Gregory Moore, a 27-year-old man from San Jose, California.

The chain apparently began when 44-year-old Michael David Shannon began tailgating a car driven by Leslie Holsten, a San Jose woman travelling with her two-year-old son. After the two cars stopped at traffic lights, Holsten refused to pull away when the light turned green, hoping to put an end to Shannon's tailgating. In response, Shannon tapped the rear bumper of Holsten's car with his truck. Outraged, Holsten put on the emergency brake and got out of her car. After a heated exchange, she slapped Shannon's face. According to the deputy district attorney, Shannon then stepped hard on the gas and shoved Holsten's car into the intersection before speeding away.

Only seconds later, Shannon found himself behind another slow-moving vehicle, this time a utility truck. The driver of the truck had slowed down to copy Shannon's licence plate number after witnessing Shannon's hit-and-run action against Holsten. Already upset from the altercation with Holsten, Shannon accelerated around the utility truck. He couldn't see what lay beyond the truck until it was too late. His vehicle slammed into a third car, this one driven by Christine Hawley. Gregory Moore, a passenger riding with Hawley, was killed instantly. ■

Road rage can be defined as an incident in which an angry or impatient motorist or passenger intentionally injures or kills another motorist, passenger or pedestrian or threatens to injure or kill another motorist, passenger or pedestrian. Anger is a common and often adaptive human experience. But the explosive and dangerous anger on display in cases of road rage shows how extreme, powerful and even uncontrollable human emotions can be in certain circumstances.

There have also been press reports of various sorts of queue rage, for instance, at airports and in supermarkets, where frustrated customers get fed up with waiting and 'explode' physically and verbally. Many public places throughout Europe warn people to be polite and civil to employees they have contact with or else face prosecution.

Of course, anger and rage are not the only emotions people experience and, more often than not, experiencing an emotion does not lead to tragic consequences. In fact, today alone, you have undoubtedly experienced several different emotions, perhaps including happiness, surprise or sadness and fear. You may even be experiencing clear, readily identified emotions as you read this chapter (hopefully boredom is not one of them).

What exactly happens in our minds and bodies when we experience an emotion? Where do emotions come from? Are emotions meaningful, or are they just noise cluttering up our better judgement? Might even negative emotions be good for us? How can we influence the emotions of others?

We will address all these issues in this chapter.

What Is Emotion?

LEARNING OBJECTIVE 1
Define emotion, and discuss the components, measurement and functions of emotion.

Psychologists have had trouble agreeing on exactly what an emotion is. Over 500 words in the English language refer to various aspects or forms of emotions, from *affect* to *mood* and *feeling*. No unified agreed definition exists. However, after years of neglect, in favour of studying cognition (namely thinking), we are seeing the emergence of the *science of emotion*. Scientists have recognized how much emotion influences cognition and vice versa. We are all *both* 'people of the heart' and 'people of the head'. Emotions are complex physiological and psychological responses to events, but they are also a source of motivation. For example, phobics attempt to control their sudden powerful emotions towards creatures (e.g. snakes) or inanimate objects (e.g. needles) or situations (e.g. heights) by assiduously avoiding them. So emotions

have a powerful influence on how we behave in many very specific situations.

Components of Emotion

Most of today's theorists define an **emotion** as an individual state that occurs in response to either an external or an internal event and that typically involves three separate but intertwined components:

> **emotion** an interpersonal state that occurs in response to either external or internal events and typically involves a physiological, cognitive and behavioural component.

- A *physiological component*. Changes in bodily arousal, such as increased heart rate, body temperature and respiration.

- A *cognitive component*. The subjective appraisal and interpretation of one's feelings and one's surrounding environment.

- A *behavioural component*. The expression of emotion through verbal or nonverbal channels, such as smiling, frowning, whining, laughing, reflecting or slouching.

When we experience an emotion, all three are at work.

Physiological Component The *physiological component* of emotion refers to the bodily arousal we feel when (perhaps unconsciously) experiencing a particular emotion, be it positive or negative. When, for example, you are nervous about giving a class presentation or going out on a first date, you may notice that your heart beats faster, your hands sweat and your mouth becomes dry. These physical manifestations of anxiety are produced by your *autonomic nervous system (ANS)*. As described in Chapter 5, the ANS is responsible for regulating various bodily functions and the activity of specific organs, glands and muscles. Other physiological changes that may occur as we experience an emotion include increased blood pressure, increased blood sugar, pupil dilation and the inhibition of intestinal action.

Because emotions vary in intensity, some emotions may be accompanied by several physiological changes, while others may involve only a few. If, for example, you are anxious about going out with someone for the first time, you will likely experience certain physiological reactions. But they will be fewer and milder than the ones you experience if you are trying to escape from a fire in a crowded concert hall. The reason for these differences has to do with the *sympathetic nervous system*. This subdivision of the ANS mobilizes internal resources and primes the organism to take swift action for survival: the *fight-or-flight response*. When waiting for a new date to arrive, your heart may beat faster and your palms may sweat. That is your body's way of signifying the importance of the situation to you. When, however, you need to flee a burning building, more emotional arousal and energy are needed. As a result, the body produces a more intense physiological response. Like fear and anxiety, emotions such as happiness, excitement and surprise also involve activation of the sympathetic nervous system. Following an intense physiological reaction, the other component of the ANS, the *parasympathetic nervous system*, works to calm the body down. This system attempts to save energy by returning the organism to a normal state. Later, we will see how various areas of the brain and the endocrine system are involved in each of these processes.

Cognitive Component The cognitive component of emotion has two parts. One is the *evaluative* thoughts (positive, neutral, negative) people have about their emotional experiences (such as 'I feel bad'). The other is their appraisal of the events (this is fun, dangerous, exciting) that are producing the emotions. Our appraisal or evaluation of an event not only helps bring about an emotional reaction but also influences how intensely we will experience that emotion. Consider coming face to face with a bear in Spain or a boar in Germany. It is one thing if the bear is just a cub and is safely behind a protective barrier at the National Zoo. In that case, you will probably appraise the situation as pleasant and experience an emotion such as happiness. It is another thing if a full-grown bear appears in front of you on a hiking trail. In that situation, you will likely appraise the situation as life-threatening and experience, among other emotions, intense fear.

In addition to appraising the situation that gives rise to a particular emotion, people also interpret and evaluate the emotion itself. This interpretation helps to shape how they experience that emotion. If you love to ride roller coasters, you will most likely interpret the bodily arousal you feel while going into a big drop as excitement and thrill. If, in contrast, you dread roller coasters but are talked into riding one by your friends, you will likely label that same bodily arousal as fear.

PSYCHOLOGY AROUND US Expressing Emotion in a Digital World

On September 19, 1982, a critical moment in the evolution of emotional expression occurred. At Carnegie Mellon University, members of the computer science department began using the latest brand-new thing – an online bulletin board – to communicate among themselves. The problem was, every now and then a discussion would explode into violent debate because someone had posted a joke or sarcastic comment that was being misinterpreted as serious by other members of the board. In response, the board users decided that they needed a symbol of some kind that digital communicators could use to indicate when they were, in fact, kidding. The users considered various symbols including (#) and \-/, before board user Scott Fahlman invented a symbol that you may find familiar: :-). As a result of the *emoticon*, the emotion behind e-mails, texts or tweets now have less chance of being misinterpreted. Many people now choose to use emoticons or acronyms like 'LOL' to improve the clarity of their communication. In fact, for some people the cold medium of the e-mail or text can only be made subtle and warm through the use of emoticons.

Behavioural Component When you experience an emotion, you express and reveal that emotion physically and behaviourally. You do so through body language, such as facial expressions, gestures and body posture, as well as through verbal expression. For example, happiness is almost always expressed with a smile (Leppänen & Hietanen, 2007). Conversely, someone who is frustrated may cross his arms and shrug his shoulders. Someone who is angry may clench her teeth and furrow her eyebrows. Someone who is sad may frown, slump and avoid eye contact. We read each other's body language to try to understand what we are feeling and thinking. The body language of famous people has been studied in detail for the emotions it reveals.

In a brilliant and highly detailed analysis of one famous person, Peter Collett (2003) from Oxford University identified six quite different smiles used often by Diana, Princess of Wales:

- *Eye-puff smile*. To widen the eyes and make people feel more protective/nurturing of her.

- *Spencer smile*. Authentic, heartfelt, genuine.

- *Pursed smile*. Occurred at times of shyness and embarrassment.

- *Dipped smile*. Involved lowering the head so the eyes look up, showing childlikeness.

- *Head-cant smile.* Tilting the head to one side to show she was unthreatening.

- *Turn-away smile.* Gives two opposing messages (approach/avoidance), which Darwin called a *hybrid expression* and is thought to be 'irresistible'.

Research suggests that there are several facial expressions that most people are able to identify accurately. Paul Ekman, a pioneer in the study of emotion and facial expressions, conducted a series of studies in which participants were asked to identify which emotion an individual was experiencing on the basis of facial cues (Cohn *et al.*, 2007; Ekman, 2003; Ekman & Friesen, 1975).

Ekman and his colleagues found six fundamental emotions that typically can be identified by research participants: anger, sadness, happiness, surprise, fear and disgust. In fact, some research suggests that the ability to identify the facial expressions for these emotions is genetically programmed (Izard, 2009, 1997, 1977). This would explain why even people from different countries and cultures readily recognize them in photographs of facial expressions (Ekman *et al.*, 1987). In this sense, many signals of string emotions are universal.

Although less fundamental to emotional expression than nonverbal emotional behaviours, the verbal expression of emotion is also important (Rimé, 2007). In one study, for example, researchers asked respondents to recall a recently experienced emotion from memory. The researchers found that more than

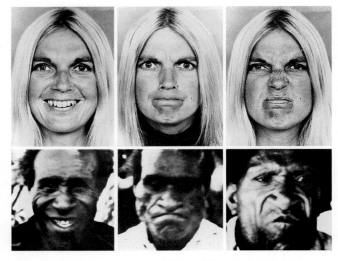

Universal recognition. In one study, Paul Ekman travelled to parts of New Guinea where he found that members of the Fore tribe could readily identify the emotions of happiness, anger and disgust expressed on a Westerner's face (*top row*). Similarly, he found that college students in the United States easily recognized the same emotions when they were expressed on a Fore tribe member's face (*bottom row*).

Source: Courtesy of Paul Ekman, Human Interaction Lab, University of California, San Francisco.

90% of the respondents had already talked with someone about that emotion (Luminet *et al.*, 2000). Indeed, many of the 'talking cures' in psychology are about understanding, reappraising and attempting to change emotional responses to people and situations.

Measurement of Emotions

Researchers typically use three kinds of information to measure an individual's emotions: (1) behavioural displays of emotion, (2) self-reports of emotion and (3) physiological reactions to situations.

Behavioural displays of emotion are most often observed by objective raters. These displays typically include obvious acts, such as fighting, fleeing or making sexual advances. Behavioural displays may also include facial and body expressions. Researchers often observe behavioural displays in role-playing situations. The researchers evoke particular emotional responses from participants by showing them a film, giving them a small gift or manipulating them in some other way (Isen, 2008, 2004, 1993). Then they measure how well the participants perform on tasks of various kinds. If you watch people watching an exciting sports match or a powerful (love or horror) film, it is not difficult to observe how similar people are in their behavioural expression of emotions.

Self-ratings are the most widely used approach to measuring a person's emotional experience. Many questionnaires and surveys ask people to provide ratings for how happy, afraid, content, anxious or depressed they are. The *Positive and Negative Affect Schedule (PANAS)*, for example, is a measure of various emotional states, such as cheerful, angry, sad, happy and timid (Watson & Tellegen, 1985). Individuals rate how much they are feeling each emotional state on a scale from 1 ('very slightly') to 5 ('extremely'). Self-report scales such as this offer a fast and convenient measure of emotional experiences. However, self-reports may be inaccurate at times. They provide only a limited picture of a person's total emotional experience, and they rely on a person's ability to properly identify and describe a complex, multi-dimensional emotional experience.

In recent years, researchers have developed several techniques for measuring *psychophysiological reactions* to stimuli. It is now possible to use such measures to assess emotional experiences (Santerre & Allen, 2007; Bradley *et al.*, 1990). This approach is based on the premise that emotions vary biologically from one another (Bradley & Lang, 2007, 2000). Psychophysiological approaches include facial electromyography and assessments of heart rate, skin conductance and the startle reflex.

- *Facial electromyography (EMG).* When a person is exposed to an emotionally charged stimulus, such as a pleasant or unpleasant picture, certain facial muscles

PSYCHOLOGY AROUND US   Voice and Emotions

Furnham & Petrova (2010) note that vocal cues are full of emotions, and these emotional overtones can be easily detected. We can distinguish between a happy and a sad voice with no difficulty. However, could you detect lying from the affective colouring of the voice? That is what *voice risk analysis* devices claim to do. They are similar to polygraphs, or lie detectors, in their function and are used to try to detect whether people tell the truth, especially over the phone. The idea behind the technology is relatively straightforward: lying is stressful, thus when a person lies their vocal patterns change. Stress-induced voice alterations are, however, not always obvious and cannot be picked up by a human ear. The changes in voice tremor are subtle and insidious but can be spotted by sensitive voice risk analysis systems. The technology is said to account for individual differences in voice tones and pitches, too. After all, some people are naturally shyer than others and may feel tense when making an honest insurance or benefit claim. Yet, it is not clear whether this technology works as a 'liar catcher' or a 'liar deterrent'. The accuracy rate is far from infallible and the final decision on whether the caller is lying or not still has to be made by a human agent. On the other hand, similarly to lie detectors, voice risk analysis systems seem to work because people believe they do. When warned about being monitored, liars' detection apprehension increases. This results in more stress and more noticeable voice-quality changes, but it also simply discourages unconfident liars from making a false claim.

contract. A facial EMG measures these contractions. Studies have found that emotional reactions to unpleasant stimuli, such as pictures of mutilated bodies, are often associated with greater activity of the muscles used in frowning (Sloan *et al.*, 2002; Lang, 1993). Conversely, when people are shown pleasant stimuli, such as scenic images or sexually provocative pictures, they display heightened activity of the facial muscles responsible for smiling.

- *Heart rate*. Reductions in heart rate have been observed when individuals are presented with unpleasant stimuli. In contrast, pleasant stimuli are associated with accelerations in heart rate (Löw *et al.*, 2008; Bradley & Lang, 2000).

- *Skin conductance*. We tend to perspire when we are emotionally aroused. One technique developed to measure emotional arousal thus involves perspiration. Researchers place a large electrode on the palm of a person's hand and determine from readings of the electrode how well the skin conducts electrical activity. High skin conductance reflects increased perspiration. Thus, a higher conductance reading means greater arousal of emotions.

- *Startle reflex*. An additional physiological indicator of emotional reactivity is the startle reflex. This reflex is an involuntary movement, such as an eye blink, that is brought on by a sudden stimulus, such as a loud burst of noise. Researchers usually measure startle reflexes by placing tiny electrodes on the muscle just below a person's eye. They then assess the magnitude of involuntary eye blinks that occur when people are startled while viewing pleasant and unpleasant pictures. Studies have revealed that eye blinks brought on by unpleasant pictures are larger than those brought on by pleasant pictures (Bradley & Lang, 2007, 1990; Mallan & Lipp, 2007; Bradley *et al.*, 1990).

The Lie Detector (Polygraph) Lie detectors have been used for well over 50 years. They have been used by employers and crime investigators. The problem, however, is the reliability of these measures. Many psychologists are very unhappy about these tests because in experimental work it has been shown that too many (as much as 10–20%) innocent people are judged guilty (of lying) and a similar number of liars remain undetected.

The polygraph attempts to measure autonomic nervous system activity by attached sensors to different parts of the body: chest, stomach and fingers. These sensors measure changes in breathing (depth and rate), cardiac activity (blood pressure) and perspiration. It is also possible to measure electrical activity in the brain (event-related potentials). The indicators only show physiological changes usually induced by strong emotions. The machine amplifies signals picked up from sensors put at specific parts of the body. It detects not lies but physical changes that are results of specific emotions (fear, anger, guilt) at a particular point and in response to a question.

People are asked *hot*, or relevant, questions as well as *cool*, or control, questions. The assumption is that for the innocent person there is no physical difference in the way he/she responds to relevant and control questions. Some people are more reactive than others. Drugs can be used to suppress autonomic nervous system activity and make any physiological recording inconclusive. People can and are trained at defeating the test with a range of techniques. Tests would therefore not only be highly unreliable but counterproductive: alienating and misclassifying the innocent and letting the guilty get away scot-free. The lie detector is still used in three different contexts: criminal investigation, security vetting and personnel selection.

It is difficult to obtain reliable data but it seems lie detectors are not used much across Europe today in the public or private sectors and in some countries governments try to enforce strict rules about their use, mainly because of problems associated with false diagnosis.

Functions of Emotions

Since ancient times, philosophers have often considered emotion inferior to reason: the mind rules the heart. Modern researchers who study emotion have, in contrast, emphasized its positive effects. William James (1842–1910), perhaps the most influential emotion researcher of the last 150 years, declared that, without emotion, consciousness and cognition would be 'void of human significance' (1890). Can you imagine riding a roller coaster without experiencing exhilaration (or fear)? How about watching your favourite movie, playing your favourite sport or spending time with your best friends without feeling some happiness or satisfaction? Without emotions, our most enjoyable activities and experiences would not seem very rewarding. Emotions can and do serve cognitive, behavioural and social functions.

Cognitive Functions One function of emotions is to help us organize our memories. As we discussed in Chapter 10, for example, memories linked to emotional content are much easier to recall. Emotions also help us to prioritize our concerns, needs or goals in a given moment (Morris, 1992). The information we gain from noticing our emotions may help us form judgements and make decisions (Gohm & Clore, 2002). A strong feeling of fear if you encounter a grizzly bear while out gathering berries in the woods can make it easy to decide which is more important to you: fleeing the bear or filling your basket with berries.

Behavioural Functions Emotions can also help us organize our behaviour. Generally speaking, we act to minimize our experience of negative emotions and maximize our experience of positive emotions. Such actions may involve basic behaviours, such as diverting our attention away from unpleasant or disgusting images in favour of more neutral or positive images. They may also involve more complex behaviours, such as *procrastination*, or putting off doing something (generally undesirable). You have probably noticed a correlation between how difficult or boring you believe working on a homework assignment will be and how long you delay before starting that assignment. In contrast, tasks that we find enjoyable or pleasurable, such as spending time with a friend, are very easy to find time for and hard to delay. In this way, our emotions can

help us organize our behaviours (although admittedly in ways that sometimes run counter to our self-interest).

Some theorists also believe that particular emotions are associated with predictable patterns of behaviour, sometimes called *action tendencies*, that help us to adapt and survive in our social and physical environments (Frijda, 2007, 1986; Lang *et al.*, 1998). Specific action tendencies associated with key emotions include:

- *Happiness*. When people who engage in rewarding behaviours or positive interactions feel happiness and joy, they will likely continue to engage in those behaviours or interactions. Happiness and joy also signal to people that particular goals have been attained (Carver, 2004).

- *Embarrassment*. This often evokes forgiveness and motivates reconciliation and adherence to social norms (Parrott, 2004, 2001). Consider, for example, a scenario in which a young employee asks an overweight co-worker when she is due, only to discover that she is not pregnant. Embarrassment will probably lead the unfortunate enquirer to apologize profusely. It may also help to ensure that he or she will not make such a careless remark again.

- *Anger*. This signals the presence of injustice and prompts aggression (as we saw at the beginning of this chapter), as well as other self-protective behaviours (Mayer & Salovey, 1997).

- *Anxiety*. This directs a person's attention towards potential threats and motivates appropriate action to avoid or cope with them (Öhman, 2000).

- *Sadness*. This may signal the loss of positive relationships and help people to seek necessary support and help from others (Oatley & Jenkins, 1996).

Social Functions Another important function of emotions appears to be coordination of relationships. Emotions form the foundations of relationships by helping us develop a sense that we like and trust another person. In one study, for example, viewers assigned more positive ratings of friendliness and competence to people who showed a sincere smile in their yearbook photographs than to those whose pictures had false smiles or no smiles (Harker & Keltner, 2001).

Emotions, even when they are negative, can also improve the quality of our relationships. Research suggests, for example, that the more a married couple talk about their feelings, the happier they are (Gottman & Levenson, 1988). In contrast, keeping our emotions inside may get in the way of our ability to form lasting relationships. One study found that participants who always kept their emotions to themselves

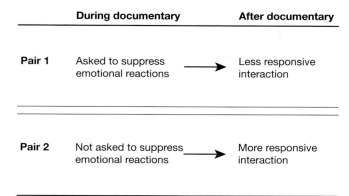

	During documentary	After documentary
Pair 1	Asked to suppress emotional reactions →	Less responsive interaction
Pair 2	Not asked to suppress emotional reactions →	More responsive interaction

FIGURE 14.1 Emotional expressiveness improves the quality of relationships. In one study of the social function of emotion, pairs of women watched a disturbing film clip. One group was asked to suppress their emotional reactions while watching the clip. The other group was not instructed to do so. After the documentary, when pairs were asked to interact with each other, those who had suppressed their emotions were less responsive and felt less rapport with their partners. The study demonstrated that suppressed emotions can lead to poor social relations.

were more likely to report problems with closeness and sharing in intimate relationships than people who talked about their emotions (Gross & John, 2003).

In an experimental study of this idea, researchers asked pairs of unacquainted women to watch a film clip designed to produce disgust, anger and sadness (Butler et al., 2003). Following the clip, the researchers asked the women to interact with each other (Figure 14.1). Half of the participants had been asked to suppress their emotional reactions to the documentary. These participants later demonstrated heightened physiological arousal and reported less rapport with their partners. Similarly, the partners of these suppressors felt less rapport and were less willing to form a friendship with the partners. This shows that being able to show, rather than repress, negative emotions actually brings about positive rewards. This finding indicates that emotional expressiveness may have a direct impact on feelings of intimacy.

Emotional Intelligence The term *emotional intelligence* (EI) can be traced back over 40 years, but a very popular book by Daniel Goleman in 1995 made the topic very popular. It seems to have replaced the term *social skills* and is used widely in business circles, suggesting it is an attribute that most employers value in their staff.

Emotional intelligence is about being aware of your own and others' emotions and being able to manage them appropriately.

Some people prefer to talk about emotional *competencies* (rather than traits or abilities), which are essentially learnt capabilities. Emotional competencies include emotional self-awareness, emotional self-regulation, social-emotional awareness, regulating emotions in others, understanding emotions, etc. If one is to include older related concepts like social skills or interpersonal competencies then it is possible

to find a literature dating back thirty years showing these skills predict occupational effectiveness and success. Further, these skills can be improved and learnt.

There remains still no agreement about what features, factors, abilities or skills do or do not form part of EI. This lack of agreement at the beginning of an academic exploration of a new concept is not unusual.

A central unresolved question is: what are the facets or components of EI? Thus, early models distinguished between the perception, appraisal and expression of emotion in self and others, the use of emotional knowledge to understand and analyse emotions as well as the reflective regulation of emotions to promote growth. Matthews *et al.* (2007) note that different researchers have talked of *emotional literacy* (which involves the knowledge and understanding of one's own emotions and how they function), *emotional fitness* (which involves trustworthiness and emotional hardiness and flexibility), *emotional depth* (which involves emotional growth and intensity) and *emotional alchemy* (which involves using emotions to discover creative opportunities).

Petrides and Furnham (2003) divide EI up into factors like self-awareness, self-regulation, self-motivation, empathy and social skills. One more popular conception by Petrides (2009) has 15 components (Table 14.1).

These 15 scales can be combined into four different related but independent factors labelled *well-being*, *self-control skills*, *emotional skills* and *social skills*.

Dispute about what to measure when trying to ascertain a person's EI is paradoxically clearer but much more passionate when it comes to this area of research. Psychologists make a basic distinction between measures of *maximum* performance (e.g. IQ tests – right or wrong answers) and measures of *typical* response (e.g. personality questionnaires with preference answers) with far-reaching implications. Self-report measurement leads to the idea of EI essentially as a personality trait (trait EI or emotional self-efficacy), whereas potential maximum-performance measurement would lead to ideas of EI as a cognitive ability (ability EI or cognitive-emotional ability). Thus, trait EI and ability EI are two *different constructs*. The primary basis for discriminating between trait EI and ability EI is to be found in the type of measurement approach one chooses to employ.

There are, therefore, two very different ways to measure EI. The first is akin to taking a personality test and indeed treats EI as a type of personality trait. The other is more like an ability test. The former method is much easier and cheaper to administer than the latter. But the real question is which is the more *accurate and reliable measure*. Studies have shown that scores from the two tests are modestly positively correlated. Researchers are still arguing over which measure is best but at the very heart of the debate is whether EI is just another personality trait or whether it can be thought of more accurately as a real part of intelligence.

TABLE 14.1 Common Facets in the Model of Emotional Intelligence

Facets	High scorers perceive themselves as being . . .
Adaptability	Flexible and willing to adapt to new conditions
Assertiveness	Forthright, frank and willing to stand up for their rights
Emotion expression	Capable of communicating their feelings to others
Emotion management (others)	Capable of influencing other people's feelings
Emotion perception (self and others)	Clear about their own and other people's feelings
Emotion regulation	Capable of controlling their emotions
Impulsiveness (low)	Reflective and less likely to give into their urges
Relationship skills	Capable of having fulfilling personal relationships
Self-esteem	Successful and self-confident
Self-motivation	Driven and unlikely to give up in the face of adversity
Social competence	Accomplished networkers with excellent social skills
Stress management	Capable of withstanding pressure and regulating stress
Trait empathy	Capable of taking someone else's perspective
Trait happiness	Cheerful and satisfied with their lives
Trait optimism	Confident and likely to look on the bright side of life

Many people in business claim that EI is more important than IQ when it comes to success. While there is not a lot of evidence to support this contention, the possible explanation for the success of high-EQ people is, according to Furnham (2008):

- High-EQ people are better at communicating their ideas, intentions and goals. They are more articulate, assertive and sensitive.

- EQ is closely associated with teamwork social skills, which are very important at work.

- Business leaders, high in EQ, build supportive climates that increase organizational commitment, which in turn leads to success.

- High-EQ leaders are perceptive and know their own and their teams' strengths and weaknesses, which enables them to leverage the former and compensate for the latter.

- EQ is related to effective and efficient copying skills, which enable people to deal with demands, pressure and stress better.

- High-EQ leaders can accurately identify what followers feel and need, as well as make themselves more inspiring and supportive. They generate more excitement, enthusiasm and optimism.

- High-EQ managers, unlike their low-EQ companions, are less prone to negative, defensive and destructive coping and decision-making styles.

Before You Go On

What Do You Know?

1. What system produces the bodily arousal associated with emotions?
2. What three types of information are most commonly used by researchers to measure emotions?
3. Name four physiological indicators of emotional state.
4. What are the major functions of emotion?
5. Distinguish between trait- and ability-based emotional intelligence.

What Do You Think?

Think about the road-rage incident described in our opening example. Describe what you think the physiological, cognitive and behavioural components of the various drivers may have been.

Where Do Emotions Come From?

LEARNING OBJECTIVE 2

Discuss the major theories of emotion, and identify the main brain structures associated with emotion.

How do emotions occur? What causes them? How have they evolved in the human species? How do they develop in each individual as he or she moves from infancy to adulthood? And what is going on in the brain while all this is happening? These are the core questions for understanding emotions, and we will turn to them now.

Theories of Emotion

Since the birth of psychology, a number of theories have been proposed to explain human emotion. They include the James–Lange theory, the Cannon–Bard theory, Schacter and Singer's two-factor theory, the cognitive-mediational theory and the facial-feedback theory. Each theory proposes a different twist on the sequence and nature of an emotional episode. In addition, evolutionary theory has important things to say about the origins of emotion.

The James–Lange Theory As we observed earlier, William James (1890) was the earliest and one of the most influential psychologists to study emotion. James took issue with the contemporaneous, conventional common-sense explanation of emotion. This view, which we still encounter today, suggests that an event triggers an emotion, which leads to physiological changes, followed by a behavioural response. Looking at the road-rage example that began this chapter, the common-sense explanation would suggest that Michael Shannon became angry in response to Leslie Holsten's driving. As a result, we can imagine that his heart started beating faster and his face became flushed and red. Once he experienced this high arousal, he began tailgating Holsten.

James (1890, 1884) argued that emotions proceed differently. He suggested that an emotion begins with (1) the perception of an environmental situation or event. Next comes (2) the elicitation of physiological and behavioural changes. These changes are then (3) processed by the cortex and converted into felt emotion. In other words, Shannon did not become angry and then, as a result, experience high physiological arousal. Instead, he experienced high physiological arousal and interpreted it as anger. James believed that our physiological response to a stimulus occurs prior to, and provides the basis for, the experience of a particular emotion.

In 1885, a Danish physiologist, Carl Lange (1834–1900), published a theory of emotion that was very similar to James's. The views of both theorists are collectively referred to as the **James–Lange theory of emotion**. Figure 14.2 compares the James–Lange theory with the two theories that we will turn to next: the Cannon–Bard theory and Schachter and Singer's two-factor theory. Michael Eysenck (2004) in his evaluation of the James–Lange theory notes this: 'The James–Lange theory provides a very limited account of

> **James–Lange theory of emotion** a theory proposing that felt emotions result from physiological changes, rather than being their cause.

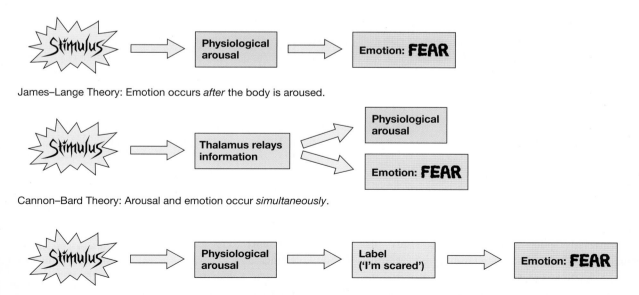

James–Lange Theory: Emotion occurs *after* the body is aroused.

Cannon–Bard Theory: Arousal and emotion occur *simultaneously*.

Schachter and Singer's Two-Factor Theory: Both physiological arousal *and* a cognitive label determine the emotion experienced.

FIGURE 14.2 Three major theories of emotion.

emotion. It is uninformative about the cognitive processes intervening between the presentation of an emotional stimulus and the onset of physiological changes' (p. 152).

The Cannon–Bard Theory The James–Lange theory of emotion produced quite a stir in the fields of psychology and physiology, and much research was published disputing various pieces of it. The leading critic of the James–Lange theory was Harvard psychologist Walter Cannon (1871–1945). Central to Cannon's criticism was the James–Lange theory's notion that *visceral organs* (i.e. our internal organs in which physiological arousal occurs, such as the heart) could produce complex emotional experiences. Pointing to various research findings, Cannon challenged this notion.

Cannon pointed out, for example, that total separation of the visceral organs from the central nervous system did not change emotional behaviour. He cited research on dogs and cats whose visceral organs had been disconnected from their central nervous systems. Even without these organs, the cats and dogs continued to display aggression and rage in the usual way. We know also that most human patients with spinal cord injuries experience emotional excitability that is similar to what they experienced prior to injury.

Cannon also challenged the James–Lange theory by pointing out that the artificial production of visceral changes did not produce clear emotions. He cited, for example,

research by the Spanish psychologist Gregorio Marañon (1924). In this research, adrenaline, a stimulant, was injected into the bloodstream of research participants. Adrenaline activates the sympathetic nervous system and produces visceral changes typical of intense emotions. Nevertheless, injection of adrenaline did not produce clear and identifiable emotional reactions in research participants.

Following his critique of the James–Lange theory, Cannon (1927) offered his own explanation of emotion. His work was later elaborated on by Philip Bard (1934), an American physiologist. The resulting theory, often referred to as the **Cannon–Bard theory of emotion**, assigns an important role to the *thalamus*, a key brain structure. When we perceive an emotionally stirring event, in this view, the thalamus *simultaneously* relays information about the event to the sympathetic nervous system and to the parts of the brain that are active in thought and decision making. As a result, the subjective experience of emotion and the activation of the sympathetic nervous system (i.e. bodily arousal) occur at the same time (see Figure 14.2 again). According to the Cannon–Bard theory, Michael Shannon would have experienced both rage and physiological arousal when he perceived Leslie Holsten blocking his way.

> **Cannon–Bard theory of emotion** a theory proposing that the subjective experience of emotion and the activation of the sympathetic nervous system (i.e. bodily arousal) occur simultaneously.

PSYCHOLOGY AROUND US   'I Know How You Feel'

If changes in blood pressure and skin temperature can reliably distinguish between the emotions of anger, fear, sadness, joy, and disgust, and if machines . . . can detect these bodily changes, then why can we not build machines that know how we feel – that read our emotions? Imagine sensors built into the steering wheel of a car to read the driver's heart rate and skin temperature. Imagine sensors built into the handles of bicycles, pilot simulators, joysticks, golf clubs, and utensils . . .

Actually, soon you will not need to imagine such technological inventions, as scientists in the new field of 'affective computing' are hard at work building such devices. One particularly interesting invention is the 'emotion mouse.' It

functions like an ordinary computer mouse, except it [also monitors] heart rate, skin temperature, hand movements, and electrical skin conductance. The computer monitors the data collected by the emotion mouse and analyzes this data to infer the user's emotional state.

If a computer can read a user's emotions, then a computer gains the potential capacity for adjusting to its user. A computer game can be made more or less challenging, a tutorial can be adjusted to decrease fear or to increase joy, or an online counseling session can provide emotional feedback regarding the feelings of a client at different points in the conversation.

(Reeve, 2001, p. 440)

Schachter and Singer's Two-Factor Theory In 1962, Stanley Schachter and Jerome Singer, social psychologists at Columbia University, published a landmark study that helped change psychology's understanding of emotion. According to Schachter and Singer (1962), earlier theories had neglected to consider the influence of cognition, or thought processes, in our emotional experiences. Physiological differences alone are too subtle to define specific

emotional states, said these researchers. It is our cognitive appraisal of the immediate situation that provides a label ('I'm scared') for our bodily feelings.

According to **Schachter and Singer's two-factor theory of emotion**, 'It is the cognition which determines whether the state of physiological arousal will be

> **Schachter and Singer's two-factor theory of emotion** a theory proposing that an emotional state is a function of both physiological arousal and cognition.

labeled as "anger," "joy," "fear," or "whatever"' (Schachter & Singer, 1962). Schachter and Signer agreed that physiological arousal is *necessary* for an emotion to occur and that it determines the intensity of the emotional experience. But they believed that it was up to our cognitive faculties to determine our specific emotional state (see Figure 14.2 again).

If we were to apply Schachter and Singer's two-factor theory to Michael Shannon's case, we would assume that his actions were determined by his level of physiological arousal. If his arousal had been mild or moderate, he might have appraised the situation differently ('Stuck in traffic again'). He might then have responded to Holsten in a mildly angry or frustrated way (perhaps cursing in the privacy of his car or raising his middle finger at her). Instead, however, we presume that he experienced intense physiological arousal and so appraised the situation in a way that led to anger ('That woman is purposely getting in my way'). As a result, he responded in ways that had fatal consequences.

What if we feel physically aroused but cannot immediately determine the cause? Two-factor theory suggests that in this situation we use cues from our surroundings to help us identify a cause. This can lead us to mislabel physical arousal from a non-emotional source as an emotion. Schachter and Singer conducted one of psychology's most famous experiments at the University of Minnesota to test this idea (Figure 14.3). They told undergraduate research participants

that the study was examining the effects of a vitamin supplement (called *Suproxin*) on vision.

When the students arrived at the laboratory, they were met by an experimenter and told that they would be receiving a small injection of Suproxin and then would complete several vision tests. The participants then received an injection of either adrenaline or a placebo (saline solution). By producing physiological arousal, the adrenaline injections mimicked sympathetic nervous system activation. Among those who received adrenaline, one-third (the *informed group*) were told they might experience side effects, such as palpitations, trembling and facial flushing. One-third (the *deceived group*) were told they would experience no side effects. Finally, one-third (the *misinformed group*) were told they would experience side effects that were not in fact likely to occur, such as headaches. All the participants in the placebo group were told they would have no side effects. After the participants were given the drug, a person (a confederate of the researchers) entered the room and acted either euphoric or angry. These manipulations created a scenario in which participants experienced bodily arousal either with or without an explanation for it.

As Schachter and Singer's two-factor theory had predicted, students who received an adrenaline injection but were not given a proper explanation for their bodily arousal (the deceived and misinformed groups) later reported

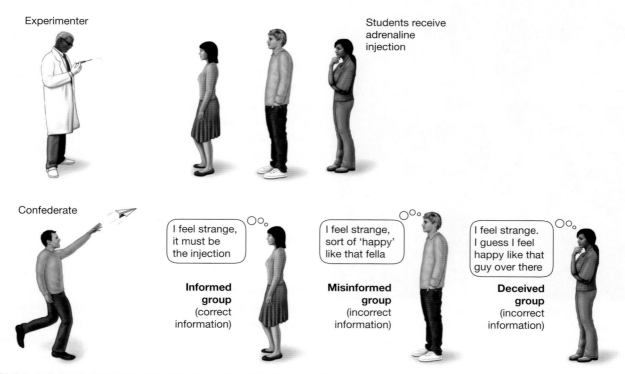

FIGURE 14.3 Testing the two-factor theory. In the absence of correct information, participants in the deceived and misinformed groups who receive the adrenaline injection concluded that they were feeling happy, like the confederate who had acted euphoric.

feelings of anger or euphoria. In contrast, students in the adrenaline condition who were told to anticipate various symptoms of sympathetic nervous system activity (informed group) did not experience anger or euphoria. They were immune to any effects of the arousal manipulation. Clearly, the label of an emotion is influenced by whether a person has an appropriate explanation for his or her arousal.

Schachter and Singer's two-factor theory redirected the focus of emotion research towards the role of cognitive factors. Indeed, a number of studies have since provided indirect evidence for their theory. In one study, for example, male participants were confronted by an attractive female (a confederate of the researchers) and asked to complete questionnaires. Some of the males met the woman while crossing the Capilano Suspension Bridge in British Columbia, Canada – a long, narrow footbridge constructed of wooden boards and wire cables suspended 100 feet above the river. These participants reported being more attracted to the female confederate than males who met the same woman on a wider, sturdier bridge only 10 feet above the river (Dutton & Aron, 1974). The researchers concluded that the men on the Capilano Bridge had experienced anxious arousal because of the height of the bridge. They had misinterpreted this arousal as sexual attraction – a finding consistent with Schachter and Singer's two-factor theory.

Echoes of the Capilano Bridge study. This young man and woman run into each other for the first time while looking out from a wooden-boarded, not-so-sturdy footbridge that stands high above the water. If surveyed by a nosy researcher, each of them would probably report being more attracted to the other than they would if they had met on a sturdier and lower (i.e. less-arousing) bridge.

Source: ©Dave & Les Jacobs/Blend Images/Corbis.

Cognitive-Mediational Theory Cognitive-mediational theory was developed by Richard Lazarus, a psychologist at the University of California, Berkeley, built on Schachter and Singer's ideas (Lazarus, 2007). However, unlike Schachter and Singer's two-factor theory, Lazarus's theory holds that cognitive appraisal affects not only how people interpret physical arousal but also the level of arousal itself. As such, his **cognitive-mediational theory of emotion** views cognitive interpretations as playing a still broader role in the experience of emotion.

> **cognitive-mediational theory of emotion** a theory proposing that cognitive interpretations, particularly appraisals, of events are the keys to experiences of emotion.

In one of his early studies, for example, Lazarus had participants watch stressful films (featuring, for instance, skin-piercing rituals among Australian tribesmen). As they watched, their autonomic nervous system activity was measured, and their subjective reports of stress were recorded. Some of the viewers were told, 'The people in this film were not hurt or distressed by what is happening.' Others were told, 'Many of the people you see in this film suffered severe pain and infection from these rituals.' By influencing the way the participants construed what was happening in the films, Lazarus and his colleagues found they could greatly change the participants' physiological activity and subjective emotional reactions. That is, appraisal serves as a *cognitive mediator* between environmental stimuli and people's reaction to those stimuli (Lazarus, 2007, 1993).

Facial-Feedback Theory We mentioned earlier, in discussing the behavioural component of emotion, that facial expressions help us express our emotions. Related to this observation is the **facial-feedback theory of emotion**. According to this perspective, our subjective experiences of emotion are actually influenced by sensory feedback we receive from the activity of our facial muscles, our **facial efference** (Izard, 2007, 1997, 1977; Tomkins, 1962). Thus, facial expressions not only express a given emotion but also intensify the physiological experience of that emotion.

> **facial-feedback theory of emotion** a theory proposing that subjective experiences of emotion are influenced by sensory feedback from facial muscular activity, or facial efference.

> **facial efference** sensory feedback from facial muscular activity.

In one study, researchers directed participants to move their facial muscles into certain positions, without directly telling them which emotions they were expressing. At the same time, the researchers monitored changes in the participants' autonomic nervous system activity through such measures as heart rate and skin conductance. The facial changes produced significant changes in autonomic nervous system arousal (Ekman *et al.*, 1983). In a related study, research participants held pens in their mouths while rating the funniness

FIGURE 14.4 Genuine versus artificial smiles. Real or Duchenne smiles reflect genuine emotion and involve muscles near the mouth and eyes (*left*). Social or artificial smiles involve only muscles near the mouth (*right*).

Source: Courtesy of Karen Huffman.

of cartoons (Strack *et al.*, 1988). This approach enabled the experimenters to manipulate the participants' facial expressions without calling attention to their facial activity or to the emotions normally associated with that activity. People directed to hold the pen in their teeth made a face similar to a smile. Those directed to hold the pen with their lips were unable to smile. Sure enough, individuals who held the pen in their teeth found the cartoons funnier than those who held the pen in their lips.

The facial-feedback theory of emotion has also been supported by studies of the *Duchenne smile*, named after French neurologist Guillaume Duchenne. Duchenne observed that smiles reflecting genuine emotion involve the activity of certain muscles near the mouth and the eyes. In contrast, more artificial 'social smiles' involve only muscles near the mouth (Figure 14.4). One experiment found that participants who displayed genuine Duchenne smiles while viewing a positive film clip displayed greater physiological arousal and experienced more positive emotion than other participants (Soussignan, 2002).

It is important to note that none of the four theories just discussed seems to explain emotion completely. As psychologist Robert Zajonc has said, 'It is unlikely that all emotions . . . are characterized by the same affective and cognitive processes . . . or have the same underlying neuroanatomical structure and neurochemical actions' (Zajonc *et al.*, 1989, p. 412). Thus, one emotional experience may result largely from a singular source, such as physiological arousal, cognitive appraisal or facial expression. Others may be the product of a combination of these factors.

Evolutionary Theory Over the past 50 years, a number of theorists have suggested that emotions are innate, hardwired responses that have evolved over millions of years, from lower species to humans (Izard, 2007; Cosmides &

Tooby, 2000). This perspective is based on the evolutionary theory of Charles Darwin, described in Chapter 1.

Darwin had noted similarities in emotional expression across and within species throughout the world. In 1872, he published *The Expression of the Emotions in Man and Animals*. In this book, he argues that emotional expression in both people and animals serves a *communicative* function that is essential to survival. Emotional expressions may, for example, warn others of danger, dissuade enemies from attacking or signal sexual receptiveness (Seyfarth & Cheney, 2003; LeDoux, 1996).

Evolutionary psychologists argue that certain emotions have been passed down through the generations because they are extremely useful. A particular condition or situation triggers an emotional programme or sub-programme that affects a person's physiology and thinking. Emotions galvanize and activate many systems together that deal with a very real problem. Emotions serve first to detect evolutionarily reliable cues then trigger reactions that have proved in the past to be good solutions to those problems.

A good example is fear: the fear of being followed, ambushed or attacked at night. This fear sets off circumstances or routines. These seem to follow a set order.

- First, you become highly attentive to particular visual or auditory cues.

- Second, your priorities and goals change: hunger, pain, thirst are suppressed, ignored and forgotten to achieve safety.

- Third, your information-gathering systems focus on very particular issues, like how to escape.

- Fourth, some simple concepts emerge or change in your mind from, say, easy or difficult to danger or safety.

- Fifth, memories of events like this are triggered.

- Sixth, there may be an attempt to communicate via a loud shout or mobile call: or indeed the opposite, finding oneself paralysed by fear and unable to utter a sound.

- Seventh, an inference or hypothesis-testing system is evoked, meaning people try to work out what is happening and what will happen next.

- Eighth, learning systems from the past are activated.

- Ninth, physiological systems enabling one to act are readied. This may be for a flight-or-fight response.

- Finally, a series of behavioural decision rules are created. Thus, the person might run or even attack.

Think of the last time you were really scared. What exactly happened? How many of the nine steps can you remember going through?

Much of the research support for an evolutionary explanation of emotion centres on the universal and innate nature of facial expressions of emotion. As we observed earlier, Paul Ekman and his colleagues have conducted a series of studies on facial expressions of emotion (Cohn *et al.*, 2007; Ekman, 2003; Ekman & Friesen, 1971). They have found that individuals from many different cultural and language backgrounds, when presented with photographs of different facial expressions, are fairly accurate at selecting the emotions being expressed. Individuals from places such as Estonia, Ethiopia, Turkey and Japan, for example, similarly recognize facial expressions of happiness, anger, fear, disgust, surprise and sadness (Ekman *et al.*, 1987). One study even found that the inhabitants of isolated villages in Papua New Guinea – who had never seen a photograph, magazine, film or television – recognized facial expressions of emotion with the same degree of accuracy as individuals from countries exposed to Western media (Ekman & Friesen, 1971).

Based on such research, a number of theorists have suggested that some innate, **basic emotions** are pre-programmed into all people. Tomkins (1962) proposes that there are eight basic emotions: surprise, interest, joy, rage, fear, disgust, shame and anguish. Indeed, it appears that infants typically display the facial expressions of such fundamental emotions very early in life (Izard, 1994). Even children who are born without sight display facial expressions similar to those of sighted children of the same age (Galati *et al.*, 2003; Goodenough, 1932).

basic emotions a group of emotions pre-programmed into all humans regardless of culture.

Emotional Development HOW WE DEVELOP

We have discussed ideas about how emotions evolved in the human species. What about how emotions develop in each individual as that person grows from infant to adult? Let's look at two contrasting theories of emotional development. One holds that emotions unfold as a consequence of neural and cognitive development. The other argues that emotions themselves help spur (i.e. cause) neural growth and the development of cognitive processes. As you will see, research on facial expressions, which we discussed in the preceding section, plays a role in both theories.

Lewis's Cognitive Theory of Emotional Development Developmental psychologist Michael Lewis has proposed a cognitive theory of emotional development suggesting that most emotions can be experienced and expressed only *after* particular cognitive abilities have developed. According to Lewis (2008, 2007, 2005, 1992), all children are born with a limited capacity for emotional experience.

That capacity expands enormously over the first three years of life, ending eventually in the development of a full range of emotions.

As you may have observed, newborn infants often move between only a few *mood states*, appearing either distressed (when hungry, startled, tired, lonely or in need of changing) or content (when satiated, rested and secure). Their emotional responses remain rather undifferentiated until they achieve certain milestones in their cognitive development. According to Lewis, those key cognitive milestones include the abilities to perceive and discriminate stimuli, to recall memories of past events and compare them with current situations and to be aware of themselves and compare themselves with others (Lewis, 2008, 2007, 2005, 1992).

By the time babies are three months of age, they show happiness and excitement at the sight of familiar objects and faces and sadness at the loss of positive stimuli, such as a parent's attention. In addition, they begin to demonstrate disgust during this time, characterized by spitting out unpleasant-tasting objects (Lewis, 2008). Between four and six months, infants begin to express anger when they are frustrated and surprise when confronted with situations that are unexpected. By 7 to 8 months, most infants display fearfulness. According to Lewis (2008), fearfulness emerges only after infants develop the ability to compare an event with an internal representation of a similar event from the past. This gives them, for example, the ability to distinguish strangers from familiar adults. Thus, by eight months of age, most infants exhibit the fundamental emotions – anger, sadness, happiness, surprise, fear and disgust – identified in studies of facial expressions (Ekman & Friesen, 1986, 1975).

For the next year of life, an infant's emotional development remains stable. No new emotions emerge, although those in the current repertoire are enhanced. From 18 to 24 months, however, children reach the cognitive milestone of paying attention to themselves. This ability eventually gives rise to *objective self-awareness*, an ability to look at themselves as objects, with a clear understanding that they are separate from other people (Lewis, 2008). Such cognitive development enables them to experience so-called *emotions of self-consciousness*, such as envy, empathy and embarrassment.

A final cluster of emotions emerges between the second and third year of life. These emotions depend on the achievement of yet another cognitive milestone – the capacity to compare one's behaviour against external or internal standards, which eventually include such points of comparison as parents, teachers and personal ideals (Lewis, 2008, 2007, 1992). These emotions, which Lewis calls *self-conscious evaluative emotions*, include pride, shame and guilt. Emotional development continues well into adolescence and beyond and is further shaped by external factors, such as cultural rules. Yet the most significant growth and achievement of emotional milestones is complete by the age of three.

Izard's Differential Emotions Theory Emotion researcher Carroll Izard does not agree that emotions emerge as a result of cognitive development. Instead, he suggests that they actually help trigger the achievement of social and cognitive milestones. In his **differential emotions theory**, Izard argues that emotions aid in the successful completion of various stages of development (Izard, 2007, 1991, 1977; Abe & Izard, 1999). Indeed, in Izard's view, emotions evolved largely to help individuals develop.

> **differential emotions theory** a theory proposing that particular emotions or sets of emotions become prominent during specific life stages as they serve stage-related developmental processes.

The theory is essentially a feedback hypothesis that suggests that emotional expressions can actually cause the emotional experiences that they signify. This can help us recognize the emotional expression in others. Thus, as we mimic or echo the emotional expression of others we can help to get to know what they are feeling.

During the third or fourth month of life, the emotional experiences of an infant and caregiver play off each other more and more. These emotional interactions give rise to two emotional milestones of infancy: the ability to regulate emotions and the formation of attachment bonds with caregivers. The infant's achievement of these emotional milestones, in turn, triggers the emergence of exploratory behaviours. Feeling secure that their parents are nearby and available, infants increasingly explore their surroundings. Similarly, Izard argues that emotional interactions of one kind or another eventually help trigger later cognitive and social achievements, such as the acquisition of moral standards, the ability to make social comparisons, the emergence of a self-concept and the ability to think abstractly (Izard, 2007; Abe & Izard, 1999).

Emotion in the Brain

 **WHAT HAPPENS IN THE** **B R A I N ?**

We noted earlier that evolutionary theory has helped shape human emotions. In the same way, thousands of years of natural selection seemed to have helped mould and re-mould the human brain, enabling it to adapt to an ever-changing environment. The brain seems not to have evolved as a single unified entity, though. Different parts appear to have evolved at different times, each at its own pace. As a result, there is no unified 'emotion centre' in the brain. Rather, the brain structures involved in emotion are located in several regions. And the neural structures that spring into action when we are, for example, confronted by a rattlesnake are different from the structures that are activated when we feel lust or love towards someone.

In 1949, neuroscientist Paul MacLean coined the term *limbic system* to describe a system of structures of the brain that seem to work together in creating emotions. The limbic system includes the thalamus, hypothalamus, hippocampus, cingulate cortex, amygdala and prefrontal cortex. This system includes many structures that are also present in less complex mammals. MacLean therefore believed that it was responsible for primitive brain functions, such as emotion, and that it, in fact, evolved in order to help humans control their emotional functioning.

In recent years, researchers have given their greatest focus to the roles of the thalamus, amygdala and cerebral cortex in the experience of emotion, particularly fear (LeDoux, 2008, 1996). As we saw in Chapter 7, the thalamus serves as a relay station for a great deal of incoming information in the brain, including emotional information. The amygdala is believed to have a direct connection with the thalamus, which allows for almost instantaneous processing of fear-related stimuli (Figure 14.5). If you were to stumble upon a snake while on a hiking trail, your thalamus would send the visual information directly to your amygdala. The amygdala would immediately produce bodily arousal and begin to prepare your body for danger.

At the same time, the thalamus would send the visual image of the snake to the visual centre of your cerebral cortex. This centre would process the information and then send its assessment to the amygdala, as well. In a sense, the initial activation of the amygdala enables your brain to initiate a fear response before you even have a chance to think about the snake in front of you! As you may notice, this order of events is consistent with the early James–Lange theory. Recall that, according to that theory, perceptions of environmental events produce physiological arousal and behavioural changes before that information is processed by the cerebral cortex.

Current research has repeatedly highlighted the importance of the amygdala, sometimes called the *hub* of fear in the brain, in the conditioning and recognition of fear. It appears, for example, that individuals with damage to their amygdalas do not easily learn fear responses to various

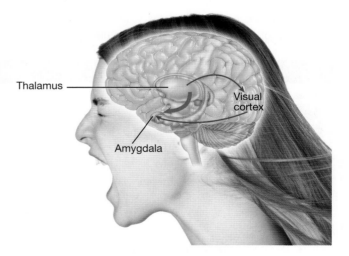

FIGURE 14.5 The brain's shortcut for fear. When sensory input arrives at the thalamus, the thalamus sends it along a fast route to the amygdala and along a slower route to the visual cortex. The shortcut direct to the amygdala allows us to react instantly before thinking (LeDoux, 2008, 1996).

Source: Masterfile.

PSYCHOLOGY AROUND US | Mixed Emotions

We often think of emotions as opposing pairs. For example, you can be either sad *or* happy; angry *or* calm. Common experience tells us, however, that often we experience *mixed emotions*, degrees and combinations of emotions that lie in between such pairs of opposites.

As you have seen in this chapter, positive and negative emotional experiences may reflect activation of different areas of the brain, particularly different areas of the prefrontal cortex (LeDoux, 1995). If so, it seems to imply that we could indeed feel both positive and negative emotions simultaneously.

Studies demonstrate clearly that such mixed emotions exist (Larsen *et al.*, 2001). In one experiment, for example,

researchers found that participants felt both happy and sad simultaneously after they had received both a smaller reward and a smaller loss than they had expected (Larsen *et al.*, 2004). Perhaps not surprisingly, researchers have also found that we are most likely to experience mixed emotions in emotionally complex situations (Larsen *et al.*, 2007, 2004).

Think about your own experiences for a moment. When have you experienced mixed emotions? Based on such experiences, what other seemingly opposite pairs of emotions might we be likely to mix?

stimuli in the laboratory. In contrast, people whose amygdalas are intact readily learn these responses (Angrilli *et al.*, 2008, 1996; Bechara *et al.*, 1995). Moreover, other research has found that the amygdala becomes active when individuals look at pictures of faces depicting fear, but not when they observe faces depicting happiness (Morris *et al.*, 1996). Conversely, people whose amygdalas are damaged cannot recognize facial expressions of fear, even though they can still recognize facial expressions of other emotions (Berntson *et al.*, 2007; Adolphs *et al.*, 1994).

Today's researchers are also paying considerable attention to the prefrontal cortex, an area of the cerebral cortex, in the study of emotions. Whereas the amygdala seems to be devoted primarily to fear, it appears that the prefrontal cortex plays a role in a range of both positive and negative emotions. One brain scan study found, for example, that participants displayed heightened activity in the right prefrontal cortex when they experienced negative emotions and in their left prefrontal cortex when they experienced positive emotions (Sutton & Davidson, 2000; Sutton *et al.*,

1997). Similarly, other studies indicated that participants with damage to the left brain had a greater incidence of depression than did individuals with damage to the right brain. Still other research found that when people who were very anxious about social situations anticipated giving a public speech the right prefrontal cortex showed increased activation (Davidson *et al.*, 2000). This pattern of findings has led some researchers to wonder whether positive and negative emotions may be governed by two independent brain systems. Further explorations in this area may help explain why some people appear to be characteristically positive and upbeat while other people have a more depressive or negative outlook on life.

Research is also beginning to suggest that the prefrontal cortex may be involved in *coordinating* emotional responses. Whereas the amygdala is responsible for the rapid processing of emotional information, particularly fear-related stimuli, the prefrontal cortex may serve the role of an emotional guide, turning emotional impulses into carefully planned and deliberate actions (Cain & LeDoux, 2008; LeDoux, 1996).

Before You Go On

What Do You Know?

6. What was the key idea in the James–Lange theory of emotion, and what were Cannon's arguments disputing this idea?

7. What element did Schachter and Singer's two-factor theory add to explanations of what determines emotional experience?

8. In what major way do Lewis and Izard disagree about the developmental relationship between cognition and emotion?

9. According to current research, what region of the brain is especially important in the experience of fear?

What Do You Think?

Recall a powerful emotional experience you have had. Which of the theories of emotion detailed in this chapter seems to best explain your experience? Is one theory sufficient?

The Range of Emotional Experiences

LEARNING OBJECTIVE 3
Discuss the emotional dimensions on which people may differ, and describe how malfunctions in emotional processes are related to psychological disorders.

Actually, there are as many emotional experiences as there are people. Do you know anyone who experiences emotions in exactly the same way you do? Probably not. People experience their emotions in a variety of ways. In extreme cases, these differences may even amount to psychological disturbances. Let's examine both differences in how people experience emotion and psychological disturbances of emotion and conclude with a discussion of current research in the field of positive emotions.

Experiencing Emotion  HOW WE DIFFER

In this section, we will look at some common patterns in how different people experience emotions. Indeed, some researchers suggest that such patterns affect how well individuals adapt to their environments We will also discuss how people differ in their ability to regulate emotions. And finally, we will ask how much gender and culture affect the experience of emotions.

Features of Emotional Responding A good deal of research has focused on three features of our emotional responding: the clarity of our emotions, the attention we pay to them and the intensity with which we feel emotions.

- Emotional *clarity* has been described as the ability to accurately identify and distinguish one's emotions (Barrett *et al.*, 2001). If we vaguely experience our emotions as being either pleasant or unpleasant, we cannot develop clear strategies for reducing or enhancing particular emotions or for navigating particular social circumstances (Gohm, 2003). If, however, we are able to accurately pinpoint and distinguish emotions (say, guilt and anger), we can better understand the causes of those emotions, the context in which they occur and the most appropriate responses to make in particular situations (Barrett *et al.*, 2007, 2001). Clarity will also be related to emotional vocabulary: for clarity we need to first be able to subtly distinguish between emotions but also have the descriptive words to label them.

- A process closely related to emotional clarity is *attention to emotion*. This has been described as a

person's tendency to take notice of, value and focus on his or her emotions and moods (Gohm, 2003). People who are aware of, and attend more to, their emotions typically have greater access to them and greater ability to use them in positive and meaningful ways. Conversely, people who tend to ignore or undervalue emotions are less able to identify or control them (Gohm, 2003). Through instruction and practice, individuals can become more skilled at attending to their emotions. Such improvements may be limited, however, by individuals' inborn sensitivity to physiological changes that occur within their bodies (Larsen, 2000). While some people try to suppress or ignore their emotional state, others do the opposite, paying very great attention to how they feel.

- **Emotional intensity** refers to the strength with which an individual typically experiences emotions. Of course, the magnitude of our emotions is related to the magnitude of the emotional stimuli that we encounter. Nevertheless, some individuals may react intensely even to a mild experience (say, a bad grade on a minor homework assignment). Others may barely respond to situations that most individuals would find extremely upsetting (such as a failing grade in a required class). Research has confirmed that individuals who report heightened levels of emotional intensity display stronger emotional responses to the same emotional stimulus than do individuals who report low intensity (Larsen & Diener, 1987). This remains to be confirmed with physiological measures.

> **emotional intensity** the characteristic strength with which an individual typically experiences emotion.

Many theorists believe that emotional intensity is stable across different kinds of emotions (Charles & Piazza, 2007; Larsen & Diener, 1987). In support of this notion, studies have found that people who react to positive events with strong positive emotions (say, great joy) also tend to react to negative with strong negative emotions (such as intense anger). Similarly, those who react to positive events with mild positive emotions react to negative events with mild negative emotions (Larsen *et al.*, 1986; Diener *et al.*, 1985).

Patterns of Emotional Responding Using a statistical technique called *cluster analysis*, emotion researcher Carol Gohm (2003) identifies four common *patterns* of emotional responding that combine different levels of emotional clarity,

PSYCHOLOGY AROUND US   Fearless

Psychologists have devoted many studies to people who experience intense fear. They have also conducted research on individuals who are afraid but nevertheless act bravely, people who are often called *courageous* (Rachman, 2004, 1989). But they have almost ignored people who experience no fear at all – individuals who go through life untouched by anxiety of any kind. Yet, they are out there. Consider the real-life case of SM, a woman referred to by these initials to protect her identity (Feinstein *et al.*, 2011). At first glance, SM seems to be a typical, everyday 44-year-old mother. In fact, however, she was born with two tiny, symmetrical black holes where

her amygdala should be. As a result, SM demonstrates complete and absolute fearlessness. Scientists have taken her to haunted houses and horror films. There, SM may exhibit a little curiosity, but she is otherwise unaffected. SM claims to be afraid of snakes, but if scientists take her to a pet store, she can pet or hold snakes with no problem. The woman has been the victim of multiple crimes and has been threatened with both a knife and a gun. Once, she was almost killed. Yet she demonstrates no lasting trauma from any of the crimes and remembers feeling more or less calm during each situation.

---

attention and intensity. She calls the clusters *hot, cool, overwhelmed* and *cerebral*.

- The *hot* cluster consists of individuals who experience their emotions intensely (high intensity), value and attend to their emotions regularly (high attention) and identify and describe their emotions readily (high clarity).

- In contrast, individuals in the *cool* cluster display low emotional intensity, attention and clarity.

- The *overwhelmed* cluster is made up of individuals who display average emotional attention, high emotional intensity and low emotional clarity.

- People in the *cerebral* cluster show high emotional clarity, average emotional attention and low emotional intensity.

According to Gohm, emotionally overwhelmed people experience the most emotional discomfort. Having intense emotions but little understanding of them, these people worry greatly about the influence of mood in their lives. Frequently, they are flooded with intense emotions that they would like to regulate. However, their inability to identify the emotions accurately makes emotion regulation difficult to achieve.

Repressive Coping Style A great deal of work has been done on repressive coping which is a coping style first described over 30 years ago (Weinberger *et al.*, 1979). The idea is that you measure people on two tests: one of anxiety and the second on social desirability (the need to portray yourself in a positive light). Those who are low on both scales are called *low anxious* and those high on both scales *high anxious* or *defensive*. The most interesting are those

called *repressors* who are high on social desirability and low on anxiety. What is interesting about these people is that they actively try to convince themselves and others that they are rarely or never prone to negative affect/feelings. While they seem to report healthy adaptation and coping, the physical evidence suggests the opposite and their hypersensitivity to anxiety-provoking information. They exaggerate their positive attributes and play down and deny their negative emotional responses.

Regulation of Emotions Because emotions have 'the capacity to either enhance or undermine effective functioning', reducing or otherwise regulating them is often necessary (Thompson, 1994, p. 25). Sometimes, for example, emotions occur at inconvenient times, are too intense or run counter to our goals. In such situations, dampening them through some form of emotion regulation may be the most desirable response. In fact, we often exert considerable control over our emotions, using various strategies to help influence what emotions we have, when we have them and how we experience them (Gross & John, 2003).

Efforts to regulate emotions begin very early in life and continue throughout the lifespan (Cicchetti *et al.*, 1991). Several factors affect the way a person comes to perceive and experience emotions. These factors include the presence or absence of stressors early in the person's life, the person's temperament and the models available in the person's family and in social settings. Depending on such factors, individuals may develop either adaptive or maladaptive styles of regulation (Linehan & Dexter-Mazza, 2008; Linehan, 1993).

Unhealthy attempts to regulate one's emotions are referred to as **emotion dysregulation** (Chapman *et al.*, 2008; Linehan, 1993). Dysregulation occurs when efforts at regulation prevent us from effectively adapting to

emotion dysregulation unhealthy attempts to regulate emotion.

our life circumstances or negatively influence our overall well-being. Some people try to control their emotions by *suppressing* them, for example. This strategy may be helpful in the short run, particularly when it decreases the intensity of a strongly negative emotion. Continuing to suppress emotions in situation after situation, however, may eventually backfire, reducing people's ability to adjust to life circumstances or to attain goals (Cole & Hall, 2008; Carver & Scheier, 1998).

It is often difficult to specify what constitutes adaptive or maladaptive emotional regulation, because emotions depend so much on context. We have already noted, for instance, that suppression of emotions is often a bad thing. Then again, there are some occasions when emotions should be suppressed or, at least, moderated. For example, although sharing private information about our emotions often helps us develop intimacy with someone, too much emotional disclosure can make a listener uncomfortable (Christophe & Rimé, 1997). Indeed, you probably can recall an instance in which you felt ill at ease while a person you hardly knew disclosed too much about him- or herself.

PSYCHOLOGY AROUND US   Emotional Labour

After an in-depth study of airline steward staff, a researcher called Hochschild (2003) wrote a book entitled *The Managed Heart: Commercialisation of human feeling*. In this book, she argues for a new concept: emotional labour. She points out that many jobs require physical and mental labour but some, uniquely, require emotional labour.

The idea is simple: service staff are required to express emotions they do not necessarily feel. They are required to smile, to be positive, to appear relaxed whatever they actually experience. This is called *surface acting*. However, in some jobs, you are almost required actually to feel the emotions that you are required to display. This is called *deep acting*. The idea is that (canny) customers can spot the false display of emotion so you have to learn the 'inside-out smile'.

Some service workers, whose emotions are 'managed and controlled' by their employers become alienated from their real feelings. The sorts of emotions are showing patience, friendliness, curiosity, while suppressing boredom, frustration and anger.

One way to control and aid expression is through the use of scripts. Service staff are encouraged to act, to learn their lines or to portray a character. This teaches them the appropriate emotion, which may, in time, become actually how they feel.

There is nothing new in scripts. Sociologists, in fact, argue that they are a good thing because they can both help workers distance themselves from their 'performance' and reduce the likelihood of a mishap. Young staff seem to like scripts. They help interactions with difficult and demanding customers and control volatile exchanges. As they become more confident, quite often staff personalize the (suggested) script with their own idiosyncrasies. Staff believe scripts help and protect them.

Similarly, uniforms can act like a stage costume. They can inform and protect. They help identify who is who. Was the uniform a barrier? Does it mark people as servile and powerless? Much depends on how smart it is, what is it that people are serving and who is the customer.

All service staff have a 'backstage' in the galley, the kitchen, even the cloakrooms. Here they can be themselves, let off steam, react how they would naturally. Behind the scenes, they can mock difficult customers. They can get their own back and enjoy the camaraderie of the oppressed.

Rest breaks are times to become the real self, to take off the 'makeup', to recover a sense of self-worth and to take some time off emotional labour.

Gender Differences in Emotion One of the more enduring stereotypes in Western society is that women are inherently more emotional than men (Fischer & Manstead, 2000). Men traditionally have been seen as calm, cool, and rational in emotional situations. In contrast, women have been viewed as being more emotionally intense and more likely to express their feelings openly. Consistent with these stereotypical views, women typically report that they express emotions more than men do and that they experience emotions more intensely (John & Gross, 2007; Gross & John, 1998). In one self-report study, for example, female participants reported experiencing stronger emotions than male participants did, as well as expressing more positive and negative emotions (Gross & John, 1998). Such differences also have been observed when researchers observe the social interactions, facial expressions and verbalizations of males and females (Brody, 1999; Dimberg & Lundquist, 1990).

Narrowing the gender gap. Although research indicates that women, on average, may experience and express emotions more intensely than men, that gender difference seems to be fading. Upon receiving their gold medals at the 2004 Olympic games, German canoeists Christian Gille and Thomasz Wylenzek expressed their pride, joy and relief with the same flow of tears (*left*) as that displayed by 2008 Olympic gold medal pole vaulter Elena Isinbaeva of Russia (*right*).

Source: Left photo: ©Kin Cheung/Reuters/Corbis. Right photo: ©Jens Buettner/epa/Corbis.

At first glance, these findings seem to support the stereotypical view that women are biologically more emotional than men. But alternative interpretations are certainly possible. It may be, for example, that when women report experiencing and expressing their emotions more intensely than men they are being influenced by display rules. **Display rules** are cultural expectations that prescribe how, when and by whom emotions should be expressed. In families and society at large, expressions of anger are more socially acceptable for males than for females. Similarly, society deems it more acceptable for females to express nurturing emotions, such as love and warmth (Safdar *et al.*, 2009).

display rules cultural expectations that prescribe how, when and by whom emotions should be expressed.

One study found that women more often conform to *feminine* display rules, including the suppression of negative emotions and the expression of positive emotions. Men more often conform to *masculine* display rules, such as the suppression of positive emotions and the expression of negative emotions (Simpson & Stroh, 2004). Another study found a relationship between participants' acceptance of societal norms and their experiences of emotion (Grossman & Wood, 1993). For example, female participants who believed that women should experience emotions more intensely than men do actually experienced their own emotions with greater intensity than male participants did.

It appears that when cultural display rules are removed from the equation, many of the male/female differences in emotionality disappear. For example, studies have found fewer differences between the emotional experiences of men and women in countries with a greater focus on female empowerment and male–female equality (Fischer *et al.*, 2004). In short, it may be that men and women are actually wired for similar patterns of emotionality but have learnt from society to experience and express their emotions differently.

Cultural and Ethnic Differences in Emotion Emotionality does not vary from culture to culture as much as one might expect. It is true that some cultures do differ in the *language* of emotionality. For example, in Gidjingali, an Australian aboriginal language, only one word, *gurakadj*, is available to describe a range of fearful emotions, from terror, horror and dread to apprehension and timidity. And in Ecuador, the Quichua people lack any word at all for remorse (Tousignant, 1984; Hiatt, 1978). However, there is, for the most part, considerable overlap from culture to culture with respect to the primary categories used to classify emotions.

When differences between cultural groups are observed, they commonly are due to differences in display rules. Ekman (1972) reports that Japanese and American participants differed in how the presence of another person affected their expression of negative emotion. When they were left alone, both Japanese and American participants displayed similar expressions of anger, disgust, fear and sadness in reaction to a negative stimulus. However, the story was very different when an experimenter remained seated in the room. Under that circumstance, the Americans continued to exhibit expressions of negative emotions, but the Japanese participants masked their negative emotions with smiles.

The Japanese participants in this study were probably conforming to a culture-specific display rule that prohibits the expression of negative emotions in the presence of a higher-status individual. In Japan's collectivist society, group harmony, cohesion and cooperation are valued first and foremost. Individual needs and individualistic traits, such as uniqueness and autonomy, are considered secondary (Matsumoto *et al.*, 1998). Thus, the Japanese participants in this study may have been smiling in the presence of the experimenter to display harmony and respect for the experimenter's status (Safdar *et al.*, 2009; Ekman, 1972; Friesen, 1972).

Among ethnic groups within the United States, studies have found few differences in the experience and expression of emotion. In a study that compared Hmong Americans and European Americans, for example, members of the two groups displayed similar physiological patterns of arousal and facial expression and reported similar emotional experiences in response to an emotion-inducing exercise (Tsai *et al.*, 2002). Similarly, other studies have found that Chinese Americans and European Americans show similar levels of physiological arousal and report similar emotions during interpersonal tasks and discussions of relationship conflicts (Tsai *et al.*, 2006, 2004, 2002).

Furnham and Petrova (2010) consider cultural differences in embarrassment. It is one of the universally felt emotions concerned with the feeling of doing something socially inappropriate, breaching the rules of etiquette. It is felt and displayed across the world in a similar manner: blushing, suddenly dropping the smile, lowering your eyes and head, sometimes giggling.

Yet some societies control their facial expressions more than others do. Russians followed closely by South Koreans and Japanese come out on top in the battle of facial muscles control, while Americans land the bottom place in the hierarchy.

The concept of *face* appears to be particularly important in business dealings with certain countries, such as China, Japan and countries of the Middle East. Members of these traditional collectivist societies try to avoid showing their weaknesses at all costs. Losing face by making a mistake, for example, means losing respect and hard-earned status. However, it is also true to say that no one in any sort of position of power would like to be directly challenged in front of their subordinates. Thus, while face saving may be a special concept in some cultural encounters, it is just as relevant in most Western business dealings.

Essentially, while people experience the same range and intensity of emotions everywhere, the way in which they learn to express them differs subtly from one culture to the next.

Disorders of Emotion

OUT OF THE ORDINARY

Earlier, we observed that people differ in the clarity, attention, intensity and regulation of their emotions. It turns out that in extreme cases these features may contribute to psychological disturbances of one kind or another.

- *Clarity of emotions.* Some people are largely unable to identify and describe their emotions, a condition commonly referred to as *alexithymia*. Researchers have found that these people often confuse their emotions with symptoms of medical problems. As a result, they have numerous bodily fears and health complaints (Cox *et al.*, 1994).

- *Attention to emotions.* People who attend to their emotions too much, a pattern called *hypervigilance*, tend to be more anxious than other people (Vujanovic *et al.*, 2007). Because of their heightened self-focus, they keep noticing signs of arousal that other people are not even aware of. They may also appraise such arousal in ways that cause them constant worry.

- *Intensity of emotions.* People who experience too little emotion may be incapable of caring deeply for and relating effectively to other people. An extreme form of this problem is found in *antisocial personality disorder*, a pattern that we will examine more in Chapters 15 and 19. People who display this pattern seem to experience little or no guilt or anxiety. They are thus more likely to violate the needs of other people and less likely to learn from the bad consequences of their actions (Cleckley, 1941).

- *Regulation of emotions.* People who cannot regulate their emotions often develop self-defeating ways of trying to bring order to their emotional lives (Bradley, 2000). As you will see in Chapters 15 and 19, for example, people with *borderline personality disorder* have intense emotions that they are unable to regulate. They may show impulsivity or even resort to self-mutilation. Many theorists view these behaviours as dysfunctional attempts to regulate intense emotional reactions (Nock & Prinstein, 2004; Gratz, 2003; APA, 2000).

PSYCHOLOGY AROUND US Overregulated

Clearly, poor regulation of one's emotions can lead to all kinds of problems. But overregulation – too much control – is no bargain either. Researchers at the University of Minnesota showed a group of students a pair of particularly disgusting movie scenes – a scene in a dirty public toilet in *Trainspotting* and a projectile vomiting scene from Monty Python's *The Meaning of Life* (Vohs et al., 2011). The experimenters instructed half of the students in the study to suppress their emotional reactions to the movie but allowed the other half to react however they pleased. After watching the movie scenes, the student participants were told they were going to play an online game in which they could blast an opponent with noise. The participants who had been asked to suppress their emotions earlier now opted to blast their opponents with substantially louder noise than did the non-suppressing participants. It appears that overregulation of emotions may catch up with people sooner or later.

Like the disorders just mentioned, just about all psychological disorders involve some degree of disturbance in emotional functioning (Gard & Kring, 2009; Yuan & Kring, 2009). For certain disorders, however, emotional disturbances seem to be the central and defining features. These disorders include the *anxiety disorders* and *mood disorders*.

Anxiety Disorders Some people experience such levels of disabling fear and anxiety that they cannot lead normal lives. They are said to have an *anxiety disorder*. Anxiety disorders are collectively the most prevalent of all mental disorders, and we will discuss them further in Chapter 19. Four prominent disorders of this kind are *phobias*, *generalized anxiety disorder*, *panic disorder* and *obsessive–compulsive disorder*.

> **phobia** a persistent and unreasonable fear of a particular object, activity or situation.

You already came across phobias in Chapter 9. A **phobia** is a persistent and unreasonable fear of a particular object, activity or situation. Everyone has areas of special fear, and it is normal for a person to be upset by some things more than other things. A phobia, however, is more intense, persistent and disruptive than such common fears (APA, 2000).

> **generalized anxiety disorder** an anxiety disorder in which people feel excessive anxiety and worry under most circumstances.

People with **generalized anxiety disorder** experience excessive anxiety under most circumstances. They seem to worry all the time. They seem to have a cognitive bias that leads them to interpret almost every situation as threatening (Beck & Weishaar, 2011).

> **panic disorder** an anxiety disorder marked by repeated and unpredictable panic attacks.

Individuals with **panic disorder** experience repeated *panic attacks*. These short bouts of panic occur suddenly and feature palpitations of the heart, tingling in the hands or feet, shortness of breath, sweating, hot and cold flushes, trembling, chest pains, faintness and dizziness. Panic-prone people are more attentive to their bodily sensations than other individuals are, experience more intense bodily sensations and are more inclined to misinterpret their sensations (Nardi et al., 2008).

As noted in Chapter 9, *obsessions* are persistent thoughts or images that seem to invade a person's consciousness. *Compulsions* are repetitive and rigid behaviours that people feel they must perform. A diagnosis of **obsessive–compulsive disorder (OCD)** is made when obsessions or compulsions are excessive, cause great distress, take up much time and interfere with daily functions. In this disorder, the obsessions cause intense anxiety, and the compulsions are aimed at preventing or reducing this anxiety.

> **obsessive–compulsive disorder (OCD)** an anxiety disorder in which obsessions or compulsions feel excessive or unreasonable, cause great distress, take up much time or interfere with daily functions.

Mood Disorders Most people's moods are transient. Their feelings of happiness or sadness tend to rise and fall in response to daily events. In contrast, the moods of people with mood disorders last a long time, colour all of their interactions with the world and interfere with normal functioning.

Depression and *mania* are the key emotions in mood disorders. **Depression** is a markedly sad state in which life seems dark and its challenges overwhelming. In contrast, **mania** is a state of frenzied energy in which people may have an exaggerated belief that they can do and accomplish anything. Most people with a mood disorder suffer only from depression, a pattern called **major depressive disorder**. Others, however, experience periods of mania that alternate with periods of depression, a pattern called **bipolar disorder**.

> **depression** a persistent sad state in which life seems dark and its challenges overwhelming.

> **mania** a persistent state of euphoria or frenzied energy.

> **major depressive disorder** a mood disorder marked by the experience of severe depression without any symptoms of mania.

> **bipolar disorder** a mood disorder in which periods of mania alternate with periods of depression.

Given what you have read in this chapter, you probably will not be surprised to hear that a variety of factors – cognitive, behavioural and biochemical, as well as emotional – combine to produce these disorders. We will be looking at them in greater detail in Chapter 19.

What About Positive Emotions?

Disorders of emotion are certainly of interest to psychologists. But what do psychologists have to say about the experience of pleasant, positive emotions? The past decade has, in fact, witnessed a striking rise in research on positive emotions. As you will recall from Chapter 1, a new trend in the field of psychology is to focus on positive psychology (Seligman & Fowler, 2011; Seligman, 2007). *Positive psychology* is the study and enhancement of positive feelings, including happiness and optimism; positive traits, such as perseverance and wisdom; positive abilities, such as interpersonal skills; and virtues that enhance the well-being of society, including altruism and tolerance. Consistent with this important new field of psychology, researchers are now conducting numerous studies on happiness. We have learnt that happiness is indeed one of the most important and adaptive of human emotions.

In fact, regarding happiness, the news seems to be quite good. Research indicates that people's lives are, in general, more upbeat than psychologists used to think. About three-quarters of people around the world say they are happy, including most of those who are poor, unemployed, elderly and disabled (Bakalar, 2010; Becchetti & Santoro, 2007). Consider the following findings:

- Wealthy people appear only slightly happier than those of modest means (Diener *et al.*, 2010; Easterbrook, 2005).

- Provided they remain healthy, people over 65 report more happiness and less negative emotion than do younger people (Mroczek & Spiro, 2007, 2005; Mroczek, 2004).

- Men and women are equally likely to declare themselves satisfied or very happy.

- Overall, only one person in ten reports being 'not too happy' (Myers, 2000; Myers & Diener, 1996).

- One in seven people reports waking up unhappy (Wallis, 2005).

The main determinants of happiness are a person's health, social relationships, personality, job situation and belief/value system.

Of course, some people are indeed happier than others. Those who are generally happy seem to remain happy from decade to decade, regardless of job changes, moves and family changes (Holder & Klassen, 2010; Becchetti & Santoro, 2007). Such people adjust to negative events and return to their usual cheerful state within a few months. Conversely, unhappy people are not cheered much in the long term even by positive events. Some theorists believe that people have a 'happiness set point' to which they consistently return, despite life's ups and downs. However, this notion is not always supported by research (Lucas, 2007).

Some studies suggest that one's sense of happiness may have a genetic component (Roysamb, 2006; Lykken & Tellegen, 1996). Indeed, one of the most dominant factors in determining happiness may be temperament. Twin studies have found that twins' ratings of happiness are generally similar (Seligman, 2002). Other researchers have reported that the single best predictor of future happiness is past happiness (Seligman, 2002). These findings may indicate that a temperamental predisposition to look at life optimistically is more important than an individual's life situation.

Research also indicates that happiness is linked to our personality characteristics and our typical ways of interpreting events. Happy people are, for example, generally optimistic, outgoing, curious and tender-minded. They also tend to possess high self-esteem, be spiritual, be goal-directed and have a sense of perseverance and of control over their lives (Fisher, 2010; Peterson *et al.*, 2007; Sahoo *et al.*, 2005).

It appears that good relationships are related to happiness and satisfaction. Married people tend to be happier than single people, although this effect may be stronger for men than for women (Myers, 2000). And in what may or may not be surprising news to you, college students who have close friends and significant others are happier than college students who do not (Diener & Seligman, 2002).

No age limit. People who are happy when younger tend to remain happy as they age. On average, older people are as likely as younger people to be happy, perhaps more so.
Source: ©Corbis.

Happiness Myths Eysenck (1990) lists a number of *myths* about the nature and cause of happiness. These include the following, which are widely believed but *wrong*:

- Happiness depends mainly on the quality and quantity of things that happen to you.

- People are less happy than they used to be.

- People with a serious physical disability are always less happy.

- Young people in the prime of life are much happier than older people.

- People who experience great happiness also experience great unhappiness.

- More intelligent people are generally happier than less intelligent people.

- Children add significantly to the happiness of married couples.

- Acquiring lots of money makes people much happier in the long run.

- Men are overall happier than women.

- Pursuing happiness paradoxically ensures you lose it.

Eysenck in his book attempts to provide explanations to debunk these myths – for example, intelligent people should be happier, as they tend to have better jobs and more stable families. But brighter people have higher expectations and may be more aware of some of the more serious problems in their society.

Before You Go On

What Do You Know?

10. What factors may influence the techniques a person uses to control his or her emotions?
11. What are display rules, and how do they affect emotional differences?
12. Extreme variations of which individual differences in emotion have been linked to psychological disorders?
13. List and describe four anxiety disorders and two mood disorders.
14. What are some of the life circumstances positively related to happiness and satisfaction?

What Do You Think?

Build your own emotional profile by estimating your levels of emotional clarity, attention, intensity and regulation. How easy or difficult do you believe it would be to change your emotional profile?

Access your interactive e-book to view a video clip for this chapter at
www.wileyopenpage.com

Summary

What Is Emotion?

LEARNING OBJECTIVE 1   Define emotion, and discuss the components, measurement and functions of emotion.

- An *emotion* is an intrapersonal state that occurs in response to an external or internal event. An emotion includes three components: a *physiological component*, a *cognitive component* and a *behavioural component*.
- To measure emotion, researchers typically use three kinds of information: people's *behavioural displays* of emotion, *self-reports of emotion* and *physiological reactions*.
- Emotions serve cognitive, behavioural and social functions.

Where Do Emotions Come From?

LEARNING OBJECTIVE 2   Discuss the major theories of emotion, and identify the main brain structures associated with emotion.

- The James–Lange theory proposes that the emotion we feel results from bodily and behavioural responses to environmental stimuli, rather than causing those responses.
- According to the Cannon–Bard theory, the perception of an emotionally stirring event simultaneously sends messages to parts of the brain responsible for the subjective experience of emotion and physiological arousal.
- Schachter and Singer's two-factor theory holds that an emotional state is a function of both physiological arousal and cognition.
- The cognitive-mediational theory proposes that cognitive interpretations, particularly appraisals, of events are the keys to the experience of emotions.
- The facial-feedback theory of emotion holds that facial expressions which occur in response to stimuli provide feedback to the brain that helps to shape emotional experience.
- Evolutionary theorists believe that emotions have been passed down because of their role in the survival of our species.
- According to Lewis's cognitive theory of emotional development, emotions unfold in infants as a consequence of neural and cognitive development, with the most significant development achieved by the age of three. In contrast, Izard's differential emotions theory holds that emotions actually help to trigger cognitive development.
- A collection of brain areas, collectively called the limbic system, play key roles in the experience of emotion. Today's brain research on emotion focuses most often on the thalamus, amygdala and cerebral cortex, particularly the prefrontal cortex.

The Range of Emotional Experiences

LEARNING OBJECTIVE 3   Discuss the emotional dimensions on which people may differ, and describe how malfunctions in emotional processes are related to psychological disorders.

- Individuals show important differences in emotional clarity, attention to emotions, emotional intensity and regulation of emotions.
- Women often report being more emotionally expressive than men and experiencing emotions more intensely. These gender differences are highly influenced by cultural display rules, however, and may not reflect inherent patterns of emotionality.
- Emotionality does not vary greatly from culture to culture.
- Extremes in the intensity, clarity, attention to, regulation of and expression of emotion may contribute to psychological disturbances.
- Anxiety disorders include phobias, generalized anxiety disorder, panic disorder and obsessive–compulsive disorder. Mood disorders include major depressive disorder and bipolar disorder.
- Researchers have linked happiness to temperament, certain personality characteristics, certain cognitive styles, high self-esteem, spirituality, goal-directed behaviour and positive relationships.

 Activities to test yourself further are available in your interactive e-book at **www.wileyopenpage.com**

TYING IT TOGETHER

 **WHAT HAPPENS IN THE BRAIN?**

- The amygdala plays a key role in the onset of emotions, particularly fear. Its activation enables the brain to initiate an immediate fear reaction before other brain areas even start to process the fear-arousing situation.
- The prefrontal cortex seems to serve as an emotion coordinator and guide, turning emotional impulses to deliberate actions.

 **OUT OF THE ORDINARY**

- Anxiety disorders are collectively the most common of all mental disorders.
- Just about all psychological disorders involve some degree of disturbance in emotional functioning.

HOW WE DIFFER

- People differ in how clearly they can identify their emotions, how attentive they are to their emotions and how intense their emotions feel.
- Women may not really be all that much more emotional than men. Rather, individuals may follow social display rules about how their particular gender should express emotions.

HOW WE DEVELOP

- The range of emotions in newborns is largely undifferentiated. Infants vacillate largely between general distress and general contentment.
- Some research suggests that the achievement of various cognitive stages enables certain emotions to emerge. Other research finds that the emergence of various emotions helps trigger cognitive and social development.

QUIZ

Quizzes to test yourself further are available in your interactive e-book at **www.wileyopenpage.com**

Key Terms

basic emotions 420
bipolar disorder 428
Cannon–Bard theory of emotion 416
cognitive-mediational theory of emotion 418
depression 428
differential emotions theory 421

display rules 426
emotion 408
emotion dysregulation 424
emotional intensity 423
facial efference 418
facial-feedback theory of emotion 418
generalized anxiety disorder 428

James–Lange theory of emotion 415
major depressive disorder 428
mania 428
obsessive–compulsive disorder (OCD) 428
panic disorder 428
phobia 428

Schachter and Singer's two-factor theory of emotion 416

FLASHCARDS

Flashcards to test yourself further are available in your interactive e-book at **www.wileyopenpage.com**

CHAPTER 15

Personality

Adapted by Adrian Furnham, University College London, UK

CHAPTER OUTLINE

- The Psychodynamic Perspective
- The Humanistic Perspective
- The Trait Perspective
- The Situationist and Interactionist Perspectives

- Biological Foundations of Personality
- Personality and Group Differences
- Personality Disorders
- Personality Assessment

 Access your interactive e-book to view a video clip for this chapter at **www.wileyopenpage.com**

What makes us who we are? What we have in common is that we are all different. We may share birthdays with famous people, we may share the same parents with siblings, we may share strong beliefs with other people and we may even look (something) like someone really famous. But we are all unique, just like our fingerprints. Yet, we can all be described along various specific dimensions or categorized into clear groups, such as introverts or extroverts.

Also, we are able to describe and sometimes predict the behaviour of others. We talk endlessly about others' personality. But what is personality? ■

Consider the following definitions.

> Personality is that which permits a prediction of what a person will do in any given situation.
>
> **Cattell (1965, p. 3)**

> Personality is a stable set of tendencies and characteristics that determine those commonalities and differences in people's psychological behaviour (thoughts, feelings, actions) that have continued in time and that may not be easily understood as the sole result of the social and biological pressures of the moment.
>
> **Maddi (1989, p. 2)**

personality the unique characteristics that account for enduring patterns of inner experience and outward behaviour.

You probably do a lot of thinking about **personality**. Are you, personality speaking, more like your mother or your father? Do you know what your dark or shadow side is?

Maybe you have also spent time thinking and talking about the varying personalities of your friends. How is it that some of your friends have such odd tastes? What pleasures can they possibly get from such strange pastimes? And what on earth do they see in their romantic partners?

Thinking about people's unique characteristics allows us to give context to their behaviour and to try to predict how they might react in a given situation.

Psychological research has historically focused on the divide between nature and nurture explanations of personality development. Increasingly, however, psychologists have come to acknowledge that these two factors *interact* to shape personality. In this chapter, we first explore different perspectives on personality – the *psychodynamic, humanistic, trait, situationist* and *interactionist* perspectives. Many of these perspectives are more of historical interest because without doubt the *trait perspective* is the dominant one in modern personality theory.

We then look at the important role played by genetic predispositions in personality and what researchers have found out about the contributions of *both* genetic and environmental factors. Next, we examine whether personality differs depending on gender and culture. And, finally, we describe various personality disorders and consider how psychologists assess personality in individuals.

In fact, there has been something of a renaissance in what is called *differential psychology* because of four things. *First*, growing agreement about the description and understanding of the basic dimensions of personality. *Second*, a greater understanding of the heritability of personality and the role of the social environment in shaping it. *Third*, an understanding of the biological processes that cause these differences

and, *fourth*, the extent to which personality predicts all sorts of outcomes like educational and work success, relationship building and maintenance as well as long-term mental and physical health.

One question people ask is how to select among different personality theories: which is best? There are various criteria one could apply. Does it describe or explain all important aspects of human behaviour simply? Is the theory clear and free of jargon? Can it be tested with precision, and what is the evidence from those who have tested it? In short, is it empirically valid? And has it stimulated others to work in the area and apply it to other aspects of life?

The Psychodynamic Perspective

LEARNING OBJECTIVE 1

Summarize the main ideas of the psychodynamic view of personality development.

The *psychodynamic model* emphasizes the unconscious, often dark desires (mainly about sex and aggression) that have to be held in check. The model was formulated by the Viennese neurologist Sigmund Freud (1856–1939) at the beginning of the 20th century. In Freud's view, the personality forms as a result of struggles between primal needs and social or moral restraints. Many other theorists who follow Freud's key principles differ from him in certain ways.

The basic assumptions of the theory are essentially these: all social behaviour is the result of fights and compromises between powerful and unconscious drives, motives and needs. Social behaviour often reflects a motive in a subtle or disguised way and the same behaviour can reflect different motives at different times with different people. People may be more or less aware of the forces driving them, and they are driven most often by sexual and aggressive instincts and urges.

The Structure of Personality

Central to Freud's ideas are his views of the conscious and unconscious mind. To Freud, the mind is a little like an iceberg. Only the top of the massive entity is visible to the outside world (Figure 15.1). Three levels of consciousness contain the information stored in our minds, but most of that information is not available to normal awareness.

1. The topmost level is the *conscious* mind. It contains the thoughts and feelings of which we are aware at any given moment.

2. The second level, just below the surface, is the *preconscious*, which contains mental content that

FIGURE 15.1 Freud's view of the mind. According to Freud, the mind has three levels of consciousness. The content stored in the unconscious level is especially important for personality development.

can be relatively easily brought into the conscious mind if it is attended to. For example, your mother's birthday or your plans for this evening remain in your preconscious until you need to use the information. At that point, the information is transferred into your conscious awareness.

3. The deepest level, the *unconscious*, contains most of the content of our minds. We are unaware of this content. And we cannot become aware of it except under special circumstances. According to this theory, the unconscious is particularly important to the development of personality.

Freud identified three central forces in personality development: basic instinctual drives (which he called the *id*), rational thoughts (the *ego*) and moral limits (the *superego*).

id according to psychoanalytic theory, the personality element representing basic instinctual drives (eating, sleeping, sex and comfort).

The **id** is present at birth. It represents basic instinctual needs and desires, such as those related to eating, sleeping, sex and comfort. These impulses are governed by the *pleasure principle*. That is, they constantly strive for gratification. Freud believed that most of these basic impulses have sexual overtones and that sexual energy, which he called *libido*, fuels the id. The id's needs are simple, and its demands to satisfy these needs are urgent. Thus, it is often described as immature and childlike. The id resides largely in the unconscious, and so is not readily available to consciousness.

As children grow older, they begin to learn that their id impulses cannot always be satisfied. The **ego** develops as a result of this learning. The ego works under the *reality principle*, the awareness that it is not always possible or acceptable to have all wants and desires met. Much like the id, the ego is responsible for satisfying impulses. But instead of demanding immediate and direct gratification, the ego first assesses what is realistically possible. Freud essentially saw the ego as a rational, problem-solving force that constantly strove to keep id-based impulses from bursting forth in a destructive manner. You may conclude that the ego is largely a product of the conscious mind. Freud, though, believed that it worked both consciously and unconsciously.

ego according to psychoanalytic theory, a personality element that works to help satisfy the drives of the id while complying with the constraints placed on behaviour by the environment.

The **superego** also forms during childhood. It is in charge of determining which impulses are acceptable to express openly and which are unacceptable. The superego develops as children observe the behaviours of those in their families and their culture. As children, we *internalize* – or unconsciously adopt – the values and norms embodied in those behaviours. At the same time, we begin to use them to evaluate ourselves. The superego's standards of right and wrong make up our moral code and remain stable over the course of our lives. Our superego may therefore be thought of as our *conscience*, an entity that leads us to feel guilt and sometimes even anxiety. Like the ego, the superego resides in both the conscious and the unconscious mind.

superego according to psychoanalytic theory, a personality element in charge of determining which impulses are acceptable to express openly and which are unacceptable; develops as we observe and internalize the behaviours of others in our culture.

According to Freud, the ego acts as a mediator between the id and superego. That is, it balances the powerful desires of the id with the moral standards of the superego. Freud believed that the three forces were always in conflict to some degree. Usually, the conflict takes place at an unconscious level. What if these conflicts are not resolved? Personality problems and even psychological disorders may result if a person is not able to find acceptable compromises.

The British clinical psychologist Don Bannister once remarked that Freud's theory was 'basically a battlefield' because the picture is of 'a dark cellar in which a well-bred lady (the superego) and a sex-crazed monkey (the id) are forever engaged in a mortal combat, the struggle being refereed by a rather nervous bank clerk (the ego).'

TABLE 15.1 Freud's Psychosexual Stages

Stage	Erogenous zone	Key conflict or experience	Symptoms of fixation
Oral (0–18 months)	Mouth	Weaning	Dependency on pleasures of the mouth; also general dependence on mother
Anal (18 months–3 years)	Anus	Toilet training	Excessive neatness, orderliness, stubbornness, stingy, controlling
Phallic (3–6 years)	Genitals	Attraction to opposite sex parent	Sexual role rigidity or confusion
Latency (6 years to puberty)	None	Repression of sexual impulses; identification with same-sex parent	No fixations for this stage
Genital (puberty–adult)	Genitals	Establishing mature sexual relations and emotional intimacy	Sexual dysfunction and unsatisfactory relationships

Freud's Psychosexual Stages

Freud believed that as the id, the ego and the superego work with and against one another, children move through stages that result in the development of personality. The two drives that influence these stages most strongly are *sexuality* and *aggression*. To Freud, these drives are the most likely to cause internal conflict. Why? Because they are the ones that most often fall under social and moral rules and the ones that are most likely to be left unsatisfied. Accordingly, the stages of development are termed **psychosexual stages**. Most are named after specific *erogenous zones*, or pleasure-producing areas of the body. As shown in Table 15.1, Freud labelled the stages *oral, anal, phallic, latency* and *genital*.

psychosexual stages according to psychoanalytic theory, stages in the development of personality – labelled oral, anal, phallic, latency and genital – are primarily influenced by sexuality and aggression.

The psychosexual stages function as learning periods. Children must successfully complete, or *resolve*, the issues of each stage to form a healthy personality. As children move into a new stage, they must cope with new demands from the environment and conflicting internal feelings. If they do not successfully resolve the conflicts that arise, they may become *fixated*, or mentally stuck, at that stage of development. Freud hypothesized that a fixation may affect all subsequent development.

Thus, some people adopt positive oral traits, like optimism. They indulge in eating, kissing, drinking and chewing gum and may become obsessed with oral hygiene. Their orality may be expressed in humour, wit or sarcasm and they may become food or wine experts. They may be speech purists or faddish eaters with very strict rules about what they eat. Those fixated at the anal phase may equally show traits like stinginess, stubbornness and a strong need for order, cleanliness, rigid punctuality and precision. The Freudian idea is that if we get fixated at any of these crucial stages we will be *marked* by certain behaviours that define our adult personality.

Freud linked fixation at different psychosexual stages to the development of distinct, sometimes abnormal, personality characteristics. For instance, Freud believed that a boy in the phallic stage focuses on his penis. What about girls? A girl focuses on her lack of a penis (so-called *penis envy*). A boy entering the phallic stage also begins to feel sexual attraction towards his mother. At the same time, he feels jealous rage towards her love interest, his father. Freud called these feelings the *Oedipus complex*, after the character in Greek mythology who inadvertently killed his father and married his mother. The boy fears that his father will punish him for his feelings, perhaps by cutting off his main zone of pleasure, his penis (so-called *castration anxiety*). These feelings, of course, are unconscious. The child's attempts to resolve the conflicts they create also occur largely at the unconscious level. If children fail to resolve such conflicts, they may suffer from neuroses. **Neurosis** is Freud's term for abnormal behaviour patterns characterized by anxiety, depression and other such symptoms.

neurosis an abnormal behaviour pattern caused by unresolved conflicts between the id, the ego and the superego.

Anxiety and Defence Mechanisms

We have seen that internal conflict, often resulting in anxiety, is central to personality development in psychoanalytic theory. Humans cannot constantly live in an unsettled state of anxiety. They must have some effective methods of handling it. This realization forms the basis for one of Anna Freud's major contributions to how human beings think about themselves: **defence mechanisms**.

defence mechanisms unconscious tactics employed by the ego to protect the individual from anxiety.

TABLE 15.2 Some Common Defence Mechanisms

Mechanism	Description	Example
Repression	Keeping unpleasant memories or thoughts buried in the unconscious	Forgetting the details of a tragic accident
Denial	Refusing to recognize an unpleasant reality	Refusing to admit an addiction
Rationalization	Creating a socially acceptable excuse to justify unacceptable behaviour	Justifying cheating on taxes because 'everyone does it'
Reaction formation	Not acknowledging unacceptable impulses and overemphasizing their opposite	Overpraising a sibling's accomplishment even though resentful
Projection	Transferring one's unacceptable qualities or impulses to others	Not trusting a colleague and believing the colleague does not trust you
Displacement	Diverting one's impulses to a more acceptable target	Yelling at family members after being yelled at by your boss
Sublimation	Channelling socially unacceptable impulses into acceptable activities	Redirecting aggressive behaviour by becoming a professional fighter
Regression	Reverting to immature ways of responding	Throwing a tantrum when frustrated
Identification	Enhancing self-esteem by imagining or forming alliances with others	Joining groups for their prestige value
Intellectualization	Ignoring troubling emotional aspects by focusing on abstract ideas or thoughts	Discussing various economic theories while ignoring the pain of losing your job

Freud described them as unconscious tactics that our egos use to protect us from anxiety. Table 15.2 lists and describes some defence mechanisms.

repression the most basic defence mechanism; the process of keeping unpleasant memories or thoughts buried deep within the unconscious mind.

Repression is the most basic defence mechanism. This strategy keeps unpleasant memories or thoughts buried deep within our unconscious minds. In that way, it protects us from the difficult and painful process of facing them. Another frequently used defence mechanism, and one that has entered into our common vocabulary, is **denial**. This occurs when a person simply refuses to recognize an existing situation. A person who gambles constantly, for example, may claim that she does not really gamble that much. Or she may claim that, even if she does, it is not a problem. It is important to remember that, as stated above, defence mechanisms are unconscious tactics. Thus, the gambler is not consciously making excuses for her behaviour when she practises denial.

denial a defence mechanism; the process of refusing to recognize an existing situation.

PSYCHOLOGY AROUND US   **Denial in Folktales**

In 'The Emperor's New Clothes,' two rogues come to town with a promise to weave a most beautiful cloth, so fine that it can be seen only by a very wise man. The emperor, who is very vain and especially fond of clothes, requests a suit to be made of this extraordinary material and pays the two rogues handsomely . . . As time passes . . . courtiers are sent [by the emperor] to report on the weaving, and eventually the emperor himself goes to see the new suit of clothes.[In fact] no cloth was being woven. Nevertheless, after each visit by the royal court, the beauty of the cloth was praised; that is, the nonexistence of the cloth was denied. Each viewer attributed his difficulty in seeing the cloth to his own stupidity, believing that if he were smarter, he would be able to see the (nonexistent) cloth. The denial is carried to an extreme when the emperor rides through the town in a grand procession, wearing the new suit. The townspeople praise the beauty of the new clothes. [Finally] a little child . . . looks at the emperor and cries aloud, 'But he hasn't got anything on!' The defense of denial, quite inappropriate for grown men, is exposed by a youngster.

(Cramer, 2006)

The Harvard-based psychiatrist Vaillant proposed a developmental hierarchy of four defence levels ranging from *pathological mechanisms* (e.g. denial and distortion), which allow the individual to alter current external experiences to remove any need to deal with reality, to *mature mechanisms* (e.g. sublimation, humour and altruism), which have been adapted throughout an individual's life in order to cope with current circumstances, helping the individual to effectively eliminate conflicting emotions and thoughts. Within these extremes, on reaching adulthood, individuals are also expected to display *immature defences* (e.g. acting out and fantasy), which reduce distress and anxiety that are caused by uncomfortable surroundings or unpleasant company, and *neurotic defences* (e.g. intellectualization and displacement). These can provide short-term benefits in coping, and individuals often have problems with relationships, work and life satisfaction.

Research into the defence mechanisms continues and may be one of the most important contributors to modern personality theory.

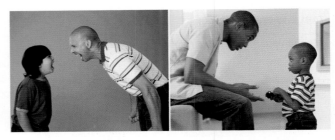

Setting the stage. Freud was among the first theorists to hold that parent–child relationships influence how people feel about themselves and how they handle intimacy as adults. It is obvious which of the interactions pictured here represents a healthier approach to correcting a child's mistake, according to Freud.

Source: Left photo: ©Image Source/Corbis. Right photo: ©Jose Luis Pelaez, Inc./Blend Images/Corbis.

Evaluating Freud's Theories

The popularity of psychoanalytic theory was at its highest in the mid-20th century. Even today, many of Freud's ideas continue to influence the development of the field (Dumont, 2010; Solms, 2007a, 2007b, 2004).

It is true that personality development does depend in part on early childhood experiences, though Freud was not clear which, and why and when they have an effect. Also, he understated the important role of heredity in personality. Some have argued that his theory of motivation was highly simplistic. Yet Freud opened up important and neglected areas, like dreaming, attitudes to authority and the study of humour. He also related personality to mental health.

However, Freud's theories have come under significant criticism in the scientific community. This criticism is largely due to the fact that the key principles of psychoanalytic theory cannot be readily tested by scientific methods. That is, many claims are not refutable and easily open to scientific investigation. This, for many psychologists, means he has been relegated to a historical footnote with regard to personality theory.

Freud based his theories on the cases of patients he treated in his private practice as a neurologist. They were a very special and unusual group, which makes it difficult to extrapolate his theories to all human beings.

When presented with puzzling symptoms, Freud pieced together clues from the patient's childhood to try to identify the cause. For example, one of his patients – a five-year-old boy called Little Hans – had developed an intense fear of horses (Freud, 1909). Freud came to believe that the boy's anxiety related to his relationship with his father. In a lengthy summary of his treatment of Hans, Freud described how he helped the father and son learn to address the repressed feelings that were leading to Hans's anxiety.

Freud's case studies, such as that of Little Hans, are effective at characterizing and classifying certain types of observed behaviours. Indeed, Freud's theories can explain almost any type of observed behaviour. For example, we might say that a man who kept getting into fist fights was redirecting angry, unresolved feelings of aggression towards his parents onto other people in his life. At the same time, we might say that another man, who was unhappy but not hostile, is repressing those same feelings of aggression. In both cases, we have explained the man's behaviour (or non-behaviour). But recall that psychologists seek to predict as well as to describe and explain. Based only on the knowledge that a man has unresolved feelings of aggression towards his parents, could we predict whether he would be prone to hostile, violent relationships? Probably not. This lack of predictive power is a key weakness of psychoanalytic theory and why it has been relegated to a footnote in modern psychological theories.

Additionally, many of Freud's observations were based on a very small and select group of upper-class individuals from 19th-century Vienna. This raises questions about the theory's generalizability, or cross-cultural validity. It also highlights the fact that Freud's ideas were based on his particular, and at times narrow, views of sexuality, parenting norms and gender roles.

At the same time, Freud's supporters argue that it is unfair to criticize psychoanalytic theory for not holding up to scientific testing. It was, after all, never intended to act as a predictive model. Rather, Freud's fundamental claim was that individuals could find meaning from looking into their past.

On the positive side, many aspects of Freud's theory remain relevant today. We are all familiar with the idea that our relationships with our parents can influence how we form intimate relationships as adults (Black & Schutte, 2006). In addition, some studies on defence mechanisms suggest that they can have important functions in both development and psychological disorders (Bouchard & Thériault, 2003).

Perhaps most importantly, Freud's ideas spurred the first inquiries into how the conscious and unconscious aspects of the mind function and how they relate to behaviour. The study of the unconscious mind has in fact accelerated since the last decade of the 20th century. As you learnt in Chapters 8 and 10 many studies indicate that much of the information processed by the mind remains unconscious and that people rely on a variety of automatic processes to function in the world.

Other Psychodynamic Theories

Over time, some of Freud's followers split away to form their own schools of thought, becoming what are called *neo-Freudians*. Three of Freud's most notable followers were Alfred Adler, Carl G. Jung and Karen Horney. The theories of the neo-Freudians departed from Freud's in important ways. But, as you read earlier, each held on to Freud's basic belief that human functioning is shaped by interacting, or *dynamic*, psychological forces.

The positive drives of personality. One-hundred-year-old artist Frances Dunham Catlett speaks about her work at a reception celebrating her 'century of creativity'. Carl Jung believed that unconscious drives towards joy and creativity are powerful forces in personality.

Source: ©Michael Macor/San Francisco Chronicle/Corbis.

Alfred Adler Alfred Adler (1870–1937) believed that social needs and conscious thoughts are more important to human behaviour than sexual needs and other unconscious motivations. Adler was particularly interested in how feelings of *inferiority* motivate behaviour. In Adler's view, almost everyone has some feelings of inferiority. These feelings come from childhood experiences of helplessness. People often make special efforts to compensate for or mask those painful feelings. Adler focused, in particular, on how feelings of inferiority are channelled into a quest for superiority. Adler's school of *individual psychology* has not had a major impact on personality theory. However, his ideas about how the need for power shapes human behaviour have gained momentum in contemporary research.

Carl Jung Carl G. Jung (1875–1961), unlike Adler, agreed with Freud's views on the importance of the unconscious. However, he added a new dimension: the *collective unconscious*. In Jung's system, the unconscious has two parts. The *personal unconscious*, formed from individual experiences, is similar to the unconscious as seen by Freud. The collective unconscious, though, is not a private entity like the personal unconscious. Instead, it is a cumulative storehouse of inherited memories shared by all humankind. Jung called these shared memories *archetypes*. According to Jung, archetypes are reflected in symbols and images that appear in the art, literature and religions of all cultures. The archetype of the hero, for example, can be found in the stories of almost any cultural tradition.

Jung's *analytical psychology* also differed from psychoanalytic theory in terms of the emphasis placed on sexuality

and aggression. Jung acknowledged the importance of these forces. But in his view, the unconscious also included drives towards joy, creativity and internal harmony (Wilde, 2011). Indeed, the search for harmony is a central theme of Jung's theory. He believed that each of us seeks to integrate the mind's various conscious and unconscious elements into a coherent whole, which he termed the *self*.

Jung emphasized the importance of opposing drives or forces with a person such as the public persona versus the private self, as well as the masculine and feminine sides of personality. Perhaps his greatest contribution to personality research has been through the most famous personality test (the Myers–Briggs Type Indicator), which measures four dimensions of human behaviour. It has been suggested that the test is so popular one is completed every second somewhere in the world.

Karen Horney Karen Horney (1885–1952), another neo-Freudian, accepted many of the basic principles of psychoanalysis but went on to develop her own orientation and school of psychoanalytic training. Horney agreed with Freud that anxiety-provoking experiences in childhood could lead to lasting psychological problems. She was particularly interested in what she called *basic anxiety*, which develops in children who experience extreme feelings of isolation and helplessness. Basic anxiety, in Horney's view, sets the stage for later neuroses.

Perhaps Horney's greatest disagreement with Freud related to cultural influences on behaviour. To Freud, the basic conflicts that shaped development were universal. Horney observed distinct differences in personality structure

PRACTICALLY SPEAKING   Jung in the Business World

In the 1940s, a mother–daughter team, Katharine Cook Briggs and Isabel Briggs Myers, created the Myers–Briggs Type Indicator (MBTI). Today, it is one of the most well-known personality tests. Employers in various job fields, employment agencies and careers advisers distribute the questionnaire to several million individuals each year (Wilde, 2011; Furnham, 2008). The test is popular because it describes how we interact with our environment as well as with other people. This knowledge can be extremely useful for a manager in charge of a team of employees from diverse backgrounds, for example.

The MBTI is based on Carl Jung's theory of personality types, and it describes personality in terms of individual preferences for perceiving and judging the world. Do you prefer a more social or solitary environment? How do you interpret the information you take in? When you make a decision, do you first think about it logically or emotionally? Are you open to several possibilities? Your answers describe your basic preferences and, theoretically, reveal a lot about the kinds of jobs you would most enjoy (Wilde, 2011; Myers *et al.*, 1998). Knowing your preferences may also provide clues about your strengths and weaknesses at work. One thing the MBTI cannot inform you or a prospective employer about is your abilities. It cannot tell you how well you will perform in a particular job.

Most psychologists warn against basing career decisions only on the MBTI (Wilde, 2011; Gardner & Martinko, 1996). The test may tell you that you meet the criteria for an introverted type, for example, but that does not mean you should avoid that sales job you were coveting. Even if you are more introverted than extraverted, you may not completely lack extraverted qualities. Moreover, success at a job does not depend just on personality traits, such as extraversion. Rather, it depends on many variables. For most jobs, a variety of different approaches can lead to success.

---

between patients from Europe and those from the United States, however. She came to believe that cultural differences played a more important role in development than traditional psychoanalytic theory acknowledged. Horney also rejected Freud's theories about penis envy. She suggested that what Freud was really detecting was women's envy of men's power – power that came from cultural norms, not inherent differences.

Before You Go On

What Do You Know?

1. In Freudian theory, what is neurosis and what causes it?
2. What is repression?
3. What are some common criticisms of psychoanalytic theory?
4. How did Jung's idea of the unconscious differ from Freud's?

What Do You Think?

Why do you think the concept of defence mechanisms has been embraced by so many theorists (even those who are not psychodynamic) and by the public?

The Humanistic Perspective

LEARNING OBJECTIVE 2

Describe the humanistic theories of Abraham Maslow and Carl Rogers.

Psychodynamic theorists, particularly Freud, generally believe that personality development is driven by forces beyond our control. Humanistic psychologists offer a different, more positive view. As you first saw in Chapter 1, they emphasize people's potential and highlight each person's consciousness, free will and other special human qualities. While humanistic psychology, sometimes called *the third force* in psychology (psychoanalysis and behaviourism being the other two) was seriously on the wane for the last decades of the 20th century, it has re-emerged in the form of *positive psychology*.

Let's consider the ideas of two key humanistic theorists: Abraham Maslow (1908–1970) and Carl Rogers (1902–1987).

Abraham Maslow

In each of us, according to Maslow, is an urge to grow and fulfil his or her potential. Personality arises from people's striving to meet their needs (Leontiev, 2008). As you saw in Chapters 1 and 13, these needs are arranged hierarchically, beginning with the need for basic physiological necessities, such as food and shelter, and becoming increasingly complex. Only after our basic needs have been met can we address more subtle needs and strive to attain more complex things. Our highest-level need is **self-actualization**, the need to fulfil our special potential as human beings. Maslow described self-actualization as 'the full use and exploitation of talents, capacities [and] potentialities' (1970, p. 150), though precisely what this means and how to measure it is unclear.

> **self-actualization** the need of humans to fulfil their full and special potential; the highest level of need in Maslow's hierarchy of needs.

He suggested that psychologists had become overly focused on biological drives and needs, overlooking the role of high-level processes and the need for more complex forms of fulfilment.

If you ask adults to name any or all of the psychologists they have ever heard of, it is not unusual to hear the name of Maslow (after Freud). Critics, however, say it is difficult to find clear evidence of his five basic needs or that they are 'activated' in the precise order that he suggests.

Unlike Freud, Maslow believed that more could be learnt from individuals who were healthy and well adjusted than from those who had psychological problems. In fact, he based his notion of self-actualized individuals on notable historical figures who appeared to lead rich and healthy lives, such as Albert Einstein and Eleanor Roosevelt. What are the characteristics that define self-actualized people? They include the ability to recognize the needs and desires of others, the willingness to respond to the uniqueness of people and situations rather than responding in mechanical or fixed ways, an emotionally deep connection with a few people, spontaneity and creativity, and the ability to resist the urge to conform while still responding to reality.

Some of Maslow's ideas have been taken up by psychologist Mihaly Csikszentmihalyi (2003, 1998). Csikszentmihalyi is interested in *peak experiences*. At such moments, people experience intense clarity of perception, feelings of joy and excitement, and a suspended sense of time and reality. Maslow thought that such moments usually occur when a person becomes engrossed in an activity, such as hearing a beautiful piece of music. These ideas have been influential in sports psychology. Darts players, for example, talk about *being in the zone*, reaching a point where they feel they cannot miss or the board seems twice as big. Csikszentmihalyi's writings on peak experiences reflect psychologists' growing interest in **positive psychology**, the study of positive experiences and healthy mental functioning that we discussed in Chapters 1 and 14 (Baumgardner & Crothers, 2009; Seligman & Csikszentmihalyi, 2000).

> **positive psychology** an area of psychology focusing on positive experiences and healthy mental functioning.

PSYCHOLOGY AROUND US   'In the Zone'

People are 'in the zone' or 'in the flow' when they lose all sense of time. They are completely entranced and captivated by an activity that they are very well suited to. It may be playing a musical instrument or taking part in a sport. It is where they have really discovered what they are good at and like doing best.

They seem to perform brilliantly well and with seemingly little effort. People in this state talk about being 'on a physical high', 'feeling in complete harmony' and 'feeling that time stopped'. They say their sense of self vanishes and that they are able to concentrate for long periods.

Carl Rogers

Carl Rogers, like Maslow, believed that human nature is fundamentally positive and that people strive for self-actualization (Rogers, 2008, 1963). However, Rogers' theory of personality centres on the concept of the *self* rather than on a hierarchy of needs. For Rogers, **self-concept** is a pattern of perception that remains consistent over time and can be used to characterize an individual. Our self-concept is related both to how we see ourselves and to how others see us. The idea that self-concept develops in part based on how we are perceived by others is important in Rogers' theory. It means that as children we need **unconditional positive regard** – acceptance without terms or conditions – from parents or other adults to develop healthy self-concepts.

> **self-concept** a pattern of self-perception that remains consistent over time and can be used to characterize an individual.

> **unconditional positive regard** acceptance without terms or conditions.

The idea of unconditional positive regard became a central part of Rogers' therapeutic practice. He believed that, over the course of development, many children form *conditions of worth*. Such children come to believe that they must meet certain standards in order to gain the love of their parents or other important figures. These standards are often rigid or harsh. And they can hold over into adulthood, acting as a negative force that prevents people from reaching their full potential. Not surprisingly, in Rogers' *client-centred therapy*, discussed in Chapter 1, he worked with clients to create an atmosphere of openness, honesty and absence of judgement. He believed that only in such an atmosphere could individuals begin to put aside the conditions of worth that lay at the root of their personal maladaptive functioning.

Evaluating Humanistic Theories

Many critics fault the humanistic theories for their overly positive focus. These theories are simplistic, say the critics, and they ignore the role of psychological dysfunction in society. They neglect the role of biology and the evidence of evolutionary psychology. In addition, it has been difficult for researchers to conduct controlled studies on such abstract concepts as self-actualization and unconditional positive regard. Further, the evidence for the efficacy of the therapies recommended by humanistic psychologists has not been very impressive.

However, humanistic theories have had a pervasive influence on the field of psychology. As we have mentioned, researchers in positive psychology are giving new attention to questions about how human beings can achieve their full potential for happiness. It remains to be seen how humanistic psychology will contribute to this ongoing discussion.

Before You Go On

What Do You Know?

5. What is self-actualization?
6. According to Rogers, what happens if children fail to regularly receive unconditional positive regard?
7. What is a key criticism of humanistic theory?

What Do You Think?

What do you think are the key qualities of a fully self-actualized person? Who would match your characterization?

The Trait Perspective

LEARNING OBJECTIVE 3

Summarize the leading trait theories, and describe how the five-factor theory has evolved from the work of Gordon Allport and Hans Eysenck.

Suppose you were asked to describe your best friend's personality. What would you say? You may use words such as *funny*, *caring* and *outgoing*. Indeed, one study revealed that there are 18,000 words to describe *personality* in the English language (Allport & Odbert, 1936). Many of these words describe personality traits. Many are considered very positive, like sincere, loyal and truthful; others are considered very negative, like cruel, mean and phoney. Indeed, the Lexical school of personality psychologists seeks to understand personality by looking at the structure of personality words in different languages. The idea is that words have developed to describe the very basic behavioural traits that have been observed over the centuries in all cultures.

Personality traits are tendencies to behave in certain ways that remain relatively constant across situations. Personality traits describe our general dispositions, and those dispositions, in turn, lead to our behaviours. If people are generally enthusiastic, for example, they may show enthusiasm by doing their homework with gusto or singing as they walk down the street. We can describe personality traits at different levels: as a trait/domain (i.e. extraversion) or as a facet (activity, sociability, risk taking) or a habit (going to parties, playing practical jokes). In doing so we can understand the structure of personality and try to get some idea of the mechanisms and processes involved.

Many of today's personality theories are based on the premise that people's personalities are made up of collections of traits. There is general agreement now, after many years of debate, about the *Big Five* dimensions of personality and interest in their origins.

personality traits tendencies to behave in certain ways that remain relatively constant across situations.

Human beings are natural trait theorists. It appears, though, that we are likely to explain our own behaviour in situational terms and others' behaviour in terms of personality traits. (This tendency, called the *fundamental attribution error*, is discussed further in Chapter 16) For example, you did not finish your paper because you were busy studying for two tests in your other classes. That guy over there did not finish his paper because he was uninterested or disorganized. Thinking about others' behaviour in terms of traits helps make their behaviour predictable and gives us a sense of how our interactions with them may go.

PSYCHOLOGY AROUND US | Blameless, But Consistent

People may not be inclined to point to their personalities to explain their own behaviours, especially their negative behaviours. But they do seem to think that they behave consistently, even when that is not the case. Political scientist Greg Markus collected information about the political behaviours and beliefs of a large group of people in 1973 and again in 1982. Markus found that the people in his study, like people everywhere, became more conservative as they got older. But, once they changed in this way, they tended to remember themselves as having been more conservative in the past. Only a third of the people he studied were able to accurately remember their past political beliefs – their memory distortions were always in the direction of their current beliefs. For example, people who had previously been in favour of the legalization of marijuana but had subsequently changed their minds downplayed the degree to which they had been for it in the first place. The moral of the study: most of us are probably much more inconsistent than we think we are.

It was trait theorists such as Gordon Allport (1897–1967) and Hans Eysenck (1916–1997) who first proposed that *central traits* affect a broad range of behaviours. There were also many others, like Raymond Cattell (1905–1998), whose work remains very important to all trait theorists. Traits are thought to cause behaviour and describe the fundamental core qualities of a person that are latent rather than clearly manifest. That is, we cannot 'see' traits, only the behaviour that results from them.

Among researchers, it is difficult to pinpoint a standard definition for central traits. Generally speaking, however, trait theorists make several assumptions:

- People have innate tendencies to respond to situations in certain ways (traits).

- These tendencies can be linked together to form broad habits (central traits).

- Such principles can be used to form the foundation of a scientifically testable theory.

A man named Jason, for example, may have many traits. He may be cheerful, friendly, lazy, disorganized and talkative. According to the early trait theorists, however, only a few of his traits dominate his behaviours, while others are at work less often. Jason may be cheerful in most situations, from home to school and from changing a light bulb to playing tennis (central trait) and lazy only when it comes to cleaning his house. We will look at the ideas of Allport and Eysenck next. Then we will move on to the influential *five-factor theory* of personality.

Gordon Allport

The influential personality theorist Gordon Allport believed that psychoanalysis 'may plunge too deep, and that psychologists would do well to give full recognition to *manifest* motives before probing the unconscious' (1968, pp. 383–384). Unlike Freud, Allport did not believe that behaviour is necessarily related to unconscious tensions. Rather, it can be quite healthy and organized. He also thought that the present is more important than the past in understanding personality. Over the course of his long and distinguished career, Allport emphasized the unity and uniqueness of the individual. Allport conducted detailed case studies that sought to reveal the unique collection of traits at play for each individual. Because much of his work was based on case studies, his ideas have sometimes been criticized by trait theorists who use empirical investigations to identify traits. Nevertheless, his work on personality factors provided the starting point for many empirical studies.

Hans Eysenck and Factor Analysis

The British psychologist Hans Eysenck was a strong proponent of using reliable statistical measures to test psychological principles. To Eysenck, it was vital to develop a theory that could be scientifically tested. As a result, he strove to develop adequate measures of personality traits. He was one of the first to do scientific studies in the area and developed and refined many tests that are extensively used today.

He was especially interested in measures of biological basis, and often challenged the popular ideas of his time. He hoped that eventually theorists would be able to identify clear correlations between traits and behaviours and underlying biological systems. Many of his predictions have proved true and he remains one of the greatest personality psychologists of the 20th century.

Eysenck made particular use of *factor analysis*. As you may recall from Chapter 12, factor analysis is a statistical method for analysing correlations among variables. Its use marked a significant turning point in the scientific study of personality theory. In the past, psychologists such as Freud and Allport had relied on case studies and on their own intuition to form ideas about personality structure. Although factor analysis can also be influenced by the decisions and interpretations of a given researcher, the method provides a much more objective way of identifying relationships between variables.

Eysenck used factor analysis to identify traits that cluster together to form fundamental dimensions of personality, which he called **superfactors** (Figure 15.2). Eysenck eventually identified three basic superfactors:

> **superfactor** a fundamental dimension of personality made up of a related cluster of personality traits.

- *Extraversion* is the best known of the three major personality dimensions that defined Eysenck's model and in some ways is at the heart of the theory. Extraverts are outgoing, sociable and impulsive. They are biologically under-stimulated and therefore seek out all sorts of stimulation. Eysenck's cortical arousal theory of extraversion states that

  - introverts are more aroused than extraverts
  - stimulation increases arousal
  - arousal related to performance is curvilinear

- the optimal level of arousal for a task is negatively related to task difficulty
- arousal related to hedonic tone is curvilinear.

So extraverts trade off accuracy for speed, they are more likely to have accidents and they are attracted to people because they are a source of stimulation, which they crave.

- *Neuroticism* is based on activation thresholds in the sympathetic nervous system or visceral brain. This is the part of the brain that is responsible for the fight-or-flight response in the face of danger. Neurotic people have a low activation threshold and when confronted with even mild stressors or anxiety-producing situations will experience negative affect and become easily upset. Neurotics are moody and prone to anxiety, depression and worrying. Those low in neuroticism are called *stable*. They are relaxed, resilient, even-tempered and calm. These manifestations can range from physiological changes in heart rate, blood pressure, cold hands, sweating and muscular tension to feelings of apprehension and nervousness to the full effects of fear and anxiety. In contrast to neuroticism or emotionally unstable and labile people, emotionally stable people have a much higher activation threshold, and thus will experience negative affect only when confronted by very major stressors.

- *Psychoticism*, the most controversial and debated of Eysenck's three superfactors. Those scoring high are often seen as tough-minded, manipulative and aggressive. High scorers are more predisposed to

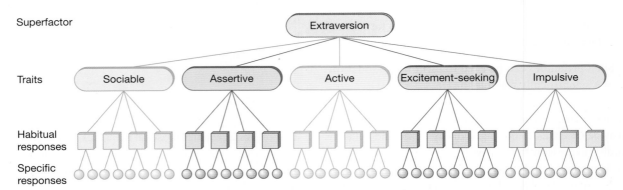

FIGURE 15.2 Eysenck's model of personality. Eysenck used factor analysis to identify traits that cluster together. He described three basic trait clusters, which he called superfactors. Each superfactor – such as extraversion, shown here – is made up of specific traits. Each trait, in turn, is made up of habitual and specific responses.

Source: Adapted with permission from Eysenck, H.J. (1976). *The Biological Basis of Personality*, p. 36. Courtesy of Charles C Thomas Publisher, Ltd., Springfield, Illinois; based on Weiten, W. (2007). *Psychology: Themes and variations* (7th ed). Belmont, CA: Thomson Wadsworth.

psychotic episodes, but also tend to manifest a higher probability of engaging in aggression and demonstrating the kind of cold, tough-mindedness that characterizes psychopathy and people more likely to engage in crime.

The past 20 years or more have witnessed a serious dispute between the pro-Eysenckians who support the Gigantic Three Eysenckian system and those who support the Big Five (see next section). The two positions are debated between proponents in conferences and journal articles.

Eysenck saw each of these superfactors – and the individual character traits of which each is composed – as existing on a continuum, with each person displaying a certain degree of each superfactor.

Although Eysenck depended on factor analysis to determine how personality traits cluster together, he gathered information on the traits themselves through the use of questionnaires. He administered his *Eysenck Personality Questionnaire* to people in hundreds of countries. The results indicated that his superfactors corresponded to basic personality types across many cultures (Eysenck, 2002, 1992, 1990).

As noted, Eysenck believed that personality traits were biologically based. Thus, he also studied the biological basis of personality traits. His belief in the biological roots of personality has been supported by a number of studies. Several investigations of twins, for example, suggest that genetics play a significant role in how individuals score on the extraversion superfactor (Pergadia *et al.*, 2006; Heath *et al.*, 1994). A number of studies of hormones, blood pressure and brain activity support the notion that biological factors are linked to the superfactors at least to some degree (Eysenck, 1990).

Furnham (2008), among others, argues that Eysenck's work was characterized by five things:

* a desire to be parsimonious
* a desire to offer explanations for the mechanisms and processes by which the traits worked
* laboratory experimentation to test his theories
* understanding how the traits worked in the applied world
* continual updating and refinement of the theory and the measures.

Eysenck's work has had an enormous influence on personality theory and research. His early emphasis on empirical research set the stage for much of the current research on personality. Eysenck's personality tests have been translated into many languages. In addition, his ideas and findings have influenced such diverse fields as education, aesthetics, politics and psychopathology. Finally, he was one of the first psychologists to systematically investigate the possible biological basis of personality traits. As we shall see, this area of investigation has become a significant force in the field.

The Five-Factor Model

A number of factor analysis studies have found more than three higher-order dimensions of personality, or superfactors (Poropat, 2009; Boyle, 2008; Saggino & Kline, 1996). As a result, many trait theorists today favour the **five-factor model**. This model identifies five major trait categories, popularly known as the *Big Five* (Figure 15.3):

* *agreeableness* (versus disagreeableness)
* *extraversion* (versus introversion)
* *neuroticism* or *emotional instability* (versus stability)
* *conscientiousness* or *dependability* (versus irresponsibility)
* *openness to experience* or *imaginativeness* (versus unimaginativeness).

> **five-factor model** an empirically derived model that proposes five major trait categories: agreeableness/disagreeableness, extraversion/introversion, neuroticism/stability, conscientiousness/irresponsibility and openness to experience/unimaginativeness.

Big Five Traits	Low Scorers	High Scorers
1 **O**penness	Practical Uncreative Incurious Conforming	Imaginative Creative Curious Independent
2 **C**onscientiousness	Disorganized Careless Lazy Late	Organized Careful Disciplined Punctual
3 **E**xtraversion	Retiring Passive Sober Reserved	Sociable Active Fun-loving Affectionate
4 **A**greeableness	Ruthless Suspicious Critical Uncooperative	Soft-hearted Trusting Lenient Helpful
5 **N**euroticism	Calm Unemotional Secure Self-satisfied	Anxious Emotional Insecure Self-pitying

FIGURE 15.3 The five-factor model of personality. Studies using factor analysis have identified five broad categories of traits, known as the Big Five. Many researchers believe that individual differences in personality can be captured by these five categories.

Adapted from Cattell (1974). Personality pinned down. *Psychology Today*, 44.

A helpful way to memorize these five factors is with the acronym OCEAN (openness, conscientiousness, extraversion, agreeableness and neuroticism).

If you look closely, you will notice that Eysenck's dimensions of extraversion and neuroticism are also found among the Big Five superfactors. His third dimension, psychoticism, does not appear in the five-factor model, however. That dimension was originally thought by Eysenck to serve as a marker of psychotic tendencies, and people with schizophrenia were indeed found to score high on this dimension. However, many people who score highly on Eysenck's psychoticism dimension do not become psychotic. In fact, they display particular traits that are found within the Big Five superfactors of agreeableness and conscientiousness (Saggino, 2000). So high psychoticism is low agreeableness and conscientiousness and high openness.

There has been a rigorous debate among the Eysenckians who insist on the Giant Three and those who like the Big Five, or the five-factor model. There are others who prefer a six- or even seven-dimensional model. It would also be unfair to leave out the very important work of Raymond Cattell who had a 16-factor theory that also remains popular today.

Despite such differences, Eysenck would probably be happy to learn that trait theory has been reenergized in recent years, thanks largely to the popularity of the five-factor model. Indeed, a great many researchers believe that individual differences in personality can be captured by the five broad categories of this theory (Ewen, 2010; Boyle, 2008; McCrae & Costa, 2003). Because of the theory's popularity with researchers, a significant body of relevant research has accumulated (Zuckerman, 2011; Cooper & Sheldon, 2002).

Spotting the superfactors. Take a look at this photograph of people passing through an airport waiting room. All of the fundamental dimensions of personality cited in the Big Five model and other theories of personality are on display in this photo. Can you identify examples of each key trait category?

Source: Baerbel Schmidt/Getty Images, Inc.

This research has attempted to answer questions about both the validity and the usefulness of the five-factor approach.

There are advantages and disadvantages to both the Giant Three and the Big Five. The Giant Three approach strives to ask *why* people differ and to bridge psychology and biology. It has findings consistent with animal research findings as well as drug studies. On the other hand, it tends to be less comprehensive and may over-emphasize biological as opposed to social and environmental factors. The Big Five seems better at description than explanation. It provides a more thorough description and assessment of personality but still there are those who argue it is not comprehensive enough.

Evaluating Trait Theories

Numerous questions have been addressed by research into trait theories. First, do traits apply to a variety of cultures? As we mentioned, Eysenck found that his superfactors described basic types in a number of countries. In addition, there is growing evidence that people in many cultures display personality types that can be captured by several, and sometimes by all, of the Big Five superfactors (Correa & Rogers, 2010; Nye *et al.*, 2008; Saucier *et al.*, 2000).

A second question involves how powerful personality traits are. Consider an interesting study conducted to determine whether people are naturally expressive or inexpressive (DePaulo *et al.*, 1992). To evaluate a person's ability to control his or her expressiveness, the experimenters asked participants to act either very expressively or very inexpressively while discussing a topic. Interestingly, even when asked to be expressive, naturally inexpressive people showed less expression than did expressive people in their natural state. Similarly, when naturally expressive subjects were asked to act inexpressively, they were still more expressive than naturally inexpressive individuals. Clearly, traits are often quite powerful. Even when people want to behave in a manner that conflicts with a particular trait, they may have trouble doing so.

A third question is whether traits remain stable across situations. The answer appears to be sometimes yes and sometimes no (but more yes than no). In a classic study conducted in the early 1980s, investigators observed college students and rated their levels of *conscientiousness* (Mischel & Peake, 1982). Were the students usually on time? Did they complete assignments when due? Did they tidy their rooms? (Recall from Figure 15.3 that conscientious people typically are organized, careful, disciplined and punctual.) The researchers found that levels of conscientiousness were relatively stable across *similar* situations but not across very different situations. That is, people who are punctual for class will likely be punctual for dates, because those situations are similar. However, individuals who are punctual may not necessarily keep their rooms clean. Although both of these situations require conscientiousness, the situations are quite different, leading to inconsistent displays of conscientiousness for some people.

In *strong* situations, where people are expected to follow social rules or etiquette (a lecture or church service, for instance), people behave much the same, but in *weak* situations where there is a much greater ability to express behaviour personality has more effect. Thus, it may be predicted that you see the real person behaving consistently more in weak situations than strong, and people being more consistent when they have more choice as to how to behave.

Yet another question is whether traits are stable over time. Studies indicate that personality traits are more stable over a short time than over a span of years (Srivastava *et al.*, 2003). People who conscientiously show up on time for an appointment today are likely to be punctual for appointments next week and next month. But today's punctuality is not as likely to predict punctuality a year or two from now.

Three processes may explain why people do not change very much. First, people react differently to the same experiences because of their personality. Next, they tend to evoke in others similar reactions. Third, we all proactively choose and change our social situations according to their ability and values.

Indeed, traits often show some inconsistency across a person's lifespan, especially as the individual travels from childhood to adulthood (Fleeson, 2007). For example, people who score highly during their teenage years on *openness* (adventurous, imaginative and untraditional) may score lower in their 50s. Researchers disagree on why such changes occur. Some believe that they reflect biologically based maturation (McCrae, 2002). Others hold that they have more to do with changes in an individual's social environment (Srivastava *et al.*, 2003). Either way, it is worth noting that once a person reaches adulthood lifespan fluctuations seem to lessen. Thus, traits become increasingly stable across the adult years (Roberts & DelVecchio, 2000; Caspi & Roberts, 1999). At the age of 30, what you see is what you get. People

get a little less extraverted and neurotic and a little more agreeable and conscientious, but not a great deal.

The *predictive value* of a model is another issue of concern to researchers. The idea that personality factors may be able to predict broad outcomes dates back many years. One longitudinal investigation found that the Big Five superfactor *conscientiousness* can help predict the length of a person's life (Kern & Friedman, 2008). In this study, a large number of children were followed for 70 years. When the children were 11 years old, their parents and teachers rated them on various personality dimensions. Over the course of the study, records were kept about these individuals and the causes of their eventual deaths. It turned out that, on average, those who had been rated as conscientious lived significantly longer than those who had not been rated as conscientious. To explain this finding, the researchers speculated that conscientiousness is related to a broad pattern of health-related behaviours, such as not smoking and not drinking – behaviours that add up over a lifetime. Similarly, research has suggested that certain personality attributes may predict marital satisfaction. One study found, for example, that high agreeableness greatly increases the chances of having a happy and satisfying marriage (Botwin *et al.*, 1997). So do conscientiousness, emotional stability and intellectual openness.

Finally, researchers have asked whether traits are inherited (Zuckerman, 2011). As suggested earlier, case studies of identical twins who have been reared apart seem to suggest that genetic factors can have a strong influence on personality. In addition, a growing number of empirical studies indicate that heredity plays a role in many dimensions of personality (Krueger *et al.*, 2008; Plomin & Caspi, 1999). Based on such studies, the heritability of personality traits has been estimated at around 40% (Pervin *et al.*, 2005). It does depend on the trait specified, and others have suggested a number as high as 60–70%. In short, it appears that genes contribute strongly to personality.

Before You Go On

What Do You Know?

8. Who were Gordon Allport and Hans Eysenck, and what were their contributions to the trait perspective?

9. What is factor analysis, and how is it tied to trait theories?

10. What are the Big Five personality factors?

11. How stable are traits over time and across situations?

What Do You Think?

Think of three famous people and predict how they each would score on the major trait categories of the five-factor model.

The Situationist and Interactionist Perspectives

LEARNING OBJECTIVE 4
Describe and differentiate the situationist and interactionist views of personality.

Traits obviously play an important role in behaviour. As we have just seen, traits can be predictive, powerful and consistent forces in our lives. But are traits the single key to behaviour? Apparently not. Clearly, there is more to behaviour than traits alone. Recall that traits show more consistency and are more predictive in the short run than in the long run and across similar situations than across dissimilar situations. How big a role do those situations play in how we behave? Personality theorists have wrestled with the relative importance of traits and situational factors over the years. For a while, a *situationist* perspective gained hold in the field. But eventually that position gave way to *interactionist* views, such as the *social-cognitive theory*.

The Situationist View

In the 1960s, psychologist Walter Mischel and other personality theorists began to embrace a view called **situ-ationism**, the notion that behaviour is governed primarily by the variables in a given social situation rather than by internal traits (Mischel, 2004). These theorists acknowledged that personality factors come into play when people are making choices, reacting to events or displaying other behaviours. Nevertheless, the theorists argued, situational 'pushes' and 'pulls' rule in most instances. They argued that personality tests were weak predictors of behaviour (with correlations rarely exceeding $r = 0.30$), and therefore situational or environmental factors must account most for differences in behaviour.

situationism the view that behaviour is governed primarily by the variables in a given situation rather than by internal traits.

The behaviourist B. F. Skinner, discussed in earlier chapters, could be said to have viewed personality from a situationist perspective. Indeed, Skinner believed that human behaviour is completely shaped by environmental factors, a position called *radical behaviourism*. What we call *personality*, Skinner saw as simply a certain consistency in what he called *response tendencies*. By that, Skinner meant that we approach life in a certain way because certain responses have been rewarding to us in the past while certain other responses have not. That is, we tend to repeat responses that have helped us gain a desired outcome or avoid an undesired one. For example, a trait theorist might look at your presence in college as a combination of intelligence, conscientiousness and perhaps a little neuroticism. Skinner would say that you studied because you found academic achievement to be rewarding or because studying kept your parents happy. Because these outcomes were sufficiently motivating, you developed a general response tendency to persist at studying.

Situationism had a strong appeal. As we already mentioned, human beings tend to explain their own behaviour in situational terms, although they tend to explain others' behaviour in terms of traits. How often have you responded 'it depends' when somebody has asked how you would handle a situation? Certainly, we do not like to think of ourselves as 'trait machines': robots who behave as if we have been programmed.

At the same time, though, we must note that there really can be no such thing as *pure* situational factors in human behaviour (Ewen, 2010). Consider, for instance, Skinner's perspective on reward. As we saw in Chapter 9, Skinner defined a *reinforcer* as something that leads you to engage in a behaviour more often. But what is a reinforcer to you may not be a reinforcer to someone else. Even in the context of reinforcement principles, it is still *people* who choose, manipulate, interpret and react to the situations – or reinforcements – they meet. Consider a particular student who puts off every single essay assignment until the very last minute. It is hard to believe that happens because the student's reinforcers always line up in that direction. Ultimately, even as we acknowledge the power and influence of situations, we must acknowledge the power and influence of people and their personalities. Thus, it is not surprising that many situationist theorists, including Walter Mischel, the perspective's early leader, eventually moved to an interactionist perspective of personality. Indeed, he is now a strong advocate for the pervasive influence of personality over time.

The Interactionist Perspective

Interactionism focuses on interactions between people and situations. At the centre of the interactionist view of personality is the idea that people influence the situations they encounter. People choose and change the social situations they encounter every day. Their personality determines how they perceive them and react to them.

interactionism the view that emphasizes the relationship between a person's underlying personality traits and the reinforcing aspects of the situations in which they choose to put themselves.

According to this model, the choices you make are functions of underlying personality traits. Think about why you enrolled at your university. Let's say, for example, that introversion played a role in your choice. You may have chosen a school or university with really small classes – a choice that you suspected would make it more comfortable for you to participate in class. Or perhaps instead you chose a school or university with really large classes – a choice that you believed would make it easier for you to go unnoticed in class. Either choice is likely to result in situational factors that produce a self-fulfilling prophecy. If you chose the school or university with big classes, for example, the large class sizes will indeed help ensure that you can remain quiet in class and continue your introverted style. This idea that individual and situational variables interact suggests a way of moving beyond the trait-versus-situation controversy.

One of the leading interactionist theories is cognitive psychologist Albert Bandura's *social learning theory* (Bandura, 2008, 2006, 1986), which you first read about in Chapter 9. Bandura is famous for introducing the concepts of modelling and self-efficacy to the study of human behaviour and personality. As you will recall, *modelling*, also known as *observational learning*, is a process by which people, especially as young children, learn to respond to particular situations by observing and imitating the behaviour of others. *Self-efficacy* refers to people's personal sense that they have the ability to achieve the goals they pursue. The higher your self-efficacy, the more likely you are to pursue a goal and, ultimately, to be reinforced by the outcome of your efforts (Maddux & Volkmann, 2010).

How do these concepts influence personality? Through a process Bandura called *reciprocal determinism*. In Bandura's way of thinking, the external environment, internal mental events (such as beliefs and expectations) and behaviour all interact with and influence one another, as shown in Figure 15.4.

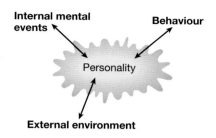

FIGURE 15.4 Bandura's theory of reciprocal determination. In Bandura's view, personality is determined by the interaction of the external environment, internal mental events and behaviour.

How, for example, would Bandura explain your current presence in university? He might note that as a child you observed your parents or friends studying or working hard. As a result, you engaged in similar behaviour when you entered the school environment. Perhaps you were praised by teachers or your parents for good grades, which reinforced that behaviour. You may in turn have developed a confident belief that you were a good student. Your high level of self-efficacy may have led you to persist in behaviours (listening, completing your homework, studying) that led to more desired reinforcements (praise, good grades, positive self-image).

The major advantage of this perspective over other theories of personality is that it is readily testable. Its special emphasis on observable variables – such as models, behaviours, goals and outcomes –makes testing it much easier than testing, say, the abstractions of humanistic theory. And

---

PSYCHOLOGY AROUND US   Influence of Movies and TV on Personality and Behaviour

Film and television are powerful media. The stories conveyed in movies and TV shows can make us laugh, cry or get angry. But can they fundamentally affect our personality or influence how we act? This is a subject of much debate among parents, psychologists and government organizations.

In one study, movie clips of violent acts were shown to university students to see whether the brain's response to aggression changes with repeated viewing. The researchers found that a region of the brain partly responsible for regulating aggression was less active after repeated exposure to violence (Kelly *et al.*, 2007). Such findings have raised concern among scientists and the public. At the same time, it is important to recognize that although the average person views 200,000 dramatized acts of violence by the age of 18, most university-aged individuals are far from violent (Finley, 2007). In short, as we noted in Chapter 9, TV and movie viewing may indeed have a potential relationship to aggressive behaviour, and perhaps to other undesirable behaviours as well. However, other

factors, such as parental and peer influences, may play an even more powerful role (Kim *et al.*, 2006; Collins, 2005).

TV programmes and films appear to have at least some influence on harmful and risky behaviour, but can they also affect us in a positive way? A study of the effect of the documentary film *Super Size Me* – an exposé on overeating in the United States – showed that undergraduates who viewed the film were more conscious about their food choices afterwards (Cottone & Byrd-Bredbenner, 2007). The study did not examine whether long-term, permanent changes in eating behaviour occurred, however.

Film and television are frequently blamed for negatively influencing the behaviour of children and adolescents. Research suggests that such attributions may indeed have merit. At the same time, however, personality and behaviour are complex, and a variety of genetic and environmental factors interact to influence who we are. In most cases, the content of movies and TV shows probably plays only a supporting role.

indeed, a vast amount of data links both modelling and self-efficacy to personality development and change across the lifespan (Hoyle, 2010; Borgen & Betz, 2008; Walsh, 2007).

With an interactionist perspective in mind, personality researchers have uncovered a new kind of consistency over the past decade: not trait consistency, not situation consistency, but *disposition-situation* consistency. They have discovered that interactive effects between dispositions (traits) and situations are common and that disposition-situation relationships often show stability (Ewen, 2010; Mischel, 2004). Such stability would be reflected by the statement, 'Tamara is more outgoing than her sister when she decides to go for a run but less outgoing than her sister when visiting a museum to please her friends.'

Before You Go On

What Do You Know?

12. What is the situationist view of personality, and what theorists played key roles in promoting it?
13. What is the interactionist view of personality, and how does Bandura's social-cognitive theory fit into this perspective?

What Do You Think?

How might Skinner and Bandura each view someone's failure to quit smoking?

Biological Foundations of Personality

LEARNING OBJECTIVE 5

Discuss the heritability of personality traits and some of the neural systems that may be involved in the expression of personality.

You have just seen that the trait-versus-situation debate has moved towards an interactionist view. As we mentioned earlier, the traditional nature/nurture debate has changed in much the same way. No longer is the question nature *or* nurture. Instead, many researchers are trying to understand the *relative* contributions of genetic and environmental factors to the development of personality. Other researchers have been investigating what brain structures and other neurological factors affect personality patterns. Let's see what they have found.

How Much Do Genetic Factors Contribute to Personality?

As we have seen throughout this book, situations in which twins are separated very early in life and raised in different families give researchers a unique opportunity to separate the effects of genetics, shared family and social environments, and non-shared environments. Perhaps the most famous of these twin adoption studies is the *Minnesota Study of Twins Reared Apart (MISTRA)* (Johnson *et al.*, 2007; Bouchard & Pedersen, 1999). This investigation focused on 59 pairs of identical twins who had been raised in different families and 47 pairs of fraternal twins raised in the same household. Recall that identical twins have exactly the same genetic structure, while fraternal twins are no more genetically similar than non-twin siblings.

The twins who participated in the study spent six days taking personality and intelligence tests. The identical twins proved to be substantially more similar on every psychological dimension than the fraternal twins (Figure 15.5). These

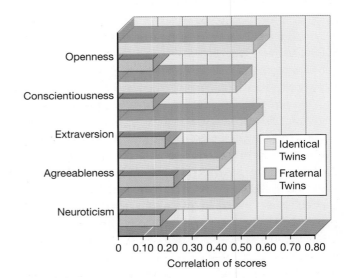

FIGURE 15.5 Heritability of the Big Five traits among twins. Studies comparing identical twins (who share 100% of their genes) and fraternal twins reveal that the Big Five personality traits have a strong genetic component (Loehlin, 1992).

results suggest that shared environments are less important than genetic factors to the development of temperament and many personality traits, although shared environments certainly do contribute (Zawadzki *et al.*, 2001).

Some broad traits appeared to have particularly strong genetic links. For example, in twin studies of personality, the superfactor *agreeableness* from the Big Five scale had an estimated heritability coefficient of 0.40. The heritability coefficient of the superfactor *openness* was estimated to be 0.55 (Bouchard, 2004). Among more specific traits, the heritability coefficient for *warmth* was estimated to be 0.23, while that for *excitement* was estimated to be 0.36 (Jang *et al.*, 1998; Loehlin, 1992).

MISTRA has been embraced by the media for its straightforward findings. It is easy, though, to *misinterpret* the meaning of heritability statistics. Based on their findings, for example, the study's authors estimated that the heritability coefficient of IQ is close to 0.70 (other studies suggest that it is closer to 0.50). Does this mean that IQ is 70% genetic and 30% environmental? No. As noted in Chapter 12, the heritability statistic is related to the total variance in a population, not to the development of IQ on an individual level. That is, a heritability coefficient of 0.70 means that 70% of all differences observed in the tested population are due to genetic factors.

Certain behavioural tendencies that are expressions of personality may also have an inherited component. For instance, genetic factors may contribute to an individual's tendency to watch television (Prescott *et al.*, 1991). Even more complex behaviours, such as the tendency to get a divorce (McGue & Lykken, 1992) and to develop alcoholism (Froehlich *et al.*, 2000; Pickens *et al.*, 1991), have been found to be partially heritable. Of course, no single gene is at work in traits or in behaviours such as these. More likely, multiple genes interact and affect an individual's broad biological systems. These systems in turn contribute to the traits or behaviours in question.

Genes clearly are important in how personality factors are expressed. But even strong proponents of a genetic model now recognize that environmental experiences also play a critical role (Zuckerman, 2011). Recall, for example, that Eysenck considered personality traits to be biologically based. He proposed the superfactor *psychoticism* to be a marker of psychotic tendencies, such as schizophrenia. Even Eysenck, however, discovered that people who displayed high levels of psychoticism did not necessarily develop schizophrenia or other related mental illness. Their environmental experiences helped determine whether they would become disabled by their genetic disposition or channel that disposition into more productive behaviours.

Personality and Biological Systems

Twin studies, as we have seen, suggest links between genes and personality. But these studies do not provide precise information about what biological systems affect personality patterns. The search for such systems dates back to Franz Joseph Gall (1758–1828). Gall developed the theory of **phrenology**, a method of assessing a person's mental and moral qualities by studying the shape of the skull. He believed he could pinpoint specific parts of the brain that were responsible for distinct personality qualities (Figure 15.6). The practice became quite widespread between 1820 and 1850.

> **phrenology** a method of assessing a person's mental and moral qualities by studying the shape of their skull.

The traditional *reading of the head* begins by first considering the overall shape of the head. A rounded head supposedly indicates a strong, confident, courageous and sometimes restless nature. A square head reveals a solid, reliable nature, deeply thoughtful and purposeful. A wide head suggests an energetic, outgoing character, while a narrower

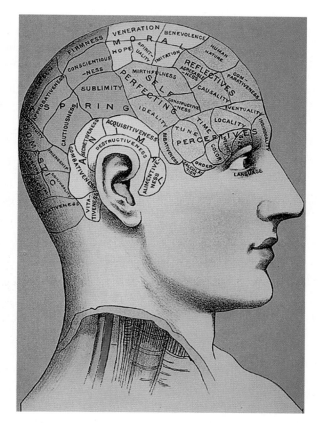

FIGURE 15.6 Bumps, lumps and personality. Franz Gall proposed that personality could be determined by measuring the bumps on a person's skull and he diagrammed the areas associated with particular personality traits. While his assumptions were wrong, his idea that brain functions are localized was true.
Source: © Bettmann/Corbis.

head suggests a more withdrawn, inward-looking nature. An ovoid shape belongs to an intellectual. You must then gently but firmly run your fingers over the skull so that you can feel the contours of the skull. One has to measure individual size of each faculty and its prominence in comparison to other parts of the head. As the brain consists of two hemispheres, each faculty can be duplicated: check both sides of the skull.

The phrenological head has over 40 regions but it depends on which list or system you read. Some with rather old-fashioned concepts, like 20 Veneration, which is respect for society, its rules and institutions; 26 Mirthfulness, which is cheerfulness and sense of humour, and 24 Sublimity, which is the love of grand concepts. There are also head regions for 1 Amativeness (sex appeal), 3 Philoprogenitiveness (parental, filial love), 10 Alimentiveness (appetite, love of food), 31 Eventuality (memory) and 5 Inhabitiveness (love of home). These areas have been further described or classified into eight sentiments or propensities.

1. The *Domestic Propensities*, which are characteristics common to man and animals and are basically responsible for one's emotions and instinctive reactions to objects and events.

2. The *Selfish Propensities* provide for man's wants and assist him in self-protection and self-preservation.

3. The *Self-regarding Sentiments* are concerned with self-interest and expressions of personality.

4. The *Perceptive Faculties* are responsible for awareness of surroundings.

5. The *Artistic Propensities* give rise to sensitivity and aptitude in art and artistic creation.

6. The *Semi-Perceptive Faculties* in such fields as literature, music and language are responsible for an appreciation of cultural surroundings.

7. The *Reflective, Reasoning* and *Intuitive Faculties* are concerned with styles of thinking.

8. The *Moral Sentiments*, including religious faculties, humanize and elevate the character.

Despite its popularity, phrenology has always been dismissed by mainstream science as quackery and pseudoscience. The idea that bumps on the head were related to personality structure and moral development was dismissed as nonsense. The evidence has been evaluated and is wanting.

The rise of neuroscience has shown how many of the claims of phrenology are fraudulent. However, there remain other popular brain myths like the idea that we only use 10% of our brain in day-to-day processing (see Chapter 5).

Gall's techniques were later shown to be inaccurate, but his ideas about the localization of brain functions and the role of the brain in personality continue to influence neuroscience. Many researchers are currently attempting to uncover how brain structures, neurotransmitters, and other factors influence personality (Strelau, 2010; Joseph, 2007). Much of this research focuses on specific personality traits, but a new line of study is also examining higher-order personality variables, such as moral inclinations and self-concept (Paprzycka, 2010).

PSYCHOLOGY AROUND US   Hardwired for Juicy Gossip?

According to some scientists, we may be built that way. In one study, researchers showed a group of participants a set of neutral, unfamiliar faces, and then shared a piece of made-up gossip about each of the faces. The gossip could be negative, positive or neutral. The researchers then showed the faces to the participants once again, but this time they were mixed in with other faces. When the faces were presented in this new manner, the researchers noted where the eye glances of the participants wandered. It turned out that their eyes focused on the faces that had nasty gossip attached to them much more that on faces that had been associated with positive or neutral gossip. All of which suggests to some observers that reality TV may be so successful partly because we are built to want to watch it, just like we slow down to look at car accidents on the motorway.

Research on Neural Systems and Personality  WHAT HAPPENS IN THE BRAIN?

Many studies suggest that certain *brain structures* help to regulate personality. As noted in previous chapters (Chapter 14, for example), the amygdala plays a key role in emotionality, motivation and the processing of negative stimuli, especially stimuli that activate fear and avoidance responses (Haas

et al., 2007; Adolphs et al., 1999). Brain-imaging studies have shown that people with damage to the amygdala have difficulty becoming conditioned to fear stimuli (LeDoux, 1999). The damage may prevent the amygdala from responding to stimuli that excite fearful responses in people without amygdala damage. Conversely, an overly active amygdala may contribute to an overly fearful personal style. According

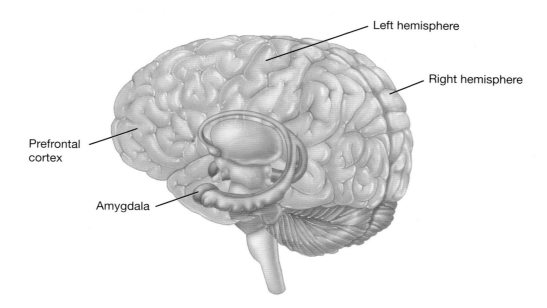

to some researchers, for example, children who display an inhibited personality – characterized by shyness and fear of the unfamiliar – have amygdalas that are *too easily* activated, causing the children to be aroused by unfamiliar situations too readily (Schwartz *et al.*, 1999).

Cerebral hemisphere dominance may also contribute in subtle ways to personality. Some studies have hinted that people whose right hemisphere is dominant experience more negative emotions and traits, such as withdrawal and inhibition. Those whose left hemisphere is dominant display more positive emotions and traits, such as extraversion (Davidson, 1998). One study found, for example, that participants who were generally sad and withdrawn had less activity in the left side of the prefrontal cortex – the part of the brain responsible, in part, for emotional reactions to stress (Davidson & Fox, 1989). Moreover, the link between hemisphere dominance and personality may appear at a very early age. Psychologists have studied the brains of infants who show high levels of distress when separated from their mothers. Results indicate that such infants tend to show heightened activity in the right-side prefrontal cortex (Harman & Fox, 1997).

Neurotransmitter activity has also been linked to some personality variables. As we saw in Chapter 8, the neurotransmitter dopamine helps regulate the *pleasure pathway* (Dreher *et al.*, 2009; Volkow & Fowler, 2000). It is central to the brain's reward systems. High dopamine activity in the reward centres has been associated with positive emotions, high energy and lack of inhibition. Conversely, low activity has been linked to anxiety, inhibition and low energy levels (Zuckerman, 2007, 1995). Similarly, low serotonin activity has been associated with depression, violent behaviour and impulsivity (Knutson *et al.*, 1998).

Hormonal activity, too, has been tied to personality. As we saw in Chapter 4, for example, Jerome Kagan conducted a famous study of inhibited children in 1994. He measured the blood cortisol levels of children as they were reacting to stressful situations. Recall that cortisol is an important hormone that helps regulate reactions to threatening experiences. Kagan found that the children with inhibited personalities tended to have higher cortisol stress reactions to unfamiliar situations.

Organizing Research Findings Many studies have looked at the link between biological processes and personality. We are still in the early phases of this work and results often have been complex and confusing. One compelling method for organizing these findings has been suggested by researchers Lee Anna Clark and David Watson. They group personality types into three broad categories of temperament, similar to the superfactors proposed by Eysenck and the Big Five theorists (Watson *et al.*, 2008; Clark & Watson, 1999).

Negative emotionality Individuals who have high levels of negative emotionality are thought to experience more negative emotions and see the world as distressing. Individuals low on this dimension are relatively peaceful and have higher levels of satisfaction.

Positive emotionality Measures of positive emotionality are thought to represent people's engagement with their environment. High scorers are social individuals who lead active lives and exhibit enthusiasm. Low scorers are shyer and have less energy and self-confidence.

Disinhibition versus constraint This dimension reflects how we regulate our emotions. People high in disinhibition have difficulty controlling their emotional responses and tend to be impulsive, living for the moment. People high in constraint live more careful and controlled lives.

Note that negative emotionality and positive emotionality are two separate dimensions. They are not necessarily at opposite ends of a spectrum. A person may score high on both, low on both or high on one and low on the other.

Scores on the three dimensions have been broadly related to particular lifestyle patterns (Figure 15.7). Individuals high in negative emotionality seem more likely to experience feelings such as anger, contempt and guilt, for example. Those high in positive emotionality tend to experience positive emotions such as joy, excitement and pride. Certain problematic lifestyle patterns have been found among individuals who score high on disinhibition. Highly impulsive and unable to act with long-term consequences in mind, these individuals tend to get poorer grades in school, perform more poorly in their jobs and engage in riskier activities, such as drinking and using illegal drugs.

Evidence suggests that biological processes may be at the root of these three dimensions. Levels of positive emotionality appear to be associated with higher dopamine activity (Clark & Watson, 1999; Depue & Collins, 1999). And levels of negative emotionality seem to be tied primarily to low serotonin activity (Clark & Watson, 1999).

The biological roots of disinhibition appear to be more complicated. Low serotonin activity seems to contribute to some features of this dimension, such as aggressiveness and substance abuse, whereas low dopamine activity contributes to thrill seeking and impulsivity, other features of the dimension. It is almost as if the individuals need to seek outside thrills to make up for deficiencies in their dopamine-activated pleasure pathways (Clark & Watson, 1999). Testosterone also comes into play in disinhibition. High levels have been associated with aggressiveness and competitiveness, prominent characteristics of the disinhibition dimension (Carré *et al.*, 2009).

Interpreting Research Findings Clearly, researchers have found links between brain functioning and personality. But we must, as always, take care in interpreting these findings. The links just discussed are not usually straightforward, and personality traits are never the result of a single biological process. The activity of one neurotransmitter – say, serotonin – is, at most, *partly* responsible for regulating a trait or emotion.

In addition, it is important to remember the difference between association and cause. The patterns of brain activity that we have observed have not been shown to provide a causal explanation of traits. Particular biological processes associated with personality may themselves result from environment and experience. As we have seen, for example, studies indicate that life experiences, even very early ones, may affect both biological make-up and personality patterns. One study of rhesus monkeys found that baby monkeys who had been abused and rejected by their mothers had lower levels of serotonin activity in adulthood. Moreover, the lower their level of serotonin activity in adulthood, the more likely they were to abuse their own offspring (Maestripieri *et al.*, 2006). Clearly, environmental factors, even at an early age, can

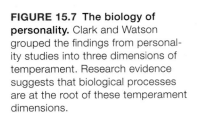

FIGURE 15.7 The biology of personality. Clark and Watson grouped the findings from personality studies into three dimensions of temperament. Research evidence suggests that biological processes are at the root of these temperament dimensions.

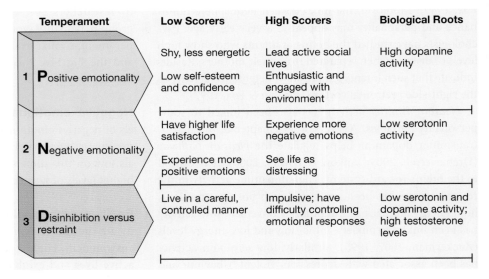

Temperament	Low Scorers	High Scorers	Biological Roots
1 **P**ositive emotionality	Shy, less energetic Low self-esteem and confidence	Lead active social lives Enthusiastic and engaged with environment	High dopamine activity
2 **N**egative emotionality	Have higher life satisfaction Experience more positive emotions	Experience more negative emotions See life as distressing	Low serotonin activity
3 **D**isinhibition versus restraint	Live in a careful, controlled manner	Impulsive; have difficulty controlling emotional responses	Low serotonin and dopamine activity; high testosterone levels

greatly affect the neurobiological system. And that impact can last a lifetime.

In summary, we must be very careful about the conclusions we draw from genetic and neurological personality research. First, we must keep in mind that the brain operates as a system and personality reflects activity in a number of brain regions, as well as the expression of multiple genes (Bouchard, 2004). Second, we must recall that one gene may interact with other genes and affect a variety of personality dimensions (Livesley *et al.*, 2003). Third, we need to recognize that the environment affects the operation and impact of both genetic and biological processes. Those processes, in turn, affect how individuals interact with their environment. All this adds up to a system of bidirectional relationships between traits, biological factors, the environment and behaviour (Maruszewski *et al.*, 2010). In the end, the only certain conclusion that can be drawn is that much more research is needed before we can truly understand the nature and causes of personality. But that research is now being done. We now have more sophisticated techniques to test our theories and, thanks to neuroscience, we are now really beginning to understand how we tick.

Before You Go On

What Do You Know?

14. What do we mean when we say that the Big Five dimension of openness has a heritability coefficient of 0.55?

15. What is thought to be the role of the amygdala in the development of inhibited personalities?

16. What are the three categories of temperament proposed by Clark and Watson?

17. Why is it necessary to be careful in interpreting research findings associating particular personality traits with particular biological substances or structures?

What Do You Think?

Many of the same brain structures are involved in both emotion and personality. Discuss what you think this suggests about the relationship between emotion and personality.

Personality and Group Differences

 HOW WE DIFFER

LEARNING OBJECTIVE 6

Explain how gender and cultural differences can affect personality.

We have focused so far on ideas about how personality unfolds. Let's turn now to the question of group differences in personality. Are male and female personalities inherently different? Do personalities differ among different cultures and subcultures? We will examine these questions now.

Gender Differences

The 1992 book *Men Are from Mars, Women Are from Venus* by John Gray has sold more than seven million copies and been translated into 40 languages. The book's premise, that men and women are entirely different, clearly struck a responsive chord. But how accurate is this notion?

Research into Gender Differences The widespread belief in inherent personality differences between men and women often is a myth. Recent broad reviews of studies on gender differences in personality, cognitive abilities and leadership have found that the similarities between men and women far outnumber the differences (Hyde, 2008, 2007, 2005). Differences among individuals of each gender are much larger than differences between males and females (Costa *et al.*, 2001).

Beyond all this, gender researchers have begun to note the importance of context in their investigations. The situational and social context of a study can greatly influence the nature and size of observed gender differences (Bussey & Bandura, 1999; Eagly & Wood, 1999). Many psychologists rightly stress that incorrect conclusions about certain gender differences can maintain stereotypes and harm both women and men at work, at home and in their professional lives (Barnett & Rivers, 2004). There is an active debate between the feminists and the evolutionary psychologists: the former tend to reject sociobiological descriptions and explanations of sex differences, claiming they are predominantly a function of culture learning.

Different Values, Different Personalities. One of these business meetings is being held in the United States and the other in Japan. The different ways in which meetings are being conducted reflect the different values and personalities at work in individualist and collectivist cultures. Goals and personal styles in an individualist culture emphasize striving for autonomy, individual achievement and high self-esteem. In contrast, those on display in a collectivist culture emphasize the community, cooperation and honouring one's family.

Source: Left photo: ©Creasource/Corbis. Right photo: ©Tokyo Space Club/Corbis.

Nevertheless, some consistent sex differences have been documented. For example, many people assume that women are more tuned in to other people (i.e. emotionally intelligent) than are men. And in fact, women, on average, tend to be more accurate than men at assessing emotion in other people (McClure, 2000). Psychologist Carol Gilligan (2004) has argued that women and men, in fact, view the world differently, although she also emphasizes that one perspective is not superior to the other. Gilligan believes that women are more attuned to interpersonal concerns when making moral decisions. Men are more likely to base such decisions on laws or abstract principles. Building on this idea, she has found that men, on average, score higher on traits that reflect individuality and autonomy. In contrast, women score higher on traits that emphasize social connectedness (Gilligan, 1982). Similarly, some investigations have indicated that women tend to display more nurturing behaviours (Feingold, 1994).

Psychologist Janet Hyde (2008, 2005) statistically compared the results of many studies relating to gender differences in personality. Hyde found only a handful of variables on which females and males differed consistently. Those that she did find, however, seem important. Levels of aggression – particularly physical aggression – were somewhat higher among males. In addition, males were quite different from females on measures of motor performance and sexuality. And males and females had strikingly different attitudes about sex in casual, uncommitted relationships – men were more open to sex in such instances. As we saw in Chapter 13, the data on gender differences in sexual attitudes may be influenced by research participants' awareness that society expects men and women to behave in certain ways sexually. Still, it is clear that, overall, differences in aggression and attitudes may contribute to differences in the expression of personality.

Why Do Gender Differences in Personality Exist?
Knowing about gender differences is similar to looking at the results of a personality assessment. Both provide descriptions but do little to explain *why* certain patterns exist and what those patterns say about future behaviour. A number of theories attempt to explain the personality differences observed in men and women. Many tests show different norms for men and women. Thus, overall, men tend to be less agreeable and neurotic than women on the Big Five. The question is why?

One theory explains these differences in sociocultural terms. After all, a person's self-concept, life goals and values all develop in a social context. According to **social role theory**, girls and boys develop different personal styles, behaviours, and skills based largely on differences in gender role expectations (Eagly & Koenig, 2006; Eagly, 1987). In other words, males and females develop the personality attributes that are best suited for the roles that they are expected by society to occupy. Many theorists believe that play behaviour in childhood helps teach gender roles and expectations. Young boys are expected to play competitive games, for example. Girls, in contrast, are encouraged to play games that emphasize nurturing and interacting with peers.

Family and social relationships may also contribute to personality differences between boys and girls. As children

> **social role theory** the theory that gender differences occur because girls and boys develop different behaviours and skills based largely on differences in gender role expectations.

interact with their families and peers, they observe how those individuals react to their behaviours. Based on others' reactions, the children form ideas about gender role expectations. Particularly important, the reactions of others teach the children what behaviours and ideas are not appropriate to their gender role (Henley, 1977). A little boy may, for example, face disapproval if he plays with dolls rather than action figures.

PSYCHOLOGY AROUND US   Trying to Break Free of Social Roles

Efforts to break free from social roles can take a toll on individuals. Researchers Jennifer K. Bosson and Joseph A. Vandello (2011) asked men to engage in a plaiting task – half of them plaited a length of rope, and half of them plaited hair. Afterwards, the men were given the choice of punching a bag or working on a puzzle. The men who plaited hair overwhelmingly opted to punch a bag. In another condition, men who were not allowed to punch a bag or engage in other aggressive behaviours reported high anxiety levels. In essence, according to Bosson and Vandello, if the men did not get an opportunity to reassert some gender-stereotyped behaviour, their sense of manliness became threatened.

Broad cultural practices are also significant in the development of male/female differences. Often, these practices reflect religious and philosophical beliefs. Traditionally, men held a position of higher power than women in most societies, and this power structure had a trickle-down effect on smaller units of behaviour. Women, for example, often were limited to certain roles, such as child rearing, domestic work and particular occupations (nurse, teacher, secretary). It may be that women were more likely to develop certain personality traits as a result of these constraints. Consider, for example, the superior abilities of women, on average, to read emotions and to perform in the social realm. Individuals who are in positions of less power or privilege may need to develop their skills at recognizing interpersonal cues and spotting the emotions of those in power (Eagly & Koenig, 2006; Tavris, 1991; Eagly, 1987). They can use such skills as they try to make sure their own needs are met.

A number of theorists further propose that cultural norms influence how men and women form their self-schemata. As we discussed in Chapter 3, *schemata* are ways we organize knowledge. A *self-schema* is an individual's cognitive framework for the knowledge he or she has about him- or herself. When we need to process new information about ourselves, we refer to these schemata for guidance. How should we react when a homeless person approaches us for money? What movie should we go to tonight? We will probably refer to our self-schemata to help us make these decisions. A number of studies suggest that the self-schemata of men and women are different in some respects. Men are more likely to have self-schemata that emphasize autonomy and independence, while women are more likely to have collectivist or relationship-based schemata (Bekker & van Assen, 2008). One team of researchers hypothesized that an individual's self-esteem would be directly related to how well he or she lived up to gender-dependent schemata (Josephs *et al.*, 1992). The researchers found that participants who believed that they equalled or surpassed most of their peers in gender-specific skills and abilities had consistently higher levels of self-esteem.

In addition to such sociocultural factors, biological factors contribute to gender differences in personality. In Chapter 5, for example, we discussed the nature and importance of the *lateralization of function* in the brain. It turns out that males and females may exhibit different degrees of hemispheric lateralization. In male brains one hemisphere is relatively dominant for various kinds of processing, while female brains tend to be more integrated (Everhart *et al.*, 2001; Saucier & Elias, 2001). Still other studies have found that the sex hormones testosterone and oestrogen, which are available in different amounts and often act differently in males and females, have major influences on behaviour and personal tendencies. Thus, many theorists believe that these hormones also contribute to gender differences in personality (Hines, 2004; Dabbs *et al.*, 2001).

In summary, it is true, on the one hand, that many of society's beliefs about male/female personality differences are incorrect or overstated. A number of psychologists worry that the Mars/Venus myth of massive gender differences serves to bolster harmful misconceptions. Highlighting differences between men and women, for example, may support prejudice and discrimination against women (Hyde, 2005). On the other hand, it is also true that there is danger in ignoring the real differences that exist between the genders. Boys and girls are vulnerable to different pressures. There seem to be widening differences in educational success and in the world of work. Denying real differences, argue a number of theorists, may downplay the unique strengths and gifts of each gender. Like issues of race, the reaction to people when gender differences are discussed has alas persuaded many psychologists either not to work in this area or else not to attempt to popularize their results.

Perhaps the most appropriate response to this debate was offered by the psychologist Diane Halpern, past president of the American Psychological Association. There may be limited differences between males and females, Halpern stated, but 'differences are not deficiencies' (Halpern, 2000).

Differences among Cultural Groups

Most personality theorists hypothesize that major individual difference variables such as intelligence and personality are in fact universal constructs. While they may vary in their expression (phenotype) as a function of culture and other psychosocial factors, basic traits are common across human kind. Some psychologists would also argue that the measurement of their specifically described traits or constructs would prove universal across all countries and cultures (in all periods) because of the universally based biological structure of personality across racial, gender and educational groups. Considerable research has been published over the years examining the genetic, biological, neurological and environmental basis (e.g. culture, ethnicity and family) of personality and has demonstrated the significant contribution of both biology and sociocultural factors in determining and shaping the expression of intelligence and personality.

There have been numerous large-scale studies looking at personality test scores in different cultures like the one led by Robert McCrae (McCrae et al., 2005). It looked at data from 50 countries as well as the differences between men and women, and age trends. What the results showed, as have others of this type, is that there are more similarities than differences in personality traits across cultures.

Around the world, each culture is characterized by its own values, beliefs and patterns of behaviours. These features help guide members of the cultural group, teaching them what they should value, how they should treat others in their group and how they should view themselves in relation to society. Cultures also form their own ideas about what is important in life. For example, the term *self-esteem*, so important in Western culture, is not even found in a number of languages. Clearly, people who live in a society that does not emphasize self-esteem are less likely to spend their lives striving for it. Similarly, in Western Europe, a person's goals and life path are often influenced by the culture's emphasis on autonomy and accomplishment, whereas Asian cultures place far more emphasis on contributing to a community and honouring one's family.

Some of the most comprehensive cross-cultural research has focused on personality development in individualist and collectivist cultures. As we observed in Chapter 14, most collectivist cultures consider the needs of the group more important than the needs of the individual. With this orientation comes a focus on the role of the individual in his or her family and on social relationships in general. In turn, the individual is more likely to strive to help maintain the social order and to exhibit humility in social interactions (Triandis, 2001; Triandis et al., 1990). Collectivist values are particularly found in African, Latin American, Asian and Middle Eastern cultures (Buda & Elsayed-Elkhouly, 1998).

In contrast, individualist cultures value individual achievement, freedom and success. The self is seen as independent, and each individual is thought to possess a unique set of psychological qualities. Unlike collectivist cultures, individualist cultures consider individual attainment more important than the needs of others. Indeed, competition between individuals is valued. Countries known for this type of structure include the United Kingdom, the Netherlands, the United States and Australia.

Cross-cultural psychologists have uncovered some interesting personality variations between collectivist and individualist cultures (Correa & Rogers, 2010; Oyserman et al., 2002a, 2002b; Schmitt et al., 2007). One large, multination study found that people in collectivist cultures tend to score higher on measures of agreeableness, for example. People from individualist cultures score higher on measures of extraversion and openness (Hofstede & McCrae, 2004).

Happiness and success may also be defined differently from culture to culture. In collectivist societies, contentment is related to harmony in interpersonal relationships, and this emphasis affects behaviour (Kitayama et al., 2000). Interpersonal behaviours are tailored to the feelings and needs of others (Kashima et al., 1992). A strong sense of cooperation shapes personal styles, behaviours, life goals and measures of success. In such a culture, a sense of accomplishment comes not from individual achievements but from strong commitment to family, community or company.

In contrast, people in more individualist cultures are less constrained by a tightly knit social network and enjoy greater personal freedom. They value their privacy and place a premium on individual rights. Interestingly, some studies have found that people in individualist cultures tend to report greater happiness than those in collectivist cultures (Kuppens et al., 2008; Diener et al., 1995). At the same time, however, individualist societies have higher rates of divorce, murder and stress-related disease than collectivist ones do (Triandis, 2001; Popenoe, 1993; Triandis et al., 1988).

People's sense of their own personalities also differs across cultures. Individuals in collectivist cultures, for example, do not use traits to describe themselves as often as those in individualist cultures do. Studies have shown that when students are asked to complete the phrase 'I am . . .', those from the United States are more likely to answer using a personal trait (e.g. 'I am friendly' or 'I am honest'). Those from cultures with a collectivist orientation are more likely to describe themselves in a social manner (e.g. 'I am a member of the psychology department') (Cousins, 1989; Triandis, 2001, 1989). In light of such findings, some theorists have argued that Western personality measures, such as the Big Five superfactors, are not very useful for studying behaviour in collectivist cultures (Church & Katigbak, 2000). It may be that traditional Westernized tests need to be supplemented by culturally specific ones.

The interplay of culture and personality is evident when people move from one environment to another. As a person becomes part of a new cultural context, he or she typically absorbs the norms and values of the society. Indeed, research has shown that when individuals move from a collectivist culture to an individualist one their personal and behavioural patterns change. That, however, does not mean that their personality changes: rather they learn to express their personality in different circumstances and environments.

One study, for example, looked at the personality traits of Chinese students who were enrolled in universities in North America (McCrae *et al.*, 1998). Those students who had been in North America the longest, and had presumably been more exposed to Western culture, showed higher levels of extraversion. They also had personality profiles more similar to those of North Americans.

Interestingly, some people who come from bicultural backgrounds seem to develop the ability to *frame switch*. In other words, they can change back and forth between cultural frameworks as necessary. This suggests that they may have internalized the belief systems of both cultures (Hong *et al.*, 2000). It is not yet clear what implications frame switching has for the ties between culture and personality. This is, however, an important question as the world moves each day towards greater cultural integration.

Culture, Socioeconomic Environment and Personality

A key aspect of culture is the socioeconomic environment. Even in the most prosperous nations, those in the lowest and highest income brackets live in very different conditions. These differences have actually increased across the world in recent years (Autor *et al.*, 2006). The relationship between socioeconomic conditions and personality traits has received relatively little attention. However, the investigations that have been conducted suggest that it is an important topic (Caspi, 2002; Caspi *et al.*, 1989). At the very least, it appears that living conditions have a direct impact on how and whether certain personality traits translate into interpersonal behaviours.

One study assessed the impulsivity of a group of 13-year-old males in the US city of Pittsburgh (Lynam *et al.*, 2000). The teens in the study came from a mixture of backgrounds, from wealthy households to poverty-stricken neighbourhoods. These backgrounds had a clear link to how individual differences in impulsivity translated to behaviours. Among boys who lived in poor neighbourhoods, those who displayed high levels of impulsivity were much more likely to engage in delinquent behaviours than those who displayed low levels of impulsivity. In contrast, among boys from high-socioeconomic-status neighbourhoods, behavioural differences between those with low and high impulsivity were small. To explain these findings, the investigators reasoned that poor neighbourhoods produce many triggers for delinquent acts. In contrast, community structures in wealthier neighbourhoods may offer limited opportunities for antisocial activities.

In short, particular personality characteristics will result in particular behaviours only if certain situational triggers also are in place.

Before You Go On

What Do You Know?

18. What personality differences between men and women have researchers identified?

19. How does social role theory explain these differences?

20. What are some of the primary differences between the values of collectivist and individualist cultures, and how do these differences affect personality?

21. How does the socioeconomic environment affect personality?

What Do You Think?

Think about the personality traits of a number of people you know. Include people of different gender and different cultural or subcultural groups. Do personalities seem to differ more on a group level or on an individual level among these acquaintances? How would you explain your observation?

Personality Disorders

LEARNING OBJECTIVE 7

Define personality disorder, and describe some of the key features of this disorder.

What does the description below tell us about Karen? Was she an unfortunate victim of circumstances? Or was her self-destructive behaviour the result of dysfunctional personal characteristics? It appears that when someone new first entered Karen's life she bubbled over with positive feelings and excitement. Invariably, this positive phase was followed by emotional outbursts and an eventual falling out. This pattern suggests that Karen may have a **personality disorder**, an inflexible pattern of inner experience and outward behaviour that causes distress or difficulty with daily functioning. Such patterns are enduring, and they differ markedly from the experiences and behaviours usually expected of people (APA, 2000).

> **personality disorder** an inflexible pattern of inner experience and outward behaviour that causes distress or difficulty with daily functioning.

PSYCHOLOGY AROUND US   The Roommate

Karen and I met when I placed an ad in a newspaper for a new roommate. At first I thought we were having fun living together . . . Then one night, about two months after she moved in, I was getting ready to go out with a friend, and Karen demanded to know where I was going. She wanted to know who I was seeing, what I was doing, and then she tried to make me feel guilty for going out.

When I came home that night, it was really scary. There was a little blood on the floor, and it made a trail that led to her bedroom door. When I banged on the door to see if she was all right, she said that she'd accidentally cut herself making a sandwich, and everything was fine.

Dealing with her was starting to take a lot out of me. Then she started dating this guy, Eric, and I thought things were getting better. Karen was spending almost no time at home, and when I did see her, she would gush about how incredibly happy she was.

I should have seen what was coming next, but, like an idiot, I didn't. Eric left her, and she was totally my problem again. She stayed home and cried for days at a time. She made me take care of her, telling me she was too depressed to do anything for herself. She even fantasized about the violent things she would do to Eric when she felt up to it. After Eric, there was Ahmad, then James, then Stefan. Always the same story, always the same ending. And always with me in the middle . . .

As we suggested earlier in this chapter, each of us has a distinct personality and specific personality traits. Yet, for most of us, this distinct personality is also flexible. We are affected by situational factors, and we learn from our experiences. As we interact with our environment, we try out various responses to see which are more effective. This flexibility is missing in people who have a personality disorder.

As in Karen's case, the effects of a personality disorder can sometimes be so subtle that they are not noticeable to others at first. It may take multiple encounters over time for the symptoms to become recognizable. Nevertheless, they have a significant impact on the individual's functioning in school, at work and in social and romantic relationships (Berenson et al., 2011; Mason & Kreger, 2010).

Psychologists are interested in personality *traits*; psychiatrists (and clinical psychologists) are interested in personality *disorders*. So psychologists talk about conscientiousness, and psychiatrists talk about obsessive–compulsive disorder. The two are clearly related. Psychologists often argue the *spectrum thesis*, which means extremes of normal personality show abnormal behaviour. This has come to be known as a phenomenon called the *spectrum hypothesis*. This suggests that abnormality is essentially characterizable by people at the far end of the trait dimensions. Just as very tall or very short people are abnormal in their height, so those extremely high or low on any personality trait dimension show very strong preferences and are maybe inflexible, even rigid, in their behaviour. Thus, it is *not* adaptive to be too *extraverted* or *stable* or *conscientious*, or even *agreeable*. However, clinical psychologists and psychiatrists, and not psychologists, have concentrated more on personality abnormality.

Psychiatrists are interested in personality functioning. They talk about personality disorders that are typified by *early onset* (recognizable in children and adolescents), *pervasive effects* (on all aspects of life) and with relatively *poor prognosis* (i.e. difficult to cure).

Psychiatrists and psychologists share some simple assumptions with respect to personality. Both argue for the *stability* of personality: 'enduring pattern', 'inflexible and pervasive' or 'stable and of long duration'. The pattern of behaviour is not a function of drug usage or some other medical condition. The personality pattern furthermore is *not* a manifestation or consequence of another mental disorder. One factor does differentiate the two. Psychiatrists tend to think in categorical terms. Psychologists, on the other hand, talk in categorical terms but measure and research in terms of dimensions. Thus, there are *ambiverts*, *mild extraverts* and *very strong extraverts*. They argue that all characteristics are normally distributed and it is clumsy and inefficient to measure categorically which throws away important information.

Both argue that the personality factors relate to *cognitive*, *affective* and *social aspects of functioning*. In other words, the disorder or traits affect how people think, feel and act. It is where a person's behaviour 'deviates markedly' from the expectations of an individual's culture that the disorder is manifest. The psychiatric manual is very clear that 'odd behaviour' is not simply an expression of habits, customs, religious or political values professed or shown by people of a particular cultural origin.

The personality disorders all have a long history and have an onset no later than early adulthood. Moreover, there are some gender differences; thus the antisocial disorder is more likely to be diagnosed in men while the borderline, histrionic and dependent personality disorders are more likely to be found in women.

Many theorists have attempted to uncover the origins of personality disorders. They have studied the roles of various factors, such as biological predispositions, early experiences of abuse and neglect and the pressures of poverty or otherwise harsh social environments (Arens *et al.*, 2011; Linehan & Dexter-Mazza, 2008; Patrick, 2007). Generally, however, the disorders are not well understood.

The American Psychiatric Association's diagnostic and classification system identifies ten personality disorders, which are described briefly in Table 15.3. You will read more about these personality disorders in Chapter 19, particularly *antisocial personality disorder* and *borderline personality disorder* – the two that have received the most clinical and research attention. At that time, you will come to appreciate just how disabling and disruptive the disorders can be.

TABLE 15.3 The Major Personality Disorders

Marked by odd or eccentric behaviour	
Paranoid	Exaggerated suspicion and distrust of others; assumption that others' motives are hostile; highly guarded and emotionally withdrawn
Schizoid	Detachment from social relationships; flat emotional expression; cold or indifferent to others
Schizotypal	Behaviour that is odd or peculiar; unusual cognitive or perceptual experiences; acute discomfort with close relationships
Involve dramatic or emotional behaviour	
Antisocial	Extreme disregard for others; relationships are dishonest, deceitful, and exploitive; typically impulsive and reckless
Borderline	Severe instability in emotion and self-concept; impulsive and self-destructive behaviour
Histrionic	Excessive need to be noticed and the centre of attention; emotions shallow and changeable; engagement with others superficial
Narcissistic	Characterized by high degree of self-interest and self-importance; callous attitude towards others
Characterized by high levels of fear and anxiety	
Avoidant	Extreme feelings of inadequacy; avoidance of social activities; inhibited personal relationships; hypersensitive to criticism
Dependent	Excessive need to be cared for by others; clinging and submissive behaviour; difficulty making decisions
Obsessive–compulsive	Preoccupied with perfectionism and control at the expense of flexibility or enjoyment; excessive devotion to work and productivity

Source: Based on American Psychiatric Association. (2000). *Diagnostic and Statistical Manual of Mental Disorders IV-TR*. Washington: APA with permission. However, the new DSM manual is about to be published and there are great changes in how psychiatrists define and describe the personality disorders. Problems in the reliability of diagnoses has meant that it likely that a number of the disorders previously described will be dropped.

Before You Go On

What Do You Know?

22. What is a personality disorder?
23. What are the ten personality disorders recognized by DSM IV-TR?

What Do You Think?

Personality disorders are popular subjects of fiction. Think about films or television programmes that you have seen, and try to find examples of characters who may be displaying personality disorders.

Personality Assessment

LEARNING OBJECTIVE 8

Describe the two major types of personality tests, and give examples of each.

Open almost any newspaper or popular magazine and you will find evidence of people's desire to understand, describe and use personality traits. Horoscopes, personality quizzes and even clairvoyants offer personality-based analyses and advice to thousands of people worldwide. It does not seem to matter that these devices have been shown to be unreliable: their popularity persists.

Of course, there are also more formal tools for assessing personality, and these tools are used in a variety of important contexts. Clinicians use personality assessment tools to learn more about their clients' problems. Researchers may use them to conduct personality research or to help select participants for their studies. Employers and careers advisers often use such tools to find out whether potential employees are suitable for various positions. Scores on traits such as conscientiousness have, for example, been used to predict absenteeism, misconduct and termination (Organ & Ryan, 1995). The personality tests used most frequently by these professionals are *personality inventories* and *projective tests*.

Personality Inventories

Very likely, you have taken a **personality inventory** at some time in your life. Personality inventories are questionnaires designed to measure various aspects of personality. The questionnaires usually consist of a series of true-or-false or agree/disagree statements. These types of assessments are sometimes called *self-report inventories* because they depend on information that respondents supply about themselves (Blais *et al.*, 2010). There are many inventories, some favoured by clinicians and others by personality psychologists. They are favoured by clinicians, employers and other professionals largely because they are easy to administer and to score and do not require subjective interpretations by test administrators. Each test requires individuals to respond to hundreds of statements that cover a broad range of feelings, behaviours and inclinations. Because of this scope, the inventories can provide a summary, or *profile*, of the various traits that comprise a personality.

> **personality inventory** a questionnaire designed to assess various aspects of personality.

PRACTICALLY SPEAKING Evaluating Personality Quizzes

Source: ©Image Source/Corbis.

Are you dating a person with a narcissistic personality? What is your 'pizza personality'? What kind of podcast are you? Personality quizzes fascinate and entertain millions of people. Magazines as varied as *Cosmopolitan* and *Time* publish personality quizzes all the time, and the Internet has numerous websites dedicated to helping you to better understand yourself.

Below are some pop-culture quiz types that you are most likely to stumble across:

- *Scenario quizzes* ask the question: When this happens, how do you react? Popular topics are love and relationships. The claim is that the answers you choose can reveal personal qualities that you may not normally attribute to yourself.
- *Preference quizzes* pose questions on a variety of topics, from your favourite colour to how you write to what time of day you like best. The claim here is that your answers illustrate enduring and broad traits such as extraversion or creativity.
- *Relational quizzes* ask you open-ended questions about how you would react to specific, imaginary events. For example, 'If you saw someone being robbed, what would you do?' The claim behind these quizzes is that your responses can tell you a great deal about your values and your *self-concept*, or how you see yourself.

Almost all psychologists recommend treating such pop-culture personality quizzes as entertainment at most. They may be fun, but they typically emerge from the minds of enterprising individuals or organizations, rarely undergo testing or research of any kind and often are misleading. Always keep in mind that you should not base important decisions on the results of such quizzes. Forming insights or views about yourself based on the results of the tests is likely to be a big mistake.

PSYCHOLOGY AROUND US   The Story Behind the Story

Earlier, you read about the Myers–Briggs Type Indicator (MBTI), one of the field's most widely used and popular personality tests, used especially in the business field. You may have assumed that this instrument, which applies the principles of Carl Jung's personality theory, was developed by skilled and learned psychologists. It was not.

The MBTI was created by a mother and her daughter – neither of whom was a psychologist. The story began when Katherine Briggs met Clarence 'Chief' Myers, the boyfriend (and, later, the husband) of her daughter Isabel. Struck by how different Chief was from anyone in her family, Katherine became interested in personality types. She began reading biographies. From those readings, she identified a list of traits on which people differ. Later, she discovered the work of Carl

Jung and adapted her categories to better conform with his constructs. Each person, Katherine believed, could be characterized somewhere along the dimensions of personality that she had identified.

Katherine and Isabel worked feverishly to find applications for their personality typology. Isabel, for example, wrote a mystery novel whose solution hinged on her mother's ideas, and she also began teaching herself the fundamentals of test construction, statistics and psychological assessment. Katherine and Isabel hoped to produce a test that would guide employment opportunities for the massive influx of women entering the workforce during World War II. Eventually, a major test publishing company took interest in their work, and the rest, as they say, is history.

TABLE 15.4 Most Commonly Used Personality and Motivation Tests in the United Kingdom

Personality/Motivation Tests	Percentage that have heard of the test
16 Personality Factor Questionnaire (16PF)	85.5
Bar-On Emotional Quotient Inventory (EQ-i)	40.3
Belbin Team Role Inventory	71.8
Big Five (NEO-PI-R)	62.5
California Personality Inventory (CPI)	46.3
Corporate Culture Questionnaire	28.2
Eysenck Personality Tests (EPI) (EPQ) (EPP)	62.8
Fundamental Interpersonal Relations Orientation Behaviour (FIRO-B)	61.3
Hogan Personality Questionnaires (HPI, HDS)	46.4
Kirton Adaptor Innovator Test (KAI)	26.3
Motivational Appraisal of Personnel Potential (MAPP)	25.1
Motivational Questionnaire	40.5
Myers–Briggs Type Indicator (MBTI)	84.2
Occupational Personality Questionnaire (OPQ)	79.8
Occupational Stress Inventory (OSI)	51.4
Orpheus Personality Test	18.2
PASAT Sales Personality Test	19.2

There are many tests to choose from. Table 15.4 contains some of the most commonly used in selection setting. These data are taken from a study by British psychologist Adrian Furnham when he asked over 500 human resources professionals about the tests they had heard of. Some are very well established and available commercially. Some have considerable evidence of their psychometric properties, while others have received far less attention from those psychologists interested in test construction.

There are many criteria for choosing one test over another. The first questions to ask concern what it is trying to measure and its theoretical foundation. Perhaps the most important question, however, is the evidence for its psychometric properties: that is validity and reliability. Other issues refer to its norms and whether it is fair and legal to be used in the way it is. There are also costs involved and whether and how participants are given feedback on their scores.

Despite the popularity of personality inventories, some concerns have been raised about their use as indicators of personality. First, the tests rely on self-reports. As we have seen, self-reports may not always be accurate (Feliciano & Gum, 2010; Gold & Castillo, 2010). If we are not fully aware of our own behaviour patterns, preferences or interests, our self-reports may not reflect our actual personal style. These tests require some amount of self-insight and self-awareness. In one study, for example, extraverted people did score highly on the extraversion scale of a personality inventory, but neurotic people did not score highly on the neuroticism scale of the same inventory (Spain *et al.*, 2000).

Another concern is that personality tests may not always be used and applied properly. Some employers, for example, use measures of conscientiousness to predict an applicant's potential job performance. But some jobs are not well suited for conscientious people, at least not overly conscientious people. An individual's performance on a job that emphasizes speed or quantity of output may be hindered by extensive checking and rechecking, for example.

Still another concern is that test takers may tailor their answers on personality inventories to try to create a good impression. This phenomenon is common enough to have its own name – **socially desirable responding** (Viswesvaran & Ones, 1999). The problem of socially desirable responding was, in fact, anticipated by the creators of the Minnesota Multiphasic Personality Inventory (MMPI), a popular assessment technique used in the USA. They built certain questions, called *validity items*, into the questionnaire to assess the likelihood that a respondent would purposely give an answer that was socially desirable rather than accurate. Suppose, for example, that an individual keeps answering 'true' to such items as 'I smile at everyone I meet' and 'false' to 'I get angry sometimes.' It is assumed that these responses, and perhaps many others as well, show socially desirable responding. In such cases, test scorers may disregard or adjust the respondents' personality scores.

socially desirable responding tailoring answers on personality inventories to try to create a good impression.

Projective Tests

projective tests personality assessment devices intended to tap a person's unconscious by presenting the person with an ambiguous stimulus and asking the person to interpret what the stimulus means.

Projective tests are quite different from personality inventories (Figure 15.8). These tests, commonly used by psychoanalytic clinicians and researchers, are intended to tap into a person's unconscious mind to detect personality styles and conflicts that are hidden beneath the surface. The most widely used and famous projective test is the *Rorschach*

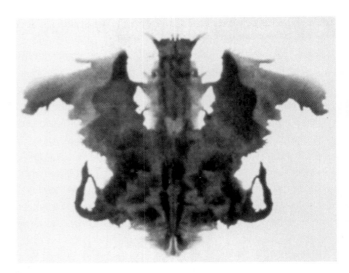

FIGURE 15.8 What do you see? Shown here is an inkblot similar to those used in the Rorschach Inkblot Test.

Inkblot Test. During the test, participants are shown a set of ten inkblots and asked to explain what they see. The ambiguous shapes of the inkblots are intended to force participants to *project* structure and meaning onto the images. The participants' responses are thought to reveal underlying psychological themes and personality issues. For example, a person who sees images of animals or weapons in the inkblots may be grappling with underlying aggressive urges.

Some clinicians believe that the Rorschach test provides useful suggestions that can enhance the effectiveness of therapy. It is widely agreed in the scientific community, however, that projective tests, such as the Rorschach, are low in validity, or accuracy (Butcher, 2010; Wood *et al.*, 2002). How such a test is scored depends on how the test administrator interprets the responses. And these interpretations may be affected by the assessor's professional biases or level of expertise. In addition to problems with validity, many have concerns about the reliability, or consistency, of projective tests. Individuals who take a Rorschach test today may offer responses very different from those they offered when they took the test last week, leading to different personality assessments. Look again at the sample in Figure 15.8. You can probably see why the Rorschach test may present difficulties.

An alternative and commonly used projective test is the *Thematic Apperception Test (TAT)*. This tool, created in the 1930s by psychologist Henry Murray, is made up of ambiguous black-and-white drawings of people in various situations. Test-takers are asked to describe and make up a story about each drawing. The uses and criticisms of the TAT are similar to those of the Rorschach. Although some systematic scoring procedures exist, most clinicians rely on their own judgements when analysing an individual's TAT responses (Masling, 2004). Additionally, it is difficult to know for certain that the stories created by individuals reflect how they are actually feeling. They may instead represent the individuals' projections of how they believe they should be feeling (Lilienfeld *et al.*, 2000).

The Rorschach and TAT tests are not the only *projective techniques* in psychology. What they have in common is that they give a person a stimulus (usually a picture; it could be a sound or smell) and then encourage them to project into or onto it their immediate, innermost and intense thoughts, feelings and desires. They say how they react to an ambiguous stimulus. The more unclear, ambiguous, vague the stimulus, the more the person projects themselves onto it.

There are essentially five categories of tests:

- *Inkblot or abstract pictures.* These can be constructed very simply by dropping a large blob of wet ink on the middle of a page folding it in half and then looking at the resultant pattern.

- *Sentence Completion.* Thus, you complete the following: 'I wished I had never . . .', 'I am . . .', 'My greatest fear is . . .', 'I am rather proud about . . .'

- *Free Drawing.* People are asked to draw certain objects, a house, a car, a parent and are then asked questions about them.

- *Solid Objects.* Dolls, block, sand: the person is asked to play with, construct or manoeuvre the object while describing what they are doing.

- *Sounds.* People listen to sounds (e.g. baby crying, car crashing) or music and describe how they react.

There are four objections to the use of these tests on scientific grounds:

- They are unreliable because different experts or scores come up with quite different interpretations. If the testers cannot agree on the meanings, we cannot get anywhere.

- They are invalid because the scores do not predict anything. In short, they do not measure what they say they are measuring.

- Context makes all the difference. The mood of the person, the characteristics of the tester, the setting of the test all affect results, which suggests they are picking up on trivial, rather than essential, underlying factors.

- The testers cannot agree on what the tests measure: attitudes, abilities, defences, motivation, deep desires.

So why do these tests still get used?

- They provide often unique and intriguing data relatively easily that cannot be obtained as cheaply and quickly elsewhere.

- Skilled and trained practitioners seem able to obtain impressive, reliable and insightful findings which they cannot get from other tests or interviews.

- The richness of the data makes other test data often look crude, colourless and constipated.

- They can complement and confirm other findings and ideas.

Before You Go On

What Do You Know?

24. How do personality inventories differ from projective assessment techniques?

25. What is socially desirable responding and how is it addressed in the MMPI?

26. What are some problems with projective assessment techniques?

What Do You Think?

There are so-called personality tests all over the Internet. Which ones have you come across? Why are most such tests uninformative and often misleading?

VIDEO

Access your interactive e-book to view a video clip for this chapter at **www.wileyopenpage.com**

Summary

The Psychodynamic Perspective

LEARNING OBJECTIVE 1 Summarize the main ideas of the psychodynamic view of personality development.

- Personality refers to the unique characteristics that account for enduring patterns of inner experience and outward behaviour.
- Sigmund Freud's psychoanalytic theory of personality depended to a large extent on his ideas about the conscious and unconscious mind. Most of the content of our minds, in Freud's view, is in the unconscious.
- Freud proposed three central forces in personality development: the id, the ego and the superego.
- In Freud's view, personality develops as children pass through a series of psychosexual stages. Each stage is characterized by strong conflicts between the id, the ego and the superego. Failure to resolve these conflicts can result in neurosis.
- Conflicts result in anxiety, and Freud believed that we use unconscious tactics called defence mechanisms to protect ourselves from this anxiety.
- Other psychodynamic theories include those of Alfred Adler, Carl G. Jung and Karen Horney.

The Humanistic Perspective

LEARNING OBJECTIVE 2 Describe the humanistic theories of Abraham Maslow and Carl Rogers.

- Humanist theorists, including Abraham Maslow and Carl Rogers, emphasized people's basic goodness and their ability to fulfil their potential.
- Maslow proposed that personality arises from people's striving to meet their needs. Human needs are arranged hierarchically, with self-actualization at the top level.
- Rogers based his theory of personality on his ideas about the importance of self-concept. He believed that children need unconditional positive regard to develop healthy self-concepts.

The Trait Perspective

LEARNING OBJECTIVE 3 Summarize the leading trait theories, and describe how the five-factor theory has evolved from the work of Gordon Allport and Hans Eysenck.

- Personality traits are tendencies to behave in certain ways that remain relatively constant across situations.

Trait theorists such as Gordon Allport and Hans Eysenck first proposed that central traits affect a broad range of behaviour.

- Allport conducted detailed case studies that sought to reveal the unique collection of traits at play for each individual.
- Eysenck, using factor analysis, identified three personality superfactors: extraversion, neuroticism and psychoticism.
- Other trait theorists proposed the five-factor theory, which identified five major trait categories: agreeableness, extraversion, neuroticism, conscientiousness and openness to experience.
- Although traits play an important role in behaviour, they can be inconsistent over time and across different situations.

The Situationist and Interactionist Perspectives

LEARNING OBJECTIVE 4 Describe and differentiate the situationist and interactionist views of personality.

- Situationism holds that behaviour is governed primarily by the variables in a given situation rather than by internal traits. The behaviourist B. F. Skinner could be said to have viewed personality from this perspective.
- Interactionism focuses on interactions between persons and situations. Albert Bandura's social-cognitive theory is an example of interactionist theory. In Bandura's view, the environment, internal mental events and behaviour all interact to affect behaviour through the process of reciprocal determinism.

Biological Foundations of Personality

LEARNING OBJECTIVE 5 Discuss the heritability of personality traits and some of the neural systems that may be involved in the expression of personality.

- Twin studies, such as the Minnesota Study of Twins Reared Apart, suggest that many personality traits have strong genetic links.
- Certain brain structures, neurotransmitters and hormones have been associated with personality variables.
- In interpreting links between genes, physiological factors and personality, it is important to remember that the relationships are complex and multidirectional.

Personality and Group Differences

LEARNING OBJECTIVE 6   Explain how gender and cultural differences can affect personality.

- Research has found many more similarities than differences between men's and women's personalities. Nevertheless, some consistent differences have been identified.
- Sociocultural factors are thought to play an important role in gender differences in personality. According to social role theory, for example, boys and girls develop different behaviours and skills based largely on the division of labour between the sexes and the resulting differences in gender role expectations.
- Cross-cultural research into personality has focused on personality development in individualist and collectivist cultures. Some traits observed in these cultures reflect differing cultural values.
- The relationship between socioeconomic conditions and personality traits has received relatively little attention. However, the investigations that have been conducted suggest that, at the very least, living conditions have a direct impact on how and whether certain personality traits translate into behaviours.

Personality Disorders

LEARNING OBJECTIVE 7   Define personality disorder, and describe some of the key features of this disorder.

- A personality disorder is an inflexible pattern of inner experience and outward behaviour that causes distress or difficulty with daily functioning.
- The American Psychological Association has outlined ten personality disorders in its guide for therapists.

Personality Assessment

LEARNING OBJECTIVE 8   Describe the two major types of personality tests, and give examples of each.

- Personality inventories are questionnaires that require individuals to respond to a series of true-or-false or agree/disagree statements designed to measure various aspects of personality.
- Projective tests are intended to tap into a person's unconscious mind by having him or her interpret ambiguous stimuli. In the case of the Rorschach Inkblot Test, the stimuli are inkblots. In the case of the Thematic Apperception Test (TAT), they are black-and-white drawings.

ACTIVITY

Activities to test yourself further are available in your interactive e-book at
www.wileyopenpage.com

TYING IT TOGETHER

WHAT HAPPENS IN THE
B R A I N ?

- Phrenologists in the 19th century believed that the shapes of people's skulls could reveal their personal and moral characteristics.
- Some studies suggest that, on average, people whose right brain hemisphere is dominant tend to be less extraverted than people with a dominant left hemisphere.

- People with high dopamine activity in their brain's reward learning pathway tend to be less inhibited, less anxious and more energetic than those with lower dopamine activity in that pathway.

HOW WE DIFFER

- Personality similarities between men and women far outnumber the differences between them.
- Two variables on which males and females tend to differ are aggression and interpersonal sensitivity. On average, males are more aggressive and females are more empathic.
- People from collectivist cultures tend to display more agreeableness. Those from individualistic cultures tend to be more extraverted and success-oriented.

HOW WE DEVELOP

- Identical twins tend to be more similar on many personality characteristics than are fraternal twins. This is true even if the identical twins have been raised apart.
- Particularly strong ties have been found between genetic inheritance and the traits of openness, extraversion, neuroticism and agreeableness.
- Freud warned of life-long fixation at an early stage of development for individuals whose oral, anal or phallic needs were not adequately met during childhood.

OUT OF THE ORDINARY

- An excessive need to be noticed, taken care of or to avoid social contacts may each reflect a type of personality disorder: histrionic, dependent and avoidant, respectively.
- Most online personality tests are, at most, a form of entertainment. Typically, they offer inaccurate and useless information about one's personality or one's clinical problems.
- Neurosis was Freud's term for psychological dysfunctioning marked by anxiety, depression or other such symptoms. The term has no official status in the clinical field today.

Quizzes to test yourself further are available in your interactive e-book at www.wileyopenpage.com

Key Terms

defence mechanisms 436
denial 437
ego 435
five-factor model 445
id 435
interactionism 448
neurosis 436

personality 434
personality disorder 460
personality inventory 462
personality traits 442
phrenology 451
positive psychology 441
projective tests 464

psychosexual
   stages 436
repression 437
self-actualization 441
self-concept 441
situationism 448
social role theory 456

socially desirable
   responding 464
superego 435
superfactor 444
unconditional positive
   regard 441

Flashcards to test yourself further are available in your interactive e-book at www.wileyopenpage.com

CHAPTER 16

Social Cognition, Social Relations and Social Functioning

Adapted by Chris McVittie, Queen Margaret University, Edinburgh, UK

CHAPTER OUTLINE

- Social Cognition: Attitudes
- Social Cognition: Attributions

- Social Relations
- Social Functioning

 Access your interactive e-book to view a video clip for this chapter at **www.wileyopenpage.com**

Social Psychology in a Storm

On 11 March 2011, at 14:46 local time (05:46 GMT), the north-east coast of Japan was struck by a massive earthquake. This earthquake, of 8.9 magnitude, was the most powerful in Japanese history and the fifth largest in the world since 1900. As well as causing major immediate damage to buildings and communities, it triggered a massive tsunami which struck about 400 km (250 miles) north-east of Tokyo. The resulting wall of water measured over 15 m (50 ft) high and travelled at speeds in excess of 800 km/h (500 mph), as fast as a jetliner. Reaching 10 km (six miles) inland, this wave swept away houses, buildings, boats and cars as it hit communities along and near the coast.

One site of major damage was the Fukushima Daiichi nuclear power plant, run by the Tokyo Electric Power Company (TEPCO) and located in the towns of Okuma and Futaba in the Futaba District of Fukushima Prefecture, Japan. TEPCO estimated that the tsunami that hit the power plant exceeded 14 m (46 ft) in height, more than twice what the plant was designed to withstand. The plant's reactor cooling systems were unable to cope with the impact of a tsunami of such magnitude, leading to partial nuclear meltdowns of units 1, 2 and 3 of the plant's six units and visible and suspected explosions and uncovering of spent fuel pools in several units. The resulting nuclear leaks led to the imposition of a 30 km (19 mile) evacuation zone around the plant, causing over 80,000 people to be forced to leave their homes.

Over one year on from the earthquake and tsunami, the devastation caused to the lives of many Japanese people is all too clear. Although the Fukushima Daiichi power plant has since been decommissioned and declared safe, dismantling of the plant is likely to continue for up to another 40 years. In the meantime, tens of thousands of people remain unable to return to their homes as a result of the imposition of a continuing evacuation zone of 20 km (12 miles) around the plant, which may only be entered under government supervision. Along and in the vicinity of the north-east coast of Japan, in excess of 20,000 people were killed in the immediate aftermath, with another 3,200 still missing to this day. In the fishing port of Yuriage, in Natori on Japan's east coast, there are ruins of a centuries-old temple that used to stand there. This port, which used to be home to 7,000 people, was totally washed away and is now marked by scars and emptiness where houses used to stand. One survivor, Tatsuya Suzuki, recently brought his children back to mourn for their mother who was lost in the disaster and to see where their family house once stood. As Mr Suzuki stated on returning to Yuriage, 'Even though one year has passed, nothing has really changed. Time has stopped for me. Time has passed for everyone and everything else, but not me. For others, the disaster may be becoming a thing of the past, but for us, it is still our reality today.' ■

The poet John Donne's famous words, 'No man is an island', highlight the interconnectedness of humankind. We live in a world of approximately seven billion people, and each and every day we influence and are influenced by others. Social psychologists devote themselves to the study of human interconnectedness. Unlike many areas of psychology, which focus on areas of individual difference, such as temperament and personality, social psychology is based on the belief that 'it is not so much the kind of person a man is as the kind of situation in which he finds himself that determines how he will act' (Milgram, 2004, p. 101).

We may think of social psychology in a general way as the scientific study of how people are affected by other people. This informal definition covers considerable territory. Many aspects of an individual's functioning can be affected by others: thoughts, feelings and behaviours may each reflect the influence of the social environment. Moreover, the influence of others can be direct or indirect.

Turning back to the consequences of the earthquake that struck Japan, it is all too easy for us to imagine the effects of such devastation on people's lives. For those caught up in the aftermath of the earthquake, influences of other people that previously were ever-present, perhaps those of loved ones as in the case of Mr Suzuki and his family, are gone for ever and sorely missed. Conversely, new influences of other people have come into play for those involved: for example, the ways in which TEPCO and the Japanese government have responded to the disaster and the consequences for all those affected. Events of this magnitude have also of course unfolded in the world's media, leading to changes in how viewers and readers are affected by and respond to the plight of others in the world around them.

Given the many ways in which people can affect one another, the pioneering psychologist Gordon Allport (1954), whom we also discussed in the previous chapter, offered a more detailed definition of social psychology that is embraced by many people in the field. That is, **social psychology** seeks to understand, explain and predict how our thoughts, feelings and behaviour are influenced by the actual, imagined or implied presence of others (Allport, 1985).

> **social psychology** an area of psychology that seeks to understand, explain and predict how people's thoughts, feelings and behaviours are influenced by the actual, imagined or implied presence of others.

Which pieces of this definition should social psychologists focus on? As we will see in this and the following chapter, this definition allows for a diverse range of work. Many social psychologists have examined the social processes and practices that result from the presence of others – be they actual, imagined or implied – and have considered the consequences of such presence for the individual. These topics we will consider in the next chapter. Here, we will examine work that has, by contrast, focused on the individual and emphasized how people themselves make sense of others in their social worlds. Much of this work comes within the topic of **social cognition**, the study of how people perceive and interpret themselves and others: for example, the attitudes people hold and the attributions that people make.

> **social cognition** the way in which people perceive and interpret themselves and others in their social world.

Other social psychologists have looked at social relations, in particular the ways in which people respond to others in contexts that potentially involve actions of helping, aggression or interpersonal attraction. In this chapter, we will discuss each of these areas and examine what happens in the brain during social functioning.

Social Cognition: Attitudes

LEARNING OBJECTIVE 1

Explain how attitudes form and change and what role they play in behaviour.

There are few things in our world that we do not evaluate in some form or another. On some evaluations, people tend to agree. For example, most people believe that poverty is bad, that horror movies are scary and that Olympic Games provide a major sporting spectacle. On other topics, people are more divided, such as the proper role of government in people's lives, the best ice cream flavour and the advisability of legalizing drugs. Psychologists refer to our relatively stable and enduring evaluations of things and people as **attitudes** (Albarracín *et al.*, 2005).

According to the **ABC model of attitudes**, attitudes have three components, as shown in Figure 16.1 (van den Berg *et al.*, 2006; Eagly & Chaiken, 1998):

- The *affective* component – how we feel towards an object.
- The *behavioural* component – how we behave towards an object.
- The *cognitive* component – what we believe about an object.

As one example of how this model of attitudes may work, let us consider attitudes held by citizens of the United States towards their safety prior to the terrorist attacks on the World Trade Center in New York on 11 September 2001. Before 11 September 2001, many Americans held the attitude that their everyday world was safe from terrorism. They felt secure (affective component), went to work each day confident that terrorism would not touch their lives (behavioural component) and believed they were safe (cognitive component). Similarly, before the earthquake in 2011, most residents of north-east Japan felt relatively safe and secure and went about their lives accordingly. Clearly, the attitudes of those living in the United States and in Japan would change markedly following the impact of these major events. Attitudes, then, can and do change. We will explain how that can happen later in this section; but first, let us discuss how attitudes form in the first place.

attitudes relatively stable and enduring evaluations of things and people.

ABC model of attitudes a model proposing that attitudes have three components: the affective component, the behavioural component and the cognitive component.

Attitudes

HOW WE DEVELOP

Early in life, parents play a major role in shaping children's beliefs and opinions about things and people (Day *et al.*, 2006). Socialization is the process by which children acquire beliefs and behaviours considered desirable or appropriate by the family to which they belong. You are reading this textbook right now because you have been socialized in a number of ways, perhaps to believe in the value of further or higher education or in the need for hard work to achieve your goals. This socialization may have occurred by direct transmission (your parents teaching you about these values) or in subtler ways. Perhaps your mother or father praised you for your grades or punished you for not doing your homework. Over time, you may generalize these individual experiences into an overall attitude about the value of what you are doing.

As children mature, their peers, their teachers and the media influence their attitudes more prominently (Prislin & Wood, 2005). Children observe their classmates and take note of the rewards and punishments those students reap from their behaviour. If a child sees a classmate rejected by the rest of the class for making disparaging remarks about a particular ethnic group, for example, the child may develop an attitude that such remarks are inappropriate and unacceptable. Similarly, seeing a favourite television character get whatever he or she wants by bullying people may foster an attitude that aggression is an acceptable way to achieve one's goals.

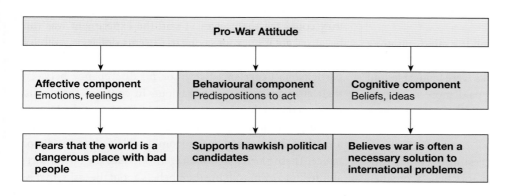

FIGURE 16.1 The ABC model of attitudes.

How Do Attitudes Change?

Once we have internalized a particular attitude, that is once we have made it our own, how rigid and long lasting is that attitude? Can people experience a change of heart? In a classic social psychology experiment in the late 1950s, researchers Leon Festinger and J. Merrill Carlsmith (1959) demonstrated that when we are subtly manipulated into doing or saying something that is contrary to our private attitudes we often change our attitudes to match the new action or statement. If, for example, a woman must make a presentation on the merits of managed-care health systems when she in fact favours healthcare reform, she may later report, and believe, that she actually favours the existing managed-care systems.

In their study, Festinger and Carlsmith had research participants engage in a number of repetitive and boring tasks, such as spending an hour slowly turning square pegs on a board or adding spools to a tray and then removing them. After the tasks were done, the experimenters told the participants that the experiment was over and that they would be allowed to go home shortly – but in truth the experiment had just begun. Each participant was then told that a new group of individuals would soon arrive – individuals who would be performing the same tedious tasks but would be told in advance that the tasks were actually fun and intriguing. The experimenter further asked each participant to help by describing the upcoming tasks as fun and exciting to one of the new individuals. (All of the new individuals were in fact confederates collaborating with the experimenters.) In almost all cases, the participants agreed to prepare the new individuals for an enjoyable experience. In addition, some of the participants were told they would be paid one dollar for helping out in this way, while others were told they would receive twenty dollars.

After presenting the positive account of the tedious tasks to the new individuals, the participants were interviewed by the experimenters about how enjoyable they themselves actually believed the tasks to be. This was, in fact, Festinger and Carlsmith's central topic of interest. Many of the participants reported that they actually had found the tasks to be quite enjoyable! Even more fascinating, it was those who had been paid one dollar for talking up the tasks who reported the tasks to be most enjoyable – not those who had been paid twenty dollars (Figure 16.2).

How could participants come to find the mind-numbing tasks of this study enjoyable? Why did those paid less money to convince someone else that the tasks were enjoyable find the tasks *more* enjoyable than those paid more money to do so? Theorists have offered two possible answers to these questions.

Cognitive Dissonance Theory Festinger (1957) proposed that when we hold two contradictory beliefs, or when

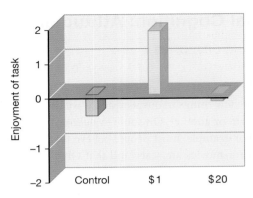

FIGURE 16.2 Cognitive dissonance. After describing a boring task as fun, participants in Festinger and Carlsmith's study were asked to rate their own enjoyment of the task on a scale of –5 to +5. Those paid $1 for praising the task rated the task as more enjoyable than those paid $20 for praising it.

Source: Adapted with permission of John Wiley & Sons, Inc., from Kowalski, R. & Westen, (2009). *Psychology* (5th edn). Hoboken, NJ: John Wiley & Sons, p. 614; based on Festinger, L. & Carlsmith, J. M. (1959). Cognitive consequences of forced compliance. *Journal of Abnormal and Social Psychology, 58,* 203–210.

we hold a belief that contradicts our behaviour, we experience a state of emotional discomfort, or **cognitive dissonance**. This state is so unpleasant that we are motivated to reduce or eliminate it. One way of removing dissonance is to modify our existing beliefs. In Festinger and Carlsmith's study, cognitive dissonance theory would hold that the conflict between the participants' initial attitudes about the tasks (that the tasks were boring and trivial) and their later behaviour (telling someone that the tasks were enjoyable) resulted in cognitive dissonance, and this unpleasant state motivated them to change their attitudes about the tasks in positive directions.

> **cognitive dissonance** a state of emotional discomfort people experience when they hold two contradictory beliefs or hold a belief that contradicts their behaviour.

But what about the differing results for the participants in the one-dollar condition and those in the twenty-dollar condition? According to dissonance theory, the participants in the twenty-dollar condition experienced less dissonance because they had sufficient justification for their behaviour. Since they were well paid to say that the tasks were enjoyable, they could tell themselves, 'I said the experiment was fun because I got money for saying it.' (Twenty dollars was quite a bit more money in the late 1950s than it is today.) Thus, these participants experienced little or no discrepancy between their attitudes and their behaviour. In contrast, those who received only a dollar for their positive statements had insufficient justification for their behaviour and so experienced a marked discrepancy and uncomfortable feelings of dissonance. These participants managed to reduce the uncomfortable feelings by modifying their beliefs about the tasks; that is, by later reporting (and indeed, believing) that the tasks were actually interesting.

Festinger's theory of cognitive dissonance has received support from literally hundreds of studies (Cooper *et al.*, 2005, 2004). Furthermore, it has significant implications for many events and strategies in real life. For example, a growing number of today's parents financially reward their children for working on their homework. The parents' hope is that such rewards will move doing homework ahead of attractive alternatives, such as texting, listening to music on iPods or playing computer games, and that the children will come willingly to complete and even to enjoy homework. However, cognitive dissonance theory warns that such strategies are likely to backfire. Children who are given explicit financial rewards, especially sizeable ones, will likely know exactly why they are doing their homework. That is, they will experience little or no dissonance between their attitude towards homework and their act of doing homework. In turn, they will not be inclined to change their unfavourable view about doing homework.

The Self-Perception Alternative Cognitive dissonance theory explains some instances of attitude change, but not others. In many cases, we seem to form and change attitudes in the absence of internal discomfort. You may think, for example, that you are alert but after yawning decide that you are tired, not because of a need to reduce emotional tension brought about by the discrepancy between the attitude ('I'm alert') and the behaviour (a yawn) but simply because the yawn was informative. Thus, psychologist Daryl Bem developed the **self-perception theory** of attitude change (Bem, 1972). This theory minimizes the role of emotional discomfort and suggests that when we are uncertain of our attitudes we simply infer what our attitudes are by observing our own behaviour, much as outsiders may observe us. According to Bem, our behaviours are often clues from which we deduce our attitudes. Thus, we may decide we like roller coasters because we keep riding them, or we may decide we hate spinach because we keep spitting it out.

self-perception theory the theory suggesting that when people are uncertain of their attitudes, they infer what the attitudes are by observing their own behaviour.

Which is correct, the cognitive dissonance or the self-perception explanation of attitude change? Historically, this has been a source of great debate in social psychology, but research has clarified that each may be more relevant in particular situations (Cooper *et al.*, 2004; Petty *et al.*, 2003; Fazio *et al.*, 1977). Festinger's theory of cognitive dissonance seems more applicable to situations in which we behave in ways that are strikingly out of character for us, whereas Bem's self-perception theory may be at work in situations where we

behave only slightly out of character or our attitudes are not all that clear to begin with.

Do Attitudes Influence Behaviour?

If we know someone's attitudes, does that mean we can predict that person's behaviour? It turns out that the attitudes people express are not necessarily related to how they actually behave (Fazio & Roskos-Ewoldsen, 2005; Cooper *et al.*, 2004; Eagly & Chaiken, 1998). In the 1930s, a time when many Americans held very negative attitudes towards the Chinese, sociologist Richard LaPiere conducted a field study in which he had a Chinese couple travel across the United States and visit over 250 hotels and restaurants (LaPiere, 1934). Although managers at over 90% of the establishments indicated in a questionnaire that they would not serve Chinese guests, only one of the establishments visited by the Chinese couple actually refused them service. In fact, most of the hotels and restaurants provided above-average service.

Of course, attitudes do sometimes predict behaviour. Research has uncovered various factors that affect the extent to which attitudes will predict behaviours (Fabrigar *et al.*,

'Believe what I do, not what I say.' Many people who endorse healthy eating and better fitness on surveys actually consume huge quantities of junk food in their daily lives.

Source: ©Michele Constantini/Photo Alto/Corbis.

2006; Fazio & Roskos-Ewoldsen, 2005; Cooper *et al.*, 2004). One of the leading factors is *attitude specificity*. The more specific an attitude, the more likely it is to predict behaviour. If a person specifically enjoys *Harry Potter* films, for example, he or she is more likely to view the latest *Harry Potter* film on the day of its release than is someone who enjoys films more generally. Another factor is *attitude strength*. Stronger attitudes predict behaviour more accurately than weak or vague attitudes.

Are People Honest about Their Attitudes?

One reason that attitudes fail to consistently predict behaviours is that people often *misrepresent* their attitudes. In fact, analyses of most self-report questionnaires, the tools usually used by researchers to measure attitudes, cannot distinguish genuine attitudes from false ones (Carels *et al.*, 2006; Cobb, 2002; Rosenberg, 1969). Why would people misrepresent their attitudes? There appear to be several reasons.

The Social Desirability Factor   Often, people state attitudes that are *socially desirable* rather than accurate. A person who privately does not trust people of a particular ethnic background, for example, may not acknowledge having this attitude for fear of being judged unfavourably by others. To eliminate the social desirability factor and measure people's attitudes, psychologists have sometimes employed a method known as the *bogus pipeline* technique (Jones & Sigall, 1971). Here, a research participant is connected to a non-functioning device that looks like a polygraph (lie-detector machine) and is told that the device can detect deception. When individuals are connected to such a device, they are more likely to report their attitudes truthfully (Nier, 2005; Roese & Jamieson, 1993).

In one bogus pipeline study, investigators asked students about socially sensitive issues, such as how frequently they drank, smoked, had sex and used illicit drugs (Tourangeau *et al.*, 1997). Participants in one group were hooked up to a device and told that it could detect inaccurate answers. This belief apparently made the participants more honest. The students hooked up to the machine reported performing socially sensitive behaviours relatively frequently. Control participants, who were not hooked up to the device, answered in more socially desirable ways, reporting lower frequencies of the behaviours in question.

Implicit Attitudes   Another problem that researchers run into when trying to measure attitudes is that people are not always *aware* of their true attitudes (Bassili & Brown,

2005). In their own minds, employers may believe that applicants of all ethnicities deserve a fair interview process. But when interviewing individuals from ethnic backgrounds other than their own, the same employers may, in fact, engage in less eye contact, maintain greater physical distance and offer less interview time than when interviewing applicants whose backgrounds are similar to their own. In such cases, the employers may have difficulty trusting people of different backgrounds, but this attitude has not reached their conscious awareness (Baron & Banaji, 2006; Bassett *et al.*, 2005; Greenwald *et al.*, 2002, 1998). When an attitude such as this lies below the level of conscious awareness, it is called an **implicit attitude**. The finding that people have implicit attitudes is reminiscent of the following observation by the famous Russian writer Fyodor Dostoyevsky (1972):

> **implicit attitude** an attitude of which the person is unaware.

> Every man has reminiscences which he would not tell to everyone but only his friends. He has other matters in his mind which he would not reveal even to his friends, but only to himself, and that in secret. But there are other things which a man is afraid to tell even to himself, and every decent man has a number of such things stored away in his mind.

As you might imagine, measuring attitudes that the holder is not aware of presents a challenge for researchers. To examine implicit attitudes, researchers have employed the *Implicit Association Test (IAT)*, which uses a person's reaction times to help discover his or her implicit attitudes. The IAT consists of three stages.

- First, a person is exposed to two broad categories: for example, *dog* and *cat*. The person is asked to categorize certain words as belonging in the *dog* category or the *cat* category: for example, *fire hydrant* and *litter tray*.

- Next, the person is asked to categorize words as either pleasant or unpleasant. These words are again fairly obvious, such as *poison* and *happiness*.

- Finally, the categories are combined, and the person is asked to identify a series of words as either more dog-related/pleasant or more cat-related/unpleasant; the categories are later reversed to be cat/pleasant and dog/unpleasant. The assumption is that if a person implicitly believes that dogs are more desirable than cats, the person should be quicker to identify pleasant words during the dog/pleasant combination, because the association between pleasant things and dogs is stronger. It will take this person slightly longer to make the dog/unpleasant association because it requires more effort. Similarly, cat people should respond quicker to the cat/pleasant combination.

You may find this logic convoluted and hard to accept. However, for example, American research has found that many white Americans who characterize themselves as not prejudiced have quicker reaction times to white American/pleasant and African-American/unpleasant identifications than to white American/unpleasant and African-American/pleasant ones. Such implicit attitudes appear to be stable over time, and they have been useful predictors of both subtle indicators of discomfort, such as turning one's eyes away during a conversation with someone of another race, and overt acts of racism, such as the use of slurs, physical violence and snubbing (Rudman & Ashmore, 2007). The IAT has also been used by researchers to detect bias against elderly people, overweight people, and other groups.

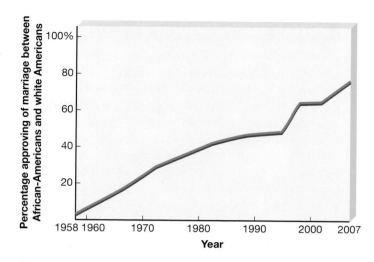

FIGURE 16.3 Prejudice over time. Americans have expressed greater approval of interracial marriage over the last 50 years, yet studies show that subtle biases remain.
Source: Gallup Poll (2007).

Stereotypes and Prejudice

Following the earthquake and tsunami in Japan, many survivors returned to villages and towns where they had previously lived, either to look for relatives who were missing or to remember happier times. We saw at the beginning of this chapter part of the story of Mr Suzuki who had taken his children back to the village of Yuriage, which had been totally destroyed by the tsunami. In talking about his experiences, one topic that Mr Suzuki discussed was the difficulties that he experienced in bringing up his children following the loss of his wife and their mother:

> My wife was very good at bringing up the kids. I am no good at it. Both my kids were inseparable from their mother before the disaster. The kids have got used to me a bit, but there are a lot of things only a mother can do for her children (Grammaticas, 2012).

In part, Mr Suzuki was talking about *stereotypes*. Most of us are familiar with the notion of **stereotypes**, generalized impressions of people or groups of people based on the social category they occupy. Stereotypes can be based on gender, age, race, geographical origin, political or religious beliefs or any other group characteristic.

Although stereotypes can be positive or negative, there is little doubt that there is a strong relationship between stereotypes and **prejudice**, negative attitudes towards individuals from another group. For example, research conducted in the United States suggests that prejudice in the form of overt racism and sexism has decreased over time (Figure 16.3) but that subtle biases remain (Sue *et al.*, 2007; Dovidio, *et al.*, 2002). Thus, as noted earlier, many white Americans who characterize themselves as not prejudiced respond to the IAT in a way that suggests they have some implicit negative attitudes towards African-Americans.

prejudice negative stereotypical attitudes towards individuals from another group.

stereotypes generalized impressions of a person or a group of people based on the social category they occupy.

Attitudes and the Power of Persuasion

Earlier, we discussed how attitudes form and change. Advertisers have taken a strong interest in these processes. In fact, vast amounts of advertising money are spent each year in attempts to persuade people to develop particular attitudes towards products or services. If you would not dream of using any computer but a MacBook Pro, or if you much prefer Coca-Cola over Pepsi (or vice versa), that attitude probably has been created in part through persuasion, the advertiser's best efforts to convince you that its product is far superior to any competitor product and that you must have it. Politicians running for office, interest groups looking to increase their influence and any number of others also use persuasive techniques regularly. Indeed, most of us have had occasion to try to persuade someone else to come round to our way of thinking.

For persuasion to occur, a few elements must be present. There must be, of course, a *message*, somebody to transmit the message (the *source*) and somebody to receive it (the *receiver*). In attempting to make a message persuasive, the source can use methods that follow either a central route or a peripheral route (Figure 16.4).

Central Route versus Peripheral Route The *central route* to persuasion emphasizes the content of the message, using factual information and logical arguments to persuade. This method requires a fair amount of effort on the part of the receiver and is more commonly used for matters of some significance. If you were trying to decide whether to buy a Mac or a PC, you might be willing to spend considerable time in careful deliberation of all the facts. After all, a computer is an expensive item and an important purchase. You may not be as interested in thinking hard about whether to buy Coco-Cola or Pepsi, though, or about which brand of shampoo to purchase.

The *peripheral route* relies on more superficial information. When you respond to peripheral appeals, you are responding to such factors as how attractive the spokesperson is and how amusing or engaging the message is. As might be expected, decisions based on central routes to persuasion are more likely to last than decisions based on the peripheral route.

Aids to Persuasion Beyond the route chosen, a number of other factors can also make a message more or less persuasive. Characteristics of the *source* are important. We are more likely to be persuaded by a source who is rated as more knowledgeable or more likable, for example. In addition, if we think of the source as more similar to us, we are more likely to be persuaded by the message. (This is part of the reason why political candidates often try to emphasize their similarities to others by speaking in hospitals, schools and shopping centres.) Finally, at least in some instances, people are more likely to find a source credible and persuasive when the source presents both sides of an issue.

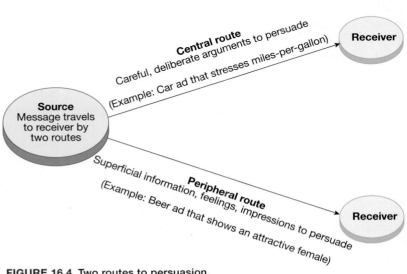

FIGURE 16.4 Two routes to persuasion.

Sometimes, the key to persuasion rests on an interaction between audience characteristics and source characteristics. If, for example, a source is trying to win the favour of an intelligent or highly motivated audience, an emphasis on logic and on supporting data is more likely to be effective. If addressing a less intelligent or less interested audience, however, the source may have more success with a glossy, superficial presentation and a good haircut.

A number of *specific techniques* can further improve the chances of successfully persuading others. Here we will mention only a few. You have probably been exposed to some of these strategies (and you may even have used some of them).

- The *foot-in-the-door technique* involves getting someone to agree to a small request and then following up with a much larger one. The idea is that the person will be inclined to grant the second request because of having granted the first one. For example, you might first ask to borrow your parents' car for an hour and then later ask to borrow it for the weekend.

- The *door-in-the-face technique* reverses this behaviour. The technique involves making an absurd first request that will obviously be turned down and following it with a more moderate request. A teenager might ask his or her parents, 'Will you buy me a motorbike?', and then follow up with 'Just kidding, but can I borrow £50?' as the parents sigh in relief.

- *Appeals to fear* can be powerful. We frequently see these appeals in antismoking campaigns and the like. In order to work, however, an appeal to fear must make receivers truly believe that something bad will happen to them if they do not comply with the source's request.

Barriers to Persuasion Other strategies can interfere with persuasion. Again, we will mention only a few.

- Forewarning an audience that you will be trying to persuade them of something will immediately raise their defences. Although listeners in this situation may make subtle shifts towards your way of thinking, they are unlikely to change their attitudes as much as individuals who are not told that they are about to hear a persuasive speech.

- Beginning with a weak argument instead of a strong one can make subsequent arguments seem weaker. Starting off a request to your professor for an extension to a deadline by arguing that you simply need to catch up on your sleep may lead the professor to interpret your subsequent (stronger) argument – that you have been up for days working on assignments for three other subjects – as more of an excuse than a valid argument.

Tools of persuasion. The organization People for the Ethical Treatment of Animals (PETA) has run many campaigns to persuade consumers to stop eating meat and go vegetarian. Which of the above approaches is more likely to help change the minds of meat eaters: the model who holds a sign while posing inside a cage (*left*) or the spokesperson who systematically presents facts and figures on the merits of a vegetarian lifestyle (*right*).

Source: Left photo: Jay Directo/AFP/Getty Images, Inc. Right photo: Tetra Images/Getty Images, Inc.

Before You Go On

What Do You Know?

1. What are the three components of attitudes, according to the ABC model?
2. How do cognitive dissonance theory and self-perception theory differ in their explanation of attitude change?
3. Why do people sometimes misrepresent their attitudes?
4. What are the central and peripheral routes to persuasion?

What Do You Think?

Watch a television advert or select a print advert and critique it according to the material in this section. For example, does the advertisement use the central or the peripheral route? Was that a good route for the advertiser to choose, considering the product being advertised?

Social Cognition: Attributions

LEARNING OBJECTIVE 2

Discuss how people make attributions to explain their own behaviour and the behaviour of others.

One ever-present topic in media news over recent years has been the global economic crisis that began in December 2007. The effects of this crisis became marked in 2008 and accelerated in the years that have followed. These effects, as reflected across numerous countries and economic zones, have included the collapse of major financial institutions, endless individual and corporate bankruptcies, decline in investor and consumer confidence, foreclosures on the homes of individuals, urgent government interventions designed to rescue major banks and rising and prolonged unemployment. Despite governmental and international efforts to alleviate some of the worst consequences, the austerity resulting from the crisis continues to play a major part in the lives of people across the world as they struggle to come to terms with difficulties in finding and remaining in paid employment, problems in retaining their homes and the continuing impact on their everyday lives of the actions of financial institutions in which they have totally lost confidence.

One way of understanding the economic crisis would be to view it as a failure of a system that proved unsustainable, at least in the short term. With such a view, the effects of the crisis would be taken to be the outcome of circumstances that prevailed in the years preceding and including 2007. This, however, is not how most people have come to make sense of the crisis. Instead of it being the result of a particular economic context, the crisis is generally viewed as resulting from the decisions and actions of particular individuals, namely the bankers involved in dealing on and perhaps manipulating the financial markets. These individuals are commonly treated as responsible for taking unwarranted risks with other people's money, and as being handsomely rewarded for taking these risks, and thereby as largely accountable for the ensuing economic collapse that continues to affect people's lives.

PSYCHOLOGY AROUND US | Careful Deliberations?

Many criminal justice systems are based on the idea that someone is innocent until proven guilty. But what do we do if our brains do not go along with that principle? According to two American lawyers, Janice Nadler and Mary-Hunter McDonnell, most social psychology experiments suggest that our tendency to blame others is based on quick, unconscious, intuitive and broad assessments of their character and their general motives in life, rather than on careful assessments of all relevant details surrounding an event or crime. Even obvious innocence may be overlooked if observers do not like an accused person.

To help emphasize this point, the lawyers conducted a study in which they developed a series of vignettes. For each vignette, a single detail was altered. For example, in a vignette about an accidental fire triggered by the storage of fertilizer, some participants were told that the protagonist in the story had been storing the fertilizer to raise orchids, whereas other participants were told the protagonist had been storing it for the eventual manufacture of methamphetamine. That one detail made all the difference in how careless, irresponsible and blameworthy the participants judged the protagonist to be. If the protagonist was perceived to be a bad guy making meth, participants found him more to blame for the fire, even if the vignette pointed to the roles played by other factors or people. In short, if people do not like someone or his or her general motives, they tend to consider the individual more blameworthy and guilty of carelessness, even if those issues are largely irrelevant to the case at hand.

In many ways, we are all lay psychologists, continually trying to explain what we see in our social worlds so that we can make sense of events and predict what will happen in the future. We attempt to figure out *why* people, including ourselves, do things. Social psychologists refer to these causal explanations as **attributions**, and they are interested in what influences our attributions and how such attributions affect our subsequent decisions, feelings and behaviours (Stewart, 2005).

attributions causal explanations of behaviour.

Dispositional and Situational Attributions

Attributions may fall into one of two categories. *Dispositional*, or *internal*, *attributions* focus on people's traits as the cause of their behaviour. In contrast, *situational*, or *external*, *attributions* focus on environmental factors as the cause of behaviour. If you fail an examination, you may make a dispositional attribution that you failed because you were not smart enough. Instead, though, you may tell yourself that the test was unfair and that your neighbour's music was so loud the night before that you could not get a good night's sleep: situational attributions.

What determines whether we make dispositional or situational attributions? Research suggests that when explaining *other* people's behaviour, we tend to rely more heavily on dispositional attributions. In a famous study in the 1960s, researchers had participants read a speech that expressed either support for or opposition to Cuban leader Fidel Castro. They then asked each participant to rate the extent to which the speechwriter was pro-Castro (Jones & Harris, 1967). Participants who read a speech supportive of Castro naturally rated the speechwriter as pro-Castro, and those who read a speech critical of Castro naturally rated the speechwriter as anti-Castro. These were dispositional attributions: the participants reasoned that the speeches reflected internal characteristics of the speechwriters. But then the participants were told that the speechwriters had been randomly assigned to write either a pro- or anti-Castro speech. In other words, the participants were given a reason to make a situational attribution rather than a dispositional one. Remarkably, even then, the participants rated speechwriters who had written supportive speeches as very pro-Castro and speechwriters who had written critical speeches as very anti-Castro (Figure 16.5).

Social psychologist Lee Ross (2001, 1977) refers to our reliance on dispositional attributions to explain the behaviour of other people as the **fundamental attribution error**. When we are almost hit by a speeding driver, we are likely to conclude that the driver is reckless and irresponsible, even though, in fact, he or she may have been racing to the hospital

fundamental attribution error the tendency to use dispositional attributions to explain the behaviour of other people.

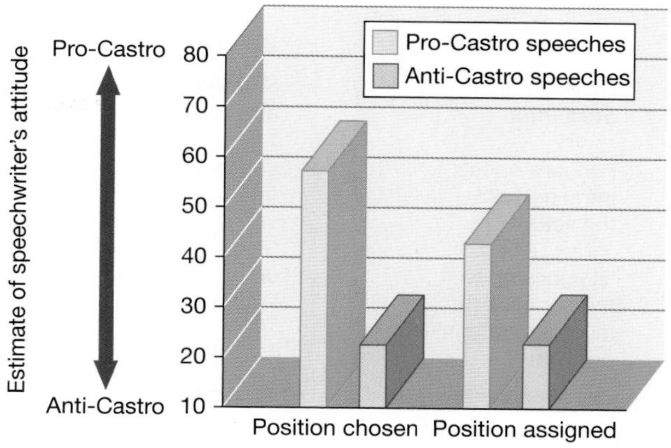

FIGURE 16.5 The fundamental attribution error. Even when told that pro-Castro or anti-Castro speechwriters had been randomly assigned their positions, research participants assumed that each speechwriter truly believed what he or she had written.

Source: Adapted from Myers, D.G. (2002). *Social Psychology* (7th ed.). New York: McGraw-Hill, Figure 3.2. © The McGraw-Hill Companies, Inc.; data from Jones, E. E. & Harris, V. A. (1967). The attribution of attitudes. *Journal of Experimental Social Psychology*, 3, 1–24.

to see a stricken child. When we meet a woman who is not very talkative, we may conclude that she is shy and introverted, when in fact she may be a normally friendly sort who has a terrible cold. When a waiter or waitress provides unsatisfactory service, we may assume that he or she is disorganized, even though the fault may lie in the restaurant's kitchen or in the policies of its management (Cowley, 2005).

In contrast, as we have already suggested, we tend to rely more heavily on situational attributions when explaining our own behaviour. Recall our example about failing an examination. Although you may make the dispositional attribution that you are not smart enough, you are more likely to make a situational attribution and blame your failure on the unfairness of the exam or your noisy neighbour. Research has repeatedly shown this tendency (Bauman & Skitka, 2010).

The Actor–Observer Effect

Social psychologists refer to the discrepancy between how we explain other people's behaviour and how we explain our own behaviour as the **actor–observer effect** (Jones & Nisbett, 1971). The idea is that as *actors* we tend to make situational attributions about our behaviours; as *observers* we tend to make dispositional attributions (Figure 16.6). Several explanations have been offered as to why this is so. For one thing, as actors, we have information about ourselves that observers do not have. We know from experience, for example, that we do not act the same way in every situation. For another thing, observers

actor–observer effect the discrepancy between how we explain other people's behaviour (dispositionally) and how we explain our own behaviour (situationally).

The Observer	The Actor
Dispositional attribution	**Situational attribution**
Focuses on the personality of the actor	Focuses attention on external factors
'He goes up to the bar a lot; he must have a drinking problem.'	'People keep picking up my drink whenever I put it down.'

FIGURE 16.6 The actor–observer effect. We tend to explain our own behaviour in terms of external factors (situational attributions), and others' behaviour in terms of their internal characteristics (dispositional attributions).

tend to focus on the actor, while actors need to focus more on situations. Think about a football game. As a fan (observer), you may watch the player with the ball closely. But if you were the player (actor), you would need to pay attention to the ball, the other players, the goal and many other aspects of your surroundings. Interestingly, if people are shown videotapes of their own behaviour – that is, if they become observers – they tend to make more dispositional attributions about the causes of their behaviour (Storms, 1973). That is, the video enables them to switch from actors to observers, and their explanations for their behaviours switch correspondingly.

As an example of the actor–observer effect, consider a class exercise developed by social psychologist Susan Fiske (2010). She tells her students, 'Rate on a scale from 1 (low) to 10 (high) to what extent each of the following are reasons you chose your university.'

- I had a wish to please my parents.
- I desired to get away from home.
- I wanted to go where my friends went.
- I liked the location of my college.
- I decided to go to a prestigious college.
- I was looking to find a marriage partner.
- I wanted a good social life.

After the students have completed these ratings, Fiske instructs them, 'Next rate all the reasons that the *typical* student at your university picked it.'

Take a break from reading, and complete this exercise yourself. Then compare your ratings of your reasons for attending your university with your ratings of other students' reasons. Did your ratings follow a pattern? If you are like most of the students in Fiske's classes, you thought the reasons on the list described the typical student's decision better than they described yours. If that is the case, your ratings illustrate the actor–observer effect. Each of the reasons on the list is a dispositional attribution, relating to something internal to the person. As Fiske observes, 'People see themselves as having rich, deep and adaptive personalities, able to express almost any [behaviour] or its opposite, depending on the circumstances. *Other* people, of course, are ruled by their personalities' (Fiske, 2010, p. 116).

Exceptions to the Rule

Despite the trend just described, we do not *always* attribute other people's behaviours to their personalities. When we know that just about everyone would react the same way in a given situation, we will likely conclude that a person's behaviour in that situation is situationally caused. When most people are robbed at gunpoint, for example, they (wisely) hand over their money. Thus, a particular robbery victim's surrender of money will usually be attributed to the powerful situational factors.

Similarly, if we are given detailed information about situational pressures, we may attribute the behaviour of other people to situational factors. Think back, once again, to the tsunami that struck the Fukushima Daiichi nuclear power plant in Japan. Rather than assuming that individuals' desires to return to their homes within the 20 km evacuation area reflect the foolish dispositions of those who are prepared to ignore the risks associated with nuclear leaks, we can understand these as the natural wishes of people who are victims of an unanticipated and unprecedented natural disaster.

Cultural background may also push certain individuals away from personality attributions and towards situational attributions when explaining the behaviours of other people. Generally, individuals from collectivistic cultures are less likely than those from individualistic cultures to explain the behaviour of other people in personality terms (Markus *et al.*, 2006). One study, for example, had Chinese and American participants explain the real-life case of a fired postal worker who shot his supervisor and other workers in Michigan (Morris & Peng, 1994). The American participants made dispositional attributions, as the fundamental attribution error would predict. They believed that the shooter was psychologically disturbed and out of touch with reality. In contrast, the Chinese participants included more situational causes in their explanations. They said, for example, that the media's glorification of violence, economic pressures and unhelpful supervisors were responsible for the shootings to at least some degree.

By the same token, we do not *always* attribute our own behaviour to situational factors. Let us say, for example, that you do poorly on an examination and complain that the questions were too hard and the grading unfair. You are, as we would expect, making a situational attribution for your poor performance. But suppose you get a good mark on the next examination. Will you explain your success by pointing out how easy the exam questions were or how generous the marking was? Not likely.

Consistent with this point, social psychologists have noted that when we explain our own behaviour we are able, and often likely, to fluctuate between situational and dispositional attributions, depending on which puts us in a better light. In other words, we tend to attribute our successes to internal causes and our failures to external ones – a phenomenon referred to as the **self-serving bias** (Johnston & Lee, 2005; Miller & Ross, 1975). Research has also indicated that the direction of our attributions can be influenced by factors such as our moods and emotions, motives, prejudices, stereotypes and cultural background (Lieberman *et al.*, 2005; Sadler *et al.*, 2005).

> **self-serving bias** the tendency people have to attribute their successes to internal causes and their failures to external ones.

Before You Go On

What Do You Know?

5. How do dispositional and situational attributions differ?
6. What is the fundamental attribution error?
7. What are some exceptions to the actor–observer effect?

What Do You Think?

How do you think empathy may affect the actor–observer effect?

Social Relations

 HOW WE DIFFER

LEARNING OBJECTIVE 3

Review major concepts in the areas of helping behaviour, aggression and interpersonal attraction.

Many social psychologists have been interested in social relations. Some have attempted to determine when people choose to help others and when they ignore others' needs. Other social psychologists have examined aggression and interpersonal attraction, trying to understand why people behave aggressively and how people come to like or love others in their social world.

Helping Behaviour

When people are in need, we tend to offer our help, as an expression of **altruism** or of another social motive. After the 9/11 terrorist attacks, for example, people gave their time, money and support to those affected by the attacks. The number of people donating blood to the Red Cross doubled in the month following the attacks, and by the end of September 2001, $115 million had been donated to the September 11 Fund (Piferi *et al.*, 2006). Social psychologists have studied various aspects of such helping behaviour.

> **altruism** self-sacrificing behaviour carried out for the benefit of others.

Why Do We Help? Altruism refers to self-sacrificing behaviour carried out for the benefit of others. To be altruistic, behaviour must be motivated by concern for people in need, without concern for oneself (Post, 2005; Puka, 2004). Thus, engaging in self-sacrificing behaviour to avoid a sense of

Responding to tragedy. Almost immediately after a series of terrorist bombs ripped through passenger trains in Madrid, Spain in 2004, killing 191 people and injuring 1,800 others, Spanish citizens such as these began lining up to donate blood to the victims. Altruism? Possibly. But social psychologists point out that egoistic motives may also be at work during the early reactions to tragedies of this kind.
Source: ©Albert Gea/Reuters/Corbis.

guilt or donating to charity for tax purposes would not be considered altruistic behaviour. Such acts, which are motivated by a desire to reduce one's own personal distress or to receive rewards, are sometimes called *egoistic helping behaviours* (Batson *et al.*, 2004, 1997; Khalil, 2004).

When we engage in helping behaviour, our motives can be entirely altruistic, entirely egoistic or a combination of both. For example, surveys have revealed that in the *immediate* aftermath of the 9/11 terrorist attacks on New York, actions such as giving blood, money and goods and offering prayers were associated with both altruistic and egoistic motives (Piferi *et al.*, 2006). People's motivations for giving ranged from wanting to ease the suffering of others to hoping to reduce their own attack-induced distress and seeking to reassure themselves that other people would also help them if they were in need. In contrast, *sustained* giving after the attacks (that is, giving after one or more years) was associated only with altruistic motives.

Research further indicates that certain factors increase the likelihood of altruistic behaviour. When people empathize and identify with the individuals in need, they are more likely to behave altruistically (Batson *et al.*, 2004, 1997; Batson & Weeks, 1996). Similarly, people tend to display more altruism when they take the perspective of victims (Mikulincer *et al.*, 2005; Underwood & Moore, 1982). Not surprisingly, then, people who are generally trusting and outward-looking and who form secure attachments in their relationships are most likely to perform altruistic behaviours (Mikulincer *et al.*, 2005; Mikulincer & Shaver, 2005).

Bystander Apathy Imagine you are in a life-threatening situation and desperately need the help of others. If you could choose, would you prefer that one or two people were nearby or that a large number of people were present? If you are like most people, you probably would prefer the larger number. After all, that would mean more potential helpers. In fact, however, this would probably be the more dangerous choice. It turns out that, in many circumstances, the more people present in a situation where help is required, the less likely it is that any one person will give that help (Fischer *et al.*, 2006; Garcia *et al.*, 2002; Batson, 1991).

On 20 October 2011, a two-year-old Chinese girl died in hospital having been in a coma since being run down in a busy Chinese market seven days earlier. Wang Yue, whose parents ran a shop in the market, had been hit by one van and subsequently run over by a second vehicle while she lay injured on the ground. Subsequent inspection of surveillance camera footage showed 18 passers-by walking past the girl, as she lay bleeding and unconscious, and making no attempt to help her. A rubbish collector who did finally intervene to move Wang Yue to the side of the street and seek assistance

was labelled a hero, but the failure of others to help her in her time of need led many to question the state of Chinese morality.

This incident, shocking enough in its own terms, gives rise to concerns that are reminiscent of those surrounding a murder that took place on 13 March 1961 in the New York borough of Queens. Reports of that murder suggested that the victim, a woman named Kitty Genovese, had been stabbed to death in a prolonged attack lasting over 30 minutes, while at least 38 neighbours and other onlookers failed to intervene. These reports led social psychologists John Darley and Bibb Latané to examine features of the situation that may have kept onlookers from providing the help required. In a series of studies examining the impact of the presence of others on helping behaviour, Darley and Latané repeatedly demonstrated that we are, in fact, more likely to intervene when we are *alone* than when others are also present. In one of their studies, for example, participants found themselves in a situation where they smelled smoke (contrived by the experimenters) while either alone or in the presence of others. When other people were present in the room, less than 40% of the participants got up to report the smoke. By contrast, 75% of the participants reported smelling smoke when no one else was in the room (Figure 16.7) (Latané & Darley, 1968). In another experiment by the two researchers, participants were placed in a situation in which they overheard a person (actually an actor) in another room having a seizure. The more people the participants believed could also hear the individual having the seizure, the less quickly they acted to help (Darley & Latané, 1968).

This phenomenon has been termed *bystander apathy*. Researchers in addition to Darley and Latané have observed group apathy of this kind under a wide variety of conditions,

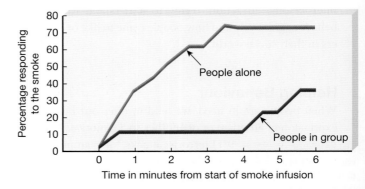

FIGURE 16.7 Bystander intervention. People are more likely to intervene to help when they are alone than in a group. In the presence of others, people feel less compelled to act, a phenomenon called bystander apathy.

Source: Adapted from Myers, D.G. (2002). *Social psychology* (7th ed.). New York: Mc-Graw Hill, Figure 12.4. Based on Darley, J.M., & Latane, B. 1968.

including situations in which a person's belongings were seemingly stolen in a library (Shaffer *et al.*, 1975), graffiti was written on a wall (Chekroun & Brauer, 2002) and drunk driving was about to take place (Rabow *et al.*, 1990).

What must occur in order for bystanders to intervene on someone else's behalf? Apparently, several steps are involved (Fischer *et al.*, 2006; Darley, 2000; Latané & Darley, 1970). Bystanders must:

- Notice the event.
- Interpret the event as an emergency.
- Feel personal responsibility for acting.
- Consider what form of assistance is needed.
- Implement action.

Some theorists have focused on the third step, *feel personal responsibility for acting*, as the key to bystander apathy. They suggest that the presence of a large number of people in an emergency situation creates a *diffusion of responsibility*. When others are present, we feel that we do not bear the full burden of responsibility, and thus we feel less compelled to act. We might also assume that someone else must be taking action. Of course, when everyone in a crisis assumes that others will be taking responsibility for constructive action, no one intervenes. In some cases, such as that of the death of Wang Yue, individual tragedy can result from lack of intervention.

Aggression

In social psychological terms, *aggression* describes a broad category of behaviours, including physical and verbal attacks, intended to do harm to another. Aggression appears to have at least some biological underpinnings. Twin studies indicate that identical twins are more likely to share the trait of violent temper than fraternal twins, suggesting a genetic component (Baker *et al.*, 2007; Rowe *et al.*, 1999; Miles & Carey, 1997). High levels of the hormone testosterone have been linked with higher levels of aggression, as have low levels of the neurotransmitter serotonin. Indeed, the people most likely to be involved with violent crime are muscular young men with below-average intelligence, high levels of testosterone and low levels of serotonin (Dabbs *et al.*, 2001).

That said, under the right circumstances, we are apparently all capable of aggressive acts. One major hypothesis explaining aggression in humans – the *frustration–aggression hypothesis* – holds that we become aggressive in response to frustration (Dollard *et al.*, 1939). Any emotional stressor that impedes our progress or prevents achievement of some goal can elicit frustration. Aggression, then, might be a cue to push harder in order to achieve that goal.

This theory was later expanded to include the notion that any unpleasant event, ranging from experiencing a bad odour or an annoying sound to hearing bad news, leads to activation of the sympathetic nervous system (Berkowitz, 1989). Recall from Chapter 14 that activation of the sympathetic nervous system is associated with both anger and fear and with the fight-or-flight response. This theory suggests that if you have translated this activation to aggressive (fight) behaviour in the past, and the outcome has had a desired effect, you will continue to engage in that aggressive behaviour.

Other factors influencing aggression probably result from both biology and environment (Figure 16.8). For example, as we have observed previously, men tend to be more aggressive than women, at least in some respects. Women are more likely to engage in acts of *relational aggression*, such as snubbing, gossiping and otherwise excluding others as a means of venting frustration or anger (Archer, 2005). However, men are more likely to engage in *direct aggression*, which includes direct physical and verbal abuse. In fact, the vast majority of violent offenders are male (Halpern, 2000). Because this disparity shows up very early in childhood, it may be at least partially attributable to biological gender differences. However, it is probably also affected by social norms within our society, where men are permitted more than women to express anger and act aggressively.

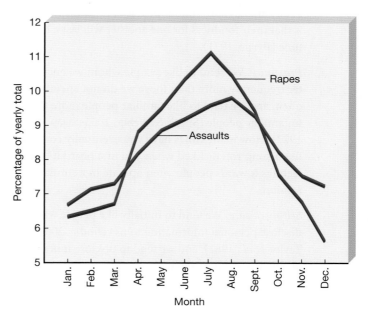

FIGURE 16.8 Aggression by time of year. Studies of data in North America and Europe over the past hundred years show that aggression is highest in the hottest months of the year.

Source: Adapted from Anderson, C, (1989). Temperature and aggression: Ubiquitous effects of heat on occurrence of human violence. *Psychological Bulletin, 106*, 74–96.

Alcohol has also been found to increase aggressive behaviour for both biological and psychological reasons. The effects of the drug may reduce inhibitions and so make people more likely to engage in violence or verbal abuse. However, people have been shown to become more aggressive even if they only think that they have consumed alcohol, suggesting that they are responding to social expectations about how people act when they have been drinking.

Interpersonal Attraction

Why are we attracted to some people and not others? What is the difference between liking someone and loving someone? These are questions central to the study of interpersonal attraction. Interpersonal attraction operates at three levels: *cognitively*, we think certain things about the other person; *affectively*, we experience particular feelings towards him or her; and *behaviourally*, we act in certain ways towards the person (Orbuch & Sprecher, 2003; Berscheid & Walster, 1978).

Liking *Liking* refers to fondness and affection for another person. Research has revealed five key factors that lead to liking someone.

- *Similarity*. The more similar to us we perceive someone to be, the more likely we are to develop a fondness for that person (Lankau *et al.*, 2005; Bates, 2002). In addition, the more similar people are, the likelier it is that their fondness for one another will last a long time (Byrne, 1971).

- *Proximity*. We tend to like people whom we encounter frequently more than those we do not encounter often, and we tend to like familiar people more than unfamiliar people (Smith & Weber, 2005; Swap, 1977). How many times have you eventually come to like a song you disliked when you first heard it? Our feelings towards people often operate in a similar fashion.

- *Self-disclosure*. We tend to initially like people who disclose personal information to us (Dindia, 2000; Taylor *et al.*, 1981), and we tend to disclose more to people whom we initially like (Certner, 1973; Worthy *et al.*, 1969).

- *Situational factors*. The situations in which we encounter other people greatly affect how much we like them. It has been suggested, for example, that we like people when we experience rewards while in their presence (Lott & Lott, 1974). Furthermore, a

New approach, new criteria. Two people meet in a speed-dating programme held on Bondi Beach in Australia. Speed dating is a form of social engagement in which large numbers of people are rotated to meet many potential partners over a series of short 3- to 8-minute 'dates'. What kinds of partners do speed daters choose most often? Those who are attractive and hold attitudes similar to those of the selectors.
Source: Sergio Dionisio/Getty Images, Inc.

shared humorous experience seems to be a powerful way of forging closeness with a stranger (Fraley & Aron, 2004; Lyttle, 2001). The playwright Oscar Wilde once said, 'Laughter is not at all a bad beginning for a friendship.'

- *Physical attractiveness*. People of all ages, even babies, prefer to look at and be near attractive people (Smith & Weber, 2005; Langlois & Stephan, 1981). Not surprisingly, then, physical attractiveness may affect likeability.

What kinds of studies have led researchers to these conclusions? Let us examine a few of the investigations into the last factor mentioned above, physical attractiveness. In a study by social psychologist Elaine Walster and her colleagues (1966), the experimenters randomly paired participants to be dates at a dance. During a break in the dance, the participants were asked to rate how much they liked their partners. Overall, the more attractive the partner, the more likeable he or she was reported to be.

In other studies, an attractive middle-aged person was judged to be more outgoing and more pleasant than a less attractive middle-aged individual (Adams & Huston, 1975); physically attractive college students were found to be more popular than less attractive ones among members of the same sex (Byrne *et al.*, 1968); and attractive fifth-grade students were rated more popular by their classmates than less attractive students (Cavior & Dokecki, 1973; 1971).

Finally, one study examined the joint impact of two factors – physical attractiveness and similarity – on liking (Byrne *et al.*, 1970). The experimenters arranged lab dates for participants, varying both attractiveness and similarity of attitudes on certain issues. Upon their arrival, the dates were sent to a student lounge to talk for 20 minutes and then instructed to return to the lab. In the laboratory, the experimenters then measured how much the date pairs liked each other by having the participants fill out a questionnaire and by observing how close together the date pair stood when they re-entered the lab. It turned out that the measures of liking were indeed related to both how attractive the dates were and how similar their attitudes were.

Loving Whereas liking someone involves a sense of fondness, loving is associated with a more extreme affection. When we *love* someone, we experience a strong, passionate attachment to that person. Some see loving as simply an extreme form of liking – with degree of attraction being the key distinction – whereas others see loving as a qualitatively different phenomenon (Watts & Stenner, 2005; Sternberg, 2004, 1987).

Let us first consider the question of what functions love serves. Freud viewed love as *sublimated sexual energy*; that is, a transformation of sexual desire into a more socially acceptable form (Fenchel, 2006). Evolutionary theorists emphasize love's role in propagating the species (Brumbaugh & Fraley, 2006; Wilson, 1981). According to these theorists, strong passionate attachments have ensured that, over time, parents would stay together and raise their children together.

Still other theorists argue that love's most important value is to help provide companionship, emotional support and even protection throughout the lifespan (Mikulincer *et al.*, 2008; Mikulincer & Goodman, 2006). Loving relationships have in fact been associated with improved health (Levin, 2000). Such relationships provide us with people to confide in – and not being able to confide our troubles to someone has been associated with a host of health problems (Pennebaker, 2004, 2003, 1990; Pennebaker *et al.*, 2004). This may be one reason why recently widowed individuals are more vulnerable to disease than individuals of similar age who have not lost a spouse (Troyer, 2006; Daggett, 2002).

What are the building blocks of love? Decades ago, social psychologist Zick Rubin (1970) emphasized three elements of love: attachment, caring and intimacy. *Attachment* refers to the individual's need or desire for the physical presence and emotional support of the other person; *caring* is a feeling of concern and responsibility for him or her; and *intimacy* involves the desire for close, confidential communication with the other individual.

Using this definition of love, Rubin (1973) designed a self-report scale that he hoped would be able to measure love and distinguish it from liking. The scale included *love* items, such as 'If I could never be with ____, I would feel miserable' and 'I feel I can confide in ____ about virtually everything', along with *like* items, such as 'I think that ____ is usually well adjusted' and '____ is the sort of person whom I myself would like to be.' In one study, Rubin had dating couples fill out this scale, alone and confidentially, focusing on their date partner in their ratings. He found that friends and lovers both scored high on the like items, but friends did not score high on the love items.

In another study, Rubin had volunteer couples come to his laboratory and sit across from each other while awaiting the start of the experiment. His assistants secretly observed the couples from behind a one-way mirror to determine which ones gazed into each other's eyes, a sign of love according to conventional wisdom. As expected, the partners who had scored high on Rubin's love scale gazed lovingly at each other more than did partners who had scored low on the scale.

Another psychologist, Robert Sternberg, whom you met back in Chapter 12, proposed the **triangular theory of love**, which holds that love is composed of *intimacy*, *passion* and *commitment* (Sternberg & Weis, 2006; Sternberg, 2004, 1986). Here, *intimacy* refers once again to feelings that promote closeness and connection, *passion* involves intense desires for union with the other person and *commitment* refers to the decision to maintain the relationship across time. According to Sternberg, the extent and quality of each of these three components determined the nature of a particular loving relationship.

> **triangular theory of love** the theory that love is composed of three elements: intimacy, passion and commitment; proposed by Robert Sternberg.

In fact, Sternberg distinguished eight kinds of love, each reflecting a particular combination of the three components (Table 16.1). For example, purely *romantic* love consists of much intimacy and passion with little commitment. In contrast, couples who experience *companionate* love are high on intimacy and commitment but low on passion. Couples who experience *consummate* love are high on all three components; and those with *empty* love are high on commitment only. Sternberg also believed these relationships change over time, peaking at different points.

A number of social psychologists propose that relationships proceed through *stages* as the participants move from the fondness and affection of liking to the intimacy and commitment of loving. One theory, for example, cites four stages: exploration, bargaining, commitment and institutionalization (Backman, 1990, 1981). In the *exploration* stage, the

TABLE 16.1 Sternberg's Eight Kinds of Love

Kind of Love	Intimacy	Passion	Commitment
Non-Love	✗	✗	✗
Liking	✓	✗	✗
Infatuated love	✗	✓	✗
Empty love	✗	✗	✓
Romantic love	✓	✓	✗
Companionate love	✓	✗	✓
Fatuous love	✗	✓	✓
Consummate love	✓	✓	✓

Source: From R. J. Sternberg (1987). *The Triangle of Love: Intimacy, passion, commitment.* New York: Basic Books. Copyright © 1987 by Basic Books. Reprinted with the permission of the author.

partners try out the possible rewards and costs of a relationship. During the *bargaining* stage, they implicitly negotiate the terms of the relationship. That is, they feel out its ground rules: which behaviours are rewarding, which cost too much and how the joint benefits of the relationship can be maximized. During the third stage, *commitment*, the partners grow increasingly dependent on each other. Finally, in the *institutionalization* stage, shared expectations emerge, and the relationship is recognized by the partners (and by others) as exclusive. Other theorists have proposed different specific stages, but most agree that relationships do tend to proceed step-by-step as they deepen from liking to loving, with each stop marked by changing understandings, behaviours and feelings (Yela, 2006; Berscheid, 1983).

PSYCHOLOGY AROUND US   Falling in Limerence

Have you been in love? If yes, what did it feel like? Did you think about the object of your affection constantly? Did you intensely fear that the person would reject you? Did you even have an aching feeling in your chest? If so, the reality may have been that you were not in love. You were in *limerence* (Tennov, 1999).

Based on interviews with over 500 individuals conducted in the 1960s and 1970s, psychologist Dorothy Tennov coined the term *limerence* to describe the ultimate, obsessive form of romantic love. According to Tennov, limerence lasts, on average, two years. A person can experience it many times, only once or never in a lifetime. The most notable component of limerence is constant, intrusive thinking about the object of affection, whom Tennov referred to as the *limerent object*, or LO (Reynolds, 1993). Tennov claimed that when people first fall into limerence, they spend about 30% of their day thinking about the LO. A few months later, they are thinking about the LO 100% of the time (*Time,* 1980).

The reality is that limerence can be problematic. Not only do romantic relationships suffer if one partner is in limerence while the other is not, but friendships and familial relationships can also become strained by the limerent's preoccupation with the LO. Some observers have even compared limerence to substance dependence.

Some psychologists believe that limerence is so disruptive it should be categorized as a psychological disorder for which people should get clinical help. They argue that people in limerence who do seek treatment are often incorrectly diagnosed with generalized anxiety disorder, depression or obsessive–compulsive disorder (OCD) (Wakin & Vo, 2008).

Some brain research supports the view that limerence is not a usual state. Neuroscientists have found that people who are newly 'in love' have activity levels of the neurotransmitter serotonin similar to the levels found in individuals with OCD. In addition, people who have fallen in love within the past six months have elevated levels of the stress hormone cortisol (Ananthaswamy, 2004).

What do you think? Is this heart-pounding state actually a psychological disorder?

Before You Go On

What Do You Know?

8. How does altruistic helping behaviour differ from egoistic helping behaviour?

9. How does the presence of other people affect the likelihood that a bystander will intervene on behalf of someone who needs help?

10. What are some of the biological underpinnings of aggressive behaviour?

11. What are the three components of Robert Sternberg's triangular theory of love and how do they interact in relationships?

What Do You Think?

Think about a relationship you have had with a friend – someone you really like. Analyse the development of that relationship with reference to each of the key factors discussed in this section.

Social Functioning  WHAT HAPPENS IN THE BRAIN?

LEARNING OBJECTIVE 4

Describe the major findings of social neuroscience about regions of the brain particularly important to our social functioning.

Throughout this book, you have seen that, with the help of brain-scanning procedures, researchers have tied many areas of psychological functioning, such as memory or emotions, to particular neural circuits – collections of neurons that communicate with each other. The study of social functioning is no different. Indeed, there has been so much work to uncover what happens in the brain when people are thinking and behaving socially that the field of study has been given a special title, *social neuroscience*, and the combination of brain regions that operate together when people function socially has also been given a special name in some circles: the *social brain*.

One of the early clues for helping researchers to identify regions of the brain that may be at work in social cognition and behaviour came from evolutionary psychology (Adolphs, 2009, 2003). Beginning with the observation that

a unique and critically important area of human functioning is social cognition – particularly the ability to infer what is going on (intentions, feeling, and thoughts) inside the minds of other people – scientists decided to pay special attention to those regions that are newer and/or bigger in human brains than in the brains of other animals. Their contention was that these regions may be the ones that play key roles in social functioning.

Not surprisingly, several of the brain regions that, according to brain scans, are very active during social cognition and behaviour are indeed particularly large in the human brain. For example, the *prefrontal cortex*, the part of the frontal cortex that is closest to the front of the head, is much larger in humans than in other animals (Figure 16.9). As we observed in Chapter 5, the entire frontal cortex is somewhat larger in the human brain than in the brains of less complex animals. But the prefrontal cortex is particularly larger (Semendeferi et al., 2002).

Social cognitions and behaviours rely on many of the psychological functions that we have examined throughout this book. They require, for example, the rapid identification of social stimuli and signals (e.g. recognition

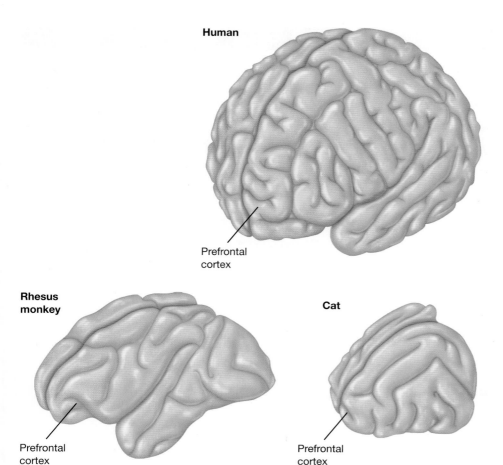

FIGURE 16.9 Across the species. The prefrontal cortex of human beings is larger than that of other animals and is, at the same time, very active during social behaviour, suggesting that it plays an important role in human social functioning.

of people), the rapid retrieval of memories (to help us remember who is a friend and who is a foe), the ability to recognize the perspective of others, anticipation of others' behaviours, experiences of emotion and empathy, and moral and other evaluations of situations (e.g. to help us decide whether prosocial behaviour is in order) (Adolphs, 2009). Thus, some of the brain regions that are highly active during social functioning turn out to be ones that we have come across in our chapters on language and thought, memory, emotion and the like. To date, social neuroscientists have identified the following brain regions as among the key players in social functioning:

- *Orbitofrontal cortex.* A subregion of the prefrontal cortex. It is involved in social reasoning, reward evaluation, reading other people and eliciting emotional states (Stuss *et al.*, 2001).

- *Ventromedial prefrontal cortex.* Another subregion of the prefrontal cortex. It plays a key role in the processing of rewards and punishments, interpreting nonverbal social information (such as facial expressions), making social and moral assessments and decisions and feeling empathy (Koenigs *et al.*, 2007; Shamay-Tsoory *et al.*, 2005).

- *Insula.* A region of the cortex that is located beneath the frontal cortex. It plays a key role in empathy and in reading others. The insula is activated when we observe others in physical or emotional pain and immediately feel that pain ourselves (Keysers & Gazzola, 2007).

- *Amygdala.* A brain region that is located in the temporal lobe. It is, as we have seen, actively involved in the control of emotions. In social functioning, it helps us to identify the emotional facial expressions of other people and to pay particular attention to stimuli that can be unpredictable, potentially rewarding or potentially punishing (Whalen *et al.*, 2009; Whalen, 1998).

We still have much to learn about how these and other regions operate together to help people function socially. Social neuroscientists are also still trying to identify the precise neural networks that enable us to so readily carry out the social cognitions and behaviours examined throughout this chapter. Considering how little researchers knew about the relationship between the brain and social functioning just a decade ago, however, the progress made and knowledge gained in recent years is quite remarkable.

Before You Go On

What Do You Know?

12. What is social neuroscience and what is the social brain?

13. Which brain regions have been identified as particularly important to our social functioning?

What Do You Think?

If you were a neuroscientist looking for parts of the brain that were important to social functioning, how would you decide where to look first?

Access your interactive e-book to view a video clip for this chapter at **www.wileyopenpage.com**

Summary

Social Cognition: Attitudes

LEARNING OBJECTIVE 1 Explain how attitudes form and change and what role they play in behaviour.

- Attitudes are relatively stable and enduring evaluations of things and people. According to the ABC model, they have affective, behavioural and cognitive components.

- Parents play a major role in shaping children's attitudes. In older children, peers, teachers and the media also exert an influence.

- Leon Festinger proposed that people change their attitudes when they experience cognitive dissonance – a state of emotional discomfort that arises when a person holds two contradictory beliefs or a belief inconsistent with his or her behaviour.
- The self-perception theory of attitude change minimizes the role of emotional discomfort and suggests that people simply infer what their attitudes are by observing their own behaviour.
- The attitudes people express are not necessarily related to their behaviour. In part, this is because people sometimes misrepresent their attitudes. They may wish to express socially desirable attitudes or they may not be aware of what their implicit attitudes really are.
- Stereotypes provide generalized impressions about people or groups based on broad social categories. Overt prejudice in the form of negative attitudes towards individuals from other groups has decreased over time in many countries but subtler implicit forms of prejudice endure.
- People use persuasion techniques to try to influence the attitudes of others. The central route to persuasion emphasizes the content of the message, while the peripheral route depends on more superficial appeals, such as the appearance of the spokesperson.

Social Cognition: Attributions

LEARNING OBJECTIVE 2 Discuss how people make attributions to explain their own behaviour and the behaviour of others.

- Attributions, or causal explanations of behaviour, can be dispositional (internal) or situational (external).
- People tend to attribute their own behaviour to situational factors and the behaviour of others to dispositional factors. The reliance on dispositional factors to explain others' behaviour is the fundamental attribution error.
- According to the actor–observer effect, this discrepancy exists because people make situational attributions as actors and dispositional attributions as observers.
- People sometimes attribute only their failures to situational factors and attribute their successes to dispositional factors, which is called the self-serving bias.

Social Relations

LEARNING OBJECTIVE 3 Review major concepts in the areas of helping behaviour, aggression and interpersonal attraction.

- Helping behaviour is of two types: altruism, which is motivated by concern for others, and egoistic helping behaviour, which is motivated by a desire to reduce one's own distress or receive rewards.
- People are more likely to engage in helping behaviour when alone than when in the presence of others. Theorists propose that the presence of others may create a diffusion of responsibility, in which no single individual feels personal responsibility for acting.
- Aggression describes a broad range of behaviours intended to do harm to another. Aggression has some biological underpinnings. In addition, the frustration–aggression hypothesis proposes that aggression arises in response to frustration.
- Factors that lead to liking another person include similarity, proximity, self-disclosure, situational factors and physical attractiveness.
- One description of love includes three elements: attachment, caring and intimacy. Another, Sternberg's triangular theory of love, holds that love is composed of intimacy, passion and commitment, which combine in varying degrees.

Social Functioning

LEARNING OBJECTIVE 4 Describe the major findings of social neuroscience about regions of the brain particularly important to our social functioning.

- Social neuroscience is the speciality of neuroscience that studies how the brain works during social functioning. Social functioning is so important and uniquely human that social neuroscientists have given the name social brain to the combination of brain areas that are particularly active in social functioning.
- The orbitofrontal cortex, ventromedial prefrontal cortex, insula and amygdala have all been identified as especially important in social functioning, and researchers continue to try to pinpoint neural connections related to social functioning.

ACTIVITY

Activities to test yourself further are available in your interactive e-book at **www.wileyopenpage.com**

TYING IT TOGETHER

WHAT HAPPENS IN THE BRAIN?

- There has been so much research on the brain's role in social functioning that there is now a branch of neuroscience called social neuroscience.
- The prefrontal cortex, much larger in humans than most animals, houses many of the structures important in social functioning.
- High levels of aggression have been linked to a combination of high-testosterone activity and low-serotonin activity.

HOW WE DIFFER

- People who are trusting, outward-looking and form secure attachments in their relationships are more likely to perform altruistic behaviours.
- Both men and women are aggressive, but males are, on average, more likely to engage in direct, physical and verbal aggression, while female aggression is more likely, on average, to be relational, such as snubbing someone.

QUIZ Quizzes to test yourself further are available in your interactive e-book at **www.wileyopenpage.com**

Key Terms

ABC model of attitudes 471
actor–observer effect 479
altruism 481
attitudes 471

attributions 479
cognitive dissonance 472
fundamental attribution
   error 479

implicit attitude 474
prejudice 475
self-perception theory 473
self-serving bias 481

social cognition 470
social psychology 470
stereotypes 475
triangular theory of love 485

FLASHCARDS Flashcards to test yourself further are available in your interactive e-book at **www.wileyopenpage.com**

CHAPTER 17

Social Forces, Group Processes and Language

Adapted by Chris McVittie, Queen Margaret University, Edinburgh, UK

CHAPTER OUTLINE

- Social Forces
- Intragroup Processes

- Intergroup Relations
- Language and Social Groups

 Access your interactive e-book to view a video clip for this chapter at **www.wileyopenpage.com**

Social Groups in Protest

On 15 October 2011, up to 3,000 people arrived in central London to participate in a demonstration against UK government austerity measures, wealth inequality and corporate greed. The demonstrators' intended target was Paternoster Square, home of the London Stock Exchange, which to them was symbolic of much of the financial activity against which they sought to protest. They were, however, denied entry to Paternoster Square and instead set up camp outside St Paul's Cathedral nearby, marking the start of what became known as the *Occupy London* protest. As the protest continued day after day, the numbers of protesters camping outside the cathedral grew and the protest spread to other sites in central London and beyond. Meanwhile, local people faced increasing difficulties in getting to their places of work, local businesses lost trade and St Paul's Cathedral had to close to visitors for the first time since World War II. Police attempts to end the demonstration through negotiation with the protesters failed to end the occupation of the Cathedral Square, leading to those responsible for the cathedral and the City of London Corporation initiating legal proceedings to require the demonstrators to leave. Following on from the resignations from their posts of two leading clergy in the cathedral, legal action was suspended. Subsequently, however, this legal action resumed following the failure of protesters, cathedral staff, police and the City of London Corporation to reach an agreement that would lead to the end of the protests. At this time, it became clear that the occupation of the square outside the Cathedral could not readily be brought to an end in a way that would serve the interests of all these groups, of local people, businesses and broader society. ∎

Events such as those that occurred at St Paul's Cathedral provide a particular focus for social psychologists in their attempts to understand and explain large-scale social actions. We might think also of the mobilization of populations in 2011 against existing regimes in Tunisia and Egypt in large-scale actions that came to be part of the *Arab Spring*, of events in Libya leading to the overthrow and subsequent death of the former dictator Colonel Muammar Gaddafi and of the riots that occurred in London and other cities in the United Kingdom during the summer of 2011. Such events, as do many more, have far-reaching social consequences for those involved, whether as leaders, members of a crowd or movement or as people who are swept along by and possibly caught up in events as they unfold. For social psychologists who study such issues, the emphasis shifts from a focus on how individuals make sense of the world around them to one of how the social world comes to influence the understandings of individual people. How, for example, do people respond to social norms or the influence that others in positions of leadership may attempt to exert in certain situations? How do groups themselves work in terms of their own dynamics and the possibly different contributions of different members? What may it mean to a person to belong to a social group that is involved in certain sorts of actions and does so in relation to other groups and their members? What functions do language and communication play in the construction of social groups and group memberships? It is to these sorts of questions that we turn in this chapter. We will begin by looking at social forces.

Social Forces

LEARNING OBJECTIVE 1

Describe how norms, social roles and obedience shape people's behaviour.

Norms and Social Roles

Recall that, during the Occupy London protest, people around the United Kingdom learnt that the actions of protesters had led to the closure of a national landmark, St Paul's Cathedral, difficulties for local businesses in conducting their usual activities and problems for London residents in leading their day-to-day lives. Such reports made many observers and media viewers feel very unsettled. One reason for their discomfort was that such behaviours seemed to represent a breakdown of recognized social order. Another reason was that the behaviours defied people's social expectations. Fellow citizens are not expected to disrupt the lives of others in pursuit of their own personal ends. These expectations arise from the norms and roles of our society.

Norms Society has many rules governing how everyone is supposed to act. These conventions, referred to as **norms**, provide order and predictability. Some norms are *explicit*, or stated openly. We all know, for example, that we are supposed to stop our car when we come to a red light. Other norms are *implicit*. These norms are not openly stated, but we are still aware of them. You probably were not taught as a child to face the front of a lift, for instance, but when is the last time you stepped into a lift where all the passengers had their backs to the doors?

> **norms** social rules about how members of a society are expected to act.

We can also classify norms as descriptive or injunctive (Larimer *et al.*, 2005, 2004; Larimer & Neighbors, 2003; Eagly & Karau, 2002). *Descriptive norms* are agreed-on expectations about what members of society *do*, while *injunctive norms* are agreed-on expectations about what members of society *ought to do*. Consider the behaviour of museum visitors, for example. The pristine appearance of the typical museum, along with signs throughout the building, regularly reminds visitors not to drop litter in this setting. Virtually all museum-goers abide by this rule, making it a descriptive norm (Kallgren *et al.*, 2000; Cialdini *et al.*, 1991). Now consider the behaviour of people walking outdoors. They, too, are expected not to drop litter; but in this arena, the no-litter norm is less explicit and more often ignored. Still, it is an expectation about what people *ought* to do, so it is an injunctive norm.

People are more likely to abide by injunctive norms if the norms are called to their attention. For example, people walking through a neighbourhood with litterbins and anti-littering signs are more likely to become aware of and follow the community's injunctive anti-littering norm. In one study of this phenomenon, researchers passed out leaflets to pedestrians. Each pedestrian received a leaflet promoting the importance of not littering, the wisdom of saving electricity by turning off lights or the responsibility of each citizen to vote (Cialdini *et al.*, 1991). Only 10% of the pedestrians who had been given the anti-littering leaflet crumpled and threw the leaflet to the ground after they had finished reading it, compared with 20% of those who had been given the 'lights out' or 'voting' leaflet.

Social Roles A **social role** is a set of norms ascribed to a person's social position – expectations and duties associated with the individual's position in the family, at work, in the community and in other settings (Glass, 2005; Alexander & Wood, 2000; Sarbin & Allen, 1968). The role of police officers, for example, is to maintain law and order. The role of

> **social role** a set of norms ascribed to a person's social position; expectations and duties associated with their position in the family, at work, in the community and in other settings.

parents is to nurture, rear and teach their children and prepare them for life outside the family.

Roles often have a positive impact on people and society. Indeed, they are critical for the smooth functioning of society. They can, however, also confine people. Just as many actors complain of being typecast and prevented from demonstrating their versatility, people in various positions are often limited by their prescribed social roles. Many observers argue, for example, that traditional Western gender roles disadvantage women.

When individuals in a particular group try to step out of the social roles assigned to members of that group, they may be met with negative reactions and evaluations (Morfei *et al.*, 2004). For example, traditional Western gender roles ascribe more *communal* characteristics to women – that is, ones associated with the welfare of other people – and more *agentic* characteristics to men – that is, those associated with assertiveness, control and confidence (Mosher & Danoff-Burg, 2008, 2005; Eagly & Koenig, 2006). In short, women in the West are expected to be caring and men to be assertive and self-assured.

One arena in which these gender roles can become especially relevant is employment. Being viewed as more caring, women have often been associated with work in caring professions such as nursing. Conversely, other occupations, for example being an airline pilot, often are portrayed as primarily taken up by men (Ashcraft, 2007). Where people do not meet these gendered expectations then it can be more difficult for them to show that they meet the expectations of the occupational role. Thus, for example, men who enter nursing have often been portrayed as gay unless they are engaged in specific parts of the occupation, such as mental health nursing, that are seen as more 'macho' (Harding, 2007). Also, men who do enter the nursing profession can be seen as uninterested in providing the routine 'housework' elements of nursing care (McKinlay *et al.*, 2010). Thus, nursing commonly is still viewed as an occupation that is primarily suited to women because they are deemed to have greater caring abilities than men.

Roles and Situational Demands: The Stanford Prison Experiment

Social roles affect not only how others think about us but also how we think about ourselves and how we act towards others. In 1971, Philip Zimbardo and his colleagues at Stanford University studied the power of roles in a study famously known as *The Stanford Prison Experiment*, although it did not actually follow an experimental design (Zimbardo, 2006, 1972; Haney *et al.*, 1973). The basement of the university's psychology department was converted into a mock prison, and 24 male students were randomly assigned to play the roles of either prisoners or guards for what was supposed to be two weeks. 'Guards' were given batons, uniforms and mirrored sunglasses and were told that it was their responsibility to run the prison. 'Prisoners' wore smocks and small chains around their ankles and were referred to by assigned numbers instead of by name. To the researchers' horror, within hours the 'guards' had settled comfortably into their new roles and had begun humiliating their 'prisoner' peers. Some actually tormented the prisoners, imposed physical punishments on them and denied bathroom privileges and food to prisoners who were deemed to have transgressed the rules, even in minor ways. The study, clearly out of hand, had to be shut down after just six days.

The Stanford Prison Experiment raised many ethical concerns in the field of psychology, primarily because the participants experienced clear psychological pain: both the prisoners, who were abused psychologically, and the guards, who were confronted with the fact that they were capable of cruelty and even sadism. Many researchers have challenged the legitimacy of the study and believe that its costs outweighed its benefits. As you read in Chapter 2, there are now ethical guidelines and review procedures that all researchers must follow when conducting studies, guidelines and procedures that would make it impossible for this same study to be conducted today. That aside, the study did underscore the power and potential dangers of certain social roles.

Roles, Gender and Social Skills

HOW WE DIFFER

There is a popular belief in Western society that, on average, women are more skilled socially than men, more sensitive emotionally, more expressive and more focused on social relationships. In fact, research has supported this notion over the years (Eagly & Koenig, 2006). In a wide range of social psychology studies, it has been found, for example, that female participants tend to read nonverbal social cues more accurately than male participants, are more expressive with their faces and bodies during interactions, feel more empathy for the emotional experiences of others and act friendlier in group discussions. For their part, male participants tend to focus more narrowly on the tasks at hand in group activities than do female participants, to emerge as leaders (as opposed to social facilitators) in group activities and to adopt more authoritarian and less participative styles when they take on leadership roles.

Why do these gender differences occur in the social realm? Although researchers do not agree upon a single explanation for gender differences in such matters, one of the most common explanations points to social roles (Eagly & Wood, 2006). As we observed above, traditional Western gender roles ascribe more communal characteristics to women – including expectations that they should be friendly, unselfish, concerned about others and emotionally expressive – and more agentic characteristics to men – including expectations that they will be assertive, independent and controlling. According to social role theory, people are inclined to behave in ways that are consistent with the expectations tied to their roles. Moreover, over the course of their lives, as people enact their social roles, their skills in the assigned realm become sharper and their corresponding attitudes more deeply ingrained. Thus, the theory goes, women learn to be more interested and skilled in the social realm than men do.

Of course, as you are well aware, traditional gender roles have been undergoing considerable change in recent decades. Enormous numbers of women, for example, compete in the world of work and many men have taken on domestic and caretaking responsibilities and adopted more people-oriented attitudes and concerns. Not surprisingly, along with these changes in roles and expectations, social psychologists have been finding fewer and smaller gender differences in their studies of social skills, empathy, leadership and the like. To be sure, such differences still exist in many research undertakings, as social role theory would predict, but there is clearly a shift occurring in the social roles available to men and to women.

Obedience

As we have seen, social norms and roles exert considerable influence on how we all act. Certainly, people do not conform to norms all of the time, nor do they always fulfil roles in ways that are commonly expected. In some situations, however, we can simply be instructed perhaps by police officers or by employers how we should act. Ordinarily we will comply with instructions that we recognize as coming from someone in another social role that confers upon them authority to give instructions. By contrast, other situations and the extent to which we should comply with the instructions given by the person in authority are rather less clear. Classic work by researcher Stanley Milgram has offered important, and unsettling, insights into situations of this kind. Milgram was studying **obedience**, which occurs when people follow direct commands, usually given by an authority figure.

obedience the act of following direct commands, usually given by an authority figure.

Milgram's Experiment Milgram's (1963) study is perhaps the most famous and controversial experiment in the history of psychology (Blass, 2007, 2004). Imagine that you have agreed to participate in this experiment. You arrive at the designated location and are met by a stern-looking man in a lab coat. The man introduces you to the mild-mannered 'Mr Wallace' and explains that the two of you are participating in a study of the effects of punishment on learning. One of you will be randomly assigned the role of 'teacher'; the other, the role of 'learner'. You are then given the 'teacher' role. Although you are not aware of it, the assignment of roles has not been random at all. 'Mr Wallace' is a collaborator in league with the experimenter, who is really only interested in your behaviour.

The experimenter takes the two of you to an adjacent room, where Mr Wallace is prepared for his role as learner. He is told to roll up his right shirtsleeve, and the investigator attaches an electrode to his wrist. His arm is strapped down 'to prevent excessive movement' and electrode paste is applied 'to prevent blisters or burns'. You are informed that the electrode is connected to a shock generator in the other room (Figure 17.1).

The two of you are told that you (as the teacher) will recite a list of word pairs. After going through the entire list, you will recite only the first word of each pair, followed by four options. Mr Wallace will indicate which option is the correct match for the first word by pulling one of four levers. If the response is incorrect, you will administer an electric shock. Mr Wallace mumbles something about having a heart condition, but that comment is more or less ignored by the experimenter.

You are taken to another room, unable to see Mr Wallace, and are seated in front of a metallic, box-shaped instrument, covered with knobs and switches and labelled 'Shock Generator'. You notice that each switch on the shock generator's control panel is identified by a voltage – ranging from

FIGURE 17.1 Milgram's learner and the shock generator. Most people believe that they would not administer shocks to a person crying out in protest, but Milgram's experiment found otherwise.

Source: ©1968 by Stanley Milgram. ©renewed 1993 by Alexandra Milgram. From the film *Obedience*, distributed by Penn State Media Sales.

15 volts to 450 volts – and a label – ranging from 'slight shock'(15 volts) to 'danger: extreme shock' (375 volts) to 'XXX' (450 volts). The experimenter explains that whenever you push down a switch Mr Wallace will receive the corresponding shock, and this shock will stop as soon as you push the switch back up.

You are to communicate with Mr Wallace through a microphone intercom, as the rooms are 'partially soundproof'. When he responds by pulling one of the four levers, one of four lights on top of the shock generator will light up. You are to administer a shock to Mr Wallace whenever he responds incorrectly. With each successive incorrect response, you are to move up one switch on the shock generator, administering what the labels suggest are increasingly powerful – and dangerous – shocks.

After Mr Wallace offers his first incorrect response, you flick the switch identified as '15 volts'. The machine springs to life, with bright red lights flashing and an ominous buzzing noise filling the air. As Mr Wallace continues to offer incorrect responses, you are instructed to administer increasingly powerful shocks. Through the wall, you can hear Mr Wallace moan and say things such as 'Get me out of here!' Any time

you express reluctance to go on, the experimenter confidently states, 'Please continue' or even, 'You have no choice: you must go on.' After a while, Mr Wallace stops responding to your word prompts. The experimenter tells you to treat the failure to respond as an incorrect response and administer another shock (you are up to 450 volts, or 'XXX', by now). Mr Wallace lets out an agonized scream and yells, 'Let me out of here! I have heart problems!' You hear and feel Mr Wallace banging on the adjacent wall. Then he is completely silent. There are no further responses to your word prompts or to the shocks you administer.

As you are reading about this study, you are probably saying to yourself that you would have refused to go on with the experiment very early on. Most people who learn about this study have that reaction. Indeed, before the study became famous, its procedures were described to psychologists, and they predicted that only 1% of participants would continue with the experiment all the way through to 450 volts. Astonishingly, Milgram found that 65% of the participants continued with the experiment all the way through to the 450 volts label, and no participant stopped before the 300 volt mark (Figure 17.2).

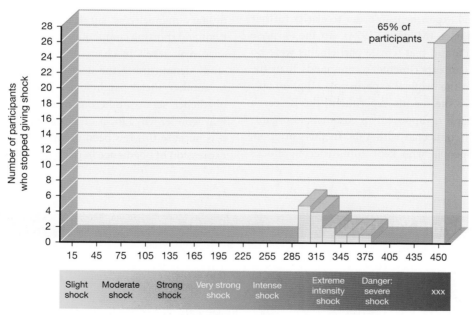

Voltage levels labelled on Milgram's shock generator

FIGURE 17.2 The results of Milgram's obedience experiment. Milgram found that no participant stopped administering shocks before the 300 volt mark and that the majority (65%) continued administering shocks to the highest level.

Source: Based on Milgram, S. (1963). Behavioural study of obedience. *Journal of Abnormal and Social Psychology, 67*, 371–378 and Weiten, W. (2007). *Psychology: Themes and variations* (7th edn). Belmont, CA: Wadsworth Figure 16-17, p. 658.

The Milgram Controversy It is no wonder that Milgram's study is one of psychology's most controversial. The study revealed something profoundly disturbing about human nature, namely that we are inclined to obey authority, even if it means betraying our own personal morality. Milgram demonstrated that it is not just a cruel and sadistic fringe of the population that can inflict pain and suffering on innocent victims; two-thirds of the population would hurt others if ordered to do so by an authority figure. Milgram (1974) went on to explain the atrocities committed by Nazi Germany within the context of his remarkable findings, although a number of theorists have questioned the appropriateness of such a leap (Miller, 2004).

Initially, many refused to believe that Milgram's findings provided an accurate representation of people's readiness to inflict suffering. Critics attacked the experiment on various grounds. Most notably, the participants in the original study were all male. Some speculated that women may be less inclined to obey commands to inflict pain on others. Additionally, a number pointed out that the study had been conducted at Yale University. Had it been carried out at a less prestigious locale, they argued, the participants may have been less likely to obey the experimenter's commands. Finally, many questioned the ethical implications of the research.

Follow-Up Studies Milgram spent the years following the publication of his controversial findings conducting variations of the original experiment in order to clarify further the nature of obedience (Milgram, 1974). To the surprise of many people, he found that female participants were no more likely to defy an experimenter's commands than the male participants in the original experiment. Milgram also set up an alternative site for his experiment, the Research Associates of Bridgeport, supposedly a commercial organization that was not connected with Yale. In this variation, the percentage of people who kept administering shocks through to 450 volts was somewhat lower than in the original experiment, but still considerable – around 50%, compared with the original 65%.

Milgram's experiments and subsequent replications demonstrated just how ready people are to obey authority, but they also clarified that certain factors *reduce* people's willingness to obey (Lüttke, 2004):

- If a confederate served as 'co-teacher' with the research participant and refused to continue, over 90% of the real participants followed suit and disobeyed as well.

- The *salience* of a victim's suffering – its obviousness – affects participants' obedience. Participants in Milgram's studies were, for example, less likely to obey when they could see the look on Mr Wallace's face with each successive shock.

- A participant's *proximity* to the victim affects obedience. When Milgram's participants were seated in the room with Mr Wallace, only about 40% of them continued to obey through 450 volts. Still less (30%) were obedient in a condition that had them placing Mr Wallace's hand on a shock plate to administer the shock.

Of course, there are many occasions in life where it is quite useful and even advantageous to obey commands. During military manoeuvres, surgical procedures, theatre productions and sporting competitions, for example, a lack of obedience may result in chaos or disaster. However, Milgram's study demonstrates the dark side of obedience. In a letter to another social psychologist, Milgram wrote, 'Certainly, obedience serves numerous productive functions, and you may wonder why I focus on its destructive potential. Perhaps it is because this has been the most striking and disturbing expression of obedience in our time' (Blass, 2004).

Before You Go On

What Do You Know?

1. What are norms and what is their function in society?
2. How do norms relate to social roles?
3. How does obedience occur in laboratory settings and what effects does the presence of others have on a person's willingness to obey?

What Do You Think?

Zimbardo's and Milgram's experiments have both been criticized on grounds of having insufficient ethical safeguards to ensure the safety and well-being of the participants. Do you think that such criticisms are fair or unfair? How would you attempt to ensure that any repeat of either study addressed the ethical concerns that have been expressed?

Intragroup Processes

LEARNING OBJECTIVE 2
Review major concepts in the areas of intragroup processes.

> **group** a collection of people in which the members are aware of and influence one another and share a common identity.

A **group** is a collection of people in which the members are aware of and influence one another and share a common identity. Group members are thus *interdependent*: that is, the behaviour of one group member affects the behaviour of the other members. Groups, of course, are commonly defined in relation to other groups; for instance, we can think of sets of social groups such as men and women, parents and children, and lecturers and students.

Group Dynamics

In order to begin our examination of what happens in social groups, we turn first to the psychological processes that are understood to occur within particular groups, namely, **intra-**

> **intragroup processes** psychological processes that occur within groups.

group processes. Let us start by considering several topics related to groups and the processes that are found within groups: *group productivity*, the *social facilitation, social loafing, group polarization* and *groupthink*.

Group Productivity One issue of interest to social psychologists is what makes groups productive. Not surprisingly, they have found that the optimal group size for productivity depends on the task at hand (Steiner, 1972).

- When a group confronts an *additive task*, its members must perform parallel actions. For example, to clear a property of snow after a storm, all members of a work crew must shovel snow. For such tasks, group productivity increases directly with group size.

- In contrast, a group faced with a *conjunctive task* is only as productive as its weakest member. If, for example, group members are hiking together up a mountain, they can travel only as fast as the slowest person in the group. In this situation, a greater number of group members does not necessarily yield better performance.

- A *disjunctive task* requires a single solution. In such undertakings, the most competent person in the group is likely to provide the solution. Larger groups are typically more productive for disjunctive tasks, because a larger group is more likely to have a superstar member who can solve the problem at hand.

- *Divisible tasks* involve the simultaneous performance of several different activities. When groups confront such tasks, no single person works on all phases of the undertaking; thus, the different strengths of group members complement one another. For divisible tasks, larger groups tend to be more productive.

Social Facilitation In many instances, our performance is enhanced when we are in the presence of others. This is one of the oldest observations in social psychology. In the late 1890s, psychologist Norman Triplett noted that cyclists tend to go faster when in the presence of other cyclists than when alone, even when they are not in competition with one another. To test his hypothesis that the presence of others can enhance individual performance, Triplett (1898) conducted an experiment in which he had children wind a fishing reel either all alone or side-by-side with other children. Triplett found that children winding side-by-side worked substantially quicker than children winding by themselves. This phenomenon was later labelled **social facilitation** and its study was expanded to include not just physical tasks but also mental tasks (such as solving puzzles and doing mathematical problems).

> **social facilitation** an effect in which the presence of others enhances performance.

As social facilitation has been studied over the years, researchers have learnt that people's performance in the presence of others is more complicated than Triplett first believed. In fact, for some tasks, and for some people, performing in the presence of others can impair, rather than enhance, performance (Uziel, 2007; Strauss, 2002; Aiello & Douthitt, 2001). Trying to make sense of these contradictory findings,

Improving each other's performance. Without realizing it, these two friends probably run faster when they jog together than when they jog alone – the result of social facilitation.

Source: Rolf Bruderer/Blend Images/Getty Images, Inc.

psychologist Robert Zajonc (1965) proposes that the presence of others elevates our arousal level, which in turn facilitates performance on simple, well-learnt tasks but interferes with performance on complicated tasks. Zajonc's theory has received support from numerous studies and observations of both humans and animals (Bargh, 2001; Platania & Moran, 2001; Zentall & Levine, 1972).

In recent years, theorists have focused less on the mere presence of others and more on individuals' *interpretations* of and *reactions* to the presence of others (Aiello & Douthitt, 2001; Bond, 2000). If, for example, individuals do not like or trust other people in their group, their own contributions to a group project may suffer. In addition, if people believe that other group members are disregarding their ideas or efforts, their own performance in the group may decline (Fiske, 2010; Paulus *et al.*, 2002, 1993).

Social Loafing

Groups are often formed in hopes that an interconnected body of people can energize and motivate every individual member. However, these hopes are not always realized. How many times when working in a group have you noticed that one or two of the group members are not pulling their weight? **Social loafing**, also known as *free riding*, refers to the phenomenon in which people exert less effort on a collective task than they would on a comparable individual task (Liden *et al.*, 2004; Latané *et al.*, 1979).

> **social loafing** a phenomenon in which people exert less effort on a collective task than they would on a comparable individual task; also known as free riding.

Social loafing seems to rear its ugly head most in large groups (Liden *et al.*, 2004). It is most likely to occur when certain group members lack motivation to contribute, feel isolated from the group, calculate the cost of contributing as too high or view their own contributions as unnecessary (Chidambaram & Tung, 2005; Shepperd, 1995, 1993). Research suggests that people from Western cultures are more inclined to display social loafing than people from Eastern cultures, and men are more likely to do so than women (Fiske, 2004).

Fortunately, social loafing can be minimized. When, for example, groups are highly *cohesive* – when group members all desire and value membership in the group – the social loafing phenomenon all but disappears (Hoigaard *et al.*, 2006; Liden *et al.*, 2004). Additionally, social loafing is reduced when group members are each explicitly reminded of their uniqueness and importance (Asmus & James, 2005), when they are given specific and challenging goals (Ling *et al.*, 2005), when the output of each member is publicly identified (Williams *et al.*, 1981) and when the members are given clear norms and comparison standards for their work (Hoigaard *et al.*, 2006; Paulus *et al.*, 2002). Finally, alertness tends to decrease social loafing, whereas fatigue tends to increase it (Hoeksema-van Orden *et al.*, 1998).

Group Polarization

Have you ever begun talking about one of your favourite bands with a bunch of friends with similar musical tastes and found yourself liking the band even more by the end of the conversation? When an initial tendency of individual group members is intensified following group discussion, **group polarization** occurs (Abrams *et al.*, 2001; Isenberg, 1986). This phenomenon is not simply an example of conformity. With group polarization, the attitudes and inclinations of the individual group members are already in place, and they become more intense and more extreme as a result of the group interaction (Cooper *et al.*, 2004).

> **group polarization** the intensification of an initial tendency of individual group members brought about by group discussion.

Group polarization has been studied most often with regard to racial and ethnic bias and social and political attitudes (Prislin & Wood, 2005; Billings *et al.*, 2000). When, for example, researchers have placed individuals with highly prejudiced attitudes in a group to discuss racial issues, the attitudes of the individuals tend to become still more prejudiced (Myers & Bishop, 1970). In similar work, it has been found that the attitudes of women with moderate leanings towards feminism become more strongly feminist following group discussions (Myers, 1975).

Groupthink

OUT OF THE **ORDINARY** Groups often come together to solve specific problems and make decisions. We noted earlier that group cohesiveness can prevent social loafing, but sometimes groups can become *too* cohesive and single-minded, and the group's decision making can lead to disaster. A classic example occurred in the early 1960s, when the United States government was determined to overthrow the communist government that Fidel Castro had instituted in Cuba. The US government had trained a small group of Cuban exiles as part of a military operation to overthrow Castro. Proponents of the plan predicted that once this small militia touched down in Cuba at the Bay of Pigs, the Cuban citizens would rise up and join them. Instead, the operation collapsed, with no support from the Cuban people and no further help from the US government. As a result of the failed invasion, anti-American sentiment around the globe increased, as did Castro's influence in Latin America and Cuba's ties with the Soviet Union.

> **groupthink** a form of faulty group decision making that occurs when group members strive for unanimity and this goal overrides their motivation to realistically appraise alternative courses of action.

Psychologist Irving Janis (1972), after examining the flawed decision-making process that went into the Bay of Pigs invasion, attributed the fiasco to **groupthink**, which he defined as a form of

A consequence of groupthink? In 2003, the space shuttle *Columbia* disintegrated during re-entry over Texas, killing all seven crew members. Just two days before the disaster, a NASA engineer had warned his supervisors of possible catastrophes on re-entry, but his message was not passed up the chain of command. How may groupthink have been involved in this mishandling of the warning?
Source: NASA/©AP/Wide World Photos.

faulty group decision-making that occurs when group members strive too hard for unanimity. The goal of achieving a consensus among all group members overrides the need to realistically appraise alternative courses of action. Clearly, groupthink can have undesired consequences (Henningsen *et al.*, 2006; Baron, 2005; Whyte, 2000).

Janis identified a number of conditions that set the stage for groupthink:

- strong similarity in group members' backgrounds and ideologies

- high group cohesiveness

- high perceived threat

- elevated stress

- insulation from outside influence

- a directive leader.

Group members experience an illusion of invulnerability and have an unquestioned belief in the group's inherent morality. Typically, group members exert direct pressure against any member who expresses strong disagreement, and members protect the group from information that may shatter the shared conviction that their decisions are effective and moral (Janis, 1982).

For example, the decision to invade Iraq in 2003 taken by the US government and supported by the UK government has since been heavily criticized on a number of grounds. Ostensibly, this invasion was undertaken in order to neutralize the threat posed by a state ruled by an authoritarian dictator (Saddam Hussein) to Western societies and Middle-Eastern neighbours through its possession of weapons of mass destruction. Following the invasion, however, exhaustive searches conducted in Iraq failed to locate any such weapons. This failure, and the consequent lack of authority for the invasion mission, has been attributed to poor intelligence provision in the period preceding the war. Dina Badie (2010), however, argues that the decision to invade Iraq can instead be understood as an instance of groupthink, in which the leaders responsible for US decision making incorrectly persuaded themselves as a group that weapons were present where none existed. Over the period before the invasion, the group's changing perceptions of the potential threat posed by Iraq and by Saddam Hussein, their reliance on ambiguous and unreliable evidence and an unwillingness to consider other possibilities led to an ultimately flawed decision.

PSYCHOLOGY AROUND US   Space Disasters and Groupthink

On the morning of January 28, 1986, the space shuttle Challenger blasted off from the Kennedy Space Center in Florida. Seventy-three seconds after lift-off, the Challenger exploded, killing all seven astronauts on board . . . Following the explosion . . . information came to light about the faulty decision-making processes . . . that [had] led to the decision to launch. Some engineers had expressed concerns about the design of the O-ring seal in the solid-fuel rocket, which could allow hot gases to leak through the joint and thereby spark an explosion. However . . . these concerns were ignored . . .

'Unfortunately little was learned from this tragic accident because many of these same errors contributed to the loss of the Columbia space shuttle, and its seven astronauts, on February 1, 2003 [the shuttle was trying to return to earth after a 16-day mission in space]. Research now shows that prior to the Columbia disaster, some NASA engineers had grave concern about the shuttle's ability to return to earth following some tile damage it [had] experienced on lift-off. On January 28, just days before the Columbia tragedy, a landing gear specialist at NASA sent an email expressing his concerns about the tile damage . . . However, high-level NASA administrators viewed the damage to the shuttle as minor – not a serious threat – and refused to respond.

(Sanderson, 2010)

Having identified the phenomenon of groupthink, Janis went on to propose measures that a group can take to safeguard against it. First, the leader of the group should encourage members to air objections and doubts and should accept criticisms of the group's judgements. Additionally, various group members should be assigned the role of devil's advocate, arguing against the group's favoured position. Finally, outside experts should be invited to group meetings and encouraged to challenge the group's core views and decisions.

Research conducted since Janis first proposed his theory suggests that groupthink is a complicated phenomenon, probably more complicated than Janis initially realized. The conditions that he believed set the stage for groupthink do not always result in unwarranted unanimity (Baron, 2005). Nor do his proposed safeguards always prevent groupthink. At the same time, research and observations clearly indicate that the phenomenon of groupthink is widespread. Not only does it often affect decision making in important policy-setting groups, as Janis recognized, but it also influences decision making in mundane and temporary groups and groups working on trivial matters (Baron, 2005; Eaton, 2001; Whyte, 2000).

Majority Influence in Groups

conformity the tendency to yield to social pressure.

Conformity is the tendency to yield to real or imagined group pressure. Over the course of many decades, numerous findings derived from real-life situations have demonstrated that in group settings people will often act in ways that are consistent with the actions of the group rather than maintaining an individual position that diverges from that of the group. For example, in an early study of political views at a US college, Newcomb (1943) found that over the course of their studies students' initial conservative views became superseded by the politically liberal views that prevailed among staff and students within the college. Moreover, these acquired liberal views endured well into late adulthood, confirmed by interviews conducted 25 and 50 years later (Alwin et al., 1991; Newcomb et al., 1967).

The question that arises is why would people in group contexts give up a personal viewpoint and understanding and instead conform with one that agrees with other members of the group? One well-known model of how and why this happens (Deutsch & Gerard, 1955) suggests that, within a social group, members of the group experience two sorts of influence that arise from belonging to the group. A first form of influence is **informational influence**. Informational influence arises where group members are uncertain

informational influence the influence based on information about the reality of a situation that provides a basis for making a judgement.

about the reality of a situation facing the group and look to others to provide accurate information that can provide a basis for making a judgement. The second form of influence is **normative influence**. Normative influence reflects not uncertainty about available information but rather individual members' need to achieve harmony or social approval from other people. Two sets of classic social psychology studies respectively demonstrate these processes of informational influence and normative influence at work.

normative influence the influence based upon a need for harmony or social approval.

Informational Social Influence You may be aware from your own experience of gazing at a bright star in a night sky that, if you gaze for long enough, the star will appear to move. The star, however, is stationary, at least so far as discernible to the naked eye, and the appearance of movement is merely an optical illusion. This effect, whereby in the absence of any reference point a stationary point of light appears to move, is known as the **autokinetic effect**. While long known to astronomers, the autokinetic effect provided the basis for a series of classic group studies conducted by Muzafer Sherif (1935, 1936).

autokinetic effect the illusion of a stationary point of light moving against a dark background.

What Sherif did was to place his participants in a completely darkened room with a single point of light situated at a distance of approximately five metres. The point of light remained stationary throughout but to the participants, who were unaware of the autokinetic effect, the light appeared to move. The participants were required to provide verbal estimates of how far the light travelled. One half of the participants first took part in individual trials, giving their own estimates, before repeating the process later in groups comprising three people. In this condition, participants who previously had provided widely divergent estimates of movement quickly agreed upon group estimates of the distance involved. The other half of the participants took part first in group trials, agreeing group estimates of distance, and thereafter underwent individual trials involving the same procedure. In these cases, participants continued to provide estimates that reflected the previously agreed group estimate.

These findings certainly demonstrated how **group norms** can emerge within groups. Group norms are rules established within groups themselves as to how members should act. There are, however, two other aspects of these findings that are of interest here. First, in such circumstances of uncertainty, there does not seem to be any need for moderation in an agreed group norm. In several studies, Sherif placed within the groups individuals who had been instructed to provide estimates of

group norms rules established within groups as to how members should act.

distance that suggested extreme movement. These individual estimates, regardless of being extreme, came to influence the group estimate that was subsequently agreed. Second, once established, group norms endured for considerable periods. A subsequent study (Jacobs & Campbell, 1961) found that agreed group norms of distance would continue long after members of an initial group were replaced by new members. Indeed, norms that were established in the early stages of a group continued even to the point when no members of the original group remained and all members had been replaced several times. Established group norms therefore, regardless of their accuracy or inaccuracy, can exert a powerful informational influence over existing group members and over any others who thereafter join the group.

Normative Social Influence Imagine that you agree to participate in a psychology experiment on *perceptual judgements*. You and six other participants are seated around a table – you are seated second from the end – and the experimenter presents two cards to the group. The card on the left, Card A, displays a single vertical line, whereas the card on the right, Card B, displays three vertical lines of various lengths (Figure 17.3). The experimenter asks each participant which of the three lines on Card B is equal in length to the line on Card A. When it is your turn, you immediately recognize that the second line on Card B matches the one on Card A. Thus, after the five participants seated ahead of you indicate that the second line on Card B is equal in length to the line on Card A, you do the same. Another set of cards is presented, and again everyone agrees. The straightforward task is moving along easily and comfortably.

Then something odd happens. On the third round, you again readily note which line on Card B matches the line on Card A – it is pretty clear that it is line 3 this time – but you are shocked to hear that the first person called upon by the

experimenter answers, 'Line 1.' You think to yourself 'He/she needs an eye test,' but then the second person responds the same as the first. You rub your eyes, blink and squint, but still you see that it is line 3 that matches the length of the line on Card A. After the five people ahead of you have all selected line 1, it is your turn to respond. What will you say?

In fact, this study, conducted by Asch (1955), was not about perceptual judgements at all but rather was an investigation of conformity. In the study, the other 'participants' were actually confederates, coached by the experimenter to give uniformly wrong answers on the third round and thereafter. Asch found that when the responses of the confederates were incorrect, as much as 75% of the real participants conformed to the group norm and gave an incorrect response.

Asch also varied the procedures in his experiment to reveal what group features might affect this 'tyranny of the majority' (Martin & Hewstone, 2001), and others have followed with similar work. One key factor is *group unanimity*. The presence of even one dissenting group member dramatically reduces the likelihood that participants will conform to an incorrect group norm (Prislin & Wood, 2005). The *size of* the group also affects its influence. Groups with fewer than four members, for example, do not seem to bring about a powerful conformity effect (Figure 17.4). Many laboratory studies on conformity have been conducted since Asch's pioneering undertaking (Abrams *et al.*, 2005, 2000). The findings of most such studies are similar to Asch's: they demonstrate the strong effects of social pressure.

Conformity and Culture  HOW WE DIFFER

Conformity is viewed very differently in individualistic and collectivistic cultures (Markus & Kitayama, 1994). People in individualistic cultures often consider conformity to be a bad thing. Typically, members of this kind of culture want to stand out and be different, to have their own identity. In contrast, those in collectivistic cultures usually value fitting in with other people. They see virtue in conforming to social norms and view conformity as an indication of maturity, respect for others and appropriate self-control. In fact, the Korean word for *conformity* means 'inner strength and maturity' (Kim & Markus, 1999).

When ordering food in a restaurant, people in the United States, an individualistic society, order whatever they desire (Kim & Markus, 1999). They may say, for example, 'I will have a Caesar salad, but light on the croutons and with the dressing on the side.' However, in Korea, a collectivistic culture, that kind of restaurant etiquette is unthinkable. It would be seen as an inability to get along with others and an insensitivity to the needs of the waiter. Thus, as you might expect, whenever Asch-like studies are conducted in collectivistic cultures, the

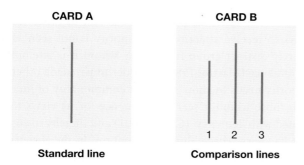

FIGURE 17.3 The perceptual judgement task in Asch's conformity study. Asch's participants were asked which line (1, 2 or 3) was the same length as the standard line. Despite the obvious and correct choice (line 2), when confederates gave the wrong answer, almost 75% of the participants conformed and gave the wrong answer too.

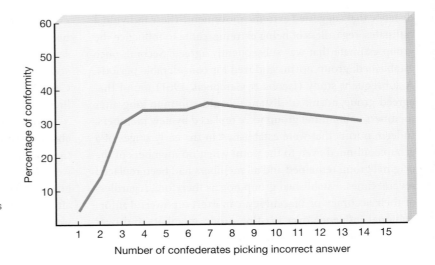

FIGURE 17.4 Group size and conformity. A key factor in conformity is group size. Asch found that the conformity effect is not strong when a group has fewer than four members.

Source: Adapted from Asch, S.E. (1955). Opinions and social pressure. *Scientific American, 193*(5), 31–35. © 1955 by Scientific American, Inc. All rights reserved. Reproduced with permission.

participants show even higher rates of conformity than do participants in the United States (Bond & Smith, 1996).

Minority Influence in Groups

Although majority views and the influence that they exert on minority members can be very powerful, these are not the only forces operating in group contexts. Even in the Asch experiments, a number of participants in each case held out against the (incorrect) majority view and thereby resisted the normative influence of the majority of group members. In some cases, members of a minority within a group can go further than simply resisting majority influence and can instead attempt to sway other members in their direction. The 1957 film *Twelve Angry Men*, directed by Sidney Lumet and starring Henry Fonda, shows one dissenting member of a jury questioning the verdict agreed upon by all other members and steadily winning each of them over in turn to agree finally upon the opposite verdict. This phenomenon, the ways in which minorities can influence group decisions, was investigated in a series of studies conducted by Serge Moscovici and colleagues.

The Moscovici Studies In these studies, often termed the *blue–green* studies, Moscovici and colleagues (Moscovici & Lage, 1976; Moscovici *et al.*, 1969) used a modified version of the Asch experimental design. Here, each group consisted of six participants, of whom four were naive participants and two were confederates of the experimenter. The task was a colour perception one in which group members simply had to state the colour of a slide that was presented to them. All slides were actually blue, although the intensity of the colour varied from slide to slide. Sometimes the two confederates would call all slides 'green', and sometimes they would call some slides 'green' and others 'blue' in accordance with their instructions from the experimenter. Moscovici found that where the confederates were consistent in their (incorrect) responses, calling all slides 'green', they managed to influence many of the responses from the other four group members who would also call some slides 'green'. Although the rate of incorrect responses from the majority group members was not as high as found in the Asch experiments, the results showed that consistent minority views can indeed influence majority opinion within the group.

Now, of course, minority opinion does not always sway the majority, even when a minority expresses its views consistently. Throughout society, there are many minorities who are unlikely to exert much influence over others and whose views are often ignored, trivialized or even ridiculed. What seems to matter here is that in order for its views to receive attention the minority is not seen as an entirely distinct group from those whom it is attempting to influence (Martin, 1988). In order to persuade others, a minority needs to show sufficient commonality of interest with those whom it seeks to influence for its views to be treated with 'leniency' (Crano, 2001) and thereby to ensure that its views receive due consideration. In the absence of any common interest or credentials, a minority may, instead of being listened to, be treated as a different and competing group. Should that situation arise, any likelihood of minority influence would be gone and the psychological outcome would instead reflect intergroup processes (considered below).

Before You Go On

What Do You Know?

4. Is the presence of others in a group likely to enhance people's contribution to tasks or lead to reduced performance?

5. What processes lead to groups reaching polarized decisions or arriving at flawed decisions through groupthink?

6. What are processes of informational influence and normative influence, and how do they result in individual group members conforming to emerging group norms?

7. What influence can a minority exert on other group members and when is this most likely to be effective?

What Do You Think?

Consider the discussions of a group to which you belong, perhaps a group of students engaged in the preparation of a presentation that is to be assessed. Are you most likely to conform to the majority views expressed within the group or will you attempt to persuade others round to your own views of how to proceed? What does this tell you about how processes affecting contributions, influence and persuasion work in such contexts?

Intergroup Relations

LEARNING OBJECTIVE 3

Describe how the processes involved in belonging to social groups work to create our social identities and how these social identities are linked to psychological well-being and intergroup contexts.

If we return to consider the Occupy London protest at St Paul's, it is immediately obvious that the circumstances leading to the protest and surrounding it involved a diverse range of different social groups with widely varying interests and concerns. The protesters who assembled there initially defined themselves as being in opposition to corporate entities and other social groups, and in opposition also to the UK government and its economic policies. As the protest continued, the context drew in also clergy, local business people, local residents and other groups who did not share wholly or even partly the aims of the protesters. For social psychologists interested in studying how these groups and their members related to each other, the topic turns from examination of processes occurring within any or all of these groups to that of how they act in relation to each other as groups and the psychological consequences for their members.

We have already seen above how processes that occur in group contexts have far-reaching effects for the members of those groups. As well, however, as influencing people within groups, setting up a context where groups with different identities and different interests come together equally makes for powerful psychological consequences. In circumstances such as those at St Paul's, it is evident even from an initial glance that the goals of the groups involved cannot all be fully met. For example, for the protesters to have achieved their aims, members of other groups would have had to have changed their actions, and they were unlikely to do so. We therefore have to look not just to what may be happening within groups for their members but also at **intergroup relations**, the relations between different social groups and their respective members. The intergroup context at St Paul's is one of competition, if not outright confrontation. What this means is that prejudice or discrimination occurring in contexts involving the interests of different groups is likely to reflect group concerns rather than negative individual dispositions or attitudes: the actions of members will favour the in-group *as a group* over the out-group *as a group*.

> **intergroup relations** the relations between different social groups and their respective members.

Realistic Group Conflict Theory

Realistic group conflict theory argues that the amount of prejudice or discrimination found to exist between particular in-groups and out-groups and their members will reflect the amount of actual or perceived conflict occurring between these groups. Thus, the greater the incompatibility of the aims of different groups in an intergroup setting, the higher will be the level of prejudice between them. In a series of studies known as the *summer camp experiments*, or the *Robbers' Cave studies*, Muzafer Sherif (1966) examined the processes involved when groups come together in competitive and non-competitive settings. The participants in

> **realistic group conflict theory** the argument that intergroup conflict reflects actual or perceived competition between in-groups and out-groups.

these studies were white middle-class American boys, all aged around 12 years old with no history of psychological difficulties and who did not previously know each other. Typically, Sherif's studies involved four phases. In phase 1, the boys could freely interact with each other and form friendships of their own choosing. Phase 2 comprised *group formation*, in which the boys were divided into two groups. These groups were devised so as to cut across any friendships that may have been formed up to that point and involved each group separately from the other participating in various sporting and other activities that served to strengthen the identities of the newly formed groups. Following this period of group formation, the third phase comprised *intergroup competition*, in which the two groups came together and engaged in a range of direct contests. Members of the winning team each received prizes such as penknives (highly attractive to 12-year-old boys!), with the winning team being awarded a trophy. By contrast, the losing group and its members received nothing. Thus, the contests were set up to ensure that only one group could be successful and receive these rewards. Unsurprisingly, these contests led to intense competition between the two groups, both in the contests themselves and in the relations between members of opposing teams generally. For instance, encounters between members of different teams were marked by abusive and derogatory name-calling, posters that threatened the other team and the collection of supplies of apples that could be used as ammunition against the other team. In order to end the escalating intergroup hostility, Sherif then introduced a fourth phase of *intergroup cooperation*, involving superordinate goals that required all members of both groups to work together instead of competing. For example, in one study the camp truck that was to be used on a day trip 'broke down' and had to be rescued by all boys pulling together to get it back on the road. Only after several such tasks did the hostilities finally cease. Thus, contact between the two groups in itself did not resolve the conflict between them, but the need for interdependence allowed for the creation of a new group identity that involved cooperation in place of previous competition and intergroup conflict.

Social Identity Theory

Actual or perceived competition, then, appears to provide a basis for conflict between groups. Other researchers, however, have argued that competition is not necessary for differences to exist between groups, and that membership of a group in itself produces psychological consequences for its members. The most influential research conducted within this approach is **social identity theory**, deriving from the work of Henri Tajfel

social identity theory the theory that our social identities arise from the social groups to which we belong.

and colleagues (e.g. Tajfel & Turner, 1986; Tajfel, 1978; Tajfel *et al.*, 1971). The basic argument of social identity theory is that, for each of us, our sense of who we are in social terms actually comes from the social groups to which we belong. We can identify ourselves therefore as students, teachers, family members, nationals of particular countries or otherwise, in terms of how we make sense of who we are by virtue of belonging to groups such as these. Although we may view ourselves at times as unique individuals, much of our social lives is bound up with the social identities that we take up from our own in-group memberships and in relation to out-groups to which we do not belong.

The origins of social identity theory are to be found in a set of studies using what became known as the **minimal group paradigm** (Billig & Tajfel, 1973; Tajfel *et al.*, 1971). In studies using the minimal group paradigm, participants were allocated to a group entirely arbitrarily and not on any meaningful basis. For example, in one study participants were asked to state a preference for the abstract paintings of one of two artists (Klee or Kandinsky) and were then told that they belonged to the Klee group or the Kandinsky group. Subsequently, however, they did not meet any other member of either group. The experimental task assigned to them was to allocate rewards or points to sets of other participants (in-group and out-group), but not to themselves, by means of a **rewards allocation matrix**. We can think of such a matrix as a set of different possibilities for allocating rewards from which an individual must choose one option. The matrices provided contained a number of columns that allowed for a range of strategies in the allocation of rewards. One column could be used to maximize the joint profit of in-group and out-group members while giving higher rewards to the out-group member. Other possibilities were designed to provide broadly equitable outcomes. A further column offered lower rewards for both in-group and out-group members but gave the relative advantage to the in-group member.

minimal group paradigm allocation of individuals to groups that have little meaning and whose members do not meet each other.

rewards allocation matrix a set of different possibilities for allocating rewards from which an individual must choose one option.

From this range of reward possibilities, which one was the participant most likely to choose, bearing in mind that he or she gained no personal advantage and had not met any other experimental participant? You may consider the most obvious choice to be one that took advantage of the maximum rewards available or, alternatively, one that appeared most fair to all involved. Perhaps surprisingly, however, neither of these options was most attractive to the participants. Commonly, in contrast to such possibilities, the participants adopted a strategy that maximized the difference between the two group members in favour of the in-group member, even when this allocation resulted in both individuals receiving less by way of reward than could have been gained otherwise. Regardless of the minimal nature of the groups, and their lack of any contact with any other in-group and out-group members, the participants sought as far as possible to boost the relative standing of the group to which they had been randomly assigned.

Now you may think that taking up an identity in terms of social relations with other students, fellow family members or in terms of particular nationalities is one thing, but identifying yourself meaningfully as a member of a group that prefers one abstract painting or which was worked out on the toss of a coin (as happened in one study) is quite another. After all, interactions with colleagues, exchanges in families in which we are related to others or identifying ourselves in terms of nationalities that are historically and geographically defined all provide meanings that are likely to endure. The results of the minimal group studies, however, suggest that this level of meaning is not necessary for social identities to become relevant. Thus, as soon as we become a member of any social group, we in appropriate circumstances will view ourselves as members of that group and act in ways that promote the interests of that group.

The findings from the minimal group studies led Tajfel and his colleagues over time to develop their theory into what became social identity theory (Tajfel & Turner, 1979). According to social identity theory, the taking up of any social identity involves three different processes. These three processes are:

- *Social categorization.* A process that divides the social world into categories or groups on the basis of perceived features such as gender, race or nationality.

- *Social identification.* The process by which an individual identifies him- or herself as belonging to a particular perceived social group.

- *Social comparison.* A process in which the individual compares the group with which he or she has identified him- or herself with other social groups.

We should note, however, that the social identity which is acquired through these processes is not simply a description of where the individual stands within a set of social relations. Social identities are highly important parts of the self because, for each of us, they make up in large part how we see ourselves in social life. For example, social identity is closely linked to self-esteem and positive well-being. If we feel that we belong to highly prized groups, then we are more likely to feel good about ourselves than if we consider ourselves to be members of groups that are socially undervalued and disadvantaged. For such reasons, in comparing the groups to which we belong with other groups, we always seek to maximize the position of the in-group and minimize that of the out-group in order to achieve favourable comparisons. Therefore, even in situations where the available groups may appear rather meaningless, as in the minimal group studies, it becomes important for members to maximize the standing of the in-group relative to the out-group. Identity is not a trivial matter, and identity is bound up with the outcomes of any intergroup context.

Social Identities in Action

Social identity theory offers us a far-reaching perspective for understanding both ourselves and the social worlds in which we live: we experience the social identities that we develop through our memberships of different groups as no less real or basic than our sense of being unique individuals and independent selves (Turner *et al.*, 1987). Let us return, once more, to considering the events at the Occupy London protest in the grounds of St Paul's Cathedral. Applying social identity theory allows us to see how what may have begun as an assembly of individual demonstrators quickly turned into an intergroup context. As individual demonstrators met up with other demonstrators, the developing situation involved a group of protesters and allowed all involved to take up a common social identity. The emerging identity came to be defined through the relationship of this in-group to relevant out-groups. The protesters' views of relevant out-groups were immediately apparent as, indeed, the grounds for the protest were their negative evaluations of the actions of the UK government in introducing austerity measures and those of the corporate realm in promoting individual greed and social inequality. In contrast to the actions of those groups, the protesters defined themselves as morally virtuous in arguing for actions to address perceived inequalities. All such elements make for social identities that can be positively valued and so promote the identities of the protesters.

In addition, as Reicher and Drury (e.g. Drury & Reicher, 2000, 1999; Reicher, 1997) point out, the social identities that we have are neither fixed nor static but instead are always in flux as the social contexts around us change. Take, for example, the social identity of being a student. What it means to be a student is likely to differ markedly as you progress through your studies. Starting off a three- or four-year course, meeting for the first time others who are doing the same and encountering students in other years, lecturers and other university staff will give rise to an initial identity of student that is likely to change as other groups become more familiar and are refined in accordance with experiences gained over time. This example illustrates how groups define and redefine their identities in response to the actions, actual or perceived, of the other groups that are relevant to them.

Crowds

One further point that we should note here is that, in terms of social identity theory, the size of any particular social group makes little difference to the social psychological processes involved. Whereas, as in the case of the original minimal group studies, the size of the group could be small or even imagined(!), social identity theory in principle is equally applicable to understanding large-scale social groups and social actions. Thus, the theory offers explanations for the behaviour of crowds, how crowds and members make sense of themselves and their actions in relation to other people and how those identities and that of the crowd and all its members can change over time. In the case of the protest at St Paul's, what it meant to be a protester would change over time in response to the actions of members of the cathedral's clergy, the City of London Corporation and the police who were attempting to end the protest or to move on the protesters. These groups similarly could define themselves and what they were doing in a changing situation and provide their own evaluations of the actions of the protesters and of how their identities were made out in relation to them. Members of the police force who attempted to control or end the demonstration were somewhat unlikely to define the relevant groups and ongoing intergroup actions in ways similar to the protesters; nonetheless, all involved could identify themselves in ways that valued their own parts highly and that enhanced their sense of self-esteem and psychological well-being.

Before You Go On

What Do You Know?

8. How does actual or perceived competition between groups lead to intergroup conflict, and how can this be resolved?

9. What processes result simply from belonging to social groups, meaningful or not, and how do these produce social identities for each of us?

10. How do members of groups compare themselves with members of other groups and how do such comparisons change over the course of social protests?

11. What are the psychological consequences of social identities?

What Do You Think?

Think about one large-scale social action, such as the Occupy London protest, that has been widely reported in the media. How easily can you identify the different social groups involved? May the media comprise one or more social groups that have an involvement in the actions, and, if so, how will that affect the social identities of all involved?

Language and Social Groups

LEARNING OBJECTIVE 4

Describe approaches to studying language in social life and the effects of communication and discourse for understanding social groups, identities and other social psychological topics.

So far in this chapter, and in the previous chapter, we have examined a wide range of explanations for how people act in the presence of others, be it actual, imagined or implied. There is, however, one recurring feature of social life that we have not as yet considered in any detail: language. Language, in its many forms, is an ever-present aspect of our lives, in how we interact with friends, family and others; how we understand the media that we read, see or hear; and how we make sense of ourselves and others in the world around us. We turn here to consider two highly influential but very different theories of the role that language plays in our social lives: *social representations theory* and *discursive psychology*.

Social Representations Theory

Social representations theory stems from the influential work of the French psychologist Serge Moscovici. In contrast to much writing in social psychology that emphasizes individual attitudes, beliefs and actions, Moscovici's (2000, 1984, 1961) long-standing interest lay in how we come to share understandings of events and phenomena with other members of the cultures and societies in which we live. Thus, a **social representation** is a representation of an element of the social world that is shared among the members of a social

social representation a representation of an element of the social world that is shared among the members of a social group.

group. In particular, Moscovici studied the ways in which scientific or theoretically based knowledge comes to be taken up in the course of everyday life among members of groups or societies, allowing what began as specialized or technical understandings to become more familiar to all of us as we talk to family, friends and others that we meet.

To illustrate how social representations allow theoretically based knowledge to become commonly familiar, let us take the example of Freud's theory of psychoanalysis. Psychoanalytic theory provides a developed account of the self in terms of psychic structures, developmental stages, unconscious motivations and the formation and defence of the self in response to inner drives and external constraints. Outside the realms of psychoanalysis (and perhaps of psychology), few will be aware of the details of the theory and the explanations that Freud offered for interpreting human behaviour. Nonetheless, we can commonly talk, or hear others talk, about concepts such as the ego, Freudian slips, the Oedipal complex and the role of the unconscious in leading to particular behaviours, without necessarily assuming that the use of these concepts reflects a comprehensive understanding of the theory. From what was, and perhaps still is, a highly complex and unfamiliar theory, numerous elements have found their way into the language commonly found among members of certain cultures and societies.

PSYCHOLOGY AROUND US   Public Representations of Climate Change

Perceptions towards climate change . . . have changed little if at all in the past nine years. The public appear to be fully aware of climate change and consider themselves to have at least the level of knowledge required to actively engage in tackling the issue, yet refrain from actually doing so. Furthermore, whilst the members of the public who consider themselves to have a level of knowledge of 'very' or 'expert' tend to source their information from academia, the majority of the public gains its information from the media and considers itself 'quite knowledgeable'. However, it clearly appears that respondents are actively engaging in some aspects of potential mitigation (e.g. recycling) but the extent to which this actually contributes to tackling global climate change compared with how effective the public consider it to be should be investigated further. The results in this work suggest that, in line with other studies, the individual considers responsibility for tackling climate change to lie with the international community, thereby distancing themselves from the issue.

(Sharples, 2010, p. 202.)

Of course, as seen in the example above of public representations of climate change, the representations that find their way into the public domain can be quite different from those held by scientists or other theorists. Moscovici (2000), however, argues that the resulting social representations should not be treated as diluted or inferior versions of knowledge that originates in the scientific realm. Quite the reverse, for to view social representations in such a way would be to ignore the functions that they play in social life. In offering a different form of understanding to that found elsewhere, social representations arise out of communications between members of social groups and allow communications within these groups that otherwise would not take place. In these ways, what starts off as unfamiliar becomes integrated into the everyday communications of members of groups and societies.

Discursive Psychology

Discursive psychology shares with social representations theory an interest in the role of language in social life. As an approach, however, it diverges from those we have considered above and in the previous chapter. For instance, discursive psychology does not study the language that people use in different situations in order to understand what is going on for them mentally, or to see what such language may tell us about social groups and shared representations. Instead, discursive psychology focuses primarily on the language that people use in its own right. Thus, discourse is viewed as the topic of study and not as a resource for uncovering what is located elsewhere, for example in terms of attitudes, cognitions, group memberships or other representations (Potter & Wetherell, 1987). Here, **discourse** refers to language as actually used, for example in everyday life, rather than to language in any dictionary sense. Thus, **discursive psychology** is the study of language as used in everyday life and its effects for psychology. It draws our attention to the ways that people talk to each other in everyday interactions and how these interactions work to construct and present particular versions of our social worlds and all that lies within them.

discourse language as actually used, not language in a dictionary sense.

discursive psychology the study of language as used in everyday life and its effects for psychology.

Now, all of this may sound quite abstract, if not complicated. What can the study of language tell us about ourselves, other people, how we act and so on? An example will help to illustrate this. We will all be familiar with the cliché that the same individual whom one person calls a *terrorist* will be called a *freedom-fighter* by others. In such instances, there is no way of arriving at one consistent description of that individual; instead, there will always be a competing **version** available for use in different contexts and different arguments. Here,

version one way of describing a social feature out of a range of possible ways of describing that same feature.

a version comprises one way of describing a social feature out of a range of possible ways of describing that same feature. Often, different speakers will produce divergent and competing versions of individuals, actions or events: this is perhaps only to be expected. What is less expected, however, is that each of us can and will produce equally different, and often inconsistent, descriptions in the course of our talk. The descriptions that we give of ourselves, of other people and of social events will inevitably vary according to the contexts in which we find ourselves and in which the descriptions are placed.

PSYCHOLOGY AROUND US   The Discursive Psychology of Prejudice

One major focus of recent discursive psychology has been the study of how individuals in their talk seek to avoid being heard as prejudiced. Rarely now do people directly express attitudes towards other social groups that may be treated as prejudiced. Studies of implicit attitudes, however, are not concerned with how people deal with the possibility of being accountable for appearing to be prejudiced. Below, we see an example of how people themselves manage this possibility in discourse.

1 Jack: [: : :] let's face it, it's not as if they're wanted here. We have enough low-

2 life here already without importing [other people's.

3 Hilda: [Jack! ((to Susan)) I'm sorry about

4 that. He's not xenophobic. It's it's not=

5 Jack: =it's not racist, no. We've never been racist, have we Hilda?

6 Hilda: No. We've got nothing against=

7 Jack: =nothing against the refugees. I have <u>every</u> sympathy for them. But you'd

8 be mad not to ask, why are they all coming <u>here</u>?

(Condor *et al.*, 2006, p. 452)

You will see some strange features (line numbering, :, [, ((, =) in the extract above. These are commonly found in discursive psychological data but we do not need to consider them here. In the extract itself, at lines 1 to 2, we see Jack expressing an attitude that describes immigrants in highly prejudiced terms. In the rest of the extract, Hilda and Jack both seek to distance themselves from this prejudiced statement, by denying that either of them is 'racist' and through Jack later saying that he has 'every sympathy' for immigrants. The effect of this talk is that they disclaim any prejudice, despite Jack's initial statement. This talk comes from a context in which Jack and Hilda are being interviewed by an interviewer (Susan) who may well challenge expressions of prejudice that are not addressed. We can therefore see how core elements of social psychology, by way of attitudes, prejudice and intergroup relations, are worked out in the context and the discourse itself and we do not need to go beyond this to understand what is happening.

Discursive psychology therefore argues that if we pay sufficiently close attention to the ways in which people use discourse in everyday life, then we can see how the central concerns of social psychology are displayed and worked out within the talk. The extract above shows one example of attitudes, intergroup relations and potential prejudice being negotiated in action. However, discursive psychologists go beyond this in arguing that we can, by studying discourse, understand how people make attributions

(Edwards & Potter, 1992), make sense of social cognition without attempting to look inside people's heads (Edwards, 1997) and see how descriptions of social groups are used in a range of ways (Verkuyten, 2005). Indeed, discursive psychology offers a different way of understanding all topics of interest to social psychologists (McKinlay & McVittie, 2008), including the very identities that we and other people take up throughout our social lives (McKinlay & McVittie, 2011).

Before You Go On

What Do You Know?

12. What is a social representation and how does it function within a social group?

13. What is discourse and why is the study of discourse important for social psychology?

14. How does discursive psychology explain attitudes, social cognitions and other features of social psychology?

What Do You Think?

Think about the descriptions found in media coverage of a major news topic, for example climate change or the economic crisis. What versions of people, actions and events are presented within that coverage? Now consider how the topic could be presented differently to provide a different version. What does this tell you about how the identities of the relevant individuals and the relations between different social groups are presented and how we can understand the psychological elements involved?

Social Psychology around Us

Early in Chapter 16 we introduced the definition of social psychology provided by Gordon Allport (1985, 1954). Allport suggested that social psychology seeks to understand, explain and predict how our thoughts, feelings and behaviour are influenced by the actual, imagined or implied presence of others. Over the course of that chapter and this one, we have examined how different social psychologists have taken up particular elements of that definition as the focus of their investigation of how we act and interact in social worlds. The topics covered have ranged from an emphasis on the individual and how he or she makes sense of the social world to a rather different focus on how social life affects each of us and has consequences for how we act and, indeed,

who we understand ourselves to be. Social psychologists who study social cognition, attitudes and attitude change, attributions and social relations all focus on individual experience as it might relate to social life. By contrast, the social psychology discussed in this chapter emphasizes broader elements of the social landscape, in the form of the social forces that we encounter, processes that operate within social groups and the impact of social group memberships, and the role of language in forming and communicating shared understandings or as a primary site for pursuing social psychology. All falling within a broad remit of social psychology, these widely varying concerns of different social psychologists have divergent outcomes for how we understand ourselves and the social world around us.

Access your interactive e-book to view a video clip for this chapter at
www.wileyopenpage.com

Summary

Social Forces

LEARNING OBJECTIVE 1   Describe how norms, social roles and obedience shape people's behaviour.

- Society establishes rules, or norms, about how people are supposed to act. Social roles are sets of norms ascribed to particular social positions and affect how we think about ourselves and act towards others. Norms and roles are critical to the smooth functioning of society but also place limits on individuals.

- Obedience involves following direct orders, usually from an authority figure. Experiments by Stanley Milgram

found that 65% of subjects continued to follow orders to administer what they believed to be dangerous electric shocks. Conformity is the tendency to yield to real or imagined group pressure.

Intragroup Processes

LEARNING OBJECTIVE 2   Review major concepts in the areas of intragroup processes.

- The social facilitation effect occurs when the presence of others enhances a person's performance. Research shows that this effect holds for simple, well-learnt tasks; but the presence of others can impair performance on more complicated tasks.

- With social loafing, people in a group expend less effort on a task than they would if performing the task alone.
- Group polarization is a phenomenon in which group discussion intensifies the already-held opinions of group members and produces a shift towards a more extreme position.
- Groups with certain characteristics – a strong similarity among members, high group cohesiveness, high perceived threat, elevated stress, insulation from outside influence and a directive leader – may become victims of groupthink, a faulty decision-making process in which group members strive for unanimity at the expense of realistically appraising alternative courses of action.
- In a social group, members experience two forms of influence. Informational influence arises when members look to other members to provide accurate information about the reality of a situation. Normative influence reflects group members' needs to achieve harmony and social approval.
- In a famous series of experiments, Solomon Asch found that 75% of research participants yielded to implicit group pressure to conform to an incorrect judgement. Conversely, in the blue–green studies, Serge Moscovici found that majority group members would often conform to the views of a minority, in cases where the minority expressed their views consistently and continued to be seen as part of the group.

Intergroup Relations

LEARNING OBJECTIVE 3   Describe how the processes involved in belonging to social groups work to create our social identities and how these social identities are linked to psychological well-being and intergroup contexts.

- In a context of intergroup relations, where different groups come together, actions such as prejudice and discrimination will reflect group concerns rather than individual dispositions or attitudes.
- Realistic group conflict theory argues that that intergroup conflict in such contexts will reflect actual or perceived competition between in-groups and out-groups. Studies by Muzafer Sherif have demonstrated how intergroup conflict arises in situations of conflict and how the resulting conflict can be resolved through superordinate tasks that require intergroup cooperation.
- A set of famous studies conducted by Henri Tajfel and colleagues has examined how processes of social categorization, social identification and social comparison produce social identities for each of us in group contexts. Social identities arise even in minimal groups, which do not have strong meanings for the participants and in which they do not encounter other members.
- The social identities that arise through our memberships of social groups are closely linked to our sense of self-esteem and psychological well-being. We experience these social identities as no less real than our sense of being unique individuals and they allow us to make sense of ourselves and the social worlds around us.

Language and Social Groups

LEARNING OBJECTIVE 4   Describe approaches to studying language in social life and the effects of communication and discourse for understanding social groups, identities and other social psychological topics.

- Social representations theory looks at how representations of the social world are shared among members of social groups. Social representations allow elements of theoretical knowledge, for example psychoanalytic theory or of the science of climate change, to become incorporated into everyday understandings and communications.
- Discourse is language as used in everyday life and not language in any dictionary sense. Discursive psychology examines how people use discourse to construct versions of people, actions or events, in particular contexts.
- One particular focus of discursive psychology has been on how individuals attend to the possibility of prejudice in their everyday talk. Discursive psychology also offers a way of understanding attitudes, social cognitions, identities and all other areas of interest to social psychology.

ACTIVITY

Activities to test yourself further are available in your interactive e-book at
www.wileyopenpage.com

TYING IT TOGETHER

OUT OF THE ORDINARY

- Belonging to social groups can have benefits in terms of providing social identities and promoting well-being. However, the processes operating in and between social groups can as easily produce negative outcomes as positive ones.
- Groupthink can occur when groups make inaccurate decisions through failing to take account of external social factors.
- Competition between in-groups and out-groups or even identification with in-groups can lead to negative attitudes and prejudice, and potentially to conflict between members of different groups.
- Discourse provides people with means for them to deny prejudice against others, despite expressing negative attitudes.

HOW WE DIFFER

- Group-based theories argue that we differ according to the social groups that we each belong to and the consequences that memberships have for our identities.
- Social representations theory suggests that we differ according to the groups to which we belong and the communications that are found in each group. Different groups will have different understandings of various issues, such as climate change.
- According to discursive psychology, we differ in the ways that we use discourse in our everyday lives to accomplish social actions. For example, different people will offer different descriptions of people in other social groups and find different ways of avoiding being viewed as prejudiced.

QUIZ

Quizzes to test yourself further are available in your interactive e-book at **www.wileyopenpage.com**

Key Terms

FLASHCARDS

Flashcards to test yourself further are available in your interactive e-book at **www.wileyopenpage.com**

CHAPTER 18

Stress, Coping and Health

Adapted by Mark Forshaw,
Adelphi Values, UK

CHAPTER OUTLINE

- What Is Stress?
- Responding to and Coping with Stress

- Stress and Health

Access your interactive e-book to view a video clip for this chapter at
www.wileyopenpage.com

Bruce has recently divorced from his wife of 20 years. He has one child, but since the divorce he moved away from the family home and is now working more than a two hours' drive away, and so he does not see his daughter as often as he would like. In addition, since turning 40 he has started to question his life more profoundly and is looking back and looking forward with some regret and fear. Behind him, he sees a failed marriage, and ahead he sees little to be happy about. He now lives alone, and in order to prevent spending long evenings in solitude he has started to work late. However, he has found that working late is not enough to get through the enormous amount of work which is now coming his way from his bosses, who see his lateness as devotion to his employment.

When he does get home, it's often late, so he buys a takeaway on the way home and a bottle of wine most nights. He used to play tennis and jog, but he does not really have the time for that any more. Recently, he has started to find it difficult to sleep because of work that is still on his mind, but he finds that the wine helps him put that into perspective somewhat. In fact, without a glass of wine he will often sit up well into the night, unable to get to sleep, thinking about his life. He has started to notice his heart beating faster than it used to, and he cannot seem to slow it down. He can hear the blood pounding in his ears, and he is sure his blood pressure is too high, but he has not got time to see the doctor. His hands and feet tingle sometimes, he has difficulty swallowing and his shoulders ache. One night he got almost no sleep, and so he called in sick the next day from work. It was a Friday, and he stayed at home all weekend, watching TV and listening to old music, which just made him feel depressed. He longed for the old days when he was happier and healthier and less worried about life in general. ∎

Can you see how Bruce has trapped himself in a set of behaviours which all build upon each other, like a spiral? This is how a well-functioning person can be sucked into becoming someone who is anxious, depressed, physically unfit, stressed and socially isolated. In this chapter, we will see how individual components of Bruce's story have been researched and what the facts are about the relationship between physical and mental health.

What Is Stress?

LEARNING OBJECTIVE 1

Define stress, and describe the ways and situations in which people experience it.

Many people think that stress and emotion are one and the same. They may say, for example, that they are *stressed out* when they really mean they are feeling emotions such as anxiety, depression or anger. In fact, stress and emotion are related, but they are not the same. Stress often triggers emotional reactions, particularly negative ones, but it has a number of other effects as well. We examine stress in the remainder of this chapter. Let's start with a discussion of what stress is and what brings it on.

Stress and Stressors

You do not need a textbook to tell you that Nina, featured below, is experiencing stress. After all, you have probably been in a similar place: too much to do, too little time, too many expectations, too little certainty about what to do next. Obviously, Nina feels stress because she has lots of work to do and is running out of time. But she also has stress connected to something otherwise pleasant – the opportunity to socialize with friends. Something as minor as an essay, as pleasant as the prospect of an evening out or as awful as a life-threatening medical condition can prompt feelings of stress.

You probably throw around the word *stress* all the time, but have you thought about what it actually means? **Stress** commonly is defined as a state brought on by any situation that threatens or appears to threaten a person's sense of well-being, thus challenging the person's ability to cope. A situation or circumstance that triggers the stress response is called a **stressor**. Stressors can be *acute* or *chronic*. An **acute stressor** is short term and has a definite endpoint, such as a near-miss in heavy traffic. A **chronic stressor** is long term and often lacks a definite endpoint, such as dealing over time with a high-pressure job.

It is our *perception* of threat that triggers the emotional state we connect to stress. If we do not perceive a situation as threatening, we will not feel particularly stressed. A number of psychological factors help to determine whether we experience a situation as threatening. Our appraisal of our ability (or inability) to cope with that situation is one such factor. A quiz in Spanish may not be threatening and stressful to a student who is up to date in the course, but a student who has been putting off assignments and is far behind will find a surprise quiz quite stressful. We will look soon at more psychological factors involved in stress, but before that let's examine the different ways that people experience stress.

stress brought on by any situation that threatens or appears to threaten a person's sense of well-being, thus challenging their ability to cope.

stressor a situation or circumstance that triggers the stress response.

acute stressor a stressful situation or circumstance that happens in the short term and has a definite endpoint.

chronic stressor a stressful situation or circumstance that happens in the long term and does not have a definite endpoint.

PSYCHOLOGY AROUND US · Just Work Harder

Nina sits at her desk, unable to concentrate. Her latest English essay is due on Wednesday, but her computer screen remains blank. All sorts of thoughts are flying through her head, and each one makes her chest tighten and makes her want to curl up into a ball and shut her eyes.

She has to leave for her job in less than an hour, and her boss has told her that if she's late again, he'll 'have to find someone more reliable'. Then there's the email she just got from her parents asking, once again, about her grades. In fact, things are not going so well at university. 'Just work harder,' her parents have told her. But the more trouble she has, the more she feels like just going out with her friends at night.

And then there's the recent break-up with her boyfriend. One night when she was late for work and in a panic, he called her and teasingly refused to let her off the phone. After a few minutes, she called him an idiot and hung up. It was not the first time she had lashed out at him, and though she tried to apologize later he said he did not want to deal with her moods any more.

Ways of Experiencing Stress

By definition, people who experience stress feel threatened and challenged. But these threats and challenges come in different forms. Certainly, soldiers in combat, students whose grades are falling and children whose parents are unhappy with them face different kinds of stress. Psychologists have in fact distinguished four kinds of stress experience: *frustration*, *pressure*, *conflict* and *danger*. These kinds of stress are not mutually exclusive.

Feeling Frustrated You finally find a parking spot, and someone pulls into it just ahead of you. You try to register for a course, and it is full. You work hard, but you get a low grade on a test. Whenever we find ourselves thwarted in the pursuit of a goal, we experience **frustration**. Life is full of frustration; it is one of our most familiar kinds of stress. Frustration can be caused by acute stressors, such as those in the situations just described, or

> **frustration** an emotion people experience when thwarted in pursuit of a goal.

PSYCHOLOGY AROUND US   Sports and Pressure

Eleven seconds remained in the 1993 NCAA Division I Men's Basketball Championship game. For the second year in a row, the University of Michigan was losing, but this time they were only down by two points. All-American Chris Webber grabbed a defensive rebound and suddenly Michigan had a chance to tie the game or even go ahead. After a stutter step, Webber brought the ball down the court. He paused for a moment, then desperately gestured for a time-out. However, Michigan had no time-outs remaining, and calling for a time-out when none remains is penalized by loss of possession of the ball and a technical foul. Whistles blew, and moments later Michigan had lost the championship once again.

What happened to Webber and to myriad other athletes who have made mental errors in high-pressure situations? When does pressure aid athletic performance and when does it impair it? These questions have been the subject of much study, and a number of explanations have been offered, but a clear understanding of the effects of pressure on athletes remains elusive (Weinberg & Gould, 2003).

We do know that performance pressure results when athletes feel strongly about the outcome of an event and believe that their own performance will have an impact on that outcome (Wallace *et al.*, 2005). We also know that this pressure can result in increased physiological and psychological arousal. But insights start to drop off when we try to predict the precise relationship between such arousal and performance.

For years, psychologists believed that the relationship probably follows the principle of the Yerkes–Dodson law. As we observed in Chapter 13, this psychological 'law', developed in 1908 by psychologists Robert Yerkes and John Dodson, holds that performances on tasks of any kind increase along with physical or mental arousal – up to a point – but, once an optimal, moderate level of arousal is passed, performances decrease more and more. Applying this law to athletic performances, it is generally believed that if an athlete is not aroused his or her performance will suffer, and that if he or she is too aroused his or her performance will also suffer. Optimal performance is thought to occur only in the presence

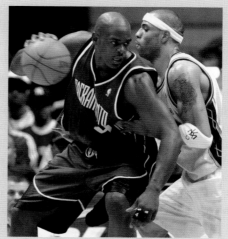

Source: ©Ray Stubblebine/Corbis.

of a moderate level of arousal (Yerkes & Dodson, 1908). Over the years, research has better supported an alternative version of the Yerkes–Dodson law, particularly in the realm of athletic performance. This alternative model holds that the level of arousal at which optimal performance occurs is a zone (not a single point) and varies from athlete to athlete. Some cross-country runners, for example, will perform best if they take naps right before a race while their teammates will do best if they listen to hard-core music, visualize their opponents and stretch intensely before the race (Hanin, 1997).

A different line of research has clarified that coaches can play a large role in helping athletes cope with performance pressure. Since anxiety tends to be lowest in athletes who believe in their performance abilities and are self-assured, coaches apparently can help by facilitating feelings of confidence – by, for example, providing frequent, genuine encouragement and by fostering a positive environment regardless of whether things have gone well or mistakes have occurred (Weinberg & Gould, 2003). Here again, however, such rules may vary from athlete to athlete. Some athletes respond better to certain coaching styles and techniques, while others respond better to alternative styles and techniques.

by chronic stressors. People who have chronic illnesses or disabilities, for example, are likely to feel frustrated that they cannot do more. All of these experiences are bound up with the notion of trying to achieve something and having a barrier to our progress. Barriers to progress generate stress.

Feeling Pressured We all encounter a certain amount of pressure, the expectation that we should act in a certain way. Pressure often comes from within. Some individuals have such high expectations of themselves that they are constantly under self-imposed stress. Think of the sources of pressure in your own life. What standards do you set for yourself academically and socially? How much pressure do you experience as a result of such expectation? Stress that comes from within is often more difficult to cope with than stress imposed by others. It may not be easy to meet the deadline for turning in a piece of coursework, but at least when you do so the pressure will be off. By contrast, if you set yourself a rigid standard of perfection, you may never find release from this internal pressure.

> **pressure** an expectation or demand that someone act in a certain way.

Pressure also varies along with the task and situation. One set of studies, for example, used the presence of an audience to provide pressure for participants who were performing a task. When the task was fairly simple, the participants were not affected by the presence of the audience – their performance was about the same, audience or no audience. When the task was more complex, however, the individuals performed significantly better without the pressure of an audience (Wan & Huon, 2005; Butler & Baumeister, 1998; Baumeister, 1984). Other research has found a strong correlation between feelings of pressure and symptoms of distress.

Feeling Conflicted Remember Nina, from our earlier example? The stress she felt was not simply the result of pressure from her parents. It also resulted in part from her desire to do two things at the same time: (1) study to earn good grades and (2) have time to go out with her friends. In situations such as this, we experience **conflict**, discomfort brought about by two or more goals or impulses that we perceive to be incompatible. There are three basic types of conflict: *approach–approach, avoidance–avoidance* and *approach–avoidance* (Figure 18.1) (Miller, 1959; Lewin, 1935).

> **conflict** discomfort brought about by two or more goals or impulses perceived to be incompatible.

- As its name implies, **approach–approach conflict** occurs when we must choose between two equally desirable options. Should we have the chocolate cake or the strawberry meringue? Should we buy the red backpack or the black one? In many cases, approach–approach conflicts are easy to resolve (you cannot really lose with either choice) and so are not especially stressful.

> **approach–approach conflict** a conflict that occurs when a person must choose between two equally desirable options.

- **Avoidance–avoidance conflict** is somewhat more stressful because here the choice is between two equally undesirable outcomes. Should you clean the garage or do the laundry? You may be tempted to do neither. If you deal with this kind of conflict by deciding to procrastinate, postpone or avoid the choice, however, you are particularly likely to experience stress (Shafir & Tversky, 2002).

> **avoidance–avoidance conflict** a conflict that occurs when a person must choose between two equally undesirable options.

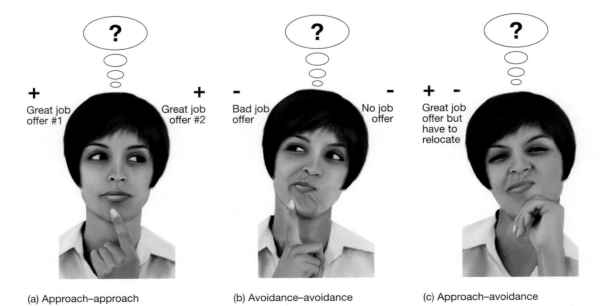

(a) Approach–approach (b) Avoidance–avoidance (c) Approach–avoidance

FIGURE 18.1 Three basic types of conflict that can lead to stress.

- In an **approach–avoidance conflict**, any available choice has both desirable and undesirable qualities, rendering us ambivalent and indecisive. In some situations, this sort of conflict may involve only one choice with both positive and negative features. For example, if Nina were to go out with her friends, she would enjoy herself, but she would not be able to work on her essay. In other situations, more than one option may be involved. Should you buy a car that is expensive but fuel-efficient, for example, or a less expensive gas-guzzler? Approach–avoidance conflicts are on display in many of our most agonizing decisions. Often people worry for some time about how to resolve them and experience considerable stress along the way.

approach–avoidance conflict a conflict that occurs when any available choice has both desirable and undesirable qualities.

Feeling Endangered

Life-threatening situations understandably produce stress, making us feel endangered. The adrenaline rush we experience when a car in front of us suddenly stops, forcing us to swerve and slam on the brakes, is characteristic of this kind of stress. Similarly, such stress is experienced by people who face combat or are trapped in a fire. Natural disasters may also be life-threatening and, in turn, stressful.

Terrorism poses a special danger to life and in turn produces stress. The deadly violence of a terrorist attack leaves survivors and those who grieve for lost loved ones with feelings of uncertainty, sadness and fear, making them vulnerable to the onset of stress disorders (Delahanty, 2007). Indeed, terrorism may have long-term psychological effects. Because of past run-ins with terrorism, a New Yorker may experience a sense of life-threatening fear at the sight of a plane in the sky, for example, or a person from Kabul may cringe at the sound of a bus backfiring.

Kinds of Stressors

Just as there are different ways of experiencing stress, there are different types of stressors. Moreover, stressors can be mild, extreme or anywhere in between. As you will see later in this chapter, what is stressful for one person may not be stressful for another. Still, several kinds of events are likely to produce feelings of stress whenever they are experienced: daily hassles, such as traffic jams; life changes, such as the loss of a job; traumatic events, such as natural disasters; chronic negative situations, such as an enduring illness; and special sociocultural conditions, such as racism. We will discuss each of these categories in turn; but it must be borne in mind that they can and do overlap or intersect.

Daily Hassles

Probably the most familiar sources of stress are **daily hassles**, the everyday annoyances that leave us feeling upset and at the end of our tether. These stressors can range from minor irritations, such as lost keys or a talkative colleague, to major problems, such as intense work pressure or conflict with a romantic partner. Some daily hassles seem to be universally upsetting, including time pressures, cash-flow problems, feelings of being cheated after purchasing something, conflicts with romantic partners, mistreatment by friends and poor evaluations at work.

daily hassles everyday annoyances that contribute to higher stress levels.

Over time, daily hassles can add up. They may become particularly stressful when they occur in combination with other stressors, leaving individuals overwhelmed (Bouteyre *et al.*, 2007; DeLongis *et al.*, 1982). A hot day may not be particularly stressful by itself, but combine it with waiting in a long line to file an application to tax your car and you may feel exasperated and depleted.

It turns out that the impact of daily hassles on health is often greater than that of a major life event (Stuart & Garrison, 2002). This is because ongoing stress may impair our immune system responses, as we shall see later. Indeed, one study found that people who face daily commutes in heavy traffic are particularly likely to miss work because of colds and influenza (Novaco *et al.*, 1990), illnesses that can result from stress-induced changes in the immune system.

Life Changes

Another common source of stress is change. Those first few weeks or months at university, for example, are usually quite stressful, even if they are also exciting, particularly for those who move away from home to study. In the first weeks, students need to decide what classes to take, where classrooms are located, what is expected of them and where to buy books (as well as how to pay for them). At the same time, they are meeting many new people. Trying to find our way in new relationships can be even more complicated and challenging than finding our way to a lecture.

Life changes, shifts in life circumstances that require adjustment of some kind, were among the first sources of stress studied. In 1967, investigators Thomas Holmes and Richard Rahe set out to develop a way to systematically measure how much stress people experience. They compiled a list of 43 events that were likely to change a person's life and therefore cause stress. These events ranged from the death of a spouse to minor violations of the law, to taking a vacation. Based on ratings by participants, the researchers assigned a point value to each event, ranging from 1 to 100 points, or *life-change units (LCUs)*. The point value for each event corresponded to the amount of upset and adjustment the event typically

life changes shifts in life circumstances that require adjustment of some kind.

Even positive changes can be stressful. Completing their airborne marriage ceremony, this man and wife kiss while freefalling. Even more conventional marriages produce a high degree of stress according to research using the Social Readjustment Rating Scales.

Source: AFP/Getty Images, Inc.

TABLE 18.1 The Social Readjustment Rating Scale. To score your susceptibility to stress on this scale, add up the life-change units for the events you experienced in the past year. Scores of 150 or less indicate little stress, 150–199 mild stress, 200–299 moderate stress and over 300 major life stress.

Life events	Life change units
Death of spouse	100
Divorce	73
Marital separation	65
Jail term (Prison Sentence)	63
Death of a close family member	63
Personal injury or illness	53
Marriage	50
Fired at work	47
Marital reconciliation	45
Retirement	45
Change in health of family member	44
Pregnancy	40
Sex difficulties	39
Gain of a new family member	39
Business readjustment	39
Change in financial state	38
Death of a close friend	37
Change to different line of work	36
Change in number of arguments with spouse	35
Mortgage or loan for major purchase	31
Foreclosure on mortgage or loan	30
Change in responsibilities at work	29
Son or daughter leaving home	29
Trouble with in-laws	29
Outstanding personal achievement	28
Spouse begins or stops work	26
Begin or end school	26
Change in living conditions	25
Revision of personal habits	24
Trouble with boss	23
Change in work hours or condition	20
Change in residence	20
Change in schools	20
Change in recreation	19
Change in church activities	19
Change in social activities	18
Mortgage or loan for lesser purchase (car, major appliance)	17
Change in sleeping habits	16
Change in number of family get-togethers	15
Change in eating habits	15
Vacation	13
Christmas	12
Minor violations of the law	11

Source: Reprinted from *Journal of Psychosomatic Research*, Vol. 11, Holmes and Rahe: 'The Social Readjustment Rating Scale,' 213–218, 1967, with permission from Elsevier.

produced. The death of a spouse received a score of 100 LCUs on the scale, for example, whereas a change in responsibilities at work was 29 LCUs, and taking a vacation came in at 13 LCUs.

With this 43-item list, called the *Social Readjustment Rating Scale (SRRS)*, Holmes and Rahe set about conducting studies on the impact of stress on people's lives. First, they had individuals complete the scale to determine how much stress they were under. Participants were asked to check off all those events that had occurred in their lives over a certain period, usually the past year. Then the total number of life-change units was added up, with the sum indicating the amount of stress the person had been under. A total score of 150 LCUs or less indicated relatively little stress, 150 to 199 indicated mild stress, 200 to 299 suggested moderate stress and over 300 pointed to major life stress. The life events from the SRRS and their ratings are listed in Table 18.1. Notice that a life-changing event need not be an undesirable one. A number of the events on the SRRS are positive, and some can be either positive or negative. A change in living conditions, for example, may reflect a move upwards or downwards in life.

Life Changes HOW WE DEVELOP Although feelings of stress may be similar for both young and old people, the life changes that evoke these feelings apparently differ widely from age group to age group. As you have just seen, the most powerful stressors (in decreasing order) on the SRRS, a largely adult scale, are death of a spouse, divorce, marital separation, jail term, death of a close family member and personal injury or illness. But what about younger age groups?

Researchers have developed special scales to measure life events and stress among university students (Renner & Mackin, 2002; Crandall *et al.*, 1992). They have found that the most stressful life event for this population is the death of a family member or friend, much like the top life stressor for other adults. Beyond this event, however, the leading life stressors for students are ones that are tied to university life. They are (again in decreasing order) having to take multiple tests, enduring finals week, applying for postgraduate courses, being a victim of crime, having several assignments due on the same day and breaking up with a boyfriend or girlfriend.

Moving to still younger individuals, researchers have found that the leading life stressors for children overlap to some degree with those of adults and university students, but, here again, they largely reflect issues unique to childhood (Ryan-Wenger *et al.*, 2005; Neff & Dale, 1996; Coddington, 1984, 1972). Across various scales, the leading stressors for school-aged children are taking tests, having excessive homework, being made fun of or bullied, feeling left out, getting bad grades, getting in trouble, arguing with family members or friends, experiencing the death or illness of someone close and doing something embarrassing.

It is worth noting that the kinds of life events that produce stress tend to shift as children develop (Vasey *et al.*, 1994). As children move from five years old to 12 years old, physical-type events (e.g. getting sick) become less stressful, behavioural events (getting into trouble) become more stressful and psychosocial events (arguing with friends) also become more stressful.

Finally, life stressors seem to change from generation to generation (Ryan-Wenger *et al.*, 2005). In the 1990s, a number of new childhood stressors worked their way into children's life stress scales, for example being bullied and experiencing violence in school. Similarly, during the 2000s, several other powerful childhood stressors have emerged, such as having too many things to do and performing poorly at sports and games.

Traumatic Events Life changes are stressful because they disrupt the routines of our lives. **Traumatic events** are more extreme disruptions; they are unexpected events that have the power to change the way we view the world. The terrorist attack on the World Trade Center on 11 September 2001 is an example of the stress-inducing power of a single, cataclysmic event. A natural disaster, such as the 2011 earthquake and tsunami in Japan, can also have such power. So can a rape or violent assault. Such events can have profound and long-lasting effects.

traumatic events unexpected events severe enough to cause extreme disruptions.

Victims may experience a sense of helplessness, depression, anxiety, numbness and disorientation (Overmier & Murison, 2005). The effects can last for years in some cases, or even persist permanently.

Although traumatic events are usually of short duration, some can be ongoing. Suffering ongoing physical or sexual abuse or living with an alcoholic spouse or parent are examples of long-lasting traumatic events. These, too, can leave victims withdrawn and experiencing recurring mental images, anxiety and depression.

Chronic Negative Situations A negative situation may become particularly stressful if it continues over a long, perhaps indefinite, period (Schmidt *et al.*, 2009). People living in a war zone, for example, confront the fearful possibility of an attack as they go about their daily lives, attending school, shopping or taking the bus to work. Similarly, people who live in poverty face constant concerns about meeting their basic needs and paying their debts. An ongoing negative home environment – marked by endless arguments with a spouse or child, for example – may produce considerable stress, and so may enduring workplace problems, such as continually feeling underpaid, unappreciated, bored or in danger of being fired (Rossi *et al.*, 2009).

Chronic job stress. Certain jobs produce chronic stress. Research reveals, for example, that physicians, particularly those whose specialties deal largely with life-threatening medical problems, often experience enormous work pressure and strain.
Source: ©Kevin Dodge/Corbis.

Long-term (chronic) illnesses can also produce much stress over time. Such illnesses may not only cause pain but also impose limitations and produce feelings of mortality and uncertainty in people's lives. The patients themselves are not the only ones affected by chronic illnesses. Their caregivers also may experience stress. In fact, research indicates that caregivers are more likely than other people to suffer from depression, drink excessively and be sleep-deprived, and less likely to engage in healthy behaviours such as exercise (O'Rourke *et al.*, 2003; Yoon, 2003).

The physical environment may also provide chronic stressors. Chronic noise, for example, often leads to tension and upset (Evans, 2001). This is one of the reasons why noisy neighbours are taken very seriously by authorities. Similarly, chronic overcrowding leads to higher bodily arousal and makes it difficult for people to calm down (Fleming *et al.*, 1987). (We will discuss bodily arousal and stress later.)

Special Sociocultural Conditions Special sociocultural conditions, such as those faced by members of ethnic minority groups who confront prejudice regularly, can be sources of stress. Minority-group members face special challenges and stressors as they try to navigate through the dominant culture. An immigrant worker, for example, has to adjust to new ways of doing things, learn a new language and often contend with poverty and the stress of a crowded living situation. In addition, members of minority groups often have to try to balance the demands of two cultures – their own and the dominant one in which they live. If they are not proficient in the language of the dominant culture, they may also experience the stress of having limited access to important channels of communication (Mino *et al.*, 2000).

Living in an atmosphere of racism – even if it occurs in subtle forms – is a particularly difficult sociocultural condition. Many members of minority groups receive the message that they are inferior. While this message is rarely stated outright, it may be on display in the lesser services, jobs and consideration that are part of their minority status. As minority group members increasingly achieve success in the dominant culture, another source of stress can emerge: they may find themselves having to decode their interactions with the dominant culture. Consider Jonathan, a black man who is working in the advertising department of a large department store. It is Jonathan's job to produce ads for a special sale of autumn clothing. His boss, who is white, does not think much of the two ideas Jonathan has proposed and tells him so. In addition to feeling disappointed and perhaps angry about the rejection of his ideas, Jonathan may experience the further stress of wondering whether his boss is reacting to his colour. The suspicions, confusion and vigilance experienced by minority group members as they navigate their way through interactions with majority group members is often invisible to those in the majority group (Profit *et al.*, 2000).

Existential Angst Something that does not quite fit with any of these categories, but at the same time permeates most if not all of them, is *existential angst*. At various life stages, and sometimes throughout, many individuals experience significant distress associated with a crisis of identity and meaning (Yalom, 1980). In fact, it is worth dwelling for a moment on the word *distress* because it contains the word *stress*, interesting in itself. When someone starts to really question what life is about, especially, for example, following isolation or loss, they can easily develop a long-term stress attached to those feelings. These feelings can develop for no apparent reason, perhaps just because of a realization, by the individual, that life is confusing and can seem to lack purpose. When people start to ask who they are, and what they are for, they experience existential angst. Many textbooks on the subject of stress will not cover this, and often you will find it only in counselling books or chapters on that issue, but it is important to understand stress as a multifaceted thing. To leave out mention of this kind of deep malaise is to miss a crucial factor in the stress that many individuals experience, especially at certain key points in life. Many would say that the so-called *mid-life crisis* is an existential one (Becker, 2006).

Before You Go On

What Do You Know?

1. What is the difference between an acute stressor and a chronic stressor?
2. What are the four types of stress experiences?
3. Define the three basic types of conflict.
4. What is the Social Readjustment Rating Scale?

What Do You Think?

What kinds of situations do you find especially stressful? How do they compare with what your friends find stressful? What do variations in the experience of stress tell us about stress and stressors?

Responding to and Coping with Stress

LEARNING OBJECTIVE 2
Explain how individual responses to stress differ, and discuss several ways in which people cope with stress.

We have looked at the kinds of experiences that cause stress. Let's turn next to what happens to people when they experience stress. Responses to stress fall into three general types: *physiological*, *emotional* and *cognitive*. As you might expect, people vary greatly in their responses.

Physiological Responses to Stress

 **WHAT HAPPENS IN THE BRAIN?**

Think about how you come to know that you are under stress. Typically, your breathing and heart rate quicken, you begin to sweat, your mouth becomes dry and your stomach tightens. What's happening is that your brain has perceived a challenge and is sending signals to your body to prepare to meet it. Sweating, dry mouth and stomach tightness are some of the immediate physical effects of stress, but these effects are actually indicators of more basic physiological responses. We examine these responses next and illustrate them in Figure 18.2.

Under fire. This marine fighting in Afghanistan yells to other marines after an IED (improvised explosive device) goes off while they are under enemy fire. Fewer individuals feel more endangered on a daily basis than combat soldiers.
Source: Joe Raedle/Getty Images, Inc.

The Fight-or-Flight Response You may remember the physiologist Walter Cannon from our earlier discussion of theories of emotion (in Chapter 14). Cannon was the first theorist to connect the bodily arousal associated with emotional responses to the need to fight or flee. According to Cannon

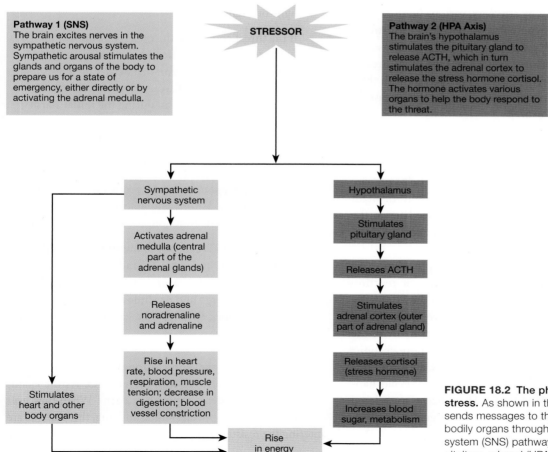

Pathway 1 (SNS) The brain excites nerves in the sympathetic nervous system. Sympathetic arousal stimulates the glands and organs of the body to prepare us for a state of emergency, either directly or by activating the adrenal medulla.

Pathway 2 (HPA Axis) The brain's hypothalamus stimulates the pituitary gland to release ACTH, which in turn stimulates the adrenal cortex to release the stress hormone cortisol. The hormone activates various organs to help the body respond to the threat.

FIGURE 18.2 The physiological response to stress. As shown in this flow chart, the brain sends messages to the endocrine glands and bodily organs through the sympathetic nervous system (SNS) pathway and the hypothalamic–pituitary–adrenal (HPA) axis.

(1932), the fight-or-flight response is a series of physiological reactions throughout the sympathetic nervous system and the endocrine system that mobilize an organism to either attack or escape an enemy. The process begins in the brain. The brain sends messages to the endocrine glands and bodily organs along two different routes. One is through the sympathetic nervous system, and the other is through the *hypothalamic–pituitary–adrenal (HPA) axis*.

When we confront a dangerous situation, within seconds the brain sends messages to the sympathetic nervous system, and these nerves directly stimulate organs of the body (the heart, for example). The nerves also influence organs indirectly by stimulating the adrenal glands (located at the top of the kidneys), particularly the inner layer of those glands, called the *adrenal medulla*. The adrenal medulla, in turn, releases the chemicals adrenaline and noradrenaline into the bloodstream, where they are carried to various organs and muscles, further arousing the organism and enabling it to fight or flee. Normally, these changes subside around 15 minutes after the threatening situation eases.

The brain also sends messages through the HPA axis (Jankord & Herman, 2008). This system acts more slowly than the sympathetic nervous system, taking minutes as opposed to seconds to have a big influence on the body. When we are confronted by stressors, various brain regions communicate with the hypothalamus, which in turn stimulates the pituitary gland, prompting the gland to release the *adrenocorticotropic hormone (ACTH)* into the bloodstream. ACTH travels to the adrenal glands and interacts with their outer covering, the *adrenal cortex*, causing the release of stress hormones called *cortisol*.

Cortisol travels to a range of the body's organs, where, among other activities, it helps elevate blood sugar levels, supply energy to the organism under stres, and protect the body from inflammation. In this way, cortisol helps prepare individuals who are under stress for their fight-or-flight response (Lupien *et al.*, 2006). As you will see later in the chapter, however, problems can arise if the cortisol level remains high for too long.

The fight-or-flight response is an early evolutionary adaptation. You can imagine how this kind of reaction may have come in handy to early humans. If they suddenly came across a sabre-toothed tiger, they were better able to either overwhelm it or escape in a hurry. But many of the stressors we face today are more subtle and more chronic: homework stress, employment pressures, relationship difficulties and any number of other conditions. What happens when a stressor is chronic? Hans Selye considered that question in forming his theory of the general adaptation syndrome.

The General Adaptation Syndrome The endocrinologist Hans Selye is credited with first talking about stress in living creatures (Selye, 1993, 1956a, 1956b, 1936). In his laboratory, Selye exposed animals to a variety of stressors. No matter what the stressor – mild shock, pain, restraint, heat, cold – he found that the animals displayed the same pattern of response – a consistent pattern that he labelled *stress* (a term he borrowed from engineers, who use it when they discuss forces that affect the structural integrity of the things they build). Selye believed we respond in much the same ways to stress, whatever its source. This insight was particularly important, because it means that, although our responses to different stressors may vary in degree, we are responding in the same basic way to all of them.

Selye also noticed that if stressors continue, the organism's body progresses through three stages of response: alarm, resistance and, finally, exhaustion. He called this three-stage response to stress the **general adaptation syndrome (GAS)**.

> **general adaptation syndrome (GAS)** a three-stage response to stress identified by Hans Selye; the stages are alarm, resistance and exhaustion.

- When an organism is first exposed to a threat, it reacts with *alarm* and becomes aroused physically as it prepares to face the challenge by fighting or fleeing. In short, the first stage of the GAS corresponds to the fight-or-flight response.

- If the threat continues, the organism's body undergoes further changes in an attempt to stabilize itself – a second wave of adaptation that Selye called *resistance*. The organism's level of arousal remains elevated, though slightly lower than during the initial alarm phase, as it adjusts to the stressor. If new stressors are introduced during this stage, the body is less able to marshal the energy needed to address them. According to Selye, this makes the body vulnerable to *diseases of adaptation*: health problems, such as high blood pressure, asthma and illnesses, associated with impaired immune function.

- If the organism is exposed to the stressor for still longer periods, its resistance gradually gives way to the third stage, *exhaustion*. In this stage, the body is depleted of energy and has little ability to resist. If the threat continues, the organism can suffer organ damage or death.

Students who have gone through final exams often have first-hand experience with Selye's GAS. As the exams approach, most students experience alarm. When they gear up and begin patterns of late-night studying, the students are entering the resistance phase. By the end of the exam period, many students feel as if they are heading towards exhaustion, and, in fact, a number catch colds or develop other illnesses at the end of the academic year.

Although the principles of Selye's theory are widely accepted today, some theorists have questioned his claim that the stress response is the same no matter what the stressor (Lupien *et al.*, 2007, 2006). They point out that although Selye used many kinds of stressors in his experiments with animals, all were physical – pain, heat, cold and so forth. This has led some theorists to suggest that the precursors of stress are much more specific than Selye thought, and in fact measurable and predictable. As we shall soon see, psychological factors also play an important part in our stress experience.

Emotional Responses to Stress

Bodily arousal is only one dimension of our reaction to stressors. When people feel threatened by an event or situation, they typically experience a change in emotions or mood as well. Indeed, researchers have found that the more stress a person experiences, the more negative his or her emotions (Lazarus, 2007, 1999, 1993). People who generally live under severe stress tend to be more anxious, depressed or otherwise upset than those who have relatively stress-free lives. Even within the course of a day, people feel more negative when short-term stressors emerge. Conversely, as daily stressors subside, people's moods take an upward turn (van Eck *et al.*, 1998). Towards the end of a week, stress often builds to a peak on Friday, in working people at least, and then peaks again on Sunday night when thoughts of the next week ahead begin again. For people who work seven days, there is often no rest period in the stresses of work. If we define *work* more widely, to include caring for children or dependants, we can easily see how many people are potentially affected by the stresses of everyday living on a continuous basis.

It was once thought that certain negative emotions – anxiety and depression – were more likely than others to emerge during stress. However, researchers have learnt that, in fact, a range of different negative emotions may accompany stress, depending on individuals' personal styles and on the stress-inducing situations. The most common emotional reactions include anxiety, fear and apprehension; dejection and grief; annoyance, anger and rage; guilt; shame; disgust; and jealousy (Lazarus, 2007, 1993, 1991; Sher, 2003).

Cognitive Responses to Stress

As we noted earlier, a key feature of stress is how we appraise both the challenging situation and our ability to handle that situation. If asked to speak publicly, for example, one person may

be excited and pleased at the opportunity, while another may be fearful and anxious (see 'What Happens in the Brain When Public Speaking Stresses Us Out' on the following page). Sometimes, as in the fear of public speaking, this appraisal is stable: that is, people tend to react consistently to the prospect of speaking before a group. In other situations, however, the appraisal depends on the person's present psychological state. We may appraise a missing car key as much more stressful when we are late for work than when we are just going out to run a few errands.

Richard Lazarus believed that emotion is aroused by a combination of two elements: an environmental event and a person's motives and beliefs. In fact, much of his early work was focused specifically on stress, and he identified two steps in how we experience stress.

- In the first step, **primary appraisal**, we assess how severe the stressor is. We may identify the stressor as a future danger (a threat), a current situation to be confronted and overcome (a challenge) or a loss or harm. The way we appraise the stressor in this first step can have important consequences for how we attempt to deal with it.

> **primary appraisal** an appraisal of a stressor to determine how severe it is; the first stage in Richard Lazarus's description of how people experience stress.

- In the second step, we evaluate our own resources and ability to cope with the threat, challenge or loss. This step is called **secondary appraisal**. Perceiving ourselves as lacking the resources to deal with a problem will elevate its threat level. Conversely, by reminding ourselves of what resources we have, we can decrease the threat level quickly.

> **secondary appraisal** an appraisal of one's personal resources and ability to cope with a stressor; the second stage in Richard Lazarus's description of how people experience stress.

One common factor in these appraisals is that the degree to which we feel in control of a situation affects how dangerous or stressful it feels. Perceptions of control (or lack of control) can greatly influence our appraisal of a stressor and, in turn, our experience of stress. People who believe that they can exert control over a particular stressor will experience less stress than individuals who feel no such control. A study of residents in a nursing home, for example, found that people who were given more control over their lives (deciding when to attend a movie, for example, or where to receive visitors) experienced less overall stress than residents given little control. Perhaps not so coincidentally, the residents with control were twice as likely to still be alive 18 months after the study began (Langer & Rodin, 2004; Rodin & Langer, 1977).

YOUR BRAIN AND BEHAVIOUR   What Happens in the Brain When we are Speaking in Public

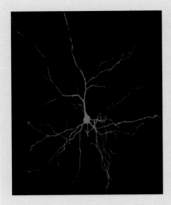

COPING WITH STRESS OVER THE LONG TERM

Activation of stress hormone systems is adaptive in the short term because they can help focus attention and increase energy sources. If negative stress goes on for too long, however, it can become detrimental to the brain. Chronic stress results in a reduction in the size of prefrontal cortex pyramidal neurons (shown here stained with a fluorescent dye). As well as diminished performance on cognitive tasks associated with this brain region.

Source: Courtesy of Dr Jason Radley.

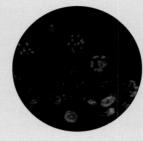

LEARNING TO ENJOY PUBLIC SPEAKING

With repeated experiences, most people find public speaking less frightening and some even begin to enjoy it. When stress has a rewarding component to it, the brain's response switches from negative to positive. Even with elevated stress hormones, neurons are not damaged and they even start to grow. Studies have shown that rewarding stress can stimulate the production of new neurons in the hippocampus (shown here stained with red fluorescent dye).

Source: Courtesy of Elizabeth Gould.

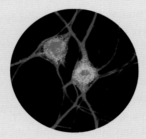

SHUTTING DOWN THE STRESS RESPONSE

To reduce the risks associated with long-term exposure to stress hormones and to enable stress systems to reset themselves for future use with new experiences, the brain has stress hormone receptors (shown here stained with a green fluorescent dye). These receptors, located in the hippocampus, prefrontal cortex and hypothalamus, work to turn the system off and restore the brain to its normal resting state.

Source: Casper Hoogenraad (Erasmus Medical Center Rotterdam, the Netherlands) and Harm Krugers (SILS-CNS, University of Amsterdam, The Netherlands). Reproduced with permission.

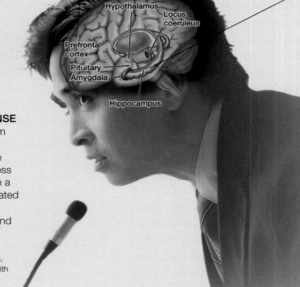

Hypothalamus
Locus coeruleus
Prefrontal cortex
Pituitary
Amygdala
Hippocampus

Source: Photo: Masterfile.

If you are like most people, you feel stressed out when you have to give a speech in public. What's happening in the brain while you are feeling this pressure? Although you are not in physical danger, your brain is responding to the presence of an audience as if you were. Brain signals activate the sympathetic nervous system – resulting in increased heart rate, sweaty palms and a dry mouth. In the brainstem, the locus coeruleus increases arousal by changing activity in its widespread projections throughout the brain. The amygdala and cortex process sensory stimuli that in turn activate stress systems. The hypothalamus sends signals to the pituitary gland to release a hormone that stimulates the adrenal glands (located on top of your kidneys) to release cortisol, the main stress hormone. This hormone helps to mobilize energy stores so that you can cope with the stressor. Finally, the hippocampus and prefrontal cortex recognize elevated levels of cortisol and send inhibitory signals to the hypothalamus to shut down the stress response. Will the audience realize how nervous you are or will you come across as cool, calm and collected?

Individual Responses to Stress

It should be clear by now that when it comes down to it, how stressed someone gets in a particular situation often depends on whom we are talking about. You probably have friends who collapse at the slightest hint of trouble and other friends who are experts in crisis management. Perhaps you have other friends who just let trouble roll off their backs without even a suggestion of worry.

Individuals are unique in many ways. Each of us has a particular biological make-up, a preferred style of interpretation and a favoured cluster of personality traits. In addition, we each operate within a particular social context. These individual differences profoundly influence our physical, emotional and cognitive responses to stress. Researchers have spent considerable energy examining four areas of individuality and their relationships to stress: *autonomic reactivity*, *explanatory style*, *personality* and *social support*.

Autonomic Reactivity and Stress Earlier, we observed that the *autonomic nervous system (ANS)*, particularly the sympathetic nervous system, plays a key role in stress reactions. When a person confronts a stressor, the ANS stimulates organs throughout the body, triggering feelings of physical arousal. As you might expect, people differ in how intensely the ANS responds to stressors. In some, the ANS tends to be highly reactive across various situations and springs into action even in response to mild stressors. In others, the ANS is less reactive and so less likely to respond even to fairly significant stressors. Such basic differences in *autonomic reactivity* may cause some people to experience stress reactions more often or more intensely than other people, even in the face of identical environmental threats (Cohen & Hamrick, 2003).

To illustrate, let's look at cardiovascular responses to stress, which include blood pressure and heart rate. In a number of studies, researchers have measured the cardiovascular reactions of individuals confronting stressors, such as difficult cognitive or social tasks (Sgoifo *et al.*, 2003; Malkoff *et al.*, 1993; Sherwood, 1993). Across a variety of situations, certain participants repeatedly display high cardiovascular reactivity, while others consistently exhibit low cardiovascular reactions.

Explanatory Style and Stress The characteristic manner in which we explain events, our *explanatory style*, can make a difference in how we appraise and respond to stressors. People with generally *optimistic* explanatory styles tend to believe that, despite setbacks, things will improve (Peterson & Steen, 2009). Those with generally *pessimistic* explanatory styles have a gloomier appraisal: they believe that if things can go wrong they usually will go wrong.

Imagine two people, each failing to make a sports team. Both feel disappointed and sad. One says to herself, 'I'll never make it. I'm such a dud. I should never have tried. It was stupid of me to think I was any good at this.' In contrast, the other individual says, 'At least I tried. If I improve my fitness in the spring, I can increase my speed and make the team next year. Meanwhile, I'll talk to the coach and find out how I can improve.' It is likely that the latter individual, the more optimistic one, will experience less stress than the former.

Research has supported the idea that optimistic and pessimistic explanatory styles influence stress reactions (Chang *et al.*, 2008; Carver & Sheier, 1999). When optimistic research participants appraise stressful situations, they are more likely than pessimists to recognize the positive features and to perceive the situations as manageable (Aspinwall *et al.*, 2001). In turn, they typically experience lower levels of stress (Chang, 2002). Similarly, it turns out that optimists are more likely to seek out social support during stressful events and to employ constructive coping techniques (Iwanaga *et al.*, 2004). Of course, few people are exclusively pessimistic or exclusively optimistic, although they may lean in one direction or other. One other potentially complicating factor is that striving to achieve can be stressful in itself. The optimist is probably more likely to strive, whereas some pessimists simply do not bother. If you do not try, you never feel the stress associated with trying!

Personality and Stress Our personalities often help set the tone for how we appraise and react to stressors (Vollrath, 2001). People who are generally timid will likely greet a stressor with more alarm than people who are generally bold. Similarly, our ongoing levels of anger, depression, curiosity and the like will influence our stress reactions.

One personality style that has received particular study is the *hardy personality*, sometimes called the *stress-resistant personality* (Maddi, 2007; Ouellette & DiPlacido, 2001). Individuals with such personalities welcome challenges and are willing to commit themselves and take control in their daily lives. Generally, they greet stressors as opportunities for growth rather than as crises and perceive stressors as less severe than non-hardy individuals. Not surprisingly, hardy people also seem to experience fewer and less intense feelings of stress (Beasley *et al.*, 2003).

At the other end of the stress continuum are people with personality styles that appear to make them more prone to stress. In the late 1950s, two cardiologists, Meyer Friedman and Raymond Rosenman (1959) reported that many of their heart patients seemed to share similar personality traits: they were consistently angry, cynical, hard-driving, impatient and time-conscious. They were also competitive, ambitious and in a hurry to do many things at once. Friedman and Rosenman

Type A a personality type characterized by competitiveness, impatience, anger and hostility.

Type B a personality type that is less aggressive, more relaxed and less hostile than Type A.

claimed that individuals with this personality style, which they labelled **Type A**, interact with the world in a way that produces continual stress (Jamal & Baba, 2003; Smith & Gallo, 2001; Friedman & Rosenman, 1959). In contrast, people who display **Type B** personalities are more relaxed, less aggressive and less worried about time. People with this personal style are thought to experience lower levels of stress. In fact, most people fall between these two extremes, leaning towards one or the other but showing features of both personality patterns.

Social Support and Stress Many studies and observations attest to the importance of social support in the experience of stress (Taylor, 2008, 2007, 2006a, 2006b). Although negative interactions with relatives and friends can be sources of significant stress (Lepore *et al.*, 1991), studies have resoundingly indicated that social relationships and support can also help prevent or reduce stress reactions (Cohen & Janicki-Deverts, 2009; Cohen, 2004).

The positive impact of social support on stress was first revealed in animal studies. In a famous investigation, for example, twin goats were subjected to a stressful conditioning task. One goat worked in isolation, and the other worked in the presence of its mother. The goat working in isolation reacted with greater anxiety and stress than did its twin goat (Liddell, 1950). In another study, a group of mice had to share a common feeding place, which created a persistent state of territorial conflict (Henry & Cassel, 1969). In one condition, the mice in the group were strangers, while in the other the mice were from the same litter. The former group showed more signs of stress than did the latter.

Studies of humans have revealed a similar role for social support in stress reactions (Taylor, 2008, 2007, 2006a, 2006b). It has been found, for example, that when faced with various job stressors, from work overload to job conflict, workers who can rely on their supervisors, colleagues, and spouses for emotional and practical support often experience less distress than workers without such support (Beehr *et al.*, 2003). Other studies suggest that having an intimate, confiding relationship with someone – be they a spouse, close friend or other individual – provides the strongest kind of social support (Cohen & Wills, 1985).

Coping with Stress

We have seen that a number of individual differences contribute to how stressed we become. Once we feel stressed, we also differ in our efforts to manage the situation. What do you do when you feel stressed? If you feel overloaded or overburdened, do you lie in bed, worrying about all that you have to do, unable to get started? Or do you start making lists and timetables? If you are in a traffic jam, do you pound the steering wheel or do you instead try to find an interesting radio station or play your favourite CD? Faced with the terrifying prospect of a chemistry examination, do you call a friend to study or light a cigarette?

Our efforts to manage, reduce or tolerate stress are called **coping**. Although most people use this term to convey constructive efforts ('I'm coping with the situation'), a coping response may be either adaptive or maladaptive in a given situation (Folkman & Moskowitz, 2004). For a person faced with failing grades, for example, going out and socializing is a less adaptive coping response than spending additional time studying. Each of us has preferred styles of coping that we tend to apply across various situations (Aldwin, 2007; Folkman & Moskowitz, 2004; Carver & Scheier, 1999). Let's look at some of the more common coping styles.

coping efforts to manage, reduce or tolerate stress.

Lashing Out As stressors pile up, people often say that they feel 'they are going to explode'. Thus, it is not surprising that some individuals do in fact explode – psychologically or physically. They react to stress by lashing out at other people

But Does It Work? This man was one of many individuals invited by a hotel chain in Spain to smash and destroy the rooms of a hotel undergoing reconstruction. Similarly, certain consulting organizations in Spain have advised clients to destroy old cars, computers, TVs or mobile phones with sledgehammers as a way of fighting stress. The approach has caught on throughout the country, but research has not found that lashing out or venting anger are necessarily effective coping strategies.

Source: Paul White/AP/Wide World Photos.

with angry words or behaviours. Around one-quarter of adults report such reactions (Kanner, 1998). For some, it is a characteristic mode of coping.

Lashing out often occurs after a series of stressors has taken place. The particular event that triggers an aggressive outburst may seem relatively mild in itself, but for the individual under siege it is the last straw. Recall our earlier example involving the beleaguered Nina, who blew up at her boyfriend during a phone conversation. His crime? He had refused to let her off the phone. Ordinarily, this teasing may not have elicited such a strong reaction. But Nina was feeling pressure from her boss, her parents and the demands of her studies. Her explosive reaction is not surprising when we consider the cumulative impact of these multiple stressors.

Angry outbursts, although sometimes understandable, are not typically a constructive way of dealing with stress. Such outbursts may harm relationships, produce psychological or physical damage and lead to additional stress. Theorists and clinicians once believed that expressions of anger were cathartic, or cleansing: that is, if people expressed their anger and 'got their frustrations out of their system' they would feel better and be able to move forward constructively. It turns out, however, that excessive or continual expressions of anger usually cause further outbursts (Tavris, 2003, 1989). In one study, experimenters induced anger in participants and then directed one group of angry participants to hit a punching bag and the other group of angry individuals to sit quietly (Bushman *et al.*, 1999). Later in the experiment, the 'punching bag' participants were found to behave much more aggressively than the 'sit quiet' individuals. It seems that, over time, aggression becomes normal to an individual who consistently acts in a belligerent way.

PSYCHOLOGY AROUND US   Cursed Response

Want a quick relief from stress? Angry outbursts may not work, but apparently shouting out your favourite swearword can help. Richard Stephens and his research group at Keele University had university students put their arms in a bucket of ice water for as long as they could (Stephens *et al.*, 2009). Some of the participants were instructed to shout out swearwords of their choosing while holding their arms in the water; others shouted out neutral words only. Which group do you think were better able to keep their arms immersed in the ice water? That's right: the swearers. In fact, they kept their arms in the water almost a minute longer than the students who repeated neutral words. Why does swearing help? The experimenters theorized that it triggers our fight-or-flight responses, which help us to deal with immediate stress and negate the link between fear of pain and pain perception. But be warned (or relieved): swearing has a much greater coping and pain-reduction effect for occasional swearers than for habitual swearers. Save your swearing for a special occasion! Like many things, we habituate after a while. Have you ever wondered why you first feel your clothing when you put it on, but after a while it's as if it were a part of you? So it is with swearing: it loses its effect after continual use.

Self-Defence In some instances, people run away from, that is physically leave, stressors through such actions as dropping a difficult class, changing jobs or ending a troubled relationship. More commonly, people try to make a *psychological getaway*. You may recall Aesop's story of the fox and the grapes. A fox was trying to get some grapes, but they were hanging too high on a vine, and he could not reach them. Eventually, after trying for most of the afternoon, the fox gave up, saying, 'They're probably sour anyway.' Leaving aside the question of why a fox wants grapes in the first place, the fox's behaviour in this story is an example of *reaction formation*: saying or doing the opposite of what one actually believes, one of Freud's defence mechanisms.

As you will remember from Chapter 15, Freud explained such behaviour in psychoanalytic terms. Today, though, the notion of defence mechanisms is widely embraced even by theorists outside the psychoanalytic model. Many psychologists believe that people often cope with stress, whether consciously or unconsciously, by engaging in defensive behaviours. These theorists also agree that the defensive behaviours often involve a high degree of self-deception.

Although everyone reacts to stressors with defensive behaviours on occasion, some people use such behaviours regularly. In fact, certain individuals display what theorists describe as a *repressive coping style* (Langens & Mörth, 2003;

Brown *et al.*, 1996). They consistently deny negative feelings and discomfort and try to push such emotions out of awareness.

It is also worth noting that defensive coping can be difficult to achieve. Research has found that people with a repressive coping style often fail to fully repress their feelings of stress (Pauls & Stemmler, 2003; Brown *et al.*, 1996). While research participants were watching an upsetting film, for example, experimenters measured their autonomic nervous system responses. Although participants with a repressive coping style reported feeling less stress than other participants did, their autonomic responses were actually higher (e.g. their heart rates and blood pressure were higher throughout the film). It may be that repressive coping behaviours mask stress rather than eliminate it. Or perhaps the higher autonomic activity associated with repressive coping indicates that such repression requires considerable physical effort. Either way, it is not surprising that people with this coping style have been found to experience more medical problems than people who use other coping styles do (Coy, 1998).

Self-Indulgence Many individuals use self-indulgent coping strategies, such as overeating, smoking cigarettes and consuming drugs and alcohol (Steptoe, 2000). Such strategies may help people feel better in the short term, but in most instances they fail to change the challenge at hand and so have little long-term benefit. In fact, such responses are often associated with poor adjustment and depression and anxiety (Folkman & Moskowitz, 2004; Aspinwall & Taylor, 1992).

If the problem at hand is transient and simple – recovering from a drive home in a blinding snowstorm, for example – the self-indulgence of having a bowl of ice cream or a beer may indeed help a stressed person to calm down. If, however, the problem is more complex – a term paper due next week – self-indulgence is unlikely to be an effective coping strategy. Eating, drinking, shopping, watching television or surfing the Internet will not make the problem go away. In fact, it may produce still greater pressure and higher stress: while one indulges, the paper's due date keeps getting closer. Moreover, certain self-indulgent strategies – such as cigarette smoking, excessive alcohol consumption, drug use and extreme overeating – have serious health effects. Nevertheless, surveys show that self-indulgence is on the rise as a coping response (Young, 2009, 2004, 1998, 1996).

Constructive Strategies It is possible, of course, to cope with stress constructively rather than lashing out at others or engaging in self-defence or self-indulgence. Psychologists

Richard Lazarus and Susan Folkman (1984) use the terms *problem-focused coping* and *emotion-focused coping* to distinguish two kinds of constructive strategies. Which of these strategies we are likely to use depends in part on the nature of the problem (Stanton *et al.*, 2009, 2002; Folkman & Moskowitz, 2004). For example, we could try to hit the road at 4:00 a.m. as a way of dealing with morning traffic, but it is probably more practical to learn how to react calmly and philosophically to rush-hour tie-ups. Conversely, when a flooding is forecast, working on calming down may not be as fruitful as deciding whether to buy some sandbags or carry everything upstairs.

In **problem-focused coping**, the person's efforts are aimed at dealing directly with the stressor in some way. A man who is repeatedly late to work, for example, may ask his boss to assign him to a different shift so that he has more time to get to work. Or he may look for a new job closer to home. Or he may devise a plan to buy a car, so that he can save time travelling to work. By dealing directly with the stressor, he can begin to reduce its effects.

> **problem-focused coping** those coping strategies focused on dealing directly with the stressor, such as by changing the stressor in some way.

But what about the noisy two-year-old next door who keeps interrupting your efforts to relax in the backyard? Or the grief resulting from the loss of a loved one? These are not stressors that readily yield to a problem-focused approach. When we can exert little control over stressors, we may instead try to change how we feel towards the stressors, thus limiting their negative effects, an approach called **emotion-focused coping** by Lazarus and Folkman (1984).

> **emotion-focused coping** those coping strategies focused on changing one's feelings about the stressor.

In some cases, emotion-focused coping may involve *cognitive reappraisal*, finding a way to reinterpret the negative aspects of a situation so that they are less upsetting (Harvey, 2008; Lechner *et al.*, 2008). People who are trying to come to terms with the death of a loved one or with some other catastrophic loss often look for ways to find positive meaning or purpose in their loss (Folkman & Moskowitz, 2004). Similarly, people may reinterpret threatening situations as challenges or tests, rather than catastrophes. The loss of a job, for example, might be viewed as a new beginning or new opportunity (Folkman & Moskowitz, 2000). As we shall see later, strong religious beliefs help some individuals make such cognitive reappraisals.

Changing how we think or feel about a stressor can also be a useful tactic for less traumatic stressors, such as tests and traffic jams. Rather than becoming increasingly upset over a traffic jam, for example, you may be able to shrug it off – saying, in effect, 'It won't be great if I'm late, but I'll survive.'

PRACTICALLY SPEAKING   How Can You Manage Stress?

Stress is often unavoidable. The traffic jams, life changes and occasional natural disasters that create stress are not going to miraculously disappear. The issue, then, is how to handle stress. Is there a way to lessen its impact so that cortisol levels, blood pressure and the like do not soar? The answer, according to many psychologists and studies, is yes (Folkman & Moskowitz, 2004). As this chapter has already begun to suggest, there are quite a few things you can do the next time you anticipate or begin to feel the heart-pounding symptoms of stress.

Exercise, Meditation and Relaxation

One of the best ways to manage physiological responses to stress is to exercise (Steptoe, 2000). In fact, it appears that people who exercise regularly reap not only physical benefits, such as lowering the activity of stress hormones (Rejeski & Thompson, 2007; Rejeski *et al.*, 1992, 1991), but also psychological benefits, such as increases in self-confidence. Similarly, research indicates that some of those who learn to quiet their thoughts and relax their muscles through meditation and relaxation training experience reductions in stress hormone activity, blood pressure and anxiety levels (Cardoso *et al.*, 2009; Stetter & Kupper, 2002).

Social Support

Seeking the support of others, whether in the form of assistance or a sympathetic ear, is another way to ease the effects of stress. Simply knowing that friends or family will be available when needed is a form of social support (Taylor, 2008, 2007, 2006a, 2006b). It appears that social support helps ease the effects of stress in at least two ways: by helping to reduce the actual number and impact of threatening situations and by providing practical, problem-focused assistance when stress does occur.

Religion

For many people, religion is of major help in dealing with stress. As we have observed in this chapter, one reason for this may be the social support that the individuals derive from religion (Folkman & Moskowitz, 2004). Religion and religious communities can, for example, serve as antidotes

Mass relaxation. These students in China receive stress relief training to help them relax during their upcoming college entrance exam.
Source: ©Xinhua Press/Corbis.

to feelings of isolation and may also provide a sense of order as people face the uncertainties of life. In addition, religious beliefs may offer explanations for stressful events that make those events seem less threatening or overwhelming to many people (Packer, 2000).

Self-Disclosure

Self-disclosure, the sharing of emotions and experiences with others, can also help people deal with stress. Up to a point, self-disclosure serves to release stress – consider the phrase *getting things off my chest* – but it is more than simply the venting of emotion. It helps people to channel emotions into a cohesive narrative, making stressors easier to process and deal with (Foa & Kozak, 1986). In addition, by putting fearful, angry or uncomfortable feelings into language and sharing them with other people, individuals are forced to think about and perhaps better address those feelings (Smyth & Pennebaker, 2001). Of course, the effectiveness of self-disclosure is tied to the ability of others to understand the problems a person is going through. Rape victims or former prisoners of war, for example, may discover that certain relatives or friends simply cannot comprehend what they are going through. In such cases, the feedback they receive ('Blimey, that's really rough, but I am sure you'll feel better soon') may feel empty, unhelpful and in some cases even painful.

Before You Go On

What Do You Know?

5. How do the sympathetic nervous system and hypothalamic–pituitary–adrenal (HPA) pathways influence our experience of stress?
6. What happens in each stage of the general adaptation syndrome (GAS)?
7. How does autonomic reactivity affect how different people experience stress?
8. How can lashing out negatively affect our management of stressors?

What Do You Think?

Do you tend to use constructive coping strategies or do your responses tend to be more maladaptive? Do you adapt your coping style to the situation or do you tend to use the same style across many different situations? How could you improve your coping style?

Stress and Health

LEARNING OBJECTIVE 3

Explain how stress can cause physical illness, and discuss situations in which stress may be beneficial.

We have seen that stress has a profound effect on bodily functioning. Thus, it should come as no surprise that researchers have found strong relationships between stress and health – or, more accurately, between stress and illness (Groër *et al.*, 2010). Scientists' appreciation of this relationship unfolded slowly. Back in the 1930s and 1940s, researchers began to recognize that certain medical illnesses were caused by an interaction of psychological factors (particularly stress-related factors) and biological factors, rather than by biological factors alone. These special illnesses were given the label *psychosomatic* or *psychophysiological diseases*. Among the most prominent were ulcers, asthma, tension and migraine headaches, and hypertension.

As the list of psychosomatic diseases grew, medical researchers began to suspect that stress may, in fact, be at work in a wide range of medical illnesses, not just in a special few. Their suspicions changed to near certainty when studies revealed that stress often contributes to coronary heart disease, the leading cause of death in the Western world. Researchers continue to investigate how stress is connected to various illnesses, as well as how stress brings about its effects on the body's systems.

Coronary Heart Disease

Coronary heart disease involves a blocking of the *coronary arteries*, the blood vessels that surround the heart and are responsible for carrying oxygen to the heart muscle. The term actually refers to several problems, including blockage of the coronary arteries and *myocardial infarction* (heart attack). Together, such problems are the leading cause of death in men over the age of 35 and women over the age of 40. Research has shown that most cases of coronary heart disease are related to an interaction of psychological factors, such as job stress, and physiological factors, such as high cholesterol, obesity, hypertension, smoking and lack of exercise (Bekkouche *et al.*, 2011; Kendall-Tackett, 2010).

Earlier, we discussed the Type A personality, which was identified by two cardiologists, Friedman and Rosenman (1959). These doctors argued that the stress-producing behaviour of people with Type A personalities makes them more likely to develop coronary heart disease. People with the more relaxed Type B behaviour pattern exhibit lower levels of stress and less coronary disease. In a pioneering study of more than three thousand men, Friedman and Rosenman (1974) separated healthy men in their forties and fifties into Type A and Type B groups and then followed their health over a period of eight years. The doctors found that more than twice as many of the Type A men developed coronary heart disease. Subsequent studies found similar correlations among women (Haynes *et al.*, 1980).

As research continued into the link between Type A behaviour and coronary heart disease, many investigators found that while a connection existed it was weaker than that reported by Friedman and Rosenman (Gallacher *et al.*, 2003). It now appears that only some of the Type A characteristics are related strongly to heart disease. In particular, research has identified the importance of negative emotions. Hostility, which includes not just feelings of anger but also enduring cognitive patterns of mistrust and cynicism, seems to be especially important (Figure 18.3) (Smith & Gallo, 2001). People who score high on measures of hostility tend to experience greater stress and to have an increased risk of developing coronary heart disease, as well as other serious medical illnesses (Elovainio *et al.*, 2011; Kendall-Tackett, 2010).

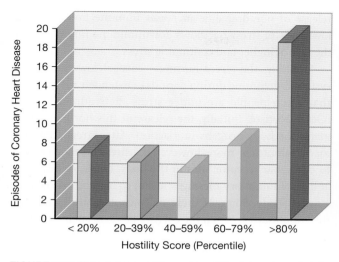

FIGURE 18.3 Type A personality and hostility. A key characteristic of the Type A personality is chronic hostility. People with this personality style interact with others in a way that produces continual high levels of stress and increases their risk of coronary heart disease.

Source: Adapted from Niaura, R., *et al.* (2002). Hostility, the metabolic syndrome and incident coronary heart disease. *Health Psychology, 21*, 588–593.

Internal combat. This scanning electron micrograph shows a cancer cell (red) being attacked by natural killer T-cells (yellow).

Source: Jean Claude Revy/ISM/Phototake.

Life Change and Illness

Earlier, we observed that in the 1960s researchers Thomas Holmes and Richard Rahe opened the door to investigations of life changes and stress when they designed the Social Readjustment Rating Scale (SRRS). The higher a person's score on the scale, as measured in life-change units (LCUs), the more stress he or she has been experiencing. With the SRRS, Holmes and Rahe decided to examine the relationship between life stress and the onset of illness. They found that the LCU scores of sick people during the year before they became ill were considerably higher than those of healthy people (Holmes & Rahe, 1989, 1967). In fact, if a person's life changes totalled more than 300 LCUs over the course of a year, that person was likely to develop a serious health problem.

The SRRS has been revised by researchers over the years. Using various scales, studies have tied a variety of life stressors to a wide range of physical problems, from upper respiratory infection to cancer (Baum *et al.*, 2011; Rook *et al.*, 2011). Generally, the greater the amount of life stress, the higher the likelihood of medical illness. Some researchers have even found a relationship between stress and death. Widows and widowers, for example, have an elevated risk of death during their period of bereavement (Rees & Lutkin, 1967).

Stress and the Immune System

Research clearly shows that stress can result in various medical disorders. But exactly how does this effect come about? What is it about stress that makes it a threat to health? An area of study called **psychoneuroimmunology** has tried to answer this question by examining the links between stress, the immune system and health (Kendall-Tackett, 2010).

The **immune system** is the body's system of organs, tissues and cells that identify and destroy foreign invaders, such as bacteria and viruses, as well as cancer cells. An important group of cells in the immune system are **lymphocytes**, white blood cells that circulate through the lymphatic system and the bloodstream. When stimulated by bacterial or viral invaders, lymphocytes act to help the body fight the invaders, often by destroying body cells that have been infected by the invaders.

Researchers believe that severe stress can negatively affect the activity of lymphocytes, slowing them down and thus reducing a person's ability to fight off viral and bacterial infections (Dhabhar, 2011) (Figure 18.4). In a pioneering study, researchers in New South Wales, Australia, compared the immune systems of 26 people whose spouses had died eight weeks earlier to those of 26 similar participants whose spouses had not died (Bartrop *et al.*, 1977). Blood samples showed that lymphocyte functioning was significantly slower in the bereaved people than in the non-bereaved individuals. Other studies have shown poor immune system functioning in people who are exposed to long-term stressors, such as people who must provide care for relatives with Alzheimer's disease (Lovell & Wetherell, 2011; Kiecolt-Glaser *et al.*, 2002a, 2002b, 1996).

psychoneuroimmunology an area of study focusing on links between stress, the immune system and health.

immune system the body's system of organs, tissues and cells that identify and destroy foreign invaders, such as bacteria and viruses, as well as cancer cells.

lymphocytes white blood cells that circulate through the body and destroy foreign invaders and cancer cells; important components of the immune system.

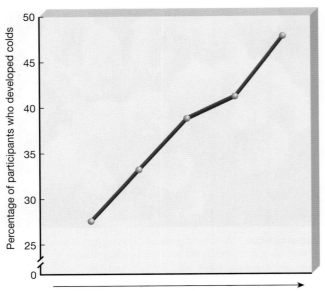

General level of psychological stress in participants' lives

FIGURE 18.4 Stress and the common cold. Researchers have examined the links between stress and illness. One study found that when healthy inoculation volunteers were exposed to a cold virus those who reported generally the highest levels of stress in their lives were most likely to come down with the cold and to develop worse symptoms.

Source: Based on Cohen, S., Tyrrell, D. A. J., & Smith, A. P. (1991). Psychological stress and susceptibility to the common cold. *New England Journal of Medicine, 325,* 609.

In short, during periods when healthy people confront unusual levels of stress, their immune systems slow down, so that they become susceptible to illness. If stress adversely affects our very capacity to fight off illness, it is not surprising that Holmes and Rahe and other researchers have found a relationship between life stress and a wide range of illnesses. Several factors seem to influence whether and when stress will lead to immune system problems. A number of biochemical changes must occur in order for stress to have such an impact. Certain behavioural changes, personality styles and social circumstances may also play a role.

Biochemical Activity Remember that when stressors first appear the sympathetic nervous system springs into action. Its activity includes an increase in the release of noradrenaline throughout the brain and body. Apparently, beyond supporting the activity of the sympathetic nervous system, noradrenaline can eventually help slow the functioning of the immune system (Groer *et al.*, 2010; Lekander, 2002). During periods of low stress, noradrenaline travels to particular lymphocyte receptors, binds to them and gives a message for the lymphocytes to increase activity. As stress rises and continues, however, the chemical travels to other receptors on the lymphocytes, binds to them and gives an inhibitory message: a signal for the lymphocytes to stop their activity. Thus, the release of noradrenaline increases immune functioning at low levels of stress but slows down immune functioning in the face of higher and continuing stress.

Similarly, the stress hormone cortisol lowers immune system functioning during periods of extended stress. Recall that when people are under stress their adrenal glands release cortisol. Initially, the release of this hormone stimulates the body's organs into action. After stress continues for 30 minutes or more, however, the stress hormone travels to particular receptor sites in the body, binds to these sites and gives inhibitory messages meant to help calm down the stressed body. Some of these receptor sites are located on the lymphocytes. When the cortisol binds to such receptors, its inhibitory messages slow down the activity of the immune system (Groer *et al.*, 2010; Bellinger *et al.*, 1994). Again, a chemical that initially helps people to deal with stress eventually acts to slow the immune system.

Another action of cortisol is to stimulate an increase in the production of *cytokines,* proteins that bind to receptors throughout the body and play a key role in the immune system. At early levels of stress, the cytokines help fight infection. But as stress continues, the continuing production and spread of cytokines leads to inflammation throughout the body (Burg & Pickering, 2011; Burg *et al.*, 2011). *Inflammation* is an immune response characterized by swelling, heat, redness and pain. Chronic inflammation of this kind may contribute to heart disease, stroke and other illnesses.

Finally, investigators have learnt that patterns of immune system responding vary from individual to individual (Marsland *et al.*, 2002). Certain individuals experience more profound immune system slowdowns in the face of stress than other individuals do. Moreover, these individual differences in immune system functioning tend to be consistent across stressful situations. Thus, some stressed persons are more likely than others to develop infections and other diseases. Let's look next at some individual factors that may be responsible for differences in immune system functioning.

Behaviour, Personality and Social Support Stress may trigger a series of behavioural changes that affect the immune system indirectly. People under chronic stress may, for example, become anxious or depressed, perhaps even develop an anxiety or mood disorder. In turn, they may eat poorly, exercise less, have trouble sleeping or smoke or drink. Such behaviours are all known to slow down the immune system (Brooks *et al.*, 2011; Kibler *et al.*, 2010). There is also a vicious circle to be aware of here. If, as a result of stress, you eat badly, sleep badly, take drugs and so on, you will start to feel terrible. Feeling terrible creates more stress, as does the awareness that you are dealing badly with your stress by smoking or drinking, for example. This adds to the stress, which leads to greater levels of sleep disturbance, drug-taking and so the cycle continues. In fact, it is more of a spiral than a circle, because with each revolution the problem gets bigger and bigger, and more and more difficult to cope with.

An individual's personality may also help determine how much the immune system is affected by stress. Studies suggest that people who typically respond to life stress with optimism, effective coping and resilience tend to experience better immune system functioning and to be better prepared to fight off illness (Kern & Friedman, 2011; Williams *et al.*, 2011). Correspondingly, those with resilient personalities tend to remain healthy after stressful events, whereas those whose personal styles are less hardy are more vulnerable to illness (Bonanno & Mancini, 2012; Ouellette & DiPlacido, 2001).

Some researchers have identified a connection between religiousness and health. Specifically, studies have found that regular church attendance is correlated with a decreased risk of death over a particular period (Ellison *et al.*, 2000). A few studies have also linked religiousness to better immune system functioning (Jackson & Bergeman, 2011). Although the relationship between church attendance and health is not well understood, it appears to result at least in part from the social support people receive from others in their religious group.

More generally, research indicates that social support helps to protect us from the effects of stress. People who have little social support and feel lonely tend to experience poorer immune functioning when stressed than other people do (Uchino & Birmingham, 2011; Cohen, 2002). Conversely, it appears that social support helps protect people from stress, poor immune system functioning and illness and helps improve recovery from illness or surgery (Matsumoto & Juang, 2008; Cohen, 2002; Kiecolt-Glaser *et al.*, 2002a, 2002b). Some studies have even suggested that patients with certain kinds of cancer who receive social support or supportive therapy may display better immune system functioning and, in turn, have more successful recoveries than patients without such social help (Dagan *et al.*, 2011; Spiegel & Fawzy, 2002).

The stress-reducing benefits of social support can be seen in the health of people who grow up in close-knit communities. One early study explored the low rate of stress-related illnesses among residents of the town of Roseto, Pennsylvania (Wolf, 1969). The death rate from coronary heart disease in this town was considerably lower than that in the general population, despite the fact that the residents' eating, smoking and exercise patterns were similar to those in communities with much higher coronary death rates. Clearly, something special was responsible for the residents' good health. That something turned out to be Roseto's positive

social environment. An Italian enclave, Roseto was home to extremely close, supportive and traditional families. Relatives, friends and local priests were always available to help out with any kind of problem. During the 1970s, Roseto's younger generation began to marry people from other backgrounds and move away. Church attendance also dropped. These social changes resulted in less social support throughout the community. Perhaps not surprisingly, the rate of heart attacks in the community increased (Greenberg, 1978).

The Benefits of Stress

It might be hard to believe, given the litany of problems that we have identified here, but stress can be positive. In fact, when Selye first identified stress as a concept, back in 1936, he actually drew a distinction between unpleasant stressors and pleasant stressors. How can a stressor be pleasant? Think about waiting for a call from someone you met at a party last night; it can be stressful, but in an exciting way. Unpleasant stressors, according to Selye, cause **distress**, the kind of unpleasant stress on which we have generally been focusing up to now. Pleasant stressors, in contrast, cause *eustress*.

> **distress** stress caused by unpleasant situations or circumstances.

A key benefit of stress is that it helps promote positive development. Some theorists' state that parents can actually stunt a baby's development by meeting all the baby's needs and that there is some optimal level of frustration that facilitates development. Researchers have suggested that similar principles apply across the lifespan. That is, adverse events and the stress that they produce can force you to confront challenges, adapt to your environment and build up strength and resilience (Tennen & Affleck, 2009, 2002; Tennen *et al.*, 2005).

Today, **eustress** is defined not in terms of the stressor but in terms of the stress level: it is the optimal level of stress that promotes physical and psychological health (Nelson & Cooper, 2005). But what exactly is an optimal level of stress? We can think about this question in a couple of ways. First, exposing yourself to a small level of stress in a controlled situation can improve your performance in a more stressful situation, a process called **inoculation**. If you call one friend to talk through what you want to say to another friend with whom you have been arguing, you are inoculating yourself.

> **eustress** the optimal level of stress needed to promote physical and psychological health.

> **inoculation** exposing oneself to a relatively low level of stress in a controlled situation in order to improve later performance in a more stressful situation.

As we have seen previously, another way of considering what constitutes an optimal level of stress involves looking at the relationship between stress and performance. As shown

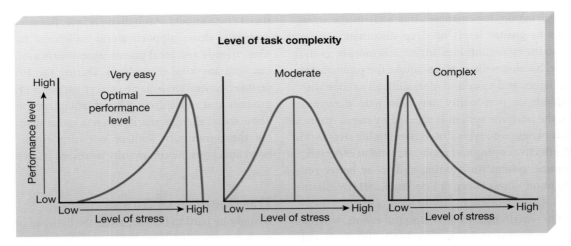

FIGURE 18.5 Stress and performance. Stress can actually benefit performance, depending on the complexity of the task. On very complex tasks, a low level of stress is optimal for performing your best; on very easy tasks, a high stress level helps you stay focused.
Source: Based on Figure 13.5, p. 528, from WEITEN. Psychology, 6E. © 2004 Wadsworth, a part of Cengage Learning, Inc. Reproduced by permission, www.cengage.com/permissions.

in Figure 18.5, researchers have found that stress can actually facilitate performance on a task, depending on the complexity of the task.

- *Performance of very easy tasks can benefit from a high level of stress.* For example, the videogame Tetris involves very little cognitive complexity and very low stakes, but as the computer starts dropping the pieces faster, it will get your attention and help you stay focused on the game.

- *A moderately difficult task benefits from a moderate level of stress.* Too low, and you will not get excited enough to perform your best. Too high, and you will be more likely to lose your focus or perform poorly.

- *For a complex task, low stress leads to the optimal performance.* Consider that next time you decide to make dinner for a few friends and do not leave quite enough time to get everything prepared before they arrive.

Well-Being and Happiness: The Opposite of Stress

In recent years, there has been a change of focus by a number of psychologists onto what is now called *positive psychology.* The emphasis is more on well-being than *abnormal psychology,* with its focus on clinical syndromes and aberrant behaviour. It is true that there are many human success stories out there about people who face up to challenges and succeed, and we can learn more from those, arguably, than by dwelling on when things fall apart. Positive psychology is all about taking value from situations and learning about good practice from others. So, what is *well-being* (or subjective well-being as it is commonly called) and how can we get some of that for ourselves?

Two of the main figures in the well-being movement in psychology are Martin Seligman and Ed Diener. Ed Diener, known by many as *Dr Happy*, is responsible for the most commonly used scale to measure subjective well-being: the *Satisfaction with Life Scale* (Diener *et al.*, 1985). This five-item measure is intended to indicate how comfortable with their existence people are and how much they feel their life is working out the way that they would want it to. This is a key indicator of happiness, and in fact Diener's recent work shows very clearly just how important being happy is: people who are happier live longer, by a substantial margin (Diener & Chan, 2011).

Martin Seligman's work focuses more on positive psychology rather than well-being per se, and in particular he is responsible for identifying specific *character strengths* or *signature strengths*, which underpin success and happiness, which societies tend to reward and value (Peterson & Seligman, 2004). This is particularly relevant when considering the issues of stress, resilience and hardiness. The character strengths include creativity, bravery, kindness, fairness and humour. It is hard to imagine a culture that would eschew such traits. They seem to be human universals, as it were. Furthermore, there is evidence that possession of many of these strengths sets a person up well for recovery from illness

(Peterson *et al.*, 2006). It is a short step from that finding to the potential for these strengths to also underpin successful coping and resistance to stress.

In an important paper, Seligman (2008) calls for a new field of medicine, which he terms *positive health*. It is Seligman's assertion that medicine, and psychology, has achieved a lot in the field of mental illness, but not so much in mental health. It was assumed, erroneously, that mental health was the absence of mental illness, but actually all that leaves is some kind of even keel, or a neutrality, rather than anything good or positive. We need more than this. As Seligman says: 'The most important theme that runs through the tantalizing positive physical health outcomes is a link between positive psychology and positive health: subjective well-being, as measured by optimism and other positive emotions, protects one from physical illness' (2008, p. 7). Even simple things, like smiling, are known to have positive effects on physical health and life success (Harker & Keltner, 2001). Of course, it is difficult to smile when everything around you is going wrong, which is where the positive psychology movement suffers its biggest problem. Knowing that happy people are healthier does not make happy people, just as knowing that stress damages the individual does not do anything to alleviate stress.

One well-researched intervention to improve happiness, and thereby reduce stress, is the *three good things* exercise (Seligman *et al.*, 2005). At the end of each day, a person writes down three good things that they are glad about in their life. It is a simple technique, but it has been shown to substantially enhance well-being. Perhaps it works because people forget to think about the good things in their lives,

because the bad things weigh them down all day long. Taking time out to reflect that life is not all bad, and keeping a record of that, puts things into some kind of perspective. There are other, equally successful, brief interventions too, including writing a letter to someone that you love or to whom you are grateful. It seems that there is something enjoyable about expressing positive emotion, be it a smile or a kind word, which reflects back on the person who expresses it.

Post-Traumatic Stress Disorder

 OUT OF THE ORDINARY

In addition to leading to physical diseases, stress can contribute to various psychological disorders, from depression to sexual dysfunctions. Moreover, it plays a central role in *post-traumatic stress disorder (PTSD)*.

In PTSD, people who have confronted an extraordinarily stressful event – combat, rape, earthquake, aeroplane crash, automobile accident – experience severe psychological symptoms lasting for months or even years. They have lingering reactions of intense fear and helplessness. They may be battered by memories, dreams or nightmares connected to the traumatic event and may repeatedly try to avoid activities, thoughts, feelings or conversations that remind them of the event. Many also feel detached from other people, some lose interest in activities that once brought enjoyment and some feel dazed. Individuals with the disorder may be easily startled, develop sleep problems and have trouble concentrating. They may also feel extreme guilt because they survived the traumatic event while others did not.

PSYCHOLOGY AROUND US | Remembering Vietnam

I cannot get the memories [of combat] out of my mind! The images come flooding back in vivid detail, triggered by the most inconsequential things, like a door slamming or the smell of stir-fried pork. Last night I went to bed, was having a good sleep for a change. Then in the early morning a storm-front passed through and there was a bolt of crackling thunder. I awoke instantly, frozen in fear. I am right back in Vietnam, in the middle of the monsoon season at my guard post. I am sure I'll get hit in the next volley and convinced I will die. My hands are freezing, yet sweat pours from my entire body. I feel each hair on the back of my neck standing on end. I cannot catch my breath and my heart is pounding. I smell a damp sulfur smell.

(Davis, 1992)

While any traumatic event can trigger PTSD, certain events are particularly likely to do so. Among the most common are combat, natural disasters, abuse and victimization (Keane *et al.*, 2009). People who are victims of terrorism, for example, or who live with the fear of terrorism, often

experience post-traumatic stress symptoms (Tramontin & Halpern, 2007).

In the United Kingdom, between 5 and 10% of people experience PTSD at some point, according to government statistics; it can be up to 22% in emergency ambulance personnel (Bennett *et al.*, 2004). Anyone who experiences an unusual trauma will be affected by it, but only some people develop PTSD. To understand the development of this disorder more fully, researchers have looked at the same stress-related factors that we have come across throughout this chapter:

- *Biological Factors.* As we have observed, stressors trigger biochemical reactions throughout the brain and body. Apparently, in the face of extraordinarily threatening stressors, some people develop particularly strong biochemical reactions, reactions that continue well beyond a short fight-or-flight period. It appears that such individuals are more likely than others to experience a PTSD (Pace & Heim, 2011; Bremner & Charney, 2010).

- *Personality.* Earlier, we observed that people with certain personality styles or coping styles are particularly likely to react to threats with stress and to develop medical problems. Similarly, such styles increase the likelihood of developing a PTSD (Burijon, 2007). It turns out, for example, people with less resilient, or less hardy, personality styles appear more likely to develop a PTSD than those with more resilient styles (Kunst, 2011; Maddi, 2007).

- *Social Support.* We have seen that inadequate social support can intensify stress reactions and slow down immune system functioning. Thus, it is not surprising that people with weak social support systems are more likely to develop a PTSD after a traumatic event (Uchino & Birmingham, 2011; Ozer *et al.*, 2003).

We will look at PTSD in greater detail in Chapter 19. In the meantime, the current discussion helps clarify once again that stress is a very powerful force. Moreover, when it is overwhelming or dealt with ineffectively, it can totally disrupt our functioning and our lives.

Before You Go On

What Do You Know?

9. How has stress been linked with coronary heart disease?
10. What is the connection between life changes and illness?
11. How does stress affect the immune system?
12. What are some beneficial effects of stress?
13. What are some symptoms of post-traumatic stress disorder (PTSD)?

What Do You Think?

Try to recall five events in your life or in the lives of your family members and friends that suggest a relationship between stress and illness. Having now read this chapter, how might you account for those events and relationships?

Access your interactive e-book to view a video clip for this chapter at **www.wileyopenpage.com**

Summary

What Is Stress?

LEARNING OBJECTIVE 1   Define stress, and describe the ways and situations in which people experience it.

- Stress is a state brought on by any situation that threatens or appears to threaten a person's sense of well-being, thus challenging the person's ability to cope. A situation that triggers the stress response is a stressor. A stressor may be acute (short term) or chronic (long term).
- People may experience stress as frustration, pressure, conflict or danger.
- Kinds of stressors include daily hassles, life changes, traumatic events, chronic negative situations and special sociocultural conditions.

Responding to and Coping with Stress

LEARNING OBJECTIVE 2   Explain how individual responses to stress differ, and discuss several ways in which people cope with stress.

- There are two main physiological pathways of stress: the sympathetic nervous system and the hypothalamic–pituitary–adrenal (HPA) axis. Both lead to activation of the fight-or-flight response, which is an immediate response to a stressor.
- Hans Selye first described the effects of chronic stress, which he called the general adaptation syndrome (GAS). The syndrome has three stages: alarm, resistance and exhaustion.
- Emotional responses to stress generally involve negative emotions.
- Individuals vary greatly in their responses to stress. Areas of difference include autonomic activity, explanatory style, personality and availability of social support.
- Coping describes efforts to manage, reduce or tolerate stress.

- Dealing with stress by lashing out at others, using defence mechanisms such as repression and engaging in self-indulgent behaviours such as smoking or drinking alcohol can be destructive when used in excess.
- More constructive coping strategies include problem-focused coping and emotion-focused coping.

Stress and Health

LEARNING OBJECTIVE 3   Explain how stress can cause physical illness, and discuss situations in which stress may be beneficial.

- Stress can increase risk for a number of health problems. People with high levels of hostility, such as those with Type A personalities, are prone to stress and appear to be at greater risk for coronary heart disease. Using the Social Readjustment Rating Scale, researchers have found that stress-producing life changes also increase the risk of illness.
- Psychoneuroimmunology is an area of study that examines the links between stress, the immune system and health. Severe stress may, for example, lower the activity of lymphocytes, a component of the immune system.
- Noradrenaline activity, cortisol activity, behaviour, personality and social support are each factors that affect how much the immune system is slowed down by stress.
- Eustress, an optimal level of stress, can promote the development of resilience and facilitate performance, especially for easy or moderately difficult tasks.
- Post-traumatic stress disorder (PTSD) is characterized by persistent, frightening thoughts or memories of a traumatic event, along with anxiety, depression and other symptoms.
- Factors that affect the likelihood of developing PTSD include biological factors, personality factors, childhood experiences and the availability of social support.

Activities to test yourself further are available in your interactive e-book at
www.wileyopenpage.com

TYING IT TOGETHER

WHAT HAPPENS IN THE BRAIN?

- The amygdala plays a key role in the onset of emotions, particularly fear. Its activation enables the brain to initiate an immediate fear reaction before other brain areas even start to process the fear-arousing situation.
- The prefrontal cortex seems to serve as an emotion coordinator and guide, turning emotional impulses to deliberate actions.
- The brain reacts to danger or stress by both activating the sympathetic nervous system and setting in motion the HPA axis.
- The release of noradrenaline and stress hormones can be helpful and protective when people experience short-term stress, but physically and psychologically debilitating when people experience high, longer-term stress.

OUT OF THE ORDINARY

- Anxiety disorders are collectively the most common of all mental disorders.
- People with high levels of hostility and certain other Type A personality characteristics are at greater risk for coronary heart disease.
- Significant life changes occurring over a limited period may contribute to a slowdown in immune system functioning and the onset of various medical problems.
- People whose personalities are less resilient and those with weak social supports seem more likely than other people to develop PTSD in the face of a traumatic event.

HOW WE DIFFER

- People differ in how clearly they can identify their emotions, how attentive they are to their emotions and how intense their emotions are.
- Women may not really be all that much more emotional than men. Rather, individuals may be following social display rules about how their particular gender should express emotions.
- People with highly reactive autonomic nervous systems (ANSs), pessimistic explanatory styles, Type A personality styles or weak social supports display, on average, more intense stress reactions than other people.
- Optimists are more likely than pessimists to seek out social support during stressful events and to employ constructive coping techniques.

HOW WE DEVELOP

- The range of emotions in newborns is largely undifferentiated. Infants vacillate largely between general distress and general contentment.
- Some research suggests that the achievement of various cognitive stages enables certain emotions to emerge. Other research finds that the emergence of various emotions helps trigger cognitive and social development.
- As children move from five years old to 12 years old, physical events (e.g. falling ill) feel less stressful to them while behavioural events (e.g. getting into trouble) and psychosocial events (e.g. arguing with friends) arouse more stress.
- The leading stressors for college students include having to take multiple tests, enduring finals week, applying to graduate school, being a victim of crime, having several assignments due on the same day and breaking up with a boyfriend or girlfriend.

QUIZ

Quizzes to test yourself further are available in your interactive e-book at
www.wileyopenpage.com

Key Terms

acute stressor 514
approach–approach
   conflict 516
approach–avoidance
   conflict 517
avoidance–avoidance
   conflict 516
chronic stressor 514
conflict 516

coping 526
daily hassles 517
distress 533
emotion-focused coping 528
eustress 533
frustration 515
general adaptation syndrome
   (GAS) 522
immune system 531

inoculation 533
life changes 517
lymphocytes 531
pressure 516
primary appraisal 523
problem-focused coping 528
psychoneuroimmunology 531
secondary appraisal 523
stress 514

stressor 514
traumatic events 519
Type A 526
Type B 526

FLASHCARDS

Flashcards to test yourself further are available in your interactive e-book at
www.wileyopenpage.com

CHAPTER 19

Psychological Disorders

Adapted by David A. Holmes, Manchester Metropolitan University, UK

CHAPTER OUTLINE

- Defining, Classifying and Diagnosing Psychological Disorders
- Models of Psychological Disorder
- Mood Disorders

- Anxiety Disorders
- Schizophrenia
- Other Psychological Disorders

 Access your interactive e-book to view a video clip for this chapter at **www.wileyopenpage.com**

Depressed and Lost

Diane Newman, a 38-year-old female, was referred to a new therapist for depression. Within three months, she had lost 15 pounds and felt constantly tired. She had withdrawn from nearly all her usual social activities and openly acknowledged thoughts of overdosing on pills. Previous psychotherapy and treatment with antidepressant medication had produced no improvement.

This change occurred shortly after the breakup of a relationship she had been having for approximately two years. She now saw herself as 'fat, unattractive, and doomed to be a spinster'. Although she had never had a wide circle of friends, the past two years had seen her social contacts become even more limited. Other than the few evenings spent with her boyfriend, she had gradually managed to enter a life of all work and no play, and was intensely lonely.

Diane lived alone and worked full-time as a paediatric nurse while pursuing a master's degree in nursing part-time. Although she was a first-class student, she had had numerous difficulties with fellow students and tutors. Her relations with staff were similarly troubled. Although she had a reputation as a good staff nurse, she had never been able to hold supervisory positions for any length of time without interpersonal conflicts.

Diane's early family history provided some clues to the source of her current difficulties. She was the eldest of three children and was frequently expected to play the role of carer for her younger siblings. She felt that her parents' love was contingent on her playing the role of 'mother's little helper'. She felt that her sister and brother had been allowed to enjoy a much more carefree childhood.

In short, Diane saw her past and present as an unhappy life of servitude, rejection and failure with no change in her future. She felt quite hopeless and therefore was considered a serious suicidal risk by her new therapist (Spitzer *et al.*, 1983). ■

Throughout this book, most of the discussions have looked at 'normal' mental functioning and behaviour. However, functioning often does go astray, as in the case of Diane Newman, where her depressed mood, isolated behaviour and negative thinking are far from functional.

You have already come across the leading psychological disorders while reading the 'Out of the Ordinary' sections throughout this book. In this chapter, it will be apparent that although most people believe they can recognize abnormal functioning it is, in fact, a difficult concept to define. Following this, the ways in which psychologists classify, assess and explain the various kinds of abnormal functioning will be examined. The next chapter will examine how mental health practitioners try to help the individuals whose behaviours, thoughts or emotions are dysfunctional – individuals known as *clients* or *patients* when seen in mental health settings.

Defining, Classifying and Diagnosing Psychological Disorders

LEARNING OBJECTIVE 1

Identify the common features of most definitions of abnormal functioning, and describe how psychological disorders are classified and diagnosed.

Diane Newman's emotions, behaviours and thoughts appear to be disturbed, the result of states referred to variously as *psychological dysfunctioning*, *psychopathology*, *psychological disorders* or *mental disorders*. The field devoted to the scientific study of psychological disorders has been historically

abnormal psychology the scientific study of psychological disorders.

referred to as **abnormal psychology** but is increasingly referred to as *psychopathology* or as a component of *clinical psychology*.

Disordered psychological functioning is a wide-ranging problem, as indicated in Figure 19.1. During their lifetime, as much as 25% of individuals in Europe experience psychological disorders (Alonso, *et al.*, 2004). The numbers and rates in other countries are similar. Furthermore, many people go through periods of great tension, upset or other forms of psychological discomfort in their lives, when they may experience some of the distress found in psychological disorders.

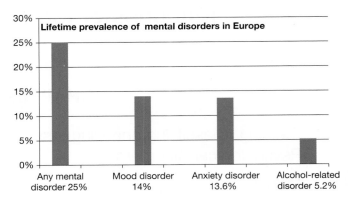

FIGURE 19.1 How many people are diagnosed with mental disorders? A quarter of people in Europe each year experience symptoms that qualify for a diagnosis of at least one mental disorder.

Defining Psychological Disorders

What is *psychological abnormality*? Although many definitions of abnormality have been proposed over the years, none is universally accepted (Pierre, 2010). However, most definitions have key features in common, often called *the four Ds*: deviance, distress, dysfunction and danger:

- *Deviance.* Behaviour, thoughts and emotions are considered abnormal when they differ from a society's ideas about proper functioning, which vary from society to society. A society that values competition and dominance may embrace aggressive behaviour, whereas one that emphasizes cooperation may consider such behaviour unacceptable and even abnormal. Moreover, a society's values may change over time, leading to a new societal view of what is psychologically abnormal. For example, a woman's participation in athletics, academia or business was considered unusual and even inappropriate a hundred years ago in Europe. Modern Europeans now value that behaviour.

- *Distress.* For many clinical theorists, behaviour, ideas or emotions must also cause distress or unhappiness before they can be considered disordered. Diane Newman feels upset and burdened most of the time by her negative feelings and thoughts and the impact they are having on her life.

- *Dysfunction.* Disordered behaviour also tends to interfere with daily functioning so that sufferers cannot take proper care of themselves, interact well with others or work effectively. As in the opening case, Diane's behaviours have contributed to social isolation, problems at work and conflicts at school.

- *Danger.* Some people with psychological dysfunctioning become dangerous to themselves or others. If, for example, individuals are consistently hostile or confused, they may put themselves, family members or friends at risk. Recall that Diane Newman's thoughts of overdosing on pills have led her therapist to consider her a serious suicide risk. It is important to note, however, that although danger is often cited as a feature of abnormal psychological functioning research indicates that it is actually the exception rather than the rule (Hiday & Burns, 2010). Despite popular views, most people who are greatly troubled or even out of touch with reality pose no immediate danger to themselves or anyone else.

As our discussion suggests, the definition of disorder or abnormality depends heavily on social norms and values. At the same time, societies often have difficulty distinguishing between an abnormality that requires help and an eccentricity that should not be the concern of other people. We are often aware of people who behave in ways considered strange, such as an individual who lives alone with dozens

Does dysfunction equal abnormality? A man sets himself on fire to protest about China's occupation of Tibet. In this context, such personal dysfunctioning does not, by itself, indicate that he is experiencing a psychological disorder.
Source: Rajesh Nirgude/©AP/Wide World Photos.

of animals and avoids other people. The behaviour of such individuals is deviant, but unless it leads to clear distress and dysfunction, most clinicians would judge it to be eccentric rather than abnormal.

PSYCHOLOGY AROUND US | Just a Bit Different

The dictionary defines an eccentric as a person who deviates from common behaviour patterns or displays odd or whimsical behaviour. Eccentrics do not typically suffer from psychological disorders. Whereas the unusual behaviour of people with disorders is thrust upon them and usually causes them suffering, eccentricity is chosen freely and provides pleasure. In short, 'Eccentrics know they're different and glory in it' (Weeks & James, 1995, p. 14).

Some very famous people were eccentrics. Writer James Joyce always carried a tiny pair of lady's bloomers, which he waved in the air to show approval. Writer Oscar Wilde in addition to wearing flamboyant clothing walked the streets of Oxford with a lobster on a leash. Alan Turing, scientist and mathematician, ate grass and used a necktie to hold up his trousers. Inventor and writer Sir George Sitwell stencilled his cows to make them look better and tried to pay his son's school fees with pigs and potatoes. Alexander Graham Bell covered the windows of his house to keep out the rays of the full moon. He also tried to teach his dog how to talk. And writer D. H. Lawrence enjoyed climbing mulberry trees in the nude.

Made for each other. A bride with real scorpions on her gown kisses her groom, who has a real centipede in his mouth. She holds the world record for staying in a cage with 3,400 scorpions for 32 days, he for staying with 1,000 centipedes for 28 days. Eccentric? Yes. Mentally disordered? Probably not.
Source: ©Sukree Sukplang/Reuters/Corbis.

To ascertain whether abnormality requires intervention or treatment three criteria are commonly applied throughout Europe:

- Significant distress or dysfunction in the individual concerned.

- Significant distress or disruption to those around them.

- Behaviour that warrants the attention of health or legal authorities.

To determine the exact form of an abnormality and thus its specific treatment requires the application of *classification* and *diagnosis*.

Classifying and Diagnosing Psychological Disorders

A *symptom* is a physical, behavioural or mental feature presented by a client that helps indicate a condition, illness or disorder. Fatigue is often a symptom of depression, for example. Similarly, poor concentration can be a symptom of anxiety, and hallucinations may indicate schizophrenia. When certain symptoms regularly occur together and follow a particular course, clinicians agree that those symptoms make up a particular mental disorder. A list of such disorders, with descriptions of the symptoms and guidelines for determining when individuals should be assigned to the categories, is known as a *classification system*.

The classification system that is used by most countries throughout the world is the **International Classification of Diseases (ICD)**, published by the World Health Organization. ICD is now in its tenth edition (ICD-10). In the United States, the **Diagnostic and Statistical Manual of Mental Disorders (DSM)** is published by the American Psychiatric Association and largely adopted across the United Kingdom and the rest of Europe as well. The current version is called DSM-IV Text Revision (DSM-IV-TR) (APA, 2000) but a new version called DSM-5, due in 2013, has many changes to the categories, symptoms and criteria (Regier *et al.*, 2011). Both DSM and ICD systems have been revised several times since they were first published, DSM in 1952 and the first version of ICD with mental disorders in 1948. DSM system has been used outside the United States and tends to dominate literature, although both systems cover very similar disorders and there are only a few differences (Table 19.1). With each revision, agreement between DSM and ICD systems increases.

International Classification of Diseases (ICD) the European-based system used by most countries to classify psychological disorders; published by the World Health Organization and currently in its tenth edition (ICD-10).

Diagnostic and Statistical Manual of Mental Disorders (DSM) the US-based classification system for psychological disorders featured in most literature; DSM-IV-TR is the current version.

TABLE 19.1 Disorders in DSM-IV-TR and ICD-10 Variations

DSM Group	Description and Examples of Disorder Group	ICD Variation
Disorders usually first diagnosed in infancy, childhood and adolescence	Disorders in this group tend to emerge before adult life, e.g. Mental retardation (Intellectual disability) Autism	Termed 'Disorders of psychological development' these are similar to DSM but 'Mental retardation' is in its own separate group
Delirium, dementia and amnestic and other cognitive disorders	These disorders are dominated by impairment in cognitive functioning, e.g. Alzheimer's disease Huntington's disease	These are very similar to DSM but are referred to as 'Organic, including symptomatic mental disorders'
Substance-related disorders	These disorders are brought about by the use of substances that affect the central nervous system, e.g. Alcohol use disorders Opioid use disorders	These are very similar to DSM but termed 'Mental and behavioural disorders due to psychoactive substance use'
Psychotic disorders	In this group of disorders, functioning deteriorates until the individual reaches a state of psychosis or loss of contact with reality, e.g. Schizophrenia	Termed 'Schizophrenia, schizotypal and delusional disorders', ICD includes a schizotypal form, which appears as a personality disorder in DSM. ICD still uses the 'Hebephrenic' subtype, termed 'Disorganised' in DSM
Mood disorders	Disorders in this group are marked by severe disturbances of mood that cause people to feel extremely and inappropriately sad or elated for extended periods, e.g. Major depressive disorder Bipolar disorders	These are very similar in ICD, though they retain the term 'affective' and depression is mainly divided into single episode versus recurrent depressive disorder

TABLE 19.1 (*Continued*)

DSM Group	Description and Examples of Disorder Group	ICD Variation
Anxiety disorders	Anxiety is the predominant disturbance in this group of disorders, e.g. Phobias Obsessive–compulsive disorder	Named 'Neurotic, stress-related and somatoform disorders' in ICD. These DSM disorders, but with the addition of depression with anxiety, all appear in ICD. However, ICD retains the term 'Neurotic' for the disorder group and includes Somatoform and Dissociative Disorders in this group (see below)
Somatoform disorders	These disorders are marked by physical symptoms that apparently are caused primarily by psychological rather than physiological factors, e.g. Somatization disorder Body dysmorphic disorder	ICD versions of these disorders are similar but are listed under DSM equivalent of Anxiety Disorders
Dissociative disorders	These disorders are characterized by significant changes in consciousness memory, identity or perception without a clear physical cause, e.g. Dissociative fugue Dissociative identity disorder	ICD versions of these disorders are similar but are listed under DSM equivalent of Anxiety Disorders
Eating disorders	People with these disorders display abnormal patterns that significantly impair their functioning, e.g. Anorexia nervosa Bulimia nervosa	ICD includes overeating amongst these disorders but groups eating disorders under a wider category of 'Behavioural syndromes associated with physiological disturbance and physical factors'
Sexual disorders and gender identity disorder	These are disorders in sexual function, behaviour or preferences, e.g. Sexual dysfunctions Paraphilias	In ICD, sexual dysfunctions are in a wider category of 'Behavioural syndromes associated with physiological disturbance and physical factors'. Gender identity and paraphilias are under the heading of 'Disorders of adult personality and behaviour' in ICD
Sleep disorders	People with these disorders display chronic sleep problems, e.g. Primary insomnia Sleep-terror disorder	In ICD, sleep disorders are under the heading of 'Behavioural syndromes associated with physiological disturbance and physical factors' but contains similar items
Impulse-control disorders	People with these disorders are chronically unable to resist impulses, drives or temptations to perform certain acts that are harmful to themselves or to others, e.g. Pathological gambling Kleptomania	The disorders listed in DSM are the same in ICD but under the heading of 'Disorders of adult personality and behaviour'
Psychological factors affecting medical condition	These disorders, also called psychophysiological disorders, result from an interaction of psychological and biological factors, e.g. Asthma Hypertension	These disorders tend to be classified as medical conditions and are only mentioned generally in both DSM and ICD under general headings such as 'Other conditions that may be a focus of clinical attention'
Personality disorders	People with these disorders display pervasive, inflexible, enduring and deviant personality traits and behaviours, i.e. Paranoid Schizoid Schizotypal Antisocial Borderline Histrionic Narcissistic avoidant Dependent Obsessive–compulsive	These have their own category in DSM but in ICD come under 'Disorders of adult personality and behaviour'. DSM 'Antisocial' is termed 'Dissocial' in ICD, 'Obsessive–Compulsive' is referred to as 'Anankastic', 'Borderline' as 'Emotionally unstable' and DSM's 'Avoidant' as 'Anxious' in ICD. ICD does not have entries for Schizotypal or Narcissistic Personality Disorders

When clinicians decide that a person's symptoms fit the criteria for a particular disorder, they are making a **diag-**

diagnosis a clinician's determination that a person's cluster of symptoms represents a particular disorder.

nosis. Most clinicians use DSM or ICD to help them diagnose their clients' problems. Assigning a diagnosis suggests that the client's pattern of dysfunction is basically the same as patterns displayed by many other people, has been researched in numerous studies and has responded to certain kinds of treatment. Clinicians can then apply what is generally known about the disorder to the client with whom they are working.

Based on her pattern of symptoms, Diane Newman would probably receive a diagnosis of a mood disorder: *major*

depressive disorder. A clinician may also take note of the fact that Diane has avoided people and social relationships throughout her life, largely because she fears being judged, and may also diagnose *avoidant personality disorder*. When people qualify for two or more diagnoses, they are said to display **comorbidity**.

Although very useful, DSM and ICD do not always lead to accurate diagnoses. A wrong diagnosis may lead to various problems, including treatments that are misguided. Some of the risks of misdiagnosis are discussed in the following box, 'Can Assessment and Diagnosis Cause Harm?'

comorbidity the condition in which a person's symptoms qualify him or her for two or more diagnoses.

PSYCHOLOGY AROUND US   Can Assessment and Diagnosis Cause Harm?

Although mental health terms such as anxiety, depression and schizophrenia are common in the media, public discourse and even daily conversations, it turns out that accurate diagnoses of psychological disorders are sometimes elusive in the clinical field. It appears that even with effective assessment techniques and carefully researched classification categories clinicians sometimes arrive at a wrong conclusion or diagnosis (Fernbach *et al.*, 2011).

Indeed, studies have revealed occasional errors in assessment and diagnosis, particularly in hospitals (Mitchell, 2010). In an often-cited study, skilled clinicians were asked to re-evaluate the diagnoses of 131 patients at a mental hospital (Lipton & Simon, 1985). Whereas 89 of the patients had originally received a diagnosis of schizophrenia, only 16 received it upon re-evaluation. And while 15 patients initially had been

given a diagnosis of mood disorder, 50 received that label on re-evaluation.

Simply classifying people can lead to unfortunate results. Diagnostic labels can become self-fulfilling prophecies. Once a diagnosis has been made, others may view and react to patients in ways that actually lead to their behaving more disordered. Furthermore, our society attaches a *stigma*, or negative prejudice, to mental disorders (Bell *et al.*, 2011; Rosenberg, 2011). People with such labels may find it hard to get a job, particularly one with a high level of responsibility, or to be accepted socially for some time.

Some clinicians have argued for doing away with assessment and diagnosis. Others, however, believe that classification and diagnosis are essential to understanding and treating disorders and that we should further research psychological disorders and improve assessment and diagnostic techniques.

Assessing Individuals for Psychological Disorders

In order to give a diagnosis, clinicians must *assess* the individual. Clinical assessment is used to precisely identify both the disordered behaviour and the best treatment approach. The hundreds of clinical assessment techniques and tools developed fall into three categories: *clinical interviews*, *observations* and *tests*.

clinical interview an assessment technique involving a face-to-face encounter between the clinician and the person being assessed.

Clinical Interviews A **clinical interview** is a face-to-face encounter (Cepeda, 2010) and is the starting point with a client for almost every practitioner.

Interviews can be either unstructured or structured or a combination of the two (Segal & Hersen, 2010). In an *unstructured* clinical interview, the clinician asks open-ended questions such as, 'What brings you here today?' The lack of structure allows the interviewer to follow leads that could not be anticipated beforehand. In a *structured* clinical interview, clinicians ask carefully prepared questions. A structured format helps guarantee that clinicians will gather the same kinds of useful information in all their interviews.

One reliable structured interview is used in conjunction with a rating scale called the *Hamilton Depression Scale*. Here, clinicians ask specific questions such as:

Have you been feeling hopeless? How bad is the feeling?

In the past week, when something good happened, did your mood brighten up?

Have you been putting yourself down this past week?

This past week, have you had thoughts that life is not worth living?

How have you been spending your time this past week?

(Williams, 1996)

Based on the client's answers to such structured questions, the clinical interviewer completes the depression scale and arrives at both a level of depression score and a clear picture of the client's depression.

Although valuable, this assessment technique has certain limitations (Chang & Krosnick, 2010). Clients may intentionally mislead interviewers, presenting themselves as less impaired or more impaired than they actually are (in the hope of gaining faster clinical attention). Similarly, they may avoid discussing particularly unflattering or flattering events (Gold & Castillo, 2010). Often, people may be *unable* to give an accurate report in their interview simply because of their problems. For example, individuals who suffer from depression view themselves very negatively and may describe themselves as poor students or inadequate parents when that is far from accurate (Feliciano & Gum, 2010). During her clinical interview, Diane Newman inaccurately described herself as overweight, unattractive, unintelligent and ineffective.

Particularly in unstructured interviews, clinicians may mistakenly influence the information they gather. Race, gender and age biases may affect their interpretations of what a client is saying (Ungar *et al.*, 2006). Similarly, a client's feelings about the interviewer's race, sex, age and appearance may affect his or her responses (Davis *et al.*, 2010).

Clinical Observations

Another strategy in the assessment of abnormal functioning is the systematic observation of behaviour. In **analogue observation**, clinicians observe clients in an artificial setting, such as a therapy office or laboratory. Such observations are often aided by special equipment, such as a video recorder or one-way mirror (Lindhiem *et al.*, 2011). Clients may role-play or solve problems in interactions with same-aged individuals or authority figures. These observations give clinicians a clearer picture of their interpersonal or assertiveness skills.

In **naturalistic observation**, practitioners observe their clients in their everyday environments, such as homes,

analogue observation the observation of individuals in an artificial setting, such as a clinical office or a laboratory.

naturalistic observation the observation of individuals in everyday settings.

schools, institutions such as hospitals and prisons or community settings. In most cases, they centre on parent–child, sibling–child or teacher–child interactions and on fearful, aggressive or disruptive behaviour (Lindheim *et al.*, 2011).

Clinical observations have limitations (Norton *et al.*, 2010). A client's behaviour may be affected by the presence of the observer (Mowery *et al.*, 2010). If students in a classroom become aware that someone is watching them, they may change their usual behaviour, trying, for example, to create a good impression (Lane *et al.*, 2011).

In **self-monitoring**, people observe themselves and record the frequency of certain behaviours, feelings or thoughts as they occur (Norton *et al.*, 2010). How often, for instance, does a man have an urge to drink alcohol or an anxious person have worrying thoughts? What circumstances bring those feelings about? Although useful, self-monitoring has certain limitations (Baranski, 2011). When people monitor themselves, they often change their behaviours unintentionally (Holifield *et al.*, 2010). Smokers, for example, often reduce the number of cigarettes they smoke when monitoring how much they smoke. Although this interferes with accurate assessment, it can be useful in treatment. Indeed, programmes to help people cut down smoking anticipate that such self-monitoring will help reduce smoking.

self-monitoring when individuals monitor their own symptoms.

Clinical Tests

Clinical tests are tools for gathering information about certain aspects of a person's mental functioning, from which broader conclusions about the person can be drawn, using any of the hundreds of clinical tests available.

clinical tests one means of gathering information about a person's psychological functioning.

Although clinicians currently use interviews and informal observation to help assess clients, most do not conduct formal testing. The tests that are most commonly used in the clinical arena are ones already examined throughout this textbook, including personality inventories (Chapter 15), intelligence tests (Chapter 12) and neuroimaging (Chapter 5).

Clinical testing may also include a *response inventory*, a test or questionnaire that measures one specific area of functioning, such as emotions or social skills (Wilson *et al.*, 2010; Osman *et al.*, 2008). Given her difficulties, Diane Newman's therapist may administer the *Beck Depression Inventory*. In this, clients rate their own level of depressive moods, thoughts and behaviours and any effect on aspects of their functioning. One item asks respondents to rate their level of suicidal ideas from 0 to 3, for example, with 0 being 'I don't have any thoughts of killing myself' and 3 being, 'I would kill myself if I had the chance.'

Models of Psychological Disorder

LEARNING OBJECTIVE 2

Describe the models frequently used by psychologists to explain disordered functioning.

Over the course of our lives, each of us has developed a perspective that helps us make sense of the things other people say and do. The perspectives that scientists use to explain phenomena are known as *models*, or *paradigms* (Kuhn, 1962). To understand how a clinical theorist explains disorders, we must know which model shapes his or her view of abnormal functioning. Thus, in this section we will examine today's most influential clinical models – the neuroscientific and cognitive-behavioural models – as well as the less empirical humanistic, existential, sociocultural and developmental psychopathology models, which include the historic psychodynamic approach (Table 19.2). In the next chapter, we will see how each model infers a differing treatment.

TABLE 19.2 Current and Historically Significant Models of Disorder

Approach	Causes of Disordered Functioning
Neuroscientific	Structural or biochemical malfunctions in the brain
Cognitive-Behavioural	Disordered behaviour acquired through a tightly interwoven mix of conditioning, modelling and cognitive principles
Humanistic/Existential	Distorted views of self prevent personal growth or decision making
Sociocultural	Societal, cultural, social and familial pressures or conflicts
Developmental Psychopathological	Early risk factors combined with poor resilience throughout life stages
Psychodynamic	Assumes unconscious conflicts claimed to be rooted in childhood

The Neuroscience Model  WHAT HAPPENS IN THE BRAIN?

Neuroscientists view abnormal behaviour as an illness brought about by a malfunctioning brain. Researchers have discovered connections between certain psychological or neurological disorders and problems in specific structures of the brain. Huntington's disease is a disorder marked by violent emotional outbursts, memory loss, suicidal thinking, involuntary body movements and absurd beliefs, which has been linked to the loss of cells in the brain region called the *striatum*.

Neuroscientists also link mental disorder to deficient or excessive activity of different neurotransmitters and abnormal hormonal activity in the endocrine system (see Chapter 5). Depression has been related to insufficient activity of the neurotransmitters *noradrenaline* and *serotonin* as well as increased levels of the hormone *cortisol*. Two currently researched factors underpinning these neural imbalances are *genetics* and *viral infections*.

Studies have found that genetic inheritance plays a key role in mood disorders, schizophrenia, intellectual disability, Alzheimer's disease and other mental disorders. In most cases, no single gene is responsible for a particular disorder (Oksenberg & Hauser, 2010), but many genes combine to produce dysfunction. The predispositions set up by such genes may in some cases require environmental triggers.

Another source of neurological dysfunction is viral infection. Some research suggests schizophrenia, a disorder marked by hallucinations and other departures from reality, may be related to exposure to certain viruses before birth or during childhood (Fox, 2010). A damaging virus may enter the brain of a foetus or young child and then remain dormant until the individual reaches puberty or young adulthood. Hormonal changes, another infection or stressful life events may then activate the virus, thereby producing the symptoms of schizophrenia. Viruses have also been linked to mood and anxiety disorders (Fox, 2010).

Extreme social disorders and the brain. Forensic psychiatrist Helen Morrison displays slices of the brain of John Wayne Gacy, who murdered at least 33 boys and young men between 1972 and 1978. In this case, post-mortem examination did not reveal a clear link between physical brain structure and the behaviour of Gacy. Other neural studies, such as those by Adrian Raine, have found abnormalities leading to aggression.

Source: M. Spencer Green/©AP/Wide World Photos.

Today, the neuroscience model of mental disorder is increasingly recognized and advancing very rapidly with research. Psychotropic medications bring relief where other approaches have failed (see Chapter 20).

However, some neuroscience proponents of this model consider biological factors and brain interventions alone to explain and treat all disordered behaviours, neglecting any complex interplay of biological factors and environmental experiences. And yet, very few contemporary neuroscientists hold extreme views and there are many disorders that are minimally influenced by the environment.

The Cognitive-Behavioural Model

Cognitive-behavioural theorists propose that psychological disorders result largely from a combination of problematic learnt behaviours and dysfunctional cognitive processes. According to this model, such behaviours and thinking processes interact with and mutually influence each other:

people use their particular ways of thinking to explain their behaviours and the events in their lives, behaviours may lead to particular thoughts, various cognitions may trigger certain behaviours and so on. Cognitive-behavioural theorists also view emotions and biological events as key variables, seeking to understand how these variables influence and interact with behaviour and cognition to produce dysfunction. But behavioural and cognitive principles lie at the heart of the model and cognitive-behavioural therapists focus largely on behaviours and cognitions in treating individuals (see Chapter 20).

It can be useful to initially examine the behavioural and cognitive components separately, reflecting the fact that, at one time, the behavioural model stood alone without the cognitive component. Then in the 1960s, theorists proposed a more cognitive-behavioural perspective. They argued that *individuals'* cognitions greatly influence and are influenced by their behaviour.

The Behavioural Perspective The behavioural perspective uses learning principles to explain how the environment changes a person's behaviour (see Chapter 9). Most learnt behaviour is constructive, but undesirable behaviour can also be learnt by the same principles of learning as adaptive behaviours. As discussed in Chapter 9, for example, phobias can occur by *classical conditioning*, in pairing a previously neutral object with an unconditioned stimulus that creates fear.

Evidence shows that disordered behaviour is learnt through *operant conditioning* processes of reward and punishment. For example, people may learn to abuse alcohol and drugs because initially such behaviours brought feelings of calm, comfort or pleasure. Others may develop or continue to display disordered eating patterns partly because of praise they receive for a thinner appearance (Wilson, 2011).

Modelling, in which we learn by observing others, can also lead to disordered behaviour. In Chapter 9, we saw how children learnt from a model to behave aggressively towards a Bobo doll, an inflatable clown (Bandura *et al.*, 1963). Similarly, children may develop maladaptive reactions because of exposure to dysfunctional models presented by their parents.

Behavioural principles can be tested in the laboratory, unlike others, such as the historical psychodynamic approach. In this, clinical symptoms have been conditioned in research participants, suggesting disorders develop through learning. In Chapter 20, we discuss how research shows that behavioural interventions are very helpful for treating specific fears, compulsive behaviours, social deficits and a wide range of other problems (Wilson, 2011).

The Cognitive Perspective According to this approach, disordered behaviour is due to cognitive problems including *maladaptive beliefs* and *illogical thinking processes*.

The pioneering clinical theorists Albert Ellis (1913–2007) and Aaron Beck have proposed that each of us holds broad beliefs about ourselves and our world that help to guide us through life and determine our reactions to the situations we encounter. However, for some, these beliefs are unjustified and unhelpful, leading them to act and react in ways that are inappropriate, with consequences for personal happiness.

Some individuals assume they are failures if they are not loved or approved of by every person they know. A successful presentation in the classroom can make them sad or anxious because one listener seemed bored. Their problematic belief helps set the stage for a life hampered by tension and disappointment.

In the Diane Newman case, she held unjustified beliefs that left her vulnerable to depression. Her case study further stated:

> Many of her [problems] seemed to stem from underlying attitudes . . . such as: 'If I care for others, they should/ must care for me,' or 'If something good happens to me, I'll have to pay for it later with pain,' or 'People either love me or hate me.

> **(Spitzer *et al.*, 1983, p. 129)**

Beck also found that some people continually think in illogical ways and keep drawing self-defeating and even pathological conclusions (Beck & Weishaar, 2011). He has identified several illogical thinking processes that are very common in depression and anxiety disorders. These include:

- *Selective perception.* Seeing only the negative features of an event.

- *Magnification.* Exaggerating the importance of undesirable events.

- *Overgeneralization.* Drawing broad negative conclusions on the basis of a single insignificant event.

Diane Newman's therapist noted repeated examples of illogical thinking that helped predispose Diane to depressive reactions:

> When she finally did get a B from her tutor, she concluded that she had failed miserably. There was no recognition of any middle ground between total academic success and total academic failure. Moreover, she tended to magnify the importance of events like this as if they were an indictment of her as a total human being.

> **(Spitzer *et al.*, 1983, p. 129)**

The cognitive perspective has appealed to a wide range of theorists. They embrace a viewpoint that sees *thought* as a key factor in both normal and dysfunctional behaviour. Research has found that people with psychological disorders often display the kinds of beliefs and errors in thinking described in cognitive theories (Sharf, 2012; Ellis, 2011).

The Humanistic and Existential Models

Humanistic and existential approaches lack evidence-based support and, along with the psychoanalytic model, are referred to as *non-empirical views* with little support for their use in clinical practice for major disorders. They are grouped together because both focus on the broader dimensions of human existence, but there are differences between them.

As discussed in Chapter 15, *humanists* believe that all of us are born with a natural inclination to self-actualize: a motive to fulfil our potential for goodness and growth (Maslow, 1970). We can achieve this if we can honestly appraise and accept our strengths and weaknesses and find positive personal values to live by. According to humanists, people who habitually deceive themselves and create a distorted view of the things that happen to them are likely to suffer some degree of psychological dysfunction.

Again, as discussed in Chapter 15, the humanist Carl Rogers thought we all have a basic need to receive *unconditional positive regard* from the other people, particularly our parents (Raskin *et al.*, 2011; Rogers, 2000, 1987, 1951). Rogers believed that children who do not receive unconditional positive regard acquire **conditions of worth**, a sense that they must meet certain standards in order to gain the love of their parents or other important figures. This relates to Diane Newman's feeling that her parents' love was conditional on her helping in the care and upkeep of the family.

> **conditions of worth** a person's perception that he or she must meet certain standards in order to gain the love of their parents or other important figures.

Harsh or rigid conditions of worth are thought to prevent a person from reaching his or her full potential. People may deny or distort thoughts and actions that do not measure up to their conditions of worth, creating a distorted view of themselves and their experiences. Eventually, they may not know what they are genuinely feeling or needing, or what values and goals will bring satisfaction to their lives, which is thought to lead to dysfunction.

Existentialists agree with humanists that human beings must have an accurate awareness of themselves and live meaningful lives in order to be well adjusted. These theorists believe that from birth we have the freedom either to confront our existence and give meaning to our lives or to run away from that responsibility.

According to existentialists, many people become intimidated by the pressures of society and look to others for guidance and authority. Surrendering their personal freedom of choice, they 'hide' from responsibility and decisions (Yalom & Josselson, 2011). They are then left with empty, inauthentic lives, anxious, frustrated and depressed.

Both humanistic and existential theories, in highlighting the challenges of psychological life, claim that this is missing from the other models (Watson *et al.*, 2011).

The broad issues of human fulfilment at the core of this model are hard to research. Only recently have any controlled studies been conducted by humanistic and existential researchers (Schneider & Krug, 2010). Such research may establish the value, if any, of these approaches.

The Sociocultural Model

Some theorists consider disordered behaviour is better understood in the light of social, cultural and familial forces. Some societies may create stresses that increase disordered functioning. Relationships are assumed between dysfunctioning and factors such as widespread social change, socioeconomic class membership, cultural background, social networks and family systems.

Social Change When a society undergoes major change, the mental health of its members can be greatly affected, such as rapid urbanization producing a rise in mental disorder. It is not yet known which features of urbanization – overcrowding, technological change, social isolation, migration and so forth – are most to blame. Similarly, societies in the throes of economic depression often display rises in rates of clinical depression and suicide (SAMHSA, 2010; Hammer, 1993).

Socioeconomic Class Studies have found that rates of psychological disorder, especially severe disorder, are much higher among members of lower socioeconomic classes than higher ones (Sareen *et al.*, 2011). Perhaps the special pressures of lower-class life help explain this relationship. Poverty is linked to many stressors, including high rates of crime, unemployment, overcrowding and even homelessness, as well as basic medical care and limited educational opportunities. Of course, other factors may account for this

The economy and mental health. Thousands of Filipino job seekers line up at a job fair in Manila. Unemployment and poverty seem to be strongly linked to psychological dysfunction.
Source: Romeo Ranoco/Reuters/Landov LLC.

relationship. People who suffer from significant mental disorders may be less effective at work, earn less money and, as a result, drift downwards to settle in a lower socioeconomic class.

Cultural Factors Many theorists believe that human behaviour, including disordered behaviour, is understood best by examining an individual's unique cultural context, including the values of that culture and the external pressures faced by members of the culture (Matsumoto & van de Vijer, 2011; Alegría, A. A. *et al.*, 2009; Alegría, M., 2007, 2004). Cultural groups that have been studied most often are ethnic and racial minority groups, along with economically disadvantaged people, women and homosexual individuals. Each of these groups faces special pressures in society that may help produce feelings of stress and, in some cases, abnormal functioning. Moreover, of course, membership of these groups often overlaps.

Women have been found to be twice as likely as men to experience depressive and anxiety disorders (Essau *et al.*, 2010). Similarly, migrant groups across Europe can have markedly higher or lower prevalence figures for certain mental illnesses. These differences are partly explained by lack of access to and take-up of mental health services (Lindert *et al.*, 2008). Racial and sexual prejudice and related problems certainly may also help explain these differences (Guimón, 2010).

Another cultural factor that has received much attention from clinical researchers and therapists in recent years is religion. Researchers have studied possible links between religious faith and mental health and have learnt that the two are often correlated. Studies have found, for example, that genuinely spiritual people tend, on average, to be less lonely, pessimistic, depressed or anxious than other people (Day, 2010). Moreover, as we observed in Chapter 18, such individuals often seem to cope better with major life stressors and appear less likely to abuse drugs or to attempt suicide.

Social Networks and Supports Many theorists focus on the social networks in which people operate, including their social and professional relationships, in terms of how communication and feedback from others affects health. Evidence has linked deficiencies in a person's social networks and their functioning (Gask *et al.*, 2011; Vega *et al.*, 2011; Paykel, 2006, 2003). People who are isolated and lack social support or intimacy in their lives have been found to be more likely to become depressed when under stress and to remain depressed longer than are people with supportive spouses or warm friendships.

Family Systems In **family systems theory**, the family is a system of interacting parts, in which family members interact with one another in consistent ways and follow rules unique to each family (Goldenberg & Goldenberg, 2011). In this, the *structure* and *communication* patterns of certain families force individual members to react in ways that would otherwise seem disturbed. If the members were to behave normally, they would severely strain the family's usual manner of operation and would actually increase their own and their family's turmoil.

> **family systems theory** the theory that each family has its own implicit rules, relationship structure and communication patterns that shape the behaviour of the individual members.

Diane Newman's family was structured so she was required to be a third parent in the family. This situation deprived her of normal childhood experiences and emotions in many ways, and so she came to view her life as one of 'servitude, rejection, and failure', and she experienced ongoing depression.

The Developmental Psychopathology Model

Developmental psychopathology relates to how psychological disorders evolve, based on both genetics and early childhood experiences. Early problematic patterns are thought to disrupt functioning as individuals move through later life stages (Cicchetti, 2010; Santostefano, 2010; Hinshaw, 2008). Developmental psychopathologists compare and contrast abnormal behaviour patterns with more normal ones, attempting to identify biological and environmental

> **developmental psychopathology** the study of how problem behaviours evolve as a function of a person's genes and early experiences and how these early issues affect the person at later life stages.

risk factors that contribute to negative outcomes and seek out factors that can help children avoid or recover from such outcomes.

> **risk factors** biological and environmental factors that contribute to problem outcomes.

Developmental psychopathologists hold that behaviour can be analysed in a variety of ways, including genetics, early environmental influences and the persons' own psychological processes.

Developmental psychologists have contributed two concepts to the field of psychology: *equifinality* and *multifinality* (Fanti & Henrich, 2010; Mitchell *et al.*, 2004). The concept of **equifinality** holds that individuals can start out from all sorts of different places but function (or dysfunction) in similar ways, owing to experiences. **Multifinality** follows the opposite principle. It suggests that children can start from the same point and wind up in any number of different psychological places.

> **equifinality** the idea that different children can start from different points and wind up at the same outcome.

> **multifinality** the idea that children can start from the same point and wind up at any number of different outcomes.

Conduct disorder is a disorder of childhood and adolescence characterized by repeated violations of others' rights, displays of aggression and destructive behaviour. This disorder offers an example for developmental principles in that various roads may lead to its development during adolescence (Litschge *et al.*, 2010). Sufferers may have been born with a difficult temperament, experienced poor parenting or developed poor social skills. As suggested by the notion of equifinality, the outcome is often similar, regardless of which risk factor is dominant.

At the same time, multifinality assures us that not every difficult baby or baby with ineffective parents will become conduct disordered. The majority will develop no pathology at all. Developmental psychopathologists research the biological, psychological or environmental events that help buffer or negate the impact of risk factors – events that help produce **resilience**, an ability to recover from or avoid the serious effects of negative circumstances (Dudley *et al.*, 2011; Flouri *et al.*, 2011; Hudziak & Bartels, 2008). Thus, it is just as critical to understand what goes right as it is to understand what goes wrong.

> **resilience** the ability to recover from or avoid the serious effects of negative circumstances.

The Psychodynamic Model

Currently, the psychodynamic model is best considered a historical approach as it is based on principles that have little or no empirical support and *psychoanalysis* is not supported by public mental health services in most of Europe. The psychodynamic approach will be described briefly here as it formed an enduring component of 19th- and early-20th-century treatment approaches and could be said to have impeded contemporary clinical approaches (see Shorter, 1997).

The psychodynamic model was developed from Sigmund Freud's theories. Psychodynamic theorists believe that a person's behaviour is determined by underlying unconscious psychological forces. Abnormal behaviours or symptoms are viewed as the consequences of conflicts between these forces or as unconscious attempts to resolve conflicts and lessen painful inner turmoil.

Freud proposed that a child's environment may prevent his or her id, ego and superego (see Chapter 15) from maturing properly or interacting effectively. Such a child is said to be *fixated* at an early stage of development. Such fixations, claimed Freud, affect all subsequent development and lead to disordered functioning.

Freud would have suggested that the family pressures Diane Newman experienced during her early years caused an imbalance of power among her id, ego and superego. The demands she experienced forced her to put aside many of her own id needs and to act in a mature, ego-dominated manner beyond her years. Freud would see childhood pressures and deprivations as possible roots for her adult depression.

Several of Freud's early colleagues disagreed with key aspects of his theories (see Chapter 15) and produced a number of psychodynamic variations (Sharf, 2012). For example, *object relations* theorists believe people are motivated primarily by a need to establish relationships with others, known as *objects*; difficulties with these relations create psychological problems (Blum, 2010; Kernberg, 2005, 1997).

As reported in Chapter 20, research has often failed to support the effectiveness of psychodynamic therapies (Prochaska & Norcross, 2010).

Before You Go On

What Do You Know?

4. What are the current major models used by psychologists to explain disordered functioning?
5. What are the major types of brain problems that are linked to disordered functioning?
6. In the view of cognitive-behavioural theorists, what kinds of problems can lead to disordered functioning?
7. How are the humanistic and existential models similar, and how do they differ?
8. What social and cultural factors have been found to be related to disordered functioning?

What Do You Think?

How would you describe your personal model for explaining why people behave as they do?

Mood Disorders  OUT OF THE ORDINARY

LEARNING OBJECTIVE 3

Differentiate major depressive disorder and bipolar disorder.

There are more than 400 disorders listed in DSM-IV-TR. The rest of this chapter will examine common disorders that are the focus of research attention, beginning with mood disorders (see also Chapter 14).

Mood changes usually come and go, as do reactions of joy or sadness to daily events. However, the moods of people with mood disorders tend to last a long time. In Diane Newman's case, her moods coloured all her interactions with the world and interfered with normal functioning.

Depression and mania are the key states in mood disorders. **Depression** is a sad state in which life seems bleak and its challenges overwhelming. **Mania**, the opposite of depression, is a state of heightened euphoria or irritability and frenzied energy, in which people may have an exaggerated belief that the world is theirs for the taking. Most people with a mood disorder suffer only from depression, a pattern found in **major depressive disorder** or in a less disabling but chronic form of depression called *dysthymic disorder*. Others experience periods of mania that alternate or intermix with periods of depression, a pattern called **bipolar disorder** in its severe form and *cyclothymic disorder* in a less severe but chronic form.

depression a persistent sad state in which life seems to lack meaning and its challenges become overwhelming.

mania a persistent state of euphoria or frenzied energy.

major depressive disorder a disorder characterized by a depressed mood that is significantly disabling and is not caused by such factors as drugs or a general medical condition.

bipolar disorder a mood disorder in which periods of mania alternate with periods of depression.

Major Depressive Disorder

People experiencing temporary sadness say they are *depressed*. Typically, they are responding to sad events, fatigue or morbid thoughts. This use of the term confuses a naturally occurring mood swing with a clinical syndrome. All of us experience dejection from time to time, but only some experience major depressive disorder. This disorder brings severe and long-lasting psychological pain that may intensify with time. Many of those who suffer from it may become unable to carry out the simplest of life's activities. Some even try to end their lives.

Using stringent criteria, data from many studies suggest that 6.7% of the population suffer from major depressive disorder during their lifetime (Waraich *et al.*, 2004). Other studies with broader criteria may put this figure much higher. Women are at least twice as likely as men to experience it. Approximately half of people with this disorder recover within six weeks, and 90% recover within a year, some without treatment (Kessler, 2002). However, most of them have at least one other episode of depression later in their lives (Taube-Schiff & Lau, 2008).

As we saw in the case of Diane Newman, severe depression has many symptoms other than sadness, and the symptoms often feed into one another. The symptoms span five areas of functioning: emotional, motivational, behavioural, cognitive and physical.

Characteristics of Depression Most people who are depressed feel sad and dejected. They describe themselves as *miserable* and *empty*. They often lose the desire to participate in their usual activities. Almost all report a lack of drive, initiative and spontaneity. Many depressed people become uninterested in life or wish to die; others wish that they could kill themselves; some attempt suicide. It has been estimated that between 6 and 15% of people who suffer from severe depression commit suicide (Taube-Schiff & Lau, 2008).

Depressed people usually are less active and less productive than others. They spend more time alone and may stay in bed for long periods. They may also move and even speak more slowly than others (Mitchell, 2010; Joiner, 2002). Most hold extremely negative views of themselves, considering themselves inadequate, undesirable, inferior and perhaps evil and blaming themselves for unfortunate events. Another cognitive symptom of depression is pessimism. Sufferers are usually convinced that nothing will ever improve, and feel helpless to change any aspect of their lives.

Finally, people who are depressed often report such physical ailments as headaches, indigestion, constipation, dizzy spells and general pain. They may also have disturbances of appetite and sleep (Mitchell, 2010; Neckelmann *et al.*, 2007).

Major depressive disorder often seems to be triggered by stressful events (Brown, 2010; Hammen *et al.*, 2009). Research has found that depressed people experience a greater number of stressful life events during the month just before the onset of a depressive episode than do other people during the same period (Monroe & Hadjiyannakis, 2002).

Today's leading explanations for major depressive disorder point to either neuroscientific, psychological or sociocultural factors. Many theorists believe that the various explanations should be combined where appropriate in order to more fully understand people with this disorder.

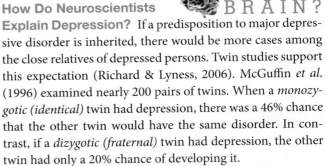

How Do Neuroscientists Explain Depression? If a predisposition to major depressive disorder is inherited, there would be more cases among the close relatives of depressed persons. Twin studies support this expectation (Richard & Lyness, 2006). McGuffin *et al.* (1996) examined nearly 200 pairs of twins. When a *monozygotic (identical)* twin had depression, there was a 46% chance that the other twin would have the same disorder. In contrast, if a *dizygotic (fraternal)* twin had depression, the other twin had only a 20% chance of developing it.

The inherited biological factor ultimately producing the disorder seems to be low activity of the neurotransmitters noradrenaline and serotonin (Goldstein *et al.*, 2011).

In the 1950s, evidence began to point to these neurotransmitters. First, several medications for high blood pressure often caused depression (Ayd, 1956) and lowered noradrenaline activity, while others lowered serotonin. Second, the first truly effective antidepressant drugs were discovered by accident but researchers later learnt they relieved depression by increasing either noradrenaline or serotonin activity (Bunney & Davis, 1965; Schildkraut, 1965).

Many studies over the past half-century have further supported the relationship between major depressive disorder and low activity of noradrenaline and/or serotonin. Neuroscience research has also linked depression to the endocrine system, specifically high levels of cortisol, the hormone released by the adrenal glands during times of stress (Neumeister *et al.*, 2005). This provides a further link between stressful events and depression.

How Do Cognitive-Behavioural Theorists Explain Depression? Cognitive-behavioural theorists consider severe depression to involve negative behaviours and thought patterns that cause and maintain the disorder (Zuckerman, 2011). Two influential cognitive-behavioural explanations centre on the phenomenon of *learned helplessness* and on the effects of *negative thinking*.

Learned helplessness Since the mid-1960s, Martin Seligman has been developing the *learned helplessness* theory of depression (Gillham *et al.*, 2011; Yu & Seligman, 2002; Seligman 1992, 1975). It holds that people become depressed when they think (1) that they no longer have control over the significant events and reinforcements in their lives and (2) that they are responsible for this helpless state. Learned helplessness was introduced in Chapter 9.

PSYCHOLOGY AROUND US | Losing Control: Learning to Feel Helpless

Mary was 25 years old and had just begun her final year at university . . . Asked to recount how her life had been going recently, Mary began to weep. Sobbing, she said that for the past year or so she felt she was losing control of her life and that recent stresses (starting lectures again, friction with her boyfriend) had left her feeling worthless and frightened. A gradual deterioration in her vision meant she had to wear glasses all day. 'The glasses make me look terrible,' she said, and 'I don't look people in the eye much any more.' Also, to her dismay, Mary had gained 20 pounds in the past year. She viewed herself as overweight and unattractive. At times she was convinced that with enough money to buy contact lenses and enough time to exercise she could overcome her depression; at other times she believed nothing would help . . . Mary saw her life deteriorating in other spheres, as well. She felt overwhelmed by university work and, for the first time in her life, had received penalties for late work . . . In addition to her dissatisfaction with her appearance and her fears about her academic future, Mary complained of a lack of friends. Her social network consisted solely of her boyfriend, with whom she was living. Although there were times she experienced this relationship as almost unbearably frustrating, she felt helpless to change it and was pessimistic about its permanence . . .

(Spitzer *et al.*, 1983, pp. 122–123)

Seligman's theory first formed when he was working with laboratory dogs. He found that when dogs were given inescapable shocks they came to learn that they had no control over the unpleasant reinforcements (shocks) in their lives. That is, they learnt that they were helpless to do anything to change negative situations. Moreover, when later placed in a new situation where they could in fact escape shocks and control their fate, the dogs continued to act as if they were generally helpless. They would just lie in their experimental boxes and accept the shocks. Seligman noted that the effects of learned helplessness greatly resembled the symptoms of human depression, and he proposed that people become depressed after developing a generalized belief that they have no control over the reinforcements in their lives.

The learned helplessness explanation of depression has been revised somewhat over the past two decades. According to a revised version of the theory, the *attribution-helplessness theory*, when people view events to be beyond their control, they ask themselves why this is so (Taube-Schiff & Lau, 2008; Abramson *et al.*, 2002, 1989, 1978). If they attribute their present lack of control to some *internal* cause (some deficiency in themselves) that is both *global* (a deficiency that is wide-ranging) and *stable* (a deficiency that will continue for a long time), they may well feel helpless to prevent future negative outcomes and they may experience depression. If they make other kinds of attributions, this reaction is unlikely.

Consider a university student whose girlfriend breaks up with him. If he attributes this loss of control to an internal cause that is both global and stable – 'It's my fault [internal]; I ruin everything I touch [global], and I always will [stable]'– he then has reason to expect loss of control in the future and may generally experience a sense of helplessness. According to the learned helplessness view, he is at high risk of depression. If the student had instead attributed the breakup to causes that were more specific ('The way I've behaved the past couple of weeks blew this relationship'), unstable ('I don't usually act like that') or external ('She never did know what she wanted'), he might not expect to lose control again and would probably not experience helplessness and depression.

Negative thinking Aaron Beck believes that negative thinking plays a key role in depression. Beck points to *dysfunctional attitudes, errors in thinking*, the *cognitive triad* and *automatic thoughts* as the keys to the clinical syndrome (Beck & Weishaar, 2011; Beck, 2002, 1991, 1967).

Beck considered people to develop *dysfunctional attitudes*, such as 'My general worth is tied to every task I perform' and 'If I fail, others will feel repelled by me.' Beck also considered that those same people often commit errors in their thinking, such as arbitrary inferences or magnification.

For Beck, the effect of continuing dysfunctional attitudes and illogical thinking eventually produces extended trains

cognitive triad a pattern of thinking in which individuals repeatedly interpret their experiences, themselves, and their futures in negative ways that lead them to feel depressed.

of negative thinking. The thinking typically takes three forms and is therefore termed the **cognitive triad**: individuals repeatedly interpret (1) *their experiences*, (2) *themselves* and (3) *their futures* in negative ways that lead them to feel depressed. That is, depressed people interpret their experiences as burdens that repeatedly defeat or deprive them. They view themselves as undesirable, worthless and inadequate and they regularly see the future as bleak (as in Figure 19.2).

automatic thoughts specific upsetting thoughts that arise unbidden.

Beck also considered depressed people to experience **automatic thoughts**, a steady train of unpleasant thoughts assuming that they are inadequate and that their situation is hopeless. Beck labelled these thoughts automatic because they happen, like a reflex, automatically. In a few hours, depressed people have hundreds of such thoughts: 'I'm worthless . . . I let everyone down . . . Everyone hates me . . . My responsibilities are overwhelming . . . I've failed as a parent . . . I'm stupid. . . . Everything is difficult for me . . . Things will never change.'

Research has supported Beck's explanation, with studies finding that depressed people hold dysfunctional attitudes, and the more of these attitudes they hold, the greater their depression (Evans *et al.*, 2005; Whisman & McGarvey, 1995). Other research has found depressed participants to recall more unpleasant experiences than positive ones, rate themselves lower than non-depressed subjects and select pessimistic statements in storytelling tests (e.g. 'I expect my plans will fail') (Ridout *et al.*, 2003).

How Do Sociocultural Theorists Explain Depression?

Sociocultural theorists propose that social forces play an important role in depression, in that depression is often triggered by outside stressors and that a lack of social support plays a role in the onset of depression (Brown, 2010; Doss *et al.*, 2008). People who are separated or divorced display higher rates of depression than married or widowed persons and people who have never been married (Weissman *et al.*, 1991). In some cases, a spouse's depression may contribute to a separation or divorce, but more often the interpersonal conflicts and lack of mutual support found in troubled relationships seem to lead to depression.

Isolated individuals without intimacy seem particularly prone to depression at times of stress (Brown, 2010; Kendler *et al.*, 2005). Some highly publicized studies in the UK several decades ago showed that women who had three or more young children, lacked a close confidante, and had no outside employment were more prone to depression after stressful life events (Brown, 2010; Brown *et al.*, 2005; Brown

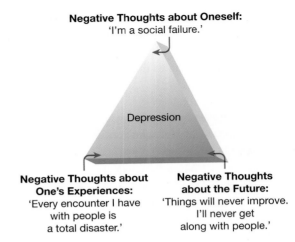

FIGURE 19.2 Cognitive triad of depression. According to Aaron Beck, a regular pattern of these three types of negative thoughts increases vulnerability to depression.

& Harris, 1978). Depressed people who lack social support also tend to remain depressed longer than those who have a supportive spouse or close friendships.

Bipolar Disorders

People with a *bipolar disorder* often describe their lives as an emotional roller coaster. They oscillate between extreme moods, experiencing both the lows of depression and the highs of mania. Unlike depression, those in a state of *mania* experience dramatic and inappropriate rises in mood. The symptoms of mania involve the same areas of functioning as depression – emotional, motivational, behavioural, cognitive and physical – but in the opposite direction.

In mania, people have active, powerful emotions in search of an outlet. Their euphoric joy or extreme agitation is out of all proportion to the context. Individuals with mania are motivated towards constant excitement, involvement and companionship, moving quickly and talking rapidly and loudly.

Individuals with mania usually show poor cognition in judgement and planning. Their indomitable optimism and drive means they dismiss dangers or those pointing them out as they spend or invest recklessly. They have unwarranted high self-esteem approaching grandiosity and are remarkably energetic, sleeping little but feeling and acting wide awake.

The two main DSM-IV-TR bipolar disorders are bipolar I and bipolar II. *Bipolar I disorder* involves severe manic and, in most (but not all) cases, major depressive episodes. There may be *alternation* of the episodes. However, this is distinct from *mixed* episodes, which move from manic to depressive symptoms and back in a day. *Bipolar II disorder* involves only milder hypomanic (*below mania*) episodes, which may alternate with major depressive episodes in time.

Globally, between 1 and 2.6% of adults suffer from a bipolar disorder (Merikangas *et al.*, 2007) and it is equally common in women and men, as well as socioeconomic classes and ethnic groups.

In the second half of the 20th century, neuroscience research has produced evidence that a combination of gene abnormalities plays a major role in the development of bipolar

disorders (Grieco & Edwards, 2010; Schulze & McMahon, 2009). They may also be linked to irregularities in the electrically charged ions that enable neurons to fire and transmit messages (El-Mallakh & Huff, 2001).

Studies have found stress to precipitate bipolar episodes in some biologically predisposed individuals (Post & Miklowitz, 2010). Positive events have also been found to precipitate bipolar disorders in those predisposed (Alloy *et al.*, 2011; Bender & Alloy, 2011; Alloy & Abramson, 2010).

Before You Go On

What Do You Know?

9. What is learned helplessness, and what is its role in depression?
10. What is the cognitive triad?
11. How does bipolar disorder differ from major depression?

What Do You Think?

Which of the explanations described in this section do you think best explains depression? Why?

Anxiety Disorders  OUT OF THE ORDINARY

LEARNING OBJECTIVE 4

Describe the various types of anxiety disorders, and explain some of their causes.

Bob: It's been an awful month. I can't seem to do anything. I don't know whether I'm coming or going. I'm afraid I'm going mad or something.

Doctor: What makes you think that?

Bob: I can't concentrate. My boss tells me to do something and I start to do it, but before I've taken five steps I don't know what I started out to do. I get dizzy and I can feel my heart beating and everything looks like it's shimmering or far away from me or something – it's unbelievable.

Doctor: What thoughts come to mind when you're feeling like this?

Bob: I just think, 'Oh, Christ, my heart is really beating, my head is swimming, my ears are ringing – I'm either going to die or go crazy.'

Doctor: What happens then?

Bob: Well, it doesn't last more than a few seconds, I mean that intense feeling. I come back down to earth, but then I'm worrying what's the matter with me all the time, or

checking my pulse to see how fast it's going, or feeling my palms to see if they're sweating.

Doctor: Can others see what you're going through?

Bob: You know, I doubt it. I hide it. I haven't been seeing my friends. You know, they say, 'Let's stop for a drink' or something after work and I give them some excuse – you know, like I have to do something around the house or with my car. I'm not with them when I'm with them anyway; I'm just sitting there worrying. My friend Jim said I was frowning all the time. So, anyway, I just go home and turn on the TV or pick up the sports page, but I can't really get into that either.

People who suffer such disabling levels of fear and anxiety that they cannot lead a normal life are said to have an *anxiety disorder*. These disorders are common with around a fifth of the adult population suffering a DSM-IV anxiety disorder (Daitch, 2011; Kessler *et al.*, 2010, 2009, 2005a).

There are several kinds of anxiety disorders: *generalized anxiety disorder* involves disconnected worry and anxiety; *social anxiety disorder* includes persistent fears of social or performance situations; *specific phobias* involve an irrational fear of a specific object, activity or situation; *panic disorder* displays recurrent attacks of terror; *obsessive–compulsive disorder* is characterized by recurrent anxiety raising thoughts and compulsions to perform repetitive actions in an effort to reduce anxiety; and *post-traumatic stress disorder (PTSD)* involves fear and related symptoms persisting after a perturbing event has ended.

Most sufferers have more than one anxiety disorder, thus Bob in the excerpt demonstrates the excessive worry found in generalized anxiety disorder and the repeated attacks of fear that mark panic disorder.

Generalized Anxiety Disorder

generalized anxiety disorder an anxiety disorder in which people feel excessive anxiety and worry under most circumstances.

People with **generalized anxiety disorder** experience excessive anxiety unrelated to their circumstances and worry about practically anything (Figure 19.3). Like Bob, they typically feel restless, tense or on edge, tire easily, have difficulty concentrating, suffer from muscle tension and have sleep problems.

The prevalence of symptoms of this disorder is less than 5% (Kessler *et al.*, 2010, 2005a; Ritter *et al.*, 2010), with twice as many women as men being diagnosed. Research has favoured cognitive-behavioural and neuroscientific explanations of the disorder.

How Do Cognitive Theorists Explain Generalized Anxiety Disorder? Cognitive theorists such as Beck suggest silent *dysfunctional assumptions underpin generalized anxiety disorder* that imply the sufferer is in imminent danger: for example, 'A situation or a person is unsafe until proven to be safe' or 'It is always best to assume the worst' (Beck & Weishaar, 2011; Beck & Emery, 1985). Similarly,

Albert Ellis (2011, 2002, 1962) claimed generally anxious individuals hold the following 'irrational' assumptions:

'It is a dire necessity for an adult human being to be loved or approved of by virtually every significant other person in his community.'

'It is awful and catastrophic when things are not the way one would very much like them to be.'

'If something is or may be dangerous or fearsome, one should be terribly concerned about it and should keep dwelling on the possibility of its occurring.'

'One should be thoroughly competent, adequate, and achieving in all possible respects if one is to consider oneself worthwhile.'

(Ellis, 1962)

More recently, specific cognitive explanations for generalized anxiety disorder have emerged. These *new wave cognitive explanations* build on the notions of Ellis and Beck and their emphasis on danger (Ritter *et al.*, 2010). In one such explanation, the *intolerance of uncertainty theory*, certain individuals consider it unacceptable that negative events may occur, even if the possibility of occurrence is very small. Given that life is filled with uncertain events, such individuals may come up against several 'unacceptable' events each day. Worrying constantly that unacceptable events are on the verge of happening, can lead to the development of generalized anxiety disorder (Dugas *et al.*, 2004).

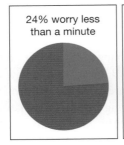    

24% worry less than a minute | 38% worry 1–10 minutes | 18% worry 10–60 minutes | 11% worry 1–2 hours | 9% worry 2 hours or more

Time devoted to worrying

FIGURE 19.3 Some people worry more than others. In one survey, 24% of college students said they spend less than one minute at a time worrying about something. In contrast, 9% worry for more than two hours.

Source: Adapted from Tallis, F., Davey, G., & Capuzzo, N. (1994). The phenomenology of non-pathological worry: A preliminary investigation. In G. Davey & F. Tallis (eds), *Worrying: Perspectives on theory, assessment and treatment* (pp. 61–89). Chichester: John Wiley & Sons, Ltd.

Much in life is uncertain, and we accept this. However, the uncertainty of waiting for a crucial text reply from a first-love partner can be extreme, as so much hangs on that one expectation. The worry that you experience in such instances of sometimes unbearable uncertainty is, according to intolerance of uncertainty theory, how people with generalized anxiety disorder feel all the time.

This theory assumes generalized anxiety disorder sufferers keep worrying in an effort to find 'correct' solutions to situations to restore certainty. However, as there is no certainty, they are always left with intolerable levels of uncertainty, triggering more worry and new efforts to find correct solutions.

In support of this approach, studies have found that people with generalized anxiety disorder display greater levels of intolerance of uncertainty than people with normal degrees of anxiety (Daitch, 2011; Dugas *et al.*, 2009, 2005, 2004). However, recent research indicates high levels of intolerance of uncertainty in other anxiety disorders (Nelson & Shankman, 2011).

How Do Neuroscientists  **WHAT HAPPENS IN THE BRAIN? Explain Generalized Anxiety Disorder?** One neuroscience explanation of generalized anxiety disorder focuses on *gamma-aminobutyric acid (GABA)*, a common and important inhibitory neurotransmitter. Thus, when GABA is received at a neuron's receptor, it reduces the neuron's ability to fire.

In normal fear reactions, key neurons throughout the brain fire more rapidly, triggering the firing of still more neurons and creating a general state of excitability throughout the brain and body, experienced as fear or anxiety. Persistent neuron firing triggers a *feedback system* that reduces the level of excitability. Some neurons release GABA, which then binds to GABA receptors instructing those neurons to stop firing. The state of excitability is thereby halted, and the experience of fear or anxiety subsides (Makkar *et al.*, 2010).

Failure of the GABA feedback system can cause fear or anxiety to go unchecked (Bremner & Charney, 2010; Roy-Byrne, 2005). Experimentally reducing GABA's ability to bind to GABA receptors produces animal subjects to react with heightened anxiety. This finding suggests that people with generalized anxiety disorder may have too few GABA receptors or their GABA receptors fail to function.

Recent research points to a more complex explanation than GABA alone, with other neurotransmitters also playing important roles (Martin & Nemeroff, 2010). As seen in Chapter 14, emotional reactions of various kinds are tied to brain *circuits*, or networks of brain structures that work together, triggering each other into action with the help of neurotransmitters and producing particular kinds of emotional reactions. The circuit that produces anxiety reactions includes the *prefrontal cortex*, *anterior cingulate* and *amygdala*. Studies have found this circuit may malfunction in generalized anxiety disorder (Schienle *et al.*, 2011; McClure *et al.*, 2007).

Social Anxiety Disorder (Social Phobia)

Many people worry about talking or performing in front of others. Entertainers, from singer Barbra Streisand to actor Anthony Hopkins, have described major bouts of anxiety before performing. Social fears of this kind are unpleasant and inconvenient, but usually the people who have them manage to function adequately, some to a very high level.

People with a **social anxiety disorder** have severe, persistent and irrational fears of social or performance situations in which embarrassment may occur. The social anxiety may be *narrow*, such as a fear of talking in public or writing in front of others, or it may be *broad*, such as a general fear of functioning poorly in front of others. In both forms, people repeatedly judge themselves as performing less adequately than they actually do.

> **social anxiety disorder** an anxiety disorder in which people feel severe, persistent and irrational fears of social or performance situations in which embarrassment may occur.

A social phobia can be disabling (Ravindran & Stein, 2011) and a person who is unable to interact with others or speak in public may fail to perform important responsibilities. One who cannot eat in public may reject dinner invitations or other social opportunities. Since most people with this phobia keep their fears secret, their social reluctance is often misinterpreted as snobbery, lack of interest or hostility.

Across studies between 7 and 12% of individuals will develop social anxiety disorder during their lifetime, with women sufferers outnumbering men by three to two (Alfano & Beidel, 2011; Kessler *et al.*, 2010). It often begins in late childhood or adolescence and may continue into adulthood.

Research finds that poor people are 50% more likely than wealthier people to display a social phobia (Sareen *et al.*, 2011). Studies have also found African and Asian ethnic groups to score higher in surveys of social anxiety (Stein & Williams, 2010; Schultz *et al.*, 2008, 2006).

Phobias

As described in Chapter 9, a **phobia** (Greek for 'fear') is a persistent and unreasonable fear of a particular object, activity or situation. Most phobias are in the

> **phobia** a persistent and unreasonable fear of a particular object, activity or situation.

category *specific phobia*, an intense fear of a specific object or situation, such as particular animals or insects, heights, enclosed spaces, thunderstorms or blood. However, as you can see in Table 19.3 there are many others. Phobias are common in our society. Surveys suggest that 9% of people suffer from at least one specific phobia in any given year (Kessler *et al.*, 2010, 2009).

Behavioural principles provide the leading explanations for specific phobias (Gamble *et al.*, 2010). According to behaviourists, *classical conditioning* is one way of acquiring fear reactions to benign objects or situations. An example would be that a fear-inducing event, such as a lightning strike (*unconditioned stimulus*), naturally elicits a reaction of fear (*unconditioned response*) in an individual. In such a situation, it is possible that a harmless object, such as raindrops (*conditioned stimulus*) – an object that had simply accompanied the frightening event – will come to elicit a fear reaction (*conditioned response*) in the person.

TABLE 19.3 The Variety of Phobias

Object	Phobia
Animals	zoophobia
Beards	pogonophobia
Being afraid	phobophobia
Blood	hematophobia
Books	bibliophobia
Churches	ecclesiaphobia
Corpses	necrophobia
Crossing a bridge	gephyrophobia
Crowds	ochlophobia
Darkness	achluophobia, nyctophobia
Demons or devils	demonophobia
Dogs	cynophobia
Dolls	pediophobia
Drugs	pharmacophobia
Enclosed spaces	claustrophobia
Eyes	ommatophobia
Faeces	coprophobia
Fire	pyrophobia
Flood	antlophobia
Flowers	anthophobia
Flying	aerophobia
Fog	homichlophobia
Fur	doraphobia
Germs	spermophobia
Ghosts	phasmophobia
God	theophobia
Graves	taphophobia
Heat	thermophobia
Heights	acrophobia
Homosexuality	homophobia
Horses	hippophobia
Ice, frost	cryophobia
Insects	entomophobia
Machinery	mechanophobia
Marriage	gamophobia

Object	Phobia
Meat	carnophobia
Mice	musophobia
Mirrors	eisoptrophobia
Money	chrometrophobia
Night	nyctophobia
Noise or loud talking	phonophobia
Odours	osmophobia
Pleasure	hedonophobia
Poison	toxiphobia
Poverty	peniaphobia
Pregnancy	maieusiophobia
Railways	siderodromophobia
Rain	ombrophobia
Rivers	potamophobia
Robbers	harpaxophobia
Satan	Satanophobia
Sexual intercourse	coitophobia
Shadows	sciophobia
Sleep	hypnophobia
Snakes	ophidiophobia
Snow	chionophobia
Speed	tachophobia
Spiders	arachnophobia
Stings	cnidophobia
Strangers	xenophobia
Sun	heliophobia
Surgery	ergasiophobia
Teeth	odontophobia
Travel	hodophobia
Trees	dendrophobia
Wasps	spheksophobia
Water	hydrophobia
Wind	anemophobia
Worms	helminthophobia
Wounds, injury	traumatophobia

Source: Van Wagner, 2007; Melville, 1978.

Another behavioural way of acquiring a fear reaction is through modelling: that is, through observation and imitation (Bandura & Rosenthal, 1966). A person may observe that others are afraid of certain objects or events and so develop fears of the same things vicariously. Consider a young boy whose mother is afraid of illnesses, doctors and hospitals. If she frequently expresses those fears, before long the boy himself may fear illnesses, doctors and hospitals. Laboratory research has indicated repeatedly that fears can indeed be acquired through classical conditioning or modelling (Wilson, 2011).

Panic Disorder

Sometimes anxiety takes the form of panic, in which sufferers may lose control of their behaviour and sometimes be unaware of what they are doing. Anyone can react with panic when a real threat looms up suddenly. A number of people, however, experience **panic attacks**, periodic, discrete bouts of panic that occur suddenly, reach a peak within 10 minutes and gradually pass. And some of those individuals have panic attacks repeatedly and often unexpectedly without apparent reason, which is termed **panic disorder**. In addition to panic attacks, people with this disorder experience changes in their thinking or behaviour as a result of the attacks. For example, they may believe that their attacks mean they are having a heart attack or losing their mind.

panic attacks periodic, short bouts of panic.

panic disorder an anxiety disorder characterized by recurrent and unpredictable panic attacks that occur without apparent provocation.

Panic disorder is often accompanied by **agoraphobia**, a fear of venturing into public places, especially when alone. Because of their panic attack history, sufferers develop a fear of being in locations where escape might be difficult or help unavailable should panic symptoms develop.

agoraphobia a phobia that makes people avoid public places or situations in which escape might be difficult or help unavailable should panic symptoms develop.

Around 2.8% of individuals suffer from panic disorder in a given year (Kessler *et al.*, 2005b). The disorder is likely to develop during late adolescence or young adulthood, and it is at least twice as common among women as among men (APA, 2000). The leading explanation for panic disorder is one that combines neuroscience and cognitive-behavioural principles.

Based on neuroscientists linking emotional reactions to brain circuits, panic attacks seem to involve the *amygdala*, *hypothalamus* and *locus coeruleus* (Etkin, 2010). Research considers that these brain areas and the associated neurotransmitters, such as noradrenaline, function improperly in people who experience panic disorder (Bremner & Charney,

2010; Burijon, 2007). Because of this malfunctioning brain circuit, sufferers are more prone to experiencing certain bodily sensations, such as breathing discomfort, fullness of the abdomen and heart palpitations.

Cognitive theorists consider sufferers to misinterpret such sensations as signs of a medical catastrophe (Wenzel, 2011; Clark & Beck, 2010; Clark, 1986). Rather than understanding the probable cause of the sensations as 'something I ate', panic-prone individuals grow increasingly worried they may be about to have a panic attack or even die. Thus, they may precipitate a panic attack as expectation becomes a self-fulfilling prophecy.

Researchers have consistently found evidence for this neuroscience/cognitive explanation of panic disorder. Sufferers of the disorder do experience more bodily sensations than other people do, react more to these sensations and are much more likely to interpret them as harmful and dangerous (Reinecke *et al.*, 2011; Wilson & Hayward, 2005; McNally, 2001).

Obsessive–Compulsive Disorder

Obsessions are persistent intrusive thoughts, ideas, impulses or images that cause anxiety. **Compulsions** are repetitive and rigid behaviours or mental acts that people feel compelled to perform in an effort to prevent or reduce anxiety. A diagnosis of **obsessive–compulsive disorder** (OCD) is made when obsessions or compulsions are severe, viewed by the person as excessive or unreasonable, cause great distress, consume considerable time or interfere with daily functions.

obsessions persistent thoughts, ideas, impulses or images that seem to invade a person's consciousness.

compulsions repetitive and rigid behaviours or mental acts that people feel compelled to perform in order to prevent or reduce anxiety.

obsessive–compulsive disorder (OCD) a mental disorder associated with repeated, abnormal, anxiety-provoking thoughts and/or repeated rigid behaviours.

Compulsive acts in this disorder are typically responses to obsessive thoughts. One study found that in most cases of OCD compulsions represent a *yielding* to obsessive doubts, ideas or urges (Akhtar *et al.*, 1975). For example, a woman who has obsessive fears of contamination may yield to that fear by performing cleaning rituals. The study also found that compulsions sometimes serve to *control* obsessions. A man with obsessive images of sexual events, for example, may try to control those images by filling his mind with compulsive verbal rituals, such as repeated expressions, phrases or chants. In all such instances, the performance of the compulsive act is intended to reduce the anxiety produced by obsessive thoughts.

As many as 2% of individuals suffer from obsessive–compulsive disorder in any given year (Kessler *et al.*, 2010;

Björgvinsson & Hart, 2008). The disorder is equally common in men and women and among people of different races and ethnic groups.

Obsessions can take the form of obsessive *wishes* (e.g. repeated wishes that one's spouse would die), *impulses* (repeated urges to yell out obscenities at work or in church), *images* (fleeting visions of forbidden sexual scenes) or *doubts* (concerns that one has made or will make a wrong decision). Like obsessions, compulsions take various forms. *Cleaning compulsions* are very common, in which individuals feel compelled to keep cleaning themselves, their clothing or their homes. The cleaning may follow ritualistic rules and be repeated dozens or hundreds of times a day, making it almost impossible to have a normal life.

PSYCHOLOGY AROUND US   Overrun by Cleanliness

Ruth complained that . . . she was spending most of her time engaged in some type of behaviour she felt driven to carry out. In addition, each ritual activity was becoming more involved and time consuming. At the time of the interview, she was washing her hands at least three or four times an hour, showering six or seven times a day, and thoroughly cleaning her apartment at least twice a day . . . Ruth stated that she felt frustrated and tired most of the time, due to the amount of effort involved in these rituals. She experienced a great deal of pain in her hands because the outer layer of skin was virtually rubbed off. Nonetheless, she felt compelled to thoroughly wash her hands and repeatedly clean her house each time she felt that she or her environment was contaminated in some way.

(Leon, 1977, pp. 127–132)

The main explanations for obsessive–compulsive disorder come from the behavioural and neuroscience models.

Cognitive–Behavioural Explanations of Obsessive–Compulsive Disorder According to one cognitive-behavioural theory, people develop their compulsions quite randomly. In a fearful situation, they happen just coincidentally to wash their hands, say, or dress a certain way. When the threat lifts, they link the improvement to that particular action, a form of superstitious behaviour. After repeated accidental associations, they believe that the action is bringing them good luck or actually changing the situation. As a result, they perform the same action repeatedly in similar situations. If they do not, they become anxious. The act becomes their method of avoiding or reducing anxiety (Steketee & Frost, 2007; Frost & Steketee, 2001).

A further cognitive-behavioural approach focuses on the relationship between obsessions and compulsions and suggests that people learn to perform compulsive acts specifically because such acts appear to reduce the anxiety aroused by their obsessions. According to this theory, some people are generally more inclined than others to experience repetitive, unwanted and intrusive thoughts, to blame themselves for such thoughts and to expect that the thoughts can cause terrible things to happen (Clark & Beck, 2010; Salkovskis, 1999, 1985). To avoid such negative outcomes, they learn to *neutralize* the thoughts, behave in ways meant to put matters right in their minds, make amends and reduce their anxiety.

Studies have found sufferers experience intrusive thoughts more often than other people, resort to more neutralizing strategies and experience reductions in anxiety after using neutralizing techniques, supporting the cognitive behavioural explanation (Shafran, 2005; Salkovskis *et al.*, 2003). Exactly why certain people experience more intrusive thoughts may have a neuroscience explanation.

How Do Neuroscientists **WHAT HAPPENS IN THE BRAIN?** **Explain Obsessive–Compulsive Disorder?** The neuroscience explanation of this disorder features two lines of neural research, abnormally low activity of the neurotransmitter serotonin and abnormal activity in key brain structures.

Serotonin's role in obsessive–compulsive disorder was evident when clinical researchers found certain antidepressant drugs reduced obsessive and compulsive symptoms (Stein & Fineberg, 2007). Since these drugs increase serotonin activity, the disorder may be caused by low serotonin activity (Spooren *et al.*, 2010).

Also, a link was found between obsessive–compulsive disorder and abnormal functioning in the *orbitofrontal cortex*, a region in the prefrontal cortex, and the *caudate nuclei*, structures located within the basal ganglia. These regions are part of a brain circuit that usually converts sensory information into thoughts and actions (Craig & Chamberlain, 2010). Neuroscientists consider these regions too active in the disorder, leading to a constant eruption of troublesome thoughts and actions (Endrass *et al.*, 2011). Additional parts of this brain circuit have been identified in recent years, including the *thalamus*, *cingulate cortex* and the *amygdala*, which may also play key roles in obsessive–compulsive disorder.

The two neuroscience approaches may be connected in that serotonin plays a very active role in the operation of the orbitofrontal cortex, caudate nuclei and other structures in the brain circuit. Thus, low serotonin activity may well disrupt the proper functioning of these brain structures.

Post-traumatic Stress Disorder (PTSD)

acute stress disorder an anxiety disorder in which fear and related symptoms are experienced soon after a traumatic event and last less than a month.

post-traumatic stress disorder (PTSD) an anxiety disorder in which fear and related symptoms continue to be experienced long after a traumatic event.

Stress reactions and psychological disorders can be linked, as when a large number of stressful events may precipitate the onset of depression. Stress is thought to have a more central role in **acute stress disorder** and **post-traumatic stress disorder (PTSD)**, as was discussed in Chapter 18.

Symptoms of Acute Stress Disorder and Post-traumatic Stress Disorder

Chapter 18 also described the roles of the *autonomic nervous system (ANS)* and the *hypothalamic–pituitary–adrenal (HPA)* axis during everyday stress reactions. If a stressful situation is unusually dangerous, we may temporarily experience levels of arousal, anxiety and depression that are far beyond those everyday stress reactions. For most people, the unusual reactions subside soon after the extreme danger passes, but, for others, the feelings of anxiety and depression and other symptoms persist long after the traumatic event. These individuals are suffering from acute stress disorder or PTSD, in reaction to a psychologically traumatic event, such as combat, rape, an earthquake, an aeroplane crash or a traffic accident.

If the lingering stress symptoms begin within four weeks of the traumatic event and last for less than a month, the diagnosis is acute stress disorder (APA, 2000). If the symptoms continue longer than a month, a diagnosis of PTSD is given. The symptoms of PTSD may begin either shortly after the traumatic event or months, even years, later.

Studies indicate that 80% of cases of acute stress disorder develop into PTSD (Burijon, 2007). Apart from the differences in onset and duration, the symptoms of acute stress disorder and PTSD are similar, with individuals experiencing high levels of ongoing anxiety and depression. They may feel overly alert (*hyperalertness*), be easily startled, have trouble concentrating and/or develop sleep problems (Ruzek *et al.*, 2011; Breslau *et al.*, 2005). They may also feel extreme guilt and helplessness because they survived the traumatic event while others did not.

Stress disorders also involve recurring thoughts, memories, dreams or nightmares connected to the traumatic event (Geraerts, 2010). Activities, thoughts, feelings or conversations related to the event are avoided (Marx & Sloan, 2005). In addition, sufferers often feel detached from other people or lose interest in activities that once brought enjoyment. They may feel confused and have trouble remembering things.

Data identifies around 3.5% of the population experiencing one of the stress disorders in any given year (Peterlin *et al.*, 2011; Taylor, 2010; Kessler *et al.*, 2009). Women are at least twice as likely as men to develop stress disorders. Around 20% of women who are exposed to a serious trauma may develop one, compared to 8% of men (Koch & Haring, 2008).

What Causes a Stress Disorder? Clearly, extraordinary trauma can cause a stress disorder. However, a stressful event alone is not the entire explanation, as only some people develop acute stress disorder or PTSD. To distinguish those who develop it from those who do not, evidence has been considered from biological processes, personalities, childhood experiences, social support systems and cultural backgrounds.

Biological and genetic factors Investigators have learnt that traumatic events often trigger change in the brain and body, leading to stress reactions and, in some cases, to stress disorders. Abnormal activity of the hormone cortisol and the neurotransmitter noradrenaline has been found in the urine, blood and saliva of combat soldiers, rape victims, concentration camp survivors and survivors of other severe stresses (Gerardi *et al.*, 2010; Delahanty *et al.*, 2005).

Studies also identify that, once a stress disorder develops, individuals experience further persistent biochemical arousal, which may eventually damage key brain areas, particularly the hippocampus and the amygdala (Bremner & Charney, 2010; Yehuda *et al.*, 2010).

Personality Research suggests that people with certain personalities, attitudes and coping styles are more prone to stress disorders (Burijon, 2007). In the aftermath of the 1999 earthquake in Bolu, Turkey, children who had been more sensitive to anxiety before the earthquake were more likely than other children to develop severe stress reactions (Kilic *et al.*, 2008). Also, individuals who perceive negative events as beyond their control tend to develop more severe stress symptoms after sexual or other kinds of criminal assaults than those who perceive greater control (Taylor, 2006).

Childhood experiences Certain childhood experiences seem to increase the risk of later acute and post-traumatic stress disorders. Poverty in childhood seems to increase the risk of these disorders when faced with later trauma. Other factors that increase this risk are: having family members who suffered from psychological disorders; experience of assault, abuse or catastrophe at an early age; or being younger than 10 when their parents separated or divorced (Yehuda *et al.*, 2010; Koch & Haring, 2008).

Social support Individuals whose social and family support systems are weak are also more likely to develop a stress disorder after a traumatic event (Uchino & Birmingham, 2011; Ozer, 2005). Rape victims who feel loved, cared for, valued and accepted by their friends and relatives recover more successfully, as do those treated with dignity and respect by the criminal justice system (Patterson, 2011).

Cultural factors  There is a growing suspicion among clinical researchers that the rates of PTSD may differ between ethnic groups. For example, studies of combat veterans from the wars in Vietnam and Iraq have found higher rates of PTSD among those of Hispanic origin than among white Western and African origin (RAND Corporation, 2010, 2008; Kulka *et al.*, 1990). Hispanic groups have been found more vulnerable in other circumstances in Europe and elsewhere (Perilla *et al.*, 2002; Robila, 2010). This may be due to part of their cultural belief system, leading those of Hispanic origin tending to view traumatic events as inevitable and unalterable, an attribution that may heighten their risk of PTSD (Perilla *et al.*, 2002). Also, Hispanic culture emphasizes social relationships and social support, which are often removed by disastrous events.

Before You Go On

What Do You Know?

12. What distinguishes the six types of anxiety disorder?
13. How and why may generalized anxiety disorder be related to uncertainty?
14. What role do conditioning and modelling play in the development of phobias?
15. What individual factors affect who will develop post-traumatic stress disorder (PTSD)?

What Do You Think?

We all feel anxious sometimes. Think of a situation that makes you anxious. How does this differ from the anxiety disorders discussed in this chapter?

Schizophrenia  OUT OF THE ORDINARY

schizophrenia a mental disorder characterized by disorganized thoughts, lack of contact with reality and sometimes hallucinations.

psychosis loss of contact with reality.

In **schizophrenia** individuals deteriorate into a world of unusual perceptions, odd thoughts, disturbed emotions and motor abnormalities. They also experience **psychosis**, in which a loss of contact with reality and an inability to perceive and respond appropriately disturbs their occupational, social and domestic functioning. They may have *hallucinations* (false sensory perceptions) or *delusions* (false beliefs), or they may withdraw into a private world. Schizophrenia is the most common form of psychosis; however, other disorders also feature psychotic symptoms (see the box below: 'The Case of Andrea Yates').

Approximately, one in every 100 people across the world suffers from schizophrenia during their lifetime (Miller & Mason, 2011; APA, 2000). Equal numbers of men and women receive this diagnosis. Almost 3% of all those who are divorced or separated will have schizophrenia in their lifetime, compared with 1% of married people and 2% of people who remain single.

The symptoms of schizophrenia can be grouped into three categories: *positive symptoms*, *negative symptoms* and *psychomotor symptoms*.

Positive Symptoms of Schizophrenia

Positive symptoms are *pathological excesses*, or bizarre additions, to a person's behaviour. *Delusions, disorganized thinking and speech, hallucinations* and *inappropriate affect* are the ones most often found in schizophrenia.

positive symptoms in the case of schizophrenia, symptoms that seem to represent pathological excesses in behaviour, including delusions, disorganized thinking and speech, hallucinations and inappropriate affect.

PSYCHOLOGY AROUND US   The Case of Andrea Yates

On the morning of 20 June 2001, television viewers watched in horror as officials escorted 36-year-old Andrea Yates to a police car. Just minutes before, she had called police and explained that she had drowned her five children in the bathtub because 'they weren't developing correctly'.

As many as 80% of mothers experience *baby blues* soon after giving birth, and between 10 and 30% display the clinical syndrome of *postpartum depression*. But apparently postpartum psychosis is an entirely different disorder – one that has become all too familiar to the public, by way of cases such as that of Andrea Yates (Doucet *et al.*, 2011; Worley, 2010).

Postpartum psychosis affects about 1 to 2 of every 1,000 mothers who have recently given birth (Posmontier, 2010). The symptoms apparently are triggered by the enormous shift in hormone levels that occur after delivery (Blackmore *et al.*, 2009). Within days or at most a few months of childbirth, the woman develops signs of losing touch with reality, such as delusions (e.g. she may become convinced that her baby is the devil); hallucinations (perhaps hearing voices); extreme anxiety, confusion and disorientation; disturbed sleep; and illogical or chaotic thoughts (e.g. thoughts about killing herself or her child).

Women with a history of bipolar disorder, schizophrenia or major depressive disorder are particularly vulnerable to the

disorder. In addition, women who have previously experienced postpartum depression or postpartum psychosis have an increased likelihood of developing it after subsequent births. Andrea Yates, for example, had developed signs of postpartum depression (and perhaps postpartum psychosis) and attempted suicide after the birth of her fourth child but responded well to a combination of medications, and so the couple decided to have a fifth child (King, 2002).

After the birth of her fifth child, the symptoms recurred, along with features of psychosis and a suicide attempt. Although she was hospitalized twice and treated with various medications, her condition failed to improve. Six months after giving birth to Mary, her fifth child, she drowned all five of her children.

Most clinicians consider that Yates was suffering postpartum psychosis. Although only a fraction of women with the disorder actually harm their children (estimates run as high as 4%), the Yates case reminds us that such an outcome is indeed possible (Posmontier, 2010) and that early detection and treatment are critical (Doucet *et al.*, 2011).

After a second trial for murder in 2007, Yates was found *not guilty by reason of insanity* and sent to a high-security mental health unit for treatment. Some months later, she was transferred to a low-security mental hospital, where she continues to receive treatment today.

PSYCHOLOGY AROUND US   Drifting into Psychosis

[Laura, a professional dancer, met her husband in Germany, and subsequently married.] They had no children [but Laura] had a dog to whom she was very devoted. The dog became sick and partially paralyzed, and the vet felt that there was no hope of recovery . . . Finally [Laura's husband asked her,] 'Should the dog be put down or not?' From that time on Laura became restless, agitated, and depressed . . . Later Laura started to complain about the neighbors. A woman who lived on the floor beneath them was knocking on the wall to irritate her. According to the husband, this woman had really knocked on the wall a few times; he had heard the noises. However, Laura became more and more concerned about it . . . Later

she . . . started to feel that the neighbors were now recording everything she said; maybe they had hidden wires in the house. She started to feel 'funny' sensations. There were many strange things happening, which she did not know how to explain; people were looking at her in a funny way in the street . . . She felt that people were planning to harm either her or her husband . . . When she looked at television, it became obvious to her that the programs referred to her life. Often the people on the programs were just repeating what she had thought. They were stealing her ideas. She wanted to go to the police and report them.

(Arieti, 1974, pp. 165–168)

delusions blatantly false beliefs that are firmly held despite evidence to the contrary.

Delusions are firmly held beliefs that have no basis in fact and, of these, *delusions of persecution* are the most common (Langdon *et al.*, 2010).

Individuals with delusions of persecution believe that they are being plotted or discriminated against, spied on, slandered, threatened, attacked or deliberately victimized. Laura believed that her neighbours were deliberately irritating her and that others were trying to harm her and her husband.

Schizophrenia includes *disorganized thinking and speech* such as **loose associations** – or **derailment**: a rapid shift from one topic to another – the sufferer believes makes sense. One man with schizophrenia, asked about his itchy arms, responded:

> **loose associations, or derailment** a common thought disorder of schizophrenia, characterized by rapid shifts from one topic to another.

> The problem is insects. My brother used to collect insects. He's now a man 5 foot 10 inches. You know, 10 is my favourite number. I also like to dance, draw, and watch television.

Individuals with schizophrenia may also experience **hallucinations**, perceptions that occur in the absence of external stimuli. *Auditory hallucinations* are the most common in schizophrenia, where sounds and voices seem to come from outside of one's head (see Holmes, 2010).

> **hallucinations** imagined sights, sounds or other sensory events experienced as if they were real.

The positive symptom *inappropriate affect* refers to emotions unsuited to the situation, such as smiling when being told terrible news or being upset in happy situations. This may also include inappropriate shifts in mood.

Negative Symptoms of Schizophrenia

Negative symptoms are *pathological deficits*, characteristics that are lacking such as: *poverty of speech, flat affect, loss of volition* and *social withdrawal* found in some cases of schizophrenia.

> **negative symptoms** in the case of schizophrenia, symptoms that seem to reflect pathological deficits, including poverty of speech, flat affect, loss of volition and social withdrawal.

Poverty of speech refers to a reduction in speech and its content. Some negative symptom sufferers think and say very little in contrast to the positive symptom of saying a lot with little meaning. In *flat affect*, individuals show very little anger, sadness, joy or other feelings, with immobile expressions, poor eye contact and monotone voices.

In *avolition*, or apathy, sufferers lack energy and interest in normal goals and fail to start or complete a course of action. The negative symptom *withdrawal* involves moving interest and focus from the social environment into their own confused ideas and fantasies, distancing them further from reality.

Psychomotor Symptoms

Psychomotor symptoms in schizophrenia may involve awkward movement or odd grimaces and gestures. The latter may have a private, perhaps ritualistic or magical meaning to the sufferer. **Catatonia** is an extreme motionless psychomotor state. In a *catatonic stupor*, individuals stop responding to their environment, remaining motionless and silent for long periods. Others exhibit *catatonic rigidity*, maintaining a rigid upright posture for hours and resisting movement or *catatonic posturing*, assuming awkward, bizarre positions for long periods. Much of this is an active state of immobility (not passively relaxed) demonstrated by *waxy flexibility*, in which they maintain postures for very long periods, into which they have been placed by someone else (see Holmes, 2010).

> **catatonia** extreme psychomotor symptoms of schizophrenia, including catatonic stupor, catatonic rigidity and catatonic posturing.

How Do Neuroscientists Explain Schizophrenia?

 WHAT HAPPENS IN THE B R A I N ?

Research supports neuroscience explanations of schizophrenia, although psychological and sociocultural factors do have a precipitating or moderating role. This is the *diathesis-stress model*, where a biological predisposition may be triggered by psychological events, personal stress or societal factors. However, schizophrenia will not develop without the biological underpinning but may develop without the external stressors (Holmes, 2010).

Genetic Factors It is accepted that people inherit a genetic predisposition to schizophrenia (Akbarian, 2010). Studies have found repeatedly that schizophrenia is more common among relatives of people with the disorder (Tamminga *et al.*, 2008) and the more closely related the existing sufferer, the greater their likelihood of developing the disorder (Figure 19.4).

Twin studies examine if both members of a pair of twins have schizophrenia, in which case they are said to be *concordant* for that trait. If genetic factors are at work in schizophrenia, identical, or *monozygotic*, twins (who share the same genes) should have a higher concordance rate for this disorder than non-identical, *dizygotic*, twins (who share only some genes). Research supports this (Higgins & George, 2007), finding if one identical twin develops schizophrenia there is a 48% chance that the other twin will do so as well. If the twins are non-identical, the second twin has approximately a 17% chance of developing the disorder.

Research has also indicated two kinds of brain abnormalities that could be inherited in schizophrenia: *biochemical abnormalities* and *abnormal brain structures*.

Biochemical Abnormalities Over the past four decades, researchers have developed the so-called *dopamine hypothesis* to help explain schizophrenia, which suggests certain neurons that use the neurotransmitter dopamine are over-active

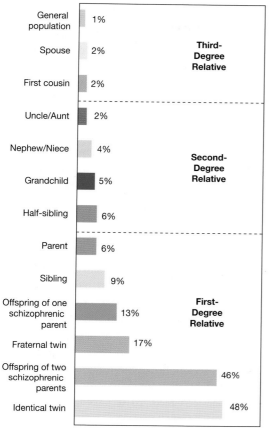

Relationship to Person with Schizophrenia

Relationship	%	
General population	1%	
Spouse	2%	Third-Degree Relative
First cousin	2%	
Uncle/Aunt	2%	
Nephew/Niece	4%	Second-Degree Relative
Grandchild	5%	
Half-sibling	6%	
Parent	6%	
Sibling	9%	
Offspring of one schizophrenic parent	13%	First-Degree Relative
Fraternal twin	17%	
Offspring of two schizophrenic parents	46%	
Identical twin	48%	

Percentage of Risk

FIGURE 19.4 Family connections. Biological relatives of people with schizophrenia have a higher risk than the general population of developing the disorder during their lifetimes. Close relatives (who have a more similar genetic make-up) have a greater risk than distant relatives.

Source: Adapted from Gottesman, I. I. (1991). *Schizophrenia Genesis: The Origins of Madness* © 1991 by W. H. Freeman and Company, p. 96. Used with permission.

(Busatto *et al.*, 2009; McGowan *et al.*, 2004). This hypothesis has undergone challenges and adjustments in recent years, but it is still the foundation for present biochemical explanations of schizophrenia.

Evidence that high dopamine activity contributes to schizophrenia came with the accidental discovery in the 1950s of **antipsychotic drugs**, effective medication that reduces the symptoms of schizophrenia. These drugs often produce muscular tremors as a side effect, like tremors seen in Parkinson's disease, a disabling neurological illness. Scientists already knew that people who suffered from Parkinson's disease had abnormally low levels of the neurotransmitter dopamine in some areas of the brain and that lack of dopamine was the reason for their uncontrollable shaking. If antipsychotic drugs produced Parkinsonian symptoms in people with schizophrenia while removing their psychotic symptoms, perhaps the drugs would reduce dopamine activity. Thus, if lowering dopamine activity helped remove the symptoms of schizophrenia, perhaps schizophrenia was related to excessive dopamine activity.

> **antipsychotic drugs** medications that help remove the symptoms of schizophrenia.

Research has since suggested that messages from dopamine-sending neurons to dopamine receptors on other neurons may be transmitted too easily or too often in schizophrenia. This fits with the theory, as certain dopamine neurons are known to play a key role in guiding attention (Sikstrom & Soderlund, 2007). Attention is severely disturbed by excessive dopamine activity and may also result in the problems of perception and thought found in schizophrenia. Research also suggests that abnormal activity of the neurotransmitters glutamate and serotonin may also play a role in schizophrenia (Bach, 2007).

Abnormal Brain Structures During the past decade, abnormalities of brain structure have been identified in schizophrenia (Brown & Thompson, 2010; Eyler, 2008). Brain scans have identified enlarged ventricles (the brain cavities that contain cerebrospinal fluid), relatively small temporal lobes and frontal lobes and abnormal blood flow in certain areas of the brain. In addition, there have been associations between schizophrenia and structural abnormalities of the hippocampus, amygdala and thalamus.

Before You Go On

What Do You Know?

16. What is a psychosis?

17. What are the positive symptoms of schizophrenia? The negative symptoms? The psychomotor symptoms?

18. What biochemical abnormalities and brain structures have been associated with schizophrenia?

What Do You Think?

We noted in this section that if one identical twin develops schizophrenia, there is a 48% chance that the other twin will do so as well. Discuss how this would support the diathesis-stress model.

Other Psychological Disorders

LEARNING OBJECTIVE 6

Discuss the features and possible causes of somatoform, dissociative and personality disorders.

This chapter will conclude by looking briefly at three additional disorder categories: somatoform disorders, dissociative disorders and personality disorders. Each of these disorder categories is problematic, with personality disorders having a great deal of overlap and, more fundamentally, somatoform and dissociative disorders being challenged for their very status as diagnostic categories (Holmes, 2010; Spanos, 1996)

Somatoform Disorders

When a presented physical ailment has no detectable medical cause, it is suggested that the sufferer may be experiencing a **somatoform disorder**, a pattern of physical complaints with largely psychosocial causes. It is assumed that individuals do not consciously want or purposely produce their symptoms: they almost always claim to believe that their symptoms are genuinely medical (Lahmann *et al.*, 2010). In conversion disorder, somatization disorder and pain disorder associated with psychological factors, clients present with a change in physical functioning. In hypochondriasis and body dysmorphic disorder, healthy individuals worry that there is

somatoform disorder a pattern of physical complaints with largely psychosocial causes; types include conversion disorder, somatization disorder, pain disorder associated with psychological factors, hypochondriasis and body dysmorphic disorder.

something physically wrong with them without medical confirmation.

Conversion Disorder In *conversion disorder*, it is suggested that a psychosocial conflict or need is converted into dramatic physical symptoms that affect voluntary motor or sensory functioning. The symptoms are pseudoneurological, resembling paralysis, blindness or loss of feeling (APA, 2000) but often only to the level of patient understanding of these conditions (Holmes, 2010). Conversion disorders are diagnosed at least twice as often in women as in men (Abbey, 2005). They usually appear suddenly, at times of extreme stress, and last a matter of weeks. The incidence of reporting these disorders is thought to be quite rare, occurring in, at most, five out of every 1,000 people.

Somatization Disorder People with *somatization disorder* present with many long-lasting physical ailments that have no apparent organic basis. These ailments include pain symptoms (such as headaches and chest pain), gastrointestinal symptoms (such as nausea and diarrhoea), sexual symptoms (such as erectile or menstrual difficulties) and neurological symptoms (such as double vision or paralysis) (APA, 2000). Sufferers may go from doctor to doctor in search of relief. Some may even seek multiple surgical procedures. They often describe their many symptoms in dramatic and exaggerated terms (Dimsdale & Creed, 2010; Creed, 2009; APA, 2000). Between 0.2 and 2% of all women may experience this disorder in any given year, compared with less than 0.2% of men (North, 2005; APA, 2000). The disorder is maintained much longer than a conversion disorder, typically for many years (Yutzy, 2007).

PSYCHOLOGY AROUND US   Baffling Symptoms

Sheila reported having abdominal pain since the age of 17, necessitating exploratory surgery that yielded no specific diagnosis. She had several pregnancies, each with severe nausea, vomiting and abdominal pain; she ultimately had a hysterectomy for a tipped uterus. Since turning 40, she has experienced dizziness and blackouts, which she eventually was told might be multiple sclerosis or a brain tumour. She continued to be bedridden for extended periods, with weakness, blurred vision and difficulty urinating. At the age of 43, she was treated for a hiatal hernia because of complaints of bloating and intolerance of a variety of foods. She also had additional hospitalizations for neurological, hypertensive and renal examinations, all of which failed to reveal a definitive diagnosis.

(Spitzer *et al.*, 1981, pp. 185, 260)

Pain Disorder Associated with Psychological Factors When psychosocial factors play a central role in the onset, severity or continuation of pain, patients may receive a diagnosis of *pain disorder associated with psychological factors*. Patients with a conversion or somatization disorder

may also experience pain, but it is the key symptom in this disorder. The disorder appears to be fairly common (Nickel *et al.*, 2010). Often it develops after an accident or during an illness that has caused genuine pain, which then appears to be maintained by the patient.

Hypochondriasis In *hypochondriasis*, there is an unfounded interpretation of bodily symptoms as signs of a serious illness. Often the symptoms are merely normal bodily changes, such as occasional coughing, sores or sweating. Between 1 and 5% of all people experience hypochondriasis (Abramowitz & Braddock, 2011; APA, 2000). Doctors report seeing many cases (Dimsdale *et al.*, 2011). As many as 7% of all patients seen by primary care doctors may display hypochondriasis (Asmundson & Taylor, 2008).

Body Dysmorphic Disorder People who experience *body dysmorphic disorder*, formerly known as *dysmorphophobia*, become deeply concerned about some imagined or minor defect in their appearance. Most often, they focus on wrinkles; spots on the skin; excessive facial hair; swelling of the face; or a misshapen nose, mouth, jaw or eyebrow (Marques *et al.*, 2011; McKay *et al.*, 2008). Others are overly concerned about the appearance of their feet, hands, breasts, penis or other bodily parts. Still others are concerned about bad odours coming from sweat, breath, genitals or the rectum (Rocca *et al.*, 2010; Phillips & Castle, 2002).

It is common in our society to worry about appearance (Figure 19.5), particularly teenagers worrying about acne, etc. The concerns of people with body dysmorphic disorder, however, are extreme. Sufferers often severely limit contact with other people, avoiding eye contact or going to great lengths to conceal their 'defects' such as always wearing sunglasses to cover their supposedly misshapen eyes (Didie *et al.*, 2010; Phillips, 2005). As many as half of people with this disorder seek plastic surgery or dermatological treatment, and often they feel worse rather than better afterwards (McKay *et al.*, 2008). Up to 5% of the Western population may suffer from the disorder (Buhlmann *et al.*, 2010; Ovsiew, 2006).

What Causes Somatoform Disorders? Theorists typically explain hypochondriasis and body dysmorphic disorders much as they explain anxiety disorders (Bouman, 2008; Noyes, 2008). Behaviourists consider these fears to be acquired through classical conditioning or modelling (Marshall *et al.*, 2007). Cognitive theorists suggest that sufferers are overly sensitive to bodily cues and misinterpret them (Witthöft & Hiller, 2010; Williams, 2004).

In contrast, the other somatoform disorders – conversion, somatization and pain disorders – are considered by contemporary approaches to be at some level contrived by the client or misinterpreted neurological complications (along the lines of the phantom limb pains experienced by amputees) (Holmes, 2010). However, psychodynamic and sociocultural approaches have attempted to explain these disorders, although these explanations, particularly the psychodynamic,

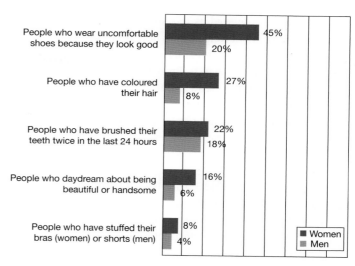

FIGURE 19.5 How do I look? People with body dysmorphic disorder may be extreme, but they are not the only ones who worry about their appearance. Surveys often indicate that substantial percentages of people keep trying to change how they look.

have little proven value and have failed to receive research support (Kirmayer & Looper, 2007; Yutzy, 2007).

Psychodynamic explanation of somatoform disorders Although only of value for historical purposes, the psychodynamic approach used Sigmund Freud's psychoanalysis for what was then termed *hysterical neurosis (somatoform type)*. His patients were mostly female and Freud considered their physical symptoms to result from an unresolved *Electra complex during their phallic stage (ages 3–5)*. Thus, in Freud's terms, the sexual feelings towards the father are not resolved by identifying with the mother and as a result these women as adults hide their sexual feelings by unconsciously converting them into physical symptoms. Although believed at the time, this approach has been discredited and some of his patients are retrospectively considered to have had undiagnosed neurological disorders (Holmes, 2010).

Sociocultural explanations  **of somatoform disorders** The term *somatization* is used when referring to the development of somatic symptoms in response to personal distress. Somatization tends to be considered inappropriate in Western countries (So, 2008; Escobar, 2004). This may reflect a bias held by Western clinicians in seeing somatic symptoms as an *inferior* way of presenting emotions.

Globally, personal distress being reported as somatic complaints is seen as acceptable in many non-Western cultures (Draguns, 2006; Kleinman, 1987). In such cultures, somatization is viewed as less stigmatizing as a reaction to stress. High rates of somatization have been found throughout the world, including China, Japan and Arab countries (Matsumoto & Juang, 2008). Individuals in Latin countries seem to display the greatest number of somatic symptoms (Escobar, 2004, 1995; Escobar *et al.*, 1998, 1992). These findings indicate that reactions to life's stressors can be influenced by culture.

Dissociative Disorders

dissociative disorder a psychological disorder characterized by a major loss of memory without a clear physical cause; types include dissociative amnesia, dissociative fugue and dissociative identity disorder.

People sometimes experience a major disruption of their memory, forgetting new information that they just learnt or old information they knew. Where this change lacks a physical cause, it is called a **dissociative disorder**, where part of the person's memory seems to be *dissociated*, or separated, from the rest (Barlow, 2011).

Although dissociative disorders are often portrayed in novels, movies and television shows, many clinicians believe that they are in fact quite rare (Pope *et al.*, 2007) and others dispute that they exist at all (Holmes, 2010; Spanos, 1996). Dissociative disorders include *dissociative amnesia, dissociative fugue* and *dissociative identity disorder*.

Dissociative Amnesia Individuals with *dissociative amnesia* claim to be unable to recall important information, possibly of an upsetting nature (APA, 2000). The loss of memory can be more extensive than normal forgetting and is claimed to be triggered by a traumatic event, although individuals documented as undergoing trauma do not report this (Holmes, 2010; Hunt, 2010). In most of those claiming amnesia, the forgotten material or events eventually return, without treatment. The 1990s witnessed many highly controversial reports of dissociative amnesia in which adults claimed to recall long-forgotten experiences of childhood abuse, perhaps encouraged by certain therapists, as in the box below: 'Repression versus False Memories'.

PSYCHOLOGY AROUND US | Repression versus False Memories

Throughout the 1990s, reports of *repressed childhood memory of abuse* being 'recovered' attracted enormous public attention. Adults presenting with a type of *dissociative amnesia* seemed to recover buried memories of sexual and physical abuse from their childhood. A woman might claim her father had sexually molested her repeatedly, another would 'recall' a neighbour making sexual advances on many occasions.

Although the number of such claims has declined in recent years, many are opposed over this issue (Birrell, 2011; Haaken & Reavey, 2010). Therapists who have helped recover these events believe that these are real memories of abuse that have been buried for years in the person's mind. Many experts have documented that the memories are actually illusions, as a result of suggestion and are false memories created in a confused vulnerable client. Opponents of the repressed memory concept hold that the details of genuine documented childhood sexual abuse are often remembered all too well, not completely wiped from the memory (Loftus & Cahill, 2007). Moreover, they point out that false memories often can be created in the laboratory by suggestion and tapping into research participants' imaginations (Spanos, 1996; Weinstein & Shanks, 2010).

Thus, the alleged recovery of childhood memories may be a powerful case of suggestibility (Loftus & Cahill, 2007). Critics note that the attention paid to the phenomenon by both clinicians and the public has led some therapists to make the diagnosis without sufficient evidence (Haaken & Reavey, 2010). Therapists may actively search for signs of early abuse in clients and even encourage clients to produce repressed memories (McNally & Geraerts, 2009), and some clients respond by unknowingly forming false memories of abuse. These apparent memories then become increasingly familiar to them as a result of repeated therapy discussions of the alleged incidents.

Occasionally, repressed memories of childhood sexual abuse emerge outside of clinical settings (Geraerts *et al.*, 2009). These cases are explained by the suggestive power of various books, articles, websites and television shows that seem to validate repressed memories of childhood abuse (Haaken & Reavey, 2010).

It is important to recognize that the experts who question the recovery of repressed childhood memories do not in any way deny the problem of child sexual abuse. Importantly, they point out that such false claims make it far more difficult for genuine cases to be believed and acted on.

Dissociative Fugue In *dissociative fugue*, individuals claim to forget their personal identities and details of their past lives but also to flee to an entirely different location.

Some individuals travel a short distance and make few social contacts in the new setting (APA, 2000). In other cases, however, the person may travel far from home, take a new name and establish a new identity, new relationships, even a new line of work and claim to have no memory of their former life (APA, 2000).

Dissociative Identity Disorder People with *dissociative identity disorder*, previously known as *multiple personality disorder*, appear to develop two or more distinct personalities, called *subpersonalities* or *alternate personalities*, each appearing to have a unique set of memories, behaviours, thoughts and emotions. At any given time, one of the subpersonalities is in control and dominates the person's functioning (Barlow, 2011). Cases of dissociative identity disorder were first reported almost three centuries ago (Rieber, 2006, 2002). Women receive this diagnosis at least three times as often as men do (APA, 2000). Diagnosis of this disorder, and its former incarnation, has received similar criticism to that of repressed memories. It is often diagnosed in suggestible patients by the same small number of therapists, whereas the majority of clinicians never come across any cases (Spanos, 1996; Holmes, 2010). The socio-cognitive view is that the extra personalities are suggested and encouraged by therapists (Spanos, 1996). The historical psychodynamic approach still maintains the personalities are due to repressed childhood abuse, although there is no evidence for this. Diagnostic approaches tend to accept the belief that one has extra personalities as the essence of the disorder.

Personality Disorders

Personality is a unique and enduring pattern of inner experience and outward behaviour that tends to be predictable and consistent. In personality disorders, these patterns are so prominent as to be dysfunctional and are remarkably inflexible and persistent.

personality disorder an inflexible pattern of inner experience and outward behaviour that causes distress or difficulty with daily functioning.

A **personality disorder** is a very rigid pattern of inner experience and outward behaviour. The pattern is seen in most of the person's interactions, tends to be lifelong and differs markedly from the experiences and behaviours usually expected of people. Such disorders typically become recognizable in adolescence or early adulthood, although some are recognized during childhood (Westen *et al.*, 2011). It has been estimated that as much as 9 to 13% of all adults may have one or more personality disorders (Paris, 2010; O'Connor, 2008).

DSM-IV-TR identifies 10 personality disorders, and ICD-10 has eight but includes other specifications. Only two of them, the *antisocial* and *borderline personality disorders* (in ICD termed *dissocial* and *emotionally unstable personality disorder* respectively), have been studied extensively, partly because they create so many problems for other people.

Antisocial Personality Disorder Those with **antisocial personality disorder** persistently disregard and violate others' rights (APA, 2000). Aside from substance-related disorders, this is the disorder most closely linked to adult criminal behaviour. Most people with antisocial personality disorder display some patterns of misbehaviour before they were 15, including truancy, running away, physical cruelty to animals or people and destroying property, often defined as *conduct disorder*. A small proportion of those with antisocial personality disorder may be diagnosed as *psychopathic* and pose a greater risk to others (see Holmes, 2010).

antisocial personality disorder a personality disorder characterized by extreme and callous disregard for the feelings and rights of others.

People with antisocial personality disorder lie repeatedly (Patrick, 2007). Most cannot work consistently at a job, are absent frequently and may leave work altogether. They are careless with money, fail to pay their debts and are impulsive, taking action without thinking of the consequences (Millon, 2011). Correspondingly, they may be irritable, aggressive and quick to start fights.

Recklessness is a common trait: they have little regard for their own safety or for that of others, even their children. They are self-centred as well, likely to have difficulty maintaining close relationships and are skilled at gaining personal profit at the expense of other people. The pain or damage they cause seldom concerns them, so clinicians claim they lack empathy or a moral conscience (Kantor, 2006). They think of their victims as weak, inferior and deserving of being manipulated or robbed.

Around 2 to 4% of the population meet the criteria for antisocial personality disorder (Paris, 2010; O'Connor, 2008; Livesley, 2001). The disorder is as much as four times more common among men than women.

Because people with this disorder are often arrested, researchers frequently find people with antisocial patterns in prison populations (Black *et al.*, 2010). In fact, at least 30% of people in prison meet the criteria for antisocial personality disorder (O'Connor, 2008).

Explanations of antisocial personality disorder

None of the various causal models fully accounts for the broad range of symptoms found in the disorder, but the behavioural and neuroscience models offer insights into particular symptoms.

Behavioural theorists consider antisocial symptoms to be learnt through modelling (Gaynor & Baird, 2007)

(Figure 19.6). Evidence of this is the high rate of antisocial personality disorder found among the parents of people with this disorder. Other behaviourists have suggested that some parents unintentionally teach antisocial behaviour by regularly rewarding a child's aggressive behaviour (Kazdin, 2005). When the child misbehaves or becomes violent in reaction to the parents' requests or orders, for example, the parents may give in to restore peace. Unintentionally, they may be rewarding the child for being stubborn and perhaps even violent.

Neurological factors include the finding that people with the disorder display lower serotonin activity than others (Patrick, 2007). Low serotonin activity is linked to both impulsivity and aggression, which are key features of antisocial personality disorder. In addition, deficient functioning has been found in the frontal lobes of people with this disorder (Morgan & Lilienfield, 2000). Such a deficiency could help explain the poor planning, inferior judgement and low empathy characteristic of this disorder.

Antisocial personalities are found to experience less anxiety and so may, thus, lack a key ingredient for learning (Blair *et al.*, 2005). This would account for a lack of learning from negative life experiences or picking up emotional cues from others. Their lack of anxiety may relate to their responding to threat or expectations of stress with low brain and bodily arousal (Perdeci *et al.*, 2010; Gaynor & Baird, 2007). Because of the low arousal, they can ignore threatening or emotional situations, and remain unaffected.

Borderline Personality Disorder Sufferers display great instability, including major shifts in mood, an unstable self-image and impulsivity. These characteristics combine to make their relationships very unstable (Mason & Kreger, 2010; APA, 2000).

Individuals with this disorder rapidly move in and out of depressive, anxious and irritable states lasting from a few

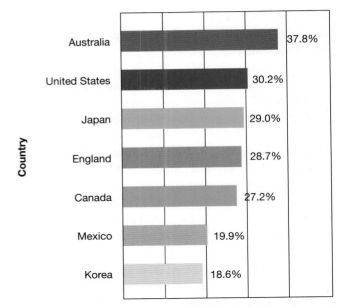

FIGURE 19.6 Antisocial behaviour, country by country. In a cross-cultural study, teenagers had to describe how imaginary characters would respond to conflicts. Almost 40% of the respondents from Australia described violent responses, compared with 30% of respondents from the United States and less than 20% of those from Korea.

Source: Adapted from Archer & McDaniel, 1995.

hours to days or longer. Their emotions seem to be always in conflict with the world around them. They are prone to bouts of extreme anger, which sometimes result in physical aggression.

They also redirect this aggression towards themselves in the form of cutting or other forms of self-harming (Whipple & Fowler, 2011). Many self-harm as a dysfunctional way of dealing with chronic feelings of emptiness, boredom and identity confusion.

PSYCHOLOGY AROUND US Self-Injury: Pain to Avoid Pain

Feelings of separation and loneliness bubbled beneath my volcanic surface. Anxiety and lack of self identity swirled in the whirlpool within. It's my fault, I did this, I'm to blame, I shouldn't be here . . .

Then, I went to work.

First a cross . . . In closing, a couple of parallel lines along my wrist . . .

My mind screamed from deep inside Dante's Inferno as the neighbours slept soundly in their beds and cats went unstartled. Blood dripped down my arm as a sign of life or something else secretly desired, I don't know. Paper towels spotted with dark red looking like a bad kitchen accident. In time, it was over and whatever psychological pain needed to be transferred to my body was complete.

I awoke the next day with alternate physical stings and pangs on my arm and my mind in conflict. Had I gone too far? . . . This was not the first time, only the most recent.

Suicidal threats and parasuicidal actions are also common. Seventy-five percent of borderline sufferers attempt suicide at least once in their lives, with around 10% actually committing suicide (Gunderson, 2011; Leichsenring *et al.*, 2011).

borderline personality disorder a personality disorder characterized by severe instability in emotions and self-concept and high levels of volatility.

Those with **borderline personality disorder** frequently form intense, conflict-ridden relationships in which their feelings are not necessarily shared by the other person. They often violate the boundaries of a relationship. Thinking in *dichotomous* (black-and-white) terms, they quickly become furious when their expectations are not met. Yet they remain very attached to the relationships, having an intense fear of being left alone (Berenson *et al.*, 2011). Sometimes they will self-harm or threaten suicide to prevent partners from leaving.

Around 2% of the general population are thought to suffer from this disorder (Paris, 2010; Sherry & Whilde, 2008), with 75% of those diagnosed being women (Gunderson, 2011).

Explanations of borderline personality disorder
Clearly, there is a relationship between borderline personality disorder and mood disorders, which would indicate biological instability in mood regulation. The sympathetic autonomic nervous system is less controlled, leading to outbursts of anger. Some explanations have tried combining concepts from differing models of disorder to form a *biosocial* theory of the disorder (Arens *et al.*, 2011; Linehan & Dexter-Mazza, 2008). According to this view, the child will have difficulty controlling arousal levels and emotions in an environment in which the child's emotions may be punished or disregarded. Such children may not learn how to properly recognize and regulate their emotional arousal or tolerate emotional distress.

Before You Go On

What Do You Know?

19. What distinguishes a pain disorder associated with psychological factors from a conversion or somatization disorder?

20. Why have dissociative disorders been criticized?

21. Describe the interpersonal difficulties involved in two personality disorders.

22. Which disorder discussed in this section is most closely linked to adult criminal behaviour?

What Do You Think?

Analyse a character from a film you have seen or a book you have read that has one of the disorders described in this section. Is the information provided in the text consistent with what you know of the character?

Access your interactive e-book to view a video clip for this chapter at
www.wileyopenpage.com

Summary

Defining, Classifying and Diagnosing Psychological Disorders

LEARNING OBJECTIVE 1 Identify the common features of most definitions of abnormal functioning, and describe how psychological disorders are classified and diagnosed.

- The study of psychological disorders is often called abnormal psychology, psychopathology or clinical psychology. Disordered psychological functioning is a wide-ranging problem.
- Definitions of psychological disorders often include the 'four Ds': deviance, distress, dysfunction and danger.

- *The Diagnostic and Statistical Manual of Mental Disorders (DSM)* (current version DSM-IV-TR) and *the International Classificatory System of Disorders* (ICD) (current version ICD-10) are the leading classificatory systems of psychological disorders.

- To assess people for psychological disorders, clinicians use various tools: structured and unstructured clinical interviews; analogue, naturalistic and self-monitoring observations; and a variety of clinical tests. Clinicians often combine information gathered from each of these sources.

Models of Psychological Disorder

LEARNING OBJECTIVE 2 Describe the models frequently used by psychologists to explain disordered functioning.

- Clinicians use several major models to explain abnormal functioning, including the neuroscience, cognitive-behavioural, sociocultural, developmental and psychopathology models and a few maintain the more historical, less empirical models.

- The neuroscience model views abnormal functioning as a result of malfunctions in brain structure or biochemical activity. Malfunctions can be caused by injuries or other factors, including genetics or viruses.

- Behavioural theorists propose that abnormal behaviours develop via the same processes as more adaptive behaviours: classical conditioning, operant conditioning and modelling. Cognitive theorists believe that abnormal functioning can result from disordered thoughts, including basic irrational assumptions, specific upsetting thoughts and illogical thinking processes. These combine to form the major cognitive behavioural model.

- According to the sociocultural model, abnormal behaviour is best understood in light of the social, cultural and familial forces brought to bear on an individual. Important factors include social change, socioeconomic class membership, cultural background, social networks and family systems.

- Developmental psychopathology theorists are interested in how psychological disorders evolve, based on both genetics and early childhood experiences, and on how those early patterns affect people's functioning as they move through later life stages.

- There are less empirical models: humanists suggest that people are vulnerable to psychological disorders when they develop inaccurate views of their worth or goals in life; existentialist therapies focus on helping clients to discover their personal freedom of choice and to take responsibility for making choices; psychodynamic theorists view abnormal functioning as the result of unconscious conflicts.

Mood Disorders

LEARNING OBJECTIVE 3 Differentiate major depressive disorder and bipolar disorder.

- The key features in mood disorders are depression – a low, sad state – and mania – a state of breathless euphoria. Most people with a mood disorder suffer only from depression.

- People with major depressive disorder suffer from a variety of symptoms, including feelings of sadness and lack of interest, low levels of activity and productivity, negative views of themselves and their lives, and physical ailments.

- Today's leading explanations for major depressive disorder point to genetic, neurological, biochemical and psychological, with the addition of sociocultural, factors. Some believe the various explanations should be combined.

- People with bipolar disorder experience the highs of mania but in many cases the lows of depression as well. In the manic state, they seek constant excitement. They tend to show poor judgement and planning, hold inflated opinions of themselves and show a great deal of energy.

- Genes and biological factors play key roles in the development of bipolar disorder, although stress and certain kinds of environmental events can precipitate episodes.

Anxiety Disorders

LEARNING OBJECTIVE 4 Describe the various types of anxiety disorders, and explain some of their causes.

- As a group, anxiety disorders are the most common mental disorder. Often, people with one type of anxiety disorder have another as well.

- In generalized anxiety disorder, individuals experience persistent feelings of worry and anxiety. An important neuroscience explanation focuses on gamma-aminobutyric acid (GABA), a neurotransmitter involved in fear reactions. Some cognitive approaches suggest this disorder arises when individuals hold certain dysfunctional or irrational assumptions; other approaches consider the sufferers' intolerance of uncertainty.

- People with social anxiety disorder display severe, persistent and irrational fears of social or performance situations. Some sociocultural and biological factors appear to be involved.

- People with phobias have a persistent and irrational fear of a specific object, activity or situation. Behavioural principles, including classical conditioning and modelling, provide the leading explanations for specific phobias.
- People with panic disorder have recurrent attacks of terror. These panic attacks are sometimes accompanied by agoraphobia, a fear of venturing into public places. A neuroscientific/cognitive explanation of the disorder focuses on physical sensations produced by malfunctioning brain circuitry, which are then misinterpreted.
- People with obsessive–compulsive disorder (OCD) feel overrun by recurrent thoughts that cause anxiety (obsessions) and by the need to perform repetitive actions to reduce this anxiety (compulsions). Cognitive-behavioural approaches focus on the role of learning in these behaviours, while neuroscientists consider abnormally low levels of serotonin or abnormal functioning in specific brain regions.
- People with post-traumatic stress disorder (PTSD) have protracted fear and related symptoms long after a traumatic event has ended. Although extraordinary trauma precipitates the disorder, not everyone who experiences trauma develops PTSD. Differences in biological processes, personalities, social support systems and to some extent cultural backgrounds can make individuals prone to the disorder.

Schizophrenia

LEARNING OBJECTIVE 5 Describe the features of schizophrenia and some of the theories of what causes it.

- Schizophrenia is a disorder in which individuals suffer unusual perceptions, odd thoughts, disturbed emotions and motor abnormalities, the core elements of which are described as psychosis, or a loss of contact with reality.
- Positive symptoms of schizophrenia are termed pathological excesses in behaviour, emotion or thinking. These include delusions, disorganized thinking and speech, hallucinations and inappropriate affect.
- Negative symptoms, or pathological deficits, include poverty of speech, flat affect, loss of volition and social withdrawal.
- People with schizophrenia also sometimes experience unusual psychomotor symptoms, which in its most extreme form is termed catatonia.
- Evidence supports a genetic predisposition to schizophrenia. Two kinds of brain abnormalities are inherited: biochemical abnormalities and abnormal brain structure.
- Neuroscience explanations of schizophrenia have substantial research support, although psychological and

sociocultural factors may help to precipitate the disorder in those with a biological predisposition.

Other Psychological Disorders

LEARNING OBJECTIVE 6 Discuss the features and possible causes of somatoform, dissociative and personality disorders.

- A somatoform disorder is a pattern of physical complaints with no known physical basis. In conversion disorder, somatization disorder and pain disorder associated with psychological factors, there is an actual change in physical functioning. In hypochondriasis and body dysmorphic disorder, people who are healthy mistakenly worry that there is something physically wrong with them.
- Theorists typically explain hypochondriasis and body dysmorphic disorders much as they explain anxiety disorders, as resulting from classical conditioning, modelling or the misinterpretation of bodily cues. Psychodynamic and sociocultural explanations have been offered for conversion, somatization and pain disorders, but these explanations have failed to receive research support.
- Changes in memory that lack a physical cause are called dissociative disorders. In dissociative amnesia, people claim to be unable to recall important information about their lives. In dissociative fugue, people not only claim to forget their identities and their past lives but also flee to a different location. In dissociative identity disorder, people present themselves as having two or more distinct personalities.
- There is much debate as to whether these disorders are sociocognitive creations by the client and encouraged by the therapist, a view which is supported by research. Others claim it emanates from some early event from which the client is psychologically escaping.
- People with antisocial personality disorder persistently disregard and violate others' rights. Because of their many negative behaviours, such as lying, impulsiveness and recklessness, they are frequently found in prison. According to behavioural theorists, this disorder can be learnt through various means. Neuroscience explanations focus on brain factors, such as low serotonin levels, deficient frontal lobe functioning and low arousal in response to warnings.
- People with borderline personality disorder display great instability, including major shifts in mood, an unstable self-image and impulsivity. This disorder is not fully understood, but probably has genetic and biological underpinnings and a recent biosocial theory proposes a combination of internal and external factors.

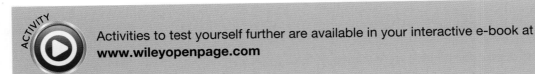

ACTIVITY

Activities to test yourself further are available in your interactive e-book at
www.wileyopenpage.com

TYING IT TOGETHER

WHAT HAPPENS IN THE
BRAIN?

- Low activity of the neurotransmitter GABA has been linked to several anxiety disorders.
- Low serotonin and low noradrenaline activity have been linked to depression.
- High dopamine activity accompanies schizophrenia.
- Improper functioning of various brain structures and brain circuits has also been linked to psychological disorders.

OUT OF THE
ORDINARY

- Around 18% of adults suffer from one or more of the anxiety disorders, making them possibly the most common of psychological disorders.
- Around 7% of adults experience major depressive disorder, whereas 1% display bipolar disorder.
- Around 1% of adults suffer from schizophrenia, but that includes 3% of all divorced or separated people.

HOW WE
DIFFER

- Poor people experience more psychological disorders than wealthy people.
- Women with depression and panic disorders outnumber men with these disorders by at least two to one.
- Those in the East tend to somatize their anxiety, whereas those in the West present psychological symptoms.
- People with high sensitivity to bodily cues are more likely to develop certain anxiety disorders and somatoform disorders.

HOW WE
DEVELOP

- Traumas and significant losses during childhood can increase the likelihood of adult depression developing.
- People who acquire dysfunctional attitudes early in life are more at risk of developing generalized anxiety disorder, social anxiety disorder and depression in adolescence or adulthood.
- Individuals whose childhoods are filled with uncontrollable events increase their risk of developing depression.
- People who develop resilience in life can overcome early risk factors for psychopathology.

QUIZ

Quizzes to test yourself further are available in your interactive e-book at
www.wileyopenpage.com

Key Terms

abnormal psychology 542
acute stress disorder 563
agoraphobia 561
analogue observation 547
antipsychotic drugs 567
antisocial personality
    disorder 571
automatic thoughts 556
bipolar disorder 553
borderline personality
    disorder 573
catatonia 566
clinical interview 546
clinical tests 547
cognitive triad 556

comorbidity 546
compulsions 561
conditions of worth 550
delusions 565
depression 553
developmental
    psychopathology 552
diagnosis 546
Diagnostic and Statistical
    Manual of Mental
    Disorders (DSM) 544
dissociative disorder 570
equifinality 552
family systems
    theory 552

generalized anxiety
    disorder 558
hallucinations 566
International Classification
    of Diseases (ICD) 544
loose associations, or
    derailment 566
major depressive disorder 553
mania 553
multifinality 552
naturalistic observation 547
negative symptoms 566
obsessions 561
obsessive–compulsive
    disorder (OCD) 561

panic attacks 561
panic disorder 561
personality disorder 571
phobia 559
positive symptoms 564
post-traumatic stress
    disorder (PTSD) 563
psychosis 564
resilience 552
risk factors 552
schizophrenia 564
self-monitoring 547
social anxiety
    disorder 559
somatoform disorder 568

Flashcards to test yourself further are available in your interactive e-book at
www.wileyopenpage.com

CHAPTER 20

Treatment of Psychological Disorders

Adapted by David A. Holmes, Manchester Metropolitan University, UK

CHAPTER OUTLINE

- Treatment in the Modern Context
- Biological Treatments
- Behavioural Therapies
- Cognitive-Behavioural Therapies

- Non-Empirical Therapies
  - Humanistic and Existential Therapies
  - Psychodynamic Approaches
- Formats of Therapy
- Does Therapy Work?
- Some Final Thoughts about the Field of Psychology

 Access your interactive e-book to view a video clip for this chapter at
www.wileyopenpage.com

Finding His Way Back

February: He cannot leave the house; George knows that for a fact. Home is the only place where he feels safe – safe from humiliation, danger, even ruin. If he were to go to work, his colleagues would somehow reveal their contempt for him. A pointed remark, a quizzical look – that's all it would take for him to get the message. If he were to go shopping at the supermarket, before long everyone would be staring at him. Surely, others would see his low mood and negative thoughts; he wouldn't be able to hide them. He dare not even go for a walk alone in the woods – his heart would probably start racing again, bringing him to his knees and leaving him breathless, incoherent and unable to get home. No, he's much better off staying in his room, trying to get through another evening of this curse called life. Thank goodness for the Internet. Were it not for his reading of news sites and postings to blogs and online forums, he would, he knows, be cut off from the world altogether.

July: George's life revolves around his circle of friends: Michael and Jason, whom he knows from the office, where he was recently promoted to director of customer relations, with Sam and Pete, his weekend tennis partners. The gang meets for dinner every week at someone's house, and they chat about life, politics and their jobs. Particularly special in George's life is Kate. They go to movies, restaurants and concerts together. She thinks George is terrific, and George finds himself beaming whenever she's around. George looks forward to work each day and his one-on-one dealings with customers. He's taking part in many activities and relationships and more fully enjoying life. ■

George's thoughts, feelings and behaviour interfered with all aspects of his life in February. Yet most of his symptoms had disappeared by July. All sorts of factors may have contributed to George's improvement: advice from friends and family members, a new job or vacation, perhaps a big change in his diet or exercise regime. Any or all of these things may have been useful, but they could not be considered **treatment**, or **therapy**. Those terms are usually reserved for special, systematic procedures designed to change abnormal behaviour into more normal behaviour. Frank (1973, pp. 2–3) considers that all forms of therapy have three essential features:

> **treatment, or therapy** systematic procedures designed to change abnormal behaviour into normal behaviour.

- A *sufferer* who seeks relief from the healer.

- A trained *healer*, whose expertise is accepted by the sufferer and his or her social group.

- A *series of contacts* between the healer and the sufferer, through which the healer tries to produce certain changes in the sufferer's emotional state, attitudes and behaviour.

> **psychotherapy** a treatment system in which a client and therapist use words and acts to overcome the client's psychological difficulties.

> **biological therapy** the use of physical and chemical procedures to help people overcome psychological difficulties.

The therapeutic process may be brought about by **psychotherapy**: in Frank's words, 'by words, acts, and rituals in which sufferer, healer, and – if there is one – group participate jointly.' Or it may be accomplished through **biological therapy**, consisting of 'physical and chemical procedures'.

In today's world, the healers are called *clinicians*, *clinical practitioners* or *therapists*. In Chapter 19 *clinicians* were said to gather information systematically to better describe, explain and predict psychological disorders. The knowledge acquired is then used by clinicians, whose role is to detect, assess and treat people with psychological disorders.

Despite Frank's straightforward definition, clinical treatment is surrounded by conflict and confusion. Carl Rogers frequently expressed the opinion that therapists are not in agreement as to their goals or aims; they are not in agreement as to what constitutes a successful outcome of their work; they cannot agree on what constitutes a failure; and that the field seems to be completely chaotic and divided.

Some clinicians view disorder as an illness and so consider therapy a procedure that helps *cure* the illness. Others see disorder as a problem in living and therapists as *teachers* of more functional behaviour and thought. Clinicians even differ on what to call the person who receives therapy. Those who see abnormality as an illness use the label *patient*, while those who view it as a problem in living refer to the *client*. This chapter will use both of these common terms interchangeably. All agree therapy of some kind is necessary and will be effective to differing degrees.

Treatment in the Modern Context

LEARNING OBJECTIVE 1

Explain who currently receives treatment for psychological problems, how they enter treatment and what general features characterize types of treatment.

Surveys suggest that more than 15% of people – children, adolescents and adults – receive therapy for psychological problems in the course of a year (NAMI, 2011). The number and variety of problems for which treatments are available have increased during the past 100 years. When Freud and his colleagues first began to conduct therapy during the late 19th and early 20th centuries, most of their patients suffered from anxiety or depression. People with schizophrenia and other more severe disorders were considered poor prospects for therapy, and treatment for them was confined to custodial care in institutions.

All of that has changed since the 1950s, with the discovery of effective medication for severe disorders. Anxiety and depression still dominate the therapy picture, but schizophrenia is now a major area for therapy. Moreover, large numbers of people with milder psychological problems, sometimes called *problems in living*, are also receiving therapy. Surveys suggest that approximately 25% of clients enter therapy largely because of problems with marital, family, job, peer, school or community relationships.

Entering and Receiving Treatment

People enter therapy, including psychological therapy and drug therapy, in various ways. Many decide on their own to consult a therapist and others may do so on the advice of a friend, family member, doctor or other professional with whom they have discussed their difficulties. Still others are persuaded into treatment by parents, spouses, teachers or employers if they are causing disruption or are in obvious distress. The legal system may formally pronounce people mentally disturbed and dangerous and commit them to a secure hospital for treatment (in the United Kingdom this is called *sectioning*, referring to the section of the Mental Health Act that covers it.)

The decision to seek therapy is not easy in most cases. Extensive studies indicate that most individuals are aware of their problems well before they look for help. Many wait more than two years after they first become aware that they have a problem. And it is estimated that half or more of people with psychological disorders never seek treatment (SoRelle, 2000). Therapy has been underutilized for a long time because some individuals who may benefited from it have not understood its value, are unlikely to think about personal problems in mental health terms or are worried about the stigma that acknowledging having psychological problems (by attending therapeutic sessions) may bring. Generally speaking, therapy seems to hold greater attraction for those who have a social network of friends with a positive attitude to therapy, who have received therapy themselves or express confidence in therapy as a solution to personal problems (SAMHSA, 2008, 2002; Kadushin, 1969).

PSYCHOLOGY AROUND US **Working Against Therapy**

The Eating Disorders Association reports that there are more than five hundred pro-anorexia Internet sites with names such as Dying to Be Thin and Starving for Perfection (Borzekowski *et al.*, 2010). Users of these sites exchange tips on how they can starve themselves and disguise their weight loss from family, friends and doctors. The sites also offer support and feedback about starvation diets. One site of this kind sponsors a contest, The Great Ana Competition, and awards a diploma to the girl who consumes the fewest calories in a two-week period. Another site endorses what it calls the Pro-Anorexia Ten Commandments: assertions such as 'Being thin is more important than being healthy' and 'Thou shall not eat without feeling guilty'.

Conducting Treatment

Psychologists often see clients presenting with problems such as anxiety, depression or relationship difficulties. Psychiatrists do see a much larger number of patients with schizophrenia, bipolar disorders and other severe disorders than do psychologists. Mental health services tend to be concentrated in urban areas in most countries and there is a shortage of practitioners in rural areas (Jackson et al., 2007; Smith et al., 2004).

Therapy takes place in all sorts of settings, from hospitals and health centres to private offices. Most clients, even those who are severely disturbed, are treated as *outpatients*. Most of the people who receive *inpatient* treatment in psychiatric hospital units have severe psychological problems (Craig & Power, 2010). There are also private routes to treatment outside national health provision for those willing and able to pay for it.

Clinicians have become increasingly concerned about the negative effects of long-term institutionalization. Thus, beginning in the 1960s, they carried out a policy of *deinstitutionalization*. This process accelerated when the economic benefits were realized and between 1955 and today the population of psychiatric institutions was reduced to less than one-tenth (Althouse, 2010).

Hospitalization today usually lasts weeks instead of months or years. When people develop severe psychological disorders, therapists now try to treat them first as outpatients, usually with medication along with other forms of therapy. If this strategy proves ineffective, the patient may be admitted to a hospital for a short period so that the condition can be monitored, diagnosed and stabilized. As soon as hospitalization has served this purpose, the patient is returned to the community.

In theory, this may be a reasonable treatment plan for people with severe psychological disorders. However, as we will discuss later, community treatment facilities have been so underfunded and understaffed over the years that they have not been able to meet the treatment needs of the majority of severely impaired people. Indeed, many thousands of people with severe psychological disorders are currently condemned to an endless cycle of hospital discharges and readmissions, the so-called *revolving door effect*.

In the clinical field today there are, by some estimates, more than 400 forms of therapy, each practised by clinicians who believe that their chosen methodology is highly effective. Typically, therapists use principles and techniques that they have been trained in and are consistent with the theoretical paradigm they have been taught. Many of these are not evidence-based. The majority of clinical psychology training is based on *cognitive-behavioural therapy* (Holmes, 2010, p. 158).

The differing approaches in Chapter 19 lead to corresponding treatment approaches for clinical practitioners with their clients. For example, Aaron Beck's cognitive approach is based on removing dysfunctional thinking patterns and responses. The majority of therapists adopt this approach in the form of cognitive-behavioural therapy, and will focus on identifying and replacing such thinking errors with adaptive thoughts and responses. The following sections will focus on biological, behavioural, cognitive-behavioural and non-empirical (humanistic, existential and psychodynamic) therapies (Table 20.1). Recall from our chapter opener, though, that all these forms of therapy have three essential features: a sufferer who seeks relief, a trained healer and a series of contacts between the two in which the healer tries to bring about changes in the sufferer's emotional state, attitudes and behaviour.

TABLE 20.1 Comparison of Treatments for Psychological Disorders

Approach	Goals of Therapy	Therapy Techniques	Strengths	Weaknesses
Biological	Improve structural or bio-chemical functioning Relieve symptoms	Psychotropic drugs Electroconvulsive therapy (ECT) Psychosurgery	Research supports as highly effective for symptoms	Side effects Not effective in small number of cases Does not address clients' non-biological problems
Behavioural	Learn more functional behaviours	Desensitization Aversion therapy Operant conditioning, including token economies Therapist modelling, including social skills training	Research supports effectiveness of treatments	Effects of treatment may not always last long after treatment stops May neglect unobservable cognitive processes
Cognitive-Behavioural	Change harmful thinking patterns to more useful ones	Rational-emotive therapy Cognitive therapy Cognitive-behavioural techniques	Considerable research support for its application to several disorders	Dysfunctional thinking may result from, not cause, abnormal functioning
Non-Empirical 1: Humanistic and Existential	Provide support for honest self-appraisal, self-acceptance and self-actualization	Client-centred and Gestalt therapy techniques Existential therapy	Recognize positive human goals Recognize distinctly human values and needs	Unsupportive and limited research to test effectiveness
Non-Empirical 2: Psychodynamic	Discover source of conflicts and resolve them	Free association Therapist analysis of resistance, transference and dreams Catharsis Working through problems	Offered first major alternative to biological treatments Sees abnormal functioning as rooted in same processes as normal functioning Model for many other psychological treatments	Research does not support effectiveness of therapies

Biological Treatments

WHAT HAPPENS IN THE BRAIN?

LEARNING OBJECTIVE 2

Describe the major biological treatments for psychological disorders.

Biological therapies use biochemical and physical methods to help people overcome their psychological problems. The practitioners who apply such approaches are usually *psychiatrists*, therapists whose training includes medical school. The three principal kinds of brain interventions are *drug therapy*, *electroconvulsive therapy* and *psychosurgery*. Drug therapy is by far the most common of these approaches.

Drug Therapy

Since the 1950s, researchers have discovered several kinds of effective **psychotropic drugs**, which can significantly reduce the symptoms of psychological disorders (Julien *et al.*, 2011). Some of these medications have been introduced in previous chapters and are used widely, either as the first-line treatment for a disorder or in conjunction with psychotherapy or other interventions.

As you can see in Table 20.2, four major psychotropic drug groups are used in therapy: antianxiety, antidepressant, antibipolar and antipsychotic drugs. **Antianxiety drugs**, also called *minor tranquilizers* or *anxiolytics*, help reduce tension and anxiety. **Antidepressant drugs** help improve the mood of people who are depressed (see the following 'When a Depressed Person Takes an Antidepressant' box). **Antibipolar drugs**, also called *mood stabilizers*, help steady the moods of those with a bipolar disorder, the condition marked by mood swings from mania to depression. And **antipsychotic drugs** help reduce the confusion, hallucinations and delusions of *psychotic disorders*, the disorders (such as schizophrenia) marked by a loss of contact with reality.

The medications have radically changed the outlook for many people with psychological disorders. However, they do not work for everyone and some worry that the drugs are being overused, in a quick-fix world. Some drugs have undesired side effects and these must be weighed against the good the drugs can do. For example, certain *antipsychotic drugs* may produce noticeable movement abnormalities, including

psychotropic drugs medications that act primarily on the brain.

antianxiety drugs psychotropic drugs that reduce tension and anxiety.

antidepressant drugs psychotropic drugs that lift the mood of depressed people.

antibipolar drugs psychotropic drugs that help stabilize the moods of people suffering from bipolar disorder.

antipsychotic drugs psychotropic drugs that help correct grossly confused or distorted thinking.

TABLE 20.2 Commonly Prescribed Psychotropic Drugs

Symptom	Type of Medication	Examples
Psychosis (loss of touch with reality)	Antipsychotics	chlorpromazine (Thorazine), clozapine (Clozaril)
Depression	Antidepressants	trazodone (Desyrel), amitriptyline (Elavil), phenelzine (Nardil), fluoxetine (Prozac), paroxetine (Paxil), sertraline (Zoloft), venlafaxine (Effexor)
Mania	Mood stabilizers	lithium (Lithonate), carbamazepine (Tegretol)
	Antipsychotics	valproate (Depakote), olanzapine (Zyprexa)
Anxiety	Anxiolytics	benzodiazepines (Valium, Xanax)
	Antidepressants	fluoxetine (Prozac)

Source: Reprinted with permission of John Wiley and Sons, Inc., from Kowalski, R., & Westen, D. (2009). *Psychology* (5th edn). Hoboken, NJ: Wiley, p. 574.

shaking, bizarre-looking contractions of the face and body, and extreme restlessness (Geddes *et al.*, 2011). However, a new group of antipsychotic drugs, called *atypical* antipsychotic drugs, have been developed that are not as likely to produce unpleasant and dangerous effects and are often more effective than conventional antipsychotic drugs (Julien *et al.*, 2011).

Neuroscientists continue to advance in their ability to map the brain and connect its functioning with human behaviour. As progress continues, they believe that they will eventually be able to pinpoint the actions of drugs and their precise areas of impact producing more effective drugs that have fewer harmful or annoying side effects.

Electroconvulsive Therapy

electroconvulsive therapy (ECT) the use of electric shock to trigger a brain seizure in hopes of relieving abnormal functioning.

Another form of biological treatment is **electroconvulsive therapy (ECT)**, a technique first developed in the 1930s. ECT is used primarily for people who have severe depression. Here, two electrodes are attached to a patient's forehead, and 65 to 140 volts of electricity are briefly passed through the brain. The procedure produces a brain seizure that lasts up to a few minutes. After an average of seven to nine ECT sessions, spaced two or three days apart, many patients feel

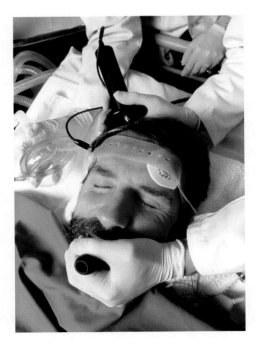

ECT today. As we can see with this patient, today's ECT treatments are conducted with considerable medical care and many safety precautions, and include helping patients sleep through the procedure.

Source: Will & Deni McIntyre/Photo Researchers, Inc.

considerably less depressed. ECT helps approximately 70% of depressed patients to improve (Perugi *et al.*, 2011).

ECT is administered today less often than it was in the past and is much more precisely controlled, producing only the minimum convulsion to be effective. However, the procedure has been found to negatively affect short-term memory (Merkl *et al.*, 2011). The majority of such memories return, but in rare cases, some people report long-term memory difficulties (Hanna *et al.*, 2009; Wang, 2007). With the growing success of antidepressant medications and certain forms of psychotherapy, fewer depressed patients now need this form of treatment. Nevertheless, ECT is still applied when people have a severe depressive episode that does not respond to other forms of treatment, which makes its high success rate all the more impressive.

In recent years, two other biological approaches have been developed that also directly stimulate the brain. These approaches are *vagus nerve stimulation* and *transcranial magnetic stimulation*. These approaches lack the generalized impact of ECT.

Vagus Nerve Stimulation The vagus nerve, the longest nerve in the human body, runs from the brain stem through the neck down the chest and on to the abdomen. In the procedure of **vagus nerve stimulation**, a surgeon implants a small device called a *pulse generator* under the skin of the chest. The surgeon then guides a wire, which extends from the pulse generator, up to the neck and attaches it to the left vagus nerve (Figure 20.1). Electrical signals travel periodically from the pulse generator through the wire to the vagus nerve. In turn, the stimulated vagus nerve delivers electrical signals to the brain.

vagus nerve stimulation a procedure in a which an implanted device sends electrical signals to the brain through the vagus nerve; used to treat severe depression.

Vagus nerve stimulation was first tried on depressed patients in 1998 and since then research has found that the procedure brings significant relief in 65% of cases (Howland *et al.*, 2011; Nahas *et al.*, 2005).

Transcranial Magnetic Stimulation In the procedure of **transcranial magnetic stimulation (TMS)**, first developed in 1985, the clinician places an electromagnetic coil on or above the patient's head. The coil sends a current into the prefrontal cortex, some parts of which are underactive in depressed individuals. TMS appears to increase neuron activity in those regions, thus helping to alleviate severe depression in about 65% of patients when administered daily for two to four weeks (Howland *et al.*, 2011; Rosenberg *et al.*, 2011).

transcranial magnetic stimulation (TMS) a procedure in which an electromagnetic coil placed on or above a person's head sends a current into the prefrontal cortex; used to treat severe depression.

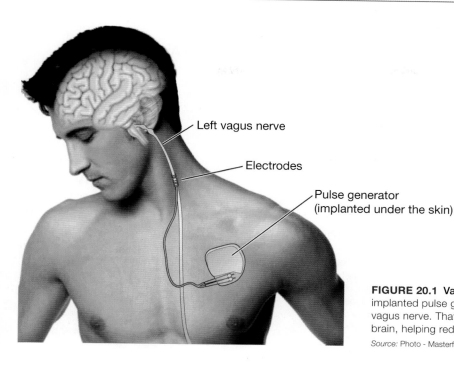

Left vagus nerve

Electrodes

Pulse generator
(implanted under the skin)

FIGURE 20.1 Vagus nerve stimulation. In this procedure, an implanted pulse generator sends electrical signals to the left vagus nerve. That nerve then delivers electrical signals to the brain, helping reduce depression in many people.
Source: Photo - Masterfile.

Psychosurgery

As mentioned previously in this text, **psychosurgery** can help some people with psychological disorders. A primitive practice of pre-civilized approaches to mental disorders was **trephining**, the prehistoric practice of chipping a hole in the skull to treat an injury or other disorder by letting out 'evil spirits' thought to be causing the disorder. Evidence indicates that trephining was used not only by prehistoric people but also by people in classical and medieval times, when 'demonic possession' re-emerged.

> **psychosurgery** brain surgery, often used in an attempt to relieve abnormal functioning.

> **trephining** prehistoric practice of chipping a hole in the skull as a treatment for various brain conditions.

Many modern forms of psychosurgery have a less intelligent predecessor, known as **lobotomy**. In this procedure, the surgeon cuts the connections between the brain's frontal lobes and the lower centres of the brain. Lobotomies were widely used for a few decades after the procedure was developed in the 1930s, particularly in cases of schizophrenia. By the late 1950s, however, it had become clear that lobotomies were not as effective as many psychosurgeons had thought. Many patients later suffered irreversible effects, including seizures, extreme listlessness, stupor and in some cases death (Barahal, 1958). Thus, use of this procedure declined during the 1960s.

> **lobotomy** surgical practice of cutting the connections between the frontal lobe and the lower centres of the brain.

Psychosurgery today is much more precise than primitive lobotomies (Holmes, 2010, p. 55). It has few negative effects, and it is beneficial for some psychological and neurological

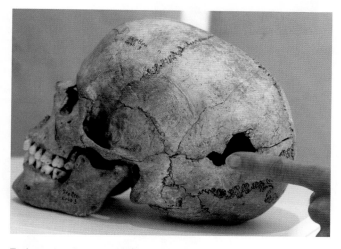

Early roots of psychosurgery? The hole in this 5,100-year-old skull indicates that the individual underwent trephining, cutting away a circular section of the skull. Some historians believe that trephination was done to release the evil spirits that were thought to be responsible for mental dysfunctioning.
Source: Winfried Rothermel/©AP/Wide World Photos.

disorders. One form of psychosurgery that is currently receiving considerable attention is **deep brain stimulation**, a procedure applied in cases of severe depression, Parkinson's disease and brain seizure disorder (epilepsy). In deep brain stimulation, a surgeon drills two tiny holes into the patient's skull and implants electrodes in areas of the brain that have

> **deep brain stimulation** a procedure in which implanted electrodes deliver constant low stimulation to a small area of the brain; used to treat severe depression, Parkinson's disease and epilepsy.

YOUR BRAIN AND BEHAVIOUR | What Happens in the Brain When a Depressed Person Takes an Antidepressant

When symptoms of depression interfere with normal functioning, physicians will sometimes prescribe the use of antidepressant medication. The most commonly prescribed antidepressants are selective serotonin reuptake inhibitors (SSRIs). The primary action of these drugs is to increase the availability of the neurotransmitter serotonin in the brain. Neurons that make serotonin are present in the brainstem raphe nuclei. These neurons send axon projections to the cortex, hippocampus and amygdala, among other regions. SSRIs have a multitude of effects on these brain regions, although the precise mechanisms by which the drugs alleviate symptoms of depression are not known. How might antidepressant drugs work?

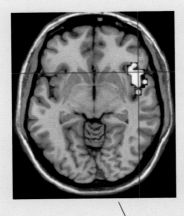

RESTORING BRAIN ACTIVITY TO NORMAL LEVELS

The prefrontal cortex of depressed individuals shows reduced activity and a lower-than-normal level of blood flow. Some studies suggest that antidepressants ultimately raise activity in this brain region (shown on this brain scan in yellow) and restore blood flow to levels observed in nondepressed individuals. Similar findings have been reported for the amygdala.

Source: Paul Keedwell, Neural markers of symptomatic improvement during antidepressant therapy in severe depression: subgenual cingulate and visual cortical responses to sad, but not happy, facial stimuli are correlated with changes in symptom score. *Journal of Psychopharmacology,* 23(7), 775–788, Figure 3, 2009. Sage Publications. ©2009 British Association for Psychopharmacology. Reprinted by permission of SAGE.

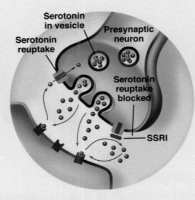

BLOCKING SEROTONIN REUPTAKE

By blocking key receptors, SSRIs prevent the reuptake, or retention, of serotonin by presynaptic neurons (shown in this illustration), thus freeing the neurotransmitter to better activate brain regions that are targets of serotonin axons, including the hippocampus and cerebral cortex. Depression relief, however, usually does not occur until someone has taken the drug for a few weeks, suggesting that some other mechanism may be responsible for improving mood.

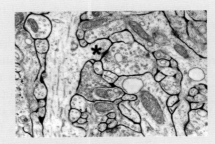

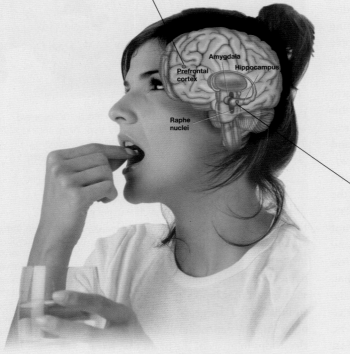

Source: MedioImages/Photodisc/Getty Images, Inc.

REJUVENATING THE MIND

Antidepressant use stimulates the production of synapses in the hippocampus (shown here in this electron micrograph, with the asterisk indicating a postsynaptic site). The hippocampus plays a role in cognitive function and in regulating anxiety (a feature in many cases of depression). The growth of new synapses may refresh this important brain region, enabling the formation of new connections to support a more positive outlook.

Source: Courtesy of Prof. Charles Nicholson, New York University School of Medicine.

been implicated in the disorder. The electrodes are connected to a battery, or pacemaker, that is implanted in the patient's chest (for men) or stomach (for women). The pacemaker powers the electrodes, sending a steady stream of low-voltage electricity to the problematic brain areas. In many cases, this repeated stimulation readjusts the person's brain activity and, over time, brings significant improvement (Blomstedt *et al.*, 2011; Hamani *et al.*, 2011; Mayberg *et al.*, 2005). Although such implants have offered promising results, at present they are still considered experimental. Thus, they are used infrequently, particularly in cases of depression, and usually only after the severe disorder has continued for years without responding to other forms of treatment.

Biological Treatments in Perspective

Today, biological treatments for psychological disorders, particularly pharmacological treatments, are highly regarded. They often bring great relief when other approaches have failed. However, the treatments have key limitations, such as significant side effects. In a number of cases, biological interventions alone are not the optimum treatment for psychological disorders, which may benefit from environmental interaction with these interventions (Kosslyn & Rosenberg, 2004).

Evidence is mounting that our brain chemistry can respond to changes in behaviour as well as vice versa. One study has found depressed individuals who responded to psychotherapy produced brain responses more similar to nondepressed individuals but depressed individuals who did not respond to psychotherapy had brain patterns that typically accompany depression (Okamoto *et al.*, 2006). In short, just as negative experiences can interact with brain activity to produce abnormal functioning, positive experiences can interact with the brain to improve functioning.

Before You Go On

What Do You Know?

4. What are the three main categories of brain interventions?
5. What are the newer methods of direct brain stimulation, and how are they used?

What Do You Think?

Are today's clinicians and their clients becoming reliant on drugs as a treatment?

Behavioural Therapies

LEARNING OBJECTIVE 3

Describe the behavioural treatments for psychological disorders.

As we saw in Chapter 19, behavioural theories and treatments are currently considered part of the *cognitive-behavioural model* combining behavioural and cognitive principles to explain and treat psychological disorders. Prior to cognitive approaches, behavioural treatments were applied on their own, and there are many occasions when behavioural interventions are sufficient to treat certain problems. Thus, this section will examine behavioural therapies exclusively before considering cognitive-behavioural therapies in the next section.

Behaviourists contend that the symptoms of a psychological disorder are learnt behaviours acquired through the same conditioning processes that produce normal behaviours (see Chapter 19). The goal of behavioural therapy is to identify the client's specific problem-causing behaviours and to replace them with more adaptive behaviours. The therapist's attitude towards the client is that of a teacher, rather than a healer. Behavioural techniques fall into three categories: *classical conditioning*, *operant conditioning* and *modelling*.

Classical Conditioning Techniques

Classical conditioning treatments are intended to change clients' dysfunctional reactions to stimuli. One treatment, described in Chapter 9, is *systematic desensitization*. This process is aimed at training people with phobias to react with calm instead of fear to the objects or situations producing anxiety (Fishman *et al.*, 2011; Wolpe, 1997, 1995, 1990). Clients first are trained in deep-muscle relaxation. Next, they construct a *fear hierarchy* in which they list objects or situations associated with their phobia, starting with the least feared and ending with the most feared. For a client with a phobia of lifts, for example, looking at a lift on the outside of a building a street away may be low on the fear hierarchy. Watching the lift doors close while inside the lift may be near the top (Figure 20.2). Finally, either in imagination or

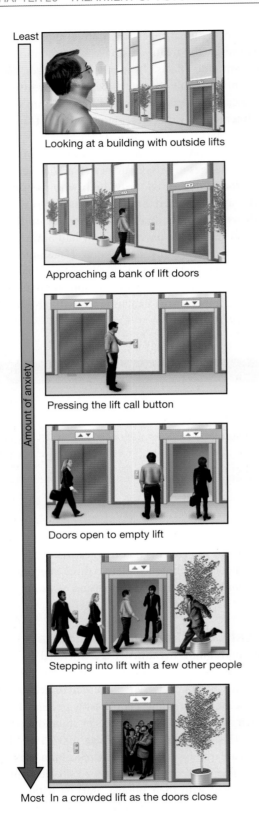

Least

Looking at a building with outside lifts

Approaching a bank of lift doors

Pressing the lift call button

Doors open to empty lift

Stepping into lift with a few other people

Most In a crowded lift as the doors close

Amount of anxiety

FIGURE 20.2 Fear hierarchy. Systematic desensitization uses classical conditioning principles to reduce a person's fears. Starting with the least stressful situation on his fear hierarchy, a man with fear of travelling in a lift is exposed to each item on the hierarchy with applying relaxation techniques.

physically, clients confront each item on the hierarchy while they are in a state of deep relaxation, starting with the least fearful and then moving on up the list, while maintaining this non-anxious state.

Research has repeatedly found that systematic desensitization and other classical conditioning techniques reduce phobic reactions more effectively than placebo treatments or no treatment at all (Olatunji *et al.*, 2011; Kraft & Kraft, 2010). These techniques have also been helpful in treating several other kinds of problems, including sexual dysfunctions, posttraumatic stress disorder, agoraphobia and asthma attacks (Koch & Haring, 2008). Because desensitization techniques expose individuals to the objects or situations they fear, and because this exposure seems so critical to effectiveness, these are often referred to as *exposure* treatments.

An opposite use of classical conditioning is known as **aversion therapy**. Here, clients *acquire* anxiety responses to stimuli that they have a maladaptive liking for. This approach has been used to reduce excessive drinking, as shown in Figure 20.3 (Owen-Howard, 2001). In repeated sessions, the clients may be given an electric shock, a nausea-producing drug or some other noxious stimulus whenever they reach for a drink. Aversion therapy has also been applied to help eliminate such undesirable behaviours as self-mutilation in autistic children, sexual paraphilias and smoking (Krueger & Kaplan, 2002). The effects of this conditioning tend to be short-lived but the avoidance may continue after this effect.

> **aversion therapy** a therapy designed to help clients to acquire anxiety responses to stimuli that they have been finding too attractive.

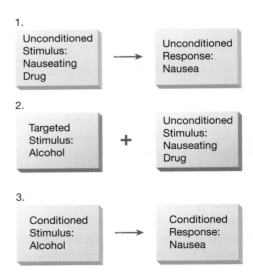

1.

| Unconditioned Stimulus: Nauseating Drug | → | Unconditioned Response: Nausea |

2.

| Targeted Stimulus: Alcohol | + | Unconditioned Stimulus: Nauseating Drug |

3.

| Conditioned Stimulus: Alcohol | → | Conditioned Response: Nausea |

FIGURE 20.3 Aversion therapy. Aversion therapy uses classical conditioning principles to create a negative response to a stimulus a person would like to avoid, such as alcohol. Here, a man savours a drink just before the effects of a nauseating drug begin.

Operant Conditioning Techniques

In operant conditioning treatments, therapists consistently provide rewards for appropriate behaviour and withhold rewards for inappropriate behaviour. This technique has been employed frequently, and successfully, with hospitalized patients experiencing psychosis (Kopelowicz *et al.*, 2007; Paul & Lentz, 1977; Ayllon & Azrin, 1965). When such patients talk coherently and behave normally, they are rewarded with food, privileges, attention or something else they value. Conversely, they receive no rewards when they speak bizarrely or display other psychotic behaviours.

Parents, teachers and therapists have successfully used operant conditioning techniques to change challenging behaviours in children, such as repeated tantrums, and to teach skills to individuals with autism or learning disabilities (Soorya *et al.*, 2011; Spiegler & Guevremont, 2003). Rewards in such cases have included food, TV and trips out etc.

Operant conditioning techniques typically work best in institutions or schools, where a person's behaviour can be reinforced systematically throughout the day. Often, a whole ward or classroom is converted into an operant conditioning arena. In many such programmes, desirable behaviour is reinforced with tokens that can later be exchanged for food, privileges or other rewards (Ayllon & Azrin, 1968). Programmes of this sort are called **token economy** programmes.

> **token economy** an operant conditioning therapy programme in which participants receive tokens (that can be traded for rewards) when they display desired behaviours.

Behavioural techniques based on operant conditioning have also been useful for depression (Lazzari *et al.*, 2011). Recall from Chapter 19 that depression is often associated with a decline in rewarding activities and withdrawal. Behaviour therapists may analyse the behaviour of such individuals to identify activities they respond to and use these to increase their participation in rewarding activities.

Modelling Techniques

Modelling therapy was introduced by the pioneering work of social learning theorist Albert Bandura (1977, 1969). In this, therapists demonstrate appropriate behaviour for clients. Then the clients, through a process of imitation and vicarious reward, begin to initiate the behaviour in their own lives. This procedure has been used to treat phobias, where therapists repeatedly display calm emotions while confronting objects that are feared by phobic clients. In this way, many clients are able to overcome their phobias (Rosenthal & Bandura, 1978; Bandura *et al.*, 1977).

Behavioural therapists have also used modelling to help people acquire or improve their social skills and assertiveness. In an approach called **social skills training**, for example, therapists point out the social deficits of clients and then role-play social situations with the clients, typically modelling more appropriate social behaviours for them. Ultimately, the clients practise the behaviours in real-life situations. In the role-playing session in the 'Acquiring the Social Touch' box below, the client is a male university student who has difficulty making dates with women.

> **social skills training** behavioural therapy technique in which therapists serve as models and teachers to help clients acquire desired social behaviours.

PSYCHOLOGY AROUND US   Acquiring the Social Touch

Client: By the way, [Pause] I don't suppose you want to go out Saturday night?

Therapist: Up to actually asking for the date you were very good. However, if I were the girl, I think I might have been a bit offended when you said, 'By the way'. It's like your asking her out is pretty casual. Also, the way you phrased the question, you were kind of suggesting to her that she doesn't want to go out with you. Pretend for the moment I'm you. Now, think how this sounds: 'There is a movie at the University theatre this Saturday that I want to see. If you don't have other plans, I'd very much like to take you.'

Client: That sounded good. Like you were sure of yourself and liked the girl too.

Therapist: Why don't you try it?

Client: You know that movie at the University? Well, I'd like to go, and I'd like to take you Saturday, if you don't have anything better to do.

Therapist: Well, that certainly was better. Your tone of voice was especially good. But the last line, 'if you don't have anything better to do', sounds like you don't think you have too much to offer. Why not run through it one more time.

Client: I'd like to see the show at the University, Saturday, and, if you haven't made other plans, I'd like to take you.

Therapist: Much better. Excellent, in fact. You were confident, forceful, and sincere.

(Rimm & Masters, 1979, p. 74)

Using a combined strategy of modelling, rehearsal, feedback and practice, therapists have successfully taught social and assertion skills to shy, passive or socially isolated people. These techniques can also help people who have a pattern of bursting out in rage or violence after building up resentment (rather than asserting themselves) over perceived social slights (Lochman *et al.*, 2010; Fisher *et al.*, 2004). The approach has also been used to improve the social skills of children and adults who experience depression, anxiety or other psychological problems (Ogden, 2011; Ishikawa *et al.*, 2010; Cooney *et al.*, 1991).

Behavioural Therapies in Perspective

Behavioural interventions are one of the most widely researched treatment approaches in the clinical field (Wilson, 2011). Moreover, behavioural approaches have been effective for numerous problems, including specific fears, social deficits and learning disabilities (Wilson, 2011).

The limitations of behavioural therapies include difficulty in maintaining improvement without further behavioural interventions, although, in many cases behavioural change is self-perpetuating. Also, behavioural therapies are less effective with some disorders, such as generalized anxiety disorder where targeting of specific behaviours for change is difficult (Wilson, 2011; O'Leary & Wilson, 1987). These are some of the reasons these interventions are now usually combined with cognitive approaches as cognitive-behavioural therapy.

Before You Go On

What Do You Know?

6. What are systematic desensitization and aversion therapy?

7. What principles and procedures are involved in a token economy programme?

8. How does social skills training work?

What Do You Think?

Does changing behaviour always fully treat disorders?

Cognitive-Behavioural Therapies

LEARNING OBJECTIVE 4

Describe cognitive-behavioural therapies for psychological disorders.

Cognitive-behavioural therapists try to help people recognize and change their faulty thinking processes and behaviour. Therapists may employ a range of cognitive strategies and behavioural techniques to help clients think, behave and feel better. Three influential cognitive-behavioural approaches are those of Albert Ellis, Aaron Beck and the *second-wave* cognitive-behavioural therapists. Ellis and Beck were pioneering cognitive therapists, and their basic approaches are essentially cognitive.

Ellis's Rational-Emotive Behavioural Therapy

In line with his belief that irrational assumptions give rise to abnormal functioning, Albert Ellis developed an approach called **rational-emotive behavioural therapy** (Ellis, 2011, 2002, 1962). Therapists using this approach first help clients identify the irrational assumptions that seem to guide their behavioural and emotional responses. Next, they help clients change those assumptions into constructive ways of viewing themselves and the world. One technique is *cognitive restructuring*, in which clients learn to replace negative interpretations with more positive thinking.

In his own practice, Ellis would point out to clients their irrational assumptions in a blunt, confrontational and often humorous way. Then he would model the use of alternative assumptions. After criticizing a young man's perfectionistic standards, for example, he might say, 'So what if you did a lousy job on that essay? It's important to realize that one lousy essay simply means one lousy essay, and no more than that!' Ellis gave clients homework assignments requiring them to observe their assumptions operating in their daily lives and think of ways to test the rationality of the dysfunctional assumptions. They were then required to rehearse new assumptions during therapy and apply them at home and work.

Rational-emotive therapists have cited numerous studies in support of this approach (Ellis, 2011, 2002). Clients with social anxiety who are treated with this therapy improve more than

> **rational-emotive behavioural therapy** Ellis's therapy technique designed to help clients discover and change the irrational assumptions that govern their emotions, behaviours and thinking.

Therapist: The point is for you to decide exactly what hypothesis or dysfunctional idea you want to work on for at least ten minutes a day, which, in your case would be the idea, again, that it's terrible for you to get rejected by a woman you find attractive. You would take this idea, and ask yourself several basic questions, in order to challenge and dispute it.

Client: What kind of questions?

Therapist: Usually, four basic questions—though they have all kinds of variations. The first one is, 'What am I telling myself?' or, 'What silly idea do I want to challenge?' And the answer, in your case, is, 'It's terrible if a woman whom I find attractive rejects me'. The

second question is, 'Is this, my hypothesis, true?' And the answer is —?

Client: Uh, well, uh. No, it isn't.

Therapist: Fine. If you had said it was true, the third question would have been, 'Where is the evidence for its being true? But since you said it isn't true, the third question is, 'Where is the evidence that it's not true?' Well —?

Client: Well, uh, it's not true because, as we said before, it may be very inconvenient if an attractive woman rejects me, but it's not more, uh, than that. It's only damned inconvenient!

(Ellis, 1962, pp. 29–30)

socially anxious clients who receive no treatment or placebo treatments (McEvoy, 2007). In addition, the approach has been applied to a wide range of other disorders (Ellis, 2011).

Beck's Cognitive Therapy

Aaron Beck independently developed a system of therapy that is similar to Ellis's rational-emotive behavioural therapy.

cognitive therapy Beck's cognitive therapy technique designed to help clients recognize and change their dysfunctional thoughts and ways of thinking.

Although he named his approach **cognitive therapy**, Beck has emphasized for decades that he also has clients experiment with new behaviours as a key feature of the approach.

This approach has been used most often for depression, although it also has been applied to problems ranging from panic disorder to personality disorders (Beck & Weishaar, 2011). With depressed

clients, Beck, like other cognitive therapists, helps clients to identify the negative thoughts and errors in logic that pervade their thinking and promote feelings of depression. The therapists also teach clients to challenge their dysfunctional thoughts, try new interpretations and apply different ways of thinking in their daily lives. In the 'Jumping to Negative Conclusions' box below, Beck guides a depressed 26-year-old postgraduate student to see the link between the way she interprets her experiences and the way she feels and to begin questioning the accuracy of her interpretations.

Around two-thirds of depressed people who are treated with Beck's cognitive approach improve. This is significantly more than those who receive no treatment and about the same as those who receive biological treatments (Beck & Weishaar, 2011; Hollon *et al.*, 2006, 2005, 2002). Research has also indicated the effectiveness of Beck-like cognitive therapy in cases of panic disorder and social anxiety disorder.

Patient: I get depressed when things go wrong. Like when I fail a test.

Therapist: How can failing a test make you depressed?

Patient: Well, if I fail I'll never get into a legal practice.

Therapist: So failing the test means a lot to you . . . Did everyone who failed get depressed enough to require treatment?

Patient: No, but it depends on how important the test was to the person.

Therapist: Right, and who decides the importance?

Patient: I do.

Therapist: Now what did failing mean?

Patient: (Tearful) That I couldn't get into a legal practice.

Therapist: And what does that mean to you?

Patient: That I'm just not smart enough.

Therapist: Anything else?

Patient: That I can never be happy.

Therapist: And how do these thoughts make you feel?

Patient: Very unhappy.

Therapist: So it is the meaning of failing a test that makes you very unhappy. [Moreover] you get yourself into a trap – by definition, failure to get into legal career equals 'I can never be happy.'

(Beck et al., 1979, pp. 145–146)

Second-Wave Cognitive-Behavioural Therapies

A growing body of research suggests that the kinds of cognitive changes proposed by Ellis, Beck and other cognitive therapists are not always possible to achieve (Sharf, 2012). Thus, a new group of cognitive-behavioural therapies, sometimes called *second-wave cognitive-behavioural therapies*, has emerged in recent years (Hollon & DiGiuseppe, 2011). These approaches help clients to *accept* many of their problematic thoughts rather than judge them, act on them or try fruitlessly to change them. The hope is that by recognizing such thoughts for what they are – just thoughts – clients will eventually be able to let them pass through their awareness without being particularly troubled by them.

One of several disorders to which this kind of approach has been applied is generalized anxiety disorder. As you read in Chapter 19, this disorder is characterized by persistent and excessive feelings of anxiety and endless worrying about numerous events and activities. Second-wave cognitive-behavioural therapists guide clients with generalized anxiety disorder to recognize and then accept their dysfunctional over-use of worrying (Newman *et al.*, 2011; Ritter *et al.*, 2010; Wells, 2010). They begin by educating the clients about the role of worrying in their disorder and have them observe their bodily arousal and cognitive responses across various situations. Over time, the clients come to appreciate the triggers of their worrying, their misconceptions about worrying and their misguided efforts to control their lives by worrying. As their insights grow, clients are expected to see the world as less threatening (and so less arousing), try out more constructive ways of dealing with arousal and, perhaps most importantly, worry less about the fact that they worry so much. Research indicates that a concentrated focus on worrying of this kind is indeed a helpful addition to the treatment of generalized anxiety disorder (Ritter *et al.*, 2010; Wells, 2010).

An established second-wave cognitive-behavioural approach is *mindfulness-based cognitive therapy*, developed by psychologist Steven Hayes and colleagues as part of their broader treatment approach called *acceptance and commitment therapy* (Antony, 2011; Treanor, 2011; Hayes *et al.*, 2004). Here therapists help clients to become mindful of their streams of thoughts, including their worries, at the very moments they are occurring and to *accept* such thoughts as mere events of the mind. Once again, by accepting their thoughts rather than trying to eliminate them the clients are expected to be less upset and affected by them.

Mindfulness-based cognitive therapy has also been applied to other psychological problems such as depression, post-traumatic stress disorder, personality disorders and substance abuse, often with promising results (Orsillo & Roemer, 2011; Hayes *et al.*, 2004). The approach borrows heavily from a form of meditation called *mindfulness meditation*, which teaches individuals to pay attention to the thoughts and feelings that flow through their minds during meditation and to accept such thoughts in a nonjudgemental way.

Cognitive-Behavioural Therapies in Perspective

Cognitive-behavioural therapy is the approach clinical psychologists are trained in and is supported by research. This evidence-based therapy has proved very effective for treating depression, social anxiety disorder, generalized anxiety disorder, panic disorder, sexual dysfunctions and a number of other psychological disorders (Beck & Weishaar, 2011; Landon & Barlow, 2004).

The limitations of cognitive-behavioural approaches include the debate as to whether cognitive dysfunction precedes or is a consequence of a disorder. In addition, it is not clear whether it is the behavioural or the cognitive features of the cognitive-behavioural approaches that are effective in these treatments. The assumption of many therapists is that the behavioural features help bring about essential cognitive changes, thus, it may be that the behavioural changes are most important. And, finally, although cognitive-behavioural therapies are certainly effective for most problems, there are a small number of exceptions (Sharf, 2012).

Before You Go On

What Do You Know?

9. What do therapists help clients to do in rational-emotive behavioural therapy?

10. What is cognitive therapy?

11. What are the goals of second-wave cognitive-behavioural therapies?

What Do You Think?

We all sometimes have irrational assumptions, though they do not usually cause psychological disorders. What irrational assumptions and thoughts do you occasionally have?

Non-Empirical Therapies

The following approaches to therapy are important in historical terms but have little research support and lack the evidence-based status necessary for current practice (Holmes, 2010). Thus, they are no longer considered mainstream therapies and, though available privately, are not part of current clinical training as therapies. However, aspects of these approaches, particularly humanistic, contribute to other services available to individuals such, as counselling.

Humanistic and Existential Therapies

LEARNING OBJECTIVE 5a

Describe the humanistic and existential approaches used as therapy for psychological disorders.

Humanistic and existential therapists assume clients deceive themselves and try to help them examine themselves and their situations more accurately and acceptingly. They would then expect that clients would then be better able to actualize their full potential as human beings by emphasizing present experiences rather than events from the client's past.

Rogers' Client-Centred Therapy Carl Rogers' original **client-centred therapy** attempts to create a positive climate in which clients can view themselves honestly and acceptingly (Raskin *et al.*, 2011). There are three important aspects to the way clients would be approached:

> **client-centred therapy** humanistic therapy was designed to help clients experience unconditional positive regard and look at themselves honestly and acceptingly.

- *Unconditional positive regard.* Full and warm acceptance of the client.

- *Accurate empathy.* Skilful listening, including restatements of the client's own comments.

- *Genuineness.* Sincere communication.

According to Rogers, clients feel accepted by their therapists in this kind of atmosphere and eventually come to recognize and value their own emotions, thoughts and behaviours. They should then theoretically be relieved of the insecurities that have been preventing self-actualization. The interaction in the 'Hearing the Client' box below shows the techniques used by Rogers.

PSYCHOLOGY AROUND US **Hearing the Client**

Client: In lectures I feel that everyone's just waiting for a chance to jump on me . . . When I meet somebody I wonder what he's actually thinking of me. Then later on I wonder how I match up to what he's come to think of me.

Therapist: You feel that you're pretty responsive to the opinions of other people.

Client: Yes, but it's things that shouldn't worry me.

Therapist: You feel that it's the sort of thing that shouldn't be upsetting, but they do get you pretty much worried anyway.

Client: There are lots of little things that aren't true . . . Things just seem to be piling up, piling up inside of me . . . It's a feeling that things were crowding up and they were going to burst.

Therapist: You feel that it's a sort of oppression with some frustration and that things are just unmanageable.

Client: In a way . . . I'm afraid I'm not very clear here but that's the way it comes.

Therapist: That's all right. You say just what you think.

(Snyder, 1947, pp. 2–24)

Client-centred therapy has not performed well in research (Sharf, 2012). Although some studies have reported improvements, most controlled research does not support this. Nevertheless, Rogers' approach has had a very positive influence on clinical interactions with clients (Raskin *et al.*, 2011; Kirschenbaum, 2004). He also provided an accepted alternative to psychodynamic therapy, helping pave the way for later approaches.

Gestalt Therapy Gestalt therapy was derived from the humanistic approach, and introduced in the 1950s by Frederick (Fritz) Perls. The Gestalt approach attempts to move clients

towards self-recognition and self-acceptance (Yontef & Jacobs, 2011). Unlike the client-centred approach, they aim to achieve this by challenging and frustrating the clients. Perls' favourite techniques included challenging, role-playing and rules.

- *Challenging.* Gestalt therapists consistently refuse to meet their clients' expectations or demands. The aim here is to help the clients to see how often they try to manipulate others into meeting their needs.

- *Role-playing.* Gestalt therapists often have clients act out various roles. A person may be instructed to be another person, an object, an alternative self or even a part of the body. Role-playing can become very intense, as individuals are encouraged to fully express their feelings. They demonstrably enact their emotions until they 'own', or accept, feelings that previously made them uncomfortable.

- *Rules.* The rules enforced by Gestalt therapists ensure that clients look at themselves in detail. For example, clients may be required to say, 'I am sad' rather than 'The situation is depressing.'

Little research has been conducted on the Gestalt approach, owing to its subjectivity (Yontef & Jacobs, 2011; Strümpfel, 2006, 2004). Gestalt techniques have been included in *emotion-focused approaches*. These emphasize attention to one's current emotional experiences as a way to reduce anxiety, depression and other psychological difficulties (Greenberg & Goldman, 2008).

Existential Therapy Existential therapists encourage clients to accept responsibility for their lives and their problems. Clients are shown their freedom to choose different paths and to change their lives (Yalom & Josselson, 2011; Schneider & Krug, 2010). Existential approaches emphasize the relationship between therapist and client and try to create an atmosphere of honesty and shared learning.

PSYCHOLOGY AROUND US Who's the Doctor?

Patient: I don't know why I keep coming here. All I do is tell you the same thing over and over. I'm not getting anywhere.

Doctor: I'm getting tired of hearing the same thing over and over, too.

Patient: Maybe I'll stop coming.

Doctor: It's certainly your choice.

Patient: What do you think I should do?

Doctor: What do you want to do?

Patient: You know what's best; you're the doctor.

Doctor: Do I act like a doctor?

(Keen, 1970, p. 200)

Like Gestalt therapists, most existential therapists do not believe in evaluating their treatments empirically (Yalom & Josselson, 2011). Thus, their approach has no empirical support.

Humanistic and Existential Therapies in Perspective Humanistic and existential approaches claim to highlight the challenges of psychological life (Watson *et al.*, 2011; Cain, 2007). They focus on self-acceptance, personal values, personal meaning and personal choice, claimed to be lacking in some disordered individuals. However, although these approaches are hard to research, a small number of studies suggest the approach could be of some benefit in a few cases (Schneider & Krug, 2010; Cain, 2007; Strümpfel, 2006).

Psychodynamic Approaches

 HOW WE DEVELOP

LEARNING OBJECTIVE 5b
Describe the psychodynamic approach to disorders.

Psychodynamic approaches assume that emotional disorder is the result of earlier emotional trauma. Psychodynamic methods ranged from classical *Freudian psychoanalysis* to briefer versions such as *short-term psychodynamic analysis* and *relational psychoanalysis*. All aim to uncover presumed past traumatic events claimed to cause inner conflicts and resolve these.

Techniques of Psychodynamic Analysis

Psychodynamic analysts claim to help clients discover their own underlying problems by using *free association, therapist interpretation, catharsis* and *working through*.

Free Association In **free association** clients are responsible for starting and leading each discussion. The analyst tells the individual to describe any thoughts or feelings that come to mind, even if they seem unimportant and the therapist then probes the client's associations in the hope that they will eventually reveal unconscious events they claim underlie the individual's problem.

> **free association** psychodynamic therapy technique of allowing clients to freely talk about whatever they want.

Interpretation Psychoanalysts share their interpretations with the client when they think the individual is ready to hear them. Psychoanalysts claim that three phenomena – *resistance, transference* and *dreams* – are of special value.

- **Resistance**. When clients cannot proceed in their free associations or change the subject, it is presumed they are avoiding something anxiety-provoking. The analyst remains vigilant for presumed unconscious resistance and may point it out to a client and interpret it.

resistance practice in which clients encounter a block in their free associations or change the subject so as to avoid a potentially painful discussion.

- **Transference**. Analysts believe clients act and feel towards the therapist as they do towards important figures in their lives, past and present. They call assumed displacement of feelings *transference*. From this, analysts attempt to help individuals understand unconscious feelings towards other key people.

transference process through which clients come to act and feel towards the therapist as they did towards important figures in their lives, past and present.

- *Dream interpretation*. Freud (1924) called dreams the 'royal road to the unconscious', although we now consider such attribution of meaning unfounded. He believed that repression and other defence mechanisms are weakened during sleep to reveal the person's unconscious instincts, needs and wishes. Freud claimed a distinction between a dream's *manifest content* (the consciously remembered content) and its *latent content* (the symbolic meaning).

Catharsis

Psychodynamic followers believe that individuals must experience **catharsis** if they are to resolve internal conflicts and overcome their problems by re-experiencing their past, repressed feelings both intellectually and emotionally.

catharsis re-experiencing of past, repressed feelings as means of settling internal conflicts and overcoming problems.

Working Through

Followers of psychoanalysis believe that to gain insight the client and analyst must *work through*, or examine, the same issues repeatedly across many sessions.

Short-Term Psychoanalysis

Freudian psychoanalysis was a very time-indulgent and expensive process, leading to some making the process shorter. In *short-term psychoanalysis*, clients would focus on a single problem, termed *dynamic focus*, such as excessive dependence on other people (Wolitzky, 2011). One or two studies have claimed some value in these approaches but only in a few cases (Wolitzky, 2011; Present *et al.*, 2008).

Relational Psychoanalysis

In contrast to Freud's approach, **relational psychoanalysis** believes analysts' reactions and beliefs should be included in the analysis process (Luborsky *et al.*, 2011). In this, it is thought that analysts should also disclose things about themselves, particularly their own reactions to patients, and attempt to have equal relationships with clients.

relational psychoanalysis a school of psychodynamic therapy holding that therapists should work to form more equal relationships with clients.

Psychodynamic Approaches in Perspective

Freud's psychoanalysis was a very early approach to mental conditions, primarily the dubiously defined *hysteria*, and thus of value in historical terms. It was one of the earliest methods to attempt a psychological, rather than biological, approach.

Empirical research, however, has failed to support the effectiveness of psychoanalysis (Wampold *et al.*, 2011; Nietzel *et al.*, 2003). For the first half of the 20th century, psychoanalysis was only supported by case studies of enthusiastic clinicians and by uncontrolled studies. Controlled investigations have only recently been attempted and only a very small number of these, mostly brief psychotherapies, have shown any value over and above placebo treatments (Prochaska & Norcross, 2010).

Before You Go On

What Do You Know?

12. What are the key characteristics therapists should display in client-centred therapy?
13. What techniques are used in Gestalt therapy?
14. What are the main goals of existential therapy?
15. Contrast three types of psychoanalysis.

What Do You Think?

Remember George, in our chapter opener? In treating George's psychological distress, where would a Gestalt therapist start? What kind of clients and what kind of problems do you think could possibly be helped by humanistic and existential approaches?

Formats of Therapy

LEARNING OBJECTIVE 6
Describe commonly used formats of therapy.

individual therapy a psychotherapy format in which the therapist sees the client alone; the oldest of the modern formats.

Individual therapy, or treatments conducted by individual therapists with individual clients, is the oldest of the modern therapy formats. Other formats include *group therapy, family and couple therapy* and *community treatment*. Therapists may apply their particular approach in each of these formats and additional strategies have also been developed for use in the non-individual formats.

Group Therapy

group therapy a psychotherapy format in which a therapist sees several clients at the same time.

In **group therapy**, a therapist sees several clients with psychological problems at the same time. Group therapy became a popular format for treating people with psychological difficulties after World War II, when growing demand for psychological services forced therapists throughout the United States and Europe to look for time-saving alternatives to individual therapy. Some therapists now specialize in group therapy, and many others conduct therapy groups as one aspect of their practice. A survey of clinical psychologists, for example, revealed that almost one-third of them practise group therapy to some degree (Norcross & Goldfried, 2005).

Typically, group members meet with a therapist and discuss the problems or concerns of one or more of the members (Burlingame & Baldwin, 2011). Groups are often created with particular client populations in mind. For example, there are groups for people with alcoholism, for people who are physically handicapped and for people who are divorced, abused or bereaved.

Irvin Yalom, a group-therapy theorist, suggests that successful forms of group therapy share certain 'curative' features (Cox *et al.*, 2008; Yalom & Leszcz, 2005):

- *Guidance.* They usually provide information and advice for members.

- *Identification.* They provide models of appropriate behaviour.

- *Group cohesiveness.* They offer an atmosphere of solidarity in which members can learn to take risks and accept criticism.

- *Universality.* Members discover that other people have similar problems.

- *Altruism.* Members develop feelings of self-worth by helping others.

- *Catharsis.* Members develop more understanding of themselves and of others and learn to express their feelings.

- *Skill building.* Members acquire or improve social skills.

One kind of group intervention in wide use today is **self-help groups**. These groups are made up of people who have similar problems and come together to help and support one another without the direct leadership of a professional clinician (White & Madara, 2012; Mueller *et al.*, 2007). Self-help groups have become increasingly popular over the past few decades. Of the many thousands of self-help groups in the United Kingdom, a significant proportion involve mental health issues.

self-help groups a format in which people who have similar problems and come together to help and support one another without the direct leadership of a professional clinician.

Self-help groups address a wide assortment of issues. Examples include alcoholism and other forms of substance abuse, compulsive gambling, bereavement, overeating, phobias, child abuse, medical illnesses, rape victimization, unemployment and divorce. Online self-help chat rooms and message boards are often similar to the traditional self-help groups and have greatly increased in number and popularity in recent years.

Self-help groups are popular for several reasons. Some participants believe clinicians and institutions have only limited time and engagement to help with their particular problems. For example, Alcoholics Anonymous, the well-known network of self-help groups for people dependent on alcohol, was developed in 1934 in response to the limitations of clinical treatments for alcoholism. Some are drawn to self-help groups because they find them less threatening and less stigmatizing than directed therapy groups.

As group formats vary from conventional therapy groups to self-help groups, it is difficult to assess their effectiveness. Some research suggests that group therapy is often of help to clients, perhaps as helpful as individual therapy (Burlingame & Baldwin, 2011; Dies, 2003). Candid feedback is usually useful for group members as long as there is a balance between positive and negative feedback.

Family Therapy

family therapy a format in which therapists meet with all members of a family in order to help the whole family to change.

Family therapy dates back to the 1950s. In this format, therapists meet with all members of a family to identify and feed back problem behaviours and interactions between the members, and try to help the whole family change (Goldenberg & Goldenberg, 2011). Most meet with family members as a group, but some choose to see them separately. In each case, the family is viewed as the unit for treatment.

Like group therapists, family therapists may follow the principles of any of the major theoretical models. Some will also adhere to the principles of family systems theory. As we saw in Chapter 19, family systems theory holds that each family has its own implicit rules, relationship structure and communication patterns that shape the behaviour of the individual members, including dysfunctional behaviour. For one family member to change, the family system may have to be changed.

Research has not reliably evaluated the effectiveness of family systems approaches (Goldenberg & Goldenberg, 2011). A few studies have claimed that as much as 65% of treated individuals improve, but others have found very low success rates. No single type of family therapy emerged as consistently more effective than the others (Alexander *et al.*, 2002).

Couple Therapy

couple therapy, or **marital therapy** a therapy format in which a therapist works with two people who are in a long-term relationship.

In **couple therapy**, also known as **marital therapy**, the therapist works with two people who are in a long-term relationship, focusing on the structure and communication patterns in their relationship (Gurman & Snyder, 2011; Baucom *et al.*, 2010, 2009). Often, this format of therapy involves a husband and wife, but the couple need not be married or even living together. Similarly, they need not be heterosexual. Indeed, some therapists specialize in working with same-sex couples.

Although some degree of discord occurs in any long-term relationship, there is growing evidence that many adults in our society experience serious marital problems. The divorce rate across Europe is now close to 50% of the marriage rate and has been climbing steadily in recent decades, partly because of legal changes and the acceptability of cohabitation without marriage (Coontz, 2004). Of those who married a few decades ago, much less than half are now still married and proclaiming their marriages to be 'very happy'. Further to this, many of those who live together without marrying seem to have similar levels of relationship disharmony (Harway, 2005).

Like group and family therapy, couple therapy may utilize any paradigm approach (Baucom *et al.*, 2010; Shadish & Baldwin, 2005). According to research, people treated in couple therapy show greater improvements in their relationships than a no-treatment condition, but no one form of couple therapy is significantly more effective than the others (Gurman & Snyder, 2011; Christensen *et al.*, 2010). Altogether, two-thirds of treated couples experience improved marital functioning. However, less than half of those who are treated achieve 'distress-free' relationships and a quarter of all treated couples eventually divorce.

Community Treatment

At one time, people with psychological disorders, especially severe disorders, had to be referred to consultants or visit institutions. Today, however, a number of **community mental health treatment** programmes offer such people services from nearby agencies. Community-based treatments include community mental health centres, community day programmes and residential services. Collectively, these agencies often play a major role in the treatment of people with severe psychological disorders, such as schizophrenia (Daly *et al.*, 2010).

community mental health treatment programmes that focus on community care, including an emphasis on prevention.

PSYCHOLOGY AROUND US   In Need of Community Care

What happens to people with schizophrenia and other severe psychological disorders in the absence of the community mental health services they need? Many return to their families and receive medication and support, but little else in the way of treatment (Barrowclough & Lobban, 2008). Around 8% receive only custodial care and medication in an institution, or alternatively nursing or rest homes (Torrey, 2001). As many as 18% are placed in residences which may be privately run, such as hostels, where supervision often is mostly provided by untrained individuals. Another 31% live in totally unsupervised settings, including rundown single-room-occupancy hotels spending their days wandering through neighbourhood streets (Burns & Drake, 2011). Large numbers become homeless (Kooyman & Walsh, 2011). And at least as many again end up in prisons because their disorders result in them breaking the law (Peters *et al.*, 2008).

A key feature of community treatment is *prevention*. Community clinicians seek out clients rather than wait for them, an approach that is often very successful (Clanton Harpine, 2011; Juhnke *et al.*, 2011). There are three types of prevention: *primary*, *secondary* and *tertiary*.

- *Primary prevention* consists of efforts to improve community functioning and policies. The goal here is to prevent psychological disorders altogether. Community health professionals facilitate improved child-care facilities in the community, offer mental health workshops on stress reduction or provide online information and support sites independently or as part of national health service provision.

- *Secondary prevention* consists of detecting and treating psychological disorders in the early stages, before they reach serious levels. Community health professionals may produce information packs for clergy, teachers or police on how to identify the early signs of psychological dysfunction and how to refer people to the right places for treatment.

- *Tertiary prevention* aims to provide effective treatment immediately so that moderate or severe disorders do not become chronic problems. Unfortunately, although community agencies are able to offer tertiary care for many people with moderate problems, stretched budgets often prevent them from providing care for the smaller number with more severe disorders (Althouse, 2010).

Before You Go On

What Do You Know?

16. What are self-help groups?

17. What is the main assumption of family systems therapy?

18. Describe primary, secondary and tertiary prevention.

What Do You Think?

Which therapy format appeals to you the most? The least? Why? Are certain formats better suited for particular problems or client personalities?

Does Therapy Work?

LEARNING OBJECTIVE 7

Summarize research on the effectiveness of therapy.

As we noted earlier, as many as four hundred forms of therapy are currently available (Corsini & Wedding, 2011). The most important question to ask about each of them is whether it really helps. **Therapy outcome studies**, which measure the effects of various treatments, typically ask one of four questions:

therapy outcome studies research that looks at the effects of various treatments.

- *Is therapy in general effective?* Studies reveal that therapy is often more helpful than no treatment or placebo treatments. Using a statistical technique called *meta-analysis*, one early review combined the results of 375 separate, controlled studies, covering a total of almost 25,000 people seen in a wide assortment of therapies (Smith *et al.*, 1980; Smith & Glass, 1977). According to this statistical analysis, shown in Figure 20.4, the average person who received treatment was better off than 75% of the untreated control clients. Other analyses have found similar relationships between treatment and improvement (Sharf, 2012; Bickman, 2005).

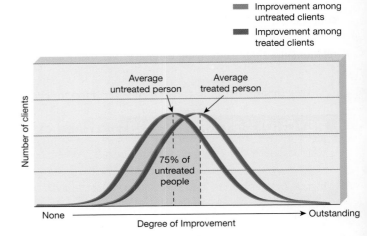

FIGURE 20.4 Is therapy generally effective? An analysis of 375 studies of treatment effectiveness shows that the average person who gets treatment of any kind is better off after treatment than a similar person who does not get treatment.

- *How effective are particular therapies?* A number of studies have found that almost all of the current major forms of therapy when evaluated are of some help to clients above placebo treatment (Prochaska & Norcross, 2010). Research comparing these therapies found that no one form of therapy generally stands out over the others (Luborsky *et al.*, 2006, 2003, 1975).

  Similar overall success rates for current therapies may indicate they share common features (Sharf, 2012; Bohart & Tallman, 2010). Surveys of highly successful therapists suggest that, regardless of their particular orientations, successful therapists tend to do similar things: (1) They provide feedback to clients. (2) They help clients focus on their own thoughts and behaviour. (3) They pay careful attention to the way they and their clients interact. (4) They try to build a sense of self-mastery in their clients (Portnoy, 2008; Korchin & Sands, 1983).

- *Are particular therapies especially effective for certain problems?* Researchers have found that particular therapies are especially effective at treating certain disorders (Beutler, 2011; Corsini & Wedding, 2011). Behavioural therapies, for example, seem to be the most effective of all treatments for phobias (Wilson, 2011). Cognitive-behavioural therapies are particularly helpful in cases of social anxiety disorder, generalized anxiety disorder, panic disorder and depression (Craske, 2010; Pontoski & Heimberg, 2010). And drug therapy is the single-most-helpful treatment for schizophrenia and bipolar disorder (Minzenberg *et al.*, 2011).

  Contemporary therapy often combines two or more approaches when treating particular disorders (Cuijpers *et al.*, 2010). Drug therapy, for example, is often combined with cognitive-behavioural therapy to treat depression or various anxiety disorders, although the superiority of such combinations over the individual approaches has not always been supported consistently by research (Otto *et al.*, 2010; Pontoski & Heimberg, 2010). In fact, it is now common for clients to be seen by two professionals: one of them is usually a psychiatrist who is able to prescribe medications and the other a clinical psychologist who conducts psychotherapy.

HOW WE DIFFER

- *Is therapy equally effective across race and gender?* Studies conducted in countries across the world have found that members of ethnic and racial minority groups typically show less improvement in clinical treatment, make less use of mental health services and stop therapy sooner than members of majority groups (Comas-Diaz, 2011, 2006; Ward, 2007). Given such findings, a number of clinicians have developed **culture-sensitive therapies**, which seek to address the unique issues faced by members of cultural minority groups. Clinicians using these approaches typically try to do the following (Brown, 2011; Comas-Diaz, 2011; Wyatt & Parham, 2007):

> **culture-sensitive therapies** approaches that seek to address the unique issues faced by members of cultural minority groups.

- Be aware of the client's cultural values.
- Be aware of the stress, prejudices and stereotypes to which minority clients are exposed.
- Be aware of the hardships faced by the children of immigrants.
- Help clients recognize the impact of both their own culture and the dominant culture on their self-views and behaviours.
- Help clients identify and express suppressed anger and pain.
- Help clients achieve a bicultural balance that feels right for them.
- Help clients raise their self-esteem – a sense of self-worth that has often been damaged by generations of negative messages.

Therapies geared to the pressures of being female, called **gender-sensitive**, or **feminist**, **therapies** follow similar principles (Calogero *et al.*, 2011). In a related vein, when working with clients who are very religious, many of today's therapists make a point of including spiritual issues in therapy (Aten *et al.*, 2011; Worthington, 2011). They may, for example, encourage clients to use their spiritual resources to help them cope (Galanter, 2010).

> **gender-sensitive, or feminist, therapies** approaches that seek to address the unique pressures of being female.

Obviously, knowledge of how particular therapies fare with particular disorders and particular populations can help therapists and clients alike make better decisions about treatment (Beutler, 2011, 2002; Beutler *et al.*, 2011). To help clinicians become more familiar with and apply such research findings, there is a movement in the United Kingdom and elsewhere called the **empirically supported**, or **evidence-based**, **treatment movement** (Sharf, 2012; Pope & Wedding, 2011; Lambert, 2010). Proponents of this movement have formed task forces that seek to identify which therapies have

> **empirically supported, or evidence-based, treatment movement** a movement to help clinicians become more familiar with and apply research findings concerning the effectiveness of particular treatments.

received clear empirical research support for particular disorders, to propose corresponding treatment guidelines and to spread such information to clinicians. Critics of the movement claim that such efforts are at times simplistic, biased and even misleading (Hagemoser, 2009; Westen *et al.*, 2005). However, the empirically supported treatment movement has become widely accepted and may result in therapies of dubious effectiveness not being supported (see Holmes, 2010).

Before You Go On

What Do You Know?
19. What does research show about whether therapy is generally effective?
20. What do effective therapists have in common?
21. What does research show about the effectiveness of particular therapies for certain problems?
22. Is therapy equally effective across race and gender?

What Do You Think?
Do you believe that all therapies should be empirically evaluated and found effective before use?

Some Final Thoughts about the Field of Psychology

It is ironic that we end this book with chapters on psychopathology and its treatments. Many people automatically think of psychopathology when they hear the term *psychology*. However, psychology is a broad field that studies a wide variety of mental processes and behaviour. In addition, all of those normal or disordered processes and behaviours tend to be rather awe-inspiring. For example, disorders of memory, such as Alzheimer's disease, may be fascinating, but normal acts of memory – encoding, storing and retrieving so many experiences and pieces of information – are no less remarkable.

Psychology is a wide-ranging and complex field consisting of many subdivisions, from sensation and perception to social psychology attempting to explain specific aspects of mental functioning from a particular angle. Collectively, these subdivisions have provided us with an impressive understanding of mental processes and behaviour. However, there is still some way to go before a complete understanding is possible.

Although subdivisions have provided specialist expertise for research, the different divisions are increasingly discovering areas of overlap and commonality. Thus, each inform the others to collectively provide a more integrated, complete and accurate understanding of mental processes and behaviour. It is now less a matter of choosing between neuroscience, cognitive psychology and social psychology to understand how and why people behave (or fail to act) when passing by, for example, the scene of an accident and more one of how the subfields jointly account for that behaviour. In short, psychology is becoming an integrated field.

Access your interactive e-book to view a video clip for this chapter at
www.wileyopenpage.com

Summary

Treatment in the Modern Context

LEARNING OBJECTIVE 1 Explain who currently receives treatment for psychological problems, how they enter treatment and what general features characterize types of treatment.

- Women once outnumbered men in therapy by four to one; men today are more willing to enter therapy.
- Psychological therapy was once only available to the wealthy, but in contemporary clinical psychology it is available to all in national health provision.

- People may enter therapy on their own or may be sectioned for treatment under the Mental Health Act (in the United Kingdom). Many never seek treatment at all.
- Professionals conducting therapy include psychologists and psychiatrists.
- Most clients are treated in the community as outpatients, but some people with severe problems are treated as inpatients in psychiatric institutions.
- All forms of therapy have three essential features: a sufferer who seeks relief, a trained healer and a series of contacts between the two in which the healer tries to bring about change in the sufferer's emotional state, attitudes and behaviour.

Biological Treatments

LEARNING OBJECTIVE 2   Describe the major biological treatments for psychological disorders.

- Drug therapy, electroconvulsive therapy (ECT) and psychosurgery are the three methods of biological treatments.
- Psychotropic drugs – including antianxiety, antidepressant, antibipolar and antipsychotic drugs – have brought relief to many, but they do not work well in a minority of cases and may have undesired side effects.
- ECT, used primarily to treat depression, is administered less often today than in the past. Two more recently developed brain stimulation treatments, vagus nerve stimulation and transcranial magnetic stimulation, have fewer wide-ranging side effects than ECT.
- Psychosurgery today is much more precise than the crude lobotomies of the past, in which the connections between the frontal lobe and the lower brain centres were severed.
- Biological treatments for psychological disorders, particularly drug treatments, are highly regarded today. However, in some cases, biological interventions are better supplemented with cognitive behavioural therapies.

Behavioural Therapies

LEARNING OBJECTIVE 3   Describe the behavioural treatments for psychological disorders.

- Behavioural treatments, aimed at replacing dysfunctional behaviours with more functional ones, are based on learning processes. Behavioural techniques fall into three categories: classical conditioning, operant conditioning and modelling.
- Systematic desensitization and aversion therapy rely on classical conditioning. Systematic desensitization is especially effective in treating phobias, while aversion therapy has been used to treat people who want to eliminate problem behaviours, such as drinking.

- Token economies follow the principles of operant conditioning and use rewards to encourage desired behaviours.
- Social skills training uses modelling to help clients acquire desired social behaviours.
- Research suggests that behavioural therapies are highly effective. Sometimes lasting change outside therapy is difficult to maintain, however, and can be less effective with disorders that are not well defined.

Cognitive-Behavioural Therapies

LEARNING OBJECTIVE 4   Describe cognitive-behavioural therapies for psychological disorders.

- Cognitive-behavioural therapists try to help people recognize and change their faulty thinking processes. Most such therapies use some behavioural techniques. Three influential cognitive-behavioural approaches are those of Albert Ellis, Aaron Beck and the second-wave cognitive-behavioural therapists.
- Ellis's rational-emotive behavioural therapy focuses on helping clients to identify their maladaptive assumptions, test them and change them.
- Beck's cognitive therapy guides clients to challenge their maladaptive attitudes, automatic thoughts and illogical thinking. Research supports the effectiveness of cognitive therapy for depression and other disorders.
- Second-wave cognitive-behavioural therapies help clients to accept their problem behaviours rather than judge them, act on them or try to change them.
- Cognitive-behavioural therapy is almost universally used today, and research suggests that this treatment is very effective. It is still not always clear, however, whether psychological disorders create or result from maladaptive thoughts.

Non-Empirical Therapies
Humanistic and Existential Approaches

LEARNING OBJECTIVE 5a   Describe the humanistic and existential approaches used as therapy for psychological disorders.

- Humanistic and existential therapists attempt to help clients regard themselves and their situations more accurately and acceptingly.
- Carl Rogers' client-centred therapy attempts to provide unconditional positive regard, accurate empathy and genuineness, in the hope that clients may come to value their own emotions, thoughts and behaviours.
- Gestalt therapists use planned frustration, role-playing and rules to help clients recognize and accept their needs and goals.

- Existentialist therapies attempt to help clients discover their personal freedom of choice and take responsibility for making choices.
- Humanistic and existential approaches lack empirical support from research. However, recent research suggests they can be of benefit to some clients.

Psychodynamic Approaches

LEARNING OBJECTIVE 5b Describe the psychodynamic approaches to psychological disorder.

- Psychodynamic approaches range from classical Freudian psychoanalysis to adaptations that followed this. Psychoanalysis attempts to get clients to uncover past traumatic events and associated inner conflicts and to resolve these.
- Psychoanalytic approaches include free association; therapist interpretation of resistance, transference and dreams; catharsis; and repeatedly working through supposed issues.
- Post-Freudian developments include short-term psychoanalysis and relational psychoanalysis.
- The psychodynamic approach is important in historical terms and was the first to offer a psychological approach. But the effectiveness of psychodynamic therapy is not supported by research.

Formats of Therapy

LEARNING OBJECTIVE 6 Describe commonly used formats of therapy.

- Individual therapy, in which practitioners meet with one client at a time, is the oldest of the modern therapy formats.
- In group therapy several clients with similar problems meet with a single therapist at the same time. Self-help groups are similar, but are conducted without the leadership of a therapist. Both types of groups can be helpful for certain clients.

- Family therapy treats all members of a family, together or individually, and therapists usually consider the family as a system. Two people in a long-term relationship can seek couple therapy to help address issues in their relationship.
- Community mental health treatment focuses on preventing abnormal functioning through (1) primary prevention, policies that reduce psychological risk in a community; (2) secondary prevention, treating minor problems before they become serious; and (3) tertiary prevention, providing prompt treatment for moderate and severe disorders so they do not become long-term problems.

Does Therapy Work?

LEARNING OBJECTIVE 7 Summarize research on the effectiveness of therapy.

- In general, receiving therapy is more likely to help people with psychological disorders than going without treatment. Research has found that each of the currently used therapies are of some use to clients, although research also indicates that particular therapies are often best suited to certain disorders.
- Successful therapists often share similar effective elements in their approaches, regardless of their particular orientations. They provide feedback, help clients focus on their own thoughts and behaviour, pay careful attention to the way they interact with clients and try to build a sense of control in their clients.
- Women and members of ethnic minority groups face pressures that sometimes contribute to psychological dysfunctioning. Culture-sensitive and gender-sensitive therapy approaches help clients become aware of and react adaptively to the gender-related and cultural pressures and issues they face.
- The empirically supported, or evidence-based, treatment movement seeks to identify which therapies have received clear research support for particular disorders, to propose corresponding treatment guidelines and to spread such information to clinicians.

ACTIVITY Activities to test yourself further are available in your interactive e-book at **www.wileyopenpage.com**

TYING IT TOGETHER

WHAT HAPPENS IN THE BRAIN?

- ECT remains one of the clinical field's most effective treatments for severe depression.
- Psychosurgical methods could be traced back to the misguided prehistoric practice of chipping a hole in a person's skull to let 'evil spirits' out.
- Research suggests that successful psychotherapy may produce changes in brain activity.
- In a small number of cases, anxiety disorders and depression treated with combinations of drug therapy and psychotherapy may not necessarily help more than either approach alone.

HOW WE DIFFER

- Women in therapy for psychological problems used to outnumber men by two to one. Now the number of women and men in therapy is about equal.
- On average, members of racial and ethnic minority groups across the world show less improvement in clinical treatment, make less use of mental health services and stop therapy sooner than members of majority groups.
- A greater proportion of those institutionalized for mental illness tend to be from lower socioeconomic groups.
- Therapy groups and self-help groups often specialize in particular populations, such as bereaved people or compulsive gamblers.

HOW WE DEVELOP

- Psychoanalysts believed that patients' current psychological disorders are always linked to traumatic childhood experiences.
- Humanistic and existential therapists assume clients deceive themselves and so try to help clients examine themselves and their situations more accurately and acceptingly.

- Existential therapists encourage clients to accept responsibility for their lives and their problems.
- Gestalt therapists often prohibit clients from focusing on past experiences.

Quizzes to test yourself further are available in your interactive e-book at
www.wileyopenpage.com

Key Terms

antianxiety drugs 583
antibipolar drugs 583
antidepressant drugs 583
antipsychotic drugs 583
aversion therapy 588
biological therapy 580
catharsis 595
client-centred
   therapy 593
cognitive therapy 591
community mental health
   treatment 597

couple therapy, or marital
   therapy 597
culture-sensitive
   therapies 599
deep brain stimulation 585
electroconvulsive
   therapy (ECT) 584
empirically supported, or
   evidence-based,
   treatment movement 599
family therapy 596
free association 594

gender-sensitive, or feminist,
   therapies 599
group therapy 596
individual therapy 596
lobotomy 585
psychosurgery 585
psychotherapy 580
psychotropic drugs 583
rational-emotive behavioural
   therapy 590
relational psychoanalysis 595
resistance 595

self-help groups 596
social skills training 589
therapy outcome studies 598
token economy 589
transcranial
   magnetic stimulation
   (TMS) 584
transference 595
treatment, or therapy 580
trephining 585
vagus nerve
   stimulation 584

Flashcards to test yourself further are available in your interactive e-book at
www.wileyopenpage.com

Glossary

ABC model of attitudes a model proposing that attitudes have three components: the affective component, the behavioural component and the cognitive component.

abnormal psychology the scientific study of psychological disorders.

absolute refractory period a short time after an action potential during which a neuron is completely unable to fire again.

absolute threshold the minimum stimulation necessary for detection by a person.

accommodation one of two ways of acquiring knowledge, defined by Piaget as the alteration of existing mental frameworks to take in new information.

action potential a sudden positive change in the electrical charge of a neuron's axon. Also known as a spike, or firing, action potentials rapidly transmit an excitatory charge down the axon.

activation-synthesis model the theory that dreams result from the brain's attempts to synthesize or organize random internally generated signals and give them meaning.

actor–observer effect the discrepancy between how we explain other people's behaviour (dispositionally) and how we explain our own behaviour (situationally).

acute stress disorder an anxiety disorder in which fear and related symptoms are experienced soon after a traumatic event and last less than a month.

acute stressor a stressful situation or circumstance that happens in the short term and has a definite endpoint.

adaptation a characteristic that improves the survival and reproductive prospects of an organism in its current environment.

adaptive theory of sleep the theory that organisms sleep for the purposes of self-preservation, to keep away from predators that are more active at night.

addiction psychological or physical compulsion to take a drug, resulting from regular ingestion and leading to maladaptive patterns of behaviour and changes in physical response.

ageusia the inability to taste.

agoraphobia a phobia that makes people avoid public places or situations in which escape might be difficult or help unavailable should panic symptoms develop.

agrammatism a neurological condition arising from damage to a brain region just anterior to Broca's area where the patient is incapable of using words in grammatical sequence.

algorithm a problem-solving strategy that always leads to a solution.

allele different variations of the same gene.

alleles variations of a gene.

altruism self-sacrificing behaviour carried out for the benefit of others.

Alzheimer's disease the most common form of dementia.

amnestic disorders organic disorders in which memory loss is the primary symptom.

amygdala the area of the brain involved in processing information about emotions, particularly fear.

amyotrophic lateral sclerosis (ALS or Lou Gehrig's disease) a neurological disease that causes degeneration of motor neurons in the spinal cord, leading to loss of movement and eventual death.

analogue observation the observation of individuals in an artificial setting, such as a clinical office or a laboratory.

anisogamy sex differences in the size of sex cells (gametes).

anorexia nervosa eating disorder in which individuals under-eat and have a distorted body image of being overweight.

anosmia the inability to smell.

anterograde amnesia the ongoing inability to form new memories after an amnesia-inducing event.

antianxiety drugs psychotropic drugs that reduce tension and anxiety.

antibipolar drugs psychotropic drugs that help stabilize the moods of people suffering from bipolar disorder.

antidepressant drugs psychotropic drugs that lift the mood of depressed people.

antipsychotic drugs psychotropic drugs that help correct grossly confused or distorted thinking.

antisocial personality disorder a personality disorder characterized by extreme and callous disregard for the feelings and rights of others.

apoptosis cell death that is preprogrammed.

approach–approach conflict a conflict that occurs when a person must choose between two equally desirable options.

approach–avoidance conflict a conflict that occurs when any available choice has both desirable and undesirable qualities.

assimilation one of two ways of acquiring knowledge, defined by Piaget as the inclusion of new information or experiences into existing schemata.

association cortex those areas of the neocortex responsible for complex functions, including higher-order sensory processing, thinking and planning.

associative learning a type of learning that involves forming associations between stimuli.

attachment a close emotional bond to another person, such as a baby to a caregiver.

attention deficit disorder (ADD) a disorder characterized by an inability to concentrate.

attention deficit hyperactivity disorder (ADHD) a disorder characterized by an inability to concentrate, accompanied by problematically high activity levels.

attitudes relatively stable and enduring evaluations of things and people.

attributions causal explanations of behaviour.

atypical development when children do not develop in line with typically developing peers.

autokinetic effect the illusion of a stationary point of light moving against a dark background.

automatic processing encoding information with little conscious awareness or effort.

automatic thoughts specific upsetting thoughts that arise unbidden.

autonomic nervous system the portion of the peripheral nervous system that includes the sympathetic and parasympathetic nervous systems.

availability heuristic judging easily recalled events as more common.

aversion therapy a therapy designed to help clients to acquire anxiety responses to stimuli that they have been finding too attractive.

avoidance–avoidance conflict a conflict that occurs when a person must choose between two equally undesirable options.

axons the part of the neuron that conducts information away from the cell body towards other neurons.

axon terminal the end of a neuron's axon that provides the output through which neurotransmitters are released.

B

babbling babies' production of meaningless sounds.

basic emotions a group of emotions pre-programmed into all humans regardless of culture.

basilar membrane structure in the cochlea where the hair cells are located.

behavioural genetics a subfield of psychology looking at the influence of genes on human behaviour.

behaviour modification a planned effort to change behaviour.

behavioural neuroscience the study of how the brain and nervous system control our behaviour.

behaviourism the systematic study and manipulation of observable behaviour.

biases distorted beliefs based on a person's subjective sense of reality.

bioecological model of intelligence Ceci's theory that intelligence is a function of the interactions among innate potential abilities, environmental context and internal motivation.

biological therapy the use of physical and chemical procedures to help people overcome psychological difficulties.

bipolar disorder a mood disorder in which periods of mania alternate with periods of depression.

body mass index (BMI) weight-to-height ratio.

body weight set point a weight that individuals typically return to even after dieting or overeating.

borderline personality disorder a personality disorder characterized by severe instability in emotions and self-concept and high levels of volatility.

bottom-up processing the perception that proceeds by transducing environmental stimuli into neural impulses that move on to successively more complex brain regions.

brainstem or medulla the area of the brain closest to the spinal cord that serves basic functions.

Broca's aphasia a neurological condition arising from damage to Broca's area where the patient is unable to produce coherent speech.

Broca's area the region of the brain located in the frontal lobe that is important for speech production.

bulimia nervosa eating disorder in which individuals binge and then engage in purging behaviour.

by-product a characteristic that emerged alongside an adaptation but is not adaptive itself.

C

Cannon–Bard theory of emotion a theory proposing that the subjective experience of emotion and the activation of the sympathetic nervous system (i.e. bodily arousal) occur simultaneously.

case study a study focusing on a single person.

catatonia extreme psychomotor symptoms of schizophrenia, including catatonic stupor, catatonic rigidity and catatonic posturing.

catharsis re-experiencing of past, repressed feelings as means of settling internal conflicts and overcoming problems.

cellular clock theory the theory suggesting that we age because our cells have built-in limits on their ability to reproduce.

cephalocaudal pattern a pattern in which growth and development proceed from top to bottom.

cerebellum the area of the brain, near the back of the head, that is important for motor coordination.

cheater an individual who receives a benefit without incurring a cost.

child-directed speech a speech characterized by exaggerated emotional responses and a slow pace that is common among caregivers communicating with babies and young children.

chromosomes strands of DNA; each human being has 46 chromosomes, distributed in pairs.

chronic stressor a stressful situation or circumstance that happens in the long term and does not have a definite endpoint.

chunking grouping bits of information together to enhance one's ability to hold that information in working memory.

circadian rhythm the pattern of sleep/wake cycles that in human beings roughly corresponds to periods of daylight and night.

client-centred therapy an approach to therapy founded by Carl Rogers, based on the notion that the client is an equal and positive gains are made by mirroring clients' thoughts and feelings in an atmosphere of unconditional positive regard.

clinical interview an assessment technique involving a face-to-face encounter between the clinician and the person being assessed.

clinical tests one means of gathering information about a person's psychological functioning.

cochlea fluid-filled structure in the inner ear containing the hair cells.

codominance in a heterozygous combination of alleles: both traits are expressed in the offspring.

cognition mental processes of thinking and knowing.

cognitive control the ability to direct thought in accordance with one's intentions.

cognitive development changes in thinking that occur over the course of time.

cognitive dissonance a state of emotional discomfort people experience when they hold two contradictory beliefs or hold a belief that contradicts their behaviour.

cognitive-mediational theory of emotion a theory proposing that cognitive interpretations, particularly appraisals, of events are the keys to experiences of emotion.

cognitive neuroscience the study of mental processes and how they relate to the biological functions of the brain.

cognitive triad a pattern of thinking in which individuals repeatedly interpret their experiences, themselves, and their futures in negative ways that lead them to feel depressed.

cognitive psychology a field of psychology that studies mental processes.

cognitive therapy Beck's cognitive therapy technique designed to help clients recognize and change their dysfunctional thoughts and ways of thinking.

cohort-sequential design a blended cross-sectional and longitudinal research design that follows at least two different age groups over time.

collectivist a culture that focuses more on the needs of the group and less on individual desires.

community mental health treatment programmes that focus on community care, including an emphasis on prevention.

comorbidity the condition in which a person's symptoms qualify him or her for two or more diagnoses.

compulsions repetitive and rigid behaviours or mental acts that people feel compelled to perform in order to prevent or reduce anxiety.

concrete operations Piagetian stage during which children are able to talk about complex relationships, such as categorization and cause and effect, but are still limited to understanding ideas in terms of real-world relationships.

conditioned response (CR) a physical response elicited by a conditioned stimulus; it is usually the same as the unconditioned response.

conditioned stimulus (CS) a neutral stimulus that eventually elicits the same response as an unconditioned stimulus with which it has been paired.

conditioned taste aversion a form of classical conditioning whereby a previously neutral stimulus (often an odour or taste) elicits an aversive reaction after it is paired with illness (nausea).

conditions of worth a person's perception that he or she must meet certain standards in order to gain the love of their parents or other important figures.

conduct disorder a clinical disorder in children and adolescents associated with emotional and behavioural problems, such as rule-breaking, trouble with limit-setting from authority figures, bullying, fighting and cruelty.

cones photoreceptors necessary for colour vision and perception of fine detail.

confirmation bias a tendency to look for information that meets our expectations when problem solving.

conflict discomfort brought about by two or more goals or impulses perceived to be incompatible.

conformity the tendency to yield to social pressure.

conservation the understanding that certain properties of an object (such as volume and number) remain the same despite changes in the object's outward appearance.

content validity the degree to which the content of a test accurately represents what the test is intended to measure.

continuous reinforcement when behaviour is reinforced every time it occurs.

control group a group that has not been or will not be exposed to the independent variable.

convergence the inward movement of the eyes to view objects close to oneself.

coping efforts to manage, reduce or tolerate stress.

corpus callosum the region of the brain that allows communication from one side of the neocortex to the other.

correlation a predictable relationship between two or more variables.

correlation coefficient a statistic expressing the strength and nature of a relationship between two variables.

couple therapy, or marital therapy a therapy format in which a therapist works with two people who are in a long-term relationship.

creativity the ability to produce ideas that are both original and valuable.

critical period a time during development after which we cannot develop certain capabilities.

cross-sectional design research comparisons of groups of different-aged people.

cuckoldry when males raise another male's offspring in the mistaken belief they are their own.

cultural psychology the study of how individual behaviour can be shaped or affected by societal processes.

cultural universality those behaviours and practices that occur across all cultures.

culture-sensitive therapies approaches that seek to address the unique issues faced by members of cultural minority groups.

D

daily hassles everyday annoyances that contribute to higher stress levels.

deafness the loss or lack of hearing.

debriefing supplying full information to participants at the end of their participation in a research study.

decay theory the theory of forgetting, suggesting memories fade over time owing to neglect or failure to access over time.

decision making evaluating and choosing from among options.

deductive reasoning the reasoning proceeding from broad basic principles applied to specific situations.

deep brain stimulation a procedure in which implanted electrodes deliver constant low stimulation to a small area of the brain; used to treat severe depression, Parkinson's disease and epilepsy.

defence mechanisms unconscious tactics employed by the ego to protect the individual from anxiety.

delusions blatantly false beliefs that are firmly held despite evidence to the contrary.

dementia severe memory problems combine with losses in at least one other cognitive function, such as abstract thinking or language.

dendrites the parts of neurons that receive input from other neurons.

denial a defence mechanism; the process of refusing to recognize an existing situation.

deoxyribonucleic acid (DNA) molecules in which genetic information is enclosed.

dependent variable the condition or event that you expect to change as a result of variations in the independent variable.

depressants a class of drugs that slow the activity of the central nervous system.

depression a persistent sad state in which life seems dark and its challenges overwhelming.

descriptive research methods studies that allow researchers to demonstrate a relationship between the variables of interest, without specifying a causal relationship.

developmental psychology the study of changes in behaviour and mental processes over time and the factors that influence the course of those changes.

developmental psychopathology the study of how problem behaviours evolve as a function of a person's genes and early experiences and how these early issues affect the person at later life stages.

developmental trajectory an approach that measures how a group or population follow a common developmental course (i.e., between chronological age and another variable).

diagnosis a clinician's determination that a person's cluster of symptoms represents a particular disorder.

Diagnostic and Statistical Manual of Mental Disorders (DSM) the US-based classification system for psychological disorders featured in most literature; DSM-IV-TR is the current version.

difference threshold or just noticeable difference the smallest difference between two stimuli necessary for detecting a difference between the two.

differential emotions theory a theory proposing that particular emotions or sets of emotions become prominent during specific life stages as they serve stage-related developmental processes.

discourse language as actually used, not language in a dictionary sense.

discourse analysis a qualitative research approach that focuses on the use of language to construct and shape the world around us.

discrete traits traits that result as the product of a single gene pairing.

discursive psychology the study of language as used in everyday life and its effects for psychology.

display rules cultural expectations that prescribe how, when and by whom emotions should be expressed.

dissociation a splitting of consciousness into two dimensions.

dissociative amnesia psychological disorder characterized by an inability to recall important information, usually of an upsetting nature, about one's life.

dissociative fugue psychological disorder characterized by loss of memory of personal identities and details of one's past life and flight to an entirely different location.

dissociative disorder a psychological disorder characterized by a major loss of memory without a clear physical cause; types include dissociative amnesia, dissociative fugue and dissociative identity disorder.

dissociative identity disorder psychological disorder characterized by the development of two or more distinct personalities.

distress stress caused by unpleasant situations or circumstances.

domain-specific the ability of a particular mental module is only present in relevant tasks.

dominant trait a trait that is expressed in a phenotype, no matter whether the genotype is homozygous or heterozygous for the trait.

dopamine neurotransmitter with various brain functions, including movement and reward learning.

double-blind procedure a study in which neither the participant nor the researcher knows what treatment or procedure the participant is receiving.

Down syndrome an inherited disorder, usually caused by the presence of extra chromosomal material on the 21st chromosome, that results in intellectual disability.

dualism a position in the philosophy of mind that states that the world consists of two distinct kinds of thing.

dyscalculia an inability to readily process mathematical computations.

dyslexia involves difficulties in learning to read not caused by deficits in general intelligence.

E

effortful processing encoding information through careful attention and conscious effort.

ego according to psychoanalytic theory, a personality element that works to help satisfy the drives of the id while complying with the constraints placed on behaviour by the environment.

egocentrism flaws in a child's reasoning based on his or her inability to take other perspectives.

electroconvulsive therapy (ECT) the use of electric shock to trigger a brain seizure in hopes of relieving abnormal functioning.

eliminativism a viewpoint within materialism which does not accept that qualia are 'things' that have an independent existence. Eliminativists attempt to get rid of such notions (eliminate them) by explaining them in purely physical terms.

emotion an interpersonal state that occurs in response to either external or internal events and typically involves a physiological, cognitive and behavioural component.

emotion dysregulation unhealthy attempts to regulate emotion.

emotion-focused coping those coping strategies focused on changing one's feelings about the stressor.

emotional intensity the characteristic strength with which an individual typically experiences emotion.

emotional intelligence an individual's ability to perceive, express, assimilate and regulate emotion.

empirical able to be tested in objective ways.

empirically supported, or evidence-based, treatment movement a movement to help clinicians become more familiar with and apply research findings concerning the effectiveness of particular treatments.

empiricism the view that our knowledge of the world should come from testing out what our senses perceive.

encoding a basic activity of memory, involving the recording of information in our brain.

endocrine, or hormonal, system the system that controls levels of hormones throughout the body.

endorphins neurotransmitters that help relieve pain and reduce emotional tension.

enkephalins naturally occurring painkilling chemicals in the brain.

epiphenomenalism an explanation for consciousness based on the idea that it emerges from physical processes but is not reducible to them.

episodic memory a person's memory of personal events or episodes from his or her life.

equifinality the idea that different individuals can start out from different places and end up with the same outcome.

equilibrium balance in a mental framework.

ethics committee a research oversight group that evaluates research to protect the rights of participants in the study.

ethology the scientific study of the evolutionary origins of behaviour.

eugenics the controversial approach that attempts to use scientific principles to guide human breeding.

eustress the optimal level of stress needed to promote physical and psychological health.

evolutionarily stable strategy a strategy that cannot be out-competed by others.

evolutionary psychology the field of study that applies evolutionary ideas, including the importance of adaption over millions of years, to the explanation of human behaviour.

evolution the process by which species modify and change over time.

experiment a controlled observation in which researchers manipulate the presence or amount of the independent variable to see what effect it has on the dependent variable.

experimental group a group that is exposed to the independent variable.

explicit memory a memory that a person can consciously bring to mind, such as one's date of birth.

extrinsic motivation engaging in a behaviour because of the influence of factors outside ourselves.

F

facial efference sensory feedback from facial muscular activity.

facial-feedback theory of emotion a theory proposing that subjective experiences of emotion are influenced by sensory feedback from facial muscular activity, or facial efference.

factor analysis a statistical method for determining whether certain items on a test correlate highly, thus forming a unified set, or cluster, of items.

family systems theory the theory that each family has its own implicit rules, relationship structure and communication patterns that shape the behaviour of the individual members.

family therapy a format in which therapists meet with all members of a family in order to help the whole family to change.

fitness variance the amount of variance in the number of offspring produced.

five-factor model an empirically derived model that proposes five major trait categories: agreeableness/disagreeableness, extraversion/introversion, neuroticism/stability, conscientiousness/irresponsibility and openness to experience/unimaginativeness.

fixation occurs when only one allele remains within a population, usually because of its adaptive benefits.

fixed interval schedule reinforcement occurs every time a specific time period has elapsed.

fixed ratio schedule reinforcement occurs after a specific number of responses.

flashbulb memory detailed and near-permanent memories of an emotionally significant event, or of the circumstances surrounding the moment we learnt about the event.

Flynn effect an observed rise in average IQ scores throughout the world over time.

forgetting the inability to recall information that was previously encoded into memory.

formal operations Piaget's final stage of cognitive development; the child achieves formal adult reasoning and the ability to think about things that do not have a concrete reality.

fovea centre of the retina, containing only cones, where vision is most clear.

free association psychodynamic therapy technique of allowing clients to freely talk about whatever they want.

free-radical theory the theory suggesting we age because special negatively charged oxygen molecules become more prevalent in our body as we get older, destabilizing cellular structures and causing the effects of ageing.

frontal cortex the lobe of the neocortex involved in many functions, including movement and speech production.

frustration an emotion people experience when thwarted in pursuit of a goal.

functional fixedness tendency to view objects as having only one function.

functionalists someone who believes that mental processes have purpose, and that the focus of study should be on how the mind adapts those purposes to changing environments.

fundamental attribution error the tendency to use dispositional attributions to explain the behaviour of other people.

G

gate control theory of pain suggests that certain patterns of neural activity can close a 'gate' to keep pain information from travelling to the parts of the brain crucial for pain perception.

gender-sensitive, or feminist, therapies approaches that seek to address the unique pressures of being female.

general adaptation syndrome (GAS) a three-stage response to stress identified by Hans Selye; the stages are alarm, resistance and exhaustion.

generalized anxiety disorder an anxiety disorder in which people feel excessive anxiety and worry under most circumstances.

genes basic building blocks of biological inheritance.

genome the entire genetic code that makes up an organism.

genotype a person's genetic inheritance.

Gestalt psychology field of psychology arguing that we have inborn tendencies to structure what we see in particular ways and to structure our perceptions into broad perceptual units.

g factor a theoretical general factor of intelligence underlying all distinct clusters of mental ability; part of Spearman's two-factor theory of intelligence.

glia the cells that, in addition to neurons, constitute the nervous system.

grounded theory an approach to qualitative research which emphasizes the need to collect data from interviews or texts and analyse those for themes which emerge from the text.

group a collection of people in which the members are aware of and influence one another and share a common identity.

group norms rules established within groups as to how members should act.

group polarization the intensification of an initial tendency of individual group members brought about by group discussion.

group therapy a psychotherapy format in which a therapist sees several clients at the same time.

groupthink a form of faulty group decision making that occurs when group members strive for unanimity and this goal overrides their motivation to realistically appraise alternative courses of action.

gustatory sense our sense of taste.

H

habituation a form of non-associative learning whereby repeated presentation of a stimulus leads to a reduction in response.

hair cells sensory receptors that convert sound waves into neural impulses.

hallucinations imagined sights, sounds or other sensory events experienced as if they were real.

hallucinogens substances that dramatically change one's state of awareness, causing powerful changes in sensory perception.

handicap principle the theory that males develop handicaps to demonstrate their genetic quality to females.

hemispheres halves of the brain.

heritability an estimate of the contribution that genetics can have on a particular trait.

heritability coefficient a correlation coefficient used to indicate the contribution of heredity to some characteristic, such as intelligence.

heritability the overall extent to which differences among people are attributable to genes.

heritable characteristics that can be transmitted to offspring.

heterosexual sexual attraction to members of the opposite sex.

heterozygous parents contribute two different alleles to offspring.

heuristics shortcut thinking strategy.

hippocampus the region of the brain that is important for certain types of learning and memory.

homeostasis a tendency of the body to maintain itself in a state of balance, or equilibrium.

hominids organisms that belong to the Hominidae family.

homosexual sexual attraction to members of one's own sex.

homozygous both parents contribute the same genetic material for a particular trait.

humanistic psychology a theory of psychology that sought to give greater prominence to special and unique features of human functioning.

Huntington's disease an inherited neurological condition that results in the death of neurons in the striatum.

hypnagogic state a pre-sleep period often characterized by vivid sensory phenomena.

hypnosis a seemingly altered state of consciousness during which individuals can be directed to act or experience the world in unusual ways.

hypothalamus the brain structure important for motivation and control of the endocrine system.

hypothesis a general statement about the way variables relate that is objectively falsifiable.

hypothetico-deductive approach a process of modern science where scientists begin with an educated guess about how the world works and then set about designing small controlled observations to support or invalidate that hypothesis.

I

id according to psychoanalytic theory, the personality element representing basic instinctual drives (eating, sleeping, sex and comfort).

identity theory a position in the philosophy of mind that holds that brain states are identical to mental states.

immune system the body's system of organs, tissues and cells that identify and destroy foreign invaders, such as bacteria and viruses, as well as cancer cells.

implicit attitude an attitude of which the person is unaware.

implicit memory a memory that a person is not consciously aware of, such as learnt reactions, motor behaviours and skills.

incentives external motives that indirectly indicate reward.

inclusive fitness the reproductive success of a particular gene in different organisms.

independent variable the condition or event that is thought to be a factor in changing another condition or event.

individualistic a culture that places the wants or desires of the person over the needs of the group.

individual therapy a psychotherapy format in which the therapist sees the client alone; the oldest of the modern formats.

inductive reasoning the reasoning process proceeding from small specific situations to more general truths.

information processing the means by which information is stored and operated internally.

informational influence the influence based on information about the reality of a situation that provides a basis for making a judgement.

information-processing model a view of memory suggesting that information moves among three memory stores during encoding, storage and retrieval.

information-processing theory developmental theory focusing on how children take in and use information from their environment.

informed consent the requirement that researchers give as much information as possible about the purpose, procedures, risks and benefits of the study so that a participant can make an informed decision about whether to participate.

innate characteristics that have biological or genetic origins.

inoculation exposing oneself to a relatively low level of stress in a controlled situation in order to improve later performance in a more stressful situation.

insight learning a sudden realization of a solution to a problem or a leap in understanding new concepts.

insomnia a sleep disorder characterized by a regular inability to fall asleep or stay asleep.

instincts innate behavioural tendencies, activated by stimuli in our environments.

intellectual disability a term describing individuals who have poor adaptive behaviour and display general intellectual functioning that is well below average.

intelligence the ability to learn, to meet the demands of the environment effectively and to understand and control one's mental activities.

intelligence quotient (IQ) Terman's measure of intelligence; the ratio of a child's mental age to his or her chronological age, multiplied by 100.

interactionism the view that emphasizes the relationship between a person's underlying personality traits and the reinforcing aspects of the situations in which they choose to put themselves.

interference theory the theory that forgetting is influenced by what happens to people before or after they take information in.

intergroup relations the relations between different social groups and their respective members.

intermittent or partial reinforcement a schedule of reinforcement where the behaviour is only followed by reinforcement some of the time.

International Classification of Diseases (ICD) the European-based system used by most countries to classify psychological disorders; published by the World Health Organization and currently in its tenth edition (ICD-10).

interpretative phenomenological analysis (IPA) an approach to qualitative research that emphasizes interpretation and aims to understand the lived experience of the participants.

intersexual selection competition via sexual display to attract members of the opposite sex.

intragroup processes psychological processes that occur within groups.

intrinsic motivation engaging in a behaviour simply for the satisfaction that is part of doing it.

introspect to study one's own mental states and feelings, hence introspection.

ion channels pores in the cell membrane that open and close to allow certain ions into and out of the cell.

J

James–Lange theory of emotion a theory proposing that felt emotions result from physiological changes, rather than being their cause.

just-so story an account of why a characteristic is adaptive that seems plausible (or in some cases entertaining or interesting) but is actually incorrect.

K

kin selection altruistic behaviour towards close relatives which increases an individual's inclusive fitness.

L

language a set of symbols used to communicate.

language comprehension the process of understanding spoken, written or signed language.

language production the process of using movement to produce speech. Language production can also encompass signing by using hand signals.

lateral geniculate nucleus (LGN) the part of the thalamus which processes visual information.

lateral hypothalamus (LH) a region of the hypothalamus important in signalling thirst and hunger.

law of effect behaviours leading to rewards are more likely to occur again, while behaviours producing unpleasantness are less likely to occur again.

learned helplessness a situation in which repeated exposure to inescapable punishment eventually produces a failure to make escape attempts.

learning a lasting change caused by experience.

learning curve a graph that shows change in performance on a learning task over time.

learning difficulty a specific deficiency in one aspect of cognitive function while other aspects function normally.

leptin a protein produced by fat cells that is important for regulating the amount of food eaten over long periods.

lexical meaning dictionary meaning of a word.

life changes shifts in life circumstances that require adjustment of some kind.

linguistic relativity hypothesis the idea that the vocabulary available for objects or concepts in a language influences how speakers of that language think about them.

lobotomy surgical practice of cutting the connections between the frontal lobe and the lower centres of the brain.

long-term memory the system that holds previously gathered information ready for retrieval and use in a new situation.

long-term potentiation (LTP) a form of synaptic change that involves increased activity in the postsynaptic cells after strong, repetitive stimulation.

longitudinal design research following the same people over a given period by administering the same tasks or questionnaires and seeing how their responses change.

loose associations, or derailment a common thought disorder of schizophrenia, characterized by rapid shifts from one topic to another.

lucid dreams dreams in which the sleeper fully recognizes that he or she is dreaming, and occasionally actively guides the outcome of the dream.

lymphocytes white blood cells that circulate through the body and destroy foreign invaders and cancer cells; important components of the immune system.

M

major depressive disorder a disorder characterized by a depressed mood that is significantly disabling and is not caused by such factors as drugs or a general medical condition.

maladaptive an adapted characteristic that no longer improves survival and reproductive prospects, owing to changes in the environment.

mania a persistent state of euphoria or frenzied energy.

materialism a philosophical position in which it is held that everything can be explained in physical/material terms.

maturation the unfolding of development in a particular sequence and timeframe.

mean the average score in a distribution.

median the score exactly in the middle of a distribution.

meme a unit of cultural selection analogous to a gene.

memory the faculty for reproducing past events and past learning.

memory span maximum number of items that can be recalled in their correct order.

menopause series of changes in hormonal function occurring in women during their 50s, which lead to the end of the menstrual cycle and reproductive capabilities.

mental age the intellectual age at which a person is functioning, as opposed to chronological age.

mental imagery thoughts that involve conjuring up internal representations of stored sensory input.

mental set the tendency to use problem-solving strategies that have worked in the past.

mental processes activities of our brain when it is engaged in thinking, observing the environment and using language.

metacognition thinking about one's thoughts.

minimal group paradigm allocation of individuals to groups that have little meaning and whose members do not meet each other.

mirror neurons the neurons located in the frontal and parietal cortices that respond similarly when an individual engages in an activity or watches someone else engage in it.

mnemonic devices techniques used to enhance the meaningfulness of information to make them more memorable.

modelling mimicking the behaviour of others.

mode the score that occurs most frequently in a distribution.

modularity a view that different processes in the brain function independently and specifically.

monism the idea that there is one type of fundamental substance from which everything else is made. This can be either *physical* substance (i.e. *materialism*) or mental substance (i.e. *idealism*).

monocular (pictorial) cues visual clues about depth and distance that can be perceived using information from only one eye.

morpheme the smallest unit of meaning in language.

motivation an internal state or condition that directs behaviour.

motives one's needs or desires.

motor skills ability to control bodily movements.

multifinality the idea that children can start from the same spot and end up in any number of other outcomes.

multiple realizability the idea that identical mental states can be realized by different brain processes (or different brain regions).

multiple sclerosis neurological disease that causes a loss of myelin on the axons of neurons.

mutations   alterations to the sequence of DNA within an organism's genome.

myelin   a fatty, white substance, formed from glial cells, that insulates the axons of many neurons.

myelination   development of fatty deposits on neurons that allow electric impulses to pass through neurons more efficiently.

N

naturalistic fallacy   the false belief that if something occurs naturally it ought to occur.

naturalistic observation   a study in which researchers directly observe people behaving as they normally do.

negative correlation   a relationship in which scores on one variable increase as scores on another variable decrease.

negative punishment   the removal of a pleasant stimulus as a consequence of a behaviour.

negative reinforcement   the removal of a negative consequence as a result of behaviour.

negative symptoms   in the case of schizophrenia, symptoms that seem to reflect pathological deficits, including poverty of speech, flat affect, loss of volition and social withdrawal.

neocortex   the largest portion of the brain, responsible for complex behaviours, including language and thought.

nerve conduction velocity (NCV)   the speed with which electrical impulses are transmitted along nerve fibres and across synapses.

neural tube   area of an embryo from which the central nervous system arises.

neurofibrillary tangles   twisted protein fibres found within the cells of the hippocampus and certain other brain areas.

neurogenesis   the production of new neurons.

neuroimaging   involves the application of various brain imaging techniques that provide images of the structure and function of awake (or not) humans either directly or indirectly; some of these techniques are invasive (e.g. PET); others non-invasive (e.g. fMRI).

neuron   a nerve cell.

neuroscience   the study of psychological functions by looking at the biological foundations of those functions; previously known as psychobiology.

neurosis   an abnormal behaviour pattern caused by unresolved conflicts between the id, the ego and the superego.

neurotechnology   the technology on which our understanding of neurons is based.

neurotransmitter receptors   proteins in the membranes of neurons that bind to neurotransmitters.

neurotransmitters   specialized chemicals that travel across synapses to allow communication between neurons.

non-associative learning   a type of learning that does not involve forming associations between stimuli.

non-REM (NREM) sleep   Stages 1 through 4 of normal sleep pattern.

nonverbal communication   body language.

noradrenaline   the neurotransmitter important for arousal and attention.

normal distribution   a symmetrical, bell-shaped distribution in which most scores are in the middle with smaller groups of equal size at either end.

normative influence   the influence based upon a need for harmony or social approval.

norms   social rules about how members of a society are expected to act.

nucleus accumbens   an area of the brain that is important for motivation and reward.

O

obedience   the act of following direct commands, usually given by an authority figure.

obesity   overweight; characterized as a body mass index of over 30.

object permanence   an infant's realization that objects continue to exist even when they are outside the infant's immediate sensory awareness.

observational learning   a type of learning that occurs without overt training but in response to watching the behaviour.

obsessions   persistent thoughts, ideas, impulses or images that seem to invade a person's consciousness.

obsessive–compulsive disorder (OCD)   an anxiety disorder in which obsessions or compulsions feel excessive or unreasonable, cause great distress, take up much time or interfere with daily functions.

occipital cortex   the lobe of the neocortex at the back of the skull, important for processing visual information.

odorants   airborne chemicals that are detected as odours.

olfactory bulb   the first region where olfactory information reaches the brain on its way from the nose.

olfactory receptor neurons   sensory receptor cells that convert chemical signals from odorants into neural impulses that travel to the brain.

olfactory sense   our sense of smell.

operant conditioning   a form of associative learning whereby behaviour is modified depending on its consequences.

operant or instrumental conditioning   a form of associative learning whereby behaviour is modified depending on its consequences.

operationalize   to develop a working definition of a variable that allows you to test it.

operations   Piagetian description of a child's ability to hold an idea in his or her mind and mentally manipulate it.

opioids   a class of drugs derived from the sap of the opium poppy.

opponent process theory   a theory holding that colour perception depends on the actions of three systems of colour opposites: blue/yellow, red/green and black/white.

optic nerve   the bundle of axons of ganglion cells that carries visual information from the eye to the brain.

oval window   a membrane separating the ossicles and the inner ear, deflection of which causes vibrations in the cochlear fluid.

overregularization   the process by which preschool children apply general grammatical rules to words that are exceptions.

oxytocin   hormone produced in pituitary gland that plays a role in different social interactions.

P

panic attacks   periodic, short bouts of panic.

panic disorder   an anxiety disorder characterized by recurrent and unpredictable panic attacks that occur without apparent provocation.

panpsychism   the view that consciousness is pervasive and exists in everything.

papillae   bumps on the tongue that contain clumps of taste buds.

parallel distributed-processing (PDP) (or connectionist) model   a theory of memory suggesting information is represented in the brain as a pattern of activation across entire neural networks.

parasympathetic nervous system   the division of the autonomic nervous system active during restful times.

parietal cortex   the lobe of the neocortex involved in processing information related to touch and complex visual information, particularly locations.

Parkinson's disease   a neurological disease that involves the death of dopaminergic neurons in the substantia nigra, leading to tremors, muscle rigidity and other motor problems.

Pavlovian or classical conditioning   a form of associative learning whereby a neutral stimulus is paired with a salient stimulus so that eventually the neutral stimulus predicts the salient stimulus.

perception   recognition and identification of a sensory stimulus.

perceptual constancy   the perception that objects are unchanging, despite shifts in the environmental stimuli we receive.

perceptual sets   readiness to interpret a certain stimulus in a certain way.

perfect (absolute) pitch   the ability to recognize or produce any note on a musical scale.

perfect correlation one in which two variables are exactly related, such that low, medium and high scores on both variables are always exactly related.

personality the unique characteristics that account for enduring patterns of inner experience and outward behaviour.

personality disorder an inflexible pattern of inner experience and outward behaviour that causes distress or difficulty with daily functioning.

personality inventory a questionnaire designed to assess various aspects of personality.

personality traits tendencies to behave in certain ways that remain relatively constant across situations.

phenotype the observable manifestation of a person's genetic inheritance.

phobia a persistent and unreasonable fear of a particular object, activity or situation.

phoneme the smallest unit of language, an individual sound.

phonology the study of how individual sounds or phonemes are used to produce language.

photoreceptors the sensory receptor cells for vision, located in the retina.

phrenology a method of assessing a person's mental and moral qualities by studying the shape of their skull.

pituitary gland the brain structure that plays a central role in controlling the endocrine system.

plasticity change in the nervous system.

Pleistocene period between two million and 10,000 years ago.

polygenic traits traits that manifest as the result of the contributions of multiple genes.

pons the area of the brain anterior to the brainstem that includes the locus coeruleus.

positive correlation a relationship in which scores on two variables increase together.

positive psychology a movement in psychology that focuses on the positive features of human functioning and examines how they might be developed more readily.

positive punishment the presentation of an unpleasant consequence following a behaviour.

positive reinforcement the presentation of a pleasant consequence following a behaviour.

positive symptoms in the case of schizophrenia, symptoms that seem to represent pathological excesses in behaviour, including delusions, disorganized thinking and speech, hallucinations and inappropriate affect.

post-traumatic stress disorder (PTSD) an anxiety disorder in which fear and related symptoms continue to be experienced long after a traumatic event.

postsynaptic potentials electrical events in postsynaptic neurons that occur when a neurotransmitter binds to one of its receptors.

pragmatics the practical aspects of language usage, including speech pace, gesturing and body language.

pragmatism an American philosophical movement that argued that our theories are evaluated by examining their practical consequences.

preconsciousness the level of awareness at which information can become readily available to consciousness if necessary.

prefrontal cortex the portion of the frontal cortex involved in higher-order thinking, such as memory, moral reasoning and planning.

prejudice negative stereotypical attitudes towards individuals from another group.

prenatal period the approximately nine months of development stretching from conception to birth.

preoperational stage according to Piaget, a developmental stage during which the child begins to develop ideas of objects in the external world and the ability to work with them in his or her mind.

pressure an expectation or demand that someone act in a certain way.

prestige bias a preference for imitating individuals judged to be prestigious.

primary appraisal an appraisal of a stressor to determine how severe it is; the first stage in Richard Lazarus's description of how people experience stress.

primary mental abilities seven distinct mental abilities identified by Thurstone as the basic components of intelligence.

primary reinforcer a reinforcer that is intrinsically pleasurable.

primary sex characteristics changes in body structure that occur during puberty that have to do specifically with the reproductive system, including the growth of the testes and the ovaries.

priming activation of one piece of information, which in turn leads to the activation of another piece and ultimately to the retrieval of a specific memory (Tulving *et al.*, 1982).

private speech a child's self-talk, which Vygotsky believed the child uses to regulate behaviour and internal experiences.

proactive interference competing information that is learnt before the forgotten material, preventing its subsequent recall.

problem-focused coping those coping strategies focused on dealing directly with the stressor, such as by changing the stressor in some way.

problem solving determining how to reach a goal.

projective tests personality assessment devices intended to tap a person's unconscious by presenting the person with an ambiguous stimulus and asking the person to interpret what the stimulus means.

property dualism the idea that there is probably only one type of substance, but this can have both physical and non-physical properties.

proximodistal pattern a pattern in which growth and development proceed from the centre to the extremities.

psychoactive drugs chemicals that affect awareness, behaviour, sensation, perception or mood.

psychoanalysis the theory, developed by Freud, suggesting our psychological functioning is the result of the dynamic interplay of forces of which we are largely unaware.

psychological literacy having the research skills and vocabulary allowing one to evaluate, communicate and apply psychological principles.

psychology the systematic study of selves and others.

psychometric approach an approach to defining intelligence that attempts to measure intelligence with carefully constructed psychological tests.

psychometrics an approach to the mind that uses tests to measure differences between people.

psychoneuroimmunology an area of study focusing on links between stress, the immune system and health.

psychosexual stages according to psychoanalytic theory, stages in the development of personality – labelled oral, anal, phallic, latency and genital – are primarily influenced by sexuality and aggression.

psychosis loss of contact with reality.

psychosurgery brain surgery, often used in an attempt to relieve abnormal functioning.

psychotherapy a treatment system in which a client and therapist use words and acts to overcome the client's psychological difficulties.

psychotropic drugs medications that act primarily on the brain.

puberty development of full sexual maturity during adolescence.

punishment an experience that produces a decrease in a certain behaviour.

Q

qualia the raw material of conscious experience. Qualia is the name philosophers use to describe the experiences that make up our consciousness. What it is like to experience the redness of a red object, for example, is a quale (singular).

R

random selection identifying a sample in such a way that everyone in the population of interest has an equal chance of being involved in the study.

rapid eye movement (REM) sleep stage of sleep associated with rapid and jagged brainwave patterns, increased heart rate, rapid and irregular breathing, rapid eye movements and dreaming.

rational-emotive behavioural therapy Ellis's therapy technique designed to help clients discover and change the irrational assumptions that govern their emotions, behaviours and thinking.

realistic group conflict theory the argument that intergroup conflict reflects actual or perceived competition between in-groups and out-groups.

recall tasks memory tasks in which people are asked to reproduce information using little or no retrieval cues.

recessive trait a trait that is only expressed if a person carries the same two genetic alleles (e.g. is homozygous for the trait).

reciprocal altruism an individual incurring a cost to help another provided the recipient will return the act in the future.

reciprocal socialization the transactional relationship between parent and child.

recognition tasks memory tasks in which people are asked to identify whether they have seen a particular item before.

reflexes programmed physical reactions to certain cues that do not require any conscious thought to perform.

rehearsal conscious repetition of information in an attempt to make sure the information is encoded.

reinforcer an experience that produces an increase in a certain behaviour.

relatedness the probability that any particular gene is shared between two individuals.

relational psychoanalysis a school of psychodynamic therapy holding that therapists should work to form more equal relationships with clients.

relative refractory period time just after the absolute refractory period during which a neuron can only fire if it receives a stimulus stronger than its usual threshold level.

reliability the degree to which a test produces the same scores over time.

replication the repeated testing of a hypothesis to ensure that the results achieved in one experiment were not due to chance.

representativeness heuristic classifying something based on how similar it seems to a typical case in a given category.

repression a process in which we unconsciously prevent some traumatic events from entering our awareness, so that we do not have to experience the anxiety or blows to our self-concept that the memories would bring.

reproductive success the number of fertile offspring an individual has.

resilience the ability to recover from or avoid the serious effects of negative circumstances.

resistance practice in which clients encounter a block in their free associations or change the subject so as to avoid a potentially painful discussion.

responses the ways we react to stimuli.

restorative theory of sleep theory that we sleep in order to allow the brain and body to restore certain depleted chemical resources and eliminate chemical wastes that have accumulated during the waking day.

reticular formation a brain structure important for sleep and wakefulness.

retina a specialized sheet of nerve cells in the back of the eye containing the sensory receptors for vision.

retinal disparity the slight difference in images processed by the retinas of the two eyes.

retrieval a basic activity of memory, involving recovery of information when we need it later.

retrieval cues words, sights or other stimuli that remind us of the information we need to retrieve from our memory.

retroactive interference learning of new information that disrupts access to previously recalled information.

retrograde amnesia the inability to remember things that occurred before an organic event.

reward-deficiency syndrome the theory that people may abuse drugs because their reward centre is not readily activated by usual life events.

reward learning pathway brain circuitry that is important for learning about rewarding stimuli.

rewards allocation matrix a set of different possibilities for allocating rewards from which an individual must choose one option.

risk factors biological and environmental factors that contribute to problematic outcomes.

rods photoreceptors most responsive at low light levels.

runaway selection the tendency for exaggerated sexual ornaments to evolve because of their attractiveness to the opposite sex.

S

sample the group of people studied in an experiment, used to stand in for an entire group of people.

scaffolding developmental adjustments that adults make to give children the help that they need, but not so much that they fail to move forward.

Schachter and Singer's two-factor theory of emotion a theory proposing that an emotional state is a function of both physiological arousal and cognition.

schemas knowledge developed from prior exposure to similar experiences or other knowledge bases.

schemata Piaget's proposed mental structures or frameworks for understanding or thinking about the world.

schizophrenia a mental disorder characterized by disorganized thoughts, lack of contact with reality and sometimes auditory hallucinations.

secondary appraisal an appraisal of one's personal resources and ability to cope with a stressor; the second stage in Richard Lazarus's description of how people experience stress.

secondary reinforcer a reinforcer that is associated with primary reinforcers.

secondary sex characteristics changes that occur during puberty and that differ according to gender, but are not directly related to sex.

selection certain variants of the characteristic will aid survival or reproduction better than others.

self-actualization the need of humans to fulfil their full and special potential; the highest level of need in Maslow's hierarchy of needs.

self-concept a pattern of self-perception that remains consistent over time and can be used to characterize an individual.

self-determination competence, relatedness and autonomy thought necessary for us to achieve our potential.

self-help groups a format in which people who have similar problems and come together to help and support one another without the direct leadership of a professional clinician.

self-monitoring when individuals monitor their own symptoms.

self-perception theory the theory suggesting that when people are uncertain of their attitudes, they infer what the attitudes are by observing their own behaviour.

self-serving bias the tendency people have to attribute their successes to internal causes and their failures to external ones.

semantic code cognitive representation of information or an event based on the meaning of the information.

semantic memory a person's memory of general knowledge of the world.

semantics the study of how meaning in language is constructed of individual words and sentences.

senile plaques sphere-shaped deposits of a protein known as beta-amyloid that form in the spaces between cells in the brain.

sensation the act of using our sensory systems to detect environmental stimuli.

sensitive period a time during development after which it becomes more difficult to develop certain capabilities.

sensitization a form of non-associative learning whereby repeated experience of a stimulus results in an increasingly bigger response to that stimulus.

sensory memory a memory involving a detailed sensory image or sound being retained for a brief period.

sensory adaptation the process whereby repeated stimulation of a sensory cell leads to a reduced response.

serotonin a neurotransmitter involved in activity levels and mood regulation.

sexual selection a form of natural selection for characteristics that improve an individual's reproductive success.

sexy sons hypothesis females will choose males who possess genes most likely to enhance their sons' reproductive success.

s factor a theoretical specific factor uniquely tied to a distinct mental ability or area of functioning; part of Spearman's two-factor theory of intelligence.

shaping introducing new behaviour by reinforcing small approximations of the desired behaviour.

sibling rivalry the competition between siblings for parental investment.

situationism the view that behaviour is governed primarily by the variables in a given situation rather than by internal traits.

sleep spindles bursts of brain activity lasting a second or two; occur during Stage 2 sleep.

social anxiety disorder an anxiety disorder in which people feel severe, persistent and irrational fears of social or performance situations in which embarrassment may occur.

social cognition the way in which people perceive and interpret themselves and others in their social world.

social contract individuals only receive a benefit when they incur a cost.

social facilitation an effect in which the presence of others enhances performance.

social identity theory the theory that our social identities arise from the social groups to which we belong.

social loafing a phenomenon in which people exert less effort on a collective task than they would on a comparable individual task; also known as free riding.

social neuroscience the study of social functioning and how it is tied to brain activity.

social psychology an area of psychology that seeks to understand, explain and predict how people's thoughts, feelings and behaviours are influenced by the actual, imagined or implied presence of others.

social representation a representation of an element of the social world that is shared among the members of a social group.

social role a set of norms ascribed to a person's social position; expectations and duties associated with their position in the family, at work, in the community and in other settings.

social role theory the theory that gender differences occur because girls and boys develop different behaviours and skills based largely on differences in gender role expectations.

social skills training behavioural therapy technique in which therapists serve as models and teachers to help clients acquire desired social behaviours.

socially desirable responding tailoring answers on personality inventories to try to create a good impression.

sociobiologists theorists who believe humans have a genetically innate concept of how social behaviour should be organized.

somatic nervous system all the peripheral nerves that send information about the senses and movement to and from the central nervous system.

somatoform disorder a pattern of physical complaints with largely psychosocial causes; types include conversion disorder, somatization disorder, pain disorder associated with psychological factors, hypochondriasis and body dysmorphic disorder.

somatosensory strip an area of the parietal cortex that processes tactile information coming from our body parts.

sound waves vibrations of the air in the frequency of hearing.

source misattribution remembering information, but not the source it came from; can lead to remembering as true information from unreliable sources.

spacing effect the facilitated encoding of material through rehearsal situations spread over time.

spatial navigation a type of learning that involves forming associations among stimuli relevant to navigating in space.

spontaneous recovery re-emergence of a conditioned response some time after extinction has occurred.

stages developmental periods that are characterized by a certain level of functioning that is qualitatively different from the functioning that characterizes other stages.

standard deviation the statistical index of how much scores vary within a group.

standardization the use of uniform procedures in administering and scoring a test.

state-dependent memory a memory retrieval facilitated by being in the same state of mind in which you encoded the memory in the first place.

stem cells undifferentiated cells that can divide to replace themselves and create new cells that have the potential to become all other cells of the body, including neurons.

stereotypes generalized impressions of a person or a group of people based on the social category they occupy.

stereotype threat an awareness of a negative stereotype that affects oneself and often leads to impairment in performance.

stimulants substances that increase the activity of the central nervous system.

stimuli an environmental trigger that changes our internal or external states.

stimulus generalization the situation in which similar stimuli elicit the same response as a conditioned stimulus after classical conditioning has occurred.

storage a basic activity of memory, involving retention of information for later use.

stress brought on by any situation that threatens or appears to threaten a person's sense of well-being, thus challenging their ability to cope.

stressor a situation or circumstance that triggers the stress response.

striatum an area of the brain that works with the substantia nigra to enable fluid movements.

subpersonalities alternative personalities developed in dissociative identity disorder, each with a unique set of memories, behaviours, thoughts and emotions.

substance dualism a position that holds that there are two distinct and independent substances that constitute our world: material things (the physical world) and immaterial things (consciousness/mind/soul).

substantia nigra the region of the brain concerned with fluidity of movement and inhibiting movements.

superego according to psychoanalytic theory, a personality element in charge of determining which impulses are acceptable to express openly and which are unacceptable; develops as we observe and internalize the behaviours of others in our culture.

superfactor a fundamental dimension of personality made up of a related cluster of personality traits.

suprachiasmatic nucleus (SCN) the small group of neurons in the hypothalamus responsible for coordinating the many rhythms of the body.

survey a study in which researchers use a questionnaire or interview participants.

sympathetic nervous system the division of the autonomic nervous system active during times of stress.

synapses transmission points between neurons.

synaptic pruning developmental reduction of neuronal connections, allowing stronger connections to flourish.

synaptic vesicles membrane-bound spheres in the axon terminals of neurons where neurotransmitters are stored before their release.

synaptogenesis the process of forming new synapses.

syntax the grammatical positioning of words in a sentence.

systematic desensitization a process used to condition extinction of phobias through gradual exposure to the feared object or situation.

T

taste buds clusters of sensory receptor cells that convert chemical signals from food, drink, etc. into neural impulses that travel to the brain.

telegraphic speech a type of speech that consists of minimalistic sentences. It characterizes early toddlerhood and is the first evidence of sentence formation.

temperament biologically based tendencies to respond to certain situations in similar ways throughout our lifetimes.

temporal cortex the area of the neocortex important for processing sounds, speech comprehension and for recognizing complex visual stimuli, such as faces.

testosterone an androgen hormone primarily found in males.

thalamus the area of the brain that serves as a relay station for incoming sensory information.

thematic analysis a basic form of qualitative analysis involving derivation of themes from a text or interview transcript.

theories ideas about laws that govern phenomena.

theory of mind a recognition that other people base their behaviours on their own perspectives, not on information that is unavailable to them.

theory of multiple intelligences the theory that there is no single, unified intelligence but instead several independent intelligences arising from different portions of the brain.

therapy outcome studies research that looks at the effects of various treatments.

token economy an operant conditioning therapy programme in which participants receive tokens (that can be traded for rewards) when they display desired behaviours.

tonotopic map the representation in the auditory cortex of different sound frequencies.

top-down processing the perception processes led by cognitive processes, such as memory or expectations.

transcranial magnetic stimulation (TMS) a procedure in which an electromagnetic coil placed on or above a person's head sends a current into the prefrontal cortex; used to treat severe depression.

transference process through which clients come to act and feel towards the therapist as they did towards important figures in their lives, past and present.

traumatic events unexpected events severe enough to cause extreme disruptions.

treatment, or therapy systematic procedures designed to change abnormal behaviour into normal behaviour.

trephining prehistoric practice of chipping a hole in the skull as a treatment for various brain conditions.

triangular theory of love the theory that love is composed of three elements: intimacy, passion and commitment; proposed by Robert Sternberg.

triarchic theory of intelligence Sternberg's theory that intelligence is made up of three interacting components: internal, external and experiential components.

trichromatic theory a theory of colour perception holding that the human eye has three sensors of colour, each of which responds to a different range of wavelengths.

tympanic membrane the eardrum.

Type A a personality type characterized by competitiveness, impatience, anger and hostility.

Type B a personality type that is less aggressive, more relaxed and less hostile than Type A.

U

unconditional positive regard acceptance without terms or conditions.

unconditioned response (UR) a physical response elicited by an unconditioned stimulus; it does not need to be learnt.

unconditioned stimulus (US) a stimulus that on its own elicits a response.

unconscious a hypothesized repository of thoughts, feelings and sensations outside human awareness, thought in some theories to have a strong bearing on human behaviour.

unconscious state the state in which information is not easily accessible to conscious awareness.

universal Darwinism the idea that natural selection will occur whenever an entity is subject to variation, selection and heredity.

universality describes a characteristic that is shared by all members of a species.

V

vagus nerve stimulation a procedure in a which an implanted device sends electrical signals to the brain through the vagus nerve; used to treat severe depression.

validity the extent to which a test accurately measures or predicts what it is supposed to measure or predict.

validity coefficient a correlation coefficient that measures validity by correlating a test score with some external criterion.

variable interval schedule reinforcement occurs after varying amounts of time.

variable ratio schedule the number of responses required for reinforcement varies.

variable the condition, event or situation that is studied in an experiment.

variation the different varieties of a characteristic within a population.

ventromedial region of the hypothalamus (VMH) a region of the hypothalamus important in signalling satiety.

version one way of describing a social feature out of a range of possible ways of describing that same feature.

visual field a term used to describe how the world looks from the point of view of the visual system. Positions in the visual field correspond with points on each retina.

voluntarism the doctrine that states that all our mental life is motivated, that our mental life is not a passive reflection of the world around us.

W

wear-and-tear theory the theory suggesting we age because use of our body wears it out.

Wernicke's aphasia a neurological condition associated with damage to Wernicke's area where a person cannot understand language.

Wernicke's area a brain region located in the temporal lobe that is important for language comprehension.

working memory a form of memory that allows the simultaneous manipulation and storage of information in the short term.

Y

Yerkes–Dodson law holds that ideal performance on a task occurs when the arousal level is optimized to the difficulty level.

Z

zone of proximal development the gap between what a child can accomplish alone and what the child can accomplish with help from others.

References

CHAPTER 1

Barash, D. P. (1979). *The Whispering Within: Evolution and the origin of human nature*. New York: Viking Press/Penguin Books.

Biswas-Diener, R. (ed.) (2011). *Positive Psychology as Social Change*. New York: Springer Science + Business Media.

Botton, A. (2006). *The Architecture of Happiness*. London: Pantheon.

Bryan, W. L. & Harter, N. (1897). Studies in the psychology of the telegraphic language. *Psychological Review, 4*, 27–53.

Buss, D. M. (1999). *Evolutionary Psychology: The new science of the mind*. Boston: Allyn & Bacon.

Buss, D. M. (ed.) (2005). *The Handbook of Evolutionary Psychology*. Hoboken, NJ: John Wiley & Sons, Inc.

Buss, D. M. (2009). The great struggles of life: Darwin and the emergence of evolutionary psychology. *American Psychologist, 64*(2), 140–148.

Cohen, S., Alper, C. M., Doyle, W. J., Adler, N., Treanor, J. J., & Turner, R. B. (2008). Objective and subjective socioeconomic status and susceptibility to the common cold. *Health Psychology, 27*(2), 268–274.

Cohen, S., Doyle, W. J., Turner, R. B., Alper, C. M., & Skoner, D. P. (2003). Emotional style and susceptibility to the common cold. *Psychosomatic Medicine, 65*, 652–657.

Confer, J. C., Easton, J. A., Fleischman, D. S., Goetz, C. D., Lewis, D. M. G., Perilloux, C., & Buss, D. M. (2010). Evolutionary psychology: Controversies, questions, prospects, and limitations. *American Psychologist, 65*(2), 110–126.

Cooper, C. L. (2010). The happiness agenda. *Stress and Health: Journal of the International Society for the Investigation of Stress, 26*(5), 349.

Garbarino, J. (2011). *The Positive Psychology of Personal Transformation: Leveraging resilience for life change*. New York: Springer Science + Business Media.

Gazzaniga, M. S. (2005). Forty-five years of split-brain research and still going strong. *Nature Reviews Neuroscience, 6*(8), 653–659.

Gazzaniga, M. S. (2010). Neuroscience and the correct level of explanation for understanding the mind: An extraterrestrial roams through some neuroscience laboratories and concludes earthlings are not grasping how best to understand the mind–brain interface. *Trends in Cognitive Sciences, 14*(7), 291–292.

Gould, S. J. & Lewontin, R. C. (1979). The sandrels of San Marco and the Panglossian paradigm: A critique of the adaptation programme. *Proceedings of the Royal Society of London, Series B, 205*, 581–598.

Headey, B. (2008). Life goals matter to happiness: A revision of set-point theory. *Social Indicators Research, 86*(2), 213–231.

Jastrow, J. (1929). Review of J. B. Watson, ways of behaviorism, psychological care of infant and child, battle of behaviorism. *Science, 69*, 455–457.

Kleiner, S. & Condor, B. (2007). *The Good Mood Diet: Feel great while you lose weight*. New York: Springboard Press.

Leahey, T. H. (2000). *A History of Psychology* (5th edn). Upper Saddle River, NJ: Prentice Hall.

Lu, L. & Shih, J. (1997) Personality and happiness: Is mental health a mediator? *Personality and Individual Differences, 22*, 249–256.

Markus, H. R., Plaut, V. C., & Lachman, M. E. (2004). Well-being in America: Core features and regional patterns. In O. G. Brim, C. D. Ryff & R. C. Kessler (eds), *How Healthy Are We? A national study of well-being at midlife* (pp. 614–650). Chicago: University of Chicago Press.

Morton, J. & Johnson, M. H. (1991). Conspec and Conlern: A 2-process theory of infant face recognition. *Psychological Review, 98*, 164–181.

Neisser, U. (1967). *Cognitive Psychology*. New York: Appleton-Century-Crofts.

Richardson, R. D. (2006). *William James: In the maelstrom of American modernism*. Boston: Houghton Mifflin.

Rossano, M. J. (2003). *Evolutionary Psychology*. Hoboken, NJ: John Wiley & Sons, Inc.

Stam, H. J. (2010). The tradition of personalism and its relationship to contemporary indeterminate functionalism. *New Ideas in Psychology, 28*(2), 143–150.

Turati, C., Di Giorgio, E., Bardi, L., & Simion, F. (2010). Holistic face processing in newborns, 3-month-old infants, and adults: Evidence from the composite face effect. *Child Development, 81*(6), 1894–1905.

CHAPTER 2

American Psychological Association. (2002). Ethical principles of psychologists and code of conduct. *American Psychologist, 57*, 1060–1073.

Aubrey, J. (2000). *Brief Lives*. Harmondsworth: Penguin.

Boyatzis, R. E. (1998). *Transforming Qualitative Information-Thematic Analysis and Code Development*. Thousand Oaks, CA: Sage.

British Psychological Society. (2009). *Code of Ethics and Conduct*. Leicester: British Psychological Society.

British Psychological Society. (2012). *Guidelines for Psychologists Working with Animals*. Leicester: British Psychological Society.

Campbell, L., Vasquez, M., Behnke, S., & Kinscherff, R. (2010). *APA Ethics Code Commentary and Case Illustrations*. Washington, DC: American Psychological Association.

Connor-Greene, P. A. (2007). Observation or interpretation: Demonstrating unintentional subjectivity and interpretive variance. *Teaching of Psychology, 34*(3), 167–171.

Damasio, A. (1994). *Descartes' Error*. New York: Grosset/Putnam.

Damasio, A. (1999). *The Feeling of What Happens: Body and emotion in the making of consciousness*. New York: Harcourt.

Damasio, A. (2003). *Looking for Spinoza: Joy, sorrow and the feeling brain*. New York: Harcourt.

Damasio, A. (2010). *Self Comes to Mind: Constructing the conscious brain*. New York: Pantheon.

Davis, R. (1992). Canada settles '63 brainwash case. *USA Today*, 19 November, p. 2A.

Denzin, N. K. (1978). *The Research Act: A theoretical introduction to sociological methods*. New York: McGraw-Hill.

Girden, E. R. & Kabacoff, R. I. (2011). *Evaluating Research Articles: From start to finish* (3rd edn). Thousand Oaks, CA: Sage Publications.

Glaser, B. G. & Strauss, A. L. (1967). *The Discovery of Grounded Theory: Strategies for qualitative research*. Chicago: Aldine.

Goodwin, C. J. (2011). *Research in Psychology: Methods and design* (6th edn). Hoboken, NJ: John Wiley & Sons, Inc.

GSS (General Social Survey). (2007). *Job Satisfaction in the United States*. Chicago: National Opinion Research Center.

Hergenhahn, B. R. (2005). *An Introduction to the History of Psychology* (5th edn). Belmont, CA: Thomson Wadsworth.

Hirschorn, M. (2007). The case for reality TV. *The Atlantic Online*, http://www.theatlantic.com/magazine/archive/2007/05/the-case-for-reality-tv/305791/, accessed 29 October 2012.

ILAR (Institute for Laboratory Animal Research). (2011). *The Guide*, http://dels.nas.edu/global/ilar/Guide, accessed 29 October 2012.

Jones, J. (1981). *Bad Blood: The Tuskegee syphilis experiment: A tragedy of race and medicine*. New York: Free Press.

Kant, I. (2003). Anthropology from a pragmatic point of view. *The History of Psychology: Fundamental questions* (pp. 127–140). New York: Oxford University Press.

Lalasz, R. (2011). Is something wrong with the scientific method? Part 1. *Cool green science (The conservation blog of the Nature Conservancy)*, http://blog.nature.org/2011/01/something-wrong-scientific-method-jonathan-hoekstra-jensen-montambault/, accessed 29 October 2012.

Leahey, T. H. (2005). Mind as a scientific object: A historical-philosophical exploration. In C. E. Erneling & D. M. Johnson (eds), *The Mind as a Scientific Object: Between brain and culture* (pp. 35–78). New York: Oxford University Press.

Lee, E., Mishna, F., & Brennenstuhl, S. (2010). How to critically evaluate case studies in social work. *Research on Social Work Practice, 20*(6), 682–689.

Locke, E. A. (2007). The case for inductive theory building. *Journal of Management, 33*(6), 867–890.

McGaha, A. C. & Korn, J. H. (1995). The emergence of interest in the ethics of psychological research with humans. *Ethics & Behavior, 5*, 147–159.

McGrath, R. E. (2011). *Quantitative Models in Psychology*. Washington: American Psychological Association.

MORI (Market Opinion Research International). (1999). Poll on animal experimentation. *New Scientist*, May.

MORI (Market Opinion Research International). (2005). Use of animals in medical research: Research study conducted for the Coalition for Medical Progress. London, http://www.ipsos-mori.com/researchpublications/researcharchive/434/MORI-Use-Of-Animals-In-Medical-Research-Survey-2005.aspx, accessed 30 October 2012.

Nagy, T. F. (2011). *Essential Ethics for Psychologists: A primer for understanding and mastering core issues*. Washington: American Psychological Association.

Pinker, S. (1994). *The Language Instinct*. New York: HarperCollins.

Pinker, S. (1997). *How the Mind Works*. New York: W. W. Norton & Co.

Pinker, S. (2002). *The Blank Slate: The modern denial of human nature*. New York: Viking.

Pinker, S. (2007). *The Stuff of Thought: Language as a window into human nature*. New York: Viking.

Pinker, S. (2010). Mind over mass media. *New York Times*, 10 June.

Popper, K. R. (1959). *The Logic of Scientific Discovery*. Oxford: Basic Books.

Popper, K. R. (1963). *Conjectures and Refutations: The growth of scientific knowledge*. London: Routledge & Kegan Paul.

Powis, T. (1990). Paying for the past: A brainwashing victim seeks compensation. *Macleans*, 19 March.

Pozner, J. L. (2010). *Reality Bites Back: The troubling truth about guilty pleasure TV*. Berkeley, CA: Seal Press.

Remler, D. K. & Van Ryzin, G. G. (2011). *Research Methods in Practice: Strategies for description and causation*. Thousand Oaks, CA: Sage Publications.

Smith, C. (1996). Sleep states, memory processes and synaptic plasticity. *Behavioural Brain Research, 78*(1), 49–56.

Sprenger, J. (2011). Hypothetico-deductive confirmation. *Philosophy Compass, 6*, 497–508.

Tartakovsky, M. (2011). Eugenics & the story of Carrie Buck. *Psych-Central*, 24 January.

Wender, P. H., Reimherr, F. W., Marchant, B. K., Sanford, M. E., Czajkowski, L. A., & Tomb, D. A. (2011). A one-year trial of methylphenidate in the treatment of ADHD. *Journal of Attention Disorders, 15*(1), 36–45.

CHAPTER 3

Adolph, K. E., Karasik, L. B., & Tamis-Lemonda, C. (2010). Motor skill. In M. H. Bornstein (ed.), *Handbook of Cultural Developmental Science* (pp. 61–88). New York: Psychology Press.

Anderson, M. L., Sisti, H. M., Curlik, D. M., II, & Shors, T. J. (2011). Associative learning increases adult neurogenesis during a critical period. *European Journal of Neuroscience, 33*(1), 175–181.

APA (American Psychiatric Association). (2000). *Diagnostic and Statistical Manual of Mental Disorders* (4th edn). Washington: American Psychiatric Association.

Apostolova, L. G. & Cummings, J. L. (2008). Neuropsychiatric aspects of Alzheimer's disease and other dementing illnesses. In S. C. Yudofsky & R. E. Hales (eds), *The American Psychiatric Publishing Textbook of Neuropsychiatry and Behavioral Neurosciences* (5th edn). Washington: American Psychiatric Publishing.

Armstrong, V., Brunet, P. M., Chao, H., Nishimura, M., Poole, H. L., & Spector, F. J. (2006). What is so critical?: A commentary on the reexamination of critical periods. *Development and Psychobiology, 45*, 326–331.

Baillargeon, R. (1987). Object permanence in 3½- and 4½-month-old infants. *Developmental Psychology, 23*, 655–664.

Baird, A. A. (2010). The terrible twelves. In P. D. Zelazo, M. Chandler, & E. Crone (eds), *Developmental Social Cognitive Neuroscience* (pp. 191–207). New York: Psychology Press.

Bartzokis, G., Lu, P. H., Tingus, K., Mendez, M. F., Richard, A., Peters, D. G., & Mintz, J. (2010). Lifespan trajectory of myelin integrity and maximum motor speed. *Neurobiology of Aging, 31*(9), 1554–1562.

Bedinghaus, T. (2010). *Top 5 Milestones in Vision Development*, http://vision.about.com/od/childrensvision/tp/vision_develop.htm, accessed 2 November 2012.

Bialystok, E. & Craik, F. I. M. (2010). Structure and process in life-span cognitive development. In W. F. Overton & R. M. Lerner (eds), *The Handbook of Life-Span Development, Vol. 1: Cognition, biology, and methods* (pp. 195–225). Hoboken, NJ: John Wiley & Sons, Inc.

Blakemore, S., Burnett, S., & Dahl, R. E. (2010). The role of puberty in the developing adolescent brain. *Human Brain Mapping, 31*(6), 926–933.

Bock, P. (2005). Infant science: How do babies learn to talk? *Pacific Northwest: The Seattle Times Magazine*, 6 March 2005.

Boldyrev, A. A. & Johnson, P. (2007). Free radicals and cell signaling in Alzheimer's disease. *Journal of Alzheimer's Disease, 11*(2), 141.

Bord-Hoffman, M. A. & Donius, M. (2005). Loss in height: When is it a problem? *AAACN Viewpoint, 1*, 14–15.

Brach, J. S., FitzGerald, S., Newman, A. B., Kelsey, S., Kuller, L., Van-Swearingen, J. M., & Kriska, A. M. (2003). Physical activity and functional status in community-dwelling older women. *Archives of Internal Medicine, 163*, 2565–2571.

Bruner, J. (1960). *The Process of Education*. Cambridge, MA: Harvard University Press.

Carpendale, J. I. M. & Lewis, C. (2010). The development of social understanding: A relational perspective. In W. F. Overton & R. M. Lerner (eds), *The Handbook of Life-Span Development, Vol. 1: Cognition, biology, and methods* (pp. 584–627). Hoboken, NJ: John Wiley & Sons, Inc.

Charles, E. P. & Rivera, S. M. (2009). Object permanence and method of disappearance: Looking measures further contradict reaching measures. *Developmental Science, 12*(6), 991–1006.

de Haan, A. D., Prinzie, P., & Dekovic, M. (2010). How and why children change in aggression and delinquency from childhood to adolescence: Moderation of overreactive parenting by child personality. *Journal of Child Psychology and Psychiatry, 51*(6), 725–733.

DeVries, R. (1969). Constancy of genetic identity in the years three to six. *Monograph of the Society for Research in Child Development, 34* (Serial No. 127).

Di Pietro, J. A. (2000). Baby and the Brain: Advances in child development. *Annual Review of Public Health, 21*(1), 455–471.

Drummond, M. (2011). Men's bodies throughout the life span. In C. Blazina & D. S. Shen-Miller (eds), *An International Psychology of Men: Theoretical advances, case studies, and clinical innovations* (pp. 159–188). New York: Routledge/Taylor & Francis Group.

Duncan, S. C., Duncan, T. E., & Strycker, L. (2006). Alcohol use from ages 9 to 16: A cohort-sequential latent growth model. *Drug and Alcohol Dependence, 81*(4), 71–81.

Edin, F., Macoveanu, J., Olesen, P., Tegnér, J., & Klingberg, T. (2007). Stronger synaptic connectivity as a mechanism behind development of working memory-related brain activity during childhood. *Journal of Cognitive Neuroscience, 19*(5), 750–760.

Elkind, D. (1978). Understanding the young adolescent. *Adolescence, 13*(49), 127–134.

Elkind, D. (2007). *The Hurried Child: Growing up too fast too soon (25th anniversary edn)*. Cambridge, MA: Da Capo Press.

Ernst, M. & Hardin, M. (2010). Neurodevelopment underlying adolescent behavior: A neurobiological model. In P. D. Zelazo, M. Chandler, & E. Crone (eds), *Developmental Social Cognitive Neuroscience* (pp. 165–189). New York: Psychology Press.

Eun, B. (2010). From learning to development: A sociocultural approach to instruction. *Cambridge Journal of Education, 40*(4), 401–418.

Fantz, R. L. (1961). The origin of form perception. *American Psychologist, 37*(2), 197–211.

Feldhusen, J. F. (2003). Lewis M. Terman: A pioneer in the development of ability tests. In B. J. Zimmerman & D. H. Schunk (eds), *Educational Psychology: A century of contributions* (pp. 155–169). Mahwah, NJ: Lawrence Erlbaum Associates.

Feldman, D. H. (2003). Cognitive development in childhood. In R. M. Lerner, M. A. Easterbrooks, & J. Mistry (eds), *Handbook of Psychology: Developmental Psychology, Vol. 6* (pp. 195–210). Hoboken, NJ: John Wiley & Sons, Inc.

Fozard, J., Wolf, E., Bell, B., Farland, R., & Podolsky, S. (1977). Visual perception and communication. In J. Birren & K. Schaie (eds), *Handbook of the Psychology of Aging*. New York: Van Nostrand Reinhold.

Freedman, V. A., Aykan, H., & Martin, L. G. (2001). Aggregate changes in severe cognitive impairment among older Americans: 1993 and 1998. *Journal of Gerontology, 56B*, S100–S111.

Freund, A. M. & Lamb, M. E. (2010). Social and emotional development across the life span. In M. E. Lamb, A. M. Freund, & R. M. Lerner (eds), *The Handbook of Life-Span Development, Vol. 2: Social and emotional development* (pp. 1–8). Hoboken, NJ: John Wiley & Sons, Inc.

Fry, C. J. (1988). Left-handedness and tongue-rolling ability. *Perceptual and Motor Skills, 67*(1), 168–170.

Gould, E. (2007). How widespread is adult neurogenesis in mammals? *Nature Reviews Neuroscience, 8*, 481–488.

Hawkley, L. C., Berntson, G. G., Engeland, C. G., Marucha, P. T., Masi, C. M., & Cacioppo, J. T. (2005). Stress, Aging, and Resilience: Can accrued wear and tear be slowed? *Canadian Psychology, 46*(3), 115–125.

Hayatbakhsh, M. R., Najman, J. M., McGee, T. R., Bor, W., & O'Callaghan, M. J. (2009). Early pubertal maturation in the prediction of early adult substance use: A prospective study. *Addiction, 104*(1), 59–66.

Herdt, G. (2010). Sex/gender, culture, and development: Issues in the emergence of puberty and attraction. In C. M. Worthman, P. M. Plotsky, D. S. Schechter, & C. A. Cummings (eds), *Formative Experiences: The interaction of caregiving, culture, and developmental psychobiology* (pp. 356–374). New York: Cambridge University Press.

Hermer-Vazquez, L., Moffet, A., & Munkholm, P. (2001). Language, space, and the development of cognitive flexibility in humans: The case of two spatial memory tasks. *Cognition, 79*, 263–299.

Hughes, M. (1975). *Egocentrism in preschool children*. Unpublished PhD thesis, University of Edinburgh.

Inhelder, B. & Piaget, J. (1979). Procedures et structures. *Archives de Psychologie, 47*, 165–176.

Jensen, L. A. (ed.) (2011). *Bridging Cultural and Developmental Approaches to Psychology: New syntheses in theory, research, and policy*. New York: Oxford University Press.

Jolly, J. L., Treffinger, D. J., Inman, T. F., & Smutny, J. F. (eds) (2011). *Parenting Gifted Children: The authoritative guide from the National Association for Gifted Children*. Waco, TX: Prufrock Press.

Kagan, J. (2010). Emotions and temperament. In M. H. Bornstein (ed.), *Handbook of Cultural Developmental Science* (pp. 175–194). New York: Psychology Press.

Kaplan, H. & Dove, H. (1987). Infant development among the Ache of eastern Paraguay. *Developmental Psychology, 23*(2), 190–198.

Kellman, P. J. & Arterberry, M. E. (1998). *The Cradle of Knowledge: Development of perception in infancy*. Cambridge, MA: MIT Press.

Kesselring, T. & Müller, U. (2011). The concept of egocentrism in the context of Piaget's theory. *New Ideas in Psychology 29*(3), 327–345.

Keverne, E. B. (2010). Neurobiology of wellbeing: A life course perspective. In C. L. Cooper, J. Field, U. Goswami, R. Jenkins, & B. J. Sahakian (eds), *Mental Capital and Wellbeing* (pp. 927–934). Hoboken, NJ: Wiley-Blackwell.

Kohlberg, L. (1963). The development of children's orientations toward a moral order: I. Sequence in the development of moral thought. *Vita Humana, 6*(1–2), 11–33.

Kohlberg, L. (1994). The claim to moral adequacy of a highest stage of moral judgment. In B. Puka (ed.), *The Great Justice Debate: Kohlberg criticism* (pp. 2–18). New York: Garland Publishing.

Kohlberg, L. (2008). The development of children's orientations toward a moral order: I. Sequence in the development of moral thought. *Human Development, 51*(1), 8–20.

Larson, E. B., Wang, L., Bowen, J. D., McCormick, W. C., Teri, L., Crane, P., & Kukull, W. (2006). Exercise is associated with reduced risk of incident dementia among persons 65 years of age and older. *Annals of Internal Medicine, 144*, 73–81.

Leuner, B., Gould, E., & Shors, T. J. (2006). Is there a link between adult neurogenesis and learning? *Hippocampus, 16*(3), 216–224.

Leuner, B., Glasper, E. R., & Gould, E. (2010). Parenting and plasticity. *Trends in Neurosciences, 33*(10), 465–473.

Lloyd, M., Burghardt, A., Ulrich, D. A., & Angulo-Barroso, R. (2010). Physical activity and walking onset in infants with Down syndrome. *Adapted Physical Activity Quarterly, 27*(1), 1–16.

Logsdon, A. (2011). Early child development: Your baby's first six month early child development. *About.com Guide: Learning disabilities*, http://learningdisabilities.about.com/od/infancyandearlychildhood/p/first6monthdeve.htm, accessed 2 November 2012.

Lorenz, K. (1970). *Studies in Animal and Human Behaviour: I*, trans. R. Martin. Oxford: Harvard University Press.

Lorenz, K. (1971). *Studies in Animal and Human Behaviour: II*, trans. R. Martin. Oxford: Harvard University Press.

Lorenz, K. (2002). Critique of the modern ethologists' attitude. In M. H. Johnson, Y. Munakata, & R. O. Gilmore (eds), *Brain Development and Cognition: A reader* (2nd edn, pp. 8–17). Malden, MA: Blackwell Publishing.

Lourenç, O. & Machado, A. (1996). In defense of Piaget's theory: A reply to 10 common criticisms. *Psychological Review, 103*, 143–164.

Mar, R. A., Tackett, J. L., & Moore, C. (2010). Exposure to media and theory-of-mind development in preschoolers. *Cognitive Development, 25*(1), 69–78.

Maurer, D. & Salapatek, P. (1976). Developmental changes in the scanning of faces by young infants. *Child Development, 47*, 523–527.

MacNamara, A., Button, A., & Collins, D. (2010). The role of the psychological characteristics in the facilitating the pathway to elite performance. *The Sport Psychologist, 24*, 52–73.

McCrink, K., & Wynn, K. (2004). Large-number addition and subtraction by 9-month-old infants. *Psychological Science, 15*(11), 776–781.

McDonald, J. H. (2010). Tongue rolling. In J. H. McDonald, *Myths of Human Genetics*. University of Delaware.

McGarrigle, J. & Donaldson, M. (1975). Conservation accidents. *Cognition, 3*, 341–350.

Meltzoff, A. N. & Moore, M. K. (1983). Newborn infants imitate adult facial gestures. *Child Development, 54*, 702–709.

Memmert, D. (2011). Creativity, expertise, and attention: Exploring their development and their relationships. *Journal of Sports Sciences, 29*(1), 93–102.

Michel, G. F. & Tyler, A. N. (2005). Critical period: A history of the transition from questions of when, to what, to how. *Development and Psychobiology, 46*, 156–162.

Miller, D. B. & O'Callaghan, J. P. (2005). Aging, stress and the hippocampus. *Ageing Research Review, 4*, 23–140.

Müller, U. & Racine, T. P. (2010). The development of representation and concepts. In W. F. Overton & R. M. Lerner (eds), *The Handbook of Life-Span Development, Vol. 1: Cognition, biology, and methods* (pp. 346–390). Hoboken, NJ: John Wiley & Sons, Inc.

Nosek, M., Kennedy, H. P., Beyene, Y., Taylor, D., Gilliss, C., & Lee, K. (2010). The effects of perceived stress and attitudes toward menopause and aging on symptoms of menopause. *Journal of Midwifery & Women's Health, 55*(4), 328–334.

Oda, A. Y. (2007). David Elkind and the crisis of adolescence: Review, critique, and applications. *Journal of Psychology and Christianity, 26*(3), 251–256.

Ornstein, P. A. & Light, L. L. (2010). Memory development across the life span. In W. F. Overton & R. M. Lerner (eds), *The Handbook of Life-Span Development, Vol. 1: Cognition, biology, and methods* (pp. 259–305). Hoboken, NJ: John Wiley & Sons, Inc.

Overton, W. F. (2010). Life-span development: Concepts and issues. In W. F. Overton & R. M. Lerner (eds), *The Handbook of Life-Span Development, Vol. 1: Cognition, biology, and methods* (pp. 1–29). Hoboken, NJ: John Wiley & Sons, Inc.

Overton, W. F. & Lerner, R. M. (eds). (2010). *The Handbook of Life-Span Development, Vol. 1: Cognition, biology, and methods.* Hoboken, NJ: John Wiley & Sons, Inc.

Paus, T., Zijdenbos, A., Worsley, K., Collins, D. L., Blumenthal, J., Giedd, J. N., *et al.* (1999). Structural maturation of neural pathways in children and adolescents: In vivo study. *Science, 283*(5409), 1908–1911.

Perluigi, M., Di Domenico, F., Giorgi, A., Schininà, M. E., Coccia, R., Cini, C., & Calabrese, V. (2010). Redox proteomics in aging rat brain: Involvement of mitochondrial reduced glutathione status and mitochondrial protein oxidation in the aging process. *Journal of Neuroscience Research, 88*(16), 3498–3507.

Phillips, J. L. (1975). *The Origins of Intellect: Piaget's theory.* London: W. H. Freeman.

Piaget, J. (1972). *Essay on Operative Logic* (2nd edn). Dunod: 75661 Paris Cedex 14.

Piaget, J. (1985). *The Equilibration of Cognitive Structures: The central problem of intellectual development* (T. Brown & K. Thampy, trans). University of Chicago Press.

Piaget, J. (2000). *Studies in Reflecting Abstraction* (R. L. Campbell, trans). Hove: Psychology Press.

Piaget, J. (2003). Part I: Cognitive development in children: Piaget: Development and learning. *Journal of Research in Science Teaching, 40,* S8–S18.

Piaget, J., le Cozannet, R., & Samson, D. (2009). La causalité chez l'enfant. *British Journal of Psychology, 100,* 207–224.

Pierpaoli, W. (ed.) (2005). *Reversal of Aging: Resetting the pineal clock.* New York: Academy of Sciences.

Plomin, R. & Daniels, D. (1987). Why are children in the same family so different from one another? *Behavioral and Brain Sciences, 10,* 1–16.

Pollak, S. D., Nelson, C. A., Schlaak, M. F., Roeber, B. J., Wewerka, S. S., Wiik, K. L., & Gunnar, M. R. (2010). Neurodevelopmental effects of early deprivation in postinstitutionalized children. *Child Development, 81*(1), 224–236.

Porges, S. W. & Carter, C. S. (2010). Neurobiological bases of social behavior across the life span. In M. E. Lamb, A. M. Freund, & R. M. Lerner (eds), *The Handbook of Life-Span Development, Vol. 2: Social and emotional development* (pp. 9–50). Hoboken, NJ: John Wiley & Sons, Inc.

Rekers, G. A. (1992). Development of problems of puberty and sex roles in adolescence. In C. E. Walker & M. C. Roberts, M. C. (eds), *Handbook of Clinical Child Psychology* (2nd edn, pp. 607–622). New York: John Wiley & Sons Inc.

Roberson-Nay, R. & Brown, R. C. (2011). Neurodevelopmental aspects of social anxiety. In C. A. Alfano & D. C. Beidel (eds), *Social Anxiety in Adolescents and Young Adults: Translating developmental science into practice* (pp. 53–71). Washington: American Psychological Association.

Rutter, M., Sonuga-Barke, E. & Castle, J. (2010). Investigating the impact of early institutional deprivation on development: Background and research strategy of the English and Romanian adoptees (ERA) study. *Monographs of the Society for Research in Child Development, 75*(1), 1–20.

Sheridan, M., Drury, S., McLaughlin, K., & Almas, A. (2010). Early institutionalization: Neurobiological consequences and genetic modifiers. *Neuropsychology Review, 20*(4), 414–429.

Super, C. M. (1976). Environmental effects on motor development: The case of African infant precocity. *Developmental Medicine & Child Neurology, 18*(5), 561–567.

Thomas, M. S. C., Annaz, D., Ansari, D., Serif, G., Jarrold, C., & Karmiloff-Smith, A. (2009). Using developmental trajectories to understand developmental disorders. *Journal of Speech, Language, and Hearing Research, 52,* 336–358.

Trawick-Smith, J. & Dziurgot, T. (2011). 'Good-fit' teacher–child play interactions and the subsequent autonomous play of preschool children. *Early Childhood Research Quarterly, 26*(1), 110–123.

Truett, K. R., Eaves, L. J., Walters, E. E., Heath A.C., Hewitt J.K., Meyer J.M., *et al.* (1994). A model system for analysis of family resemblance in extended kinships of twins. *Behavior Genetics, 24*(1), 35–49.

Vygotsky, L. (1978). *Mind in Society: Development of higher psychological processes.* Cambridge, MA: Harvard University Press.

Vygotsky, L. S. (1991). Genesis of the higher mental functions. In P. Light, S. Sheldon, & M. Woodhead (eds), *Learning to Think* (pp. 32–41). Florence: Taylor & Francies/Routledge.

Vygotsky, L. S. (2004). Imagination and creativity in childhood. *Journal of Russian & East European Psychology, 42*(1), 7–97.

Wertsch, J. V. (1985). *Vygotsky and the social formation of mind.* Cambridge, MA: Harvard University Press.

Wimmer, H. & Perner, J. (1983). Beliefs about beliefs: Representation and constraining function of wrong beliefs in young children's understanding of deception. *Cognition, 12*(1), 103–128.

Wynn, K. (1992). Addition and subtraction by human infants. *Nature, 358*(6389), 749–750.

Wynn, K. (2002). Do infants have numerical expectations or just perceptual preferences? Comment. *Developmental Science, 5*(2), 207–209.

Zelazo, P. D. & Lee, W. S. C. (2010). Brain development: An overview. In W. F. Overton & R. M. Lerner (eds), *The Handbook of Life-Span Development, Vol. 1: Cognition, biology, and methods* (pp. 89–114). Hoboken, NJ: John Wiley & Sons, Inc.

CHAPTER 4

Ahern, E. C., Lyon, T. D., & Quas, J. A. (2011). Young children's emerging ability to make false statements. *Developmental Psychology, 47,* 61–66.

Ainsworth, M. D. (1967). *Infancy in Uganda: Infant care and the growth of love.* Baltimore: Johns Hopkins University Press.

Ainsworth, M. D. (1985). Patterns of attachment. *Clinical Psychologist, 38*(2), 27–29.

Ainsworth, M. S. (1993). Attachment as related to mother–infant interaction. *Advances in Infancy Research, 8,* 1–50.

Ainsworth, M. S. (2010). Security and attachment. In R. Volpe (ed.), *The Secure Child: Timeless lessons in parenting and childhood education* (pp. 43–53). Greenwich, CT: IAP Information Age Publishing.

Aldwin, C. M., Yancura, L. A., & Boeninger, D. K. (2010). Coping across the life span. In M. E. Lamb, A. M. Freund, & R. M. Lerner (eds), *The Handbook of Life-Span Development, Vol. 2: Social and emotional development* (pp. 298–340). Hoboken, NJ: John Wiley & Sons, Inc.

Allen, B. (2011a). The use and abuse of attachment theory in clinical practice with maltreated children, part I: Diagnosis and assessment. *Trauma, Violence, & Abuse, 12*(1), 3–12.

Allen, B. (2011b). The use and abuse of attachment theory in clinical practice with maltreated children, part II: Treatment. *Trauma, Violence, & Abuse, 12*(1), 13–22.

Allen, K. R. & Demo, D. H. (1995). The families of lesbians and gay men: A new frontier in family research. *Journal of Marriage and the Family, 57,* 111–127.

Arnett, J. J. (2007) Emerging adulthood: What is it, and what is it good for? *Child Development Perspectives, 1*(2), 68–73.

Arnett, J. J., Kloep, M., Hendry, L. B., & Tanner, J. L. (2011). *Debating Emerging Adulthood: Stage or process*. Oxford: Oxford University Press.

Baird, G., Simonoff, E., Pickles, A., Chandler, S., Loucas, T., Meldrum, D., & Charman, T. (2006) Prevalence of disorders of the autism spectrum in a population cohort of children in South Thames: The Special Needs and Autism Project (SNAP). *Lancet 368*(9531), 210–215.

Baltes, P. B. (1997). On the incomplete architecture of human ontogenesis: Selection, optimisation, and compensation as foundations of developmental theory. *American Psychologist, 52*, 366–381.

Baltes, P. B. & Smith, J. (2008). The fascination of wisdom: Its nature, ontogeny, and function. *Perspectives on Psychological Science, 3*, 56–64.

Bates, J. E., Schermerhorn, A. C., & Goodnight, J. A. (2010). Temperament and personality through the life span. In M. E. Lamb, A. M. Freund, & R. M. Lerner (eds), *The Handbook of Life-Span Development, Vol. 2: Social and emotional development* (pp. 208–253). Hoboken, NJ: John Wiley & Sons, Inc.

Baumrind, D. (1991). The influence of parenting style on adolescent competence and substance use. *Journal of Early Adolescence, 11*, 56–95.

Baumrind, D., Larzelere, R. E., & Owens, E. B. (2010). Effects of preschool parents' power assertive patterns and practices on adolescent development. *Parenting: Science and Practice, 10*(3), 157–201.

Blatchford, P. & Baines, E. (2010). Peer relations in school. In Littleton, K., Wood, C., & Staarman, K. (eds), *International Handbook of Psychology in Education* (pp. 178–227). Emerald Group Publishing Limited.

Bowlby, J. (1958). The nature of the child's tie to his mother. *International Journal of Psychoanalysis, 39*, 1–23.

Bowlby, J. (1969). *Attachment and Loss, Vol. 1: Attachment*. New York: Basic Books.

Bretherton, I. (1992). The origins of attachment theory: John Bowlby and Mary Ainsworth. *Developmental Psychology, 28*, 759–775.

Bronfenbrenner, U. (1989). Ecological systems theory. *Annals of Child Development, 6*, 185–246.

Burman, E. (2008). *Deconstructing Developmental Psychology* (2nd edn). London, Routledge.

Carlo, G., Koller, S. H., Eisenberg, N., Da Silva, M. S., & Frohlich, C. B. (1996). A cross-national study on the relations among prosocial moral reasoning, gender role orientations, and prosocial behaviours. *Developmental Psychology, 32*, 231–240.

Carstensen, L. L. (1995). Evidence for a life-span theory of socioemotional selectivity. *Current Directions in Psychological Science, 4*(5), 151–156.

Carstensen, L. L. & Mikels, J. A. (2005). At the intersection of emotion and cognition: Aging and the positivity effect. *Current Directions in Psychological Science, 14*, 117–121.

Carstensen, L. L., Isaacowitz, D. M., & Charles, S. T. (1999). Taking time seriously: A theory of socioemotional selectivity. *American Psychologist, 54*, 165–181.

Caspi, A. (1998). Personality development across the life course. In W. Damon & N. Eisenberg (eds), *Handbook of Child Psychology: Vol. 3, Social, emotional, and personality development* (5th edn, pp. 311–388). New York: John Wiley & Sons, Ltd.

Chan, S. M. (2010). Aggressive behaviour in early elementary school children: Relations to authoritarian parenting, children's negative emotionality and coping strategies. *Early Child Development and Care, 180*(9), 1253–1269.

Chao, R. (2001). Extending research on the consequences of parenting style for Chinese Americans and European Americans. *Child Development, 2*, 1832–1843.

Chess, S. & Thomas, A. (1996). *Temperament: Theory and practice*. New York: Brunner-Mazel.

Cicchetti, D. (2010a). A developmental psychopathology perspective on bipolar disorder. In D. J. Miklowitz & D. Cicchetti (eds), *Understanding Bipolar Disorder: A developmental psychopathology perspective* (pp. 1–32). New York: Guilford Press.

Cicchetti, D. (2010b). Developmental psychopathology. In M. E. Lamb, A. M. Freund, & R. M. Lerner (eds), *The Handbook of Life-Span Development, Vol. 2: Social and emotional development* (pp. 511–589). Hoboken, NJ: John Wiley & Sons, Inc.

Clark, J. J. (2010). Life as a source of theory: Erik Erikson's contributions, boundaries, and marginalities. In T. W. Miller (ed.), *Handbook of Stressful Transitions across the Lifespan* (pp. 59–83). New York: Springer Science + Business Media.

Clarke, A. & Clarke, A. (1998). *Early Experience and the Life Path*. London: Jessica Kingsley.

Clarke-Stewart, A. & Dunn, J. (eds) (2006). *Families Count: Effects on child and adolescent development*. New York: Cambridge University Press.

Cowan, P. A. & Cowan, C. P. (2002). Interventions as tests of family systems theories: Marital and family relationships in children's development and psychopathology. *Development and Psychopathology, 14*(4), 731–759.

Crisp, M. (2001). Sticks & stones: 'New Kid' puts comic spin on a serious situation. *Sunday News*, April 8, (Lancaster, PA), p. H-1.

Cuffe, S. P., McKeown, R. E., Addy, C. L., & Garrison, C. Z. (2005). Family and psychosocial risk factors in a longitudinal epidemiological study of adolescents. *Journal of the American Academy of Child and Adolescent Psychiatry, 44*, 121–129.

Cukan, A. (2001). *Confronting a culture of cruelty*. General feature release. United Press International.

Curtiss, S. (1981). Dissociations between language and cognition: Cases and implications. *Journal of Autism and Developmental Disorders, 11*, 15–30.

Dawson, T. L. (2002). New tools, new insights: Kohlberg's moral judgement stages revisited. *International Journal of Behavioral Development, 26*(2), 154–166.

Demo, D. H., Allen, K. R., & Fine, M. A. (eds) (2000). *Handbook of Family Diversity*. New York: Oxford University Press.

Dudley, K. J., Li, X., Kobor, M. S., Kippin, T. E., & Bredy, T. W. (2011). Epigenetic mechanisms mediating vulnerability and resilience to psychiatric disorders. *Neuroscience and Biobehavioral Reviews, 35*(7), 1544–1551.

Edelstein, B. A., Stoner, S. A., & Woodhead, E. (2008). Older adults. In M. Hersen & J. Rosqvist (eds), *Handbook of Psychological Assessment: Case conceptualization and treatment, Vol. 1: Adults*. Hoboken, NJ: John Wiley & Sons, Inc.

Eisenberg, N. & Mussen, P. H. (1989) *The Roots of Prosocial Behaviour in Children*. Cambridge: Cambridge University Press.

Elkind, D. (1967). Egocentrism in adolescence. *Child Development, 38*(4), 1025–1034.

Elrod, S. S. (2010). Seniors return to retirement jobs. *Senior Citizen Journal*, 18 November.

Erikson, E. H. (1959). Identity and the life cycle: Selected papers. *Psychological Issues, 1*, 1–171.

Erikson, E. H. (1984). Reflections on the last stage: And the first. *Psychoanalytic Study of Children, 39*, 155–165.

Erikson, E. H. (1985). *The Life Cycle Completed: A review*. New York: W. W. Norton.

Etaugh, C. (2008). Women in the middle and later years. In F. L. Denmark & M. A. Paludi (eds), *Psychology of Women: A handbook of issues and theories* (2nd edn, pp. 271–302). Westport, CT: Praeger Publishers/Greenwood Publishing Group.

Fanti, K. A. & Henrich, C. C. (2010). Trajectories of pure and co-occurring internalizing and externalizing problems from age 2 to age 12: Findings from the national institute of child health and human development study of early child care. *Developmental Psychology, 46*(5), 1159–1175.

FAS (Focus Adolescent Services). (2008). *Teen violence*, http://www.focusas.com/Violence.html, accessed 5 November 2012.

Flouri, E., Hickey, J., Mavroveli, S., & Hurry, J. (2011). Adversity, emotional arousal, and problem behaviour in adolescence: The role of non-verbal cognitive ability as a resilience promoting factor. *Child and Adolescent Mental Health, 16*(1), 22–29.

Frank, T. L., Turenshine, H., & Sullivan, S. J. (2010). Birth order's effect on personality, intelligence, and achievement: Same-family siblings. Conference Abstract. Annual Convention of American Psychology Association.

Freund, A. M. & Lamb, M. E. (2010). Social and emotional development across the life span. In M. E. Lamb, A. M. Freund, & R. M. Lerner (eds), *The Handbook of Life-Span Development, Vol. 2: Social and emotional development* (pp. 1–8). Hoboken, NJ: John Wiley & Sons, Inc.

Frey, K. S., Hirschstein, M. K., Snell, J. L., Edstrom, L. V., MacKenzie, E. P., & Broderick, C. J. (2005). Reducing playground bullying and supporting beliefs: An experimental trial of the Steps to Respect program. *Developmental Psychology, 41*, 479–491.

Gadsden, V. & Ray, A. (2003). Father's role in children's academic achievement and early literacy. *ERIC Clearinghouse on Early Education and Parenting*, http://www. ericdigests.org/2004-3/role.html, accessed 15 December 2012.

Garandeau, C. & Cillessen, A. H. N. (2006). From indirect aggression to invisible aggression: A conceptual view on bullying and peer group manipulation. *Aggression and Violent Behaviour, 11*, 612–625.

Gibbs, J. C., Basinger, K. S., Grime, R. L., & Snarey, J. R. (2007). Moral judgment development across cultures: Revisiting Kohlberg's universality claims. *Developmental Review, 27*, 443–500.

Gilligan, C. (1993). *In a Different Voice.* Cambridge, MA: Harvard University Press.

González, A. R. A., Escobar-Córdoba, F., & Castañeda, G. C. (2007). Factores de riesgo para violencia y homicidio juvenil. [Risk factors for juvenile violence and homicide.] *Revista Colombiana de Psiquia-tria, 36*(1), 78–97.

Gonzalez, T. (2010). Review of why kids kill: Inside the minds of school shooters. *Professional School Counseling, 13*(5), 281–282.

Hartup, W. W. (1996). The company they keep: Friendships and their developmental significance. *Child Development, 67*, 1–13.

Hendry, L. B. & Kloep, M. (2007). Conceptualising emerging adulthood: Inspecting the emperor's new clothes? *Child Development Perspectives, 1*(2), 74–79.

Hendry, L. B. & Kloep, M. (2010). How universal is emerging adulthood? An empirical example. *Journal of Youth Studies, 13*(2), 169–179.

Henderson, H. A. & Wachs, T. D. (2007). Temperament theory and the study of cognitive-emotion interactions across development. *Developmental Review, 27*, 396–427.

Hill, N.E., Castellino, D. R., Lansford, J. E., Nowlin, P., Dodge, K. A., Bates, J. E., & Pettit, G. S. (2004). Parent academic involvement as related to school behaviour, achievement, and aspirations: Demographic variations across adolescence. *Child Development, 75*, 1491–1509.

Hinshaw, S. P. (2002). Process, mechanism, and explanation related to externalizing behavior in developmental psychopathology. *Journal of Abnormal Child Psychology, 30*, 431–446.

Hinshaw, S. P. (2008). Developmental psychopathology as a scientific discipline: Relevance to behavioral and emotional disorders of childhood and adolescence. In T. P. Beauchaine & S. P. Hinshaw (eds), *Child and Adolescent Psychopathology* (pp. 3–26). Hoboken, NJ: John Wiley & Sons, Inc.

Holcomb, T. F. (2010). Transitioning into retirement as a stressful life event. In T. W. Miller (ed.), *Handbook of Stressful Transitions across the Lifespan* (pp. 133–146). New York: Springer Science + Business Media.

Howes, C. (1999). Attachment relationships in the context of multiple caregivers. In J. Cassidy & P. R. Shaver (eds), *Handbook of Attachment: Theory, research, and clinical applications* (pp. 671–687). New York: Guilford Press.

Hudziak, J. & Bartels, M. (2008). Genetic and environmental influences on wellness, resilience, and psychopathology: A family-based approach for promotion, prevention, and intervention. In J. J. Hudziak (ed.), *Developmental Psychopathology and Wellness: Genetic and environmental influences* (pp. 267–286). Arlington, VA: American Psychiatric Publishing.

Hughes, D. A. (2009). *Attachment-Focused Parenting: Effective strategies to care for children.* New York: W. W. Norton.

Jacobs, A. K. (2008). Components of evidence-based interventions for bullying and peer victimization. In R. G. Steele, T. D. Elkin, & M. C. Roberts (eds), *Handbook of Evidence-Based Therapies for Children and Adolescents: Bridging science and practice.* New York: Springer.

Jaffee, S. R., Moffit, T. E., Caspi, A., & Taylor, A. (2003). Life with (or without) father: The benefits of living with two biological parents depend on the father's antisocial behaviour. *Child Development, 74*, 109–126.

Jaswal, V. K., Carrington Croft, A., Setia, A. R., & Cole, C. A. (2010). Young children have a specific, highly robust bias to trust testimony. *Psychological Science, 21*(10), 1541–1547.

Jefferson, T., Herbst, J. H., & McCrae, R. R. (1998). Associations between birth order and personality traits: Evidence from self-report and observer ratings. *Journal of Research in Personality, 32*, 498–502.

Jensen, L. A. (ed.) (2011). *Bridging Cultural and Developmental Approaches to Psychology: New syntheses in theory, research, and policy.* New York: Oxford University Press.

Kagan, J. (2001). Biological constraint, cultural variety, and psychological structures. In A. Harrington (ed.), *Unity of Knowledge: The convergence of natural and human science* (pp. 177–190). New York: New York Academy of Sciences.

Kagan, J. (2008). Behavioral inhibition as a risk factor for psychopathology. In T. P. Beauchaine & S. P. Hinshaw (eds), *Child and Adolescent Psychopathology* (pp. 157–179). Hoboken, NJ: John Wiley & Sons, Inc.

Kagan, J. (2010). Emotions and temperament. In M. H. Bornstein (ed.), *Handbook of Cultural Developmental Science* (pp. 175–194). New York: Psychology Press.

Kluger, J. (2007). The power of birth order. *Time*, 29 October.

Kohlberg, L. (1963). The development of children's orientations toward a moral order: I: Sequence in the development of moral thought. *Vita Humana, 6*(1–2), 11–33.

Kohlberg, L. (1994). The claim to moral adequacy of a highest stage of moral judgment. In B. Puka (ed.), *The Great Justice Debate: Kohlberg criticism* (pp. 2–18). New York: Garland Publishing.

Kohlberg, L. (2008). The development of children's orientations toward a moral order: I: Sequence in the development of moral thought. *Human Development, 51*(1), 8–20.

Krebs, D. L. & Denton, K. (2006). Explanatory limitations of cognitive-developmental approaches to morality. *Psychological Review, 113*, 672–675.

Kroger, J., Martinussen, M., & Marcia, J. E. (2010). Identity status change during adolescence and young adulthood: A meta-analysis. *Journal of Adolescence, 33*(5), 683–698.

Lahey, B. B. & Waldman, I. D. (2007). Personality dispositions and the development of violence and conduct problems. In D. J. Flannery, A. T. Vazsonyi, & I. D. Irwin (eds), *The Cambridge Handbook of Violent Behavior and Aggression* (pp. 260–287). New York: Cambridge University Press.

Lamb, M. E. (2010). How do fathers influence children's development? Let me count the ways. In M. E. Lamb (ed.), *The Role of the Father in Child Development* (5th edn, pp. 1–26). Hoboken, NJ: John Wiley & Sons, Inc.

Lamb, M. E. & Day, R. D. (eds) (2004). *Conceptualizing and Measuring Father Involvement.* Mahwah, NJ: Lawrence Erlbaum Associates.

Laslett, P. (1994). The Third Age, the Fourth Age and the Future. *Ageing and Society, 14*(3), 436–447, http://journals.cambridge.org/action/display Abstract;jsessionid=46B9A35929BEA0542C9B86B46BC24D1A.jour nals?fromPage=online&aid=2019044, accessed 22 March 2012.

Leung, K., Lau, S., & Lam, W. L. (1998). Parenting styles and academic achievement: A crosscultural study. *Merrill-Palmer Quarterly, 44*, 157–172.

Levinson, D. (1986a). *The Seasons of a Man's Life.* Random House Publishing.

Levinson, D. J. (1986b). Conception of adult development. *American Psychologist, 41*(1), 3–13.

Lewis, C. & Lamb M. E. (2003). Fathers' influences on child development: The evidence from two-parent families. *European Journal of Psychology of Education, 18*(2), 211–228.

Litschge, C. M., Vaughn, M. G., & McCrea, C. (2010). The empirical status of treatments for children and youth with conduct problems: An overview of meta-analytic studies. *Research on Social Work Practice, 20*(1), 21–35.

Locke, L. M. & Prinz, R. J. (2002). Measurement of parental discipline and nurturance. *Clinical Psychology Review, 22*, 895–929.

Maccoby, E. E. (2000). Parenting and its effects on children: On reading and misreading behaviour genetics. *Annual Review of Psychology, 51*, 1–27.

Main, M. & Solomon, J. (1990). Discovery of a new, insecure-disorganized/disoriented attachment pattern. In T. B. Brazelton & M. Yogman (eds), *Affective Development in Infancy* (pp. 121–160). Norwood, NJ: Ablex.

Main, M., Hesse, E., & Kaplan, N. (2005). Predictability of attachment behavior and representational processes at 1, 6, and 19 years of age: The Berkeley longitudinal study. In K. E. Grossmann, K. Grossmann, & E. Waters (eds), *Attachment from Infancy to Adulthood: The major longitudinal studies* (pp. 245–304). New York: Guilford Press.

Marcia, J. E. (1994). The empirical study of ego identity. In H. A. Bosma, T. L. G. Graafsma, H. D. Grotevant, & D. J. de Levita (eds), *Identity and Development: An interdisciplinary approach* (pp. 67–80). Thousand Oaks, CA: Sage Publications.

Marcia, J. E. (2007). Theory and measure: The identity status interview. In M. Watzlawik & A. Born (eds), *Capturing Identity: Quantitative and qualitative methods* (pp. 1–14). Lanham, MD: University Press of America.

Marcia, J. E. (2010). Life transitions and stress in the context of psychosocial development. In T. W. Miller (ed.), *Handbook of Stressful Transitions across the Lifespan* (pp. 19–34). New York: Springer Science + Business Media.

Mascaro, O. & Sperber, D. (2009). The moral, epistemic, and mindreading components of children's vigilance towards deception. *Cognition, 112*, 367–380.

Mitchell, C. M., Kaufman, C. E., & Beals, J. (2004). Equifinality and multifinality as guides for prevention interventions: HIV risk/protection among American Indian young adults. *Journal of Primary Prevention, 25*(4), 491–510.

Mueser, K. T., Crocker, A. G., Frisman, L. B., Drake, R. E., Covell, N. H., & Essock, S. M. (2006). Conduct disorder and antisocial personality disorder in persons with severe psychiatric and substance use disorders. *Schizophrenia Bulletin, 32*(4), 626–636.

Munekata, H. & Ninomiya, K. (1985). Development of prosocial moral judgements. *Japanese Journal of Educational Psychology, 33*, 157–164.

Murray, J. & Farrington, D. P. (2010). Risk factors for conduct disorder and delinquency: Key findings from longitudinal studies. *Canadian Journal of Psychiatry/La Revue Canadienne De Psychiatrie, 55*(10), 633–642.

Nelson, J. K. & Bennett, C. S. (2008). Introduction: Special issue on attachment. *Clinical Social Work Journal, 36*, 3–7.

Newland, L. A. & Coyle, D. D. (2010). Fathers' role as attachment figures: An interview with Sir Richard Bowlby. *Early Child Development and Care, 180*(1–2), 25–32.

Newton, P., Reddy, V., & Bull, R. (2000). Children's everyday deception and performance on false-belief tasks. *British Journal of Developmental Psychology, 18*, 297–317.

NFI (National Fatherhood Initiative). (2009). *The Father Factor: Facts of fatherhood*, http://www.fatherhood.org/media/consequences-of-father-absence-statistics, accessed 9 December 2012.

Nishina, A., Juvonen, J., & Witkow, M. R. (2005). Sticks and stones may break my bones, but names will make me feel sick. The psychosocial, somatic, and scholastic consequences of peer harassment. *Journal of Clinical Child and Adolescent Psychology, 34*(1), 37–48.

O'Connor, T. G. (2002). Annotation: The 'effects' of parenting reconsidered: Findings, challenges, and applications. *Journal of Child Psychology and Psychiatry, 43*, 555–572.

Office for National Statistics (2010). *UK Population Estimate*, http://www.ons.gov.uk/ons/publications/all-releases.html?definition=tcm:77-22371, accessed 3 November 2012.

Oppenheim, D., Sagi, A., & Lamb, M.E. (1988). Infant–adult attachments on the kibbutz and their relation to socioemotional development four years later. *Developmental Psychology, 24*, 427–433.

Osgood, D. W., Foster, E. M., Flanagan, C., & Ruth, G. R. (2005). *On Your Own without a Net: The transition to adulthood for vulnerable populations.* University of Chicago Press.

Panko, T. L. (2005). *Pathways from childhood conduct problems to adult criminality.* Student paper at Rochester Institute of Technology.

Patterson, C. J. (2000). Family relationships of lesbians and gay men. *Journal of Marriage and the Family, 62*, 1052–1069.

Pellegrini, A. D. & Blatchford, P. (2002). The development and educational significance of breaktime in school. *Psychologist, 15*, 59–62.

Phinney, J. S. & Baldelomar, O. A. (2011). Identity development in multiple cultural contexts. In L. A. Jensen (ed.), *Bridging Cultural and Developmental Approaches to Psychology: New syntheses in theory, research, and policy* (pp. 161–186). New York: Oxford University Press.

Piaget, J. (1965). *The Moral Judgement of the Child.* New York: Free Press.

Piaget, J. (1985). *The Equilibration of Cognitive Structures: The central problem of intellectual development* (T. Brown & K. Thampy, Trans). Chicago: University of Chicago Press.

Pong, S., Johnston, J., & Chen, V. (2010). Authoritarian parenting and Asian adolescent school performance: Insights from the U.S. and Taiwan. *International Journal of Behavioral Development, 34*(1), 62–72.

Rigby, K. & Bauman, S. (2010). How school personnel tackle cases of bullying. In S. R. Jimerson, S. M. Swearer, & D. L. Espelage (eds), *Handbook of Bullying in Schools: An international perspective* (pp. 455–467). New York: Routledge/Taylor & Francis Group.

Rubino, G. (2011). *Couples without children vs. couples with children.* eHow: Relationships & Family, http://www.ehow.com/info_7904316_couples-children-vs-couples-children.html, accessed 5 November 2012.

Rutter, M. (1981). *Maternal Deprivation Reassessed* (2nd edn). Harmondsworth: Penguin.

Sameroff, A. J. & Chandler, M. J. (1975). Reproductive risk and the continuum of caretaking casualty. In Harrowitz, F. D., Scarr-Salapatek, S., & Siegel, G. (eds), *Review of Child Development Research*, pp. 187–244, Vol. 4. University of Chicago Press.

Santostefano, S. (2010). Developmental psychopathology: Self, embodiment, meaning: A holistic-systems perspective. In W. F. Overton & R. M. Lerner (eds), *The Handbook of Life-Span Development, Vol. 1: Cognition, biology, and methods* (pp. 792–836). Hoboken, NJ: John Wiley & Sons, Inc.

Skinner, N. F. & Fox-Francoeur, C. (2010). Personality implications of adaption-innovation: V: Birth order as a determinant of cognitive style. *Social Behavior and Personality, 38*(2), 237–240.

Skuse, D. H. (1993) Extreme deprivation in early childhood. In D. Bishop & K. Mogford (eds), *Language Development in Exceptional Circumstances* (pp. 29–46). Hove: Lawrence Erlbaum Associates.

Smith, P. K. (2010). Bullying in primary and secondary schools: Psychological and organizational comparisons. In S. R. Jimerson, S. M. Swearer, & D. L. Espelage (eds), *Handbook of Bullying in Schools: An international perspective* (pp. 137–150). New York: Routledge/Taylor & Francis Group.

Smith, P. K. & Slonje, R. (2010). Cyberbullying: The nature and extent of a new kind of bullying, in and out of school. In S. R. Jimerson, S. M. Swearer, & D. L. Espelage (eds), *Handbook of Bullying in Schools: An international perspective* (pp. 249–262). New York: Routledge/Taylor & Francis Group.

Smith, P. K., Mahdavi, J., Carvalho, M., Fisher, S., Russell, S., & Tippet, N. (2008) Cyberbullying: Its nature and impact in secondary schools. *Journal of Child Psychology and Psychiatry, 49*(4), 376–385.

Snarey, J. R. (1985). Cross-cultural universality of social-moral development: A critical review of Kohlbergian research. *Psychological Bulletin, 97*, 202–232.

Sodian, B. (1991). The development of deception in young children. *British Journal of Developmental Psychology, 9*, 173–188.

Solantaus, T. & Salo, S. (2005). Paternal postnatal depression: Fathers emerge from the wings. *Lancet, 365*, 2158–2159.

Sternberg, R. J. (1998). A balance theory of wisdom. *Review of General Psychology, 2*(4), 347–365.

Takahashi, K. (1990). Are the key assumptions of the 'strange situation' procedure universal? A view from Japanese research. *Human Development, 33*, 23–30.

Talwar, V. & Lee, K. (2002). Development of lying to conceal a transgression: Children's control of expressive behaviour during verbal deception. *International Journal of Behavioral Development, 26*, 436–444.

Talwar, V., Murphy S., & Lee, K. (2007). White lie-telling in children. *International Journal of Behavioral Development, 31*, 1–11.

Tamis-LeMonda, C. & Cabrera, N. (eds) (2002). *Handbook of Father Involvement*. Mahwah, NJ: Lawrence Erlbaum Associates.

Taylor, J., Iacono, W. G., & McGue, M. (2000). Evidence for a genetic etiology of early-onset delinquency. *Journal of Abnormal Psychology, 109*, 634–643.

Thompson, A. M. (1986). Adam: A severely deprived Colombian orphan: A case report. *Journal of Child Psychology and Psychiatry, 27*(5), 689–695.

Townsend, F. (2000). Birth order and rebelliousness: Reconstructing the research in *Born to Rebel. Politics and the Life Sciences, 19*(2), 135–156.

Turiel, E. (2010). The development of morality: Reasoning, emotions, and resistance. In W. F. Overton & R. M. Lerner (eds), *The Handbook of Life-Span Development, Vol. 1: Cognition, biology, and methods* (pp. 554–583). Hoboken, NJ: John Wiley & Sons, Inc.

Twemlow, S. W., Fonagay, P., Sacco, F. C. (2003). Modifying social aggression in schools. *Journal of Applied Psychoanalytical Studies, 5*(2), 211–222.

Veríssimo, M., Santos, A. J., Vaughn, B. E., Torres, N., Monteiro, L., & Santos, O. (2011). Quality of attachment to father and mother and number of reciprocal friends. *Early Child Development and Care, 181*(1), 27–38.

Volz, J. (2000). Successful aging: The second 50. *APA Monitor, 31*, 24–28.

Walker, L. J. (2006). Gender and morality. In M. Killen & J. G. Smetana (eds), *Handbook of Moral Development* (pp. 93–115). Mahwah, NJ: Lawrence Erlbaum Associates.

Weaver, C. M., Borkowski, J. G., & Whitman, T. L. (2008). Violence breeds violence: Childhood exposure and adolescent conduct problems. *Journal of Community Psychology, 36*(1), 96–112.

Weinraub, M., Horvath, D. L., & Gringlas, M. B. (2002). Single parenthood. In M. H. Bornstein (ed.), *Handbook of Parenting: Vol. 3: Being and becoming a parent* (2nd edn, pp. 109–140). Mahwah, NJ: Lawrence Erlbaum Associates.

Welsh, E., Buchanan, A., Flouri, E., & Lewis, J. (2004). *'Involved' Fathering and Child Well-Being: Fathers' involvement with secondary school age children*. National Children's Bureau for the Rowntree Foundation Parenting in Practice series.

CHAPTER 5

Abosch, A. & Cosgrove, G. R. (2008). Biological basis for the surgical treatment of depression. *Neurosurgical Focus, 25*(1), E2.

Anderson, S. W., Bechara, A., Damasio, H., Tranel, D., & Damasio, A. R. (1999). Impairment of social and moral behavior related to early damage in human prefrontal cortex. *Nature Neuroscience, 2*(11), 103–107.

Angulo, M. C., Le Meur, K., Kozlov, A. S., Charpak, S., & Audinat, E. (2008). GABA: A forgotten gliotransmitter. *Progress in Neurobiology, 86*, 297–303.

Archer, T. (2011). Physical exercise alleviates debilities of normal aging and Alzheimer's disease. *Acta Neurologica Scandinavica, 123*, 221–238.

Archer, T. (2012). Influence of traumatic exercise on traumatic brain injury deficits: scaffolding effect. *Neurotoxicity Research, 21*(4), 418–434.

Archer, T. & Fredriksson, A. (2011). Delayed exercise-induced functional and neurochemical partial restoration following MPTP. *Neurotoxicity Research, 21*(2), 210–21.

Archer, T. & Fredriksson, A. (2010). Physical exercise attenuates MPTP-induced deficits in mice. *Neurotoxicity Research, 18*(3–4), 313–327.

Archer, T., Fredriksson, A., & Johansson, B. (2011a). Exercise alleviates parkinsonism. Clinical and laboratory evidence. *Acta Neurologica Scandinavica, 123*, 73–84.

Archer, T., Fredriksson, A., Schütz, E., & Kostrewa, R. M. (2011b). Influence of physical exercise on neuroimmunological functioning and health: Aging and stress. *Neurotoxicity Research, 20*(1), 69–83.

Archer, T. & Kostrzewa, R. M. (2011). Physical exercise alleviates ADHD symptoms: Regional deficits and developmental trajectory. *Neurotoxicity Research, 21*(2), 195–209.

Archer, T., Kostrzewa, R. M., Beninger, R. J., & Palomo, T. (2010). Staging perspectives in neurodevelopmental aspects of neuropsychiatry: Agents, phases and ages at expression. *Neurotoxicity Research, 18*(3–4), 287–305.

Archer, T., Svensson, K., & Alricsson, M. (2012). Physical exercise ameliorates deficits induced by traumatic brain injury. *Acta Neurologica Scandinavica, 125*(5), 293–302.

Barnabé-Heider, F. & Frisén, J. (2008). Stem cells for spinal cord repair. *Cell Stem Cell, 3*, 16–24.

Bédard, P. & Sanes, J. N. (2009). Gaze and hand position effects on finger movement related human brain activation. *Journal of Neurophysiology, 101*(2), 834–842.

Borg, J., Roe, C., Nordenbo, A., Andelic, N., de Boussard, C., & Geigerstam, J. L. (2011). Trends and challenges in the early rehabilitation of patients with traumatic brain injury: A Scandinavian perspective. *American Journal of Physical Medicine & Rehabilitation, 90*, 65–73.

Botvinick, M.M., Braver, T. S., Barch, D. M., Carter, C. S., & Cohen, J. D. (2001). Conflict monitoring and cognitive control. *Psychological Review, 108*, 624–652.

Brain Injury Group. (2012). *Brain Injury Facts & Figures: 'The Unfortunate Truth'*, http://www.braininjurygroup.co.uk/facts-&-figures.htm, accessed 10 November 2012.

Cameron, H. A. & McKay, R. D. (2001). Adult neurogenesis produces a large pool of new granule cells in the dentate gyrus. *Journal of Comparative Neurology, 435*, 406–417.

Cenci, M. A. (2007). Dopamine dysregulation of movement control in L-DOPA-induced dyskinesia. *Trends in Neuroscience, 30*, 236–243.

Clark, P. J., Kohman, R. A., Miller, D. S., Bhattacharya, T. K., Brzezinska, W. J., & Rhodes, J. S. (2011). Genetic influences on exercise-induced adult hippocampal neurogenesis across 12 divergent mouse strains. *Genes, Brain and Behavior, 10*(3), 345–53. DOI: 10.1111/j.1601-183X.2010.00674.x.

Cooke, B. M. & Woolley, C. S. (2005). Gonadal hormone modulation of dendrites in the mammalian CNS. *Journal of Neurobiology, 64*, 34–46.

Costa-Mattioli, M., Sossin, W. S., Klann, E., & Sonenberg, N. (2009). Translational control of long-lasting synaptic plasticity and memory. *Neuron, 61*, 10–26.

Damasio, H., Tranel, D., Grabowski, T., Adolphs, R., & Damasio, A. (2004). Neural systems behind word and concept retrieval. *Cognition, 92*, 179–229.

Donaldson, Z. R. & Young, L. J. (2008). Oxytocin, vasopressin, and the neurogenetics of sociality. *Science, 322*, 900–904.

Fordyce, D. E. & Wehner, J. M. (1993). Physical activity enhances spatial learning performance with associated alteration in hippocampal protein kinase C activity in C57BL/6 and DBA/2 mice. *Brain Research, 619*, 111–119.

Franklin, R. J. & Ffrench-Constant, C. (2008). Remyelination in the CNS: From biology to therapy. *Nature Reviews Neuroscience, 9*, 839–855.

Fredriksson, A., Stidsdotter, I. M., Hurtig, A., Ewalds-Kvist, B., & Archer, T. (2011). Running wheel activity restores MPTP-induced deficits. *Journal of Neural Transmission, 118*(3), 407–420.

Gazzaniga, M. S. (2005). Forty-five years of split-brain research and still going strong. *Nature Reviews Neuroscience, 6*(8), 653–659.

Goto Y. & Grace, A. A. (2008). Limbic and cortical information processing in the nucleus accumbens. *Trends in Neurosciences, 31*, 552–558.

Gould, E. (2007). Structural plasticity. In P. Andersen, R. Morris, D. Amaral, T. Bliss & J. O'Keefe (eds), *The Hippocampus Book*. New York: Oxford University Press.

Grahn, J. A., Parkinson, J. A., & Owen, A. M. (2008). The cognitive functions of the caudate nucleus. *Progress in Neurobiology, 86*, 141–155.

Graziano, M. S. (2006). The organization of behavioral repertoire in motor cortex. *Annual Review of Neuroscience, 29*, 105–134.

Gross, C. G. (2005). Processing the facial image: A brief history. *American Psychologist, 60*, 755–763.

Heller, A. C., Amar, A. P., Liu, C. Y., & Apuzzo, M. L. (2006). Surgery of the mind and mood: A mosaic of issues in time and evolution. *Neurosurgery, 59*, 720–733.

Hovakimyan, M., Haas, S. J., Schmitt, O., Gerber, B., Wree, A., & Andressen, C. (2008). Mesencephalic human neural progenitor cells transplanted into the adult hemiparkinsonian rat striatum lack dopaminergic differentiation but improve motor behavior. *Cells Tissues Organs, 188*, 373–383.

Isacson, O. & Kordower, J. H. (2008). Future of cell and gene therapies for Parkinson's disease. *Annals of Neurology, 2*, S122–138.

Jankovic, J. & Aguilar, L. G. (2008). Current approaches to the treatment of Parkinson's disease. *Neuropsychiatric Disease and Treatment, 4*, 743–757.

Johnson, S. C., Farnworth, T., Pinkston, J. B., Bigler, E. D., & Blatter, D. D. (1994). Corpus callosum surface area across the human adult lifespan: Effect of age and gender. *Brain Research Bulletin, 35*(4), 373–377.

Jones, E. G. (2007). Neuroanatomy: Cajal and after Cajal. *Brain Research Reviews, 55*, 248–255.

Kannangara, T. S., Lucero, M. J., Gil-Mohapel, J., Drapala, R. J., Simpson, J. M., Christie, B. R., & van Praag, H. (2011). Running reduces stress and enhances cell genesis in aged mice. *Neurobiology of Aging, 32*, 2279–2286.

Knott, G. W., Holtmaat, A., Wilbrecht, L., Welker, E., & Svoboda, K. (2006). Spine growth precedes synapse formation in the adult neo-cortex in vivo. *Nature Neuroscience, 9*, 1117–1124.

Kramer, A. F., Hahn, S., Cohen, N. J., Banich, M. T., McAuley, E., Harrison, C. R., Chason, J., Vakil, E., Bardell, L., Boileau, R. A., & Colcombe, A. (1999). Ageing, fitness and neurocognitive function. *Nature, 400*(6743), 418–419.

Kuhn, H. G., Dickinson-Anson, H., & Gage, F. H. (1996). Neurogenesis in the dentate gyrus of the adult rat: Age-related decrease of neuronal progenitor proliferation. *Journal of Neuroscience, 16*, 2027–2033.

Lashley, K. S. (1929). *Brain Mechanisms and Intelligence: A quantitative study of injuries to the brain.* University of Chicago Press.

Laslo, P., Lipski, J., Nicholson, L. F., Miles, G. B., & Funk, G. D. (2001). GluR2 AMPA receptor subunit expression in motoneurons at low and high risk for degeneration in amyotrophic lateral sclerosis. *Experimental Neurobiology, 169*, 461–471.

LeDoux, J. (2007). The amygdala. *Current Biology, 17*, R868–874.

Leuner, B., Gould, E., & Shors, T. J. (2006). Is there a link between adult neurogenesis and learning? *Hippocampus, 16*(3), 216–224.

Levi-Montalcini, R. (1988). *In Praise of Imperfection: My life and work.* New York: Basic Books.

Lowry, C. A., Hale, M. W., Evans, A. K., Heerkens, J., Staub, D. R., Gasser, P. J., & Shekhar, A. (2008). Serotonergic systems, anxiety, and affective disorder: Focus on the dorsomedial part of the dorsal raphe nucleus. *Annals of the New York Academy of Sciences, 1148*, 86–94.

Luo, L. & O'Leary, D. D. (2005). Axon retraction and degeneration in development and disease. *Annual Review of Neuroscience, 28*, 127–156.

Mannen, T., Iwata, M., Toyokura, Y., & Nagashima, K. (1982). The Onufs' nucleus and the external anal sphincter muscles in amyotrophic lateral sclerosis and Shy-Drager syndrome. *Acta Neuropathologica, 58*, 255–260.

Marín, O. & Rubenstein, J. L. (2003). Cell migration in the forebrain. *Annual Review of Neuroscience, 26*, 441–483.

McEwen, B. S. (2001). Plasticity of the hippocampus: Adaptation to chronic stress and allostatic load. *Annals of the New York Academy of Sciences, 933*, 265–277.

Moser, E. I., Kropff, E., & Moser, M. B. (2008). Place cells, grid cells, and the brain's spatial representation system. *Annual Review of Neuroscience, 31*, 69–89.

Nestler, E. J. (2004). Molecular mechanisms of drug addiction. *Neuropharmacology, 1*, 24–32.

Paulsen, J. S. (2009, January 3). Functional imaging in Huntington's disease. *Experimental Neurobiology.* [Epub ahead of print.]

Pereira, A. C., Huddleston, D. E., Brickman, A. M., Sosunov, A. A., Hen, R., McKhann, G. M., Sloan, R., Gage, F. H., Brown, T. R., & Small, S. A. (2007). An in vivo correlate of exercise-induced neurogenesis in the adult dentate gyrus. *Proceedings of the National Academy of Sciences of the United States of America, 104*, 5638–5643.

Perneczky, R., Drzezga, A., Boecker, H., Ceballos-Baumann, A. O., Granert, O., Förstl, H., Kurz, A., & Häussermann, P. (2008). Activities of daily living, cerebral glucose metabolism, and cognitive reserve in Lewy body and Parkinson's disease. *Dementia and Geriatric Cognitive Disorders, 26*, 475–481.

Rafii, M. S. & Aisen, P. S. (2009). Recent developments in Alzheimer's disease therapeutics. *BMC Medicine, 7*, 7.

Seeck, M., Mainwaring, N., Ives, J., Blume, H., Dubuisson, D., Cosgrove, R., Mesulam, M. M., & Schomer, D. L. (1993). Differential neural activity in the human temporal lobe evoked by faces of family members and friends. *Annals of Neurology, 34*, 369–372.

Sheline, Y. I., Gado, M. H., & Kraemer, H. C. (2003). Untreated depression and hippocampal volume loss. *American Journal of Psychiatry, 160*, 1516–1518.

Soto, D., Hodsoll, J., Rotshtein, P., & Humphreys, G. W. (2008). Automatic guidance of attention from working memory. *Trends in Cognitive Sciences, 12*, 342–348.

Squire, L. R., Stark, C. E., & Clark, R. E. (2004). The medial temporal lobe. *Annual Review of Neuroscience, 27*, 279–306.

Srivastava, A. S., Malhotra, R., Sharp, J., & Berggren, T. (2008). Potentials of ES cell therapy in neurodegenerative diseases. *Current Pharmaceutical Design, 14*, 3873–3879.

Steller, H. (1995). Mechanisms and genes of cellular suicide. *Science, 267*, 1445–1449.

Stranahan, A. M., Khalil, D., & Gould, E. (2006). Social isolation delays the positive effects of running on adult neurogenesis. *Nature Neuroscience, 9*, 526–533.

Stranahan, A. M., Khalil, D., & Gould, E. (2007). Running induces widespread structural alterations in the hippocampus and entorhinal cortex. *Hippocampus, 17*, 1017–1022.

Takahashi, J., Takagi, Y., & Saiki, H. (2009). Transplantation of embryonic stem cell-derived dopaminergic neurons in MPTP-treated monkeys. *Methods in Molecular Biology, 482*, 199–212.

Urry, H. L., Nitschke, J. B., Dolski, I., Jackson, D. C., Dalton, K. M., Mueller, C. J., Rosenkranz, M. A., Ryff, C. D., Singer, B. H., & Davidson, R. J. (2004). Making a life worth living: Neural correlates of well-being. *Psychological Science, 15*(6), 367–372.

Viggiano, D., Ruocco, L. A., Arcieri, S., & Sadile, A. G. (2004). Involvement of norepinephrine in the control of activity and attentive processes in animal models of attention deficit hyperactivity disorder. *Neural Plasticity, 11*, 133–149.

CHAPTER 6

Alexander, R. D. (1987). *The Biology of Moral Systems.* Hawthorne, NY: Aldine de Gruyter.

Axelrod, R. & Hamilton, W. D. (1981). The evolution of cooperation. *Science, 221*, 1390–1396.

Bales, K. L. & Carter, C. S. (2003). Developmental exposure to oxytocin facilitates partner preferences in male prairie voles. *Behavioral Neuroscience, 117*, 854–859.

Barclay, P. (2008). Enhanced recognition of defectors depends on their rarity. *Cognition, 107*, 817–828.

Barclay, P. (2010). Altruism as a courtship display: Some effects of third-party generosity on audience perceptions. *British Journal of Psychology, 101*, 123–135.

Barclay, P. & Lalumière, M. L. (2006). Do people differentially remember cheaters? *Human Nature, 17*, 98–113.

Baron-Cohen, S. (2003). *The Essential Difference.* London: Penguin Books.

Barrett, L. & Dunbar, R. I. M. (1994). Not now, dear, I'm busy. *New Scientist, 142*, 30–34.

Barton, R. A., Aggleton, J., & Grenyer, R. (2003). Evolutionary coherence of the mammalian amygdala. *Proceedings of the Royal Society B, 270*, 539–544.

Bateman, A. J. (1948). Intra-sexual selection in *Drosophila. Heredity, 2*, 349–368.

Baumgartner, T., Heinrichs, M., Vonlanthen, A., Fischbacher, U., & Fehr, E. (2008). Oxytocin shapes the neural circuitry of trust and trust adaptation in humans. *Neuron, 58*, 639–650.

Berté, N. A. (1988). K'ekchi horticultural labor exchange: Productive and reproductive implications. In L. Betzig, M. Borgerhoff Mulder, & P. Turke (eds), *Human Reproductive Behaviour: A Darwinian perspective* (pp. 83–96). Cambridge: Cambridge University Press.

Betzig, L. & Turke, P. (1986). Food sharing on Ifaluk. *Current Anthropology, 27*, 397–400.

Blackmore, S. (1999). *The Meme Machine*. Oxford: Oxford University Press.

Boyd, R. & Richerson, P. J. (1985). *Culture and the Evolutionary Process*. Chicago, IL: Chicago University Press.

Burnham, T. C., Chapman, J. F., Gray, P. B., McIntyre, M. H., Lipson, S. F., & Ellison, P. T. (2003). Men in committed, romantic relationships have lower testosterone. *Hormones and Behavior, 44*, 119–122.

Buss, D. M. (1989). Sex differences in human mate preferences: Evolutionary hypotheses tested in 37 cultures. *Behavioural and Brain Sciences, 12*, 1–49.

Buss, D. M. (2000). The evolution of happiness. *American Psychologist, 55*(1), 15–23.

Buss, D. M. & Schmitt, D. P. (1993). Sexual strategies theory: An evolutionary perspective on human mating. *Psychological Review, 100*, 204–32.

Campbell, A. (1999). Staying alive: Evolution, culture, and women's intrasexual aggression. *Behavioural and Brain Sciences, 22*, 203–252.

Chiappe, D., Brown, A., & Dow, B. (2004). Cheaters are looked at longer and remembered in social exchange situations. *Evolutionary Psychology, 2*, 108–120.

Chomsky, N. (1957). *Syntactic Structures*. The Hague: Mouton & Co.

Chomsky, N. (1991). Linguistics and cognitive science: Problems and mysteries. In A. Kasher (ed.), *The Chomskyan Turn* (pp. 26–53). Cambridge, MA: Basil Blackwell.

Cosmides, L. & Tooby, J. H. (1992). Cognitive adaptations for social exchange. In J. H. Barkow, L. Cosmides, & J. H. Tooby (eds), *The Adapted Mind* (pp. 163–228). Oxford: Oxford University Press.

Cosmides, L. & Tooby, J. H. (1996). Are humans good intuitive statisticians after all? Rethinking some conclusions from the literature on judgement under uncertainty. *Cognition, 58*, 1–73.

Costa, P. T. & McCrae, R. (1992). Four ways five factors are basic. *Personality and Individual Differences, 13*, 653–665.

Daly, M. & Wilson, M. (1995). Discriminant parental solicitude and the relevance of evolutionary models to the analysis of motivational systems. In M. S. Gazzaniga (ed.), *The Cognitive Neurosciences* (pp. 1269–1286). Cambridge, MA: MIT Press.

Darwin, C. (1859). *On the Origin of Species*. London: Murray.

Darwin, C. (1871). *The Descent of Man and Selection in Relation to Sex*. London: Murray.

Dawkins, R. (1976). *The Selfish Gene*. Oxford: Oxford University Press.

Deacon, T. (1997). *The Symbolic Species: The coevolution of language and the human brain*. Harmondsworth: Allen Lane.

DeBruine, L. M. (2002). Facial resemblance enhances trust. *Proceedings of the Royal Society B, 269*, 1307–1312.

Dennett, D. (1995). *Darwin's Dangerous Idea: Evolution and the meanings of life*. New York: Simon & Schuster.

Domes, G., Heinrichs, M., Michel, A., Berger, C., & Herpertz, S. C. (2007). Oxytocin improves 'mindreading' in humans. *Biological Psychiatry, 6*, 731–733.

Dunbar, R. I. M. (1993). The co-evolution of neocortex size, group size and language in humans. *Behavioral and Brain Sciences, 16*, 681–735.

Dunbar, R. I. M. (1996). *Grooming, Gossip, and the Evolution of Language*. London, Faber & Faber.

Dunbar, R. I. M. (1998). The social brain hypothesis. *Evolutionary Anthropology, 6*, 178–190.

Dunbar, R. I. M., Duncan, N., & Marriott, A. (1997). Human conversational behaviour. *Human Nature, 8*, 231–246.

Durham, W. H. (1991). *Coevolution: Genes, culture and human diversity*. Stanford, CA: Stanford University Press.

Farrelly, D. (2011). Cooperation as a signal of genetic or phenotypic quality in female mate choice? Evidence from preferences across the menstrual cycle. *British Journal of Psychology, 102*, 406–430.

Farrelly, D. & Turnbull, N. (2008). The role of reasoning domain on face recognition: Detecting violations of social contract and hazard management rules. *Evolutionary Psychology, 6*, 523–537.

Farrelly, D., Lazarus, J., & Roberts, G. (2007). Altruists attract. *Evolutionary Psychology, 5*, 313–329.

Fiddick, L. (2004). Domains of deontic reasoning: Resolving the discrepancy between the cognitive and moral reasoning literatures. *Quarterly Journal of Experimental Psychology, 57A*, 447–474.

Fisher, R. A. (1930). *The Genetical Theory of Natural Selection*. Oxford: Clarendon Press.

Gangestad, S. W. & Thornhill, R. (1997). Human sexual selection and developmental instability. In J. A. Simpson & D. T. Kenrick (eds), *Evolutionary Social Psychology* (pp. 169–195). Mahwah, NJ: Lawrence Erlbaum Associates.

Geary, D. C. (2000). Evolution and proximate expression of human paternal investment. *Psychological Bulletin, 126*, 55–77.

Gintis, H., Smith, E. A., & Bowles, S. (2001). Costly signaling and cooperation. *Journal of Theoretical Biology, 213*, 103–119.

Gould, S. J. (1987). *The Limits of Adaptation: Is language a spandrel of the human brain?* Paper presented to the Cognitive Science Seminar, Center for Cognitive Science, MIT, Cambridge, MA.

Gray, P. B., Chapman, J. F., Burnham, T. C., McIntyre, M. H., Lipson, S. F., & Ellison, P. T. (2004). Human male pair bonding and testosterone. *Human Nature, 15*, 119–131.

Griskevicius, V., Tybur, J. M., Sundie, J. M., Cialdini, R. B., Miller, G. F., & Kenrick, D. T. (2007). Blatant benevolence and conspicuous consumption: When romantic motives elicit strategic costly signals. *Journal of Personality and Social Psychology, 93*, 85–102.

Gurven, M. (2004). Reciprocal altruism and food sharing decisions among hunter-gatherers. *Behavioral Ecology and Sociobiology, 56*, 366–380.

Hames, R. (1988). The allocation of parental care among the Ye'kwana. In L. Betzig, M. Borgerhoff Mulder, & P. Turke (eds), *Human Reproductive Behaviour: A Darwinian perspective* (pp. 237–252). Cambridge: Cambridge University Press.

Hamilton, W. D. (1964). The genetical evolution of social behaviour I and II. *Journal of Theoretical Biology, 7*, 1–52.

Henrich, J. & Gil-White, F. J. (2001). The evolution of prestige: Freely conferred deference as a mechanism for enhancing the benefits of cultural transmission. *Evolution and Human Behaviour, 22*, 165–196.

Iredale, W., Van Vugt, M., & Dunbar, R. I. M. (2008). Showing off in humans: Male generosity as a mating signal. *Evolutionary Psychology, 6*, 386–392.

Jensen-Campbell, L. A., Graziano, W. G., & West, S. G. (1995). Dominance, prosocial orientation, and female preferences: Do nice guys really finish last? *Journal of Personality and Social Psychology, 68*, 427–440.

Jonason, P. K., Cetrulo, J. F., Madrid, J. M., & Morrison, C. (2009). Gift-giving for courtship or mate-retention? Insights from animal models. *Evolutionary Psychology, 7*, 89–103.

Kahneman, D. (2011). *Thinking, Fast and Slow*. London: Penguin.

Kenrick, D. T. & Keefe, R. C. (1992). Age preferences in mates reflects sex differences in reproductive strategies. *Behavioural and Brain Sciences, 15*, 75–133.

Kosfeld, M., Heinrichs, M., Zak, P. J., Fischbacher, U., & Fehr, E. (2005). Oxytocin increases trust in humans. *Nature, 435*, 673–676.

Lander, E. S., Linton, L. M., Birren, B., Nusbaum, C., Zody, M. C., Baldwin, J., Devon, K., Dewar, K., Doyle, M., FitzHugh, W. *et al.* (2001). Initial sequencing and analysis of the human genome. *Nature, 409*, 860–921.

Madsen, E. A., Tunney, R. J., Fieldman, G., Plotkin, H. C., Dunbar, R. I. M., Richardson, J. M. *et al.* (2007). Kinship and altruism: A cross-cultural experimental study. *British Journal of Psychology, 98,* 339–360.

Mazur, A. & Booth, A. (1998). Testosterone and dominance in men. *Behavioral and Brain Sciences, 21,* 353–397.

Mazur, A., Susman, E. J., & Edelbrock, S. (1997). Sex differences in testosterone response to a video game contest. *Evolution & Human Behavior, 18,* 317–326.

McGuire, M., Troisi, A., & Raleigh, M. M. (1997). Depression in an evolutionary context. In S. Baron-Cohen (ed.), *The Maladapted Mind* (pp. 255–282). Hove: Psychology Press.

McNamara, J. M., Stephens, P. A., Dall, S. R. X., & Houston, A. I. (2009). Evolution of trust and trustworthiness: Social awareness favours personality differences. *Proceedings of the Royal Society B, 276,* 605–613.

Mealey, L., Daood, C., & Krage, M. (1996). Enhanced memory for faces of cheaters. *Ethology and Sociobiology, 17,* 119–128.

Mehl, B. & Buchner, A. (2008). No enhanced memory for faces of cheaters. *Evolution and Human Behavior, 29,* 35–41.

Miller, G. F. (2000). *The Mating Mind: How sexual choice shaped the evolution of human nature.* London: William Heinemann.

Miller, G. F. (2007). Sexual selection for *moral virtues. Quarterly Review of Biology, 82,* 97–125.

Mock, D. W., Drummond, H., & Stinson, C. H. (1990). Avian siblicide. *American Scientist, 78*(5), 438–449.

Nesse, R. M. & Williams, G. C. (1995). *Evolution and Healing: The new science of Darwinian medicine.* London: Weidenfeld & Nicolson.

Nettle, D. (2006). The evolution of personality variation in humans and other animals. *American Psychologist, 61,* 622–631.

Nettle, D. (2007). Individual differences. In R. I. M. Dunbar & L. Barrett (eds), *Oxford Handbook of Evolutionary Psychology* (pp. 479–490). Oxford: Oxford University Press.

Nowak, M. A. & Sigmund, K. (1998). Evolution of indirect reciprocity by image scoring. *Nature, 393,* 573–577.

Oates, K. & Wilson, M. (2002). Nominal kinship cues facilitate altruism. *Proceedings of the Royal Society B, 269,* 105–109.

Oda, R. (1997). Biased face recognition in the prisoner's dilemma game. *Evolution and Human Behavior, 18,* 309–315.

Packer, C. (1977). Reciprocal altruism in *Papio anubis. Nature, 265,* 441–443.

Penke, L., Denissen, J. J. A., & Miller, G. F. (2007). The evolutionary genetics of personality. *European Journal of Personality, 21,* 549–587.

Petrie, M., Halliday, T., & Sanders, C. (1991). Peahens prefer peacocks with elaborate trains. *Animal Behaviour, 41,* 323–331.

Pinker, S. (1994). *The Language Instinct.* New York: Morrow.

Pinker, S. & Bloom, P. (1990). Natural language and natural selection. *Behavioral and Brain Sciences, 13,* 707–784.

Price, J. S., Sloman, L., Gardner, R., Gilbert, P., & Rodhe, P. (1994). The social competition hypothesis of depression. *British Journal of Psychiatry, 164,* 309–35.

Rizzolatti, G., Fadiga, L., Fogassi, L., & Gallese, V. (1996). Premotor cortex and the recognition of motor actions. *Cognitive Brain Research, 3,* 131–141.

Roberts, G. (1998). Competitive altruism: From reciprocity to the handicap principle. *Proceedings of the Royal Society B, 265,* 427–431.

Roney, J. R., Mahler, S. V., & Maestripieri, D. (2003). Behavioral and hormonal responses of men to brief interactions with women. *Evolution and Human Behavior, 24,* 365–375.

Scott-Phillips, T. C., Dickins, T. E., & West, S. A. (2011). Evolutionary theory and the ultimate/proximate distinction in the human behavioural sciences. *Perspectives on Psychological Science, 6,* 38–47.

Sear, R. & Mace, R. (2008). Who keeps children alive? A review of the effects of kin on child survival. *Evolution and Human Behaviour, 29*(1), 1–18.

Singh, D. (1993). Adaptive significance of female physical attractiveness: Role of waist-to-hip ratio. *Journal of Personality and Social Psychology, 65,* 292–307.

Smith, E. A. & Bleige Bird, R. (2000). Turtle hunting and tombstone opening: Public generosity as costly signaling. *Evolution and Human Behaviour, 21,* 245–262.

Smith, M. S., Kish, B. J., & Crawford, C. B. (1987). Inheritance of wealth as human kin investment. *Ethology and Sociobiology, 8,* 171–182.

Stone, V., Cosmides, L., Tooby, J., Kroll, N., & Knight, R. T. (2002). Selective impairment of reasoning about social exchange in a patient with bilateral limbic system damage. *Proceedings of the National Academy of Sciences of the United States of America, 99,* 11531–11536.

Sugiyama, L. S., Tooby, J., & Cosmides, L. (2002). Cross-cultural evidence of cognitive adaptations for social exchange among the Shiwiar of Ecuadorian Amazonia. *Proceedings of the National Academy of Sciences of the United States of America, 99,* 11537–11542.

Swanson, L. W. & Petrovich, G. D. (1998). What is the amygdala? *Trends in Neurosciences, 21,* 323–331.

Tessman, I. (1995). Human altruism as a courtship display. *Oikos, 74,* 157–158.

Theodoridou, A., Rowe, A. C., Penton-Voak, I. S., & Rogers, P. J. (2009). Oxytocin and social perception: Oxytocin increases perceived facial trustworthiness and attractiveness. *Hormones & Behavior, 56,* 128–132.

Tinbergen, N. (1951). *The Study of Instinct.* Oxford, Oxford University Press.

Tomasello, M. (1999). *The Cultural Origins of Human Cognition.* Cambridge, MA: Harvard University Press.

Tooby, J. H. & Cosmides, L. (1990). The past explains the present: Emotional adaptations and the structure of ancestral environments. *Ethology and Sociobiology, 11,* 375–424.

Tooby, J. H. & Cosmides, L. (1992). Psychological foundations of culture. In J. H. Barkow, L. Cosmides, & J. H. Tooby (eds), *The Adapted Mind* (pp. 19–136). Oxford: Oxford University Press.

Tovee, M. J. & Cornelissen, P. L. (2001). Female and male perceptions of female physical attractiveness in front view and profile. *British Journal of Psychology, 92,* 391–402.

Trivers, R. L. (1971). The evolution of reciprocal altruism. *Quarterly Review of Biology, 46,* 35–57.

Trivers, R. L. (1972). Parental investment and sexual selection. In B. Campbell (ed.), *Sexual Selection and the Descent of Man* (pp. 139–179). Chicago, IL: Aldine.

Trivers, R. L. (1974). Parent–offspring conflict. *American Zoologist, 14,* 249–264.

van Leengoed, E., Kerker, E., & Swanson, H. H., (1987). Inhibition of postpartum maternal behaviour in the rat by injecting an oxytocin antagonist into the cerebral ventricles. *Journal of Endocrinology, 12,* 275–282.

Wason, P. C. (1966). Reasoning. In B. M. Foss (ed.), *New Horizons in Psychology* (pp. 135–151). Harmondsworth: Penguin.

Wilkinson, G. W. (1984). Reciprocal food sharing in the vampire bat. *Nature, 308,* 181–184.

Williams, G. C. (1966). *Adaptation and Natural Selection: A critique of some current evolutionary thought.* Princeton, NJ: Princeton University Press.

Wilson, E. O. (1975). *Sociobiology: The new synthesis.* Harvard University Press.

Wilson, E. O. (1978). *On Human Nature.* Cambridge, MA: Harvard University Press.

Wilson, M. & Daly, M. (1985). Competitiveness, risk-taking and violence: The young male syndrome. *Ethology and Sociobiology, 6,* 59–73.

Zahavi, A. (1975). Mate selection: A selection for a handicap. *Journal of Theoretical Biology, 53,* 205–214.

Zahavi, A. (1995). Altruism as a handicap: The limitations of kin selection and reciprocity. *Avian Biology, 26,* 1–3.

CHAPTER 7

Accolla, R., Bathellier, B., Petersen, C. C., & Carleton, A. (2007). Differential spatial representation of taste modalities in the rat gustatory cortex. *Journal of Neuroscience, 27,* 1396–1404.

al Absi, M. & Rokke, P. D. (1991). Can anxiety help us tolerate pain? *Pain, 46,* 43–51.

Axelrod, F. B. (2004). Familial dysautonomia. *Muscle & Nerve, 29,* 352–363.

Bakin, J. S., South, D. A., & Weinberger, N. M. (1996). Induction of receptive field plasticity in the auditory cortex of the guinea pig during instrumental avoidance conditioning. *Behavioral Neuroscience, 110*, 905–913.

Balaraman, S. (1962). Color vision research and the trichromatic theory: A historical review. *Psychological Bulletin, 59*, 434–448.

Banks, M. S. & Salapatek, P. (1983). Infant visual perception. In M. M. Haith & J. J. Campos (eds), *Handbook of Psychology* (pp. 435–571). New York: John Wiley & Sons.

Bartoshuk, L. M., Duffy, V. B., & Miller, I. J. (1994). PTC/PROP tasting: Anatomy, psychophysics, and sex effects. *Physiology Behavior, 56*(6), 1165–1171.

Bartoshuk, L. M., Duffy, V. B., Reed, D., & Williams, A. (1996). Supertasting, earaches and head injury: Genetics and pathology alter our taste worlds. *Neuroscience and Biobehavioral Reviews, 20*(1), 79–87.

Battmer, R. D., Linz, B., & Lenarz, T. (2009). A review of device failure in more than 23 years of clinical experience of a cochlear implant program with more than 3,400 implantees. *Otology & Neurotology, 30*, 455–463.

Bermudez, P., Lerch, J. P., Evans, A. C., & Zatorre, R. J. (2009). Neuroanatomical correlates of musicianship as revealed by cortical thickness and voxel-based morphometry. *Cerebral Cortex, 19*, 1583–1596.

Berry, J. W., Poortinga, Y. H., Segall, M. H., & Dasen, P. R. (1992). *Cross-Cultural Psychology, Research and Applications*. New York: Cambridge University Press.

Billock, V. A. & Tsou, B. H. (2010). Seeing forbidden colors. *Scientific American, 302*(2), 72–77.

Björkman, B., Arnér, S., & Hydén, L. C. (2008). Phantom breast and other syndromes after mastectomy: Eight breast cancer patients describe their experiences over time: A 2-year follow-up study. *Journal of Pain 9*, 1018–1025.

Blakemore, S. J., Wolpert, D., & Frith C. (2000). Why can't you tickle yourself? *Neuroreport, 11*(11), R11–R16.

Breivik, H., Collett, B., Ventrafridda, V. Cohen, R., & Gallacher, D. (2006). Survey of chronic pain in Europe: Prevalence, impact on daily life, and treatment. *European Journal of Pain, 10*, 287–333.

Brislin, R. W. & Keating, C. F. (1976). Cultural differences in the perception of a three-dimensional Ponzo illusion. *Journal of Cross-Cultural Psychology, 7*, 397–412.

Buchsbaum, G. & Gottschalk, A. (1983). Trichromacy, opponent colours coding and optimum colour information transmission in the retina. *Proceedings of the Royal Society of London Series B, Containing Papers of a Biological Character, 220*, 89–113.

Buck, L. B. (1996). Information coding in the vertebrate olfactory system. *Annual Review of Neuroscience, 19*, 517–544.

Calder, A. J., Beaver, J. D., Davis, M. H., van Ditzhuijzen, J., Keane, J., & Lawrence, A. D. (2007). Disgust sensitivity predicts the insula and pallidal response to pictures of disgusting foods. *European Journal of Neuroscience, 25*, 3422–3428.

Cetas, J. S., Saedi, T., & Burchiel, K. J. (2008). Destructive procedures for the treatment of nonmalignant pain: A structured literature review. *Journal of Neurosurgery, 109*, 389–404.

Dalton, P. (2000). Psychophysical and behavioral characteristics of olfactory adaptation. *Chemical Senses, 25*, 487–492.

de Villers-Sidani, E., Chang, E. F., Bao, S., & Merzenich, M. M. (2007). Critical period window for spectral tuning defined in the primary auditory cortex (A1) in the rat. *Journal of Neuroscience, 27*, 180–189.

Djordjevic, J., Jones-Gotman, M., De Sousa, K., & Chertkow, H. (2008). Olfaction in patients with mild cognitive impairment and Alzheimer's disease. *Neurobiology of Aging, 29*, 693–706.

Doty, R. I. (1986). Odor-guided behavior in mammals. *Experientia, 42*, 257–271.

Dubé, A. A., Duquette, M., Roy, M., Lepore, F., Duncan, G., & Rainville, P. (2009). Brain activity associated with the electrodermal reactivity to acute heat pain. *Neuroimage, 45*, 169–180.

Farah, M. J., Levinson, K. L., & Klein, K. L. (1995). Face perception and within-category discrimination in prosopagnosia. *Neuropsychologia, 33*, 661–674.

Farbman, A. I. (1997). Injury-stimulated neurogenesis in sensory systems. *Advances in Neurology, 72*, 157–161.

Galanter, E. (1962). Contemporary psychophysics. *The Journal of Applied Psychology, 92*, 1524–1541.

Garcia, E., Godoy-Izquierdo, D., Godoy, J. F., Perez, M., & Lopez-Chicheri, I. (2007). Gender differences in pressure pain threshold in a repeated measures assessment. *Psychology: Health & Medicine, 12*, 567–579.

Gazzaniga, M. S. (1995). The visual analysis of shape and form. *The Cognitive Neurosciences* (pp. 339–350). Cambridge, MA: MIT Press.

Goldstein, E. B. (2010). *Sensation and Perception* (8th edn). Belmont, CA: Wadsworth.

Gosselin, F. & Schyns, P. G. (2003). Superstitious perceptions reveal properties of internal representations. *Psychological Science, 14*(5), 505–509.

Goubet, N., Strasbaugh, K., & Chesney, J. (2007). Familiarity breeds content? Soothing effect of a familiar odor on full-term newborns. *Journal of Developmental and Behavioral Pediatrics, 28*, 189–194.

Grandin, T. & Scariano, M. (1986). *Emergence: Labelled autistic*. Novato, CA: Arena.

Halpern, B. P. (2002). Taste. In S. Yantis & H. Pashler (eds), *Stevens' Handbook of Experimental Psychology: Vol. 1: Sensation and Perception* (3rd edn; pp. 653–690). New York: John Wiley & Sons.

Haxel, B. R., Grant, L., & Mackay-Sim, A. (2008). Olfactory dysfunction after head injury. *Journal of Head Trauma Rehabilitation, 23*, 407–413.

Henry, M. J. & McAuley, J. D. (2010). On the prevalence of congenital amusia. *Music Perception, 27*, 413–418.

Heron, G., McQuaid, M., & Morrice, E. (1995). The Pulfrich effect in optometric practice. *Ophthalmic and Physiological Optics, 21*, 425–429.

Hubel, D. H. & Wiesel, T. N. (1959). Receptive fields of single neurones in the cat's striate cortex. *Journal of Physiology, 148*, 574–591.

Hughes, L. F., McAsey, M. E., Donathan, C. L., Smith, T., Coney, P., & Struble, R. G. (2002). Effects of hormone replacement therapy on olfactory sensitivity: Cross-sectional and longitudinal studies. *Climacteric, 5*, 140–150.

Hupé, J. M., Bordier, C., & Dojat, M. (2011). The neural bases of grapheme-color synesthesia are not localized in real color-sensitive areas. *Cerebral Cortex*. DOI: 10.1093/cercor/bhr236 (online ahead of full publication).

Hyde, M. & Power, D. (2006). Some ethical dimensions of cochlear implantation for deaf children and their families. *Journal of Deaf Studies and Deaf Education, 11*, 102–111.

Johnson, K. (2002). Neural basis of haptic perception. In S. Yantis & H. Pashler (eds), *Stevens' Handbook of Experimental Psychology: Vol. 1: Sensation and Perception* (3rd edn; pp. 537–583). New York: John Wiley & Sons.

Kakigi, R., Hoshiyama, M., Shimojo, M., Naka, D., Yamasaki, H., Watanabe, S., Xiang, J., Maeda, K., Lam, K., Itomi, K., & Nakamura, A. (2000). The somatosensory evoked magnetic fields. *Progress in Neurobiology, 61*, 495–523.

Kaufman, L. & Rock, I. (1989). The moon illusion thirty years later. In M. Hershenson (ed.), *The Moon Illusion* (pp. 193–234). Hillsdale, NJ: Lawrence Erlbaum Associates.

Kelman, L. (2007). The triggers or precipitants of the acute migraine attack. *Cephalalgia, 27*, 394–402.

Knox, P. J. Simmers, A. J., Gray, L. S., & Cleary, M. (2012). An exploratory study: Prolonged periods of binocular stimulation can provide an effective treatment for childhood amblyopia. *Investigative Ophthalmology and Visual Science, 53*(2), 817–824.

Knudson, E. I. (2004). Sensitive periods in the development of the brain and behavior. *Journal of Cognitive Neuroscience, 16*, 1412–1425.

Koivisto Hursti, U. K. (1999). Factors influencing children's food choice. *Annals of Medicine, 1*, 26–32.

Komiyama, O., Wang, K., Svensson, P., Arendt-Nielsen, L., Kawara, M., & De Laat, A. (2009). Ethnic differences regarding sensory, pain, and reflex responses in the trigeminal region. *Clinical Neurophysiology, 120*, 384–389.

Kuboshima-Amemori, S. & Sawaguchi, T. (2007). Plasticity of the primate prefrontal cortex. *Neuroscientist, 13*, 229–240.

Lagercrantz, H. & Changeux, J. P. (2009). The emergence of human consciousness: From fetal to neonatal life. *Pediatric Research, 65*(3), 255–260.

Lanting, C. P., de Kleine, E., & van Dijk, P. (2009). Neural activity underlying tinnitus generation: Results from PET and fMRI. *Hearing Research, 255*, 1–13.

Leekam, S., Nieto, C., Libby, S. J., Wing, L., & Gould, J. (2007). Describing the sensory abnormalities of children and adults with autism. *Journal of Autism and Developmental Disorders, 37*(5), 894–910.

Lehrer, J. (2007). *Proust was a Neuroscientist*. Boston: Houghton Mifflin Harcourt.

Leventhal, E. A., Leventhal, H., Shacham, S., & Easterling, D. V. (1989). Active coping reduces reports of pain from childbirth. *Journal of Consulting and Clinical Psychology, 57*, 365–371.

Li, W., Howard, J. D., Parrish, T. B., & Gottfried, J. A. (2008). Aversive learning enhances perceptual and cortical discrimination of indiscriminable odor cues. *Science, 319*, 1842–1845.

Liem, D. G. & Mennella, J. A. (2003). Heightened sour preferences during childhood. *Chemical Senses, 28*, 173–180.

Liu, F., Xu, Y., Patel, A. D., Francart, T., & Jiang, C. M. (2012). Differential recognition of pitch patterns in discrete and gliding stimuli in congenital amusia: Evidence from Mandarin speakers. *Brain and Cognition, 79*, 209–215.

McEwen, D. P., Jenkins, P. M., & Martens, J. R. (2008). Olfactory cilia: Our direct neuronal connection to the external world. *Current Topics in Developmental Biology, 85*, 333–370.

Mech, L. D. & Boitani, L. (2003). *Wolves: Behavior, ecology, and conservation*. University of Chicago Press.

Melzack, R. (1999). From the gate to the neuromatrix. *Journal of Pain, 6*, S121–126.

Mesulam, M. M. (1981). A cortical network for directed attention and unilateral neglect. *Annals of Neurology, 10*, 309–325.

Milner, A. D. & Goodale, M. A. (1995). *The Visual Brain in Action*. Oxford University Press.

Munger, B. L. & Ide, C. (1988). The structure and function of cutaneous sensory receptors. *Archives of Histology and Cytology, 51*, 1–34.

Nishitani, S., Miyamura, T., Tagawa, M., Sumi, M., Takase, R., Doi, H., Moriuchi, H., & Shinohara, K. (2009). The calming effect of a maternal breast milk odor on the human newborn infant. *Neuroscience Research, 63*, 66–71.

Norgren, R., Hajnal, A., & Mungarndee, S. S. (2006). Gustatory reward and the nucleus accumbens. *Physiology & Behavior, 89*, 531–553.

Numazaki, M. & Tominaga, M. (2004). Nociception and TRP channels. *Current Drug Targets: CNS and Neurological Disorders, 3*, 479–485.

Nunn, J. A., Gregory, L. J., Brammer, M., Williams, S. C. R., Parslow, D. M., Morgan, M. J., Morris, R. G., Bullmore, E. T., Baron-Cohen, S., & Gray, J. A. (2002). Functional magnetic resonance imaging of synesthesia: Activation of V4/V8 by spoken words. *Nature Neuroscience, 5*(4), 371–375.

Pause, B. M., Sojka, B., Krauel, K., Fehm-Wolfsdorf, G., & Ferstl, R. (1996). Olfactory information processing during the course of the menstrual cycle. *Biological Psychology, 44*, 31–54.

Peretz, I., Cummings, S., & Dubé, M. P. (2007). The genetics of congenital amusia (tone deafness): A family-aggregation study. *American Journal of Human Genetics, 81*, 582–588.

Petrescu, N. (2008). Loud music listening. *McGill Journal of Medicine, 11*, 169–176.

Racine, M., Tousignant-Laflamme, Y., Kloda, L. A., Dion, D., Dupuis, G., & Choinière, M. (2012). A systematic literature review of 10 years of research on sex/gender and experimental pain perception: Part 1: Are there really differences between women and men? *Pain, 153*(3), 602–618.

Ramachandran, V. S. (2005). Plasticity and functional recovery in neurology. *Clinical Medicine, 5*, 368–373.

Reddy, L. & Kanwisher, N. (2006). Coding of visual objects in the ventral stream. *Current Opinion in Neurobiology, 16*, 408–414.

Robertson, A. E. & Simmons, D. R. (2012). The relationship between sensory sensitivity and autistic traits in the general population. *Journal of Autism and Developmental Disorders* (26 July, Epub ahead of print).

Rosenstein, D. & Oster, H. (1988). Differential facial responses to four basic tastes in newborns. *Child Development, 59*, 1555–1568.

Sacks, O. (1985). *The Man Who Mistook His Wife for a Hat: And other clinical tales*. New York: Touchstone.

Schienle, A., Schäfer, A., & Vaitl, D. (2008). Individual differences in disgust imagery: A functional magnetic resonance imaging study. *Neuroreport, 19*, 527–530.

Schiffman, H. R. (1996). *Sensation and perception* (4th edn). New York: John Wiley & Sons.

Shargorodsky, J., Curhan, S. G., Curhan, G. C., & Eavey, R. (2010). Change in prevalence of hearing loss in US adolescents. *JAMA, 304*(7), 772–778.

Sharma, A., Nash, A. A., & Dorman, M. (2009). Cortical development, plasticity and re-organization in children with cochlear implants. *Journal of Communication Disorders, 42*, 272–279.

Spence, C. (2011). Cross-modal correspondences: A tutorial review. *Attention, Perception & Psychophysics, 73*, 971–995.

Sugita, M. (2006). Taste perception and coding in the periphery. *Cellular and Molecular Life Sciences, 63*, 2000–2015.

Ulrich, R. S. (1984). View through a window may influence recovery from surgery. *Science, 224*, 420–421.

Ungerleider, L. G. & Haxby, J. V. (1994). 'What' and 'where' in the human brain. *Current Opinion in Neurobiology, 4*, 157–165.

Wieser, H. G. (2003). Music and the brain. Lessons from brain diseases and some reflections on the 'emotional' brain. *Annals of the New York Academy of Sciences, 999*, 76–94.

Wilson, D. A. (2001). Receptive fields in the rat piriform cortex. *Chemical Senses, 26*(5), 577–584.

Yahr, P. (1977). Social subordination and scent-marking in male Mongolian gerbils. *Animal Behaviour, 25*(2), 292–297.

Zatorre, R. J. (2003). Absolute pitch: A model for understanding the influence of genes and development on neural and cognitive function. *Nature Neuroscience, 6*, 692–695.

CHAPTER 8

Acebo, C., Sadeh, A., Seifer, R., Tzischinsky, O., Hafer, A., & Carskadon, M. A. (2005). Sleep/wake patterns derived from activity monitoring and maternal report for healthy 1- to 5-year-old children. *Sleep, 28*, 1568–1577.

Acosta, M. C., Haller, D. L., & Schnoll, S. H. (2005). Cocaine and stimulants. In R. J. Frances, A. H. Mack, & S. I. Miller (eds), *Clinical Textbook of Addictive Disorders* (3rd edn). New York: Guilford Press.

Anderson, C. & Platten, C. R. (2011). Sleep deprivation lowers inhibition and enhances impulsivity to negative stimuli. *Behavioural Brain Research, 217*(2), 463–466.

APA (American Psychiatric Association). (2000). *Diagnostic and Statistical Manual of Mental Disorders* (4th edn), Text Revision. Washington: American Psychiatric Association.

Auld, J. M. (2007). Review of hypnosis and communication in dental practice. *Australian Journal of Clinical & Experimental Hypnosis, 35*(2), 248–250.

Baars, B. J. (2003). How brain reveals mind: Neuroimaging supports the central role of conscious experience. *Journal of Consciousness Studies, 10*, 100–114.

Baars, B. J. & Gage, N. M. (2010). *Cognition, Brain, and Consciousness: Introduction to cognitive neuroscience* (2nd edn). San Diego: Elsevier Academic Press.

Baars, B. J., Banks, W. P., & Newman, J. B. (eds) (2003). *Essential Sources in the Scientific Study of Consciousness*. Cambridge, MA: MIT Press.

Barnier, A. J. & Council, J. R. (2010). Hypnotizability matters: The what, why, and how of measurement. In S. J. Lynn, J. W. Rhue, & I. Kirsch (eds), *Handbook of Clinical Hypnosis* (2nd edn; pp. 47–77). Washington: American Psychological Association.

Bastien, C. (2011). Insomnia: Neurophysiological and neuropsychological approaches. *Neuropsychology Review, 21*(1), 22–40.

Benarroch, E. E. (2008). The midline and intralaminar thalamic nuclei: Anatomic and functional specificity and implications in neurologic disease. *Neurology, 71*, 944.

Benarroch, E. E. (2011). The midline and intralaminar thalamic nuclei: Anatomic and functional specificity and implications in neurologic disease (Update). *Neurology, 74*.

Bertini, M., Ferrara, M., DeGennaro, L., Moroni, F., DeGasperis, M., Babiloni, C., Rossini, P. M., Vecchio, F., & Curcio, G. (2007). Directional information flows between brain hemispheres during pre-sleep wake and early sleep stages. *Cerebral Cortex, 17*(8), 1970–1978.

Blagrove, M., Bell, E., & Wilkinson, A. (2010). Association of lucid dreaming frequency with Stroop task performance. *Dreaming, 20*(4), 280–287.

Bliwise, D. L. (2010). The pit (of sleeplessness) and the pendulum (of regulation). *Sleep Medicine, 11*(1), 7–8.

Blum, K., Braverman, E. R., Holder, J. M., Lubar, J. F., Monastra, V. J., Miller, D., *et al.* (2000). Reward deficiency syndrome: A biogenetic model for the diagnosis and treatment of impulsive, addictive, and compulsive behaviors. *Journal of Psychoactive Drugs, 32* (Suppl.), 1–68.

Blumberg, M. S. & Seelke, A. M. H. (2010). The form and function of infant sleep: From muscle to neocortex. In M. S. Blumberg, J. H. Freeman, & S. R. Robinson (eds), *Oxford Handbook of Developmental Behavioral Neuroscience* (pp. 391–423). New York: Oxford University Press.

Bollinger, T., Bollinger, A., Oster, H., & Solbach, W. (2010). Sleep, immunity, and circadian clocks: A mechanistic model. *Gerontology, 56*(6), 574–580.

Carskadon, M. A. (ed.) (2002). *Adolescent Sleep Patterns: Biological, social and psychological influences.* New York: Cambridge University Press.

Cartwright, R. D. (2010). *The Twenty-Four Hour Mind: The role of sleep and dreaming in our emotional lives.* New York: Oxford University Press.

Chalmers, D. J. (1996). *The Conscious Mind: In search of a fundamental theory.* Oxford: Oxford University Press.

Churchland, P. M. (1988). *Matter and Consciousness* (revised edition). Cambridge, MA: The MIT Press.

Colvin, M. K. & Gazzaniga, M. S. (2007). Split-brain cases. In M. Velmans & S. Schneider (eds), *The Blackwell Companion to Consciousness.* (pp. 181–193). Malden: Blackwell Publishing.

Covino, N. A. & Pinnell, C. M. (2010). Hypnosis and medicine. In S. J. Lynn, J. W. Rhue, & I. Kirsch (eds), *Handbook of Clinical Hypnosis* (2nd edn; pp. 551–573). Washington: American Psychological Association.

Crisp, S. (2010). *How much sleep do children need?* NetDoctor, http://www.netdoctor.co.uk/health_advice/facts/childrensleep.htm, accessed 26 November 2012.

Crowley, S. J., Acebo, C., & Carskadon, M. A. (2007). Sleep, circadian rhythms, and delayed phase in adolescence. *Sleep Medicine, 8,* 602–612.

Curzi-Dascalova, L. & Challamel, M. J. (2000). Neurophysiological basis of sleep development. In G. M. Loughlin, J. L. Carroll, & C. L. Marcus (eds), *Sleep and Breathing in Children: A developmental approach* (pp. 3–37). New York: Marcel Dekker.

Czigler, I. & Winkler, I. (eds) (2010). *Unconscious Memory Representations in Perception.* Amsterdam, Netherlands: John Benjamins Publishing Company.

Damasio, A. (2010). *Self Comes to Mind: Constructing the conscious brain.* New York: Pantheon.

Danovi, S. A. (2010). Circadian rhythms: In the heat of the night. *Nature Reviews Neuroscience, 11*(12), 788.

Delaney, P. F., Sahakyan, L., Kelley, C. M., & Zimmerman, C. A. (2010). Remembering to forget: The amnesic effect of daydreaming. *Psychological Science, 21*(7), 1036–1042.

Dement, W. C. & Vaughan, C. (1999). *The Promise of Sleep: A pioneer in sleep medicine explores the vital connection between health, happiness, and a good night's sleep.* New York: Dell.

Dennett, D. C. (1991). *Consciousness Explained.* New York: Little Brown & Co.

Dennett, D.C. (1996). Facing backwards on the problem of consciousness. *Journal of Consciousness Studies, 3*(1), 4–6.

Diekelmann, S. & Born, J. (2010). Slow wave sleep takes the leading role in memory reorganization. *Nature Reviews Neuroscience, 11*(3), 218.

Dienes, Z., Brown, E., Hutton, S., Kirsch, I., Mazzoni, G., & Wright, D. B. (2009). Hypnotic suggestibility, cognitive inhibition, and dissociation. *Consciousness and Cognition: An International Journal, 18*(4), 837–847.

Dogu, O. & Pressman, M. R. (2011). Identification of sleepwalking gene(s): Not yet, but soon? *Neurology, 76*(1), 12–13.

Doweiko, H. E. (2006). *Concepts of Chemical Dependency* (6th edn). Belmont, CA: Thomson Brooks/Cole.

Dworak, M., McCarley, R. W., Kim, T., Kalinchuk, A. V., & Basheer, R. (2010). Sleep and brain energy levels: ATP changes during sleep. *Journal of Neuroscience, 30*(26), 9007–9016.

Edelstein, B. A., Stoner, S. A., & Woodhead, E. (2008). Older adults. In M. Hersen & J. Rosqvist (eds), *Handbook of Psychological Assessment: Case conceptualization and treatment. Vol. 1: Adults.* Hoboken, NJ: John Wiley & Sons, Inc.

Elisha, P. (2011). Psyche and soma in the work of Sigmund Freud: Theoretical foundations. In P. Elisha (ed.), *The Conscious Body: A psychoanalytic exploration of the body in therapy* (pp. 65–97). Washington: American Psychological Association.

El-Sheikh, M. (ed.) (2011). *Sleep and Development: Familial and sociocultural considerations.* New York: Oxford University Press.

Empson, J. (2002). *Sleep and Dreaming* (3rd edn). Basingstoke: Palgrave MacMillan.

Erlacher, D. & Schredl, M. (2010). Practicing a motor task in a lucid dream enhances subsequent performance: A pilot study. *Sport Psychologist, 24*(2), 157–167.

Espie, C. A. (2002). Insomnia: Conceptual issues in the development, persistence, and treatment of sleep disorders in adults. *Annual Review of Psychology, 53,* 215–243.

Fedotchev, A. I. (2011). Modern nondrug methods of human sleep regulation. *Human Physiology, 37*(1), 113–120.

Fogel, S. M., Smith, C. T., Higginson, C. D., & Beninger, R. J. (2011). Different types of avoidance behavior in rats produce dissociable post-training changes in sleep. *Physiology & Behavior, 102*(2), 170–174.

Fredericks, L. E. (2001). *The Use of Hypnosis in Surgery and Anesthesiology: Psychological preparation of the surgical patient.* Springfield, IL: Charles C. Thomas Publisher.

Freud, S. (2010). *The Interpretation of Dreams* (trans. J. Strachey). New York: Basic Books.

Gais, S., Hüllemann, P., Hallschmid, M., & Born, J. (2006). Sleep-dependent surges in growth hormone do not contribute to sleep-dependent memory consolidation. *Psychoneuroendocrinology, 31*(6), 786–791.

García-García, F., De, L. H., Juárez-Aguilar, E., Regalado-Santiago, C., Millán-Aldaco, D., Blanco-Centurión, C., & Drucker-Colín, R. (2011). Growth hormone improves hippocampal adult cell survival and counteracts the inhibitory effect of prolonged sleep deprivation on cell proliferation. *Brain Research Bulletin, 84*(3), 252–257.

Garcia-Rill, E., Charlesworth, A., Heister, D., Ye, M., & Hayer, A. (2008). The developmental decrease in REM sleep: The role of transmitters and electrical coupling. *Sleep: Journal of Sleep and Sleep Disorders Research, 31*(5), 673–690.

Gazzaniga, M. S. (2005). Forty-five years of split-brain research and still going strong. *Nature Reviews Neuroscience, 6*(8), 653–659.

Gazzaniga, M. S. (2010). Neuroscience and the correct level of explanation for understanding the mind: An extraterrestrial roams through some neuroscience laboratories and concludes earthlings are not grasping how best to understand the mind–brain interface. *Trends in Cognitive Sciences, 14*(7), 291–292.

Gfeller, J. D. & Gorassini, D. R. (2010). Enhancing hypnotizability and treatment response. In S. J. Lynn, J. W. Rhue, & I. Kirsch (eds), *Handbook of Clinical Hypnosis* (2nd edn; pp. 339–355). Washington: American Psychological Association.

Gibbons, D. E. & Lynn, S. J. (2010). Hypnotic inductions: A primer. In S. J. Lynn, J. W. Rhue, & I. Kirsch (eds), *Handbook of Clinical Hypnosis*

(2nd edn; pp. 267–291). Washington: American Psychological Association.

Glaser, J. & Kihlstrom, J. F. (2005). Compensatory automaticity: Unconscious volition is not an oxymoron. In R. R. Hassin, J. S. Uleman, & J. A. Bargh (eds), *The New Unconscious: Oxford series in social cognition and social neuroscience*. New York: Oxford University Press.

Gonzalez, Y. (2010). The impact of nightmares on the treatment of a 10-year-old girl. *Journal of Infant, Child & Adolescent Psychotherapy, 9*(4), 151–161.

Goswami, M., Pandi-Perumal, S. R., & Thorpy, M. J. (eds) (2010). *Narcolepsy: A clinical guide*. Totowa, NJ: Humana Press.

Green, J. P. (2010). Hypnosis and smoking cessation: Research and application. In S. J. Lynn, J. W. Rhue, & I. Kirsch (eds), *Handbook of Clinical Hypnosis* (2nd edn; pp. 593–614). Washington: American Psychological Association.

Gunzelmann, G., Moore, L. R., Gluck, K. A., Van Dongen, H., & Dinges, D. F. (2011). Fatigue in sustained attention: Generalizing mechanisms for time awake to time on task. In P. L. Ackerman (ed.), *Cognitive Fatigue: Multidisciplinary perspectives on current research and future applications* (pp. 83–101). Washington: American Psychological Association.

Halliday, G. (2004). Dreamwork and nightmares with incarcerated juvenile felons. *Dreaming, 14*(1), 30–42.

Hammond, D. C. (2008). Hypnosis as sole anesthesia for major surgeries: Historical & contemporary perspectives. *American Journal of Clinical Hypnosis, 51*(2), 101–121.

Haney, M. (2008). Neurobiology of stimulants. In H. D. Kleber & M. Galanter (eds), *The American Psychiatric Publishing Textbook of Substance Abuse Treatment* (4th edn). Arlington, VA: American Psychiatric Publishing.

Harrison, Y. & Horne, J. A. (2000). The impact of sleep deprivation on decision making: A review. *Journal of Experimental Psychology: Applied, 6,* 236–249.

Hart, C., Ksir, C., & Oakley, R. (2010). *Drugs, Society, and Human Behavior.* New York: McGraw-Hill.

Higgins, E. S. & George, M. S. (2007). *The Neuroscience of Clinical Psychiatry: The pathophysiology of behavior and mental illness.* Philadelphia, PA: Wolters Kluwer/Lippincott Williams & Wilkins.

Higgins, S. T., Heil, S. H., & Lussier, J. P. (2004). Clinical implications of reinforcement as a determinant of substance use disorders. *Annual Review of Psychology, 55,* 431–461.

Hilgard, E. R. (1992). Dissociation and theories of hypnosis. In E. Fromm & M. R. Nash (eds), *Contemporary Hypnosis Research.* New York: Guilford Press.

Hobson, J. A. (2005). Sleep is of the brain, by the brain and for the brain. *Nature, 437,* 1254–1256.

Hobson, J. A. (2009). REM sleep and dreaming: Towards a theory of protoconsciousness. *Nature Reviews Neuroscience, 10*(11), 803–813.

Hobson, J. A. & McCarley, R. W. (1977). The brain as dream state generator: An activation-synthesis hypothesis of the dream process. *American Journal of Psychiatry, 134,* 1335–1348.

Hobson, J. A., Pace-Schott, E., & Stickgold, R. (2003). Dreaming and the brain: Toward a cognitive neuroscience of conscious states. In E. F. Pace-Schott, M. Solms, M. Blagrove, & S. Harnad (eds), *Sleep and Dreaming: Scientific advances and reconsiderations* (pp. 1–50). New York: Cambridge University Press.

Hobson, J. A., Sangsanguan, S., Arantes, H., & Kahn, D. (2011). Dream logic: The inferential reasoning paradigm. *Dreaming, 21*(1), 1–15.

Hobson, J. A., Stickgold, R., & Pace-Schott, E. F. (1998). The neuro-psychology of REM sleep dreaming. *Neuroreport: An International Journal for the Rapid Communication of Research in Neuroscience, 9*(3), R1–R14.

Hopkin, K. (2010). Some nerve. *The Scientist, 24*(9), 52.

Horne, J. (2010). Primary insomnia: A disorder of sleep, or primarily one of wakefulness? *Sleep Medicine Reviews, 14*(1), 3–7.

Hymowitz, N. (2005). Tobacco. In R. J. Frances, A. H. Mack, & S. I. Miller (eds), *Clinical Textbook of Addictive Disorders* (3rd edn). New York: Guilford Press.

Irwin, M. (2001). Neuroimmunology of disordered sleep in depression and alcoholism. *Neuropsychopharmacology, 25*(suppl. 5), S45–S49.

Ivanenko, A. & Johnson, K. P. (2010). Sleep disorders. In M. K. Dulcan (ed.), *Dulcan's Textbook of Child and Adolescent Psychiatry* (pp. 449–461). Arlington, VA: American Psychiatric Publishing, Inc.

Jackson, F. (1986). What Mary didn't know. *Journal of Philosophy, 83,* 291–295.

Jansson-Fröjmark, M., Harvey, A. G., Lundh, L., Norell-Clarke, A., & Linton, S. J. (2011). Psychometric properties of an insomnia-specific measure of worry: The anxiety and preoccupation about sleep questionnaire. *Cognitive Behaviour Therapy, 40*(1), 65–76.

Jaussent, I., Dauvilliers, Y., Ancelin, M., Dartigues, J., Tavernier, B., Touchon, J., & Besset, A. (2011). Insomnia symptoms in older adults: Associated factors and gender differences. *American Journal of Geriatric Psychiatry, 19*(1), 88–97.

Jefferson, D. J. (2005). America's most dangerous drug. *Newsweek, 146* (6), 40–48.

Johannsdottir, K. R. & Herdman, C. M. (2010). The role of working memory in supporting drivers' situation awareness for surrounding traffic. *Human Factors, 52*(6), 663–673.

Johnson, C. H., Elliott, J., Foster, R., Honma, K. I., & Kronauer, R. (2004). Fundamental properties of circadian rhythms. In J. C. Dunlap, J. J. Loros, & DeCoursey, P. J. (eds), *Chronobiology: Biological timekeeping.* Sunderland, MA: Sinauer Associates, Inc.

Jones, S. R., Fernyhough, C., & Larøi, F. (2010). A phenomenological survey of auditory verbal hallucinations in the hypnagogic and hypnopompic states. *Phenomenology and the Cognitive Sciences, 9*(2), 213–224.

Kalsbeek, A., Fliers, E., Hofman, M. A., Swaab, D. F., & Buijs, R. M. (2010). Vasopressin and the output of the hypothalamic biological clock. *Journal of Neuroendocrinology, 22*(5), 362–372.

Kannape, O. A., Schwabe, L., Tadi, T., & Blanke, O. (2010). The limits of agency in walking humans. *Neuropsychologia, 48*(6), 1628–1636.

Karni, A., Tanne, D., Rubenstien, B. S., Askenasy, J. J. M., & Sagi, D. (1994). Dependence on REM sleep of overnight improvement of a perceptual skill. *Science, 265*(5172), 679–682.

Kauert, G. & Iwersen-Bergmann, S. (2004). Illicit drugs as cause of traffic crashes: Focus on cannabis. *Sucht (German Journal of Addiction Research and Practice), 50*(5), 327–333.

Kihlstrom, J. F. (2007). Consciousness in hypnosis. In P. D. Zelazo, M. Moscovitch, & E. Thompson (eds), *The Cambridge Handbook of Consciousnes* (pp. 445–479). New York: Cambridge University Press.

Kihlstrom, J. F., Mulvaney, S., Tobias, B. A., & Tobis, I. P. (2000). The emotional unconscious. In E. Eich, J. F. Kihlstrom *et al.* (eds), *Cognition and Emotion.* London : Oxford University Press.

Kopasz, M., Loessl, B., Hornyak, M., Riemann, D., Nissen, C., Piosczyk, H., & Voderholzer, U. (2010). Sleep and memory in healthy children and adolescents: A critical review. *Sleep Medicine Reviews, 14*(3), 167–177.

Kosten, T. R., Sofuoglu, M., & Gardner, T. J. (2008). Clinical management: Cocaine. In H. D. Kleber & M. Galanter (eds), *The American Psychiatric Publishing Textbook of Substance Abuse Treatment* (4th edn). Washington: American Psychiatric Publishing.

Lack, L. C. & Bootzin, R. R. (2003). Circadian rhythm factors in insomnia and their treatment. In M. L. Perlis, & K. L. Lichstein (eds), *Treating Sleep Disorders: Principles and practice of behavioral sleep medicine.* New York: John Wiley & Sons.

Lavie, P. (2001). Sleep–wake as a biological rhythm. *Annual Review of Psychology, 52,* 277–303.

Legault, G., Delay, S., & Madore, A. (2010). Identification of a rapid eye movement sleep window for learning of the win-shift radial arm maze task for male Sprague–Dawley rats. *Journal of Sleep Research, 19*(4), 508–515.

Lewis, M. (2010). The emergence of consciousness and its role in human development. In W. F. Overton & R. M. Lerner (eds), *The Handbook of Life-Span Development: Vol. 1: Cognition, biology, and methods* (pp. 628–670). Hoboken, NJ: John Wiley & Sons, Inc.

Llinás, R. R. & Ribary, U. (2001). Consciousness and the brain: The thalamo-cortical dialogue in health and disease. *Annals of the New York Academy of Sciences, 929*, 166–175.

Loessl, B., Valerius, G., Kopasz, M., Hornyak, M., Riemann, D., & Voderholzer, U. (2008). Are adolescents chronically sleep-deprived? An investigation of sleep habits of adolescents in the southwest of Germany. *Child: Care, Health and Development, 34*, 549–556.

Lundqvist, T. (2005). Cognitive consequences of cannabis use: Comparison with abuse of stimulants and heroin with regard to attention, memory and executive functions. *Pharmacology, Biochemistry, and Behavior, 81*, 330–391.

Lynn, S. J., Rhue, J. W., & Kirsch, I. (eds) (2010). *Handbook of Clinical Hypnosis* (2nd edn). Washington: American Psychological Association.

Mandler, J. M. (2004). *Foundations of the Mind.* New York: Oxford University Press.

Manelis, A., Hanson, C., & Hanson, S. J. (2011). Implicit memory for object locations depends on reactivation of encoding-related brain regions. *Human Brain Mapping, 32*(1), 32–50.

Mathew, R. J., Wilson, W. H., Humphreys, D., Lowe, J. V., & Weithe, K. E. (1993). Depersonalization after marijuana smoking. *Biological Psychiatry, 33*(6), 431–441.

Mellinger, D. I. (2010). Hypnosis and the treatment of anxiety disorders. In S. J. Lynn, J. W. Rhue, & I. Kirsch (eds), *Handbook of Clinical Hypnosis* (2nd edn; pp. 359–389). Washington: American Psychological Association.

Mental Health Foundation (2011). *Sleep matters: The impact of sleep on health and wellbeing,* http://www.mentalhealth.org.uk/publications/sleep-report/, accessed 26 November 2012.

Moorcroft, W. H. (2003). *Understanding Sleep and Dreaming.* New York: Springer.

Nagel, T. (1974). What is it like to be a bat? *Philosophical Review LXXXIII, 4*, 435–450.

Naish, P. L. N. (2010). Hypnosis and hemispheric asymmetry. *Consciousness and Cognition: An International Journal, 19*(1), 230–234.

Neuman, Y. & Nave, O. (2010). Why the brain needs language in order to be self-conscious. *New Ideas in Psychology, 28*(1), 37–48.

Oakley, D. A. & Halligan, P. W. (2010). Psychophysiological foundations of hypnosis and suggestion. In S. J. Lynn, J. W. Rhue, & I. Kirsch (eds), *Handbook of Clinical Hypnosis* (2nd edn; pp. 79–117). Washington: American Psychological Association.

Ohayon, M. M. (2008). From wakefulness to excessive sleepiness: What we know and still need to know. *Sleep Medicine Reviews, 12*(2), 129–141.

Olness, K. & Kohen, D. P. (2010). Childhood problems. In A. F. Barabasz, K. Olness, R. Boland, & S. Kahn (eds), *Medical Hypnosis Primer: Clinical and research evidence* (pp. 33–39). New York: Routledge/Taylor & Francis Group.

Orzel-Gryglewska, J. (2010). Consequences of sleep deprivation. *International Journal of Occupational Medicine and Environmental Health, 23*(1), 95–114.

Palumbo, S. R. (1978). *Dreaming and Memory: A new information processing model.* New York: Basic Books.

Payne, P. (2010). Why teenagers stay up late. *The Washington Post, 133*(267).

Place, U. T. (1956). Is consciousness a brain process? *British Journal of Psychology, 47*, 44–50.

Punjabi, N. M. (2008). The epidemiology of adult obstructive sleep apnea. *Proceedings of the American Thoracic Society, 5*, 136–143.

Rainville, P., Duncan, G. H., Price, D. D., Carrier, B., & Bushnell, M. C. (1997). Pain affect encoded in human anterior cingulate but not somatosensory cortex. *Science, 277*(5328), 968–971.

Rainville, P., Hofbauer, R. K., Bushnell, M. C., Duncan, G. H., & Price, D. D. (2002). Hypnosis modulates activity in brain structures involved in the regulation of consciousness. *Journal of Cognitive Neuroscience, 14*(6), 887–901.

Rainville, P., Hofbauer, R. K., Paus, T., Duncan, G. H., Bushnell, M. C., & Price, D. D. (1999). Cerebral mechanisms of hypnotic induction and suggestion. *Journal of Cognitive Neuroscience, 11*(1), 110–125.

Ratey, J. J. (2001). *A User's Guide to the Brain: Perception, attention, and the four theaters of the brain.* New York: Random House.

Revonsuo, A. (2010). *Consciousness: The science of subjectivity.* New York: Psychology Press.

Rial, R. V., Akaârir, M., Gamundí, A., Nicolau, C., Garau, C., Aparicio, S., & Esteban, S. (2010). Evolution of wakefulness, sleep and hibernation: From reptiles to mammals. *Neuroscience and Biobehavioral Reviews, 34*(8), 1144–1160.

Sadeh, A., Mindell, J. A., Luedtke, K., & Wiegand, B. (2009). Sleep and sleep ecology in the first 3 years: A web-based study. *Journal of Sleep Research, 18*(1), 60–73.

Sadler, P. & Woody, E. (2010). Dissociation in hypnosis: Theoretical frameworks and psychotherapeutic implications. In S. J. Lynn, J. W. Rhue, & I. Kirsch (eds), *Handbook of Clinical Hypnosis* (2nd edn; pp. 151–178). Washington: American Psychological Association.

Sahraie, A., Hibbard, P. B., Trevethan, C. T., Ritchie, K. L., & Weiskrantz, L. (2010). Consciousness of the first order in blindsight. *Proceedings of the National Academy of Sciences of the United States of America, 107*(49), 21217–21222.

SAMHSA (Substance Abuse and Mental Health Services Administration). (2008). *Patterns of Mental Health Service Utilization and Substance Use among Adults, 2000 and 2001.* Washington: SAMHSA.

Sankupellay, M., Wilson, S., Heussler, H. S., Parsley, C., Yuill, M., & Dakin, C. (2011). Characteristics of sleep EEG power spectra in healthy infants in the first two years of life. *Clinical Neurophysiology, 122*(2), 236–243.

Schon, J. (2003). Dreams and dreaming: Perspectives over the century. *Psychoanalytic Psychotherapy in South Africa, 11*(2), 1–23.

Schooler, J. W. (2011). Introspecting in the spirit of William James: Comment on Fox, Ericsson, and Best (2011). *Psychological Bulletin, 137*(2), 345–350.

Schultz, T. F. & Kay, S. A. (2003). Circadian clocks in daily and seasonal control of development. *Science, 301*(5631), 326–327.

Searle, J. (1997). *The Mystery of Consciousness.* London: Granta.

Sheldon, S. A. M. & Moscovitch, M. (2010). Recollective performance advantages for implicit memory tasks. *Memory, 18*(7), 681–697.

Siegel, J. M. (2005). Clues to the functions of mammalian sleep. *Nature, 437*, 1264–1271.

Singer, J. L. (2003). Daydreaming, consciousness, and self-representations: Empirical approaches to theories of William James and Sigmund Freud. *Journal of Applied Psychoanalytic Studies, 5*, 461–483.

Smith, C. (1996). Sleep states, memory processes and synaptic plasticity. *Behavioural Brain Research, 78*(1), 49–56.

Smith, C. (2006). Symposium V: Sleep and learning: New developments. *Brain and Cognition, 60*(3), 331–332.

Spanos, N. P. (1996). *Multiple Identities & False Memories: A Sociocognitive Perspective.* Washington: American Psychological Association.

Sperry, R. W. (1982). Some effects of disconnecting the cerebral hemispheres. *Science, 217*(4566), 1223–1226.

Sperry, R. W. (1998). A powerful paradigm made stronger. *Neuropsychologia, 36*(10), 1063–1068.

Super, C. M. & Harkness, S. (1972). The infant's niche in rural Kenya and metropolitan America. In L. Adler (ed.), *Issues in Cross-Cultural Research.* New York: Academic Press.

Super, C. M. & Harkness, S. (2002). Culture structures the environment for development. *Human Development, 45*, 270–274.

Taylor, D. J., McCrae, C. M., Gehrman, P., Dautovich, N., & Lichtein, K. L. (2008). Insomnia. In M. Hersen & J. Rosqvist (eds), *Handbook of Psychological Assessment: Case conceptualization and treatment. Vol. 1: Adults.* Hoboken, NJ: John Wiley & Sons, Inc.

Thakkar, M. M. & Datta, S. (2010). The evolution of REM sleep. In P. McNamara, R. A. Barton, & C. L. Nunn (eds), *Evolution of Sleep: Phylogenetic and functional perspectives* (pp. 197–217). New York: Cambridge University Press.

Theodorou, S. & Haber, P. S. (2005). The medical complications of heroin use. *Current Opinions in Psychiatry, 18*(3), 257–263.

Thompson, R. F. (2000). *The Brain: A neuroscience primer* (3rd edn). New York: Worth Publishers.

Van der Werf, Y. D., Jolles, J., Witter, M. P., & Uylings, H. B. M. (2003). Contributions of thalamic nuclei to memory functioning. *Cortex, 39*, 1047–1062.

Van der Werf, Y. D., Witter, M. P., & Groenewegen, H. J. (2002). The intralaminar and midline nuclei of the thalamus. Anatomical and functional evidence for participation in processes of arousal and awareness. *Brain Research Reviews, 39*, 107–140.

Vertes, R. P. & Eastman, K. E. (2003). The case against memory consolidation in REM sleep. In E. F. Pace-Schott, M. Solms, M. Blagrove, & S. Harnad (eds), *Sleep and Deaming: Scientific advances and reconsiderations*. New York: Cambridge University Press.

Waterhouse, J. M. & DeCoursey, P. J. (2004). The relevance of circadian rhythms for human welfare. In J. C. Dunlap, J. J. Loros, & DeCoursey, P. J. (eds), *Chronobiology: Biological timekeeping*. Sunderland, MA: Sinauer Associates.

Weiskrantz, L. (2000). Blindsight: Implications for the conscious experience of emotion. In R. D. Lane & L. Nadel (eds), *Cognitive Neuro-Science of Emotion*. London: Oxford University Press.

Weiskrantz, L. (2002). Prime-sight and blindsight. *Consciousness and Cognition: An International Journal, 11*(4), 568–581.

Weiskrantz, L. (2009). Is blindsight just degraded normal vision? *Experimental Brain Research, 192*(3), 413–416.

Wickwire, E. M., Jr., Roland, M. M. S., Elkin, T. D., & Schumacher, J. A. (2008). Sleep disorders. In D. Reitman (ed.), *Handbook of Psychological Assessment: Case conceptualization, and treatment: Vol. 2: Children and adolescents*. Hoboken, NJ: John Wiley & Sons, Inc.

Wolfson, A. R. & Richards, M. (2011). Young adolescents: Struggles with insufficient sleep. In M. El-Sheikh (ed.), *Sleep and Development: Familial and socio-cultural considerations* (pp. 265–298). New York: Oxford University Press.

Worthman, C. M. (2011). Developmental cultural ecology of sleep. In M. El-Sheikh (ed.), *Sleep and Development: Familial and socio-cultural considerations* (pp. 167–194). New York: Oxford University Press.

Yoon, I. Y., Kripke, D. F., Elliott, J. A., Youngstedt, S. D., Rex, K. M., & Hauger, R. L. (2003). Age-related changes of circadian rhythms and sleep–wake cycles. *Journal of the American Geriatrics Society, 51*(8), 1085–1091.

Zelazo, P. D. (2004). The development of conscious control in childhood. *Trends in Cognitive Sciences, 8*, 12–17.

CHAPTER 9

Adams, C. D. (1982). Variations in the sensitivity of instrumental responding to reinforcer devaluation. *Quarterly Journal of Experimental Psychology, 34B*, 77–98.

Attwell, P. J. E., Rahman, S., & Yeo, C. H. (2001). Acquisition of eyeblink conditioning is critically dependent upon normal function in cerebellar cortical lobule HVI. *Journal of Neuroscience, 21*, 5715–5722.

Baeyens, F., Eelen, P., & Crombez, G. (1995). Pavlovian associations are forever: On classical conditioning and extinction. *Journal of Psychophysiology, 9*, 127–141.

Bandura, A. (1978). Social learning theory of aggression. *Journal of Communication, 28*, 12–29.

Bandura, A., Ross, D., & Ross, S. A. (1961). Transmission of aggression through imitation of aggressive models. *Journal of Abnormal and Social Psychology, 63*, 575–582.

Bliss, T. V. & Lomo, T. (1973). Long-lasting potentiation of synaptic transmission in the dentate area of the anaesthetized rabbit following stimulation of the perforant path. *Journal of Physiology, 232*, 331–356.

Breland, K. & Breland, M. (1961). The misbehaviour of organisms. *American Psychologist, 16*, 681–684.

Brosnan, S. F. & De Waal, F. B. (2003). Monkeys reject unequal pay. *Nature, 425*(6955), 297–299.

Bush, G., Valera, E. M., & Seidman, L. J. (2005). Functional neuroimaging of attention-deficit/hyperactivity disorder: A review and suggested future directions. *Biological Psychiatry, 57*(11), 1273–1284.

Clements, C. M. & Sawhney, D. K. (2000). Coping with domestic violence: Control attributions, dysphoria, and hopelessness. *Journal of Traumatic Stress, 13*(2), 219–240.

Cooper, S. J. (2005). Donald O. Hebb's synapse and learning rule: A history and commentary. *Neuroscience and Biobehavioral Reviews, 28*(8), 851–874.

Davey, G. C. L. (1992). Characteristics of individuals with fear of spiders. *Anxiety Research, 4*, 299–314.

De Houwer, J., Thomas, S., & Baeyens, F. (2001). Associative learning of likes and dislikes: A review of 25 years of research on human evaluative conditioning. *Psychological Bulletin, 127*(6), 853–869. DOI: 10.1037//0033-2909.127.6.853.

DeCasper, A. J. & Spence, M. J. (1986). Prenatal maternal speech influences newborns' perception of speech sounds. *Infant Behavior & Development, 9*(2), 133–150.

DeFelipe, J. (2002). Sesquicentenary of the birthday of Santiago Ramón y Cajal, the father of modern neuroscience. *Trends in Neurosciences, 2*(9), 481–484.

Edwards, S. & Salkovskis, P. M. (2006). An experimental demonstration that fear, but not disgust, is associated with return of fear in phobias. *Journal of Anxiety Disorders, 20*(1), 58–71.

Field, A. P. & Nightingale, Z. C. (2009). Test of time: What if little Albert had escaped? *Clinical Child Psychology and Psychiatry, 14*, 311–319.

Fridlund, A. J., Beck, H. P., Goldie, W. D., & Irons, G. (2012). Little Albert: A neurologically impaired child. *History of Psychology, 15*(4), 302–327.

Gantt, W. H. (1980). Review of the shaping of behaviorism. *Pavlovian Journal of Biological Science, 15*(1), 42–44.

Garcia, J., Lasiter, P. S., Bermudez-Rattoni, F., & Deems, D. A. (1985). A general theory of aversion learning. *Annals of the New York Academy of Sciences, 443*, 8–21.

Gaston, K. E. (1978). Interocular transfer of a visually mediated conditioned food aversion in chicks. *Behavioral Biology, 24*(2), 272–278.

Geary, D. C. (1996). Sexual selection and sex differences in mathematical abilities. *Behavioural and Brain Sciences, 19*, 229–284.

Gingrich, K. J. & Byrne, J. H. (1985). Simulation of synaptic depression, post-tetanic potentiation, and presynaptic facilitation of synaptic potentials from sensory neurons mediating gill-withdrawal reflex in *Aplysia. Journal of Neurophysiology, 53*(3), 652–669.

Godden, D. R. & Baddeley, A. D. (1975). Context-dependent memory in two natural environments: On land and underwater. *British Journal of Psychology, 66*, 325–331. DOI: 10.1111/j.2044-8295.1975.tb01468.x.

Greely, H., Sahakian, B., Harris, J., Kessler, R. C., Gazzaniga, M., Campbell, P., & Farah, M. J. (2008). Towards responsible use of cognitive-enhancing drugs by the healthy. *Nature, 456*, 702–705.

Gutbezahl, J. (1997). Mathematics performance and underperformance: Effects of gender and confidence. *Dissertation Abstracts International Section A: Humanities and Social Sciences, 57*(7), 2924.

Hawkins, R. D., Cohen, T. E., & Kandel, E. R. (2006). Dishabituation in *Aplysia* can involve either reversal of habituation or superimposed sensitization. *Learning & Memory, 13*, 397–403.

Herd, S. A., Banich, M. T., & O'Reilly, R. C. (2006). Neural mechanisms of cognitive control: An integrative model of Stroop task performance and fMRI data. *Journal of Cognitive Neuroscience, 18*(1), 22–32.

Heyes, C. M., Dawson, G. R., & Nokes, T. (1992). Imitation in rats: Initial responding and transfer evidence. *Quarterly Journal of Experimental Psychology, 45B*, 81–92.

Hill, D. E., Yeo, R. A., Campbell, R. A., Hart, B., Vigil, J., & Brooks, W. (2003). Magnetic resonance imaging correlates of attention-deficit/hyperactivity disorder in children. *Neuropsychology, 17*(3), 496–506.

Hoeft, F., Hernandez, A., McMillon, G., Taylor-Hill, H., Martindale, J. L., Meyler, A., Keller, T. A., Siok, W. T., Deutsch, G. K., Just, M. A., Whitfield-Gabrieli, S., & Gabrieli, J. D. (2006). Neural basis of dyslexia: A comparison between dyslexic and nondyslexic children equated for reading ability. *Journal of Neuroscience, 26*(42), 10700–10708.

Johnson, J. G., Cohen, P., Smailes, E. M., Kasen, S., & Brook, J. S. (2002). Television viewing and aggressive behavior during adolescence and adulthood. *Science, 295*, 2468–2471.

Kalivas, P. W. & Nakamura, M. (1999). Neural systems for behavioral activation and reward. *Current Opinions in Neurobiology, 9*, 223–227.

Kandel, E. R. (2001). The molecular biology of memory storage: A dialogue between genes and synapses. *Science, 294*, 1030–1038.

Killcross, S. & Coutureau, E. (2003). Coordination of actions and habits in the medial prefrontal cortex of rats. *Cerebral Cortex, 13*(4), 400–408.

Kirschner, P. A. & Karpinski, A. C. (2010). Facebook® and academic performance. *Computers in Human Behavior, 26*(6), 1237–1245.

Krützen, J. M., Heithaus, M. R., Connor, R. C., Bejder, L., & Sherwin, W. B. (2005). Cultural transmission of tool use in bottlenose dolphins. *Proceedings of the National Academy of Sciences, 102*(25), 8939–8943.

LeDoux, J. E. (2000). Emotion circuits in the brain. *Annual Review of Neuroscience, 23*, 155–184.

LeDoux, J. (2003). The emotional brain, fear, and the amygdala. *Cellular and Molecular Neurobiology, 23*(4–5), 727–738.

Lee, A. K. & Wilson, M. A. (2002). Memory of sequential experience in the hippocampus during slow wave sleep. *Neuron, 36*(6), 1183–1194.

Leuner, B., Falduto, J., & Shors, T. J. (2003). Associative memory formation increases the observation of dendritic spines in the hippocampus. *Journal of Neuroscience, 23*, 659–665.

Leuner, B., Gould, E., & Shors, T. J. (2006). Is there a link between adult neurogenesis and learning? *Hippocampus, 16*(3), 216–224.

Loewi, O. (1957). On the background of the discovery of neuro-chemical transmission. *Journal of Mt Sinai Hospital, NY, 24*(6), 1014–1016.

Louie, K. & Wilson, M. A. (2001). Temporally structured replay of awake hippocampal ensemble activity during rapid eye movement sleep. *Neuron, 29*(1), 145–156.

Maguire, E. A., Gadian, D. G., Johnsrude, I. S., Good, C. D., Ashburner, J., Frackowiak, R. S., & Frith, C. D. (2000). Navigation-related structural change in the hippocampi of taxi drivers. *Proceedings of the National Academy of Sciences, 97*(8), 4398–4403.

Maguire, E. A., Woollett, K., & Spiers, H. J. (2006). London taxi drivers and bus drivers: A structural MRI and neuropsychological analysis. *Hippocampus, 16*(12), 1091–101.

Maren, S. (2005). Synaptic mechanisms of associative memory in the amygdala. *Neuron, 47*, 783–786.

Matsumoto, M. & Hikosaka, O. (2009). Two types of dopamine neuron distinctly convey positive and negative motivational signals. *Nature,* May 17.

Mirescu, C. & Gould, E. (2006). Stress and adult neurogenesis. *Hippocampus, 16*(3), 233–238.

Moriceau, S. & Sullivan, R. M. (2006). Maternal presence serves as a switch between learning and attraction in infancy. *Nature Neuroscience, 9*, 1004–1006.

Morris, R. G. (1990). Toward a representational hypothesis of the role of hippocampal synaptic plasticity in spatial and other forms of learning. *The Cold Spring Harbor Symposia on Quantitative Biology, 55*, 161–173.

Moser, M. B., Trommald, M., & Andersen, P. (1994). An increase in dendritic spine density on hippocampal CA1 pyramidal cells following spatial learning in adult rats suggests the formation of new synapses. *Proceedings of the National Academy of Sciences, 91*(26), 12673–12675.

Nakamichi, N., Kato, E., Kojima, Y., & Itoigawa, N. (1998). Carrying and washing of grass roots by free-ranging Japanese macaques at Katsuyama. *Folia Primatologica, 69*, 35–40.

O'Keefe, J. (1990). A computational theory of the hippocampal cognitive map. *Progress in Brain Research, 83*, 301–312.

O'Malley, A., O'Connell, C., & Regan, C. M. (1998). Ultrastructural analysis reveals avoidance conditioning to induce a transient increase in hippocampal dentate spine density in the 6 hour post-training period of consolidation. *Neuroscience, 87*, 607–613.

Ophira, E., Nassb, C., & Wagner, A. D. (2009). Cognitive control in media multitaskers. *Proceedings of the National Academy of Sciences of the United States of America, 106*, 15583–15587.

Parkinson, J. A., Cardinal, R. N., & Everitt, B. J. (2000). Limbic cortical-ventral striatal systems underlying appetitive conditioning. *Progress in Brain Research, 126*, 263–85. DOI: 10.1016/S0079-6123(00)26019-6.

Pavlov, I. P. (1927). *Conditioned Reflexes: An investigation of the physiological activity of the cerebral cortex.* New York: Dover.

Porsolt, R. D. (2000). Animal models of depression: Utility for transgenic research. *Reviews in the Neurosciences, 11*, 53–58.

Porter, R. H. & Winberg, J. (1999). Unique salience of maternal breast odors for newborn infants. *Neuroscience and Biobehavioral Reviews, 23*(3), 439–449.

Price, G. R., Holloway, I., Räsänen, P., Vesterinen, M., & Ansari, D. (2007). Impaired parietal magnitude processing in developmental dyscalculia. *Current Biology, 17*(24), R1042–1043.

Qiu, A., Crocetti, D., Adler, M., Mahone, E. M., Denckla, M. B., Miller, M. I., & Mostofsky, S. H. (2009). Basal ganglia volume and shape in children with attention deficit hyperactivity disorder. *American Journal of Psychiatry, 166*(1), 74–82.

Quirk, G. J., Garcia, R., & González-Lima, F. (2006). Prefrontal mechanisms in extinction of conditioned fear. *Biological Psychiatry, 60*, 337–343.

Ramnani, N., Toni, I., Josephs, O., Ashburner, J., & Passingham, R. E. (2000). Learning- and expectation-related changes in the human brain during motor learning. *Journal of Neurophysiology, 84*, 3026–3036.

Rosenzweig, M. R., & Bennett, E. L. (1996). Psychobiology of plasticity: Effects of training and experience on brain and behavior. *Behavioural Brain Research, 78*(1), 57–65.

Sapolsky, R. & Share, L. (2004). A pacific culture among wild baboons: Its emergence and transmission. *Plos Biology, 2*(4), E106.

Scelfo, B., Sacchetti, B., & Strata, P. (2008). Learning-related long-term potentiation of inhibitory synapses in the cerebellar cortex. *Proceedings of the National Academy of Sciences, 105*, 769–774.

Seligman, M. E., Weiss, J., Weinraub, M., & Schulman, A. (1980). Coping behavior: Learned helplessness, physiological change and learned inactivity. *Behavioral Research Therapy, 18*, 459–512.

Shaw, P., Eckstrand, K., Sharp, W., Blumenthal, J., Lerch, J. P., Greenstein, D., Clasen, L., Evans, A., Giedd, J., & Rapoport, J. L. (2007). Attention deficit/hyperactivity disorder is characterized by a delay in cortical maturation. *Proceedings of the National Academy of Sciences, 104*, 19649–19654.

Shors, T. J. (2009). Saving new brain cells. *Scientific American, 300*, 46–52.

Skinner, B. F. (1958). Diagramming schedules of reinforcement. *Journal of the Experimental Analysis of Behavior, 1*, 67–68.

Skinner, B. F. & Morse, W. H. (1958). Fixed-interval reinforcement of running in a wheel. *Journal of the Experimental Analysis of Behavior, 1*, 371–379.

Smith, S. M. (1984). A comparison of two techniques for reducing context-dependent forgetting. *Memory & Cognition, 12*, 477–482.

Smith, S. M. & Rothkopf, E. Z. (1984). Contextual enrichment and distribution of practice in the classroom. *Cognition & Instruction, 1*, 341–358.

Smith, A. B., Taylor, E., Brammer, M., Halari, R., & Rubia, K. (2008). Reduced activation in right lateral prefrontal cortex and anterior cingulate gyrus in medication-naïve adolescents with attention deficit hyperactivity disorder during time discrimination. *Journal of Child Psychology and Psychiatry, and Allied Disciplines 49*(9), 977–985.

Steele, C. M. & Aronson, J. (1995). Stereotype threat and the intellectual test performance of African Americans. *Journal of Personality and Social Psychology, 69*(5), 797–811.

Steele, C. M. & Aronson, J. A. (2004). Stereotype threat does not live by Steele and Aronson (1995) alone. *American Psychologist, 59*(1), 47–48.

Stoet, G. & Geary, D. C. (2012). Can stereotype threat explain the gender gap in mathematics performance and achievement? *Review of General Psychology, 16*(1), 93–102.

Symonds, M. & Hall, G. (2012). Avoidance, anxiety, and aversion in the clinical setting: The role of classical conditioning. In M. Haselgrove &

L. Hogarth (eds), *Clinical Applications of Learning Theory* (pp. 27–47). Hove: Psychology Press.

Tassi, P., Rohmer, O., Schimchowitsch, S., Eschenlauer, A., Bonnefond, A., Margiocchi, F., Poisson, F., & Muzet, A. (2010). Living alongside railway tracks: Long-term effects of nocturnal noise on sleep and cardiovascular reactivity as a function of age. *Environment International, 36*(7), 683–689.

Thorndike, E. L. (1933). A proof of the law of effect. *Science, 77*(1989), 73–175.

Tolman, E. C. & Gleitman, H. (1949). Studies in spatial learning: Place and response learning under different degrees of motivation. *Journal of Experimental Psychology, 39*, 653–659.

Treisman, A. M. & Kanwisher, N. G. (1998). Perceiving visually presented objects: Recognition, awareness, and modularity. *Current Opinions in Neurobiology, 8*, 218–226.

Weiss, J. M. & Glazer, H. I. (1975). Effects of acute exposure to stressors on subsequent avoidance-escape behavior. *Psychosomatic Medicine, 37*, 499–521.

Whitlock, J. R., Heynen, A. J., Shuler, M. G., & Bear, M. F. (2006). Learning induces long-term potentiation in the hippocampus. *Science, 313*, 1093–1097.

Windholz, G. (1987). Pavlov as a psychologist: A reappraisal. *Pavlovian Journal of Biological Science, 22*(3), 103–112.

Wolosin, S. M., Richardson, M. E., Hennessey, J. G., Denckla, M. B., & Mostofsky, S. H. (2009). Abnormal cerebral cortex structure in children with ADHD. *Human Brain Mapping, 30*, 175–184.

Woollett, K. & Maguire, E. A. (2011). Acquiring 'the Knowledge' of London's layout drives structural brain changes. *Current Biology, 21*(24), 2109–2114.

Yin, H. H., Ostlund, S. B., & Balleine, B. W. (2008). Reward-guided learning beyond dopamine in the nucleus accumbens: The integrative functions of cortico-basal ganglia networks. *European Journal of Neuroscience, 28*(8), 1437.

CHAPTER 10

APA (American Psychiatric Association). (2000). *Diagnostic and Statistical Manual of Mental Disorders* (4th edn). Washington: American Psychiatric Association.

Apostolova, L. G. & Cummings, J. L. (2008). Neuropsychiatric aspects of Alzheimer's disease and other dementing illnesses. In S. C. Yudofsky & R. E. Hales (eds), *The American Psychiatric Publishing Textbook of Neuropsychiatry and Behavioral Neurosciences* (5th edn; pp. 935–968). Washington: American Psychiatric Publishing.

Artero, S., Ancelin, M., Portet, F., Dupuy, A., Berr, C., Dartigues, J., Tzourio, C., Rouaud, O., Poncet, M., Pasquier, F., Auriacombe, S., Touchon, J., & Ritchie, K. (2008). Risk profiles for mild cognitive impairment and progression to dementia are gender specific. *Journal of Neurology, Neurosurgery & Psychiatry, 79*(9), 979–984.

Atkinson, R. C. (1975). Mnemotechnics in second-language learning. *American Psychologist, 30*(8), 821–828.

Backhaus, J., Hoeckesfeld, R., Born, J., Hohagen, F., & Junghanns, K. (2008). Immediate as well as delayed post learning sleep but not wakefulness enhances declarative memory consolidation in children. *Neurobiology of Learning & Memory, 89*, 76–80.

Baddeley, A. D. (2004). The psychology of memory. In A. D. Baddeley, M. D. Kopelman, & B. A. Wilson (eds), *The Essential Handbook of Memory Disorders for Clinicians* (pp. 1–14). Chichester: John Wiley & Sons.

Baddeley, A. (2010). Long-term and working memory: How do they interact? In L. Bäckman & L. Nyberg (eds), *Memory, Aging and the Brain: A festschrift in honour of Lars-Göran Nilsson* (pp. 7–23). New York: Psychology Press.

Baddeley, A. D. & Hitch, G. (1974). Working memory. In G. H. Bower (ed.), *The Psychology of Learning and Motivation: Advances in research and theory*: Vol. 8 (pp. 47–89). New York: Academic Press.

Barnes, L. L., Wilson, R. S., Bienias, J. L., Schneider, J. A., Evans, D. A., & Bennett, D. A. (2005). Sex differences in the clinical manifestations of Alzheimer disease pathology. *Archives of General Psychiatry, 62*(6), 685–691.

Barnier, A. J., McConkey, K. M., & Wright, J. (2004). Posthypnotic amnesia for autobiographical episodes: Influencing memory accessibility and quality. *International Journal of Clinical and Experimental Hypnosis, 52*, 260–279.

Basak, C., Boot, W. R., Voss, M. W., & Kramer, A. F. (2008). Can training in a real-time strategy video game attenuate cognitive decline in older adults? *Psychology and Aging, 23*(4), 765–777.

Berr, C., Wancata, J., & Ritchie, K. (2005). Prevalence of dementia in the elderly in Europe. *European Neuropsychopharmacology, 15*(4), 463–471.

Bower, G. H. (1981). Mood and memory. *American Psychologist, 36*(2), 129–148.

Bower, G. H. (2008). The evolution of a cognitive psychologist: A journey from simple behaviors to complex mental acts. *Annual Review of Psychology, 59*, 1–27.

Brewer, W. F. & Treyens, J. C. (1981). Role of schemata in memory for places. *Cognitive Psychology, 13*, 207–230.

Cahill, L., Prins, B., Weber, M., & McGaugh, J. L. (1994). Beta-adrenergic activation and memory for emotional events. *Nature, 371*(6499), 702–704.

Cardena, E. & Gleaves, D. H. (2007). Dissociative disorders. In M. Hersen, S. M. Turner, & D. C. Beidel (eds), *Adult Psychopathology and Diagnosis* (5th edn; pp. 473–503). Hoboken, NJ: John Wiley & Sons, Inc.

Cavallini, E., Pagnin, A., & Vecchi, T. (2003). Aging and everyday memory: The beneficial effect of memory training. *Archives of Gerontology and Geriatrics, 37*(3), 241–257.

Changeux, J. (2011). The epigenetic variability of memory: Brain plasticity and artistic creation. In S. Nalbantian, P. M. Matthews, & J. L. McClelland (eds), *The Memory Process: Neuroscientific and humanistic perspectives* (pp. 55–72). Cambridge, MA: MIT Press.

Chein, J. M., Moore, A. B., & Conway, A. R. A. (2011). Domain-general mechanisms of complex working memory span. *Neuroimage, 54*(1), 550–559.

Chen, G., Zou, X., Watanabe, H., van Deursen, J. M., & Shen, J. (2010). CREB binding protein is required for both short-term and long-term memory formation. *Journal of Neuroscience, 30*(39), 13066–13077.

Chin, J. H., Ma, L., MacTavish, D., & Jhamandas, J. H. (2007). Amyloid beta protein modulates glutamate-mediated neurotransmission in the rat basal forebrain: Involvement of presynaptic neuronal nicotinic acetylcholine and metabotropic glutamate receptors. *Journal of Neuroscience, 27*(35), 9262–9269.

Christman, S. D. & Propper, R. E. (2010). Episodic memory and interhemispheric interaction: Handedness and eye movements. In G. M. Davies & D. B. Wright (eds), *Current Issues in Applied Memory Research* (pp. 185–205). New York: Psychology Press.

Conway, M. A. (2005). Memory and the self. *Journal of Memory and Language, 53*, 594–628.

Corkin, S. (1984). Lasting consequences of bilateral medial temporal lobectomy: Clinical course and experimental findings in H. M. *Seminars in Neuroscience, 4*, 249–259.

Courage, M. L., Howe, M. L., Ilkowska, M., Engle, R. W., Kossowska, M., Orehek, E., & Brzezicka, A. (2010). Individual differences in working memory and higher-ordered processing: The commentaries. In A. Gruszka, G. Matthews, & B. Szymura (eds), *Handbook of Individual Differences in Cognition: Attention, memory, and executive control* (pp. 419–436). New York: Springer Science + Business Media.

Cowan, N. & Chen, Z. (2009). How chunks form in long-term memory and affect short-term memory limits. In A. S. C. Thorn & M. P. A. Page (eds.), *Interactions between short-term and long-term memory in the verbal domain* (pp. 86–107). New York: Psychology Press.

Craik, F. I. M. & Lockhart, R. S. (1972). Levels of processing: A framework for memory research. *Journal of Verbal Learning and Verbal Behavior, 11*, 671–684.

Denver, J. Y., Lane, S. M., & Cherry, K. E. (2010). Recent versus remote: Flashbulb memory for 9/11 and self-selected events from the reminiscence bump. *International Journal of Aging & Human Development, 70*(4), 275–297.

Devenport, J. L., Kimbrough, C. D., & Cutler, B. L. (2009). Effectiveness of traditional safeguards against erroneous conviction arising from mistaken eyewitness identification. In B. L. Cutler (ed.), *Expert Testimony on the Psychology of Eyewitness Identification* (pp. 51–68). New York: Oxford University Press.

Dudai, Y. (2011). The engram revisited: On the elusive permanence of memory. In S. Nalbantian, P. M. Matthews, & J. L. McClelland (eds), *The Memory Process: Neuroscientific and humanistic perspectives* (pp. 29–40). Cambridge, MA: MIT Press.

Edery-Halpern, G. & Nachson, I. (2004). Distinctiveness in flashbulb memory: Comparative analysis of five terrorist attacks. *Memory, 12*(2), 147–157.

Erdelyi, M. H. (2010). The ups and downs of memory. *American Psychologist, 65*(7), 623–633.

Erten-Lyons, D., Woltjer, R. L., Dodge, H., Nixon, R., Vorobik, R., Calvert, J. F., Leahy, M., Montine, T., & Kaye, J. (2009). Factors associated with resistance to dementia despite high Alzheimer disease pathology. *Neurology, 72*(4), 354–360.

Eysenck, M. W., Matthews, G., Nęcka, E., Chuderski, A., Schweizer, K., & Szymura, B. (2010). Individual differences in attention: The commentaries. In A. Gruszka, G. Matthews, & B. Szymura (eds), *Handbook of Individual Differences in Cognition: Attention, memory, and executive control* (pp. 283–292). New York: Springer Science + Business Media.

Fioravante, D. & Byrne, J. H. (2011). Protein degradation and memory formation. *Brain Research Bulletin, 85*(1–2), 14–20.

Forgas, J. P. (2008). Affect, cognition, and social behavior: The effects of mood on memory, social judgments, and social interaction. In M. A. Gluck, J. R. Anderson, & S. M. Kosslyn (eds), *Memory and Mind: A festschrift for Gordon H. Bower* (pp. 261–279). Mahwah, NJ: Lawrence Erlbaum Associates.

Gathercole, S. E. (1998). The development of memory. *Journal of Child Psychology and Psychiatry, 39*, 3–27. DOI: 10.1111/1469-7610.00301.

Gilchrist, A. L. & Cowan, N. (2010). Conscious and unconscious aspects of working memory. In I. Czigler & I. Winkler (eds), *Unconscious Memory Representations in Perception* (pp. 1–35). Amsterdam, Netherlands: John Benjamins Publishing Company.

Glaser, V., Carlini, V. P., Gabach, L., Ghersi, M., de Barioglio, S. R., Ramirez, O. A., & Latini, A. (2010). The intra-hippocampal leucine administration impairs memory consolidation and LTP generation in rats. *Cellular and Molecular Neurobiology, 30*(7), 1067–1075.

Greene, R. L. (1989). Spacing effects in memory: Evidence for a two-process account. *Journal of Experimental Psychology: Learning, Memory, and Cognition, 15*(3), 371–377.

Hambrick, D. Z. & Engle, R. W. (2003). The role of working memory in problem solving. In J. E. Davidson & R. J. Sternberg (eds), *The Psychology of Problem Solving* (pp. 176–206). New York: Cambridge University Press.

Hasher, L. & Zacks, R. T. (1979). Automatic and effortful processes in memory. *Journal of Experimental Psychology: General, 108*(3), 356–388.

Hawley, W. R., Grissom, E. M., & Dohanich, G. P. (2011). The relationships between trait anxiety, place recognition memory, and learning strategy. *Behavioural Brain Research, 216*(2), 525–530.

Hochman, J. (2001). A basic online search on the eidetic with PsycINFO, MEDLINE and ERIC. *Journal of Mental Imagery, 25*(1–2), 99–215.

Hochman, J. (2010). The eidetic: An image whose time has come? *Journal of Mental Imagery, 34*(1–2), 1–9.

Hofmann, W., Friese, M., Schmeichel, B. J., & Baddeley, A. D. (2011). Working memory and self-regulation. In K. D. Vohs & R. F. Baumeister (eds), *Handbook of Self-Regulation: Research, theory, and applications* (2nd edn; pp. 204–225). New York: Guilford Press.

Hoveida, R., Alaei, H., Oryan, S., Parivar, K., & Reisi, P. (2011). Treadmill running improves spatial memory in an animal model of Alzheimer's disease. *Behavioural Brain Research, 216*(1), 270–274.

Hunt, N. C. (2010). *Memory, War and Trauma*. New York: Cambridge University Press.

Hyman, I. E., Jr. & Kleinknecht, E. E. (1999). False childhood memories: Research, theory, and applications. In L. M. Williams & V. L. Banyard (eds), *Trauma & Memory* (pp. 175–188). Thousand Oaks, CA: Sage Publications.

Jacoby, L. L., Bishara, A. J., Hessels, S., & Toth, J. P. (2005). Aging, subjective experience, and cognitive control: Dramatic false remembering by older adults. *Journal of Experimental Psychology: General, 134*(2), 131–148.

Jeneson, A., Kirwan, C. B., Hopkins, R. O., Wixted, J. T., & Squire, L. R. (2010). Recognition memory and the hippocampus: A test of the hippocampal contribution to recollection and familiarity. *Learning & Memory, 17*(1), 63–70.

Jonides, J., Lewis, R. L., Nee, D. E., Lustig, C. A., Berman, M. G., & Moore, K. S. (2008). The mind and brain of short-term memory. *Annual Review of Psychology, 59*, 193–224.

Jonides, J., Sylvester, C. C., Lacey, S. C., Wager, T. D., Nichols, T. E., & Awh, E. (2003). Modules of working memory. In R. H. Kluwe, G. Lüer, & F. Rösler (eds), *Principles of Learning and Memory* (pp. 113–134). Cambridge, MA: Birkhäuser.

Just, M. A. & Carpenter, P. A. (2002). A capacity theory of comprehension: Individual differences in working memory. In T. A. Polk & C. M. Seifert (eds), *Cognitive Modeling* (pp. 131–177). Cambridge, MA: MIT Press.

Kennedy, Q., Mather, M., & Carstensen, L. L. (2004). The role of motivation in the age-related positivity effect in autobiographical memory. *Psychological Science, 15*(3), 208–214.

Kensinger, E. A. & Corkin, S. (2003). Memory enhancement for emotional words: Are emotional words more vividly remembered than neutral words? *Memory & Cognition, 31*(8), 1169–1180.

Kensinger, E. A., Ullmann, M. T., & Corkin, S. (2001). Bilateral medial temporal lobe damage does not affect lexical or grammatical processing. Evidence from amnesic patient H. M. *Hippocampus, 11*(4), 347–360.

Kessels, R. P. C. & Postma, A. (2002). Verbal interference during encoding and maintenance of spatial information in working memory. *Current Psychology Letters: Behaviour, Brain & Cognition, 9*, 39–46.

Kihlström, J. F. (2001). *Dissociative Disorders*. New York: Kluwer Academic/Plenum.

Kihlström, J. F. (2006). Repression: A unified theory of a will-o'-the-wisp. *Behavioral and Brain Sciences, 29*(5), 523.

Lashley, K. S. (1948). Brain mechanisms and intelligence, 1929. In W. Dennis (ed.), *Readings in the History of Psychology* (pp. 557–570). East Norwalk, CT: Appleton-Century-Crofts.

LeDoux, J. E. & Doyère, V. (2011). Emotional memory processing: Synaptic connectivity. In S. Nalbantian, P. M. Matthews, & J. L. McClelland (eds), *The Memory Process: Neuroscientific and humanistic perspectives* (pp. 153–171). Cambridge, MA: MIT Press.

Lemonick, M. D. (2007). Why we get disgusted. *Time Magazine,* May 24, http://www.time.com/time/printout/0,8816,1625167,00.html, accessed 30 November 2012.

Lindsay, D. S., Hagen, L., Read, J. D., Wade, K. A., & Garry, M. (2004). True photographs and false memories. *Psychological Science, 15*(3), 149–154.

Loewenstein, R. J. (2007). Dissociative identity disorder: Issues in the iatrogenesis controversy. In D. Spiegel, E. Vermetten, & M. Dorahy (eds), *Traumatic Dissociation: Neurobiology and treatment*. Washington: American Psychiatric Publishing.

Loftus, E. F. (2005). Planting misinformation in the human mind: A 30-year investigation of the malleability of memory. *Learning & Memory, 12*(4), 361–366.

Loftus, E. F. & Ketcham, K. (1991). *Witness for the Defense*. New York: St. Martin's Press.

Loftus, E. F. & Loftus, G. R. (1980). On the permanence of stored information in the human brain. *American Psychologist, 35*(5), 409–420.

Loftus, E. F., Miller, D. G., & Burns, H. J. (1978). Semantic integration of verbal information into a visual memory. *Journal of Experimental Psychology: Human Learning and Memory, 4*(1), 19–31.

Lovheim, H., Sandman, P., Karlsson, S., & Gustafson, Y. (2009). Sex differences in the prevalence of behavioral and psychological symptoms of dementia. *International Psychogeriatrics, 21*(3), 469–475.

Luh, C. W. (1922). The conditions of retention. *Psychological Monographs, 31*(3), i–87.

Lynch, G., Granger, R., & Staubli, U. (1991). Long-term potentiation and the structure of memory. In W. C. Abraham, M. Corballis, & K. G. White (eds), *Memory Mechanisms: A tribute to G. V. Goddard* (pp. 3–26). Hillsdale, NJ: Lawrence Erlbaum Associates, Inc.

Macleod, M. D., Saunders, J., & Chalmers, L. (2010). Retrieval-induced forgetting: The unintended consequences of unintended forgetting. In G. M. Davies & D. B. Wright (eds), *Current Issues in Applied Memory Research* (pp. 50–71). New York: Psychology Press.

Magnussen, S., Greenlee, M. W., Baumann, O., & Endestad, T. (2010). Visual perceptual memory: Anno 2008. In L. Bäckman & L. Nyberg (eds), *Memory, Aging and the Brain: A festschrift in honour of Lars-Göran Nilsson* (pp. 53–75). New York: Psychology Press.

Markowitsch, H. J., Welzer, H., & Emmans, D. (2010). *The Development of Autobiographical Memory*. New York: Psychology Press.

Martin, N. (2009). The roles of semantic and phonological processing in short-term memory and learning: Evidence from aphasia. In A. S. C. Thorn & M. P. A. Page (eds), *Interactions between Short-Term and Long-Term Memory in the Verbal Domain* (pp. 220–243). New York: Psychology Press.

Mather, M. (2009). When emotion intensifies memory interference. In B. H. Ross (ed.), *The Psychology of Learning and Motivation: Vol. 51* (pp. 101–120). San Diego: Elsevier Academic Press.

Matthews, P. M. (2011). The mnemonic brain: Neuroimaging, neuro-pharmacology, and disorders of memory. In S. Nalbantian, P. M. Matthews, & J. L. McClelland (eds), *The Memory Process: Neuroscientific and humanistic perspectives* (pp. 99–127). Cambridge, MA: MIT Press.

Maybery, M. T. & Do, N. (2003). Relationships between facets of working memory and performance on a curriculum-based mathematics test in children. *Educational and Child Psychology, 20*(3), 77–92.

Mazzoni, G., Heap, M., & Scoboria, A. (2010). Hypnosis and memory: Theory, laboratory research, and applications. In S. J. Lynn, J. W. Rhue, & I. Kirsch (eds), *Handbook of Clinical Hypnosis* (2nd edn; pp. 709–741). Washington: American Psychological Association.

McClelland, J. L. (2011). Memory as a constructive process: The parallel distributed processing approach. In S. Nalbantian, P. M. Matthews, & J. L. McClelland (eds), *The Memory Process: Neuroscientific and humanistic perspectives* (pp. 129–155). Cambridge, MA: MIT Press.

McGaugh, J. L. (2003). *Memory and Emotion: The making of lasting memories*. New York: Columbia University Press.

McGaugh, J. L. (2006). Make mild moments memorable: Add a little arousal. *Trends in Cognitive Sciences, 10*(8), 345–347.

Mecklinger, A., Brunnemann, N., & Kipp, K. (2011). Two processes for recognition memory in children of early school age: An event-related potential study. *Journal of Cognitive Neuroscience, 23*(2), 435–446.

Meyer-Luehmann, M., Spires-Jones, T., Prada, C., Garcia-Alloza, M., de Calignon, A., Rozkalne, A., Koenigsknecht-Talboo, J., Holtzman, D. M., Bacskai, B. J., & Hyman, B. T. (2008). Rapid appearance and local toxicity of amyloid-β plaques in a mouse model of Alzheimer's disease. *Nature, 451*(7179), 720–724.

Miller, G. A. (1956). The magical number seven, plus or minus two: Some limits on our capacity for processing information. *Psychological Review, 63*(2), 81–97.

Nee, D. E., Berman, M. G., Moore, K. S., & Jonides, J. (2008). Neuroscientific evidence about the distinction between short- and long-term memory. *Current Directions in Psychological Science, 17*(2), 102–106.

Neuschatz, J. S., Preston, E. L., & Toglia, M. P. (2005). Comparison of the efficacy of two name-learning techniques: Expanding rehearsal and name-face imagery. *American Journal of Psychology, 118*, 79–101.

O'Connor, T., Sadleir, K. R., Maus, E., Velliquette, R. A., Zhao, J., Cole, S. L., & Vassar, R. (2008). Phosphorylation of the translation initiation factor eIF2alpha increases BACE1 levels and promotes amyloidogenesis. *Neuron, 60*(6), 988–1009.

Öztekin, I., McElree, B., Staresina, B. P., & Davachi, L. (2009). Working memory retrieval: Contributions of the left prefrontal cortex, the left posterior parietal cortex, and the hippocampus. *Journal of Cognitive Neuroscience, 21*(3), 581–593.

Park, D. C. & Reuter-Lorenz, P. (2009). The adaptive brain: Aging and neurocognitive scaffolding. *Annual Review of Psychology, 60*, 173–196.

Piper, A. & Merskey, H. (2004). The persistence of folly: A critical examination of dissociative identity disorder: Part I: The excesses of an improbable concept. *Canadian Journal of Psychiatry, 49*(9), 592–600.

Postle, B. R. (2003). Context in verbal short-term memory. *Memory & Cognition, 31*(8), 1198–1207.

Postle, B. R. (2009). Mechanisms underlying the short-term retention of information. In F. Rösler, C. Ranganath, B. Röder, & R. H. Kluwe (eds), *Neuroimaging of Human Memory: Linking cognitive processes to neural systems* (pp. 213–226). New York: Oxford University Press.

Pressley, M., Levin, J. R., & Delaney, H. D. (1982). The mnemonic keyword method. *Review of Educational Research, 52*(1), 61–91.

Raaijmakers, J. G. & Shiffrin, R. M. (1992). Models for recall and recognition. *Annual Review of Psychology, 43*, 205–234.

Raaijmakers, J. G. W. & Shiffrin, R. M. (2002). Models of memory. In H. Pashler & D. Medin (eds), *Stevens' Handbook of Experimental Psychology: Vol. 2: Memory and cognitive processes* (3rd edn; pp. 43–76). Hoboken, NJ: John Wiley & Sons, Inc.

Ramirez, J. J., Poulton, W. E., Knelson, E., Barton, C., King, M. A., & Klein, R. L. (2011). Focal expression of mutated tau in entorhinal cortex neurons of rats impairs spatial working memory. *Behavioural Brain Research, 216*(1), 332–340.

Ramponi, C., Richardson-Klavehn, A., & Gardiner, J. M. (2007). Component processes of conceptual priming and associative cued recall: The roles of preexisting representation and depth of processing. *Journal of Experimental Psychology: Learning, Memory & Cognition, 33*, 843–862.

Rathbone, C. J., Moulin, C. J. A., & Conway, M. A. (2009). Autobiographical memory and amnesia: Using conceptual knowledge to ground the self. *Neurocase, 15*(5), 405–418.

Raugh, M. R. & Atkinson, R. C. (1975). A mnemonic method for learning a second-language vocabulary. *Journal of Educational Psychology, 67*(1), 1–16.

Richardson, A. (2011). Memory and imagination in romantic fiction. In S. Nalbantian, P. M. Matthews, & J. L. McClelland (eds), *The Memory Process: Neuroscientific and humanistic perspectives* (pp. 277–296). Cambridge, MA: MIT Press.

Rolls, E. T. (2011). Functions of human emotional memory: The brain and emotion. In S. Nalbantian, P. M. Matthews, & J. L. McClelland (eds), *The Memory Process: Neuroscientific and humanistic perspectives* (pp. 173–191). Cambridge, MA: MIT Press.

Rosenzweig, M. R. (1996). Aspects of the search for neural mechanisms of memory. *Annual Review of Psychology, 47*, 1–32.

Sadock, B. J. & Sadock, V. A. (2007). *Kaplan & Sadock's Synopsis of Psychiatry* (10th edn). Philadelphia: Lippincott Williams & Wilkins.

Sanberg, C. D., Jones, F. L., Do, V. H., Dieguez Jr., D., & Derrick, B. E. (2006). 5-HT1a receptor antagonists block perforant path-dentate LTP induced in novel, but not familiar, environments. *Learning & Memory, 13*(1), 52–62.

Schacter, D. L. (2001). *The Seven Sins of Memory: How the mind forgets and remembers*. New York: Houghton.

Schwanenflugel, P. J., Akin, C., & Luh, W. (1992). Context availability and the recall of abstract and concrete words. *Memory & Cognition, 20*(1), 96–104.

Schwarting, R. K. W. (2003). The principle of memory consolidation and its pharmacological modulation. In R. H. Kluwe, G. Lüer, & F. Rösler (eds), *Principles of Learning and Memory* (pp. 137–153). Cambridge, MA: Birkhäuser.

Selkoe, D. J. (1991). Amyloid protein and Alzheimer's disease. *Scientific American, 265*, 68–78.

Selkoe, D. J. (2000). The origins of Alzheimer's disease: A is for amyloid. *JAMA, 283*(12), 1615–1617.

Selkoe, D. J. (2011). Alzheimer's disease. *Cold Spring Harbor Perspectives in Biology, 3*(7).

Silva, A. J. (2011). Molecular genetic approaches to memory consolidation. In S. Nalbantian, P. M. Matthews, & J. L. McClelland (eds), *The Memory Process: Neuroscientific and humanistic perspectives* (pp. 41–54). Cambridge, MA: MIT Press.

Sizemore, C. C. (1991). *A Mind of My Own: The woman who was known as 'Eve' tells the story of her triumph over multiple personality disorder.* New York: William Morrow.

Smith, J. C, Nielson, K. A., Woodard, J. L., Seidenberg, M., Durgerian, S., Antuono, P., & Rao, S. M. (2011). Interactive effects of physical activity and APOE-e4 on semantic memory activation in healthy elders. *NeuroImage, 54*(1), 635–644.

Sperling, G. (1960). The information available in brief visual presentation. *Psychological Monographs, 74*(11), 29.

Squire L. R. (1992). Memory and the hippocampus: A synthesis from findings with rats, monkeys, and humans. *Psychological Review, 99*(2): 195–231.

Squire, L. R. & Schacter, D. L. (eds) (2002). *Neuropsychology of Memory* (3rd edn). New York: Guilford Press.

Stickgold, R. (2011). Memory in sleep and dreams: The construction of meaning. In S. Nalbantian, P. M. Matthews, & J. L. McClelland (eds), *The Memory Process: Neuroscientific and humanistic perspectives* (pp. 73–95). Cambridge, MA: MIT Press.

Sun, M. (ed.) (2007). *New Research in Cognitive Sciences.* Hauppauge, NY: Nova Science Publishers.

Sweatt, J. D. (2010). *Mechanisms of Memory* (2nd edn). San Diego: Elsevier Academic Press.

Talarico, J. M. & Rubin, D. C. (2003). Confidence, not consistency, characterizes flashbulb memories. *Psychological Science, 14*(5), 455–461.

Talarico, J. M. & Rubin, D. C. (2007). Flashbulb memories are special after all; in phenomenology, not accuracy. *Applied Cognitive Psychology, 21*(5), 557–578.

Talarico, J. M. & Rubin, D. C. (2009). Flashbulb memories result from ordinary memory processes and extraordinary event characteristics. In O. Luminet & A. Curci (eds), *Flashbulb Memories: New issues and new perspectives* (pp. 79–97). New York: Psychology Press.

Thigpen, C. H. & Cleckley, H. M. (1957). *The Three Faces of Eve.* New York: McGraw-Hill.

Thomas, A. K., Hannula, D. E., & Loftus, E. F. (2007). How self-relevant imagination affects memory for behaviour. *Applied Cognitive Psychology, 21*(1), 69–86.

Thompson, R. F. (2000). *The Brain: A neuroscience primer* (3rd edn). New York: Worth Publishers.

Tillmann, B., Peretz, I., & Samson, S. (2011). Neurocognitive approaches to memory in music: Music is memory. In S. Nalbantian, P. M. Matthews, & J. L. McClelland (eds), *The Memory Process: Neuroscientific and humanistic perspectives* (pp. 377–394). Cambridge, MA: MIT Press.

Trout-Ervin, E. (1990). Application of keyword mnemonics to learning terminology in the college classroom. *Journal of Experimental Education, 59*(1), 31–41.

Tsukiura, T., Sekiguchi, A., Yomogida, Y., Nakagawa, S., Shigemune, Y., Kambara, T., & Kawashima, R. (2011). Effects of aging on hippocampal and anterior temporal activations during successful retrieval of memory for face–name associations. *Journal of Cognitive Neuroscience, 23*(1), 200–213.

Tulving, E. (1974). Cue-dependent forgetting. *American Scientist, 62*, 74–82.

Tulving, E., Schacter, D. L., & Stark, H. A. (1982). Priming effects in word fragment completion are independent of recognition memory. *Journal of Experimental Psychology: Learning, Memory and Cognition, 8*(4), 336–342.

Turkington, C. & Harris, J. R. (2009). *The Encyclopedia of Memory and Memory Disorders* (3rd edn). New York: Facts on File/Infobase Publishing.

Vidal, F. (2011). Memory, movies, and the brain. In S. Nalbantian, P. M. Matthews, & J. L. McClelland (eds), *The Memory Process:*

Neuroscientific and humanistic perspectives (pp. 395–415). Cambridge, MA: MIT Press.

Voss, J. L. (2009). Long-term associative memory capacity in man. *Psychonomic Bulletin & Review, 16*(6), 1076–1081.

Wang, X. (2005). Discovering spatial working memory fields in pre-frontal cortex. *Journal of Neurophysiology, 93*(6), 3027–3028.

Was, C. A. (2010). The persistence of content-specific memory operations: Priming effects following a 24-h delay. *Psychonomic Bulletin & Review, 17*(3), 362–368.

Wells, G. L. & Loftus, E. F. (2003). Eyewitness memory for people and events. In A. M. Goldstein (ed.), *Handbook of Psychology: Forensic psychology: Vol. 11* (pp. 149–160). Hoboken, NJ: John Wiley & Sons, Inc.

West, R. L., Bagwell, D. K., & Dark-Freudeman, A. (2008). Self-efficacy and memory aging: The impact of a memory intervention based on self-efficacy. *Aging, Neuropsychology, and Cognition, 15*(3), 302–329.

Wilson, B. A. & Wearing, D. (1995). Prisoner of consciousness: A state of just awakening following Herpes Simplex Encephalitis. In R. Campbell & M. A. Conway (eds), *Broken Memories: Case studies in memory impairment* (pp. 14–30). Oxford: Blackwell.

Winningham, R. G. (2010). *Train Your Brain: How to maximize memory ability in older adulthood.* Amityville, NY: Baywood Publishing Co.

Wixted, J. T. (2004). The psychology and neuroscience of forgetting. *Annual Review of Psychology, 55*, 235–269.

Wixted, J. T. (2005). A theory about why we forget what we once knew. *Current Directions in Psychological Science, 14*, 6–9.

Wixted, J. T. (2010). The role of retroactive interference and consolidation in everyday forgetting. In S. Della Sala (ed.), *Forgetting* (pp. 285–312). New York: Psychology Press.

Wixted, J. T. & Squire, L. R. (2010). The role of the human hippocampus in familiarity-based and recollection-based recognition memory. *Behavioural Brain Research, 215*(2), 197–208.

Zhu, B., Chen, C., Loftus, E. F., Lin, C., He, Q., Chen, C., & Dong, Q. (2010). Individual differences in false memory from misinformation: Cognitive factors. *Memory, 18*(5), 543–555.

CHAPTER 11

Acredolo, L. & Goodwyn, S. (1988). Symbolic gesturing in normal infants. *Child Development, 59*, 450–466.

APA (American Psychiatric Association). (2000). *Diagnostic and Statistical Manual of Mental Disorders* (4th edn). Washington: American Psychiatric Association.

Aschersleben, G., Hofer, T., & Jovanovic, B. (2008). The link between infant attention to goal-directed action and later theory of mind abilities. *Developmental Science, 11*(6), 862–868.

Aslin, R. N., Jusczyk, P., & Pisoni, D. B. (1998). Speech and auditory processing during infancy: Constraints on and precursors to language. In D. Kuhn & R. S. Siegler (eds), *Handbook of Child Psychology: Vol. 2: Cognition, perception, and language* (5th edn; pp. 147–198). New York: John Wiley & Sons.

Baer, L., Rauch, S. L., Ballantine, T., Martuza, R., *et al.* (1995). Cingulotomy for intractable obsessive-compulsive disorder: Prospective long-term follow-up of 18 patients. *Archives of General Psychiatry, 52*(5), 384–392.

Bensafi, M., Sobel, N., & Khan, R. M. (2007). Hedonic-specific activity in piriform cortex during odor imagery mimics that during odor perception. *Journal of Neurophysiology, 98*(6), 3254–3262.

Berenbaum, H. & Barch, D. (1995). The categorization of thought disorder. *Journal of Psycholinguistic Research, 24*, 349–376.

Bloom, L. (1970). *Language Development: Form and function in emerging grammars.* Cambridge, MA: MIT Press.

Bornstein, M. H., Tal, J., Rahn, C., Galperin, C. Z., Pacheux, M., Lamour, M., Toda, S., Azuma, H., Ogino, M., & Tamis-LeMonda, C. S. (1992). Functional analysis of the contents of maternal speech to infants of 5 and 13 months in four cultures: Argentina, France, Japan, and the United States. *Developmental Psychology, 28*, 593–603.

Bourne, L. E., Dominowski, R. L., & Loftus, W. F. (1979). *Cognitive Processes.* Englewood Cliffs, NJ: Prentice Hall.

Carlsson, A. & Lindqvist, M. (1963). Effect of chlorpromazine and haloperidol on the formation of 3-methoxytyramine and normetanephrine in mouse brain. *Acta Pharmacology, 20,* 140.

Carter, C. S., Botvinick, M. M., & Cohen, J. D. (1999). The contribution of the anterior cingulate cortex to executive processes in cognition. *Reviews in the Neurosciences, 10*(1), 49–57.

Catrambone, R. (1998). The subgoal learning model: Novel problems. *Journal of Experimental Psychology: General, 127,* 355–376.

Chandler, M. J. & Carpendale, J. I. (1998). Inching toward a mature theory of mind. In M. Ferrari & R. J. Sternberg (eds), *Self-Awareness: Its Nature and Development* (pp. 148–190). New York: Guilford Press.

Chomsky, N. (1964). The development of grammar in child language: Formal discussion. *Monographs of the Society for Research in Child Development, 29,* 35–39.

Clements, A. M., Rimrodt, S. L., Abel, J. R., Blankner, J. G., Mostofsky, S. H., Pekar, J. J., Denckla, M. B., & Cutting, L. E. (2006). Sex differences in cerebral laterality of language and visuospatial processing. *Brain Language, 98*(2), 150–158.

Coltheart, M. (2005). Modeling reading: The dual-route approach. In M. J. Snowling & C. Hulme (eds), *The Science of Reading: A handbook* (pp. 6–23). Oxford: Oxford University Press.

Connolly, T. & Zeelenberg, M. (2002). Regret in decision making. *Current Directions in Psychological Science, 11*(6), 212–216.

Cooper, R. P. & Aslin, R. N. (1994). Developmental differences in infant attention to the spectral properties of infant-directed speech. *Child Development, 65,* 1663–1677.

Covington, M. A., He, C., Brown, C., Naçi, L., McClain, J. T., Fjordbak, B. S., Semple, J., & Brown, J. (2005). Schizophrenia and the structure of language: The linguist's view. *Schizophrenia Research, 77,* 85–98.

Critchley, H. D., Elliott, R., Mathias, C. J., & Dolan, R. J. (2000). Neural activity relating to generation and representation of galvanic skin conductance responses: A functional magnetic resonance imaging study. *Journal of Neuroscience, 20*(8), 3033–3040.

Damasio, A. R. & Geschwind, N. (1984). The neural basis of language. *Annual Review of Neuroscience, 7,* 127–147.

Davies, I. R. & Corbett, G. G. (1997). A cross-cultural study of colour grouping: Evidence for weak linguistic relativity. *British Journal of Psychology, 88*(3), 493–517.

Dietrich, C., Swingley, D., & Werker, J. F. (2007). Native language governs interpretation of salient speech sound differences at 18 months. *Proceedings of the National Academy of Sciences, 104*(41), 16027–16031.

Edwards, W. (1977). How to use multiattribute utility measurement for social decision making. *IEEE Transactions in Systems Management and Cybernetics, 17,* 326–340.

Edwards, W. & Newman, J. R. (1986). Multiattribute choice. In H. R. Arkes & K. R. Hammond (eds), *Judgment and Decision Making: An interdisciplinary reader.* Cambridge, MA: Cambridge University Press.

Eimas, P. D. (1975). Developmental studies in speech perception. In L. B. Cohen & P. Salapatek (eds), *Infant Perception: From sensation to cognition* (pp. 193–231). New York: Academic Press.

Eimas, P., Siqueland, E. R., Jusczyk, P., & Vigorito, J. (1971). Speech perception in infants. *Science, 171*(3968), 303–306.

Elliott, J. (2007). Professor researches cell phone usage among college students. *Phys.Org,* http://www.physorg.com/ news91732046.html, accessed 3 December 2012.

Ely, R. (1997). Language and literacy in the school years. In J. Berko Gleason (ed.), *The Development of Language* (4th edn; pp. 398–439). Boston: Allyn & Bacon.

Fenske, J. N. & Schwenk, T. L. (2009). Obsessive compulsive disorder: Diagnosis and management. *American Family Physician, 80,* 239–245.

Fenson, L., Dale, P., Reznick, S., Bates, E., Thal, D., & Pethick, S. (1994). Variability in early communicative development. *Monographs of the Society for Research in Child Development, 59*(242), 1–185.

Fernald, A., Taeschner, T., Dunn, J., Papousek, M., Boysson-Bardies, B., & Fukui, I. (1989). A cross-language study of prosodic modifications in mothers' and fathers' speech to preverbal infants. *Journal of Child Language, 16,* 477–502.

Foster, J. D. (2009). Mass murder is nothing to fear. *Psychology Today.* Downloaded on 11 July 2009 from: http://www.psychology-today.com/blog/the-narcissus-in-all-us/200903/mass-murder-is-nothing-to-fear.

Garvey, C. (1974). Requests and responses in children's speech. *Journal of Child Language, 2,* 41–60.

Gernsbacher, M. A. & Kaschak, M. P. (2003). Neuroimaging studies of language production and comprehension. *Annual Review of Psychology, 54,* 91–114.

Gigerenzer, G. (2004). Fast and frugal heuristics: The tools of bounded rationality. In D. J. Koehler & N. Harvey (eds), *Blackwell Handbook of Judgment and Decision Making.* Malden, MA: Blackwell Publishing.

Gigerenzer, G. & Goldstein, D. G. (1996). Reasoning the fast and frugal way: Models of bounded rationality. *Psychological Review, 103,* 650–669.

Goff, D. C. & Coyle, J. T. (2001). The emerging role of glutamate in the pathophysiology and treatment of schizophrenia. *American Journal of Psychiatry, 158,* 1367–1377.

Goldberg, A. E. (2008). Universal grammar? Or prerequisites for natural language? *Behavioral and Brain Sciences, 31*(5), 522–523.

Goldberg, R. F., Perfetti, C. A., & Schneider, W. (2006). Perceptual knowledge retrieval activates sensory brain regions. *Journal of Neuroscience: The official journal of the Society for Neuroscience, 26*(18), 4917–4921.

Goldin-Meadow, S. (1999). The role of gesture in communication and thinking. *Trends in Cognitive Sciences, 3*(11), 419–429.

González, J., Barros-Loscertales, A., Pulvermüller, F., Meseguer, V., Sanjuán, A., Belloch, V. & Avila, C. (2006). Reading cinnamon activates olfactory brain regions. *Neuroimage, 32*(2), 906–912.

Gourzis, P., Katrivanou, A., & Beratis, S. Symptomatology of the initial prodromal phase in schizophrenia. *Schizophrenia Bulletin, 28*(3):415–429, 2002.

Halle, M. (1990). Phonology. In D. Osherson and H. Lasnick, *An Invitation to Cognitive Science: Vol. 1: Language.* Cambridge, MA: MIT Press.

Harley, T. A. (2010). *Talking the Talk: Language, psychology and science.* Hove: Psychology Press.

Hart, B. & Risley, T. R. (1995). *Meaningful Differences in Everyday Parenting and Intellectual Development in Young American Children.* Baltimore: Paul H. Brookes.

Hirata, S. (2009). Chimpanzee social intelligence: Selfishness, altruism, and the mother–infant bond. *Primates, 50,* 2–11.

Holyoak, K. J. & Morrison, R. G. (eds) (2005). *The Cambridge Handbook of Thinking and Reasoning.* New York: Cambridge University Press.

Ingram, D. (1986). Phonological development: Production. In P. Fletcher & M. Garman (eds), *Language Acquisition* (2nd edn; pp. 223–239). Cambridge, MA: Cambridge University Press.

Johnson, J. S. & Newport, E. L. (1989). Critical period effects in second language learning: The influence of maturational state on the acquisition of English as a second language. *Cognitive Psychology, 21,* 60–99.

Kahneman, D. & Tversky, A. (1979). Prospect theory: An analysis of decision making under risk. *Econometrica, 47,* 263–291.

Keane, M. (2008). Texting overtakes voice in mobile phone usage. *Wired,* 29 September, at http://www.wired.com/epicenter/2008/09/texting-overtak.

Keller, D., Siegrist, M., & Gutscher, H. (2006). The role of the affect and availability of heuristics in risk communication. *Risk Analysis, 26,* 631–639.

Kessler, R. C., Ruscio, A. M., Shear, K., & Wittchen, H. (2009). Epidemiology of anxiety disorders. In M. M. Antony & M. B. Stein (eds), *Oxford Handbook of Anxiety and Related Disorders* (pp. 19–33). New York: Oxford University Press.

Kosslyn, S. M., Ball, T. M., & Reiser, B. J. (1978). Visual images preserve metric spatial information: Evidence from studies of image scanning. *Journal of Experimental Psychology: Human perception and performance, 4,* 46–60.

Kyle, J. G. (1980). Auditory deprivation from birth: Clarification of some issues. *British Journal of Audiology, 14*(1), 34–36.

Lahey, B. B., Kupfer, D. L., Beggs, V. E., & Landon, D. (1982). Do learning-disabled children exhibit peripheral deficits in selective attention? An analysis of eye movements during reading. *Journal of Abnormal Child Psychology, 10*(1), 1–10.

Lakhan, S. E. (2007). Neuropsychological generation of source amnesia: An episodic memory disorder of the frontal brain, http://cnx.org/content/m14401/1.1, accessed 4 December 2012.

Larach, V. W., Zambroni, R. T., Mancini, H. R., Mancini, R. R., & Gallado, R. T. (1997). New strategies for old problems: Tardive dyskinesia (TD): Review and report on severe TD cases treated with clorapine, with 12, 8 and 5 years of video follow-up. *Schizophrenic Research, 28,* 231–246.

Linville, P. W., Fischer, G. W., & Fischhoff, B. (1993). AIDS risk perceptions and decision biases. In J. B. Pryor & G. D. Reeder (eds), *The Social Psychology of HIV Infection.* Hillsdale, NJ: Lawrence Erlbaum Associates.

Magee, J. C. & Teachman, B. A. (2007). Why did the white bear return? Obsessive-compulsive symptoms and attributions for unsuccessful thought suppression. *Behaviour Research and Therapy, 45*(12), 2884–2898.

Maratsos, M. (2000). More overregularizations after all: New data and discussion on Marcus, Pinker, Ullman, Hollander, Rosen & Xu. *Journal of Child Language, 27*(1), 183–212.

Masataka, N. (1998). Motherese in Japanese sign language by 6-month-old hearing infants. *Developmental Psychology, 34,* 241–246.

McKelvie, S. J. & Drumheller, A. (2001). The availability heuristic with famous names: A replication. *Perceptual & Motor Skills, 92*(2), 507–516.

Mellers, B., Schwartz, A., Ho, K., & Ritov, I. (1997). Decision affect theory: Emotional reactions to the outcomes of risky options. *Psychological Science, 8,* 423–429.

Mellers, B., Schwartz, A., & Cooke, A. D. J. (1998). Judgment and decision making. *Annual Review of Psychology, 49,* 447–477.

Miller, G. (1978). The acquisition of word meaning. *Child Development, 49,* 999–1004.

Novick, L. R. & Bassok, M. (2005). Problem solving. In K. J. Holyoak & R. G. Morrison (eds), *The Cambridge Handbook of Thinking and Reasoning.* New York: Cambridge University Press.

O'Craven, K. M. & Kanwisher, N. (2000). Mental imagery of faces and places activates corresponding stimulus-specific brain regions. *Journal of Cognitive Neuroscience, 12*(6), 1013–1023.

Oppenheimer, D. M. (2004). Spontaneous discounting of availability in frequency judgment tasks. *Psychological Science, 15*(2), 100–105.

Patil, S. T., Zhang, L., Martenyi, F., Lowe, S. L., Jackson, K. A., Andreev, B. V., Avedisova, A. S., Bardenstein, L. M., Gurovich, I. Y., Morozova, M. A., Mosolov, S. N., Neznanov, N. G., Reznik, A. M., Smulevich, A. B., Tochilov, V. A., Johnson, B. G., Monn, J. A., & Schoepp, D. D. (2007). Activation of mGlu2/3 receptors as a new approach to treat schizophrenia: A randomized Phase 2 clinical trial. *Nature Medicine, 13,* 1102–1107.

Payne, J. W. & Bettman, J. R. (2004). Walking with the scarecrow: The information-processing approach to decision research. In D. J. Koehler & N. Harvey (eds), *Blackwell Handbook of Judgment and Decision Making.* Malden, MA: Blackwell Publishing.

Pinker, S. & Jackendoff, R. (2005). The faculty of language: What's special about it? *Cognition, 95*(2), 201–236.

Piskulic, D., Olver, J. S., Norman, T. R., & Maruff, P. (2007). Behavioural studies of spatial working memory dysfunction in schizophrenia: A quantitative literature review. *Psychiatry Research, 150*(2), 111–121.

Pobric, G., Mashal, N., Faust, M., & Lavidor, M. (2008). The role of the right cerebral hemisphere in processing novel metaphoric expressions: A transcranial magnetic stimulation study. *Journal of Cognitive Neuroscience, 20*(1), 170–181.

Redelmeier, D. A., Katz, J., & Kahneman, D. (2003). Memories of colonoscopy: A randomized trial. *Pain, 104*(1–2), 187–194.

Regier, D. A., Narrow, W. E., Rae, D. S., Manderscheid, R. W., Locke, B. Z., & Goodwin, F. K. (1993). The de facto US mental and addictive disorders service system: Epidemiologic catchment area prospective 1-year prevalence rates of disorders and services. *Archives of General Psychiatry, 50*(2), 85–94.

Reid, P. J. (2009). Adapting to the human world: Dogs' responsiveness to our social cues. *Behavioral Processes, 80,* 325–33.

Reznick, J. S. & Goldfield, B. A. (1992). Rapid change in lexical development in comprehension and production. *Developmental Psychology, 28,* 406–416.

Rizzolatti, G. & Fabbri-Destro, M. (2008). The mirror system and its role in social cognition. *Current Opinion in Neurobiology, 18*(2), 179–184.

Rupke, S. J., Blecke, D., & Renfrow, M. (2006). Cognitive therapy for depression. *American Family Physician, 73*(1), 83–86.

Rymer, R. (1994). *Genie: A scientific tragedy.* New York: Harper Paperbacks.

Sabbagh, M. A., Bowman, L. C., Evraire, L. E., & Ito, J. M. B. (2009). Neurodevelopmental correlates of theory of mind in preschool children. *Child Development, 80*(4), 1147–1162.

Sachs, J. (2009). Communication development in infancy. In J. B. Gleason (ed.), *The Development of Language* (7th edn; pp. 40–60). Columbus, OH: Allyn & Bacon.

Sanford, A. J., Fray, N., Stewart, A., & Moxey, L. (2002). Perspective in statements of quantity, with implications for consumer psychology. *Psychological Science, 13,* 130–134.

Schwartz, B. L. (2005). *The Paradox of Choice.* New York: Harper Perennial.

Schwartz, G., Ward, A. H., Monterosso, J., Lyubomirsky, S., White, K., & Lehman, D. (2002). Maximizing versus satisficing: Happiness is a matter of choice. *Journal of Personality and Social Psychology, 83,* 1178–1197.

Senechal, M. & LeFevre, J. (2001). Storybook reading and parent teaching: Links to language and literacy development. In P. R. Britto & J. Brooks-Gunn (eds), *New Directions in Child Development: No. 92: The role of family literacy environments in promoting young children's emerging literacy skills* (pp. 39–52). San Francisco: Jossey-Bass.

Shin, L. M., Orr, S. P., Carson, M. A., Rauch, S. L., Macklin, M. L., Lasko, N. B., *et al.* (2004). Regional cerebral blood flow in the amygdala and medial prefrontal cortex during traumatic imagery in male and female Vietnam veterans with PTSD. *Archives of General Psychiatry, 61*(2), 168–176.

Simon, H. A. (1957). *Models of Man.* New York: John Wiley & Sons, Inc.

Simon, H. (1990). Invariants of human behavior. *Annual Review of Psychology, 4,* 1–19.

Skinner, B. F. (1957). *Verbal Behavior.* Englewood Cliffs, NJ: Prentice Hall.

Slovic, P. (1990). Choice. In D. N. Osherson & E. E. Smith (eds), *Thinking: An invitation to cognitive science: Vol. 3.* Cambridge, MA: MIT Press.

Soomro, G. M., Altman, D., Rajagopal, S., & Oakley-Browne, M. (2008). Selective serotonin re-uptake inhibitors (SSRIs) versus placebo for obsessive compulsive disorder (OCD). *Cochrane Database of Systematic Reviews (Online),* (1), CD001765.

Stanovich, K. E. (2008). *How to Think Straight about Psychology* (8th edn). Boston: Allyn & Bacon.

Sullivan, P. F., Kendler, K. S., & Neale, M. C. (2003). Schizophrenia as a complex trait: Evidence from a meta-analysis of twin studies. *Archives of General Psychiatry, 60*(12), 1187–1192.

Tager-Flusberg, H. (2001). Putting words together: Morphology and syntax in the preschool years. In J. Berko Gleason (ed.), *The Development of Language* (5th edn; pp. 116–212). Boston, MA: Allyn & Bacon.

Takano, K. & Tanno, Y. (2009). Self-rumination, self-reflection, and depression: Self-rumination counteracts the adaptive effect of self-reflection. *Behavior Research and Therapy, 47*(3), 260–264.

Talwar, V. & Lee, K. (2008). Little liars: Origins of verbal deception in children. In S. Itakura & K. Fujita (eds), *Origins of the Social Mind: Evolutionary and developmental views* (pp. 157–178). New York: Springer Science + Business Media.

Talwar, V., Gordon, H. M., & Lee, K. (2007). Lying in the elementary school years: Verbal deception and its relation to second-order belief understanding. *Developmental Psychology, 43*(3), 804–810.

Tandon, R., Belmaker, R. H., Gattaz, W. F., Lopez-Ibor, J. J., Okasha, A., Singh, B., *et al.* (2008). World Psychiatric Association Pharmacopsychiatry Section statement on comparative effectiveness of antipsychotics in the treatment of schizophrenia. *Schizophrenia Research, 100*(1–3), 20–38.

Thagard, P. & Kroon, F. W. (2006). Emotional consensus in group decision making. *Mind & Society, 5*(1), 85–104.

Tversky, A. (1972). Elimination by aspects: A theory of choice. *Psychological Review, 79*, 281–299.

Tversky, A. & Kahneman, D. (1974). Judgment under uncertainty: Heuristics and biases. *Science, 185*(4157), 1124–1131.

Tversky, A. & Kahneman, D. (1993). Probabilistic reasoning. In A. I. Goldman (ed.), *Readings in Philosophy and Cognitive Science*. Cambridge, MA: MIT Press.

Wallace, V., Menn, L., & Yoshinaga-Itano, C. (1999). Is babble the gateway to speech for all children? A longitudinal study of children who are deaf or hard of hearing. *Volta Review, 100*, 121–148.

Ward, J. (2010). *The Student's Guide to Cognitive Neuroscience* (2nd edn). Hove: Psychology Press.

Wason, P. C. (1960). On the failure to eliminate hypotheses in a conceptual task. *Quarterly Journal of Experimental Psychology, 12*, 129–140.

Wellman, H. M. & Hickling, A. K. (1994). The mind's 'I': Children's conception of the mind as an active agent. *Child Development, 65*, 1564–1580.

Werker, J. F. (1989). Becoming a native listener: A developmental perspective on human speech perception. *American Scientist, 77*(1), 54–59.

Whorf, B. L. (1956). *Language, Thought, and Reality*. Cambridge, MA: MIT Press.

Zola, S. M. (1998). Memory, amnesia, and the issue of recovered memory: Neurobiological aspects. *Clinical Psychology Review, 18*(8), 915–932.

CHAPTER 12

Alegre, A. (2011). Parenting styles and children's emotional intelligence: What do we know? *Family Journal, 19*(1), 56–62.

Ambady, N., Paik, S. K., Steele, J., Owen-Smith, A., & Mitchell, J. P. (2004). Deflecting negative self-relevant stereotype activation: The effects of individuation. *Journal of Experimental Social Psychology, 40*(3), 401–408.

Ambady, N., Shih, M., Kim, A., & Pittinsky, T. L. (2001). Stereotype susceptibility in children: Effects of identity activation on quantitative performance. *Psychological Science, 12*(5), 385–390.

APA (American Psychiatric Association). (2000). *Diagnostic and Statistical Manual of Mental Disorders* (4th edn). Washington: American Psychiatric Association.

Ardelt, M. (2011). Wisdom, age, and well-being. In K. W. Schaie & S. L. Willis (eds), *Handbook of the Psychology of Aging* (7th edn; pp. 279–291). San Diego: Elsevier Academic Press.

Arnold, D. H., Zeljo, A., Doctoroff, G. L., & Ortiz, C. (2008). Parent involvement in preschool: Predictors and the relation of involvement to pre-literacy development. *School Psychology Review, 37*(1), 74–90.

Ash, J. & Gallup, G. G., Jr. (2008). Brain size, intelligence, and paleoclimatic variation. In G. Geher & G. Miller (eds), *Mating Intelligence: Sex, relationships, and the mind's reproductive system* (pp. 313–335). Mahwah, NJ: Lawrence Erlbaum Associates.

Avery, R. D. *et al.* (1994). Mainstream science on intelligence. *The Wall Street Journal*, editorial p. 356, 13 December.

Barnett, S. M. & Ceci, S. J. (2005). The role of transferable knowledge in intelligence. *Cognition and Intelligence: Identifying the mechanisms of the mind* (pp. 208–224). New York: Cambridge University Press.

Bass, B. M. (2002). Cognitive, social, and emotional intelligence of transformational leaders. In R. E. Riggio, S. E. Murphy, & F. J. Pirozzolo (eds), *Multiple Intelligences and Leadership* (pp. 105–118). Mahwah, NJ: Lawrence Erlbaum Associates.

Beckett, C., Castle, J., Rutter, M., & Sonuga-Barke, E. (2010). Institutional deprivation, specific cognitive functions, and scholastic achievement: English and Romanian adoptees (ERA) study findings. *Monographs of the Society for Research in Child Development, 75*(1), 125–142.

Beghetto, R. A. & Kaufman, J. C. (2010). Broadening conceptions of creativity in the classroom. In R. A. Beghetto & J. C. Kaufman (eds), *Nurturing Creativity in the Classroom* (pp. 191–205). New York: Cambridge University Press.

Biswas-Diener, R. (ed.) (2011). *Positive Psychology as Social Change*. New York: Springer Science + Business Media.

Bowden, S. C., Saklofske, D. H., & Weiss, L. G. (2011). Invariance of the measurement model underlying the Wechsler adult intelligence scale-IV in the United States and Canada. *Educational and Psychological Measurement, 71*(1), 186–199.

Brackett, M. A., Rivers, S. E., & Salovey, P. (2011). Emotional intelligence: Implications for personal, social, academic, and workplace success. *Social and Personality Psychology Compass, 5*(1), 88–103.

Bradley, R. H. & Caldwell, B. M. (1984). The HOME inventory and family demographics. *Developmental Psychology, 20*(2), 315–320.

Bradley, R. H., Caldwell, B. M., & Corwyn, R. F. (2003). The child care HOME inventories: Assessing the quality of family child care homes. *Early Childhood Research Quarterly, 18*(3), 294–309.

Bratko, D., Butkovic, A., & Chamorro-Premuzic, T. (2010). The genetics of general knowledge: A twin study from Croatia. *Personality and Individual Differences, 48*(4), 403–407.

Cain, N., Davidson, P., Dosen, A., Garcia-Ibañez, J., Giesow, V., Hillery, J., & Torr, J. (2010). An international perspective of mental health services for people with intellectual disability. In N. Bouras & G. Holt (eds), *Mental Health Services for Adults with Intellectual Disability: Strategies and solutions* (pp. 37–53). New York: Psychology Press.

Canivez, G. L. & Watkins, M. W. (2010). Exploratory and higher-order factor analyses of the Wechsler Adult Intelligence Scale: Fourth edition (WAIS-IV): Adolescent subsample. *School Psychology Quarterly, 25*(4), 223–235.

Carroll, J. B. (1993). *Human Cognitive Abilities*. Cambridge: Cambridge University Press.

Castejon, J. L., Perez, A. M., & Gilar, R. (2010). Confirmatory factor analysis of project spectrum activities: A second-order g factor or multiple intelligences? *Intelligence, 38*(5), 481–496.

Ceci, S. J. (1991). How much does schooling influence general intelligence and its cognitive components? A reassessment of the evidence. *Developmental Psychology, 27*(5), 703–722.

Ceci, S. J. & Kanaya, T. (2010). 'Apples and oranges are both round': Furthering the discussion on the Flynn effect. *Journal of Psychoeducational Assessment, 28*(5), 441–447.

Ceci, S.J. & Liker, J.K. (1986). A day at the races: A study of IQ, expertise, and cognitive complexity. Journal of *Experimental Psychology: General 115*(3), Sep 1986, 255–266

Ceci, S. J. & Williams, W. M. (1997). Schooling, intelligence, and income. *American Psychologist, 52*(10), 1051–1058.

Ceci, S. J. & Williams, W. M. (2007). Little g: Prospects and constraints. *European Journal of Personality, 21*(5), 716–718.

Ceci, S. J. & Williams, W. M. (2010). *The Mathematics of Sex: How biology and society conspire to limit talented women and girls*. New York: Oxford University Press.

Cherniss, C. (2010). Emotional intelligence: Toward clarification of a concept. *Industrial and Organizational Psychology: Perspectives on science and practice, 3*(2), 110–126.

Choi, Y. Y., Shamosh, N. A., Cho, S. H., DeYoung, C. G., Lee, M. J., Lee, J., *et al.* (2008). Multiple bases of human intelligence revealed by cortical thickness and neural activation. *Journal of Neuroscience, 28*(41), 10323–10329.

Cole, M., Gay, J., & Glick, J. (1967). A cross-cultural study of clustering in free recall. *Psychonomic Bulletin, 1*(2), 18.

Cramond, B., Kim, K. H., & VanTassel-Baska, J. (2010). The relationship between creativity and intelligence. In J. C. Kaufman & R. J. Sternberg (eds), *The Cambridge Handbook of Creativity* (pp. 395–412). New York: Cambridge University Press.

Deary, I. J. (2001). *Intelligence: A very short introduction*. Oxford: Oxford University Press.

Deary, I. J. & Stough, C. (1996). Intelligence and inspection time: Achievements, prospects, and problems. *American Psychologist, 51*(6), 599–608.

Deary, I. J., Whiteman, M. C., Starr, J. M., Fox, H. C., & Whalley, L. J. (2004). The impact of childhood intelligence on later life: Following up the

Scottish mental surveys of 1932 and 1947. *Journal of Personality and Social Psychology, 86*(1), 130–147.

Demaree, H. A., Burns, K. J., & DeDonno, M. A. (2010). Intelligence, but not emotional intelligence, predicts Iowa gambling task performance. *Intelligence, 38*(2), 249–254.

Dube, E. F. (1982). Literacy, cultural familiarity, and 'intelligence' as determinants of story recall. In U. Neisser (ed.), *Memory Observed: Remembering in natural contexts* (pp. 274–292). New York: Freeman.

Duncan, J. (2001). Frontal lobe function and the control of visual attention. In J. Braun, C. Koch, & J. L. Davis (eds), *Visual Attention and Cortical Circuits* (pp. 69–88). Cambridge, MA: MIT Press.

Duncan, J., Seitz, J. R., Kolodny, J., Bor, D., Herzog, H., Ahmed, A., Newell, F. N., & Emslie, H. (2000). A neural basis for general intelligence. *Science, 289*(5478), 457–460.

Dusseljee, J. C. E., Rijken, P. M., Cardol, M., Curfs, L. M. G., & Groenewegen, P. P. (2011). Participation in daytime activities among people with mild or moderate intellectual disability. *Journal of Intellectual Disability Research, 55*(1), 4–18.

Edgin, J. O., Pennington, B. F., & Mervis, C. B. (2010). Neuropsychological components of intellectual disability: The contributions of immediate, working, and associative memory. *Journal of Intellectual Disability Research, 54*(5), 406–417.

Fancher, R. E. (2004). The concept of race in the life and thought of Francis Galton. In A. S. Winston (ed.), *Defining Difference: Race and racism in the history of psychology* (pp. 49–75). Washington: American Psychological Association.

Fancher, R. E. (2009). Scientific cousins: The relationship between Charles Darwin and Francis Galton. *American Psychologist, 64*(2), 84–92.

Feist, G. J. (2010). The function of personality in creativity: The nature and nurture of the creative personality. In J. C. Kaufman & R. J. Sternberg (eds), *The Cambridge Handbook of Creativity* (pp. 113–130). New York: Cambridge University Press.

Feldhusen, J. F. (2003). Lewis M. Terman: A pioneer in the development of ability tests. In B. J. Zimmerman & D. H. Schunk (eds), *Educational Psychology: A century of contributions* (pp. 155–169). Mahwah, NJ: Lawrence Erlbaum Associates.

Feldman, M. W. & Lewontin, R. C. (2008). Race, ancestry, and medicine. In B. A. Koenig, S. S. Lee, & S. S. Richardson (eds), *Revisiting Race in a Genomic Age* (pp. 89–101). Piscataway, NJ: Rutgers University Press.

Fish, J. M. (ed.) (2002). *Race and Intelligence: Separating science from myth.* Mahwah, NJ: Lawrence Erlbaum Associates Publishers.

Flynn, J. R. (2000). *How to Defend Humane Ideals: Substitutes for objectivity.* Lincoln, NE: University of Nebraska Press.

Flynn, J. R. (2007). *What is intelligence? Beyond the Flynn effect.* New York: Cambridge University Press.

Flynn, J. R. (2008). *Where Have All the Liberals Gone? Race, class, and ideals in America.* New York: Cambridge University Press.

Ford, D. Y. (2008). Intelligence testing and cultural diversity: The need for alternative instruments, policies, and procedures. In J. L. VanTassel-Baska (ed.), *Alternative Assessments with Gifted and Talented Students* (pp. 107–128). Waco, TX: Prufrock Press.

Fowers, B. J. (2003). Reason and human finitude: In praise of practical wisdom. *American Behavioral Scientist, 47*(4), 415–426.

Fowers, B. J. (2005). *Virtue and Psychology: Pursuing excellence in ordinary practices* (pp. 107–128). Washington: American Psychological Association.

Freund, P. A. & Holling, H. (2011). Who wants to take an intelligence test? Personality and achievement motivation in the context of ability testing. *Personality and Individual Differences, 50*(5), 723–728.

Furnham, A. (2001). Self-estimates of personality. *Personality and Individual Differences, 31,* 1381–1405.

Furnham, A. (2008). *50 Psychology Ideas You Really Need to Know.* London: Quercus.

Furnham, A. (2009). The validity of a new, self-report measure of multiple intelligence. *Current Psychology: A Journal for Diverse Perspectives on Diverse Psychological Issues, 28*(4), 225–239.

Furnham, A. & Monsen, J. (2009). Personality traits and intelligence predict academic school grades. *Learning and Individual Differences, 19*(1), 28–33.

Galton, F. (1948). Co-relations and their measurement, chiefly from anthropometric data, 1888. In W. Dennis (ed.), *Readings in the History of Psychology* (pp. 336–346). East Norwalk, CT: Appleton-Century-Crofts.

Ganzach, Y. (2003). Intelligence, education, and facets of job satisfaction. *Work and Occupations, 30*(1), 97–122.

Ganzach, Y. & Pazy, A. (2001). Within occupation sources of variance in incumbent perception of job complexity. *Journal of Occupational and Organizational Psychology, 74*(1), 95–108.

Gardner, H. (1993). *Multiple intelligences: The theory in practice.* New York: Basic Books.

Gardner, H. (2004). *Frames of Mind: The theory of multiple intelligences.* New York: Basic Books.

Gardner, H. (2008). Who owns intelligence? In M. H. Immordino-Yang (ed.), *The Jossey-Bass Reader on the Brain and Learning* (pp. 120–132). San Francisco: Jossey-Bass.

Gardner, H. (2011). Changing minds: How the application of the multiple intelligences (MI) framework could positively contribute to the theory and practice of international negotiation. In F. Aquilar & M. Galluccio (eds), *Psychological and Political Strategies for Peace Negotiation: A cognitive approach* (pp. 1–14). New York: Springer Science + Business Media.

Gardner, H, & Traub, J. (2010). A debate on 'multiple intelligences'. In D. Gordon (ed.), *Cerebrum 2010: Emerging ideas in brain science* (pp. 34–61). Washington: Dana Press.

Gardner, H. & White, J. (2010). Is the theory of multiple intelligences valid? In B. Slife (ed.), *Clashing Views on Psychological Issues* (16th edn; pp. 198–216). New York: McGraw-Hill.

Georgas, J. (2003). Cross-cultural psychology, intelligence, and cognitive processes. In J. Georgas, L. G. Weiss, F. J. R. van de Vijver, & D. H. Saklofske (eds), *Culture and Children's Intelligence: Cross-cultural analysis of the WISC-III* (pp. 23–37). San Diego: Academic Press.

Gläscher, J., Rudrauf, D., Colom, R., Paul, L. K., Tranel, D., Damasio, H., & Adolphs, R. (2010). Distributed neural system for general intelligence revealed by lesion mapping. *Proceedings of the National Academy of Sciences of the United States of America, 107*(10), 4705–4709.

Goleman, D. (1995). *Emotional Intelligence.* New York: Bantam Books.

Goleman, D. (2006). *Social Intelligence: The new science of human relationships.* New York: Bantam Books.

Gottfredson, L. J. (1997), Mainstream science on intelligence (editorial). *Intelligence, 24,* 13–23.

Gow, A. J., Johnson, W., Pattie, A., Brett, C. E., Roberts, B., Starr, J. M., & Deary, I. J. (2011). Stability and change in intelligence from age 11 to ages 70, 79, and 87: The Lothian birth cohorts of 1921 and 1936. *Psychology and Aging, 26*(1), 232–240.

Grabner, R. H., Stern, E., & Neubauer, A. C. (2003). When intelligence loses its impact: Neural efficiency during reasoning in a familiar area. *International Journal of Psychophysiology, 49*(2), 89–98.

Harris, J. C. (2010). *Intellectual Disability: A guide for families and professionals.* New York: Oxford University Press.

Hart, C., Ksir, C., & Oakley, R. (2010). *Drugs, Society, and Human Behavior.* New York: McGraw-Hill.

Hartman, D. E. (2009). Test review: Wechsler adult intelligence scale IV (WAIS IV): Return of the gold standard. *Applied Neuropsychology, 16*(1), 85–87.

Harvey, M., Novicevic, M., & Keissling, T. (2002). Development of multiple IQ maps for use in the selection of impatriate managers. *International Journal of Intercultural Relations, 26,* 493–524.

Hazlett, H. C., Hammer, J., Hooper, S. R., & Kamphaus, R. W. (2011). Down syndrome. In S. Goldstein & C. R. Reynolds (eds), *Handbook of Neurodevelopmental and Genetic Disorders in Children* (2nd edn; pp. 362–381). New York: Guilford Press.

Hegarty, P. (2007). From genius inverts to gendered intelligence: Lewis Terman and the power of the norm. *History of Psychology, 10*(2), 132–155.

Hennessey, B. A. (2010). The creativity–motivation connection. In J. C. Kaufman & R. J. Sternberg (eds), *The Cambridge Handbook of Creativity* (pp. 342–365). New York: Cambridge University Press.

Herrnstein, R. J. & Murray, C. A. (1994). *The Bell Curve: Intelligence and class structure in American life*. New York: Free Press.

Hodapp, R. M. & Dykens, E. M. (2003). Mental retardation (intellectual disabilities). In E. J. Mash & R. A. Barkley (eds), *Child Psychopathology* (2nd edn). New York: Guilford Press.

Hunt, E. (2011). *Human Intelligence*. New York: Cambridge University Press.

Johnson, W. (2010). Review of intelligence and how to get it: Why schools and cultures count. *Gifted Child Quarterly, 54*(1), 72.

Johnson, W., Bouchard, T. J., Jr., Krueger, R. F., McGue, M., & Gottesman, I. I. (2004). Just one *g*: Consistent results from three test batteries. *Intelligence, 32*(1), 95–107.

Joia, L. A. & Lemos, B. (2010). Relevant factors for tacit knowledge transfer within organisations. *Journal of Knowledge Management, 14*(3), 410–427.

Karama, S., Colom, R., Johnson, W., Deary, I. J., Haier, R., Waber, D. P., & Evans, A. C. (2011). Cortical thickness correlates of specific cognitive performance accounted for by the general factor of intelligence in healthy children aged 6 to 18. *Neuroimage, 55*(4), 1443–1453.

Karelitz, T. M., Jarvin, L., & Sternberg, R. J. (2010). The meaning of wisdom and its development throughout life. In W. F. Overton & R. M. Lerner (eds), *The Handbook of Life-Span Development, Vol. 1: Cognition, biology, and methods* (pp. 837–881). Hoboken, NJ: John Wiley & Sons, Inc.

Kaufman, A. S. (2000). Wechsler, David. In A. E. Kazdin (ed.), *Encyclopedia of Psychology: Vol. 8.* (pp. 238–239). Washington: American Psychological Association.

Kaufman J. C. (ed.) (2009). *Intelligent Testing: Integrating psychological theory and clinical practice*. New York: Cambridge University Press.

Kaufman, A. S. & Doppelt, J. E. (1976). Analysis of WISC-R standardization data in terms of the stratification variables. *Child Development, 47*(1), 165–171.

Kaufman, J. C. & Sternberg, R. J. (eds) (2010). *The Cambridge Handbook of Creativity*. New York: Cambridge University Press.

Kohn, M. L. & Schooler, C. (1973). Occupational experience and psychological functioning: An assessment of reciprocal effects. *American Sociological Review, 38*(1), 97–118.

Kuncel, N. R., Hezlett, S. A., & Ones, D. S. (2004). Academic performance, career potential, creativity, and job performance: Can one construct predict them all? *Journal of Personality and Social Psychology, 86*(1), 148–161.

Kuncel, N. R., Ones, D. S., & Sackett, P. R. (2010). Individual differences as predictors of work, educational, and broad life outcomes. *Personality and Individual Differences, 49*(4), 331–336.

Larsen, L., Hartmann, P., & Nyborg, H. (2008). The stability of general intelligence from early adulthood to middle-age. *Intelligence, 36*(1), 29–34.

Lazar, I. & Darlington, R. B. (1982). Lasting effects of early education: A report from the consortium for longitudinal studies. *Monographs of the Society for Research in Child Development, 47*(2–3), 1–151.

Lee, E. S. (1961). Negro intelligence and selective migration. In J. J. Jenkins & D. G. Paterson (eds), *Studies in Individual Differences: The search for intelligence* (pp. 669–676). East Norwalk, CT: Appleton-Century-Crofts.

Leslie, M. (2000). The vexing legacy of Lewis Terman. *Stanford Magazine*, July/August 2000, 1–21.

Lewontin, R. (1976). Science and politics: An explosive mix. *Psyc-CRITIQUES, 21*(2), 97–98.

Lewontin, R. (1982). *Human Diversity*. New York: Scientific American Library.

Lewontin, R. (2001). Gene, organism and environment. *Cycles of Contingency: Developmental systems and evolution* (pp. 59–66). Cambridge, MA: MIT Press.

Lounsbury, J. W., Sundstrom, E., Loveland, J. M., & Gibson, L. W. (2003). Intelligence, 'big five' personality traits, and work drive as predictors of course grade. *Personality and Individual Differences, 35*(6), 1231–1239.

Lounsbury, J. W., Fisher, L. A., Levy, J. J., & Welsh, D. P. (2009). An investigation of character strengths in relation to the academic success of college students. *Individual Differences Research, 7*(1), 52–69.

Lubart, T. (2010). Cross-cultural perspectives on creativity. In J. C. Kaufman & R. J. Sternberg (eds), *The Cambridge Handbook of Creativity* (pp. 265–278). New York: Cambridge University Press.

Lubinski, D. (2004). Introduction to the special section on cognitive abilities: 100 years after Spearman's (1904) 'General Intelligence': Objectively determined and measured. *Journal of Personality and Social Psychology, 86*(1), 96–111.

Lynn, A. B. (2008). *The EQ Interview: Finding employees with high emotional intelligence*. New York: AMACOM.

Lynn, R. & Meisenberg, G. (2010). National IQs calculated and validated for 108 nations. *Intelligence, 38*(4), 353–360.

Mandelman, S. D., Tan, M., Kornilov, S. A., Sternberg, R. J., & Grigorenko, E. L. (2010). The metacognitive component of academic self-concept: The development of a triarchic self-scale. *Journal of Cognitive Education and Psychology, 9*(1), 73–86.

Martin, C. M. (2008). A meta-analytic investigation of the relationship between emotional intelligence and leadership effectiveness. *Dissertation Abstracts International Section A: Humanities and social sciences, 69*(2), 530.

Martin, J. A. (2010). Genetic causes of mental retardation. In R. C. Dryden-Edwards & L. Combrinck-Graham (eds), *Developmental Disabilities from Childhood to Adulthood: What works for psychiatrists in community and institutional settings* (pp. 127–142). Baltimore: Johns Hopkins University Press.

Mason, J. M., Kerr, B. M., Sinha, S., & McCormick, C. (1990). Shared book reading in an early start program for at-risk children. *National Reading Conference Yearbook, 39*, 189–198.

Maul, A. (2011). The factor structure and cross-test convergence of the Mayer–Salovey–Caruso model of emotional intelligence. *Personality and Individual Differences, 50*(4), 457–463.

Mayer, J. D. (2008). Personal intelligence. *Imagination, Cognition and Personality, 27*(3), 209–232.

Mayer, J. D. (2009). Personal intelligence expressed: A theoretical analysis. *Review of General Psychology, 13*(1), 46–58.

Mayer, J. D., Salovey, P., Caruso, D. R., & Sitarenios, G. (2003). Measuring emotional intelligence with the MSCEIT V2.0. *Emotion, 3*(1), 97–105.

McCormick, C. E. & Mason, J. M. (1986). Intervention procedures for increasing preschool children's interest in and knowledge about reading. In W. H. Teale & E. Sulzby (eds), *Emergent Literacy: Writing and reading* (pp. 90–115). Norwood, NJ: Ablex.

McVicker Hunt, J. M. (1982). Toward equalizing the developmental opportunities of infants and preschool children. *Journal of Social Issues, 38*(4), 163–191.

Murphy, N. A. & Hall, J. A. (2011). Intelligence and interpersonal sensitivity: A meta-analysis. *Intelligence, 39*(1), 54–63.

Myerson, J., Rank, M. R., Raines, F. Q., & Schnitzler, M. A. (1998). Race and general cognitive ability: The myth of diminishing returns to education. *Psychological Science, 9*(2), 139–142.

Nair, E. (2003). Hindsight lessons aka experiential wisdom: A review of the XXV ICAP. *Applied Psychology: An international review, 52*(2), 165–174.

Neisser, U. (ed.) (1998). *The Rising Curve: Long-term gains in IQ and related measures*. Washington: American Psychological Association.

Nelson, C. A. (2007). A neurobiological perspective on early human deprivation. *Child Development Perspectives, 1*, 13–18.

Nelson, C. A., Furtado, E. A., Fox, N. A., & Zeanah, C. H., Jr. (2009). The deprived brain. *American Scientist, 97*(3), 222–229.

Neubauer, A. C. & Fink, A. (2003). Fluid intelligence and neural efficiency: Effects of task complexity and sex. *Personality and Individual Differences, 35*(4), 811–827.

Neubauer, A. C. & Fink, A. (2010). Neuroscientific approaches to the study of individual differences in cognition and personality. In A. Gruszka, G. Matthews, & B. Szymura (eds), *Handbook of Individual Differences in Cognition: Attention, memory, and executive control* (pp. 73–85). New York: Springer Science + Business Media.

Nisbett, R. E. (2009). *Intelligence and How to Get It: Why schools and cultures count*. New York: W. W. Norton.

Olsen, L. & DeBoise, T. (2007). Enhancing school readiness: The Early Head Start model. *Children and Schools, 29*, 47–50.

Owens, J. & Massey, D. S. (2011). Stereotype threat and college academic performance: A latent variables approach. *Social Science Research, 40*(1), 150–166.

Pan, Y., Wang, K., & Aragam, N. (2011). NTM and NR3C2 polymorphisms influencing intelligence: Family-based association studies. *Progress in Neuro-Psychopharmacology & Biological Psychiatry, 35*(1), 154–160.

Pietschnig, J., Voracek, M., & Formann, A. K. (2010). Mozart effect–Shmozart effect: A meta-analysis. *Intelligence, 38*(3), 314–323.

Plomin, R. & Spinath, F. M. (2004). Intelligence: Genetics, genes, and genomics. *Journal of Personality and Social Psychology, 86*(1), 112–129.

Posner, M. I., Petersen, S. E., Fox, P. T., & Raichle, M. E. (2002). Localization of cognitive operations in the human brain. In D. J. Levitin (ed.), *Foundations of Cognitive Psychology: Core readings* (pp. 819–830). Cambridge, MA: MIT Press.

Posner, M., Petersen, S. F., Fox, P. T., & Raichle, M. E. (2009). Localization of cognitive operations in the human brain. In *Foundations of Psychological Thought: A history of psychology* (pp. 279–294). Thousand Oaks, CA: Sage Publications.

Pungello, E. P., Kainz, K., Burchinal, M., Wasik, B. H., Sparling, J. J., Ramey, C. T., & Campbell, F. A. (2010). Early educational intervention, early cumulative risk, and the early home environment as predictors of young adult outcomes within a high-risk sample. *Child Development, 81*(1), 410–426.

Raichle, M. E. (2005). Imaging the human brain: Reflections on some emerging issues. In U. Mayr, E. Awh, & S. W. Keele (eds), *Developing Individuality in the Human Brain: A tribute to Michael I. Posner* (pp. 109–123). Washington: American Psychological Association.

Raid, G. H. & Tippin, S. M. (2009). Assessment of intellectual strengths and weaknesses with the Stanford–Binet intelligence scales: Fifth edition (SB5). In J. A. Naglieri & S. Goldstein (eds), *Practitioner's Guide to Assessing Intelligence and Achievement* (pp. 127–152). Hoboken, NJ: John Wiley & Sons, Inc.

Ramey, C. T. & Ramey, S. L. (2007). Early learning and school readiness: Can early intervention make a difference? In G. W. Ladd (ed.), *Appraising the Human Developmental Sciences: Essays in honor of Merrill-Palmer Quarterly* (pp. 329–350). Detroit: Wayne State University Press.

Rauscher, F. H., Shaw, G. L., & Ky, K. N. (1993). Music and spatial-task performance. *Nature, 365*, 611.

Reed, T. E. & Jensen, A. R. (1992). Conduction velocity in a brain nerve pathway of normal adults correlates with intelligence level. *Intelligence, 16*(3–4), 259–272.

Reynolds, C. R., Chastain, R. L., Kaufman, A. S., & McLean, J. E. (1987). Demographic characteristics and IQ among adults: Analysis of the WAISR standardization sample as a function of the stratification variables. *Journal of School Psychology, 25*(4), 323–342.

Richards, G. (2004). 'It's an American Thing': The 'race' and intelligence controversy from a British perspective: Defining difference: Race and racism in the history of psychology (pp. 137–169). Washington: American Psychological Association.

Ripple, C. H., Gilliam, W. S., Chanana, N., & Zigler, E. (1999). Will fifty cooks spoil the broth? The debate over entrusting Head Start to the states. *American Psychologist, 54*(5), 327–343.

Roberts, R. D., MacCann, C., Matthews, G., & Zeidner, M. (2010). Emotional intelligence: Toward a consensus of models and measures. *Social and Personality Psychology Compass, 4*(10), 821–840.

Runco, M. A. (2004). Creativity. *Annual Review of Psychology, 55*, 657–687.

Runco, M. A. (2010). Divergent thinking, creativity, and ideation. In J. C. Kaufman & R. J. Sternberg (eds), *The Cambridge Handbook of Creativity* (pp. 413–446). New York: Cambridge University Press.

Rushton, J. P. (2009). Brain size as an explanation of national differences in IQ, longevity, and other life-history variables. *Personality and Individual Differences, 48*(2), 970–977.

Sackett, P. R. & Shen, W. (2010). Subgroup differences on cognitive tests in contexts other than personnel selection. In J. L. Outtz (ed.), *Adverse Impact: Implications for organizational staffing and high stakes selection* (pp. 323–346). New York: Routledge/Taylor & Francis Group.

Salovey, P., Mayer, J. D., Caruso, D., & Lopes, P. N. (2003). Measuring emotional intelligence as a set of abilities with the Mayer–Slovey–Caruso emotional intelligence test. In S. J. Lopez & C. R. Snyder (eds), *Positive Psychological Assessment: A handbook of models and measures* (pp. 251–265). Washington: American Psychological Association.

Sangwan, S. (2001). Ecological factors as related to IQ of children. *Psycho-Lingua, 31*(2), 89–92.

Sassi, R. B. (2011). Got a raise? Thank your kindergarten teacher. *Journal of the American Academy of Child & Adolescent Psychiatry, 50*(1), 2.

Schooler, C. (2001). The intellectual effects of the demands of the work environment. In R. J. Sternberg & E. L. Grigorenko (eds), *Environmental Effects on Cognitive Abilities* (pp. 363–380). Mahwah, NJ: Lawrence Erlbaum Associates.

Schooler, C., Mulatu, M. S., & Oates, G. (2004). Occupational self-direction, intellectual functioning, and self-directed orientation in older workers: Findings and implications for individuals and societies. *American Journal of Sociology, 110*(1), 161–197.

Seashore, H., Wesman, A., & Doppelt, J. (1950). The standardization of the Wechsler intelligence scale for children. *Journal of Consulting Psychology, 14*(2), 99–110.

Shaw, P., Greenstein, D., Lerch, J., Clasen, L., Lenroot, R., Gogtay, N., Evans, A., Rapoport, J., & Giedd, J. (2006). Intellectual ability and cortical development in children and adolescents. *Nature, 440*(7084), 619–620.

Shaw, P., Kabani, N. J., Lerch. J. P., Eckstrand, K., Lenroot, R., Gogtay, N., Greenstein D., Clasen, L., Evans, A., Rapoport, J. L., Giedd, J. N., & Wise, S. P. (2008). Neurodevelopmental trajectories of the human cerebral cortex. *Journal of Neuroscience, 28*(14), 3586–3594.

Shayer, M. & Adhami, M. (2010). Realizing the cognitive potential of children 5–7 with a mathematics focus: Post-test and long-term effects of a 2-year intervention. *British Journal of Educational Psychology, 80*(3), 363–379.

Shih, M., Pittinsky, T. L., & Ambady, N. (1999). Stereotype susceptibility: Identity salience and shifts in quantitative performance. *Psychological Science, 10*(1), 80–83.

Sidhu, M., Malhi, P. & Jerath, J. (2010). Intelligence of children from economically disadvantaged families: Role of parental education. *Psychological Studies, 55*(4), 358–364.

Siegler, R. S. (2003). Thinking and intelligence. In M. H. Bornstein, L. Davidson, C. L. M. Keyes, & K. A. Moore (eds), *Well-Being: Positive development across the life course* (pp. 311–320). Mahwah, NJ: Lawrence Erlbaum Associates.

Silvia, P. J. (2008). Another look at creativity and intelligence: Exploring higher order models and probable confounds. *Personality and Individual Differences, 44*(4), 1012–1021.

Simonton, D. K. (2010). Research notes: The curious case of Catharine Cox (Miles): The 1926 dissertation and her Miles–Wolfe (1936) follow-up. *History of Psychology, 13*(2), 205–206.

Smith, L. B. (2010). More than concepts: How multiple integrations make human intelligence. In D. Mareschal, P. C. Quinn, & S. E. G. Lea (eds), *The Making of Human Concepts* (pp. 335–363). New York: Oxford University Press.

Sokal, M. M. (2010). Scientific biography, cognitive deficits, and laboratory practice. James McKeen Cattell and early American experimental psychology, 1880–1904. *Isis, 101*(3), 531–554.

Spearman, C. (1904). 'General intelligence': Objectively determined and measured. *American Journal of Psychology, 15*(2), 201–293.

Spearman, C. (1927). *The Nature of Intelligence and the Principles of Cognition* (2nd edn). Oxford: Macmillan.

Spearman, C. (1937). *Psychology down the Ages*. Oxford: Macmillan.

Spearman, C. (1939). Thurstone's work reworked. *Journal of Educational Psychology, 30*(1), 1–16.

Steele, C. M. & Aronson, J. (1995). Stereotype threat and the intellectual test performance of African Americans. *Journal of Personality and Social Psychology, 69*(5), 797–811.

Steele, C. M. & Aronson, J. A. (2004). Stereotype threat does not live by Steele and Aronson (1995) alone. *American Psychologist, 59*(1), 47–48.

Stein, Z., Susser, M., Saenger, G., & Marolla, F. (1972). Nutrition and mental performance. *Science, 178,* 708–713.

Sternberg, R. J. (2003). *Wisdom, Intelligence, and Creativity Synthesized.* New York: Cambridge University Press.

Sternberg, R. J. (2007). Who are the bright children? The cultural context of being and acting intelligent. *Educational Researcher, 36*(3), 148–155.

Sternberg, R. J. (2008). The balance theory of wisdom. In M. H. Immordinoang (ed.), *The Jossey-Bass Reader on the Brain and Learning* (pp. 133–150). San Francisco: Jossey-Bass.

Sternberg, R. J. (2010). Teaching for creativity. In R. A. Beghetto & J. C. Kaufman (eds), *Nurturing Creativity in the Classroom* (pp. 394–414). New York: Cambridge University Press.

Sternberg, R. J., Conway, B. E., Ketron, J. L., & Bernstein, M. (1981). People's conceptions of intelligence. *Journal of Personality and Social Psychology, 41*(1), 37–55.

Sternberg, R. J., Grigorenko, E. L., & Bundy, D. A. (2001). The predictive value of IQ. *Merrill-Palmer Quarterly, 47*(1), 1–41.

Sternberg, R. J., Jarvin, L., & Grigorenko, E. L. (2011). *Explorations in Giftedness.* New York: Cambridge University Press.

Sternberg, R. J., Wagner, R. K., Williams, W. M., & Horvath, J. A., *et al.* (1995). Testing common sense. *American Psychologist, 50*(11), 912–927.

Sturmey, P. (2008). Adults with intellectual disabilities. In M. Hersen & J. Rosqvist (eds), *Handbook of Psychological Assessment, Case Conceptualization, and Treatment: Vol. 1: Adults.* Hoboken, NJ: John Wiley & Sons, Inc.

Tang, C. Y., Eaves, E. L., Ng, J. C., Carpenter, D. M., Mai, X., Schroeder, D. H., & Haier, R. J. (2010). Brain networks for working memory and factors of intelligence assessed in males and females with fMRI and DTI. *Intelligence, 38*(3), 293–303.

Terman, L. M. (1925). *Genetic Studies of Genius: Mental and physical traits of a thousand gifted children.* Oxford: Stanford University Press.

Terman, L. M. & Merrill, M. A. (1937). *Measuring Intelligence: A guide to the administration of the new revised Stanford–Binet tests of intelligence.* Oxford: Houghton Mifflin.

Thompson, W. F., Husain, G., & Schellenberg, E. G. (2001). Arousal, mood, and the Mozart effect. *Psychological Science, 12*(3), 248–251.

Thorndike, E. L. (1920). The reliability and significance of tests of intelligence. *Journal of Educational Psychology, 11*(5), 284–287.

Thorndike, E. L. (1921). Intelligence and its measurement. *Journal of Educational Psychology, 12,* 41–50.

Thurstone, L. L. (1938). *Primary Mental Abilities.* Chicago: University of Chicago Press.

Tirri, K. & Nokelainen, P. (2008). Identification of multiple intelligences with the multiple intelligence profiling questionnaire III. *Psychology Science, 50*(2), 206–221.

Tomes, Y. I. (2010). Culture and psychoeducational assessment: Cognition and achievement. In E. García-Vásquez, T. D. Crespi, & C. A. Riccio (eds), *Handbook of Education, Training, and Supervision of School Psychologists in School and Community: Vol. 1: Foundations of professional practice* (pp. 167–183). New York: Routledge/Taylor & Francis Group.

Toth, K. & King, B. H. (2010). Intellectual disability (mental retardation). In M. K. Dulcan (ed.), *Dulcan's Textbook of Child and Adolescent Psychiatry* (pp. 151–171). Arlington, VA: American Psychiatric Publishing.

Tranel, D., Manzel, K., & Anderson, S. W. (2008). Is the prefrontal cortex important for fluid intelligence? A neuropsychological study using matrix reasoning. *Clinical Neuropsychologist, 22*(2), 242–261.

Trembath, D., Balandin, S., Stancliffe, R. J., & Togher, L. (2010). Employment and volunteering for adults with intellectual disability. *Journal of Policy and Practice in Intellectual Disabilities, 7*(4), 235–238.

Tulsky, D. S. & O'Brien, A. R. (2008). The history of processing speed and its relationship to intelligence. In J. DeLuca & J. H. Kalmar (eds), *Information Processing Speed in Clinical Populations* (pp. 1–28). Philadelphia: Taylor & Francis.

Tulsky, D. S., Saklofske, D. H., & Ricker, J. H. (2003). Historical overview of intelligence and memory: Factors influencing the Wechsler scales. In D. S. Tulsky, D. H. Saklofske, G. J. Chelune, R. K. Heaton, & R. J. Ivnik (eds), *Clinical Interpretation of the WAIS-III and WMS-III* (pp. 7–41). San Diego: Academic Press.

USDHHS (US Department of Health & Human Services). (2011). *Head Start impact study and follow-up: 2000–2011.* Washington: Author.

Vernon, P. A. (1990). An overview of chronometric measures of intelligence. *School Psychology Review, 19*(4), 399–410.

Vernon, P. A., Wickett, J. C., Bazana, P. G., & Stelmack, R. M. (2000). The neuropsychology and psychophysiology of human intelligence. In *Handbook of Intelligence* (pp. 245–264). New York: Cambridge University Press.

Visser, B., Ashton, M., & Vernon, P. (2006). Beyond *g*: Putting multiple intelligence theory to the test. *Intelligence, 34,* 487–502.

Watkins, M. W. (2010). Structure of the Wechsler intelligence scale for Children: Fourth edition among a national sample of referred students. *Psychological Assessment, 22*(4), 782–787.

Wechsler, D. (1961). Cognitive, conative, and non-intellective intelligence. In J. J. Jenkins & D. G. Paterson (eds), *Studies in Individual Differences: The search for intelligence* (pp. 651–660). East Norwalk, CT: Appleton-Century-Crofts.

Weiss, L. G. (2010). Considerations on the Flynn effect. *Journal of Psychoeducational Assessment, 28*(5), 482–493.

Wicherts, J. M. & Dolan, C. V. (2010). Measurement invariance in confirmatory factor analysis: An illustration using IQ test performance of minorities. *Educational Measurement: Issues and Practice, 29*(3), 39–47.

Williams, W. M., Papierno, P. B., Makel, M. C., & Ceci, S. J. (2004). Thinking like a scientist about real-world problems: The Cornell Institute for research on children science education program. *Journal of Applied Developmental Psychology, 25*(1), 107–126.

Wilson, G. (1989). *The Great Sex Divide.* London: Peter Owen.

Wissler, C. (1961). The correlation of mental and physical tests. In J. J. Jenkins & D. G. Paterson (eds), *Studies in Individual Differences: The search for intelligence* (pp. 32–44). East Norwalk, CT: Appleton-Century-Crofts.

Yang, S. & Sternberg, R. J. (1997). Taiwanese Chinese people's conceptions of intelligence. *Intelligence, 25*(1), 21–36.

Zeidner, M. (1990). Perceptions of ethnic group modal intelligence: Reflections of cultural stereotypes or intelligence test scores? *Journal of Cross-Cultural Psychology, 21*(2), 214–231.

Zigler, E. & Berman, W. (1983). Discerning the future of early childhood intervention. *American Psychologist, 38*(8), 894–906.

CHAPTER 13

Abramowitz, J. S. (2008). Is nonparaphilic compulsive sexual behavior a variant of OCD? In J. S. Abramowitz, D. McKay, & S. Taylor (eds), *Obsessive-Compulsive Disorder: Subtypes and spectrum conditions.* Oxford: Elsevier.

Admon, Y. (2009). *Rising criticism of child bride marriages in Saudi Arabia.* The Middle East Media Research Institute, http://www.memri.org/report/en/0/0/0/0/0/0/131/3216.htm, accessed 10 December 2012.

Althof, S. E. (2007). Treatment of rapid ejaculation: Psychotherapy, pharmacotherapy, and combined therapy. In S. R. Leiblum (ed.), *Principles and Practice of Sex Therapy* (4th edn; pp. 212–240). New York: Guilford Press.

Andreasen, N. C. & Black, D. W. (2006). *Introductory Textbook of Psychiatry* (4th edn). Washington: American Psychiatric Publishing.

APA (American Psychiatric Association). (2000). *Diagnostic and Statistical Manual of Mental Disorders* (4th edn). Washington: American Psychiatric Association.

Arias-Carrión, Ó. & Pöppel, E. (2007). Dopamine, learning, and reward-seeking behavior. *Acta Neurobiologiae Experimentalis (Warsaw), 67*(4), 481–488.

Bach, A. K., Wincze, J. P., & Barlow, D. H. (2001). Sexual dysfunction. In D. H. Barlow (ed.), *Clinical Handbook of Psychological Disorders:*

A step-by-step treatment manual (3rd edn; pp. 562–608). New York: Guilford Press.

Bailey, J. M. & Pillard, R. C. (1991). A genetic study of male sexual orientation. *Archives of General Psychiatry, 48*(12), 1089–1096.

Bakker, A., van Kestren, P. J., Gooren, L. J. G., & Bezemer, P. D. (1993). The prevalence of transsexualism in the Netherlands. *Acta Psychiatrica Scandinavica, 87*, 237–238.

Bancroft, J. (2005). The endocrinology of sexual arousal. *Journal of Endocrinology, 186*(3), 411–427.

Bancroft, J., Loftus, J., & Long, J. S. (2003). Distress about sex: A national survey of women in heterosexual relationships. *Archives of Sexual Behavior, 32*(3), 193–208.

Barrett, J., Abbott, D. H., & George, L. M. (1993). Sensory cues and the suppression of reproduction of subordinate female marmoset monkeys. *Journal of Reproduction and Fertility, 97*(1), 301–310.

Baumeister, R. F., Catanese, K. R., & Vohs, K. D. (2001). Is there a gender difference in strength of sex drive? Theoretical views, conceptual distinctions, and a review of relevant evidence. *Personality and Social Psychology Review, 5*, 242–273.

Bendelius, J. (2004). Prevention: The best way to help our kids avoid the obesity epidemic. *School Nurse News, 21*(3), 32–33.

Berkman, N. D., Bulik, C. M., Brownley, F. A., Lohr, K. N., Sedway, T. A., Rooks, A., & Gartlener, S. (2006). *Management of Eating Disorders.* University of North Carolina.

Berman, J. R. (2005). Physiology of female sexual function and dysfunction. *International Journal of Impotence Research, 17*(suppl. 1), S44–S51.

Berridge, K. C. (2007). The debate over dopamine's role in reward: The case for incentive salience. *Psychopharmacology, 191*(3), 391–431.

Berridge, K. & Kringelbach, M. (2008). Affective neuroscience of pleasure: Reward in humans and animals. *Psychopharmacology, 199*(3), 457–480.

Bevins, R. A. (2001). Novelty seeking and reward: Implications for the study of high-risk behaviors. *Current Directions in Psychological Science, 10*(6), 189–193.

Bieber, I., Dain, H. J., Dince, P. R., Drellich, M. G., Grand, H. G., Gundlach, R. H., & Bieber, T. B. (1962). *Homosexuality: A psychoanalytic study.* New York: Basic Books.

Björnholm, M., Münzberg, H., Leshan, R. L., Villanueva, E. C., Bates, S. H., Louis, G. W., & Myers, Martin G., Jr. (2007). Mice lacking inhibitory leptin receptor signals are lean with normal endocrine function. *Journal of Clinical Investigation, 117*(5), 1354–1360.

Blanchard, R. (2001). Fraternal birth order and the maternal immune hypothesis of male homosexuality. *Hormonal Behavior, 40*(2), 105–114.

Blanchard, R. (2004). Quantitative and theoretical analyses of the relation between older brothers and homosexuality in men. *Journal of Theoretical Biology, 230*(2), 173–187.

Blumenfeld, P., Kempler, T., & Krajcik, J. (2006). Motivation and cognitive engagement in learning environments. In R. K. Sawyer (ed.), *The Cambridge Handbook of the Learning Sciences* (pp. 475–488). Cambridge, MA: Cambridge University Press.

Boecker, H., Sprenger T., Spilker, M. E., Henriksen, G., Koppenhoefer, M., Wagner, K. J., Valet, M., Berthele, A., & Tolle, T. R. (2008). The runner's high: Opioidergic mechanisms in the human brain. *Cerebral Cortex, 18*(11), 2523–2531.

Bowne, W. B., Julliard, K., Castro, A. E., Shah, P., Morgenthal, C. B., Ferzli, G. S., *et al.* (2006). Laparoscopic gastric bypass is superior to adjustable gastric band in super morbidly obese patients. *Archives of Surgery, 141*, 683–689.

Broad, K. D., Curley, J. P., & Keverne, E. B. (2006). Mother–infant bonding and the evolution of mammalian social relationships. *Philosophical Transactions of the Royal Society of London: Series B, 361*(1476), 2199–2214.

Brown, T. M. & Fee, E. (2003). Sexual behavior in the human male. *American Journal of Public Health, 93*(6).

Buhrich, N., Bailey, M. J., & Martin, N. G. (1991). Sexual orientation, sexual identity, and sex-dysmorphic behaviors in male twins. *Behavior Genetics, 21*(1), 75–96.

Bullough, V. L. (2004). Sex will never be the same: The contributions of Alfred C. Kinsey. *Archives of Sexual Behavior, 33*(3), 277–286.

Burger King (2012). Burger King USA Nutritionals, http://www.bk.com/cms/en/us/cms_out/digital_assets/files/pages/MenuNutritionInformation.pdf, accessed 7 December 2012.

Byers, E. S., Purdon, C., & Clark, D. A. (1998). Sexual intrusive thoughts of college students. *Journal of Sex Research, 35*, 359–369.

Cameron, A., Rosen, R. C., & Swindle, R. W. (2005). Sexual and relationship characteristics among an internet-based sample of U.S. men with and without erectile dysfunction. *Journal of Sex & Marital Therapy, 31*(3), 229–242.

Carlezon, W. A., Jr. & Thomas, M. J. (2009). Biological substrates of reward and aversion: A nucleus accumbens activity hypothesis. *Neuropharmacology, 56* (suppl. 1), 122–132.

Carroll, R. A. (2007). Gender dysphoria and transgender experiences. In S. R. Leiblum (ed.), *Principles and Practice of Sex Therapy* (4th edn; pp. 477–508). New York: Guilford Press.

CDC (Centers for Disease Control and Prevention). (2008). *Sexually Transmitted Disease Surveillance, 2007.* Atlanta, GA: US Department of Health and Human Services.

CDC (Centers for Disease Control and Prevention). (2009). *Health, United States, 2008, Table 75,* http://www.cdc.gov/nchs/data/hus/hus09.pdf, accessed 7 December 2012.

CDC (Centers for Disease Control and Prevention). (2011). *HIV Among Youth,* http://www.cdc.gov/hiv/youth/index.htm, accessed 10 December 2012.

Childress, A. R., Ehrman, R. N., Wang, Z., Li, Y., Sciortino, N., Hakun, J., *et al.* (2008). Prelude to passion: Limbic activation by 'unseen' drug and sexual cues. *PloS ONE, 3*(1), e1506.

Christakis, N. A. & Fowler, J. H. (2007). The spread of obesity in a large social network over 32 years. *New England Journal of Medicine, 357*, 370–379.

Christou, N. V., Look, D., & Maclean, L. D. (2006). Weight gain after short- and long-limb gastric bypass in patients followed for longer than 10 years. *Annals of Surgery, 244*(5), 734–740.

Clark, R. E., Broadbent, N. J., & Squire, L. R. (2008). The hippocampus and spatial memory: Findings with a novel modification of the water maze. *Journal of Neuroscience, 27*(25), 6647–6654.

Cochran, W. G., Mosteller, F., & Tukey, J. W. (1953). Some statistical problems of the Kinsey Report. *Journal of the American Statistical Association, 48*, 673–716.

Cohen-Kettenis, P. T. (2001). Gender identity disorder in DSM? *Journal of the American Academy of Child & Adolescent Psychiatry, 40*(4), 391–391.

Colson, S. D., Meek, J. H., & Hawdon, J. M. (2008). Optimal positions for the release of primitive neonatal reflexes stimulating breastfeeding. *Early Human Development, 84*(7), 441–449.

Connolly, K. (2007). Brother and sister fight Germany's incest laws. *The Guardian,* Tuesday, February 27, 2007.

Cramer, R. J., Golom, F. D., LoPresto, C. T., & Kirkley, S. M. (2008). Weighing the evidence: Empirical assessment and ethical implications of conversion therapy. *Ethics & Behavior, 18*(1), 93–114.

Dailard, C. (2001). Sex education: Politicians, parents, teachers and teens. *Issues in Brief, 2*, 1–4.

Dansinger, M. L., Gleason, J. A., Griffith, J. L., Selker, H. P., & Schaefer, E. J. (2005). Comparison of the Atkins, Ornish, Weight Watchers, and Zone diets for weight loss and heart disease risk reduction: A randomized trial. *Journal of the American Medical Association, 293*(1), 43–53.

De Araujo, I. E. T., Rolls, E. T., Kringelbach, M. L., McGlone, F., & Phillips, N. (2005). Taste–olfactory convergence, and the representation of pleasantness of flavour, in the human brain. *European Journal of Neuroscience, 18*, 2059–2068.

DeLamater, J. & Karraker, A. (2009). Sexual functioning in older adults. *Current Psychiatry Reports, 11*(1), 6–11.

Dhillon, H., Zigman, J. M., Ye, C., Lee, C. E., McGovern, R. A., Tang, V., *et al.* (2006). Leptin directly activates SF1 neurons in the VMH, and this action by leptin is required for normal body-weight homeostasis. *Neuron, 49*(2), 191–203.

Diener, E. & Seligman, M. E. P. (2002). Research report: Very happy people. *Psychological Science, 13*(1), 81–84, http://pcl.missouri.edu/jeff/sites/pcl.missouri.edu.jeff/files/Diener.pdf, accessed 10 December 2012.

Dugger, B. N., Morris, J. A., Jordan, C. L., & Breedlove, S. M. (2007). Androgen receptors are required for full masculinization of the ventromedial hypothalamus (VMH) in rats. *Hormones and Behavior, 51*(2), 195–201.

Durante, K. M. & Li, N. P. (2009). Oestradiol level and opportunistic mating in women. *Proceedings of the Royal Society of London: Series B, 5*(2), 19–182.

Durkin, K. F. & Hundersmarck, S. (2008). Pedophiles and child molesters. In E. Goode & D. A. Vail (eds), *Extreme Deviance* (pp. 144–150). Thousand Oaks, CA: Pine Forge Press/Sage Publications.

Eckert, E. D., Bouchard, T. J., Bohlen, J., & Heston, L. L. (1986). Homosexuality in monozygotic twins reared apart. *British Journal of Psychiatry, 148*, 421–425.

Eisenberger, N. I., Lieberman, M. D., & Williams, K. D. (2003). Does rejection hurt? An fMRI study of social exclusion. *Science, 302*, 290–292.

Ellis, B. J. & Symons, D. (1990). Sex differences in sexual fantasy: An evolutionary psychological approach. *Journal of Sex Research, 27*, 527–555.

Erlanson-Albertsson, C. (2005). Appetite regulation and energy balance. *Acta Paediatrica (Norway) 94*(448), 40–41.

Eysenck, H. J. (1990). Biological dimensions of personality. In L. A. Pervin (ed.), *Handbook of Personality: Theory and research* (pp. 244–276). New York: Guilford Press.

Fancher, R. E. (1996). *Mind in Conflict: Pioneers in psychology* (pp. 393–394). New York: W. W. Norton.

Farooqi, I. S., Wangensteen, T, Collins, S., Kimber, W, Matarese, G., Keogh, J. M., *et al.* (2007). Clinical and molecular genetic spectrum of congenital deficiency of the leptin receptor. *New England Journal of Medicine, 356*(3), 237–247.

Favaro, A., Santonastaso, P., Monteleone, P., Bellodi, L., Mauri, M., Rotondo, A., *et al.* (2008). Self-injurious behavior and attempted suicide in purging bulimia nervosa: Associations with psychiatric comorbidity. *Journal of Affective Disorders, 105*(1–3), 285–289.

Feldman, H. A., Longcope, C., Derby, C. A., Johannes, C. B., Araujo, A. B., Coviello, A. D., *et al.* (2002). Age trends in the level of serum testosterone and other hormones in middle-aged men: Longitudinal results from the Massachusetts male aging study. *Journal of Clinical Endocrinology & Metabolism, 87*(2), 589–598.

Fernandes, M., Atallah, A. N., Soares, B. G., Humberto, S., Guimarães, S., Matos, D., *et al.* (2007). Intragastric balloon for obesity. *Cochrane Database of Systematic Reviews (Online), 1*, CD004931.

Finer, L. B. (2007). Trends in premarital sex in the United States: 1954–2003. *Public Health Reports, 122*, 73–78.

Fisher, H., Aron, A., & Brown, L. L. (2005). Romantic love: An fMRI study of a neural mechanism for mate choice. *Journal of Comparative Neurology, 493*(1), 58–62.

Frank, J., Mistretta, P., & Will, J. (2008). Diagnosis and treatment of female sexual dysfunction. *American Family Physician, 77*(5), 635–642.

Friedlander, S. L., Larkin, E. K., Rosen, C. L., Palermo, T. M., & Redline, S. (2003). Decreased quality of life associated with obesity in school-aged children. *Archives of Pediatrics & Adolescent Medicine, 157*(12), 1206–1211.

Friedman, K. E., Reichmann, S. K., Costanzo, P. R., Zelli, A., Ashmore, J. A., Musante, G. J., *et al.* (2005). Weight stigmatization and ideological beliefs: Relation to psychological functioning in obese adults. *Obesity Research, 13*(5), 907–916.

Gagnon, J. H. (1975). Sex research and social change. *Archives of Sexual Behavior, 4*(2), 111–141.

Gallese, V., Fadiga, L., Fogassi, L., & Rizzolatti, G. (1996). Action recognition in the premotor cortex. *Brain, 119*(2), 593–609.

Gilger, L. (2007). Wow! A world wiener winner: Californian stuffs way to new record in Tempe hot dog eating contest. *The Tribune*, Mesa, AZ.

Godart, N. M., Berthoz, S., Rein, Z. et al. (2006). Does the frequency of anxiety and depressive disorders differ between diagnostic subtypes of anorexia nervosa and bulimia? *International Journal of Eating Disorders, 39*, 772–778.

Grassian, S. (1983). Psychopathological effects of solitary confinement. *American Journal of Psychiatry, 140*, 1450–1454.

Hackworth, M. (2007). Kobayashi loses: Hot dog title captured by Californian. *Sierra Star*, Oakhurst, CA.

Hagan, M. M., Chandler, P. C., Wauford, P. K., Rybak, R. J., & Oswald, K. D. (2003). The role of palatable food and hunger as trigger factors in an animal model of stress-induced binge eating. *International Journal of Eating Disorders, 34*(2), 183–97.

Haldeman, D. C. (1994). The practice and ethics of sexual orientation conversion. *Journal of Consulting and Clinical Psychology, 62*(2), 221–227.

Haney, M. (2008). Neurobiology of stimulants. In H. D. Kleber & M. Galanter (eds), *The American Psychiatric Publishing Textbook of Substance Abuse Treatment* (4th edn). Arlington, VA: American Psychiatric Publishing.

Hartmann, U. & Waldinger, M. D. (2007). Treatment of delayed ejaculation. In S. R. Leiblum (ed.),. *Principles and Practice of Sex Therapy* (4th edn; pp. 241–276). New York: Guilford Press.

Harvey, N. L., Srinivasan, R. S., Dillard, M. E., Johnson, N. C., Witte, M. H., Boyd, K., *et al.* (2005). Lymphatic vascular defects promoted by Prox1 haploinsufficiency cause adult-onset obesity. *Nature Genetics, 37*(10), 1072–1081.

Hayaki, J., Friedman M. A., & Brownell, K. D. (2002). Emotional expression and body dissatisfaction. *International Journal of Eating Disorders, 31*, 57–62.

Hebl, M. R. & Mannix, L. M. (2003). The weight of obesity in evaluating others: A mere proximity effect. *Personality and Social Psychology Bulletin, 29*(1), 28–38.

Heiman, J. R. (2007). Orgasmic disorders in women. In S. R. Leiblum (ed.), *Principles and Practice of Sex Therapy* (4th edn; pp. 84–123). New York: Guilford Press.

Hepp, U., Klaghofer, R., Burkhard, K., & Buddeberg, C. (2002). Treatment history of transsexual patients: A retrospective follow-up study. *Nervenarzt, 73*(3), 283–288.

Hines, M. & Kaufman, F. R. (1994). Androgen and the development of human sex-typical behavior: Rough-and-tumble play and sex of preferred playmates in children with congenital adrenal hyperplasia (CAH). *Child Development, 65*(4), 1042–1053.

Hinton, E. C., Holland, A. J., Gellatly, M. S., Soni, S., & Owen, A. M. (2006). An investigation into food preferences and the neural basis of food-related incentive motivation in Prader–Willi syndrome. *Journal of Intellectual Disability Research, 50*(9), 633–642.

Hoek, H. W. & van Hoeken, D. (2003). Review of the prevalence and incidence of eating disorders. Published online in Wiley InterScience. DOI: 10.1002/eat. 1022.

Holland, A. J., Treasure, J., Coskeran, P., Dallow, J., Milton, N., & Hillhouse, E. (1993). Measurement of excessive appetite and metabolic changes in Prader–Willi syndrome. *International Journal of Obesity and Related Metabolic Disorders, 17*, 527–532.

Holstege, G., Georgiadis, J. R., Paans, A. M., Meiners, L. C., & Graaf, F. H. (2003). Brain activation during human male ejaculation. *Experimental Brain Research, 23*(27), 9185–9193.

Holt-Lunstad, J., Birmingham, W., & Jones, B. Q. (2008). Is there something unique about marriage? The relative impact of marital status, relationship quality, and network social support on ambulatory blood pressure and mental health. *Annals of Behavioral Medicine, 35*(2), 239–244.

Hommel, J. D., Trinko, R., Sears, R. M., Georgescu, D., Liu, Z. W., Gao, X. B., Thurmon, J. J., Marinelli, M., & DiLeone, R. J. (2006). Leptin receptor signaling in midbrain dopamine neurons regulates feeding. *Neuron, 51*, 801–810.

Huang, P. L. (2005). Unraveling the links between diabetes, obesity, and cardiovascular disease. *Circulation Research, 96*, 1129–1131.

Hudson, J. I., Hiripi, E., Pope, H. G., Jr., & Kessler, R. C. (2007). The prevalence and correlates of eating disorders in the national comorbidity survey replication. *Biological Psychiatry, 61*(3), 348–358.

Jannini, E. & Lenai, A. (2005). Ejaculatory disorders: Epidemiology and current approaches to definition, classification and subtyping. *World Journal of Urology, 23*, 68–75.

Johnson, A. & Earle, T. (1987). *The Evolution of Human Societies*. Stanford, CA: Stanford University Press.

Jones, B. E. (2003). Arousal systems. *Frontiers in Bioscience, 8*, 438–451.

Kamiji, M. M., Troncon, L. E., Suen, V. M., & de Oliveira, R. B. (2009). Gastrointestinal transit, appetite, and energy balance in gastrectomized patients. *American Journal of Clinical Nutrition, 89*(1), 231–239.

Kaplan, H. S. (1977). Hypoactive sexual desire. *Journal of Sex & Marital Therapy, 3*(1), 3–9.

Kaplan, R. M. & Kronick, R. G. (2006). Marital status and longevity in the United States population. *Journal of Epidemiology & Community Health, 60*(9), 760–765.

Karama, S., Lecours, A. R., Leroux, J., Bourgouin, P., Beaudoin, G., Joubert, S., et al. (2002). Areas of brain activation in males and females during viewing of erotic film excerpts. *Human Brain Mapping, 16*(1), 1–13.

Keel, P. & Haedt, A. (2008). Evidence based psychosocial treatments for eating disorders. *Journal of Clinical Child and Adolescent Psychiatry, 37*, 39–61.

Kinsey, A. C., Pomeroy, W. B., & Martin, C. E. (1948). *Sexual Behavior in the Human Male*. Philadelphia, PA: W. B. Saunders.

Kinsley, C. H., Bardi, M., Karelina, K., Rima, B., Christon, L., Frieden-berg, J., et al. (2008). Motherhood induces and maintains behavioral and neural plasticity across the lifespan in the rat. *Archives of Sexual Behavior, 37*(1), 43–56.

Komaki, J. (2004). Water can induce better spatial memory performance than food in radial maze learning by rats. *Japanese Psychological Research, 46*(1), 65–71.

Kudwa, A. E., Michopoulos, V., Gatewood, J. D., & Rissman, E. F. (2006). Roles of estrogen receptors alpha and beta in differentiation of mouse sexual behavior. *Neuroscience, 138*(3), 921–928.

LaGraize, S. C., Borzan, J., Rinker, M. M., Kopp, J. L., & Fuchs, P. N. (2004). Behavioral evidence for competing motivational drives of nociception and hunger. *Neuroscience Letters, 372*(1/2), 30–34.

Långström, N. & Seto, M. C. (2006). Exhibitionist and voyeuristic behavior in a Swedish national population survey. *Archives of Sexual Behavior, 35*, 27–435.

Laumann, E. O., Gagnon, J. H., Michael, R. T., & Michaels, S. (1994). *The Social Organization of Sexuality*. Chicago: University of Chicago Press.

Laumann, E. O., Nicolosi, A., Glasser, D. B., Paik, A., Gingell, C., Moreira, E., et al. (2005). Sexual problems among women and men aged 40–80 years: Prevalence and correlates identified in the Global Study of Sexual Attitudes and Behaviors. *International Journal of Impotence Research, 17*, 39–57.

Laumann, E. O., Paik, A., & Rosen, R. C. (1999). Sexual dysfunction in the United States: Prevalence and predictors. *Journal of the American Medical Association, 281*(6), 537–544.

Lawson, R. (1987). Scandal in the Adventist-funded program to 'heal' homosexuals: Failure, sexual exploitation, official silence, and attempts to rehabilitate the exploiter and his methods. Paper presented at the annual convention of the American Sociological Association, Chicago.

Leavitt, G. C. (1989). Disappearance of the incest taboo: A cross-cultural test of general evolutionary hypotheses. *American Anthropologist, 91*(1), 116–131.

Ledikwe, J. H., Ello-Martin, J. A., & Rolls, B. J. (2005). Portion sizes and the obesity epidemic. *Journal of Nutrition, 135*, 905–909.

Leiblum, S. R. (2007). Sex therapy today: Current issues and future perspectives. In S. R. Leiblum (ed.), *Principles and Practice of Sex Therapy* (4th edn; pp. 3–22). New York: Guilford Press.

Lemmon, K. & Moore, C. (2007). The development of prudence in the face of varying future rewards. *Developmental Science, 10*(4), 502–511.

LeVay, S. (1991). A difference in hypothalamic structure between heterosexual and homosexual men. *Science, 253*, 1034–1037.

Levin, B. E., Routh, V. H., Kang, L., Sanders, N. M., & Dunn-Meynell, A. (2004). Neuronal glucosensing: What do we know after 50 years? *Diabetes, 53*(10), 2521–2528.

Lieberson, A. D. (2004). How long can a person survive without food? *Scientific American*, http://www.scientificamerican.com/article.cfm?id=how-long-can-a-person-sur, accessed 7 December 2012.

Litman, J. (2005). Curiosity and the pleasures of learning: Wanting and liking new information. *Cognition & Emotion, 19*(6), 793–814.

LoPiccolo, J. (1995). Sexual disorders and gender identity disorders. In R. J. Comer (ed.), *Abnormal Psychology* (2nd edn). New York: W. H. Freeman.

LoPiccolo, J. & Stock, W. E. (1987). Sexual function, dysfunction, and counseling in gynecological practice. In Z. Rosenwaks, F. Benjamin, & M. L. Stone (eds), *Gynecology*. New York: Macmillan.

LoPiccolo, J. (2004). Sexual disorders affecting men. In L. J. Haas (ed.), *Handbook of Primary Care Psychology* (pp. 485–494). New York: Oxford University Press.

Luker, K. (2007). *When Sex Goes to School: Warring views on sex and sex education since the sixties*. New York: W. W. Norton.

Lumeng, J. C. & Hillman, K. H. (2007). Eating in larger groups increases food consumption. *Archives of Disease in Childhood, 92*(5), 384–387.

Maggini, C. (2000). Psychobiology of boredom. *CNS Spectrums, 5*(8), 24–27.

Makino, M., Tsuboi, K., & Dennerstein, L. (2004). Prevalence of eating disorders: A comparison of Western and non-Western countries. *Medscape General Medicine, 6*(3), 49.

Markowitz, L. E., Dunne, E. F., Saraiya, M., Lawson, H. W., Chesson, H., & Unger, E. R. (2007). Quadrivalent human papillomavirus vaccine: Recommendations of the Advisory Committee on Immunization. *Morbidity and Mortality Weekly Report, 56*(10), March 16.

Marshall, W. L., Serran, G. A., Marshall, L. E., & O'Brien, M. D. (2008). Sexual deviation. *Handbook of Psychological Assessment, Case Conceptualization, and Treatment: Vol. 1: Adults* (pp. 590–615). Hoboken, NJ: John Wiley & Sons Inc.

Maslow, A. (1970). *Motivation and Personality* (2nd edn). New York: Harper & Row.

Masters, W. H. & Johnson, V. E. (1966). *Human Sexual Response*. Oxford: Little, Brown.

Masters, W. H. & Johnson, V. E. (1970). *Human Sexual Inadequacy*. New York: Bantam Books.

Masters, W. H. & Johnson, V. (1979). *Homosexuality in Perspective*. Boston: Little, Brown.

Maurice, W. L. (2007). Sexual desire disorders in men. In S. R. Leiblum (ed.), *Principles and Practice of Sex Therapy* (4th edn; pp. 181–211). New York, Guilford Press.

McLaren, L. (2007). Socioeconomic status and obesity. *Epidemiological Reviews, 29*(1), 29–48.

Meister, B. (2000). Control of food intake via leptin receptors in the hypothalamus. *Vitamins and Hormones, 59*, 265–304.

Messinger, D. & Fogel, A. (2007). The interactive development of social smiling. *Advances in Child Development and Behavior, 35*, 327–366.

Miller, L. C., Putcha, A., & Pederson, W. C. (2002). Men's and women's mating preferences: Distinct evolutionary mechanisms? *Current Directions in Psychological Science, 11*, 88–93.

Mischel, W., Shoda, Y., & Rodriguez, M. L. (1989). Delay of gratification in children. *Science, 244*, 933–938.

Miyagawa, Y., Tsujimura, A., Fujita, K., Matsuoka, Y., Takahashi, T., Takao, T., et al. (2007). Differential brain processing of audiovisual sexual stimuli in men: Comparative positron emission tomography study of the initiation and maintenance of penile erection during sexual arousal. *Neuroimage, 36*(3), 830–842.

Mogan, J. (1984). Obesity: Prevention is the treatment. *Patient Education and Counseling, 6*(2), 73–76.

Moll, P. P., Burns, T. L., & Lauer, R. M. (1991). The genetic and environmental sources of body mass index variability: The Muscatine ponderosity family study. *American Journal of Human Genetics, 49*, 1243–1255.

Monteiro, C. A., Moura, E. C., Conde, W. L., & Popkin, B. M. (2004). Public health reviews: Socioeconomic status and obesity in adult populations of developing countries: A review. *Bulletin of the World Health Organization, 84*(12), 940–946.

Mosher, W. D., Chandra, A., & Jones, J. (2005). Sexual behavior and selected health measures: Men and women 15–44 years of age, United States, 2002. *Advance Data, 362*, 1–55.

Mouras H., Stoléru, S., Moulier, V., Pélégrini-Issac, M., Rouxel, R., Grandjean, B., Glutron, D., & Bittoun, J. (2008). Activation of mirror neuron system by erotic video clips predicts degree of induced erection: An fMRI study. *Neuroimage, 42*, 1142–1150.

Murphy, T. (1992). Redirecting sexual orientation: Techniques and justifications. *Journal of Sex Research, 29*, 501–523.

Murray, H. (1938). *Explorations in Personality*. New York: Oxford University Press.

NAAFA (National Association to Advance Fat Acceptance). (2009). *Workplace issues*, http://www.naafaonline.com/dev2/the_issues/worklife.html, accessed 10 December 2012.

NIH (National Institutes of Health). (2009). Aim for a healthy weight: Body Mass Index Table. *Obesity Guidelines*. Bethesda, MD: Author.

Novin, D., Sanderson, J. D., & Vanderweele, D. A. (1974). The effect of isotonic glucose on eating as a function of feeding condition and infusion site. *Physiology & Behavior, 13*(1), 4.

Olsson, S. E. & Moller, A. R. (2003). On the incidence and sex ratio of transsexualism in Sweden. *Archives of Sexual Behavior, 32*(4), 381–386.

Orikasa, C., Kondo, Y., & Sakuma, Y. (2007). Transient transcription of the somatostatin gene at the time of estrogen-dependent organization of the sexually dimorphic nucleus of the rat preoptic area. *Endocrinology, 148*, 1144–1149.

Pasquet, P. & Apfelbaum, M. (1994). Recovery of initial body weight and composition after long-term massive overfeeding in men. *American Journal of Clinical Nutrition, 60*(6), 861–863.

Pattison, E. & Pattison, M. (1980). 'Ex-gays': Religiously mediated change in homosexuals. *American Journal of Psychiatry, 137*, 1553–1562.

Peplau, L. A. (2003). Human sexuality: How do men and women differ? *Current Directions in Psychological Science, 12*, 37–41.

Petrovich, G. D., Setlow, B., Holland, P. C., & Gallagher, M. (2002). Amygdalohypothalamic circuit allows learned cues to override satiety and promote eating. *Journal of Comparative Physiology, 22*(19), 8748–8753.

Pettersen, G., Rosenvinge, J. H., & Ytterhus, B. (2008). The 'double life' of bulimia: Patients' experiences in daily life interactions. *Eating Disorders, 16*(3), 204–211.

Pew Forum. (2003). *Religious Beliefs Underpin Opposition to Homosexuality*. Washington: Pew Research Center.

Philipson, T. (2001). The world-wide growth in obesity: An economic research agenda. *Health Economics, 10*, 1–7.

Pliner, P., Bell, R., Hirsch, E. S., & Kinchla, M. (2006). Meal duration mediates the effect of 'social facilitation' on eating in humans. *Appetite, 46*(2), 189–98.

Plum, L., Belgardt, B. F., & Brüning, J. C. (2006). Central insulin action in energy and glucose homeostasis. *Journal of Clinical Investigation, 116*(7), 1761–1766.

Poirier, P., Giles, T. D., Bray, G. A., Hong, Y., & Stern, J. S. (2006). Obesity and cardiovascular disease: Pathophysiology, evaluation, and effect of weight loss: An update of the 1997 American Heart Association Scientific Statement on Obesity and Heart Disease from the Obesity Committee of the Council on Nutrition, Physical Activity, and Metabolism. *Circulation, 113*, 898–918.

Porter, R. & Winberg, J. (1999). Unique salience of maternal breast odors for newborn infants. *Neuroscience & Biobehavioral Reviews, 23*(3), 439–449.

Price, R. A. & Gottesman, I. I. (1991). Body fat in identical twins reared apart: Roles for genes and environment. *Behavior Genetics, 21*(1), 22903.

Probst, M., Goris, M., Vandereycken, W., Pieters, G., Vanderlinden, J., Van Coppenolle, H., *et al.* (2004). Body composition in bulimia nervosa patients compared to healthy females. *European Journal of Nutrition, 43*(5), 288–296.

Puhl, R. M., Moss-Racusin, C. A, Schwartz, M. B., & Brownell, K. D. (2008). Weight stigmatization and bias reduction: Perspectives of overweight and obese adults. *Health Education Research, 23*(2), 347–358.

Rahman, Q. (2005). The neurodevelopment of human sexual orientation. *Neuroscience & Biobehavioral Reviews, 29*(7), 1057–1066.

Raskin, K., de Gendt, K., Duittoz, A., Liere, P., Verhoeven, G., Tronche, F., *et al.* (2009). Conditional inactivation of androgen receptor gene in the nervous system: Effects on male behavioral and neuroendocrine responses. *Journal of Neuroscience, 29*(14), 4461–4470.

Rigaud, D., Trostler, N., Rozen, R., Vallot, T., & Apfelbaum, M. (1995). Gastric distension, hunger, and energy intake after balloon implantation in severe obesity. *International Journal of Obesity and Related Metabolic Disorders, 19*(7), 489–495.

Rizzolatti, G. & Craighero, L. (2004). The mirror-neuron system. *Annual Review of Neuroscience, 27*, 169–192.

Robinson, T. E. & Berridge, K. C. (2001). Incentive-sensitization and addiction. *Addiction (England), 96*(1), 103–114.

Roche, B. & Quayle, E. (2007). Sexual disorders. In D. W. Woods & J. W. Kanter (eds), *Understanding Behavior Disorders: A contemporary behavioral perspective*. Reno, NV: Context Press.

Rolls, E. T. (2007). Sensory processing in the brain related to the control of food intake. *Proceedings of the Nutrition Society, 66*(1), 96–112.

Roman, C. & Reilly, S. (2007). Effects of insular cortex lesions on conditioned taste aversion and latent inhibition in the rat. *European Journal of Neuroscience, 26*(9), 2627–2632.

Roman, C., Lin, J., & Reilly, S. (2009). Conditioned taste aversion and latent inhibition following extensive taste preexposure in rats with insular cortex lesions. *Brain Research, 1259*, 68–73.

Romano, S. J., Halmi, K.A., Sarkar, N. P., Koke, S. C., & Lee, J. S.(2002). A placebo controlled study of fluoxtine in continued treatment of bulimia nervosa after successful acute fluoxetine treatment. *American Journal of Psychiatry, 159*, 96–102.

Roughgarden, J. (2004). *Evolution's Rainbow: Diversity, gender, and sexuality in nature and people*. Berkley, CA: University of California Press.

Ryan, R. M. & Deci, E. L. (2002). Overview of self-determination theory: An organismic-dialectical perspective. In E. L. Deci & R. M. Ryan (eds), *Handbook of Self-Determination Research* (pp. 3–33). Rochester, NY: University of Rochester Press.

Sadock, B. J. & Sadock, V. A. (2008). *Kaplan and Sadock's Synopsis of Psychiatry*. Philadelphia: Lippincott Williams and Wilkins.

Schmitt, F. F & Lahroodi, R. (2008). The epistemic value of curiosity. *Educational Theory, 58*(2), 125–149.

Schneider, T. A., Butryn, T. M., Furst, D. M., & Masucd, M. A. (2007). A qualitative examination of risk among elite adventure racers. *Journal of Sports Behavior, 408*, 330–337.

Sheldon, K. M., Ryan, R. M., Deci, E. L., & Kasser, T. (2004). The independent effects of goal contents and motives on well-being: It's both what you pursue and why you pursue it. *Personality and Social Psychology Bulletin, 30*(4), 475–486.

Sheppird, S. F. (2009). *100 Questions & Answers about Anorexia Nervosa*. Burlington, MA: Jones & Bartlett Learning.

Shmuelof, L. & Zohary, E. (2007). Watching others' actions: Mirror representations in the parietal cortex. *Neuroscientist, 13*, 667–672.

Shoda, Y., Mischel, W., & Peake, P. K. (1990). Predicting adolescent cognitive and self-regulatory competencies from preschool delay of gratification: Identifying diagnostic conditions. *Developmental Psychology, 26*(6): 978–986.

Simon, J., Braunstein, G., Nachtigall, L., Utian, W., Katz, M., Miller, S., *et al.* (2005). Testosterone patch increases sexual activity and desire in surgically menopausal women with hypoactive sexual desire disorder. *Journal of Clinical Endocrinology and Metabolism, 90*(9), 5226–5233.

Smith, D. (2004). Love that dare not squeak its name. *The New York Times*, http://www.nytimes.com/2004/02/07/arts/love-that-dare-not-squeak-its-name.html, accessed 10 December 2012.

Sørensen, T. I., Holst, C., Stunkard, A. J., & Skovgaard, L. T. (1992). Correlations of body mass index of adult adoptees and their biological and adoptive relatives. *International Journal of Obesity and Related Metabolic Disorders, 16*(3), 227–236.

Steinhausen, H. C. (2002). The outcome of anorexia in the 20th century. *American Journal of Psychiatry, 159*, 1284–1293.

Stoléru, S., Gregoire, M. C., Gerard, D., Decety, J., Lafarge, E., Cinotti, L., et al. (1999). Neuroanatomical correlates of visually evoked sexual arousal in human males. *Archives of Sexual Behavior, 28*, 1–21.

Stricker, E. M. & Zigmond, M. J. (1986). Brain monoamines, homeostasis, and adaptive behavior. In F. E. Bloom (ed.), *Handbook of Physiology: Vol. 4: Intrinsic regulatory systems of the brain* (pp. 677–696). Bethesda, MD: American Physiological Society.

Swain, J. E., Lorberbaum, J. P., Kose, S., & Strathearn, L. (2007). Brain basis of early parent–infant interactions: Psychology, physiology, and in vivo functional neuroimaging studies. *Journal of Child Psychology and Psychiatry, and Allied Disciplines, 48(3–4)*: 262–287.

Toates, F. (2009). An integrative theoretical framework for understanding sexual motivation, arousal, and behavior. *Journal of Sex Research, 46(2)*, 168–193.

Triandis, H. C. (2002). Individualism-collectivism and personality. *Journal of Personality, 69(6)*, 907–924.

Waite, L. J., Laumann, E. O., Das, A., & Schumm, L. P. (2009). Sexuality: Measures of partnerships, practices, attitudes, and problems in the national social life, health, and aging study. *Journals of Gerontology: Series B, 64B*(suppl. 1), i56–i66, DOI: 10.1093/geronb/gbp038.

Warziski, M. T., Sereika, S. M., Styn, M. A., Music, E., & Burke, L. E. (2008). Changes in self-efficacy and dietary adherence: The impact on weight loss in the PREFER study. *Journal of Behavioral Medicine, 31(1)*, 81–92.

Weiss, J. (2000). *To Have and to Hold: Marriage, the baby boom, and social change.* Chicago: University of Chicago Press.

Wenseleers, T., Helanterä, H., Hart, A., & Ratnieks, F. L. (2004). Worker reproduction and policing in insect societies: An ESS analysis. *Journal of Evolutionary Biology, 17(5)*, 1035–1047.

Williams, T. J., Pepitone, M. E., Christensen, S. E., Cooke, B. M., Huberman, A. D., Breedlove, N. J., *et al.* (2000). Finger-length ratios and sexual orientation. *Nature, 404*, 455–456.

Wilson, G. T. & Shafran, R. (2005). Eating disorders guidelines from NICE. *Lancet, 365*, 79–81.

Wincze, J. P., Bach, A. K., & Barlow, D. H. (2008). Sexual dysfunction. *Clinical Handbook of Psychological Disorders: A step-by-step treatment manual* (4th edn; pp. 615–661). New York: Guilford Press.

Woods, S. C., Lutz, T. A., Geary, N., & Langhans, W. (2006). Pancreatic signals controlling food intake: Insulin, glucagon, and amylin. *Philosophical Transactions of the Royal Society of London: Series B, 361(1471)*, 1219–1235.

Wynne, K., Stanley, S., & Bloom, S. (2004). The gut and regulation of body weight. *Journal of Clinical Endocrinology and Metabolism, 89(6)*, 2576–2582.

Yadav, R., Suri, M., Mathur, R., & Jain, S. (2009). Effect of ventromedial nucleus of hypothalamus on the feeding behavior of rats. *Journal of Clinical Biochemical Nutrition, 44*(May), 247–252.

Yerkes R. M. & Dodson, J. D. (1908). The relation of strength of stimulus to rapidity of habit-formation. *Journal of Comparative Neurology and Psychology, 18*, 459–482.

Young, L. R. & Nestle, M. (2007). Portion sizes and obesity: Responses of fast-food companies. *Journal of Public Health Policy, 28(2)*, 238–248.

Zucker, K. J. & Bradley, S. J. (2005). Gender identity and psychosexual disorders. In J. M. Weiner & M. K. Dulcan (eds), *American Psychiatric Publishing Textbook of Child and Adolescent Psychiatry* (3rd edn). Washington: American Psychiatric Publishing.

CHAPTER 14

Abe, J. A. & Izard, C. E. (1999). The developmental functions of emotions: An analysis in terms of differential emotions theory. *Cognition and Emotion, 13*, 523–549.

Adolphs, R., Tranel, D., Damasio, H., & Damasio, A. (1994). Impaired recognition of emotion in facial expressions following bilateral damage to the human amygdala. *Nature, 372*, 669–672.

Angrilli, A., Bianchin, M., Radaelli, S., Bertagnoni, G., & Pertile, M. (2008). Reduced startle reflex and aversive noise perception in patients with orbitofrontal cortex lesions. *Neuropsychologia, 46(4)*, 1179–1184.

Angrilli, A., Mauri, A., Palomba, D., Flor, H., Birbaumer, N., Sartori, G., & di Paola, F. (1996). Startle reflex and emotion modulation impairment after a right amygdala lesion. *Brain, 119*, 1991–2000.

APA (American Psychiatric Association). (2000). *Diagnostic and Statistical Manual of Mental Disorders* (4th edn). Washington: American Psychiatric Association.

Bakalar, N. (2010). Happiness may come with age, study says. *The New York Times, 31 May*, http://www.nytimes.com/2010/06/01/health/research/01happy.html?_r=0, accessed 13 December 2012.

Bard, P. (1934). The neuro-humoral basis of emotional reactions. In C. Murchinson (ed.), *Handbook of General Experimental Psychology* (pp. 264–311). Worcester, MA: Clark University Press.

Barrett, L. F., Gross, J. J., Christensen, T. C., & Benvenuto, M. (2001). Knowing what you're feeling and knowing what to do about it: Mapping the relation between emotion differentiation and emotion regulation. *Cognition and Emotion, 15*, 713–724.

Barrett, L. F., Mesquita, B., Ochsner, K. N., & Gross, J. J. (2007). The experience of emotion. *Annual Review of Psychology, 58*, 373–403.

Becchetti, L & Santoro, M. (2007). The income–unhappiness paradox: A relational goods/Baumol disease explanation. In P. L. Porta & L. Bruni (eds), *Handbook on the Economies of Happiness*. Northampton, MA: Edward Elgar Publishing.

Bechara, A., Tranel, D., Damasio, H., Adolphs, R., Rockland, C., & Damasio, A. R. (1995). Double dissociation of conditioning and declarative knowledge relative to the amygdala and hippocampus in humans. *Science, 269*, 1115–1118.

Beck, A. T. & Weishaar, M. (2011). Cognitive therapy. In R. J. Corsini & D. Wedding (eds), *Current Psychotherapies* (9th edn). Florence, KY: CENGAGE Learning.

Berntson, G. G., Bechara, A., Damasio, H., Tranel, D., & Cacioppo, J. T. (2007). Amygdala contribution to selective dimensions of emotion, *2(2)*, 123–129.

Bradley, M. M. & Lang, P. J. (2000). Measuring emotion: Behavior, feeling, and physiology. In R. D. Lane & L. Nadel (eds), *Cognitive Neuroscience of Emotion* (pp. 242–276). New York: Oxford University Press.

Bradley, M. M. & Lang, P. J. (2007). Emotion and motivation. In J. T. Cacioppo, L. G. Tassinary, & G. G. Berntson (eds), *Handbook of Psychophysiology* (3rd edn; pp. 581–607). New York: Cambridge University Press.

Bradley, M. M., Cuthbert, B. N., & Lang, P. J. (1990). Startle reflex modification: Emotion or attention? *Psychophysiology, 27*, 513–522.

Bradley, S. J. (2000). *Affect Regulation and the Development of Psychopathology.* New York: Guilford Press.

Brody, L. R. (1999). *Gender, Emotion and the Family.* Cambridge, MA: Harvard University Press.

Butler, E. A., Egloff, B., Wilhelm, F. H., Smith, N. C., Erickson, E. A., & Gross, J. J. (2003). The social consequences of expressive suppression. *Emotion, 3(1)*, 48–67.

Cain, C. K. & LeDoux, J. E. (2008). Emotional processing and motivation: In search of brain mechanisms. In A. J. Elliot (ed.), *Handbook of Approach and Avoidance Motivation* (pp. 17–34). New York: Psychology Press.

Cannon, W. B. (1927). The James–Lange theory of emotions: A critical examination and an alternative theory. *The American Journal of Psychology, 39(1)*, 106–124.

Carver, C. S. (2004). Self-regulation of action and affect. In R. F. Baumeister & K. D. Vohs (eds), *Handbook of Self-Regulation: Research, theory, and applications* (pp. 13–39). New York: Guilford Press.

Carver, C. S. & Scheier, M. F. (1998). *On the Self-Regulation of Behavior.* New York: Cambridge University Press.

Chapman, A. L., Leung, D. W., & Lynch, T. R. (2008). Impulsivity and emotion dysregulation in borderline personality disorder, *22(2)*, 148–164.

Charles, S. T. & Piazza, J. R. (2007). Memories of social interactions: Age differences in emotional intensity. *Psychology and Aging, 22(2)*, 300–309.

Christophe, V. & Rimé, B. (1997). Exposure to the social sharing of emotion: Emotional impact, listener responses and secondary social sharing. *European Journal of Social Psychology, 27*(1), 37–54.

Cicchetti, D., Ganiban, J., & Barnett, D. (1991). Contributions from the study of high-risk populations to understanding the development of emotion regulation. In J. Garber & K. A. Dodge (eds), *The Development of Emotion Regulation and Dysregulation* (pp. 15–48). New York: Cambridge University Press.

Cleckley, H. (1941). *The Mask Of Sanity: An attempt to reinterpret the so-called psychopathic personality*. Oxford: Mosby.

Cohn, J. F., Ambadar, Z., & Ekman, P. (2007). Observer-based measurement of facial expression with the facial action coding system. In J. A. Coan & J. J. B. Allen (eds), *Handbook of Emotion Elicitation and Assessment* (pp. 203–221). New York: Oxford University Press.

Cole, P. M. & Hall, S. E. (2008). Emotion dysregulation as a risk factor for psychopathology. In T. P. Beauchaine & S. P. Hinshaw (eds), *Child and Adolescent Psychopathology* (pp. 265–298). Hoboken, NJ: John Wiley & Sons, Inc.

Collett, P. (2003.) *The Book of Tells*, London: Doubleday.

Cosmides, L. & Tooby, J. (2000). Evolutionary psychology and the emotions. In M. Lewis & J. M. Haviland-Jones (eds), *Handbook of Emotions* (2nd edn; pp. 91–115). New York: Guilford Press.

Cox, B. J., Kuch, K., Parker, J. D. A., Shulman, I. D., *et al.* (1994). Alexithymia in somatoform disorder patients with chronic pain. *Journal of Psychosomatic Research, 38*(6), 523–527.

Davidson, R. J., Jackson, D. C., & Kalin, N. H. (2000). Emotion, plasticity, context, and regulation: Perspectives from affective neuroscience. *Psychological Bulletin, 126*, 890–909.

Diener, E., Sandvik, E., & Larsen, R. (1985). Age and sex effects for emotional intensity. *Developmental Psychology, 21*, 542–546.

Diener, E. & Seligman, M. E. P. (2002). Research report: Very happy people. *Psychological Science, 13*(1), 81–84, http://pcl.missouri.edu/jeff/sites/pcl.missouri.edu.jeff/files/Diener.pdf, accessed 10 December 2012.

Diener, E., Ng, W., Harter, J., & Arora, R. (2010). Wealth and happiness across the world: Material prosperity predicts life evaluation, whereas psychosocial prosperity predicts positive feeling. *Journal of Personality and Social Psychology, 99*(1), 52–61.

Dimberg, U. & Lundquist, L. (1990). Gender differences in facial reactions to facial expressions. *Biological Psychology, 30*, 151–159.

Dutton, D. G. & Aron, A. P. (1974). Some evidence for heightened sexual attraction under conditions of high anxiety. *Journal of Personality and Social Psychology, 23*, 510–517.

Easterbrook, G. (2005). The real truth about money. *Time, 165*(3), January 17, A32–A34.

Ekman, P. (1972). Universal and cultural differences in facial expressions of emotions. In J. Cole (ed.), *Nebraska Symposium on Motivation, 1971: Vol. 19*. Lincoln: University of Nebraska Press.

Ekman, P. (2003). *Emotions Revealed: Recognizing faces and feelings to improve communication and emotional life*. New York: Times Books.

Ekman, P., & Friesen, W. V. (1971). Constants across cultures in the face and emotion. *Journal of Personality and Social Psychology, 17*(2), 124–129.

Ekman, P. & Friesen, W. V. (1975). *Unmasking the Face: A guide to recognizing emotions from facial clues*. Oxford: Prentice Hall.

Ekman, P. & Friesen, W. V. (1986). A new pan-cultural facial expression of emotion. *Motivation and Emotion, 10*, 159–168.

Ekman, P., Friesen, W. V., O'Sullivan, M., Chan, A., *et al.* (1987). Universals and cultural differences in the judgments of facial expressions of emotion. *Journal of Personality and Social Psychology, 53*, 712–717.

Ekman, P., Levenson, R. W., & Friesen, W. V. (1983). Autonomic nervous system activity distinguishes among emotions. *Science, 221*, 1208–1210.

Eysenck, M. (1990). *Happiness: Facts and myths*. Hove: Lawrence Erlbaum Associates.

Eysenck, M. (2004). *Psychology: An international perspective*. Hove: Psychology Press.

Feinstein, J. S., Adolphs, R., Damsio, A., & Tranel, D. (2011). The human amygdala and the induction and experience of fear. *Current Biology, 21*(1), 34–38.

Fischer, A. H. & Manstead, A. S. R. (2000). The relation between gender and emotions in different cultures. In A. H. Fischer (ed.), *Gender and Emotion: Social psychology perspectives* (pp. 71–94). New York: Cambridge University Press.

Fischer, A. H., Rodriguez Mosquera, P. M., van Vianen, A. E. M., & Manstead, A. S. R. (2004). Gender and culture differences in emotion. *Emotion, 4*(1), 87–94.

Fisher, C. D. (2010). Happiness at work. *International Journal of Management Reviews, 12*(4), 384–412.

Friesen, W. V. (1972). *Cultural differences in facial expressions in a social situation: An experimental test of the concept of display rules*. Unpublished doctoral dissertation, University of California, San Francisco.

Frijda, N. H. (1986). *The Emotions*. Cambridge, MA: Cambridge University Press.

Frijda, N. H. (2007). *The Laws of Emotion*. Mahwah, NJ: Lawrence Erlbaum Associates.

Furnham, A. (2008). *Personality and Intelligence at Work*. London: Routledge.

Furnham, A. & Petrova, E. (2010). *Business Language in Business*. Basingstoke: Palgrave MacMillan.

Galati, D., Sini, B., Schmidt, S., & Tinti, C. (2003). Spontaneous facial expressions in congenitally-blind and sighted children aged 8–11. *Journal of Visual Impairment and Blindness, 97*, 418–428.

Gard, D. E. & Kring, A. M. (2009). Emotion in the daily lives of schizophrenia patients: Context matters. *Schizophrenia Research, 115*(2–3), 379–380.

Gohm, C. L. (2003). Mood regulation and emotional intelligence: Individual differences. *Journal of Personality and Social Psychology, 84*, 594–607.

Gohm, C. L. & Clore, G. L. (2002). Four latent traits of emotional experience and their involvement in well-being, coping, and attributional style. *Cognition and Emotion, 16*, 495–518.

Goleman, D. (1995). *Emotional Intelligence*. New York: Bantam Books.

Goleman, D. (1998). *Working with Emotional Intelligence*. New York: Bantam Books.

Goodenough, F. L. (1932). Expression of the emotions in a blind-deaf child. *Journal of Abnormal and Social Psychology, 27*, 328–333.

Gottman, J. M. & Levenson, R. W. (1988). The social psychophysiology of marriage. In P. Noller & M. A. Fitzpatrick (eds), *Perspectives on Marital Interaction* (pp. 182–200). Clevedon: Multilingual Matters.

Gratz, K. L. (2003). Risk factors for and functions of deliberate self-harm: An empirical and conceptual review. *Clinical Psychology: Science and practice, 10*(2), 192–205.

Gross, J. J. & John, O. P. (1998). Mapping the domain of expressivity: Multimethod evidence for a hierarchical model. *Journal of Personality and Social Psychology, 74*(1), 170–191.

Gross, J. J. & John, O. P. (2003). Individual differences in two emotion regulation processes: Implications for affect, relationships, and well-being. *Journal of Personality and Social Psychology, 85*(2), 348–362.

Grossman, M. & Wood, W. (1993). Sex differences in intensity of emotional experience: A social role interpretation. *Journal of Personality and Social Psychology, 65*, 1010–1022.

Harker, L. & Keltner, D. (2001). Expressions of positive emotion in women's college yearbook pictures and their relationship to personality and life outcomes across adulthood. *Journal of Personality and Social Psychology, 80*(1), 112–124.

Hiatt, L. R. (1978). Classification of the emotions. In L. R. Hiatt (ed.), *Australian Aboriginal Concepts* (pp. 182–187). Princeton, NJ: Humanities Press.

Hochschild, A. R. (2003) *The Managed Heart: Commercialisation of human feeling*. Berkley, CA: University of California Press.

Holder, M. D. & Klassen, A. (2010). Temperament and happiness in children. *Journal of Happiness Studies, 11*(4), 419–439.

Isen, A. M. (1993). Positive affect and decision making. In M. Lewis & J. M. Haviland (eds), *Handbook of Emotions* (pp. 261–277). New York: Guilford Press.

Isen, A. M. (2004). Some perspectives on positive feelings and emotions: Positive affect facilitates thinking and problem solving. In A. Manstead, N. Frijda, & A. Fischer (eds), *Feelings and Emotions: The Amsterdam symposium* (pp. 263–281). New York: Cambridge University Press.

Isen, A. M. (2008). Positive affect and decision processes: Some recent theoretical developments with practical implications. In C. P. Haugtvedt, P. M. Herr, & F. R. Kardes (eds), *Handbook of Consumer Psychology* (pp. 273–296). New York: Taylor & Francis Group/Lawrence Erlbaum Associates.

Izard, C. E. (1977). *Human Emotions*. New York: Plenum Press.

Izard, C. E. (1991). *The Psychology of Emotions*. New York: Plenum.

Izard, C. E. (1994). Innate and universal facial expressions: Evidence from developmental and cross-cultural research. *Psychological Bulletin, 115*, 288–299.

Izard, C. E. (1997). Emotions and facial expressions: A perspective from differential emotions theory. In J. A. Russell & J. M. Fernandez-Dols (eds), *The Psychology of Facial Expression* (pp. 57–77). New York: Cambridge University Press.

Izard, C. E. (2007). Basic emotions, natural kinds, emotion schemas, and a new paradigm. *Perspectives on Psychological Science, 2*, 260–280.

Izard, C. E. (2009). Emotion theory and research: Highlights, unanswered questions, and emerging issues. *Emotion Theory and Research, 60*, 1–25.

James, W. (1884). What is emotion? *Mind, 19*, 188–205.

James, W. (1890). *The Principles of Psychology*. New York: Holt.

John, O. P. & Gross, J. J. (2007). Individual differences in emotion regulation. In J. J. Gross (ed.), *Handbook of Emotion Regulation* (pp. 351–371). New York: Guilford Press.

Lang, P. J. (1993). The three systems approach to emotion. In N. Birbaumer & A. Öhman (eds), *The Organization of Motion* (pp. 18–30). Toronto: Hogrefe-Huber.

Lang, P. J., Bradley, M. M., & Cuthbert, B. N. (1998). Emotion, motivation, and anxiety: Brain mechanisms and psychophysiology. *Biological Psychiatry, 44*, 1248–1263.

Larsen, J. T., McGraw, A. P. & Cacioppo, J. T. (2001). Can people feel happy and sad at the same time? *Journal of Personality and Social Psychology, 81*(4), 684–696.

Larsen, J. T., McGraw, A. P., Mellers, B. A., & Cacioppo, J. T. (2004). The agony of victory and thrill of defeat: Mixed emotional reactions to disappointing wins and relieving losses. *Psychological Science, 15*(5), 325–330.

Larsen, J. T., To, Y. M., & Fireman, G., (2007). Children's understanding and experience of mixed emotions. *Psychological Science, 18*(2), 186–191.

Larsen, R. J. (2000). Toward a science of mood regulation. *Psychological Inquiry, 11*, 129–141.

Larsen, R. J. & Diener, E. (1987). Affect intensity as an individual difference characteristic: A review. *Journal of Research in Personality, 21*, 1–39.

Larsen, R. J., Diener, E., & Emmons, R. A. (1986). Affect intensity and reactions to daily life events. *Journal of Personality and Social Psychology, 51*, 803–814.

Lazarus, R. S. (1993). From psychological stress to the emotions: A history of changing outlooks. *Annual Review of Psychology, 44*, 1–21.

Lazarus, R. S. (2007). Stress and emotion: A new synthesis. In A. Monat, R. S. Lazarus, & G. Reevy (eds), *The Praeger Handbook on Stress and Coping: Vol. 1* (pp. 33–51). Westport, CT: Praeger Publishers/Greenwood Publishing Group.

LeDoux, J. E. (1995). Emotions: Clues from the brain. *Annual Review of Psychology, 46*, 209–235.

LeDoux, J. E. (1996). *The Emotional Brain: The mysterious underpinnings of emotional life*. New York: Simon & Schuster.

LeDoux, J. E. (2008). Remembrance of emotions past. In M. H. Immordino-Yang (ed.), *The Jossey-Bass Reader on the Brain and Learning* (pp. 151–179). San Francisco: Jossey-Bass.

Leppänen, J. M. & Hietanen, J. K. (2007). Is there more in a happy face than just a big smile? *Visual Cognition, 15*(4), 468–490.

Lewis, M. (1992). *Shame: The exposed self*. New York: Free Press.

Lewis, M. (2005). Origins of the self-conscious child. In W. R. Crozier & L. E. Alden (eds), *The Essential Handbook of Social Anxiety for Clinicians* (pp. 81–98). Hoboken, NJ: John Wiley & Sons, Inc.

Lewis, M. (2007). Self-conscious emotional development. In J. L. Tracy, R. W. Robins, & J. P. Tangney (eds), *The Self-Conscious Emotions: Theory and research* (pp. 134–149). New York: Guilford Press.

Lewis, M. (2008). The emergence of human emotions. In M. Lewis, J. M. Haviland-Jones, & L. Feldmann Barrett (eds), *Handbook of Emotions* (3rd edn; pp. 304–319). New York: Guilford Press.

Linehan, M. M. (1993). *Cognitive-Behavioral Treatment of Borderline Personality Disorder*. New York: Guilford Press.

Linehan, M. M. & Dexter-Mazza, E. (2008). Dialectical behavior therapy for borderline personality disorder. In D. H. Barlow (ed.), *Clinical Handbook of Psychological Disorders: A step-by-step treatment manual* (4th edn; pp. 365–420). New York: Guilford Press.

Löw, A., Lang, P. J., Smith, J. C., & Bradley, M. M. (2008). Both predator and prey: Emotional arousal in threat and reward. *Psychological Science, 19*(9), 865–873.

Lucas, R. E. (2007). Adaptation and the set point model of subjective well-being: Does happiness change after major life events? *Current Directions in Psychological Science, 16*(2), 75–79.

Luminet, O., Bouts, P., Delie, F., Manstead, A. S. R., & Rimé, B. (2000). Social sharing of emotion following exposure to a negatively valenced situation. *Cognition and Emotion, 14*(5), 661–688.

Lykken, D. & Tellegen, A. (1996). Happiness is a stochastic phenomenon. *Psychological Science, 7*(3), 186–189.

Mallan, K. M. & Lipp, O. V. (2007). Does emotion modulate the blink reflex in human conditioning? Startle potentiation during pleasant and unpleasant cues in the picture–picture paradigm. *Psychophysiology, 44*, 737–748.

Marañon, G. (1924). Contribution à l'etude de l'action emotive de l'adrénalin. *Revue Française d'Endocrinologie, 2*, 301–325.

Matsumoto, D., Takeuchi, S., Andayani, S., Kouznetsova, N., & Krupp, D. (1998). The contribution of individualism vs. collectivism to cross-national differences in display rules. *Asian Journal of Social Psychology, 1*, 147–165.

Matthews, G., Zeidner, M., & Roberts, R. (2007). *The Science of Emotional Intelligence*. Oxford: Oxford University Press.

Mayer, J. D. & Salovey, P. (1997). What is emotional intelligence? In P. Salovey & D. Sluyter (eds), *Emotional Development and Emotional Intelligence: Educational implications* (pp. 3–31). New York: Basic Books.

Morris, J. S., Frith, C. D., Perrett, D. I., Rowland, D., *et al.* (1996). A differential neural response in the human amygdala to fearful and happy facial expressions. *Nature, 383*(6603), 812–815.

Morris, W. N. (1992). A functional analysis of the role of mood in affective systems. In M. S. Clark (ed.), *Emotion* (pp. 256–293). Thousand Oaks, CA: Sage Publications.

Mroczek, D. K. (2004). Positive and negative affect at midlife. In O. G. Brim, C. D. Ryff, & R. C. Kessler (eds), *How Healthy Are We? A national study of well-being at midlife* (pp. 205–226). Chicago: University of Chicago Press.

Mroczek, D. K. & Spiro, A. (2005). Change in life satisfaction during adulthood: Findings from the Veterans Affairs normative aging study. *Journal of Personality and Social Psychology, 88*(1), 189–202.

Mroczek, D. K. & Spiro, A. (2007). Personality change influences mortality in older men. *Psychological Science, 18*(5), 371–376.

Myers, D. G. (2000). The funds, friends, and faith of happy people. *American Psychologist, 55*(1), 56–67.

Myers, D. G. & Diener, E. (1996). The pursuit of happiness. *Scientific American, 274*(5), 70–72.

Nardi, A. E., Valenca, A. M., Nascimento, I., Freire R.C., *et al.* (2008). A caffeine challenge test in panic disorder patients, their healthy first-degree relatives and healthy controls. *Depression and Anxiety, 25*, 847–853.

Nock, M. K. & Prinstein, M. J. (2004). A functional approach to the assessment of self-mutilative behavior. *Journal of Consulting and Clinical Psychology, 72,* 885–890.

Oatley, K. & Jenkins, J. M. (1996). *Understanding Emotions.* Malden, MA, and Oxford, UK: Blackwell.

Öhman, A. (2000). Fear and anxiety: Evolutionary, cognitive, and clinical perspectives. In M. Lewis & J. M. Haviland-Jones (eds), *Handbook of Emotions* (2nd end; pp. 573–593). New York: Guilford Press.

Parrott, W. G. (2001). Implications of dysfunctional emotions for understanding how emotions function. *Review of General Psychology, 5,* 180–186.

Parrott, W. G. (2004). The nature of emotion. In M. B. Brewer & M. Hewstone (eds), *Emotion and Motivation* (pp. 5–20). Malden, MA: Blackwell Publishing.

Peterson, C., Ruch, W., Beermann, U., Park, N., & Seligman, M. E. P. (2007). Strengths of character, orientations to happiness, and life satisfaction. *Journal of Positive Psychology, 2*(3), 149–156.

Petrides, K. V. (2009). *Technical Manual for the Trait Emotional Intelligence Questionnaires (TEIQue).* London: London Psychometric Laboratory.

Petrides, K. V. & Furnham, A. (2003). Trait emotional intelligence. *European Journal of Personality, 17,* 39–57.

Rachman, S. J. (1989). *Fear and Courage.* New York: W. H. Freeman.

Rachman, S. J. (2004). Fear and courage: A psychological perspective. *Social Research, 71*(1), 149–176.

Reeve, J. M. (2001). *Understanding Motivation and Emotion* (3rd edn). Fort Worth, TX. Harcourt College Publications.

Rimé, B. (2007). The social sharing of emotion as an interface between individual and collective processes in the construction of emotional climates. *Journal of Social Issues, 63,* 307–322.

Roysamb, E. (2006). *Personality and Well-Being: Handbook of personality and health* (pp. 115–134). New York: John Wiley & Sons.

Safdar, S., Friedlmeier, W., Matsumoto, D., Yoo, S. H., Kwantes, C. T., Kakai, H., *et al.* (2009). Variations of emotional display rules within and across cultures: A comparison between Canada, USA, and Japan. *Canadian Journal of Behavioural Science, 41*(1), 1–10.

Sahoo, F. M., Sahoo, K., & Harichandan, S. (2005). Five big factors of personality and human happiness. *Social Science International, 21*(1), 20–28.

Santerre, C. & Allen, J. J. B. (2007). Methods for studying the psychophysiology of emotion. In J. Rottenberg & S. L. Johnson (eds), *Emotion and Psychopathology: Bridging affective and clinical science.* Washington: American Psychological Association.

Schachter, S. & Singer, J. (1962). Cognitive, social, and physiological determinants of emotional state. *Psychological Review, 69,* 379–399.

Seligman, M. E. P. (2002). *Authentic Happiness.* London: Random House.

Seligman, M. E. P. (2007). Coaching and positive psychology. *Australian Psychologist, 42*(4), 266–267.

Seligman, M. E. P. & Fowler, R. D. (2011). Comprehensive soldier fitness and the future of psychology. *American Psychologist, 66*(1), 82–86.

Seyfarth, R. M. & Cheney, D. L. (2003). Meaning and emotion in animal vocalizations. In P. Ekman, J. J. Campos, J. J. Davidson, R. J. de Waal, & B. M. Frans (eds), *Emotions Inside Out: 130 years after Darwin's: The expression of the emotions in man and animals* (pp. 32–55). New York: New York University Press.

Simpson, P. A. & Stroh, L. K. (2004). Gender differences: Emotional expression and feelings of personal inauthenticity. *Journal of Applied Psychology, 89,* 715–721.

Sloan, D. M., Bradley, M. M., Dimoulas, E., & Lang, P. J. (2002). Looking at facial expressions: Dysphoria and facial EMG. *Biological Psychology, 60*(2–3), 79–90.

Soussignan, R. (2002). Duchenne smile, emotional experience, and autonomic reactivity: A test of the facial-feedback hypothesis. *Emotion, 2,* 52–74.

Strack, F., Martin, L. L., & Stepper, S. (1988). Inhibiting and facilitating conditions of the human smile: A non-obtrusive test of the facial-feedback hypothesis. *Journal of Personality and Social Psychology, 54,* 768–777.

Sutton, S. K. & Davidson, R. J. (2000). Prefrontal brain electrical asymmetry predicts the evaluation of affective stimuli, *38*(13), 1723–1733.

Sutton, S. K., Ward, R. T., Larson, C. L., Holden, J. E., Perlman, S. B., & Davidson, R. J. (1997). Asymmetry in prefrontal glucose metabolism during appetitive and aversive emotional states: An FDG-PET study. *Psychophysiology, 34,* S89.

Thompson, R. A. (1994). Emotion regulation: A theme in search of a definition. *Monographs of the Society for Research in Child Development, 59,* 25–52.

Tomkins, S. S. (1962). *Affect, Imagery, and Consciousness.* New York: Springer Publishing.

Tousignant, M. (1984). *Pena* in the Ecuadorian Sierra: A psychoanthropological analysis of sadness. *Culture, Medicine, and Psychiatry, 8,* 381–398.

Tsai, J. L., Chentsova-Dutton, Y., Freire-Bebeau, L., & Przymus, D. E. (2002). Emotional expression and physiology in European Americans and Hmong Americans. *Emotion, 2,* 380–397.

Tsai, J. L., Levenson, R. W., & McCoy, K. (2006). Cultural and temperamental variation in emotional response. *Emotion, 6,* 484–497.

Tsai, J. L., Simeonova, D. I., & Watanabe, J. T. (2004). Somatic and social: Chinese Americans talk about emotion. *Personality and Social Psychology Bulletin, 30,* 1226–1238.

Vohs, K. D., Glass, B. D., Maddox, W. T., & Markman, A. B. (2011). Ego depletion is not just fatigue: Evidence from a total sleep deprivation experiment. *Social Psychological and Personality Science, 2*(2), 166–173.

Vujanovic, A. A., Zvolensky, M. J., Bernstein, A., Feldner, M. T., & McLeish, A. C. (2007). A test of the interactive effects of anxiety sensitivity and mindfulness in the prediction of anxious arousal, agoraphobic cognitions, and body vigilance. *Behaviour Research and Therapy, 45*(6), 1393–1400.

Wallis, C. (2005). The new science of happiness. *Time, 165*(3), A2–A9.

Watson, D. & Tellegen, A. (1985). Towards a consensual structure of mood. *Psychological Bulletin, 98,* 219–235.

Weinberger, D. A., Schwartz, G. E., & Davidson R. J. (1979). Low-anxious, high-anxious, and repressive coping style: psychometric patterns and behavioral and physiological responses to stress. *Journal of Abnormal Psychology, 88,* 369–801.

Yuan, J. W. & Kring, A. M. (2009). Dysphoria and the prediction and experience of emotion. *Cognition and Emotion, 23*(6), 1221–1232.

Zajonc, R. B., Murphy, S. T., & Inglehart, M. (1989). Feeling and facial efference: Implications of the vascular theory of emotion. *Psychological Review, 96,* 395–416.

CHAPTER 15

Adolphs, R., Russell, J., & Tranel, D. (1999). A role for the human amygdala in recognizing emotional arousal from unpleasant stimuli. *Psychological Science, 10,* 167–171.

Allport, G. (1968). *The Person in Psychology.* Boston: Beacon Press.

Allport, G. W. & Odbert, H. S. (1936). Trait-names: A psycholexical study. *Psychological Monographs, 47,* 171.

APA (American Psychiatric Association). (2000). *Diagnostic and Statistical Manual of Mental Disorders* (4th edn). Washington: American Psychiatric Association.

Arens, E. A., Grabe, H., Spitzer, C., & Barnow, S. (2011). Testing the biosocial model of borderline personality disorder: Results of a prospective 5-year longitudinal study. *Personality and Mental Health, 5*(1), 29–42.

Autor, D., Katz, L., & Kearney, M. (2006). The polarization of the US labor market. *American Economic Review, 96,* 189–194.

Bandura, A. (1986). Social foundations of thought and action: A social cognitive theory. Englewood Cliffs, NJ: Prentice Hall.

Bandura, A. (2006). Toward a psychology of human agency. *Perspectives on Psychological Science, 1,* 164–180.

Bandura, A. (2008). Reconstrual of 'free will' from the agentic perspective of social cognitive theory. In J. Baer, J. C. Kaufman, & R. F. Baumeister (eds), *Are We Free? Psychology and free will* (pp. 86–127). New York: Oxford University Press.

Barnett, R. & Rivers, C. (2004). *Same Difference: How gender myths are hurting our relationships, our children, and our jobs*. New York: Basic Books.

Baumgardner, S. R. & Crothers, M. K. (2009). *Positive Psychology*. Upper Saddle River, NJ: Prentice Hall/Pearson Education.

Bekker, M. H. J. & van Assen, M. A. L. M. (2008). Autonomy-connectedness and gender. *Sex Roles, 59*(7–8), 532–544.

Berenson, K. R., Downey, G., Rafaeli, E., Coifman, K. G., & Paquin, N. L. (2011). The rejection–rage contingency in borderline personality disorder. *Journal of Abnormal Psychology, 120*(3), 681–690.

Black, K. A. & Schutte, E. D. (2006). Recollections of being loved: Implications of childhood experiences with parents for young adults' romantic relationships. *Journal of Family Issues, 27*, 1459–1480.

Blais, M. A., Baity M. R., & Hopwood C. J. (eds) (2010). *Clinical Applications of the Personality Assessment Inventory*. New York: Routledge/Taylor & Francis Group.

Borgen, F. H. & Betz, N. E. (2008). Career self-efficacy and personality: Linking career confidence and the healthy personality. *Journal of Career Assessment, 16*(1), 22–43.

Bosson, J. K. & Vandello, J. A. (2011). Precarious manhood and its links to action and aggression. *Current Directions in Psychological Science, 20*, 82–86.

Botwin, M. D., Buss, D. M., & Shackelford, T. K. (1997). Personality and mate preferences: Five factors in mate selection and marital satisfaction. *Journal of Personality, 65*, 107–136.

Bouchard, G. & Thériault, V. J. (2003). Defense mechanisms and coping strategies in conjugal relationships: An integration. *International Journal of Psychology, 38*(2), 79–90.

Bouchard, T., Jr. (2004). Genes, environment, and personality. *Science, 264*, 1700–1701.

Bouchard, T. & Pedersen N. (1999). Twins reared apart: Nature's double experiment. In M. LaBuda & E. Grigorenko (eds), *On the Way to Individuality: Current methodological issues in behavior genetics* (pp. 71–93). Commack, NY: Nova Science Press.

Boyle, G. J. (2008). Critique of the five-factor model of personality. In G. J. Boyle, G. Matthews, & D. H. Saklofske (eds), *The SAGE Handbook of Personality Theory and Assessment: Vol. 1: Personality theories and models.* (pp. 295–312). Sage Publications.

Buda, R. & Elsayed-Elkhouly, S. M. (1998). Cultural differences between Arabs and Americans: Individualism–Collectivism revisited. *Journal of Cross-Cultural Psychology, 29*, 487–492.

Bussey, K. & Bandura, A. (1999). Social cognitive theory of gender development and differentiation, *Psychological Review, 106*, 676–713.

Butcher, J. N. (2010). Personality assessment from the nineteenth to the early twenty-first century: Past achievements and contemporary challenges. *Annual Review of Clinical Psychology, 6*, 1–20.

Carré, J. M., Putnam, S. K., & McCormick, C. M. (2009). Testosterone responses to competition predict future aggressive behaviour at a cost to reward in men. *Psychoneuroendocrinology, 34*(4), 561–570.

Caspi, A. (2002). Social selection, social causation, and developmental pathways: Empirical strategies for better understanding how individuals and environments are linked across the life course. In L. Pulkkinen & A. Caspi (eds), *Paths to Successful Development: Personality in the life course* (pp. 281–301). Cambridge: Cambridge University Press.

Caspi, A. & Roberts, B. W. (1999). Personality change and continuity across the life course. In L. A. Pervin & O. P. John (eds), *Handbook of Personality Theory and Research: Vol. 2* (pp. 300–326). New York: Guilford Press.

Caspi, A., Bem, D. J., & Elder, G. H., Jr. (1989). Continuities and consequence of interactional styles across the life course. *Journal of Personality, 57*, 375–406.

Cattell, R. B. (1965). *The Scientific Analysis Personality*. London: Penguin.

Church, A. T. & Katigbak, M. S. (2000). Trait psychology in the Philippines. *American Behavioral Scientist, 44*, 73–94.

Clark, L. & Watson, D. (1999). Temperament: A new paradigm for trait psychology. In L. A. Pervin & O. P. John (eds), *Handbook of Personality* (2nd edn; pp. 399–423). New York: Guilford Press.

Collins, R. L. (2005). Sex on television and its impact on American youth: Background and results from the RAND television and adolescent sexuality study. *Child and Adolescent Psychiatric Clinics of North America, 14*(3), 371–385.

Cooper, M. L. & Sheldon, M. S. (2002). Seventy years of research on personality and close relationships: Substantive and methodological trends over time. *Journal of Personality, 70*, 783–812.

Correa, A. A. & Rogers, R. (2010). Cross-cultural applications of the PAI. In M. A. Blais, M. R. Baity, & C. J. Hopwood (eds), *Clinical Applications of the Personality Assessment Inventory* (pp. 135–148). New York: Routledge/Taylor & Francis Group.

Costa, P. T., Jr., Terracciano, A., & McCrae, R. R. (2001). Gender differences in personality traits across cultures: Robust and surprising findings. *Journal of Personality and Social Psychology, 81*, 322–331.

Cottone, E. & Byrd-Bredbenner, C. (2007). Knowledge and psychosocial effects of the film *Super Size Me* on young adults. *Journal of the American Dietetic Association, 107*(7), 1197–1203.

Cousins, S. D. (1989). Culture and selfhood in Japan and the U.S. *Journal of Personality and Social Psychology, 56*, 124–131.

Cramer, P. (2006). *Protecting the Self: Defense mechanisms in action*. New York: Guilford Press.

Csikszentmihalyi, M. (1998). *Finding Flow: The psychology of engagement with everyday life*. New York: Basic Books.

Csikszentmihalyi, M. (2003). *Good Business: Leadership, flow, and the making of meaning*. New York: Penguin Books.

Dabbs, J. M., Jr., Bernieri, F. J., Strong, R. K., Campo, R., & Milun, R. (2001). Going on stage: Testosterone in greetings and meetings. *Journal of Research of Personality, 35*(1), 27–40.

Davidson, R. J. (1998). Affective style and affective disorders: Perspectives from affective neuroscience. *Cognition and Emotion, 12*, 307–330.

Davidson, R. J. & Fox, N. A. (1989). Frontal brain asymmetry predicts infants' response to maternal separation. *Journal of Abnormal Psychology, 98*, 127–131.

DePaulo, B. M., Blank, A. L., Swaim, G. W., & Hairfield, J. G. (1992). Expressiveness and expressive control. *Personality and Social Psychology Bulletin, 18*, 276–285.

Depue, R. & Collins, P. F. (1999). Neurobiology of the structure of personality: Dopamine, facilitation of incentive motivation, and extraversion. *Behavioral and Brain Sciences, 22*, 491–569.

Diener, E., Diener, M., & Diener, C. (1995). Factors predicting the subjective well-being of nations. *Journal of Personality and Social Psychology, 69*, 851–864.

Dreher, J., Kohn, P., Kolachana, B., Weinberger, D. R., & Berman, K. F. (2009). Variation in dopamine genes influences responsivity of the human reward system. *Proceedings of the National Academy of Sciences, 106*(2), 617–622.

Dumont, F. (2010). *A History of Personality Psychology: Theory, science, and research from Hellenism to the twenty-first century*. New York: Cambridge University Press.

Eagly, A. H. (1987). *Sex Differences in Social Behavior: A social-role interpretation*. Hillsdale, NJ: Lawrence Erlbaum Associates.

Eagly, A. H. & Koenig, A. M. (2006). Social role theory of sex differences and similarities: Implication for prosocial behavior. In K. Dindia & D. J. Canary (eds), *Sex Differences and Similarities in Communication* (2nd edn; pp. 161–177). Mahwah, NJ: Lawrence Erlbaum Associates.

Eagly, A. H. & Wood, W. (1999). The origins of sex differences in human behavior: Evolved dispositions versus social roles. *American Psychologist, 54*, 408–423.

Everhart, D. E., Shucard, J. L., Quatrin, T., & Shucard, D. W. (2001). Sex-related differences in event-related potentials, face recognition, and facial affect processing in prepubertal children. *Neuropsychology, 15*, 329–341.

Ewen, R. B. (2010). *An Introduction to Theories of Personality* (7th edn). New York: Psychology Press.

Eysenck, H. J. (1990). Biological dimensions of personality. In L. A. Pervin (ed.), *Handbook of Personality: Theory and research* (pp. 244–276). New York: Guilford Press.

Eysenck, H. J. (1992). Four ways five-factors are not basic. *Personality and Individual Differences, 13*, 667–673.

Eysenck, H. J. (2002). *The Dynamics of Anxiety and Hysteria: An experimental application of modern learning theory to psychiatry*. New Brunswick, NJ: Transaction Publishers.

Feingold, A. (1994). Gender differences in personality: A meta-analysis. *Psychological Bulletin, 116*, 429–456.

Feliciano, L. & Gum, A. M. (2010). Mood disorders. In D. L. Segal & M. Hersen (eds), *Diagnostic Interviewing* (pp. 153–176). New York: Springer Publishing Co.

Finley, L. L. (2007). *The Encyclopedia of Juvenile Violence* (p. 291). Westport, CT: Greenwood Publishing Group.

Fleeson, W. (2007). Situation-based contingencies underlying trait-content manifestation in behavior. *Journal of Personality, 75*(4), 825–862.

Freud, S. (1909). Analysis of a phobia in a five-year-old boy. *S. E., 10*, 5–149.

Froehlich, J. C., Zink, R. W., Li, T., & Christian, J. C. (2000). Analysis of heritability of hormonal responses to alcohol in twins: Beta-endorphin as a potential biomarker of genetic risk for alcoholism. *Alcoholism: Clinical and Experimental Research, 24*(3), 265–277.

Furnham, A. (2008). *Personality and Intelligence at Work: Exploring and explaining individual differences at work*. Hove: Psychology Press/Taylor & Francis.

Gardner, W. L. & Martinko, M. J. (1996). Using the Myers–Briggs Type Indicator to study managers: A literature review and research agenda. *Journal of Management, 22*(1), 45–83.

Gilligan, C. (1982). *In a Different Voice: Psychological theory and women's development*. Cambridge, MA: Harvard University Press.

Gilligan, C. (2004). Recovering psyche: Reflections on life-history and history. *Annual of Psychoanalysis, 32*, 131–147.

Gold, S. N. & Castillo, Y. (2010). Dealing with defenses and defensiveness in interviews. In D. L. Segal & M. Hersen (eds), *Diagnostic Interviewing* (pp. 89–102). New York, Springer Publishing.

Gray, J. (1992). *Men Are from Mars, Women Are from Venus*. New York: Thorsons.

Haas, B. W., Omura, K., Constable, R. T., & Canli, T. (2007). Emotional conflict and neuroticism: Personality-dependent activation in the amygdala and subgenual anterior cingulate. *Behavioral Neuroscience, 121*(2), 249–256.

Halpern, D. F. (2000). *Sex Differences in Cognitive Abilities* (3rd edn). Mahwah, NJ: Lawrence Erlbaum Associates.

Harman, C. & Fox, N. A. (1997). Frontal and attentional mechanisms regulating distress experience and expression during infancy. In N. A. Krasnegor, G. R. Lyon, & P. S. Goldman-Rakic (eds), *Development of the Prefrontal Cortex: Evolution, neurobiology, and behavior* (pp. 191–208). Baltimore: Paul H. Brookes Publishing.

Heath, A. C., Madden, P. A., Cloninger, C. R., & Martin, N. G. (1994). Genetic and environmental structure of personality. In C. R. Cloninger (ed.), *Personality and Psychopathology*. Washington: American Psychiatric Press.

Henley, N. M. (1977). *Body Politics: Power, sex, and nonverbal communication*. Englewood Cliffs, NJ: Prentice Hall.

Hines, M. (2004). Androgen, estrogen and gender. In A. Eagly, A. Beall, & R. Sternberg (eds), *The Psychology of Gender* (2nd edn; pp. 9–37). New York: Guilford Press.

Hofstede, G. & McCrae, R. R. (2004). Culture and personality revisited: Linking traits and dimensions of culture. *Cross-Cultural Research, 38*, 52–88.

Hong, Y., Morris, M. W., Chiu, Y., & Benet-Martinez, V. (2000). Multicultural minds: A dynamic constructivist approach to culture and cognition. *American Psychologist, 55*, 709–717.

Hoyle, R. H. (ed.) (2010). *Handbook of Personality and Self-Regulation*. Hoboken, NJ: Wiley-Blackwell.

Hyde, J. S. (2005). The gender similarities hypothesis. *American Psychologist, 60*, 581–592.

Hyde, J. S. (2007). New directions in the study of gender similarities and differences. *Current Directions in Psychological Science, 16*(5), 259–263.

Hyde, J. S. (2008). Men are from earth, women are from earth: The gender similarities hypothesis. *General Psychologist, 43*(1), 1.

Jang, K., McCrae, R., Angleitner, A., Riemann, R., & Livesley, W. (1998). Heritability of facet-level traits in a cross-cultural twin sample: Support for a hierarchical model of personality. *Journal of Personality and Social Psychology, 74*, 1556–1565.

Johnson, W., Bouchard, T. J., Jr., McGue, M., Segal, N. L., Tellegen, A., Keyes, M., *et al.* (2007). Genetic and environmental influences on the verbal-perceptual-image rotation (VPR) model of the structure of mental abilities in the Minnesota study of twins reared apart. *Intelligence, 35*(6), 542–562.

Joseph, S. V. (2007). A study of the amplitudes and latencies of the brain stem and cortical auditory evoked potentials (AEP) in relation to the personality dimension of extraversion. ProQuest Information & Learning: US. *Dissertation Abstracts International: Section B: The Sciences and Engineering, 68*(6), 4133.

Josephs, R. A., Markus, H., & Tarafodi, R. W. (1992). Gender and self-esteem. *Journal of Personality and Social Psychology, 63*, 391–402.

Kashima, Y., Siegal, M., Tanaka, K., & Kashima, E. S. (1992). Do people believe behaviours are consistent with attitudes? Towards a cultural psychology of attribution processes. *British Journal of Social Psychology, 31*, 111–124.

Kelly, C. R., Grinband, J., & Hirsch, J. (2007). Repeated exposure to media violence is associated with diminished response in an inhibitory fronto-limbic network. *PLoS ONE, 2*(12), e1268.

Kern, M. L. & Friedman, H. S. (2008). Do conscientious individuals live longer? A quantitative review. *Health Psychology, 27*(5), 505–512.

Kim, J. L., Collins, R. L., Kanouse, D. E., Elliott, M. N., Berry, S. H., Hunter, S. B., Miu, A., & Kunkel, D. (2006). Sexual readiness, household policies, and other predictors of adolescents' exposure to sexual content in mainstream entertainment television. *Media Psychology, 8*(4), 449–471.

Kitayama, S., Markus, H. R., & Kurokawa, M. (2000). Culture, emotion, and well-being: Good feelings in Japan and the United States. *Cognition and Emotion, 14*, 93–124.

Knutson, B., Wolkowitz, O., Cole, S., Chan, T., Moore, E., Johnson, R., *et al.* (1998). Selective alteration of personality and social behavior by serotonergic intervention. *American Journal of Psychiatry, 155*, 373–379.

Krueger, R. F., South, S., Johnson, W., & Iacono, W. (2008). The heritability of personality is not always 50%: Gene–environment interactions and correlations between personality and parenting. *Journal of Personality, 76*(6), 1485–1522.

Kuppens, P., Realo, A., & Diener, E. (2008). The role of positive and negative emotions in life satisfaction judgment across nations. *Journal of Personality and Social Psychology, 95*(1), 66–75.

LeDoux, J. E. (1999). The power of emotions. In R. Conlan (ed.), *States of Mind: New discoveries about how our brains make us who we are* (pp. 123–149). New York: John Wiley & Sons.

Leontiev, D. A. (2008). Maslow yesterday, today, and tomorrow. *Journal of Humanistic Psychology, 48*(4), 451–453.

Lilienfeld, S. O., Wood, J. M., & Garb, H. N. (2000). The scientific status of projective techniques. *Psychological Science in the Public Interest, 1*, 27–66.

Linehan, M. M. & Dexter-Mazza, E. (2008). Dialectical behavior therapy for borderline personality disorder. In D. H. Barlow (ed.), *Clinical Handbook of Psychological Disorders: A step-by-step treatment manual* (4th edn; pp. 365–420). New York: Guilford Press.

Livesley, W., Jang, K., & Vernon, P. (2003). Genetic basis of personality structure. In T. Millon & M. J. Lerner (eds), *Handbook of Psychology: Vol. 5: Personality and social psychology* (pp. 59–84). Hoboken, NJ: John Wiley & Sons, Inc.

Loehlin, J. C. (1992). *Genes and Environment in Personality Development*. Newbury Park, CA: Sage Publications.

Lynam, D., Caspi, A., Moffitt, T., Wikstrom, P., Loeber, R., & Novak, S. (2000). The interaction between impulsivity and neighborhood context on offending: The effects of impulsivity are stronger in poorer neighborhoods. *Journal of Abnormal Psychology, 109*, 563–574.

Maddi, S. (1989). *Personality Theories: A comparative analysis*. Chicago: Dorsey Press.

Maddux, J. E. & Volkmann, J. (2010). Self-efficacy. In R. H. Hoyle (ed.), *Handbook of Personality and Self-Regulation* (pp. 315–331). Hoboken, NJ: Wiley-Blackwell.

Maestripieri, D., Higley, J., Lindell, S., Newman, T., McCormack, K., & Sanchez, M. (2006). Early maternal rejection affects the development of monoaminergic systems and adult abusive parenting in rhesus macaques (*Macaca mulatta*). *Behavioral Neuroscience, 120*, 1017–1024.

Maruszewski, T., Fajkowska, M., & Eysenck, M. W. (2010). Introduction: An integrative view of personality. In T. Maruszewski, M. Fajkowska, & M. Eysenck (eds), *Personality from Biological, Cognitive, and Social Perspectives: Warsaw lectures in personality and social psychology*. Clifton Corners, NY: Eliot Werner Publications.

Masling, J. (2004). A storied test. *PsycCRITIQUES*. No pages.

Maslow, A. (1970). *Motivation and Personality* (2nd edn). New York: Harper & Row.

Mason, P. T. & Kreger, R. (2010). *Stop Walking on Eggshells: Taking your life back when someone you care about has borderline personality disorder* (2nd edn). Oakland, CA: New Harbinger Publications.

McClure, E. B. (2000). A meta-analytic review of sex differences in facial expression processing and their development in infants, children, and adolescents. *Psychological Bulletin, 126*, 424–453.

McCrae, R. R. (2002). The maturation of personality psychology: Adult personality development and psychological well-being. *Journal of Research in Personality, 36*(4), 307–317.

McCrae, R. & Costa, P. (2003). *Personality in Adulthood: A five-factor theory perspective* (2nd edn). New York: Guilford.

McCrae, R. R., Terracciano, A., & 78 Members of the Personality Profiles of Cultures Project. (2005). Universal features of personality traits from the observer's perspective: Data from 50 cultures. *Journal of Personality and Social Psychology, 88*, 547–561.

McCrae, R. R., Yik, M. S. M., Trapnell, P. D., Bond, M. H., & Paulhus, D. L. (1998). Interpreting personality profiles across cultures: Bilingual, acculturation and peer rating studies of Chinese undergraduates. *Journal of Personality and Social Psychology, 74*, 1041–1055.

McGue, M. & Lykken, D. T. (1992). Genetic influence on risk of divorce. *Psychological Science, 3*(6), 368–373.

Mischel, W. (2004). Toward an integrative science of the person. *Annual Review of Psychology, 55*, 1–22.

Mischel, W. & Peake, P. K. (1982). Beyond deja vu in the search for cross-situational consistency. *Psychological Review, 89*, 730–755.

Myers, I., McCaulley, M., Quenk, N. L., & Hammer, A. L. (1998). *MBTI Manual: A guide to the development and use of the Myers–Briggs type indicator* (3rd edn). Palo Alto, CA: Consulting Psychologists Press.

Nye, C. D., Roberts, B. W., Saucier, G., & Zhou, X. (2008). Testing the measurement equivalence of personality adjective items across cultures. *Journal of Research in Personality, 42*(6), 1524–1536.

Organ, D. & Ryan, K. (1995). A meta-analytic review of attitudinal and dispositional predictors of organizational citizenship behavior. *Personnel Psychology, 48*, 775–802.

Oyserman, D., Coon, H. M., & Kemmelmeier, M. (2002a). Rethinking individualism and collectivism: Evaluation of theoretical assumptions and meta-analyses. *Psychological Bulletin, 128*, 3–72.

Oyserman, D., Kemmelmeier, M., & Coon, H. M. (2002b). Cultural psychology: A New Look: Reply to Bond (2002), Fiske (2002), Kitayama (2002), and Miller (2002). *Psychological Bulletin, 128*, 110–117.

Paprzycka, K. (2010). Is neurobiology of personality inevitable? A philosophical perspective. In T. Maruszewski, M. Fajkowska, & M. W. Eysenck (eds), *Personality from Biological, Cognitive, and Social Perspectives* (pp. 13–27). Clinton Corners, NY: Eliot Werner Publications.

Patrick, C. J. (2007). Antisocial personality disorder and psychopathy. In W. O'Donohue, K. A. Fowler, & S. O. Lilienfeld (eds), *Personality Disorders: Toward the DSM–V* (pp. 109–166). Thousand Oaks, CA: Sage Publications.

Pergadia, M., Madden, P., Lessov, C., Todorov, A., Bucholz, K., Martin, N., & Heath, A. (2006). Genetic and environmental influences on extreme personality dispositions in adolescent female twins. *Journal of Child Psychology and Psychiatry, 47*, 902–915.

Pervin, L. A., Cervone, D., & John, O. P. (2005). *Personality: Theory and research* (9th edn). New York: John Wiley & Sons, Inc.

Pickens, R., Svikis, D., McGue, M., Lykken, D., Heston, L., & Clayton, P. (1991). Heterogeneity in the inheritance of alcoholism. *Archives of General Psychiatry, 48*, 19–28.

Plomin, R. & Caspi, A. (1999). Behavioral genetics and personality. In L. A. Pervin & O. P. John (eds), *Handbook of Personality: Theory and research*. New York: Guilford Press.

Popenoe, D. (1993). American family decline 1960–1990: A review and appraisal. *Journal of Marriage and the Family, 55*, 527–544.

Poropat, A. E. (2009). A meta-analysis of the five-factor model of personality and academic performance. *Psychological Bulletin, 135*(2), 322–338.

Prescott, C., Johnson, R. C., & McArdle, J. (1991). Genetic contributions to television viewing. *Psychological Science, 2*, 430–431.

Roberts, B. W. & DelVecchio, W. F. (2000). The rank-order consistency of personality from childhood to old age: A quantitative review of longitudinal studies. *Psychological Bulletin, 126*, 3–25.

Rogers, C. R. (1963). Actualizing tendency in relation to 'motives' and to consciousness. In M. R. Jones (ed.), *Nebraska Symposium on Motivation* (pp. 1–24). Oxford: University of Nebraska Press.

Rogers, C. R. (2008). The actualizing tendency in relation to 'motives' and to consciousness. In B. E. Levitt (ed.), *Reflections on Human Potential: Bridging the person-centered approach and positive psychology* (pp. 17–32). Ross-on-Wye: PCCS Books.

Saggino, A. (2000). The big three or the big five? A replication study. *Personality and Individual Differences, 28*, 879–886.

Saggino, A. & Kline, P. (1996). The location of the Myers–Briggs type indicator in personality factor space. *Personality and Individual Differences, 21*, 591–597.

Saucier, D. M. & Elias, L. J. (2001). Lateral and sex differences in manual gesture during conversation. *Laterality, 6*, 239–245.

Saucier, G., Hampson, S. E., & Goldberg, L. R. (2000). Cross-language studies of lexical personality factors. In S. E. Hampson (ed.), *Advances in Personality Psychology: Vol. 1* (pp. 1–36). Hove: Psychology Press.

Schmitt, D. P., Allik, J., McCrae, R. R., & Benet-Martínez, V. (2007). The geographic distribution of big five personality traits: Patterns and profiles of human self-description across 56 nations. *Journal of Cross-Cultural Psychology, 38*(2), 173–212.

Schwartz, C. E., Snidman, N., & Kagan, J. (1999), Adolescent social anxiety as an outcome of inhibited temperament in childhood. *Journal of the American Academy of Child and Adolescent Psychiatry, 38*, 1008–1015.

Seligman, M. P. & Csikszentmihalyi, M. (2000). Positive psychology. *American Psychologist, 55*, 5–14.

Solms, M. (2004). Is the brain more real than the mind? In A. Casement (ed.), *Who Owns Psychoanalysis?* (pp. 323–342). London: Karnac Books.

Solms, M. (2007a). Freud returns. In F. E. Bloom (ed.), *Best of the Brain from Scientific American* (pp. 35–46). Washington: Dana Press.

Solms, M. (2007b). The interpretation of dreams and the neurosciences. In L. Mayes, P. Fonagy, & M. Target (eds), *Developmental Science and Psychoanalysis: Integration and innovation: Developments in psychoanalysis*. London, England: Karnac Books.

Spain, J., Eaton, L., & Funder, D. (2000). Perspectives on personality: The relative accuracy of self versus others in the prediction of emotion and behavior. *Journal of Personality, 68*, 837–867.

Srivastava, S., John, O. P., Gosling, S. D., & Potter, J. (2003). Development of personality in early and middle adulthood: Set like plaster or persistent change? *Journal of Personality and Social Psychology, 84*, 1041–1053.

Strelau, J. (2010). How far are we in searching for the biological background of personality? In T. Maruszewski, M. Fajkowska, & M. Eysenck (eds), *Personality from Biological, Cognitive, and Social Perspectives*. Clifton Corners, NY: Eliot Werner Publications.

Tavris, C. (1991). The mismeasure of woman: Paradoxes and perspectives in the study of gender. In J. D. Goodchilds (ed.), *Psychological Perspectives on Human Diversity in America* (pp. 87–136). Washington: American Psychological Association.

Triandis, H. C. (1989). Cross-cultural studies of individualism and collectivism. In J. Berman (ed.), *Nebraska Symposium* (pp. 41–130). Lincoln: University of Nebraska Press.

Triandis, H. C. (2001). Individualism–collectivism and personality. *Journal of Personality, 69*(6), 907–924.

Triandis, H. C., Botempo, R., Villareal, M., Asai, M., & Lucca, N. (1988). Individualism and collectivism: Cross-cultural perspectives on self in group relationships. *Journal of Personality and Social Psychology, 54*, 332–336.

Triandis, H. C., McCusker, C., & Hui, C. H. (1990). Multimethod probes of individualism and collectivism. *Journal of Personality and Social Psychology, 59*, 1006–1020.

Viswesvaran, C. & Ones, D. (1999). Meta-analysis of fakability estimates: Implications for personality measurement. *Educational and Psychological Measurement, 54*, 197–210.

Volkow, N. & Fowler, J. (2000). Addiction, a disease of compulsion and drive: Involvement of the orbitofrontal cortex. *Cerebral Cortex, 10*, 318–325.

Walsh, W. B. (2007). Introduction: Special section on self-efficacy, interests, and personality. *Journal of Career Assessment, 15*(2), 143–144.

Watson, D., Clark, L. A., & Chmielewski, M. (2008). Structures of personality and their relevance to psychopathology: II. Further articulation of a comprehensive unified trait structure. *Journal of Personality, 76*(6), 1545–1586.

Wilde, D. J. (2011). *Jung's Personality Theory Quantified*. New York: Springer-Verlag Publishing.

Wood, J. M., Garb, H. N., Lilienfeld, S. O., & Nezworski, M. T. (2002). Clinical assessment. *Annual Review of Psychology, 53*(1), 519–543.

Zawadzki, B., Strelau W., Oniszczenko, W., Roemann, R., & Angleitner, A. (2001). Genetic and environmental influences on temperament. *European Psychologist, 6*, 272–286.

Zuckerman, M. (1995). Good and bad humors: Biochemical bases of personality and its disorders. *Psychological Science, 6*, 325–332.

Zuckerman, M. (2007). Sensation seeking and risk. *Sensation Seeking and Risky Behavior* (pp. 51–72). Washington: American Psychological Association.

Zuckerman, M. (2011). *Personality Science: Three approaches and their applications to the causes and treatment of depression* (pp. 123–148). Washington: American Psychological Association.

CHAPTER 16

Adams, G. R. & Huston, T. L. (1975). Social perception of middle-aged persons varying in physical attractiveness. *Developmental Psychology, 11*, 657–658.

Adolphs, R. (2003). Cognitive neuroscience of human social behaviour. *Nature Reviews Neuroscience, 4*(3), 165–178.

Adolphs, R. (2009). The social brain: Neural basis of social knowledge. *Annual Review of Psychology, 60*, 693–716.

Albarracín, D., Johnson, B. T., & Zabba, N. O. (eds) (2005). *The Handbook of Attitudes*. Mahwah, NJ: Lawrence Erlbaum Associates.

Allport, G. W. (1954). *The Nature of Prejudice*. Oxford: Addison-Wesley.

Allport, G. W. (1985). The historical background of social psychology. In G. Lindzey & E. Aronson (eds), *Handbook of Social Psychology: Vol. 1* (3rd edn; pp. 1–46). New York: Random House.

Ananthaswamy, A. (2004). Hormones converge for couples in love. *New Scientist*, http://www.newscientist.com/article/dn4957-hormones-converge-for-couples-in-love.html, accessed 16 December 2012.

Archer, J. (2005). Are women or men the more aggressive sex? In S. Fein, G. R. Goethals, & M. J. Sandstrom (eds), *Gender and Aggression: Interdisciplinary perspectives*. Mahwah, NJ: Lawrence Erlbaum Associates.

Backman, C. W. (1981). Attraction in interpersonal relationships. In M. Rosenberg & R. Turner (eds), *Social Psychology: Sociological perspectives*. New York: Basic Books.

Backman, C. W. (1990). Attraction in interpersonal relationships. In M. Rosenberg & R. H. Turner (eds), *Social Psychology: Sociological perspectives* (pp. 235–268). New Brunswick, NJ: Transaction Publishers.

Baker, L. A., Jacobson, K. C., Raine, A., Lozano, D. I., & Bezdjian, S. (2007). Genetic and environmental bases of childhood antisocial behavior: A multiinformant twin study. *Journal of Abnormal Psychology, 116*, 219–235.

Baron, A. S. & Banaji, M. R. (2006). The development of implicit attitudes: Evidence of race evaluations from ages 6 and 10 and adulthood. *Psychological Science, 17*(1), 53–58.

Bassett, R. L., Smith, A., Thrower, J., Tindall, M., Barclay, J., Tiuch, K., *et al.* (2005). One effort to measure implicit attitudes toward spirituality and religion. *Journal of Psychology and Christianity, 24*(3), 210–218.

Bassili, J. N. & Brown, R. D. (2005). Implicit and explicit attitudes: Research, challenges, and theory. In D. Albarracín, B. T. Johnson, & M. P. Zanna (eds), *The Handbook of Attitudes* (pp. 543–574). Mahwah, NJ: Lawrence Erlbaum Associates.

Bates, R. (2002). Liking and similarity as predictors of multi-source ratings. *Personnel Review, 31*(5), 540–552.

Batson, C. D. (1991). *The Altruism Question: Towards a social psychological answer*. Hillsdale, NJ: Lawrence Erlbaum Associates.

Batson, C. D. & Weeks, J. L. (1996). Mood effects of unsuccessful helping: Another test of the empathy-altruism hypothesis. *Personality and Social Psychology Bulletin, 22*, 148–157.

Batson, C. D., Ahmad, N., & Stocks, E. L. (2004). Benefits and liabilities of empathy-induced altruism. In A. G. Miller (ed.), *The Social Psychology of Good and Evil* (pp. 359–385). New York: Guilford Press.

Batson, C. D., Sanger, K., Garst, E., Kang, M., Rubchinsky, K., & Dawson, K. (1997). Is empathy-induced helping due to self-other merging? *Journal of Personality and Social Psychology, 73*, 495–509.

Bauman, C. W. & Skitka, L. J. (2010). Making attributions for behaviors: The prevalence of correspondence bias in the general population. *Basic and Applied Social Psychology, 32*(3), 269–277.

Bem, D. J. (1972). Self-perception theory. In L. Berkowitz (ed.), *Advances in Experimental Social Psychology: Vol. 6*. New York: Academic Press.

Berkowitz, L. (1989). Frustration–aggression hypothesis: Examination and reformulation. *Psychological Bulletin, 106*, 59–73.

Berscheid, E. (1983). Interpersonal attraction. In G. Lindzey & E. Aronson (eds), *Handbook of Social Psychology* (3rd edn). Reading, MA: Addison-Wesley.

Berscheid, E. & Walster, E. H. (1978). Interpersonal attraction. In G. Lindzey & E. Aronson (eds), *Handbook of Social Psychology: Vol. 2* (pp. 413–484). New York: Random House.

Brumbaugh, C. C. & Fraley, R. C. (2006). The evolution of attachment in romantic relationships. In M. Mikulincer & G. S. Goodman (eds), *Dynamics of Romantic Love: Attachment, caregiving, and sex* (pp. 71–101). New York: Guilford Press.

Byrne, D. (1971). *The Attraction Paradigm*. New York: Academic Press.

Byrne, D., Ervin, C., & Lamberth, J. (1970). Continuity between the experimental study of attraction and real-life computer dating. *Journal of Personality and Social Psychology, 16*, 157–165.

Byrne, D., London, O., & Reeves, K. (1968). The effects of physical attractiveness, sex, and attitude similarity on interpersonal attraction. *Journal of Personality, 36*, 259–271.

Carels, R. A., Cacciapaglia, H. M., Rydin, S., Douglass, O. M., & Harper, J. (2006). Can social desirability interfere with success in a behavioral weight loss program? *Psychology & Health, 21*(1), 65–78.

Cavior, N. & Dokecki, P. R. (1971). Physical attractiveness self concept: A test of Mead's hypothesis. *Proceedings of the Annual Convention of the American Psychological Association, 6*, 319–320.

Cavior, N. & Dokecki, P. R. (1973). Physical attractiveness, perceived attitude similarity, and academic achievement as contributors to interpersonal attraction among adolescents. *Developmental Psychology, 9*(1), 44–54.

Certner, B. C. (1973). Exchange of self-disclosures in same-sexed groups of strangers. *Journal of Consulting and Clinical Psychology, 40*, 292–297.

Chekroun, P. & Brauer, M. (2002). The bystander effect and social control behavior: The effect of the presence of others on people's reactions to norm violations. *European Journal of Social Psychology, 32*(6), 853–866.

Cobb, M. D. (2002). Unobtrusively measuring racial attitudes: The consequences of social desirability effects. ProQuest Information & Learning. *Dissertation Abstracts International Section A: Humanities and Social Sciences, 62*(8), 2869.

Cooper, J., Kelly, K. A., & Weaver, K. (2004). Attitudes, norms, and social groups. In M. B. Brewer, & M. Hewstone (eds), *Social Cognition* (pp. 244–267). Malden, MA: Blackwell Publishing.

Cooper, J., Mirabile, R., & Scher, S. J. (2005). Actions and attitudes: The theory of cognitive dissonance. In T. C. Brock & M. C. Green (eds), *Persuasion: Psychological insights and perspectives* (2nd edn; pp. 63–79). Thousand Oaks, CA: Sage Publications.

Cowley, E. (2005). Views from consumers next in line: The fundamental attribution error in a service setting. *Journal of the Academy of Marketing Science, 33*(2), 139–152.

Dabbs., J. M., Jr., Riad, J. K., & Chance, S. E. (2001). Testosterone and ruthless homicide. *Personality and Individual Differences, 31*(4), 599–603.

Daggett, L. M. (2002). Living with loss: Middle-aged men face spousal bereavement. *Qualitative Health Research, 12*(5), 625–639.

Darley, J. M. (2000). Bystander phenomenon. In A. E. Kazdin (ed.), *Encyclopedia of Psychology: Vol. 1* (pp. 493–495). Washington: American Psychological Association.

Darley, J. M. & Latané, B. (1968). Bystander intervention in emergencies: Diffusion of responsibility. *Journal of Personality and Social Psychology, 8*, 377–383.

Day, D. M., Peterson-Badali, M., & Ruck, M. D. (2006). The relationship between maternal attitudes and young people's attitudes toward children's rights. *Journal of Adolescence, 29*(2), 193–207.

Dindia, K. (2000). Sex differences in self-disclosure, reciprocity of self-disclosure, and self-disclosure and liking: Three meta-analyses reviewed. In S. Petronio (ed.), *Balancing the Secrets of Private Disclosures* (pp. 21–35). Mahwah, NJ: Lawrence Erlbaum Associates.

Dollard, J., Miller, N. E., Doob, L. W., Mowrer, O. H., & Sears, R. R. (1939). *Frustration and Aggression*. New Haven, CT: Yale University Press.

Dostoyevsky, F. (1972). *Notes from the Underground* (trans. J. Coulson). London: Penguin.

Dovidio, J. F., Gaertner, S. L., Kawakami, K., & Hodson, G. (2002). Why can't we all just get along? Interpersonal biases and interracial distrust. *Cultural Diversity and Ethnic Minority Psychology, 8*, 88–102.

Eagly, A. H., & Chaiken, S. (1998). Attitude structure and function. In D. T. Gilbert, S. T. Fiske, & G. Lindzey (eds), *The Handbook of Social Psychology* (4th edn; pp. 269–322). New York: McGraw-Hill.

Fabrigar, L. R., Petty, R. E., Smith, S. M., & Crites, S. L., Jr. (2006). Understanding knowledge effects on attitude-behavior consistency: The role of relevance, complexity, and amount of knowledge. *Journal of Personality and Social Psychology, 90*(4), 556–577.

Fazio, R. H. & Roskos-Ewoldsen, D. (2005). Acting as we feel: When and how attitudes guide behavior. In T. C. Brock & M. C. Green (eds), *Persuasion: Psychological insights and perspectives* (2nd edn; pp. 41–62). Thousand Oaks, CA: Sage Publications.

Fazio, R. H., Zanna, M. P., & Cooper, J. (1977). Dissonance and self perception: An integrative view of each theory's proper domain of application. *Journal of Experimental Social Psychology, 13*, 464–479.

Fenchel, G. H. (2006). *Psychoanalytic Reflections on Love and Sexuality*. Lanham, MD: University Press of America.

Festinger, L. (1957). *A Theory of Cognitive Dissonance*. Stanford, CA: Stanford University Press.

Festinger, L. & Carlsmith, J. M. (1959). Cognitive consequences of forced compliance. *Journal of Abnormal and Social Psychology, 58*, 203–210.

Fischer, P., Greitemeyer, T., Pollozek, F., & Frey, D. (2006). The unresponsive bystander: Are bystanders more responsive in dangerous emergencies? *European Journal of Social Psychology, 36*(2), 267–278.

Fiske, S. T. (2010). Interpersonal stratification: Status, power, and subordination. In S. T. Fiske, D. T. Gilbert, & G. Lindzey (eds), *Handbook of Social Psychology: Vol. 2* (5th edn; pp. 941–982). Hoboken, NJ: John Wiley & Sons, Inc.

Fraley, B. & Aron, A. (2004). The effect of a shared humorous experience on closeness in initial encounters. *Personal Relationships, 11*, 61–78.

Garcia, S. M., Weaver, K., Moskowitz, G. B., & Darley, J. M. (2002). Crowded minds: The implicit bystander effect. *Journal of Personality and Social Psychology, 83*(4), 843–853.

Grammaticas, D. (2012). Grief of Japan's tsunami survivors. Available at: http://www.bbc.co.uk/news/world-asia-china-17295912.

Greenwald, A. G., Banaji, M. R., Rudman, L. A., Farnham, S. D., Nosek, B. A., & Mellott, D. S. (2002). A unified theory of implicit attitudes, stereotypes, self-esteem, and self-concept. *Psychological Review, 109*(1), 3–25.

Greenwald, A. G., McGhee, D. E., & Schwartz, J. L. K. (1998). Measuring individual differences in implicit cognition: The implicit association test. *Journal of Personality and Social Psychology, 74*, 1464–1480.

Halpern, D. F. (2000). *Sex Differences in Cognitive Abilities* (3rd edn). Mahwah, NJ: Lawrence Erlbaum Associates.

Johnston, C. & Lee, C. M. (2005). Children's attributions for their own versus others' behavior: Influence of actor versus observer differences. *Journal of Applied Developmental Psychology, 26*(3), 314–328.

Jones, E. E. & Harris, V. A. (1967). The attribution of attitudes. *Journal of Experimental Social Psychology, 3*, 1–24.

Jones, E. E. & Nisbett, R. E. (1971). *The Actor and the Observer: Divergent perceptions of the causes of behavior*. Morristown, NJ: General Learning Press.

Jones, E. E. & Sigall, H. (1971). The bogus pipeline: A new paradigm for measuring affect and attitude. *Psychological Bulletin, 76*, 349–364.

Keysers, C. & Gazzola, V. (2007). Integrating simulation and theory of mind: From self to social cognition. *Trends in Cognitive Sciences, 11*(5), 194–196.

Khalil, E. L. (2004). What is altruism? *Journal of Economic Psychology, 25*(1), 97–123.

Koenigs, M., Young, L., Adolphs, R., Tranel, D., Cushman, F., Hauser, M., *et al.* (2007). Damage to the prefontal cortex increases utilitarian moral judgements. *Nature, 446*(7138), 908–911.

Langlois, J. H. & Stephan, C. W. (1981). Beauty and the beast: The role of physical attractiveness in the development of peer relations and social behavior. In S. S. Brehm, S. M. Kassin, & F. X. Gibbons (eds), *Developmental Social Psychology*. New York: Oxford University Press.

Lankau, M. J., Riordan, C. M., & Thomas, C. H. (2005). The effects of similarity and liking in formal relationships between mentors and protégés. *Journal of Vocational Behavior, 67*(2), 252–265.

LaPiere, R. (1934). Attitudes versus actions. *Social Forces, 13*, 230–237.

Latané, B. & Darley, J. M. (1968). Group inhibition of bystander intervention in emergencies. *Journal of Personality and Social Psychology, 10*, 215–221.

Latané, B. & Darley, J. M. (1970). *The Unresponsive Bystander: Why doesn't he help?* Englewood Cliffs, NJ: Prentice-Hall.

Levin, J. (2000). A prolegomenon to an epidemiology of love: Theory, measurement, and health outcomes. *Journal of Social & Clinical Psychology, 19*(1), 117–136.

Lieberman, M. D., Jarcho, J. M., & Obayashi, J. (2005). Attributional inference across cultures: Similar automatic attributions and different controlled corrections. *Personality and Social Psychology Bulletin, 31*(7), 889–901.

Lott, A. J. & Lott, B. E. (1974). The role of reward in the formation of positive interpersonal attitudes. In T. L. Huston (ed.), *Foundation of Interpersonal Attraction* (pp. 171–189). New York: Academic Press.

Lyttle, J. (2001). The effectiveness of humor in persuasion: The case of business ethics training. *Journal of General Psychology, 128*(2), 206–216.

Markus, H., Uchida, Y., Omoregie, H., Townsend, S., & Kitayama, S. (2006). Going for the gold: Models of agency in Japanese and American contexts. *Psychological Science, 17*, 103–112.

Mikulincer, M. & Goodman, G. S. (eds). (2006). *Dynamics of Romantic Love: Attachment, caregiving, and sex*. New York: Guilford Press.

Mikulincer, M. & Shaver, P. R. (2005). Attachment security, compassion, and altruism. *Current Directions in Psychological Science, 14*(1), 34–38.

Mikulincer, M., Shaver, P. R., & Gillath, O. (2008). *A Behavioral Systems Perspective on Compassionate Love: The science of compassionate love: Theory, research, and applications* (pp. 225–256). Hoboken, NJ: Wiley-Blackwell.

Mikulincer, M., Shaver, P. R., Gillath, O., & Nitzberg, R. A. (2005). Attachment, caregiving, and altruism: Boosting attachment security increases compassion and helping. *Journal of Personality and Social Psychology, 89*(5), 817–839.

Miles, D. R. & Carey, G. (1997). Genetic and environmental architecture on human aggression. *Journal of Personality and Social Psychology, 72*(1), 207–217.

Milgram, S. (2004). *Obedience to Authority.* New York: Perennial Classics.

Miller, D. T. & Ross, M. (1975). Self-serving biases in the attribution of causality: Fact or fiction? *Psychological Bulletin, 82,* 213–225.

Morris, M. & Peng, K. (1994). Culture and cause: American and Chinese attributions for social and physical events. *Journal of Personality and Social Psychology, 67,* 949–971.

Nier, J. A. (2005). How dissociated are implicit and explicit racial attitudes? A bogus pipeline approach. *Group Processes & Intergroup Relations, 8*(1), 39–52.

Orbuch, T. L. & Sprecher, S. (2003). Attraction and interpersonal relationships. In J. Delamater (ed.), *Handbook of Social Psychology* (pp. 339–362). New York: Kluwer Academic/Plenum Publishers.

Pennebaker, J. (1990). *Opening Up: The healing power of confiding in others.* New York: William Morrow.

Pennebaker, J. W. (2003). The social, linguistic and health consequences of emotional disclosure. In J. Suls & K. A. Wallston (eds), *Social Psychological Foundations of Health and Illness* (pp. 288–313). Malden, MA: Blackwell Publishing.

Pennebaker, J. W. (2004). Theories, therapies, and taxpayers: On the complexities of the expressive writing paradigm. *Clinical Psychology: Science and practice, 11*(2), 138–142.

Pennebaker, J. W., Kiecolt-Glaser, J., & Glaser, R. (2004). Disclosure of traumas and immune function: Health implications for psychotherapy. In R. M. Kowalski & M. R. Leary (eds), *The Interface of Social and Clinical Psychology: Key readings* (pp. 301–312). New York: Psychology Press.

Petty, R. E., Wheeler, S. C., & Tormala, Z. L. (2003). Persuasion and attitude change. In T. Millon & M. J. Lerner (eds.), *Handbook of Psychology: Personality and social psychology,* Vol. 5 (pp. 353–382). Hoboken, NJ: John Wiley & Sons Inc.

Piferi, R. L., Jobe, R. L., & Jones, W. H. (2006). Giving to others during national tragedy: The effects of altruistic and egoistic motivations on long-term giving. *Journal of Social and Personal Relationships, 23,* 171–184.

Post, S. G. (2005). Altruism, happiness, and health: It's good to be good. *International Journal of Behavioral Medicine, 12*(2), 66–77.

Prislin, R. & Wood, W. (2005). Social influence in attitudes and attitude change. In D. Albarracin, B. T. Johnson, & N. O. Zabba (eds), *The Handbook of Attitudes* (pp. 671–705). Mahwah, NJ: Lawrence Erlbaum Associates.

Puka, B. (2004). Altruism and character. In D. K. Lapsley & D. Narvaez (eds), *Moral Development, Self, and Identity* (pp. 161–187). Mahwah, NJ: Lawrence Erlbaum Associates.

Rabow, J., Newcomb, M. D., Monto, M. A., & Hernandez, A. C. (1990). Altruism in drunk driving situations: Personal and situational factors in intervention. *Social Psychology Quarterly, 53*(3), 199–213.

Reynolds, S. E. (1993). 'Limerence': A new word and concept. *Psychotherapy: Theory, research and practice, 20*(1), 107–111.

Roese, N. J. & Jamieson, D. W. (1993). Twenty years of bogus pipeline research: A critical review and meta-analysis. *Psychological Bulletin, 114,* 363–375.

Rosenberg, M. J. (1969). The conditions and consequences of evaluation apprehension. In R. Rosenthal & R. L. Rosnow (eds), *Artifact in Behavioral Research* (pp. 279–349). New York: Academic Press.

Ross, L. (1977). The intuitive psychologist and his shortcomings: Distortions in the attribution process. In L. Berkowitz (ed.), *Advances in Experimental Social Psychology: Vol. 10.* New York: Academic Press.

Ross, L. (2001). Getting down to fundamentals: Lay dispositionism and the attributions of psychologists. *Psychological Inquiry, 12,* 37–40.

Rowe, D. C., Almeida, D. M., & Jocabson, K. C. (1999). School context and genetic influences on aggression in adolescence. *Psychological Science, 10*(3), 277–280.

Rubin, Z. (1970). Measurement of romantic love. *Journal of Personality and Social Psychology, 16,* 265–273.

Rubin, Z. (1973). *Liking and Loving.* New York: Holt, Rinehart & Winston.

Rudman, L. A. & Ashmore, R. D. (2007). Discrimination and the Implicit Association Test. *Group Processes and Intergroup Relations, 10,* 359–372.

Sadler, M. S., Lineberger, M., Correll, J., & Park, B. (2005). Emotions, attributions, and policy endorsement in response to the September 11th terrorist attacks. *Basic and Applied Social Psychology, 27*(3), 249–258.

Semendeferi, K., Lu, A., Schenker, N., & Damasio, H. (2002). Humans and great apes share a large frontal cortex. *Nature Neuroscience, 5*(3), 272–276.

Shaffer, D. R., Rogel, M., & Hendrick, C. (1975). Intervention in the library: The effect of increased responsibility on bystanders' willingness to prevent a theft. *Journal of Applied Social Psychology, 5*(4), 303–319.

Shamay-Tsoory, S., Tomer, R., Berger, B. D., Goldsher, D., & Aharon-Peretz, J. (2005). Impaired 'affective theory of mind' is associated with right ventromedial prefrontal damage. *Cognitive and Behavioral Neurology, 18*(1), 55–67.

Smith, R. A. & Weber, A. L. (2005). Applying social psychology in everyday life. In F. W. Schneider, J. A. Gruman, & L. M. Coutts (eds), *Applied Social Psychology: Understanding and addressing social and practical problems* (pp. 75–99). Sage Publications.

Sternberg, R. J. (1986). A triangular theory of love. *Psychological Review, 93,* 119–135.

Sternberg, R. J. (1987). Liking versus loving: A comparative evaluation of theories. *Psychological Bulletin, 102,* 331–345.

Sternberg, R. J. (2004). A triangular theory of love. In H. T. Reis & C. E. Rusbult (eds), *Close Relationships: Key readings* (pp. 213–227). Philadelphia: Taylor & Francis.

Sternberg, R. J. & Weis, K. (2006). *The New Psychology of Love.* New Haven, CT: Yale University Press.

Stewart, A. E. (2005). Attributions of responsibility for motor vehicle crashes. *Accident Analysis & Prevention, 37*(4), 681–688.

Storms, M. S. (1973). Videotape of the attribution process: Reversing actors' and observers' points of view. *Journal of Personality and Social Psychology, 27,* 165–175.

Stuss, D. T., Gallup, G. G., Jr., & Alexander, M. P. (2001). The frontal lobes are necessary for 'theory of mind'. *Brain: A Journal of Neurology, 124*(2), 279–286.

Sue, D. W., Capodilupo, C. M., & Torino, G. C. (2007). Racial microaggressions in everyday life: Implications for clinical practice. *American Psychologist, 62,* 271–286.

Swap, W. C. (1977). Interpersonal attraction and repeated exposure to rewarders and punishers. *Personality and Social Psychology Bulletin, 3,* 248–251.

Taylor, D. A., Gould, R. J., & Brounstein, P. J. (1981). Effects of personalistic self-disclosure. *Personality and Social Psychology Bulletin, 7,* 487–492.

Tennov, D. (1999). *Love and Limerence: The experience of being in love* (2nd edn). Chelsea, MI: Scarborough House.

Time. (1980). Let's fall in limerence. *Time Magazine,* http://www.time.com/time/magazine/article/0,9171,952554,00.html, accessed 16 December 2012.

Tourangeau, R., Smith, T. W., & Rasinski, K. A. (1997). Motivation to report sensitive behaviors on surveys: Evidence from a bogus pipeline experiment. *Journal of Applied Social Psychology, 27,* 209–222.

Troyer, J. M. (2006). Post-bereavement experiences of older widowers: A qualitative investigation. ProQuest Information & Learning: US. *Dissertation Abstracts International Section A: Humanities and social sciences, 66*(8), 3051.

Underwood, B. & Moore, B. (1982). Perspective-taking and altruism. *Psychological Bulletin, 91,* 143–173.

van den Berg, H., Manstead, A. S. R., van der Pligt, J., & Wigboldus, D. H. J. (2006). The impact of affective and cognitive focus on attitude formation. *Journal of Experimental Social Psychology, 42*(3), 373–379.

Wakin, A. & Vo, D. B. (2008). *Love-Variant: The Wakin-Vo I.D.R. model of limerence*, http://www.persons.org.uk/ptb/persons/pil/pil2/wakinvo%20paper.pdf, accessed 16 December 2012.

Walster, E., Aronson, E., & Abrahams, D. (1966). On increasing the persuasiveness of a low prestige communicator. *Journal of Experimental Social Psychology, 2*, 73–79.

Watts, S. & Stenner, P. (2005). The subjective experience of partnership love: A Q methodological study. *British Journal of Social Psychology, 44*(1), 85–107.

Whalen, P. J. (1998). Fear, vigilance, and ambiguity: Initial neuroimaging studies of the human amygdala. *Current Directions in Psychological Science, 7*(6), 177–188.

Whalen, P. J., Davis, F. C., Oler, J. A., Kim, H., Kim, M. J., & Neta, M. (2009). Human amygdala responses to facial expressions of emotion. In P. J. Whalen & E. A. Phelps (eds), *The Human Amygdala* (pp. 265–288). New York: Guilford Press.

Wilson, G. (1981). *The Coolidge Effect: An evolutionary account of human sexuality*. New York: William Morrow.

Worthy, M., Gary, A. L., & Kahn, G. M. (1969). Self-disclosure as an exchange process. *Journal of Personality and Social Psychology, 13*, 59–63.

Yela, C. (2006). The evaluation of love: Simplified version of the scales for Yela's tetrangular model based on Sternberg's model. *European Journal of Psychological Assessment, 22*(1), 21–27.

CHAPTER 17

Abrams, D., Hogg, M. A., & Marques, J. M. (2005). *A Social Psychological Framework for Understanding Social Inclusion and Exclusion: The social psychology of inclusion* (pp. 1–23). New York: Psychology Press.

Abrams, D., Marques, J. M., Bown, N., & Henson, M. (2000). Pro-norm and anti-norm deviance within and between groups. *Journal of Personality and Social Psychology, 78*(5), 906–912.

Abrams, D., Wetherell, M., Cochrane, S., Hogg, M. A., & Turner, J. C. (2001). Knowing what to think by knowing who you are: Self-categorization and the nature of norm formation, conformity and group polarization. In M. A. Hogg & D. Abrams (eds), *Intergroup Relations: Essential readings* (pp. 270–288). New York: Psychology Press.

Aiello, J. R. & Douthitt, E. A. (2001). Social facilitation from Triplett to electronic performance monitoring. *Group Dynamics: Theory, research, and practice, 5*, 163–180.

Alexander, M. G. & Wood, W. (2000). Women, men, and positive emotions: A social role interpretation. In A. H. Fischer (ed.), *Gender and Emotion: Social psychological perspectives* (pp. 189–210). New York: Cambridge University Press.

Allport, G. W. (1954). *The Nature of Prejudice*. Oxford: Addison-Wesley.

Allport, G. W. (1985). The historical background of social psychology. In G. Lindzey & E. Aronson (eds), *Handbook of Social Psychology: Vol. 1* (3rd edn; pp. 1–46). New York: Random House.

Alwin, D. F., Cohen, R. L., & Newcomb, T. M. (1991). *Political Attitudes over the Life-Span: The Bennington women after fifty years*. Madison, WI: University of Wisconsin Press.

Asch, S. E. (1955). Opinions and social pressure. *Scientific American, 193*(5), 31–35.

Ashcraft, K. L. (2007). Appreciating the 'work' of discourse: Occupational identity and difference as organizing mechanisms in the case of commercial airline pilots. *Discourse and Communication, 1*, 9–36.

Asmus, C. L. & James, K. (2005). Nominal group technique, social loafing, and group creative project quality. *Creativity Research Journal, 17*(4), 349–354.

Badie, D. (2010). Groupthink, Iraq and the war on terror: Explaining US policy shift towards Iraq. *Foreign Policy Analysis, 6*, 277–296.

Bargh, J. A. (2001). The psychology of the mere. In J. A. Bargh & D. K. Apsley (eds), *Unraveling the Complexities of Social Life: A festschrift in honor of Robert B. Zajonc* (pp. 25–37). Washington: American Psychological Association.

Baron, R. S. (2005). So right it's wrong: Groupthink and the ubiquitous nature of polarized group decision making. In M. P. Zanna (ed.), *Advances in Experimental Social Psychology: Vol. 37* (pp. 219–253). San Diego: Elsevier Academic Press.

Billig, M. & Tajfel, H. (1973). Social categorisation and similarity in intergroup behaviour. *European Journal of Social Psychology, 3*, 27–52.

Billings, L. S., Vescio, T. K., & Biernat, M. (2000). Race-based social judgment by minority perceivers. *Journal of Applied Social Psychology, 30*(2), 221–240.

Blass, T. (2004). *The Man Who Shocked the World: The life and legacy of Stanley Milgram*. New York: Basic Books.

Blass, T. (2007). Unsupported allegations about a link between Milgram and the CIA: Tortured reasoning in a question of torture. *Journal of the History of the Behavioral Sciences, 43*, 199–203.

Bond, C. F., Jr. (2000). Social facilitation. In A. E. Kazdin (ed.), *Encyclopedia of Psychology: Vol. 7* (pp. 338–440). Washington: American Psychological Association.

Bond, R. & Smith, P. B. (1996). Culture and conformity: A meta-analysis of studies using Asch's (1952b, 1956) line judgment task. *Psychological Bulletin, 119*, 111–137.

Chidambaram, L. & Tung, L. L. (2005). Is out of sight, out of mind? An empirical study of social loafing in technology-supported groups. *Information Systems Research, 16*(2), 149–168.

Cialdini, R. B., Kallgren, C. A., & Reno, R. R. (1991). A focus theory of normative conduct: A theoretical refinement and reevaluation of the role of norms in human behavior. In M. P. Zanna (ed.), *Advances in Experimental Social Psychology: Vol. 24* (pp. 201–234). New York: Academic Press.

Condor, S., Figgou, L., Abell, J., Gibson, S., & Stevenson, C. (2006). 'They're not racist:::': Prejudice denial, mitigation and suppression in dialogue. *British Journal of Social Psychology, 45*, 441–462.

Cooper, J., Kelly, K. A., & Weaver, K. (2004). Attitudes, norms, and social groups. In M. B. Brewer & M. Hewstone (eds), *Social Cognition* (pp. 244–267). Malden, MA: Blackwell Publishing.

Crano, W. D. (2001). Social influence, social identity, and ingroup leniency. In C. W. K. de Dreu & N. K. de Vries (eds), *Group Consensus and Minority Influence: Implications for innovation* (pp. 122–143). Oxford: Blackwell.

Deutsch, M., & Gerard, H. B. (1955). A study of normative and informational social influences upon individual judgment. *Journal of Abnormal and Social Psychology, 51*, 629–636.

Drury, J. & Reicher, S. (1999). The intergroup dynamics of collective empowerment: Substantiating the social identity model of crowd behaviour. *Group Processes and Intergroup Relations, 2*, 1–22.

Drury, J. & Reicher, S. (2000). Collective action and psychological change: The emergence of new social identities. *British Journal of Social Psychology, 39*, 579–604.

Eagly, A. H. & Karau, S. J. (2002). Role congruity theory of prejudice toward female leaders. *Psychological Review, 109*, 573–598.

Eagly, A. H. & Koenig, A. M. (2006). Social role theory of sex differences and similarities: Implication for prosocial behavior. In K. Dindia & D. J. Canary (eds), *Sex Differences and Similarities in Communication* (2nd edn; pp. 161–177). Mahwah, NJ: Lawrence Erlbaum Associates.

Eagly, A. H., & Wood, W. (2006). Three ways that data can misinform: Inappropriate partialling, small samples, and anyway, they're not playing our song. *Psychological Inquiry, 17*(2), 131–137.

Eaton, J. (2001). Management communication: The threat of group-think. *Corporate Communications, 6*(4), 183–192.

Edwards, D. (1997). *Discourse and Cognition*. London: Sage.

Edwards, D. & Potter, J. (1992). *Discursive Psychology*. London: Sage.

Fiske, S. T. (2004). *Social Beings: A core motives approach to social psychology*. Hoboken, NJ: John Wiley & Sons, Inc.

Fiske, S. T. (2010). Interpersonal stratification: Status, power, and subordination. In S. T. Fiske, D. T. Gilbert, & G. Lindzey (eds), *Handbook of Social Psychology: Vol. 2* (5th edn; pp. 941–982). Hoboken, NJ: John Wiley & Sons, Inc.

Glass, J. (2005). Sociological perspectives on work and family. In S. M. Bianchi, L. M. Casper, & B. R. King (eds), *Work, Family, Health, and Well-Being* (pp. 215–229). Mahwah, NJ: Lawrence Erlbaum Associates.

Harding, T. (2007). The construction of men who are nurses as gay. *Journal of Advanced Nursing, 60*, 636–644.

Haney, C., Banks, C., & Zimbardo, P. (1973). Interpersonal dynamics in a simulated prison. *International Journal of Criminology & Penology, 1*, 69–97.

Henningsen, D. D., Henningsen, M. L. M., Eden, J., & Cruz, M. G. (2006). Examining the symptoms of groupthink and retrospective sensemaking. *Small Group Research, 37*(1), 36–64.

Hoeksema-van Orden, C. Y. D., Gaillard, A. W. K., & Buunk, B. P. (1998). Social loafing under fatigue. *Journal of Personality and Social Psychology, 75*, 1179–1190.

Hoigaard, R., Säfvenbom, R., & Tonnessen, F. E. (2006). The relationship between group cohesion, group norms, and perceived social loafing in soccer teams. *Small Group Research, 37*(3), 217–232.

Isenberg, D. J. (1986). Group polarization: A critical review and meta-analysis. *Journal of Personality and Social Psychology, 50*, 1141–1151.

Jacobs, R. & Campbell, D. T. (1961). The perpetuation of an arbitrary tradition through several generations of a laboratory microculture. *Journal of Abnormal and Social Psychology, 62*, 649–658.

Janis, I. L. (1972). *Victims of Groupthink: A psychological study of foreign-policy decisions and fiascoes.* Boston: Houghton Mifflin.

Janis, I. L. (1982). *Groupthink.* Boston: Houghton Mifflin.

Kallgren, C. A., Reno, R. R., & Cialdini, R. B. (2000). A focus theory of normative conduct: When norms do and do not affect behavior. *Personality and Social Psychology Bulletin, 26*, 1002–1012.

Kim, H. & Markus, H. R. (1999). Deviance or uniqueness, harmony or conformity? A cultural analysis. *Journal of Personality and Social Psychology, 77*, 785–800.

Larimer, M. E. & Neighbors, C. (2003). Normative misperception and the impact of descriptive and injunctive norms on college student gambling. *Psychology of Addictive Behaviors, 17*(3), 235–243.

Larimer, M. E., Kilmer, J. R., & Lee, C. M. (2005). College student drug prevention: A review of individually-oriented prevention strategies. *Journal of Drug Issues, 35*(2), 431–456.

Larimer, M. E., Turner, A. P., Mallett, K. A., & Geisner, I. M. (2004). Predicting drinking behavior and alcohol-related problems among fraternity and sorority members: Examining the role of descriptive and injunctive norms. *Psychology of Addictive Behaviors, 18*(3), 203–212.

Latané, B., Williams, K., & Harkins, S. G. (1979). Many hands make light the work: The cause and consequences of social loafing. *Journal of Personality and Social Psychology, 37*, 822–832.

Liden, R. C., Wayne, S. J., Jaworski, R. A., & Bennett, N. (2004). Social loafing: A field investigation. *Journal of Management, 30*(2), 285–304.

Ling, K., Beenen, G., Ludford, P., Wang, X., Chang, K., Li, Z., Cosley, D., Frankowski, D., Terveen, L., Rashid, A. M., Resnick, P. & Kraut, R. (2005). Using social psychology to motivate contributions to online communities. *Journal of Computer-Mediated Communication, 10*, 10.

Lüttke, H. B. (2004). Experimente unter dem milgram-paradigma. *Gruppendynamik Und Organisationsberatung, 35*(4), 431–464.

Markus, H. R. & Kitayama, S. (1994). A collective fear of the collective: Implications for selves and theories of selves. *Personality and Social Psychology Bulletin, 20*, 568–579.

Martin, R. (1988). Ingroup and outgroup minorities: Differential impact upon public and private response. *European Journal of Social Psychology, 18*, 39–52.

Martin, R. & Hewstone, M. (2001). Conformity and independence in groups: Majorities and minorities. In M. A. Hogg & R. S. Tindale (eds), *Blackwell Handbook of Social Psychology: Group processes* (pp. 209–234). Malden, MA: Blackwell.

McKinlay, A., Cowan, S., McVittie, C., & Ion, R. (2010). Student nurses' gender-based accounts of men in nursing. *Procedia: Social and Behavioral Sciences, 5*, 345–349.

McKinlay, A. & McVittie, C. (2008). *Social Psychology and Discourse.* Oxford: Wiley-Blackwell

McKinlay, A. & McVittie, C. (2011). *Identities in Context: Individuals and discourse in action.* Oxford: Wiley-Blackwell.

Milgram, S. (1963). Behavioral study of obedience. *Journal of Abnormal and Social Psychology, 67*, 371–378.

Milgram, S. (1974). *Obedience to Authority: An experimental view.* New York: Harper & Row.

Miller, A. G. (2004). What can the Milgram obedience experiments tell us about the holocaust? Generalizing from the social psychology laboratory. In A. G. Miller (ed.), *The Social Psychology of Good and Evil* (pp. 193–239). New York: Guilford Press.

Morfei, M. Z., Hooker, K., Carpenter, J., Mix, C., & Blakeley, E. (2004). Agentic and communal generative behavior in four areas of adult life: Implications for psychological well-being. *Journal of Adult Development, 11*(1), 55–58.

Moscovici, S. (1961). *La Psychanalyse: Son image et son public.* Paris: Presses Universitaires de France.

Moscovici, S. (1984). *Psychologie Sociale.* Paris: Presses Universitaires de France.

Moscovici, S. (2000). Social representations: Explorations in social psychology. Oxford: Blackwell.

Moscovici, S. & Lage, E. (1976). Studies in social influence: III. Majority vs. minority influence in a group. *European Journal of Social Psychology, 6*, 149–174.

Moscovici, S., Lage, E., & Naffrechoux, M. (1969). Influence of a consistent minority on the responses of the majority in a colour perception task. *Sociometry, 32*, 365–380.

Mosher, C. E. & Danoff-Burg, S. (2005). Agentic and communal personality traits: Relations to attitudes toward sex and sexual experiences. *Sex Roles, 52*(1–2), 121–129.

Mosher, C. E. & Danoff-Burg, S. (2008). Agentic and communal personality traits: Relations to disordered eating behavior, body shape concern, and depressive symptoms. *Eating Behaviors, 9*(4), 497–500.

Myers, D. G. (1975). Discussion-induced attitude polarization. *Human Relations, 28*(8), 699–714.

Myers, D. G. & Bishop, G. D. (1970). Discussion effects on racial attitudes. *Science, 169*, 778–779.

Newcomb, T. M. (1943). *Personality and Social Change.* New York: Dryden.

Newcomb, T. M., Koening, K. E., Flacks, R., & Warwick, D. P. (1967). *Persistence and Change: Bennington College and its students after 25 years.* New York: John Wiley & Sons.

Paulus, P. B., Dugosh, K. L., Dzindolet, M. T., Coskun, H., & Putnam, V. L. (2002). Social and cognitive influences in group brainstorming: Predicting production gains and losses. In W. Stroebe & M. Hewston (eds), *European Review of Social Psychology: Vol. 12* (pp. 299–325). Chichester: John Wiley & Sons.

Paulus, P. B., Dzindolet, M. T., Poletes, G., & Camacho, L. M. (1993). Perception of performance in group brainstorming: The illusion of group productivity. *Personality and Social Psychology Bulletin, 19*, 78–79.

Platania, J. & Moran, G. P. (2001). Social facilitation as a function of mere presence of others. *Journal of Social Psychology, 141*(2), 190–197.

Potter, J. & Wetherell, M. (1987). *Discourse and Social Psychology: Beyond attitudes and behaviour.* London: Sage.

Prislin, R. & Wood, W. (2005). Social influence in attitudes and attitude change. In D. Albarracín, B. T. Johnson, & N. O. Zabba (eds), *The Handbook of Attitudes* (pp. 671–705). Mahwah, NJ: Lawrence Erlbaum Associates.

Reicher, S. (1997). Social identity and social change: Rethinking the context of social psychology. In W. P. Robinson (ed.), *Social Groups and Identities: Developing the legacy of Henri Tajfel* (pp. 317–336). London: Butterworth.

Sanderson, C. A. (2010). *Social Psychology.* Hoboken, NJ: John Wiley & Sons.

Sarbin, T. R. & Allen, V. L. (1968). Role theory. In G. Lindzey & E. Aronson (eds), *Handbook of Social Psychology: Vol. 1* (2nd edn; pp. 488–567). Reading, MA: Addison-Wesley.

Sharples, D. M. (2010). Communicating climate science: Evaluating the UK public's attitude to climate change. *Earth & Environment, 5*, 185–205.

Shepperd, J. A. (1993). Productivity loss in performance groups: A motivation analysis. *Psychological Bulletin, 113*, 67–81.

Shepperd, J. A. (1995). Remedying motivation and productivity loss in collective settings. *Current Directions in Psychological Science, 4*, 131–134.

Sherif, M. (1935). A study of some social factors in perception. *Archives of Psychology, 27*, 1–60.

Sherif, M. (1936). *The Psychology of Social Norms*. New York: Harper.

Sherif, M. (1966). *In Common Predicament: Social psychology in intergroup conflict and cooperation*. Boston, MA: Houghton Mifflin.

Steiner, I. D. (1972). *Group Process and Productivity*. New York: Academic Press.

Strauss, B. (2002). Social facilitation in motor tasks: A review of research and theory. *Psychology of Sport and Exercise, 3*(3), 237–256.

Tajfel, H. (1978). Intergroup behaviour: II. Group perspectives. In H. Tajfel & C. Fraser (eds), *Introducing Social Psychology* (pp. 423–445). Harmondsworth, UK: Penguin.

Tajfel, H., Billig, M. G., Bundy, R. P., & Flament, C. (1971). Social categorization and intergroup behaviour. *European Journal of Social Psychology, 1*, 149–178.

Tajfel, H. & Turner, J. C. (1979). An integrative theory of intergroup conflict. In W. G. Austin & S. Worchel (eds), *The Social Psychology of Intergroup Relations* (pp. 33–47). Monterey, CA: Brooks Cole.

Tajfel, H. & Turner, J. C. (1986). The social identity theory of intergroup behaviour. In S. Worchel & W. G. Austin (eds), *Psychology of Intergroup Relations* (pp. 7–24). Chicago: Nelson-Hall.

Triplett, N. (1898). The dynamogenic factors in pace-making and competition. *American Journal of Psychology, 9*, 507–533.

Turner, J. C., Hogg, M. A., Oakes, P. J., Reicher, S. D., & Wetherell, M. S. (1987). *Rediscovering the Social Group: A self-categorization theory*. Oxford: Blackwell.

Uziel, L. (2007). Individual differences in the social facilitation effect: A review and meta-analysis. *Journal of Research in Personality, 41*, 579–601.

Verkuyten, M. (2005). Accounting for ethnic discrimination: A discursive study among minority and majority group members. *Journal of Language and Social Psychology, 24*, 66–92.

Whyte, G. (2000). Groupthink. In A. E. Kazdin (ed.), *Encyclopedia of Psychology: Vol. 4* (pp. 35–38). Washington: American Psychological Association.

Williams, K. D., Harkins, S. G., & Latané, B. (1981). Identifiability as a deterrent to social loafing: Two cheering experiments. *Journal of Personality and Social Psychology, 40*, 303–311.

Zajonc, R. B. (1965). Social facilitation. *Science, 149*, 269–274.

Zentall, T. R. & Levine, J. M. (1972). Observational learning and social facilitation in the rat. *Science, 178*, 1220–1221.

Zimbardo, P. G. (1972). Psychology of imprisonment. *Transition/Society, 9*(6), 4–8.

Zimbardo, P. G. (2006). A situationist perspective on the psychology of evil: Understanding how good people are transformed into perpetrators. In R. Falk, I. Gendzier, & R. J. Lifton (eds), *Crimes of War: Iraq* (pp. 366–369). New York: Nation Books.

CHAPTER 18

Aldwin, C. M. (2007). *Stress, Coping, and Development: An integrated perspective* (2nd edn). New York: Guilford Press.

Aspinwall, L. G. & Taylor, S. E. (1992). Modeling cognitive adaptation: A longitudinal investigation of the impact of individual differences and coping on college adjustment and performance. *Journal of Personality and Social Psychology, 63*(6), 989–1003.

Aspinwall, L. G., Richter, L., & Hoffman, R. R., III. (2001). *Understanding How Optimism Works: An examination of optimists' adaptive moderation of belief and behavior: Optimism & pessimism: Implications for theory, research, and practice* (pp. 217–238). Washington: American Psychological Association.

Bartrop, R. W., Lockhurst, E., Lazarus, L., Kiloh, L. G., & Penny, R. (1977). Depressed lymphocyte function after bereavement. *Lancet, 1*, 834–836.

Baum, A., Trevino, L. A., & Dougall, A. L. (2011). Stress and the cancers. In R. J. Contrada & A. Baum (eds), *The Handbook of Stress Science: Biology, psychology, and health* (pp. 411–423). New York: Springer Publishing.

Baumeister, R. F. (1984). Choking under pressure: Self-consciousness and the paradoxical effects of incentives on skilled performance. *Journal of Personality and Social Psychology, 46*, 610–620.

Beasley, M., Thompson, T., & Davidson, J. (2003). Resilience in responses to life stress: The effects of coping style and cognitive hardiness. *Personality and Individual Differences, 34*(1), 77–95.

Becker, D. (2006). Therapy for the middle-aged: The relevance of existential issues. *American Journal of Psychotherapy, 60*, 87–99.

Beehr, T. A., Farmer, S. J., Glazer, S., Gudanowski, D. M., & Nair, V. N. (2003). The enigma of social support and occupational stress: Source congruence and gender role effects. *Journal of Occupational Health Psychology, 8*(3), 220–231.

Bekkouche, N. S., Holmes, S., Whittaker, K. S., & Krantz, D. S. (2011). Stress and the heart: Psychosocial stress and coronary heart disease. In R. J. Contrada & A. Baum (eds), *The Handbook of Stress Science: Biology, psychology, and health*. New York: Springer Publishing.

Bellinger, D. L., Madden, K. S., Felten, S. Y., & Felten, D. L. (1994). Neural and endocrine links between the brain and the immune system. In C. S. Lewis, C. O'Sullivan, & J. Barraclough (eds), *The Psychoimmunology of Cancer: Mind and body in the fight for survival*. Oxford: Oxford University Press.

Bennett, P., Williams, Y., Page, N., Hood K., & Woollard, M. (2004). Levels of mental health problems among UK emergency ambulance workers. *Emergency Medicine Journal, 21*, 235–236.

Bonanno, G. A. & Mancini, A. D. (2012). Beyond resilience and PTSD: Mapping the heterogeneity of responses to potential trauma. *Psychological Trauma: Theory, research, practice, and policy, 4*, 74–83.

Bouteyre, E., Maurel, M., & Bernaud, J.-L. (2007). Daily hassles and depressive symptoms among first year psychology students in France: The role of coping and social support. *Stress and Health: Journal of the International Society for the Investigation of Stress, 23*(2), 93–99.

Bremner, J. D. & Charney, D. S. (2010). Neural circuits in fear and anxiety. In D. J. Stein, E. Hollander, & B. O. Rothbaum (eds), *Textbook of Anxiety Disorders* (2nd edn; pp. 55–71). Arlington, VA: American Psychiatric Publishing.

Brooks, L., McCabe, P., & Schneiderman, N. (2011). Stress and cardio-metabolic syndrome. In R. J. Contrada & A. Baum (eds), *The Handbook of Stress Science: Biology, psychology, and health* (pp. 399–409). New York: Springer Publishing.

Brown, L. L., Tomarken, A. J., Orth, D. N., Loosen, P. T., Kalin, N. H., & Davidson, R. J. (1996). Individual differences in repressive-defensiveness predict basal salivary cortisol levels. *Journal of Personality and Social Psychology, 70*(2), 362–371.

Burg, M. M. & Pickering, T. G. (2011). The cardiovascular system. In R. J. Contrada & A. Baum (eds), *The Handbook of Stress Science: Biology, psychology, and health* (pp. 37–45). New York: Springer Publishing.

Burg, M. M., Soufer, A., Lampert, R., Collins, D., & Soufer, R. (2011). Autonomic contribution to endothelin-1 increase during laboratory anger-recall stress in patients with coronary artery disease. *Molecular Medicine, 17*(5–6), 495–501.

Burijon, B. N. (2007). *Biological Bases of Clinical Anxiety*. New York: W. W. Norton.

Bushman, B. J., Baumeister, R. F., & Stack, A. D. (1999). Catharsis, aggression, and persuasive influence: Self-fulfilling or self-defeating prophecies? *Journal of Personality and Social Psychology, 76*(3), 367–376.

Butler, J. L. & Baumeister, R. F. (1998). The trouble with friendly faces: Skilled performance with a supportive audience. *Journal of Personality and Social Psychology, 75*(5), 1213–1230.

Cannon, W. B. (1932). *Effects of Strong Emotions*. Chicago: University of Chicago Press.

Cardoso, R., Souza, E. D., & Camano, L. (2009). *Meditation in Health: Definition, operationalization, and technique: Stress and quality of working life: The positive and the negative* (pp. 143–166). Charlotte, NC: Information Age Publishing.

Carver, C. S. & Scheier, M. (1999). Optimism. In C. R. Snyder (ed.), *Coping: The psychology of what works*. New York: Oxford University Press.

Chang, E. C. (2002). Optimism–pessimism and stress appraisal: Testing a cognitive interactive model of psychological adjustment in adults. *Cognitive Therapy and Research, 26*(5), 675–690.

Chang, R., Chang, E. C., Sanna, L. J., & Hatcher, R. L. (2008). *Optimism and Pessimism as Personality Variables Linked to Adjustment: The SAGE handbook of personality theory and assessment: Vol. 1: Personality theories and models* (pp. 470–485). Thousand Oaks, CA: Sage Publications.

Coddington, R. D. (1972). The significance of life events as etiologic factors in the disease of children, II: A study of a normal population. *Journal of Psychosomatic Research, 16*, 205–213.

Coddington, R. D. (1984). Measuring the stressfulness of a child's environment. In J. H. Humphrey (ed.), *Stress in Childhood*. New York: AMS Press.

Cohen, S. (2002). Psychosocial stress, social networks, and susceptibility to infection. In H. G. Koenig & H. J. Cohen (eds), *The Link between Religion and Health: Psychoneuroimmunology and the faith factor* (pp. 101–123). New York: Oxford University Press.

Cohen, S. (2004). Social relationships and health. *American Psychologist, 59*(8), 676–684.

Cohen, S. & Hamrick, N. (2003). Stable individual differences in physiological response to stressors: Implications for stress-elicited changes in immune related health. *Brain, Behavior, and Immunity, 17*(6), 407–414.

Cohen, S. & Janicki-Deverts, D. (2009). Can we improve our physical health by altering our social networks? *Perspectives on Psychological Science, 4*(4), 375–378.

Cohen, S. & Wills, T. A. (1985). Stress, social support, and the buffering hypothesis. *Psychological Bulletin, 98*(2), 310–357.

Coy, T. V. (1998). The effect of repressive coping style on cardiovascular reactivity and speech disturbances during stress. US: ProQuest Information & Learning. *Dissertation Abstracts International: Section B: The sciences and engineering, 58*(8), 4512.

Crandall, C. S., Preisler, J. J., & Aussprung, J. (1992). Measuring life events stress in the lives of college students: The Undergraduate Stress Questionnaire (USQ). *Journal of Behavioral Medicine, 15*(6), 627–662.

Dagan, M., Sanderman, R., Schokker, M. C., Wiggers, T., Baas, P. C., van Haastert, M., & Hagedoorn, M. (2011). Spousal support and changes in distress over time in couples coping with cancer: The role of personal control. *Journal of Family Psychology, 25*(2), 310–318.

Davis, M. (1992). Analysis of aversive memories using the fear potentiated startle paradigm. In N. Butters & L. R. Squire (eds), *The Neuropsychology of Memory* (2nd edn). New York: Guilford Press.

Delahanty, D.L. (2007). Are we prepared to handle the mental health consequences of terrorism? *American Journal Psychiatry, 164*(2), 189–91.

DeLongis, A., Coyne, J. C., Dakof, G., Folkman, S., & Lazarus, R. S. (1982). The impact of daily hassles, uplifts and major life events to health status. *Health Psychology, 1*(2), 119–136.

Dhabhar, F. S. (2011). Effects of stress on immune function: Implications for immunoprotection and immunopathology. In R. J. Contrada & A. Baum (eds), *The Handbook of Stress Science: Biology, psychology, and health*. New York: Springer Publishing.

Diener, E. & Chan, M. Y. (2011). Happy people live longer: Subjective well-being contributes to health and longevity. *Applied Psychology: Health and well-being, 3*(1), 1–43.

Diener, E., Emmons, R. A., Larsen, R. J., & Griffin, S. (1985). The Satisfaction with Life Scale. *Journal of Personality Assessment, 49*, 71–75.

Ellison, C. G., Hummer, R. A., Cormier, S., & Rogers, R. G. (2000). Religious involvement and mortality risk among African American adults. *Research on Aging, 22*(6), 630–667.

Elovainio, M., Merjonen, P., Pulkki-Råback, L., Kivimäki, M., Jokela, M., Mattson, N., & Keltikangas-Järvinen, L. (2011). Hostility, metabolic syndrome, inflammation and cardiac control in young adults: The young Finns study. *Biological Psychology, 87*(2), 234–240.

Evans, G. W. (2001). Environmental stress and health. In A. Baum, T. A. Revenson, & J. E. Singer (eds), *Handbook of Health Psychology* (pp. 365–385). Mahwah, NJ: Lawrence Erlbaum Associates.

Fleming, I., Baum, A., Davidson, L., Rectanus, E., & McArdle, S. (1987). Chronic stress as a reactivity factor in physiologic reactivity to challenge. *Health Psychology, 11*, 221–237.

Foa, E. & Kozak, M. (1986). Emotional processing of fear: Exposure to corrective information. *Psychological Bulletin, 99*, 20–35.

Folkman, S. & Moskowitz, J. T. (2000). Positive affect and the other side of coping. *American Psychologist, 55*, 647–654.

Folkman, S. & Moskowitz, J. T. (2004). Coping: Pitfalls and promise. *Annual Review of Psychology, 55*, 745–774.

Friedman, M. & Rosenman, R. (1959). Association of a specific overt behavior pattern with increases in blood cholesterol, blood clotting time, incidence of arcus senilis and clinical coronary artery disease. *Journal of the American Medical Association, 169*, 1286–1296.

Friedman, M. & Rosenman, R. (1974). *Type A Behavior and Your Heart*. New York: Knopf.

Gallacher, J. E. J., Sweetnam, P. M., Yarnell, J. W. G., Elwood, P. C., & Stansfeld, S. A. (2003). Is type A behavior really a trigger for coronary heart disease events? *Psychosomatic Medicine, 65*(3), 339–346.

Greenberg, J. (1978). The Americanization of Roseto. *Science News, 113*, 378–382.

Groër, M., Meagher, M. W., & Kendall-Tackett, K. (2010). An overview of stress and immunity. In K. Kendall-Tackett (ed.), *The Psychoneuroimmunology of Chronic Disease: Exploring the links between inflammation, stress, and illness* (pp. 9–22). Washington: American Psychological Association.

Hanin, Y. L. (1997). Emotions and athletic performance: Individual zones of optimal functioning. *European Yearbook of Sport Psychology, 1*, 29–72.

Harker, L. & Keltner, D. (2001). Expressions of positive emotion in women's college yearbook pictures and their relationship to personality and life outcomes across adulthood. *Journal of Personality and Social Psychology, 80*, 112–124.

Harvey, J. H. (2008). Growth through loss and adversity in close relationships. In S. Joseph & P. A. Linley (eds), *Trauma, Recovery, and Growth: Positive psychological perspectives on posttraumatic stress* (pp. 125–143). Hoboken, NJ: John Wiley & Sons, Inc.

Haynes, S. G., Feinleib, M., & Kannel, W. B. (1980). The relationship of psychosocial factors to coronary heart disease in the Framingham study: III: Eight-year incidence of coronary heart disease. *American Journal of Epidemiology, 111*(1), 37–58.

Henry, J. P. & Cassel, J. C. (1969). Psychosocial factors in essential hypertension: Recent epidemiologic and animal experimental evidence. *American Journal of Epidemiology, 90*(3): 171–200.

Holmes, T. H. & Rahe, R. H. (1967). The Social Readjustment Rating Scale. *Journal of Psychosomatic Research, 11*, 213–218.

Holmes, T. H. & Rahe, R. H. (1989). The Social Readjustment Rating Scale. In T. H. Holmes & E. M. David (eds), *Life Change, Life Events, and Illness: Selected papers*. New York: Praeger.

Iwanaga, M., Yokoyama, H., & Seiwa, H. (2004). Coping availability and stress reduction for optimistic and pessimistic individuals. *Personality and Individual Differences, 36*(1), 11–22.

Jackson, B. R. & Bergeman, C. S. (2011). How does religiosity enhance well-being? The role of perceived control. *Psychology of Religion and Spirituality, 3*(2), 149–161.

Jamal, M. & Baba, V. V. (2003). Type A behavior, components, and outcomes: A study of Canadian employees. *International Journal of Stress Management, 10*(1), 39–50.

Jankord, R. & Herman, J. P. (2008). Limbic regulation of hypothalamo–pituitary–adrenocortical function during acute and chronic stress. *Annals of the New York Academy of Sciences, 1148*, 64–73.

Kanner, B. (1998). Are you normal? Turning the other cheek. *American Demographics, 20*, 39.

Keane, T. M., Marx, B. P., & Sloan, D. M. (2009). *Post-Traumatic Stress Disorder: Definition, prevalence, and risk factors: Post-traumatic stress disorder: Basic science and clinical practice* (pp. 1–19). Totowa, NJ: Humana Press.

Kendall-Tackett, K. (2010). Depression, hostility, posttraumatic stress disorder, and inflammation: The corrosive health effects of negative mental states. *The Psychoneuroimmunology of Chronic Disease: Exploring the links between inflammation, stress, and illness* (pp. 113–131). Washington: American Psychological Association.

Kern, M. L. & Friedman, H. S. (2011). Personality and pathways of influence on physical health. *Social and Personality Psychology Compass, 5*(1), 76–87.

Kibler, J. L., Joshi, K., & Hughes, E. E. (2010). Cognitive and behavioral reactions to stress among adults with PTSD: Implications for immunity and health. In K. Kendall-Tackett (ed.), *The Psychoneuroimmunology of Chronic Disease: Exploring the links between inflammation, stress, and illness* (pp. 133–158). Washington: American Psychological Association.

Kiecolt-Glaser, J. K., Glaser, R., Gravenstein, S., Malarkey, W. B., & Sheridan, J. (1996). Chronic stress alters the immune response to influenza virus vaccine in older adults. *Proceedings of the National Academy of Sciences, 93,* 3043–3047.

Kiecolt-Glaser, J., McGuire, L., Robles, T. F., & Glaser, R. (2002a). Psychoneuroimmunology and psychosomatic medicine: Back to the future. *Psychosomatic Medicine, 64*(1), 15–28.

Kiecolt-Glaser, J., McGuire, L., Robles, T. F., & Glaser, R. (2002b). Psychoneuroimmunology: Psychological influences on immune function and health. *Journal of Consulting and Clinical Psychology, 70*(3), 537–547.

Kunst, M. J. J. (2011). Affective personality type, post-traumatic stress disorder symptom severity and post-traumatic growth in victims of violence. *Stress and Health: Journal of the International Society for the Investigation of Stress, 27*(1), 42–51.

Langens, T. A. & Mörth, S. (2003). Repressive coping and the use of passive and active coping strategies. *Personality and Individual Differences, 35*(2), 461–473.

Langer, E. J. & Rodin, J. (2004). *The Effects of Choice and Enhanced Personal Responsibility for the Aged: A field experiment in an institutional setting: The interface of social and clinical psychology: Key readings* (pp. 339–348). New York: Psychology Press.

Lazarus, R. S. (1991). Progress on a cognitive-motivational-relational theory of emotion. *American Psychologist, 46*(8), 819–834.

Lazarus, R. S. (1993). From psychological stress to the emotions: A history of changing outlooks. *Annual Review of Psychology, 44,* 1–21.

Lazarus, R. S. (1999). *Stress and Emotion: A new synthesis.* New York: Springer Publishing.

Lazarus, R. S. (2007). Stress and emotion: A new synthesis. In A. Monat, R. S. Lazarus, & G. Reevy (eds), *The Praeger Handbook on Stress and Coping: Vol. 1* (pp. 33–51). Westport, CT: Praeger Publishers/Greenwood Publishing Group.

Lazarus, R. S. & Folkman, S. (1984). *Stress, Appraisal, and Coping.* New York: Springer Publishing.

Lechner, S. C., Stoelb, B. L., & Antoni, M. H. (2008). *Group-Based Therapies for Benefit Finding in Cancer: Trauma, recovery, and growth: Positive psychological perspectives on posttraumatic stress* (pp. 207–231). Hoboken, NJ: John Wiley & Sons, Inc.

Lekander, M. (2002). Ecological immunology: The role of the immune system in psychology and neuroscience. *European Psychiatry, 7*(2), 98–115.

Lepore, S. J., Evans, G. W., & Palsane, M. N. (1991). Social hassles and psychological health in the context of chronic crowding. *Journal of Health and Social Behavior, 32*(4), 357–367.

Lewin, K. (1935). *A Dynamic Theory of Personality.* New York: McGraw-Hill.

Liddell, H. S. (1950). *Animal Origins of Anxiety: Feelings and emotions: The mooseheart symposium* (pp. 181–188). New York: McGraw-Hill.

Lovell, B. & Wetherell, M. A. (2011). The cost of caregiving: Endocrine and immune implications in elderly and non elderly caregivers. *Neuroscience and Biobehavioral Reviews, 35*(6), 1342–1352.

Lupien, S. J., Maheu, F., Tu, M., Fiocco, A., & Schramek, T. E. (2007). The effects of stress and stress hormones on human cognition: Implications for the field of brain and cognition. *Brain and Cognition, 65*(3), 209–237.

Lupien, S. J., Ouelle-Morin, I., Hupback, A., Walker, D., Tu, M. T., & Buss, C. (2006). Beyond the stress concept: Allostatic load: A developmental biological and cognitive perspective. In: D. Cicchetti (ed.), *Handbook Series on Developmental Psychopathology* (pp. 784–809). New York: John Wiley & Sons.

Maddi, S. R. (2007). The story of hardiness: Twenty years of theorizing, research, and practice. In A. Monat, R. S. Lazarus, & G. Reevy (eds), *The Praeger Handbook on Stress and Coping: Vol. 2* (pp. 327–340). Westport, CT: Praeger Publishers/Greenwood Publishing Group.

Malkoff, S. B., Muldoon, M. F., Zeigler, Z. R., & Manuck, S. B. (1993). Blood platelet responsivity to acute mental stress. *Psychosomatic Medicine, 55*(6), 477–482.

Marsland, A. L., Bachen, E. A., Cohen, S., Rabin, B., & Manuck, S. B. (2002). Stress, immune reactivity and susceptibility to infectious disease. *Physiology & Behavior, 77*(4–5), 711–716.

Matsumoto, D. & Juang, L. (2008). *Culture and Psychology* (4th edn). Victoria, Australia: Thomson Wadsworth.

Miller, N. E. (1959). Liberalization of basic S-R concepts: Extensions to conflict behavior, motivation, and social learning. In S. Koch (ed.), *Psychology: A study of a science: Vol. 2.* New York: McGraw-Hill.

Mino, I., Profit, W. E., & Pierce, C. M., (2000). Minorities and stress. In G. Fink (ed.), *Encyclopedia of Stress: Vol. 3* (pp. 771–776). New York: Academic Press.

Neff, E. J. A. & Dale, J. C. (1996). Worries of school-age children. *Journal of the Society of Pediatric Nurses, 1,* 27–32.

Nelson, D. & Cooper, C. (2005). Stress and health: A positive direction. *Stress and Health, 21,* 73–75.

Novaco, R. W., Stokols, D., & Milanesi, L. (1990). Objective and subjective dimensions of travel impedance as determinants of commuting stress. *American Journal of Community Psychology, 18,* 231–257.

O'Rourke, N., Cappeliez, P. & Guindon, S. (2003). Depressive symptoms and physical health of caregivers of persons with cognitive impairment: Analysis of reciprocal effects over time. *Journal of Aging and Health, 15*(4), 688–712.

Ouellette, S. C. & DiPlacido, J. (2001). Personality's role in the protection and enhancement of health: Where the research has been, where it is stuck, how it might move. In A. Baum, T. A. Revenson, & J. E. Singer (eds), *Handbook of Health Psychology.* Mahwah, NJ: Lawrence Erlbaum.

Overmier, B. J. & Murison, R. (2005). Trauma and resulting sensitization effects are modulated by psychological factors. *Psychoneuroendocrinology, 30,* 965–973.

Ozer, E. J., Best, S. R., Lipsey, T. L., & Weiss, D. S. (2003). Predictors of post-traumatic stress disorder and symptoms in adults: A meta analysis. *Psychology Bulletin, 129*(1), 52–73.

Pace, T. W. W. & Heim, C. M. (2011). A short review on the psychoneuroimmunology of posttraumatic stress disorder: From risk factors to medical comorbidities. *Brain, Behavior, and Immunity, 25*(1), 6–13.

Packer, S. (2000). Religion and stress. In G. Fink (ed.), *Encyclopedia of Stress: Vol. 3* (pp. 348–355). New York: Academic Press.

Pauls, C. A. & Stemmler, G. (2003). Repressive and defensive coping during fear and anger. *Emotion, 3*(3), 284–302.

Peterson, C. & Seligman, M. E. P. (2004). *Character Strengths and Virtues: A handbook and classification.* Washington: APA Press.

Peterson, C. & Steen, T. A. (2009). Optimistic explanatory style. In S. J. Lopez & C. R. Snyder (eds), *Oxford Handbook Of Positive Psychology* (2nd edn) (pp. 313–321). Oxford: Oxford University Press.

Peterson, C., Park, N., & Seligman, M. E. P. (2006). Greater strengths of character and recovery from illness. *Journal of Positive Psychology, 1,* 17–26.

Profit, W. E., Mino, I., & Pierce, C. M. (2000). Stress in blacks. Available at: http://books.google.co.uk/books?id=NutwE33f_IIC&pg=PA326&lpg=PA326&dq=stress+in+blacks&source=bl&ots=GbpXUUhNMx&sig=skJM9EjjWwU7NjrVhoxLfH8vAGI&hl=en&sa=X&ei=T38GUdiQFMKg0QX27IF4&ved=0CGAQ6AEwBg" \l "v=onepage&q=stress%20in%20blacks&f=false.

Rees, W. D. & Lutkin, S. G. (1967). Mortality of bereavement. *British Medical Journal, 4,* 13–16.

Rejeski, W. J. & Thompson, A. (2007). *Historical and Conceptual Roots of Exercise Psychology: Essential readings in sport and exercise psychology* (pp. 332–347). Champaign, IL: Human Kinetics.

Rejeski, W. J., Gregg, E., Thompson, A., & Berry, M. (1991). The effects of varying doses of acute aerobic exercise on psychophysiological stress responses in highly trained cyclists. *Journal of Sport & Exercise Psychology, 13*(2), 188–199.

Rejeski, W. J., Thompson, A., Brubaker, P. H., & Miller, H. S. (1992). Acute exercise: Buffering psychosocial stress responses in women. *Health Psychology, 11*(6), 355–362.

Renner, M. J. & Mackin, R. S. (2002). *A Life Stress Instrument for Classroom Use: Handbook for teaching introductory psychology: Vol. 3: With an emphasis on assessment* (pp. 236–238). Mahwah, NJ: Lawrence Erlbaum Associates.

Rodin, J. & Langer, E. J. (1977). Long-term effects of a control-relevant intervention with the institutionalized aged. *Journal of Personality and Social Psychology, 35*(12), 897–902.

Rook, K. S., August, K. J., & Sorkin, D. H. (2011). Social network functions and health. In R. J. Contrada & A. Baum (eds), *The Handbook of Stress Science: Biology, psychology, and health* (pp. 123–135). New York: Springer Publishing.

Rossi A. M., Quick J. C., and Perrewe P. L. (eds) (2009). *Stress and Quality of Working Life: The positive and the negative.* Charlotte, NC: Information Age Publishing.

Ryan-Wenger, N. A., Sharrer, V. W., & Campbell, K. K. (2005). Changes in children's stressors over the past 30 years. *Pediatric Nursing, July/August.*

Schmidt, M. V., Scharf, S. H., Sterlemann, V., Ganea, K., Liebl, C., Holsboer, F., & Müller, M. B. (2009). High susceptibility to chronic social stress is associated with a depression-like phenotype. *Psychoneuroendocrinology, 35*, 635–643.

Seligman, M. E. P. (2008). Positive health. *Applied Psychology, 57*, 3–18.

Seligman, M. E. P., Steen, T. A., Park, N., & Peterson, C. (2005). Positive psychology progress: Empirical validation of interventions. *American Psychologist, 60*, 410–421.

Selye, H. (1936). A syndrome produced by diverse nocuous agents. *Nature, 138*, 32.

Selye, H. (1956a). Stress and psychobiology. *Journal of Clinical & Experimental Psychopathology, 17*, 370–375.

Selye, H. (1956b). *The Stress of Life.* New York: McGraw-Hill.

Selye, H. (1993). *History of the Stress Concept: Handbook of stress: Theoretical and clinical aspects* (2nd edn; pp. 7–17). New York: Free Press.

Sgoifo, A., Braglia, F., Costoli, T., Musso, E., Meerlo, P., Ceresini, G., & Troisi, A. (2003). Cardiac autonomic reactivity and salivary cortisol in men and women exposed to social stressors: Relationship with individual ethological profile. *Neuroscience and Biobehavioral Reviews, 27*(1–2), 179–188.

Shafir, E. & Tversky, A. (2002). *Decision making: Foundations of cognitive psychology: Core readings* (pp. 601–620). Cambridge, MA: MIT Press.

Sher, L. (2003). Daily hassles, cortisol, and depression. *Australian and New Zealand Journal of Psychiatry, 37*(3), 383–384.

Sherwood, A. (1993). *Use of Impedance Cardiography in Cardiovascular Reactivity Research: Cardiovascular reactivity to psychological stress & disease* (pp. 157–199). Washington: American Psychological Association.

Smith, T. W. & Gallo, L. C. (2001). Personality traits as risk factors for physical illness. In A. Baum, T. A. Revenson, & J. E. Singer (eds), *Handbook of Health Psychology* (pp. 139–173). Mahwah, NJ: Lawrence Erlbaum Associates.

Smyth, J. M. & Pennebaker, J. W. (2001). What are the health effects of disclosure? In A. Baum, T. A. Revenson, & J. E. Singer (eds), *Handbook of Health Psychology* (pp. 339–348). Mahwah, NJ: Lawrence Erlbaum Associates.

Spiegel, D. & Fawzy, F. I. (2002). Psychosocial interventions and prognosis in cancer. In H. G. Koenig & H. J. Cohen (eds), *The Link between Religion and Health: Psychoneuroimmunology and the faith factor* (pp. 84–100). New York: Oxford University Press.

Stanton, A. L., Parsa, A., & Austenfeld, J. L. (2002). *The Adaptive Potential of Coping through Emotional Approach: Handbook of positive psychology* (pp. 148–158). New York: Oxford University Press.

Stanton, A. L., Sullivan, S. J., & Austenfeld, J. L. (2009). Coping through emotional approach: Emerging evidence for the utility of processing and expressing emotions in responding to stressors. *Oxford Handbook of Positive Psychology* (2nd edn; pp. 225–235). New York: Oxford University Press.

Stephens, R., Atkins, J., & Kingston, A. (2009). Swearing as a response to pain. *NeuroReport: For rapid communication of neuroscience research, 20*(12), 1056–1060.

Steptoe, A. (2000). Health behavior and stress. In G. Fink (ed.), *Encyclopedia of Stress: Vol. 2* (pp. 322–326). New York: Academic Press.

Stetter, F. & Kupper, S. (2002). Autogenic training: A meta-analysis of clinical outcome studies. *Applied Psychophysiology and Biofeedback, 27*, 45–98.

Stuart, T. D. & Garrison, M. E. B. (2002). The influence of daily hassles and role balance on health status: A study of mothers of grade school children. *Women & Health, 36*(3), 1–11.

Tavris, C. (1989). *Anger: The misunderstood emotion.* New York: Touchstone Books/Simon & Schuster.

Tavris, C. (2003). *Uncivil Rights: The cultural rules of anger: Violence and society: A reader* (pp. 3–14). Upper Saddle River, NJ: Prentice Hall/Pearson Education.

Taylor, S. E. (2006a). *Health Psychology* (6th edn). New York: McGraw-Hill.

Taylor, S. E. (2006b). Tend and befriend: Biobehavioral bases of affiliation under stress. *Current Directions in Psychological Science, 15*(6), 273–277.

Taylor, S. E. (2007). *Social Support: Foundations of health psychology* (pp. 145–171). New York: Oxford University Press.

Taylor, S. E. (2008). *From Social Psychology to Neuroscience and Back: Journeys in social psychology: Looking back to inspire the future* (pp. 39–54). New York: Psychology Press.

Tennen, H. & Affleck, G. (2002). *Benefit-Finding and Benefit-Reminding: Handbook of positive psychology* (pp. 584–597). New York: Oxford University Press.

Tennen, H. & Affleck, G. (2009). *Assessing Positive Life Change: In search of meticulous methods: Medical illness and positive life change: Can crisis lead to personal transformation?* (pp. 31–49). Washington: American Psychological Association.

Tennen, H., Affleck, G., & Armeli, S. (2005). Personality and daily experience revisited. *Journal of Personality, 73*(6), 1465–1484.

Tramontin, M. & Halpern, J. (2007). The psychological aftermath of terrorism: The 2001 World Trade Center attack. In E. K. Carll (ed.), *Trauma Psychology: Issues in violence, disaster, health, and illness: Vol. 1.* Westport, CT: Praeger Publishers.

Uchino, B. N. & Birmingham, W. (2011). Stress and support processes. In R. J. Contrada & A. Baum (eds), *The Handbook of Stress Science: Biology, psychology, and health.* New York: Springer Publishing.

van Eck, M., Nicolson, N. A., & Berkhof, J. (1998). Effects of stressful daily events on mood states: Relationship to global perceived stress. *Journal of Personality and Social Psychology, 75*(6), 1572–1585.

Vasey, M. W., Crnic, K. A., & Carter, W. G. (1994). Worry in childhood: A developmental perspective. *Cognitive Therapy Research, 18*(6), 529–549.

Vollrath, M. (2001). Personality and stress. *Scandinavian Journal of Psychology, 42*(4), 335–347.

Wallace, H. M., Baumeister, R. F., & Vohs, K. D. (2005). Audience support and choking under pressure: A home disadvantage? *Journal of Sports Sciences, 23*(4), 429–438.

Wan, C. Y. & Huon G. F. (2005). Performance degradation under pressure in music: An examination of attentional processes. *Psychology of Music, 33*, 155–172.

Weinberg, R. S. & Gould, D. (2003). *Foundations of Sport and Exercise Psychology.* Champaign, IL: Human Kinetics.

Williams, P. G., Smith, T. W., Gunn, H. E., & Uchino, B. N. (2011). Personality and stress: Individual differences in exposure, reactivity, recovery, and restoration. In R. J. Contrada & A. Baum (eds), *The Handbook of Stress Science: Biology, psychology, and health.* New York: Springer Publishing.

Wolf, S. (1969). Psychosocial factors in myocardial infarction and sudden death. *Circulation, 39*, 74–83.

Yalom, I. (1980). *Existential Psychotherapy.* New York: Basic Books.

Yerkes, R. M. & Dodson, J. D. (1908). The relation of strength of stimulus to rapidity of habit-formation. *Journal of Comparative Neurology and Psychology, 18*, 459–482.

Yoon, H. (2003). Factors associated with family caregiver's burden and depression in Korea. *International Journal of Aging & Human Development, 57*(4), 291–311.

Young, K. S. (1996). Psychology of computer use: XL: Addictive use of the Internet: A case that breaks the stereotype. *Psychological Reports, 79*(3), 899–902.

Young, K. S. (1998). Internet addiction: The emergence of a new clinical disorder. *CyberPsychology & Behavior, 1*(3), 237–244.

Young, K. S. (2004). Internet addiction: A new clinical phenomenon and its consequences. *American Behavioral Scientist, 48*(4), 402–415.

Young, K. S. (2009). *Assessment and treatment of Internet addiction: The Praeger international collection on addictions: Vol. 4: Behavioral addictions from concept to compulsion* (pp. 217–234). Santa Barbara, CA: Praeger/ABC-CLIO.

CHAPTER 19

Abbey, S. E. (2005). Somatization and somatoform disorders. In J. L. Levenson (ed.), *The American Psychiatric Publishing Textbook of Psychosomatic Medicine* (pp. 271–296). Washington: American Psychiatric Publishing.

Abramowitz, J. S. & Braddock, A. E. (2011). *Hypochondriasis and Health Anxiety.* Cambridge, MA: Hogrefe Publishing.

Abramson, L. Y., Alloy, L. B., Hankin, B. L., Haeffel, G. J., MacCoon, D. G., & Gibb, B. E. (2002). Cognitive vulnerability: Stress models of depression in a self-regulatory and psychobiological context. In I. H. Gotlib & C. L. Hammen (eds), *Handbook of Depression* (pp. 268–294). New York: Guilford Press.

Abramson, L. Y., Metalsky, G. I., & Alloy, L. B. (1989). Hopelessness depression: A theory-based subtype of depression. *Psychological Review, 96*(2), 358–372.

Abramson, L. Y., Seligman, M. E., & Teasdale, J. D. (1978). Learned helplessness in humans: Critique and reformulation. *Journal of Abnormal Psychology, 87*(1), 49–74.

Akbarian, S. (2010). Epigenetics of schizophrenia. In N. R. Swerdlow (ed.), *Behavioral Neurobiology of Schizophrenia and Its Treatment* (pp. 611–628). New York: Springer-Verlag Publishing.

Akhtar, S., Wig, N. H., Verma, V. K., Pershod, D., & Verma, S. K. (1975). A phenomenological analysis of symptoms in obsessive-compulsive neuroses. *British Journal of Psychiatry, 127,* 342–348.

Alegría, A. A., Petry, N. M., Hasin, D. S., Liu, S., Grant, B. F., & Blanco, C. (2009). Disordered gambling among racial and ethnic groups in the US: Results from the National Epidemiologic Survey on Alcohol and Related Conditions. *CNS Spectrums, 14*(3), 132–142.

Alegría, M., Mulvaney-Day, N., Torres, M., Polo, A., Cao, Z., & Canino, G. (2007). Prevalence of psychiatric disorders across Latino subgroups in the United States. *American Journal of Public Health, 97*(1), 68–75.

Alegría, M., Takeuchi, D., Canino, G., Duan, N., Shrout, P., Meng, X. L., *et al.* (2004). Considering context, place and culture: The National Latino and Asian American Study. *International Journal of Methods in Psychiatric Research, 13*(4), 208–220.

Alfano C. A. & Beidel D. C. (eds) (2011). *Social Anxiety in Adolescents and Young Adults: Translating developmental science into practice.* Washington: American Psychological Association.

Alloy, L. B. & Abramson, L. Y. (2010). The role of the behavioral approach system (BAS) in bipolar spectrum disorders. *Current Directions in Psychological Science, 19*(3), 189–194.

Alloy, L. B., Uroševic, S., Abramson, L. Y., Jager-Hyman, S., Nusslock, R., Whitehouse, W. G., & Hogan, M. (2011). Progression along the bipolar spectrum: A longitudinal study of predictors of conversion from bipolar spectrum conditions to bipolar I and II disorders. *Journal of Abnormal Psychology,* no pages.

Alonso, J., Angermeyer, M. C., Bernert, S. *et al.* (2004). Prevalence of mental disorders in Europe: Results from the European Study of the Epidemiology of Mental Disorders (ESEMeD) project. *Acta Psychiatrica Scandinavica, 109*(suppl. 420): 21–27.

APA (American Psychiatric Association). (2000). *Diagnostic and Statistical Manual of Mental Disorders* (4th edn), Text Revision. Washington: American Psychiatric Association.

Archer, D. & McDaniel, P. (1995). Violence and gender: Differences and similarities across societies. In R. B. Ruback & N. A. Weiner (eds), *Interpersonal Violent Behaviors: Social and cultural aspects.* New York: Springer.

Arens, E. A., Grabe, H., Spitzer, C., & Barnow, S. (2011). Testing the biosocial model of borderline personality disorder: Results of a prospective 5-year longitudinal study. *Personality and Mental Health, 5*(1), 29–42.

Arieti, S. (1974). *Interpretation of Schizophrenia.* New York: Basic Books.

Asmundson, G. J. G. & Taylor, S. (2008). Health anxiety and its disorders. In M. Hersen & J. Rosqvist (eds), *Handbook of Psychological Assessment, Case Conceptualization, and Treatment: Vol. 1: Adults* (pp. 701–727). Hoboken, NJ: John Wiley & Sons, Inc.

Ayd, F. J., Jr. (1956). A clinical evaluation of frenquel. *Journal of Nervous and Mental Disease, 124,* 507–509.

Bach, P. A. (2007). Psychotic disorders. In D. W. Woods & J. W. Kanter (eds), *Understanding Behavior Disorders: A contemporary behavioral perspective.* Reno, NV: Context Press.

Bandura, A. & Rosenthal, T. (1966). Vicarious classical conditioning as a function of arousal level. *Journal of Personality and Social Psychology, 3,* 54–62.

Bandura, A., Ross, D., & Ross, S. (1963). Imitation of film-mediated aggressive models. *Journal of Abnormal and Social Psychology, 66,* 3–11.

Baranski, J. V. (2011). Sleep loss and the ability to self-monitor cognitive performance. In P. L. Ackerman (ed.), *Cognitive Fatigue: Multidisciplinary perspectives on current research and future applications* (pp. 67–82). Washington: American Psychological Association.

Barlow, M. R. (2011). Memory for complex emotional material in dissociative identity disorder. *Journal of Trauma & Dissociation, 12*(1), 53–66.

Beck, A. T. (1967). *Depression: Clinical, experimental and theoretical aspects.* New York: Harper & Row.

Beck, A. T. (1991). Cognitive therapy: A 30-year retrospective. *American Psychologist, 46*(4), 368–375.

Beck, A. T. (2002). Cognitive models of depression. In R. L. Leahy & E. T. Dowd (eds), *Clinical Advances in Cognitive Psychotherapy: Theory and applications.* New York: Springer.

Beck, A. T. & Emery, G. (1985). *Anxiety Disorders and Phobias: A cognitive perspective.* New York: Basic Books.

Beck, A. T. & Weishaar, M. (2011). Cognitive therapy. In R. J. Corsini & D. Wedding (eds), *Current Psychotherapies* (9th edn). Florence, KY: CENGAGE Learning.

Bell, L., Long, S., Garvan, C., & Bussing, R. (2011). The impact of teacher credentials on ADHD Stigma Perceptions. *Psychology in the Schools, 48*(2), 184–197.

Bender, R. E. & Alloy, L. B. (2011). Life stress and kindling in bipolar disorder: Review of the evidence and integration with emerging biopsychosocial theories. *Clinical Psychology Review, 31*(3), 383–398.

Berenson, K. R., Downey, G., Rafaeli, E., Coifman, K. G., & Paquin, N. L. (2011). The rejection–rage contingency in borderline personality disorder. *Journal of Abnormal Psychology, 120*(3), 681–690.

Birrell, P. (2011). Review of *Memory Matters: Contexts for understanding sexual abuse recollections. Journal of Trauma & Dissociation, 12*(1), 107–109.

Björgvinsson, T. & Hart, J. (2008). Obsessive-compulsive disorder. In M. Hersen & J. Rosqvist (eds), *Handbook of Psychological Assessment, Case Conceptualization, and Treatment: Vol. 1: Adults* (pp. 237–262). Hoboken, NJ: John Wiley & Sons, Inc.

Black, D. W., Gunter, T., Loveless, P., Allen, J., & Sieleni, B. (2010). Antisocial personality disorder in incarcerated offenders: Psychiatric comorbidity and quality of life. *Annals of Clinical Psychiatry, 22*(3), 113–120.

Blackmore, E. R., Craddock, N., Walters, J., & Jones, I. (2009). Is the perimenopause a time of increased risk of recurrence in women with a history of bipolar affective postpartum psychosis? A case series. *Archives of Women's Mental Health, 11*(1), 75–78.

Blair, J., Mitchell, D., & Blair, K. (2005). *The Psychopath: Emotion and the brain.* Malden, MA: Blackwell Publishing.

Blum, H. P. (2010). Object relations in clinical psychoanalysis. *International Journal of Psychoanalysis, 91*(4), 973–976.

Bouman, T. K. (2008). Hypochondriasis. In J. S. Abramowitz, D. McKay, & S. Taylor (eds), *Obsessive-Compulsive Disorder: Subtypes and spectrum conditions*. Oxford: Elsevier.

Bremner, J. D. & Charney, D. S. (2010). Neural circuits in fear and anxiety. In D. J. Stein, E. Hollander, & B. O. Rothbaum (eds), *Textbook of Anxiety Disorders* (2nd edn; pp. 55–71). Arlington, VA: American Psychiatric Publishing.

Breslau, N., Roth, T., Burduvali, E., Kapke, A., Schults, L., & Roehrs, T. (2005). Sleep in lifetime posttraumatic stress disorder: A community-based polysomnographic study: Correction. *Archives of General Psychiatry, 62*(2), 172.

Brown, G. G. & Thompson, W. K. (2010). Functional brain imaging in schizophrenia: Selected results and methods. In N. R. Swerdlow (ed.), *Behavioral Neurobiology of Schizophrenia and Its Treatment* (pp. 181–214). New York: Springer-Verlag Publishing.

Brown, G. W. (2010). Psychosocial origins of depressive and anxiety disorders. In D. Goldberg, K. S. Kendler, & P. J. Sirovatka (eds), *Diagnostic Issues in Depression and Generalized Anxiety Disorder: Refining the research agenda for DSM-V* (pp. 303–331). Washington: American Psychiatric Association.

Brown, G. W. & Harris, T. O. (1978). *Social Origins of Depression: A study of psychiatric disorder in women*. London: Tavistock.

Brown, R. J., Schrag, A., & Trimble, M. R. (2005). Dissociation, childhood interpersonal trauma, and family functioning in patients with somatization disorder. *American Journal of Psychiatry, 162*(5), 899–905.

Buhlmann, U., Glaesmer, H., Mewes, R., Fama, J. M., Wilhelm, S., Brähler, E., & Rief, W. (2010). Updates on the prevalence of body dysmorphic disorder: A population-based survey. *Psychiatry Research, 178*(1), 171–175.

Bunney, W. E. & Davis, J. M. (1965). Norepinephrine in depressive reactions: A review. *Archives of General Psychiatry, 13*(6), 483–493.

Burijon, B. N. (2007). *Biological Bases of Clinical Anxiety*. New York: W. W. Norton.

Busatto, G. F., Zanetti, M. V., Schaufelberger, M. S., & Crippa, J. A. S. (2009). Brain anatomical abnormalities in schizophrenia: Neurodevelopmental origins and patterns of progression over time. In W. F. Gattaz & G. Busatto (eds), *Advances in Schizophrenia Research 2009* (pp. 113–148). New York: Springer Science + Business Media.

Cepeda, C. (2010). *Clinical Manual for the Psychiatric Interview of Children and Adolescents*. Arlington, VA: American Psychiatric Publishing.

Chang, L. & Krosnick, J. A. (2010). Comparing oral interviewing with self-administered computerized questionnaires: An experiment. *Public Opinion Quarterly, 74*(1), 154–167.

Cicchetti, D. (2010). Developmental psychopathology. In M. E. Lamb, A. M. Freund, & R. M. Lerner (eds), *The Handbook of Life-Span Development: Vol. 2: Social and emotional development* (pp. 511–589). Hoboken, NJ: John Wiley & Sons, Inc.

Clark, D. A. & Beck, A. T. (2010). *Cognitive Therapy of Anxiety Disorders: Science and practice*. New York: Guilford Press.

Clark, D. M. (1986). A cognitive approach to panic. *Behaviour Research and Therapy, 24*(4), 461–470.

Craig, K. J. & Chamberlain, S. R. (2010). The neuropsychology of anxiety disorders. In D. J. Stein, E. Hollander, & B. O. Rothbaum (eds), *Textbook of Anxiety Disorders* (2nd edn; pp. 87–102). Arlington, VA: American Psychiatric Publishing.

Creed, F. (2009). Somatization and pain syndromes. In E. A. Mayer & M. C. Bushnell (eds), *Functional Pain Syndromes: Presentation and pathophysiology* (pp. 227–244). Seattle, WA: IASP Press.

Daitch, C. (2011). *Anxiety Disorders: The go-to guide for clients and therapists*. New York: W. W. Norton.

Davis, R. E., Couper, M. P., Janz, N. K., Caldwell, C. H., & Resnicow, K. (2010). Interviewer effects in public health surveys. *Health Education Research, 25*(1), 14–26.

Day, J. M. (2010). Religion, spirituality, and positive psychology in adulthood: A developmental view. *Journal of Adult Development, 17*(4), 215–229.

Delahanty, D. L., Nugent, N. R., Christopher, N. C., & Walsh, M. (2005). Initial urinary epinephrine and cortisol levels predict acute PTSD symptoms in child trauma victims. *Psychoneuroendocrinology, 30*(2), 121–128.

Didie, E. R., Kuniega-Pietrzak, T., & Phillips, K. A. (2010). Body image in patients with body dysmorphic disorder: Evaluations of and investment in appearance, health/illness, and fitness. *Body Image, 7*(1), 66–69.

Dimsdale, J. E. & Creed, F. H. (2010). The proposed diagnosis of somatic symptom disorders in *DSM-V* to replace somatoform disorders in *DSM-IV*: A preliminary report. *Journal of Psychosomatic Research, 68*(1), 99–100.

Dimsdale, J., Sharma, N., & Sharpe, M. (2011). What do physicians think of somatoform disorders? *Psychosomatics, 52*(2), 154–159.

Doss, B. D., Mitchell, A. E., & De la Garza-Mercer, F. (2008). Marital distress. In M. Hersen & J. Rosqvist (eds), *Handbook of Psychological Assessment, Case Conceptualization, and Treatment: Vol. 1: Adults* (pp. 563–589). Hoboken, NJ: John Wiley & Sons, Inc.

Doucet, S., Jones, I., Letourneau, N., Dennis, C., & Blackmore, E. R. (2011). Interventions for the prevention and treatment of postpartum psychosis: A systematic review. *Archives of Women's Mental Health, 14*(2), 89–98.

Draguns, J. G. (2006). Culture in psychopathology: Psychopathology in culture: Taking a new look at an old problem. In T. G. Plante (ed.), *Mental Disorders of the New Millennium: Vol. 2: Public and social problems*. Westport, CT: Praeger Publishers.

Dudley, K. J., Li, X., Kobor, M. S., Kippin, T. E., & Bredy, T. W. (2011). Epigenetic mechanisms mediating vulnerability and resilience to psychiatric disorders. *Neuroscience and Biobehavioral Reviews, 35*(7), 1544–1551.

Dugas, M. J., Buhr, K., & Ladouceur, R. (2004). The role of intolerance of uncertainty in the etiology and maintenance of generalized anxiety disorder. In R. G. Heimberg, C. L. Turk, & D. S. Mennin (eds), *Generalized Anxiety Disorder: Advances in research and practice* (pp. 143–164). New York: Guilford Press.

Dugas, M. J., Francis, K., & Bouchard, S. (2009). Cognitive behavioural therapy and applied relaxation for generalized anxiety disorder: A time series analysis of change in worry and somatic anxiety. *Cognitive Behaviour Therapy, 38*(1), 29–41.

Dugas, M. J., Marchand, A., & Ladouceur, R. (2005). Further validation of a cognitive-behavioral model of generalized anxiety disorder: Diagnostic and symptom specificity. *Journal of Anxiety Disorders, 19*(3), 329–343.

Ellis, A. (1962). *Reason and Emotion in Psychotherapy*. Secaucus, NJ: Lyle Stuart.

Ellis, A. (2002). The role of irrational beliefs in perfectionism. In G. L. Flett & P. L. Hewitt (eds) *Perfectionism: Theory, research, and treatment* (pp. 217–229). Washington: American Psychological Association.

Ellis, A. (2011). Rational emotive behavior therapy. In R. J. Corsini & D. Wedding (eds), *Current Psychotherapies* (9th edn). Florence, KY: CENGAGE Learning.

El-Mallakh, R. & Huff, M. O. (2001). Mood stabilizers and ion regulation. *Harvard Review of Psychiatry, 9*(1), 23–32.

Endrass, T., Kloft, L., Kaufmann, C., & Kathmann, N. (2011). Approach and avoidance learning in obsessive-compulsive disorder. *Depression and Anxiety, 28*(2), 166–172.

Escobar, J. I. (1995). Transcultural aspects of dissociative and somatoform disorders. *Psychiatric Clinics of North America, 18*(3), 555–569.

Escobar, J. I. (2004). Transcultural aspects of dissociative and somatoform disorders. *Psychiatric Times, 21*(5), 10.

Escobar, J. I., Canino, G., Rubio-Stipec, M., & Bravo, M. (1992). Somatic symptoms after a natural disaster: A prospective study. *American Journal of Psychiatry, 149*(7), 965–967.

Escobar, J. I., Gara, M., Silver, R. C., Waitzkin, H., Holman, A., & Compton, W. (1998). Somatisation disorder in primary care. *British Journal of Psychiatry, 173*, 262–266.

Essau, C. A., Lewinsohn, P. M., Seeley, J. R., & Sasagawa, S. (2010). Gender differences in the developmental course of depression. *Journal of Affective Disorders, 127*(1–3), 185–190.

Etkin, A. (2010). Functional neuroanatomy of anxiety: A neural circuit perspective. *Current Topics in Behavioral Neurosciences, 2*, 251–277.

Evans, J., Heron, J., Lewis, G., Araya, R., & Wolke, D. (2005). Negative self-schemas and the onset of depression in women: Longitudinal study. *British Journal of Psychiatry, 186*(4), 302–307.

Eyler, L. T. (2008). Brain imaging. In K. T. Mueser & D. V. Jeste (eds), *Clinical Handbook of Schizophrenia* (pp. 35–43). New York: Guilford Press.

Fanti, K. A. & Henrich, C. C. (2010). Trajectories of pure and co-occurring internalizing and externalizing problems from age 2 to age 12: Findings from the national institute of child health and human development study of early child care. *Developmental Psychology, 46*(5), 1159–1175.

Feliciano, L. & Gum, A. M. (2010). Mood disorders. In D. L. Segal & M. Hersen (eds), *Diagnostic Interviewing* (pp. 153–176). New York: Springer Publishing.

Fernbach, P., Darlow, A., & Sloman, S. (2011). When good evidence goes bad: The weak evidence effect in judgment and decision-making. *Cognition, 119*(3), 459–467.

Flouri, E., Hickey, J., Mavroveli, S., & Hurry, J. (2011). Adversity, emotional arousal, and problem behaviour in adolescence: The role of non-verbal cognitive ability as a resilience promoting factor. *Child and Adolescent Mental Health, 16*(1), 22–29.

Fox, D. (2010). The insanity virus. *Discover, 31*(5), http://discovermagazine.com/2010/jun/03-the-insanity-virus/, accessed 19 December 2012.

Frost, R. O. & Steketee, G. (2001). Obsessive-compulsive disorder. In H. S. Friedman (ed.), *Specialty Articles from the Encyclopedia of Mental Health*. San Diego: Academic Press.

Gamble, A. L., Harvey, A. G., & Rapee, R. M. (2010). Specific phobia. In D. J. Stein, E. Hollander, & B. O. Rothbaum (eds), *Textbook of Anxiety Disorders* (2nd edn; pp. 525–541). Arlington, VA: American Psychiatric Publishing, Inc.

Gask, L., Aseem, S., Waquas, A., & Waheed, W. (2011). Isolation, feeling 'stuck' and loss of control: Understanding persistence of depression in British Pakistani women. *Journal of Affective Disorders, 128*(1–2), 49–55.

Gaynor, S. T. & Baird, S. C. (2007). Personality disorders. In D. W. Woods & J. W. Kanter (eds), *Understanding Behavior Disorders: A contemporary behavioral perspective*. Reno, NV: Context Press.

Geraerts, E. (2010). Posttraumatic memory. In G. M. Rosen & B. C. Frueh (eds), *Clinician's Guide to Posttraumatic Stress Disorder* (pp. 77–95). Hoboken, NJ: John Wiley & Sons, Inc.

Geraerts, E., Lindsay, D. S., Merckelbach, H., Jelicic, M., Raymaekers, L., Arnold, M. M., & Schooler, J. W. (2009). Cognitive mechanisms underlying recovered-memory experiences of childhood sexual abuse. *Psychological Science, 20*(1), 92–98.

Gerardi, M., Rothbaum, B. O., Astin, M. C., & Kelley, M. (2010). Cortisol response following exposure treatment for PTSD in rape victims. *Journal of Aggression, Maltreatment & Trauma, 19*(4), 349–356.

Gillham, J., Adams-Deutsch, Z., Werner, J., Reivich, K., Coulter-Heindl, V., Linkins, M., & Seligman, M. E. P. (2011). Character strengths predict subjective well-being during adolescence. *Journal of Positive Psychology, 6*(1), 31–44.

Gold, S. N. & Castillo, Y. (2010). Dealing with defenses and defensiveness in interviews. In D. L. Segal & M. Hersen (eds), *Diagnostic Interviewing* (pp. 89–102). New York, Springer Publishing.

Goldenberg, I. & Goldenberg, H. (2011). Family therapy. In R. J. Corsini & D. Wedding (eds), *Current Psychotherapies* (9th edn). Florence, KY: CENGAGE Learning.

Goldstein, D. J., Potter, W. Z., Ciraulo, D. A., & Shader, R. I. (2011). Biological theories of depression and implications for current and new treatments. In D. A. Ciraulo & R. I. Shader (eds), *Pharmacotherapy of Depression* (2nd edn; pp. 1–32). New York: Springer Science + Business Media.

Grieco, R. & Edwards, L. (2010). *The Other Depression: Bipolar disorder* (2nd edn). New York: Routledge/Taylor & Francis Group.

Guimón, J. (2010). Prejudice and realities in stigma. *International Journal of Mental Health, 39*(3), 20–43.

Gunderson, J. G. (2011). Borderline personality disorder. *New England Journal of Medicine, 364*(21), 2037–2042.

Haaken, J. & Reavey, P. (2010). Why memory still matters: Disturbing recollections. In J. Haaken & P. Reavey (eds), *Memory Matters: Contexts for understanding sexual abuse recollections* (pp. 1–13). New York: Routledge/Taylor & Francis Group.

Hammen, C., Kim, E. Y., Eberhart, N. K., & Brennan, P. A. (2009). Chronic and acute stress and the prediction of major depression in women. *Depression and Anxiety, 26*(8), 718–723.

Hammer, T. (1993). Unemployment and mental health among young people: A longitudinal study. *Journal of Adolescence, 16*(4), 407–420.

Hiday, V. A. & Burns, P. J. (2010). Mental illness and the criminal justice system. In T. L. Scheid & T. N. Brown (eds), *A Handbook for the Study of Mental Health: Social contexts, theories, and systems* (2nd edn; pp. 478–498). New York: Cambridge University Press.

Higgins, E. S. & George, M. S. (2007). *The Neuroscience of Clinical Psychiatry: The pathophysiology of behavior and mental illness*. Philadelphia: Wolters Kluwer/Lippincott Williams & Wilkins.

Hinshaw, S. P. (2008). Developmental psychopathology as a scientific discipline: Relevance to behavioral and emotional disorders of childhood and adolescence. In T. P. Beauchaine & S. P. Hinshaw (eds), *Child and Adolescent Psychopathology*. Hoboken, NJ: John Wiley & Sons, Inc.

Holifield, C., Goodman, J., Hazelkorn, M., & Heflin, L. J. (2010). Using self-monitoring to increase attending to task and academic accuracy in children with autism. *Focus on Autism and Other Developmental Disabilities, 25*(4), 230–238.

Holmes, D. A. (2010). *Abnormal, Clinical and Forensic Psychology*. Harlow: Pearson Education.

Hudziak, J. & Bartels, M. (2008). Genetic and environmental influences on wellness, resilience, and psychopathology: A family-based approach for promotion, prevention, and intervention. In J. J. Hudziak (ed.), *Developmental Psychopathology and Wellness: Genetic and environmental influences*. Arlington, VA: American Psychiatric Publishing.

Hunt, N. C. (2010). *Memory, War and Trauma*. New York: Cambridge University Press.

Joiner, T. E., Jr. (2002). Depression in its interpersonal context. In I. H. Gotlib & C. L. Hammen (eds), *Handbook of Depression* (pp. 295–313). New York: Guilford Press.

Kantor, M. (2006). The psychopathy of everyday life. In T. G. Plante (ed.), *Mental Disorders of the New Millennium: Vol. 1: Behavioral issues*. Westport, CT: Praeger Publishers.

Kazdin, A. E. (2005). *Parent Management Training: Treatment for oppositional, aggressive, and antisocial behavior in children and adolescents*. New York: Oxford University Press.

Kendler, K. S., Myers, J., & Prescott, C. A. (2005). Sex differences in the relationship between social support and risk for major depression: A longitudinal study of opposite-sex twin pairs. *American Journal of Psychiatry, 162*(2), 250–256.

Kernberg, O. F. (1997). Convergences and divergences in contemporary psychoanalytic technique and psychoanalytic psychotherapy. In J. K. Zeig (ed.), *The Evolution of Psychotherapy: The third conference*. New York: Brunner/Mazel.

Kernberg, O. F. (2005). Object relations theories and technique. In E. S. Person, A. M. Cooper, & G. O. Gabbard (eds), *The American Psychiatric Publishing Textbook of Psychoanalysis* (pp. 57–75). Washington: American Psychiatric Publishing.

Kessler, R. C. (2002). Epidemiology of depression. In I. H. Gotlib & C. L. Hammen (eds), *Handbook of Depression* (pp. 23–42). New York: Guilford Press.

Kessler, R. C., Berglund, P., Demler, O., Jin, R., & Walters, E. E. (2005a). Lifetime prevalence and age-of-onset distributions of DSM-IV disorders in the National Comorbidity Survey Replication. *Archives of General Psychiatry, 62*(6), 593–602.

Kessler, R. C., Chiu, W. T., Demler, O., & Walters, E. E. (2005b). Prevalence, severity, and comorbidity of twelve-month DSM-IV disorders in the National Comorbidity Survey Replication (NCS-R). *Archives of General Psychiatry, 62*(6), 617–627.

Kessler, R. C., Ruscio, A. M., Shear, K., & Wittchen, H. (2009). Epidemiology of anxiety disorders. In M. M. Antony & M. B. Stein (eds), *Oxford Handbook of Anxiety and Related Disorders* (pp. 19–33). New York: Oxford University Press.

Kessler, R. C., Ruscio, A. M., Shear, K., & Wittchen, H. (2010). Epidemiology of anxiety disorders. In M. B. Stein & T. Steckler (eds), *Behavioral Neurobiology of Anxiety and Its Treatment* (pp. 21–35). New York: Springer Science + Business Media.

Kilic, E. Z., Kilic, E., & Yilmaz, S. (2008). Is anxiety sensitivity a predictor of PTSD in children and adolescents? *Journal of Psychosomatic Research, 65*(1), 81–86.

King, L. (2002, March 19). Interview with Russell Yates. *Larry King Live, CNN*.

Kirmayer, L. J. & Looper, K. J. (2007). Somatoform disorders. In M. Hersen, S. M. Turner, & D. C. Beidel (eds), *Adult Psychopathology and Diagnosis* (5th edn; pp. 410–472). Hoboken, NJ: John Wiley & Sons, Inc.

Kleinman, A. (1987). Anthropology and psychiatry: The role of culture in cross-cultural research on illness. *British Journal of Psychiatry, 151*, 447–454.

Koch, W. J. & Haring, M. (2008). Posttraumatic stress disorder. In M. Hersen & J. Rosqvist (eds), *Handbook of Psychological Assessment, Case Conceptualization, and Treatment: Vol. 1: Adults* (pp. 263–290). Hoboken, NJ: John Wiley & Sons, Inc.

Kuhn, T. S. (1962). *The Structure of Scientific Revolutions*. Chicago: University of Chicago Press.

Kulka, R. A., Schlesenger, W. E., Fairbank, J. A., Hough, R. L., Jordan, B. K., Marmar, C. R., *et al.* (1990). *Trauma and the Vietnam War Generation: Report of findings from the National Vietnam Veterans Readjustment Study*. New York: Brunner/Mazel.

Lahmann, C., Henningsen, P., & Noll-Hussong, M. (2010). Somatoforme schmerzen: Ein überblick. *Psychiatria Danubina, 22*(3), 453–458.

Lane, K. L., Menzies, H. M., Bruhn, A. L., & Crnobori, M. (2011). *Managing Challenging Behaviors in Schools: Research-based strategies that work*. New York: Guilford Press.

Langdon, R., Ward, P., & Coltheart, M. (2010). Reasoning anomalies associated with delusions in schizophrenia. *Schizophrenial Bulletin, 36*(2), 321–330.

Leichsenring, F., Leibing, E., Kruse, J., New, A. S., & Leweke, F. (2011). Borderline personality disorder. *The Lancet, 377*(9759), 74–84.

Leon, G. R. (1977). *Case Histories of Deviant Behavior* (2nd edn). Boston: Allyn & Bacon.

Lindert, J., Schouler-Ocak, M., Heinz, A., & Priebe, S. (2008). Mental health, health care utilisation of migrants in Europe. *Journal of European Psychiatry, 23*, 14–20.

Lindhiem, O., Bernard, K., & Dozier, M. (2011). Maternal sensitivity: Within-person variability and the utility of multiple assessments. *Child Maltreatment, 16*(1), 41–50.

Linehan, M. M. & Dexter-Mazza, E. (2008). Dialectical behavior therapy for borderline personality disorder. In D. H. Barlow (ed.), *Clinical Handbook of Psychological Disorders: A step-by-step treatment manual* (4th edn; pp. 365–420). New York: Guilford Press.

Lipton, A. A. & Simon, F. S. (1985). Psychiatric diagnosis in a state hospital: Manhattan State revisited. *Hospital & Community Psychiatry, 36*(4), 368–373.

Litschge, C. M., Vaughn, M. G., & McCrea, C. (2010). The empirical status of treatments for children and youth with conduct problems: An overview of meta-analytic studies. *Research on Social Work Practice, 20*(1), 21–35.

Livesley, W. J. (ed.) (2001). *Handbook of Personality Disorders*. New York: Guilford Press.

Loftus, E. F. & Cahill, L. (2007). Memory distortion: From misinformation to rich false memory. In J. S. Nairne (ed.), *The Foundations of Remembering: Essays in honor of Henry L. Roediger, III*. New York: Psychology Press.

Makkar, S., Zhang, S., & Cranney, J. (2010). Behavioral and neural analysis of GABA in the acquisition, consolidation, reconsolidation, and extinction of fear memory. *Neuropsychopharmacology, 35*, 1625–1652.

Marques, L., LeBlanc, N., Weingarden, H., Greenberg, J. L., Traeger, L. N., Keshaviah, A., & Wilhelm, S. (2011). Body dysmorphic symptoms: Phenomenology and ethnicity. *Body Image, 8*(2), 163–167.

Makkar, S., Zhang, S., & Cranney, J. (2010). Behavioral and neural analysis of GABA in the acquisition, consolidation, reconsolidation, and extinction of fear memory. *Neuropsychopharmacology, 35*, 1625–1652.

Marshall, T., Jones, D. P. H., Ramchandani, P. G., Stein, A., & Bass, C. (2007). Intergenerational transmission of health benefits in somatoform disorders. *British Journal of Psychiatry, 191*(4), 449–450.

Martin, E. I. & Nemeroff, C. B. (2010). The biology of generalized anxiety disorder and major depressive disorder: Commonalities and distinguishing features. In D. Goldberg, K. S. Kendler, & P. J. Sirovatka (eds), *Diagnostic Issues in Depression and Generalized Anxiety Disorder: Refining the research agenda for DSM-V* (pp. 45–70). Washington: American Psychiatric Association.

Marx, B. P. & Sloan, D. M. (2005). Peritraumatic dissociation and experimental avoidance as predictors of posttraumatic stress symptomatology. *Behavioral Research and Therapy, 43*(5), 569–583.

Maslow, A. (1970). *Motivation and Personality* (2nd edn). New York: Harper & Row.

Mason, P. T. & Kreger, R. (2010). *Stop Walking on Eggshells: Taking your life back when someone you care about has borderline personality disorder* (2nd edn). Oakland, CA: New Harbinger Publications.

Matsumoto, D. & Juang, L. (2008). *Culture and Psychology* (4th edn). Victoria, Australia: Thomson Wadsworth.

Matsumoto, D. & van de Vijver, F. J. R. (eds) (2011). *Cross-Cultural Research Methods in Psychology*. New York: Cambridge University Press.

McClure, E. B., Monk, C. S., Nelson, E. E., Parrish, J. M., Adler, A., Blair, R. J., *et al.* (2007). Abnormal attention modulation of fear circuit function in pediatric generalized anxiety disorder. *Archives of General Psychiatry, 64*, 97–106.

McGowan, S., Lawrence, A. D., Sales, T., Quested, D., & Grasby P. (2004). Presynaptic dopaminergic dysfunction in schizophrenia: A positron emission tomography [18F] fluorodopa study. *Archives of General Psychiatry, 61*, 134–142.

McGuffin, P., Katz, R., Watkins, S., & Rutherford, J. (1996). A hospital-based twin register of the heritability of DSM-IV unipolar depression. *Archives of General Psychiatry, 53*, 129–136.

McKay, D., Gosselin, J. T., & Gupta, S. (2008). Body dysmorphic disorder. In J. S. Abramowitz, D. McKay, & S. Taylor (eds), *Obsessive-Compulsive Disorder: Subtypes and spectrum conditions*. Oxford: Elsevier.

McNally, R. J. (2001). Vulnerability to anxiety disorders in adulthood. In R. E. Ingram & J. M. Price (eds), *Vulnerability to Psychopathology: Risk across the lifespan* (pp. 304–321). New York: Guilford Press.

McNally, R. J. & Geraerts, E. (2009). A new solution to the recovered memory debate. *Perspectives on Psychological Science, 4*(2), 126–134.

Melville, J. (1978). *Phobias and Obsessions*. New York: Penguin.

Merikangas, K. R., Akiskal, H. S., Angst, J., Greenberg, P. E., Hirschfeld, R. M. A., Petukhova, M., *et al.* (2007). Lifetime and 12-month prevalence of bipolar spectrum disorder in the National Comorbidity Survey Replication. *Archives of General Psychiatry, 64*(5), 543–552.

Miller, R. & Mason, S. E. (2011). *Diagnosis: Schizophrenia: A comprehensive resource for consumers, families, and helping professionals* (2nd edn). New York: Columbia University Press.

Millon, T. (2011). *Disorders of Personality: Introducing a DSM/ICD spectrum from normal to abnormal* (3rd edn). Hoboken, NJ: John Wiley & Sons, Inc.

Mitchell, A. J. (2010). Overview of depression scales and tools. In A. J. Mitchell & J. C. Coyne (eds), *Screening for Depression in Clinical Practice: An evidence-based guide* (pp. 29–56). New York: Oxford University Press.

Mitchell, C. M., Kaufman, C. E., Beals, J., *et al.* (2004). Equifinality and multifinality as guides for prevention interventions: HIV risk/protection among American Indian young adults. *Journal of Primary Prevention, 25*(4), 491–510.

Monroe, S. M. & Hadjiyannakis, K. (2002). The social environment and depression: Focusing on severe life stress. In I. H. Gotlib & C. L. Hammen (eds), *Handbook of Depression: Research and treatment* (pp. 314–340). New York: Guilford Press.

Morgan, A. B. & Lilienfeld, S. O. (2000). A meta-analytic review of the relation between antisocial behavior and neuropsychological measures of executive function. *Clinical Psychology Review, 20*, 113–136.

Mowery, J. M., Miltenberger, R. G., & Weil, T. M. (2010). Evaluating the effects of reactivity to supervisor presence on staff response to tactile prompts and self-monitoring in a group home setting. *Behavioral Interventions, 25*(1), 21–35.

Neckelmann, D., Mykletun, A., & Dahl, A. A. (2007). Chronic insomnia as a risk factor for developing anxiety and depression. *Sleep, 30*(7), 873–880.

Nelson, B. D. & Shankman, S. A. (2011). Does intolerance of uncertainty predict anticipatory startle responses to uncertain threat? *International Journal of Psychophysiology, 81*(2), 107–115.

Neumeister, A., Charney, D. S., & Drevets, W. C. (2005). Hippocampus, VI: Depression and the hippocampus. *American Journal of Psychiatry, 162*(6), 1057.

Nickel, R., Ademmer, K., & Egle, U. T. (2010). Manualized psychodynamic-interactional group therapy for the treatment of somatoform pain disorders. *Bulletin of the Menninger Clinic, 74*(3), 219–237.

North, C. S. (2005). Somatoform disorders. In E. H. Rubin & C. F. Zorumski (eds), *Adult Psychiatry* (2nd edn; pp. 261–274). Oxford: Blackwell Publishing.

Norton, P. J., Grills-Taquechel, A., & Raouf, M. (2010). Assessing adults. In D. W. Nangle, D. J. Hansen, C. A. Erdley, & P. J. Norton (eds), *Practitioner's Guide to Empirically Based Measures of Social Skills* (pp. 87–98). New York: Springer Publishing.

Noyes, R. (2008). Hypochondriasis. In M. Gelder, N. Andreasen, J. Lopez-Ibor, & J. Geddes (eds), *New Oxford Textbook of Psychiatry: Vol. 2* (2nd edn). New York: Oxford University Press.

O'Connor, B. P. (2008). Other personality disorders. In M. Hersen & J. Rosqvist (eds), *Handbook of Psychological Assessment, Case Conceptualization, and Treatment: Vol. 1: Adults* (pp. 438–462). Hoboken, NJ: John Wiley & Sons, Inc.

Oksenberg, J. R. & Hauser, S. L. (2010). Mapping the human genome with new found precision. *Annals of Neurology, 67*(6), A8–10.

Osman, A., Barrios, F. X., Gutierrez, P. M., Williams, J. E., & Bailey, J. (2008). Psychometric properties of the Beck Depression Inventory-II in nonclinical adolescent samples. *Journal of Clinical Psychology, 64*(10), 83–102.

Ovsiew, F. (2006). Hysteria in neurological practice: The somatoform and dissociative disorders. In D. V. Jeste & J. H. Friedman (eds), *Psychiatry for Neurologists* (pp. 67–80). Totowa, NJ: Humana Press.

Ozer, E. J. (2005). The impact of violence on urban adolescents: Longitudinal effects of perceived school connection and family support. *Journal of Adolescent Research, 20*(2), 167–192.

Paris, J. (2010). Estimating the prevalence of personality disorders in the community. *Journal of Personality Disorders, 24*(4), 405–411.

Patrick, C. J. (2007). Antisocial personality disorder and psychopathy. In W. O'Donohue, K. A. Fowler, & S. O. Lilienfeld (eds), *Personality Disorders: Toward the DSM-V* (pp. 109–166). Thousand Oaks, CA: Sage Publications.

Patterson, D. (2011). The linkage between secondary victimization by law enforcement and rape case outcomes. *Journal of Interpersonal Violence, 26*(2), 328–347.

Paykel, E. S. (2003). Life events: Effects and genesis. *Psychological Medicine, 33*(7), 1145–1148.

Paykel, E. S. (2006). Editorials: Depression: Major problem for public health. *Epidemiologiae Psichiatria Sociale, 15*(1), 4–10.

Perdeci, Z., Gulsun, M., Celik, C., Erdem, M., Ozdemir, B., Ozdag, F., & Kilic, S. (2010). Aggression and the event-related potentials in antisocial personality disorder. *Klinik Psikofarmakoloji Bülteni, 20*(4), 300–306.

Perilla, J. L., Norris, F. H., & Lavizzo, E. A. (2002). Ethnicity, culture, and disaster response: Identifying and explaining ethnic differences in PTSD six months after Hurricane Andrew. *Journal of Social and Clinical Psychology, 21*, 20–45.

Peterlin, B. L., Rosso, A. L., Sheftell, F. D., Libon, D. J., Mossey, J. M., & Merikangas, K. R. (2011). Post-traumatic stress disorder, drug abuse and migraine: New findings from the national comorbidity survey replication (NCS-R). *Cephalalgia, 31*(2), 235–244.

Phillips, K. A. (2005). Placebo-controlled study of pimozide augmentation of fluoxetine in body dysmorphic disorder. *American Journal of Psychiatry, 162*(2), 377–379.

Phillips, K. A. & Castle, D. J. (2002). Body dysmorphic disorder. In D. J. Castle & K. A. Phillips (eds), *Disorders of Body Image.* Petersfield: Wrightson Biomedical Publishing.

Pierre, J. M. (2010). The borders of mental disorder in psychiatry and DSM: Past, present, and future. *Journal of Psychiatric Practice, 16*(6), 375–386.

Pope, H. G., Jr., Poliakoff, M. B., Parker, M. P., Boynes, M., & Hudson, J. I. (2007). Is dissociative amnesia a culture-bound syndrome? Findings from a survey of historical literature. *Psychological Medicine, 37*(2), 225–233.

Posmontier, B. (2010). The role of midwives in facilitating recovery in postpartum psychosis. *Journal of Midwifery & Women's Health, 55*(5), 430–437.

Post, R. M. & Miklowitz, D. J. (2010). The role of stress in the onset, course, and progression of bipolar illness and its comorbidities: Implications for therapeutics. In D. J. Miklowitz & D. Cicchetti (eds), *Understanding Bipolar Disorder: A developmental psychopathology perspective* (pp. 370–413). New York: Guilford Press.

Prochaska, J. O. & Norcross, J. C. (2010). *Systems of Psychotherapy: A transtheoretical analysis* (7th edn). Pacific Grove, CA: Brooks/Cole.

RAND Corporation. (2008). 1 in 5 Iraq, Afghanistan vets has PTSD, major depression. *Science Blog.* Retrieved May 19, 2008, http://www.science blog.com/cms/1-5-iraq-afghanistan-vet-has-ptsd-major-depression -rand-15954.html, accessed 19 December 2012.

RAND Corporation. (2010). *Studies' Estimates of PTSD Prevalence Rates for Returning Service Members Vary Widely: Research Briefs.* Santa Monica, CA: RAND Corporation.

Raskin, N. J., Rogers, C., & Witty, M. (2011). Person-centered therapy. In R. J. Corsini & D. Wedding (eds), *Current Psychotherapies* (9th edn), Florence, KY: CENGAGE Learning.

Ravindran, L. N. & Stein, M. B. (2011). Pharmacotherapy for social anxiety disorder in adolescents and young adults. In C. A. Alfano & D. C. Beidel (eds), *Social Anxiety in Adolescents and Young Adults: Translating developmental science into practice* (pp. 265–279). Washington: American Psychological Association.

Regier D. A., Narrow W. E., Kuhl E. A., & Kupfer D. J. (eds) (2011). *The Conceptual Evolution of DSM-5.* Arlington, VA: American Psychiatric Publishing.

Reinecke, A., Cooper, M., Favaron, E., Massey-Chase, R., & Harmer, C. (2011). Attentional bias in untreated panic disorder. *Psychiatry Research, 185*(3), 387–393.

Richard, I. H. & Lyness, J. M. (2006). An overview of depression. In D. V. Jeste & J. H. Friedman (eds), *Psychiatry for Neurologists* (pp. 33–42). Totowa, NJ: Humana Press.

Ridout, N., Astell, A. J., Reid, I. C., Glen, T., & O'Carroll, R. E. (2003). Memory bias for emotional facial expressions in major depression. *Cognition and Emotion, 17*(1), 101–122.

Rieber, R. W. (2002). The duality of the brain and the multiplicity of minds: Can you have it both ways? *History of Psychiatry 13*(49), 3–18.

Rieber, R. W. (2006). *The Bifurcation of the Self: The history and theory of dissociation and its disorders.* New York: Springer Science + Business Media.

Ritter, M. R., Blackmore, M. A., & Heimberg, R. G. (2010). Generalized anxiety disorder. In D. McKay, J. S. Abramowitz, & S. Taylor (eds),

Cognitive-Behavioral Therapy for Refractory Cases: Turning failure into success (pp. 111–137). Washington: American Psychological Association.

Robila, M. (2010). *Eastern European Immigrant Families*. Oxford: Routledge.

Rocca, P., Aimetti, M., Giugiario, M., Pigella, E., Romano, F., Crivelli, B., & Bogetto, F. (2010). The complaint of oral malodour: Psychopathological and personality profiles. *Psychotherapy and Psychosomatics, 79*(6), 392–394.

Rogers, C. R. (1951). *Client-Centered Therapy*. Boston: Houghton Mifflin.

Rogers, C. R. (1987). Rogers, Kohut, and Erickson: A personal perspective on some similarities and differences. In J. K. Zeig (ed.), *The Evolution of Psychotherapy*. New York: Brunner/Mazel.

Rogers, C. R. (2000). Interview with Carl Rogers on the use of the self in therapy. In M. Baldwin (ed.), *The Use of Self in Therapy* (2nd edn; pp. 29–38). Binghamton, NY: Haworth.

Rosenberg, L. (2011). Mental health first aid: A "radical efficiency" in health promotion. *Journal of Behavioural Health Services & Research, 38*(2), 143–145.

Roy-Byrne, P. P. (2005). The GABA-benzodiazepine receptor complex: Structure, function, and role in anxiety. *Journal of Clinical Psychiatry, 66*(suppl. 2), 14–20.

Ruzek, J. I., Schnurr, P. P., Vasterling, J. J., & Friedman, M. J. (eds) (2011). *Caring for Veterans with Deployment-Related Stress Disorders*. Washington: American Psychological Association.

Salkovskis, P. M. (1985). Obsessional-compulsive problems: A cognitive-behavioural analysis. *Behavioral Research and Therapy, 23*, 571–584.

Salkovskis, P. M. (1999). Understanding and treating obsessive-compulsive disorder. *Behavioral Research and Therapy, 37*(suppl. 1), S29–S52.

Salkovskis, P. M., Thorpe, S. J., Wahl, K., Wroe, A. L., & Forrester, E. (2003). Neutralizing increases discomfort associated with obsessional thoughts: An experimental study with obsessional patients. *Journal of Abnormal Psychology, 112*(4), 709–715.

SAMHSA (Substance Abuse and Mental Health Services Administration). (2010). Mental health and mental disorders. In NIMH (National Institute of Mental Health), *Healthy People 2010*. Washington, DC: Department of Health and Human Services.

Santostefano, S. (2010). Developmental psychopathology: Self, embodiment, meaning: A holistic-systems perspective. In W. F. Overton & R. M. Lerner (eds), *The Handbook of Life-Span Development: Vol. 1: Cognition, biology, and methods* (pp. 792–836). Hoboken, NJ: John Wiley & Sons, Inc.

Sareen, J., Afifi, T. O., McMillan, K. A., & Asmundson, G. J. G. (2011). Relationship between household income and mental disorders: Findings from a population-based longitudinal study. *Archives of General Psychiatry, 68*(4), 419–426.

Schienle, A., Hettema, J. M., Cáceda, R., & Nemeroff, C. B. (2011). Neurobiology and genetics of generalized anxiety disorder. *Psychiatric Annals, 41*(2), 113–123.

Schildkraut, J. J. (1965). The catecholamine hypothesis of affective disorders: A review of supporting evidence. *American Journal of Psychiatry, 122*(5), 509–522.

Schneider, K. J. & Krug, O. T. (2010). *Existential–Humanistic Therapy*. Washington: American Psychological Association.

Schultz, L. T., Heimberg, R. G., & Rodebaugh, T. L. (2008). Social anxiety disorder. In M. Hersen & J. Rosqvist (eds), *Handbook of Psychological Assessment, Case Conceptualization, and Treatment: Vol. 1: Adults* (pp. 204–236). Hoboken, NJ: John Wiley & Sons, Inc.

Schultz, L. T., Heimberg, R. G., Rodebaugh, T. L., Schneier, F. R., Liebowitz, M. R., & Telch, M. J. (2006). The Appraisal of Social Concerns scale: Psychometric validation with a clinical sample of patients with social anxiety disorder. *Behavior Therapy, 37*(4), 393–405.

Schulze, T. G. & McMahon, F. J. (2009). The genetic basis of bipolar disorder. In C. A. Zarate Jr. & H. K. Manji (eds), *Bipolar Depression: Molecular neurobiology, clinical diagnosis and pharmacotherapy* (pp. 59–76). Cambridge, MA: Birkhäuser.

Segal D. L. & Hersen M. (eds) (2010). *Diagnostic Interviewing*. New York: Springer Publishing.

Seligman, M. E. P. (1975). *Helplessness*. San Francisco: W. H. Freeman.

Seligman, M. E. P. (1992). Power and powerlessness: Comments on 'cognates of personal control'. *Applied & Preventive Psychology, 1*(2), 119–120.

Shafran, R. (2005). Cognitive-behavioral models of OCD. In J. S. Abramowitz & A. C. Houts (eds), *Concepts and Controversies in Obsessive-Compulsive Disorder*. New York: Springer Science + Business Media.

Sharf, R. S. (2012). *Theories of Psychotherapy & Counseling: Concepts and cases* (5th edn). Pacific Grove, CA: Brooks/Cole.

Sherry, A. & Whilde, M. R. (2008). Borderline personality disorder. In M. Hersen & J. Rosqvist (eds), *Handbook of Psychological Assessment, Case Conceptualization and Treatment: Vol. 1: Adults* (pp. 403–437). Hoboken, NJ: John Wiley & Sons, Inc.

Shorter, E. (1997). *A History of Psychiatry: From the era of the asylum to the age of Prozac*. Chichester: John Wiley & Sons.

Sikstrom, S. & Soderlund, G. (2007). Stimulus-dependent dopamine release in attention-deficit/hyperactivity disorder. *Psychological Review, 114*(4), 1047–1075.

So, J. K. (2008). Somatization as cultural idiom of distress: Rethinking mind and body in a multicultural society. *Counselling Psychology Quarterly, 21*(2), 167–174.

Spanos, N. P. (1996). *Multiple Identities & False Memories: A sociocognitive perspective*. Washington: American Psychological Association.

Spitzer, R. L., Skodol, A., Gibbon, M., & Williams, J. B. W. (1983). *Psychopathology: A case book*. New York: McGraw-Hill.

Spitzer, R. L., Skodol, A., Gibbon, M., & Williams, J. B. W. (1981). *DSM-III Case Book*. Washington: American Psychiatric Press.

Spooren, W., Lesage, A., Lavreysen, H., Gasparini, F., & Steckler, T. (2010). Metabotropic glutamate receptors: Their therapeutic potential in anxiety. In M. B. Stein. & T. Steckler (eds), *Behavioral Neurobiology of Anxiety and Its Treatment* (pp. 391–413). New York: Springer Science + Business Media.

Stein, D. J. & Fineberg, N. A. (2007). *Obsessive-Compulsive Disorder*. Oxford: Oxford University Press.

Stein, D. J. & Williams, D. (2010). Cultural and social aspects of anxiety disorders. In D. J. Stein, E. Hollander, & B. O. Rothbaum (eds), *Textbook of Anxiety Disorders* (2nd edn; pp. 717–729). Arlington, VA: American Psychiatric Publishing.

Steketee, G. & Frost, R. O. (2007). *Treatment of Compulsive Hoarding*. New York: Oxford University Press.

Tamminga, C. A., Shad, M. U., & Ghose, S. (2008). Neuropsychiatric aspects of schizophrenia. In S. C. Yudofsky & R. E. Hales (eds), *The American Psychiatric Publishing Textbook of Neuropsychiatry and Behavioral Neurosciences* (5th edn). Washington: American Psychiatric Publishing.

Taube-Schiff, M. & Lau, M. A. (2008). Major depressive disorder. In M. Hersen & J. Rosqvist (eds), *Handbook of Psychological Assessment, Case Conceptualization, and Treatment: Vol. 1: Adults* (pp. 319–351). Hoboken, NJ: John Wiley & Sons, Inc.

Taylor, S. E. (2006). Tend and befriend: Biobehavioral bases of affiliation under stress. *Current Directions in Psychological Science, 15*(6), 273–277.

Taylor, S. E. (2010). Health psychology. In R. F. Baumeister & E. J. Finkel (eds), *Advanced Social Psychology: The state of the science* (pp. 697–731). New York: Oxford University Press.

Uchino, B. N. & Birmingham, W. (2011). Stress and support processes. In R. J. Contrada & A. Baum (eds), *The Handbook of Stress Science: Biology, psychology, and health*. New York: Springer Publishing.

Ungar, W. J., Mirabelli, C., Cousins, M., & Boydell, K. M. (2006). A qualitative analysis of a dyad approach to health-related quality of life measurement in children with asthma. *Social Science and Medicine, 63*(9), 2354–2366.

Van Wagner, K. (2007). Phobia list: An A to Z list of phobias. *About.com*. Retrieved 22 July 2008, from http://psychology.about.com/ od/. phobias/a/phobialist.htm.

Vega, W. A., Ang, A., Rodriguez, M. A., & Finch, B. K. (2011). Neighborhood protective effects on depression in Latinos. *American Journal of Community Psychology, 47*(1–2), 114–126.

Waraich, P., Goldner, E. M., Somers, J. M., & Lorena Hsu, L. (2004). Prevalence and incidence studies of mood disorders: A systematic review of the literature. *Canadian Journal of Psychiatry, 49*(2), 124–138.

Watson, J. C., Goldman, R. N., & Greenberg, L. S. (2011). Humanistic and experiential theories of psychotherapy. In J. C. Norcross, G. R. VandenBos, & D. K. Freedheim (eds), *History of Psychotherapy: Continuity and change* (2nd edn; pp. 141–172). Washington: American Psychological Association.

Weeks, D. & James, J. (1995). *Eccentrics: A study of sanity and strangeness.* New York: Villard.

Weinstein, Y. & Shanks, D. R. (2010). Rapid induction of false memory for pictures. *Memory, 18*(5), 533–542.

Weissman, M. M., Livingston, B. M., Leaf, P. J., Florio, L. P., & Holzer, C., III. (1991). Affective disorders. In L. N. Robins & D. A. Regier (eds), *Psychiatric Disorders in America: The Epidemiologic Catchment Area Study.* New York: Free Press.

Wenzel, A. (2011). Panic attacks. In *Anxiety in Childbearing Women: Diagnosis and treatment* (pp. 73–90). Washington: American Psychological Association.

Westen, D., Betan, E., & Defife, J. A. (2011). Identity disturbance in adolescence: Associations with borderline personality disorder. *Development and Psychopathology, 23*(1), 305–313.

Whipple, R. & Fowler, J. C. (2011). Affect, relationship schemas, and social cognition: Self-injuring borderline personality disorder inpatients. *Psychoanalytic Psychology, 28*(2), 183–195.

Whisman, M. A. & McGarvey, A. L. (1995). Attachment, depressotypic cognitions, and dysphoria. *Cognitive Therapy and Research, 19*(6), 633–650.

Williams, J. B. (1996). *Structured Interview Guide for the Hamilton Depression Rating Scale (SIGH-D).* New York: New York State Psychiatric Institute.

Williams, P. G. (2004). The psychopathology of self-assessed health: A cognitive approach to health anxiety and hypochondriasis. *Cognitive Therapy and Research, 28,* 629–644.

Wilson, G. T. (2011). Behavior therapy. In R. J. Corsini & D. Wedding (eds), *Current Psychotherapies* (9th edn). Florence, KY: CENGAGE Learning.

Wilson, K. A. & Hayward, C. (2005). A prospective evaluation of agoraphobia and depression symptoms following panic attacks in a community sample of adolescents. *Journal of Anxiety Disorders, 19*(1), 87–103.

Wilson, K. R., Jordan, J. A., Kras, A. M., Tavkar, P., Bruhn, S., Asawa, L. E., & Trask, E. (2010). Adolescent measures. In D. W. Nangle, D. J. Hansen, C. A. Erdley, & P. J. Norton (eds), *Practitioner's Guide to Empirically Based Measures of Social Skills* (pp. 327–381). New York: Springer Publishing.

Witthöft, M. & Hiller, W. (2010). Psychological approaches to origins and treatments of somatoform disorders. *Annual Review of Clinical Psychology, 6,* 257–283.

Worley, L. L. M. (2010). Review of *Understanding postpartum psychosis: A temporary madness. Psychosomatics: Journal of Consultation Liaison Psychiatry, 51*(2), 181.

Yalom, I. & Josselson, R. (2011). Existential psychotherapy. In R. J. Corsini & D. Wedding (eds), *Current Psychotherapies* (9th edn). Florence, KY: CENGAGE Learning.

Yehuda, R., Flory, J. D., Pratchett, L. C., Buxbaum, J., Ising, M., & Holsboer, F. (2010). Putative biological mechanisms for the association between early life adversity and the subsequent development of PTSD. *Psychopharmacologia, 212*(3), 405–417.

Yu, D. L. & Seligman, M. E. P. (2002). Preventing depressive symptoms in Chinese children. *Prevention and Treatment, 5,* no pages.

Yutzy, S. H. (2007). Somatoform disorders. In S. C. Yudofsky, J. A. Bourgeois, & R. E. Hales (eds), *The American Psychiatric Publishing Board Prep and Review Guide for Psychiatry* (pp. 235–243). Washington: American Psychiatric Publishing.

Zuckerman, M. (2011). *Personality Science: Three approaches and their applications to the causes and treatment of depression* (pp. 123–148). Washington: American Psychological Association.

CHAPTER 20

Alexander, J. F., Sexton, T. L., & Robbins, M. S. (2002). The developmental status of family therapy in family psychology intervention science. In H. A. Liddle, D. A. Santiseban, R. F. Levant, & J. H. Bray (eds), *Family Psychology: Science-based interventions* (pp. 17–40). Washington: American Psychological Association.

Althouse, R. (2010). Jails are nation's largest institutions for mentally ill. *National Psychologist, 19*(6), 1–5.

Antony, M. M. (2011). Recent advances in the treatment of anxiety disorders. *Canadian Psychology/Psychologie Canadienne, 52*(1), 1–9.

Aten, J. D., McMinn, M. R., & Worthington, E. L., Jr. (2011). *Spiritually Oriented Interventions for Counseling and Psychotherapy.* Washington: American Psychological Association.

Ayllon, T. & Azrin, N. H. (1965). The measurement and reinforcement of behavior of psychotics. *Journal of the Experimental Analysis of Behavior, 8*(6), 357–383.

Ayllon, T. & Azrin, N. (1968). *The Token Economy: A motivational system for therapy and rehabilitation.* East Norwalk, CT: Appleton-Century-Crofts.

Bandura, A. (1969). *Principles of Behavior Modification.* Oxford: Holt, Rinehart & Winston.

Bandura, A. (1977). Self-efficacy: Toward a unifying theory of behavioral change. *Psychological Review, 84*(2), 191–215.

Bandura, A., Adams, N. E., & Beyer, J. (1977). Cognitive processes mediating behavioral change. *Journal of Personality and Social Psychology, 35*(3), 125–139.

Barahal, H. S. (1958). 1000 prefrontal lobotomies: A five to ten year follow-up study. *Psychiatric Quarterly, 32,* 653–690.

Barrowclough, C. & Lobban, F. (2008). Family intervention. In K. T. Mueser & D. V. Jeste (eds), *Clinical Handbook of Schizophrenia* (pp. 214–225). New York: Guilford Press.

Baucom, B. R., Atkins, D. C., Simpson, L. E., & Christensen, A. (2009). Prediction of response to treatment in a randomized clinical trial of couple therapy: A 2-year follow-up. *Journal of Consulting and Clinical Psychology, 77*(1), 160–173.

Baucom, D. H., Epstein, N. B., Kirby, J. S., & LaTaillade, J. J. (2010). Cognitive-behavioral couple therapy. In K. S. Dobson (ed.), *Handbook of Cognitive-Behavioral Therapies* (3rd edn; pp. 411–444). New York: Guilford Press.

Beck, A. T. & Weishaar, M. (2011). Cognitive therapy. In R. J. Corsini & D. Wedding (eds), *Current Psychotherapies* (9th edn). Florence, KY: CENGAGE Learning.

Beck, A. T., Rush, A. J., Shaw, B. F., & Emery, G. (1979). *Cognitive Therapy of Depression.* New York: Guilford Press.

Beutler, L. E. (2002). The dodo bird is extinct. *Clinical Psychology: Science and practice, 9*(1), 30–34.

Beutler, L. E. (2011). Prescriptive matching and systematic treatment selection. In J. C. Norcross, G. R. VandenBos, & D. K. Freedheim (eds), *History of Psychotherapy: Continuity and change* (2nd edn; pp. 402–407). Washington: American Psychological Association.

Beutler, L. E., Harwood, T. M., Kimpara, S., Verdirame, D., & Blau, K. (2011). Coping style. *Journal of Clinical Psychology, 67*(2), 176–183.

Bickman, L. (2005). A common factors approach to improving mental health services. *Mental Health Services Research, 7*(1), 1–4.

Blomstedt, P., Sjöberg, R. L., Hansson, M., Bodlund, O., & Hariz, M. I. (2011). Deep brain stimulation in the treatment of depression. *Acta Psychiatrica Scandinavica, 123*(1), 4–11.

Bohart, A. C. & Tallman, K. (2010). Clients: The neglected common factor in psychotherapy. In B. L. Duncan, S. D. Miller, B. E. Wampold, & M. A. Hubble (eds), *The Heart and Soul of Change: Delivering what works in therapy* (2nd edn; pp. 83–111). Washington: American Psychological Association.

Borzekowski, D. L. G., Schenk, S., Wilson, J. L., & Peebles, R. (2010). e-ana and e-mia: A content analysis of pro-eating disorder web sites. *American Journal of Public Health, 100*(8), 1526–1534.

Brown, L. S. (2011). Client diversity in psychotherapy. In J. C. Norcross, G. R. VandenBos, & D. K. Freedheim (eds), *History of Psychotherapy: Continuity and change* (2nd edn; pp. 475–483). Washington: American Psychological Association.

Burlingame, G. M. & Baldwin, S. (2011). Group therapy. In J. C. Norcross, G. R. VandenBos, & D. K. Freedheim (eds), *History of Psychotherapy: Continuity and change* (2nd edn; pp. 505–515). Washington: American Psychological Association.

Burns, T. & Drake, B. (2011). Mental health services for patients with schizophrenia. In D. R. Weinberger & P. J. Harrison (eds), *Schizophrenia* (3rd edn). Hoboken, NJ: Blackwell-Wiley.

Cain, D. J. (2007). What every therapist should know, be and do: Contributions from humanistic psychotherapies. *Journal of Contemporary Psychotherapy, 37*(1), 3–10.

Calogero, R. M., Tantleff-Dunn, S., and Thompson, J. K. (eds) (2011). *Self-Objectification in Women: Causes, consequences, and counteractions.* Washington: American Psychological Association.

Christensen, A., Atkins, D. C., Baucom, B., & Yi, J. (2010). Marital status and satisfaction five years following a randomized clinical trial comparing traditional versus integrative behavioral couple therapy. *Journal of Consulting and Clinical Psychology, 78*(2), 225–235.

Clanton Harpine, E. (2011). *Group-Centered Prevention Programs for At-Risk Students.* New York: Springer Science + Business Media.

Comas-Diaz, L. (2006). Cultural variation in the therapeutic relationship. In C. D. Goodheart, A. E. Kazdin, & R. J. Sternberg (eds), *Evidence-Based Psychotherapy: Where practice and research meet* (pp. 81–105). Washington: American Psychological Association.

Comas-Diaz, L. (2011). Multicultural psychotherapies. In R. J. Corsini & D. Wedding (eds), *Current Psychotherapies* (9th edn). Florence, KY: CENGAGE Learning.

Cooney, N. L., Kadden, R. M., Litt, M. D., & Getter, H. (1991). Matching alcoholics to coping skills or interactional therapies: Two-year follow-up results. *Journal of Consulting and Clinical Psychology, 59*(4), 598–601.

Coontz, S. (2004). The world historical transformation of marriage. *Journal of Marriage and Family, 66*(4), 974–979.

Corsini R. J. & Wedding, D. (eds) (2011). *Current Psychotherapies* (9th edn). Florence, KY: CENGAGE Learning.

Cox, P. D., Vinogradov, S., & Yalom, I. D. (2008). Group therapy. In R. E. Hales, S. C. Yudofsky, & G. O. Gabbard (eds), *The American Psychiatric Publishing Textbook of Psychiatry* (5th edn; pp. 1329–1373). Arlington: American Psychiatric Publishing.

Craig, T. & Power, P. (2010). Inpatient provision in early psychosis. In P. French, J. Smith, D. Shiers, M. Reed, & M. Rayne (eds), *Promoting Recovery in Early Psychosis: A practice manual* (pp. 17–26). Hoboken, NJ: Wiley-Blackwell.

Craske, M. G. (2010). Evaluation. In *Cognitive-Behavioral Therapy* (pp. 115–126). Washington: American Psychological Association.

Cuijpers, P., van Straten, A., Hollon, S. D., & Andersson, G. (2010). The contribution of active medication to combined treatments of psychotherapy and pharmacotherapy for adult depression: A meta-analysis. *Acta Psychiatrica Scandinavica, 121*(6), 415–423.

Dies, R. R. (2003). Group psychotherapies. In A. S. Gurman & S. B. Messer (eds), *Essential Psychotherapies: Theory and practice* (2nd edn). New York: Guilford Press.

Ellis, A. (1962). *Reason and Emotion in Psychotherapy.* Secaucus, NJ: Lyle Stuart.

Ellis, A. (2002). The role of irrational beliefs in perfectionism. In G. L. Flett & P. L. Hewitt (eds), *Perfectionism: Theory, research, and treatment* (pp. 217–229). Washington, DC: American Psychological Association.

Ellis, A. (2011). Rational emotive behavior therapy. In R. J. Corsini & D. Wedding (eds), *Current Psychotherapies* (9th edn). Florence, KY: CENGAGE Learning.

Fisher, P. H., Masia-Warner, C., & Klein, R. G. (2004). Skills for social and academic success: A school-based intervention for social anxiety disorder in adolescents. *Clinical Child and Family Psychology Review, 7*(4), 241–249.

Fishman, D. B., Rego, S. A., & Muller, K. L. (2011). Behavioral theories of psychotherapy. In J. C. Norcross, G. R. VandenBos, & D. K. Freedheim (eds), *History of Psychotherapy: Continuity and change* (2nd edn; pp. 101–140). Washington: American Psychological Association.

Frank, J. D. (1973). *Persuasion and Healing* (revised edn). Baltimore: Johns Hopkins University Press.

Freud, S. (1924). The loss of reality in neurosis and psychosis. In *Sigmund Freud's Collected Papers: Vol. 2* (pp. 272–282). London: Hogarth Press.

Galanter, M. (2010). Spirituality in psychiatry: A biopsychosocial perspective. *Psychiatry: Interpersonal and Biological Processes, 73*(2), 145–157.

Geddes, J. R., Stroup, T. S., & Lieberman, J. A. (2011). Comparative efficacy and effectiveness in the drug treatment of schizophrenia. In D. R. Weinberger & P. J. Harrison (eds), *Schizophrenia* (3rd edn). Hoboken, NJ: Blackwell-Wiley.

Goldenberg, I. & Goldenberg, H. (2011). Family therapy. In R. J. Corsini & D. Wedding (eds), *Current Psychotherapies* (9th edn). Florence, KY: CENGAGE Learning.

Greenberg, L. & Goldman, R. N. (2008). *Emotion-Focused Couples Therapy.* Washington: American Psychological Association.

Gurman, A. S. & Snyder, D. K. (2011). Couple therapy. In J. C. Norcross, G. R. VandenBos, & D. K. Freedheim (eds), *History of Psychotherapy: Continuity and change* (2nd edn; pp. 485–496). Washington: American Psychological Association.

Hagemoser, S. D. (2009). Braking the bandwagon: Scrutinizing the science and politics of empirically supported therapies. *Journal of Psychology: Interdisciplinary and applied, 143*(6), 601–614.

Hamani, C., Diwan, M., Raymond, R., Nobrega, J. N., Macedo, C. E., Brandão, M. L., & Fletcher, P. J. (2011). Reply to: Electrical brain stimulation in depression: Which target(s)? *Biological Psychiatry, 69*(4), e7–e8.

Hanna, D., Kershaw, K., & Chaplin, R. (2009). How specialist ECT consultants inform patients about memory loss. *Psychiatric Bulletin, 33*(11), 412–415.

Harway, M. (ed.) (2005). *Handbook of Couples Therapy.* New York: John Wiley & Sons.

Hayes, S. C., Follette, V. M., & Linehan, M. M. (eds). (2004). *Mindfulness and Acceptance: Expanding the cognitive-behavioral tradition.* New York: Guilford Press.

Hollon, S. D. & DiGiuseppe, R. (2011). Cognitive theories of psychotherapy. In J. C. Norcross, G. R. VandenBos, & D. K. Freedheim (eds), *History of Psychotherapy: Continuity and change* (2nd edn; pp. 203–241). Washington: American Psychological Association.

Hollon, S. D., DeRubeis, R. J., Shelton, R. C., Amsterdam, J. D., Salomon, R. M., O'Reardon, J. P., et al. (2005). Prevention of relapse following cognitive therapy v. medications in moderate to severe depression. *Archives of General Psychiatry, 62*, 417–422.

Hollon, S. D., Haman, K. L., & Brown, L. L. (2002). Cognitive behavioral treatment of depression. In I. H. Gotlib & C. L. Hammen (eds), *Handbook of Depression* (pp. 383–403). New York: Guilford Press.

Hollon, S. D., Stewart, M. O., & Strunk, D. (2006). Enduring effects for cognitive behavior therapy in the treatment of depression and anxiety. *Annual Review of Psychology, 57*, 285–315.

Holmes, D. A. (2010). *Abnormal, Clinical and Forensic Psychology.* Harlow: Pearson Education.

Howland, R. H., Shutt, L. S., Berman, S. R., Spotts, C. R., & Denko, T. (2011). The emerging use of technology for the treatment of depression and other neuropsychiatric disorders. *Annals of Clinical Psychiatry, 23*(1), 48–62.

Ishikawa, S., Iwanaga, M., Yamashita, B., Sato, H., & Sato, S. (2010). Long-term effects of social skills training on depressive symptoms in children. *Japanese Journal of Educational Psychology, 58*(3), 372–384.

Jackson, H., Judd, F., Komiti, A., Fraser, C., Murray, G., Robins, G., & Wearing, A. (2007). Mental health problems in rural contexts: What are the barriers to seeking help from professional providers? *Australian Psychologist, 42*(2), 147–160.

Juhnke, G. A., Granello, D. H., & Granello, P. F. (2011). *Suicide, Self-Injury, and Violence in the Schools: Assessment, prevention, and intervention strategies.* Hoboken, NJ: John Wiley & Sons, Inc.

Julien, R. M., Advokat, C. D., & Comaty, J. (2011). *Primer of Drug Action* (12th edn). New York: Worth Publishers.

Kadushin, C. (1969). *Why People Go to Psychiatrists*. Oxford: Atherton Press.

Keen, E. (1970). *Three Faces of Being: Toward an existential clinical psychology*. By the Meredith Corp. Reprinted by permission of Irvington Publishers.

Kirschenbaum, H. (2004). Carl Rogers's life and work: An assessment on the 100th anniversary of his birth. *Journal of Counseling and Development, 82*(1), 116–124.

Koch, W. J. & Haring, M. (2008). Posttraumatic stress disorder. In M. Hersen & J. Rosqvist (eds), *Handbook of Psychological Assessment, Case Conceptualization, and Treatment: Vol. 1: Adults* (pp. 263–290). Hoboken, NJ: John Wiley & Sons, Inc.

Kooyman, I. & Walsh, E. (2011). Societal outcomes in schizophrenia. In D. R. Weinberger & P. J. Harrison (eds), *Schizophrenia* (3rd edn). Hoboken, NJ: Blackwell-Wiley.

Kopelowicz, A., Liberman, R. P., & Zarate, R. (2007). Psychosocial treatments for schizophrenia. In P. E. Nathan & J. M. Gorman (eds), *A Guide to Treatments that Work* (3rd edn; pp. 243–269). New York: Oxford University Press.

Korchin, S. J. & Sands, S. H. (1983). Principles common to all psychotherapies. In C. E. Walker (ed.), *The Handbook of Clinical Psychology*. Homewood, IL: Dow Jones-Irwin.

Kosslyn, S. M. & Rosenberg, R. S. (2004). *Psychology: The brain, the person, the world* (2nd edn). Harlow: Pearson Education Limited.

Kraft, D. & Kraft, T. (2010). Use of in vivo and in vitro desensitization in the treatment of mouse phobia: Review and case study. *Contemporary Hypnosis, 27*(3), 184–194.

Krueger, R. G. & Kaplan, M. S. (2002). Behavioral and psychopharmacological treatment of the paraphilic and hypersexual disorders. *Journal of Psychiatric Practice, 8*(1), 21–32.

Lambert, M. J. (2010). *Prevention of Treatment Failure: The use of measuring, monitoring, and feedback in clinical practice*. Washington: American Psychological Association.

Landon, T. M. & Barlow, D. H. (2004). Cognitive-behavioral treatment for panic disorder: Current status. *Journal of Psychiatric Practices, 10*(4), 211–226.

Lazzari, C., Egan, S. J., & Rees, C. S. (2011). Behavioral activation treatment for depression in older adults delivered via videoconferencing: A pilot study. *Cognitive and Behavioral Practice, 40*, 39–53.

Lochman, J. E., Barry, T., Powell, N., & Young, L. (2010). Anger and aggression. In D. W. Nangle, C. A. Erdley, & P. J. Norton (eds), *Practitioner's Guide to Empirically Based Measures of Social Skills* (pp. 155–166). New York: Springer Publishing.

Luborsky, E. B., O'Reilly-Landry, M., & Arlow, J. A. (2011). Psychoanalysis. In R. J. Corsini & D. Wedding (eds), *Current Psychotherapies* (9th edn). Florence, KY: CENGAGE Learning.

Luborsky, L., Rosenthal, R., Diguer, L., Andrusyna, T. P., Levitt, J. T., Seligman, D. A., Berman, J. S., & Krause, E. D. (2003). Are some psychotherapies much more effective than others? *Journal of Applied Psychoanalytic Studies, 5*(4), 455–460.

Luborsky, L., Singer, B., & Luborsky, L. (1975). Comparative studies of psychotherapies. *Archives of General Psychiatry, 32*, 995–1008.

Luborsky, L. B., Barrett, M. S., Antonuccio, D. O., Shoenberger, D., & Stricker, G. (2006). What else materially influences what is represented and published as evidence? In J. C. Norcross, L. E. Beutler, & R. F. Levant (eds), *Evidence-Based Practices in Mental Health: Debate and dialogue on the fundamental questions* (pp. 257–298). Washington: American Psychological Association.

Mayberg, H. S., Lozano, A. M., Voon, V., McNeely, H. E., Seminowicz, D., Hamani, C., et al. (2005). Deep brain stimulation for treatment-resistant depression. *Neuron, 45*, 651–660.

McEvoy, P. M. (2007). Effectiveness of cognitive behavioural group therapy for social phobia in a community clinic: A benchmarking study. *Behavioral Research and Therapy, 45*(12), 3030–3040.

Merkl, A., Schubert, F., Quante, A., Luborzewski, A., Brakemeier, E., Grimm, S., & Bajbouj, M. (2011). Abnormal cingulate and prefrontal cortical neurochemistry in major depression after electroconvulsive therapy. *Biological Psychiatry, 69*(8), 772–779.

Minzenberg, M. J., Yoon, J. H., & Carter, C. S. (2011). Schizophrenia. In R. E. Hales, S. C. Yudofsky, & G. O. Gabbard (eds), *Essentials of Psychiatry* (3rd edn; pp. 111–150). Arlington, VA: American Psychiatric Publishing.

Mueller, S. E., Petitjean, S., Boening, J., & Wiesbeck, G. A. (2007). The impact of self-help group attendance on relapse rates after alcohol detoxification in a controlled study. *Alcohol and Alcoholism, 42*(2), 108–112.

Nahas, Z., Marangell, L. B., Husain, M. M., Rush, A. J., Sackeim, H. A., Lisanby, S. H., et al. (2005). Two-year-outcome of vagus nerve stimulation (VNS) for treatment of major depressive episodes. *Journal of Clinical Psychiatry, 66*(9), 1097–1104.

NAMI (National Alliance on Mental Illness). (2011). *Mental Illness: Facts and numbers*. Arlington, VA: Author.

Newman, M. G., Castonguay, L. G., Borkovec, T. D., Fisher, A. J., Boswell, J. F., Szkodny, L. E., & Nordberg, S. S. (2011). A randomized controlled trial of cognitive-behavioral therapy for generalized anxiety disorder with integrated techniques from emotion-focused and interpersonal therapies. *Journal of Consulting and Clinical Psychology, 79*(2), 171–181.

Nietzel, M. T., Bernstein, D. A., Milich, R. S., & Kramer, G. (2003). *Introduction to Clinical Psychology* (6th edn). Upper Saddle River, NJ: Pearson Education.

Norcross, J. C. & Goldfried, M. R. (eds). (2005). *Handbook of Psychotherapy Integration* (2nd edn). New York: Oxford University Press.

O'Leary, K. D. & Wilson, G. T. (1987). *Behavior Therapy: Application and outcome* (2nd edn). Englewood Cliffs, NJ: Prentice Hall, Inc.

Ogden, T. (2011). Sosial ferdighetsopplæring for barn og ungdom. *Tidsskrift for Norsk Psykologforening, 48*(1), 64–68.

Okamoto, Y., Kinoshita, A., Onoda, K., Yoshimura, S., Matsunaga, M., Takami, H., Yamshita, H., Ueda, K., Suzuki, S., & Yamawaki, S. (2006). Functional brain basis of cognition in major depression. *Japanese Journal of Psychonomic Science, 25*, 237–243.

Olatunji, B. O., Huijding, J., de Jong, P. J., & Smits, J. A. J. (2011). The relative contributions of fear and disgust reductions to improvements in spider phobia following exposure-based treatment. *Journal of Behavior Therapy and Experimental Psychiatry, 42*(1), 117–121.

Orsillo, S. M. & Roemer, L. (2011). *The Mindful Way through Anxiety: Break free from chronic worry and reclaim your life*. New York: Guilford Press.

Otto, M. W., McHugh, R. K., & Kantak, K. M. (2010). Combined pharmacotherapy and cognitive-behavioral therapy for anxiety disorders: Medication effects, glucocorticoids, and attenuated treatment outcomes. *Clinical Psychology: Science and practice, 17*(2), 91–103.

Owen-Howard, M. (2001). Pharmacological aversion treatment of alcohol dependence: I: Production and prediction of conditioned alcohol aversion. *American Journal of Drug and Alcohol Abuse, 27*(3), 561–585.

Paul, G. L. & Lentz, R. (1977). *Psychosocial Treatment of the Chronic Mental Patient*. Cambridge, MA: Harvard University Press.

Perugi, G., Medda, P., Zanello, S., Toni, C., & Cassano, G. B. (2011). Episode length and mixed features as predictors of ECT nonresponse in patients with medication-resistant major depression. *Brain Stimulation, 5*(1), 18–24.

Peters, R. H., Sherman, P. B., & Osher, F. C. (2008). Treatment in jails and prisons. In K. T. Mueser & D. V. Jeste (eds), *Clinical Handbook of Schizophrenia* (pp. 354–364). New York: Guilford Press.

Pontoski, K. E. & Heimberg, R. G. (2010). The myth of the superiority of concurrent combined treatments for anxiety disorders. *Clinical Psychology: Science and practice, 17*(2), 107–111.

Pope, K. & Wedding, D. (2011). Contemporary challenges and controversies. In R. J. Corsini & D. Wedding (eds), *Current Psychotherapies* (9th edn). Florence, KY: CENGAGE Learning.

Portnoy, D. (2008). Relatedness: Where existential and psychoanalytic approaches converge. In K. J. Schneider (ed.), *Existential-Integrative Psychotherapy: Guideposts to the core of practice* (pp. 268–281). New York: Routledge/Taylor & Francis Group.

Present, J., Crits-Christoph, P., Gibbons, M. B. C., Hearon, B., Ring-Kurtz, S., Worley, M., *et al.* (2008). Sudden gains in the treatment of generalized anxiety disorder. *Journal of Clinical Psychology, 64*(1), 119–126.

Prochaska, J. O. & Norcross, J. C. (2010). *Systems of Psychotherapy: A transtheoretical analysis* (7th edn). Pacific Grove, CA: Brooks/Cole.

Raskin, N. J., Rogers, C., & Witty, M. (2011). Person-centered therapy. In R. J. Corsini & D. Wedding (eds), *Current Psychotherapies* (9th edn). Florence, KY: CENGAGE Learning.

Rimm, D. C. & Masters, J. C. (1979). *Behavior Therapy: Techniques and empirical findings* (2nd edn). New York: Academic Press.

Ritter, M. R., Blackmore, M. A., & Heimberg, R. G. (2010). Generalized anxiety disorder. In D. McKay, J. S. Abramowitz, & S. Taylor (eds), *Cognitive-Behavioral Therapy for Refractory Cases: Turning failure into success* (pp. 111–137). Washington: American Psychological Association.

Rosenberg, O., Isserles, M., Levkovitz, Y., Kotler, M., Zangen, A., & Dannon, P. N. (2011). Effectiveness of a second deep TMS in depression: A brief report. *Progress in Neuro-Psychopharmacology & Biological Psychiatry, 35*(4), 1041–1044.

Rosenthal, T. L. & Bandura, A. (1978). Psychological modeling: Theory and practice. In S. L. Garfield & A. E. Bergin (eds), *Handbook of Psychotherapy and Behavior Change: An empirical analysis* (2nd edn; pp. 621–658). New York: John Wiley & Sons.

SAMHSA (Substance Abuse and Mental Health Services Administration). (2002). *National Survey on Drug Use and Health: 2002.* Washington: Author.

SAMHSA (Substance Abuse and Mental Health Services Administration). (2008). *Patterns of Mental Health Service Utilization and Substance Use among Adults: 2000 and 2001.* Washington: Author.

Schneider, K. J. & Krug, O. T. (2010). *Existential–Humanistic Therapy.* Washington: American Psychological Association.

Shadish, W. R. & Baldwin, S. A. (2005). Effects of behavioral marital therapy: A meta-analysis of randomized controlled trials. *Journal of Consulting and Clinical Psychology, 73*(1), 6–14.

Sharf, R. S. (2012). *Theories of Psychotherapy & Counseling: Concepts and cases* (5th edn). Pacific Grove, CA: Brooks/Cole.

Smith, L. D., Peck, P. L., & McGovern, R. J. (2004). Factors contributing to the utilization of mental health services in a rural setting. *Psychological Reports, 95*(2), 435–442.

Smith, M. L. & Glass, G. V. (1977). Meta-analysis of psychotherapy outcome studies. *American Psychologist, 32*(9), 752–760.

Smith, M. L., Glass, G. V., & Miller, T. I. (1980). *The Benefits of Psychotherapy.* Baltimore: Johns Hopkins University Press.

Snyder, W. V. (1947). *Casebook of Non-directive Counseling.* Boston: Houghton Mifflin.

Soorya, L. V., Carpenter, L. A., & Romanczyk, R. G. (2011). Applied behavior analysis. In E. Hollander, A. Kolevzon, & J. T. Coyle (eds), *Textbook of Autism Spectrum Disorders* (pp. 525–535). Arlington, VA: American Psychiatric Publishing.

SoRelle, R. (2000). Nearly half of Americans with severe mental illness do not seek treatment. *Circulation Electronic Pages,* 101: e66, http://circ.ahajournals.org/content/101/5/e66.extract, accessed 21 December 2012.

Spiegler, M. D. & Guevremont, D. C. (2003). *Contemporary Behavior Therapy.* Belmont, CA: Thomson/Wadsworth.

Strümpfel, U. (2004). Research on Gestalt therapy. *International Gestalt Journal, 27*(1), 9–54.

Strümpfel, U. (2006). *Therapie der Gefühle: Forschungsbefunde zur Gestalttherapie.* Cologne, Germany: Edition Humanistiche Psychologie.

Torrey, E. F. (2001). *Surviving Schizophrenia: A manual for families, consumers, and providers* (4th ed.). New York: HarperCollins.

Treanor, M. (2011). The potential impact of mindfulness on exposure and extinction learning in anxiety disorders. *Clinical Psychology Review, 31*(4), 617–625.

Wampold, B. E., Hollon, S. D., & Hill, C. E. (2011). Unresolved questions and future directions in psychotherapy research. In J. C. Norcross, G. R. VandenBos, & D. K. Freedheim (eds), *History of Psychotherapy: Continuity and change* (2nd edn; pp. 333–356). Washington: American Psychological Association.

Wang, S. S. (2007, December 4). The graying of shock therapy. *Wall Street Journal Online.* Retrieved 14 August 2008, from http://online.wsg.com/public/article_print/SB119673737406312767.html.

Ward, J. (2007). We are all Larry David. *New Yorker,* http://www.newyorker.com/talk/2007/10/29/071029ta_talk_ward, accessed 21 December 2012.

Watson, J. C., Goldman, R. N., & Greenberg, L. S. (2011). Humanistic and experiential theories of psychotherapy. In J. C. Norcross, G. R. VandenBos, & D. K. Freedheim (eds), *History of Psychotherapy: Continuity and change* (2nd edn; pp. 141–172). Washington: American Psychological Association.

Wells, A. (2010). Metacognitive therapy: Application to generalized anxiety disorder. In D. Sookman & R. L. Leahy (eds), *Treatment Resistant Anxiety Disorders: Resolving impasses to symptom remission* (pp. 1–29). New York: Routledge/Taylor & Francis Group.

Westen, D., Dutra, L., & Shedler, J. (2005). Assessing adolescent personality pathology: Quantifying clinical judgment. *British Journal of Psychiatry, 186*(3), 227–238.

White, B. J. & Madara, E. J. (eds) (2012). *Self-Help Group Sourcebook Online,* www.mentalhelp.net/selfhelp, accessed 21 December 2012.

Wilson, G. T. (2011). Behavior therapy. In R. J. Corsini & D. Wedding (eds), *Current Psychotherapies* (9th edn). Florence, KY: CENGAGE Learning.

Wolitzky, D. L. (2011). Psychoanalytic theories of psychotherapy. In J. C. Norcross, G. R. VandenBos, & D. K. Freedheim (eds), *History of Psychotherapy: Continuity and change* (2nd edn; pp. 65–100). Washington: American Psychological Association.

Wolpe, J. (1990). *The Practice of Behavior Therapy* (4th edn). Elmsford, NY: Pergamon Press.

Wolpe, J. (1995). Reciprocal inhibition: Major agent of behavior change. In W. T. O'Donohue & L. Krasner (eds), *Theories of Behavior Therapy: Exploring behavior change.* Washington: American Psychological Association.

Wolpe, J. (1997). Thirty years of behavior therapy. *Behavior Therapy, 28*(4), 633–635.

Worthington, E. L., Jr. (2011). Integration of spirituality and religion into psychotherapy. In J. C. Norcross, G. R. VandenBos, & D. K. Freedheim (eds), *History of Psychotherapy: Continuity and change* (2nd edn; pp. 533–543). Washington: American Psychological Association.

Wyatt, G. W. & Parham, W. D. (2007). The inclusion of culturally sensitive course materials in graduate school and training programs. *Psychotherapy: Theory, research, practice, and training, 22*(suppl. 2), 461–468.

Yalom, I. & Josselson, R. (2011). Existential psychotherapy. In R. J. Corsini & D. Wedding (eds), *Current Psychotherapies* (9th edn). Florence, KY: CENGAGE Learning.

Yalom, I. D. & Leszcz, M. (2005). *The Theory and Practice of Group Psychotherapy* (5th edn). New York: Basic Books.

Yontef, G. & Jacobs, L. (2011). Gestalt therapy. In R. J. Corsini & D. Wedding (eds), *Current Psychotherapies* (9th edn). Florence, KY: CENGAGE Learning.

Name Index

Wiesel, T. N. 191
Wieser, H. G. 186
Wilde, D. J. 439, 440
Wilkinson, G. W. 148
Williams, D. 559
Williams, G. C. 140, 158
Williams, J. B. 547
Williams, K. D. 498
Williams, P. G. 533, 569
Williams, T. J. 396
Williams, W. M. 343, 360, 361
Wills, T. A. 526
Wilson, B. A. 300
Wilson, D. A. 173
Wilson, E. O. 140, 154
Wilson, G. 361, 485
Wilson, G. T. 390, 549, 561, 590
Wilson, K. A. 561
Wilson, K. R. 547
Wilson, M. 146, 147, 148
Wilson, M. A. 259
Wimmer, H. 63
Winberg, J. 264, 377

Wincze, J. P. 396
Windholz, G. 242
Winkler I. 217
Winningham, R. G. 299
Wissler, C. 350
Witthöft, M. 569
Wixted, J. T. 287, 290, 293, 296, 297
Wolf, S. 533
Wolfson, A. R. 226
Wolitzky, D. L. 595, 599
Wolosin, S. M. 267
Wolpe, J. 587
Wood, J. M. 464
Wood, W. 426, 455, 457, 471, 492, 493, 498, 501
Woods, S. C. 385
Woody, E. 218
Woollett, K. 254
Woolley, C. S. 127
Worley, L. L. M. 565
Worthington, E. L., Jr. 599
Worthman, C. M. 220, 226
Worthy, M. 484

Wyatt, G. W. 599
Wynn, K. 59
Wynne, K. 384

Y

Yadav, R. 384, 385
Yahr, P. 170
Yalom, I. 520, 551, 594
Yalom, I. D. 596
Yan, R. 390
Yang, S. 359
Yehuda, R. 563, 564
Yela, C. 486
Yerkes, R. M. 379, 515
Yin, H. H. 253
Yontef, G. 593, 594
Yoon, H. 520
Yoon, I. Y. 220
Young, K. S. 528
Young, L. J. 114
Young, L. R. 387
Yu, D. L. 555

Yuan, J. W. 428
Yutzy, S. H. 568, 569

Z

Zacks, R. T. 277
Zahavi, A. 145, 149
Zajonc, R. B. 419, 498
Zatorre, R. J. 185
Zawadzki, B. 451
Zeelenberg, M. 327
Zeidner, M. 360
Zelazo, P. D. 57, 215
Zentall, T. R. 498
Zhu, B. 294
Zigler, E. 363
Zigmond, M. J. 378
Zimbardo, P. G. 493
Zohary, E. 392
Zola, S. M. 330
Zucker, K. J. 394
Zuckerman, M. 446, 447, 451, 453, 554

Subject Index